trotman

Brian Heap

38th edition

Degree Course Offers

2008 entry

Winning your place
at university – the
essential guide

Mander Portman Woodward

Degree Course Offers 2008

In order to ensure that *Degree Course Offers* retains its reputation as the definitive guide for students wishing to study at UK universities, thousands of questionnaires are distributed, months of research and analysis undertaken, and painstaking data checking and proofing carried out.

Every effort has been made to maintain absolute accuracy in providing course information and to ensure that the entire book is as up-to-date as possible. However, changes are constantly taking place in higher education so it is important for readers to check carefully with prospectuses and websites before submitting their applications. The author, compilers and publishers cannot be held responsible for any inaccuracies in information supplied to them by third parties or contained in resources and websites listed in the book.

We hope you find this 38th edition useful, and would welcome your feedback as to how we can ensure the 39th edition is even better.

Editorial and Publishing Team
Author Brian Heap
Compilation and Data Processing Dianah Ellis, Henry Ellis
Editorial Mina Patria, Publishing Director; Jo Jacomb, Editorial Manager;
Ian Turner, Production Editor
Production Ken Ruskin, Head of Manufacturing and Logistics; James Rudge, Production Artworker
Advertising Sales Tom Lee, Commercial Director; Sarah Talbot, Head of Advertising;
Kerry Lyon, Senior Sales Executive
(contact team on 020 8334 1617 or e-mail advertising@trotman.co.uk)
Sales and Marketing Stefan Reynolds, Book Sales Manager

This 38th edition published in 2007 by Trotman an imprint of
Crimson Publishing
Westminster House, Kew Road,
Richmond, Surrey TW9 2ND
www.crimsonpublishing.co.uk
© Brian Heap and Trotman 2007

A CIP record for this book is available from the British Library

ISBN 978 1 84455 123 1

Typeset by Florence Production Ltd, Stoodleigh, Devon
Printed and bound in Great Britain by Cambridge University Press

Founded in 1973, **Mander Portman Woodward (MPW)** is one of the UK's best known groups of independent sixth-form colleges with centres in London, Birmingham and Cambridge. It offers over 40 subjects at AS and A2 with no restrictions on subject combinations and a maximum class size of eight.

MPW has one of the highest numbers of university placements each year of any independent school in the country. It has developed considerable expertise over the years in the field of applications strategy and is frequently consulted by students facing some of the more daunting challenges that may arise in areas such as getting into Oxbridge, Medicine or Law. This expertise is available to a wider audience in the form of **MPW Guides** on higher education and the seminars that are run for sixth-formers at its London centre. We are grateful to Trotman for publishing the Guides and hope that this latest edition of **Degree Course Offers** will prove as popular and useful as ever.

If you would like to know more about MPW or MPW Guides, please telephone us on 020 7835 1355 or visit our website, www.mpw.co.uk.

Choosing Your University And Degree Course... And Completing Your UCAS Form?

Why not contact Brian Heap, the author of *Degree Course Offers*, *Choosing Your Degree Course and University* and *University Scholarships, Awards and Bursaries* for a personal interview or a telephone consultation for advice on such issues as:

- Choosing A-level subjects (which are the best subjects and for which courses!)
- Degrees and Diploma courses (making the right choice from a list of thousands!)
- Completing your UCAS form (will the admissions tutor remember your personal statement?)
- Choosing the right university or college (the best ones for you and your courses)

For details of services and consultation fees contact:
The Higher Education Advice and Planning Service

tel: 01386 859355 email: heaps@dial.pipex.com

QUOTES

'This guide contains useful, practical information for all university applicants and those advising them. I heartily recommend it'
Dr John Dunford, General Secretary, Assocation of School and College Leaders, 2005

'An invaluable guide to helping students and their advisers find their way through the maze of degree courses currently on offer'
Kath Wright, President, Association for Careers Education and Guidance, 2005

No one is better informed or more experienced than Brian Heap in mediating this range of information to university and college applicants'
Careers Education and Guidance, October 2005

'The course-listings bible'
The Guardian, June 2005

'After consulting this you won't be able to say "I didn't know!" For every school library'
The Teacher, Nov 2003

'A must buy . . . one of the best single reference sources to degree course offers available'
Career Guidance Today, July 2003

'The most comprehensive guide is Degree Course Offers by Brian Heap'
John Clare in The Daily Telegraph, April 2003

'Degree Course Offers is an excellent resource and contains the type of information that prospective students and their parents need to know when making decisions about degree courses'
Mandy Telford, NUS National President, April 2003

'This guide gives a valuable and objective insight into the country's universities'
Will Straw, President, Oxford University Student Union, April 2003

'The Bible for university applicants provides detailed information on pretty much every course in the land'
The Northern Echo, April 2003

'Going to university is one of the biggest investment decisions you will ever make in your own future. In order to make the right choices, you need to be armed with fair and accurate information of the wide variety of institutions and courses open to you. Brian Heap's Degree Course Offers is an excellent source of information'
Rt Hon Charles Clarke MP, Secretary of State for Education and Skills, March 2003

'I am well aware of how helpful previous editions of Degree Course Offers have been to students who can sometimes find the process of university applications somewhat daunting. It is very positive to see that there is such a comprehensive and readable guide available to them'
Margaret Hodge MP, Minister of State for Lifelong Learning, Further Education and Higher Education, March 2003

'The author and publisher know the HE market extremely well . . . careers advisers will find this book an invaluable resource as they guide applicants through the maze of courses, institutions and admissions requirements in the UK higher education system'
Careers Adviser, June 2002

'Brian Heap, the guru on university admissions'
The Independent, May 2001

University of Worcester

STUDY AT THE UNIVERSITY OF WORCESTER

- Wide range of subjects on offer at Degree, Foundation Degree and HND level

- Excellent facilities including Digital Arts Centre and Sports Complex

- Lively modern campus with a good range of accommodation available

- Nationally recognised professional courses in management, teacher training and nursing

- Full and part-time study options

- Friendly and supportive atmosphere

Come and See for Yourself!
Open Day - Sunday 24 June 2007
Open Day - Sunday 23 September 2007

To find out more or to request a free prospectus

Call: 01905 855141
E-mail: study@worc.ac.uk
Or visit: www.worcester.ac.uk

IT'S YOUR WORLD.
WHAT WILL YOU CHANGE?

Middlesex
University

[ART AND DESIGN

MIDDLESEX UNIVERSITY]

- BA Honours Applied Arts
- BA Honours Design
- BA Honours Design and Technology
- BA Honours Fashion
- BA Honours Fashion Design, Styling and Promotion
- BA Honours Film Studies
- BA Honours Film, Video, Interactive Arts
- BA Honours Fine Art
- BA Honours Fine Art and Critical Theory
- BA Honours Graphic Design
- BA Honours History of Art with English Literature
- BA Honours History of Art with Media and Cultural Studies
- BA Honours Interior Architecture: Design and Practice
- BA Honours Jewellery
- BA Honours Fashion Jewellery and Accessories
- BA Honours Illustration
- BA Honours Interior Architecture and Design
- BA Honours Photography
- BA Honours Product Design
- BA Honours Sonic Arts
- BA Honours Textiles – Applied Print
- BA Honours Textiles – Weave, Mixed Media and Knit
- BSc Honours Engineering Product Design

020 8411 5555

www.mdx.ac.uk

MIDDLESEX UNIVERSITY IN LONDON

CONTENTS

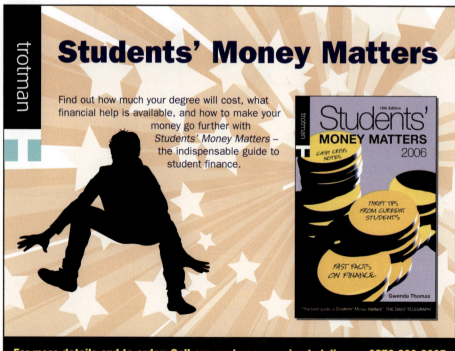

Northern School of Contemporary Dance

A unique dance training institution offering a select group of students the opportunity to develop and excel as dance artists in a conservatoire environment.

The School if a Higher Education College providing a Foundation Course in Contemporary Dance, a BPA (Hons) Degree in Contemporary Dance and an innovative Graduate Diploma Programme which now includes two distinct pathways:

• A highly successful graduate apprenticeship scheme which offers placements with some of the UK's leading dance companies.

• Verve, an exciting graduate dance company offering intensive performance experience and professional skills development.

For course and audition information contact:

T: +44 (0) 113 219 3000
E: info@nscd.ac.uk
www.nscd.ac.uk

The Northern School of Contemporary Dance is affiliated to the Conservatoire for Dance and Drama. HE provision is validated by the University of Kent.

Choosing Your University And Degree Course... And Completing Your UCAS Form?

Why not contact Brian Heap, the author of *Degree Course Offers*, *Choosing Your Degree Course and University* and *University Scholarships, Awards and Bursaries* for a personal interview or a telephone consultation for advice on such issues as:

- Choosing A-level subjects (which are the best subjects and for which courses!)
- Degrees and Diploma courses (making the right choice from a list of thousands!)
- Completing your UCAS form (will the admissions tutor remember your personal statement?)
- Choosing the right university or college (the best ones for you and your courses)

For details of services and consultation fees contact:
The Higher Education Advice and Planning Service

tel: 01386 859355 email: heaps@dial.pipex.com

AUTHOR'S ACKNOWLEDGEMENTS

I acknowledge gratefully the efforts of university and college registrars, schools liaison staff, faculty and departmental heads and admissions tutors in providing detailed information about their courses.

I should also like to thank in particular Tony Charlton and Richard Pope of UCAS, the Engineering Council UK, Sarah Hannaford of the University of Cambridge Admissions Office, Clare Woodcock of the University of Oxford Public Relations Office, Leslie Currie, Head of Admissions at the University of Bath, and Dr Roger Ash, Head of Admissions at the University of Bradford, for providing me with up-to-date information on admissions procedures. In addition, my thanks are due to Professor Ian Johnson of Nottingham University Medical School for details of the UKCAT scheme, Dr Kevin Stannard of Cambridge International Examinations for information on the Cambridge Pre-U Diploma, and also to the Higher Education Funding Council (England, Scotland and Wales) for permission to publish information relating to research ratings and teaching quality assessments. In addition, I should like to express special thanks to the Higher Education Statistics Agency (HESA) for access to its Data Report and Reference Volume *First Destinations*, and to the Quality Assurance Agency for information on subject assessment reports. I should also like to thank those admissions tutors, teachers and their pupils who have sent me interview reports and other information which has provided useful supplementary data for the book.

Every effort has been made to maintain absolute accuracy in providing course information and to ensure that the entire book is as up-to-date as possible. However, changes are constantly taking place in higher education so it is important for readers to check carefully with prospectuses and websites before submitting their applications.

I also wish to thank Dianah Ellis for her continuing editorial advice, and the many readers who have written to me about the problems they have encountered in choosing courses and places to study. Such information adds to a valuable store of knowledge which can be passed on, thereby creating a better understanding of mutual difficulties.

Finally, my thanks to Jane Heap of Putney High School (staff) for checking on course changes and also to my wife Rita for her administrative help (and patience!) through 37 years of publication.

Brian Heap
January 2007

ABOUT THIS BOOK

Choosing a career or course of study is not easy. There is much that applicants need to know in order to make decisions that are right for them as individuals, and each year they will spend a great deal of time exploring various options. One option is higher education, although entry to degree and diploma courses can be highly competitive, and applicants need good advice on how to choose courses. Comprehensive and comparative information about selection policies and the range of courses available, therefore, is an essential part of this process. To assist applicants, *Degree Course Offers* (now in its 38th year) aims to provide a **first stop** reference for applicants choosing courses of higher education by providing information from official sources.

The purpose of this book is to provide essential information for all students preparing to go to university or college in 2008. It covers information about all stages of choosing degree course subjects, universities and colleges including:

* How to select the degree subject that is right for you
* The courses offered, what they involve and how they are taught
* How difficult or easy it will be to secure an offer of a place at your chosen institution(s)
* How to prepare your personal statement for the UCAS application
* How to cope in August if your grades don't match your offer
* Information about UK universities for international students, and the acceptability of international qualifications.

The subject tables in **Chapter 8** list:

* Target offers for honours degree courses in A-level grades and/or UCAS tariff points
* IB offers for degree courses
* Foundation degrees and Higher National Diploma courses
* Subject information
* Useful websites
* Course variations
* Top universities and colleges (Research)
* Sandwich degree courses
* The number of applicants per place
* The numbers (where available) of UK, EU, non-EU and mature applicants at individual universities
* Advice to applicants and help in completing Section 10 (the personal statement) of the UCAS application
* Some misconceptions students have about courses
* Applicants' impressions of open days and interviews
* Reasons for rejection at interview
* Universities with vacancies in Clearing in 2006
* Offers to applicants repeating A-levels
* New graduates' destinations and employment
* Other degree courses for consideration.

NEW FOR THIS EDITION

* **How Much Will It Cost?** A new chapter providing information about university tuition fees, sources of help towards them, and the availability of university scholarships and bursaries for undergraduate students
* **An enlarged chapter** listing universities and colleges requiring applicants to take admissions or aptitude tests as part of the admissions process, such as the recently introduced UK Clinical Aptitude Test (UKCAT) for Medicine and Dentistry.
* **Lists of universities with vacancies in Clearing in 2006** to help applicants assess their chances of a possible place after their AL and AS results.

Degree Course Offers is updated each year from information supplied by admissions staff in universities and colleges. It is collated between October and March of each academic year for publication in the spring, so providing up-to-date advice on admissions policies and details of new courses for the next application cycle starting in the following September.

In **Chapter 8** the offers, made in terms of UCAS tariff points or grade alone, are often wide-ranging in order to suit both the needs of individual applicants and also the requirements of universities and subject departments. These are the targets at which applicants should aim. However, offers can vary and are subject to change, so it is essential for applicants always to refer to websites for the very latest information.

Used in conjunction with *Choosing Your Degree Course and University* (the companion title to this book), *Degree Course Offers* takes the student through the entire guidance process for higher education. Once again, therefore, it provides in a single volume a comprehensive survey of selection information and guidance for applicants to higher education at a time when they need it most.

Note Every effort is made to ensure accuracy throughout this book. It is important, however, that readers always check websites and prospectuses carefully for any late changes in offers, admissions policies or courses, and contact admissions officers of their chosen institutions, should queries arise.

Brain Heap
January 2007

1 | YOUR FIRST DECISIONS

HIGHER EDUCATION OR NOT?

Why do you want to go on to higher education? If you are taking GCE Advanced (AL) and Advanced Subsidiary (AS) qualifications, this is an important question to ask. Last year (2006) the total number of applicants was 504,748, with 389,505 acceptances, for full-time first degree and diploma courses in the United Kingdom. Law, Psychology, Pre-clinical Medicine, Management Studies and Design Studies were the five most popular subjects. However, higher education is just one of two options you have. The other is employment and perhaps it is important to note that higher education is not necessarily the best option for everyone. It is, however, one which is appropriate for many and, therefore, should not be rejected lightly. Higher education is likely to open many doors and give you opportunities for work and leisure that otherwise you might not have. Also, very often and quite accidentally, it can lead into careers that you might not have considered before.

Most courses in higher education lead to a degree or a diploma and for either you will have to make a *subject choice*. This can be difficult because the universities alone offer over 1200 degree subjects and over 50,000 courses within the UCAS scheme. You have two main options:

A   Choosing a course that is either similar to, or the same as, one (or more) of your examination subjects, or related to an interest outside the school curriculum, such as Anthropology, American Studies, Archaeology. See **Section A** below.

B   Choosing a course in preparation for a future career, for example Medicine, Architecture, Engineering. See **Section B** below and also **Appendix 2**.

SECTION A

Choosing your course by examination subjects

Deciding your degree or diploma course on the basis of your A-level (or equivalent) subjects is a reasonably safe option. Already you are familiar with the subjects and what they involve, and you may well look forward to studying at least one to a much greater depth over the next few years. If the long-term career prospects concern you, don't worry – a degree course isn't necessarily a training for a job. If you are taking science subjects, they can lead naturally on to a range of scientific careers, although many scientists follow non-science careers such as law and accountancy. If you are taking arts or social science subjects, remember that training for most non-scientific careers can start once you have your degree. When choosing your degree course it is important to consider what A-level subjects you are taking as universities may 'require' or 'prefer' certain subjects for entry to some courses. To make sure you have the right subjects, check the course subject requirements in university/college prospectuses or on their websites. Finally, when choosing AS-level subjects students sometimes prefer to select those with a similar subject base, for example four science subjects or four arts or humanities subjects. However, some institutions welcome one, or even two, contrasting subjects (for example, Bradford, Brunel, Imperial London, the London medical schools), provided the required A-level subjects are also offered. Subjects and policies are likely to vary depending on subject requirements for specific degree courses.

These subjects do not stand on their own, in isolation. Each subject you are taking is one of a much larger family. Each has many similarities to subjects studied in degree and diploma courses that you might never have considered, so before you decide finally on taking a subject to degree level read through the lists of A-level subjects below, each followed by examples of degree courses in the same subject field.

Here you will find some examples of degree courses with similarities to the A-level subjects you might be taking. (These lists are also useful if you have to consider alternative courses after the examination results are published!)

Accountancy See Section B.

Ancient history Archaeology, Biblical Studies, Classics and Classical Civilisation, Classical Greek, Latin, Middle and Near Eastern Studies.

Applied ICT See Section B (Computing).

Archaeology See Section B.

Art and design; Applied art and design Art, Furniture Design, Graphic Design, Textile Design, Theatre Design, Three Dimensional Design, Typography and Graphic Communication. See also Section B.

Biology; Applied science See Section B.

Business; Applied business See Section B.

Chemistry; Applied science See Section B.

Classics and Classical Civilisation Ancient History, Archaeology, Classical Greek, Classics, Latin.

Computing; Applied ICT See Section B.

Dance; Performing arts/Performing studies See Section B.

Design technology; Applied art and design; Engineering Engineering, Industrial Design, Product Design. See also Section B.

Drama and theatre studies; Performing arts See Section B.

Economics; Applied business Accountancy, Banking, Business Administration, Business Economics, Business Studies, Development Studies, Estate Management, Financial Services, Management Science, Politics, Quantity Surveying, Social Studies, Statistics.

Electronics; Engineering Computing, Engineering (Aeronautical, Aerospace, Communication, Computer, Software, Systems), Mechatronics, Multimedia Technology, Medical Electronics. See also Section B.

English language and literature Drama, Information and Library Studies/Management, Journalism, Theatre Studies.

Environmental sciences; Applied science Biological Sciences, Biology, Earth Sciences, Ecology, Environmental Hazards, Forestry, Geography, Geology, Land Management, Marine Biology, Oceanography, Plant Sciences, Wildlife Conservation, Zoology.

French International Business Studies, International Hospitality Management, Law with French Law.

Geography Development Studies, Earth Sciences, Environmental Science, Estate Management, Forestry, Geographical Information Science, Geology, Land Economy, Meteorology, Oceanography, Surveying, Town and Country Planning, Urban Studies, Water Science.

Geology See Section B.

German International Business Studies, International Hospitality Management, Law with German Law.

Government/Politics Development Studies, Economics, Government, Industrial Relations, International Politics, Law, Politics, Public Administration, Social Policy, Sociology, Strategic Studies.

History American Studies, International Relations, Law, Religious Studies.

Home economics Food Science, Hospitality Management, Nutrition.

Languages Apart from French and German – and Spanish for some universities – it is not usually necessary to have completed an A-level language course before studying the many languages (over 60) offered at degree level for example, Chinese, Japanese, Scandinavian Studies.

Law See Section B.

Mathematics Accountancy, Actuarial Mathematics, Aeronautical Engineering, Astrophysics, Building Science and Technology, Business Management, Chemical Engineering, Civil Engineering, Computational Science, Computer Systems Engineering, Control Systems Engineering, Cybernetics, Economics, Electrical/Electronic Technology, Engineering Science, Ergonomics, Geophysics, Management Science, Materials Science and Technology, Mechanical Engineering, Metallurgy, Meteorology, Naval Architecture, Physics, Quantity Surveying, Statistics, Systems Analysis, Telecommunications.

Media studies; Media communication and production See Section B.

Music See Section B.

Philosophy Divinity, History of Science, Psychology, Religious Studies.

Physical education and sport Chiropractic, Coaching Science, Dance Studies, Exercise and Health, Exercise Science, Golf Studies, Health Care/Education/Psychology/Science, Human Life Science, Nursing, Occupational Health and Safety, Occupational Therapy, Osteopathy, Outdoor Pursuits, Physical Education, Physiotherapy, Sport and Exercise Science, Sport and Health, Sport Coaching, Sport Equipment Design, Sport Management, Teaching (Primary) (Secondary).

Physics; Applied science Aeronautical Engineering, Architecture, Astronomy, Astrophysics, Automotive Engineering, Biomedical Engineering, Biophysics, Chemical Physics, Civil Engineering, Communications Engineering, Computer Science, Cybernetics, Education, Electrical/Electronic Engineering, Engineering Science, Ergonomics, Geophysics, Materials Science and Technology, Mechanical Engineering, Medical Physics, Meteorology, Nanotechnology, Naval Architecture, Oceanography, Optometry, Photonics, Planetary Science, Quantum Informatics, Renewable Energy, Telecommunications Engineering.

Psychology See Section B.

Religious studies Archaeology, Anthropology, Biblical Studies, Divinity, Philosophy, Psychology, Theology.

Social policy; Sociology; Health and social care Economics, Human Geography, Psychology, Social Work, Sociology. See also Section B.

Statistics Business Studies, Informatics. See also Mathematics (above) and Section B (Mathematics-related careers).

Travel and tourism; Leisure studies See Section B.

SECTION B
Choosing your course by career interests
An alternative strategy for deciding on the subject of your degree or diploma course is to relate it to your career interests. However, even though you may have set your mind on a particular career, it is important to remember that sometimes there are others which are very similar to your planned career. The following lists give examples of career areas, each followed by examples of some relevant degree subjects.

Accountancy Actuarial Science, Banking, Business Studies, Economics, Financial Services, Management Science.

Actuarial work Accountancy, Banking, Insurance.

Agricultural careers Agriculture and Countryside Management, Agricultural Engineering, Agricultural Surveying, Animal Sciences, Biological Sciences, Ecology, Environmental Science, Estate Management, Forestry, Horticulture, Plant Sciences, Surveying.

Animal careers Agricultural Sciences, Biological Sciences, Equine Science/Studies/Management, Veterinary Science, Zoology.

Archaeology Ancient History, Anthropology, Classical Civilisation and Classics, History of Art and Architecture.

Architecture Building, Civil Engineering, Construction Engineering and Management, Structural Engineering.

Art and Design careers Advertising, Architecture, Education (Art), Industrial Design, Landscape Architecture, Three Dimensional Design.

Astronomy Astrophysics, Mathematics, Physics.

Audiology Education of the Deaf, Nursing, Speech and Language Therapy.

Banking/Insurance Accountancy, Business Studies, Economics, Financial Services.

Biology-related careers Agricultural Sciences, Biochemistry, Ecology, Education, Environmental Health, Environmental Science, Genetics, Immunology, Medicine, Microbiology, Pharmacy, Plant Science, Physiology.

Book Publishing Advertising, Business Studies, Communications, Creative Writing, Journalism, Media Communication, Photography, Printing, Publishing, Science Communication, Web and Multimedia.

Brewing Biochemistry, Chemistry, Food Science.

Broadcasting Film and TV Studies, Journalism, Media Studies, Media and Communications Studies.

Building Architecture, Building Services Engineering, Building Surveying, Civil Engineering, Estate Management, General Practice Surveying, Land Surveying, Quantity Surveying.

Business Accountancy, Advertising, Banking, E-Commerce, Economics, Estate Management, Hospitality Management, Human Resource Management, Housing Management, Industrial Relations, Insurance, Logistics, Marketing, Public Relations, Supply Chain Management, Transport Management, Tourism.

Cartography Geographical Information Science, Geography, Land Surveying.

Catering Consumer Studies, Dietetics, Food Science, Hospitality Management, Nutrition.

Chemistry-related careers Agricultural Science, Biochemistry, Botany, Ceramics, Chemical Engineering, Colour Chemistry, Education, Geochemistry, Materials Science and Technology, Pharmacology, Pharmacy, Physiology, Technologies (for example Food, Plastics).

Computing Artificial Intelligence, Business Studies, Electronic Engineering, Mathematics, Microelectronics, Physics, Telecommunications.

Construction Architecture, Building, Building Services Engineering, Civil Engineering, Landscape Architecture, Quantity Surveying, Surveying, Town and Country Planning.

Dance Drama, Movement Studies, Performance/Performing Arts, Physical Education, Theatre Studies.

Dentistry Biochemistry, Dental Materials, Dental Technician, Equine Dentistry, Medicine, Nursing, Pharmacy.

Drama Dance, Education, Movement Studies, Teaching, Theatre Management.

Education British Sign Language, Conductive Education, Psychology, Social Work, Speech and Language Therapy, Youth Studies.

Engineering Engineering (including Chemical, Civil, Computing, Control, Electrical, Energy, Environmental, Food Process, Manufacturing, Mechanical, Microelectronics, Nuclear, Product Design, Software, Telecommunications), Geology and Geotechnics, Mathematics, Physics.

Estate Management Architecture, Building, Civil Engineering, Economics, Forestry, Housing Studies, Landscape Architecture, Property Development, Town and Country Planning.

Food and Accommodation Culinary Arts, Dietetics, Home Economics, Housing Management, Nutrition.

Food Science and Technology Biochemistry, Brewing, Chemistry, Culinary Arts, Dietetics, Food and Nutrition, Food Safety Management, Food Technology, Home Economics, Nutrition.

Forestry Arboriculture, Biological Sciences, Countryside Management, Ecology, Environmental Science, Plant Sciences, Rural Resource Management, Tropical Forestry, Urban Forestry.

Furniture Design Furniture Production, History of Art and Design, Three Dimensional Design, Timber Technology.

Geology-related careers Chemistry, Earth Sciences, Engineering (Civil, Minerals), Environmental Sciences, Geochemistry, Geography, Land Surveying, Soil Science.

Graphic Design Advertising, Photography, Printing.

Health and Safety careers Biomedical Sciences, Community and Health Studies, Environmental Health, Exercise and Health Science, Fire Science Engineering, Health Promotion, Health Sciences, Nursery Nursing, Occupational Safety and Health, Paramedic Science, Public Health, Public Services Management. (See also **Medical careers**.)

Horticulture Agriculture, Botany, Landscape Architecture, Plant Science.

Hospitality Management Business and Management, Events and Facilities Management, Food Science, Food Technology, Heritage Management, Hospitality Business Management, Human Resource Management, International Hospitality Management, Leisure Services Management, Travel and Tourism Management.

Housing Architecture, Estate Management, General Practice Surveying, Social Administration, Town and Country Planning.

Law Business Studies, Commercial Law, Consumer Law, Criminal Justice, European Law, Government and Politics, International History, Land Management, Legal Studies, Sociology.

Leisure and Recreation Countryside Management, Dance, Drama, Fitness Science, Hospitality Management, International Tourism Management, Movement Studies, Music, Physical Education, Sport Development, Sport and Leisure Management, Sports Management, Theatre Studies, Travel and Tourism.

Library and Information Management Administration, Business Information Systems, Information and Communication Studies, Information and Library Studies, Information Management, Information Sciences and Technology, Museum and Galleries Studies, Publishing.

Marketing Advertising, Business Studies, Consumer Science, E-Marketing, International Business, Printing and Packaging, Psychology, Public Relations, Travel and Tourism.

Materials Science/Metallurgy Automotive Materials, Chemistry, Engineering, Glass Science and Technology, Materials Technology, Mineral Surveying, Physics, Polymer Science, Sports Materials, Textile Science.

Mathematics-related careers Accountancy, Actuarial Science, Banking, Business Decision Mathematics, Business Studies, Computer Studies, Economics, Education, Engineering, Financial Mathematics, Mathematical Physics/Sciences, Physics, Quantity Surveying, Statistics.

Medical careers Anatomy, Biochemistry, Biological Sciences, Chiropractic, Dentistry, Genetics, Human Physiology, Medical Sciences/Medicine, Nursing, Occupational Therapy, Orthoptics, Osteopathy, Pharmacology, Pharmacy, Physiotherapy, Radiography, Social Sciences, Speech and Language Therapy, Sports Biomedicine.

Microelectronics Computer Studies, Electrical/Electronic Engineering.

Music Drama, Performance/Performing Arts, Theatre Studies.

Nautical careers Marine Engineering, Naval Architecture, Nautical Studies, Oceanography, Offshore Engineering.

Naval Architecture Marine Engineering, Maritime Studies, Offshore Engineering.

Nursing Anatomy, Applied Biology, Biochemistry, Biological Sciences, Biology, Dentistry, Education, Environmental Health and Community Studies, Health Studies, Human Biology, Medicine, Midwifery, Occupational Therapy, Orthoptics, Physiotherapy, Psychology, Podiatry, Radiography, Social Administration, Speech and Language Therapy. (See also **Medical careers**.)

Nutrition Dietetics, Food Science and Technology, Nursing.

Occupational Therapy Art, Nursing, Orthoptics, Physiotherapy, Psychology, Speech and Language Therapy.

Optometry (Ophthalmic Optics) Applied Physics, Orthoptics, Physics.

Photography/Film/TV Animation, Communication Studies (some courses), Digital Video Design, Documentary Communications, Film and Media, Graphic Art, Media Studies, Moving Image, Multimedia, Photography.

Physical Education Exercise Sciences, Fitness Science, Leisure and Recreation Management, Sport and Recreational Studies, Sports Science.

Physiotherapy Chiropractic, Exercise Science, Nursing, Orthoptics, Osteopathy, Physical Education.

Physics-related careers Applied Physics, Astronomy, Astrophysics, Education, Engineering (Civil, Electrical, Mechanical), Medical Instrumentation, Optometry (Ophthalmic Optics).

Production Technology Engineering (Mechanical, Manufacturing), Materials Science.

Property and Valuation Management Architecture, Estate Management, Quantity Surveying, Urban Land Economics.

Psychology Applied Social Studies, Cognitive Science, Occupational Therapy, Psychology (Clinical, Developmental, Educational, Experimental, Occupational, Social), Social Work.

Public Administration Applied Social Studies, Business Studies, Social Administration, Social Policy, Youth Studies.

Quantity Surveying Accountancy, Architecture, Building, Civil Engineering, Surveying (Building, Land and Valuation).

Radiography Anatomy, Audiology, Biological Sciences, Medical Photography, Nursing, Orthoptics, Photography, Physiology, Physiotherapy.

Silversmithing/Jewellery Three Dimensional Design.

Social Work Anthropology, Journalism, Politics and Government, Public Administration, Religious Studies, Social Administration, Sociology, Town and Country Planning, Youth Studies.

Speech and Language Therapy Audiology, Education (Special Education), Nursing, Occupational Therapy, Psychology, Radiography.

Statistics Business Studies, Economics, Informatics, Mathematics, Operational Research, Population Sciences.

Technology Applied Chemistry, Chemistry, Dental Technology, Food Science and Technology, Paper Science, Polymer Science, Timber Technology.

Textile Design Art, Clothing Studies, Fashion Design, Interior Design, Textile Management.

Theatre Design Drama, Interior Design, Leisure and Recreational Studies, Theatre Management, Theatre Studies.

Three Dimensional Design Architecture, Industrial Design, Interior Design, Theatre Design.

Town and Country Planning Architecture, Environmental Science, Estate Management, Geography, Leisure and Recreational Management, Planning Studies, Population Sciences, Statistics, Transport Management.

Transport Business Studies, Town and Country Planning.

Typography and Graphic Communication Graphic Design, Packaging Design, Printing, Publishing.

Veterinary careers Agricultural Sciences, Agriculture, Animal Sciences, Equine Dentistry, Equine Science, Medicine, Pharmacology, Pharmacy, Veterinary Medicine, Veterinary Nursing, Zoology.

COURSE TYPES AND DIFFERENCES

When choosing an honours (or ordinary) degree course, the first factors to consider are the course and subject requirements or preferences. Courses in the same subject at different universities and colleges can have different subject requirements so it is important to check the acceptability of your GCE A/AS and GCSE subjects (or equivalent) for your preferred courses. (See also the **Table of Equivalent Offers** in **Chapter 7** for information on the International, European and French Baccalaureates, Scottish Highers and the Irish Leaving Certificate, and **Appendix 1** for international qualifications.) Specific GCE A/AS-levels, and in some cases, GCSE subjects may be stipulated.

You will then need to decide on the type of course you want to follow. The way in which honours degree courses are arranged varies between institutions (see **Chapter 3**). For example, a subject might be offered as a single subject course (a single honours degree), or as a two-subject course (a joint honours degree), or as one of two, three or four subjects (a combined degree) or a major-minor degree (75 and 25% of each subject respectively). Courses also can vary considerably in their content. Many universities and colleges of higher education have modularised their courses which means you can choose modules of different subjects, so 'building' your course within specified 'pathways' with the help and approval of your course tutor. It also means that you are likely to be assessed after completing each module, rather than in your last year for all your previous years' learning. In almost every course the options and modules offered include some which reflect the research interests of individual members of staff. In some courses subsidiary subjects are available as minor courses alongside a single honours course. In an increasing number of courses these additional subjects include a European language, and the importance of this cannot be over-emphasised with the United Kingdom's membership of the European Union.

Many institutions have introduced credit accumulation and transfer arrangements especially in Scotland. This means that students are awarded credits for modules or units of study they have successfully completed which are accumulated towards a certificate, diploma or first degree.

When choosing your course it is important to remember that one course is not better than another – it is just different. The best course for you is the one which best suits **you**. To give some indication of the differences between courses, see **Course variations** in **Chapter 8**, and more fully in *Choosing Your Degree Course and University* (see **Appendix 3**). After provisionally choosing your courses, read the prospectuses again carefully to be sure that you understand what is included in the three, four or more years of study. Each institution differs in its course content even though the course titles may be the same and courses differ in other ways, for example, in their:

* subject/module options
* methods of assessment (eg unseen examinations, continuous assessment, project work, dissertations)
* contact time with tutors
* how they are taught (for example, frequency and size of lectures, seminars)
* practicals; field work requirements
* library, laboratory and studio facilities
* amount of free study time available.

These are useful points of comparison between courses in different institutions when you are making final course choices. Other important factors when comparing courses include the availability of opportunities for studying and working abroad during your course, and professional body accreditation of courses leading to certain professional careers (see **Appendix 2**).

SANDWICH DEGREE COURSES

Media coverage on student debt and the recent introduction of tuition fees (see **Chapter 4**) highlight the importance of sandwich courses. Many of these courses are on offer, in which industrial, commercial and public sector placements take place in the third year of a four-year degree course. Aston University reports that those working in industry and commerce may expect to earn £11,000 to £12,000 during their year out and, in very many cases, will have job offers from their firms when they graduate. During the placement year their tuition fees will be reduced by 50% whilst student loans will still apply. It should also be noted that many Higher National Diploma courses offer sandwich placements. For details of sandwich courses refer to the subject tables in **Chapter 8** and university/college websites and prospectuses.

Once you have chosen your course subject(s) the next step is to find out about the universities and colleges offering courses in your subject area. The next chapter, **Choosing Your University or College** provides information to help you do this.

see you there

To make the right choice of university, you need the right information.

We could give you a whole host of compelling reasons to choose Coventry - an innovative University in a thriving city.

We could talk about our courses - designed together with some of the biggest names in industry, giving you the best chance of success. We could tell you about how much we're investing to ensure you receive only the very best teaching and leading edge facilities.

Or we could talk about the city - like the University – built on a spirit of reinvention and enterprise – and the surrounding area is surprisingly good too.

But if you'd like to see for yourself, log on to **www.coventry.ac.uk** for further information.

Or call our admissions team on **024 7615 2222.**

Coventry University

WHICH UNIVERSITY? WHICH COLLEGE?

How do you decide?

Since your main objective for going into higher education is to obtain a degree or diploma, your course choice must take priority over deciding on a particular university or college. You have three, four or five years of study ahead and you need to choose a subject that will keep you interested. Motivation, therefore, is the most important factor. It is well worth realising that every year a large number of students – some 18% – drop out of their chosen courses before the end of the first year because the course or university or college life are very different from what they expected.

Finding a university or college that is right for you means that you have to spend time finding out about the institutions offering your chosen courses from their prospectuses and websites. This research is important because another contributory cause for students' unhappiness or drop-out is insufficient knowledge about the location of the universities and colleges they select. Many applicants have little idea of where those institutions are or what their environment is really like, and the discovery on arrival can unsettle even the well-motivated!

Most applicants look for places or courses with good reputations but they should be very cautious in following this approach. The word 'reputation' suggests that one place or course is better than another. It is true that some universities such as Oxford or Cambridge or London are well known, but this is no criterion of quality. Many applicants are concerned about employers' perceptions of their chosen university or college but it is likely that most employers are just as concerned with the quality of applicant and not necessarily with his or her place of study. Similarly, the quality of teaching is often regarded as important – which it is – although it is dangerous to assume that the most popular institutions have the best teachers! University league tables can be misleading since teaching staff in universities are not 'inspected'. These tables, therefore, do not reflect the enthusiasm and flair of university staff in communicating their subject, as most students come to realise! Whenever you have a chance, ask the students on the course for their views. Even so, it cannot be stressed enough that you will be expected to work on your own for a considerable part of the course.

The information in this chapter, therefore, is intended to help you find out about universities and colleges and the questions (see below) you should ask about them. The following chapter **University Course Profiles** gives you information about the types of courses they offer and how they are organised. This is important information that you need to know when choosing your university/college because these factors affect, for example, the amount of choice you have in what you study, and the opportunities you have for sandwich placements. You therefore need to read **Chapters 2** and **3** in conjunction so that you can find the university or college that is right for you.

The main objective when choosing the right place, however, is for applicants to try to identify the 'character' of each institution in which they are interested. This 'character' is a mix of factors which will determine whether or not an institution is 'right' for you and these factors can be identified by answering the following questions:

* Where is the institution located? Is it in town or on a self-contained campus?
* How far or close is it to home? (This is an increasingly important factor because of travel costs and their impact on your student loan.)
* What courses are on offer?
* How are studies organised?
* How good are the study facilities – libraries, laboratories, computers, teaching equipment?
* How many students are there?
* What leisure opportunities are there?
* What is the social life like?
* What are the tuition fees?
* How much does it cost to live in halls of residence, or in private accommodation?
* How much does it cost to travel to the university or college from student accommodation?
* Are there any bursaries or scholarships for undergraduates in your subject area?

The best way to choose what and where to study is to start by reading prospectuses and checking websites as these provide detailed information about all aspects of courses and facilities for students in universities and colleges. Readers wanting to compare institutions and courses are advised to refer to *Choosing Your Degree Course and University* (see **Appendix 3**) which provides information on individual subject areas and enables useful comparisons to be made between institutions offering the same course subjects.

The general rule for institution choice must be to regard universities and colleges as not better than the next, but different. Often your choice will be dictated by **location** (town, city, rural) or by **size** (large or small), by **distance** from home or by **travel** factors (particularly the ease or difficulty of reaching the university or college by public transport) and, of course, the availability of your preferred course.

It is important to note that, whilst financial help is available to all disadvantaged students at all universities, many universities also offer additional scholarships, bursaries and other awards covering a wide range of subject areas, often on the basis of academic excellence. See **Chapter 4**, and also *University Scholarships, Awards and Bursaries* (see **Appendix 3**) for full details of these awards for UK, EU and overseas students.

Another point worth noting concerns the older Scottish universities in which admission is generally to a faculty and not to a specific course or department. Students often study three subjects in Year 1 and either two or three in Year 2. Honours courses normally take four years although admission to the second year of the course is sometimes possible (see **Chapter 7**).

After reading the prospectuses and checking websites, visit some of the institutions that interest you. Many have open days and the dates of these are available from sixth form tutors, careers advisers and direct from the institutions concerned. Alternatively, applicants may write directly to the university or college and make arrangements for a personal visit.

Below are lists of universities, institutes and colleges of higher education, specialist colleges, and further education colleges offering higher education degree and diploma courses. Also provided are contact details for further information. Because of changes which continually take place in higher education, for example in the names of institutions, numbers and locations of campuses, readers should check websites and prospectuses for up-to-date information.

SECTION 1: UNIVERSITIES

Listed below are universities in the United Kingdom that offer degree and diploma courses at higher education level. Applications to these institutions are submitted through UCAS except for part-time courses, private universities and colleges, and further education courses. For current information refer to the websites shown and also to the UCAS *Directory* (for a full list of universities and colleges in UCAS) and to the UCAS *Big Guide* for a comprehensive list of degree and diploma courses (see **Appendix 3**).

Aberdeen A city-centre university on Scotland's east coast. *(University of Aberdeen, University Office, King's College, Regent Walk, Aberdeen, Grampian, Scotland AB24 3FX. Tel 01224 272000; Student Recruitment and Admissions Service 01224 272090/1; www.abdn.ac.uk)*

Abertay Dundee A modern city-centre campus. *(University of Abertay Dundee, 40 Bell Street, Dundee, Scotland DD1 1HG. Tel 01382 308000; www.abertay.ac.uk)*

Aberystwyth A coastal university with a striking campus. *(University of Wales, Aberystwyth, Old College, King Street, Aberystwyth, Ceredigion, Wales SY23 2AX. Tel 01970 623111; www.aber.ac.uk)*

American InterContinental Situated in central London, AIU London is a private university charging termly tuition fees from £4000. It is accredited in the UK by the Open University and is in the membership of the Quality Assurance Agency. *(American InterContinental University – London, 110 Marylebone High Street, London W1U 4RY. Tel 020 7467 5600; www.aiulondon.ac.uk)*

Anglia Ruskin Two campuses in Cambridge and Chelmsford, a smaller campus at Benfleet, and over 20 partner colleges throughout East Anglia and north-east London. *(Anglia Ruskin University, Bishop Hall Lane, Chelmsford, Essex CM1 1SQ. Tel 0845 271 3333; www.anglia.ac.uk)*

Arts London The University consists of four Colleges of Art and Design (Camberwell, Chelsea, Central Saint Martins (including Byam Shaw School of Art) and Wimbledon), the London College of Communication and the London College of Fashion. *(University of the Arts London, 65 Davies Street, London W1K 5DA. Tel 020 7514 6000; www.arts.ac.uk)*

Aston A green campus university in the centre of Birmingham with academic, sporting and social activities on site. *(Aston University, Aston Triangle, Birmingham B4 7ET. Tel 0121 204 3000; www.aston.ac.uk)*

Bangor A central site in Bangor on the Menai Straits with partner institutions throughout North Wales. *(University of Wales, Bangor, Gwynedd, Wales LL57 2DG. Tel 01248 351151; Undergraduate Admissions 01248 382017; www.bangor.ac.uk)*

Bath A rural campus outside Bath with college-based programmes available in Bath itself and throughout Wiltshire. *(University of Bath, Claverton Campus, Bath, Somerset BA2 7AY. Tel 01225 388388; Admissions Office 01225 386959; www.bath.ac.uk)*

Bath Spa A new university (2005) located on two campuses near Bath. *(Bath Spa University, Newton Park, Newton St Loe, Bath, Somerset BA2 9BN. Tel 01225 875875; www.bathspa.ac.uk)*

Bedfordshire This is a new university, formed in August 2006 from the merger of Luton University and the Bedford campus of De Montfort University. The main campus is in the centre of Luton. *(University of Bedfordshire, Park Square, Luton, Bedfordshire LU1 3JU. Tel 01234 400400; www.beds.ac.uk)*

Belfast (Queen's) A large campus situated in the south of the city. *(Queen's University of Belfast, University Road, Belfast, Northern Ireland BT7 1NN. Tel 028 9024 5133; Admissions 028 9097 5081; www.qub.ac.uk)*

Birmingham A 'red-brick' university on the Edgbaston site to the south of the city, with a second campus at Selly Oak. *(University of Birmingham, Edgbaston, Birmingham B15 2TT. Tel 0121 414 3344; Admissions 0121 415 8900; www.bham.ac.uk)*

Be unique

Bath Spa University could help you change your future.
We offer teaching of the highest quality across a wide range of
courses, from Foundation Degrees to Master's programmes.
We provide an inspiring and supportive environment -
our campuses are stunning. And, of course, Bath is a superb city.

To find out more about a unique University where each
student is valued as an individual, contact us now.
We have Open Days in May and October.

Tel: 01225 875 875
email: enquiries@bathspa.ac.uk
www.bathspa.ac.uk

let's change our future

Bolton A new (2005) university, situated on two campuses close to the town centre. (*University of Bolton, Deane Road, Bolton, Lancashire BL3 5AB. Tel 01204 900600; www.bolton.ac.uk*)

Bournemouth A compact university site in a large coastal resort, with seven partner colleges in the region also offering courses. (*Bournemouth University, Talbot Campus, Fern Barrow, Poole, Dorset BH12 5BB. Tel 01202 524111; www.bournemouth.ac.uk*)

Bradford The University's main campus is close to the city centre, with the management centre two miles away. (*University of Bradford, Richmond Road, Bradford, West Yorkshire BD7 1DP. Tel 01274 233081; Course Enquiries 01274 232323; www.brad.ac.uk*)

Brighton Situated on the south coast, the University has campuses in Brighton, Eastbourne and Hastings. University-validated courses are offered at several partner colleges. (*University of Brighton, Mithras House, Lewes Road, Brighton, East Sussex BN2 4AT. Tel 01273 600900; www.brighton.ac.uk*)

Brighton and Sussex Medical School (*BSMS Teaching Unit, University of Sussex, Brighton, East Sussex BN1 9PX; Tel 01275 644644; www.bsms.ac.uk*)

Bristol A city university with halls of residence in Stoke Bishop and Clifton. (*University of Bristol, Senate House, Tyndall Avenue, Bristol BS8 1TH. Tel 0117 928 9000; www.bris.ac.uk*)

Bristol UWE Three campuses to the north-east of the city centre with additional study centres in Bath, Gloucester and Swindon. Links with the Bristol Old Vic Theatre School and the Royal West of England Academy. (*University of the West of England, Frenchay Campus, Coldharbour Lane, Bristol BS16 1QY. Tel 0117 965 6261; www.uwe.ac.uk*)

Brunel A compact campus to the west of London at Uxbridge. Brunel also validates courses at the London School of Theology. (*Brunel University, Uxbridge, Middlesex UB8 3PH. Tel 01895 274000; Admissions 01895 265265; www.brunel.ac.uk*)

Buckingham A small independent university on a town campus some 40 miles north of London offering two-year (eight-term) degrees. (*University of Buckingham, Hunter Street, Buckingham MK18 1EG. Tel 01280 814080; www.buckingham.ac.uk*)

Cambridge Twenty-nine undergraduate colleges located throughout the city. **Colleges** Lucy Cavendish, New Hall and Newnham (women only); the following admit both men and women undergraduates: Christ's, Churchill, Clare, Corpus Christi, Downing, Emmanuel, Fitzwilliam, Girton, Gonville and Caius, Homerton, Jesus, King's, Magdalene, Pembroke, Peterhouse, Queens', Robinson, St Catharine's, St John's, Selwyn, Sidney Sussex, Trinity, Trinity Hall. Also Hughes Hall, St Edmund's and Wolfson (graduates and mature undergraduates). (Enquiries should be addressed to the *Tutor for Admissions, ... College, Cambridge* or to the *Cambridge Admissions Office, Fitzwilliam House, 32 Trumpington Street, Cambridge CB2 1QY. Tel 01223 333308; www.cam.ac.uk*)

Canterbury Christ Church A new university (2005) located near the city centre. (*Canterbury Christ Church University, North Holmes Road, Canterbury, Kent CT1 1QU. Tel: 01227 767700; www.canterbury.ac.uk*)

Cardiff The Cathays Park campus of the University is located in the city centre, with the Heath Park campus a mile to the south. (*Cardiff University, Cardiff, Wales CF10 3XQ. Tel 029 2087 4000; www.cardiff.ac.uk*)

Central Lancashire The University is located on a small campus in the city centre and also has campuses at Penrith and Carlisle. It also has 15 partner colleges. (*University of Central Lancashire, Preston PR1 2HE. Tel 01772 201201; www.uclan.ac.uk*)

Chester A new university (2005) located on a campus in Chester, with a second campus in Warrington. (*Chester University, Parkgate Road, Chester CH1 4BJ. Tel 01244 511000; www.chester.ac.uk*)

Chichester A small new university (2005) at Chichester and Bognor Regis on the south coast, and other sites at Crawley and the Isle of Wight.

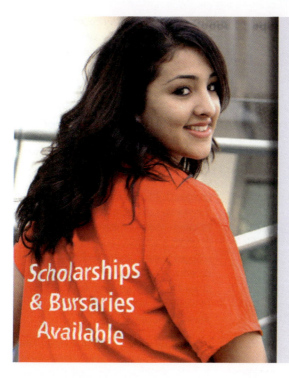

(University of Chichester, College Lane, Chichester, West Sussex PO19 6PE. Tel 01243 816000; www.chi.ac.uk)

City The University is situated in central London; Foundation courses are offered at a local college of further education. *(City University, Northampton Square, London EC1V 0HB. Tel 020 7040 5060; www.city.ac.uk)*

Coventry The University has a number of teaching centres throughout the city with courses offered in six partner colleges. *(Coventry University, Priory Street, Coventry CV1 5FB. Tel 024 7688 7688; www.cov.ac.uk)*

Cumbria A new university (August 2007) created by the merger of St Martin's College and Cumbria Institute of the Arts. *(University of Cumbria, Fusehill Street, Carlisle, Cumbria CA1 2HH. Tel 01228 616234; Enquiries 0845 606 1144; www.cumbria.ac.uk)*

De Montfort The University has two sites in Leicester. *(De Montfort University, The Gateway, Leicester LE1 9BH. Tel 0116 255 1551; Enquiries 08459 454647; www.dmu.ac.uk)*

Derby The University has two campuses: one is close to Derby city centre and the second at Buxton. It also has a wide network of partner colleges. *(University of Derby, Kedleston Road, Derby DE22 1GB. Tel 01332 590500; Course Enquiries 08701 202330; www.derby.ac.uk)*

Dundee A city-centre campus, with the Medical School and School of Nursing located at Ninewells Hospital to the west of the city. *(University of Dundee, Nethergate, Scotland DD1 4HN. Tel 01382 383000; Admissions and Student Recruitment 01382 344160; www.dundee.ac.uk)*

Durham Two sites, the main one in Durham city; the second, at Stockton, has two colleges on the Queen's Campus. *(University of Durham, Old Shire Hall, Old Elvet, Durham DH1 3HP. Tel 0191 334 2000; www.dur.ac.uk)*

East Anglia A parkland campus outside Norwich. *(University of East Anglia, Norwich NR4 7TJ. Tel 01603 456161; www.uea.ac.uk)*

East London Three campuses in London at Stratford, Docklands and Barking. Foundation degrees are offered at Barking, Newham and Redbridge Colleges. *(University of East London,*

Docklands Campus, 4–6 University Way, London E16 2RD. Tel 020 8223 3000; Admissions 020 8223 3333; www.uel.ac.uk)

Edge Hill A new university (2005) with its main campus on the outskirts of Ormskirk near Liverpool. *(Edge Hill University, Ormskirk Campus, St Helens Road, Ormskirk, Lancashire L39 4QP. Tel 01695 575171; www.edgehill.ac.uk)*

Edinburgh A city university consisting of the University Central Area in the city centre and the University King's Buildings on a site a mile to the south. *(University of Edinburgh, Student Recruitment and Admissions, 57 George Square, Edinburgh, Scotland EH8 9JU. Tel 0131 650 4360; www.ed.ac.uk)*

Essex A parkland campus two miles from Colchester. The University and the South East Essex College Partnership also provides degree schemes at the new Southend campus. The University validates degrees offered by Writtle College. *(University of Essex, Wivenhoe Park, Colchester, Essex CO4 3SQ. Tel 01206 873333; Undergraduate Enquiries 01206 872002; www.essex.ac.uk)*

Exeter Two sites in Exeter: the Streatham campus is the largest, and the St Luke's campus is a mile away. A third campus is situated a short distance from Falmouth in Cornwall. *(University of Exeter, Northcote House, The Queen's Drive, Exeter, Devon EX4 4QJ. Tel 01392 661000; www.ex.ac.uk)*

Glamorgan A single campus university and partnership arrangements with colleges in England and Wales. *(University of Glamorgan, Treforest, Pontypridd, Mid-Glamorgan, Wales CF37 1DL. Tel 0800 716925; www.glam.ac.uk)*

Glasgow The main campus is in the west end of the city, with a second base on the Crichton campus in Dumfries. Glasgow School of Art and the Scottish Agricultural College in Ayr are associated institutions. *(University of Glasgow, Glasgow, Strathclyde, Scotland G12 8QQ. Tel 0141 330 2000; www.gla.ac.uk)*

Glasgow Caledonian A city-centre campus; courses are also offered through four associated institutions. *(Glasgow Caledonian University, Cowcaddens Road, Glasgow, Strathclyde, Scotland G4 0BA. Tel 0141 331 3000; www.gcal.ac.uk)*

Gloucestershire Three campuses in Cheltenham and one in Gloucester. *(University of Gloucestershire, The Park, Cheltenham, Gloucestershire GL50 2RH. Tel 08707 210210; www.glos.ac.uk)*

Greenwich The main campus is the Maritime Greenwich campus, a second at Avery Hill Park, Eltham in south London and a third at Medway at Chatham Maritime. There are also eight partner colleges in east London and Kent. *(University of Greenwich, Maritime Greenwich Campus, Old Royal Naval College, Park Row, Greenwich, London SE10 9LS. Tel 0800 005006; www.gre.ac.uk)*

Heriot-Watt A large parkland campus seven miles west of Edinburgh, and the Scottish Borders campus at Galashiels 35 miles to the south. *(Heriot-Watt University, Edinburgh, Riccarton, Edinburgh, Lothian, Scotland EH14 4AS. Tel 0131 449 5111; www.hw.ac.uk)*

Hertfordshire Two campuses in Hatfield; courses also offered through a consortium of four Hertfordshire colleges. *(University of Hertfordshire, College Lane, Hatfield, Hertfordshire AL10 9AB. Tel 01707 284800; www.herts.ac.uk)*

Huddersfield A town-centre university with links to over 30 colleges of further education throughout the north of England. *(University of Huddersfield, Queensgate, Huddersfield HD1 3DH. Tel 01484 422288; www.hud.ac.uk)*

Hull The main campus is located in Hull, some two miles from the city centre, with a smaller campus in Scarborough. *(The University of Hull, Admissions Office, Cottingham Road, Hull, East Yorkshire HU6 7RX. Tel 01482 346311; www.hull.ac.uk)*

Hull York Medical School *(Admissions Section, University of York, Heslington, York YO10 5DD. Tel 08701 202323)*

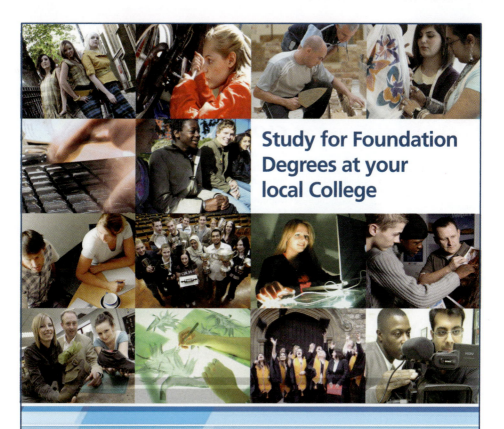

Study for Foundation Degrees at your local College

Imperial London The College will become an independent university, separate from the University of London, in July 2007. The central site is in South Kensington, with Applied Business Management courses based at the Wye campus at Ashford in Kent, and Medicine at St Mary's Hospital, Paddington and Charing Cross Hospital, Hammersmith. *(Imperial College London, South Kensington, London SW7 2AZ. Tel 020 7594 8001; www.imperial.ac.uk)*

Keele A small university on a green campus five miles from Stoke-on-Trent. *(The University of Keele, Keele, Staffordshire ST5 5BG. Tel 01782 621111; Admissions 01782 584005; www.keele.ac.uk)*

Kent A spacious campus near Canterbury, and a second in Chatham shared with the University of Greenwich. There are also three associated institutions – Mid Kent, South Kent and Canterbury Colleges. *(University of Kent, Recruitment and Admissions, Canterbury, Kent CT2 7NZ. Tel 01227 827272; www.kent.ac.uk)*

Kingston Four campuses in and around the town with easy access to London. *(Kingston University, Student Information and Advice Centre, 40–46 Surbiton Road, Kingston upon Thames, Surrey KT1 2HX. Tel 020 8547 7053; www.kingston.ac.uk)*

Lampeter A small university in a rural town in west Wales. *(University of Wales, Academic Registry, Lampeter, Ceredigion, Wales SA48 7ED. Tel 01570 422351; www.lamp.ac.uk)*

Lancaster Parkland site three miles south of the city centre. *(University, Bailrigg, Lancaster LA1 4YW. Tel 01524 65201; www.lancs.ac.uk)*

Leeds The University is sited on a campus in the centre of the city. *(University of Leeds, Leeds LS2 9JT. Tel 0113 243 1751; Course Enquiries 0113 243 2336; www.leeds.ac.uk)*

Leeds Metropolitan Two main campuses, one in the city and a second in Headingley on the outskirts of Leeds. There are two smaller campuses in Harrogate and Ripon. *(Leeds*

Metropolitan University, Civic Quarter, Leeds LS1 3HE. Tel 0113 283 3113; www.leedsmet.ac.uk)

Leicester The compact campus is located on the edge of the city. (University of Leicester, University Road, Leicester LE1 7RH. Tel 0116 252 2522; www.le.ac.uk)

Lincoln The Brayford and Cathedral campuses are in the city, with the Riseholme Park campus some five miles away; there is also a campus in Hull. (University of Lincoln, Brayford Pool, Lincoln LN6 7TS. Tel 01522 882000; www.lincoln.ac.uk)

Liverpool A large city-centre campus. (University of Liverpool, Liverpool L69 3BX. Tel 0151 794 2000; www.liv.ac.uk)

Liverpool Hope A new university (2005) outside Liverpool. (Liverpool Hope University, Hope Park, Liverpool L16 9JD. Tel 0151 291 3000; Admissions 0151 291 3295; www.hope.ac.uk)

Liverpool John Moores Three campuses in and around the city. (Liverpool John Moores University, Roscoe Court, 4 Rodney Street, Liverpool L1 2TZ. Tel 0151 231 5090; www.jmu.ac.uk)

London – Birkbeck (Birk) The College is situated in Bloomsbury in the London University precinct. (Birkbeck, University of London, Malet Street, Bloomsbury, London WC1E 7HX. Tel 08456 010174; www.bbk.ac.uk)

London – Central School of Speech and Drama Main campus at the Embassy Theatre. (Central School of Speech and Drama, Embassy Theatre, 64 Eton Avenue, Swiss Cottage, London NW3 3HY. Tel 020 7722 8183; www.cssd.ac.uk)

London – Goldsmiths (Gold) The College is located in south-east London. (Goldsmiths, University of London, Lewisham Way, New Cross, London SE14 6NW. Tel 020 7919 7171; www.goldsmiths.ac.uk)

London – Heythrop College (Hey) The College is located on a site in central London. (Heythrop College, University of London, Kensington Square, London W8 5HQ. Tel 020 7795 6600; www.heythrop.ac.uk)

London – Institute in Paris The Institute's Department of French Studies and Centre of Professional English operates in partnership with Queen Mary and Royal Holloway Colleges.

(University of London Institute in Paris, 9–11 rue de Constantine, 75340 Paris Cedex 07. Tel 00 33 1 44 11 73 83; www.ulip.lon.ac.uk)

London – King's College (King's) Three main campuses: Strand, Waterloo and London Bridge. (School of Biomedical and Health Sciences, Medicine and Dental Institute, Hodgkin Building, Guy's Campus, London Bridge, London SE1 1UL. Tel 020 7848 6511; Strand campus (a) School of Humanities: Tel 020 7848 2374; (b) School of Law: Tel 020 7848 2503; (c) School of Physical Sciences and Engineering: Tel 020 7873 2271; Florence Nightingale School of Nursing and Midwifery, James Clerk Maxwell Building, 57 Waterloo Road, London SE1 8WA. Tel 020 7848 4698; King's College London, Strand, London WC2R 2LS. Tel 020 7836 5454; www.kcl.ac.uk)

London – Queen Mary (QM) A city campus in the East End of London. (Barts and the London School of Medicine and Dentistry, Turner Street, London E1 2AD. Tel 020 7377 7611; Queen Mary, University of London, Mile End Road, London E1 4NS. Tel 020 7882 5555; www.qmul.ac.uk)

London – Royal Holloway (RH) A large campus with halls of residence located at Egham, some 19 miles from central London and three miles from Windsor. (Royal Holloway, University of London, Egham Hill, Egham, Surrey TW20 0EX. Tel 01784 434455; www.rhul.ac.uk)

London – Royal Veterinary College (RVC) The College is located in north London. (Royal Veterinary College, University of London, Royal College Street, London NW1 0TU. Tel 020 7468 5149; www.rvc.ac.uk)

London – St George's Located on a compact site in south-west London, St George's has extensive links with many hospitals and practices, and with Kingston University and Royal Holloway London. (St George's, University of London, Cranmer Terrace, Tooting, London SW17 0RE. Tel 020 8725 5201/0499; www.sgul.ac.uk)

London – London School of Economics and Political Science (LSE) A central London site near the Aldwych. LSE entrance examination may be required: see **Chapter 6**. (London School of Economics and Political Science, University of

London, PO Box 13401, Houghton Street, London WC2A 2AE. Tel 020 7955 7125/7769; www.lse.ac.uk)

London – School of Oriental and African Studies (SOAS) The School is located in Bloomsbury and Islington. (School of Oriental and African Studies, University of London, Thornhaugh Street, Russell Square, London WC1H 0XG. Tel 020 7637 2388; www.soas.ac.uk)

London – School of Pharmacy The School has a central London site near to the London University precinct. (School of Pharmacy, University of London, 29–39 Brunswick Square, London WC1N 1AX. Tel 020 7753 5800; www.pharmacy.ac.uk)

London – University College London (UCL) The College is located in Bloomsbury in the London University precinct. (University College London, Gower Street, London WC1E 6BT. Tel 020 7679 2000; www.ucl.ac.uk)

London Metropolitan Two campuses, one in north London (with the largest (new) science laboratory in Europe) and one in the City, and six partner colleges. (London Metropolitan University, 166–220 Holloway Road, London N7 8DB. Tel 020 7423 0000; Admissions 020 7133 4200; www.londonmet.ac.uk)

London South Bank Campuses at Southwark, Whipps Cross Hospital in east London and at the Harold Wood Hospital in Essex. (London South Bank University, 103 Borough Road, London SE1 0AA. Tel 020 7815 7815; www.lsbu.ac.uk)

Loughborough A large rural single-site campus one mile from the town centre. (Loughborough University, Loughborough, Leicestershire LE11 3TU. Tel 01509 263171; www.lboro.ac.uk)

Manchester A large university precinct one mile south of the city centre. (University of Manchester, Oxford Road, Manchester M13 9PL. Tel 0161 306 6000; www.man.ac.uk)

Manchester Metropolitan Five sites in Manchester and two in Cheshire, at Alsager and Crewe. (The Manchester Metropolitan University, All Saints Building, Manchester M15 6BH. Tel 0161 247 2000; www.mmu.ac.uk)

Middlesex Five campuses are located in the north of London, each focusing on a different subject area. (Middlesex University, North London Business Park, Oakleigh Road, London N11 1QS. Tel 020 8411 5000; Admissions 020 8411 5555; www.mdx.ac.uk)

Napier Four main campuses located in the centre and to the south-west of Edinburgh. (Napier University, Edinburgh, Craiglockart Campus, Edinburgh, Scotland EH14 1DJ. Tel 08452 606060; www.napier.ac.uk)

Newcastle A university campus in the city centre. (Newcastle University, 6 Kensington Terrace, Newcastle upon Tyne NE1 7RU. Tel 0191 222 6000; www.ncl.ac.uk)

Newport The University has two campuses, in Newport and Caerleon. (University of Wales, Newport, Caerleon Campus, PO Box 101, Newport, South Wales NP18 3YH. Tel 01633 430088; Admissions 01633 432030; www.newport.ac.uk)

Northampton This new university (2005) is located on two campuses close to the town centre. (University of Northampton, Park Campus, Boughton Green Road, Northampton NN2 7AL. Tel 0800 358 2232; www.northampton.ac.uk)

Northumbria Three campuses in and around Newcastle and one in Carlisle. (Northumbria University, Ellison Place, Newcastle upon Tyne NE1 8ST. Tel 0191 232 6002; www.northumbria.ac.uk)

Nottingham A large campus university to the west of the city. (The University of Nottingham, University Park, Nottingham NG7 2RD. Tel 0115 951 5151; www.nottingham.ac.uk)

Nottingham Trent The Clifton campus is four miles from the city and caters for Education, Humanities and Science whilst Brackenhurst, near Southwell, focuses on land-based subjects. (The Nottingham Trent University, Burton Street, Nottingham NG1 4BU. Tel 0115 941 8418; www.ntu.ac.uk)

Open University The UK's largest university for part-time higher education, providing supported distance learning for undergraduate (and postgraduate) students who must be over 18. Application and registration is made direct to the OU, and not through UCAS (at present). (The Open University, Student Registration and Enquiry

Service, PO Box 197, Milton Keynes MK7 6BJ. Tel 08453 006090; www.open.ac.uk)

Oxford Thirty colleges and seven private halls admitting undergraduates throughout the city. **Colleges** Balliol, Brasenose, Christ Church, Corpus Christi, Exeter, Harris Manchester (mature students only), Hertford, Jesus, Keble, Lady Margaret Hall, Lincoln, Magdalen, Mansfield, Merton, New, Oriel, Pembroke, Queen's, St Anne's, St Catherine's, St Edmund Hall, St Hilda's (women only, but has voted to admit men), St Hugh's, St John's, St Peter's, Somerville, Trinity, University, Wadham, Worcester. **Permanent private Halls** Blackfriars, Campion Hall (men only), Greyfriars, Regent's Park College, St Benet's Hall, St Stephen's House, Wycliffe. *(Enquiries should be addressed to The Tutor for Admissions . . . . College, Oxford, or to The Oxford Colleges Admissions Office, Wellington Square, Oxford OX1 2JD. Tel 01865 288000; www.ox.ac.uk)*

Oxford Brookes A campus university to the east of the city with 10 partner institutions and 10 overseas institutions. *(Oxford Brookes University, Headington Campus, Gipsy Lane, Oxford OX3 0BP. Tel 01865 741111; www.brookes.ac.uk)*

Paisley Three campuses, in Paisley, Ayr and Dumfries. *(University of Paisley, High Street, Paisley, Strathclyde, Scotland PA1 2BE. Tel 0141 848 3000; www.paisley.ac.uk)*

Peninsula College of Medicine and Dentistry Campuses at Exeter and Plymouth Universities. *(Peninsula Medical School, The John Bull Building, Tamar Science Park, Research Way, Plymouth, Devon PL6 8BU. Tel 01752 437444; www.pms.ac.uk)*

Plymouth Three campuses – Plymouth, Exeter (Art and Design) and Exmouth (Education); courses are also offered at 16 partner colleges. *(University of Plymouth, Drake Circus, Plymouth PL4 8AA. Tel 01752 600600; www.plym.ac.uk)*

Portsmouth The main campus is close to the town centre; courses are also taught at four colleges in Hampshire and Surrey. *(University of Portsmouth, University House, Winston Churchill*

Avenue, Portsmouth, Hampshire PO1 2UP. Tel 023 9284 8484; www.port.ac.uk)

Reading A large rural campus on the edge of the city. *(University of Reading, White Knights, PO Box 217, Reading, Berkshire RG6 6AH. Tel 0118 987 5123; www.rdg.ac.uk)*

Richmond, The American International University in London A private university with degrees validated by the Open University and accredited to the Middle States Association of Colleges and Schools in the USA. There are four entry points to courses in each academic year. *(Richmond, The American International University in London, Queens Road, Richmond upon Thames, Surrey TW10 6JP. Tel 020 8332 8200; Admissions 020 8332 9000; www.richmond.ac.uk)*

Robert Gordon Two campuses in and near the city centre. *(The Robert Gordon University, Schoolhill, Aberdeen, Grampian, Scotland AB10 1FR. Tel 01224 262000; Admissions 01224 262728; www.rgu.ac.uk)*

Roehampton The University, located in south-west London, close to Richmond Park, consists of four Colleges: Southlands, Digby Stuart, Froebel and Whitelands. *(Roehampton University, Erasmus House, Roehampton Lane, London SW15 5PU. Tel 020 8392 3000; Admissions 020 8392 3232; www.roehampton.ac.uk)*

St Andrews A town-centre university. *(University of St Andrews, College Gate, St Andrews, Fife, Scotland KY16 9AJ. Tel 01334 476161; www.st-and.ac.uk)*

Salford A city-centre campus university for all courses, except for Midwifery at Bury and Nursing at Eccles. *(The University of Salford, The Crescent, Salford, Greater Manchester M5 4WT. Tel 0161 295 5000; www.salford.ac.uk)*

Sheffield A campus university close to the city centre. *(University of Sheffield, Western Bank, Sheffield, South Yorkshire S10 2TN. Tel 0114 222 2000, Medical School 0114 271 2142; www.sheffield.ac.uk)*

Sheffield Hallam Three campuses are in the city centre, with two some two miles away. *(Sheffield Hallam University, City Campus, Howard Street, Sheffield, South Yorkshire S1 1WB.*

Tel 0114 225 5555; www.shu.ac.uk)

Southampton The University has six main campuses in Southampton and Winchester. *(University of Southampton, University Road, Southampton SO17 1BJ. Tel 023 8059 5000; www.soton.ac.uk)*

Southampton Solent A new university (2005) close to the city centre. *(Southampton Solent University, East Park Terrace, Southampton, Hampshire SO14 0YN. Tel 023 8031 9000; www.solent.ac.uk)*

Staffordshire Sites at Stafford, Stoke and Lichfield. *(Staffordshire University, College Road, Stoke on Trent, Staffordshire ST4 2DE. Tel 01782 294000; www.staffs.ac.uk)*

Stirling A rural campus of 310 acres. *(University of Stirling, Stirling, Central Scotland FK9 4LA. Tel 01786 473171; Admissions 01786 467044; www.stir.ac.uk)*

Strathclyde Main campus in Glasgow city centre, with the Jordanhill campus to the west of the city. *(The University of Strathclyde, 16 Richmond Street, Glasgow, Scotland G1 1XQ. Tel 0141 552 4400; www.strath.ac.uk)*

Sunderland Main campus in the city centre, with the Sir Tom Cowie campus across the river accommodating the Business School and Informatics Centre. *(University of Sunderland, Student Gateway, City Campus, Chester Road, Sunderland SR1 3SD. Tel 0191 515 3000; www.sunderland.ac.uk)*

Surrey A modern campus a mile from the city centre. Some foundation year teaching in local colleges. *(University of Surrey, Guildford, Surrey GU2 7XH. Tel 01483 300800; 01483 689305; www.surrey.ac.uk)*

Sussex A single site campus four miles from Brighton. *(University of Sussex, Sussex House, Falmer, Brighton, Sussex BN1 9RH. Tel 01273 606755; www.sussex.ac.uk)*

Swansea A parkland site outside the city. *(Swansea University, Singleton Park, Swansea, Wales SA2 8PP. Tel 01792 205678; Admissions 01792 295111; www.swan.ac.uk)*

Teesside A city-centre campus in Middlesbrough. Links with colleges in Teesside, Bishop Auckland

and Derwentside. *(University of Teesside, Borough Road, Middlesbrough, Tees Valley TS1 3BA. Tel 01642 218121; www.tees.ac.uk)*

Thames Valley Based on four sites in west London and five associated colleges. *(Thames Valley University, St Mary's Road, Ealing, London W5 5RF. Tel 020 8579 5000; Admissions 0800 036 8888; www.tvu.ac.uk)*

UCE Birmingham Eight teaching sites located around the city, each focusing on one subject. Four franchised colleges in Birmingham and Warwickshire also offer courses. *(University of Central England in Birmingham, Perry Bar, Birmingham B42 2SU. Tel 0121 331 5000; www.uce.ac.uk)*

Ulster Four campuses – in Coleraine, Jordanstown, Belfast and Londonderry. *(University of Ulster, Cromore Road, Coleraine, County Londonderry, Northern Ireland BT52 1SA. Tel 08700 400700; www.ulster.ac.uk)*

Warwick A single site campus three miles south-west of Coventry. *(University of Warwick, Coventry, Warwickshire CV4 7AL. Tel 024 7652 3523; Admissions 024 7652 3723; www.warwick.ac.uk)*

Westminster Four campuses (Cavendish, Marylebone and Regent in central London and Harrow) and eight associated colleges including the Trinity College of Music. *(University of Westminster, Headquarters Building, 309 Regent Street, London W1B 2UW. Tel 020 7911 5000; www.wmin.ac.uk)*

Winchester A new university (2005) situated close to the centre of the city. *(Winchester University, West Hill, Winchester, Hampshire SO22 4NR. Tel 01962 841515; www.winchester.ac.uk)*

Wolverhampton Two campuses in Wolverhampton and others in Walsall and Telford. *(University of Wolverhampton, Wulfruna Street, Wolverhampton, West Midlands WV1 1SB. Tel 01902 321000; www.wlv.ac.uk)*

Worcester A small new university (2005) located on a campus a short distance from the city centre. *(Worcester University, Henwick Grove, Worcester WR2 6AJ. Tel 01905 855000; www.worc.ac.uk)*

York A parkland campus situated on the outskirts of the city and a second campus in the city centre. *(University of York, Heslington, York YO10 5DD. Tel 01904 430000; www.york.ac.uk)*

York St John This new university (2006) is located on an eight-acre site facing York Minster, five minutes' walk from York city centre. *(York St John University, Lord Mayor's Walk, York YO31 7EX. Tel 01904 716598; www.yorksj.ac.uk)*

SECTION 2: UNIVERSITY COLLEGES AND COLLEGES AND INSTITUTES OF HIGHER EDUCATION.

Changes are taking place fast in this higher education sector, with several colleges becoming universities in the last year. Changes are also taking place in the further education sector (see Section 6) to give more degree course opportunities. All this means that you can study for a degree or diploma in a wide range of colleges, and it is important that you read prospectuses and check websites carefully and go to open days to find out as much as you can about them and about their courses which interest you.

Applications for full-time courses at the institutions listed below are through UCAS. Refer to the UCAS *Directory* and the UCAS *Big Guide* for details (see **Appendix 3**).

Bell College Almada Street, Hamilton, Lanarkshire, Scotland ML3 0JB. Tel 01698 283100; www.bell.ac.uk

Birmingham College of Food, Tourism and Creative Studies Summer Row, Birmingham, West Midlands B3 1JB. Tel 0121 604 1000; www.bcftcs.ac.uk

Bishop Grosseteste College Newport, Lincoln LN1 3DY. Tel 01522 527347; www.bgc.ac.uk

Bradford College Great Horton Road, Bradford, West Yorkshire BD7 1AY. Tel 01274 433333; www.bradfordcollege.ac.uk

Buckinghamshire Chilterns University College Queen Alexandra Road, High Wycombe, Buckinghamshire HP11 2JZ. Tel 01494 605060; www.bcuc.ac.uk

Colchester Institute Sheepen Road, Colchester, Essex CO3 3LL. Tel 01206 518777; www.colchester.ac.uk

Creative Arts University College The University College for the Creative Arts at Canterbury, Epsom, Farnham, Maidstone and Rochester, Oakwood Park, Maidstone, Kent ME16 8AG. Tel 01622 620000; www.ucreative.ac.uk

East Lancashire Institute of Higher Education (at Blackburn College), Feilden Street, Blackburn BB2 1LH. Tel 01254 292594; www.blackburn.ac.uk

Falmouth University College Woodlane, Falmouth, Cornwall TR11 4RH. Tel 01326 211077; www.falmouth.ac.uk

Harper Adams University College Newport, Shropshire TF10 8NB. Tel 01952 820280; www.harper-adams.ac.uk

Leeds Trinity and All Saints College Brownberrie Lane, Horsforth, Leeds LS18 5HD. Tel 0113 283 7100; Admissions 0113 283 7123; www.tasc.ac.uk

Marjon – The College of St Mark and St John Derriford Road, Plymouth, Devon PL6 8BH. Tel 01752 636700; Admissions 01752 636890; www.marjon.ac.uk

Newman College of Higher Education Genners Lane, Bartley Green, Birmingham, West Midlands B32 3NT. Tel 0121 476 1181; www.newman.ac.uk

North East Wales Institute of Higher Education Plas Coch Campus, Mold Road, Wrexham, Clwyd, Wales LL11 2AW. Tel 01978 290666; www.newi.ac.uk

Queen Margaret University College Clerwood Terrace, Corstorphine, Edinburgh EH12 8TS. Tel 0131 317 3000; www.qmuc.ac.uk

St Martin's College, Lancaster; Ambleside; Carlisle; London Now part of University of Cumbria (see Section 1)

St Mary's University College Waldegrave Road, Strawberry Hill, Twickenham, Middlesex TW1 4SX. Tel 020 8240 4000; www.smuc.ac.uk (not in UCAS)

St Mary's University College 191 Falls Road, Belfast, Northern Ireland BT12 6FE. Tel 028 9032 7678; www.stmarys-belfast.ac.uk

Stranmillis University College Stranmillis Road, Belfast, Northern Ireland BT9 5DY. Tel 028 9038 1271; www.stran.ac.uk

Suffolk University Campus Ipswich, Suffolk IP4 1LT. Tel 01473 255885; www.suffolk.ac.uk

Swansea Institute of Higher Education Mount Pleasant, Swansea, Wales SA1 6ED. Tel 01792 481000; www.sihe.ac.uk

Trinity College Carmarthen College Road, Carmarthen, Wales SA31 3EP. Tel 01267 676767; www.trinity-cm.ac.uk

UHI Millennium Institute (UHI): The UHI is based on a partnership of colleges and research institutes, each with its own distinctive character. Full-time undergraduate courses are provided by the following partner colleges (for addresses see Section 7). Institutions are shown by initials in the tables in **Chapter 8**: Argyll College (AC), Highland Theological College (HTC), Inverness College (IC), Lews Castle College (LCC), Lochaber College (LOC), Moray College (MC), Ness Foundation (NF), North Atlantic Fisheries College (NAFC), North Highland College (NHC), Orkney College (OC), Perth College (PC), Sabhal Mor Ostaig (SMO), Scottish Association for Marine Science (SAMS) and Shetland College (SC). Enquiries to the Registry. *(UHI Millennium Institute, Executive Office, Ness Walk, Inverness, Scotland IV3 5SQ. Tel 01463 279000; www.uhi.ac.uk)*

University of Wales Institute, Cardiff PO Box 377, Llandaff Campus, Western Avenue, Cardiff, Wales CF5 2SG. Tel 029 2041 6070; www.uwic.ac.uk

SECTION 3: COLLEGES OF AGRICULTURE AND HORTICULTURE

Some colleges are in the UCAS scheme for some or all of their courses (see UCAS *Directory* for details). Apply direct to colleges for courses outside UCAS.

NB Degree and diploma courses in Agriculture and Horticulture are also offered by some universities and some university colleges (see Sections 1 and 2) and also by some further education colleges (see Sections 6 and 7).

Askham Bryan College Askham Bryan, York YO23 3FR. Tel 01904 772211; www.askham-bryan.ac.uk

Berkshire College of Agriculture (BCA) Hall Place, Burchetts Green, Maidenhead, Berkshire SL6 6QR. Tel 01628 824444; www.bca.ac.uk

Bicton College of Agriculture East Budleigh, Budleigh Salterton, Devon EX9 7BY. Tel 01395 562400; www.bicton.ac.uk

Bishop Burton College York Road, Bishop Burton, Beverley, East Yorkshire HU17 8QG. Tel 01964 553000; www.bishopburton.ac.uk

Cambridgeshire College of Agriculture and Horticulture Landbeach Road, Milton, Cambridge CB4 6DB. Tel 01223 860701.

Capel Manor College Bullsmore Lane, Enfield, Middlesex EN1 4RQ. Tel 08456 122122; www.capel.ac.uk

College of Agriculture, Food and Rural Enterprise (CAFRE) Greenmount Campus, 22 Greenmount Road, Antrim, Northern Ireland BT41 4PU. Tel 08000 284291; www.cafre.ac.uk

Duchy College Cornwall College Duchy College, Rosewarne Campus, Camborne, Cornwall TR14 0AB. Tel 01209 722100; www.duchy.ac.uk

East Durham and Houghall Community College Houghall Centre, Durham DH1 3SG. Tel 0191 518 8222; www.edhcc.ac.uk

Harper Adams University College Newport, Shropshire TF10 8NB. Tel 01952 820280; www.harper-adams.ac.uk (See also Section 2)

Hartpury College (an Associate Faculty of Bristol UWE) Hartpury House, Hartpury, Gloucester GL19 3BE. Tel 01452 700283/702132; www.hartpury.ac.uk

Myerscough College (an Associate College of the University of Central Lancashire) Myerscough Hall, St Michael's Road, Bilsborrow, Preston, Lancashire PR3 0RY. Tel 01995 642222; www.myerscough.ac.uk

Otley College Charity Lane, Otley, Ipswich, Suffolk IP6 9EY. Tel 01473 785543; www.otleycollege.ac.uk

Pershore Group of Colleges (includes Pershore College and Holme Lacy College) Pershore Campus, Avonbank, Pershore, Worcestershire WR10 3JP. Tel 01386 552443; www.pershore.ac.uk

Reaseheath College Reaseheath, Nantwich, Cheshire CW5 6DF. Tel 01270 625131; Course Information 01270 613242; www.reaseheath.ac.uk

Rodbaston College Penkridge, Staffordshire ST19 5PH. Tel 01785 712209; www.rodbaston.com

Royal Agricultural College Cirencester, Gloucestershire GL7 6JS. Tel 01285 652531; www.rac.ac.uk

Scottish Agricultural College (SAC) Student Recruitment and Admissions Office, SAC Ayr Campus, Auchincruive Estate, Ayr KA6 5HW. Tel 0800 269453; www.sac.ac.uk

Shuttleworth College Old Warden Park, Biggleswade, Bedfordshire SG18 9EA. Tel 01767 626222; www.shuttleworth.ac.uk

Sparsholt College Hampshire Sparsholt, Winchester, Hampshire SO21 2NF. Tel 01962 776441; www.sparsholt.ac.uk

Warwickshire College Warwick New Road, Leamington Spa, Warwickshire CV32 5JE. Tel 01926 318000/0800 783 6767; www.warkscol.ac.uk

Welsh College of Horticulture Northop, Mold, Flintshire, Wales CH7 6AA. Tel 01352 841000; www.wcoh.ac.uk

Writtle College (an Associate College of Essex University) Chelmsford, Essex CM1 3RR. Tel 01245 424200; www.writtle.ac.uk

SECTION 4: COLLEGES OF ART

Many colleges of art are in UCAS for some or all of their courses (see the UCAS *Directory* for details). Some have now merged with universities – check with the UCAS *Directory* and prospectuses for details. Note that Art and Design courses are also offered by universities and higher and further education colleges. Apply direct to colleges for courses outside UCAS.

Architectural Association School of Architecture 36 Bedford Square, London WC1B 3ES. Tel 020 7887 4000; www.aaschool.ac.uk

Arts Institute at Bournemouth Wallisdown, Poole, Dorset BH12 5HH. Tel 01202 533011; www.aib.ac.uk

Camberwell College of Arts (University of the Arts London) Peckham Road, London SE5 8UF. Tel 020 7514 6302; www.camberwell.arts.ac.uk

Central Saint Martins College of Art and Design (University of the Arts London) Southampton Row, Holborn, London WC1B 4AP. Tel 020 7514 7022; www.csm.arts.ac.uk

Chelsea College of Art and Design (University of the Arts London) 16 John Islip Street, London SW1P 4JU. Tel 020 7514 7751; www.chelsea.arts.ac.uk

City and Guilds of London Art School 124 Kennington Park Road, London SE11 4DJ. Tel 020 7735 2306; www.cityandguildsartschool.ac.uk

Cleveland College of Art and Design Green Lane, Linthorpe, Middlesbrough TS5 7RJ. Tel 01642 288000; Student Recruitment 01642 288888; www.ccad.ac.uk

Creative Arts (UC) University College for the Creative Arts at Canterbury, Epsom, Farnham, Maidstone and Rochester, Oakwood Park, Maidstone, Kent ME16 8AG. Tel 01622 620000; www.ucreative.ac.uk

Cumbria Institute of the Arts Now part of University of Cumbria (see Section 1)

Dartington College of Arts Dartington Hall Estate, Totnes, Devon TQ9 6EJ. Tel 01803 862224; www.dartington.ac.uk

Dewsbury College (incorporating Batley School of Art and Design) Halifax Road, Dewsbury, West Yorkshire WF13 2AS. Tel 01924 436221; www.dewsbury.ac.uk

Edinburgh College of Art Lauriston Place, Edinburgh, EH3 9DF. Tel 0131 221 6000; www.eca.ac.uk

Choosing Your University And Degree Course... And Completing Your UCAS Form?

Why not contact Brian Heap, the author of *Degree Course Offers, Choosing Your Degree Course and University* and *University Scholarships, Awards and Bursaries* for a personal interview or a telephone consultation for advice on such issues as:

- Choosing A-level subjects (which are the best subjects and for which courses!)
- Degrees and Diploma courses (making the right choice from a list of thousands!)
- Completing your UCAS form (will the admissions tutor remember your personal statement?)
- Choosing the right university or college (the best ones for you and your courses)

For details of services and consultation fees contact:
The Higher Education Advice and Planning Service

tel: 01386 859355 email: heaps@dial.pipex.com

Glamorgan Centre for Art and Design Technology Glyntaff Road, Glyntaff, Pontypridd, Glamorgan, Wales CF37 4AT. Tel 01443 663309; www.gcadt.ac.uk

Glasgow School of Art 167 Renfrew Street, Glasgow, Strathclyde G3 6RQ. Tel 0141 353 4500; www.gsa.ac.uk

Gray's School of Art (Robert Gordon University) School Hill, Aberdeen, Grampian, Scotland AB10 1FR. Tel 01224 262000; www.rgu.ac.uk

Heatherley's School of Fine Art 80 Upcerne Road, London SW10 0SH. Tel 020 7351 4190; www.heatherleys.org

Herefordshire College of Art and Design Folly Lane, Hereford HR1 1LT. Tel 01432 273359; www.hereford-art-col.ac.uk

Leeds College of Art and Design Jacob Kramer Building, Blenheim Walk, Leeds LS2 9AQ. Tel 0113 202 8000; www.leeds-art.ac.uk

London College of Communication (University of the Arts London) Elephant and Castle, London SE1 6SB. Tel 020 7514 6500; www.lcc.arts.ac.uk

London College of Fashion (University of the Arts London) 20 John Princes' Street, London W1G 0BJ. Tel 020 7514 7500; www.fashion.arts.ac.uk

Norwich School of Art and Design Francis House, 3–7 Redwell Street, Norwich, Norfolk NR2 4SN. Tel 01603 610561; www.nsad.ac.uk

Plymouth College of Art and Design Tavistock Place, Plymouth, Devon PL4 8AT. Tel 01752 203434; www.pcad.ac.uk

Ravensbourne College of Design and Communication Walden Road, Chislehurst, Kent BR7 5SN. Tel 020 8289 4900; www.rave.ac.uk

Sotheby's Institute of Art 30 Bedford Square, Bloomsbury, London WC1B 3EE. Tel 020 7462 3232; www.sothebysinstitutelondon.com

Wimbledon College of Art (University of the Arts London) Merton Hall Road, London SW19 3QA. Tel 020 7514 9641; Admissions 020 7514 9687; www.wimbledon.ac.uk

Winchester School of Art (part of Southampton University) Park Avenue, Winchester, Hampshire SO23 8DL. Tel 023 8059 4741; www.wsa.soton.ac.uk

SECTION 5: COLLEGES OF DANCE, DRAMA, MUSIC AND SPEECH

Some colleges are in UCAS for some or all of their courses (see UCAS *Directory* for details). Apply direct to colleges for courses outside UCAS. Note that Music, Dance and Drama are also offered by universities and higher education colleges.

Arts Educational Schools London Cone Ripman House, 14 Bath Road, London W4 1LY. Tel for acting 020 8987 6655; for musical theatre 020 8987 6666; www.artsed.co.uk

Birmingham Conservatoire Paradise Place, Birmingham B3 3HG. Tel 0121 331 5901/2; www.conservatoire.uce.ac.uk

Birmingham School of Acting The Link Building, Paradise Place, Birmingham, West Midlands B3 3HJ. Tel 0121 262 6800; www.bssd.ac.uk

Bristol Old Vic Theatre School 1–2 Downside Road, Clifton, Bristol BS8 2XF. Tel 0117 973 3535; www.oldvic.ac.uk

Drama Centre London (part of Central Saint Martins: see University of the Arts London) First Floor, Saffron House, 10 Back Hill, London EC1R 5LQ. Tel 020 7514 8778; www.csm.arts.ac.uk/drama

East 15 Acting School Hatfields, Rectory Lane, Loughton, Essex IG10 3RY. Tel 020 8508 5983; www.east15.ac.uk

GSA Conservatoire Millmead Terrace, Guildford, Surrey GU2 4YT. Tel 01483 560701; www.conservatoire.org

Guildhall School of Music and Drama Silk Street, Barbican, London EC2Y 8DT. Tel 020 7628 2571; www.gsmd.ac.uk

Laban (Trinity Laban) Creekside, London SE8 3DZ. Tel 020 8691 8600; www.laban.org

Leeds College of Music 3 Quarry Hill, Leeds, West Yorkshire LS2 7PD. Tel 0113 222 3400; Course Enquiries 0113 222 3416; www.lcm.ac.uk

Liverpool Institute for Performing Arts (LIPA)
Mount Street, Liverpool L1 9HF. Tel 0151 330
3000; www.lipa.ac.uk

**London Academy of Music and Dramatic Art
(LAMDA)** 155 Talgarth Road, London W14 9DA.
Tel 020 8834 0500; www.lamda.org.uk

Mountview Academy of Theatre Arts Ralph
Richardson Memorial Studios, Clarendon Road,
Wood Green, London N22 6XF. Tel 020 8881
2201; www.mountview.ac.uk

Northern School of Contemporary Dance 98
Chapeltown Road, Leeds LS7 4BH.
Tel 0113 219 3000; www.nscd.ac.uk.

Rose Bruford College Lamorbey Park Campus,
Burnt Oak Lane, Sidcup, Kent DA15 9DF.
Tel 020 8308 2600; www.bruford.ac.uk

Royal Academy of Dance 36 Battersea Square,
London SW11 3RA. Tel 020 7326 8000;
www.rad.org.uk

Royal Academy of Dramatic Art (RADA) 62–64
Gower Street, London WC1E 6ED. Tel 020 7636
7076; Prospectus 020 7908 4710; www.rada.org

Royal Academy of Music Marylebone Road,
London NW1 5HT. Tel 020 7873 7373;
www.ram.ac.uk

Royal Ballet School 46 Floral Street, Covent
Garden, London WC2E 9DA. Tel 020 7845 7073;
www.royal-ballet-school.org.uk

Royal College of Music Prince Consort Road,
London SW7 2BS. Tel 020 7589 3643;
www.rcm.ac.uk

Royal Northern College of Music 124 Oxford Road,
Manchester M13 9RD. Tel 0161 907 5200;
www.rncm.ac.uk

Royal Scottish Academy of Music and Drama 100
Renfrew Street, Glasgow, Strathclyde, Scotland
G2 3DB. Tel 0141 332 4101; www.rsamd.ac.uk

Royal Welsh College of Music and Drama Castle
Grounds, Cathays Park, Cardiff, Wales CF10 3ER.
Tel 029 2034 2854; www.rwcmd.ac.uk

Trinity College of Music (Trinity Laban) King
Charles Court, Old Royal Naval College,
Greenwich, London SE10 9JK. Tel 020 8305 4444;
www.tcm.ac.uk

SECTION 6: FURTHER EDUCATION AND OTHER COLLEGES OFFERING HIGHER EDUCATION COURSES

The following colleges appear under various
subject headings in the tables in **Chapter 8** and
some are in UCAS for some of their courses. See
prospectuses and websites for application details.

Abingdon and Witney College Abingdon Campus,
Wootton Road, Abingdon, Oxfordshire OX14 1GG.
Tel 01235 555585; www.abingdon-witney.ac.uk

Accrington and Rossendale College Sandy Lane,
Accrington, Lancashire BB5 2AW. Tel 01254
389933; Information and Guidance 01254
354354; www.accross.ac.uk

Aylesbury College Oxford Road, Aylesbury,
Buckinghamshire HP21 8PD. Tel 01296 588588;
www.aylesbury.ac.uk

Barnet College Wood Street, Barnet, Hertfordshire
EN5 4AZ. Tel 020 8200 8300; Enrolment/Course
Information 020 8266 4000; www.barnet.ac.uk

Barking College Dagenham Road, Romford,
Essex RM7 0XU. Tel 01708 770000;
www.barkingcollege.ac.uk

Barnsley University Centre Central Registry,
PO Box 266, Church Street, Barnsley, South
Yorkshire S70 2AN. Tel 01226 606262;
www.barnsley.hud.ac.uk

Basingstoke College of Technology Worting Road,
Basingstoke, Hampshire RG21 8TN. Tel 01256
354141; www.bcot.ac.uk

Bedford College Cauldwell Street, Bedford MK42
9AH. Tel 01234 291000; Admissions 08000
740234; www.bedford.ac.uk

Bexley College Tower Road, Belvedere, Kent
DA17 6JA. Tel 01322 442331;
www.bexley.ac.uk

Bishop Auckland College Woodhouse Lane, Bishop
Auckland, County Durham DL14 6JZ. Tel 01388
443000; Course Enquiries 08000 926506;
www.bacoll.ac.uk

Blackburn College (partner college of East
Lancashire (IHE)) Feilden Street, Blackburn,
Lancashire BB2 1LH. Tel 01254 55144; Student
Hotline 01254 292929; www.blackburn.ac.uk

Blackpool and the Fylde College Palatine Road, Blackpool, Lancashire FY1 4DW. Tel 01253 352352; www.blackpool.ac.uk

Bournemouth and Poole College Customer Enquiry Centre, North Road, Poole, Dorset BH14 0LS. Tel 01202 205205; www.thecollege.co.uk

Bournville College Bristol Road South, Northfield, Birmingham, West Midlands B31 2AJ. Tel 0121 483 1000; Course Enquiries 0121 483 1111; www.bournville.ac.uk

Bracknell and Wokingham College College Information Centre, Church Road, Bracknell, Berkshire RG12 1DJ. Tel 0845 330 3343; www.bracknell.ac.uk

Braintree College Church Lane, Braintree, Essex CM7 5SN. Tel 01376 321711; Course Enquiries 01376 557020; www.braintree.ac.uk

Boston College Skirbeck Road, Boston, Lincolnshire PE21 6JF. Tel 01205 365701; Course Information 01205 313218; www.boston.ac.uk

Bridgwater College Bath Road, Bridgwater, Somerset TA6 4PZ. Tel 01278 455464; Course Enquiries 01278 441234; www.bridgwater.ac.uk

British College of Osteopathic Medicine Lief House, 120–122 Finchley Road, London NW3 5HR. Tel 020 7435 6464; www.bcom.ac.uk

British School of Osteopathy 275 Borough High Street, London SE1 1JE. Tel 020 7407 0222; Student Recruitment 020 7089 5316; www.bso.ac.uk

Brockenhurst College Lyndhurst Road, Brockenhurst, Hampshire SO42 7ZE. Tel 01590 625555; www.brock.ac.uk

Bromley College of Further and Higher Education Rookery Lane, Bromley, Kent BR2 8HE. Tel 020 8295 7000; Course Enquiries 020 8295 7001; www.bromley.ac.uk

Brooklands College Heath Road, Weybridge, Surrey KT13 8TT. Tel 01932 797700; Course Information 01932 797797; www.brooklands.ac.uk

Brooksby Melton College Ashfordby Road, Melton Mowbray, Leicestershire LE13 0HJ. Tel 01664 850850; Course Enquiries 01664 855444; www.brooksbymelton.ac.uk

Burnley College Shorey Bank, off Ormerod Road, Burnley, Lancashire BB11 2RX. Tel 01282 711200; Student Services 01282 711222; www.burnley.ac.uk

Burton College Student Services, Lichfield Street, Burton on Trent, Staffordshire DE14 3RL. Tel 01283 494400; www.burton-college.ac.uk

Bury College Woodbury Centre, Market Street, Bury, Manchester BL9 0BG. Tel 0161 280 8280; Course Information 08000 925900; www.burycollege.ac.uk

Calderdale College Francis Street, Halifax, West Yorkshire HX1 3UZ. Tel 01422 399399; www.calderdale.ac.uk

Cambridge Regional College Kings Hedges Road, Cambridge CB4 2QT. Tel 01223 532240; www.camre.ac.uk

Canterbury College New Dover Road, Canterbury, Kent CT1 3AJ. Tel 01227 811111; Learning Advice/Courses 01227 811188; www.cant-col.ac.uk

Carlisle College Information Unit, Victoria Place, Carlisle, Cumbria CA1 1HS. Tel 01228 822703; www.carlisle.ac.uk

Carmel College Prescot Road, St Helens, Merseyside WA10 3AG. Tel 01744 452200; www.carmel.ac.uk

Carshalton College Nightingale Road, Carshalton, Surrey SM5 2EJ. Tel 020 8544 4444; www.carshalton.ac.uk

Castle College Nottingham Maid Marian Way; Nottingham NG1 6AB. Tel 08458 450500; www.castlecollege.ac.uk

CECOS London College 2–10 Osborn Street, London E1 6TD. Tel 020 7426 0167/8; www.cecos.co.uk

Cheadle and Marple Sixth Form College Marple Campus, Hibbert Lane, Marple, Stockport, Cheshire SK6 7PA. Tel 0161 484 6600; Admissions 0161 484 6602; www.camsfc.ac.uk

Chelmsford College Moulsham Street, Chelmsford, Essex CM2 0JQ. Tel 01245 265611; www.chelmsford-college.ac.uk

Chesterfield College Infirmary Road, Chesterfield, Derbyshire S41 7NG. Tel 01246 500500; www.chesterfield.ac.uk

Chichester College Westgate Fields, Chichester, West Sussex PO19 1SB. Tel 01243 786321; www.chichester.ac.uk

City of Bath College Student Advice Centre, Avon Street, Bath, Somerset BA1 1UP. Tel 01225 312191; Prospectuses 01225 328666; www.citybathcoll.ac.uk

City College Brighton and Hove Pelham Street, Brighton, East Sussex BN1 4FA. Tel 01273 667788; Course Advisers 01273 667759; www.ccb.ac.uk

City College, Birmingham Freepost MID 1755, Birmingham B33 0BR. Tel 0121 741 1000; Course Enquiries 08450 501144; www.citycol.ac.uk

City of Bristol College Bedminster Centre, Marksbury Road, Bristol BS3 5JL. Tel 0117 312 5000; www.cityofbristol.ac.uk

City College, Coventry Butts, Coventry CV1 3GD. Tel 024 7679 1000; Course Information 0800 616202; www.covcollege.ac.uk

City College, Manchester Whitworth Street, Manchester M1 3HB. Tel 0800 013 0123; www.ccm.ac.uk

City College, Norwich Ipswich Road, Norwich, Norfolk NR2 2LJ. Tel 01603 773311; www.ccn.ac.uk

City and Islington College The Marlborough Building, 383 Holloway Road, London N7 0RN. Tel 020 7700 9200; www.candi.ac.uk

City of Sunderland College Bede Centre, Durham Road, Sunderland, Tyne and Wear SR3 4AH. Tel 0191 511 6060; HE Admissions 0191 511 6260; www.citysun.ac.uk

City of Westminster College 25 Paddington Green, London W2 1NB. Tel 020 7723 8826; www.cwc.ac.uk

City of Wolverhampton College Paget Road Campus, Paget Road, Wolverhampton, West Midlands WV6 0DU. Tel 01902 836000; www.wolverhamptoncollege.ac.uk

Cliff College Calver, Hope Valley, Derbyshire S32 3XG. Tel 01246 584200/20; www.cliffcollege.org

College of North East London Tottenham Centre, High Road, Tottenham, London N15 4RU. Tel 020 8802 3111; Course Information 020 8442 3055; www.conel.ac.uk

College of North West London Dudden Hill Lane, London NW10 2XD. Tel 020 8208 5000; Course Information 020 8208 5050; www.cnwl.ac.uk

Coleg Llandrillo Cymru Llandudno Road, Rhos on Sea, Colwyn Bay, Wales LL28 4HZ. Tel 01492 546666; Admissions 01492 542339; www.llandrillo.ac.uk

Coleg Menai Ffriddoedd Road, Bangor, Gwynedd, Wales LL57 2TP. Tel 01248 370125; www.menai.ac.uk

Coleg Sir Gâr Graig Campus, Sandy Road, Pwll, Llanelli, Wales SA15 4DN. Tel 01554 748000; www.colegsirgar.ac.uk

College of West Anglia Tennyson Avenue, King's Lynn, Norfolk PE30 2QW. Tel 01553 761144; www.col-westanglia.ac.uk

Cornwall College Tregonnisey Road, St Austell, Cornwall PL25 4DJ. Tel 01726 226626; www.cornwall.ac.uk

Craven College High Street, Skipton, North Yorkshire BD23 1JY. Tel 01756 791411; www.craven-college.ac.uk

Cricklade College Charlton Road, Andover, Hampshire SP10 1EJ. Tel 01264 360000; www.cricklade.ac.uk

Croydon College College Road, Croydon CR9 1DX. Tel 020 8760 5914; www.croydon.ac.uk

Darlington College Central Park, Haughton Road, Darlington DL1 1DR. Tel 01325 503050; Information 01325 503030; www.darlington.ac.uk

Dearne Valley College Manvers Park, Wath upon Dearne, Rotherham, South Yorkshire S63 7EW. Tel 01709 513333; www.dearne-coll.ac.uk

Derby College Prince Charles Avenue, Mackworth, Derby DE22 4LR. Tel 01332 520200 or 0800 280289; www.derby-college.ac.uk

Derwentside College Consett Campus, Park Road, Consett, County Durham DH8 5EE. Tel 01207 585900; www.derwentside.ac.uk

Dudley College The Broadway, Dudley, West Midlands DY1 4AS. Tel 01384 363277; Course Enquiries 01384 363319; www.dudleycol.ac.uk

Dunstable College Kingsway, Dunstable, Bedfordshire LU5 4HG. Tel 01582 477776; Enquiries 0845 355 2525; www.dunstable.ac.uk

Ealing, Hammersmith and West London College Gliddon Road, Barons Court, London W14 9BL. Course Information Centre 0800 980 2185; www.westlondoncollege.ac.uk

East Berkshire College Langley Campus, Station Road, Langley, Berkshire SL3 8BX. Tel 01753 793338; Course Information 08009 230423; www.eastberks.ac.uk

East Devon College Admissions Department, Bolham Road, Tiverton, Devon EX16 6SH. Tel 01884 235264; www.edc.ac.uk

East Durham and Houghall Community College Burnhope Way Centre, Burnhope Way, Peterlee, County Durham SR8 1NU. Tel 0191 518 2000; www.edhcc.ac.uk

East Riding College Beverley Campus, Gallows Lane, Beverley, East Riding of Yorkshire HU17 7DT. Tel 0845 120 0037; www.eastridingcollege.ac.uk

East Surrey College Gatton Point North, Claremont Road, Redhill, Surrey RH1 2JX. Tel 01737 788444; www.esc.ac.uk

Eastleigh College Chestnut Avenue, Eastleigh, Hampshire SO50 5FS. Tel 023 8091 1000; www.eastleigh.ac.uk

Easton College Easton, Norwich, Norfolk NR9 5DX. Tel 01603 731200; www.easton.ac.uk

Enfield College 73 Hertford Road, Enfield, Middlesex EN3 5HA. Tel 020 8443 3434; www.enfield.ac.uk

European Business School London Regent's College, Inner Circle, Regent's Park, London NW1 4NS. Tel 020 7487 7505; www.ebslondon.ac.uk

European School of Osteopathy Boxley House, The Street, Boxley, Maidstone, Kent ME14 3DZ. Tel 01622 671558; www.eso.ac.uk

Exeter College Exeter Business School, Victoria House, 33–36 Queen Street, Exeter EX4 3SR. Tel 01392 205222; www.exe-col.ac.uk

Fareham College Bishopsfield Road, Fareham, Hampshire PO14 1NH. Tel 01329 815229; www.fareham.ac.uk

Farnborough College of Technology Boundary Road, Farnborough, Hampshire GU14 6SB. Tel 01252 407028; www.farn-ct.ac.uk

Filton College Filton Avenue, Filton, Bristol BS34 7AT. Tel 0117 931 2121; www.filton.ac.uk

Furness College Channelside, Barrow-in-Furness, Cumbria LA14 2PJ. Tel 01229 825017; www.furness.ac.uk

Gateshead College Durham Road, Low Fell, Gateshead NE9 5BN. Tel 0191 490 0300; www.gateshead.ac.uk

Gloucestershire College of Arts and Technology Gloucester Campus, Brunswick Road, Gloucester GL1 1HU. Tel 01452 532000; www.gloscat.ac.uk

Grantham College Stonebridge Road, Grantham, Lincolnshire NG31 9AP. Tel 01476 400200; Course Information 08000 521577; www.grantham.ac.uk

Great Yarmouth College Southtown, Great Yarmouth, Norfolk NR31 0ED. Tel 01493 655261; www.gyc.ac.uk

Greenwich School of Management Meridian House, Royal Hill, Greenwich, London SE10 8RD. Tel 020 8516 7800; www.greenwich-college.ac.uk

Grimsby Institute of Further and Higher Education Nuns Corner, Laceby Road, Grimsby, North East Lincolnshire DN34 5BQ. Tel 01472 311222; Course Information 0800 315002; www.grimsby.ac.uk

Guildford College Stoke Park Campus, Stoke Road, Guildford, Surrey GU1 1EZ. Tel 01483 448500; www.guildford.ac.uk

Hackney Community College Shoreditch Campus, Falkirk Street, London N1 6HQ. Tel 020 7613 9123; www.hackney.ac.uk

Hadlow College Hadlow, Tonbridge, Kent TN11 0AL. Tel 01732 850551; Course Enquiry Unit 0500 551434 (free); www.hadlow.ac.uk

Halesowen College Whittingham Road, Halesowen, West Midlands B63 3NA. Tel 0121 602 7777; www.halesowen.ac.uk

Harlow College Valizy Avenue, Harlow, Essex CM20 3LH. Tel 01279 868000; www.harlow-college.ac.uk

Harrow College Harrow on the Hill Campus, Lowlands Road, Harrow, Middlesex HA1 3AQ. Tel 020 8909 6000; www.harrow.ac.uk

Hastings College of Arts and Technology Archery Road, St Leonards on Sea, East Sussex TN38 0HX. Tel 01424 442222; Student Services 01424 458458; www.hastings.ac.uk

Havering College Ardleigh Green Road, Hornchurch, Essex RM11 2LL. Tel 01708 462801; www.havering-college.ac.uk

Henley College Coventry Henley Road, Bell Green, Coventry, West Midlands CV2 1ED. Tel 024 7662 6300/0800 252772; www.henley-cov.ac.uk

Herefordshire College of Technology Folly Lane, Hereford HR1 1LS. Tel 08000 321986; www.hereford-tech.ac.uk

Hertford Regional College Scotts Road, Ware, Hertfordshire SG12 9JF. Tel 01922 411411; www.hertreg.ac.uk

Highbury College, Portsmouth Dovercourt Road, Portsmouth, Hampshire PO6 2SA. Tel 023 9231 3373; www.highbury.ac.uk

Hillcroft College South Bank, Surbiton, Surrey KT6 6DF. Tel 020 8399 2688; www.hillcroft.ac.uk

Holborn College Woolwich Road, London SE7 8LN. Tel 020 8317 6000; www.holborncollege.ac.uk

Hopwood Hall College Rochdale Campus, St Mary's Gate, Rochdale OL12 6RY. Tel 01706 345346; www.hopwood.ac.uk

Huddersfield Technical College New North Road, Huddersfield, West Yorkshire HD1 5NN. Tel 01484 536521; www.huddcoll.ac.uk

Hull College The Queen's Gardens Centre, Wilberforce Drive, Hull, East Yorkshire HU1 3DG. Tel 01482 329943; www.hull-college.ac.uk

Huntingdonshire Regional College California Road, Huntingdon PE29 1BL. Tel 01480 379100; www.huntingdon.ac.uk

Isle of Wight College Medina Way, Newport, Isle of Wight PO30 5TA. Tel 01983 526631; www.iwightc.ac.uk

Keighley College Cavendish Street, Keighley, West Yorkshire BD21 3DF. Tel 01535 618600; www.keighley.ac.uk

Kendal College (The College of the South Lakes) Milnthorpe Road, Kendal, Cumbria LA9 5AY. Tel 01539 814700; Admissions 01539 814709; www.kendal.ac.uk

Kidderminster College Market Street, Kidderminster, Worcestershire DY10 1LX. Tel 01562 820811; www.kidderminster.ac.uk

Kingston College Kingston Hall Road, Kingston upon Thames, Surrey KT1 2AQ. Tel 020 8546 2151; www.kingston-college.ac.uk

Kingston Maurward College Kingston Maurward, Dorchester, Dorset DT2 8PY. Tel 01305 215000; Course Enquiries 01305 215032/215025; www.kmc.ac.uk

Knowsley Community College Kirkby Campus, Cherryfield Drive, Kirkby L32 8SF. Tel 0151 477 5708/08451 551055; www.knowsleycollege.ac.uk

Lakes College, West Cumbria Hallwood Road, Lillyhall Business Park, Workington, Cumbria CA14 4JN. Tel 01946 839300; www.lcwc.ac.uk

Lambeth College 45 Clapham Common South Side, London SW4 9BL. Tel 020 7501 5010; Course Information 020 7501 5000; www.lambeth.ac.uk

Lancaster and Morecambe College Morecambe Road, Lancaster LA1 2TY. Tel 01524 66215; www.lmc.ac.uk

Lansdowne College 40–44 Bark Place, London W2 4AT. Tel 020 7616 4400; www.lansdownecollege.com

Leeds College of Building North Street, Leeds, West Yorkshire LS2 7QT. Tel 0113 222 6000; Student Services 0113 222 6002; www.lcb.ac.uk

Leeds College of Technology Cookridge Street, Leeds, West Yorkshire LS2 8BL. Tel 0113 297 6300; Course Information 0113 297 6464; www.lct.ac.uk

Leeds Thomas Danby Roundhay Road, Leeds, West Yorkshire LS7 3BG. Tel 0113 249 4912; www.leedsthomasdanby.ac.uk

Leek College Stockwell Street, Leek, Staffordshire ST13 6DP. Tel 01538 398866; www.leek.ac.uk

Leicester College Freemen's Park Campus, Aylestone Road, Leicester LE2 7LW. Tel 0116 224 2240; www.leicestercollege.ac.uk

Leo Baeck College The Sternberg Centre, 80 East End Road, London N3 2SY. Tel 020 8349 5600; www.lbc.ac.uk

Lewisham College Lewisham Way, London SE4 1UT. Tel 020 8692 0353/0800 834545; www.lewisham.ac.uk

Lincoln College Monks Road, Lincoln LN2 5HQ. Tel 01522 876000; www.lincolncollege.ac.uk

Liverpool Community College Bankfield Road, Liverpool L13 0BQ. Tel 0151 709 3079; www.liv-coll.ac.uk

London College, UCK Admissions Office, Kensington Campus, Victoria Gardens, Notting Hill Gate, London W11 3PE. Tel 020 7243 4000; www.lcuck.org.uk

London School of Commerce Chaucer House, White Hart Yard, London SE1 1NX. Tel 020 7357 0077; www.lsclondon.co.uk

Loughborough College Radmoor Road, Loughborough, Leicestershire LE11 3BT. Tel 0845 166 2950; www.loucoll.ac.uk

Lowestoft College St Peters Street, Lowestoft, Suffolk NR32 2NB. Tel 0800 854695; www.lowestoft.ac.uk

Macclesfield College Park Lane, Macclesfield, Cheshire SK11 8LF. Tel 01625 410000; Information/Enrolment 01625 410002/50; www.macclesfield.ac.uk

Manchester College of Arts and Technology Openshaw Campus, Ashton Old Road, Openshaw, Manchester M11 2WH. Tel 08000 688585; www.mancat.ac.uk

Matthew Boulton College of Further and Higher Education Jennens Road, Birmingham, West Midlands B4 7PS. Tel 0121 446 4545; www.matthew-boulton.ac.uk

Mid-Cheshire College Hartford Campus, Chesterford Road, Northwich, Cheshire CW8 1LJ. Tel 01606 74444; www.midchesh.ac.uk

Mid-Kent College Horsted Centre, Maidstone Road, Chatham, Kent ME5 9UQ. Tel 01634 830633; Course Information 01634 402020; www.midkent.ac.uk

Middlesbrough College Roman Road, Linthorpe, Middlesbrough TS5 5JP. Tel 01642 333333; Course Information 01642 296600; www.middlesbro.ac.uk

Milton Keynes College Chaffron Way Campus, Woughton Campus West, Leadenhall, Milton Keynes, Buckinghamshire MK6 5LP. Tel 01908 684444; www.mkcollege.ac.uk

Moulton College West Street, Moulton, Northampton NN3 7RR. Tel 01604 491131; www.moulton.ac.uk

Neath Port Talbot College Dwr-y-Felin Road, Neath SA10 7RF. Tel 01639 648000; www.nptc.ac.uk

Nelson and Colne College Scotland Road, Nelson, Lancashire BB9 7YT. Tel 01282 440200; www.nelson.ac.uk

Nescot (North East Surrey College of Technology) Reigate Road, Ewell, Epsom, Surrey KT17 3DS. Tel 020 8394 3038; www.nescot.ac.uk

New College (Formerly North East Worcestershire College) Peakman Street, Redditch, Worcestershire B98 8DW. Tel 01527 570020; www.ne-worcs.ac.uk

New College Durham Framwellgate Moor Campus, Framwellgate Moor, County Durham DH1 5ES. Tel 0191 375 4210; www.newdur.ac.uk

New College Nottingham The Adams Building, Stoney Street, The Lace Market, Nottingham NG1 1NG. Tel 0115 910 0100; www.ncn.ac.uk

New College, Swindon New College Drive, Swindon, Wiltshire SN3 1AH. Tel 01793 611470; www.newcollege.ac.uk

New College, Telford King Street, Wellington, Telford, Shropshire TF1 1NY. Tel 01952 641892; www.newcollegetelford.ac.uk

Newbury College Monks Lane, Newbury, Berkshire RG14 7TD. Tel 01635 845000; www.newbury-college.ac.uk

Newcastle College Rye Hill Campus, Scotswood Road, Newcastle upon Tyne NE4 5BR. Tel 0191 200 4000; www.ncl-coll.ac.uk

Newcastle-under-Lyme College Liverpool Road, Newcastle-under-Lyme, Staffordshire ST5 2DF. Tel 01782 715111; www.nulc.ac.uk

Newham College of Further Education East Ham Campus, High Street South, London E6 6ER. Tel 020 8257 4000; www.newham.ac.uk

North East Institute of Further and Higher Education Trostan Avenue Building, Ballymena, Co Antrim, Northern Ireland BT43 7BN. Tel 028 2565 2871; www.nei.ac.uk

North Hertfordshire College Monkswood Way, Stevenage, Hertfordshire SG1 1LA. Tel 01462 424239; Courses 01462 424239; www.nhc.ac.uk

North Lindsey College Kingsway, Scunthorpe, North Lincolnshire DN17 1AJ. Tel 01724 281111; www.northlindsey.ac.uk

North Nottinghamshire College Carlton Road, Worksop, Nottinghamshire S81 7HP. Tel 01909 504504; Student Services 01909 504500; www.nnc.ac.uk

North Trafford College Talbot Road, Stretford, Manchester M32 0XH. Tel 0161 866 7000; www.ntc.ac.uk

North Warwickshire and Hinckley College Hinckley Road, Nuneaton, Warwickshire CV11 6BH. Tel 024 7624 3000; www.nwhc.ac.uk

Northampton College Booth Lane, Northampton NN3 3RF. Tel 01604 734567/0845 300 4401; www.northamptoncollege.ac.uk

Northbrook College, Sussex West Durrington Campus, Littlehampton Road, Durrington, Worthing, West Sussex BN12 6NU. Tel 08001 836060; www.northbrook.ac.uk

Northumberland College College Road, Ashington, Northumberland NE63 9RG. Tel 01670 841200; www.northland.ac.uk

Norton Radstock College South Hill Park, Radstock, Somerset BA3 3RW. Tel 01761 433161; www.nortcoll.ac.uk

Oaklands College St Albans Smallford Campus, Hatfield Road, St Albans, Hertfordshire AL4 0JA. Tel 01727 737000; Helpline 01727 737080; www.oaklands.ac.uk

Oldham College Rochdale Road, Oldham, Lancashire OL9 6AA. Tel 0161 624 5214/ 0800 269480; www.oldham.ac.uk

Orpington College of Further Education The Walnuts, Orpington, Kent BR6 0TE. Tel 01689 899700; www.orpington.ac.uk

Otley College Charity Lane, Otley, Ipswich, Suffolk IP6 9EY. Tel 01473 785543; www.otleycollege.ac.uk

Oxford and Cherwell Valley College Banbury Campus, Broughton Road, Banbury, Oxfordshire OX16 9QA. Tel 01865 551755; www.ocvc.ac.uk

Park Lane College, Leeds Park Lane, Leeds LS3 1AA. Admissions 0113 216 2200; Course/General Enquiries 0845 045 7275; www.parklanecoll.ac.uk

Pembrokeshire College (Coleg Sir Benfro) FREEPOST, Course Enquiries and Admissions, Pembrokeshire College, Haverfordwest, Pembrokeshire SA61 1SZ. Tel 0800 716236; www.pembrokeshire.ac.uk

Peterborough Regional College Park Crescent, Peterborough, Cambridgeshire PE1 4DZ. Tel 01733 767366; www.peterborough.ac.uk

Plumpton College Ditchling Road, Near Lewes, East Sussex BN7 3AE. Tel 01273 890454; www.plumpton.ac.uk

Plymouth College of Further Education Kings Road Centre, Devonport, Plymouth, Devon PL1 5QG. Tel 01752 305300; www.pcfe.ac.uk

Portsmouth College Tangier Road, Portsmouth, Hampshire PO3 6PZ. Tel 023 9266 7521; www.portsmouth-college.ac.uk

Redbridge College Little Heath, Barley Lane, Romford, Essex RM6 4XT. Tel 020 8548 7484; www.redbridge-college.ac.uk

Redcar and Cleveland College Corporation Road, Redcar TS10 1EZ. Tel 01642 473132; www.cleveland.ac.uk

Regents Business School London Inner Circle, Regent's Park, London NW1 4NS. Tel 020 7477 2990; www.rbslondon.ac.uk

Richmond upon Thames College Egerton Road, Twickenham, Middlesex TW2 7SJ. Tel 020 8607 8000; www.rutc.ac.uk

Riverside College Halton Kingsway Campus, Kingsway, Widnes, Cheshire WA8 7QQ. Tel 0151 257 2020; www.riverside.ac.uk

Rodbaston College Rodbaston, Penkridge, Stafford ST19 5PH. Tel 01785 712209; www.rodbaston.ac.uk

Rotherham College of Arts and Technology Town Centre Campus, Eastwood Lane, Rotherham, South Yorkshire S65 1EG. Tel 01709 362111/08080 722777; www.rotherham.ac.uk

Royal Forest of Dean College Five Acres Campus, Bury Hill, Coleford, Gloucestershire GL16 7JT. Tel 01594 833416; www.rfdc.ac.uk

Royal National College for the Blind College Road, Hereford HR1 1EB. Tel 01432 265725; www.rncb.ac.uk

Runshaw College (FE) Langdale Road, Leyland, Lancashire PR25 3DQ; (HE) Euxton Lane, Chorley, Lancashire PR7 6AD. Tel 01772 642040; www.runshaw.ac.uk

Ruskin College, Oxford Walton Street, Oxford OX1 2HE. Tel 01865 310713; www.ruskin.ac.uk

SAE Institute United House, North Road, London N7 9DP. Tel 020 7609 2653; www.sae.edu

St George's, England Broomham Hall, Rye Road, Guestling, Hastings, East Sussex TN35 4LT. Tel 01424 813696; www.stgeorgesengland.com

St Helens College Town Centre Campus, Brook Street, St Helens, Merseyside WA10 1PZ. Tel 01744 733766; www.sthelens.ac.uk

Salford College Worsley Campus, Walkden Road, Worsley M28 7QD. Tel 0161 702 8272; Central Admissions 0161 211 5001/2/3; www.salford-col.ac.uk

Salisbury College Southampton Road, Salisbury, Wiltshire SP1 2LW. Tel 01722 344344; www.salisbury.ac.uk

Sandwell College Central Enquiries, Oldbury Campus, Pound Road, Oldbury, West Midlands B68 8NA. Tel 0800 622006; www.sandwell.ac.uk

SEEVIC College Runnymede Chase, Benfleet, Essex SS7 1TW. Tel 01268 756111; www.seevic-college.ac.uk

Selby College Abbot's Road, Selby, North Yorkshire YO8 8AT. Tel 01757 211000; www.selby.ac.uk

Sheffield College PO Box 345, Sheffield S2 2YY. Tel 0114 260 3603 (Course Hotline); www.sheffcol.ac.uk

Shrewsbury College of Arts and Technology London Road, Shrewsbury, Shropshire SY2 6PR. Tel 01743 342342; www.shrewsbury.ac.uk

Skelmersdale and Ormskirk Colleges Westbank Campus, Yewdale, Skelmersdale, Lancashire WN8 6JA. Tel 01695 728744; Enquiries 01695 52300; www.skelmersdale.ac.uk

Solihull College Blossomfield Road, Solihull, West Midlands B91 1SB. Tel 0121 678 7001/2; www.solihull.ac.uk

Somerset College of Arts and Technology Wellington Road, Taunton, Somerset TA1 5AX. Tel 01823 366331; www.somerset.ac.uk

South Birmingham College Hall Green Campus, Cole Bank Road, Hall Green, Birmingham, West Midlands B28 8ES. Tel 0121 694 5000; www.sbirmc.ac.uk

South Cheshire College Dane Bank Avenue, Crewe, Cheshire CW2 8AB. Tel 01270 654654; www.s-cheshire.ac.uk

South Devon College Newton Road, Torquay, Devon TQ2 5BY. Tel 08000 380123; www.southdevon.ac.uk

South Downs College College Road, Waterlooville, Hampshire PO7 8AA. Tel 023 9279 7979; www.southdowns.ac.uk

South East Derbyshire College Field Road, Ilkeston, Derbyshire DE7 5RS. Tel 0115 849 2020; www.sedc.ac.uk

South Kent College The Grange, Shorncliffe Road, Folkestone, Kent CT20 2NA. Tel 01303 858220; www.southkent.ac.uk

South Leicestershire College Station Road, Wigston, Leicestershire LE18 2DW. Tel 0116 288 5051; www.slcollege.ac.uk

South Nottingham College Greythorne Drive, West Bridgford, Nottingham NG2 7GA. Tel 0115 914 6400; www.snc.ac.uk

South Thames College Wandsworth High Street, London SW18 2PP. Tel 020 8918 7000; Course Enquiries 020 8918 7777; www.south-thames.ac.uk

South Trafford College Manchester Road, West Timperley, Altrincham, Cheshire WA14 5PQ. Tel 0161 952 4600; Course Information 0161 952 4686/7; www.stcoll.ac.uk

South Tyneside College St George's Avenue, South Shields NE34 6ET. Tel 0191 427 3500/3900; www.stc.ac.uk

Southampton City College St Mary Street, Southampton, Hampshire SO14 1AR. Tel 023 8048 4848/023 8057 7400; www.southampton-city.ac.uk

Southend Campus (Essex University at South East Essex College) Luker Road, Southend-on-Sea, Essex SS1 1ND. Tel 01702 220400; www.southend.ac.uk

Southgate College High Street, Southgate, London N14 6BS. Tel 020 8982 5050; www.southgate.ac.uk

Spelthorne College Church Road, Ashford, Middlesex TW15 2XD. Tel 01784 248666; www.spelthorne.ac.uk

Southport College Mornington Road, Southport, Merseyside PR9 0TT. Tel 01704 500606; www.southport.ac.uk

Southwark College Waterloo Centre, The Cut, London SE1 8LE. Tel 020 7815 1600; www.southwark.ac.uk

Stafford College Earl Street, Stafford ST16 2QR. Tel 01785 223800; www.staffordcoll.ac.uk

Staffordshire University Regional Federation (SURF) Staffordshire University, College Road, Stoke on Trent ST4 2DE. Tel 01782 292753; www.surf.ac.uk

Stamford College Drift Road, Stamford, Lincolnshire PE9 1XA. Tel 01780 484300; www.stamford.ac.uk

Stephenson College Coalville Thornborough Road, Coalville, Leicestershire LE67 3TN. Tel 01530 836136; www.stephensoncoll.ac.uk

Stockport College of Further and Higher Education Wellington Road South, Stockport, Greater Manchester SK1 3UQ. Tel 0161 958 3100; Admissions 0845 230 3102; www.stockport.ac.uk

Stourbridge College Hagley Road Centre, Hagley Road, Stourbridge, West Midlands DY8 1QU. Tel 01384 344344; www.stourbridge.ac.uk

Stratford-upon-Avon College The Willows North, Alcester Road, Stratford-upon-Avon, Warwickshire CV37 9QR. Tel 01789 266245; www.stratford.ac.uk

Strode College Church Road, Street, Somerset BA16 0AB. Tel 01458 844444; www.strode-college.ac.uk

Strode's College High Street, Egham, Surrey TW20 9DR. Tel 01784 437506; www.strodes.ac.uk

Stroud College in Gloucestershire Stratford Road, Stroud, Gloucestershire GL5 4AH. Tel 01453 763424; Customer Services 01453 761126; www.stroud.ac.uk

Sussex Downs College Eastbourne Campus, Cross Levels Way, Eastbourne, East Sussex BN21 2UF. Tel 01323 637637; www.sussexdowns.ac.uk

Sutton Coldfield College 34 Lichfield Road, Sutton Coldfield, West Midlands B74 2NW. Tel 0121 362 1121; www.sutcol.ac.uk

Swansea College (Coleg Abertawe) Tycoch Road, Tycoch, Swansea SA2 9EB. Tel 01792 284000/0800 174084; www.swancoll.ac.uk

Swindon College Regent Circus, Swindon, Wiltshire SN1 1PT. Tel 01793 498308/0800 731 2250; www.swindon-college.ac.uk

Tameside College Beaufort Road, Ashton-under-Lyne, Lancashire OL6 6NX. Tel 0161 908 6789; www.tameside.ac.uk

Tamworth and Lichfield College Croft Street, Upper Gungate, Tamworth, Staffordshire B79 8AE. Tel 01827 310202; www.tamworth.ac.uk

Telford College of Arts and Technology Haybridge Road, Wellington, Telford, Shropshire TF1 2NP. Tel 01952 642200; Student Services; 01952 642237; www.tcat.ac.uk

Thanet College Ramsgate Road, Broadstairs, Kent CT10 1PN. Tel 01843 605040; Admissions 01843 605049; www.thanet.ac.uk

Thurrock and Basildon College Woodview, Grays, Essex RM16 2YR. Tel 0845 601 5746; www.tab.ac.uk

Totton College Calmore Road, Totton, Hampshire SO40 3ZX. Tel 023 8087 4874; www.totton.ac.uk

Tresham Institute of Further and Higher Education St Mary's, Kettering, Northamptonshire NN15 7BS. Tel 0845 658 8990; www.tresham.ac.uk

Truro College College Road, Truro, Cornwall TR1 3XX. General Enquiries 01872 267000; HE Admissions 01872 267061; www.trurocollege.ac.uk

Tyne Metropolitan College Embleton Avenue, Wallsend NE28 9NJ. Tel 0191 229 5000; www.tynemet.ac.uk

University Centre Doncaster The Hub, Doncaster DN1 2RF. Tel 01302 553553; Course Enquiries 0800 358 7575; www.don.ac.uk

Upper Bann Institute Portadown Campus, 36 Lurgan Road, Portadown, Armagh, Northern Ireland BT63 5BL. Tel 029 3839 7777; www.ubi.ac.uk

Uxbridge College Park Road, Uxbridge, Middlesex UB8 1NQ. Tel 01895 853333; www.uxbridge.ac.uk

Wakefield College Margaret Street, Wakefield, West Yorkshire WF1 2DH. Tel 01924 789111; www.wakefield.ac.uk

Walford and North Shropshire College Oswestry Campus, Shrewsbury Road, Oswestry, Shropshire SY11 4QB. Tel 01691 688000; www.wnsc.ac.uk

Walsall College PO Box 4203, St Paul's Street, Walsall, West Midlands WS1 1WY. Tel 01922 657000; www.walcat.ac.uk

Waltham Forest College Forest Building, Forest Road, Walthamstow, London E17 4JB. Tel 020 8501 8000; www.waltham.ac.uk

Warrington Collegiate Winwick Road, Warrington, Cheshire WA2 8QA. Tel 01925 494494; www.warr.ac.uk

West Cheshire College Handbridge Centre, Eaton Road, Handbridge, Chester CH4 7ER. Tel 01244 670600; Course Information 0151 356 7800; www.west-cheshire.ac.uk

West Herts College Watford Hempstead Road, Watford, Hertfordshire WD17 3EZ. Information and Guidance 01923 812345; www.westherts.ac.uk

West Kent College Brook Street, Tonbridge, Kent TN9 2PW. Tel 01732 358101; www.wkc.ac.uk

West Nottinghamshire College Derby Road, Mansfield, Nottinghamshire NG18 5BH. Tel 01623 627191; HE Enquiries 01623 413639/0800 100 3626; www.westnotts.ac.uk

West Suffolk College Out Risbygate, Bury St Edmunds, Suffolk IP33 3RL. Tel 01284 701301; www.westsuffolk.ac.uk

West Thames College London Road, Isleworth, Middlesex TW7 4HS. Tel 020 8326 2000; Course Enquiries 020 8326 2020; www.west-thames.ac.uk

Westminster Kingsway College St James's Park Centre, Castle Lane, London SW1E 6DR. Tel 08700 609800; Course Information 08700 609801; www.westking.ac.uk

Weston College Knightstone Road, Weston super Mare, Somerset BS23 2AL. Tel 01934 411411; www.weston.ac.uk

Weymouth College Cranford Avenue, Weymouth, Dorset DT4 7LQ. Tel 01305 761100; Course Applications 0870 060 9800/1; www.weymouth.ac.uk

Wigan and Leigh College PO Box 53, Parsons Walk, Wigan WN1 1RS. Tel 01942 761600; Course Enquiries 01942 761111; www.wigan-leigh.ac.uk

Wiltshire College Cocklebury Road, Chippenham, Wiltshire SN15 3QD. Tel 01249 464644; www.wiltscoll.ac.uk

Wirral Metropolitan College Conway Park Campus, Europa Boulevard, Conway Park, Birkenhead, Wirral, Merseyside CH41 4NT. Tel 0151 551 7777; www.wmc.ac.uk

Worcester College of Technology Deansway, Worcester WR1 2JF. Tel 01905 725555; www.wortech.ac.uk

Yeovil College Mudford Road, Yeovil, Somerset BA21 4DR. Tel 01935 423921; www.yeovil.ac.uk

York College Tadcaster Road, York, North Yorkshire YO24 1UA. Tel 01904 770200; www.yorkcollege.ac.uk

Yorkshire Coast College of Further and Higher Education Lady Edith's Drive, Scarborough, North Yorkshire YO12 5RN. Tel 01723 372105; www.yorkshirecoastcollege.ac.uk

College Ystrad Mynach Twyn Road, Ystrad Mynach, Hengoed, Wales CF82 7XR. Tel 01443 810054; www.ystrad-mynach.co.uk

SECTION 7: FURTHER EDUCATION COLLEGES IN SCOTLAND OFFERING HIGHER EDUCATION COURSES

The following colleges appear under various subject headings in the tables in **Chapter 8**. Contact the colleges direct for details of courses and method of application.

Aberdeen College Gallowgate Centre, Gallowgate, Aberdeen, Grampian AB25 1BN. Tel 01224 612000; Information and Booking Centre 01224 612330; www.abcol.ac.uk

Adam Smith College St Brycedale Campus, St Brycedale Avenue, Kirkcaldy, Fife, Scotland KY1 1EX. Tel 01592 268591; Course Hotline 0800 413280; www.adamsmith.ac.uk

Angus College Keptie Road, Arbroath, Angus DD11 3EA. Tel 01241 432600; www.angus.ac.uk

Anniesland College Hatfield Campus, 19 Hatfield Drive, Glasgow G12 0YE. Tel 0141 357 3969; www.anniesland.ac.uk

Argyll College (UHI partner college – see Section 2) West Bay, Dunoon, Argyll PA23 7HP. Tel 08452 309969; www.argyllcollege.ac.uk

Ayr College Dam Park, Ayr, Strathclyde KA8 0EU. Tel 01292 265184; Admissions 0800 199798; www.ayrcoll.ac.uk

Banff and Buchan College Henderson Road, Fraserburgh, Grampian AB43 9GA. Tel 01346 586100; www.banff-buchan.ac.uk

Barony College Parkgate, Dumfries, Dumfries and Galloway DG1 3NE. Tel 01387 860251; www.barony.ac.uk

Borders College Head Office, Melrose Road, Galashiels, Lothian TD1 2AF. Tel 08700 505152; www.borderscollege.ac.uk

Cardonald College 690 Mosspark Drive, Glasgow, G52 3AY. Tel 0141 272 3333; www.cardonald.ac.uk

Central College of Commerce 300 Cathedral Street, Glasgow, G1 2TA. Information Unit 0141 552 3941; www.centralcollege.ac.uk

Clydebank College Kilbowie Road, Clydebank, G81 2AA. Tel 0141 952 7771; www.clydebank.ac.uk

Coatbridge College Kildonan Street, Coatbridge, Lanarkshire ML5 3LS. Tel 01236 422316; Admissions 01236 436000; www.coatbridge.ac.uk

Crichton Campus (Universities of Glasgow and Paisley, Bell and Dumfries and Galloway Colleges) Rutherford McGowan Buildings, Dumfries, Scotland DG1 4ZL. Tel 01387 702001; Admissions 01387 702131; www.crichtoncampus.ac.uk

Cumbernauld College Tryst Road, Cumbernauld, Glasgow, Strathclyde G67 1HU. Tel 01236 731811; www.cumbernauld.ac.uk

Dumfries and Galloway College Herries Avenue, Heathhall, Dumfries DG1 3QZ. Tel 01387 261261; www.dumgal.ac.uk

Dundee College Kingsway Campus, Old Glamis Road, Dundee, Tayside DD3 8LE. Tel 01382 834834; Enquiry Service 01382 834800; www.dundeecoll.ac.uk

Edinburgh's Telford College 350 West Granton Road, Edinburgh, EH5 1QE. Tel 0131 559 4000; www.ed-coll.ac.uk

Forth Valley College Falkirk Campus, Grangemouth Road, Falkirk FK2 9AD. Tel 01234 403000; www.forthvalley.ac.uk

Glasgow College of Nautical Studies 21 Thistle Street, Glasgow, G5 9XB. Tel 0141 565 2500; www.glasgow-nautical.ac.uk

Glasgow Metropolitan College 60 North Hanover Street, Glasgow, Strathclyde G1 2BP. Tel 0141 566 6222; www.gmc.ac.uk

Highland Theological College (UHI partner college – see Section 2) High Street, Dingwall IV15 9HA. Tel 01349 780000; www.htc.uhi.ac.uk

Inverness College (UHI partner college – see Section 2) 3 Longman Road, Longman South, Inverness, Highland IV1 1SA. Tel 01463 273000; www.inverness.uhi.ac.uk

James Watt College Finnart Street, Greenock, Strathclyde PA16 8HF. Tel 01475 724433; Student Information Centre 0800 587 2277; www.jameswatt.ac.uk

Jewel and Esk Valley College Eskbank Campus, Newbattle Road, Eskbank, Dalkeith, Midlothian EH22 3AE. Tel 0131 660 1010; Information Services 08458 500060; www.jevc.ac.uk

Kilmarnock College Holehouse Road, Kilmarnock, Strathclyde KA3 7AT. Tel 01563 523501; www.kilmarnock.ac.uk

Langside College 50 Prospecthill Road, Glasgow, Strathclyde G42 9LB. Tel 0141 649 4991; Student Services 0141 636 6066; www.langside.ac.uk

Lauder College Halbeath, Dunfermline, Fife KY11 8DY. Tel 01383 845000; www.lauder.ac.uk

Lews Castle College (Colaisde A' Chaisteil) (UHI partner college – see Section 2) Stornoway, Isle of Lewis HS2 0XR. Tel 01851 770000; www.lews.uhi.ac.uk

Lochaber College (UHI partner college – see Section 2) An Aird, Fort William, Inverness, Scotland PH33 6AN. Tel 01397 874000; www.lochaber.uhi.ac.uk

Moray College (UHI partner college – see Section 2) Moray Street, Elgin, Moray IV30 1JJ. Tel 01343 576216; www.moray.ac.uk

Ness Foundation (UHI partner college – see Section 2) Ness House, Dochfour Business Centre, Dochgarroch, Inverness IV3 8GY. Tel 01463 220407; www.ness-foundation.org.uk

North Atlantic Fisheries College (UHI partner college – see Section 2) Port Arthur, Scalloway, Shetland ZE1 0UN. Tel 01595 772000; www.nafc.ac.uk

North Glasgow College 110 Flemington Street, Springburn, Glasgow G21 4BX. Tel 0141 558 9001; www.north-gla.ac.uk

North Highland College (UHI partner college – see Section 2) Ormlie Road, Thurso, Caithness KW14 7EE. Tel 01847 889000; www.nhcscotland.com

Oatridge College Information Unit, Ecclesmachan, Broxburn, Lothian EH52 6NH. Tel 01506 864800; www.oatridge.ac.uk

Orkney College (UHI partner college – see Section 2) Kirkwall, Orkney KW15 1LX. Tel 01856 569000; www.orkney.uhi.ac.uk

Perth College (UHI partner college – see Section 2) Crieff Road, Perth, Scotland PH1 2NX. Tel 01738 877000; Admissions Office, Freepost, Perth PH1 2BR. Tel 08452 701177; www.perth.ac.uk

Reid Kerr College Admission Unit, Renfrew Road, Paisley, Renfrewshire PA3 4DR. Tel 0141 581 2222; Course Enquiries 08000 527343; www.reidkerr.ac.uk

Sabhal Mor Ostaig (UHI partner college – see Section 2) Sleat, Isle of Skye, Scotland IV44 8RQ. Tel 01471 888000; www.smo.uhi.ac.uk

Scottish Association for Marine Science (UHI partner college – see Section 2) Dunstaffnage Marine Laboratory, Oban, Argyll PA37 1QA. Tel 01631 559000; www.sams.ac.uk

Shetland College (UHI partner college – see Section 2) Gremista, Lerwick, Shetland ZE1 0PX. Tel 01595 771000; www.shetland.uhi.ac.uk

South Lanarkshire College Admissions Unit/Advice Centre, Main Street, East Kilbride G74 4JY. Tel 01355 270750; www.south-lanarkshire-college.ac.uk

Stevenson College Edinburgh Bankhead Avenue, Edinburgh, Lothian EH11 4DE. Tel 0131 535 4600; Course Enquiries 0131 535 4700; www.stevenson.ac.uk

Stow College, Glasgow 43 Shamrock Street, Glasgow, Strathclyde G4 9LD. Tel 0141 332 1786; www.stow.ac.uk

West Lothian College Almondvale Crescent, Livingston, West Lothian EH54 7EP. Tel 01506 418181; Information 01506 427605; www.west-lothian.ac.uk

To find out more about the universities and their courses, now turn to **Chapter 3: University Course Profiles**.

UNIVERSITIES AND THEIR COURSES

Choosing a degree subject is one step of the way to higher education (see **Chapter 1**), choosing a university or college is the next stage. However, in addition to such features as location, entry requirements, accommodation (see **Chapter 2**), students' facilities and the subjects offered, many universities differ in the way they organise and teach their courses. The course profiles below aim to identify the main course features of each of the universities and to provide some brief notes about the types of courses they offer and how they differ.

The ways in which students are taught differ between universities and often between subjects even at the same university. Modularisation is now quite common because of the flexibility it offers the student to choose a range of topics within their subject choice. Each course comprises modules of study, some are compulsory, some are optional, and some are 'free units' which allow the student to study a subject totally unrelated to their chosen course, for example a foreign language or management. Each module often has a credit rating and students are awarded this value of credits for each module they successfully complete (ie they pass the assessment). For a three-year honours degree students usually need 360 points. Courses which are not modular are often those for vocational subjects which must conform to the course requirements of professional bodies.

Although universities have their own distinct identities and course characteristics, they have many similarities. Apart from full-time and sandwich courses, one-year Foundation courses are also offered in many subjects which can help the student to either convert or build on existing qualifications to enable them to start a degree programme. All universities also offer one-year International Foundation courses for overseas students to provide a preliminary introduction to courses and often to provide English language tuition.

Foundation courses, however, must not be confused with Foundation degrees which normally require two years' full-time study, or longer for part-time study. They are also often taught in local colleges and may be taken part-time to allow students to continue to work. Successful completion of a Foundation degree can lead into the second or final year of related honours degree courses when offered by the university validating the Foundation degree. Two-year Higher National Diplomas will also qualify for entry into the second or final year of degree courses. These, too, are often offered at universities as well as colleges of further education and partnership colleges linked to universities.

Part-time degrees and courses in lifelong learning or distance learning are also often available and details of these can be found on university websites and in prospectuses. Some universities publish separate prospectuses for part-time courses.

The following is a list of universities and a brief outline for each of the ways in which their undergraduate courses are structured and provided, and of the range of courses they provide. For full details see university websites and prospectuses.

PROFILES

Aberdeen Students applying for the MA degree in Arts and Social Sciences are admitted to a degree rather than a subject. Students select from a range of courses in the first year, leading up to the final choice of subject and honours course in the fourth year. The BSc degree is also flexible but within the Science framework. Engineering students follow a common core course in Years 1 and 2, specialising in Year 3. There is less flexibility, however, in some vocational courses such as Accountancy, Law and Medicine. For some degree programmes, highly qualified applicants may be admitted to the second year of the course. Other courses cover Divinity and Religious Studies, Education, Law, Medicine and Sciences.

Abertay Dundee Courses have a strong vocational bias and are offered in the Schools of Computing, Business, Science and Engineering and Social and Health Sciences. Four-year courses are offered on a modular basis. Sandwich courses may be either thick (one-year placement) or thin (two six-month placements) and placements are usually at the end of the second and/or third years.

Aberystwyth The University offers single, joint and major-minor honours courses on a modular basis. In Part 1 (Year 1) core topics related to the chosen subject are studied alongside optional subjects. This arrangement allows some flexibility for change when choosing final degree subjects in Part 2 (Years 2 and 3). Some students take a year in industry or commerce between Years 2 and 3. Courses include Accountancy and Business, Agriculture, the Arts and Humanities, Computer Science, Education, Law, Mathematics, the Sciences, Sport and Theatre and TV Studies.

American Intercontinental This private university offers courses in Business, Finance, Interior Design, Media Production and Visual Communication.

Anglia Ruskin Courses are modular which enables students to choose from a range of subject topics in addition to the compulsory subject core modules. Single and combined honours courses are offered, with some opportunities to study abroad and many programmes have a strong vocational focus. Courses include Business Studies, Computer Science, Education, Engineering, Law, Nursing, Psychology, Social Sciences and the Sciences.

Arts London The University is Europe's largest institution offering courses in Art and Design, Communication and Performing Arts, focusing on creativity and practice in a large number of specialist fields.

Aston The University offers modular courses in single honours degrees (one subject), joint honours (two subjects, usually in related areas) and in combined honours and interdisciplinary studies in which programmes are organised across different subjects. Combined honours courses may be weighted 50%-50% and major-minor programmes weighted 67% for the major element and 33% for the minor. A distinctive feature of Aston is that most degrees allow students to spend the third year on a one-year sandwich placement; 70% of students follow sandwich courses or study abroad programmes, leading to a high percentage of employed graduates. Courses are taught in the Schools of Engineering and Applied Science, Languages and European Studies, Life and Health Sciences and in the Aston Business School.

Bangor Modular courses are offered in single and joint honours programmes. A broad and flexible programme is taken in Level 1 (Year 1) with the opportunity to study modules outside the chosen subject including a language. This is followed by greater specialisation in Levels 2 and 3. Courses include Agriculture and Forestry, Arts subjects, Business and Management, Computer Science and Electronics, Education, Health Studies, Music, Psychology, Sciences, Ocean Sciences, Social Sciences, Sport and Religious Studies. Contrary to popular belief, two-thirds of the students come from outside Wales and all courses are taught in English.

Bath The academic year is divided into two semesters with single and combined honours degrees composed of core units and optional units, allowing students some flexibility in shaping their courses with 10–12 units taken each year. A central feature of all programmes is the opportunity to take a sandwich course as part of the degree: this is usually taken as either one 12-month placement or two periods of six months. Courses are offered in the Faculties of Engineering and Design, Humanities and Social Sciences, Science and the Schools of Business and Health.

Bath Spa Most courses – for single awards, specialised awards and combined awards – are part of a flexible modular scheme with students taking six modules each year. Some modules are compulsory but there is a good range of optional modules. Courses on offer include Biology, Business and Management, Creative Studies, Cultural Studies, Dance, Design Technology, Drama, Education, English Literature and Creative Studies in English, Food Studies, Geography, Health Studies, History, Media and Communications, Music, Psychology, Sociology and Study of Religions.

Bedfordshire This new university offers BA and BSc undergraduate, Foundation and Extended degrees in Advertising, Marketing and Public Relations, Art and Design, Biosciences, Business, Computing, Language and Communication, Law, Media, Nursing, Psychology, Social Sciences, Sport and Leisure and Tourism. Most of the courses are vocational, some of which offer a placement year in industry or commerce.

Belfast (Queen's) The academic year is divided into two semesters of 15 weeks each (12 teaching weeks and three examination weeks), with degree courses (pathways) normally taken over three years of full-time-study. Six modules are taken each year (three in each semester) and, in theory, a degree can involve any combination of six Level 1 modules. Single, joint and combined honours courses are offered and, in addition, major-minor combinations; some courses include sandwich placements. Courses cover Agriculture and Food Science, Education, Engineering, Humanities and Social Sciences, Management and Economics, Law and Medicine and Health Sciences.

Birmingham Courses cover Arts subjects (including Drama), Business and Commerce, Education, Engineering, Law, Medicine and Dentistry and Health Sciences. Single subject and joint honours courses are offered. In joint honours courses the two chosen subjects may have common ground or can be very disparate, for example technology and a modern language. Some major/minor combinations are also possible. The modular system provides opportunities for students to study a subject outside their main degree.

Bolton Courses are offered in Art and Design, Built Environment, Business Studies, Computing and Electronics, Cultural and Creative Studies, Education, Engineering, Health and Social Studies, Product Design, Psychology and Sport, Leisure and Tourism. Teaching and learning takes place through a mixture of lectures, practicals, seminars and small tutorial groups. Many courses are based on a modular structure.

Bournemouth The University offers undergraduate degrees leading to BA, BSc and LLB. The programmes, which are mainly vocational and include sandwich placements, often carry professional recognition. The academic schools cover Business, Conservation Sciences, Design, Engineering and Computing, Health and Community Studies, Law and Media.

Bradford Single, joint and major/minor courses are offered, many of which are vocational, leading to professional accreditation, and include sandwich placements in industry and commerce. Other courses offer work shadowing placements. Language options are available to all students irrespective of their chosen degree course. Subjects are taught in the Schools of Archaeological, Geographical and Environ-mental Sciences, Engineering Design and Technology, Informatics, Health, Life Sciences, Management, Social and International Studies and Lifelong Learning.

Brighton BA, BSc and BEng courses are offered, 90% with industrial placements including some in Europe, the USA and Canada. Courses include Art and Architecture, Education and Sport, Health, Management and Information Sciences and Science and Engineering. Brighton and Sussex Medical School students are based at the Falmer campus for the first two years, with academic and clinical studies integrated from Year 1, and thereafter in the education centre at the Royal Sussex County Hospital in Brighton.

Bristol The University offers single and joint honours programmes, mostly of three or four years and, except for Dentistry, Medicine and Veterinary Science, they are based on a modular structure. Students on single honours courses have open units allowing optional choices from a range of subjects. Lectures play an important part in teaching and are supported by tutorials and seminars which, in Arts and Social Sciences, tend to dominate the final year. Other subject areas offered in Sciences and Engineering (some courses include a year abroad), Arts, Social Sciences and Law.

Bristol UWE The University offers single and joint honours courses organised on a modular basis which gives flexibility in the choice of options. Many courses include sandwich placements and, in addition, students have the opportunity to undertake a period of study in another EU country. The language centre is open to all students. Courses cover a full range of subjects in the Faculties of Media and Design, Applied Sciences, Built Environment, Computing, Education, Engineering and Mathematical Sciences, Health and Social Care, Humanities, Law, Languages and Social Sciences, the Bristol Business School and Hartpury College (offering Agricultural and Equine Business courses).

Brunel All courses are made up of self-contained modules enabling students, within their scheme of studies, to choose a broad range of topics or greater specialisation as they prefer. Some modern language modules may be taken, depending on the timetable of the chosen subjects. Almost all degree courses are available in a three-year full-time mode or in four-year thick or thin sandwich courses which combine academic work with industrial experience. Some exchange schemes also operate in Europe and the USA. Degree programmes cover Arts and Humanities subjects, Biological Sciences, Business and Management, Design, Education, Engineering, Health and Social Care, Human Sciences, Law, Mathematical Sciences, Performing Arts and Sport Sciences.

Buckingham The University is an educational charity with its main income provided by the students who pay full tuition fees. A unique feature is the two-year degree programme which starts in January although some courses start in September and may extend to 2¼ years, and some last three years. Courses are offered in Business, Humanities, Law, International Studies and Sciences.

Cambridge The University offers undergraduate courses in Arts and Sciences and postgraduate degree programmes. Three-year degree courses (Triposes) provide a broad introduction to the subject followed by options at a later stage, and are divided into Part 1 (one or two years) and Part 2. In some Science and Engineering courses there is a fourth year (Part 3). In college-based teaching sessions (supervisions), essays are set for discussion to support university lectures, seminars and practicals. The Cambridge clinical studies part of the Medicine degree has been extensively revised and the three-year course took its first intake in 2005.

Canterbury Christ Church A wide range of BA and BSc courses are on offer in addition to a wide choice of combined courses. Subjects cover American Studies, Applied Criminology, Art, Bioscience, Business, Computing, Digital and Cultural Arts and Media, Early Childhood Studies, English, Film, Radio and TV Studies, Forensic Investigation, French, Geography, Health Studies, History, Legal Studies, Marketing, Media Studies, Music, Psychology, Religious Studies, Science in the Environment, Social Science, Sport and Exercise Psychology, Sport Science, Theology and Tourism.

Cardiff All students taking the very flexible BA degree study three subjects in the first year and then follow a single or joint honours course in their chosen subject(s), or a degree in the additional subject. Similarly, BSc Econ courses offer the option to transfer to an alternative degree course at the end of Year 1, depending on the subjects originally chosen. Many degree schemes have a vocational and professional content with a period of attachment in industry, and there are well established links with universities abroad. Degrees schemes are offered by 27 Schools covering Architecture and Planning, Arts and Humanities subjects, Business, Computer Science, Earth, Ocean and Planetary Sciences, Engineering, Healthcare Studies, Law, Media Studies, Medicine, Dentistry and Nursing, Music, Optometry, Pharmacy, Psychology, Religious Studies, Sciences, Social Sciences and Welsh Studies.

Central Lancashire The University has four Faculties – Cultural, Legal and Social Studies, Health, Science, and Design and Technology. Subjects are taught in a series of modules which gives maximum flexibility in the final choice of degree course. Students may specialise or keep their options open with a choice of single honours, joint or combined honours, or they can choose three subjects in Year 1 and reduce to two in the second and third years. Some sandwich courses are offered.

Chester Single and combined courses are offered in a wide range of subjects on the Chester campus. Over 60 subjects are offered including Art and Design, Drama and Theatre Studies, Business and Social Studies courses and Nutrition and Health Care. The Warrington campus offers well established courses in Media (Radio, TV, Music) and Journalism in addition to Computer Science and Sports courses.

Chichester Degree subjects can be studied in major, joint or minor programmes. All undergraduate courses comprise a number of individual short course units/modules, taught and assessed separately. Each degree course consists of compulsory and optional modules enabling students to follow their own interests. BA courses are offered in a range of subjects covering Dance, English, Fine Art, History, Media Studies, Music, Performing Arts, Sports Studies and Theology at Chichester, and Business, Education and Tourism at the Bognor Regis campus.

City The University offers a wide range of three-year and four-year programmes leading to degrees in Arts, Business and Management, Computing, Engineering and Mathematical Sciences, Health Sciences, Law and Social Sciences. Some Schools and Departments provide a common first year, allowing students to make a final decision on their degree course at the end of the first year. Some sandwich courses are optional, others compulsory. Students in some subject areas may apply to study abroad.

Coventry Courses are offered in the Schools of Art and Design, Business, Engineering, Health and Social Sciences, Mathematical and Information Sciences and Science and the Environment. Many courses are industry-linked and offer sandwich placements in industry and commerce, with some opportunities to study abroad. Individual programmes of study are usually made up of compulsory modules, core options from a prescribed list and free choice modules.

Cumbria This new university is expected to be created in 2007 from a merger of St Martins University College and Cumbria Institute of the Arts. At the former, courses cover Business, Counselling, Drama, Education (Primary and Secondary), English, Fine Art, Geography, Health and Social Care, IT, Mathematics, Outdoor and Recreational Studies, Philosophy, PE, Social Science, Sport and Youth and Community Studies. Cumbria Institute of the Arts provides courses in Art, Design, Media, Film Studies, Dance and Drama and Journalism.

De Montfort The Faculties of Art and Design, Business and Law, Computing Science and Engineering, Health and Life Sciences and Humanities offer single honours programmes and an extensive joint honours programme in which two subjects are chosen to be studied equally. Courses are modular, some assessed by coursework only, or by a combination of coursework and examination and a few by examination only. It is possible to change a selected module early in the year.

Derby Courses in Derby are offered across three Schools – Arts, Design and Technology, Business and Education, Health and Sciences, whilst at the Buxton campus Foundation degrees and Higher National Diploma courses are offered as well as some BA and BSc degrees. There is also a comprehensive joint honours programme offering two subjects and combined honours courses with a choice of up to three subjects. Major/minor courses are also available.

Dundee Courses are offered in Accountancy, Architecture and Planning, Art and Design, Arts, Education, Engineering, Law, Medicine and Dentistry, Nursing, Sciences and Social Sciences. A flexible modular system is offered in which Arts and Social Science students have a choice of up to three or four subjects in Year 1 leading to greater specialisation as students progress through the next three years. A similar system applies to courses in Life Sciences and Physical Sciences. In Engineering a common core curriculum operates in Level 1 and in the first half of Level 2.

Durham Degree options include single and joint honours courses to which subsidiary subjects can be added. There are named routes in Natural Sciences and courses in Combined Arts and Social Sciences in which students may design their own degree course by choosing several subjects from a wide range. Courses cover the Arts, Business, Computer Science, Education, Engineering, Law, Medicine, Science and Social Science.

East Anglia There are 18 Schools of Study spanning the Humanities, Social Sciences, Health and professional disciplines. Many Schools are interdisciplinary or multidisciplinary, allowing students to combine a specialist study with complementary subjects and optional units. Some courses include study abroad in Europe, North America and Australasia.

East London The University offers some 130 single honours degrees and 50 subjects which form part of the combined honours programme. Courses provide a flexibility of choice and are based on a modular structure with compulsory and optional course units. Courses are offered in Architecture, Art and Design, Business, Computing, Engineering, Health Sciences, Humanities, Law, Media, Social Sciences, Sciences and Sport. A very large number of extended degrees are also available for applicants who do not have the normal university entrance requirements.

Edge Hill This new university has three-year programmes in Business, English, Film, Geographical Sciences, History, Law, Media, Midwifery, Nursing, Performance Studies, Social and Psychological Sciences, Sport and Teacher Training.

Edinburgh Courses are offered in Humanities and the Social Sciences, Medicine and Veterinary Medicine and in Science and Engineering. Depending on the choice of degree, three or more subjects are taken in the first year followed by second level courses in at least two of these subjects in Year 2, thus allowing a range of subjects to be studied at degree level. There is a considerable choice of subjects although there may be restrictions in the case of high-demand subjects such as English and Psychology. General or ordinary degrees take three years and honours degrees take four years. Joint honours degrees are also offered.

Essex There are 17 undergraduate departments grouped in Schools of Study covering Humanities and Comparative Studies, Social Sciences, Law and Sciences and Engineering. In Year 1 students take four or five courses including modules for their chosen degree. In Year 2 they may follow their chosen degree or choose another degree, including combined and joint courses. The four-year BA and some Law degrees include a year abroad and/or industrial placements.

Exeter Subjects are offered in the Schools of Biological Sciences, Business and Economics, Classics, Ancient History and Theology, Education and Lifelong Learning, Engineering, Computer Science and Mathematics, English, Geography, Archaeology and Earth Resources, Historical, Political and Sociological Studies, Law, Modern Languages, the Institute of Arab and Islamic Studies and the Peninsula Medical School. In some courses it is possible to study for up to a year in Europe, North America, Australia or New Zealand.

Glamorgan Many of the courses are vocational and can be studied as single or joint honours courses or major-minor degrees. Courses are offered in the fields of Art and Design, Built Environment, Business, Computing and Mathematics, Education, Engineering, English and Creative Writing, Geography and the Environment, Health Sciences, Life and Physical Sciences, Humanities and Social Sciences, Law, Policing and Crime, Media and Drama Studies and Sport.

Glasgow Applicants choose a Faculty and a degree from the Faculties of Arts, Education, Engineering, Law and Financial Studies, Medicine, Science, Social Science and Veterinary Medicine. Flexible arrangements allow students to build their own degree programme from all the courses on offer. Honours degrees normally take four years, with the decision for honours taken at the end of Year 2 (not automatic). General degrees take three years except for those involving a foreign language.

Glasgow Caledonian The University offers a wide range of vocational full-time and sandwich courses organised in the Schools of the Built and Natural Environment, Computing and Mathematical Sciences, Engineering Science and Design, Health and Social Care, Law and Social Sciences, Life Sciences, Nursing, Midwifery and Community Health and the Caledonian Business School.

Gloucestershire There are three main Faculties: Arts and Education, Business and Social Sciences and Environment and Leisure. Modular, single and joint courses are offered, many with work placements and some with exchange schemes with institutions in the USA. Many students are home-based.

Greenwich Courses cover Architecture and Construction, Business, Chemical and Life Sciences, Computing and Mathematical Sciences, Earth and Environmental Sciences, Education and Training, Engineering, Languages, Health and Social Care, Humanities and Social Sciences and Law. There is also a flexible and comprehensive combined honours degree programme offering two joint subjects of equal weight or, alternatively, major-minor combinations.

Heriot-Watt The year is divided into three ten-week terms with four modules taken each term. The six Schools cover the Built Environment, Engineering and Physical Sciences, Management and Languages, Mathematical and Computer Sciences, Textiles and Design and Life Sciences.

Hertfordshire Honours and sandwich degrees are offered in a range of courses in Art and Design, Business, Computer Science, Education, Engineering, Humanities, Law, Life and Physical Sciences, Geography, Music, Sport, Nursing and Health subjects, Psychology and Social Studies and many courses are vocational. There is also an extensive combined modular programme in which students choose three subjects in Year 1, followed by specialisation in Years 2 and 3.

Huddersfield The modular approach to study provides a flexible structure to all courses which are offered as full-time or sandwich options. All students also have the opportunity to study a modern language either as a minor option or by studying part-time through the Modern Languages Centre. Most courses are vocational and include such subjects as Accountancy and Business, Architecture, Art and Design, Computing, Education, Engineering, Geography and Environmental Sciences, Food Sciences, Hospitality and Tourism, Human and Health Sciences, Law, Marketing, Music and Sciences.

Hull The academic year is divided into two semesters with all full-time courses made up of core and optional modules. There is also a free elective scheme which allows students to take one module each year outside their main subject. A 'Languages for All' programme is available for all students irrespective of their degree course subject. The wide range of subjects offered include Arts and Humanities, Business, Computing, Drama, Economics, Education, Engineering, Law, Medicine, Music, Nursing, Physical Sciences, Social Sciences and Sport.

Imperial London The University offers Science and Engineering programmes leading to BSc, BEng, MSci and MEng degrees, and MB, BS and BSc programmes in the School of Medicine. Science courses are offered primarily in one principal subject, but flexibility is provided by the possibility to transfer at the end of the first year and by the choice of optional subjects in the later years of the course. Joint honours courses are offered in the Departments of Biological Sciences, Chemistry and Mathematics. A Humanities programme is also open to all students with a wide range of options whilst the Tanaka Business School offers Management courses which form an integral part of undergraduate degrees.

Keele Flexibility is provided through either interdisciplinary single honours degrees, bringing together a number of topics in an integrated form, or dual honours degrees in which two principal subjects are studied to degree level to the same depth as a single honours course. In addition, all students take a first-year course in Complementary Studies and may also study a foreign language. Courses are offered in Arts subjects, Biosciences and Physical Sciences, Economics, Education, Law, Management Science, Media, Music and Social Sciences.

Kent Single honours courses can include the option of taking up to 25% of the degree in another subject, or to change the focus of a degree at the end of the year. Two subjects are studied on a 50/50 basis in joint honours courses and there are also major/minor honours degrees. Degrees are offered in Accountancy and Business courses, Arts subjects, Biological and Physical Sciences, Computer Science, Drama and Theatre and Film Studies, Languages, Law, Music Technology, Pharmacy, Psychology, Religious Studies and Social Sciences.

Kingston Single and joint honours courses are offered within a modular structure, with the opportunity to take a language option in French, German, Italian, Japanese, Mandarin Chinese, Russian or Spanish. Several courses are available as a minor field, for example, Business, which adds an extra dimension to the chosen degree. Subjects are offered in the Faculties of Art, Design and Music, Arts and Social Sciences, Business, Health and Social Care Sciences, Science, Technology and in the School of Education. Exchange schemes are offered with 72 universities in Europe and five in the USA.

Lampeter Single and joint honours courses are offered, together with combined honours programmes in which three subjects are taken. All students can apply to study abroad in Canada or the USA during their second year. Over 40 subjects are offered covering Arts, Humanities, Film and Media Studies, the Environment and Business. There is considerable flexibility in course choice. In Year 1 (Part 1) all students take three subjects (two subjects alongside the main subject). In Years 2 and 3 course units can be taken in one subject but two units can be taken in a second subject (not always one studied in the first year). Combined and non-standard degrees are possible including the option to 'choose your own course'.

Leeds A very wide range of courses are on offer in most subject areas (Leeds is a pioneer of joint honours degrees). In the first year joint honours students normally divide their time equally between three subjects with a wide choice of the third or elective subject in the first year. In many cases, students can transfer to a different course at the end of the first year and delay their final choice of degree. A wide range of subjects is offered in Arts and Humanities, Science and Engineering, Social Sciences and in the Management School.

Leeds Metropolitan Many of the degrees are vocational with links to industry and commerce. Courses are modular with core studies and optional modules. Degree programmes are offered in the Faculties of Arts and Society, Information and Technology, Health, Sport and Recreation, the Leslie Silver International Faculty and the Leeds Business School.

Leicester The single honours courses are offered in all the main disciplines and are taken by 75% of students. The main subject of study may be supported by one or two supplementary subjects taken in the first, and sometimes the second, year. Joint honours courses are also offered. A three-year Combined Studies degree is also available in which three subjects are studied, one taken for two years only. Apart from Medicine, all programmes have a common modular structure with compulsory modules and a wide choice of optional modules.

Lincoln Faculties include those of Applied Computing Sciences, Art, Architecture and Design, Business and Law, Health, Life and Social Sciences, Medical Sciences and Media and Humanities. Single and joint subject degrees are offered on a modular basis, with many subjects offering the chance to study abroad.

Liverpool The University offers degrees in the Faculties of Arts, Engineering, Medicine, Science, Social and Environmental Studies and Veterinary Science. Apart from courses with a clinical component, programmes are modular. In some cases they include placements in industry or in another country whilst a 'Languages for All' scheme offers European languages. A combined honours programme in Arts gives students the chance to choose three subjects in Year 1, reducing to two subjects in Years 2 and 3. A similar combined honours course in Social and Environmental studies is also offered.

Liverpool Hope Single honours courses leading to degrees of BA and BSc are offered and there is also a wide range of options by way of two combined subjects. Course combinations are available in Business,

Computing, Dance, Drama, Education, English, Environmental Management, Film Studies, Fine Art and Design, Geography, Health, History, Human Biology, Irish Studies, Law, Leisure, Marketing, Music, Media, Politics, Psychology, Sociology, Sports Studies, Theology and Religious Studies, Tourism, and War and Peace Studies.

Liverpool John Moores Courses are offered in the Faculties of Business and Law, Education, Community and Leisure, Health and Applied Social Sciences, Media, Arts and Social Science, Science and Technology and the Environment. The majority of courses provide the opportunity for work-based learning or for a year-long industrial placement.

London (Birkbeck) Part-time evening courses are offered for mature students wishing to read for first and higher degrees. Courses are offered in the Faculties of Arts, Science, Social Science and Continuing Education.

London (Central School of Speech and Drama) The School offers a broad range of courses in the Theatre Arts. It is also linked to the Webber Douglas Academy of Dramatic Art to provide a range of courses leading to careers in classical and contemporary theatre, film and TV. Courses include Acting, Costume Construction, Stage Design, Prop making, Puppetry, Stage Management, Theatre Lighting and Sound Design.

London (Goldsmiths) Programmes are offered in Art, Drama and Media, the Arts, Education and Social Sciences. Like most London University degrees, the majority of undergraduate degrees are made up of course units giving some flexibility. Twelve units are taken over three years.

London (Heythrop) Nine BA courses are offered in Philosophy and Theology. The supportive and learning environment is enhanced by one-to-one tutorials for all students throughout their courses.

London (Institute in Paris) A single honours course in French Studies is offered to English-speaking students, taught almost entirely in French. Students graduate after their three-year course with a University of London BA and study in France for the whole of their course.

London (King's) The College offers more than 200 degree programmes covering Humanities, Law, Physical Sciences and Social Science and Public Policy at the Strand campus, Health and Life Sciences, Nursing and Midwifery and Social Science at Waterloo, and Biomedical Sciences, Medicine and Dentistry at the Guy's or King's Denmark Hill and St Thomas's campuses. The degree course structure varies with the subject chosen and consists of single honours (one subject), joint honours (two subjects), combined honours (a choice of over 60 programmes) and major/minor courses.

London (London School of Economics and Political Science) The School offers courses not only in Economics and Political Science but also in a wide range of Social Science subjects taught in 19 Departments. Programmes are offered as single honours, joint honours or major/minor courses. LSE entrance examination may be required (see **Chapter 6**).

London (Queen Mary) The College offers courses in the Arts and Humanities, Biological and Physical Sciences, Business Management and Economics, Computer Science, Engineering, Languages, Materials Science, Mathematics, Medicine and Social Sciences. In most subjects, students choose compulsory and optional course units which allow for some flexibility in planning a course to suit individual interests.

London (Royal Holloway) The College offers single, joint and major/minor honours degrees in three Faculties – Arts, History and Social Sciences, and Science. Study abroad is a feature of many courses and all students can compete for international exchanges.

London (Royal Veterinary College) Two courses are offered in Veterinary Medicine and Veterinary Sciences, the latter not qualifying graduates to practise as veterinary surgeons.

London (School of Oriental and African Studies) This is the only higher education institution in the UK specialising in the study of Asia, Africa and the Near and Middle East. Single subject degrees include compulsory and optional units with two-thirds of the total units studied in the chosen subject and the remaining units or 'floaters' from a complementary course offered at SOAS or another college of the University. In addition, two-subject degrees give great flexibility in the choice of units, enabling students to personalise their degrees to match their interests.

London (School of Pharmacy) The School offers the Master of Pharmacy degree. Except for hospital and extramural projects, all the teaching takes place on the Bloomsbury campus.

London (University College) Subjects are organised in Faculties – Arts and Humanities, Social and Historical Sciences (with a flexible course unit system), Fine Art (the Slade School), Law, Built Environment (the Bartlett), Engineering Sciences, Mathematical and Physical Sciences and Life Sciences. In addition, there is the School of Medicine. The School of Slavonic and East European Studies also offers degrees which focus on developing a high level of proficiency in speaking, writing and understanding the chosen language.

London Metropolitan Single and joint honours courses are made up of compulsory and optional modules allowing students some flexibility to follow their particular interests. Courses are offered in Accountancy and Business, Art and Architecture, Arts, Humanities and Languages, Computing, Economics and Finance, Education, Health and Human Sciences and Law.

London South Bank Subject areas cover Arts and Human Sciences including Law and Psychology, Business, Computing and Information Management, Engineering, Science and the Built Environment and Health and Social Care. All courses have flexible modes of study and many vocational courses offer sandwich placements.

Loughborough Academic programmes cover Art and Design, Business, Computer Science, Economics, Engineering, European Studies and Politics, Humanities, Sciences, Social Science and Sport. Degree programmes combine compulsory and optional modules and some transfers between courses are possible. Additional language study is possible in French, German or Spanish (including beginners' courses), for students on most courses. Sandwich degree courses with a year's paid work experience in industry result in high graduate employment. World-class sporting facilities and an unrivalled reputation in sporting success attract applicants at junior international level and above.

Manchester The University offers single and joint honours courses which are divided into course units, some of which are compulsory and others optional, and some are taken from a choice of subjects offered by other Schools and Faculties. A comprehensive Combined Studies degree enables students to choose course units from Arts, Humanities, Social Sciences and Sciences, and this provides the flexibility for students to alter the emphasis of their studies from year to year. Degree programmes are offered in the Faculties of Engineering and Physical Sciences, Humanities, Life Sciences and Medical and Human Sciences.

Manchester Metropolitan Degree programmes are offered in the Faculties of Art and Design, Community Studies and Education, Food, Clothing and Hospitality Management, Humanities, Law and Social Science, Science and Engineering and the Manchester Metropolitan Business School. A large number of courses involve industrial and commercial placements. It is also possible to take combined honours degrees selecting a combination of two or three subjects. Many programmes have a modular structure with compulsory and optional core modules.

Middlesex Single and joint honours courses are offered on a modular basis, most programmes having an optional work placement. Courses cover Art and Design, Biological and Health Sciences, Business and Management, Computing and IT, Dance, Drama and Music, English and Mass Communication, Humanities and Cultural Studies, Social Sciences and Teaching and Education.

Napier Students choose between single, joint (two subject) degrees and customised degrees which can include a range of subjects. Courses are offered in Alternative Medicine and Complementary Therapies,

Built Environment and Civil Engineering, Business Management and Financial Services, Communication and Creative Industries, Computing and IT, Life Sciences, Nursing and Midwifery and Social Sciences.

Newcastle Degree programmes are available in the Faculties of Arts, Biological Sciences, Business and Law, Engineering, Medical Sciences, Physical Sciences and Social Sciences. Single, joint and combined honours programmes are offered, in some cases providing students with the opportunity to either defer their choice of final degree or transfer to other subjects at a later stage. In the Combined Studies BA and BSc courses it is possible to combine the study of up to three different subjects which can be studied over two or three years.

Newport The University consists of seven Schools – Art and Design, Humanities, Business, Computing and Engineering, Social Studies, Education and the Centre for Community and Lifelong Learning. Courses include single and joint honours and major/minor studies; they vary in structure but many are based on a modular system.

Northampton Courses are offered in seven schools: Applied Sciences (Computing, Mechanical and Electrical/Electronic Engineering), Business, Education, Health, Social Sciences, Arts (including Fine Art and Design) and Land-based subjects at Moulton College. Courses are offered as single, combined and joint honours programmes.

Northumbria A wide range of courses is offered with an emphasis on vocational studies, covering Art and Design, Arts subjects, Built Environment, Business and Financial Management, Computing, Education and Sport, Engineering, Health and Social Care, Humanities, Languages, Law, Mathematics, Nursing and Midwifery, Psychology and Sciences. Single and joint honours courses are offered, and a combined honours course allows a choice of up to three subjects.

Nottingham Single and joint honours courses are available, with some sandwich courses. Programmes are modular with compulsory and optional modules, the latter giving some flexibility in the selection of topics from outside the chosen subject field. Degree programmes are offered in the Faculties of Arts, Education, Engineering, Law and Social Sciences, Medicine and Health Sciences and Science.

Nottingham Trent Degree programmes are offered in Art and Design, Business, Computing and Technology, Economics, Education, Humanities, Law, Sciences and Social Sciences. Many courses are vocational with industrial and commercial placements and some students are also able to spend a semester (half an academic year) studying at a partner university in Europe, the USA or Australia.

Open University Six hundred degree and diploma courses are offered covering Business, Economics, Education, Engineering, Environmental Studies, Health Studies, Law, Mathematics, Philosophy, Politics, Psychology, Science, Social Sciences and Technology. Students study at home and are sent learning materials by the OU and maintain contact with their tutors by email, post and telephone.

Oxford Candidates apply to a college and for a single or joint honours programme. Courses are offered with a core element plus a variety of options. Weekly contact with a college tutor assists students to tailor their courses to suit personal interests. Arts students are examined twice, once in the first year (Preliminary examinations) and at the end of the course (Final Honours School). Science students are similarly examined although in some subjects examinations also take place in the second year.

Oxford Brookes Single honours courses are offered with modules chosen from a field of study or, alternatively, combined honours courses in which two subjects are chosen. These subjects may be in related or unrelated subjects. There is also a Combined Studies degree in which students 'build' their own degree by taking approved modules from a range of the subjects offered by the University.

Paisley The University is a leading provider of vocational education in the region offering industry-relevant and career-focused courses and many programmes include periods of paid work placements. There are also some European and US study opportunities. Courses are offered in the Business School and the Schools of Computing, Education, Engineering and Science, Health, Nursing and Midwifery and Media, Language and Music.

Plymouth A broad portfolio of degree courses is available including Medicine at the Peninsula Medical School – a partnership with Exeter University. Other courses cover Agriculture, Art and Design, Biological and Physical Sciences, Built Environment, Business and Financial Management, Computing, Drama, Education, Engineering, Health and Social Sciences, Humanities, Languages, Law, Marine Studies, Mathematics and Sport Studies. Single honours courses are offered with many vocational programmes offering work placements.

Portsmouth The Faculties of the Environment, Social Sciences, Science, Technology and the Portsmouth Business School offer single and joint honours courses. Sandwich programmes are also available in many subjects and there is also an opportunity for all students to learn a foreign language. Many courses are planned on a modular basis which allows students to defer specialisation until after their first year.

Reading Faculties of Arts and Humanities and Economics and Social Sciences provide flexible arrangements for students. A teaching system operates in Year 1 in which students can take modules in their chosen subject and in two or three other subjects. At the end of the first year they may transfer from single honours to joint honours courses or change to another subject.

Richmond, The American International University in London Courses in Art, Design and Media, Communication, Computing Engineering, Economics, Engineering (with George Washington University, USA), Finance, History, International Relations, Marketing, Political Science, Psychology and Sociology are offered with entry in September, January, May or June.

Robert Gordon The University offers a wide range of vocational courses including Accountancy and Business, Architecture, Art and Design, Computer Science, Engineering, Law, Nursing, Occupational Therapy, Pharmacy, Physiotherapy, Radiography, Sciences, Social Sciences and Sports Science. Many courses offer work placements and there are some opportunities to study abroad in Europe, Canada and the USA.

Roehampton The University manages its academic programmes in eight Schools – Arts and Business, Social Sciences and Computing, Education Studies, English and Modern Languages, Humanities and Cultural Studies, Initial Teacher Education, Sports Science and Psychological and Therapeutic Studies. All programmes operate within a modular and semester-based structure.

St Andrews A very wide range of subjects is offered across the Faculties of Arts, Divinity, Medicine and Science. A flexible programme is offered in the first two years when students take several subjects. The decision of honours degree subject is made at the end of Year 2 when students choose between single or joint honours degrees for the next two years. A broadly-based general degree programme is also offered lasting three years.

Salford The University offers BA, BSc and BEng degrees with teaching methods depending on the degree. There is a wide range of professionally accredited programmes many involving work placements. All undergraduates may study a foreign language. Subjects include Accountancy and Business, Art and Design, Computer Science, Drama, Engineering, Humanities, Journalism, Leisure and Tourism, Languages, Music, Nursing, Physiotherapy, Psychology, Sciences, Social Sciences and Sport Science.

Sheffield The teaching year consists of two semesters (two periods of 15 weeks). Courses are fully modular, with the exceptions of Dentistry and Medicine. Students register for a named degree course which has a number of core modules, some optional modules chosen from a prescribed range of topics and some unrestricted modules chosen from any at the University. Programmes offered include Accounting and Business, Arts and Humanities, Computer Science, Engineering and Materials Science, Languages, Law, Nursing, Psychology, Sciences, Social Sciences and Town and Country Planning.

Sheffield Hallam A large number of vocational courses are offered in addition to those in Arts, Humanities and Social Sciences. The University is the largest provider of sandwich courses in the UK with most courses offering work placements, usually between the second and third years. Most students are able to study an additional language from French, German, Italian, Spanish and Japanese.

Southampton A wide range of courses is offered in the Faculties of Law, Arts and Social Sciences, Engineering, Science and Mathematics and Medicine, Health and Life Sciences. Programmes are generally for three years. All students have the chance to study a language as part of their degree and there are many opportunities for students to study abroad or on Erasmus-Socrates exchange programmes whether or not they are studying modern languages.

Southampton Solent Courses are offered in the Faculties of Technology, Media, Arts and Society and the Southampton Business School. Subjects cover Art and Design, Business and Finance including Accountancy, Marketing and Personnel, Computing, Construction, Engineering and Technology, the Environment, Human and Social Sciences and Law, Leisure, Sport and Tourism, Maritime Studies and Media, Film and Journalism.

Staffordshire The Stafford campus focuses on courses in Computing, Engineering, Technology and Health Studies whilst at Stoke programmes are offered in Art and Design, Law, Business, Humanities, Social Sciences and Science subjects. Single and joint honours awards are available, some of which are for four years and include a work placement year. Part-time courses are also offered.

Stirling A flexible system operates in which students can delay their final degree choice until midway through the course. The University year is divided into two 15-week semesters, from September to December and February to May with a reading/study block and exams at the end of each semester. Innovative February entry is possible to some degree programmes. There are 250 degree combinations with the opportunity to study a range of disciplines in the first two years. In addition to single and combined degrees, there is a general degree which allows for greater breadth of choice. Subjects range across the Arts, Social Sciences and Sciences.

Strathclyde A credit-based modular system operates with a good degree of flexibility in course choices. The University offers many vocational courses in the Faculties of Engineering, Science and the Strathclyde Business School. There are also degree programmes in Arts subjects, Education, Law and the Social Sciences.

Sunderland There are five Schools of study: Arts, Media and Culture, Business, Computer Science and Technology and single, joint honours and sandwich courses. A modular programme provides maximum flexibility in choosing appropriate subjects. Some placements are possible in Canada, USA, Australia, New Zealand, India and Europe and there is a large number of mature and local students.

Surrey Degree programmes are offered in the Arts, Biomedical and Molecular Sciences, Electronics and Physical Sciences, Engineering, Health and Medical Sciences, Human Sciences and Management. Some 80% of students spend a professional training year as part of their course and in some cases there are placements abroad. There is also a part-time BSc degree in Professional Development through work-based learning.

Sussex Teaching is structured around five Schools of study, the Brighton and Sussex Medical School and the Science and Technology Policy Research Unit. Courses cover a wide range of subjects in Humanities, Life Sciences, Science and Technology, Social Sciences and Cultural Studies. Students are registered in a School depending on the degree taken. The flexible structure allows students to interrupt their degree programme to take a year out.

Swansea Courses are offered in Arts and Social Sciences, Business, Economics and Law, Engineering, Languages, Medicine and Health Sciences and Science. Degree courses are modular with the opportunity to take some subjects outside the chosen degree course. Part-time degrees are available and study-abroad arrangements are possible in several subject areas.

Teesside Single and combined honours degrees are offered with the major subject occupying two thirds of the course and the minor option one third. There is a wide choice of vocational courses, many with sandwich arrangements in industry, commerce and the professions. Courses are offered in the Arts, Business, Engineering, Law, Media, Social Sciences and Sport with large Schools of Health and Social Care and Computing and Mathematics. There is a high mature student intake.

Thames Valley Subjects offered cover Business, Management and Law, Tourism, Hospitality and Leisure, Music, Media and Creative Technologies and Health and Human Sciences. Credit-rated single and joint honours courses are offered, many with year-long work placements between Years 2 and 3. There are some study-abroad arrangements in Europe, Canada and the USA and there is a large mature student intake.

UCE Birmingham Courses are offered through the Birmingham Institute of Art and Design, the Business School, the School of Computing, the School of Jewellery and the Faculties of the Built Environment, Education, Health and Community Care, Law, Humanities and Social Sciences and the Technology Innovation Centre. Many courses have a vocational focus and include sandwich placements. Music is offered through the Birmingham Conservatoire, a music college of international standing. There is also an extensive International Exchange Programme, with many courses abroad being taught in English.

Ulster Faculties of Arts, Business and Management, Engineering and Built Environment, Life and Health Sciences and Social Sciences offer a wide range of courses. There are various styles of learning supported by formal lectures and many courses include periods of work placement.

Warwick Courses are offered by Departments in the Faculty of Arts, Science and Social Studies, the Warwick Business School, the Warwick Institute of Education and the Leicester Warwick Medical School. Students may choose single subject degrees or combine several subjects in a joint degree. Options offered in each course provide flexibility in the choice of subjects although courses are not fully modularised. Many degrees offer the opportunity to study abroad and work placements on some science courses.

Westminster Courses cover Architecture and the Built Environment, Biosciences, Business Management, Complementary Therapies, Computer Sciences, Electronics, English and Linguistics, Languages, Law, Media and Arts and Design and Psychology and Social Sciences. Undergraduate courses are modular and taught over two semesters. The University has a broad network of partnerships within the EU which enables students to include a period of study abroad as part of their degree.

Winchester Single and two-subject courses are offered consisting of either one subject, or two subjects studied equally (a joint honours degree) or a 75%–25% split by way of a main and subsidiary honours degree. Courses are offered in American Studies, Archaeology, Business, Dance, Drama and Performance, Education, English and Creative Writing, Film Studies, History, Horticulture, Journalism and Media Studies, Marketing, Psychology, Sport Science, Theology and Tourism.

Wolverhampton A large number of specialist and joint honours degrees are offered and many have work placements at home or abroad. Except for courses linked to specific professional requirements, programmes are modular providing flexibility of choice. Courses include Art and Design, Arts and Humanities, Business Studies, Computer Science, Education, Engineering, Environmental Studies, Film and Media, Health Studies, Law, Nursing, Sciences and Social Studies.

Worcester The courses are grouped into six departments: Applied Sciences, Geography and Archaeology, Arts, Humanities and Social Sciences, the Institute of Education, the Institute of Health and Social Care, the School of Sports Science and the Worcester Business School.

York There is a flexible range of subject options in a range of combined courses. The 'Languages for All' programme enables any student to take a course in any one of 14 languages, in addition to which there are several opportunities to build a period abroad into a degree course. Courses are offered in Archaeology, Arts subjects, Computer Science, Economics, Education, Electronics, Health Sciences, Languages, Management, Medicine, Music, Psychology, Sciences and Social Sciences.

York St John Specialist degrees and joint honours courses are offered in American Studies, Business, Communication, Counselling, Design, Education, English, Film Studies, History, Information Technology, Media Studies, Occupational Therapy, Performance Physiotherapy, Psychology, Sport and Theology.

TUITION FEES AND OTHER COSTS

Tuition fees are now charged for honours and ordinary degree courses in England, Wales and Northern Ireland. The level of tuition fees charged for courses is decided annually by each individual university or college.

Most universities have set the annual fees for first degree courses for 2007/8 at £3000. However, the universities listed below have set the following fees:

* Greenwich £2500; £2000 for students from partner schools and colleges; £3000 for Pharmacy degrees
* London Metropolitan £2000
* Northampton £2500
* Thames Valley £2700

In Scotland's universities the annual tuition fee for 2007/8/9/10 has been set at £1700, and at £2700 for courses in Medicine. However, these fees are subject to annual increases in line with inflation.

You may also have additional charges, depending on your course of study. For example, studio fees for Art courses could reach £250 per year, while for other courses, such as Architecture, Science and Engineering there could be charges for equipment. Additionally, there could also be charges for fieldwork trips, study abroad and vacation courses. To find out your likely yearly course costs, in addition to your tuition fees, check with your subject department.

It is also important to check your fee status if you are planning a sandwich course involving either unpaid or paid placements. You can receive a salary of up to £12,000 doing a one-year placement but check your fee status carefully and consult the relevant websites listed below.

Useful websites www.direct.gov.uk/studentfinance
www.saas.gov.uk
www.studentfinancewales.co.uk
www.studentfinanceni.co.uk

HELP TOWARDS TUITION FEES

Loans Students will not have to pay the fees before starting their courses or while they are studying: instead they will be eligible to apply for a student loan. These range from £3000 to £6000 depending on whether they will live at home or away from home, in or outside London. Loans must be repaid after leaving university when earnings exceed £15,000.

Maintenance grants These government grants are available depending on the student's household income. They are paid on a sliding scale to students where the family income is between £17,500 and £37,425, the maximum grant is £2700 per annum. These grants are not repayable.

University bursaries These are paid in cases of financial need: all universities charging course fees are obliged to offer some bursaries to students receiving maintenance grants. See the list of universities later in this chapter for the value of their bursaries.

Other financial help Some universities also offer additional bursaries to encourage applications from the locality. These may be available to students applying from partner schools or colleges and living in certain postcode areas, in some cases to the brothers and sisters of current students at the university, or to students who have been in care or are homeless. These awards are not repayable.

In addition, students on some Health-related courses, for example Dental Hygiene, Nursing, Occupational Therapy, Physiotherapy, Radiography will be eligible for NHS bursaries. Other bursaries are also payable for programmes funded through the General Social Care Council and also for shortage subjects for those on teacher training courses.

After starting the course, Access to Learning funds are available to help students in financial hardship or through emergency payments for unexpected financial crises. Hardship funds are also offered in very special cases, particularly for students with children or for single parents, mature students and, in particular, disabled students who may also claim disability allowance. These payments are made in instalments or as a lump sum or as a short-term loan.

Scholarships These are merit-based and are often competitive although some universities offer valuable scholarships to any new entrant who has achieved top grades at A-level. Scholarships vary considerably and are often subject-specific, offered through faculties or departments, so check the availablity of any awards with the subject departmental head. Additionally, there are often music, choral and organ awards, and scholarships and bursaries for sporting achievement.

LIVING COSTS

Most students spend their first year in university accommodation, the costs of which differ between universities. Halls of residence vary in the facilities they provide, and may offer single or shared study bedrooms, in some cases en suite, with meals in some cases included. Average rent prices for one week vary depending on the location of the university, ranging from £40 in some parts of the country to £70 in London.

The following is a very generalised breakdown of how living expenses might be allocated on a monthly basis:

* Rent	£300
* Utility bills (water, gas, electricity)	£30
* Telephone calls	£30
* Food/housekeeping	£170
* Local travel	£45
* Insurance	£5
* Books/stationery	£40
* Clothing	£30
* Miscellaneous (healthcare etc)	£40
* Socialising/leisure	£90
Monthly total	**£780**
Total for academic year	**£7800**

Finally, remember that price reductions are available to students at some shops, cinemas, museums and galleries and on local bus and train travel. Contact the National Union of Students for details.

Full details of bursaries and scholarships can be found in *University Scholarships, Awards and Bursaries* (see **Appendix 3**)

UNIVERSITIES' BURSARIES AND AWARDS

The list below gives brief information about the value of bursaries offered to students receiving maintenance grants as well as brief notes on the availablity of scholarships. An annual 'cost of living' figure is also given although this must only be regarded as approximate since much depends on the individual student's preferences in terms of accommodation and lifestyle.

Aberdeen *Fees:* see www.student-support-saas.gov.uk. Entrance and subject-specific awards available. *Living costs:* £6000.

Abertay Dundee *Fees:* see www.student-support-saas.gov.uk. *Bursaries:* mature student bursaries. Some financial awards and assistance for mature students. *Living costs:* £5000.

Aberystwyth *Bursaries:* £200–£1000 (see www.studentfinancewales.co.uk). Widening Participation bursaries to students from low-income families. Entrance scholarships and a large number of other awards. *Living costs:* £6000.

Anglia Ruskin *Bursaries:* £900. Academic progress awards £1000, £500; £500 for all students for 1st, 2nd and 3rd years of study. Foundation and sport awards. *Living costs:* £6800.

Arts London *Bursaries:* standard bursaries of £300 and Access bursaries of up to £1000. *Living costs:* £10,000.

Aston *Bursaries:* up to £750; £1000 allowance for students on placement. Subject-specific scholarships for some degree courses £750. *Living costs:* £7000.

Bangor *Bursaries:* £50–£3000 (see www.studentfinancewales.co.uk). Subject-specific and music awards for Welsh students. *Living costs:* £5500. 'One of the cheapest places in Britain to be a student' (*Independent*).

Bath *Bursaries:* £300–£1500. Several subject-specific, sport and choral awards available. *Living costs:* £7500.

Bath Spa *Bursaries:* up to £1500. Subject-specific scholarships of £1000 for some courses. *Living costs:* £6500.

Bedfordshire *Bursaries:* contact the University. *Living costs* £6500.

Belfast (Queen's) *Bursaries:* £500–£1000. Entrance, organ, sport and some special awards for students with financial difficulties. *Living costs:* £7500.

Birmingham *Bursaries:* £800. Students from low-income backgrounds achieving 340 UCAS points – £1200. Subject-specific, music and sport awards. *Living costs:* £7500.

Bolton *Bursaries:* £50–£300. Awards for students from partner institutions. *Living costs:* £5500.

Bournemouth *Bursaries:* £1000. Some scholarships open to all students. *Living costs:* £8000.

Bradford *Bursaries:* all students on full or partial grants will receive £500 (1st year), £700 (2nd year), £900 (3rd year). Engineering, science and cricket awards. *Living costs:* £7500.

Brighton *Bursaries:* £500–£1000. Disabled athletics scholarships (£1000) and some sports scholarships open to all students. *Living costs:* £8000.

Bristol *Bursaries:* £1000–£1200; also bursaries for students from local schools. A large number of subject-specific scholarships are available. *Living costs:* £6000–£8500.

Bristol UWE *Bursaries:* £750–£1250. Access courses students £1250. Memorial bursary for financially-restricted students taking Computer Science. Music, sport and a small number of subject-specific awards. *Living costs:* £6000–£8000.

Brunel *Bursaries:* £200–£300 (students on part-time courses £150). Several scholarships open to all students; scholarships also for students from low income or socio-economic groups, ethnic minorities, disabled students and for students in the Widening Participation scheme covering schools in local areas. *Living costs:* £8000.

Buckingham *Fees:* £15,000 per degree course (two years or three years). Some awards available for students resident in neighbouring counties. *Living costs:* £7500.

Cambridge *Bursaries:* Up to £3000. Some funds for students with disabilities. Scholarships and College awards open to all students. *Living costs:* £7000.

Canterbury Christ Church *Bursaries:* £400–£800. Musical scholarships. *Living costs:* £7000.

Cardiff *Bursaries:* £300–£1000 (see www.studentfinancewales.co.uk). Some awards for disabled students. Subject-specific scholarships available including Welsh applicant awards. *Living costs:* £7700. 'A low-cost university' (NUS).

Central Lancashire *Bursaries:* £1000 to all students from homes in which the principal earner's income is less than £60,000. Some academic and golf scholarships. *Living costs:* £6500.

Chester *Bursaries:* £450–£1350. Music, choral and sport scholarships available. *Living costs:* £7500.

Chichester *Bursaries:* £250–£1000. Sports scholarships. *Living costs:* £8000.

City *Bursaries:* £1000 for students receiving the full maintenance grant. Some charities award grants for students in need of financial assistance. Some special grants for living costs. Some scholarships available. *Living costs:* £9500.

Coventry *Bursaries*: £5000. Academic awards and 'Star' scholarships for certain courses. *Living costs:* £7200.

Cumbria *Bursaries:* £200–£1200. *Living costs:* £6500.

De Montfort *Bursaries:* £300–£500. Some academic and opportunity scholarships available. *Living costs:* £8000.

Derby *Bursaries:* £200–£800. Some Compact bursaries and awards for students living in the DE postcode area from low-income families. *Living costs*: £6800.

Durham *Bursaries:* £600–£3000. Choral, organ, cricket and subject awards. *Living costs:* £5000.

TIP
Use email rather than mobile phones to contact friends.

East Anglia *Bursaries:* some scholarships available. *Living costs:* £7000.

East London *Bursaries:* £300 for students receiving the full maintenance grant. On completion of the first semester, £500 of vouchers or credits to be spent with a range of agreed suppliers. Achievement and progress bursaries. *Living costs:* £9500.

Edge Hill *Bursaries:* £500–£1000 for those on state support and £1000 to new students with brothers or sisters already on courses at the university. Also Excellence scholarships. *Living costs:* £5500.

Edinburgh *Fees:* see www.student-support-saas.gov.uk. Subject-related awards and scholarships for Scottish students. *Living costs:* £7000.

Essex *Bursaries:* £1250–£3000. Bursaries for refugees and children of refugees and an award to mature students returning to study after several years and resident in south-east Essex. Mathematics and sport scholarships available. *Living costs:* £7700.

Exeter *Bursaries:* £50–£2000. Several scholarships available for students from the south-west and also choral and organ scholarships. *Living costs:* £7000.

Glamorgan *Bursaries:* £300 (see www.studentfinancewales.co.uk). Widening Participation grants. Several scholarships available. *Living costs:* £7500.

Glasgow Fees: see www.student-support-saas.gov.uk. Sport, organ and choral scholarships. *Living costs:* £7000.

Glasgow Caledonian Fees: see www.student-support-saas.gov.uk. Sport bursaries. *Living costs:* £7000.

Gloucestershire *Bursaries:* 30% of maintenance grant plus £300 for those on the full grant living outside Gloucestershire. £100 for new students from Compact schools. Annual rebate of 10% of fees to those who progress to the next level of their course. *Living costs:* £6700.

Greenwich *Fees:* MPharm £3000; all other degree programmes £2500. Partner colleges £2000. *Bursaries:* £300 for MPharm students on the full maintenance grant. £500 for mature students and for other students dependent on satisfactory progress. *Living costs:* £8000.

Heriot-Watt *Fees:* see www.student-support-saas.gov.uk. Several scholarships available. *Living costs:* £6300.

Hertfordshire *Bursaries:* 50% of the maintenance grant up to a total of £1350. Academic and Science and Engineering awards for entrants with 280–340 UCAS points. *Living costs:* £6500.

Huddersfield *Bursaries:* £500–£1000. Some subject-specific awards available. *Living costs:* £5700.

Hull *Bursaries:* £500–£1000. Part-time study bursaries. Subject-specific scholarships and awards available to students from local areas. A large number of scholarships available. *Living costs:* £6500.

Imperial London *Bursaries:* £100–£4000. Holligrave scholarships for students from educationally and financially disadvantaged backgrounds. Subject scholarships available. *Living costs:* £10,000.

Keele *Bursaries:* £300 towards fees; bursaries also for students from backgrounds with little or no tradition of higher education and for students from rural areas who need to live on campus because of transport difficulties (£500 for each year of study). Ethnic minority bursaries. Keele-link bursaries for students from partner schools. Some scholarships and bursaries open to all students. *Living costs:* £9000.

TIP
Get books from the library or secondhand shops.

Kent *Bursaries:* £250–£1000. Academic excellence, sport and music scholarships. *Living costs:* £9000.

Kingston *Bursaries:* £300–£1000. Scholarships for students from associate colleges and awards for students taking shortage subjects in the School of Education. *Living costs:* £9000.

Lampeter *Bursaries:* see www.studentfinancewales.co.uk. Scholarships and other awards available. *Living costs:* £5500.

Leeds *Bursaries:* £300–£1300. Special awards for students in financial difficulties. Further scholarships available. *Living costs:* £9000.

Leeds Metropolitan *Fees:* £2000. Sports bursaries. *Living costs:* £9000.

Leicester *Bursaries:* £50–£1300. First-year and subject-specific scholarships. *Living costs:* £7500.

Lincoln *Bursaries:* up to £600 depending on maintenance support; £500 for each year completed; £500 Faculty award. *Living costs:* £7500.

Liverpool *Bursaries:* £1000–£4000. Attainment scholarships in a range of scientific and engineering subjects. *Living costs:* £8800.

Liverpool Hope *Bursaries:* £700–£1000. £400 for students not entitled to a maintenance grant. Some achievement and excellence awards. *Living costs:* £8800.

Liverpool John Moores *Bursaries:* £1000 for all students in receipt of a maintenance grant. Some A-level result and subject awards. *Living costs:* £8800.

London (Goldsmiths) *Bursaries:* £100–£1000. Scholarships for students from the London area. Academic and music scholarships. *Living costs:* £10,000.

London (Heythrop) *Bursaries:* £300–£1300. *Living costs:* £10,000.

London (King's) *Bursaries:* 50% of maintenance grant. Scholarships available. *Living costs:* £10,000.

London (London School of Economics and Political Science) *Bursaries:* up to £2500. Some scholarships available. *Living costs:* £10,000.

London (Queen Mary) *Bursaries:* £800–£1000; up to £4000 for high achievers. Some scholarships available. *Living costs:* £10,000.

London (Royal Holloway) *Bursaries:* £500 for all students receiving less than full grants. Bursaries for students wishing to join the Royal Army Veterinary Corps. *Living costs:* £10,000.

London (School of Pharmacy) *Bursaries:* contact the School. *Living costs:* £10,000.

London (St George's) *Bursaries:* £150–£1200. *Living costs:* £10,000.

London (School of Oriental and African Studies) *Bursaries:* £400–£700. *Living costs:* £10,000.

London (University College London) *Bursaries:* 50% of the maintenance grant. Denys Holland scholarship for students experiencing financial difficulty. Academic scholarships available. *Living costs:* £10,000.

London Metropolitan *Bursaries:* pro-rata amounts payable depending on the maintenance grant; minimum bursary £300. Bursary for students with a family member enrolled at the University. *Living costs:* £10,000.

London South Bank *Bursaries:* minimum £300. All students receive £500 in the first year and £750 in years 2 and 3. Competitive scholarships for students from one of four local colleges and some ethnic minority awards. Science and Engineering scholarships. *Living costs:* £10,000.

Loughborough *Bursaries:* £1300 (maximum) with other bursaries fixed on a sliding scale dependent on the level of the maintenance grant. Higher bursaries for students over 21. Over 100 renewable and merit-based scholarships worth 25% of the tuition fee. Military sponsorships. *Living costs:* £6500.

Manchester *Bursaries:* up to £1000 for students with a family annual income below £26,000. Advantage scholarship of £5000 for all students with three grade As at A-level from households with an annnual income of £17,500 or less. Several other scholarships based on academic merit. *Living costs:* £8500.

Manchester Metropolitan *Bursaries:* £100–£1000. *Living costs:* £8500.

Middlesex *Bursaries:* dependent on the level of the maintenance grant; £300 minimum. Merit-based scholarships. *Living costs:* £9000–£10,000.

Napier *Fees:* see www.student-support-saas.gov.uk. Scholarships for students from state schools. *Living costs:* £7000.

Newcastle Bursaries: £600–£1200. A wide range of merit-based scholarships. *Living costs:* £7600.

Newport *Bursaries:* see www.studentfinancewales.co.uk. Bursaries for some students in the School of Education, partner schools and those seeking childcare support. *Living costs:* £5500.

Northampton *Fees:* £2500. *Bursaries:* £500 for students paying the full tuition fee depending on family income and/or home postcode. Additional funds are available from the Access to Learning Fund, the Emergency Loan Fund and the Bridging Loan Fund. Awards range from £300 to £3500. Other merit awards are also offered. *Living costs:* £6500.

Northumbria *Bursaries:* minimum £300 for all students receiving the full maintenance grant. Some scholarships available. *Living costs:* £7600.

Nottingham *Bursaries:* £250–£100 depending on the level of the maintenance grant. 'First in the Family' and other awards and scholarships. *Living costs:* £7000.

Nottingham Trent *Bursaries:* £200–£800 for students on partial state support plus £250 per annum for those on full state support with a family and an NG postcode; £2000 merit-based scholarships for those on full state support. Part-time and other merit scholarships. *Living costs:* £7000.

Oxford *Bursaries:* £4000 in year 1 and £3000 in years 2 and 3 for students on the maximum maintenance grant. Other bursaries for those on partial grants. Scholarships and college awards offered. *Living costs:* £8500.

Oxford Brookes *Bursaries:* £200–£1230 depending on the level of the maintenance grant. Some subject scholarships. *Living costs:* £8000.

Paisley *Fees:* see www.student-support-saas.gov.uk. A small number of scholarships. *Living costs:* £7000.

Plymouth *Bursaries:* £300–£500 for students in schools and colleges receiving educational maintenance allowances; also bursaries for mature students. Some sport scholarships. *Living costs:* £7000.

Portsmouth *Bursaries:* up to £800. *Living costs:* £7000.

Reading *Bursaries:* £325–£1300. Entrance scholarships for some degree courses. *Living costs:* £6000.

Robert Gordon *Fees:* see www.student-support-saas.gov.uk. *Living costs:* £4500.

Roehampton *Bursaries:* £500. Some scholarships available. *Living costs:* £7500.

St Andrews *Fees:* see www.student-support-saas.gov.uk. A number of scholarships available. *Living costs:* £7500.

Salford *Bursaries:* £650 plus £1000 for a year abroad. Several scholarships. *Living costs:* £7500.

Sheffield *Bursaries:* £400–£600 for students with high grades at A-level, those from Outreach and Access to Medicine schemes. A range of scholarships available. *Living costs:* £7000.

Sheffield Hallam *Bursaries:* £300–£700. Memorial bursaries for students from South Yorkshire and North Humberside. *Living costs:* £7000.

Southampton *Bursaries:* £500–£1000. Additional bursaries for some students from Hampshire and the Isle of Wight; 30 bursaries of £1000 for students on the six-year BMed programme. Scholarships based on academic excellence. *Living costs:* £7500.

Southampton Solent *Bursaries:* £250–£1000. Living costs: £7500.

Staffordshire *Bursaries:* up to £1300. Awards for students from partner colleges in Staffordshire, Cheshire and Shropshire and for some students over 21 enrolling on Level 1 courses. *Living costs:* £7500.

Stirling *Fees:* see www.student-support-saas.gov.uk. Sports schoalrships. *Living costs:* £5500.

Strathclyde *Fees:* see www.student-support-saas.gov.uk. Sports scholarships and Engineering awards. *Living costs:* £6000.

Sunderland *Bursaries:* £500. Some Engineering scholarships. *Living costs:* £5500.

Surrey *Bursaries:* £300–£1000. Scholarships for some shortage subjects and/or based on academic criteria. *Living costs:* £6500.

Sussex *Bursaries:* £1000 for students on the full maintenance grant. Several merit-based scholarships available. *Living costs:* £7000.

Swansea *Bursaries:* see www.studentfinancewales.co.uk. New-entrant scholarships and Millennium scholarships based on merit, disability or special needs worth £1125. Subject-specific scholarships. *Living costs:* £5500.

Teesside *Bursaries:* £500–£1300 for students on full or partial maintenance grants. £500 for all new students except those on specially funded courses; 250 subject/merit-based scholarships for Year 1 students up to a maximum of £1000. Elite Athletic bursary. *Living costs:* £5500.

Thames Valley *Fees:* £2700. *Bursaries:* £1000 for students on a maintenance grant, £500 for all other new UK or EU students. *Living costs:* £9000.

UCE Birmingham *Bursaries:* £500 for all students receiving a maintenance grant. Music and choral scholarships and several subject-specific awards. *Living costs:* £7000.

Ulster *Bursaries:* up to £1000. Some merit-based scholarships. *Living costs:* £5500.

Warwick *Bursaries:* up to £3000. Music and sports scholarships. *Living costs:* £6500.

Westminster *Bursaries:* £300 (up to £1365 for students with dependents). Some scholarships available for Foundation and part-time courses. *Living costs:* £9400.

Winchester *Bursaries:* £300 plus a Winchester scholarship for all students (£300 to £400 annually). Scholarships for students from partner schools and for those who have been under childcare arrangements since the age of 14. Also awards for living and day-to-day expenses for some students. *Living costs:* £7500.

Wolverhampton *Bursaries:* up to £1300 plus £1000 discount on fees for students on 'Aim Higher' route. Some Excellence scholarships in Science and Engineering. *Living costs:* £6000.

TIP

Set a spending limit on your nights out.

Worcester *Bursaries:* up to £500. Excellence scholarships awarded at the end of Year 1. *Living costs:* £6000.

York *Bursaries:* £600–£1400. Several subject-specific awards. *Living costs:* £6500.

York St John *Bursaries:* £1000–£1500. *Living costs:* £6500.

5 | APPLICATIONS

ENTRY REQUIREMENTS

Before applying to universities and colleges, applicants should check that by the time they plan to start their course they will have the required qualifications. Details of entry requirements are available direct from the universities and colleges. Applicants will need to fulfil:

(i)   the **general** entry requirements for courses;

(ii)   any **specific** subject requirements to enter a particular course, for example, study of specified GCE A- and/or AS-levels, Scottish Highers/Advanced Highers, GCSEs, Scottish Standard Grades, or BTEC qualifications (for example, National Diploma, National Certificate). The course requirements are set out in prospectuses and on websites.

(iii)   any **age**, **health**, **Criminal Records Bureau (CRB) clearance** or **other** requirements for entry to particular courses and universities and colleges. For entry to some specific courses such as Medicine and Nursing, offers are made subject to health screening for hepatitis B, for example, and immunisation requirements. Owing to recent Government regulations, some universities will now insist on a minimum age at entry of 18 years. Also, for some courses, CRB clearance is required, so check university and college websites and prospectuses for these particular course requirements.

(iv)   **admissions tests** which are now required by a number of universities for a range of subjects, including Dentistry, Law, Medicine and Veterinary Science/Medicine. Offers of places made by these universities are dependent on an applicant's performance in the relevant test. It is important to find out full details about universities' course requirements for possible admissions tests well before submitting the UCAS application and to make all the necessary arrangements for registering and taking any required admissions tests. Check university/college and admissions tests websites for the latest information. See also **Chapter 6**.

Potential applicants should ask the advice of teachers, careers advisers and university and college advisers before submitting their application.

APPLICATIONS FOR UNIVERSITY AND COLLEGE COURSES THROUGH UCAS

UCAS, the organisation responsible for managing applications to higher education courses in the UK, deals with applications for admission to full-time and sandwich first degree, Foundation degree, Diploma of Higher Education and Higher National Diploma courses and some full-time Higher National Certificate courses in nearly all universities (but not the Open University), university colleges, colleges and institutes of higher education, specialist colleges and some further education colleges.

Full details of application procedures and all course information can be found on the UCAS website www.ucas.com. This information is also available in the UCAS publications *How to Apply Online* and the *Directory* which can be obtained from UCAS Application Requests, UCAS, Rosehill, New Barn Lane, Cheltenham, Glos GL52 3LZ, Tel 0870 112 2200.

Applications are usually submitted electronically by using **UCAS Apply**, a secure web-based application system, particularly useful for independent home or international users. Application can also be made by the CD ROM-based Electronic Application System (EAS) available in schools, colleges, Connexions offices or British Council offices. All applications should be made online direct to UCAS but in some circumstances paper applications can still be made.

Applications are submitted from 1 September (except for Art and Design courses via Route B, see below). The first closing date is 15 October for applications to Oxford or Cambridge Universities and for courses in Medicine, Dentistry and Veterinary Medicine or Veterinary Science. The final closing date for applications (including Art and Design, Route A) from UK and EU students is 15 January. Late applications for all courses may be considered up to 30 June.

On the UCAS application, you may have up to five course choices unless you are applying for Dentistry (courses A200, A203, A204, A205 and A206), Medicine (courses A100, A101, A102, A103, A104 and A106) or Veterinary Science/Medicine (courses D100 and D101). For these courses only four choices are permitted.

Each university or college makes an offer through the UCAS system. UCAS does not make offers, or recruit on behalf of universities and colleges. It does not advise applicants on their choice of subject although it does publish material which applicants may find useful.

Applicants may receive an 'unconditional' offer in the case of those who already hold the required qualifications, or, for those awaiting examination results, a 'conditional' offer or a rejection. When all replies are received from universities or colleges, applicants may finally hold up to two offers: a first choice (firm) offer and an insurance offer. Those rejected by all universities or who withdraw their applications may decide to use **UCAS Extra**. Applicants are told when they become eligible for **UCAS Extra** and can refer themselves on-line via **UCAS Track** on www.ucas.com from mid March until 12 July. This scheme enables applicants to make additional course choices, one at a time, where vacancies still exist. Courses available on **UCAS Extra** will be highlighted on **Course Search** on www.ucas.com. Applicants not placed through this system will be eligible to re-apply through the Clearing Scheme from mid August.

Confirmation starts on the day when the A-level examination results are released. Clearing vacancy lists are also published on A-level results day. Applicants who have met the conditions of their offers for their firm choice will receive confirmation from their university or college and may still be accepted even if their results are slightly lower than those stipulated in the original offer. If rejected by their firm choice university/college applicants will have their places confirmed by their insurance choice institution providing they have obtained the right grades. Applicants who are unsuccessful with both their institutions will be eligible to go into Clearing in which they can select an appropriate course in the same or a different institution where places are available. Each year up to 40,000 applicants obtain places through Clearing.

UCAS timetable

1 September	UCAS begins accepting applications.
15 October	Deadline for applications to Oxford or Cambridge and courses leading to a professional qualification in Medicine, Dentistry or Veterinary Science to reach UCAS.
15 January	Deadline for UK and EU applications to reach UCAS.
16 January–30 June	Late applications received by UCAS are forwarded to the institutions for consideration at their discretion. Applications received after 30 June (Art and Design Route B after 12 June) are processed through the Clearing Scheme.
14 March	Applicants without offers, who have been rejected by all universities or colleges or who have declined all offers received, will be alerted to a new

	service by UCAS. They will receive an 'Extra Passport' which will enable them to contact institutions with vacancies, one at a time. Institutions with vacancies will list courses on the UCAS website. Details of this service will be included in the 'Advice for Applicants' leaflet sent to applicants.
24 March	Applications due at UCAS for Route B Art and Design courses. Applicants are advised to submit these, if possible, by 7 March.
5 May	Applicants who have received all their decisions from universities and colleges by the end of March are asked to reply to their offers by this date.
6 June	Applicants receiving decisions from all their choices by 9 May must reply to their offers by this date.
12 June	Last date for receiving late Route B Art and Design applications.
30 June	Last date for receiving late applications. After this date applications are Clearing only.
Mid July	Clearing entry forms begin to be issued to eligible applicants.
8 August	Scottish SQA results published.
17 August	GCE A-level and AS-level results published. Clearing vacancy information available. (See **What To Do on Results Day . . . and After** below.)

PLEASE NOTE:

* You are not required to reply to any university/college offers until you have received your last decision.
* Do not send a firm acceptance to more than one offer.
* Do not try to alter a firm acceptance.
* Send a Withdrawal slip to UCAS at once if you decide not to go to university/college this year.
* Remember to tell the institutions and UCAS if you change your address, or change your examination board(s), subjects or arrangements.

APPLICATIONS FOR ART AND DESIGN COURSES

Applications for Art and Design courses are submitted via one or both of two routes which are of equal status.

Route A Courses will be identified on **Course Search** on the UCAS website, by a letter **A** after the course code. Route A courses are also identified in a separate box in the UCAS *Directory*. Applicants may enter up to **five** choices and the closing date for receipt of applications at UCAS is 15 January although early application is recommended since portfolios have to be inspected. Applications through this route will be considered simultaneously by the institutions listed. Applicants in Route A for Fine Art courses at the Ruskin School of Fine Art, Oxford must submit their application and forms by 15 October. Details from the Ruskin School of Drawing and Fine Art, 74 High Street, Oxford OX1 4BG.

Route B Courses will be identified on **Course Search** on the UCAS website, by a letter **B** after the course code. Route B courses are also identified in a separate box in the UCAS *Directory*. Additionally **all** Route B course codes have a letter **E** within them. **Three** applications may be submitted between 1 January and 24 March and early application, no later than 8 March, is recommended. Applicants will be asked to indicate on an interview preference form the order in which they wish to be interviewed by the institutions to which they have applied and applications will be considered in that order.

Applicants may apply through both routes if they wish, but can then use no more than three of the maximum five choices on Route B applications.

APPLICATIONS FOR LAW COURSES

Applicants for some specified undergraduate Law programmes at the Universities of Birmingham, Bristol, Cambridge, Durham, Exeter, Glasgow, London (King's), (UCL), Manchester Metropolitan, Nottingham and Oxford will have to sit the National Admissions Test for Law (LNAT). See **Chapter 6** and see also the LNAT website (www.lnat.ac.uk) for full details of which Law courses require applicants to sit the LNAT and for information about registration fees, sample papers, test dates and test centres. Applicants are advised to fill in their UCAS application before registering or taking the LNAT but it is important to check the deadlines for registering for, and sitting, the test. If you apply for Law at an LNAT-participating university but fail to take the test in time, your application will be rejected by the university. It is important to note that applicants must enter their UCAS number on the LNAT registration form by specified deadlines (check for 2007/2008 dates) and that applicants' LNAT scores cannot be sent to the universities to which they have applied until this has been done and all LNAT fees have been paid.

If you are applying for any other Law courses which are not listed on the LNAT website, or by the universities themselves with the LNAT as a requirement, there is no need for you to sit the LNAT.

APPLICATIONS FOR MEDICINE AND DENTISTRY COURSES

The admissions process for Medicine and Dentistry is currently undergoing great change so it is vital that you check university websites for course requirements for their medical and dental schools. Students applying for these subjects are usually required to sit the UK Clinical Aptitude Test (UKCAT) or the BioMedical Admissions Test (BMAT). You will need the most up-to-date information about taking the UKCAT or BMAT admissions tests (for example, about registration deadlines, test dates, test centres, practice papers) by checking their websites frequently (www.ukcat.ac.uk and www.bmat.org.uk). See also **Chapter 6**.

APPLICATIONS FOR VETERINARY SCIENCE/MEDICINE AND PHYSIOLOGICAL SCIENCES

The BioMedical Admissions Test (BMAT) is required for entry to specified Veterinary Sciences/Medicine courses at the University of Bristol Veterinary School, the University of Cambridge and the Royal Veterinary College. It is also required by the University of Oxford for its Physiological Sciences course.

Applicants have to register for the BMAT and must check the website (www.bmat.org.uk) for the latest information about BMAT entry closing dates, test centres, fees and test dates. See also **Chapter 6**.

APPLICATIONS FOR MUSIC COURSES AT CONSERVATOIRES

The Conservatoires UK Admissions Service (CUKAS) handles applications for practical Music courses. Applications can be made simultaneously to a maximum of six of the conservatoires listed below. Full details of the Service are given on the CUKAS website (www.cukas.ac.uk). The Conservatoires taking part in this online admissions system are:

* Birmingham Conservatoire www.conservatoire.uce.ac.uk
* Leeds College of Music www.lcm.ac.uk
* Royal College of Music www.rcm.ac.uk
* Royal Northern College of Music www.rncm.ac.uk
* Royal Scottish Academy of Music and Drama www.rsamd.ac.uk
* Royal Welsh College of Music and Drama www.rwcmd.ac.uk
* Trinity College of Music www.tcm.ac.uk

See also the **Music** table of interview requirements/tests in **Chapter 6**.

APPLICATIONS FOR NURSING AND MIDWIFERY COURSES

Degree course applications for these subjects are processed by UCAS in the usual way. The Nursing and Midwifery Admissions Service (NMAS) is merging with UCAS and applications for entry to diploma-level pre-registration Nursing and Midwifery courses at universities and colleges will also be made through UCAS from 2008. Check www.nmas.ac.uk for the latest information.

APPLICATIONS FOR SOCIAL WORK COURSES

Applications for courses should be made through UCAS. Details about social work careers and courses are available from www.socialworkcareers.co.uk. See **Appendix 2: Professional Associations** for other relevant websites.

THE UCAS APPLICATION

Two important aspects of the UCAS application concern Sections 3 and 10. In Section 3 all your university/college choices (a maximum of five) are to be listed in the order in which they are listed in the UCAS *Directory*, not in order of choice. Secondly, you should not mix your subjects. For example, in popular subject areas such as English, History or Physiotherapy, it is safer to show total commitment by applying for all courses in the same subject and not to include second and/or third subject alternatives on the form. (See advice in separate tables in **Chapter 8** for Medicine, Dentistry and Veterinary Science/Medicine.)

A brief glance at the subject tables in **Chapter 8** will give you some idea of the popularity of various courses. In principle, institutions want the best applicants available so if there are large numbers of applicants the offers made will be higher. For Medicine, offers in terms of A-level grades usually reach AAB or higher, and for Veterinary Science/Medicine AAB. Conversely, for the less popular subjects such as Chemistry or Manufacturing Engineering, the offers can be much lower – down to CC and even CD or equivalent points.

Similarly, some institutions are more popular (not necessarily better) than others. Again, this popularity can be judged easily in the tables in **Chapter 8**: the higher the offer, the more popular the institution. Quite often 'popular' universities are those located in attractive towns or cities such as Bristol, Exeter, Warwick, Bath or York. Additionally, some institutions have established a good 'reputation' for various reasons, for example, Oxford, Cambridge and Durham. Conversely and unfortunately, some universities have confused applicants with unfamiliar names and no immediate identity as to their location, such as De Montfort and Brunel. More applicants would apply to these excellent institutions if their knowledge of geography was more extensive!

When you have chosen your courses and your institutions, look again at the offers the latter usually make and compare these with the grades projected by your teachers on your UCAS reference. *It is most important to maximise your chances of a place by choosing institutions which might make you a range of offers.* When all universities have considered your application you can hold only two offers (one firm and one insurance offer) and naturally it is preferable for one to be lower than the other in case you do not achieve the offer grades or equivalent points for your first choice of university or college.

The other section of the UCAS application that deserves careful thought is Section 10 (*Personal Statement*). This seems simple enough but it is the only part of the application where you can put in a personal bid for a place! In short, you are asked to give relevant background information about yourself, your interests and your choice of course and career. Give yourself plenty of time to prepare Section 10 – if you have a Record of Achievement you could use it as a guide – as this part of your application could make all the difference to getting an offer or not.

Motivation to undertake your chosen course is very important. You can show this by giving details of any work experience and work shadowing you have done (and for History courses, for example, details of visits to places of historical interest). It is a good idea to begin your statement with such evidence explaining how your interest in your chosen subject has developed. In the subject tables in **Chapter 8** under '**Advice to applicants and planning the UCAS personal statement**', advice is given on what you might include in Section 10. You should also include various activities in which you have been involved in the last three or four years. Get your parents and other members of the family to refresh your memory – it is easy to forget something quite important. You might consider planning out this section in a series of sub-sections – and if you have a lot to say, be brief. The sub-sections can include:

* **School activities** Are you a prefect, chairperson or treasurer of a society? Are you involved in supervisory duties of any kind? Are you in a school team? Which team? For how long? (Remember, team means any team: sports, chess, debating, even business.)
* **Intellectual activities** Have you attended any field or lecture courses in your main subjects? Where? When? Have you taken part in any school visits? Do you play in the school orchestra or have you taken part in a school drama production – on or off stage? Do you go to the theatre, art galleries or concerts?
* **Out-of-school activities** This category might cover many of the topics above, but it could also include any community work you do, or Duke of Edinburgh's Awards, the Combined Cadet Force (CCF), sport, music and drama activities etc. The countries you have visited might also be mentioned – for example, any exchange visits with friends living abroad.
* **Work experience** Details of part-time, holiday or Saturday jobs could be included here, particularly if they have some connection with your chosen course. Some applicants plan ahead and arrange to visit firms and discuss career interests with various people who already work in their chosen field. For some courses such as Veterinary Science, work experience is essential, and it certainly helps for others, for example Medicine and Business courses.
* **Key Skills** These cover numeracy, communication and information technology (the basics) and also advanced skills involving teamwork, problem solving and improving your own learning. If you are not offering the Key Skills Certificate then evidence of your strengths in these areas may be mentioned in the school or college reference or you may include examples in your personal statement relating to your out-of-school activities.

Finally, plan your UCAS application carefully. You may write short statements if you wish. It is not essential to write in prose except perhaps if you are applying for English or language courses in which case your statement will be judged grammatically! Take a copy to use as a trial and a copy of your complete application to keep by you for reference if you are called for interview. Almost certainly you will be questioned on what you have written. (If you have to make a paper application remember, also, to write or print legibly in black ink (not green or blue as these colours do not copy well). Your application will be reproduced at UCAS and copies sent out to each university/college you have listed. As these copies will be only about two-thirds the size of the original it is important to present your information so that it can be easily read. To help the admissions tutor, use paragraphs and, again, if you are completing a paper application, write between, not on the lines, preferably printing your statement.)

Admissions tutors always stress the importance of the confidential report written by your head teacher or form tutors. Most schools and colleges will make some effort to find out why you want to apply for a particular course, but if they do not ask, do not take it for granted that they will know! Consequently, although you have the opportunity to write about your interests on the form, it is still a good idea to tell your teachers about them. Also, if you have to work at home under difficult conditions or if you have any medical problem, your teachers must be told since these points should be mentioned on the report.

Deferred entry

Although application is usually made in the autumn of the year preceding the proposed year of entry, admissions tutors may be prepared to consider an application made two years before entry, so that the applicant can, perhaps, gain work experience or spend a period abroad. Policies on deferred entry may differ from department to department, so you should check with admissions tutors before applying. Simply remember that there is no guarantee that you will get the grades you need or a place at the university of your first choice at the first attempt! If not, you may need to repeat A-levels and try again. It may be better not to apply for deferred entry until you are certain in August of your grades and your place.

APPLICATIONS TO THE UNIVERSITY OF CAMBRIDGE

The only major difference between the Cambridge admissions process and the normal UCAS arrangements is the date by which applications must be submitted. To allow early decisions for the benefit of other universities, the UCAS application and a Cambridge Application Form (CAF) must be submitted by 15 October at the latest: the UCAS application to UCAS in Cheltenham and the CAF to Cambridge. This allows some interviewing to start in October although the majority of interviews take place in December. Examples of written work may be requested prior to the interview and/or a short test may be set at the interview itself. This practice, however, varies between colleges and subjects (see **Chapter 6**). In January applicants receive either an offer conditional upon certain grades in examinations to be taken the following summer, or a rejection.

Decisions are made on the basis of academic record, reference, personal statement, submitted work/test results and interviews. The conditions set are grades to be obtained in examinations such as A-levels, Scottish Highers/Advanced Highers or the International Baccalaureate. Offers made by some Cambridge University colleges may also include Sixth Term Examination Papers (STEP) in mathematics (see **Chapter 6** under Mathematics).

The STEPs are taken in June and copies of past papers and the Regulations and Syllabuses can be obtained from OCR Publications, PO Box 5050, Annersley, Nottingham NG15 0DL; Tel 0870 870 6622.

NB Many of the University's colleges now use tests as part of the selection process for specific courses. See the University website and **Chapter 6** for information you need to know before completing and submitting your application.

College policies

All colleges which admit undergraduates use the selection procedures described in **Chapter 6**. However, there will be some minor variations in policy between the various colleges, within each college and also between subjects. Further information about the policies of any particular college can be found in the Cambridge *Undergraduate Prospectus* and may also be obtained from the admissions tutor of the college concerned. No college operates a quota system for any subject except Medicine and Veterinary Medicine, for which there are strict quotas for the University from which places are allocated to each college.

Full details of the admissions procedures are contained in the current Cambridge *Undergraduate Prospectus*. Copies of the prospectus are available from Cambridge Admissions Office, Fitzwilliam House, 32 Trumpington Street, Cambridge CB2 1QY, or via the website www.cam.ac.uk/admissions.

APPLICATIONS TO UNIVERSITY OF OXFORD

Application procedures to Oxford are similar to all other universities except that candidates applying to Oxford must submit a UCAS application and an Oxford Application Form by 15 October 2007 for those applying for entry in October 2008 or for deferred entry in October 2009, and admissions are carried out on a college basis. Candidates can name a college of preference and may be allocated second and third preference colleges, but if they do not have a specific college in mind, they can make an open application. This means that they will be allocated a college through a computer programme which takes account of their chosen course and the approximate number of applicants per place that each college has received that year (and gender in the case of the one women-only college).

For some subjects at some colleges at Oxford, applicants are required to sit aptitude or admissions tests (for example, the History Aptitude Test, the National Admissions Test for Law (LNAT) and the BioMedical Admissions Test (BMAT)) or to provide essays or a portfolio for interview. See **Chapter 6** for more information and contact the Oxford Colleges Admissions Office for full details. All candidates are considered carefully on their individual merits. Tutors take into account a range of information from the candidate's application including details of their academic record and the reference in order to assess a candidate's suitability and potential for his or her proposed course. Candidates applying for some courses may be required to submit samples of marked school work by early November, and/or to take a short written test when they are in Oxford for interview (see **Chapter 6**). The majority of candidates applying to Oxford are invited for interview at the beginning of December and this is an integral part of the selection procedure. Candidates will be interviewed at their college of preference and also may be interviewed by other colleges. Colleges co-operate and pool candidates to ensure that the most able candidates are offered places. Successful candidates who have not completed their school-leaving examinations will be made conditional offers based on their forthcoming examinations such as A-levels, Scottish Highers, Advanced Highers, International Baccalaureate, European Baccalaureate and other European and international qualifications. Decisions are notified to candidates via UCAS by the end of January. Candidates are welcome to attend open days which are held at all of the colleges and a number of departments, usually during the summer term or in September.

MATURE APPLICANTS

There are a great many mature students following first degree courses in UK universities and colleges. The following is a list of key points a group of mature students found useful in exploring and deciding on a university course:

* Check with your nearest university or college to find out about the courses they can offer, for example degrees, diplomas, full-time, part-time.
* Some institutions will require examination passes in some subjects, others may not.
* An age limit may apply for some vocational courses, for example Medicine, Dentistry and Teaching.
* If entry requirements are an obstacle, prospective students should approach their local colleges for information on Access or Open College courses. These courses are fast-growing in number and popularity, offering adults an alternative route into higher education other than A-levels. They are usually developed jointly by colleges of further education and the local higher education institution.
* Demands of the course – how much time will be required for study? What are the assignments and the deadlines to be met? How is your work assessed – unseen examinations, continuous assessment, practicals?
* The demands on finance – cost of the course – loan needed – loss of earnings – drop in income if changing to another career – travel requirements – accommodation – need to work part-time for income?
* The availability and suitability of the course – geographical location – competition for places – where it will lead – student support services, for example childcare, library;
* What benefits will you derive? Fulfilment, transferable skills, social contacts, sense of achievement, enjoyment, self-esteem, career enhancement?

* Why would employers want to recruit you? Ability to adapt to the work scene, realistic and balanced approach, mature attitude to work?
* Why would employers not want to recruit you? Salary expectations, inability to fit in with younger colleagues, limited mobility? However, some employers particularly welcome older graduates: Civil Service, local authorities, Health Service, religious, charitable and voluntary organisations, teaching, social/probation work, careers work, housing.

AND FINALLY . . . BEFORE YOU SEND IN YOUR APPLICATION

CHECK that you have passes at Grade C or higher in the GCSE (or equivalent) subjects required for the course at the institutions to which you are applying. FAILURE TO HAVE THE RIGHT GCSE SUBJECTS OR THE RIGHT NUMBER OF GRADE C PASSES OR HIGHER IN GCSE WILL RESULT IN A REJECTION.

CHECK that you are taking (or have taken) the GCE A- and AS-level (or equivalent) subjects required for the course at the institution to which you are applying. FAILURE TO BE TAKING OR HAVE TAKEN THE RIGHT A-LEVELS WILL ALSO RESULT IN A REJECTION.

CHECK that the GCE A-levels and other qualifications you are taking will be accepted for the course for which you are applying. Some subjects and institutions do not stipulate any specific A-levels, only that you are required to offer two or three subjects at GCE A-level. In the view of some admissions tutors NOT ALL GCE A-LEVELS CARRY THE SAME WEIGHT.

CHECK that you can meet the requirements for all relevant admissions/interview tests.

CHECK that you have made all the necessary arrangements for sitting any required admissions tests.

CHECK that you can meet any age, health and CRB requirements for entry to your listed courses.

WHAT TO DO ON RESULTS DAY . . . AND AFTER

BE AT HOME! Do not arrange to be away when your results are published. If you do not achieve the grades you require, you will need to follow an alternative course of action and make decisions that could affect your life during the next few years. Do not expect others to make these decisions for you.

If you achieve the grades or points which have been offered you will receive confirmation of a place, but this may take a few days to reach you. Once your place is confirmed contact the accommodation office at the university or college and inform them that you will need a place in a hall of residence or other accommodation.

If you achieve grades or points much higher than you expected – higher than the offer you have received – and you are already holding one or two places, you are not entitled to ignore these offers and try for a place at another 'better' university or college. If, however, you have decided definitely to change courses advise the university or college immediately.

If your grades or points are higher than you expected and you are not holding any offers you can telephone or e-mail the admissions tutor at the universities and colleges which rejected you and request that they might reconsider you.

If you just miss your offers then telephone or email the universities and colleges to see if they can still offer you a place. ALWAYS HAVE YOUR UCAS REFERENCE NUMBER AVAILABLE WHEN YOU CALL. Their decisions may take a few days. You should check the universities and colleges in your order of preference. Your first choice must reject you before you contact your second choice.

If you have not applied to any university or college earlier in the year then you can apply through the Clearing Scheme which runs from the middle of July. Check the tables in **Chapter 8** to identify which institutions normally make offers matching your results, then telephone or email the institution to see if they have any vacancies before completing your Clearing form.

If you learn finally that you do not have a place you will receive automatically a Clearing form to enable you to re-apply. Before you complete this form follow the instructions above.

If an institution has vacancies they will ask you for your grades. If they can consider you they will ask you for your Clearing form. You can only be considered by one institution at a time.

If you have to re-apply for a place, check the vacancies on the UCAS website (www.ucas.com), in the national press and through your local careers office. If there are vacancies in your subject, check with the university or college that these vacancies have not been taken.

REMEMBER – There are many thousands of students just like you. Admissions tutors have a mammoth task checking how many students will be taking up their places since not all students whose grades match their offers finally decide to do so!

IF YOU HAVE AN OFFER AND THE RIGHT GRADES BUT ARE NOT ACCEPTING THAT OR AN ALTERNATIVE PLACE – TELL THE UNIVERSITY OR COLLEGE. Someone else is waiting for your place!

You may have to make many telephone calls to institutions before you are successful. It may even be late September before you know you have a place so BE PATIENT AND STAY CALM!

TAKING A GAP YEAR

Choosing your course is the first decision you need to make, the second is choosing your university and then, for an increasing number, the third is deciding whether or not to take a gap year. But there lies the problem. Because of the very large number of things to do and places to go, you'll find that you almost need a gap year to choose the right one (although a read through *Taking a Year Off* by Margaret Flynn is a good place to start)!

Planning ahead is important but, in the end, bear in mind that you might be overtaken by events, not least in failing to get the grades you need for a place on the course or at the university you were counting on. This could mean repeating A-levels and re-applying, which in turn could mean waiting for interviews and offers and, possibly, deferring the start of your 'gap' until February or March.

Once you have decided to go, however, it's a question of whether you will go under your own steam or through a gap year agency. Unless you are streetwise, or preferably 'world wise', then an agency offers several advantages. Some agencies may cover a broad field of opportunities whilst others will focus on a specific region and activity, such as the African Conservation Experience, offering animal and plant conservation work in game and nature reserves in southern Africa.

When making the choice, some students will always prefer a 'do-it-yourself' arrangement. However, there are many advantages to going through specialist agencies. They can not only offer a choice of destinations and opportunities but also provide a lot of essential and helpful advice before your departure on issues such as health precautions and insurance. Support is also available in the case of accidents or illnesses when a link can be established between the agency and parents.

Good luck!

6 | ADMISSIONS TESTS, SELECTION OF APPLICANTS AND INTERVIEWS

The selection of applicants takes many forms. The use of predicted A-level grades (and, later, points and AS-grades) has been current practice since 1966. However, with the increase in the number of candidates for places, particularly in the popular subjects, and the rise in the numbers of students achieving higher grades, increasing importance is now attached to other aspects of the application form. The applicant's academic progress through earlier examinations, the school reference and the personal statement now receive greater consideration, particularly in the case of competitive courses, and, in addition, tests and questionnaires to be completed before interview, and further tests at the interview stage are now increasingly used. These include:

ADMISSIONS TESTS FOR LAW, MEDICINE, DENTISTRY AND VETERINARY SCIENCE/MEDICINE

The National Admissions Test for Law (LNAT)
The LNAT is an on-screen test for applicants to specified undergraduate Law programmes at the Universities of Birmingham, Bristol, Cambridge, Durham, Exeter, Glasgow, London (King's), (UCL), Manchester Metropolitan, Nottingham and Oxford. See Law below, and Law in the subject tables in **Chapter 8**. Applicants need to check the universities' websites and the LNAT website (www.lnat.ac.uk) for the UCAS codes for the courses requiring applicants to take the LNAT.

Details of the LNAT (which includes multiple-choice and essay questions), practice papers, registration dates, test dates, test centres and fees are all available on the LNAT website (see above). See **Chapter 5** for information about applications for Law courses and the LNAT website for the latest information.

The UK Clinical Aptitude Test (UKCAT)
The UKCAT is a new clinical aptitude test currently used by the majority of medical and dental schools in the selection of applicants for Medicine and Dentistry, alongside their existing selection processes.

The tests are not curriculum-based and do not have a science component. No revision is necessary, there is no textbook and no course of instruction. In the first instance, the UKCAT is a test of cognitive skills involving problem-solving and critical reasoning. With over 150 test centres, it is an on-screen test (not paper-based), and is marked electronically. The cost is £50 and some bursaries are available. Further details (including the most recent list of universities requiring applicants to take the UKCAT) are found on the website www.ukcat.ac.uk. See also the Dentistry and Medicine subject tables in **Chapter 8**, the entries for Dentistry and Medicine below, and **Chapter 5** for application details.

The BioMedical Admissions Test (BMAT)
This is a pen-and-paper admissions test taken by applicants to specified Medicine, Veterinary Medicine and related courses at the Universities of Cambridge, Manchester and Oxford, and at the Royal Veterinary College, Imperial College London and University College London. A list of exactly which courses require the BMAT is available on the BMAT website (www.bmat.org.uk) and also on university websites and in their prospectuses. It is important to note the BMAT early closing date for entries and the test dates. The two-hour test consists of three sections:

* Aptitude and skills
* Scientific knowledge and application
* Writing task.

Applicants sit the test only once and pay one entry fee no matter how many courses they apply for, but if they re-apply to universities the following year they will need to re-take the BMAT and pay another fee. Past question papers are available on the BMAT website, and a study guide is also available on www.heinemann.co.uk/bmat.

Results of the BMAT are first sent to the universities, and then to the BMAT test centres. Candidates need to contact their test centres direct for their results. See Dentistry, Medicine and Veterinary Science below and their subject tables in **Chapter 8**.

DEGREE SUBJECT LISTS OF UNIVERSITIES AND COLLEGES USING TESTS AND ASSESSMENTS

The following list of degree subjects will provide a guide to universities and colleges that use admissions tests and assessments. These may include:

* Questionnaires or tests to be completed by applicants prior to interview and/or offer.
* Examples of school work to be submitted prior to interview and/or offer.
* Written tests at interview.
* Mathematical tests at interview.
* Practical tests at interview.
* A response to a passage at interview.
* Thinking Skills Assessment (TSA) tests. These are aimed at testing critical thinking and problem-solving skills and are used by many of the Cambridge University colleges. See www.tsa.ucles.org.uk and www.cam.ac.uk/admissions/undergraduate/tests for further details.
* National Admissions Test for Law (LNAT). See www.lnat.ac.uk for further information and also **Chapter 5** under Law.
* Mathematics – Sixth Term Examination Papers (STEP), details from www.ocr.org.uk and see **Chapter 5**.
* The UK Clinical Aptitude Test (UKCAT). See above and **Chapter 5** for further information and also under Medicine and Dentistry below. Details also from www.ukcat.ac.uk.
* BioMedical Admissions Test (BMAT). See above for further information and also under Medicine, Dentistry and Veterinary Sciences below and **Chapter 5**. Details also from www.bmat.org.uk.

Cambridge University advises that changes may occur in their selection procedures and that candidates should check for changes at www.cam.ac.uk/admissions/undergraduate/apply.

Specimen tests are on the Oxford University website at www.admissions.ox.ac.uk/interviews/tests.

The information given below has been provided by universities and colleges: check their prospectuses and websites for full details of their interview and test requirements and if in doubt, contact admissions tutors.

Accountancy
Buckingham Written test for non-English-speaking applicants.

Anglo Saxon, Norse and Celtic
Cambridge (Hughes Hall and Lucy Cavendish): Test at interview; (Churchill, Fitzwilliam, Girton, Gonville and Caius, Queens', St John's, St Edmund's, Wolfson): Interview only. All other colleges require essays

to be submitted before interview.

Anthropology
Cambridge See under **Archaeology**.
Oxford See under **Archaeology**.

Arabic
Salford (Arbc Engl Transl Interp - for native speakers of Arabic) Applicants may be required to sit Arabic or English language tests.

Archaeology
Bournemouth Test for mature applicants.
Cambridge (Arch Anth) (Clare, Emmanuel, Girton, King's, Robinson, Hughes Hall, Lucy Cavendish): Test at interview; (Churchill, Robinson, Trinity): Preparatory study at interview; (Fitzwilliam, Gonville and Caius, Jesus, St Edmund's, Wolfson): Interview only. All other colleges require essays to be submitted before interview.
Oxford (Arch Anth) (All colleges offering the subject): Two recently marked essays, preferably in different subjects, plus a statement of no more than 300 words setting out your interests in archaeology and social, cultural and biological anthropology required before interview. No test at interview.
Oxford (Class Arch Anc Hist) (All colleges offering the subject): Two recent marked essays. No test at interview.

Architecture
Some universities may require applicants to complete drawing tests at the time of application and prior to interview. Most universities require art portfolios at interview.

Bradford (Coll) Questionnaire and samples of work before interview. Literacy and numeracy test at interview.
Cambridge (Downing, Emmanuel, Fitzwilliam, Girton, Jesus, King's, Magdalene, Newnham, Peterhouse, Queens', Selwyn, Sidney Sussex, Trinity, Trinity Hall, St Edmund's, Wolfson): Interview only. Essays to be submitted before interview; (Lucy Cavendish): Test at interview. All colleges require a portfolio.
Cardiff Samples of work to be sent before interview.
Dundee Samples of work required before interview.
Huddersfield, **London Met** Portfolio of work required.
Liverpool The interview will be based on the portfolio of work.
London South Bank Samples of work to be sent before interview.
Sheffield Art portfolio required for applicants without A-level Art.
Westminster Samples of work required before interview.

Art courses
All institutions will require candidates to provide a portfolio of work for discussion at interview.

Bournemouth (Comp Vis Animat) Maths, logic and life-drawing tests.
Bournemouth (AI) Practical test.
Oxford (Fine Art) (All colleges offering the subject): No written work required. Portfolio to be submitted by mid-November (see prospectus). Drawing examination. Two drawings in pencil or pencil and ink from a number of possible subjects.
Oxford and Cherwell Valley (Coll) A drawing examination is taken by all candidates who are interviewed (two drawings in pencil or pen and ink).
Matthew Boulton (CFHE) Literacy and numeracy tests.
Ravensbourne (CDC) Oral examination.

Biochemistry
London South Bank Degree subject-based test at interview.
Oxford (All colleges offering the subject): No written work required. No written tests.

Biological Sciences
London South Bank Degree subject-based test at interview.
Oxford (St Hilda's): Practical test, interpreting written work or data. (All other colleges offering the subject): No written work required. No written tests

Biomedical Science
Portsmouth Test of motivation and knowledge of the subject, the degree and careers to which it leads.

Building/Construction
Bradford (Coll) Questionnaire before interview, literacy and numeracy tests at interview.
London South Bank (Bld Serv Eng) Degree subject-based test and numeracy test at interview.

Business Courses
Arts London (CFash) School work to be submitted before interview. Degree subject-based test and numeracy test at interview.
Bolton Literacy and numeracy tests.
Buckingham English test for applicants without English as a first language.
Newcastle Some short-listed applicants will be given a variety of assessment tests at interview.
Matthew Boulton (CFHE) Literacy and numeracy tests.
South Trafford (Coll) Literacy and numeracy tests at interview.

Chemistry
London South Bank Degree subject-based test.
Oxford No written work required. No written tests.

Classical Studies
Birmingham Language aptitude test for students without a language at GCSE.

Classics (See also under **Archaeology**)
Cambridge (St Edmund's, Wolfson): Interviews only; (Emmanuel, Jesus, New Hall): Preparatory study at interview; (Churchill, Clare, Corpus Christi, Girton, New Hall, Peterhouse, St Catharine's, St John's, Trinity Hall, Hughes Hall, Lucy Cavendish): Test at interview; (All colleges except Hughes Hall, Lucy Cavendish, St Edmund's, Wolfson): Essays to be submitted before interview.
Oxford (All colleges offering the subject): Two recently marked essays normally in areas related to Classics. Written tests at interview (for details see prospectus).

Classics and English
Oxford (All colleges offering the subject) Course I: One essay relevant to Classics. (See also under **English**) Course II: One essay relevant to Classics or English. Written test at interview (for details see prospectus).

Classics and Modern Languages
Oxford (All colleges offering the subject): Two Classics essays required. Two modern language essays required, one in the language.

Communication Studies
Buckingham English test for non-English-speaking applicants.

Computer Science
Abertay Dundee (Comp Arts) Portfolio of work required. Practical tests at interview.
Blackburn (Coll) Questionnaire and test before interview.
Cambridge (Gonville and Caius): Preparatory study at interview; (Robinson, Trinity, Hughes Hall): Test at interview; (St Edmund's, Wolfson): Interview only; (all colleges with the exception of Trinity, Hughes Hall, St Edmund's): TSA tests; (Churchill): May use STEP for conditional offers; (Magdalene): STEP used for conditional offers.
Cumbria Literacy test at interview.

Liverpool John Moores Questionnaire before interview. Literacy test at interview.
London (Gold) Degree subject-based test.
London (QM) Mathematical test at interview.
Manchester (CAT) Literacy and numeracy tests.
Matthew Boulton (CFHE) Literacy and numeracy tests.
Oxford (All colleges offering the subject): See **Mathematics** below.
West Thames (Coll) Degree subject-based test and numeracy test.

Dance/Drama
All institutions with courses in which performance is involved will require an audition.

Chichester (Perf Arts) Group practical test.
Liverpool (LIPA) See under **Dance/Dance Studies** in **Chapter 8** (Interview advice and questions)

Dentistry
The following universities require UKCAT for specified courses – check www.ukcat.ac.uk: **Cardiff, Dundee, Glasgow, London (King's), (QM), Manchester, Newcastle, Sheffield**.

Bristol Degree subject-based test. (A short ten-minute test on a dental-related subject. No prior knowledge of Dentistry required, merely an awareness of the issues relating to the profession. Clarity of expression is important.)
Manchester BMAT for BDS Pre-dental year entry.

NB Check websites of all universities offering Dentistry courses for their latest admissions requirements and also see www.ukcat.ac.uk and www.bmat.org.uk.

Dietetics
London Met Interview and essay.

Drama
London (Gold) Written work required at interview.

Earth Sciences (Geology)
Oxford No essays required. No written tests at interview.

Economics
Buckingham English test for non-English-speaking applicants.
Cambridge (Churchill, Fitzwilliam, Jesus, Magdalene, Newnham, St John's, Trinity): Preparatory study at interview; (Clare, Corpus Christi, Pembroke, Sidney Sussex, Hughes Hall, Lucy Cavendish): Test at interview; (Emmanuel, Fitzwilliam, Girton, Gonville and Caius, King's, New Hall, Newnham, St John's, Selwyn, Trinity Hall, Wolfson): TSA; (Christ's, Churchill, Downing, Emmanuel, Homerton, Magdalene, Peterhouse): Essays to be submitted before interview; (Queens', St Catharine's, St Edmund's): Interview only.
Oxford (Econ Mgt) (All colleges offering the subject): Two essays required to be submitted before interview. Applicants should submit essays appropriate to these subjects. One-hour written test at interview (plus 15 minutes' reading time) designed to test comprehension, writing and problem-solving skills. See www.admissions.ox.ac.uk/interviews/tests/EM.pdf.
Lancaster Workshop.
London (LSE) Has its own admissions test – the LSE Entrance Examination – that is used for some applicants with non-standard backgrounds. The test is not subject or course specific.

Education Studies (See also under **Teacher Training**)
Cambridge (Christ's, Churchill, Emmanuel, Gonville and Caius, Homerton, Magdalene, Robinson, St John's, Trinity Hall): Essays to be submitted before interview; (Churchill, Magdalene, Trinity): Preparatory study at interview; (Clare, Girton, Jesus, New Hall, Queens', Selwyn, St Edmund's, Wolfson): Interview only; (Hughes Hall, Lucy Cavendish): Test at interview.

Durham (Primary Teaching) Key skills tests at interview.

Engineering

Blackburn (Coll) Questionnaire and tests before interview.

Bradford (Coll) (Elec Eng; Electron Eng; Instr Contr Eng; Mat Eng; Mech and Manuf Eng) Mathematical test at interview.

Bristol (Eng Des) A-level-based test.

Cambridge (Christ's, Pembroke): Interview only; (Churchill, Gonville and Caius, Magdalene, Peterhouse, Robinson, Hughes Hall, Lucy Cavendish, St Edmund's, Wolfson): Test at interview; (Trinity): Essays to be submitted before interview; (Clare, Corpus Christi, Downing, Emmanuel, Fitzwilliam, Girton, Homerton, Jesus, King's, New Hall, Newnham, Queens', St John's, Selwyn, Sidney Sussex, Trinity Hall, Wolfson): TSA.

London South Bank (Bld Serv Eng; Civ Eng; Elec Eng; Mech Eng) Degree subject-based test and numeracy test at interview.

Oxford (Eng Sci; Eng Comp Sci; Eng Econ Mgt; Eng Econ Mgt) No essays required. No written tests.

Southampton Literacy and numeracy tests for Foundation course applicants.

Southampton Solent Mathematical test at interview.

UCE Birmingham Mature students without GCSE English and/or mathematics are required to take a literacy and/or numeracy test.

English

Anglia Ruskin Samples of written work required.

Blackpool and Fylde (Coll) Samples of work before interview.

Bristol, UCE Birmingham Samples of work required.

Buckingham English test for non-English-speaking applicants.

Cambridge (All colleges except Downing, King's, Pembroke, Hughes Hall, Lucy Cavendish, St Edmunds, Wolfson): Essays to be submitted before interview; (all colleges except Christ's, Gonville and Caius, Queens', St John's, Trinity, Trinity Hall): Test at interview; (Emmanuel, Robinson): Preparatory study at interview.

Newport (Crea Writ) Samples of creative writing before interview.

Oxford (English) (All colleges offering the subject): Written work and test requirements currently under review; (St Hilda's): Samples of work required before interview. A-level-based test at interview.

Oxford (Engl Modn Langs) (All colleges offering the subject): See **English** above. A 30-minute test in the foreign language.

Portsmouth (Engl Crea Writ; Crea Writ Dr) All applicants will be required to submit a short piece of creative writing to the admissions office. This should be between 400 and 500 words long and should include the following words and use each one twice: Shell, Flicker, Knit, Coin, Compose, Lark, Stream, Root. All the words must be used and each word must be used in a different context and/or with a different meaning on each occasion. Language should be used imaginatively and accurately.

Southampton Examples of written work required from Access students.

European and Middle Eastern Languages (See under Modern and Medieval Languages)

Equine Science

Lincoln Applicants are required to show that they can ride to BHS Level 2 or equivalent.

European Studies

London (Gold) Informal conversation in the relevant language (French, German or Spanish).

Film Studies

Bournemouth A 20-page screen-play required before interview.

Bournemouth (AI) Portfolio. Practical test of short film stills.

Creative Arts (UC) Portfolio at interview.

Liverpool John Moores Questionnaire and test before interview.

Newport Portfolio of work.
Roehampton Essays taken to interview and discussed.
Westminster Questionnaire to be completed and samples of work required before interview.

French (See also under **Modern and Medieval Languages**)

Oxford (Jesus, St John's, St Hilda's): Essays to be submitted before interview. (Jesus): Response to a passage at interview; (Jesus, St John's, St Hilda's): French grammar test.

Geography

Cambridge (Christ's, Churchill, Clare, Corpus Christi, Emmanuel, Fitzwilliam, Girton, Homerton, Jesus, King's, Magdalene, New Hall, Newnham, Trinity Hall): Essays to be submitted before interview; (Downing, Gonville and Caius, Queen's, St John's, Selwyn, Sidney Sussex, Trinity, St Edmund's, Wolfson): Interview only; (Churchill, Emmanuel, Robinson, St Catharine's): Preparatory study at interview; (Fitzwilliam, New Hall, Hughes Hall, Lucy Cavendish): Test at interview.
Cardiff Test for some joint courses.
Oxford (All colleges offering the subject): Two marked pieces of written work. No written test at interview; (St Hilda's): Short written article to discuss.

German (See also under **Modern and Medieval Languages**)

Aston, **Liverpool John Moores** Written test at interview.

History

Bangor Samples of work only required from mature applicants without conventional qualifications.
Buckingham English test for non-English-speaking applicants.
Liverpool Test for mature applicants.
Liverpool John Moores Mature students not in education must submit an essay.
London (Gold) Samples of written work from non-standard applicants and from those without academic qualifications.
Oxford (Hist (Anc Modn); Hist Econ; Hist Pol) (All colleges offering the subject): All applicants take the History Aptitude Test (www.history.ox.ac) in early November (see prospectus). Those called for interview send an essay by the end of November. No written test at interview.
Oxford (Hist Modn Langs) Short 30-minute test in the language.
Roehampton Essays taken to interview and discussed.

History of Art

Cambridge (Christ's, Churchill, Clare, Corpus Christi, Emmanuel, Homerton, King's, Magdalene, New Hall, Newnham, Pembroke, St John's, Sidney Sussex, Trinity, Trinity Hall): Essays to be submitted before interview; (Downing, Fitzwilliam, Girton, Gonville and Caius, Jesus, Peterhouse, Queens', Robinson, Selwyn, St Edmund's, Wolfson): Interview only; (Hughes Hall, Lucy Cavendish): Test at interview.
Oxford (All colleges offering the subject): Two pieces required: (a) a marked essay from an A-level or equivalent course, and (b) a brief account of no more than 750 words responding to an item of art or design to which the applicant has had first-hand access with a photograph or photocopy of the item provided if possible. No written test at interview although the applicant may be presented with photographs or artefacts for discussion at interview. Submitted written work may also be discussed at interview.

Hospitality Management

Leicester (Coll) Literacy and numeracy test.

Human Sciences

Oxford (All colleges offering the subject): Two recent marked essays or project reports, relevant to the Human Sciences course, written as part of the school or college course. No written test at interview.

Italian
Cardiff Test for some joint courses.

Land Economy
Cambridge (Christ's, Clare, Fitzwilliam, Homerton, King's, Magdalene, Newnham, Peterhouse, Queens'): Essays to be submitted before interview; (Downing, Girton, Gonville and Caius, Queens', Robinson, St Catharine's, St John's, Selwyn, Sidney Sussex, Trinity, Trinity Hall, St Edmund's, Wolfson): Interview only; (Jesus, Magdalene, Newnham): Preparatory study at interview; (Newnham, Lucy Cavendish): TSA; (Hughes Hall): Test at interview.

Law
The following universities require applicants to take the LNAT for specified courses. Check university websites and www.lnat.ac.uk and see also **Chapter 5** and the Law subject table in **Chapter 8**: **Birmingham**, **Bristol**, **Cambridge** (all colleges), **Durham**, **Exeter**, **Glasgow**, **London (King's)**, **(UCL)**, **Manchester Metropolitan**, **Nottingham**, **Oxford** (all colleges) for specified courses:

Bolton Own diagnostic test used (logic and reasoning).
Bradford (Coll) Academic tests at interview for mature students.
Bristol Check with the Law Department for LNAT requirements.
Cambridge (Christ's, Corpus Christi, Emmanuel, Homerton, Magdalene, Peterhouse, Robinson, Wolfson): Essays to be submitted before interview; (Churchill, Clare, Corpus Christi, Girton, Gonville and Caius, Homerton, Jesus, Pembroke, Robinson, Trinity, St Edmund's): Test at interview; (Emmanuel, Jesus, Magdalene, New Hall, St Catharine's, Selwyn, Trinity Hall): Preparatory study at interview. All applicants take the LNAT.
Oxford (All colleges offering the subject): All applicants take the LNAT. (Law Law St Euro) LNAT plus, at interview, a short oral test in the modern language for students taking a joint language, except for those taking European Legal Studies. No other written work required except for Harris Manchester College.
UCE Birmingham Questionnaire to be completed and an IQ test.

Materials Science
Oxford (Mat Sci; Mat Econ Mgt) No written work required. No written test at interview.

Mathematics
Cambridge (All colleges except Homerton, Hughes Hall, Lucy Cavendish, St Edmund's, Wolfson): Mathematics STEP; (Churchill (possibly), Corpus Christi, Girton, King's, Magdalene (possibly), New Hall, Peterhouse (possibly), Robinson, Trinity, Hughes Hall): Test at interview; (St Edmund's): Interview only.
Liverpool John Moores Literacy and numeracy tests.
Oxford (Maths; Maths Comp Sci; Maths Stats) (All colleges offering the subjects): Overseas candidates unable to attend for interview may be required to submit written work. A 2½ hour written test is set at interview. See prospectus.
Oxford (Maths Phil) (All colleges offering the subject): Two essays showing capacity for reasoned argument and clear writing, not expected to be on a philosophical subject.

Media Studies
Bell (Coll) (Journal) Test covers public affairs and writing ability.
Blackpool and Fylde (Coll) Samples of work before interview.
Bournemouth 250-word essay.
Bournemouth and Poole (Coll) Degree subject-based test at interview.
City, Glasgow Caledonian Written test at interview.
Bolton, Leicester (Coll) Samples of work at interview.
Brighton (Spo Journal – for those called to interview: contact admissions tutor).

City Spelling, punctuation, grammar, general knowledge tests and an essay assignment. Tests given on current affairs and use of English.

Coventry Interview and portfolio.

Hull (Coll) Essay required before interview.

Liverpool John Moores Questionnaire to be completed before interview. Degree subject-based test at interview.

Napier (Journal) Samples of work before interview.

Newport Portfolio of work.

Westminster Questionnaire to be completed before interview.

Medicine

NB Some medical schools have not announced their admissions test requirements at the time of going to press and others are likely to use other admissions tests, such as the Graduate Australian Medical Schools Admissions Test (GAMSAT) and the Medical Schools Admissions Test (MSAT) for graduate-entry Medicine courses. Applicants are advised to check the websites of all universities and medical schools offering Medicine for their latest admissions requirements, including admissions and aptitude tests, and to check www.bmat.org.uk and www.ukcat.ac.uk for the latest information.

BMAT is required by **Cambridge** (All colleges), **Imperial London**, **London (UCL)**, **Manchester** (for the six-year Medicine and Foundation courses only), **Oxford** (All colleges).

GAMSAT is required by **London (St George's)**, **Nottingham**, **Swansea** (for graduate entry).

MSAT is required by **London (King's)**, **(QM)**.

UKCAT is required by the following universities and medical schools:

Aberdeen, Brighton and Sussex Medical School, Cardiff, Dundee, Durham and Newcastle, East Anglia, Edinburgh, Glasgow, Hull York Medical School, Keele, Leeds, London (King's), (QM), (St George's) (not used for MBBS 5 and MBBS 6), **Leicester Warwick, Manchester, Newcastle, Nottingham, Oxford** (graduate entry Medicine degree only), **Peninsula Medical School, Sheffield, Southampton, St Andrews**.

Modern and Medieval Languages (See also under **Oriental Studies** and separate languages)

Cambridge (All colleges except Fitzwilliam, Hughes Hall, Lucy Cavendish, St Edmund's, Wolfson): Essays to be submitted before interview; (All colleges except St Edmund's): Test at interview; (Emmanuel, New Hall, Robinson, St John's, Trinity): Preparatory study at interview; (St Edmund's): Interview only.

Liverpool The interview will last approximately 20 minutes with part of it in the language(s) to be studied. Occasionally the applicant may be asked to sit a short grammar test.

Oxford (All colleges offering the subjects): Two marked essays for each language being studied. Two 30-minute tests at interview for each language to be studied (not in languages to be taken from scratch). The tests are designed to assess grammar and not vocabulary.

Oxford (Modn Lang Ling) The essay to be submitted should involve linguistic analysis if the A-level being studied involves this.

Oxford (Euro Mid E Langs) (All colleges offering the subject): Two recent marked essays, one in the European language. Short written test in the European language at interview.

Music

All institutions will organise auditions for applicants.

Bangor Candidates offered the option of an audition.

Cambridge (All colleges except New Hall, Newnham, Queens', Sidney Sussex, Hughes Hall, Lucy Cavendish, St Edmund's, Wolfson): Essays to be submitted before interview; (Churchill, Clare, Fitzwilliam, Girton, Homerton, Jesus, King's, New Hall, Pembroke, Peterhouse, Robinson, St Catharine's, Selwyn, Trinity, Hughes Hall): Test at interview; (Clare, Emmanuel, Newnham, Robinson): Preparatory study at interview; (Downing, Queens', Sidney Sussex, St Edmund's, Wolfson): Interview only; (Lucy Cavendish): TSA.

Coventry Proforma used prior to interview. Some students rejected at this stage.

TABLE OF INTERVIEW REQUIREMENTS FOR MUSIC COURSES

Key
P = Performance
K = Keyboard tests
E = Essay
S = Sight-singing

A = Aural
H = Harmony and Counterpoint (Written)
X = Extracts for analysis or 'guessing the composer', dates etc.

Bangor*	PAX (bring example)	**Liverpool Hope**	PKH
Barnsley (Coll)	A	**London (Gold)**	PKH
Bath Spa	PKXA	**London (King's)**	PASK
Birmingham	PSKHXA	**London (RAcMus)**	PKHX
Bristol	PSKHEXA	**London (RCMus)**	PKEXH
Cambridge (Hom)*	PKE (bring example)	**London (RH)**	PHEXA
		Manchester (RNCM)	PAX
Cardiff	PE	**Newcastle**	PHXA
Chichester	P	**Oxford**	PHAK
City	PASKE	**Roehampton**	PKH
Colchester (Inst)	PKSX	**Royal Scottish (RSAMD)**	PSA
Derby	PE	**Royal Welsh (CMus/Dr)**	PSA
Durham	PKXA	**Salford**	PKEH
East Anglia	PKHEXA	**Sheffield**	PEAH
Edinburgh	PKHEA	**Southampton**	P
Glasgow	PS	**South Birmingham (Coll)**	P
Huddersfield	PH	**Surrey**	PH or X
Lancaster	PAH	**UCE Birmingham**	PAH
Leeds	PX	**Ulster**	P
Liverpool	PK	**Wolverhampton**	PE
		York	PEKHX

* Examples may include essays, harmony and counterpoint compositions. Performance tests/auditions are standard practice for music courses in all universities and colleges.

Liverpool Candidates may be asked to undertake a variety of aural tests, the performance of a prepared piece of music and some sight-reading when called for interview.

London (Gold) Degree subject-based test.

Manchester (CAT) Numeracy and literacy test.

Napier Audition and theory test.

Oxford (All colleges offering the subject): One marked sample of harmony and/or counterpoint and two marked essays on any areas or aspects of music. Candidates may submit a portfolio of compositions (these are non-returnable). Performance tests at interview; (St Hilda's): Performance, keyboard and sight-reading tests.

St Helens (Coll) (Mus Tech) Test.

UCE Birmingham Some subject-based and practical tests.

Natural Sciences (Biological)

Cambridge (Christ's, Fitzwilliam, Gonville and Caius, Jesus, King's, Newnham, Pembroke, St Catharine's, Selwyn): Interview only; (Churchill, Clare, Downing, Emmanuel, Girton, Homerton, Queens', St John's, Sidney Sussex, Trinity Hall, Wolfson): TSA; (New Hall, Trinity, Hughes Hall, Lucy Cavendish): Test at interview; (Corpus Christi, Homerton, Peterhouse, Robinson, St Edmund's): Essays to be submitted before interview; (Emmanuel, Magdalene, Robinson): Preparatory study at interview.

Natural Sciences (Physical)
Cambridge (Churchill, Clare, Downing, Emmanuel, Fitzwilliam, Girton, Homerton, New Hall, Newnham, Peterhouse, Queens, St John's, Sidney Sussex, Trinity Hall, St Edmund's, Wolfson): TSA; (Christ's, Gonville and Caius, Jesus, Magdalene, Pembroke, St Catharine's, Selwyn): Interview only; (Corpus Christi, King's, Robinson, Trinity, Hughes Hall, Lucy Cavendish): Test at interview; (Emmanuel): Preparatory study at interview; (Homerton): Essays to be submitted before interview.

Nursing
Bolton Literacy test.
Bristol UWE Questionnaire/test before interview.
City Written test.
Derby Literacy and numeracy tests at interview.
Dundee Literacy test.
Liverpool A group of candidates is given a task to undertake during which applicants are assessed for their ability to work in a team, maturity, communication skills and their level of involvement.
London South Bank Literacy and numeracy tests at interview.
UCE Birmingham Literacy and numeracy tests at interview.
York Literacy and numeracy tests.

Occupational Therapy
Bristol UWE Questionnaire/test before interview.

Optometry
Bradford (Coll) Literacy and numeracy tests.

Oriental Studies
Cambridge (Christ's, Churchill, Clare, Downing, Emmanuel, Fitzwilliam, Gonville and Caius, Jesus, Magdalene, New Hall, Newnham, Pembroke, Peterhouse, St Catharine's, St John's, Selwyn, Trinity, Trinity Hall): Essays to be submitted before interview; (Churchill, Clare, Corpus Christi, Fitzwilliam, Girton, King's, Magdalene, Peterhouse, Sidney Sussex, Trinity Hall, Hughes Hall, Lucy Cavendish): Test at interview; (Homerton, Queens', St Edmund's, Wolfson): Interview only; (Robinson, St John's): Preparatory study at interview.
Oxford (All colleges offering the subject): Two essays, preferably of different kinds. Essays in a European language are acceptable. No prior knowledge of Oriental languages required. Occasional written tests.

Osteopathy
British Sch of Ost At interview, A-level, literacy, numeracy, logic and reasoning-based tests plus a practical aptitude test.

Paramedic Science
Coventry Stress Test.

Performing Arts (See under **Dance/Drama**)

Pharmacology/Pharmaceutical Sciences
Portsmouth Test of motivation, knowledge of the subject and of the degree and the careers to which they lead.

Pharmacy
Liverpool John Moores Literacy and numeracy tests.
Portsmouth (A-level students) Test of motivation and knowledge of Pharmacy as a profession. (Other applicants) Test of chemistry and biology, plus literacy and numeracy tests.

Philosophy
Cambridge (All colleges except Lucy Cavendish, St Edmund's, Wolfson): Test at interview; (Churchill, Downing, Emmanuel, Homerton, King's, Magdalene, Peterhouse, Trinity, Wolfson): Essays to be submitted before interview; (St Edmund's): Interview only; (Lucy Cavendish): TSA.

Leeds, **London (UCL)**, **Oxford**, **Warwick** Written test at interview.

Liverpool Samples of written work may be requested in cases where there is a question of the applicant's ability to cope with the academic skills required of them.

Oxford (Phil Modn Langs) (All colleges offering the subject): Two essays required, one in the proposed language unless it is intended to start a language from scratch. A 30-minute test in the modern language at interview. (Phil) A one-hour test to assess the ability to reason analytically and to use language accurately. (Phil Theol) Written work as for Theology (see under **Religious Studies**). Written test at interview as for **Philosophy**.

Oxford (PPE) (All colleges offering the subject): Two pieces of marked written work. Those studying a related subject (philosophy, politics, economics, sociology, 19th/20th century history) should submit an essay in that subject. If studying more than one of these subjects the essays from two different subjects can be submitted. One-hour written test at interview (plus 15 minutes' reading time). No prior knowledge of philosophy, politics or economics required.

Physical Education

All institutions will require practical tests at interview.

Chichester Physical test.

Liverpool John Moores Literacy and numeracy tests and gym assessment.

Manchester (CAT) Communications test.

Physics

Bristol A-level and degree subject-based tests.

Oxford (All colleges offering the subject) Information available at www.physics.ox.ac.uk; (Corpus Christi, Jesus, St Hilda's): A-level-based test; (St John's): Mathematics-for-Physics test.

Physics and Philosophy

Oxford (All colleges offering the subject) Two pieces of written work relating to philosophy or otherwise involving careful, reasoned arguments. No written tests. No philosophy tests.

Physiological Sciences/Physiology

Oxford (All colleges offering the subject) BMAT.

Physiotherapy

Liverpool A group of candidates is given a task to undertake, during which they are assessed for their ability to work in a team, maturity, communication skills and their level of involvement.

Robert Gordon Practical testing varies from year to year.

Podiatry

Matthew Boulton (CFHE) Literacy and numeracy tests.

Politics (See also under **Social and Political Sciences**)

Buckingham English test for non-English-speaking applicants.

Liverpool John Moores Mature students not in education must submit an essay.

London (Gold) Essays to be submitted before interview.

Oxford (Keble): Written test at interview.

Psychology

Bangor Access course entry students may be asked to submit an essay.

Birmingham Written tests at interview.

Liverpool John Moores Written tests at interview.

Manchester Written tests at interview.

Manchester Met/Manchester (CAT) (Psy p/t) Samples of work before interview, numeracy and literacy tests at interview,

Oxford (Expmtl Psy) (All colleges offering the subject): No written work required. One-hour test (15 minutes' reading time) at interview. Applicants comment or answer questions on a scientific article.

Oxford (Psy Phil Physiol) To study Philosophy as part of PPP, two pieces of recent written work will be required. Written test at interview (see Expmtl Psy above).

Roehampton Questionnaire before interview; test at interview.

Radiography

Bangor Literacy and numeracy tests at interview.

Liverpool (Diag Radiog Radiothera) The group of candidates is given a task to undertake, during which they are assessed for their ability to work in a team, maturity, communication skills and their level of involvement.

Religious Studies

Cambridge (Theol Relig St) (All colleges except Churchill, Clare, Gonville and Caius, Sidney Sussex, Hughes Hall, Lucy Cavendish, St Edmund's): Essays to be submitted before interview; (Clare, Corpus Christi, Fitzwilliam, Girton, Peterhouse, Hughes Hall, Lucy Cavendish): Test at interview; (Emmanuel, Magdalene, Selwyn): Preparatory study at interview; (Gonville and Caius, Sidney Sussex, St Edmund's): Interview only.

Oxford (Theology) (All colleges offering the subject): Two essays to be submitted including one which must be ordinary marked homework of less than 2500 words. If possible, the pieces should reflect work done in Year 13. The work should be prose and should ideally contain evaluative as well as descriptive components.

Russian (See also under **Modern and Medieval Languages**)

Oxford (Jesus): A-level-based test at interview; (St John's): Russian grammar test; (St Hilda's): IQ test.

Social and Political Sciences

Cambridge (All colleges except Clare, Gonville and Caius, Jesus, Queens', St Catharine's, Hughes Hall, Lucy Cavendish): Essays to be submitted before interview; (Churchill, Emmanuel, Magdalene, Robinson): Preparatory study at interview; (Clare, Gonville and Caius, Hughes Hall, Lucy Cavendish): Test at interview; (Jesus, Queens', St Catharine's, St Edmund's): Interview only.

Social Policy

London (LSE) Two essays to be submitted before interview.

Social Work

Anglia Ruskin Samples of written work required.

Birmingham, Brunel, De Montfort, Durham New (Coll), London (Gold), Worcestershire New (Coll) Written test at interview.

Bristol UWE Questionnaire before interview.

Derby Literacy and numeracy tests at interview.

Dundee Literacy test.

London (Gold) Basic mathematics test at interview.

London Met Pre-interview literacy test and if successful, an interview.

London South Bank Literacy and numeracy tests.

Sheffield Literacy and numeracy tests.

UCE Birmingham Some tests are set at interview.

Spanish (See also under **Modern and Medieval Languages**)

Oxford (Jesus): Essays to be submitted before interview. A-level-based test at interview; (St John's): Spanish grammar test.

Speech Sciences

Manchester Met Two essays and a questionnaire.

Sheffield Listening test and problem-solving.

Teacher Training

Anglia Ruskin Literacy test at interview.

Bath Spa, **Brighton**, **Chichester**, **Cumbria**, **De Montfort**, **Gloucestershire**, **Liverpool John Moores**, **Nottingham Trent**, **Plymouth**, **Roehampton**, **Sunderland**, **Trinity Carmarthen (Coll)**, **Worcester**, **York St John** Written test at interview.

Bristol UWE, **Newport**, **St Mary's (Coll)** Literacy and mathematical tests at interview.

Brunel Literacy, mathematical and practical tests depending on subject.

Chester Literacy and numeracy tests.

Dundee, **Liverpool John Moores** Literacy and numeracy tests.

Durham Key skills test.

Gloucestershire Mathematical test at interview.

Liverpool John Moores Mathematical test at interview.

London South Bank Literacy and numeracy tests.

Nottingham Trent Practical presentation.

Plymouth Mathematical test at interview.

St Mary's (Coll) Practical tests for PE applicants.

Wigan and Leigh (Coll) Mathematical test at interview.

Winchester Literacy test at interview.

Veterinary Science/Medicine

London (RVC) BMAT.

Cambridge (All colleges except Homerton, King's, Peterhouse, Hughes Hall): BMAT; (Emmanuel, Robinson): Preparatory study at interview.

Liverpool Candidates are asked to write an essay on a veterinary topic prior to interview.

Myerscough (Coll) (Vet Nurs) Subject-based test at interview.

SELECTION OF APPLICANTS

University and college departmental admissions tutors are responsible for selecting candidates, basing their decisions on the policies of acceptable qualifications established by each institution and, where required, applicants' performance in admissions tests. There is little doubt that academic achievement, aptitude and promise are the most important factors although other subsidiary factors may be taken into consideration. The outline which follows provides information on the way in which candidates are selected for degree and diploma courses:

* Grades obtained by the applicant in GCE, A-level and AS-level examinations and the range of subjects studied may be considered. In the subject tables of **Chapter 8** some universities have indicated the levels they seek in some subjects.
* Applicant's performance in aptitude and admissions tests, as required by universities and colleges.
* Academic record of the applicant throughout his or her school career, especially up to A-level and AS-levels, Highers, Advanced Highers or other qualifications and the choice of subjects. If you are taking general studies at A-level or AS-level confirm with the admissions tutor that this is acceptable.
* Time taken by the applicant to obtain good grades at GCSE/Standard Grade and A-level and AS-levels/Highers/Advanced Highers.
* Forecast or the examination results of the applicant at A-level and AS-level and head teacher's report.
* The applicant's intellectual development; evidence of ability and motivation to follow the chosen course.
* The applicant's range of interests, both in and out of school; aspects of character and personality.
* The vocational interests, knowledge and experience of the applicant particularly if they are choosing vocational courses.

INTERVIEWS

Fewer applicants are now interviewed than in the past but even if you are not called you should make an effort to visit your chosen universities and/or colleges before you accept any offer. Interviews may be arranged simply to give you a chance to see the institution and the department and to meet the staff and students. Alternatively, interviews may be an important part of the selection procedure for specific courses such as Law, Medicine and Teaching. If they are, you need to prepare yourself well.

Most interviews last approximately 20–30 minutes and you may be interviewed by more than one person. For practical subjects such as Music and Drama almost certainly you will be asked to perform, and for artistic subjects, to take examples of your work. For some courses you may also have a written or other test at interview: see **Degree Subject Lists of Universities and Colleges using Tests and Assessments** above.

How best can you prepare yourself?

Firstly, as one applicant advised, 'Go to the interview – at least you'll see the place.'

Secondly, on the question of dress, try to turn up looking smart (it may not matter, but it can't be wrong). Two previous applicants were more specific: 'Dress smartly but sensibly so you are comfortable for travelling and walking round the campus.'

More general advice was also important:

* 'Prepare well – interviewers are never impressed by applicants who only sit there with no willingness to take part.'
* 'Read up the prospectus and course details. Know how their course differs from any other you have applied for and be able to say why you prefer theirs.'
* 'They always ask if you have any questions to ask them: prepare some!'

Questions which you could ask might focus on the ways in which work is assessed, the content of the course, field work, work experience, teaching methods, accommodation and, especially for vocational courses, contacts with industry, commerce or the professions. However, don't ask questions which are already answered in the prospectus!

These are only a few suggestions and other questions may come to mind during the interview which, above all, should be a two-way flow of information. It is also important to keep a copy of your UCAS application (especially Section 10) for reference since your interview will probably start with a question about something you have written.

Interviewers usually will want to know why you have chosen the subject and why you have chosen their particular institution. They will want to see how motivated you are, how much care you have taken in choosing your subject, how much you know about your subject, what books you have read. If you have chosen a vocational course they will want to find out how much you know about the career it leads to, and whether you have visited any places of work or had any work experience. If your chosen subject is also an A-level subject you will be asked about your course and the aspects of the course you like the most.

Try to relax. For some people interviews can be an ordeal; most interviewers know this and will make allowances. The following extract from the Oxford prospectus will give you some idea of what admissions tutors look for:

* 'Interviews serve various purposes and no two groups of tutors will conduct them in the same way or give them exactly the same weight. Most tutors wish to discover whether a candidate has done

more than absorb passively what he/she has been taught. They try to ascertain the nature and strength of candidates' intellectual interests and their capacity for independent development. They are also likely to ask about applicants' other interests outside their school curriculum. This is partly because between two candidates of equal academic merit, preference will be given to the one who has the livelier interests or activities, and partly because it is easier to learn about candidates when they talk about what interests them most.

* 'Interviews are in no sense hostile interrogations. Those candidates who show themselves to be honest, thoughtful and unpretentious will be regarded more favourably than those who try to impress or take the view that it is safest to say as little as possible. We do not expect candidates to be invariably mature and judicious.'

In the tables in **Chapter 8** (**Selection interviews**, **Interview advice and questions** and **Reasons for Rejection**) you will also find examples of questions which have been asked in recent years for which you might prepare, and non-academic reasons why applicants have been rejected! You will also find some impressions of applicants' experiences of open days and interviews they have attended (**Applicants' impressions**). These impressions may not be yours when you visit a university or college, but they do give you an idea of what you might find.

HOW TO USE THE SUBJECT TABLES

The subject tables in the next chapter represent the core of the book, listing degree and Higher National Diploma courses offered by all universities and colleges. These tables are designed to provide you with the information you need so that you can match your abilities and interests with your chosen degree subject, prepare your application and find out how applicants are selected for courses.

The information in the subject tables is provided in sequence under the following headings:

* Subject requirements/preferences (GCSE/A-level)
* Your target offers
* Alternative offers (IB offers, Scottish offers)
* Foundation degrees
* Higher National Diploma courses
* Subject information
* Course variations
* Universities and colleges teaching quality
* Top universities and colleges (research)
* Sandwich degree courses
* Number of applicants per place

* Number of UK/EU/non-EU and mature applicants
* Advice to applicants and planning the UCAS personal statement
* Misconceptions about this course
* Selection interviews
* Interview advice and questions
* Applicants' impressions
* Reasons for rejection (non-academic)
* Universities with vacancies in Clearing (2006)
* Offers to applicants repeating A-levels
* Graduate destinations and employment
* Other degree subjects for consideration

When selecting a degree course it is important to try to judge the points score or grades that you are likely to achieve and compare them with the offers listed under **Your target offers**. However, even though you might be capable of achieving the right grades, there is no guarantee that you will receive an offer since other factors in your application, such as the personal statement, will be taken into consideration.

University departments frequently re-adjust their offers, depending on the numbers of candidates applying, so **you must not assume that the offers and policies published now will necessarily apply to courses starting in 2008 or thereafter**. However, you can assume that the offers published in this book represent the general academic levels at which you should aim.

Below are explanations of the information given under the headings in the subject tables. It is important that you read these carefully so that you understand how they can help you to choose and apply for courses that are right for you.

COURSE OFFERS INFORMATION

Subject requirements/preferences

This information is given as a general guide on the GCSE (grades A*–C) and A-level (or equivalent) subjects required or preferred by universities and colleges offering degree courses in the subject area. GCSE requirements/preferences are listed first after the subheading '**GCSE**' and A-levels follow after the heading '**AL**'. In some cases, specific grades are required/preferred. Check prospectuses and websites of universities and colleges for course requirements.

Your target offers

Universities and colleges offering degree courses in the subject area are listed in descending order according to the number of UCAS tariff points they are likely to require applicants to achieve. The UCAS tariff total is listed down the left-hand side of the page, and to the right appear all the institutions (in alphabetical order) likely to make offers in this region. (More information on the UCAS tariff and how to calculate your offers is provided on page 103 and on the inside back cover of this book. Please also read the information in the **Important Note** box below.)

For each institution listed, the following information may be given:

Name of institution

Note that the name of an institution's university college or campus may be given in brackets after the institution title, for example **London (King's)** or **Kent (Medway)**. Where the institution is not a University, further information about its status may also be given to indicate the type of college – for example **(CHE)** to mean College of Higher Education or **(CAg)** to mean College of Agriculture. This is to help readers to differentiate between the types of colleges and to help them identify any specialisation a college may have – for example art or agriculture. A full list of abbreviations used is given under the heading **Institution Abbreviations** towards the end of this chapter.

Grades/points offer

After the institution name, a line of offers information is given showing the offer likely to be made by the institution for the courses indicated in brackets at the end of the line. Offers, however, may vary between applicants and the published grades and/or points offers should be regarded as targets to aim for and not necessarily the actual grades or points required. Offers may be reduced after the publication of A-level results particularly if a university or college is left with many spare places. However, individual course offers are abridged and should be used as a first source of reference and comparison only. It is not possible to publish all the variables relevant to each offer including the number of units required (see Tip below). **Applicants must check prospectuses and websites for full details of all offers and courses**. Depending on the details given by institutions, the offers may provide information as follows:

* **Grades**: The specific grades, or average grades, required at GCE A-level or at A-level plus AS-level. A-level grades are always presented in capital letters; AS-levels are shown in lower case – so the offer BBBc would indicate three grade Bs at A-level, plus an additional AS-level at grade C. Where necessary, the abbreviation 'AL' is used to indicate A-level; 'AS' to indicate AS-level. Offers are usually shown in terms of three A-level grades although some institutions accept two grades with the same points total or, alternatively, two A-level grades accompanied by AS-level grades. Two AS-levels may generally be regarded as equivalent to one A-level, and one Double Award A-level as equivalent to two standard A-levels.
  NB Unit grade information, introduced into the admissions system for entry in 2007, is most likely to be required by universities where a course is competitive, or where taking a specific unit is necessary or desirable for entry. Check with institutions' websites for their latest information.
* **UCAS Tariff points**: the number (or range) of tariff points. GCE A- and AS-levels have a unit value in the UCAS tariff system (see below). Where two sets of tariff points are shown, for example 180–220 points, offers are usually made within this points range. Note that, in some cases, an institution may require a points score which is higher than the specified grade offer given. This can be for a number of reasons – for example, you may not be offering the standard subjects that would have been stipulated in a grades offer. In such cases additional points may be added by way of AS-levels, Key

Skills etc. Check with prospectuses and websites or contact the university or college for further information.

In addition to asking for certain grades or points an institution may stipulate the number of units required or preferred, for example, 12 units (= 2AL or 1AL+2AS) or 18 units (= 3AL or 2AL+2AS). (See institutions' websites and prospectuses.)

The Cambridge Pre-U Diploma is a new examination equivalent to A-levels and the IB which is at present under consultation and will be offered for the first time in 2010 with coursework starting in 2008. Full details of this examination are given in **Appendix 4**.)

Admissions tests for Law, Medicine and Veterinary Science/Medicine: where admissions tests form part of a university's offer for any of these subjects, this is indicated on the offers line in the subject tables for the relevant university. This is shown by '+LNAT' (for Law), '+BMAT' or '+UKCAT' (for Medicine), and '+BMAT' (for Veterinary Science/Medicine). For example, the offers lines could read as follows:

Birmingham – AAA +LNAT (Law; Law Bus St)

Edinburgh – AABb +UKCAT (inc chem+1 from maths/phys/biol; AS biol min) (Medicine)

Imperial London – AABb +BMAT (inc biol/chem+sci/maths) (Medicine)

Entry and admissions tests will be required for 2008/9 by a number of institutions for a range of subjects including Dentistry: see **Chapter 6** for more information and check university websites and prospectuses.

Course title(s)

Finally, at the end of the offers line, an abbreviated form of the course title(s) to which the offers information refers is provided, also in brackets. The abbreviations used (see **Course abbreviations** below) closely relate to the course titles shown in the institutions' prospectuses. When the course gives the opportunity to study abroad (for example, in Continental Europe, Australia, North America) the abbreviated name of the relevant country is shown after the abbreviated course title. For example:

Lancaster – BBB–BBC (Env Sci N Am/Aus)

When experience in industry is provided as part of the course (not necessarily a sandwich course) this is indicated on the offers line by including 'Ind' after the abbreviated course title. For example:

Bristol – BBB (Pharmacol; Pharmacol Ind)

Southampton – ABBb 370 pts (MEng Civ Eng Ind; Civ Eng Euro; Env Eng courses; Civ Eng Archit)

Sometimes the information in the offers line relates to more than one course (see Southampton above). In such cases, each course title is separated with a semicolon. When a number of joint courses exist in combination with a major subject, they may be presented using a list separated by slashes – for example '(Euro Mgt with Fr/Ger/Ital/Span)' indicates European Management with French or German or Italian or Spanish. Some titles may be followed by the word 'courses' – for example, (Geog courses):

Swansea – 300 pts (Geog courses)

This means that the information on the offer refers not only to the single honours course in Geography, but also to Geography joint honours and/or combined courses.

Courses awaiting validation are usually publicised in prospectuses etc., but are not included in these tables since there is no guarantee that they will run. You should check with the university that a non-validated course will run.

The courses included on the offers line are examples of the courses available at that university or college. You will need to check prospectuses and websites for a complete list of the institution's single, joint, combined or major/minor degree courses available in the subject.

OFFERS LINES EXPLAINED

320 pts [University/College name] – BBCc **or** BBccc (Fr Ger)
For the joint course in French and German, the University requires grades of BBC (280 pts) at A-level plus AS-level grade c (40 pts) making a total of 320 points or, alternatively, BB (200 pts) at A-level plus AS-level grades ccc (120 pts), making the same total.

220 pts [University/College name] – 220–280 pts (Geography)
For Geography, the University usually requires 220 UCAS tariff points, but offers may range up to 280 UCAS tariff points.

200 pts [University/College name] – 200–240 pts (Env Sci Ecol)
For the course in Environmental Science and Ecology the offer is in the range of 200 to 240 pts; 200 pts may be achieved in a number of ways – for example, with CCE or BDee at A-level or a 12-unit Double Award at CD + an A-level grade D or 2 AS-levels grade dd. Institutions differ in their requirements for the ways in which the points offer can be achieved: check with websites and prospectuses for their exact requirements.

To help you understand the information provided under the 'UCAS tariff points requirements' heading, the box above provides a few examples with their meaning explained underneath.

Alternative offers

Where institutions specify grade requirements for alternative qualifications, these are provided under the headings listed below. Institutions are very happy to make offers to candidates offering IB, Irish Leaving Certificate, Scottish qualifications and qualifications offered by overseas applicants and the fact that they are not all listed here simply indicates that they do not all publicise a standard offer for these qualifications. For more information, applicants should compare the grades/tariff information given under **Your target offers** with the equivalents given in the **Equivalent Offers** table below or contact the institution direct.

IB offers

For comparison of entry requirements, applicants with IB qualifications should check the A-level offers required for their course and then refer to the Equivalent Offers table in this chapter. The figures under this subheading indicate the number or range of International Baccalaureate (IB) Diploma points likely to be requested in an offer. A range of points indicates variations between single and joint honours courses. Applicants should check with the universities for any requirements for points gained from specific Higher and Subsidiary level subjects.

At the time of going to press, a new UCAS IB tariff was being introduced. However, a number of universities have indicated that they do not expect to use it in the immediate future. The **Equivalent Offers** table below gives the IB UCAS tariff equivalents currently used by the majority of universities and colleges, but applicants offering the IB should check with prospectuses and websites and, if in doubt, contact admissions tutors for the latest information on IB offers.

Scottish offers

For comparison of entry requirements, applicants with Scottish qualifications should check the A-level offers required for their course and then refer to the **Equivalent Offers** table in this chapter. The grades in this table indicate the Scottish Highers grades likely to be requested in an offer. Full details of entry to courses in Scotland are published annually in the Entrance Guide to Higher Education in Scotland (also referred to as the 'Scottish Guide') published by UCAS/Universities Scotland and available from UCAS

Distribution, Rosehill, New Barn Lane, Cheltenham, Gloucestershire GL52 3LZ; Tel 01242 544610; e-mail distribution@ucas.ac.uk.

Scottish honours degrees normally take four years. However, students with very good qualifications may be admitted into the second year of courses (Advanced entry). In some cases it may be even be possible to enter the third year. The policies at each of the universities are as follows:

Aberdeen Advanced entry possible for many courses, but not for Education, Law or Medicine.
Abertay Dundee No advanced entry.
Dundee Advanced entry possible for many courses, but not Art, Education, Law or Medicine.
Edinburgh Only in very unusual cases is entry to the second year accepted.
Glasgow No advanced entry except in some cases for Engineering and Sciences, but not for Accountancy, Arts or Social Science courses.
Glasgow Caledonian No advanced entry.
Napier Advanced entry to Stages 2, 3 or 4 of a programme, particularly for those with an HNC/HND or those with (or expecting to obtain) good grades in Advanced Highers or A-levels.
St Andrews Advanced entry for some courses.
Stirling Advanced entry for some courses.
Strathclyde Advanced entry for some courses.

IMPORTANT NOTE ON THE COURSE OFFERS INFORMATION

The information provided in **Chapter 8** is presented as a first reference source as to the target levels required. Institutions may alter their standard offers in the light of the qualifications offered by applicants.

The offers they publish do not constitute a contract and are not binding on prospective students: changes may occur between the time of publication and the time of application in line with market and student demand.

The points levels shown on the left-hand side of the offers listings are for ease of reference for the reader: not all universities will be making offers using the UCAS tariff points system and it cannot be assumed that they will accept a points equivalent to the grades they have stipulated.

Check university and college prospectuses, and also their websites, for their latest information before submitting your application.

OTHER HIGHER EDUCATION COURSES IN THE SUBJECT FIELD
Foundation degrees
This subheading lists universities and colleges offering Foundation degrees in the subject field. Foundation degrees are employment-related higher education qualifications bringing higher education and business closer together to meet the needs of employers. The degrees are at a lower level than honours degrees and can be studied on a part-time basis or full-time over two years. Entry requirements for these courses vary, but many institutions request between 60 and 100 UCAS tariff points. Full details of institutions offering all courses can be obtained from the Department for Education and Skills (www.dfes.gov.uk) or from www.foundationdegree.org.uk.

Higher National Diploma courses

This subheading lists universities and colleges offering HND courses in the subject area. Higher National Diplomas (HNDs) offer an alternative route to students wishing to enter higher education but not to study for a Bachelor's degree. They usually last two years, and tend to focus on the vocational elements of the subject. Successful completion of an HND can lead to second or third year entry to a related degree.

CHOOSING YOUR COURSE

The information under this heading (to be read in conjunction with **Chapter 1**) covers factors that are important to consider in order to make an informed decision on which courses to apply for. The information is organised under the following subheadings:

Subject information

This subheading provides a general overview of the subject area, together with a selection of website addresses of organisations that can provide relevant careers or course information. Additional relevant website addresses are provided under the subject table heading in **Appendix 2**.

Course variations

In any degree subject area there are often many variations between the content and format of the courses on offer. Under this subheading is a short list of courses offered to demonstrate the variety of course options available. The courses included have been chosen to provide the reader with more ideas for course choice in each subject area – they are not necessarily selected on the basis of quality and many of the courses listed may also be offered by a number of universities and colleges other than those listed in the table.

Universities and colleges teaching quality

The Teaching Quality Information website (www.tqi.ac.uk) provides official information about the quality of higher education in the United Kingdom to help prospective students and their advisers make informed choices about what and where to study. Information is available for each subject taught at each university and college (and for some further education colleges). The Quality Assurance Agency (www.qaa.ac.uk) reviews the quality and standards of all universities and colleges and official reports of their reviews are available on their website.

Top universities and colleges (Research)

In 2001 an assessment exercise was carried out to rate university research on a scale of 1 (lowest) to 5* (highest). The institutions that achieved the highest ratings (5 or 5*) in the relevant subject area have been listed under this heading. However, be aware that some universities may not offer undergraduate courses in these subjects and that the next Research Assessment Exercise will take place in 2008.

Sandwich degree courses

Institutions offering sandwich courses (see **Chapter 1**) are listed here. Check with the institutions too, since new courses may be introduced or withdrawn depending on industrial or commercial arrangements.

ADMISSIONS INFORMATION

Under this heading, information gathered from the institutions on their admissions policies has been provided. This should be very useful when planning your application.

Number of applicants per place (approx)

These figures show the approximate number of applicants initially applying for each place before any offers are made. It should be noted that any given number of applicants represents candidates who have also applied for up to four other university and college courses.

Number of applicants (a UK b EU (non-UK) c non-EU d mature)

In some subject areas some universities have provided details of the actual breakdown of numbers of applicants under the following headings: UK, EU (non-UK), non-EU (overseas), mature (over 21).

Advice to applicants and planning the UCAS personal statement

This subheading offers guidelines on information that could be included in the personal statement section of your UCAS application. In most cases, applicants will be required to indicate why they wish to follow a particular course and, if possible, to provide positive evidence of their interest.

Misconceptions about this course

Admissions tutors are given the opportunity to set the record straight by clarifying aspects of their course they feel are often misunderstood by students, and in some cases, advisers!

Selection interviews

Institutions that normally use the interview as part of their selection procedure are listed here. Those institutions adopting the interview procedure will usually interview only a small proportion of applicants. Mature and Access students are often interviewed. See also **Chapter 6**.

Interview advice and questions

This subheading includes information from institutions on what candidates might generally expect the interview to cover, and examples of the types of interview questions posed in recent years. Also refer to **Chapter 6**: this provides information on tests and assessments which are used in selecting students.

Applicants' impressions (A=Open days; B=Interview days)

Extracts from applicants' reports on visits to open days and interviews.

Reasons for rejection (non-academic)

Academic ability is the major factor in the selection (or rejection) of applicants. Under this subheading, admissions tutors give other reasons for rejecting applicants.

AFTER-RESULTS ADVICE

Under this heading, information for helping you decide what to do after the examination results are published is provided (see also the section on **What to do on Results Day . . . and After** in **Chapter 5**). Details refer to the main subject area unless otherwise stated in brackets.

Universities with vacancies in Clearing (2006)

In this section universities are listed which had vacancies for courses in the table's subject field in 2006. This information may help applicants to assess their chances of a possible place after the AL and AS results are published but it should be noted that the majority of vacancies advertised in Clearing are for Combined or joint subject courses. Check the list of Clearing vacancies published in the national press for all universities, colleges and institutes of higher education.

Offers to applicants repeating A-levels

This subheading gives details of whether second-time offers made to applicants repeating their exams may be '**higher**', '**possibly higher**' or the '**same**' as those made to first-time applicants.. The information refers to single honours courses. It should be noted that circumstances may differ between candidates – some will be repeating the same subjects taken in the previous year, while others may be taking different subjects. Offers will also be dictated by the grades you achieved on your first sitting of the examinations. Remember, if you were rejected by all your universities and have achieved good grades, contact them by telephone on results day – they may be prepared to revise their decision. This applies particularly to medical schools.

GRADUATE DESTINATIONS AND EMPLOYMENT

The information under this heading has been provided by the Higher Education Statistics Agency (HESA) and is taken from their report *Destinations of Leavers from Higher Education 2004/5*. The report can be obtained from HESA, 95 Promenade, Cheltenham, Gloucestershire GL50 1HZ; Tel 01242 211155; e-mail customer.services@hesa.ac.uk.

Details are given of the total number of graduates surveyed whose destinations have been recorded – not the total number who graduated in that subject. Employment figures relate to those in full-time permanent paid employment after six months in a variety of occupations not necessarily related to their degree subject (short-term and unpaid employment figures are not included). 'Further Study' includes research into a subject-related field, higher degrees, private study or, alternatively, career training involving work and further study. The 'assumed unemployed' category refers to those students who were believed to be unemployed for various reasons (eg travelling, personal reasons) or those students still seeking permanent employment six months after graduating.

TIP
The website **www.prospects.ac.uk** also provides information about current career prospects for graduates in their chosen subject.

OTHER DEGREE SUBJECTS FOR CONSIDERATION

This heading includes some suggested alternative courses that have similarities to the courses listed in the subject table.

DECODING THE INFORMATION IN CHAPTER 8

THE UCAS TARIFF SYSTEM

The UCAS tariff system allocates points for grades achieved in a range of qualifications. Detailed information on the tariff system is provided at www.ucas.com/candq/tariff, but a brief outline is given in the table below.

GCEs	Grade	A	B	C	D	E
	AS-level tariff points	60	50	40	30	20
	A-level (Single Award) tariff points	120	100	80	60	40
	A-level (Double Award) tariff points	AA: 240	BB: 200	CC: 160	DD: 120	EE: 80
		AB: 220	BC: 180	CD: 140	DE: 100	
Free-standing maths	Grade	A	B	C	D	E
	Tariff points	20	17	13	10	7
Scottish Qualification	Grade	A	B	C	D	
	Higher Level tariff points	72	60	48	42	
	Advanced Higher Level tariff points	120	100	80	72	
Irish Leaving Certificate	Grade	A	B	C	D	
	Higher Level tariff points	A1: 90	B1: 71	C1: 52	D1: 33	
		A2: 77	B2: 64	C2: 45	D2: 26	
			B3: 58	C3: 39	D3: 20	
Key Skills (number, IT and communication)	Level	4	3	2		
	Tariff points *per unit*	30	20	10		
Advanced Extension Awards	Grade	Distinction		Merit		
	Tariff points	40		20		

Tariff points are also awarded for other qualifications, including:

* **BTEC National Awards, Certificates and Diplomas**: ranging from 40 points for a Pass in a National Award to 360 points for a triple Distinction in a Diploma.
* **CACHE Diploma in Childcare and Education**: ranging from 40 points for an E in Practical to 240 points for AA in Theory.
* **Diploma in Foundation Studies**: Pass=165 points; Merit=225 points; Distinction=285 points.
* **Music qualifications**: ranging from 5 points for a Pass in Grade 6 Theory to 75 points for a Distinction in Grade 8 Practical (as shown in the **Music** table in Chapter 8).
* **OCR National Certificates and Diplomas**: ranging from 40 points for a Pass in a Certificate to 360 points for a D1 in an Extended Diploma.

However, although an institution may give an offer in the form of a UCAS tariff total, it may not allow candidates to use points from all the above qualifications to contribute towards the total – always check with the institution direct. For example, it is common for institutions to stipulate to students that the tariff total must be achieved by way of A-levels or from a combination of A-levels and AS-levels – in which case they may specify a number of units using the system outlined below.

GCE AS-level	3 units
GCE A-level	6 units
GCE Double Award A-level	12 units

Most degree courses will require a minimum of 12 units although 15, 18 or 21 units may be stipulated. Key Skills are sometimes, but not always, included: check with the institutions direct for further details.

TIP

The key points are summarised on the **How to calculate your offers** section on the inside back cover of this book. Just fold it out for quick reference while you are looking at **Chapter 8**.

EQUIVALENT OFFERS

There is no nationally agreed set of equivalences as yet between qualifications and across all universities in the UK. Each institution makes its own decisions on the levels of offers in various subjects, depending on the popularity of the course and/or the quality of the individual applicant.

The following table, therefore, must only be used as a general guide to equivalences between A-levels, UCAS tariff points and other qualifications. Applicants should compare the A-level grades/A-level tariff points in the subject tables in **Chapter 8** with the approximate points shown in the International Baccalaureate (IB) (these are not UCAS tariff points), Irish Leaving Certificate and grades in the Scottish Highers columns. It is essential that all applicants contact their chosen institutions to check the specific grades/points to be achieved in the required subjects of the qualifications they expect to offer.

TABLE OF EQUIVALENT OFFERS

GCE A-level Grades and Tariff points	Scottish Highers Grades (see Ch.6)	IB Diploma Points	Irish Leaving Certificate Higher Level Grades	Points	EB	French Bacca- laureate
AAA (360)	AAAAA	36–42	A1A1A1A1BB	560–570		15
AAB (340)	AAABB	34–36	AAABBB	495–555	85%	14/15
ABB (320)	AABBB	32–34	AABBBB	480–540		13/14
BBB (300)	ABBBC–BBBCC	30–32	BBBBBB	450–510	75%	12/13
BBC (280)	AABB	28–30	BBBBCC	420–480	70%	11/12
BCC (260)	BBBB	28–30	BBBCCC	405–465/360–410	65%	
CCC (240)	ABCC	27–28	BBBCC–CCCC	345–395	60%	
CCD (220)	BBBC	27–28	BBCCC	330–380		
CDD (200)	BBCC	26–27	BCCCC	315–365		
DDD (180)	BCCC–CCCC	24–26	CCCCC	300–350		
DDE (160)	BBC	22–24	CCCCD	285–335		
DEE (140)	BBC–CCC	22–24	CCCCD	285–335		
DD (120)	BCC–CCC	20	BCCC	255–295		
DE (100)	CCC–CC	18–20	CCC	240–280		
EE (80)	CCC–CC	18	CCC	240–280		

INSTITUTION ABBREVIATIONS

The following abbreviations are used to indicate specific institutions or types of institution:

Ac	Academy
AI	Arts Institute
AMD	Academy of Music and Drama
Birk	Birkbeck College (London University)
CA	College of Art(s)
CAD	College of Art and Design
CAg	College of Agriculture
CAgH	College of Agriculture and Horticulture
CAST	College of Arts, Science and Technology
CAT	College of Advanced Technology or Arts and Technology
CComm	College of Communication
CDC	College of Design and Communication
CFash	College of Fashion
CFE	College of Further Education
CAFRE	College of Agriculture, Food and Rural Enterprise
CFTCS	College of Food, Tourism and Creative Studies
CHE	College of Higher Education
CHFE	College of Higher and Further Education
CHort	College of Horticulture
CMus	College of Music
CMusDr	College of Music and Drama
Coll	College
Consv	Conservatoire (Birmingham)
Court	Courtauld Institute (London University)
CSAD	College and School of Art and Design
CT	College of Technology
CTA	College of Technology and Arts
Gold	Goldsmiths (London University)
Hey	Heythrop College (London University)
Hom	Homerton College (Cambridge University)
IA	Institute of Art(s)
IAD	Institute of Art and Design
IHE	Institute of Higher Education
Inst	Institute
King's	King's College (London University)
LIPA	Liverpool Institute of Performing Arts
LSE	School of Economics and Political Science (London University)
Met	Metropolitan
MS	Medical School
QM	Queen Mary (London University)
RAcMus	Royal Academy of Music
RCMus	Royal College of Music
RegColl	Regional College
RH	Royal Holloway (London University)
RNCM	Royal Northern College of Music
RSAMD	Royal Scottish Academy of Music and Drama
RVC	Royal Veterinary College (London University)

SA	School of Art
SAD	School of Art and Design
Sch	School
SchSpDr	School of Speech and Drama
SOAS	School of Oriental and African Studies (London University)
TrCMus	Trinity College of Music
UC	University College
UCL	University College (London University)
Univ	University
UWIC	University of Wales Institute (Cardiff)

COURSE ABBREVIATIONS

The following abbreviations are used to indicate course titles:

Ab	Abrahamic	**Amen**	Amenity
Abrd	Abroad	**Analys**	Analysis
Acc	Accountancy/Accounting	**Analyt**	Analytical
Accs	Accessories	**Anat**	Anatomy/Anatomical
Acoust	Acoustics/Acoustical	**Anim**	Animal
Acpntr	Acupuncture	**Animat**	Animation
Acq	Acquisition	**Animatron**	Animatronics
Act	Actuarial	**Anth**	Anthropology
Actg	Acting	**Antq**	Antique(s)
Actn	Action	**App(s)**	Applied/Applicable/
Actr	Actor		Applications
Actvt(s)	Activity/Activities	**Appr**	Appropriate
Add	Additional	**Aqua**	Aquaculture/Aquatic
Adlscn	Adolescence	**Ar**	Area
Adlt	Adult	**Arbc**	Arabic
Admin	Administration/Administrative	**Arbor**	Arboriculture
Adt	Audit	**Arch**	Archaeology
Adv	Advertising	**Archit**	Architecture
Advc	Advice	**Aroma**	Aromatherapy
Advnc	Advanced	**Artfcts**	Artefacts
Advntr	Adventure	**Artif**	Artificial
Aero	Aeronautical/Aeronautics	**As**	Asian
Aerodyn	Aerodynamics	**Ass**	Assessment
Aeromech	Aeromechanical	**Assoc**	Associated
Aerosp	Aerospace	**Assyr**	Assyriology
Aeroth	Aerothermal	**Ast**	Asset
Af	Africa(n)	**Astnaut**	Astronautics/Astronautical
Affrs	Affairs	**Astro**	Astrophysics
Age	Ageing`	**Astron**	Astronomy
Agncy	Agency	**A-Sxn**	Anglo-Saxon
Agric	Agriculture/Agricultural	**Ated**	Accelerated
Agrofor	Agroforestry	**Atlan**	Atlantic
Agron	Agronomy	**Atmos**	Atmospheric
Aircft	Aircraft	**Attrctns**	Attractions
Airln	Airline	**Auc**	Auctioneering
Airpt	Airport	**Aud Vid**	Audio Video
Am	American	**Aud**	Audio

Audiol	Audiology	**Cap**	Capital
Audtech	Audiotechnology	**Cardio**	Cardiology
Aus	Australia(n)	**Carib**	Caribbean
Auth	Author/Authoring/Authorship	**Cart**	Cartography
Auto	Automotive	**Cat**	Catering
Autom	Automated/Automation	**CATS**	Credit Accumulation and Transfer
Automat	Automatic		Scheme
Autombl	Automobile	**Cdtng**	Conditioning
Avion	Avionics	**Cell**	Cellular
Avn	Aviation	**Celt**	Celtic
Ay St	Ayurvedic Studies	**Cent**	Century
		Ceram	Ceramics
Bch	Beach	**Cert**	Certificate
Bd	Based	**Ch Mgt**	Chain Management
Bdwk	Bodywork	**Chc**	Choice
Bhv	Behaviourial	**Chch**	Church
Bib	Biblical	**Chem**	Chemistry
Bio Ins	Bio Instrumentation	**Cheml**	Chemical
Bioarch	Bioarchaeology	**Chin**	Chinese
Bioch	Biochemistry/Biochemical	**Chld**	Child/Children/Childhood
Biodiv	Biodiversity	**Chn**	Chain
Bioelectron	Bioelectronics	**Chng**	Change
Biogeosci	Biogeoscience	**Choreo**	Choreography
Bioinform	Bioinformatics	**Chr**	Christian(ity)
Biokin	Biokinetics	**Chtls**	Chattels
Biol	Biological/Biology	**Cits**	Cities
Biom	Biometry	**Civ**	Civilisation/Civil
Biomed	Biomedical/Biomedicine	**Class**	Classical
Biomol	Biomolecular	**Clim**	Climate/Climatic
Bio-org	Bio-organic	**Clin**	Clinical
Biophys	Biophysics	**Cllct**	Collect/Collecting
Bioproc	Bioprocess	**Clnl**	Colonial
Biorg	Bio-organic	**Cloth**	Clothing
Biotech	Biotechnology	**Cmdy**	Comedy
Bld	Build/Building	**Cmn**	Common
Blt	Built	**Cmnd**	Command
Bookbind	Bookbinding	**Cmpn**	Companion
Br	British	**Cmpsn**	Composition
Braz	Brazilian	**Cmpste**	Composite
Brew	Brewing	**Cmwlth**	Commonwealth
Brit	British	**Cncr**	Cancer
Brnd	Brand	**Cnflct**	Conflict
Broad	Broadcast	**Cnma**	Cinema/Cinematics
Bty	Beauty	**Cnslg**	Counselling
Bulg	Bulgarian	**Cnsltncy**	Consultancy
Bus	Business	**Cnt**	Central
Byz	Byzantine	**Cntnt**	Content
		Cntry	Country/Countryside
Callig	Calligraphy	**Cntxt**	Context
Can	Canada/Canadian	**Coach**	Coaching

Cog	Cognitive		Cxt	Context
Col	Colour		Cyber	Cybernetics/Cyberspace
Comb	Combined		Cybertron	Cybertronics
Combus	Combustion		Cz	Czech
Comm(s)	Communication(s)			
Commer	Commerce/Commercial		Dan	Danish
Commun	Community		Decn	Decision
Comp	Computer(ised/-aided)		Decr	Decorative/Decoration
Compar	Comparative		Def	Defence
Complem	Complementary		Defer	Deferred Choice
Comput	Computation/al		Deg	Degree
Con	Context		Demcr	Democratic
Concur	Concurrent		Dept	Department
Cond	Conductive		Des	Design(er)
Condit	Conditioning		Desr	Desirable
Cons	Conservation		Dev	Development/
Constr	Construction			Developmental
Consum	Consumer		Devsg	Devising
Cont	Contour		Df	Deaf
Contemp	Contemporary		Diag	Diagnostic
Contnl	Continental		Diet	Dietetics/Dietitian
Contr	Control		Dif	Difficulties
Conv	Conveyancing		Dig	Digital
Corn	Cornish		DipSW	Diploma in Social Work
Corp	Corporate/Corporation		Dir	Direction/Director/
Cos	Cosmetic			Directing
Cosmo	Cosmology		Dis	Diseases
Cr	Care		Disab	Disability
Crcs	Circus		Disas	Disaster
Crdc	Cardiac		Discip	Disciplinary
Crea	Creative/Creation		Diso	Disorders
Crfts	Crafts/Craftsmanship		Disp	Dispensing
Crim	Criminal/Criminology		Dist	Distributed/Distribution
Crimin	Criminological		Distil	Distillation/Distilling
Crit	Criticism/Critical		Div	Divinity
Crm	Crime		d/l	distance learning
Cro	Croatian		Dnstry	Dentistry
Crr	Career		Dntl	Dental
Crs	Course		Doc	Document/Documentary
Crsn	Corrosion		Dom	Domestic/Domesticated
Cru	Cruise		Dr	Drama
Cstl	Coastal		Drg	Drawing
Cstm	Costume		Dscrt	Discrete
Ctln	Catalan		Dscvry	Discovery
Ctlys	Catalysis		Dsply	Display
Cty/s	City/Cities		Dtbs	Databases
Ctzn	Citizenship		Dth	Death
Culn	Culinary		Dvc	Device
Cult	Culture/Cultural		Dvnc	Deviance
Cur	Curation		Dynmcs	Dynamics

Ecol	Ecology/Ecological		**Exer**	Exercise
Ecomet	Econometrics		**Exhib**	Exhibition
e-Commer	E-Commerce		**Exp**	Export
Econ	Economics/Economies		**Explor**	Exploration
Ecosys	Ecosystem(s)		**Explsn**	Explosion
Ecotech	Ecotechnology		**Expltn**	Exploitation
Ecotour	Ecotourism		**Expmtl**	Experimental
Ecotox	Ecotoxicology		**Expnc**	Experience
Edit	Editorial		**Expr**	Expressive
Educ	Education		**Ext**	Extended
Educr	Educare		**Extr**	Exterior
Efcts	Effects		**Extrm**	Extreme
EFL	English as a Foreign Language			
Egypt	Egyptian/Egyptology		**Fac**	Faculty
Elec	Electrical		**Facil**	Facilities
Electroacout	Electroacoustics		**Fam**	Family
Electromech	Electromechanical		**Fash**	Fashion
Electron	Electronics		**Fbr**	Fibre
Ely	Early		**Fctn**	Fiction
Emb	Embryo		**Fd**	Food
Embd	Embedded		**Fdn**	Foundation
Embr	Embroidery		**Fin**	Finance/Financial
Emp	Employment		**Finn**	Finnish
Ener	Energy		**Fish**	Fisheries
Eng	Engineering		**Fit**	Fitness
Engl	English		**Fld**	Field
Engn	Engine		**Flor**	Floristry
Ent	Enterprise		**FMaths**	Further Mathematics
Enter	Entertainment		**Fmly**	Family
Entre	Entrepreneur/Entrepreneurship		**Foot**	Footwear
Env	Environment/Environmental		**For**	Foreign
Eql	Equal		**Foren**	Forensic
Eqn	Equine		**Foss**	Fossil(s)
Eqstrn	Equestrian		**Fr**	French
Equip	Equipment		**Frchd**	Franchised
Equit	Equitation		**Frcst**	Forecasting
Ergon	Ergonomics		**Frm**	Farm
Est	Estate		**Frshwtr**	Freshwater
Eth	Ethics		**Frsty**	Forestry/Forest
Eth-Leg	Ethico-Legal		**Frtlty**	Fertility
Ethn	Ethnic		**Fst Trk**	Fast Track
Ethnol	Ethnology		**Fstvl**	Festival
Ethnomus	Ethnomusicology		**Ftbl**	Football
EU	European Union		**Ftre**	Feature(s)
Euro	European		**Furn**	Furniture
Eval	Evaluation		**Fut**	Futures
Evnglstc	Evangelistic			
Evnts	Events		**Gael**	Gaelic
Evol	Evolution(ary)		**Gam**	Gambling
Ex	Executing		**Gard**	Garden

Gem	Gemmology		**Hrdrs**	Hairdressing
Gen	General		**Hrs**	Horse
Genet	Genetics		**Hse**	House
Geochem	Geochemistry		**Hspty**	Hospitality
Geophys	Geophysical		**Htl**	Hotel
Geosptl	Geospatial		**Hum**	Human(ities)
Geotech	Geotechnics		**Hung**	Hungarian
Ger	German/Germany		**Hydrog**	Hydrography
Gerc	Germanic		**Hydrol**	Hydrology
Gk	Greek		**Hyg**	Hygiene
GIS	Geographical Information Systems			
Glf	Golf		**Iber**	Iberian
Glf Crs	Golf Course		**Ice**	Icelandic
Gllry	Gallery/Galleries		**ICT**	Information and Communications
Glob	Global(isation)			Technology
Gmg	Gaming		**Id**	Ideas
Gmnt	Garment		**Idnty**	Identity
Gms	Games		**Illus**	Illustration
Gmtc	Geomatic		**Imag**	Image/Imaging/Imaginative
Gndr	Gender		**Immun**	Immunology/Immunity
Gnm	Genome/Genomics		**Impair**	Impairment
Gov	Government		**Inc**	Including
Govn	Governance		**Incln**	Inclusion/Inclusive
Graph	Graphic		**Ind**	Industrial/Industry
Grgn	Georgian		**Indep St**	Independent Study
Grn	Green		**Inf**	Information
gs	general studies		**Infec**	Infectious/Infection
			Infml	Informal
Hab	Habitat		**Inform**	Informatics
Hard	Hardware		**Infra**	Infrastructure
Haz	Hazard		**Inftq**	Informatique
Heal	Healing		**Injry Prvntn**	Injury Prevention
Heb	Hebrew		**Innov**	Innovation
Herb	Herbal		**Ins**	Insurance
Herit	Heritage		**Inst**	Institution(al)
Hisp	Hispanic		**Instln**	Installation
Hist	History/Historical		**Instr**	Instrument/Instrumentation
Hlnds	Highlands		**Int**	International
Hlth	Health		**Intcult**	Intercultural
Hlthcr	Healthcare		**Integ**	Integrated
HlthSC	Health and Social Care		**Intel**	Intelligent/Intelligence
Hm	Home		**Inter**	Interior
Hol	Holistic		**Interact**	Interactive
Hom	Homeopathic		**Interd**	Interdisciplinary
Homin	Hominid		**Interp**	Interpretation
Horol	Horology		**Intlctl**	Intellectual
Hort	Horticulture		**Intnet**	Internet
Hosp	Hospital		**Intrmdl**	Intermodal
Hous	Housing		**Inv**	Investment
HR	Human Resources		**Invn**	Innovation

Invstg	Investigating/Investigation	**Lsr**	Laser
Ir	Irish	**Ltg**	Lighting
Is	Issues	**Ltr**	Later
Isl	Islands	**Lv**	Live
Islam	Islamic	**Lvstk**	Livestock
Isrl	Israeli		
IT	Information Technology	**Mach**	Machine(ry)
Ital	Italian	**Mait**	Maitrise Internationale
ITE	Initial Teacher Education	**Mak**	Making
ITT	Initial Teacher Training	**Manuf**	Manufacturing
		Map	Map/Mapping
Jap	Japanese	**Mar**	Marine
Jew	Jewish	**Marit**	Maritime
Jewel	Jewellery	**Mark**	Market(ing)
Journal	Journalism	**Masch**	Maschinenbau
Jud	Judaism	**Mat**	Materials
Juris	Jurisprudence	**Mathem**	Mathematical
Just	Justice	**Maths**	Mathematics
		Mbl	Mobile
Kntwr	Knitwear	**Mdl**	Modelling
Knwl	Knowledge	**Measur**	Measurement
Kor	Korean	**Mecha**	Mechatronics
		Med	Medicine/cal
Lab	Laboratory	**Medcnl**	Medicinal
Lang(s)	Language(s)	**Mediev**	Medieval
Las	Laser	**Medit**	Mediterranean
Lat	Latin	**Metal**	Metallurgy/Metallurgical
Lcl	Local	**Meteor**	Meteorology/Meteorological
LD	Learning Disabilities	**Meth**	Method(s)
Ldrshp	Leadership	**Mgr**	Manager
Lea	Leather	**Mgrl**	Managerial
Leg	Legal	**Mgt**	Management
Legis	Legislative	**Microbiol**	Microbiology/Microbiological
Leis	Leisure	**Microbl**	Microbial
Lf	Life	**Microcomp**	Microcomputer/
Lfstl	Lifestyle		Microcomputing
Lgc	Logic	**Microelec**	Microelectronics
Lib	Library	**Midwif**	Midwifery
Lic de Geog	Licence de Geographie	**Min**	Mining
Lic	Licensed	**Miner**	Minerals
Lif	Life(style)	**Mkup**	Make-up
Ling	Linguistics	**Mling**	Multilingual
Lit	Literature/Literary	**Mltry**	Military
Litcy	Literacy	**MML**	Master of Modern Languages
Lnd	Land(scape)	**Mndrn**	Mandarin
Lndbd	Land-based	**Mnrts**	Minorities
Lns	Lens	**Mnstry**	Ministry
Log	Logistics	**Mnswr**	Menswear
Lrng	Learning	**Mntl Hlth**	Mental Health
Ls	Loss	**Mntnce**	Maintenance

Mny	Money
Mod	Modular
Model	Modelmaking
Modl	Modelling
Modn	Modern
Modnty	Modernity
Mol	Molecular
Monit	Monitoring
Mov	Movement/Moving
Mrchnds	Merchandise
Mrchnt	Merchant
Mrl	Moral
Mtl	Metal(s)
Mtn	Motion
Mtlsmth	Metalsmithing
Mtr	Motor
Mtrcycl	Motorcycle
Mtrspo	Motorsports
Multid	Multidisciplinary
Multim	Multimedia
Mus	Music(ian)
Muscskel	Musculoskeletal
Musl	Musical
Musm	Museum
N Am	North America
Nano	Nanoscale/Nanoscience
Nanotech	Nanotechnology
Nat	Natural
Navig	Navigation
Nclr	Nuclear
Nds	Needs
Neg	Negotiated
Net	Network
Neuro	Neuroscience
Neuropsy	Neuropsychology
News	Newspaper
NGO	Non-Governmental Organisation
NI	Northern Ireland/Northern Irish
NMedia	New Media
Norw	Norwegian
Nrs	Norse
Nucl	Nuclear
Nurs	Nursing
Nursy	Nursery
Nutr	Nutrition(al)
Nvl	Naval
Objs	Objects
Obs	Observational

Occ	Occupational
Ocean	Oceanography
Ocn	Ocean
Oeno	Oenology
Ofce	Office
Off	Offshore
Offrd	Off-road
Okl	Oklahoma
Onc	Oncology
On-Ln	On-Line
Op(s)	Operation(s)
Oph	Ophthalmic
Oprtg	Operating
Opt	Optical
Optim	Optimisation
Optn/s	Optional/Options
Optoel	Optoelectronics
Optom	Optometry
OR	Operational Research
Ord	Ordinary
Org	Organisation
Orgnc	Organic
Orgnsms	Organisms
Orn	Ornithology
Orntl	Oriental
Orth	Orthoptics
Orthot	Orthotics
Oseas	Overseas
Ost	Osteopathy
Out Act	Outdoor Activity
Out	Outdoor
Ovrs	Overseas
P	Primary
Pacif	Pacific
Pack	Packaging
PActv	Physical Activity
Pal	Palaeobiology
Palae	Palaeoecology/ Palaeontology
Paramed	Paramedic(al)
Parasit	Parasitology
Parl	Parliamentary
Pat	Patent
Path	Pathology
Pathobiol	Pathobiological
Pathogen	Pathogenesis
Patt	Pattern
Pblc	Public
Pce	Peace

PE	Physical Education	**Prdcl**	Periodical
Per	Person/Personal	**Precsn**	Precision
Perf	Performance	**Pref**	Preferable
Perfum	Perfumery	**Prehist**	Prehistory
Pers	Personnel	**Prem**	Premises
Persn	Persian	**Prim Cr**	Primary Care
Petrol	Petroleum	**Proc**	Process
Pharm	Pharmacy	**Prod**	Product/Production/Produce
Pharmacol	Pharmacology	**Prof**	Professional/Professions
Pharml	Pharmaceutical	**Prog**	Programme/Programming
Phil	Philosophy	**Proj**	Project
Philgy	Philology	**Prom**	Promotion
Phn	Phone	**Prop**	Property/ies
Photo	Photography/Photographic	**Pros**	Prosthetics
Photojrnl	Photojournalism	**Prot**	Protection
PhotoM	Photomedia	**Prplsn**	Propulsion
Photon	Photonic(s)	**Prsts**	Pursuits
Phys	Physics	**Prt**	Print
Physio	Physiotherapy	**Prtcl**	Particle
Physiol	Physiology/Physiological	**Prtd**	Printed
Physl	Physical	**Prtg**	Printing/Printmaking
Plan	Planning	**Pst**	Post
Planet	Planetary	**Pstrl**	Pastoral
Plas	Plastics	**Psy**	Psychology
Play	Playwork	**Psybiol**	Psychobiology
Plc	Police	**Psyling**	Psycholinguistics
Plcg	Policing	**Psysoc**	Psychosocial
Plmt	Placement	**p/t**	part-time
Plnt	Plant	**Ptcl**	Particle
Plntsmn	Plantsmanship	**Pub**	Publishing
Plt	Pilot	**Pvt**	Private
Pltry	Poultry	**Pwr**	Power
PMaths	Pure Mathematics	**Pwrcft**	Powercraft
Pntg	Painting		
Pod	Podiatry/Podiatric	**Qntm**	Quantum
Pol	Politics/Political/Policy	**Qry**	Quarry
Polh	Polish	**Qtrnry**	Quaternary
Pollut	Pollution	**QTS**	Qualified Teacher Status
Poly	Polymer/Polymeric	**Qual**	Quality
Pop	Popular	**Quant**	Quantity/Quantitative
Popn	Population		
Port	Portuguese	**Rad**	Radio
PPE	Philosophy, Politics and Economics	**Radiog**	Radiography
	or Politics, Philosophy and	**Radiothera**	Radiotherapy
	Economics	**Rbr**	Rubber
Ppl	People	**Rce**	Race
Ppr	Paper	**Rcycl**	Recycling
Pptry	Puppetry	**Rdtn**	Radiation
PR	Public Relations	**Realsn**	Realisation
Prac	Practice/Practical	**Rec**	Recording

Reclam	Reclamation		**Script**	Scriptwriting
Recr	Recreation		**Scrn**	Screen
Reg	Regional		**Scrnwrit**	Sreenwriting
Regn	Regeneration		**Scrts**	Securities
Rehab	Rehabilitation		**Scrty**	Security
Rel	Relations		**Sctr**	Sector
Relgn	Religion		**Sculp**	Sculpture
Relig	Religious		**Sdlry**	Saddlery
Reltd	Related		**Sdwh**	Sandwich
Rem Sens	Remote Sensing		**SE**	South East
Ren	Renaissance		**Sec**	Secretarial
Renew	Renewable		**Semicond**	Semiconductor
Reqd	Required		**Serb Cro**	Serbo-Croat
Res	Resources		**Serv**	Services
Resid	Residential		**Set**	Settings
Resoln	Resolution		**Sfty**	Safety
Resp	Response		**Sgnl**	Signal
Restor	Restoration		**Ship**	Shipping
Rev	Revenue		**Simul**	Simulation
Rflxgy	Reflexology		**Sk**	Skills
Rgby	Rugby		**Sln**	Salon
Rgstrn	Registration		**Slov**	Slovak/Slovene/Slavonic
Rl	Real		**Sls**	Sales
Rlblty	Reliability		**Sml**	Small
Rltd	Related		**Smtc**	Semitic
Rnwl	Renewal		**Snc**	Sonic
Robot	Robotics		**Snd**	Sound
Rom	Roman		**Soc**	Social
Romn	Romanian		**Sociol**	Sociology
Rsch	Research		**SocioLeg**	Socio-Legal
Rsprty	Respiratory		**Socling**	Sociolinguistics
Rsrt	Resort		**Soft**	Software
Rstrnt	Restaurant		**Soty**	Society
Rtl	Retail		**Sov**	Soviet
Rts	Rights		**Sp**	Speech
Rur	Rural		**Span**	Spanish
Russ	Russian		**Spat**	Spatial
			Spc	Space
S	Secondary		**SPD**	Surface Pattern Design
Sansk	Sanskrit		**Spec Efcts**	Special Effects
Sat	Satellite		**Spec**	Special(isms/-ist)
Sbstnce	Substance		**Sply**	Supply
Scand	Scandinavian		**Spo**	Sports
Schlstc	Scholastic		**Sprtd**	Supported
Schm	Scheme		**Sprtng**	Supporting
Sci	Science/Scientific		**Srf**	Surf(ing)
Scnc	Scenic		**Srgy**	Surgery
Scngrph	Scenographic		**SS**	Solid-state
Scot	Scottish		**St Reg**	State Registration
Scr	Secure		**St**	Studies

Stats	Statistics	**Tr**	Trade
Std	Studio	**Trad**	Traditional
Stg	Stage	**Trans**	Transport(ation)
Stgs	Settings	**Transl**	Translation
Stnds	Standards	**Trav**	Travel
Str	Stringed	**Trfgrs**	Turfgrass
Strat	Strategic	**Trg**	Training
Strg	Strength	**Trnrs**	Trainers
Struct	Structural/Structures	**Trpcl**	Tropical
Stt	State	**Trstrl**	Terrestrial
Supptd	Supported	**Tstmnt**	Testament
Surf	Surface	**Ttl**	Total
Surg	Surgery	**Turk**	Turkish
Surv	Surveying	**Twn**	Town
Sust	Sustainability/	**Typo**	Typographical/Typography
	Sustainable		
Swed	Swedish	**Ukr**	Ukrainian
Sxlty	Sexuality	**Un**	Union
Sys	System(s)	**Undwtr**	Underwater
Systmtc	Systematic	**Unif**	Unified
		Urb	Urban
Tap	Tapestry	**USA**	United States of America
Tax Rev	Taxation and Revenue	**Util**	Utilities/Utilisation
Tcnqs	Techniques		
Teach	Teaching	**Val**	Valuation
Tech	Technology/Technician	**Vcl**	Vocal
Technol	Technological	**Veh**	Vehicle
TEFL	Teaching English as a Foreign	**Vib**	Vibration
	Language	**Vict**	Victorian
Telecomm	Telecommunications	**Vid**	Video
TESOL	Teaching English to	**Viet**	Vietnamese
	Speakers of Other	**Virol**	Virology
	Languages	**Vis**	Visual(isation)
Testmt	Testament	**Vit**	Viticulture
Tex	Textiles	**Vkg**	Viking
Thea	Theatre	**Vnu**	Venue
Theol	Theology	**Voc**	Vocational
Theor	Theory/Theoretical	**Vol**	Voluntary
Ther	Therapeutic	**Vrtbrt**	Vertebrate
Thera	Therapy	**Vrtl Rlty**	Virtual Reality
Tht	Thought	**Vsn**	Vision
Tiss	Tissue	**Vstr**	Visitor
Tm	Time		
Tmbr	Timber	**Wdlnd**	Woodland
Tnnl	Tunnel/Tunnelling	**Welf**	Welfare
Tns	Tennis	**Wldlf**	Wildlife
Topog	Topographical	**Wls**	Wales
Tour	Tourism	**Wn**	Wine
Tox	Toxicology	**Writ**	Writing/Writer
Tr Stand	Trading Standards	**Wrld**	World

Wrlss	Wireless		**Ycht**	Yacht
Wst	Waste(s)		**Yng**	Young
Wstn	Western		**Yth**	Youth
Wtr	Water		**Zool**	Zoology
Wtrspo	Watersports			
WWWeb	World Wide Web		**3D**	Three-dimensional

ACCOUNTANCY/ACCOUNTING

(see also **Finance**)

NB The points totals shown to the left of the institutions are for ease of reference only. It must not be assumed that tariff points are always used by institutions or that they can be substituted for an offer in grades. The level of an offer is not necessarily indicative of the quality of a course.

COURSE OFFERS INFORMATION

Subject requirements/preferences **GCSE** Mathematics is usually essential and English often preferred for all courses. **Aberdeen, Dundee, Edinburgh, Glasgow** English, mathematics and a foreign language. **Belfast (Queen's), Birmingham, Brighton, East Anglia, Exeter, Kingston, Lancaster, Liverpool John Moores, Newcastle, Nottingham, Oxford Brookes, Portsmouth, Sheffield, Sheffield Hallam, Southampton** Mathematics grade A or B. **Exeter** Grade A English. **Leeds, London (LSE)** Grade A mathematics. **Loughborough** Mathematics grade B. **Southampton** Good range of grades A and B. **Warwick** Seven subjects at grades A–B inc mathematics and English. **AL** Mathematics may be required.

Your target offers

360 pts and above
    Belfast (Queen's) – AAA (Law Acc)
    Warwick – AABb **or** AAbbb (Acc Fin)

340 pts Bath – AAB (Acc Fin)
    Belfast (Queen's) – AAB (Acc; Acc Fr/Ger/Span; Acc Inf Sys)
    Exeter – AAB–BBB 340–300 pts (Acc Fin; Acc Fin Euro; Bus Acc; Bus Acc Euro)
    Lancaster – AAB (Acc Adt Fin)
    Manchester – AAB–ABB (Acc; Acc Econ; Acc; Acc Fin; Acc Law)
    Newcastle – AAB (Bus Acc Fin)
    Southampton – AAB 340 pts (Acc Fin; Acc Econ)

320 pts Aston – 320–340 pts (Acc Mgt)
    Birmingham – ABB–BBCa **or** BBcc 320–340 pts (Acc Fin)
    Bristol – ABB–BBB (Acc Fin; Acc Mgt; Econ Acc)
    Cardiff – ABB (Acc; Acc Mgt; Acc Euro Lang; Bank Fin; Acc Econ; Acc Fin)
    Glasgow – ABB–AAA (Acc Fin)
    Kent – 320 pts (Law Acc Fin)
    Lancaster – ABB (Acc Econ; Acc Fin; Acc Fin Comp Sci; Acc Fin Maths)
    Leeds – ABB (Acc Law; Acc Comp; Acc Inf Sys)
    London (LSE) – ABB (Acc Fin)
    London (RH) – 320–340 pts (Mgt Acc)
    Loughborough – 320 pts (Acc Fin Mgt; Econ Acc; Maths Acc Fin Mgt)
    Manchester – ABB (Mgt (Acc Fin))
    Newcastle – ABB–BBB (Acc Inf Sys; Acc Comp Sci; Acc Maths; Acc Stats)
    Nottingham – ABB (Fin Acc Mgt)
    Reading – 320–350 pts (Acc Mgt; Acc Econ)
    Sheffield – ABB–BBB (Acc Fin Mgt; Acc Fin Mgt Bus; Acc Fin Mgt Econ; Acc Fin Mgt Inf Mgt; Acc Fin Maths)

300 pts East Anglia – BBB–BBC 300–280 pts (Acc Fin; Acc Law; Acc Mgt)
    Edinburgh – BBB (Bus St Acc; Econ Acc; Law Acc)
    Leeds – BBB (Acc Fin; Acc Mgt)

Liverpool – BBB 300 pts (Accounting)
Strathclyde – ABC–BBB (Acc courses)
280 pts **Bournemouth** – 280 pts (Acc Fin; Acc Tax; Acc Law; Acc Bus)
Brunel – 280 pts or equiv (Fin Acc)
City – 280–300 pts (Econ Acc)
Durham (Stockton) – BBC (Acc Fin)
Essex – 280–260 pts (Acc Mgt; Acc Fin; Fin Mgt)
Northumbria – 280 pts (Accounting)
Oxford Brookes – BBC (Acc Fin)
Swansea – 280 pts (Acc courses)
Ulster – BBC 280 pts (Accounting)
Westminster – 280 pts (Acc Bus Mgt)
260 pts **Aberystwyth** – 260 pts (Acc Fin)
Chester – 260 pts (Acc Fin)
Coventry – 260 pts (Acc Econ; Acc)
Heriot-Watt – BCC 260 pts (Acc Fin; Acc Bus Law)
Hull – 260 pts (Acc; Acc (Int); Acc (Prof Exp); Acc Fin Mgt; Bus Econ)
Keele – 260–320 pts (Acc Fin)
Kent – 260 pts (Br Fr Acc Fin; Acc Fin; Acc Fin Ind; Acc Fin Comp; Acc Fin Fr Bus St; Acc Fin Ger; Acc Fin Bus; Acc Fin Econ; Acc Fin Mgt Sci; Fin Maths)
Oxford Brookes – BCC (Acc Comb Hons)
Westminster – 260–280 pts (Bus St (Prof Acc))
240 pts **Aberdeen** – CCC **or** aabb (Acc courses)
Abertay Dundee – CCC (Accounting)
Bangor – 240–280 pts (Acc Fin)
Bradford – CCC 240 pts (Acc Fin)
Buckingham – 240 pts (Acc Econ; Acc Fin Mgt; Acc Fr/Span; Acc Inf Sys)
De Montfort – 240 pts (Acc Fin; Acc Bus; Acc Comp; Acc Law)
Dundee – CCC (Acc; Acc Bus Fin; Acc Mgt Inf Sys; Acc Lang)
Gloucestershire – 240 pts (Acc Fin Mgt)
Heriot-Watt – CCC (Econ Acc)
Hertfordshire – 240 pts (Acc Fin; Acc Mgt Inf Sys)
Kingston – 240–280 pts (Acc Fin)
Nottingham Trent – 240 pts (Acc Fin)
Robert Gordon – CCC (Acc Fin)
Salford – CCC 240–260 pts (Fin Acc)
Sheffield Hallam – 240 pts (Acc; Acc Fin Mgt; Bus Acc)
Stirling – CCC (Acc courses)
220 pts **Abertay Dundee** – CCD 220 pts (Acc Fin)
Bolton – 220 pts (Accountancy)
Brighton – 220 pts (Acc Fin; Acc Law; Int Fin Cap Mark St)
Edge Hill – 220 pts (Accountancy)
Glamorgan – 220 pts (Acc Fin; Acc Mgt; Int Acc)
Liverpool John Moores – 220 pts (Acc Fin)
UCE Birmingham – 220–200 pts (Acc; Acc joint courses)
200 pts **Anglia Ruskin** – 200 pts (Acc Fin)
Bristol UWE – 200–260 pts (Acc Fin)
Huddersfield – 200 pts (Acc Fin; Acc)
Lincoln – 200 pts (Acc Fin courses)
Manchester Met – 200–260 pts (Acc Fin)
Middlesex – 200–240 pts (Acc Fin)
Newport – 200 pts (Accounting)
Plymouth – 200 pts (Acc Fin)
Portsmouth – 200–240 pts (Acc; Acc Bus; Acc Bus Law; Acc Fin; Acc Bus Sys)
180 pts **Cardiff (UWIC)** – 180 pts (Acc; Acc Econ)
Central Lancashire – 180 pts (Acc Fin St)

Derby – 180–220 pts (Acc Bus Psy; Acc Comp Inf Sys; Acc Fin; Mgt Acc)
Glasgow Caledonian – BC (Acc courses)
Northampton – 180–220 pts (Acc; Acc Fin)
Staffordshire – 180–240 pts (Acc; Acc Bus; Acc Econ; Acc Inf Sys)
Teesside – 180–220 pts (Acc Fin; Acc Law)

160 pts **Bedfordshire** – 160–200 pts (Acc; Acc Law)
Canterbury Christ Church – 160 pts (Bus St Acc; Mark Acc)
Central Lancashire – 160 pts (Acc courses except under **180 pts**)
East London – 160 pts (Acc Fin; Acc; Bus Inf Sys Acc)
Farnborough (CT) – 160–200 pts (Acc Fin)
Greenwich – 160–180 pts (Acc Fin)
London Met – 160–200 pts (Acc Fin; Acc Bank)
London South Bank – CC (Acc Fin)
Napier – CC (Accounting)
North East Wales (IHE) – 160 pts (Bus Acc)
Paisley – CC (Acc; Bus Acc)
Southampton Solent – 160–220 pts (Accountancy)
Thames Valley – 160 pts (Acc Fin)
Wolverhampton – 160–220 pts (Acc Fin)
Worcester – 160 pts (Bus Mgt (Fin Acc))

120 pts **Bradford (Coll)** – 120 pts (Acc Law)
80 pts **Holborn (Coll)** – 80 pts (Accountancy)
London (Birk) – 80 pts (p/t Acc Mgt)
Norwich City (Coll) – 80 pts (Acc Fin)
Swansea (IHE) – 80 pts (Accounting)

Leeds Met – contact University
Regents Bus Sch London – check with Business School (Int Fin Acc)

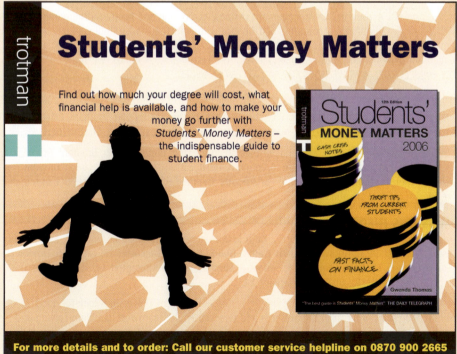

Alternative offers

IB offers Aberdeen 30 pts; Aberystwyth 29 pts; Aston 34 pts; Bath 35 pts; Birmingham 34 pts; Brighton 26 pts; Bristol 32–34 pts; Bristol UWE 24–28 pts; Brunel 30 pts; City 30–35 pts; Dundee 29 pts; East Anglia 30–32 pts; Essex 30 pts; Exeter 35–32 pts; Glasgow 30 pts; Keele 28–30 pts; Kent 30–33 pts; Lancaster 34 pts; Liverpool 32 pts; London (LSE) 36 pts, (QM) 30 pts; Loughborough 36 pts; Manchester 33 pts; Manchester Met 24 pts; Newcastle 33–35 pts; Nottingham 32 pts; Reading 33 pts; Salford 28 pts; Sheffield 33–32 pts; Southampton 35 pts; Staffordshire 26 pts; Stirling 30 pts; Warwick 36 pts. *Scottish offers* See **Chapter 7**.

OTHER HIGHER EDUCATION COURSES IN THE SUBJECT FIELD

Foundation degrees (contact the institutions for details) Croydon (Coll); Darlington (Coll); Doncaster (Univ Centre); Lambeth (Coll); London South Bank; Northampton; Plymouth (CHE); Westminster Kingsway (Coll).

Higher National Diploma courses Croydon (Coll); Durham New (Coll); Gloucestershire; London Met; Mid-Cheshire (Coll); Norwich City (Coll); Plymouth (CFE); Salford; Swansea (IHE); Thames Valley; UHI Millennium Inst; Walsall (Coll); see also under **Finance**.

CHOOSING YOUR COURSE (SEE ALSO CH.1)

Subject information Degree courses include economics, statistics, accounting and law, with some courses emphasising the use of computers. All vocational courses are designed to comply with the regulations of professional bodies. In the case of Accountancy, most degree courses will give partial exemptions from the examinations of some or all the accountancy institutions. Students should check with universities and colleges which professional bodies offer exemptions for their courses before applying. All courses provide a sound preparation for entry to the profession, although many graduates entering careers in accountancy will do so after taking degree courses in other subjects. **Useful websites** www.acca.co.uk; www.cimaglobal.org.uk; www.cipfa.org.uk; www.tax.org.uk; www.icaew.co.uk; www.bized.ac.uk.

Course variations Accounting for Management (Aston); Accounting and Taxation (Bournemouth); Law and Accountancy (Edinburgh); Accounting and Finance with French Business Studies (Kent); Accounting and Information Systems (Leeds); Accounting and Business (London Met); Finance, Accounting and Management (Nottingham); Business Management (Professional Accounting) (Westminster). *NOW CHECK PROSPECTUSES AND WEBSITES FOR ANY RECENT CHANGES.*

Universities and colleges teaching quality See www.tqi.ac.uk; www.qaa.ac.uk.

Top universities and colleges (Research) Aston; Bangor; Bristol; Bristol UWE; Durham; Edinburgh; Essex; Exeter; Glasgow; London (LSE)*; Manchester; Newcastle; Paisley; Stirling; Strathclyde.

Sandwich degree courses Abertay Dundee; Aberystwyth; Aston; Bournemouth; Bradford; Brunel; City; De Montfort; Glamorgan; Gloucestershire; Greenwich; Hertfordshire; Huddersfield; Loughborough; Manchester Met; Northumbria; Plymouth; Portsmouth; Sheffield Hallam; Staffordshire; UCE Birmingham; Ulster; Westminster; Wolverhampton.

ADMISSIONS INFORMATION

Number of applicants per place (approx) Bath 5; Birmingham 9; Bristol 23; Dundee 5; East Anglia 17; Essex 7; Exeter 18; Glasgow 10; Heriot-Watt 7; Hull 8; Kent 10; Lancaster 20; Leeds 25; London (LSE) 16; Loughborough 12; Oxford Brookes 9; Salford 8; Sheffield 40; Southampton 13; Staffordshire 3; Stirling 20; Strathclyde 10; Ulster 10; Warwick 14.

Advice to applicants and planning the UCAS personal statement Universities look for good communication skills, interest in the business and financial world, teamwork, problem-solving and computing experience. On the UCAS application you should be able to demonstrate your knowledge of accountancy and to give details of any work experience or work shadowing undertaken. Try to arrange meetings with accountants, or work shadowing or work experience in accountants' offices, commercial or industrial firms, town halls, banks or insurance companies and describe the work you have done. Obtain information from the main accountancy professional bodies (see **Appendix 2**). Refer to current affairs which have stimulated your interest from articles in the *Financial Times, The Economist* or the business and financial sections of the weekend press. **Buckingham** Commitment to follow the course. Details of any extra-curricular activities illustrating personal development are also useful. **London South Bank** Full chronological history – no gaps. **Staffordshire** Applicants with two A-levels should contact the Business School.

Misconceptions about this course Many students believe that you need to be a brilliant mathematician (A-level mathematics is rarely required) but you do have to be numerate and enjoy numbers. Many under-estimate the need for a high level of attention to detail. **Buckingham** Some students think it's a maths course. **Salford** Some applicants believe the course is limited to financial knowledge when it also provides an all-round training in management skills.

Selection interviews Some Aberystwyth, Anglia Ruskin, Bristol, Buckingham, Cardiff, De Montfort, Dundee, Kent, Lincoln, Liverpool John Moores, London (LSE), Staffordshire, Stirling, Sunderland, Wolverhampton.

Interview advice and questions Be prepared to answer questions about why you have chosen the course, the qualities needed to be an accountant, and why you think you have these qualities! You should also be able to discuss any work experience you have had and to describe the differences in the work of chartered, certified, public finance and management accountants. **Buckingham** If students are from a non-English-speaking background, they are asked to write an essay. If their maths results are weak they may be asked to do a simple arithmetic test. Mature students with no formal qualifications are usually interviewed and questioned about their work experience. See also **Chapter 6**.

Reasons for rejection (non-academic) Poor English. Lack of interest in the subject because they realise they have chosen the wrong course! No clear motivation. Course details not researched. **London South Bank** Punctuality, neatness, enthusiasm and desire to come to London South Bank not evident.

AFTER-RESULTS ADVICE
Universities with vacancies in Clearing (2006) Aberdeen; Abertay Dundee; Aberystwyth; Anglia Ruskin; Bangor; Bolton; Bournemouth; Bradford; Brighton; Bristol UWE; Brunel; Buckingham; Central Lancashire; City; Coventry; De Montfort; Derby; Dundee; East Anglia; East London; Essex; Glamorgan; Glasgow Caledonian; Gloucestershire; Greenwich; Heriot-Watt; Hertfordshire; Huddersfield; Hull; Keele; Kent; Kingston; Leicester; Lincoln; Liverpool John Moores; London (RH); London Met; London South Bank; Loughborough; Manchester Met; Middlesex; Napier; Newcastle; Newport; Northampton; Nottingham Trent; Paisley; Plymouth; Portsmouth; Reading; Robert Gordon; Salford; Sheffield; Sheffield Hallam; Southampton; Southampton Solent; Staffordshire; Stirling; Strathclyde; Sunderland; Swansea; Teesside; Thames Valley; UCE Birmingham; Ulster; Westminster; Wolverhampton. Check all Colleges and Institutes of Higher Education.

Offers to applicants repeating A-levels Higher Belfast (Queen's) (none), Brunel, Glasgow, Hull, Manchester Met; **Possibly higher** Brighton, Bristol UWE, Central Lancashire, East Anglia, Leeds, Newcastle, Oxford Brookes, Sheffield Hallam; **Same** Aberystwyth, Anglia Ruskin, Bangor, Bradford, Brighton, Buckingham, Cardiff, De Montfort, Derby, Dundee, East London, Heriot-Watt, Huddersfield, Liverpool John Moores, Loughborough, Napier, Newcastle, Northumbria, Salford, Staffordshire, Stirling, Sunderland, UCE Birmingham, Wolverhampton.

GRADUATE DESTINATIONS AND EMPLOYMENT (2005 HESA)
Graduates surveyed 2640 **Employed** 1265 **In further study** 200 **Assumed unemployed** 175.

OTHER DEGREE SUBJECTS FOR CONSIDERATION
Actuarial Studies; Banking; Business Studies; Economics; Financial Services; Insurance; International Securities and Investment Banking; Mathematics; Quantity Surveying; Statistics.

ACTUARIAL SCIENCE/STUDIES

NB The points totals shown to the left of the institutions are for ease of reference only. It must not be assumed that tariff points are always used by institutions or that they can be substituted for an offer in grades. The level of an offer is not necessarily indicative of the quality of a course.

COURSE OFFERS INFORMATION

Subject requirements/preferences GCSE Most institutions require grades A/B in mathematics. **Southampton** 50% passes at grade A or above in mathematics and science. **AL**. Mathematics usually required, possibly with a specific grade.

Your target offers

360 pts **and above**
   City – AAA (Act Sci; Act Sci Ind/Abrd)
   London (LSE) – AAA–AAB (Act Sci)
340 pts **Belfast (Queen's)** – AAB (Act St)
   Southampton – AAB (Econ Act Sci; Maths Act St)
320 pts **Kent** – 320 pts (Act Sci)
300 pts **Heriot-Watt** – ABC 1st yr entry (Act Maths Stats)
260 pts **Swansea** – 260–300 pts (Act St; Act St Acc; Act St Abrd)

Alternative offers
IB offers City 35 pts; Kent 33 pts; London (LSE) 36 pts; Southampton 35 pts.
Scottish offers See **Chapter 7**.

CHOOSING YOUR COURSE (SEE ALSO CH.1)

Subject information Actuaries deal with the evaluation and management of financial risks, particularly those associated with insurance companies and pension funds. Although students are not necessarily committed to a career as an actuary on graduation, many go on to be trainees and since the course is vocational, students will gain partial or full exemptions from some of the examinations of the Institute and Faculty of Actuaries, leading to one of the highest paid careers. **City** The first degree in this subject was offered in 1974. **Kent** The course is ideal if you are good at mathematics and you are curious about financial matters. **Useful website** www.actuaries.org.uk.

Course variations Actuarial Science with a Year in Industry (business placement) (City); Economics with Actuarial Sciences (Southampton); Actuarial Studies with Accounting (Swansea). *NOW CHECK PROSPECTUSES AND WEBSITES FOR ANY RECENT CHANGES.*

Universities and colleges teaching quality See www.tqi.ac.uk; www.qaa.ac.uk.

Top universities and colleges (Research) Kent; London (LSE); Southampton.

ADMISSIONS INFORMATION

Number of applicants per place (approx) City 6; Heriot-Watt 5; Kent 6; London (LSE) 7; Southampton 5; Swansea 9.

Advice to applicants and planning the UCAS personal statement Demonstrate your knowledge of this career and its training, and mention any contacts you have made with an actuary. (See **Appendix 2** for contact details of professional associations for further information.) Any work experience or shadowing in insurance companies should be mentioned, together with what you have learned about the problems facing actuaries. **Swansea** You must show motivation and sheer determination for training as an actuary which is long and tough (up to three or four years after graduation). Mathematical flair, an ability to communicate and an interest in business are paramount.

Misconceptions about this course There is a general lack of understanding of actuaries' career training and of the career itself.

Selection interviews **Some** Heriot-Watt, Kent, Southampton, Swansea.

Interview advice and questions In view of the demanding nature of the training, it is important to have spent some time discussing this career with an actuary in practice. Questions, therefore, may focus on the roles of the actuary and the qualities you have to succeed. You should also be ready to field questions about your mathematics course and the aspects of it you most enjoy. **Swansea** The interview does not determine who will be accepted or rejected but only the level of the offer made. See also **Chapter 6**.

Reasons for rejection (non-academic) **Kent** Poor language skills.

AFTER-RESULTS ADVICE
Universities with vacancies in Clearing (2006) All universities.

Offers to applicants repeating A-levels **Higher** City; **Same** Heriot-Watt, Southampton.

GRADUATE DESTINATIONS AND EMPLOYMENT (2005 HESA)
No data available.

OTHER DEGREE COURSE SUBJECTS FOR CONSIDERATION
Accountancy; Banking; Business Studies; Economics; Financial Risk Management; Financial Services; Insurance; Mathematics; Money, Banking and Finance; Statistics.

AFRICAN and CARIBBEAN STUDIES

NB The points totals shown to the left of the institutions are for ease of reference only. It must not be assumed that tariff points are always used by institutions or that they can be substituted for an offer in grades. The level of an offer is not necessarily indicative of the quality of a course.

COURSE OFFERS INFORMATION
Subject requirements/preferences **GCSE** Grade A–C in mathematics. **Birmingham** English and mathematics. **AL** A language subject or demonstrated proficiency in a second language.

Your target offers
280 pts **Birmingham** – BBC 260 pts (Af St; Af St Am Can St; Af St Anth; Af St Dev)
260 pts **London (SOAS)** – BCC (Af Lang Cult; Af St Ling; Af St Mgt; Hs Arbc; Swhl Mgt)
200 pts **Bristol UWE** – 200–260 pts (Carib St Psy; Carib St Bus; Carib St Pol; Carib St Int Rel)
160 pts **London Met** – 160 pts (Carib St courses)

London (Birk) – Check with admissions tutor (Af St courses; Hs; Swhl)

Alternative offers
IB offers Birmingham 32 pts; Bristol UWE 26–32 pts; London (SOAS) 30 pts.
Scottish offers See **Chapter 7**.

CHOOSING YOUR COURSE (SEE ALSO CH.1)
Subject information African Studies courses tend to be multi-disciplinary covering several subject areas and can include anthropology, history, geography, sociology, social psychology and languages. Most courses focus on Africa and African languages (Amharic (Ethiopia), Hausa (Nigeria), Somali (Horn of Africa), Swahili (Somalia and Mozambique), Yoruba (Nigeria, Sierra Leone, Ghana and Senegal), and Zulu (South Africa)). **London Met** offer a range of courses focusing on the Caribbean. **Useful websites** www.british-museum.ac.uk; www.africanstudies.org; www.black-history-month.co.uk.

Course variations A choice of five African languages (London (SOAS)); Caribbean Studies in a range of joint course including Business, International Relations and Psychology (Bristol UWE). *NOW CHECK PROSPECTUSES AND WEBSITES FOR ANY RECENT CHANGES.*

Universities and colleges teaching quality See www.tqi.ac.uk; www.qaa.ac.uk.

For information on how to read the Subject Tables, see **Chapter 7**.

Top universities and colleges (Research) Birmingham; London (SOAS).

ADMISSIONS INFORMATION

Number of applicants per place (approx) Birmingham 5.

Advice to applicants and planning the UCAS personal statement Describe any visits you have made to African or Caribbean countries or why you wish to study this subject. Embassies in London may be able to provide information about the history, geography, politics, economics and the culture of the countries in which you are interested. Keep up-to-date with political developments in Africa or Caribbean countries. Discuss any aspects which interest you.

Interview advice and questions Questions are likely on your choice of country or geographical region, your knowledge of it and your awareness of some of the political and social problems that exist. See also **Chapter 6**.

AFTER-RESULTS ADVICE

Universities with vacancies in Clearing (2006) Birmingham; London (SOAS).

GRADUATE DESTINATIONS AND EMPLOYMENT (2005 HESA)

Graduates surveyed 20 **Employed** 10 **In further study** 5 **Assumed unemployed** 5.

OTHER DEGREE SUBJECTS FOR CONSIDERATION

Anthropology; Geography; History; Languages; Sociology.

AGRICULTURAL SCIENCES/AGRICULTURE

(including **Agricultural Business Management, Countryside Conservation, Crop Science and Rural Resources Management;** see also **Animal Science, Forestry, Horticulture, Landscape Architecture** and **Surveying**)

NB The points totals shown to the left of the institutions are for ease of reference only. It must not be assumed that tariff points are always used by institutions or that they can be substituted for an offer in grades. The level of an offer is not necessarily indicative of the quality of a course.

COURSE OFFERS INFORMATION

Subject requirements/preferences **GCSE** English and mathematics usually required. Practical experience may be required by some universities. Check with admissions tutors. **Newcastle** Mathematics grade B. **AL** A science is required for some courses. **Other Belfast (Queen's)** Three months' practical farming required.

NB Many agricultural courses are offered at colleges on sites separate from the universities.

Your target offers
320 pts Newcastle – ABB (Agri-Bus Mgt)
300 pts Edinburgh – BBB (Ecol Sci (Frsty))
          Stirling – BBB 2nd yr entry (Frshwtr Sci; Cons Sci; Aquacult)
280 pts Belfast (Queen's) – 280 pts (Lnd Use Env Mgt)
          Newcastle – BBC–BCC (Agric; Rur Res Mgt; Frm Bus Mgt; Orgnc Fd Prod; Agron)
          Reading – 280 pts (Agric Bus Mgt; Rur Res Mgt; Agric)
260 pts Belfast (Queen's) – BCC–CCC (Agric Tech)
          Nottingham – BCC–CCC (Agric; Crop Sci)
240 pts Aberdeen – CCC (Agric Sci; Agric Bus Mgt; Wldlf Mgt)
          Bangor – 240–260 pts (Env Cons; Agric Cons Env)
220 pts Stirling – CCD 1st yr entry (Aquacult; Frshwtr Sci; Cons Sci)
210 pts Aberystwyth – 210 pts (Agric Bus St)
200 pts Aberystwyth – 200 pts (Sust Rur Dev; Cntry Recr Tour; Cntry Mgt; Cntry Cons)
180 pts Aberystwyth – 180 pts (Agric; Agric Cntry Cons; Agric Cntry Mgt; Agric Mark)

Nottingham Trent – 180 pts (Env Cons Cntry Mgt)
Salford – 180 pts (Aqua Sci)
160 pts **Bristol UWE (Hartpury)** – 160–200 pts (Agric Bus Mgt; Agric Cons; Agric Lnd Mgt; Dy Hrd Mgt)
Greenwich –160 pts (Land Mgt; Int Agric)
Harper Adams (UC) – 160–240 pts (Agric Anim Sci; Agric Lnd Farm Mgt; Agric Mark; Agric Mech; Agric Crop Mgt; Agric Env Mgt; Agric Fd Qual Mgt; Rur Ent Lnd Mgt; Cntry Mgt; Cntry Env Mgt; Sust Res Mgt)
Plymouth – 160–200 pts (Wldlf Cons)
Royal (CAg) – 160 pts (Agric; Agric (Orgnc Frm) (Anim Mgt) (Lnd Mgt) (Crop Prod))
SAC (Scottish CAg) – 160 pts (Agri Sci; Agric; Agric (Crop Sci) (Rur Ent) (Anim Sci); Rur Bus Mgt (Agric))
Wolverhampton – 160–220 pts (Cntry Sust Lnd Mgt)
140 pts **Bishop Burton (Coll)** – 140 pts (Wldlf Cntry Cons)
Derby – DDD 140–180 pts (Cons Cntry Mgt)
Writtle (Coll) – 140–160 pts (Agric; Agric Bus Mgt; Rur Res Mgt; Cons Env; Wldlf Mgt; Spo Trf Sci Mgt; Agric Env)
120 pts **Liverpool John Moores** – 120–140 pts (Wldlf Cons)
Sparsholt (Coll) – DD (Aquacult Fish Mgt)
100 pts **and below**
Blackpool and Fylde (Coll) – 100 pts (Rur Ent Mgt)
UHI Millennium Inst (LCC) – (Rur Dev St via HND, HNC, DipHE, CertHE)

Alternative offers

IB offers Aberdeen 28 pts; Aberystwyth 26 pts; Bristol UWE (Hartpury) 28–30 pts; Newcastle 28 pts; Nottingham 28–30 pts; Reading 29 pts; Royal (CAg) 26–28 pts; Stirling 26 pts.
Scottish offers See **Chapter 7**.

For information on how to read the Subject Tables, see **Chapter 7**.

OTHER HIGHER EDUCATION COURSES IN THE SUBJECT FIELD

Foundation degrees (contact the institutions for details) Aberystwyth; Askham Bryan (Coll); Bicton (Coll); Bishop Burton (Coll); Bristol UWE (Hartpury); CAFRE; Capel Manor (Coll); Central Lancashire; Derby; Duchy (Coll); Harper Adams (UC); Kingston Maurward (Coll); Myerscough (Coll); Northampton; Plumpton (Coll); Sparsholt (Coll); Warwickshire (Coll); Wiltshire (Coll); Wolverhampton; Writtle (Coll).

Higher National Diploma courses

120 pts and below

Aberystwyth; Anglia Ruskin; Askham Bryan (Coll); Bath; Brighton; Bristol UWE (Hartpury); Buckinghamshire Chilterns (UC); CAFRE; Capel Manor (Coll); Central Lancashire; Cornwall (Coll); Easton (Coll); Glamorgan; Harper Adams (UC); SAC (Scottish CAg); Sparsholt (Coll); Sunderland; UHI Millennium Inst (LCC); West Anglia (Coll); Wiltshire (Coll); Warwickshire (Coll); Writtle (Coll).

CHOOSING YOUR COURSE (SEE ALSO CH.1)

Subject information Courses in Agriculture recognise that modern farming practice requires sound technical and scientific knowledge, together with appropriate management skills, and most courses focus to a greater or lesser extent on all these skills. Your choice of course depends on your particular interest and aims: some courses will give greater priority than others to practical application. Many students will come from an agricultural background, but for others work experience will be deemed necessary by most institutions. The range of courses in the table above points to the diversity of the subject which, at one time, was simply aimed at farming. Such specialisations require careful consideration since many students regard them as vocational preparation for a future career and work experience beforehand is essential. **Useful websites** www.defra.gov.uk; www.countryside.gov.uk; www.ccw.gov.uk; www.rase.org.uk; www.scienceyear.com; www.iah.bbsrc.ac.uk; www.lantra.co.uk; www.nfuonline.com; www.nfyfc.org.uk; www.iagre.org.

Course variations Agriculture and Mechanisation (Harper Adams (UC)); Countryside Recreation and Tourism (Aberystwyth); Wildlife Conservation (Liverpool John Moores); Organic Food Production (Newcastle); Aquaculture (Stirling). *NOW CHECK PROSPECTUSES AND WEBSITES FOR ANY RECENT CHANGES.*

Universities and colleges teaching quality See www.tqi.ac.uk; www.qaa.ac.uk.

Top universities and colleges (Research) Aberdeen; Bangor; Nottingham; Reading; Stirling.

Sandwich degree courses Aberystwyth; Bangor; Harper Adams (UC); Nottingham Trent; Royal (CAg); Sparsholt (Coll); UHI Millennium Inst (LCC).

ADMISSIONS INFORMATION

Number of applicants per place (approx) Aberystwyth (Agric courses) 2–3; Bangor (Agric Cons Env) 4; Liverpool John Moores 3; Newcastle 6; Nottingham 4; Royal (CAg) (Agric) 2.

Advice to applicants and planning the UCAS personal statement First-hand farming experience is necessary for some courses and obviously important for all. Check prospectuses and websites. Describe the work done. Details of experience of work with agricultural or food farms (production and laboratory work), garden centres, even with landscape architects, could be appropriate. Keep up-to-date with European agricultural and fishing policies and mention any interests you have in these areas. Read farming magazines and discuss any articles which have interested you. You may even have had first-hand experience of the serious problems facing farmers. **Bangor** (Agric Cons Env) Evidence of broad interest in land use and conservation. **Derby** (Cons Cntry Mgt) Interest or experience in practical conservation work. Ability to work both independently or as a member of a team is important. (See **Appendix 2**.)

Selection interviews Yes Bristol UWE (Hartpury); **Some** Bangor, Belfast (Queen's), Bishop Burton (Coll), Derby, Edinburgh, Harper Adams (UC), Plymouth, Royal (CAg).

Interview advice and questions Agriculture is in the news, especially in relation to the consequences of the considerable problems facing farmers, particularly concerning dairy farmers and milk prices, the consequences of the foot and mouth epidemic, its origins and treatment. You should be up-to-date with political and scientific issues concerning the farming community in general and how these problems might be resolved. You are likely to be questioned on your own farming background (if relevant) and your farming experience. Questions asked in the past have included: What special agricultural interests do you have? What types of farms have you worked on? Farming publications that you read and agricultural shows visited? **Bangor** (Agric Cons Env) No tests at interview; (Rur Res Mgt) What is meant by the term 'sustainable development'? What is the UK Biodiversity Action Plan? Are farmers custodians of the countryside? What are the potential sources of non-fossil-fuel electricity generation? **Derby** (Cons Cntry Mgt) Discussion about fieldwork experience. See also **Chapter 6**.

Reasons for rejection (non-academic) Insufficient motivation. Too immature. Unlikely to integrate well. Lack of practical experience with crops or animals.

AFTER-RESULTS ADVICE
Universities with vacancies in Clearing (2006) All universities and colleges should be contacted.

Offers to applicants repeating A-levels **Possibly higher** Edinburgh, Newcastle (Agric), Plymouth (Agric); **Same** Bangor (Agric Cons Env), Bishop Burton (Coll), Bristol UWE (Hartpury), Derby, Harper Adams (UC), Nottingham, Plymouth, Royal (CAg), Writtle (Coll).

GRADUATE DESTINATIONS AND EMPLOYMENT (2005 HESA)
Graduates surveyed 725 **Employed** 425 **In further study** 70 **Assumed unemployed** 40.

OTHER DEGREE SUBJECTS FOR CONSIDERATION
Agroforestry; Animal Sciences; Biochemistry; Biological Sciences; Biology; Biotechnology; Chemistry; Conservation Management; Crop Science; Ecology (Biological Sciences); Environmental Sciences; Estate Management (Surveying); Food Science and Technology; Forestry; Horticulture; Land Surveying; Landscape Architecture; Plant Sciences; Veterinary Science; Wood Science; Zoology.

AMERICAN STUDIES
(see also Latin American Studies)

NB The points totals shown to the left of the institutions are for ease of reference only. It must not be assumed that tariff points are always used by institutions or that they can be substituted for an offer in grades. The level of an offer is not necessarily indicative of the quality of a course.

COURSE OFFERS INFORMATION
Subject requirements/preferences **GCSE Dundee**, **Edinburgh**, English, foreign language, mathematics and science. **East Anglia** English and history at grade A or B. **AL** English, history or other arts subject may be required.

Your target offers
360 pts   and above
      Manchester – AAA–ABB (Am St; Am Lat Am St)
320 pts   Birmingham – ABB (Am Can St courses)
      East Anglia – ABB–BBB 320–300 pts (Am Lit Crea Writ)
      Kent – 320 pts (Am St (Art Film))
      Lancaster – ABB (Am St Yr USA; Am St Org St)
      London (King's) – ABB (Am St; Am St Yr Abrd; Film Am St)
      Nottingham – ABB–BBB **or** 3AL+AS (Am St Hist; Am St Lat Am St; Am Engl St)
      Sussex – ABB–BBB **or** 360–340 pts 3AL+1AS (Am St courses)
      Warwick – ABB–BBBc **or** AB/BBbbc (Compar Am St; Engl Am Lit)
300 pts   Belfast (Queen's) – BBB–BBC (Am St)

Dundee – 300 pts 2nd yr entry (Am St courses; Transat St courses)
East Anglia – BBB–BBC 300–280 pts (Am St)
Essex – BBB–BBC 300–280 pts (Am (US) St; Am St (US Lat Am St); Crimin Am St; Am St Film)
Hull – 300 pts (Am St)
Leicester – BBB–AAB 300–340 pts (Am St Yr USA)
London (Gold) – 300 pts (Engl Am Lit)
Loughborough – 300 pts (Engl N Am Lit Film)

280 pts **East Anglia** – BBC–BCC (Am Hist Engl Hist; Am Hist Pol)
Hull – BBC (Am St Hist; Am St Lang; Am St Film St; Am St Phil; Am St Crea Writ; Am St Engl; Am St Gndr St)
Kent – 280 pts (Am St (Hist) (Lit))
Leicester – BBC–AAB (Am St; Am St USA)
Liverpool – BBC–BBB 280–300 pts (Compar Am St)
London (King's) – BBC+AS **or** BBbbc (US Lat Am St)
Swansea – 280 pts (Am St)

260 pts **Keele** – 260–320 pts (Am St)
Leicester – 260–320 pts (Comb courses)
Northumbria – 260 pts (Br Am Cult)

240 pts **Aberystwyth** – 240 pts (Irish Am St; Am St)
Dundee – 240 pts 1st yr entry (Am St courses; Transat St courses)
Kent – 240 pts (Br Am Pol St)
Portsmouth – 240–300 pts (Am St; Am St Hist)
Ulster – CCC 240 pts (Am St courses)

220 pts **Lincoln** – CCD 220 pts (Am St courses)
Liverpool John Moores – 220 pts (Am St courses)
Winchester – 220 pts (Am St courses; Am Lit courses)

200 pts **Cumbria** – 200 pts approx (Am St Comb)
Manchester Met – 200 pts (Am St joint courses)
Plymouth – 200 pts (Am St courses)

190 pts **London Met** – 190 pts (Am St)

180 pts **Derby** – 180 pts (Am St)
Lampeter – open admission policy (Am St)
Northampton – 180–220 pts (Am St)

160 pts **Canterbury Christ Church** – CC (Am St; Am St USA/Can)
Central Lancashire – 160–240 pts (Am St Comb Hons; Film Rad Am St; Am St)
London Met – 160–200 pts (Am St joint courses)
Middlesex – 160–200 pts (Am St courses)
Wolverhampton – 160–220 pts (Am St courses)
Sunderland – 160 pts (Am St courses)
Worcester – 160–200 pts (Am St courses)
York St John – 160 pts (Am St courses)

140 pts **Derby** – 140–180 pts (Am St Comb Hons)

Alternative offers
IB offers Aberystwyth 29 pts; Birmingham 34 pts; Dundee 29 pts; East Anglia 30 pts; Essex 32 pts; Keele 28–32 pts; Kent 28 pts; Lancaster 34 pts; Leicester 32 pts; Liverpool 32 pts; London (King's) 35 pts; Manchester Met 28 pts; Nottingham 32–34 pts; Sussex 34 pts; Warwick 32–36 pts.
Scottish offers See **Chapter 7**.

OTHER HIGHER EDUCATION COURSES IN THE SUBJECT FIELD
Foundation degrees (contact institution for details) Northampton.

CHOOSING YOUR COURSE (SEE ALSO CH.1)
Subject information American Studies courses normally cover American history, politics and literature, although in most courses there are opportunities to study in specialist fields such as drama, film

studies, history of art, linguistics, politics or sociology. In some universities a year, term or semester in the USA (or Canada) is compulsory or optional whilst at other institutions the course lasts three years without a placement abroad. **Useful website** www.historynet.com.

Course variations American and Canadian Studies (Birmingham); Transatlantic Studies (Dundee); American Studies (Art and Film) (Kent); British and American Policy Studies (Kent); English and North American Literature and Film (Loughborough); British and American Cultures (Northumbria). *NOW CHECK PROSPECTUSES AND WEBSITES FOR ANY RECENT CHANGES.*

Universities and colleges teaching quality See www.tqi.ac.uk; www.qaa.ac.uk.

Top universities and colleges (Research) Keele; Liverpool; Nottingham*; Sussex.

Sandwich degree courses De Montfort.

ADMISSIONS INFORMATION

Number of applicants per place (approx) Birmingham 6; Dundee 5; East Anglia 7; Essex 6; Hull 15; Keele 7; London (King's) 10; Nottingham 12; Swansea 2; Warwick 14;.

Advice to applicants and planning the UCAS personal statement Visits to America should be described and any knowledge or interests you have of the history, politics, economics and the culture of the USA should be included on the UCAS application. The US Embassy in London may be a useful source of information. American magazines and newspapers are good reference sources and books written by Alistair Cooke (*America* – BBC Publications) will also give a good insight to life in the USA. **Birmingham** (Am Can St) Applicants should demonstrate an intelligent interest in both North American literature and history in their personal statement. We look for enthusiasm about the US Canadian Studies course. Tell us why you are excited and interested in our subject area; at least half of your personal statement should focus on how and why your interest has developed, for example through extra-curricular reading, projects, films, academic study. **East Anglia** Wide-ranging engagement with American culture. **Swansea** We look for well-rounded and motivated students. We also look for strength in the more traditional humanities subjects though we are prepared to be flexible.

Misconceptions about this course Swansea Some candidates feel that American Studies is a soft option. While we study many topics which students find interesting, we are very much a humanities-based degree course incorporating more traditional subjects like history, literature and English. Our graduates also find that they are employable in the same jobs as those students taking other degrees.

Selection interviews Yes Birmingham, Derby, East Anglia, Hull, Lampeter, Sussex, Warwick, Winchester; **Some** Birmingham, De Montfort, Dundee, Kent.

Interview advice and questions Courses often focus on history and literature so expect some questions on any American literature you have read and also on aspects of American history, arts and culture. You may also be questioned on visits you have made to America (or Canada) and your impressions. Current political issues might also be raised, so keep up-to-date with the political scene. **Birmingham** Access course and mature students are interviewed and also those students with strong applications but whose achieved grades do not meet entrance requirements. **Derby** The purpose of the interview is to help applicants understand the interdisciplinary nature of the course. **East Anglia** Admissions tutors want to see how up-to-date is the applicant's knowledge of American culture. **Swansea** Our interviews are very informal, giving students the chance to ask questions about the course. See also **Chapter 6**.

Reasons for rejection (non academic) If personal reasons prevent year of study in America. **Birmingham** Lack of commitment to the course. **Swansea** Lack of knowledge covering literature, history and politics.

AFTER-RESULTS ADVICE

Universities with vacancies in Clearing (2006) Aberystwyth; Birmingham; Central Lancashire; Derby; East Anglia; Essex; Hull; Keele; Kent; Lampeter; Lancaster; Leicester; Liverpool; Liverpool John Moores;

London (Gold); London Met; Manchester; Manchester Met; Middlesex; Northampton; Northumbria; Plymouth; Portsmouth; Southampton; Sunderland; Swansea; Ulster; Wolverhampton; Winchester; Worcester.

Offers to applicants repeating A-levels Higher Essex, Warwick, Winchester; **Possibly higher** Nottingham; **Same** Birmingham, Derby, Dundee, East Anglia, Hull, Swansea.

GRADUATE DESTINATIONS AND EMPLOYMENT (2005 HESA)
Graduates surveyed 750 **Employed** 400 **In further study** 110 **Assumed unemployed** 55.

OTHER DEGREE SUBJECTS FOR CONSIDERATION
Business Studies; Cultural Studies; English Literature; Film Studies; Government; History; International History; International Relations; Latin-American Literature/Studies; Politics.

ANATOMICAL SCIENCE/ANATOMY
(see also **Physiology**)

NB The points totals shown to the left of the institutions are for ease of reference only. It must not be assumed that tariff points are always used by institutions or that they can be substituted for an offer in grades. The level of an offer is not necessarily indicative of the quality of a course.

COURSE OFFERS INFORMATION
Subject requirements/preferences GCSE Mathematics usually required. **Cambridge** Grade As in most subjects. **Leeds** Mathematics grade B. **AL** One or two science subjects usually required.

Your target offers
360 pts and above
          Cambridge – AAA (Nat Sci (Anat))
340 pts Manchester – AAB–BBC (Anat Sci; Anat Sci Ind Exp; Anat Sci Modn Lang)
320 pts Cardiff – ABB–BBB (Biomed Sci (Anat))
300 pts Bristol – BBB (Anat Sci; Hum Muscskel Sci; Anat Sci Vet Anat)
          Dundee – 300–240 pts (Anat Sci; Anat Physiol Sci)
          Nottingham – BBB (Neuroscience)
280 pts Edinburgh – BBC (Neuroscience)
          Glasgow – BBC–CCC (Anat; Neuro)
          Liverpool – 280–300 pts (Anat Hum Biol)
260 pts Belfast (Queen's) – BCC–CCC (Anatomy)

Alternative offers
IB offers Bristol 32 pts; Cambridge 38–42 pts; Dundee 26 pts; Glasgow 28 pts.
Scottish offers See **Chapter 7**.

CHOOSING YOUR COURSE (SEE ALSO CH.1)
Subject information Anatomy is the study of the structural basis of living creatures. Courses proceed by way of observation and dissection supported by histology and embryology and at **Bristol** can involve a year in industry in which students undertake biomedical research. The subject leads to a range of careers in various laboratories, in government establishments, the NHS, pharmaceutical and food industries. It can also lead to postgraduate studies in physiotherapy, nursing, osteopathy and, in exceptional cases, in medicine and dentistry. **Useful websites** www.scienceyear.com; www.innerbody.com; www.instantanatomy.net; www.netanatomy.com.

Course variations Anatomical Science with a Year in Industry (Bristol); Human Musculoskeletal Science (Bristol); Biomedical Science and Anatomy (Cardiff); Anatomy and Physiology (Dundee); Neuroscience (Edinburgh). *NOW CHECK PROSPECTUSES AND WEBSITES FOR ANY RECENT CHANGES.*

Universities and colleges teaching quality See www.tqi.ac.uk; www.qaa.ac.uk.

Top universities and colleges (Research) Birmingham; Bristol*; Cambridge; Leeds; Liverpool*.

Sandwich degree courses: Bristol; Cardiff; Manchester.

ADMISSIONS INFORMATION

Number of applicants per place (approx) Bristol 7; Cardiff 8; Dundee 6; Liverpool 7.

Advice to applicants and planning the UCAS personal statement Give reasons for your interest in this subject (usually stemming from school work in biology). Discuss any articles in medical and other scientific journals which have attracted your attention and any new developments in medicine related to anatomical science. **Liverpool** Genuine interest in a dissection-based course. Motivation to the practical study of anatomy.

Selection interviews **Yes** Cambridge; **Some** Cardiff, Dundee.

Interview advice and questions Questions are likely on your particular interests in biology and anatomy, why you wish to study the subject and your future career intentions. See also **Chapter 6**.

Reasons for rejection (non-academic) **Liverpool** Unfocused applications with no evidence of basic knowledge of the course.

AFTER-RESULTS ADVICE

Universities with vacancies in Clearing (2006) Dundee; Glasgow; Leeds.

Offers to applicants repeating A-levels **Higher** Bristol, Dundee, Sheffield; **Possibly higher** Liverpool; **Same** Cardiff.

GRADUATE DESTINATIONS AND EMPLOYMENT (2005 HESA)
(Including **Physiology**)

Graduates surveyed 2545 **Employed** 1545 **In further study** 625 **Assumed unemployed** 150.

OTHER DEGREE SUBJECTS FOR CONSIDERATION
Biological Sciences; Biology; Genetics; Microbiology; Neuroscience; Osteopathy; Physiology; Physiotherapy.

ANIMAL SCIENCES

(including **Equine Science/Studies and Wildlife Conservation;** see also **Agricultural Sciences/Agriculture, Biological Sciences, Biology, Psychology, Veterinary Science/Medicine, Zoology**)

NB The points totals shown to the left of the institutions are for ease of reference only. It must not be assumed that tariff points are always used by institutions or that they can be substituted for an offer in grades. The level of an offer is not necessarily indicative of the quality of a course.

COURSE OFFERS INFORMATION
Subject requirements/preferences **GCSE Reading** Mathematics grade B. Also check any weight limits on equitation modules. **AL** One or two science subjects required for scientific courses, biology and chemistry preferred.

Your target offers
360 pts and above
      Cambridge – AAA (Nat Sci)
320 pts Birmingham – ABB–BBB (Biol Sci (Anim Biol))
      Bristol – ABB–BBB (Anim Bhv Welf)
      Sheffield – ABB (MBiol Sci Anim Bhv)

132 | Animal Sciences

300 pts **Bristol** – BBB **or** BBbbb (Vet Pathogen)
Exeter – BBB–CCC (Anim Bhv)
London (RVC) – BBB (BSc Vet Sci – **not** a qualification to practise as a vet)
Newcastle – BBB–BB (Anim Sci (Cmpn Anim St) (Lvstk Tech))
Sheffield – BBB (BSc Anim Bhv)

280 pts **Aberystwyth** – 280 pts (Anim Bhv)
Glasgow – BBC–CCC (Anim Biol)
Leeds – 280–300 pts (Zool Anim Sci)
Reading – 280 pts 3AL+AS **or** 260 pts 3AL (Anim Sci)

260 pts **Nottingham** – BCC–CCC (Anim Sci; Anim Sci Cert Euro)

240 pts **Aberystwyth** – 240 pts (Eqn Sci; Anim Sci; Eqn Hum Spo Sci)
Central Lancashire (Penrith) – 240 pts (Anim Cons Sci)
Chester – 240–260 pts (Anim Bhv courses)
Lincoln – 240 pts (Eqn Sci; Anim Bhv Sci)

220 pts **Anglia Ruskin** – 220 pts (Anim Welf; Anim Bhv; Anim Bhv Psy)
Askham Bryan (Coll) – CCD (Anim Mgt Sci)
Brighton – 220 pts (Eqn Spo Perf)
Bristol UWE (Hartpury) – 220–160 pts (Anim Sci)
Gloucestershire – 220 pts (Anim Biol)
Liverpool John Moores – 220 pts (Anim Bhv)
Nottingham Trent (Brackenhurst) – 220 pts (Eqn Spo Sci; Eqn Spo Sci (Eqstrn); Eqn Psy)
Stirling – CCD (Anim Biol)

200 pts **Bristol UWE (Hartpury)** – 200–240 pts (Eqn Spo Sci; Eqn Sci; Eqn Dntl Sci)
Napier – 200 pts (Anim Biol)

180 pts **Lincoln** – 180 pts (Anim Mgt Welf; Eqn Spo Sci)
Northampton – 180–220 pts (App Anim St Eqn Mgt)
Nottingham Trent (Brackenhurst) – DDD 180 pts (Wldlf Cons; Anim Sci)
Staffordshire – 180–240 pts (Anim Biol Cons)

160 pts **Bristol UWE (Hartpury)** – 160 pts (Anim Bhv Welf; Eqn Bus Mgt)
Canterbury Christ Church – CC (Anim Sci)
Greenwich/Hadlow (Coll) – DDE 160 pts (Anim Mgt; Eqn Mgt)
Harper Adams (UC) – 160–240 pts (Anim Bhv Welf; Anim Sci)
Plymouth – 160–200 (Anim Sci; Anim Sci (Bhv Welf))
Royal (CAg) – 160 pts (Agric (Anim Mgt); Int Eqn Agric Mgt)
SAC (Scottish CAg) – CC (Anim Sci; Agric (Anim Sci); App Biosci (Anim Sci); Rur Recr Tour Mgt (Eqn St))
Warwickshire (Coll) – 160 (Eqn Sci; Eqn St; Spo Sci (Eqn Hum); Eqn St Bus Mgt)
Wolverhampton – 160–220 pts (Anim Cr Mgt; Anim)
Writtle (Coll) – 160–280 pts (Anim Sci; Anim Mgt; Eqn Sci; Eqn St; Eqn Brdng Stud Mgt; Eqn St Bus Mgt)

140 pts **Bishop Burton (Coll)** – 140 pts (App Anim Sci; App Anim Bhv Trg; Eqn Sci Mgt)
Liverpool John Moores – 140–180 pts (Wldlf Cons)
Napier – CD (Anim Biol)

120 pts **Sparsholt (Coll)** – 120 pts (Anim Mgt; Eqn St)
Worcester – 120 pts (Anim Biol courses)

80 pts **Bournemouth** – 80 pts (Anim Sci)
CAFRE – 80 pts (Eqn St)

Huddersfield – contact University (Anim Hlth Sci)

Alternative offers

IB offers Aberystwyth 26–28 pts; Brighton 26 pts; Bristol 34 pts; Bristol UWE (Hartpury) 28–39 pts; Cambridge 38–42 pts; Chester 30 pts; Exeter 33–26 pts; Glasgow 26 pts; Newcastle 28–32 pts; Nottingham 24–30 pts; Reading 30 pts; Staffordshire 28 pts; Stirling 26 pts.
Scottish offers See **Chapter 7**.

UNIVERSITY COURSES AT DUCHY COLLEGE

Study in Cornwall and take advantage of Duchy College's new facilities and excellent industry links.

Foundation Degrees available in:
- Equine Behaviour & Training
- Equine Sports Performance & Coaching
- Veterinary Nursing

All our university courses are approved by the University of Plymouth, so you get a University degree at a small, friendly and supportive college.

We also offer Foundation Degrees in:
- Agriculture
- Countryside & the Environment
- Food Studies and Manufacturing Technology
- Horticulture
- Outdoor Education
- Sport
- Police Studies

Upon graduation you could progress onto the final year of a related honours degree at the University of Plymouth Applications being taken now

t. 01579 372233
e. uni@duchy.ac.uk
w. www.duchy.ac.uk

*£2000 annual tuition fees with £500 fee waiver

College Mission "Creating opportunities for all through high quality education and training."

tuition fees from just £1500*

UNIVERSITY OF PLYMOUTH · COLLEGES CORNWALL COLLEGE

COMBINED UNIVERSITIES IN CORNWALL

Part of The **CORNWALL COLLEGE** GROUP

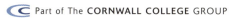

OTHER HIGHER EDUCATION COURSES IN THE SUBJECT FIELD

Foundation degrees (contact the institutions for details) Aberystwyth; Abingdon and Witney (Coll); Askham Bryan (Coll); Bicton (Coll); Bishop Burton (Coll); Bridgwater (Coll); Bristol UWE (Hartpury); Brooksby Melton (Coll); Capel Manor (Coll); Central Lancashire; Cornwall (Coll); Derby; Duchy (Coll); Greenwich; Hadlow (Coll); Harper Adams (UC); Kingston Maurward (Coll); Moulton (Coll); Myerscough (Coll); Nescot; Nottingham Trent; Otley (Coll); Plumpton (Coll); Reaseheath (Coll); Shuttleworth (Coll); Solihull (Coll); Sparsholt (Coll); Suffolk (Univ Campus); Warwickshire (Coll); Wiltshire (Coll); Writtle (Coll).

Higher National Diploma courses

120 pts and below

Aberystwyth; Anglia Ruskin; Askham Bryan (Coll); Bath; Berkshire (CAg); Bishop Burton (Coll); Brighton; Bristol UWE (Hartpury); Brooksby Melton (Coll); Buckinghamshire Chilterns (UC); CAFRE; Capel Manor (Coll); Central Lancashire (Newton Rigg); Chester; Chichester; Craven (Coll); De Montfort (Anim Sci); Easton (Coll); Filton (Coll); Glamorgan; Greenwich; Harper Adams (UC); Hertfordshire; Hopwood Hall (Coll); Nescot; Northumberland (Coll); Park Lane Leeds (Coll); Plymouth; SAC (Scottish CAg); St Helens (Coll); Solihull (Coll); Sparsholt (Coll); UHI Millennium Inst; Warwickshire (Coll); West Anglia (Coll); Wiltshire (Coll); Wolverhampton; Worcester (UC); Writtle (Coll).

CHOOSING YOUR COURSE (SEE ALSO CH.1)

Subject information Animal Sciences is a broad-based subject involving both farm and companion animals. The range of specialisms is reflected in the table of courses above and can focus on animal nutrition and health, animal biology, behaviour, ecology and welfare. In addition, many courses specialise in equine science, studies and management. **Useful websites** www.rspca.org.uk; www.iah.bbsrc.ac.uk; www.bhs.org.uk; www.wwf.org.uk; www.bsas.org.uk.

Course variations Veterinary Pathogenesis (Bristol); Animal Behaviour and Welfare (Harper Adams (UC)); Veterinary Science (London (RVC)); Animal Science (Companion Animal Studies) (Newcastle); Equine Sport Science (Nottingham Trent); International Equine and Agricultural Management (Royal (CAg)); Animal Behaviour (Sheffield); Equine Breeding and Stud Management (Writtle (Coll)). *NOW CHECK PROSPECTUSES AND WEBSITES FOR ANY RECENT CHANGES.*

Universities and colleges teaching quality See www.tqi.ac.uk; www.qaa.ac.uk.

Top universities and colleges (Research) Sheffield*; see also **Agricultural Sciences/Agriculture**.

Sandwich degree courses Harper Adams (UC); Writtle (Coll).

ADMISSIONS INFORMATION

Number of applicants per place (approx) Aberystwyth 6; Bristol 7; Harper Adams (UC) 5; Leeds 6; Newcastle 9 (all courses); Nottingham 6; Nottingham Trent (Eqn Spo Sci) 4; Reading 10; Royal (CAg) 4.

Advice to applicants and planning the UCAS personal statement Describe any work you have done with animals which generated your interest in this subject. Work experience in veterinary practices, on farms or with agricultural firms would be useful. Read agricultural/scientific journals for updates on animal nutrition or breeding. For Equine courses, details of practical experience in the horse industry (eg BHS examinations, Pony Club tests) should be included. **Bristol** A very rigorous scientific academic course; close contact with horses. **Leeds** Farm experience is helpful but not a requirement. **Lincoln** (Eqn Spo Sci) Give full details of all practical riding experience. **Plymouth** (Wldlf Cons) We look for a demonstrated genuine interest in wildlife, for example voluntary work in nature conservation or habitat management.

Misconceptions about this course Students are not always aware that horse studies courses cover science, business management, nutrition, health and breeding. **Bishop Burton (Coll)** (Eqn Sci Mgt) Some students erroneously believe that neither riding skills nor a science background are required for this course. Animal Management courses also extend to exotic species and livestock. It may also involve difficult decisions, for example for the benefit of the animal or the species rather than for the sensibilities of those involved.

Selection interviews Yes Bristol, Cambridge, Lincoln, Newcastle, Nottingham (depends on application), Plymouth, Royal (CAg), SAC (Scottish CAg), Writtle (Coll); Some Bishop Burton (Coll), Bristol UWE (Hartpury), Harper Adams (UC), Stirling, York.

Interview advice and questions Questions are likely about your experience with animals and your reasons for wishing to follow this science-based subject. Other questions asked in recent years have included: What do your parents think about your choice of course? What are your views on battery hens and the rearing of veal calves? The causes of foot and mouth disease and the on-going BSE question may also feature. Equine courses: students should check the level of riding ability expected (eg BHS stage 2 or PC B-test level). Check the amount of riding, jumping and competition work on the course. Lincoln (Eqn Spo Sci) Applicants required to show that they can ride to national Level 2. Experience with animals in general. See also Chapter 6.

Reasons for rejection (non-academic) Uncertainty as to why applicants chose the course. Too immature. Unlikely to integrate well.

AFTER-RESULTS ADVICE

Universities with vacancies in Clearing (2006) Aberdeen; Aberystwyth; Anglia Ruskin; Belfast; Birmingham; Bournemouth; Brighton; Bristol UWE (Hartpury); Canterbury Christ Church; Central Lancashire; Chester; East Anglia; Glamorgan; Gloucestershire; Greenwich; Kent; Leeds; Lincoln; Liverpool John Moores; London (RVC); Middlesex; Napier; Newcastle; Northampton; Nottingham; Nottingham Trent; Plymouth; Reading; Sheffield; Southampton; Staffordshire; Stirling; Wolverhampton; Worcester.

Offers to applicants repeating A-levels Possibly higher Nottingham; Same Anglia Ruskin, Bishop Burton (Coll), Bristol UWE (Hartpury), Chester, Harper Adams (UC), Leeds, Liverpool John Moores, Plymouth, Royal (CAg), Stirling.

GRADUATE DESTINATIONS AND EMPLOYMENT (2005 HESA)
Graduates surveyed 430 Employed 230 In further study 55 Assumed unemployed 25.

OTHER DEGREE SUBJECTS FOR CONSIDERATION
Agriculture; Biology; Food Science; Veterinary Science; Zoology.

ANTHROPOLOGY

(including Social Anthropology; see also Archaeology)

NB The points totals shown to the left of the institutions are for ease of reference only. It must not be assumed that tariff points are always used by institutions or that they can be substituted for an offer in grades. The level of an offer is not necessarily indicative of the quality of a course.

COURSE OFFERS INFORMATION

Subject requirements/preferences GCSE Mathematics usually required. Aberdeen, St Andrews English, mathematics or science and a foreign language required. Cambridge Grade A in most subjects preferred. Sussex Modern language grade A for language courses. AL A pass required in some joint course subjects.

Your target offers
360 pts and above
         Cambridge – AAA (Arch Anth))
         Durham – AAA (Nat Sci (Anth))
         Oxford – Offers vary eg AAA–AAB (Arch Anth)
340 pts Bristol – AAB–BBB (Arch Anth)
         Durham – AAB (Anth Comb Arts; Anth Comb Soc Sci)

East Anglia – AAB–BBB (Arch Anth Art Hist; Arch Anth Art Hist Yr Aus)
London (UCL) – AAB–BBB+AS (Anth; Anth Geog)

320 pts **Durham** – ABB (Anthropology)
Edinburgh – ABB–BBB (Soc Anth courses)
Glasgow – ABB–BBB (BA Anth)
London (LSE) – ABB (Anth Law)
London (SOAS) – ABB (Soc Anth)
Manchester – ABB–BBB (Soc Anth; Soc Anth Sociol; Soc Anth Crimin; Arch Anth)
St Andrews – ABB (Soc Anth courses)

300 pts **Belfast (Queen's)** – BBB (Soc Anth)
Birmingham – BBB–BBC (Anthropology)
Dundee – BBB–CCC 320–260 pts (Foren Anth)
Durham – BBB (Anth Arch)
Liverpool – BBB (Evol Anth)
London (Gold) – BBB (Anth; Anth Media; Anth Sociol)
London (LSE) – BBB (Soc Anth)
Sussex – BBB **or** 340 pts 3AL+1AS (Anth courses)
Swansea – 300–260 pts (Egypt courses)

280 pts **Durham** – BBC (Anth Sociol; Biol Anth)
Glasgow – BBC–CCC (BSc Anth)
Lancaster – BBC (Anth Relig)
Southampton – BBC 280 pts (App Soc Sci (Anth))

260 pts **Brunel** – 260 pts (Soc Anth; Psy Soc Anth; Soc Anth Sociol)
Durham – BCC (Med Anth)
Hull – 260–280 pts (Sociol Anth courses)

240 pts **Aberdeen** – CCC **or** aabb (Anthropology)
Kent – 240 pts (Anth; Soc Anth Lang/Yr Abrd; Biol Anth; Med Anth)
Oxford Brookes – CCC **or** CCcc (Anthropology)

220 pts **Liverpool John Moores** – CCD (Pal Evol; Evol Anth; Foren Anth)
200 pts **Bristol UWE** – 200–240 pts (Biol Anth)
180 pts **Lampeter** – open admissions policy (Anth; Relig St Anth; Arch Anth)
160 pts **East London** – 160 pts (Anth courses)
Roehampton – 160–200 pts (Anth; Biol Anth courses; Soc Anth courses)

Alternative offers

IB offers Aberdeen 30 pts; Birmingham 30–32 pts; Bristol UWE 24–26 pts; Brunel 28 pts; Cambridge 38–42 pts; Dundee 29 pts; Kent 27 pts; Lancaster 32–33 pts; London (Gold) 32 pts, (LSE) 36 pts, (SOAS) 36 pts, (UCL) 34–36 pts; Oxford 38–42 pts; Manchester 34 pts; St Andrews 32–36 pts; Sussex 32 pts.
Scottish offers See **Chapter 7**.

CHOOSING YOUR COURSE (SEE ALSO CH.1)

Subject information Anthropology is a study of people's behaviour, beliefs and institutions and the diverse societies in which they live, and is concerned with the biological evolution of human beings. It also involves our relationships with other primates, the structure of communities and the effects of diet and disease on human groups. Alternatively, social or cultural anthropology covers aspects of social behaviour in respect of family, kinship, marriage, gender, religion, political structures, law, psychology and language. **Useful websites** www.british-museum.ac.uk; www.therai.org.uk.

Course variations Archaeology and Anthropology (Bristol); Biological Anthropology (Bristol UWE); Forensic Anthropology (Dundee); Combined Social Sciences (Durham); Medical Anthropology (Kent). *NOW CHECK PROSPECTUSES AND WEBSITES FOR ANY RECENT CHANGES.*

Universities and colleges teaching quality See www.tqi.ac.uk; www.qaa.ac.uk.

Top universities and colleges (Research) Belfast (Queen's); Cambridge; Durham; Edinburgh; Kent; London (Gold), (LSE)*, (SOAS), (UCL)*; Manchester; Oxford; Roehampton; St Andrews; Sussex.

Sandwich degree courses Bristol UWE; Brunel.

ADMISSIONS INFORMATION

Number of applicants per place (approx) Belfast (Queen's) 10; Cambridge 2; Durham 14; Hull 11; Kent 6; Liverpool John Moores 4; London (Gold) 7, (LSE) (Anth Law) 9, (Soc Anth) 9, (SOAS) 10, (UCL) 3; Oxford Brookes 8; Sussex 10.

Advice to applicants and planning the UCAS personal statement Visits to museums should be discussed, for example, museums of anthropology (London, Cambridge). Describe any aspect of the subject which interests you (including books you have read) and how you have pursued this interest. Give details of any overseas travel. Since this is not a school subject, you will need to convince the selectors of your knowledge and interest. **St Andrews** Give reasons for choosing course and evidence of interest, sporting and extracurricular activities and positions of responsibility.

Selection interviews **Yes** Cambridge, Durham, East Anglia, Hull, London (Gold), (UCL) mature students, Oxford, Oxford Brookes; **Some** London (LSE), Roehampton; **No** Bristol.

Interview advice and questions This is a broad subject and questions will tend to emerge as a result of your interests in aspects of anthropology or social anthropology and your comments on your personal statement. Past questions have included: What stresses are there among the nomads of the North African desert? What is a society? What is speech? If you dug up a stone axe what could you learn from it? What are the values created by a capitalist society? Discuss the role of women since the beginning of this century. **Cambridge, Oxford** See **Chapter 6** and under **Archaeology**.

Reasons for rejection (non-academic) Lack of commitment. Inability to deal with a more philosophical (less positivist) approach to knowledge.

AFTER-RESULTS ADVICE

Universities with vacancies in Clearing (2006) Aberdeen; Birmingham; Bristol UWE; Brunel; East Anglia; East London; Glamorgan; Hull; Kent; Lampeter; Lancaster; Liverpool John Moores; London (Gold), (SOAS); Manchester; Middlesex; Nottingham Trent; Roehampton; Southampton.

Offers to applicants repeating A-levels **Possibly higher** Durham, Oxford Brookes; **Same** Liverpool John Moores, London (UCL), Roehampton.

GRADUATE DESTINATIONS AND EMPLOYMENT (2005 HESA)

Graduates surveyed 600 **Employed** 280 **In further study** 110 **Assumed unemployed** 45.

OTHER DEGREE SUBJECTS FOR CONSIDERATION

Archaeology; Egyptology; Heritage Studies; History; Human Sciences; Political Science; Psychology; Religious Studies; Social Science; Sociology.

ARABIC AND NEAR AND MIDDLE EASTERN STUDIES

NB The points totals shown to the left of the institutions are for ease of reference only. It must not be assumed that tariff points are always used by institutions or that they can be substituted for an offer in grades. The level of an offer is not necessarily indicative of the quality of a course.

COURSE OFFERS INFORMATION

Subject requirements/preferences **GCSE Leeds** Grade A–C in a foreign language required, grade A in Arabic. **Cambridge, Oxford** Grade A in most subjects preferred. **Edinburgh** English, mathematics or science and a foreign language required. **AL** A modern language is usually required.

Your target offers
360 pts and above

> **Cambridge** – AAA (Orntl St (Assyr); Orntl St Comb (Arbc) (Assyr) (Persn) (Egypt); Mid E Islam St Arbc)
>
> **Oxford** – Offers vary eg AAA–AAB (Orntl St (Arbc) (Arbc Islam Art Arch) (Arbc Islam St Hist) (Arbc Lang); Egypt; Egypt Anc Nr E St; Arbc Modn Mid E St; Persn Lang; Persn Islam St Hist; Persn Islam Art Arch; Turk courses)

320 pts **Exeter** – ABB–BBC 320–280 pts (Arbc; Arbc Islam St; Mid E St Arbc)

> **St Andrews** – ABB (Mid E St courses; Arbc Econ; Arbc Lat)

300 pts **Edinburgh** – BBB (Arbc courses inc Arbc Persn, Persn Pol, Persn Soc Anth)

> **Swansea** – 300–260 pts (Egypt courses)

280 pts **Leeds** – BBC–BCC (Arbc courses; Mid E St Pol; Mid E St Sociol; Arbc Mid E St; Arbc St; Islam St)

> **London (King's)** – BBC+AS (Turk Modn Gk St)
>
> **London (SOAS)** – BBC–BCC (Arbc; Arbc courses; Arbc Cult St; Arbc Islam St; Anc Near E St)
>
> **Manchester** – BBC–BCC (Mid E St Modn Lang; Arbc Islam St; Arbc St; Mid E Langs; Turk St; Turk Islam St; Persn St; Persn Islam St; Heb Jew St)
>
> **Westminster** – 280 pts (Arbc courses)

260 pts **Birmingham** – BCC 240 pts (Islam St)

200 pts **Salford** – 200 pts (Arbc/Engl Transl Interp for Arabic speakers; contact admissions tutor)

180 pts **Lampeter** – open admissions policy (Islam St)

160 pts **Central Lancashire** – 160 pts (Islam St)

> **London (Birk)** – Check with admissions tutor (Arbc courses)

Alternative offers

IB offers Birmingham 30 pts; Cambridge 38–42 pts; Exeter 30 pts; London (SOAS) 32 pts; Oxford 38–42 pts; St Andrews 32–36 pts.
Scottish offers See **Chapter 7**.

CHOOSING YOUR COURSE (SEE ALSO CH.1)

Subject information Arabic is one of the world's most widely used languages, spoken by more than 300 million people in 21 countries in the Middle East. Links between Britain and Arabic-speaking countries have increased considerably in recent years and most of the larger UK organisations with offices in the Middle East have only a relatively small pool of Arabic-speaking graduates from whom they can recruit future employees each year. Islamic Studies focuses on a faith which has much in common with Christianity and Judaism and is the second largest religion in the world which extends from Africa to the East Indies and is centred on the Middle East. **Useful websites** www.cilt.org.uk; www.iol.org.uk; www.bbc.co.uk/languages; www.languageadvantage.com; www.languagematters.co.uk; www.reed.co.uk/multilingual; www.metimes.com; www.merip.org; www.memri.org; www.mideasti.org.

Course variations Arabic and Islamic Studies (Exeter); Persian Studies (Manchester); Arabic/English Translation and Interpreting for Arab applicants (Salford). *NOW CHECK PROSPECTUSES AND WEBSITES FOR ANY RECENT CHANGES.*

Universities and colleges teaching quality See www.tqi.ac.uk; www.qaa.ac.uk.

Top universities and colleges (Research) Cambridge; Edinburgh; London (SOAS); Manchester; Oxford.

ADMISSIONS INFORMATION

Number of applicants per place (approx) Birmingham 3; Cambridge (Orntl St) 3; Leeds 6; London (SOAS) 5; Salford 5.

Advice to applicants and planning the UCAS personal statement Describe any visits to, or your experience of living in, Arabic-speaking countries. Develop a knowledge of Middle Eastern cultures, history and politics and mention these topics on the UCAS application. Provide evidence of language-learning skills and experience. **St Andrews** Reasons for choosing course and evidence of interest.

Sporting/extra-curricular activities and positions of responsibility. **Salford** Experience of use and interest in foreign languages. Experience of foreign countries. (Arbc/Engl Transl Interp) Arab applicants are normally expected to have passed their secondary school leaving certificate and to demonstrate an acceptable command of English. English and European applicants should also be able to speak Arabic.

Selection interviews Yes Cambridge, Exeter, Leeds, Oxford; **Some** Salford.

Interview advice and questions You will need to be able to justify your reasons for wanting to study Arabic or other languages and to discuss your interest in, and awareness of, cultural, social and political aspects of the Middle East. **Cambridge, Oxford** See **Chapter 6** under **Modern and Medieval Languages**. **Salford** (Arbc/Engl Transl Interp) Applicants may be required to sit Arabic language tests. See also **Chapter 6**.

AFTER-RESULTS ADVICE
Universities with vacancies in Clearing (2006) London (SOAS); Manchester; Salford; Westminster.

Offers to applicants repeating A-levels Higher Leeds, St Andrews; **Same** Exeter, Salford.

GRADUATE DESTINATIONS AND EMPLOYMENT (2005 HESA)
Graduates surveyed 70 **Employed** 30 **In further study** 15 **Assumed unemployed** 10.

OTHER DEGREE SUBJECTS FOR CONSIDERATION
Anthropology; Archaeology; Classical Studies; Hebrew; History; Persian; Politics; Turkish.

ARCHAEOLOGY

NB The points totals shown to the left of the institutions are for ease of reference only. It must not be assumed that tariff points are always used by institutions or that they can be substituted for an offer in grades. The level of an offer is not necessarily indicative of the quality of a course.

COURSE OFFERS INFORMATION
Subject requirements/preferences GCSE Mathematics or science usually required for BSc courses. **Bournemouth** CC or above in science plus English. **Bristol** A–C chemistry. **Cambridge**, **Oxford** Grade A in most subjects preferred. **Edinburgh** (Env Arch) Mathematics required. **Edinburgh**, **Liverpool** Latin or Greek preferred. **Lampeter** Geography or related science. **London (UCL)** Strong GCSE background. **AL** Chemistry or a science required for Conservation courses.

Your target offers
360 pts and above
        Cambridge – AAA (Arch Anth)
        Durham – AAA (Nat Sci (Arch))
        Oxford – Offers vary eg AAA–AAB (Arch Anth; Class Arch Anc Hist)
340 pts Bristol – AAB–BBB (Arch Anth)
        Durham – AAB (Arch Comb Soc Sci; Arch Comb Hons Arts)
        East Anglia – AAB–BBB (Arch Anth Art Hist; Arch Anth Art Hist Aus/N Am)
        York – AAB–ABB (Arch; Bioarch; Arch Hist)
320 pts Cardiff – ABB (Arch Mediev Hist)
        Exeter – 320–300 pts (Hist Arch Euro St)
        Glasgow – ABB–BBB (BA Arch; Arch St)
        London (UCL) – ABB+AS–BBB+AS (Arch; Arch Class Class Art; Egypt Arch; Arch Hist Art)
        Nottingham – ABB (Arch Engl Lang; Arch Geog)
        Sheffield – ABB–BBC (Arch courses)
        Sheffield – ABB (Class Hist Arch)
        Warwick – ABB–BBBc (Anc Hist Class Arch)
300 pts Cardiff – BBB (Arch; Arch Anc Hist; Arch (Hum); Cons Objs Musm Arch)

Durham – BBB (Arch; Anth Arch; Anc Hist Arch)
Edinburgh – BBB (1 sitting) (Arch courses; Arch Scot Ethnol)
Exeter – BBB–BBC **or** BBbb **or** BCcc 300–320 pts (Arch; Anc Hist Arch; Hist Arch; Hist Arch Euro St)
Leicester – 300–360 pts (Anc Hist Arch; Hist Arch; Geog Arch)
London (RH) – BBB (Class Arch; Class Arch Ital)
London (UCL) – BBB (Vkg St)
Manchester – BBB (Arch; Arch Anth)
Newcastle – BBB–BCC (Arch; Anc Hist Arch)
St Andrews – BBB (Anc Hist Arch; Mediev Hist Arch)
Sheffield – BBB (Arch courses except under **320 pts**)
Southampton – BBB (Arch; Arch Geog; Arch Hist)
Swansea – 300 pts (Egyptology)

280 pts **Belfast (Queen's)** – BBC–BBB (BA Arch; Arch Palae; Env Arch)
Birmingham – BBC 280 pts (Arch; Arch Anc Hist)
Bristol – BBC (Arch; Arch Sci)
Chester – 280 pts (Arch courses)
Glasgow – BBC–CCC (BSc Arch; Arch Geog; Arch St)
Hull – 280 pts (Geog Arch; Hist Arch)
Kent – 280 pts (Hist Arch St)
Leicester – 280 pts (Archaeology)
Liverpool – BBC 280 pts (Arch; Egypt; Arch Anc Civ; Egypt Arch; Geog Arch; Anc Hist Arch)
London (King's) – BBC **or** BBbbc (Class Arch)
Nottingham – BBC (Vkg St; Arch; Arch Art Hist; Arch Class Civ; Arch Hist)

260 pts **Bradford** – 260–280 pts (Arch Sci; Arch; Bioarch; Foren Arch Sci)
Kent – 260 pts (Class Arch St courses)
Leicester – 260–320 pts (Arch Comb courses)
London (SOAS) – BCC (Hist Art Arch)
Reading – 260–280 pts 3AL+AS **or** 260 pts 3AL (BSc Arch courses)

240 pts **Aberdeen** – CCC (Scot Arch)
Bradford – 240 pts (Geog Arch)
Central Lancashire – 240 pts (Archaeology)
Swansea – 240–300 pts (Egypt joint courses)

220 pts **Bangor** – 220–260 pts (Herit Arch Hist; Welsh Hist Arch)
Winchester – 220 pts (Arch courses)

180 pts **Lampeter** – open admission policy (Arch; Arch (Env) (Foren) (Prac) (Wrld Cult); Anc Hist Arch; Arch Anth)
Portsmouth – 180 pts (Pal Evol)

160 pts **Bournemouth** – 160 pts (Fld Arch; Arch Prehist; Mar Arch; Arch Foren Sci)

Central Lancashire – 160 pts (Comb Hons (Arch))
140 pts   Worcester – 140–160 pts (Arch Herit St courses; Arch Land St)

Alternative offers
IB offers Birmingham 30–32 pts; Bristol 30–36 pts; Chester 30 pts; East Anglia 32–34 pts; Exeter 30–34 pts; Glasgow 28 pts; Kent 28–29 pts; Leicester 34 pts; Liverpool 30 pts; London (King's) 32 pts, (RH) 32 pts, (SOAS) 30 pts; Newcastle 30–32 pts; Nottingham 30–34 pts; Oxford 38–42 pts; Reading 30 pts; Sheffield 32 pts; Southampton 28 pts; York 34 pts.
Scottish offers See **Chapter 7**.

OTHER HIGHER EDUCATION COURSES IN THE SUBJECT FIELD
Foundation degrees (contact the institutions for details) Bournemouth; Truro (Coll).

Higher National Diploma courses Bournemouth; Truro (Coll).

CHOOSING YOUR COURSE (SEE ALSO CH.1)
Subject information Courses in Archaeology differ between institutions but the majority focus on the archaeology of Europe, the Mediterranean and Middle Eastern countries and on the close examination of discoveries of prehistoric communities and ancient, medieval and post-medieval societies. Hands-on experience is involved in all courses as well as a close study of the history of the artefacts themselves and, in some courses, an appreciation of the application of science. **Useful websites** www.britarch.ac.uk; www.english-heritage.org.uk; www.artefact.co.uk; www.prehistoric.org.uk; www.british-museum.ac.uk; www.archaeologists.net.

Course variations Forensic and Archaeological Science (Bradford); Combined Social Sciences (Durham); Combined Honours in Archaeology or Egyptology (Liverpool); Archaeology and Scottish Ethnology (Edinburgh); Archaeology, Anthropology and Art History with a Year in Australia (East Anglia); Classical and Archaeological Studies (Kent); Egyptology (London (UCL)). *NOW CHECK PROSPECTUSES AND WEBSITES FOR ANY RECENT CHANGES.*

Universities and colleges teaching quality See www.tqi.ac.uk; www.qaa.ac.uk.

Top universities and colleges (Research) Belfast (Queen's); Bradford; Cambridge*; Cardiff; Durham; Exeter; Leicester; Liverpool; London (UCL); Oxford*; Reading; Sheffield; Southampton.

Sandwich degree courses Bradford.

ADMISSIONS INFORMATION
Number of applicants per place (approx) Birmingham 7; Bradford 4; Bristol 7; Cambridge 2; Cardiff 6; Durham 6; Lampeter 2; Leicester 4; Liverpool 12, (Egypt) 5; London (UCL) 5; Newcastle 14; Nottingham 11; Oxford (success rate 41%); Sheffield 5; Southampton 9; York 10.

Advice to applicants and planning the UCAS personal statement First-hand experience of 'digs' and other field work should be described. The Council for British Archaeology (see **Appendix 2**) can provide information on where digs are taking place. Describe any interests in fossils and museum visits as well as details of any visits to current archaeological sites. Your local university archaeological department or central library will also provide information on contacts in your local area (each county council employs an archaeological officer). Since this is not a school subject, the selectors will be looking for good reasons for your choice of subject. **Birmingham** Applications from mature students welcome. Although useful, previous experience of archaeology is not necessary. **Bournemouth** Show willingness to participate in excavations. **Bristol** Gain practical field experience and discuss this in the personal statement. A demonstration of serious commitment to the discipline through extra-curricular activities (fieldwork, museum experience) can compensate for exam results that may be less strong than desirable. **Durham** Archaeological experience useful but not necessary. **Lampeter** Experience useful but not essential. **Liverpool** (Egypt) Interest in ancient Egypt developed through reading, TV and Internet. Course covers archaeology and writings of Ancient Egypt. Be aware of the work of career archaeologists, eg sites and monuments officers, field officers and find researchers (often specialists in particular materials, eg pottery, glass, metalwork). **Oxford** No prior knowledge of archaeology or anthropology required but an enthusiasm for the study of humans and their material culture is expected, preferably from both arts and science viewpoints. (See also under **Anthropology**.) **Southampton** Give evidence of practical experience. **York** We look for interested and interesting students. (See also **Appendix 2**.)

Misconceptions about this course **Bristol** We are not an élitist course: 75% of applicants and students come from state schools and non-traditional backgrounds. **Liverpool** (Egypt) Some students would have been better advised looking at courses in Archaeology or Ancient History and Archaeology which offer major pathways in the study of Ancient Egypt.

Selection interviews **Yes** Bangor, Bournemouth, Bradford, Cambridge, Durham, East Anglia, Glasgow, Lampeter, Liverpool (Egypt), London (UCL), Newcastle, Newport, Nottingham, Oxford, Southampton (mature students), Swansea; **Some** Birmingham, Cardiff, Derby, Sheffield, Truro (Coll); **No** Bristol.

Interview advice and questions Questions will be asked about any experience you have had in visiting archaeological sites or taking part in digs. Past questions have included: How would you interpret archaeological evidence, for example a pile of flints, coins? What is stratification? How would you date archaeological remains? What recent archaeological discoveries have been made? How did you become interested in archaeology? With which archaeological sites in the UK are you familiar? **Birmingham** Questions may cover recent archaeological events. **Cambridge**, **Oxford** (see **Chapter 6**). **Oxford** (Class Arch Anc Hist) Candidates may be shown pictures, objects or other material for discussion. **York** What are your views on the archaeology programmes on TV? What would you do with a spare weekend? See also **Chapter 6**.

Applicants' impressions (A=Open day; B=Interview day) **Birmingham** (A) A tour of the department, campus and sample lectures. **Liverpool** (B) A talk about the course followed by the interview. I was asked to identify a pot and answer questions on archaeology, such as the treatment of bones. An offer was made at the end of the interview. **Swansea** (B) I had a 30-minute interview (one interviewer) with questions on why I chose the course.

Reasons for rejection (non-academic) (Mature students) Inability to cope with essay-writing and exams. **Bournemouth** Health and fitness important for excavations. **Liverpool** (Egypt) Applicant misguided on choice of course – Egyptology used to fill a gap on the UCAS application.

AFTER-RESULTS ADVICE

Universities with vacancies in Clearing (2006) Aberdeen; Bangor; Belfast; Birmingham; Bournemouth; Bradford; Cardiff; Central Lancashire; Chester; East Anglia; Glasgow; Hull; Kent; Lampeter; Leicester; London (RH), (SOAS); Manchester; Newcastle; Nottingham; Reading; Southampton; Winchester; Worcester; York.

Offers to applicants repeating A-levels **Same** Birmingham, Bradford, Chester, Derby, Durham, Lampeter, Leicester, Liverpool (Egypt), London (UCL), Newport, Sheffield, Winchester.

GRADUATE DESTINATIONS AND EMPLOYMENT (2005 HESA)
Graduates surveyed 1210 **Employed** 515 **In further study** 275 **Assumed unemployed** 105.

OTHER DEGREE SUBJECTS FOR CONSIDERATION
Ancient History; Anthropology; Classical Studies; Classics; Geology; Heritage Studies; History; History of Art and Architecture; Medieval History.

ARCHITECTURE

(including **Architectural Technology and Interior Architecture;** see also **Building**)

NB The points totals shown to the left of the institutions are for ease of reference only. It must not be assumed that tariff points are always used by institutions or that they can be substituted for an offer in grades. The level of an offer is not necessarily indicative of the quality of a course.

COURSE OFFERS INFORMATION

Subject requirements/preferences GCSE English in all cases required. **Bath** All subjects at grade A or B with mathematics at grade A, double science or A-level physics. **Cardiff** Physics or science preferred; seven/eight subjects grade A–C, A/B for mathematics and English. **East London, Greenwich, London South Bank** Art or design. **Edinburgh** Mathematics, physics grade A/B + art. **Glasgow** English, mathematics grade A or B. **Huddersfield** Six subjects above grade C. **Manchester Met** Seven subjects at grade A or B. **Newcastle** Mathematics grade A or B if not at A-level. **Nottingham** Mathematics or physics. **Oxford Brookes** Science. **Robert Gordon** English and mathematics or science. **Strathclyde** Science. **AL** Mathematics and/or physics required or preferred for some courses. Art is not usually a requirement but many schools of architecture prefer it and a portfolio of art work is often requested and in some cases a drawing test will be set.

Your target offers

360 pts and above
>> **Bath** – AAA–AAB (Archit St)
>> **Cambridge** – AAA (Architecture)
>> **Cardiff** – AAA (Archit St)
>> **Newcastle** – AAA–ABB (Archit St)
>> **Nottingham** – AAA (Architecture)

340 pts **Sheffield** – AAB (Archit; Archit Land)

320 pts **Heriot-Watt** – ABB 2nd yr entry (Archit Eng)
>> **Kingston** – 320 pts (Architecture)
>> **Liverpool** – ABB 320 pts (Architecture)
>> **London (UCL)** – ABB+AS (Architecture)
>> **Manchester** – ABB (Architecture)
>> **Manchester** – ABB–BBC (Blt Nat Env courses)
>> **Manchester Met** – ABB 320 pts (Architecture)
>> **Plymouth** –320 pts (Architecture)

300 pts **Archit Assoc Sch London** – BBB 300 pts (Architecture)
>> **Belfast (Queen's)** – BBB–BBC (Architecture)
>> **Brighton** – 300 pts (Architecture)
>> **Edinburgh** – BBB (Archit St; Archit Des; Archit Hist; Archit Hist Arch)
>> **Leeds** – BBB–CCC (Archit Eng)
>> **Nottingham** – BBB (Archit Env Des)
>> **Oxford Brookes** – BBB **or** BBe (Architecture)
>> **Strathclyde** – BBB (MEng Archit Eng)
>> **Westminster** – 300 pts (Archit; Archit (Archit Eng) (Inter Des) (Urb Des))

280 pts **Dundee** – BBC (Architecture)
>> **Glasgow (SA)** – BBC (Archit St)
>> **Kent** – 280 pts (Architecture)
>> **Northumbria** – 280 pts (Archit Des Mgt)
>> **Nottingham Trent** – 280 pts (Architecture)
>> **Strathclyde** – BBC (Archit St; Archit St Euro St)
>> **Ulster** – 280 pts (Architecture)

260 pts **Anglia Ruskin** – 260 pts (Architecture)
>> **Central Lancashire** – 260 pts (Archit Tech)
>> **Edinburgh (CA)** – 260 pts (Architecture)

Loughborough – 260 pts (Archit Eng Des Mgt)
Ulster – 260 pts (Archit Tech Mgt)
240 pts **Bristol UWE** – 240–320 pts (Archit Plan)
De Montfort – 240 pts (Archit; Archit Des Tech Prod)
Glasgow – CCC (Civ Eng Archit)
Greenwich – 240 pts (Architecture)
Huddersfield – 240 pts (Archit Int Archit; Archit Tech)
Lincoln – 240 pts (Architecture)
Liverpool John Moores – 240 pts (Architecture)
Northumbria – 240 pts (Archit Tech)
Nottingham – CCC (Archit Env Eng)
Plymouth – 240 pts (Archit Des Struct; Archit Tech Env)
Portsmouth – 240–300 pts (Architecture)
Robert Gordon – CCC (Archit; Archit Tech; Inter Archit)
UCE Birmingham – 240 pts (Architecture)
230 pts **Napier** – 230 pts (Archit Tech; Archit Des Civ Eng)
Sheffield Hallam – 230 pts (Archit Env Des; Archit Tech)
220 pts **Anglia Ruskin** – 220 pts (Archit Tech)
Bolton – 220 pts (Archit Tech)
East London – 220–260 pts (Architecture)
Nottingham Trent – 220 pts (Archit Tech)
Westminster – 220 pts (Archit Tech)
200 pts **Bristol UWE** – 200–240 pts (Archit Tech Des)
180 pts **Brighton** – 180 pts (Archit Tech)
Cardiff (UWIC) – 180 pts (Archit Des Tech)
Coventry – 180 pts (Archit Des Tech)
Derby – 180–200 pts (Archit Cons; Archit Tech Dig Innov; Archit Des courses; Archit Vnu Des Dig Innov)
Northampton – 180–220 pts (Archit Tech)
160 pts **Bedfordshire** – 160–240 pts (Inter Archit)
Creative Arts (UC) – 160 pts (Architecture)
London Met – 160–200 pts (Archit St; Archit)
London South Bank – CC (Archit; Archit Tech; Archit Eng)
Loughborough – CC (Archit Eng Des Mgt Fdn)
Middlesex – 160 pts (Inter Des)
Wolverhampton – 160–220 pts (Inter Archit Des; Archit St courses)
140 pts **Glamorgan** – 140–180 pts (Archit Tech; Archit Herit Cons)
120 pts **North East Wales (IHE)** – 120 pts (Archit Des Tech)
100 pts **Southampton Solent** – 120 pts (Archit Tech)

Leeds Met – contact University

Alternative offers
IB offers Bath 35 pts; Brighton 30–28 pts; Bristol UWE 24–28 pts, (Archit Tech) 24–28 pts; Cambridge 38–42 pts; Dundee 30 pts; Kent 31 pts; Liverpool 34 pts; London (UCL) 34 pts; Manchester 33 pts; Manchester Met 32 pts; Newcastle 37 pts; Nottingham 36 pts; Sheffield 35 pts.
Scottish offers See **Chapter 7**.

OTHER HIGHER EDUCATION COURSES IN THE SUBJECT FIELD
Foundation degrees (contact the institutions for details) Bolton; Derby; Northumbria; Oldham (Coll).

Higher National Diploma courses
100 pts and below
Blackpool and Fylde (Coll); Bournemouth; Bradford (Coll); Derby; Greenwich; Pembrokeshire (Coll); Wigan and Leigh (Coll).

Higher National Diploma courses (Architectural Technology) Anglia Ruskin; Bell (Coll); Brighton; Cardiff (UWIC); Northampton; Northumbria; Robert Gordon.

CHOOSING YOUR COURSE (SEE ALSO CH.1)

Subject information Courses in Architecture provide a broad education consisting of technological subjects covering structures, construction, materials and environmental studies. Project-based design work is an integral part of all courses and in addition, history and social studies will also be incorporated into degree programmes. After completing the first three years leading to a BA (Hons), students aiming for full professional status take a further two-year course leading to the BA (Arch) degree and after a year in an architect's practice, the final professional examinations are taken. Architectural technicians support the work of architects and may be involved in project management, design presentations and submissions to planning authorities. **Useful websites** www.riba.org; www.ciat.org.uk; www.architecture.com.

Course variations Architectural Technology and Design (Bristol UWE); Architectural History and Archaeology (Edinburgh); Architectural and Heritage Conservation (Glamorgan); Architecture with International Architecture (Huddersfield); Architectural and Environmental Design (Nottingham). *NOW CHECK PROSPECTUSES AND WEBSITES FOR ANY RECENT CHANGES.*

Universities and colleges teaching quality See www.tqi.ac.uk; www.qaa.ac.uk.

Top universities and colleges (Research) Bath; Cardiff; Heriot-Watt; Sheffield.

Sandwich degree courses (inc Architectural Technology) Bath; Belfast (Queen's); Brighton; Bristol UWE; Cardiff; Edinburgh (CA); Glasgow (SA); Northumbria; Nottingham Trent; Plymouth; Robert Gordon; Sheffield Hallam; Ulster.

ADMISSIONS INFORMATION

Number of applicants per place (approx) Archit Assoc Sch London 2; Bath 22; Belfast (Queen's) 9; Cambridge 10; Cardiff 12; Cardiff (UWIC) 2; Creative Arts (UC) 4; Dundee 6; Edinburgh 18; Glasgow 16; London (UCL) 16; London Met 13; Manchester Met 25; Newcastle 11; Nottingham 30; Oxford Brookes 15; Robert Gordon 8; Sheffield 20; Strathclyde 10.

Advice to applicants and planning the UCAS personal statement You should describe any visits to historical or modern architectural sites and give your opinions. Contact architects in your area and try to obtain work shadowing or work experience in their practices. Describe any such work you have done. Develop a portfolio of drawings and sketches of buildings and parts of buildings (you will probably need this for your interview). Show evidence of your reading on the history of architecture in Britain and modern architecture throughout the world. Discuss your preferences among the work of leading 20th century world architects. **Archit Assoc Sch London** We look for students with plenty of creativity and motivation. **Cardiff** A good academic base is required, preferably indicating a balance of skills in visual arts, sciences, writing and research. Experience in art and/or design is an advantage. Evidence of work experience in an architect's practice important. **De Montfort** Evidence of work experience and an emphasis on freehand pencil drawing. (See **Appendix 2**.)

Misconceptions about this course Some applicants believe that architectural technology is the same as architecture. Some students confuse architecture with architectural engineering.

Selection interviews The majority of universities and colleges interview or inspect portfolios for Architecture and most require a portfolio of art work. **Yes** Archit Assoc Sch London, Bradford, Brighton, Cambridge, Cardiff, Coventry, Derby, East London, Edinburgh, Huddersfield, Kingston, Liverpool, London (UCL), London South Bank, Newcastle, Nottingham, Sheffield; **Some** Dundee.

Interview advice and questions Most Architecture departments will expect to see evidence of your ability to draw; portfolios are often requested at interview and, in some cases, drawing tests are set prior to the interview. You should have a real awareness of architecture with some knowledge of historical styles as well as examples of modern architecture. If you have gained some work experience then you will be asked to describe the work done in the architect's office and any site visits you have made. Questions in the past have included the following: What is the role of the architect in society? Is the London Eye an eyesore? Discuss one historic and one 20th century building you admire. Who is your favourite architect? What sort of buildings do you want to design? Do you like the University buildings? Do you read any architectural journals? What are your views on the

Millennium Dome? What is the role of an architectural technologist? **Cambridge (Robinson)** Candidates who have taken, or are going to take, A-level art should bring with them their portfolio of work (GCSE work is not required). All candidates, including those who are not taking A-level art, should bring photographs of any three-dimensional material. Those not taught art should bring a sketch book (for us to assess drawing abilities) and analytical drawings of a new and old (pre-1900) building and a natural and human-made artefact. We are interested to see any graphic work in any medium that you would like to show us – please do not feel you should restrict your samples to only those with architectural reference. All evidence of sketching ability is helpful to us. **(NB** All colleges at Cambridge and other university departments of architecture will seek similar evidence.) **Sheffield** Art portfolio for those without AL/GCSE art. See also **Chapter 6**.

Applicants' impressions (A=Open day; B=Interview day) Bath (A) A four-hour open day. Talks on course and tour of the department, halls and university. Informative – very helpful. **Kingston** (B) A 20-minute interview, very casual. I got a very favourable impression of the teaching quality in the department. The course has an artistic, rather than a maths, emphasis. A good place to study if you want to be near London without being in the city. **Portsmouth** (B) An informal group interview took place and portfolios were discussed.

Reasons for rejection (non-academic) Weak evidence of creative skills. Folio of art work does not give sufficient evidence of design creativity. Insufficient evidence of interest in architecture. Unwillingness to try freehand sketching. **Archit Assoc Sch London** Poor standard of work in the portfolio.

AFTER-RESULTS ADVICE
Universities with vacancies in Clearing (2006) Belfast (Queen's); Bolton; Bournemouth; Bristol UWE; Greenwich; Huddersfield; Liverpool John Moores; Manchester; Nottingham; Westminster.

Offers to applicants repeating A-levels Higher Huddersfield; **Possibly higher** Brighton, De Montfort, Glasgow, Newcastle; **Same** Archit Assoc Sch London, Bath, Belfast (Queen's), Cardiff, Cardiff (UWIC), Creative Arts (UC), Derby, Dundee, Greenwich, Heriot-Watt, Kingston, Liverpool John Moores, London Met, London South Bank, Manchester Met, Nottingham, Oxford Brookes, Robert Gordon, Sheffield, UCE Birmingham.

GRADUATE DESTINATIONS AND EMPLOYMENT (2005 HESA)
Graduates surveyed 1375 **Employed** 790 **In further study** 185 **Assumed unemployed** 50.

OTHER DEGREE SUBJECTS FOR CONSIDERATION
Building; Building Surveying; Civil Engineering; Construction; Estate Management; Heritage Management; History of Art and Architecture; Housing; Interior Architecture; Interior Design; Landscape Architecture; Property Development; Quantity Surveying; Surveying; Town and Country Planning; Urban Studies.

ART AND DESIGN (General)
(including Advertising, Creative Arts, Design Management, Design Technology, Multimedia Design, Visual Arts, Web Design; see also Media Studies)

NB The points totals shown to the left of the institutions are for ease of reference only. It must not be assumed that tariff points are always used by institutions or that they can be substituted for an offer in grades. The level of an offer is not necessarily indicative of the quality of a course.

This table covers a range of subjects under the heading of Art and Design. Degree courses are grouped together in subject tables in the following categories: **Art and Design (General)**, **Art and Design (Fashion)**, **Art and Design (Fine Art)**, **Art and Design (Graphic Design)**, **Art and Design (Industrial/Product Design)**, **Art and Design (Three Dimensional Design)**, **History of Art**. Alternatively, refer to the **Course Index** at the back of the book. It should be noted that degree courses in Photography are listed in a separate subject table, Printing, Packaging and Publishing courses are listed in **Business Courses** and Textile courses are in **Art and Design (Fashion)**.

COURSE OFFERS INFORMATION

Subject requirements/preferences Entry requirements for Art and Design courses vary between institutions and courses (check prospectuses and websites). Most courses require an Art and Design Foundation course. AL grades or points may be required plus five GCSE subjects at grades A–C, or a recognised equivalent. A portfolio of work demonstrating potential and visual awareness will also be required.

Your target offers

340 pts **Manchester** – AAB–BBC (Art Arch Anc Wrld)
Reading – AAB (Art Psy)

300 pts **Bournemouth** – BBB (Comp Vis Animat)
Brunel – 300 pts (Multim Tech Des)
Dundee –300 pts 2nd yr entry (Interact Media Des)
Lancaster – BBB–BBC (Crea Arts)
Reading – 300 pts (Art Phil)

280 pts **Kent** – 280 pts (Vis Perf Arts)
Leeds – BBC (Contemp Art Prac; Perf Des)
London (Gold) – BBC (Des Innov)
Reading – 280 pts (Art Film Thea)

260 pts **Bradford** – 260 pts (Comp Animat Spec Efcts)
Loughborough – 260–300 pts (Ind Des Tech)
Nottingham Trent – 260 pts (Imag Dsply Tech)
Richmond (Am Int Univ) – 260 pts (Crea Arts Comm)
Sheffield Hallam – 260 pts (Des Tech)

240 pts **Bradford** – 240 pts (Des Comp Gms)
Brighton – 240 pts (Des Tech Educ QTS)
De Montfort – 240 pts (Des Crfts; Des Mgt Innov; Interact Des; Animat Des; Gm Art Des)
Dundee – 240 pts 1st yr entry (Interact Media Des)
Huddersfield – 240 pts (Multim Des; Vrtl Rlty Des Animat)
Lincoln – 240 pts (Adv Art Dir; Animat)
Middlesex – 240 pts (Des Tech courses)
Northumbria – CCC (Multim Des)
Nottingham Trent – 240 pts (Des Film TV; Thea Des)
Plymouth – 240 pts (Dig Arts Tech)
Stranmillis (UC) – CCC (Tech Des Educ)
UCE Birmingham/Birmingham (IAD) – 240–100 pts (Mgt Des Comm; Art Des; Vis Comm)

230 pts **Loughborough** – 230 pts (Vis Comm courses)

220 pts **Brighton** – 220 pts (Hist Des Cult Soty; Hist Decr Arts Crfts)
Edge Hill – 220 pts (Animation)
Liverpool Hope – 220 pts (Design)

200 pts **Bath Spa** – 200–240 pts (Crea Arts)
Bradford – 200 pts (Vrtl Des Innov)
Gloucestershire – 200 pts **or** Fdn Art (Advertising)
Liverpool John Moores – 200 pts (Multim Arts)
Manchester Met – 200 pts (Contemp Crfts)
Middlesex – 200 pts (Snc Arts)
Napier – 200 pts (Des Fut)
Newport – 200 pts (Adv Des)

180 pts **Anglia Ruskin** – 180 pts (Tm Bsd Art Adv Des)
Central Lancashire – 180 pts (Sust Des)
Cumbria – CDE/DD (Educ Art Des QTS)
Dundee – 180 pts (Art; Des)
Derby – BC **or** DDdd (Crea Expr Thera)
Hull – 180–240 pts (Dig Arts; Des Dig Media)
Kingston – 180–220 pts (Vis Mat Cult)

Northampton – 180–240 pts (Adv Des; Adv PR; Crea Des Mark)

160 pts **Bedfordshire** – 160 pts (Art Des)

Bishop Grosseteste (Coll) – CC (Educ St Art QTS)

Blackpool and Fylde (Coll) – 160 pts (Inf Illus; Sci Nat Hist Illus)

Bolton – 160 pts (Art Des; Animat Illus; Des Innov)

Canterbury Christ Church – CC (Std Media Drg Tech; Dig Cult Arts Media)

Cardiff (UWIC) – 160 pts (Art Crea Writ; Art Phil)

Central Lancashire – 160 pts (AV Media; Art Hist Vis Cult courses)

Central Lancashire – 160–240 pts (Web Multim courses)

Creative Arts (UC) – 160 pts (Des Brnd Mark; Adv Brnd Mgt)

Cumbria – CC (Multim Des Dig Anim; Contemp App Arts)

Dartington (CA) – 160–200 pts (Art Perf)

East London – 160 pts (Vis Theor Mark Des)

Glamorgan – 160 pts (Des Media; Art Prac)

Glasgow (SA) – CC (Des Vis Comm)

Greenwich – 160 pts (Des Tech; Commun Arts Des)

Hertfordshire – 160 pts (Modl Des Modlc Efcts; Art Des)

Lincoln – 160 pts (Cons Restor)

London South Bank – CC (Des Tech)

Manchester Met – 160 pts (Interact Arts; Des Art Dir; Des Tech)

Middlesex – 160–200 pts (Design)

Newman (CHE) – 160–240 pts (Art Educ)

Paisley – CC (Dig Art)

Portsmouth – 160–240 pts (Comp Animat; Des Interact Media)

Robert Gordon – 160–180 pts (Des Dig Media)

Salford – 160 pts (Des Mgt Crea Ind; Des Fut; Vis Arts)

Sheffield Hallam – 160 pts (Des Tech)

Teesside – 160–200 pts (Crea Adv Prom; Des; Des Mark)

Thames Valley – 160 pts (Dig Arts; Dig Animat; Crea Adv)

Ulster – 160 pts (Des; Art Des)

Wolverhampton – 160–220 pts (Des Multim; Des)

Worcester – 160 pts (Comm Des; Art Des)

York St John – CC 160 pts (Des Prac)

140 pts **Edinburgh (CA)** – 140 pts (Art Des)

Staffordshire – 140–200 pts (Interact Adv; Art Des courses)

Sunderland – 140 pts (Arts Des; Animat Des)

Trinity Carmarthen (Coll) – 140 pts (Art Des)

Wolverhampton – 140–200 pts (Design)

120 pts **Cleveland (CAD)** – 120 pts (Enter Des Crfts)

De Montfort – 120–180 pts (Des Tech)

North East Wales (IHE) – 120–80 pts (Des; Multim Des; App Arts; Animat (Des))

Southampton Solent – 120 pts (Multim Des; Des St; Des Tech)

Stockport (CFHE) – 120–240 pts (Des Vis Arts (Multim (Des) (Adv))

100 pts **and below or other selection criteria (Foundation course, interview and portfolio inspection)**

Abertay Dundee; Archit Assoc Sch London; Arts London (Camberwell CA), (Central Saint Martins CAD), (Chelsea CAD), (CFash); Barnsley (Univ Centre); Bedfordshire; Bournemouth (AI); Bradford (Coll); Brighton; Bristol UWE; Cardiff (UWIC); Carmarthenshire (Coll); Chichester; Colchester (Inst); Creative Arts (UC); Cumbria; Dartington (CA); Derby; Dundee; Edinburgh (CA); Falmouth (UC); Forth Valley (Coll); Glamorgan; Glasgow (SA); Hertfordshire; Kingston; Leeds (CAD); Liverpool John Moores; Liverpool (LIPA); London (CMus); London (Gold); London Met; London South Bank; Loughborough; Lowestoft (Coll); Manchester City (Coll); Marjon (Coll); Middlesex; Napier; Nescot; Newman (CHE); North East Wales (IHE); Northbrook (Coll); Northumbria; Norwich (SAD); Nottingham Trent; Paisley; Portsmouth; Ravensbourne (CDC); Reading; Robert Gordon; St Helens (Coll); Salford; Solihull (Coll);

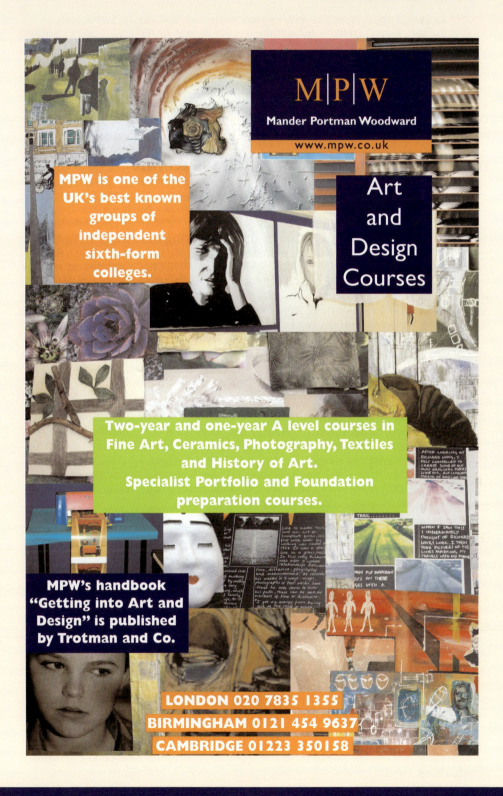

Southend Campus Essex; Southampton/Winchester (SA); Staffordshire; Suffolk (Univ Campus); Swansea (IHE); Swindon (Coll); Teesside; West Herts (Coll); Westminster; Wiltshire (Coll); Yorkshire Coast (CFHE).

Leeds Met – contact University

Alternative offers
IB offers Bristol UWE 30 pts; Dundee 24 pts; Lancaster 30–33 pts; Manchester Met 28 pts; Salford 26 pts; Staffordshire 28 pts.
Scottish offers See **Chapter 7**.

OTHER HIGHER EDUCATION COURSES IN THE SUBJECT FIELD

Foundation degrees (contact institutions for details) Arts London (Camberwell CA), (CFash), (CComm); Barnet (Coll); Barnfield (Coll); Barnsley (Univ Centre); Bath City (Coll); Bath Spa; Bedfordshire; Bicton (Coll); Blackpool and Fylde (Coll); Bournemouth (AI); Bournemouth and Poole (Coll); Bradford (Coll); Brighton and Hove City (Coll); Burnley (Coll); Cardiff (Coll); Cavendish (Coll); Chesterfield (Coll); Cleveland (CAD); Colchester (Inst); Cornwall (Coll); Creative Arts (UC); Croydon (Coll); Darlington (CT); De Montfort; Derby; Dewsbury (Coll); Dunstable (Coll); East Lancashire (IHE); Grimsby (IFHE); Hastings (Coll); Herefordshire (CAD); Hertfordshire; Hopwood Hall (Coll); Huddersfield; Hull (Coll); Hugh Baird (Coll); Huntingdon (Coll); Leeds (CAD); Leeds Met; Leicester (Coll); London Met; Manchester City (Coll); Mid-Cheshire (Coll); Milton Keynes (Coll); Newcastle (Coll); Newham (Coll); Newport; North East Wales (IHE); North West Kent (Coll); Northumberland (Coll); Nottingham New (Coll); Oldham (Coll); Park Lane Leeds (Coll); Preston (Coll); Richmond (CmC); Runshaw (Coll); St Helens (Coll); Salisbury (Coll); Shrewsbury (CAT); South Devon (Coll); South Nottingham (Coll); South Tyneside (Coll); Staffordshire; Suffolk (Univ Campus); Sunderland; Sunderland City (Coll); Sussex Downs (Coll); Tameside (Coll); Teesside; Truro (Coll); West Anglia (Coll); West Herts (Coll); Weston (Coll); Weymouth (Coll); Wiltshire (Coll); Winchester; Writtle (Coll); York St John; Yorkshire Coast (CFHE).

Higher National Diploma courses
100 pts   and below approx + portfolio
Barnet (Coll); Barnsley (Univ Centre); Bath Spa; Birmingham (IAD); Brighton; Bristol City (Coll); Burton (Coll); Canterbury Christ Church; Carmarthenshire (Coll); Central Lancashire; Colchester (Inst); East Surrey (Coll); Forth Valley (Coll); Glasgow Met (Coll); Hertfordshire; Mid-Cheshire (Coll); Middlesex; Newcastle (Coll); Newham (CFE); Portsmouth; Sheffield (Coll); Solihull (Coll); South Kent (Coll); South Nottingham (Coll); Swindon (Coll); Thames Valley; Warwickshire (Coll); West Thames (Coll); York (Coll).

CHOOSING YOUR COURSE (SEE ALSO CH.1)

Subject information This table provides a list of art and design courses which covers a wide range of creative activities for entry to Foundation studies which are required before embarking on degree courses (check with institution). Many of these courses cover aspects of fine art, graphic or three dimensional design, but to a less specialised extent than those listed in the other Art tables. Travel and visits to art galleries and museums strongly recommended by many universities and colleges. **Useful websites** www.artscouncil.org.uk; www.designcouncil.org.uk; www.britart.com; www.theatredesign.org.uk; www.worldofinteriors.co.uk; www.artefact.co.uk; www.arts.ac.uk; www.dandad.org; www.csd.org.uk.

Course variations Computer Animation and Special Effects (Bradford); History of Design, Culture and Society (Brighton); Conservation and Restoration (Lincoln); Contemporary Crafts (Manchester Met); Design Management for the Creative Industries (Salford). *NOW CHECK PROSPECTUSES AND WEBSITES FOR ANY RECENT CHANGES.*

Universities and colleges teaching quality See www.tqi.ac.uk; www.qaa.ac.uk.

Top universities and colleges (Research) Bournemouth; Brighton; London (Gold), (UCL); Newport; Sheffield Hallam; Ulster.

ADMISSIONS INFORMATION

Number of applicants per place (approx) Arts London (Camberwell CA) 2; (Chelsea CAD) 2; Bath Spa (Crea Art) 5; Birmingham 20; Blackpool and Fylde (Coll) (Inf Illus) 2, (Sci Nat Hist Illus) 2; Bournemouth (Comp Vis Animat) 16; Brunel 5; Canterbury Christ Church 3; Central Lancashire 4; Chichester 3; Colchester (Inst) 4; Cumbria 5; Dartington (CA) 4; Derby 4; Dundee 5; Glamorgan 7; Gloucestershire 8; Kent 3; Leeds (CAD) 5; London (Gold) 10; Manchester Met 10; Newman (CHE) 5; Newcastle 23; Northampton (Adv Des) 4, (Crea Des Mark) 5; Norwich (SAD) 3; Nottingham Trent (Des Film TV) 25; Portsmouth 3, (Des Interact Media) 13; Robert Gordon 5; Sheffield Hallam 15; Southampton Solent 1; Sunderland 8; Swansea (IHE) 5; Teesside 2; UCE Birmingham/Birmingham (IAD) (Vis Comm) 10; West Herts (Coll) 3; York St John 3.

Advice to applicants and planning the UCAS personal statement Admissions tutors look for a wide interest in aspects of art and design. Discuss the type of work and the range of media you have explored through your studies to date. Refer to visits to art galleries and museums and give your opinions of the styles of painting and sculpture, both historical and present-day. Mention art-related hobbies. **Bath Spa** Personal statements which clarify relevant work done in addition to formal exam work (eg creative writing). **Staffordshire** (Des Mgt) Creativity, problem-solving, cultural awareness, communications skills. **Sunderland** Good drawing skills and sketch book work. Creative and analytical thinking. See also **Appendix 2**.

Misconceptions about this course **Bath Spa** (Crea St) Some applicants apply for one subject only not realising it is a joint honours programme. **Creative Arts (UC)** Few applicants seem to know what design management is. **Kent** (Vis Perf Arts) It is not a fine arts course. **Nottingham Trent** School sixth formers are often unaware of the importance of a level zero or Foundation course preceding BA Art and Design courses; (Des TV) This is a practical art and design programme, not a Media Studies course.

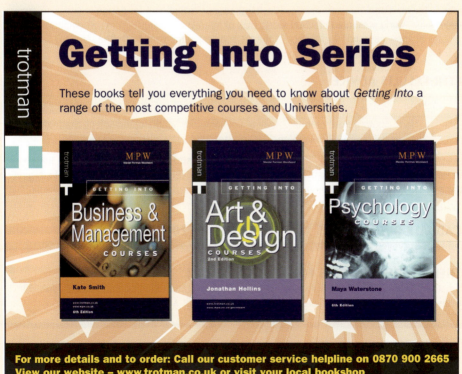

152 | Art and Design (General)

Selection interviews **Yes** Most courses (see under Interview advice and questions); **Some** Chester, Lincoln, Staffordshire.

Interview advice and questions All courses require a portfolio inspection. Admissions tutors will want to see both breadth and depth in the applicant's work and evidence of strong self-motivation. They will also be interested to see any sketch books or note books. However, they do not wish to see similar work over and over again! A logical, ordered presentation helps considerably. Large work, especially three-dimensional work, can be presented by way of photographs. Video or film work should be edited to a running time of no more than 15 minutes. Examples of written work may also be provided. Past questions have included: How often do you visit art galleries and exhibitions? Discuss the last exhibition you visited. What are the reactions of your parents to your choice of course and career? How do they link up with art? Do you feel that modern art has anything to contribute to society compared with earlier art? Is a brick a work of art? Show signs of life – no apathy! Be eager and enthusiastic. **Coventry** What have been the most significant aspects of your art course? **Ulster** Candidates should be able to communicate clearly and through discussion, to show an awareness of current developments, and to convey enthusiasm for their chosen subject. See also **Chapter 6**.

Applicants' impressions (A=Open day; B=Interview day) **Arts London (Camberwell CA)** (A; Art Fdn) A well-organised, friendly 15-minute interview with one interviewer. Why Camberwell? Has your art teacher been supportive? Which contemporary artists do you like? Which recent exhibitions have you seen? (A) Students were present at the Open Day to advise us. **Portsmouth** (B; Art Fdn) A tour of the department in groups of ten took place whilst the staff looked at the portfolios. Two people then interviewed groups of five to seven students. I felt it was a bit inhibiting if you wanted to ask personal questions. A question was asked on 'What do you think we are looking for?' Also random questions about everyday life. **Southampton Solent** (B) A one-to-one interview. An inspection of the portfolio was followed by questions on it. I was asked who won the Turner Prize and to talk about a particular piece of work I had created, my hobbies and my future career hopes.

Reasons for rejection (non-academic) (Des Mgt) Lack of enthusiasm for design issues or to acquire design skills. Poorly presented practical work. Lack of interest or enthusiasm in contemporary visual arts. Lack of knowledge and experience of the art and design industry. **Bath Spa** (Crea St) Some applicants want a particular subject emphasis which we can't offer.

AFTER-RESULTS ADVICE

Universities with vacancies in Clearing (2006) Bath Spa; Bolton; Bournemouth; Bristol UWE; Brunel; Canterbury Christ Church; Chester; Chichester; Cumbria; Derby; Huddersfield; Kingston; London (Gold); Middlesex; Northampton; Northumbria; Reading; Roehampton; Southampton Solent; Staffordshire; Teesside; Thames Valley; UCE Birmingham; Westminster; Worcester; check all institutions.

Offers to applicants repeating A-levels **Higher** Brunel; **Possibly higher** Brighton; **Same** Blackpool and Fylde (Coll), Canterbury Christ Church, Chester, Colchester (Inst), Dundee, Leeds, Lincoln, Napier, Newcastle, Richmond (Am Int Univ), Salford, Staffordshire, Sunderland, UCE Birmingham/Birmingham (IAD), York St John.

GRADUATE DESTINATIONS AND EMPLOYMENT (2005 HESA)

Graduates surveyed 8690 **Employed** 5080 **In further study** 575 **Assumed unemployed** 90.

OTHER DEGREE SUBJECTS FOR CONSIDERATION

Animation; Architecture; Art Gallery Management; Communication Studies; Computer Studies; Film Studies; History of Art; Media Studies; Photography; see other **Art and Design** tables.

ART AND DESIGN (Fashion)

(including Clothing, Fashion Marketing, Knitwear, Surface Decoration and Textile Courses)

NB The points totals shown to the left of the institutions are for ease of reference only. It must not be assumed that tariff points are always used by institutions or that they can be substituted for an offer in grades. The level of an offer is not necessarily indicative of the quality of a course.

COURSE OFFERS INFORMATION

Subject requirements/preferences See under **Art and Design (General)**.

Your target offers

320 pts **Southampton/Winchester (SA)** – ABB (Tex Fash Fbr)

300 pts **Leeds** – BBB (Fash Des)
Manchester – ABC (Tex Des Des Mgt courses; Des Mgt Fash Rtl)

260 pts **East London** – 260–220 pts (Fash Des Mark)
Leeds – BCC (Tex Des)

240 pts **De Montfort** – 240 pts (Cont Fash; Rtl Buy (Tex); Fash Des; Fash Tech; Tex Des)
Dundee – 240 pts (Tex Des)
Heriot-Watt (Scottish Borders) – CCC (Fash Des Ind; Des Tex; Cloth Des Manuf; Tex Fash Des Mgt)
Huddersfield – 240–320 pts (Fash Tex Buy; Fash Tex Mgt; Fash Tex Rtl; Fash Media Prom; Fash Des Tex; Tex Des Fash Inter)
Lincoln – 240 pts (Fash St courses)
Manchester Met – 240 pts (Fash Buy; Int Fash Mark)
Northumbria – 240 pts (Fash; Fash Mark)
Nottingham Trent – 240 pts (Fash Tex Mgt; Fash Des; Fash Knit Des Knit Tex; Fash Mark Comm; Tex Des)
UCE Birmingham/Birmingham (IAD) – 240 pts (Fash Des; Tex Des courses; Fash Rtl Mgt)
Westminster – CCC (Fash Merch Mgt)

220 pts **Anglia Ruskin** – 220–225 pts (Fash Des)
Arts London (CFash) – 220 pts (Fash Mgt)
Creative Arts (UC) – 220 pts (Fash Prom Imag)

200 pts **Bath Spa** – 200–240 pts (Crea Arts)
Bolton – 200 pts (Tex Des)
Central Lancashire – 200–160 pts (Fash courses)
Coventry – 200–220 pts (Fashion)
Hertfordshire – 200 pts (Fashion)
Manchester Met – 200 pts (Textiles)

180 pts **Northampton** – 180–220 pts (Fashion)
Southampton Solent – 180 pts (Writ Fash Cult)

160 pts **Bedfordshire** – 160 pts (Fash Tex Des)
Central Lancashire – 160 pts (AV Media Fash Brnd Prom)
Cumbria – CC (Surf Des)
Derby – 160 pts (Fash St)
Edinburgh (CA) – DDE (Des App Arts (Fash))
Glasgow Caledonian – CC (Fash Bus)
Liverpool John Moores – 160–200 pts (Fash Tex Des)
London Met – 160 pts (Tex Des Inter Prod)
Manchester Met – 160 pts (Fash; Cloth Des Tech; Fash Des Tech; Emb; Tex Tech Fash)
Newport – 160 pts (Fash Des)
Portsmouth – 160 pts (Fash Tex Ent)
Salford – 160–100 pts (Fashion)
Southend Campus Essex – 160–180 pts (Fash Des)
Teesside – 160–200 (Fash Ent)

Ulster – 160 pts (Tex Fash Des)
Wolverhampton – 160–220 pts (Des Inter Tex)
140 pts **Staffordshire** – 140–200 pts (Surf Patt Des)
York St John – 140 pts (Des Prac Bus Mgt)
120 pts **Bournemouth (AI)** – 120 pts (Fash St; Cstm Scrn Stg)
Cleveland (CAD) – 120 pts (Fash Ent; Tex Surf Des)
Derby – 120 pts (Tex Des)
Southampton Solent – 120 pts (Fashion)
Stockport (CFHE) – 120–240 pts (Des Vis Arts (Contemp Tex Surf Des))
100 pts **and below or other relevant criteria (Foundation course, interview and portfolio inspection)**
Arts London (Central Saint Martins CAD), (CFash), (Wimbledon CA); Barnsley (Univ Centre); Basingstoke (CT); Bedfordshire; Bolton; Bournemouth (AI); Bradford (Coll); Brighton; Bristol UWE; Buckinghamshire Chilterns (UC); Cardiff (UWIC); Colchester (Inst); Creative Arts (UC); Croydon (Coll); Dundee; East Lancashire (IHE); Edinburgh (CA); Falmouth (UC); Glasgow Caledonian; Great Yarmouth (Coll); Herefordshire (CAD); Kingston; Leeds (CAD); Leicester (Coll); London (Gold); Loughborough; Mid-Cheshire (Coll); Middlesex; North East Wales (IHE); Northampton; Northbrook (Coll); Norwich (SAD); Oxford and Cherwell Valley (Coll); Plymouth; Portsmouth; Ravensbourne (CDC); Robert Gordon; Rose Bruford (Coll); Somerset (Coll); Southampton/Winchester (SA); Sutton Coldfield (Coll); Swansea (IHE); Thames Valley; UHI Millennium Inst (SC); Waltham Forest (Coll); West Thames (Coll); Westminster; Wirral Met (Coll); Yorkshire Coast (CFHE).

Alternative offers
IB offers Manchester Met 24–28 pts; Salford 26 pts; Staffordshire 28 pts..
Scottish offers See **Chapter 7**.

OTHER HIGHER EDUCATION COURSES IN THE SUBJECT FIELD

Foundation degrees (contact the institutions for details) Arts London (CFash); Barnfield (Coll); Bath City (Coll); Bath Spa; Bolton; Bournemouth (AI); Chesterfield (Coll); Cleveland (CAD); Creative Arts (UC); Croydon (Coll); Derby; Derby (Coll); Dewsbury (Coll); Dunstable (Coll); East Lancashire (IHE); Hastings (Coll); Havering (CFHE); Herefordshire (CAD); Hull (Coll); Leicester (Coll); Liverpool (CmC); Manchester (CAT); Mid-Cheshire (Coll); Newham (Coll); Plymouth (CAD); South Kent (Coll); Wolverhampton.

Higher National Diploma courses
100 pts **and below approx + portfolio**
Anglia Ruskin; Arts London (CFash); Barnet (Coll); Bath Spa; Birmingham City (Coll); Bolton; Bournemouth (AI); Bradford (Coll); Cambridge Reg (Coll); Carmarthenshire (Coll); City of Birmingham (Coll); City of Manchester (Coll); Cleveland (CAD); Coventry City (Coll); Craven (Coll); Crawley (Coll); Croydon (Coll); Cumbria; De Montfort; Dewsbury (Batley (SAD)); Doncaster (Univ Centre); Dudley (Coll) (Fash); East Lancashire (IHE); Glamorgan; Glasgow (CC); Gloucestershire (CAT); Havering (Coll); Herefordshire (CAD); Lincoln; Llandrillo Cymru (Coll); Manchester Met; Mid-Cheshire (Coll); Middlesex; Newcastle (Coll); North Warwickshire/ Hinckley (Coll); Northbrook (Coll); Northampton; Norwich (SAD); Nottingham Trent; Nottingham New (Coll); Oxford and Cherwell Valley (Coll); People's (Coll); Plymouth (CAD); Portsmouth; Salford; Salisbury (Coll); Shrewsbury (CAT); Solihull (Coll); South Downs (Coll); South Nottingham (Coll); Southampton City (Coll); Southampton Solent; Southwark (Coll); Stafford (Coll); Tameside (Coll); UCE Birmingham/Birmingham (IAD); UHI Millennium Inst; Walsall (Coll); West Thames (Coll); Wigan and Leigh (Coll); York (Coll); Yorkshire Coast (CFHE).

CHOOSING YOUR COURSE (SEE ALSO CH.1)

Subject information An Art Foundation course usually precedes Fashion Design courses which involve drawing and design, research, pattern cutting and garment construction for clothing for men, women and children. Courses may also cover design for textiles, commercial production and marketing. Some institutions have particularly good contacts with industry and are able to arrange sponsorships for students. **Useful websites** www.fashion.net; www.londonfashionweek.co.uk; www.texi.org.

Course variations Surface Design (Cumbria); International Fashion Marketing (Manchester Met); Fashion Knitwear Design courses (Nottingham Trent); Textile Fashion and Fibre (Southampton/Winchester (SA)); Fashion Merchandise Management (Westminster). *NOW CHECK PROSPECTUSES AND WEBSITES FOR RECENT CHANGES.*

Universities and colleges teaching quality See www.tqi.ac.uk; www.qaa.ac.uk.

Top universities and colleges (Research) See **Art and Design (General)**.

Sandwich degree courses Brighton; Central Lancashire; De Montfort; East London; Glasgow Caledonian; Heriot-Watt; Huddersfield; Nottingham Trent.

ADMISSIONS INFORMATION

Number of applicants per place (approx) Arts London (Central Saint Martins CAD) 5, (CFash) (Fash Mgt) 20; Bournemouth (AI) 6; Brighton 6; Bristol UWE 4; Central Lancashire 4; Creative Arts (UC) 8, (Fash Prom) 4; De Montfort 5; Derby (Tex Des) 2; Heriot-Watt (Scottish Borders) 6; Huddersfield 4; Kingston 5; Leeds (CAD) 4; Liverpool John Moores 6; London (Gold) 5; Loughborough 5; Manchester Met 3; Middlesex 5; Northampton 4; Northumbria 8; Nottingham Trent 8, (Tex Des) 3; Southend Campus Essex 2; Staffordshire 3; UCE Birmingham/Birmingham (IAD) (Tex Des) 4; Wolverhampton 2.

Advice to applicants and planning the UCAS personal statement A well-written legible statement is sought, clearly stating an interest in fashion and how prior education and work experience relate to your application. You should describe any visits to exhibitions, and importantly, your views and opinions. Describe any work you have done ('making' and 'doing' skills, if any, for example, pattern-cutting, sewing) or work observation in textile firms, fashion houses, even visits to costume departments in theatres can be useful. These contacts and visits should be described in detail, showing your knowledge of the types of fabrics and production processes. Give opinions on trends in haute couture, and show awareness of the work of others. Provide evidence of materials handling (see also **Appendix 2**). **Arts London (CFash)** (Fash Comm Prom) Give details of written work (school magazine etc), work placement in media (journalism, broadcasting etc). **Bournemouth (AI)** (Cost Scrn Stg) Ability in sewing, drawing (life and design), knowledge and interest in English literature, theatre and costume for film, TV and theatre. Foundation Art course preferred. **Creative Arts (UC)** Show good knowledge of the contemporary fashion scene. **Huddersfield** (Cost Tex) Interest in historical costume and theatre. See also under **Art and Design (Graphic Design)**.

Misconceptions about this course **Creative Arts (UC)** Some students expect the Fashion degree to include textiles; (Tex) Some applicants feel that it's necessary to have experience in textiles – this is not the case. The qualities sought in the portfolio are analytical drawing, good colour sense and a sensitivity to materials.

Selection interviews Most institutions interview and require a portfolio of work. You should be familiar with current fashion trends and the work of leading designers. **Brighton** Application route B recommended for students on pre-degree courses.

Interview advice and questions Questions mostly originate from student's portfolio. **Bournemouth (AI)** (Cost Scrn Stg) Questionnaire and project prior to interview. **Creative Arts (UC)** Describe in detail a specific item in your portfolio and why it was selected. **UCE Birmingham/Birmingham (IAD)** (Tex Des) What do you expect to achieve from a degree in Fashion? See also **Art and Design (General)**. See also **Chapter 6**.

Reasons for rejection (non-academic) Portfolio work not up to standard. Not enough research. Not articulate at interview. Lack of sense of humour and inflexibility. Narrow perspective. Lack of resourcefulness, self-motivation and organisation. Complacency, lack of verbal, written and self-presentation skills. **Bournemouth (AI)** (Cost Scrn Stg) Not enough experience in designing or making clothes. See also **Art and Design (General)**.

AFTER-RESULTS ADVICE

Universities with vacancies in Clearing (2006) See **Art and Design (General)**.

Offers to applicants repeating A-levels **Same** Bournemouth (AI), Creative Arts (UC), Huddersfield, Manchester Met, Nottingham Trent, Southend Campus Essex, Staffordshire, UCE Birmingham/Birmingham (IAD).

GRADUATE DESTINATIONS AND EMPLOYMENT (2005 HESA)
See under **Art and Design (General)**.

OTHER DEGREE SUBJECTS FOR CONSIDERATION
History of Art; Retail Management; Theatre Design.

ART AND DESIGN (Fine Art)
(including **Printing, Printmaking** and **Sculpture**)

NB The points totals shown to the left of the institutions are for ease of reference only. It must not be assumed that tariff points are always used by institutions or that they can be substituted for an offer in grades. The level of an offer is not necessarily indicative of the quality of a course.

COURSE OFFERS INFORMATION
Subject requirements/preferences See **Art and Design (General)**.

Your target offers

360 pts and above
  Oxford – Offers vary eg AAA–AAB (Fine Art)
320 pts **Southampton/Winchester (SA)** – ABB 320 pts (Fine Art Prac Theor)
300 pts **Edinburgh** – BBB (Fine Art)
  Leeds – BBB (Fine Art)
  London (UCL/Slade CA) – BBB+AS minimum (Fine Art)
  Newcastle – BBB–BCC (Fine Art)
280 pts **Aberystwyth** – 280 pts (Fine Art Scngraph St)
  Leeds – BBC (Contemp Art Prac)
260 pts **Aberystwyth** – BCC 260 pts (Fine Art; Fine Art Art Hist)
  Chester – 260 pts (Fine Art)
  Lancaster – BCC (Fine Art)
  Reading – 260 pts (Art Hist Art)
240 pts **De Montfort** – 240 pts (Fine Art)
  Huddersfield – 240 pts (Fine Art; Fine art (Drg Pntg); Fine Art Contemp Writ)
  Lincoln – 240 pts (Fine Art)
  Northumbria – 240 pts (Fine Art)
  Nottingham Trent – 240 pts (Fine Art)
  UCE Birmingham/Birmingham (IAD) – 240 pts (Fine Art)
220 pts **Anglia Ruskin** – 220–225 pts (Fine Art)
  Chichester – 220 pts (Fine Art)
  East Lancashire (IHE) – CCD (Fine Art (Integ Media))
  Liverpool Hope – 220 pts (Fine Art Des courses; Crea Perf Arts)
  Oxford Brookes – CCD **or** CDcc 220 pts (Fine Art)
  Plymouth – 220–300 pts Fdn Art (Fine Art; Fine Art Art Hist)
205 pts **Reading** – 205 pts (Fine Art)
200 pts **Coventry** – 200–220 pts (Fine Art; Fine Art Illus)
  Cumbria – 200 pts (Fine Art)
  Hertfordshire – 200 pts (Fine Art)
  Liverpool John Moores – 200–160 pts (Fine Art)
  Sheffield Hallam – 200 pts (Fine Art)
180 pts **Anglia Ruskin** – 180 pts (Fine Art Prtg)

Edinburgh (CA) – 180 pts (Fine Art)
Northampton – 180–240 pts (Fine Art; Fine Art Ptng courses)
160 pts **Bedfordshire** – 160 pts (Fine Art)
Blackpool and Fylde (Coll) – 160 pts (Fine Art Prof Prac)
Bolton – 160 pts (Fine Arts)
Bournemouth (AI) – 160 pts (Fine Art)
Canterbury Christ Church – CC (Fine Art)
Cardiff (UWIC) – 160 pts (Art Art Hist)
Cumbria – CC 160 pts (Fine Art)
Dartington (CA) – 160–200 pts (Fine Art)
Derby – 160 pts (Fine Art)
Glasgow (SA) – CC (Fine Art (Env Art Sculp) (Pntg Prtg))
London Met – 160 pts (Fine Art)
Manchester Met – 160 pts (Fine Art)
Newport – 160 pts (Fine Art)
Portsmouth – 160 pts (Fine Art)
Southend Campus Essex – 160–180 pts (Fine Art)
Southampton Solent – 160 pts (Fine Art; Fine Art Media)
Swindon (Coll) – 160–200 pts (Fine Art)
Ulster – 160 pts (Fine App Arts)
Wolverhampton – 160–220 pts (Fine Art)
York St John – 160 pts (Contemp Fine Art Prac)
Yorkshire Coast (CFHE) – 160–240 pts (Fine Art)
140 pts **Staffordshire** – 140–200 pts (Fine Art)
Sunderland – 140 pts (Fine Art)
120 pts **Brighton** – 120 pts (Fine Art Ptng/Prtg; Sculp)
Buckinghamshire Chilterns (UC) – 120 pts (Fine Art)
Cleveland (CAD) – 120 pts (Fine Art)
100 pts **and below or other selection criteria (Foundation course, interview and portfolio inspection)**
Arts London (Camberwell CA), (Central Saint Martins CAD), (Chelsea CAD), (Wimbledon CA); Barnsley (Univ Centre); Bath Spa; Bradford (Coll); Bristol UWE; Cardiff (UWIC); Central Lancashire; Cleveland (CAD); Colchester (Inst); Creative Arts (UC); Croydon (Coll); Dewsbury (Coll); Dundee; East London; Falmouth (UC); Filton (Coll); Gloucestershire; Herefordshire (CAD); Hull (Scarborough); Kingston; Liverpool John Moores; London (Gold), (UCL-Slade SA); London Met; Loughborough; Middlesex; North East Wales (IHE); Northampton; Northbrook (Coll); Norwich (SAD); Oxford and Cherwell Valley (Coll); Robert Gordon; Salford; Solihull (Coll); Southend Campus Essex; South Nottingham (Coll); Southampton/Winchester (SA); Southport (Coll); Suffolk (Univ Campus); Swansea (IHE); Thames Valley; Trinity Carmarthen (Coll); UHI Millennium Inst (MC); West Thames (Coll); Westminster; Wiltshire (Coll); Wirral Met (Coll).

Leeds Met – contact University

ALTERNATIVE OFFERS
IB offers Aberystwyth 29 pts; Chichester 28 pts; Lancaster 30 pts; London (UCL) 32 pts; Newcastle 28–30 pts; Staffordshire 28 pts.
Scottish offers See **Chapter 7**.

OTHER HIGHER EDUCATION COURSES IN THE SUBJECT FIELD
Foundation degrees (contact the institutions for details) Arts London (Central Saint Martins CAD); Brighton and Hove City (Coll); Cornwall (Coll); Croydon (Coll); Dunstable (Coll); Hastings (Coll); Havering (Coll); Herefordshire (CAD); Kendal (Coll); Milton Keynes (Coll); Newcastle (Coll); North Devon (Coll); Nottingham New (Coll); Oldham (Coll); Plymouth (CAD); Somerset (CAT); South Tyneside (Coll); Suffolk (Univ Campus); Tyne Met (Coll); Yeovil (Coll).

For information on how to read the Subject Tables, see **Chapter 7**.

Higher National Diploma courses
100 pts and below approx + portfolio
Anglia Ruskin; Blackpool and Fylde (Coll); Brighton; Buckinghamshire Chilterns (UC); Cambridge Reg (Coll); Canterbury Christ Church; Carmarthenshire (Coll); Craven (Coll); Cumbria (Fine Art); Dudley (Coll); Filton (Coll); Gloucestershire (CAT); Halesowen (Coll); Havering (Coll); Lancaster and Morecambe (Coll); Liverpool (CmC); Macclesfield (Coll); Middlesex; Newcastle (Coll); Newcastle under Lyme (Coll); Newham (Coll); Northbrook (Coll); Nottingham New (Coll); Plymouth (CAD); St Helens (Coll); Sheffield (Coll); Somerset (CAT); South Birmingham (Coll); South Kent (Coll); South Nottingham (Coll); Southampton Solent; Stafford (Coll); Stourbridge (Coll); Suffolk (Univ Campus); Tameside (Coll); UCE Birmingham/Birmingham (IAD); West Anglia (Coll); West Thames (Coll); Weston (Coll); Weymouth (Coll); Wolverhampton; Worcsetershire New (Coll); Yeovil (Coll).

CHOOSING YOUR COURSE (SEE ALSO CH.1)

Subject information Fine Art courses can involve a range of activities such as painting, illustration and sculpture and often fine art media – electronic media, film, video, photography and print – although course options will vary between institutions. As in the case of most Art degrees, admission to courses usually requires a one-year Foundation Art course before applying. **Useful websites** www.artcyclopedia.com; www.fine-art.com; www.nationalgallery.org.uk; www.britisharts.co.uk; www.tate.org.uk.

Course variations Fine Art and Art History (Aberystwyth); Fine Art Printmaking (Anglia Ruskin); Fine Art: New Media (Chester); Fine Art and Illustration (Coventry); Contemporary Art Practice (Leeds); Typography (Reading). *NOW CHECK PROSPECTUSES AND WEBSITES FOR ANY RECENT CHANGES.*

Universities and colleges teaching quality See www.tqi.ac.uk; www.qaa.ac.uk.

Top universities and colleges (Research) See **Art and Design (General)**.

ADMISSIONS INFORMATION

Number of applicants per place (approx) Arts London (Chelsea CAD) 5, Wimbledon (CA) (Sculp) 3; Bath Spa 8; Bournemouth (AI) 6; Bristol UWE 3; Cardiff (UWIC) 3; Central Lancashire 4; Cleveland (CAD) 2; Creative Arts (UC) 2; Cumbria 4; De Montfort 5; Derby 3; Dundee 5; Falmouth (UC) 5; Gloucestershire 5; Hertfordshire 6; Hull (Scarborough) 2; Kingston 9; Lincolnshire and Humberside 4; Liverpool John Moores 3; London (Gold) 10, (UCL/Slade SA) 26; London Met 11; Loughborough 4; Manchester Met 4; Middlesex 3; Newcastle 30; Northampton 3; Northumbria 4; Norwich (SAD) 3; Nottingham Trent 5; Oxford (success rate 17%); Portsmouth 6; Robert Gordon 5; Sheffield Hallam 4; Solihull (Coll) 4; Staffordshire 3; Sunderland 3; UCE Birmingham/Birmingham (IAD) 6; UHI Millennium Inst (MC) 2; Wirral Met (Coll) 3.

Admissions tutors' advice Brighton Application route B recommended for applicants on pre-degree courses.

Advice to applicants and planning the UCAS personal statement Since this is a subject area that can be researched easily in art galleries, you should discuss not only your own style of work and your preferred subjects but also your opinions on various art forms, styles and periods. Keep up-to-date with public opinion on controversial issues. Give your reasons for wishing to pursue a course in Fine Art. **Aberystwyth** If you are not taking the subject at A-level we look for attendance at evening classes for art. Visits to galleries and related hobbies, for example reading, cinema, music, literature should be mentioned. Show the nature of your external involvement in art. Not interested in potted life-history or lists of irrelevant jobs. **Arts London (Chelsea CAD)** We look for visual and plastic skills, conceptual development. **Staffordshire** We look for creativity, problem-solving, cultural awareness, communication skills and commitment. (See also **Appendix 2**.)

Misconceptions about this course That Fine Art is simply art and design. Sixth form applicants are often unaware of the importance of a Foundation Art course before starting a degree programme. **Bournemouth (AI)** Applicants need to make the distinction between fine art and illustration.

For a quick reference offers calculator, fold out the inside back cover.

Selection interviews Most institutions interview and require a portfolio of work. **Arts London (Chelsea CAD)** Interviews with portfolios and essays. **Oxford** Portfolio to be submitted by 15th November. Drawing examination taken by all interviewed candidates (two drawings in pencil or pen and ink).

Interview advice and questions Questions asked on portfolio of work. Be prepared to answer questions on your stated opinions on your UCAS application and on current art trends and controversial topics reported in the press. Discussion covering the applicant's engagement with contemporary fine art practice. Visits to exhibitions, galleries etc. Ambitions for their own work. Who is your favourite living artist and why? **UHI Millennium Inst (MC)** Applicants are asked to produce a drawing in response to a set topic. See also under **Art and Design (General)**. See also **Chapter 6**.

Reasons for rejection (non-academic) Lack of a fine art specialist portfolio. No intellectual grasp of the subject – only interested in techniques.

AFTER-RESULTS ADVICE

Universities with vacancies in Clearing (2006) See **Art and Design (General)**.

Offers to applicants repeating A-levels **Same** Anglia Ruskin, Arts London (Central Saint Martins CAD), Cumbria, Manchester Met, Nottingham Trent, Staffordshire, Sunderland, UCE Birmingham/Birmingham (IAD), UHI Millennium Inst (MC).

GRADUATE DESTINATIONS AND EMPLOYMENT (2005 HESA)

Graduates surveyed 2535 **Employed** 960 **In further study** 345 **Assumed unemployed** 285.

OTHER DEGREE SUBJECTS FOR CONSIDERATION

Art Gallery Management; History of Art; see other **Art and Design** tables.

ART AND DESIGN (Graphic Design)

(including Animation, Graphic Communication, Illustration, Printmaking, Typography and Visual Communication; see also Art and Design (General), (Fine Art) and Film, Radio, Video and TV Studies)

NB The points totals shown to the left of the institutions are for ease of reference only. It must not be assumed that tariff points are always used by institutions or that they can be substituted for an offer in grades. The level of an offer is not necessarily indicative of the quality of a course.

COURSE OFFERS INFORMATION

Subject requirements/preferences See under **Art and Design (General)**.

Your target offers
300 pts **Leeds** – BBB (Graph Comm Des)
Reading – 300 pts (Des Graph Comm)
280 pts **Brighton** – 280 pts (Graph Des; Illus)
Reading – 280–340 pts (Typo comb hons)
240 pts **Chester** – 240–260 pts (Graph Des)
De Montfort – 240 pts (Graph Des; Graph Des Illus; Graph Des Photo)
Dundee – 240 pts (Graph Des)
Huddersfield – 240 pts (Crea Imag (Des) (Adv) (Illus) (Mtn Graph Animat))
Lincoln – 240 pts (Graph Des; Illus; Interact Scrnbd Graph)
Northumbria – 240 pts (Graph Des)
Nottingham Trent – 240 pts (Graph Des)
UCE Birmingham/Birmingham (IAD) – 240 pts (Vis Comm)
230 pts **Greenwich** – 230 pts (Graph Dig Des)
220 pts **Anglia Ruskin** – 220–225 pts (Graph Des; Graph Typo Des Illus; Graph Web Des)

Plymouth – 220–300 pts (Des (Graph Comm Typo) (Illus) (Photo))
200 pts **Bournemouth (AI)** – 200 pts (Graph Des)
Coventry – 200–220 pts (Illus; Graph Des; Graph Des Illus St)
Gloucestershire – 200 pts (Graph Des)
Hertfordshire – 200 pts (Graph Des Illus)
Newport – 200 pts (Graph Des)
Westminster – BB (Graph Inf Des)
180 pts **Bedfordshire** – DDD 180 pts (Graph Des; Graph Des Adv)
Northampton – 180 pts (Graph Comm; Illus)
160 pts **Blackpool and Fylde (Coll)** – DDE 160 pts (Graph Des; Inf Illus; Sci Nat Hist Illus)
Bolton – 160 pts (Graph Des)
Bournemouth (AI) – 160 pts (Illus; Graph Des)
Cumbria – CC 160 pts (Graph Des)
Derby – 160 pts (Graph Des; Illus)
Glamorgan – 160–180 pts (Graph Comm)
Kingston – 160 pts (Graph Des; Illus Animat; Graph Comm)
Liverpool John Moores – 160–200 pts (Graph Arts; Multim Arts)
Manchester Met – 160 pts (Illus Animat)
Portsmouth – 160–240 pts (Illus; Animat; Comm Des)
Salford – 160–100 pts (Graph Des)
Southend Campus Essex – 160–180 pts (Graph Des)
Swindon (Coll) – 160–200 pts (Graph Des; Illus; Arch Illus; New Media)
Teesside – 160–220 pts (Graph Des; Graph Arts)
Ulster – 160 pts (Des Vis Comm)
Wolverhampton – 160–220 pts (Animat; Graph Comm; Illus)
140 pts **Staffordshire** – 140–200 pts (Graph Des; Animat)
Sunderland – 140 pts (Graph Comm Des; Illus Des; Animat Des)
120 pts **Loughborough** – 120 pts (Vis Comm (Graph Comm) (Illus))
North East Wales (IHE) – 120–80 pts (Graph Des; Illus; Animat)
Southampton Solent – 120 pts (Graph Des; Graph Imag Mkg)
Stockport (CFHE) – 120–240 pts (Des Vis Arts (Graph Des) (Illus) (Adv))
100 pts **and below or other selection criteria (Foundation course, interview and portfolio inspection)**
Arts London (Camberwell CA), (CComm), (Central Saint Martins CAD), (Chelsea CAD); Barnsley (Univ Centre); Bath Spa; Bedfordshire; Bradford (Coll); Brighton; Bristol UWE; Buckinghamshire Chilterns (UC); Cambridge Reg (Coll); Cardiff (UWIC); Central Lancashire; Colchester (Inst); Creative Arts (UC); Croydon (Coll); Dundee; East Lancashire (IHE); East London; Edinburgh (CA); Falmouth (UC); Filton (Coll); Glasgow Caledonian; Glasgow Met (Coll); Gloucestershire; Herefordshire (CAD); Heriot-Watt; Hertford Reg (Coll); Hertfordshire; James Watt (Coll); Kingston; Leeds (CAD); London Met; Lowestoft (Coll); Menai (Coll); Middlesex; North East Wales (IHE); Northbrook (Coll); Norwich (SAD); Oxford and Cherwell Valley (Coll); Ravensbourne (CDC); Robert Gordon; Salisbury (Coll); Solihull (Coll); South Devon (Coll); Southampton/Winchester (SA); Suffolk (Univ Campus); Swansea (IHE); Thames Valley; West Herts (Coll); Westminster; Wiltshire (Coll).

Leeds Met – contact University
Southampton/Winchester (SA) – (Graph Arts - contact admissions tutor)

Alternative offers
IB offers Brighton – not suitable; Salford 24 pts; Staffordshire 28 pts.
Scottish offers See **Art and Design (General)** and **Chapter 7**.

OTHER HIGHER EDUCATION COURSES IN THE SUBJECT FIELD
Foundation degree courses (contact the institutions for details) Arts London (CComm); Barnet (Coll); Bristol City (Coll); Cleveland (CAD); Cornwall (Coll); Creative Arts (UC); Croydon (Coll); Derby; Dewsbury (Coll); Doncaster (Univ Centre); Dunstable (Coll); Durham New (Coll); Ealing, Hammersmith

and West London (Coll); Hastings (Coll); Herefordshire (CAD); Kingston; Milton Keynes (Coll); Newcastle (Coll); North Devon (Coll); Norwich (SAD); Plymouth (CAD); Richmond (Coll); Runshaw (Coll); St Helens (Coll); Sheffield (Coll); Somerset (CAT); South Devon (Coll); Stockport (CFHE); Suffolk (Univ Campus); Thames Valley; West Herts (Coll); Weymouth (Coll).

Higher National Diploma courses
100 pts   and below approx + portfolio

Arts London (Central Saint Martins CAD); Barking (Coll); Barnet (Coll); Barnsley (Univ Centre); Bedfordshire; Birmingham City (Coll); Bournemouth (AI); Bradford (Coll); Brighton; Bristol City (Coll); Buckinghamshire Chilterns (UC); Cambridge Reg (Coll); Cardiff (UWIC); Carmarthenshire (Coll); Central Lancashire; Cleveland (CAD); Craven (Coll); Creative Arts (UC); Cumbria; De Montfort; Dewsbury (Batley (SAD)); Doncaster (Univ Centre); Dudley (Coll); Dumfries and Galloway (Coll); East Lancashire (IHE); East Surrey (Coll); Edinburgh (CA); Farnborough (CT); Filton (Coll); Forth Valley (Coll); Gloucester (CAT); Greenwich; Hastings (CAT); Havering (Coll); Henley (Coll); Isle (Coll); Isle of Wight (Coll); James Watt (Coll); Leicester (Coll); Lincoln; Loughborough; Lowestoft (Coll); Manchester City (Coll); Mid Cheshire (CFHE); Newcastle (Coll); North Warwickshire (Coll); Northampton; Northbrook (Coll); Norwich (SAD); Nottingham New (Coll); Oxford and Cherwell Valley (Coll); Perth (Coll); Plymouth (CAD); Portsmouth; St Helens (Coll); Salford; Salisbury (Coll); Sandwell (Coll); Shrewsbury (CAT); Solihull (Coll); Somerset (CAT); South Birmingham (Coll); South Nottingham (Coll); Southampton Solent; Southwark (Coll); Stafford (Coll); Stockport (CFHE); Strode (Coll); Suffolk (Univ Campus); Sutton Coldfield (Coll); Swindon (Coll); Thames Valley; UCE Birmingham; UHI Millennium Inst; Warrington (Coll); Warwickshire (Coll); West Herts (Coll); West Thames (Coll); Weston (Coll); Weymouth (Coll); Wigan and Leigh (Coll); Wiltshire (Coll); Wolverhampton; Worcester (CT); Worcestershire New (Coll); York (Coll); Yorkshire Coast (CFHE).

CHOOSING YOUR COURSE (SEE ALSO CH.1)

Subject information Graphic Design students are probably the most fortunate in terms of the range of career opportunities open to them on graduation. These include advertising, book and magazine illustration, film, interactive media design, typography, packaging, photography and work in publishing and television. An Art Foundation course is usually taken before entry to degree courses. **Useful websites** www.graphicdesign.about.com; www.graphic-design.com; www.allgraphicdesign.com.

Course variations Graphic and Web Design (Anglia Ruskin); Scientific and Natural History Illustration (Blackpool and Fylde (Coll)); Archaeological Illustration (Swindon (Coll)); Graphic Arts (Teesside); Graphic Information Design (Westminster). *NOW CHECK PROSPECTUSES AND WEBSITES FOR ANY RECENT CHANGES.*

Universities and colleges teaching quality See www.tqi.ac.uk; www.qaa.ac.uk.

Sandwich degree courses Glamorgan; Gloucestershire; Huddersfield; Staffordshire.

ADMISSIONS INFORMATION

Number of applicants per place (approx) Anglia Ruskin (Illus) 3; Arts London (Central Saint Martins CAD) 4; Bath Spa 9; Bournemouth (AI) 6; Bristol UWE 4; Cardiff (UWIC) 5; Central Lancashire 5; Colchester (Inst) 3; Coventry 6; Creative Arts (UC) 5; Derby 5; East Lancashire (IHE) 2; Glamorgan 3; Hertfordshire 6; Kingston 8; Lincoln 5; Liverpool John Moores 7; Loughborough 5; Manchester Met 8; Middlesex 3; Napier 7; Northampton 3; Northumbria 8; Norwich (SAD) 4; Nottingham Trent 6; Ravensbourne (CDC) 9; Solihull (Coll) 3; Southend Campus Essex 2; Staffordshire 3; Swansea (IHE) 10; Teesside 5; Wolverhampton 5.

Advice to applicants and planning the UCAS personal statement Discuss your special interest in this field and any commercial applications that have impressed you. Discuss the work you are enjoying at present and the range of media that you have explored. Show your interests in travel, architecture, the arts, literature, film, current affairs (see also **Appendix 2** for contact details of relevant professional associations). **Arts London (Central Saint Martins CAD)** Personality is an important factor. **Creative**

Arts (UC) Look for ability to discuss applicant's own work openly and critically (including sketchbooks). Awareness of the place of design in society.

Misconceptions about this course Bath Spa Some students think that they can start the course from A-levels, that a course in Illustration is simply 'doing small drawings' and that Graphic Design is a soft option with little academic work.

Selection interviews All institutions interview and require a portfolio of work.

Interview advice and questions Questions may be asked on recent trends in graphic design from the points of view of methods and designers and, particularly, art and the computer. Questions usually are asked on applicant's portfolio of work. **Nottingham Trent** Why Graphic Design? Why this course? Describe a piece of graphic design which has succeeded. See also **Art and Design (General)**. See also **Chapter 6**.

Reasons for rejection (non-academic) Not enough work in portfolio. Inability to think imaginatively. Lack of interest in the arts in general. Lack of drive. Tutor's statement indicating problems. Poorly constructed personal statement. Inability to talk about your work. Lack of knowledge about the chosen course. See also **Art and Design (General)**.

AFTER-RESULTS ADVICE
Universities with vacancies in Clearing (2006) See **Art and Design (General)**.

Offers to applicants repeating A-levels Same Bath Spa, Bournemouth (AI), Blackpool and Fylde (Coll), Cardiff (UWIC), Creative Arts (UC), Lincoln, Manchester Met, Nottingham Trent, Salford, Southend Campus Essex, Staffordshire.

GRADUATE DESTINATIONS AND EMPLOYMENT (2005 HESA)
See **Art and Design (General)**.

OTHER DEGREE SUBJECTS FOR CONSIDERATION
Art Gallery Management; History of Art and other Art courses (see other **Art and Design** tables).

ART AND DESIGN (Industrial/Product Design)
(including **Footwear Design, Furniture Design, Interior Architecture, Interior Design, Multimedia Product Design, Museum Design, Theatre Design** and **Transport Design**)

NB The points totals shown to the left of the institutions are for ease of reference only. It must not be assumed that tariff points are always used by institutions or that they can be substituted for an offer in grades. The level of an offer is not necessarily indicative of the quality of a course.

COURSE OFFERS INFORMATION
Subject requirements/preferences See under **Art and Design (General)**.

Your target offers

320 pts	**Glasgow** – ABB (MEng Prod Des Eng)
	Nottingham – ABB–BCC (Prod Des Manuf)
	Sussex – ABB–BBB 360–330 pts (Prod Des 4 yr)
300 pts	**Aston** – BBB–BCC (Eng Prod Des; Ind Prod Des; Sust Prod Des)
	Belfast (Queen's) – BBB (MEng Prod Des Dev)
	Brunel – 300 pts (Multim Tech Des)
	Dundee – 300–240 pts (Innov Prod Des; Interact Media Des)
	Leeds – BBB (Prod Des)
	Oxford Brookes – BBB/BB (Inter Archit Des Prac)
	Strathclyde – BBB (Prod Des Eng)
280 pts	**Brighton** – 280 pts (Prod Des; Inter Archit; Des Tech)
	Cardiff (UWIC) – 280 pts (Inter Archit)

Glasgow (SA) – BBC (Prod Des)
Liverpool – BBC 280 pts (Prod Des Multim)
Sussex – BBC **or** 310 pts (Prod Des 3 yr)

260 pts Brunel – 260 pts (Ind Des Tech; Ind Des; Vrtl Prod Des; Des Spo; Prod Des Eng)
Central Lancashire – 260 pts (Inter Des; Prod Des)
Coventry – 260 pts (Ind Prod Des)
Loughborough – 260–300 pts (Prod Des Tech; Ind Des Tech)
Manchester Met – 260–300 pts (Inter Des)

240 pts Central Lancashire – 240 pts (Prod Des)
De Montfort – 240 pts (Prod Des; Ind Des; Inter Des; Furn Des; Ftwr Des)
Glasgow – CCC (BEng Prod Des Eng)
Huddersfield – 240 pts (Inter Des; Prod Des; Trans Des)
Kent – 240 pts (Inter Des; Inter Archit)
Leeds – CCC (Perf Des)
Lincoln – 240 pts (Musm Exhib Des; Inter Des; Prod Des; Furn)
London Met – 240 pts (Inter Des Tech)
London South Bank – CCC (Prod Des Env)
Loughborough – 240 pts (App Des (Prod Perf Sfty))
Middlesex – 240–260 pts (Prod Des; Inter Archit Des; Des Tech)
Northumbria – 240 pts (Trans Des; Inter Des)
Nottingham Trent – 240 pts (Furn Prod Des; Thea Des; Prod Des; Inter Archit Des)
Robert Gordon – CCC (Prod Des)
Rose Bruford (Coll) – CCC 240 pts (Ltg Des)
Sheffield Hallam – 240 pts (Des Modl; Furn Des; Pack Graph Des; Interact Prod Des; Trans Des)
Strathclyde – CCC (Prod Des Innov)
UCE Birmingham/Birmingham (IAD) – CCC (Furn Des; Inter Des; Prod Des (Ind Des))

220 pts Anglia Ruskin – 220–225 pts (Inter Des)
Bournemouth – 220–300 pts (Prod Des; Ind Des)
Bradford – 220 pts (Ind Des; Auto Des Tech)
Bristol UWE – 220–240 pts (Crea Prod Des)
Central England/Birmingham (IAD) – 220 pts (Eng Prod Des)
Heriot-Watt – CCD (Integ Prod Des)

200 pts Bangor – 200–220 pts (Des Tech)
Bradford – 200–240 pts (Vrtl Des Innov; Ind Des)
Bristol UWE – 200–240 pts (Prod Des Innov)
Coventry – 200–240 pts (Trans Des; Consum Prod Des; Boat Des; Veh Des)
Creative Arts (UC) – 200 pts (Prod Des Sust Fut)
Hertfordshire – 200 pts (Inter Spat Des; Prod Des)
Liverpool John Moores – 200–160 pts (Inter Des; Prod Des Dig Mark)
Plymouth – 200–300 pts (3D Des (Furn Inter Des) (Prod Des))
Portsmouth – 200 pts (Prod Des courses)

180 pts Belfast (Queen's) – BC (BEng Prod Des Dev)
Bournemouth – 180–240 pts (Inter Des)
Cardiff (UWIC) – BC (Prod Des)
Liverpool (LIPA) – 180 pts (Thea Perf Des)
Napier – BC–CC (Consum Prod Des; Inter Archit)
Northampton – 180–220 pts (Prod Des; Inter Des)
Portsmouth – 180–240 pts (Inter Des)
Salford – 180–160 pts (Prod Des)
Sunderland – 180 pts (Prod Des)

160 pts Bedfordshire – 160–240 pts (Inter Des; Inter Archit)
Derby – 160 pts (Inter Archit; Prod Des Innov Mark)
East London – 160 pts (Prod Des Fut)
Falmouth (UC) – CC 160 pts (Spat Des (Inter Land))

Glamorgan – 160 pts (Inter Des; Prod Des)
Kingston – 160 pts (Prod Furn Des)
London Met – 160 pts (Inter Archit Des; Inter Des Tech; Furn Prod Des)
Teesside – 160–200 pts (Inter Archit Des; Prod Des courses)
Ulster – 160 pts (Inter Des; Ind Des)
Wolverhampton – 160–220 pts (Inter Des)
Writtle (Coll) – 160 pts (Inter Des)

140 pts **Bell (Coll)** – CD 140 pts (Prod Des; Prod Des Mtrspo)
Bolton – 140 pts (Auto Prod Des; Consum Prod Des)
Salford – 140 pts (Inter Des; Spo Equip Des)
Staffordshire – 140–200 pts (Prod Des courses; Trans Des)
Swansea (IHE) – 140 pts (Ind Des)
Wolverhampton – 140–200 pts (Des Tech; Prod Des Innov)

120 pts **London South Bank** – DD (Ind Des; Eng Prod Des)
Southampton Solent – 120 pts (Prod Des Mark; Des St Inter)

100 pts **and below or other selection criteria (Foundation course, interview and portfolio inspection)**
Arts London (Central Saint Martins CAD), (Chelsea CAD), (Wimbledon CA); Barking (Coll); Basford Hall; Bath Spa; Bedfordshire; Bolton; Buckinghamshire Chilterns (UC); Central Lancashire; Cleveland (CAD); Colchester (Inst); Creative Arts (UC); Croydon (Coll); Dundee; Easton (Coll); Edinburgh (CA); Falmouth (UC); Farnborough (CT); Forth Valley (Coll); Glasgow Caledonian; Glasgow Met (Coll); Glasgow (SA); James Watt (Coll); Kingston; Leeds (CAD); Liverpool Hope; Liverpool (LIPA); London (Central Sch SpDr); London South Bank; Manchester (CAT); Middlesex; North East Wales (IHE); Northumbria; Paisley; Plymouth; Ravensbourne (CDC); Robert Gordon; Royal Welsh (CMusDr); Shrewsbury (CAT); Southend Campus Essex; Southampton Solent; Staffordshire; Suffolk (Univ Campus); Trinity Carmarthen (Coll); West Herts (Coll); Worcestershire New (Coll).

Leeds Met – contact University

Alternative offers
IB offers Brighton 28–30 pts; Bristol UWE 28 pts; Brunel 28 pts; Kent 27 pts; Loughborough 30–32 pts; Salford 26 pts; Staffordshire 28 pts.
Scottish offers See **Chapter 7**.

OTHER HIGHER EDUCATION COURSES IN THE SUBJECT FIELD

Foundation degrees (contact the institutions for details) Arts London (Chelsea CAD), (CComm); Belfast (Queen's); Bishop Burton (Coll); Bolton; Bournemouth (AI); Dewsbury (Coll); East Lancashire (IHE); Farnborough (CT); Gateshead (Coll); London Met; Milton Keynes (Coll); Newcastle (Coll); North Down and Aird (IFHE); Northumberland (Coll); Suffolk (Univ Campus); Truro (Coll).

Higher National Diploma courses
100 pts **and below approx + portfolio**
Anglia Ruskin; Arts London (CFash); Barking (Coll); Basford Hall (Coll); Bell (Coll); Bishop Burton (CAg); Blackpool and Fylde (Coll); Bournemouth; Bridgwater (Coll); Bristol City (Coll); Buckinghamshire Chilterns (UC); Cardiff (UWIC); Carmarthenshire (Coll); Central Lancashire; Cornwall (Coll); Creative Arts (UC); Croydon (Coll); Derby; Glamorgan; Glasgow Met (Coll); Huddersfield; James Watt (Coll); Leeds (CAD); Leicester (Coll); Lincoln; London (Central Sch SpDr); London Met; London South Bank; Newcastle (Coll); Northampton; Northbrook (Coll); Oxford and Cherwell Valley (Coll); Pembrokeshire (Coll); Plymouth; Rycotewood (Coll); St Helens (Coll); Salford; Shrewsbury (Coll); Somerset (CAT); Swindon (Coll); Walsall (CAT); West Thames (Coll); Wiltshire (Coll); Wolverhampton; Writtle (Coll).

CHOOSING YOUR COURSE (SEE ALSO CH.1).

Subject information The field of industrial design is extensive and degree studies are usually preceded by an Art Foundation course. Product Design is one of the most common courses in which technological studies (involving materials and methods of production) are integrated with creative design in the production of a range of household and industrial products. Other courses on offer include Furniture Design, Interior, Theatre, Museum and Exhibition, Automotive and Transport Design. **Useful website** www.ergonomics.org.uk.

Course variations Transport Design (Coventry); Interiors and Spatial Design (Hertfordshire); Product and Furniture Design (Kingston); Museum and Exhibition Design (Lincoln); Industrial Design and Technology (Loughborough); Interior Architecture and Design (Nottingham Trent); Sport Equipment Design (Salford); Sustainable Product Design (Sussex). *NOW CHECK PROSPECTUSES AND WEBSITES FOR ANY RECENT CHANGES.*

Universities and colleges teaching quality See www.tqi.ac.uk; www.qaa.ac.uk.

Top universities and colleges (Research) See under **Art and Design (General)**.

Sandwich degree courses Aston; Bournemouth; Bradford; Brighton; Bristol UWE; Brunel; Coventry; De Montfort; Glamorgan; Glasgow Caledonian; Huddersfield; Nottingham Trent; Robert Gordon; Sussex; Wolverhampton.

ADMISSIONS INFORMATION

Number of applicants per place (approx) Abertay Dundee 6; Arts London (Central Saint Martins CAD) 2, (Chelsea CAD) 2; (Wimbledon CA) 2; Aston 6; Bath Spa 4; Bolton 1; Brunel 4; Cardiff (UWIC) 6; Central Lancashire 7; Colchester (Inst) 4; Coventry 5; Creative Arts (UC) (Inter Des) 4; De Montfort 5; Derby 2; Lincoln (Musm Exhib Des) 4; London (Central Sch SpDr) 5; Loughborough 9; Manchester Met 2; Middlesex (Inter Des) 4; Napier 6; Northampton (Prod Des) 2; Northumbria 4; Nottingham Trent (Inter Archit Des) 7, (Prod Des) 5; Portsmouth 3; Ravensbourne (CDC) (Inter Des) 4, (Prod Des) 7; Salford 6; Sheffield 4; Shrewsbury (CAT) 6; Staffordshire 3; Swansea (IHE) 3; Teesside 3; UCE Birmingham/Birmingham (IAD) (Furn Des) 4, (Prod Des) 3, (Int Des) 9.

Advice to applicants and planning the UCAS personal statement Your knowledge of design in all fields should be described, including any special interests you may have, for example in domestic, rail and road aspects of design, and visits to exhibitions, motor shows. **School/College reference** Tutors should make it clear that the applicant's knowledge, experience and attitude match the chosen course – not simply higher education in general. **Creative Arts (UC)** (Inter Des) Admissions tutors look for knowledge of interior design and interior architecture, experience in 3D-design projects (which include problem-solving and sculptural demands), model-making experience in diverse materials, experience with 2D illustration and colour work, and knowledge of computer-aided design. Photography is also helpful. **Derby** Basic computer knowledge useful. **Lincoln** (Musm Exhib Des) Drawing (freehand and constructed). Model-making and CAD/computer skills. See also **Art and Design (Graphic Design)**.

Misconceptions about this course **Arts London (Wimbledon CA)** (Thea Des) The course is sometimes confused with Theatre Architecture or an academic course in Theatre Studies. **Lincoln** (Musm Exhib Des) This is a design course, not a museum course. **Portsmouth** (Inter Des) Some students think that this is about interior decorating after Laurence Llewelyn-Bowen! **UCE Birmingham/Birmingham (IAD)** (Inter Des) Some applicants believe that it is an interior decoration course (carpets and curtains).

Selection interviews Most institutions will interview and require a portfolio of work. **Some** Salford, Staffordshire.

Interview advice and questions Applicants' portfolios of art work form an important talking-point throughout the interview. Applicants should be able to discuss examples of current design and new developments in the field and answer questions on the aspects of industrial design which interest them. **Creative Arts (UC)** No tests. Discuss any visits to modern buildings and new developments, eg British Museum Great Court or the Louvre Pyramid. See also **Art and Design (General)**. See also **Chapter 6**.

Applicants' impressions (A=Open day; B=Interview day) **Bournemouth** (Prod Des; B) They inspected the work of those being interviewed. They pinned pieces of my own work on a board and looked at the work of other students. I was tested on maths, design and analytical skills. There was a general talk about the course and the university, but I had no chance to look around. **Portsmouth** (Prod Des; B) There was a brief informal interview, a talk about the course and a tour of the department. A very helpful day.

Reasons for rejection (non-academic) Not hungry enough! Mature students without formal qualifications may not be able to demonstrate the necessary mathematical or engineering skills. Poor quality and organisation of portfolio. Lack of interest. Inappropriate dress. Lack of enthusiasm. Insufficient portfolio work (eg exercises instead of projects). Lack of historical knowledge of interior design. Weak oral communication. **Creative Arts (UC)** Not enough 3D model-making. Poor sketching and drawing. See also **Art and Design (General)**.

AFTER-RESULTS ADVICE

Universities with vacancies in Clearing (2006) See **Art and Design (General)**.

Offers to applicants repeating A-levels Same Bournemouth, Creative Arts (UC), Nottingham Trent, Salford, Staffordshire, UCE Birmingham/Birmingham (IAD).

NEW GRADUATE DESTINATIONS AND EMPLOYMENT (2005 HESA)
See **Art and Design (General)**.

OTHER DEGREE SUBJECTS FOR CONSIDERATION
Art Gallery Management; History of Art and subjects in other **Art and Design** tables.

ART AND DESIGN (3D Design)

(including **Ceramics, Design Crafts, Glassmaking, Jewellery, Metalwork, Silversmithing, Plastics** and **Woodwork;** see also **Art and Design (General)**)

NB The points totals shown to the left of the institutions are for ease of reference only. It must not be assumed that tariff points are always used by institutions or that they can be substituted for an offer in grades. The level of an offer is not necessarily indicative of the quality of a course.

COURSE OFFERS INFORMATION

Subject requirements/preferences See **Art and Design (General)**.

Your target offers

240 pts **Lincoln** – 240 pts (Contemp Decr Crfts)
Nottingham Trent – 240 pts (Decr Arts)
Sheffield Hallam – 240 pts (Mtl Jewel)
UCE Birmingham/Birmingham (IAD) – 240 pts (Jewel Silver)
220 pts **Plymouth** – 220–300 pts (3D Des)
200 pts **Cumbria** – 200 pts approx (Contemp App Arts)
De Montfort – 200 pts (Des Crfts)
Hertfordshire – 200 pts (App Arts)
160 pts **Bournemouth (AI)** – 160 pts (Modl Des Media; 3D Des)
Canterbury Christ Church – 160 pts (Fine Art (Ceram))
Derby – 160 pts (3D Des)
Glasgow (SA) – CC (Des (Ceram))
Manchester Met – 160 pts (3D Des)
Portsmouth – 160–240 pts (3D Des)
Wolverhampton – 160–220 pts (3D Contemp App Arts (Ceram) (Glass); 3D Des (Wd Mtl Plas) (Jewel Silver) (Furn))
140 pts **Edinburgh (CA)** – 140 pts (Des App Arts (Glass) (Ceram) (Jewel) (Silver))
Salford – 140 pts (Dig 3D Des)
Staffordshire – 140–200 pts (3D Des (Ceram); Surf Des Ceram)
Sunderland – 140 pts (Glass Archit Glass Ceram)

120 pts **North East Wales (IHE)** – 120–80 pts (App Arts (Ceram) (Glass) (Jewel Mtl) (Wd Plas))

100 pts **and below or other selection criteria (Foundation course, interview and portfolio inspection)**

Arts London (Camberwell CA), (Central Saint Martins CAD); Bath Spa; Brighton; Buckinghamshire Chilterns (UC); Cardiff (UWIC); Central Lancashire; Cleveland (CAD); Colchester (Inst); Coventry; Creative Arts (UC); Croydon (Coll); Cumbria; Dundee; Edinburgh (CA); Falmouth (UC); Herefordshire (CAD); Hertford Reg (Coll); Hertfordshire; Leeds Met; London Met; Loughborough; Loughborough (Coll); Menai (Coll); Middlesex; North East Wales (IHE); Northumbria; Oxford and Cherwell Valley (Coll); Portsmouth; Ravensbourne (CDC); Robert Gordon; Staffordshire; Teesside; Westminster; Worcestershire New (Coll).

Leeds Met – contact University

Alternative offers
IB offers Staffordshire 28 pts.
Scottish offers See **Chapter 7**.

OTHER HIGHER EDUCATION COURSES IN THE SUBJECT FIELD

Foundation degrees (contact the institutions for details) Barnfield (Coll); Bishop Burton (Coll); Bournemouth and Poole (Coll); Bristol City (Coll); Capel Manor (Coll); Cornwall (Coll); Croydon (Coll); Grimsby (IFHE); Hastings (Coll); Herefordshire (CAD); Hull (Coll); Leeds (CAD); London Arts (CC); London Met; Myerscough (Coll); Newcastle (Coll); North Devon (Coll); Northbrook (Coll); Oxford and Cherwell Valley (Coll); Plymouth (CAD); Salisbury (Coll); Sheffield Hallam; Somerset (CAT); South Devon (Coll); Suffolk (Univ Campus); Truro (Coll); Weymouth (Coll); Writtle (Coll); Yeovil (Coll).

Higher National Diploma courses
140 pts UCE Birmingham.
100 pts **and below approx + portfolio**

Barking (Coll); Birmingham (IAD); Bournemouth (AI); Brighton; Bristol City (Coll); Burnley; Carmarthenshire (Coll); Creative Arts (UC); Cumbria (IA); De Montfort; Dewsbury (Batley (SAD)); Dudley (Coll); Dundee; Glasgow Met (Coll); Leeds Met; Leicester (Coll); London Met; Lowestoft (Coll); Manchester City (Coll); Newcastle (Coll); Northbrook (Coll); North Warwickshire/Hinckley (Coll); Nottingham New (Coll); Oxford and Cherwell Valley (Coll); Plymouth (CAD); St Helens (Coll); Sheffield (Coll); South Nottingham (Coll); Southend Campus Essex; Suffolk (Univ Campus); Sutton Coldfield (Coll); Swansea (IHE); Swindon (Coll); Warwickshire (Coll); West Thames (Coll); Wigan and Leigh (Coll); York (Coll).

CHOOSING YOUR COURSE (SEE ALSO CH.1)

Subject information This group of courses is mainly three dimensional, focusing on creative design involving jewellery, silverware, ceramics, glass, wood and plastics. Some institutions offer broad three dimensional studies courses while others provide the opportunity to study very specialised subjects such as stained glass, gemology and horology. Students normally take an Art Foundation course prior to degree level studies. **Useful website** www.ergonomics.org.uk.

Course variations Decorative Arts (Nottingham Trent); 3D Design (Wood, Metal and Plastics) (Wolverhampton). *NOW CHECK PROSPECTUSES AND WEBSITES FOR ANY RECENT CHANGES.*

Universities and colleges teaching quality See www.tqi.ac.uk; www.qaa.ac.uk.

ADMISSIONS INFORMATION

Number of applicants per place (approx) Arts London (Camberwell CA) 2, (Ceram) 3, (Central Saint Martins CAD) (Ceram) 2, (Jewel) 2; Bath Spa 3; Brighton 3; De Montfort 3; Dundee 5; Creative Arts (UC) 4; Manchester Met 5; Middlesex (3D Des) 4, (Jewel) 4; Nottingham Trent (Decr Arts) 4; Portsmouth 3; Ravensbourne (CDC) 110 first-choice applicants; Staffordshire (Des Crfts) 3; Swansea (IHE) 3; UCE Birmingham/Birmingham (IAD) 4, (Jewel) 5; Wolverhampton (3D Des (Wd Mtl Plas)) 4.

Advice to applicants and planning the UCAS personal statement Describe your art studies and your experience of different types of materials used. Discuss your special interest in your chosen field. Compare your work with that of professional artists and designers and describe your visits to museums, art galleries, exhibitions etc. **Bournemouth (AI)** (3D Des) Applicants will be expected to submit a portfolio of recent work to demonstrate drawing skills, visual awareness, creativity and innovation, showing examples of 3D work in photographic or model form. See also **Art and Design (Graphic Design)**.

Selection interviews All institutions will interview and require a portfolio of work.

Interview advice and questions Questions focus on the art work presented in the student's portfolio. See also **Art and Design (General)**. See also **Chapter 6**.

Reasons for rejection (non-academic) Lack of pride in their work. No ideas. See also **Art and Design (General)**.

AFTER-RESULTS ADVICE
Universities with vacancies in Clearing (2006) See **Art and Design (General)**.

Offers to applicants repeating A-levels **Same** Brighton, Creative Arts (UC), Dundee, Manchester Met, Nottingham Trent, UCE Birmingham/Birmingham (IAD).

GRADUATE DESTINATIONS AND EMPLOYMENT (2005 HESA)
See **Art and Design (General)**.

OTHER DEGREE SUBJECTS FOR CONSIDERATION
Design Technology; see other **Art and Design** tables.

ARTS (General/Combined/ Humanities/Modular)

(including **Arts Management** and **Cultural Studies**)

NB The points totals shown to the left of the institutions are for ease of reference only. It must not be assumed that tariff points are always used by institutions or that they can be substituted for an offer in grades. The level of an offer is not necessarily indicative of the quality of a course.

COURSE OFFERS INFORMATION
Subject requirements/preferences **GCSE Aberdeen**, **Dundee**, **Edinburgh**, **Glasgow**, **St Andrews** English, mathematics or science and foreign language. **De Montfort** Seven/eight subjects at grades A–C. **AL** Some joint courses may require a specified A-level subject.

Your target offers
The offers listed below are average offers. Specific offers will vary depending on the popularity of the subjects in combination.

340 pts **Durham** – AAB (Comb Arts)
       Manchester – AAB–BBC (Combined courses)
       Newcastle – AAB–ABB (BA Comb St)
330 pts **Southampton** – 330 pts (Comb Hons Arts Hum courses)
320 pts **Birmingham** – ABB 320 pts (Cult Soty Comm (Euro))
       Cardiff – ABB 320 pts (Cult Crit)
       Glasgow – ABB–BBB (Gen Hum)
       Glasgow (Crichton) – ABB (Hum; Crea Cult St)
       St Andrews – ABB–BBC (Arts)
300 pts **Belfast (Queen's)** – BBB (Cult Media St)

Dundee – BBB–CCC (Arts Soc Sci)

East Anglia – BBB–BBC (Cult Phil Pol; Cult Lit Pol; Soty Cult Media)

Edinburgh – BBB (Hum Soc Sci)

Leeds – BBB (Cult St Jap; Cult St)

Nottingham – ABC–BBB (Soc Cult St)

St Andrews – BBB (MA General)

Strathclyde – BBB (Commun Arts)

Surrey – 300 pts (Cult Media Comm)

280 pts **Birmingham** – 280pts (Media Cult Soty)

Essex – 280–260 pts (Hum Comb Hons)

Kent – 280 pts (Contemp Arts)

Lancaster – BBC (Cnsltncy Ind Rsch)

Leeds – BBC (Cult St Fr/Ger/Ital/Port/Russ)

Liverpool – 280–380 pts (BA Arts Comb Hons)

260 pts **Leicester** – BCC–BBC 260–320 pts (Comb St/joint courses)

Strathclyde – BCC–BB (Arts Soc Sci)

240 pts **Aberdeen** – CCC (Scot Cult St)

Belfast (Queen's) – CCC (Comb Arts)

Bristol UWE – 240–320 pts (Media Cult St)

Chester (Warrington) – 240 pts (Cult St)

Glamorgan – 240–280 pts (Cult St)

Kent – 240–260 pts (Cult St courses)

Manchester Met – CCC–DD 240–120 pts (varies with subj choices) (Comb/Joint Hons)

Sheffield Hallam – 240 pts (Comb St – offer varies with subjs)

Ulster – CCC–CCD 240–220 pts (Arts Comb Hons; Hum)

Westminster – CCC/BC (Comb Hons)

220 pts **Bradford** – 220 pts (Comb St)

Brighton – 220 pts (Cult Hist St)

De Montfort – 220–180 pts (Arts Mgt)

Heriot-Watt – CCD (Comb St)

Oxford Brookes – CCD **or** CDcc (Arts Mgt Admin)

200 pts **Bath Spa** – 200–240 pts (Cult St)

Bedfordshire – CDD 200 pts (Hum Mod)

Central Lancashire – 200–180 pts varies (Comb Hons)

Huddersfield – 200 pts (Cult Media Soty)

Manchester Met – 200 pts (Arts Cult Ent joint courses)

Napier – 200 pts (Cult Media Soty)

Roehampton – 200 pts (BA Comb Hons)

Salford – CDD 200 pts (Comb Hons courses)

Worcester – CDD–DEE 200–140 pts (Comb St)

190 pts **London Met** – 190 pts 2AL+AS (Arts Mgt)

180 pts **Bradford** – 180–220 pts (Interd Hum St)

Colchester (Inst) – DDD 180 pts (Comb St; Hum)

Lampeter – open admissions policy (Comb Hons)

Liverpool (LIPA) – 180 pts (Arts Mus Enter Mgt)

Manchester Met – 180 pts (Cult St)

Roehampton – 180 pts (Humanities)

Wolverhampton – DDD 180 pts (Comb St)

160 pts **Bath Spa** – CC 160 pts (Crea St)

Birmingham – CC (Comb St)

Bournemouth (AI) – CC (Arts Evnt Mgt)

Canterbury Christ Church – CC (Hum Comb Hons)

Cumbria – CC 160 pts (Contemp App Arts courses)

Dartington (CA) – 160–200 pts (Arts Cult Mgt)

Derby – 160–200 pts (Comb Hons)

    East London – 160 pts (Cult St courses)
    Glamorgan – 160–200 pts (Hum Comb St)
    Greenwich – 160 pts (Humanities)
    Hertfordshire – 160–240 pts (Comb Mod; Hum)
    London Met – 160 pts (Hum; Arts Mgt)
    London South Bank – CC (Comb St; Arts Mgt)
    Newport – 160 pts (Humanities)
    Peterborough Reg (Coll) – 160 pts (Comb St)
    Robert Gordon – CC (Comb St)
    St Mary's (Coll) – 160–180 pts (Cult St)
    Strathclyde – CC (Commun Arts)
    Sunderland – 160 pts (Hum joint courses)
    Thames Valley – DDE–DEE 160–140 pts (Humanities)
    West Suffolk (Coll) – CC 160 pts (Humanities)
    Wolverhampton – 160–220 pts (Arts)
140 pts **Bath Spa** – CD 140 pts (Comb St)
    Lincoln – DEE 140 pts (Comb St)
    London (CMusMedia) – 140 pts (Arts Evnts Mgt)
    Marjon (Coll) – 140–200 pts (Contemp Cult Media Soty)
    Queen Margaret (UC) – CD 140 pts (Comb Hons)
    Trinity Carmarthen (Coll) – 140 pts (Arts)
120 pts **North East Wales (IHE)** – 120 pts (Humanities)
    West Anglia (Coll) – 120 pts (Humanities)
100 pts **and below**
    Boston (Coll) – (Arts)
    Bradford (Coll) – 80 pts (Comb St)
    Bridgwater (Coll) – (Comb Hons)
    Chesterfield (Coll) – (Comb Hons)
    Hull – 80 pts (Arts Hum)
    London (Birk) – 80 pts for under 21s (over 21 varies) (p/t Hum and Engl/Fr/Ger; Hum Hisp St; Hum Hist Art; Hum Hist; Hum Media St; Hum Phil)
    London (Gold) – 80 pts (Sociol Cult St – contact admissions tutor)
    Norwich City (Coll) – 80 pts (Comb courses)
    Somerset (CAT) – (Comb Arts)
    Swansea – (Hum – for mature students)
    Swansea (IHE) – 80 pts (Comb Hons; Hum)
    Wigan and Leigh (Coll) – (Comb Hons)
    Wirral Met (Coll) – 80 pts (Cult St)

    Leeds Met – contact University
    Open University – contact University (Humanities)

Alternative offers
IB offers Birmingham 32 pts; Essex 30–28 pts; Glasgow 30 pts; Kent 27 pts; Liverpool 30–35 pts; Manchester 35–30 pts; Manchester Met 28 pts; Newcastle 34 pts.
Scottish offers See **Chapter 7**.

OTHER HIGHER EDUCATION COURSES IN THE SUBJECT FIELD

Foundation degrees (contact institution for details) Bedfordshire; Canterbury Christ Church; Colchester (Inst); Norwich (SAD); Suffolk (Univ Campus); Truro (Coll).

CHOOSING YOUR COURSE (SEE ALSO CH.1)

Subject information Many different subjects are offered in combined or modular arrangements. These courses are particularly useful for those applicants who have difficulty in deciding on one specialist subject to follow, allowing students to 'mix and match' according to their interests and often enabling them to embark on new subjects. **Useful websites** www.artscouncil.org.uk; www.scottisharts.org.uk; www.arts.org.uk.

Course variations Combined Honours courses (Durham, Leicester and Newcastle); Culture and Media Studies (Bristol UWE); Cultural Criticism (Cardiff); Arts Management (De Montfort); Cultural Studies and History (Kent). *NOW CHECK PROSPECTUSES AND WEBSITES FOR ANY RECENT CHANGES.*

Universities and colleges teaching quality See www.tqi.ac.uk; www.qaa.ac.uk.

ADMISSIONS INFORMATION

Number of applicants per place (approx) Birmingham 5; Dundee 13 (ave); Durham (Comb Arts) 7; Heriot-Watt 3; Leeds 15; Liverpool 6; Newcastle 7; Oxford Brookes 14; Staffordshire (Comb St) 5; Strathclyde 9; Swansea (IHE) 3; Thames Valley 4; Trinity Carmarthen (Coll) 3.

Advice to applicants and planning the UCAS personal statement Refer to chosen subject tables. **Bath Spa** (Crea St) Looks for personal statements which clarify relevant work done outside the school syllabus (eg creative writing). **Bradford** (Interd Hum St) Indications of interest in addressing academic work to contemporary issues. **De Montfort** (Arts Mgt) Give information about practical experience and a personal interest in one or more areas of the arts. Show a mature attitude on arts/culture and be an original thinker. **Liverpool** (Comb Hons Arts) We look for evidence of a broad interest across a range of subjects. **Nottingham Trent** Refer to work experience, reasons for choice of subject, career ambitions.

Misconceptions about this course Bath Spa (Crea St) Some applicants wish to specialise in one subject not realising it is a joint honours course. **Liverpool** Some students deterred because they believe that the Combined Honours course is too general. This is not so. The degree certificate shows the names of the two subjects taken to honours degree level.

Selection interviews Yes Aberdeen, Bath Spa, Brighton, Bristol UWE, Brunel, Colchester (Inst), De Montfort, Dundee, Durham, Gloucestershire, Greenwich, Lincoln, London Met, Manchester Met, Northampton, Roehampton, St Mary's (Coll), Trinity Carmarthen (Coll), Wirral Met (Coll), Worcester; **Some** Birmingham (Comb courses inc Drama), Central Lancashire, Liverpool.

Interview advice and questions Questions will focus on your chosen subjects. See under separate subject tables. **Bath Spa** (Cult St) No test at interview – general questions. **De Montfort** (Arts Mgt) What do you understand to be the role of the Arts Council of England? What recent arts events have you seen/enjoyed? See also **Chapter 6**.

Reasons for rejection (non-academic): Lack of clarity of personal goals.

AFTER-RESULTS ADVICE

Universities with vacancies in Clearing (2006) Check all institutions.

Offers to applicants repeating A-levels Higher Glamorgan, Huddersfield, St Andrews; **Possibly higher** Bristol UWE, Leeds, Newcastle, Roehampton, St Mary's (Coll); **Same** Anglia Ruskin, Bath Spa, Birmingham, Brunel, De Montfort, Derby, Durham, Gloucestershire, Greenwich, Kingston, Leicester, Lincoln, Liverpool, London Met, Manchester Met, Northampton, Portsmouth, Staffordshire, Swansea (IHE), Wolverhampton, Worcester.

GRADUATE DESTINATIONS AND EMPLOYMENT (2005 HESA)
No data available.

OTHER DEGREE SUBJECTS FOR CONSIDERATION
See under **Social Studies/Science**.

ASIA-PACIFIC STUDIES

(including **East and South Asian Studies;** see also **Chinese, Japanese** and **Languages)**

NB The points totals shown to the left of the institutions are for ease of reference only. It must not be assumed that tariff points are always used by institutions or that they can be substituted for an offer in grades. The level of an offer is not necessarily indicative of the quality of a course.

COURSE OFFERS INFORMATION

Subject requirements/preferences GCSE A language subject grade A–C. **Leeds** Seven/eight subjects, grades A and B in mathematics. **London (SOAS)** For Vietnamese a good reading knowledge of French is required. **Sheffield** (E As St Bus St) Grade B mathematics. **AL** A language or a second joint subject may be required.

Your target offers

360 pts and above

Cambridge – AAA (Orntl St)

Oxford – Offers vary eg AAA–AAB (Orntl St Sansk Hindi)

300 pts **Edinburgh** – BBB 300 pts (Sansk; Sansk Gk; Sansk Lat; Sansk Ling)

Leeds – BBB (As Pacif St Econ; As Pacif St; As Pacif St Mgt; As Pacif St Span; SE As St Span)

Sheffield – BBB–BBC **or** BBcc **or** BBab (E As St; E As St Mgt; E As St Hist; Kor St; Kor St Jap; Kor St Mgt)

280 pts **Leeds** – BBC (As Pacif St with Fr/Ger; As Pacif St Hist; As Pacif St Pol; As Pacif St Int Rel)

260 pts **London (SOAS)** – BCC (S As St; Sansk courses; Urdu courses; Hindi; Nepali courses; Thai courses; Viet courses)

180 pts **Central Lancashire** – 180 pts (As Pacif St)

160 pts **London Met** – 160–200 pts (As Pacif St courses)

Alternative offers

IB offers Leeds 30 pts; London (SOAS) 30 pts; Sheffield 29 pts.

Scottish offers See **Chapter 7**.

CHOOSING YOUR COURSE (SEE ALSO CH.1)

Subject information These courses focus on the study of the cultures and the languages of this region of the world, such as Korean, Sanskrit, Thai, Vietnamese. **Useful website** www.dur.ac.uk/oriental. museum.

Course variations Asia-Pacific Studies with Chinese or Japanese (Leeds); Hindi, Nepali, Urdu and Thai (London (SOAS)); Korean Studies and Japanese (Sheffield). *NOW CHECK PROSPECTUSES AND WEBSITES FOR ANY RECENT CHANGES.*

Universities and colleges teaching quality See www.tqi.ac.uk; www.qaa.ac.uk.

Top universities and colleges (Research) Cambridge*; Edinburgh; Leeds; London (SOAS); Oxford.

Sandwich degree courses Central Lancashire.

ADMISSIONS INFORMATION

Number of applicants per place (approx) London (SOAS) 4, (Thai) 2, (Burm) 1.

Advice to applicants and planning the UCAS personal statement Connections with, and visits to, South and South East Asia should be mentioned. You should give some indication of what impressed you and your reasons for wishing to study these subjects. An awareness of the geography, culture and politics of the area also should be shown on the UCAS application. **Leeds** Show your skills in learning a foreign language (if choosing a language course), interest in current affairs of the region, experience of travel and self-discipline.

Selection interviews Yes Cambridge, Oxford.

Interview advice and questions General questions are usually asked that relate to applicants' reasons for choosing a degree course in this subject area and to their background knowledge of the various cultures. See also **Chapter 6**.

AFTER-RESULTS ADVICE

Universities with vacancies in Clearing (2006) Check all institutions.

GRADUATE DESTINATIONS AND EMPLOYMENT (2005 HESA)

Graduates surveyed 45 **Employed** 30 **In further study** 5 **Assumed unemployed** 0.

OTHER DEGREE SUBJECTS FOR CONSIDERATION

Anthropology; Development Studies; Far Eastern languages; Geography; History; International Relations; Politics; Social Studies.

ASTRONOMY/ASTROPHYSICS

NB The points totals shown to the left of the institutions are for ease of reference only. It must not be assumed that tariff points are always used by institutions or that they can be substituted for an offer in grades. The level of an offer is not necessarily indicative of the quality of a course.

COURSE OFFERS INFORMATION

Subject requirements/preferences **GCSE Edinburgh, Hertfordshire, St Andrews** English and a foreign language. **London (QM)** Average of grade B in all subjects. **AL** Mathematics and physics usually required.

Your target offers
360 pts and above
  Cambridge – AAA (Nat Sci (Astro))
  Sussex – AAA–AAB 390–350 pts (MPhys Astro)
340 pts Birmingham – AAB–ABB (Phys Astro; Phys Prtcl Phys; Phys Spc Rsch; Cosmo)
  Durham – AAB (BSc Phys Astron)
  London (QM) – 340 pts (MSci Astro; Astron)
  London (UCL) – AAB–BBB+AS (Astron; Astro; Astron Phys; Planet Sci)
  Manchester – AAB–ABB (Phys Astro)
  St Andrews – AAB 2nd yr entry (Astrophysics)
  Southampton – 340 pts (Phys Astron)
  Surrey – AAB (MEng Spc Tech Planet Explor)
320 pts Belfast (Queen's) – ABB (MSci Phys Astro)
  Bristol – ABB–BBB (Phys Astro)
  Leeds – ABB (MPhys Phys Astro)
  Leicester – ABB–CCC 320–280 pts (Phys Astro; Maths Astron; Phys Spc Sci Tech)
  York – ABB (MPhys) BBB (BSc) (Phys Astro)
300 pts Cardiff – ABC pts (MPhys Phys Astron; MPhys Astro)
  Edinburgh – BBB (Astrophysics)
  Leeds – BBB (BSc Phys Astro)
  Liverpool – ABC 300 pts (Astrophysics)
  Liverpool John Moores – ABC 300 pts (MPhys Astrophysics)
  London (King's) – BBB–BBbbb 260 pts (Phys Astro)
  London (RH) – BBB (MSci Astro)
  Nottingham – BBB (Phys Astron)
  St Andrews – BBB 1st yr entry (Astrophysics)
  Sheffield – ABC (Astron courses)
  Surrey – BBB (MPhys) BCC (BSc) (Phys Nucl Astro; BEng Spc Tech Planet Explor)
280 pts Aberystwyth – 280 pts (Spc Sci Robot)

For information on how to read the Subject Tables, see **Chapter 7**.

Central Lancashire – BBC (Astrophysics)
Exeter – 280 pts (Phys Astro)
Kent – BBC (Astron Spc Sci Astro)
Lancaster – BBC (Phys Astro Cosmo)
Liverpool John Moores – BBC (Phys Astron)
London (QM) – 280 pts (BSc Astro; Astron)
London (RH) – BBC-BCC (BSc Astrophysics)
Reading – 280 pts (Phys Unvrs)
260 pts **Cardiff** – BCC (BSc Astrophysics)
Glasgow – BCC (Astron Maths; Astron Phys)
Swansea – 260–280 pts (Phys Prtcl Phys Cosmo)
240 pts **Belfast (Queen's)** – CCC/BB (BSc Phys Astro)
Hertfordshire – 240 pts (Astro; Astro Sci Comp)
Keele – 240–260 pts (Astrophysics)
220 pts **Nottingham Trent** – 220 pts (Astron Chem; Astron Comp; Astron Maths; Astron Phys)
200 pts **Glamorgan** – 200 pts (Astron Spc)

Alternative offers
IB offers Birmingham 30–32 pts; Cambridge 38–42 pts; Keele 26–28 pts; Kent 30 pts; London (King's) 32 pts, (QM) 30–32 pts, (RH) 28–30 pts, (UCL) 32–36 pts; St Andrews 36 pts; Sussex 36 pts.
Scottish offers See **Chapter 7.**

CHOOSING YOUR COURSE (SEE ALSO CH.1)

Subject information All Astronomy-related degrees are built on a core of mathematics and physics which, in the first two years, is augmented by an introduction to the theory and practice of astronomy or astrophysics. Astronomy emphasises observational aspects of the science and includes a study of the planetary system whilst Astrophysics tends to pursue the subject from a more theoretical stand-point. Other courses often combine Mathematics or Physics with Astronomy. **Useful websites** www.ras.org.uk; www.scicentral.com.

Course variations Space Science and Robotics (Aberystwyth); Planetary Science (London (UCL)); Space Technology and Planetary Exploration (Surrey); Physics with Particle Physics and Cosmology (Swansea). *NOW CHECK PROSPECTUSES AND WEBSITES FOR RECENT CHANGES.*

Universities and colleges teaching quality See www.tqi.ac.uk; www.qaa.ac.uk.

Top universities and colleges (Research) See **Physics**.

Sandwich degree courses Hertfordshire.

ADMISSIONS INFORMATION

Number of applicants per place (approx) Bristol 9; Cardiff 6; Central Lancashire (Astro) 12; Durham 3; Hertfordshire 5; Leicester 12; London (QM) 6, (RH) 6, (UCL) 5; Newcastle 7.

Advice to applicants and planning the UCAS personal statement Books and magazines you have read on astronomy and astrophysics are an obvious source of information. Describe your interests and why you have chosen this subject. Visits to observatories would also be important. (See also **Appendix 2.)**

Misconceptions about this course Career opportunities are not as limited as some students think. These courses involve an extensive study of maths and physics, opening many opportunities for graduates such as geodesy, rocket and satellite studies and engineering specialisms.

Selection interviews **Yes** Bristol, Cambridge, London (UCL), Newcastle; **Some** Cardiff.

Interview advice and questions You will probably be questioned on your study of physics and the aspects of the subject you most enjoy. Questions in the past have included: Can you name a recent development in physics which will be important in the future? Describe a physics experiment, indicating any errors and exactly what it was intended to prove. Explain weightlessness. What is a black hole? What are the latest discoveries in space? See also **Chapter 6**.

AFTER-RESULTS ADVICE
Universities with vacancies in Clearing (2006) Aberystwyth; Belfast; Cardiff; Central Lancashire; Glamorgan; Glasgow; Hertfordshire; Hull; Keele; Kent; Kingston; Lancaster; Leeds; Leicester; Liverpool; Liverpool John Moores; London (King's), (QM), (RH); Manchester; Nottingham; Nottingham Trent; Reading; Sheffield; Southampton; Surrey, Sussex; Swansea; York.

Offers to applicants repeating A-levels Higher St Andrews; **Same** Cardiff, London (UCL), Newcastle.

GRADUATE DESTINATIONS AND EMPLOYMENT (2005 HESA)
Graduates surveyed 215 **Employed** 80 **In further study** 75 **Assumed unemployed** 15.

OTHER DEGREE SUBJECTS FOR CONSIDERATION
Aeronautical/Aerospace Engineering; Computer Science; Earth Sciences; Geology; Geophysics; Mathematics; Meteorology; Mineral Sciences; Oceanography; Physics.

BIOCHEMISTRY

NB The points totals shown to the left of the institutions are for ease of reference only. It must not be assumed that tariff points are always used by institutions or that they can be substituted for an offer in grades. The level of an offer is not necessarily indicative of the quality of a course.

COURSE OFFERS INFORMATION
Subject requirements/preferences GCSE Bath Approx five grade As, five grade Bs. **Birmingham** Eight subjects A*, A or B (minimum C in English/mathematics, grade B some sciences). **Bristol** Mostly grades A or B. **Cambridge, Oxford** Grade A in most subjects preferred. **Cardiff** Seven subjects grade A or B. **Edinburgh** Mathematics grade B. **Kingston** A or B in sciences. **Leeds** Nine to ten subjects A*, A or B including mathematics. **London (RH)** Minimum five As and Bs in sciences and mathematics. **Southampton** Grade C in mathematics. **Surrey** A cluster of A* and As creates a good impression. **Swansea** Mainly A/B grades especially in the sciences. **AL** Chemistry required plus biology or another science subject.

Your target offers

360 pts and above
        Cambridge – AAA (Nat Sci (Bioch))
        Oxford – Offers vary eg AAA–AAB (Mol Cell Bioch)
        Warwick – ABBc (Biochemistry)

340 pts **Bath** – AAB (Bioch courses)
        Bristol – AAB–ABB (Bioch; Bioch Med Bioch; Bioch Mol Biol Biotech)
        East Anglia – AAB 320 pts (Bioch Aus)
        London (UCL) – AAB (Biochemistry)
        Manchester – AAB–BBB (Bioch Ind Exp; Bioch Modn Lang)
        Nottingham – AAB–BBB **or** 2AL+2AS (Bioch; Bioch Genet; Bioch Biol Chem)
        York – AAB–ABB (Bioch; Bioch Yr Euro)

320 pts **Birmingham** – ABB–BBB (Bioch; Bioch Euro; Med Bioch; Bioch Biotech)
        Cardiff – ABB–BBB 320–280 pts (Bioch; Mol Biosci)
        Durham – ABB (Mol Biol Bioch)
        East Anglia – ABB (Bioch N Am)
        Exeter – ABB–BBC 320–280 pts (Biol Medcnl Chem; Biol Medcnl Chem Ind)
        Imperial London – ABB (Bioch; Bioch Mgt; Bioch Rsch Abrd; Bioch Yr Ind)
        Lancaster – ABB (Bioch N Am/Aus; Bioch Genet)
        Leeds – ABB (Med Bioch)
        Leicester – ABB–BBB 320–300 pts (Biol Sci (Bioch))

Newcastle – ABB–BBB (Bioch Immun; Bioch)
St Andrews – ABB–BBB (Biochemistry)
Sheffield – ABB (Bioch courses)
Southampton – ABB 320 pts (Biochemistry)
300 pts **Bristol** – BBB (Immun; Virol Immun)
Dundee – 300–240 pts (Bioch; Bioch Pharmacol; Bioch Physiol Sci)
East Anglia – BBB–BBC (Bioch; Cell Mol Bioch; Bioch Euro)
Edinburgh – BBB (Biochemistry)
Lancaster – BBB–BBC (Bioch; Bioch Biomed; Bioch Genet)
Leeds – BBB (Bioch Chem Fd Sci; Bioch; Bioch Mol Biol)
Leicester – 300–360 pts (Bioch; Med Bioch)
London (King's) – BBB **or** BBbb (Bioch; Med Bioch)
London (RH) – BBB (Bioch; Bioch Psy; Bioch Sci Comm; Med Bioch)
Reading – 300 pts (Biochemistry)
Sussex – BBB–BBC 330–310 pts (Biochemistry)
280 pts **Aberystwyth** – 280 pts (Biochemistry)
Aston – BBC–CCC (Biosci Proc; Biol Chem)
Essex – 280–240 pts (Bioch; Mol Med Bioch)
Glasgow – BBC–CCC (Bioch; Med Bioch)
Liverpool – BBC–BBB 280–300 pts (Bioch; Bioch Yr Ind)
London (QM) – 280 pts (Bioch Microbiol; Bioch Foren Sci)
Strathclyde – BBC (Bioch Immun; Bioch Microbiol; Bioch Pharmacol)
Swansea – 280–300 pts (Bioch; Med Bioch; Bioch Ital)
260 pts **Belfast (Queen's)** – BCC/AB (Biochemistry)
Bradford – 260 pts (Med Bioch)
Brunel – BCC–BBC 260–280 pts (Biomed Sci (Bioch))
Nottingham – BCC–CCD (Nutr Biochem)
Surrey – BCC 260 pts (Bioch; Bioch (Med) (Neuro) (Pharmacol) (Tox))
240 pts **Aberdeen** – 240 pts (Biochemistry)
Bangor – 240–280 pts (Biomed Sci)
Heriot-Watt – CCC 2nd yr entry (Biochemistry)
Keele – 240–260 pts (Bioch courses)
Kent – CCC (Bioch; Bioch Euro)
Portsmouth – 240–280 pts (Bioch; Bioch Microbiol)
220 pts **Liverpool John Moores** – 220 pts (Bioch; App Bioch; Bioch Foren Sci; Bioch Microbiol; App Med Bioch; Med Bioch)
200 pts **Central Lancashire** – 200 pts (Bioch Foren Sci)
Greenwich – 200 pts (Biosci (Med Bioch); Mol Biol)
Hertfordshire – 200 pts (Bioch; Bioch Euro/N Am)
Huddersfield – 200 pts (Bioch; Med Bioch)
Kingston – 200–240 pts (Bioch; Med Bioch)
Nottingham Trent – 200 pts (Bioch; Bioch Microbiol)
Salford – 200 pts (Bioch Sci; Bioch Sci USA)
180 pts **Bristol UWE** – 180–220 pts (App Bioch; Mol Biol)
Heriot-Watt – DDD (Biochemistry)
Staffordshire – 180–240 pts (Bioch Microbiol)
160 pts **Bristol UWE** – 160–200 pts (Biol Medcnl Chem)
Central Lancashire – 160 pts (Bioch Comb Hons)
London Met – 160 pts (Biochemistry)
London South Bank – CC (Biosci (Bioch))
Westminster – CC (Bioch; Bioch Microbiol)
Wolverhampton – 160–220 pts (Bioch; Medcnl Bioch; Bioch Fd Sci; Bioch Mol Biol)
120 pts **East London** – 120 pts (Biochemistry)
Essex – 120 pts (Bioch; Mol Med Bioch 4yr courses)
Paisley – DD **or** bbc (Biol Bioch)
80 pts **London (Birk)** – 80 pts for under 21s (over 21s varies) (p/t Bioch Sci)

Alternative offers

IB offers Aberdeen 28 pts; Aberystwyth 26 pts; Bath 34 pts; Birmingham 32–34 pts; Cambridge 38–42 pts; Dundee 29 pts; East Anglia 30 pts; Exeter 30–34 pts; Glasgow 28 pts; Keele 26–28 pts; Lancaster 32–34 pts; Leicester 32–34 pts; Liverpool 28–32 pts; London (King's) 32 pts, (QM) 30–32 pts; Manchester 32–35 pts; Newcastle 32–35 pts; Nottingham 32–34 pts; Oxford 38–42 pts; Reading 30 pts; St Andrews 31 pts; Salford 24 pts; Sheffield 33 pts; Staffordshire 28 pts; Sussex 32 pts; Warwick 34 pts; York 35 pts.

Scottish offers See **Chapter** 7.

OTHER HIGHER EDUCATION COURSES IN THE SUBJECT FIELD

Higher National Diploma courses Coventry; Hertfordshire; Riverside Halton (Coll); Stockport (CFHE); Truro (Coll); Wolverhampton.

CHOOSING YOUR COURSE (SEE ALSO CH.1)

Subject information Biochemistry is the study of life processes at molecular level. It plays a role in many aspects of life, with applications in health and medicine, pharmaceuticals, biotechnology, environmental science and agriculture. Most courses are extremely flexible and have common first years. Modules could include genetics, immunology, blood biochemistry, physiology and biotechnology. The option to choose other courses features at many universities. Many courses allow for a placement in industry in the UK or in Europe or North America. **Useful websites** www.biochemistry.org; www.scienceyear.com; see also **Biological Sciences** and **Biology**.

Course variations Biochemistry with a Year in North America or Australia (East Anglia); Biochemistry and Genetics (Lancaster); Nutritional Biochemistry (Nottingham); Biochemical Sciences in the USA (Salford); Medical Biochemistry (Surrey). *NOW CHECK PROSPECTUSES AND WEBSITES FOR ANY RECENT CHANGES.*

Universities and colleges teaching quality See www.tqi.ac.uk; www.qaa.ac.uk.

Top universities and colleges (Research) Bristol; Cambridge*; Durham; Edinburgh; Imperial London; Leeds; Leicester; London (King's); Manchester; Oxford; Sussex.

Sandwich degree courses Aston; Bath; Bristol; Bristol UWE; Cardiff; Coventry; East London; Essex; Huddersfield; Kent; Kingston; Liverpool John Moores; London South Bank; Manchester; Northumbria; Nottingham Trent; Sheffield Hallam; Surrey; Sussex; York.

ADMISSIONS INFORMATION

Number of applicants per place (approx) Aberystwyth 5; Bath 7; Birmingham 5; Bradford 7; Bristol 8; Cardiff 6; Central Lancashire 9; Coventry 10; Dundee 6; Durham 6; East Anglia 10; East London 5; Edinburgh 8; Essex 5; Imperial London 6; Keele 7; Leeds 10; London (RH) 8, (UCL) 8; Newcastle 7; Nottingham 14; Oxford (success rate 57%); Salford 4; Southampton 5; Staffordshire 6; Strathclyde 7; Surrey 3; Warwick 6; York 10.

Advice to applicants and planning the UCAS personal statement It is important to show by reading scientific journals that you have interests in chemistry and biology beyond the exam syllabus. Focus on one or two aspects of biochemistry that interest you. Attend scientific lectures (often arranged by universities on open days), find some work experience if possible, and use these to show your understanding of what biochemistry is. Give evidence of your communication skills and time management. Further information may be obtained from the Institute of Biology and the Royal Society of Chemistry (see **Appendix 2**). **Bath** Internal transfer between degree programmes possible; do not make multiple applications (contact admissions tutor). **Oxford** Candidates are expected to have an informed interest in the subject, originating from news items or magazine articles. **St Andrews** Evidence of interest and reasons for choosing the course; sport and extra-curricular activities, posts of responsibility. **Southampton** Evidence of work experience. **Surrey** More about applicants' interests and aspirations, less about what they think the subject is. **Swansea** Evidence of interest in the subject beyond their formal studies and that some thought has been given to their future career. **Wolverhampton** Good communication skills and motivation.

Misconceptions about this course York Students feel that being taught by two departments could be a problem but actually it increases their options.

Selection interviews Yes Birmingham (Clearing only), Bradford, Brunel, Cambridge, East Anglia, East London, Keele (mature students only), Kingston, Leeds, London (RH), (UCL), London South Bank, Oxford, Portsmouth (mature students only), Surrey, Warwick; **Some** Aberystwyth (mature students only), Bath, Cardiff, Liverpool John Moores, Salford, Sheffield, Staffordshire, Wolverhampton.

Interview advice and questions Questions will be asked on your study of chemistry and biology and any special interests. They will also probe your understanding of what a course in Biochemistry involves and the special features offered by the university. In the past questions have been asked covering Mendel, genetics, RNA and DNA. **Liverpool John Moores** Informal interviews. It would be useful to bring samples of coursework to the interview. **See also Chapter 6.**

Reasons for rejection (non-academic) Borderline grades plus poor motivation. Failure to turn up for interviews or answer correspondence. Inability to discuss subject. Not compatible with A-level predictions or references. **Birmingham** Lack of total commitment to Biochemistry, for example intention to transfer to Medicine without completing the course.

AFTER-RESULTS ADVICE

Universities with vacancies in Clearing (2006) Aberdeen; Aberystwyth; Bangor; Belfast; Birmingham; Bradford; Bristol UWE; Dundee; East Anglia; Essex; Exeter; Glasgow; Edinburgh; Imperial London; Keele; Kent; Kingston; Lancaster; Leeds; Leicester; Liverpool John Moores; London (King's), (QM), (RH); Manchester Met; Nottingham; Oxford Brookes; Reading; Salford; Sheffield; Southampton; Surrey; Sussex; Swansea; Warwick; York.

Offers to applicants repeating A-levels Higher East Anglia, Leeds, Leicester, Nottingham, St Andrews, Strathclyde, Surrey, Warwick; **Possibly higher** Bath, Bristol, Brunel, Central Lancashire, Keele, Kent, Lancaster, Newcastle; **Same** Aberystwyth, Aston (Comb Hons), Birmingham, Bradford, Cardiff, Dundee, Heriot-Watt, Hull, Liverpool, Liverpool John Moores, London (RH), (UCL), Salford, Sheffield, Staffordshire, Wolverhampton, York.

GRADUATE DESTINATIONS AND EMPLOYMENT (2005 HESA)

Graduates surveyed 1220 **Employed** 445 **In further study** 450 **Assumed unemployed** 90.

OTHER DEGREE SUBJECTS FOR CONSIDERATION

Agricultural Sciences; Agriculture; Biological Sciences; Biology; Biotechnology; Botany; Brewing; Chemistry; Food Science; Genetics; Medical Sciences; Medicine; Microbiology; Neuroscience; Nursing; Nutrition; Pharmaceutical Sciences; Pharmacology; Pharmacy; Plant Science.

BIOLOGICAL SCIENCES

(Including **Biomedical Science, Ecology, Forensic Science, Immunology** and **Neurosciences;** see also **Anatomical Science/Anatomy, Biochemistry, Biology, Biotechnology, Genetics, Microbiology, Plant Sciences, Zoology)**

NB The points totals shown to the left of the institutions are for ease of reference only. It must not be assumed that tariff points are always used by institutions or that they can be substituted for an offer in grades. The level of an offer is not necessarily indicative of the quality of a course.

COURSE OFFERS INFORMATION

Subject requirements/preferences GCSE Birmingham Grade B in five relevant subjects. **Cambridge, Oxford** Grade A in most subjects preferred. **Edinburgh** Mathematics grade B. **Leeds** Mainly grade As, minimum grade B in mathematics, science and English. **London (Birk)** Mathematics and chemistry grade C, **(King's)** Grade C chemistry or combined science. **Nottingham** Grade A or B required for dual science or biology, chemistry, mathematics and English. **Reading** Grade B mathematics, science and

French. **Swansea** Majority of A/B grades especially in the sciences. **York** The general requirement for a foreign language may be waived. **AL** Chemistry required plus one or two other science subjects, often including biology. Mathematics may be accepted in place of a science subject.

Your target offers

360 pts **and above**
　　Cambridge – AAA (Nat Sci (Biol Biomed Sci) (Neuro) (Path) (Plant Sci))
　　Oxford – Offers vary eg AAA–AAB (Biol Sci)
　　Warwick – ABBc (Biol Sci)

340 pts **East Anglia** – AAB–ABB (Biol Sci N Am/Aus; Ecol N Am/Aus)
　　Imperial London – AAB (Biomed Sci)
　　London (UCL) – AAB+AS–BBB+AS (Biomed Sci; Neuro)
　　Manchester – AAB–BBC (Neuro; Cog Neuro Psy; Biomed Sci; Biol Comp Sci; Lf Sci)

330 pts **Sussex** – 330 pts (Cog Neuro)

320 pts **Birmingham** – ABB–BBC (Biol Sci courses; Bioinform; Med Sci)
　　Cardiff – ABB–BBB (Biomed Sci (Neuro); Biomed Sci; Mol Biosci; Ecol)
　　Durham – ABB (Ecol; Mol Biol Bioch)
　　East Anglia – ABB 320 pts (Ecol with N Am/Aus; Biol Sci with N Am/Aus)
　　Exeter – ABB–BBB (Biol Sci; Hum Biosci)
　　Lancaster – ABB (Ecol N Am/USA; Biol Sci N Am/USA)
　　Leicester – ABB 320 pts (MBiol Biol Sci)
　　London (RH) – ABB–BBB 320–300 pts (Biomed Sci; Ecol Env)
　　Manchester – ABB (MEng Biomed Mat Sci Ind)
　　Newcastle – ABB–BBB (Biomed Sci; Med Microbiol Immun; Biol Sci)
　　Nottingham – ABB–BBB (Neuro Bioch; Neuro Pharmacol)
　　St Andrews – ABB–BBB (Biomol Sci; Ecol Cons; Evol Biol; Env Biol; Biol courses; Neuro)
　　Sheffield – ABB or ABab (Biomed Sci; Biomed Sci Ent; Dev Cell Biol; Func Gnm Stem Cell Sci; Neuro)
　　Sussex – ABB–BBB 360–340 pts (Med Neuro; Mol Med)
　　York – ABB (Ecol Cons Env)

300 pts **Aston** – BBB–BBC (Biomed Sci)
　　Bristol – BBB (Med Microbiol; Neuro; Immun; Virol Immun)
　　Dundee – 300–240 pts (Spo Biomed; Physiol Sci; Neuro; Biomed Sci)
　　Durham – BBB (Biomed Sci)
　　East Anglia – BBB–BBC 300–280 pts (Ecol; Ecol Euro; Biol Sci; Biol Sci Euro; Ecol Biol; Biomed)
　　Edinburgh – BBB (Biol Sci; Neuro; Biol Sci Mgt; Ecol Sci; Ecol; Immun)
　　Exeter – BBB–BBC (Biol Medcnl Chem; Biol Med Chem Ind)
　　Lancaster – BBB–BBC 300–280 pts (Biol Sci; Biol Sci Biomed; Biomed Med Stats; Ecol)
　　Leeds – BBB 300 pts (Neuro Hum Phsiol; Nanotech; Med Sci; Ecol Env Biol; Biol Sci)
　　Leicester – BBB 300 pts (BSc Biol Sci courses)
　　Lincoln – 300 pts (Biovet Sci)
　　Liverpool – BBB 300 pts (Biovet Sci)
　　London (King's) – BBB **or** BBbb **or** ACac (Biomed Sci; Biomol Sci; Neuro)
　　London (QM) – 300–280 pts (Biomed Sci)
　　London (RVC) – BBB (Vet Sci – not a qualification to practise as a vet)
　　Reading – 300 pts (Biol Sci; Biol Sci Ind; Biomed Sci; App Ecol Cons)
　　Sheffield – BBB (Ecology)
　　Southampton – BBB 300 pts (Biomed Sci)
　　Stirling – BBB 2nd yr entry (Ecol; Cons Biol; Aquacult; Frshwtr Sci)
　　Surrey – BBB–BCC 300–260 pts (Biomed Sci; Bioch (Neuro); Biomed Sci+Fdn Yr)

280 pts **Aberystwyth** – 280 pts (Lf Sci; Anim Bhv; Biol Bioinform)
　　Anglia Ruskin – 280 pts (Foren Sci courses)
　　Aston – BBC 280 pts (Infec Immun)
　　Belfast (Queen's) – BBC–BCC (Biomed Sci)

Birmingham – BBC 280 pts (Biomed Mat Sci)
Bournemouth – 280 pts (Foren Cr Scn Sci)
Bradford – 280 pts (Foren Arch Sci)
Brunel – 280 pts (Biomed Sci; Biomed Sci (Foren))
Essex – BBC–CCC 280–240 pts (Biol Sci; Biomed Sci; Ecol)
Glasgow – BBC–CCC (App Biosci; Biomed Sci; Biomol Sci; Immun; Neuro)
Liverpool – BBC–BBB 280–300 pts (Biol Sci; Biol Med Sci; Lf Sci App Med)
Manchester – BBC (BSc Biomed Mat Sci)
Strathclyde – BBC (Biol Sci; Biomed Sci; Immun Microbiol; Immun Pharmacol)
Swansea – 280–300 pts (Biol Sci joint courses)
Ulster – 280 pts (Biomed Sci)

260 pts   **Aberdeen** – 260 pts (Ecol; Parasit; Neuro Psy; Immun; Biomed Sci)
Belfast (Queen's) – BCC/AB (Biol Sci)
Bradford – 260 pts (Clin Sci; Biomed Sci; Biosci; Foren Sci; Med Microbiol; Foren Med Sci; Bioarch)
Central Lancashire – 260 pts (Foren Sci courses)
Gloucestershire – 260 pts (Biol Sci)
Hull – 260–300 pts (Biomed Sci)
Keele – 260–300 pts (Foren Sci)
Kent – 260 pts (Biol Anth; Foren Sci; Foren Sci Ind; Foren Sci Comp Apps; Foren Chem)
London (St George's) – BCC 260 pts (Biomed Sci)
Northumbria – 260 pts (Foren Sci)
Oxford Brookes – BCC **or** BCbc (Biomed Sci; Ecol)
Plymouth – 260 pts (Hum Biosci)
Ulster – 260 pts (Mol Biosci)
Wolverhampton – 260–320 pts (App Biomed Sci; Biomed Sci)

240 pts   **Abertay Dundee** – CCC 240 pts (Foren Sci)
Bangor – 240–280 pts (App Trstrl Mar Ecol; Biomed Sci; Ecol)
Bristol UWE – 240–260 pts (Foren Sci; Foren Biol)
Heriot-Watt – CCC 240 pts 2nd yr entry (Biol Sci; Brew Distil)
Hull – CCC–BBC 240–280 pts (Biomed Mol Sci)
Keele – 240–260 pts (Biomed Sci; Neuro)
Lincoln – 240 pts (Foren Sci)
London (St George's) – 240 pts (Biomed Inform)
Northumbria – 240 pts (Biomed Sci; Biomed Sci Chem; Hum Biosci)
Nottingham Trent – 240 pts (Foren Sci; App Biomed Sci)
Portsmouth – 240–280 pts (Biomed Sci)
Wolverhampton – 240 pts (Biol Sci; Biomed Sci)

220 pts   **Bradford** – 220 pts (App Ecol)

Brighton – 220 pts (Biol Sci; Biomed Sci; Biogeog; App Biomed Sci)
Chester – 220 pts (Foren Biol courses; Biomed Sci)
Coventry – 220–240 pts (Biol Foren Sci; Foren Invstg St; Biol Sci; Biomed Sci)
De Montfort – 220–240 pts (Biomed Sci)
Glamorgan – 220–260 pts (Foren Sci)
Kingston – 220–200 pts (Biomed Sci; Foren Sci Invstg Analys)
Liverpool John Moores – 220–260 pts (Foren Sci courses; Biomed Sci)
Nottinham Trent – 220 pts (Foren Ecol)
Sheffield Hallam – 220 pts (Biomed Sci; Foren Eng; Cell Mol Biosci; Foren Biosci)
Stirling – CCD/BC 1st yr entry (Ecol; Aquacult; Frshwtr Sci; Cons Sci)
200 pts **Abertay Dundee** – CDD (Biomed Sci)
Anglia Ruskin – 200 pts (Biomed Sci; Biol Sci; Ecol Cons)
Bradford – 200 pts (Clin Tech)
Cardiff (UWIC) – 200 pts (Spo Biomed Nutr; Biomed Sci Mol Biol; Biomed Sci Foren Tox)
Central Lancashire – 200–240 pts (Neuro; Biomed Sci)
Cumbria – 200 pts (Educ Biol St QTS)
Glasgow Caledonian – CDD (Foren Invstg)
Hertfordshire – 200 pts (Biomed Sci)
Hull (Scarborough) – 200–240 pts (Ecology)
Lincoln – 200 pts (Biomed Sci; App Biomed Sci)
Manchester Met – 200–280 pts (Wldlf Ecol Bhv; Ecol; Biomed Sci Foren Biol; Biol Biomed Psy; Foren Sci Comb)
Middlesex – 200–240 pts (Biol Sci courses; Biomed Sci)
Napier – 200 pts (Biol Sci; Immun Tox)
Nottingham Trent – 200 pts (Ecol; Env Mgt)
Plymouth – 200 pts (Biol Sci; Hum Biosci)
Salford – 200–180 pts (Biol Sci; Biol Sci Fr/USA; Biomol Sci; Env Biosci)
Teesside – 200–260 pts (Foren Invstg Consum Law; Crim Scn Sci; Foren Biol)
180 pts **Bell (Coll)** – 180 pts (App Biosci Biotech)
Bristol UWE – 180–220 pts (App Biol Sci; Env Foren; Biomed Sci; Biovet Sci)
De Montfort – 180–160 pts (Foren Sci)
Glasgow Caledonian – DDD (Biomed Sci; Hum Biosci; Hum Biol Sociol Psy; Cell Mol Biol)
Greenwich – 180 pts (Biol Sci)
Heriot-Watt – DDD 180 pts 1st yr entry (Brew Distil)
Portsmouth – 180–240 pts (Pal Evol)
Staffordshire – 180–240 pts (Foren Sci; Foren Sci Crim; Foren Sci Psy; Biol Foren Sci; Biomed Sci)
160 pts **Bedfordshire** – 160 pts (Biomed Sci)
Canterbury Christ Church – 160 pts (Biosciences)
Derby – 160–180 pts (Ecol; Hum Sci; Foren St courses)
Greenwich – 160 pts (Foren Sci)
Harper Adams (UC) – 160–240 pts (Biovet Sci)
London Met – 160 pts (Biol Sci; Foren Sci; Med Biosci; App Biomed Sci; Biomed Sci)
London South Bank – CC (Foren Sci)
Nottingham Trent – 160–170 pts (Biol Sci)
Robert Gordon – CC (Biomed Sci; Foren Sci; Foren Sci Law)
Roehampton – 160–220 pts (Biol Sci; Biomed Sci; Hum Biosci)
SAC (Scottish CAg) – CC (App Biosci)
Westminster – CC (Biol Sci; Biomed Sci)
Wolverhampton – 160–220 pts (Foren Sci courses; Foren Mol Biol; Ecol; Analyt Sci)
140 pts **Liverpool** – 140 pts (Biol Sci Fdn)
120 pts **East London** – 120 pts (Biomed Sci; Foren Sci)
Essex – 120 pts (Biol Sci 4 yrs; Ecol 4 yrs; Cell Mol Biol 4 yrs)
North East Wales (IHE) – 120 pts (Foren Sci; Foren Sci Crim Just)
Paisley – DD **or** bbc (Foren Sci; Biomed Sci)

For information on how to read the Subject Tables, see **Chapter 7**.

Worcester – 120 pts (Ecology)

80 pts   **London (Birk)** – 80 pts for under 21s (**over** 21 varies) (p/t Biol Sci Biomed)

Leeds Met – contact University

Alternative Offers

IB offers Aberdeen (Biomed Sci) 32 pts; Aberystwyth 26 pts; Birmingham 32–34 pts; Bristol 33 pts; Bristol UWE 26–28 pts; Brunel 30 pts; Cambridge 38–42 pts; Chester 30 pts; De Montfort 24 pts; Dundee 29 pts; East Anglia 30 pts; Essex 26–30 pts; Exeter 30–34 pts; Glasgow 28 pts; Keele 26–28 pts; Lancaster 32–34 pts; Leicester 32 pts; Liverpool 28–32 pts; London (King's) 32 pts, (QM) 30–32 pts, (RH) 34 pts, (UCL) 36 pts; Manchester 32–35 pts; Manchester Met 28 pts; Newcastle 32–35 pts; Nottingham 30–34 pts; Oxford 38–42 pts; Reading 30–32 pts; Salford 24 pts; Sheffield 33 pts; Southampton 30 pts; Stirling 26 pts; Staffordshire 28 pts; Surrey 30–32 pts; Warwick 34 pts; York 34 pts.
Scottish offers See **Chapter 7**.

OTHER HIGHER EDUCATION COURSES IN THE SUBJECT FIELD

Foundation degrees (contact the institutions for details) Askham Bryan (Coll); Bedford (Coll); Bedfordshire; Bridgwater (Coll); Central Lancashire; City and Islington (Coll); Gloucestershire; London (QM); Nescot; North Devon (Coll); North East Wales (IHE); Nottingham Trent; Preston (Coll); Riverside Halton (Coll); Sheffield (Coll); Weymouth (Coll); Wigan and Leigh (Coll).

Higher National Diploma courses

100 pts   Abertay Dundee; Adam Smith (Coll); Bell (Coll); Brighton; Bromley (Coll); Cardiff (UWIC); Central Lancashire; Cornwall (Coll); Coventry; De Montfort; Greenwich; Halton (Coll); Henley (Coll); Huddersfield; Manchester Met; Matthew Boulton (CFHE); Myerscough (Coll); Napier; Nottingham Trent; Paisley; Robert Gordon; SAC (Scottish CAg); Sheffield Hallam; Stratford-upon-Avon (Coll); Sunderland; Sutton Coldfield (Coll); Westminster; Wolverhampton; Worcester. See also **Biology**.

CHOOSING YOUR COURSE (SEE ALSO CH.1)

Subject information Biological Sciences (in some universities referred to as Biosciences) cover a very wide subject field and, as for Biochemistry and Biology courses, many modular programmes are offered with a common first year allowing final decisions to be made later in the course. Since most subjects are research-based, students undertake their own projects in the final year. Sandwich courses are offered at many institutions enabling students to gain paid experience in industry and commerce, often resulting in permanent employment on graduation. **Useful websites** www.immunology.org; www.ibms.org; www.scienceyear.com; www.scientral.com; www.forensic.gov.uk; www.bbsrc.ac.uk; see also **Biochemistry** and **Biology**.

Course variations Biomedical Materials Science (Birmingham, Manchester); Education and Biological Studies (Cumbria); Immunology Sciences (Manchester); Combined Studies (Newcastle); Functional Genomics and Stem Cell Science (Sheffield); Forensic Science and Criminology (Staffordshire). *NOW CHECK PROSPECTUSES AND WEBSITES FOR ANY RECENT CHANGES.*

Universities and colleges teaching quality See www.tqi.ac.uk; www.qaa.ac.uk.

Top universities and colleges (Research) Aberdeen; Aston; Bath; Birmingham; Bradford; Brighton; Bristol; Cambridge; Cardiff; Dundee*; Durham; East Anglia; Edinburgh; Glasgow; Imperial London; Leeds; Leicester*; Liverpool; London (King's), (RH), (UCL); Manchester*; Newcastle*; Nottingham; Oxford; St Andrews; Sheffield*; Southampton; Sussex; Ulster*; Warwick; York.

Sandwich degree courses See under **Biology**.

ADMISSIONS INFORMATION

Number of applicants per place (approx) Aston (Biomed Sci) 8; Bristol 8, (Neuro) 10; Cardiff 8; Durham 11; East Anglia (Biol Sci) 15; Edinburgh 8; Essex 8; Lancaster (Biol Sci) 12; Leeds (Med Sci) 25; Leicester 7; London (King's) 7, (QM) 8, (St George's) 15; Newcastle 14; Nottingham 11; Oxford (success rate 43%); Portsmouth (Biomed Sci) 4; Southampton 5; Stirling 7; York 9.

Advice to applicants and planning the UCAS personal statement Read scientific journals and try to extend your knowledge beyond the A-level syllabus. Discuss your special interests, for example, microbiology, genetics or zoology (read up thoroughly on your interests since questions could be asked at interview). **Birmingham** (Biomed Mat Sci) Applicants should show a genuine interest in medicine. They should be able to demonstrate good oral and written communication skills and be competent at handling numerical data. **De Montfort** Evidence of outgoing personality (sport, community work, part-time job). Statement of interest simply in a 'pure' science career is a *negative* factor. (Foren Sci) Meticulous interest in the law. An ability to keep going under pressure. **Surrey** Voluntary attendance on courses, work experience, voluntary work, holiday jobs. See **Appendix 2**.

Misconceptions about this course Anglia Ruskin (Foren Sci) Students are not aware that modules in management and quality assurance are taken as part of the course. **Birmingham** We offer a range of degree labels each with different UCAS codes, for example Biol Sci Genet, Biol Sci Microbiol: all have the same first year and students can freely transfer between them. It is not necessary to apply for more than one except Biol Sci Euro. (Med Sci) Applicants often use this course as an insurance for a vocational course (usually Medicine). If they are unsuccessful for their first choice, they occasionally find it difficult to commit themselves to Medical Sciences and do not perform as well as their academic performance would predict. **Cardiff** Some students mistakenly believe that they can transfer to Medicine. **De Montfort** (Foren Sci) Students are often unaware of how much of the work is analytical biology and chemistry: they think they spend their time visiting crime scenes. **London (St George's)** It is not possible to transfer to Medicine after the first year of the Biomedical Science course. Students may be able to transfer to Year 3 of the Medical course on completion of the BSc degree. **Swansea** (Med Sci) Some applicants think the course is a form of medical training – it isn't. Alternatively, some think that they can transfer after only two years of study with us to the Medical School at Cardiff. They can't but it is possible to take a special final, ie third year in our degree and then be accepted into the second year of the Cardiff Medical School (subject to Cardiff's admissions procedure). (Biol Sci deferred entry) Some applicants think that this is a degree in its own right. In fact after the first year, students have to choose one of the other degrees offered by the School of Biological Sciences. However, this course allows students an extra year in which to consider their final specialisation. (Biol Sci two subj) Some students think that they can choose any combination of subjects. The possible combinations at present cover Bioch Genet Zool, Env Biol Genet and Genet Mar Biol or Genet Zool.

Selection interviews Yes Bangor, Bristol, Bristol UWE, Durham, East Anglia, Essex, Greenwich, Hull, London (RH), (UCL), London South Bank, Manchester, Newcastle, Nottingham, Oxford, Oxford Brookes, Stirling, Strathclyde, Sunderland, Surrey (Biomed Sci), Sussex, Swansea (Med Sci), Warwick; **Some** Aston, Birmingham, Cardiff, De Montfort, Derby, Kent, Liverpool John Moores, London (St George's), Roehampton, Salford, Sheffield, Sheffield Hallam, Staffordshire, Wolverhampton, York.

Interview advice and questions You are likely to be asked about your main interests in biology and your choice of specialisation in the field of biological sciences or, for example, about the role of the botanist, specialist microbiologist in industry, your understanding of biotechnology or genetic engineering. Questions likely to be asked on field courses attended. If you have a field course workbook, take it to interview. **Birmingham** (Biomed Sci) Applicants are invited to interview to assess their suitability for the chosen course. Basic questions relating to the content of their current course will be asked. Those with strong enthusiasm for the subject and considered to be an ideal candidate may be given a reduced points offer. **London (St George's)** (Biomed Sci) What career path do you envisage for yourself with this degree? **Oxford** Applicants are expected to demonstrate their ability to understand whatever facts they have encountered and to discuss a particular aspect of biology in which they are interested (interviews rigorous but sympathetic). See also **Chapter 6**.

Applicants' impressions (A=Open day; B=Interview day) Oxford (B) There were three interviews, very daunting. I felt fairly pressurised with constant questions and with little time to think about the answers. I didn't have much time to look around the department, only the College. The interview process seemed fairly rushed, with not too much time to meet undergraduates. Oxford is worth a try if your grades are good enough, even if it's only to prove you can get an interview at one of the top universities. **Oxford** (Worcester) (B) There were two interviewers at the first interview and one at the second. The first interview lasted half an hour with questions relating to my specific interests in biology. The second interview lasted 15 minutes with questions involving problem-solving and interpreting graphs. Both interviews were very well organised and, although I felt under pressure, staff were all very friendly and approachable. I was able to meet students who were also very helpful.

AFTER-RESULTS ADVICE

Universities with vacancies in Clearing (2006) Aberdeen; Abertay Dundee; Aberystwyth; Aston; Bangor; Belfast; Birmingham; Brighton; Bradford; Bristol UWE; Brunel; Cardiff; Chester; City; Derby; Dundee; East Anglia; Essex; Exeter; Gloucestershire; Greenwich; Hertfordshire; Hull; Imperial London; Kent; Kingston; Lancaster; Leeds; Leicester; Liverpool; Liverpool John Moores; London (QM); Northumbria; Nottingham; Nottingham Trent; Oxford Brookes; Portsmouth; Reading; Salford; Sheffield; Stirling; Sussex; Swansea; Warwick; York.

Offers to applicants repeating A-levels Higher Bristol, Bristol UWE, Durham, East Anglia, Hull, London (St George's), Newcastle, St Andrews, Sheffield; **Possibly higher** Aston, Essex, Lancaster, Leeds (Ecol Env Biol), Manchester Met; **Same** Anglia Ruskin, Birmingham, Cardiff, Chester, De Montfort, Derby, Exeter, Heriot-Watt, Kingston, Leeds, Lincoln, Liverpool John Moores, London (RH), Napier, Oxford Brookes, Plymouth, Robert Gordon, Roehampton, Salford, Sheffield Hallam, Wolverhampton, Worcester, York.

GRADUATE DESTINATIONS AND EMPLOYMENT (2005 HESA)

See under **Biology**.

OTHER DEGREE SUBJECTS FOR CONSIDERATION

Anatomy; Biochemistry; Biology; Biotechnology; Botany; Chemistry; Consumer Sciences; Ecology; Environmental Health; Environmental Science; Forensic Science; Genetics; Genomics; Immunology; Microbiology; Molecular and Cellular Biology; Pharmaceutical Sciences; Pharmacology; Pharmacy; Physiology; Plant Sciences; Psychology; Sport and Exercise Science; Toxicology; Virology; Zoology.

BIOLOGY

(including **Applied, Cancer, Environmental, Forensic, Human, Marine and Molecular Biology, and Pathology;** see also **Biological Sciences, Biotechnology** and **Zoology**)

NB The points totals shown to the left of the institutions are for ease of reference only. It must not be assumed that tariff points are always used by institutions or that they can be substituted for an offer in grades. The level of an offer is not necessarily indicative of the quality of a course.

COURSE OFFERS INFORMATION

Subject requirements/preferences GCSE Mathematics and English stipulated in some cases. **Bangor** Five subjects grade A, grade C minimum in mathematics and English language. **Bristol** Reasonable balance of grade As. **Brunel** Grade B chemistry or combined sciences. **Cambridge, Oxford** Grade A in most subjects preferred. **London (QM)** Mathematics, chemistry grade A–C if not at A-level. **Newcastle** (App Biol) Grade B in chemistry, mathematics or integrated science, if not offered at A-level. **Roehampton** Grade A or B in double science, mathematics, English. **Swansea** Majority grade Bs or better. **AL** Biology and chemistry important, other science subjects may be accepted.

Your target offers
360 pts and above
        Bath – AAA–AAB (MBiol Mol Cell Biol)
        Cambridge – AAA varies between colleges (Nat Sci (Biol Biomed Sci))
        Durham – AAA (Nat Sci (Biol))
        London (UCL) – AAA+AS–AAB+AS (Palaeobiology)
        Warwick – ABBc (Chem Biol)
340 pts **Manchester** – AAB–BBC (Biol courses; Cell Biol courses; Mol Biol courses)
        Nottingham – AAB–ABB (Biology)

320 pts **Birmingham** – ABB–BBB 320–300 pts (Hum Biol; Env Biol courses)
Bristol – ABB–BBB (Biol; Geol Biol; Biol Maths; Palae Evol)
Cardiff – ABB–BBB 320–300 pts (Biology)
Durham – ABB (Biol; Cell Biol; Mol Biol Bioch; Biol Ind)
Imperial London – 320 pts (Biol; Biol Mgt; Biol Yr Euro/Ind/Rsch)
Lancaster – ABB (Cell Biol; Env Biol N Am/Aus)
London (RH) – ABB–BBB (Biol; Mol Biol; Biol Psy; Biol Sci Comm)
London (UCL) – ABB+AS (Biol; Cell Biol; Env Biol; Biol Emb Frtlty Dev)
Sheffield – ABB–BBB **or** ABbb (MBiol Biol; Biol Cons Biodiv; Biol Modn Lang; Biol Yr Abrd)
Southampton – ABB (Mar Biol)
York – ABB–BBB (Biol; Biol Yr Ind/Euro; Mol Cell Biol; Biol Educ)

300 pts **Bristol** – BBB (Cncr Biol; Immun; Virol Immun)
Central Lancashire – 300 pts (Foren Biol)
Dundee – 300 2nd yr entry (Biol; Mol Biol; Microbiol; Zool)
East Anglia – BBB–BBC (Cell Mol Biol; Genet Mol Biol)
Edinburgh – BBB (Dev Biol; Microbiol Infec; Mol Biol)
Exeter (Cornwall) – BBB–BBC 300–280 pts (Cons Biol Ecol)
Lancaster – BBB–BBC (Env Biol; Cell Biol; Cell Biol Biomed)
Leicester – BBB–BBC (Psy Biol)
Leeds – BBB (Biol; Biol Chem; Biol Fd Sci; Biol Hist Phil Sci; Biol Mgt; Biol Maths; Biol Stats)
London (King's) – BBB (Biomed Sci)
Loughborough – 300 pts (Hum Biol)
Newcastle – ABB–BBB (Biol; App Biol; Biol Chem; Biol Psy; Biol Mar Biol)
St Andrews – ABC–BBB (Biol; Bhv Biol; Evol Biol; Hum Biol; Mar Biol; Mol Biol; Cell Biol)
Sheffield – BBB (Biology)
Southampton – BBB (Mar Biol Ocean; Biol; Biol Ocean)
Stirling – BBB 2nd yr entry (Biology)
Surrey – BBB–BCC (Microbiology)
Sussex – BBB–BBC 320–310 pts (Biol; Biol Fr/Ger/Span)

280 pts **Aberystwyth** – 280 pts (Anim Bhv; Biol Bioinform; Biol Spo Sci; Env Biol; Mar Frshwtr Biol; Biol)
Aston – BBC 280 pts (Cell Mol Biol; App Hum Biol; Infec Immun; Hum Biol)
Essex – 280–240 pts (Mar Frshwtr Biol; Cell Mol Biol)
Exeter – BBC–BCC 280–260 pts (Biol Medcnl Chem)
Exeter (Truro Coll) – BBC (Cons Biol Ecol)
Glasgow – BBC–CCC (Hum Biol; Infec Biol; Mar Frshwtr Biol; Biol Chem)
Liverpool – BBC–BBB 280–300 pts (Mar Biol; Mol Biol; Trpcl Dis Biol; Env Biol; Biol Med Sci; Anat Hum Biol)
London (QM) – 280 pts (Biol; Env Biol; Evol Biol; Mar Frshwtr Biol)
Plymouth – 280 pts (Mar Biol; Mar Biol Cstl Ecol; Mar Biol Ocean; Env Biol)
Strathclyde – BBC (Foren Biol)
Surrey – BBC (Integ Sci)
Swansea – 280–300 pts (Biol; Mar Biol)

260 pts **Aberdeen** – 260 pts (Biol; Dev Biol; Cons Biol; Env Biol)
Bangor – 260–300 pts (Mar Biol; App Mar Biol)
Belfast (Queen's) – BCC/AB (Env Biol; Mar Biol; Mol Biol)
Bradford – 260 pts (Cncr Biol; Cell Mol Path)
Central Lancashire – 260–300 pts (Foren Biol)
Gloucestershire – 260 pts (Biology)
Loughborough – 260 pts (Hum Biol)
Nottingham – BCC–CCC (App Biol; Env Biol)
Oxford Brookes – BCC **or** BCbc (Biol; Cons Biol; Hum Biol; Cell Mol Biol)
Plymouth – 260 pts (Hum Biol Psy)
Southampton – BCC 260 pts (Mar Biol Ocean)
Ulster – 260 pts (Biology)

Wolverhampton – 260–320 pts (Hum Biol Microbiol)

240 pts **Bangor** – 240–280 pts (Biol; Mar Biol Zool; Mar Biol Ocean)

Bristol UWE – 240–260 pts (Foren Biol)

Chester – 240 pts (Foren Biol)

Dundee – 240 pts 1st yr entry (Mol Biol; Biol; Microbiol; Zool)

Hull – 240–260 pts (Biol; Hum Biol; Mar Frshwtr Biol)

Keele – CCC 240–260 pts (Biology)

Kent – CCC (Foren Biol; Biol)

Northumbria – 240 pts (App Biol; Biol Foren Biol)

Portsmouth – 240–280 pts (Biol; Mol Biol; Mar Biol; Mar Biol Pollut Ecosys; Foren Biol Biomol Sci; Foren Biol Bioch; Env Biol; Pal Evol)

Salford – 240 pts (Pros Orth)

Strathclyde – CCC (Pros Orth)

220 pts **Brighton** – 220 pts (Biogeography)

Chester – 220 pts (Biol courses except under 240 pts)

Gloucestershire – 220 pts (Biol; Anim Biol)

Hull – 220 pts (Cstl Mar Biol)

Lincoln – 220 pts (Cons Biol (Anim Bhv))

Liverpool Hope – 220 pts (Hum Biol)

Liverpool John Moores – 220 pts (Biol; Biol Geog)

Sheffield Hallam – 220 pts (Hum Biol)

Stirling – CCD/BC (Biol; Mar Biol; Aquacult; Frshwtr Sci; Cons Sci)

200 pts **Anglia Ruskin** – 200–140 pts (Med Biol; Mar Biol courses; Nat Hist Wldlf Biol)

Bath Spa – 200–240 pts (Biology)

Bolton – 200 pts (Biology)

Central Lancashire – 200–260 pts (Mol Biol Bioch; Med Biol)

Glamorgan – 200 pts (Astrobiology)

Hertfordshire – 200 pts (App Biol; App Biol Euro/N Am; Mol Biol Genet)

Huddersfield – 200 pts (Hum Biol; Med Biol; Biol (Mol Cell))

Manchester Met – 200–280pts (Biol; Cell Mol Biol; Hum Biol; Biol N Am; Biomed Sci Foren Biol)

Napier – 200 pts (Env Biol; Mar Frshwtr Biol; Anim Biol; Foren Biol)

Nottingham Trent – 200–180 pts (Biol Bus)

180 pts **Bristol UWE** – 180–220 pts (Hum Biol; Spo Biol; Cons Biol; Env Biol)

Derby – 180–200 pts (Biol; Biol Abrd; Biol comb hons)

Edge Hill – 180 pts (Biology)

Glamorgan – 180–220 pts (Biol; Hum Biol)

Glasgow Caledonian – DDD (Hum Biol Sociol Psy; Cell Mol Biol; Microbiol)

Heriot-Watt – DDD 180 pts 1st yr entry (Brew Distil; App Mar Biol)

Kingston – 180–220 pts (Biol; Mar Frshwtr Biol; Foren Biol; Hum Biol; Cell Mol Biol)

Northampton – 180–220 pts (Biol; Biol Cons; Hum Biol)

Salford – 180 pts (Hum Biol Hlth Sci; Hum Biol Infec Dis; Biomol Pharm Sci)

Staffordshire – 180–240 pts (Biol; Hum Biol; Biol Spo Hlth; Biol Foren Sci; Hum Biol Psy; Foren Biol)

Teesside – 180–240 pts (App Biol)

160 pts **Abertay Dundee** – CC (Foren Psybiol)

Bournemouth – 160 pts (App Biol; Env Cons Biol)

Canterbury Christ Church – CC (Env Biol)

Harper Adams (UC) – 160 pts (Biovet Sci)

Kent – 160 pts (Fdn Biol)

London Met – 160 pts (Hum Biol; Microbiol)

London South Bank – CC (Biosci (Hum Biol); App Biol)

Newman (CHE) – CC 160 pts (BEd/BSc Biol)

Queen Margaret (UC) – 160 pts (Hum Biol)

Roehampton – 160–200 pts (Biol Psy; Biol Anth; Cons Biol)

For information on how to read the Subject Tables, see **Chapter 7**.

St Mary's (Coll) – 160–200 pts (Hum Biol courses)
Westminster – CC (App Biol; Foren Biol; Mol Biol Genet)
Wolverhampton – 160–220 pts (Ecol; Biol Geog; Foren Mol Biol; Anim Biol)
120 pts Bedfordshire – 120–160 pts (Hum Biol)
East London – 120 pts (App Biol)
Essex – 120 pts (Mar Frshwtr Biol 4 yrs; Cell Mol Biol 4 yrs)
Paisley – DD or bbc (Biol; Env Biol; Biol Bioch; Biol Multim; Biol Psy; Biol Zool; Biol Immun; Biol Microbiol)
Suffolk (Univ Campus) – 120–180 pts (Hum Biol; Spo Sci)
Worcester – 120–200 pts (Hum Biol courses)
80 pts Bishop Burton (Coll) – 80 pts (Wldlf Cntry Cons)
London (Birk) – 80 pts for under 21s (over 21 varies) (p/t Mol Biol)

Leeds Met – contact University

Alternative offers
IB offers Aberdeen 28 pts; Aberystwyth 26 pts; Bath 34 pts; Birmingham 32–34 pts; Bristol UWE 26–28 pts; Cambridge 38–42 pts; Chester 30 pts; Dundee 29 pts; East Anglia 30 pts; Essex 26–30 pts; Glasgow 28 pts; Keele 26–28 pts; Kent 26 pts; Liverpool 28–32 pts; London (QM) 30–32 pts, (RH) 34 pts, (UCL) 34–38 pts; Manchester 32–35 pts; Manchester Met 28 pts; Newcastle 32–35 pts; Nottingham 31–32 pts; Oxford 38–42 pts; St Andrews 31 pts; Salford 24 pts; Sheffield 32–36 pts; Southampton 30 pts; Staffordshire 28 pts; Stirling 26 pts; Surrey 30 pts; Sussex 32 pts; Warwick 34 pts.
Scottish offers See Chapter 7.

OTHER HIGHER EDUCATION COURSES IN THE SUBJECT FIELD
Foundation degrees (contact the institutions for details) Anglia Ruskin; Bedfordshire; Cornwall (Coll); Harlow (Coll); Nottingham Trent; Truro (Coll).

Higher National Diploma courses
100 pts and below
Bedfordshire; Bell (Coll); Blackpool and Fylde (Coll); Brighton; Cardiff (UWIC); Central Lancashire; Cornwall (Coll); Coventry; De Montfort; Dudley (Coll); Exeter (Truro Coll); Greenwich; Henley (Coll); Hertfordshire; Lincoln; London South Bank; Napier; Nescot; Nottingham New (Coll); People's (Coll); Riverside Halton (Coll); Robert Gordon; SAC (Scottish CAg); Sparsholt (Coll); Staffordshire; Stockport (CFHE); Ulster; Westminster; Wolverhampton; Worcester; Writtle (Coll); see also **Biological Sciences**.

CHOOSING YOUR COURSE (SEE ALSO CH.1)
Subject information The science of biology is a broad and rapidly developing subject that increasingly affects our lives. Biologists address the challenges faced by human populations such as disease, conservation and food production, and the continuing advances in such areas as genetics and molecular biology that have applications in medicine and agriculture. Many sandwich courses are available. **Useful websites** www.iob.org; www.scienceyear.com; www.bbsrc.ac.uk; see also **Biochemistry**.

Course variations Human Biology (Birmingham); Immunology (Bristol); Palaeontology and Evolution (Bristol); Conservation Biology and Ecology (Exeter); Brewing and Distilling (Heriot-Watt); Coastal Marine Biology (Hull); Tropical Disease Biology (Liverpool); Combined Studies (Newcastle); Biology and Forensic Biology (Northumbria); Biology of Fertility and Embryo Development (UCL London). *NOW CHECK PROSPECTUSES AND WEBSITES FOR ANY RECENT CHANGES.*

Universities and colleges teaching quality See www.tqi.ac.uk; www.qaa.ac.uk.

Top universities and colleges (Research) Bristol; Cambridge; Cardiff; Durham; Edinburgh; Imperial London; Leeds; Leicester; London (King's), (UCL); Manchester; Oxford; Sheffield*.

Sandwich degree courses Aston; Bath; Bradford; Bristol; Bristol UWE; Coventry; East London; Glamorgan; Greenwich; Harper Adams (UC); Hertfordshire; Huddersfield; Kent; Kingston; Liverpool John Moores; London South Bank; Manchester; Oxford Brookes; Surrey; Sussex; Ulster; Wolverhampton; York.

ADMISSIONS INFORMATION

Number of applicants per place (approx) Aberdeen 8; Aberystwyth 5; Aston 6; Bath 7; Birmingham 7; Bradford 7; Bristol 7; Cardiff 8; Dundee 6; Durham 11; Exeter 6; Hull 4; Kent 10; Imperial London 4; Leeds 6; Leicester 15; London (King's) 5; (RH) 5; Newcastle (Mar Biol) 15, (App Biol) 9; Nottingham 9; Oxford Brookes 13; Salford 3; Southampton 14, (Mar Biol) 8; Stirling 15; Sussex 4; Swansea (Mar Biol) 8, (Env Biol) 3, (Biol) 4; York 9.

Advice to applicants and planning the UCAS personal statement Bath Internal transfer between degree programmes possible; do not make multiple applications (contact admissions tutor). **Bristol** (Biol Geol) Looks for experience in the ecological field. **Swansea** Evidence needed of subject interest beyond formal studies and that some thought has been given to their future careers (see **Appendix 2**). See also under **Biochemistry** and **Biological Sciences**.

Misconceptions about this course Sussex Many students think that a biology degree limits you to being a professional scientist which is not the case. **York** Some fail to realise that chemistry beyond GCSE is essential. Mature students often lack the confidence to consider the course.

Selection interviews Yes Bangor, Bath, Birmingham, Bradford (informal, after offer), Cambridge, Durham, East Anglia, Essex, Hertfordshire, Kent, Kingston, London (RH), (UCL), London South Bank, Nottingham (depends on application), Oxford see **Biological Sciences**, SAC (Scottish CAg), Sheffield Hallam, Southampton, Staffordshire, Surrey, Swansea, Writtle (Coll); **Some** Aston, Bath Spa, Derby, Dundee, Liverpool John Moores, London (King's), Roehampton, Salford, Sheffield, Stirling, Wolverhampton, York.

Interview advice and questions Questions are likely to focus on your studies in biology, on any work experience or any special interests you may have in biology outside school. In the past, questions have included: Is the computer like a brain and, if so, could it ever be taught to think? What do you think the role of the environmental biologist will be in the next 40–50 years? Have you any strong views on vivisection? You have a micro-organism in the blood: you want to make a culture. What conditions should be borne in mind? What is a pacemaker? What problems will a giraffe experience? How does water enter a flowering plant? Compare an egg and a potato. Discuss a family tree of human genotypes. Discuss fish farming in Britain today. **Liverpool John Moores** Informal interview. It is useful to bring samples of coursework to the interview. **York** Why biology? How do you see your future? See also **Chapter 6**.

Applicants' impressions (A=Open day; B=Interview day) Bath (B) There was only one 30-minute interview with a few probing questions on why I had chosen the course and what my interests were. The department seemed well-organised, well-equipped and high quality. There were no opportunities to speak to students. I would strongly recommend this department: but the interview is important, so read around the subject. **Durham** (A) The open day consisted of a talk by the master of the college and a tour by student union reps. A further three-day visit was planned. **London (UCL)** (B) There was one 20-minute fairly relaxed interview with questions on 'What makes you tick?' and 'What do you see yourself doing in 10 years' time?' A second-year student took us on a tour of the university.

Reasons for rejection (non-academic) Mainly academic. **Bath Spa** Poor mathematical and scientific knowledge. **Oxford** He appeared to have so much in his head that he tended to express his ideas in too much of a rush. He needs to slow down a bit and take more time to select points that are really pertinent to the questions.

AFTER-RESULTS ADVICE

Universities with vacancies in Clearing (2006) Aberdeen; Abertay Dundee; Aberystwyth; Aston; Bangor; Belfast; Birmingham; Bolton; Bristol UWE; Canterbury Christ Church; Cardiff; Chester; Coventry; Derby; Dundee; East Anglia; East London; Essex; Glamorgan; Gloucestershire; Hertfordshire; Hull; Keele; Kent; Kingston; Lancaster; Leeds; Leicester; Lincoln; Liverpool; Liverpool John Moores; London (QM), (RH); London South Bank; Loughborough; Manchester Met; Middlesex; Napier Newcastle; Northampton; Northumbria; Nottingham; Nottingham Trent; Oxford Brookes; Paisley; Plymouth; Portsmouth; Roehampton; Salford; Sheffield; Southampton; Staffordshire; Stirling; Surrey; Swansea; Warwick; Westminster; Wolverhampton; Worcester; York.

Offers to applicants repeating A-levels **Higher** Cardiff, East London, London (King's), St Andrews, Strathclyde; **Possibly higher** Aston, Bath, Bradford, Durham, Leeds, London (RH), Nottingham, Portsmouth; **Same** Aberystwyth, Anglia Ruskin, Bangor, Bedfordshire, Brunel, Chester, Derby, Dundee, Heriot-Watt, Hull, Liverpool John Moores, London (UCL), London South Bank, Manchester Met, Napier, Newcastle, Oxford Brookes, Plymouth, Roehampton, Salford, Sheffield, Southampton, Staffordshire, Stirling, Teesside, Ulster, Wolverhampton, York.

GRADUATE DESTINATIONS AND EMPLOYMENT (2005 HESA)
Graduates surveyed 3195 **Employed** 1455 **In further study** 760 **Assumed unemployed** 230.

OTHER DEGREE SUBJECTS FOR CONSIDERATION
Anatomy; Biochemistry; Biological Sciences; Biotechnology; Chemistry; Dentistry; Ecology; Environmental Health; Environmental Science/Studies; Food Science; Genomics; Health Studies; Medicine; Midwifery; Nursing; Nutrition; Optometry; Orthoptics; Pharmaceutical Sciences; Pharmacology; Pharmacy; Physiology; Physiotherapy; Plant Sciences; Radiography; Speech and Language Therapy; Zoology.

BIOTECHNOLOGY
(including **Medical Engineering**)

NB The points totals shown to the left of the institutions are for ease of reference only. It must not be assumed that tariff points are always used by institutions or that they can be substituted for an offer in grades. The level of an offer is not necessarily indicative of the quality of a course.

COURSE OFFERS INFORMATION
Subject requirements/preferences GCSE Mathematics grade A–C. **Birmingham** Grade A*–B in five relevant subjects, grade B in mathematics and biology. **Edinburgh** Mathematics grade B. **Leeds** Nine or 10 subjects at grade A*, A or B including mathematics grade B. **AL** Courses vary but one, two or three subjects from chemistry, biology, physics and mathematics may be required.

Your target offers
340 pts **Bath** – AAB (MEng Med Eng)
Bristol – AAB (Bioch Mol Biol Biotech)
Imperial London – AAB (Biomed Eng)
London (UCL) – AAB+AS–ABB+AS (Biotechnology)
Manchester – AAB–BBB (Biotech (Ent); Biotech (Ent) Ind)
320 pts **Birmingham** – ABB–BBB (Biomed Eng; Biol Sci (Biotech))
Cardiff – ABB 320–300 pts (Biotechnology)
Imperial London – ABB (BSc Biotech; Biotech Yr Ind/Rsch)
Newcastle – ABB–BBB (Biotech; Bioproc Eng)
300 pts **Aston** – BBB–ABB (Chem Tech Des)
Bradford – 300 pts (MEng Med Eng)
Edinburgh – BBB (Biotechnology)
Leeds – BBB 300 pts (Biotechnology)
London (QM) – 300–260 pts (MEng Med Eng; Biomed Mat Sci Eng)
Nottingham – BBB (Biomed Mat Sci)
Sheffield – BBB–BCC **or** BBbb–BBcc (Med Sys Eng; Biomat Sci Tiss Eng; Biomed Eng)
Surrey – BBB (MEng Med Eng)
280 pts **Aberdeen** – BBC 2nd yr entry (Biotech (App Mol Biol))
Aston – BBC–CCC (Med Prod Des)
Cardiff – BBC 280–240 pts (BEng Med Eng)
Glasgow – BBC–CCC (Biotechnology)
Leeds – BBC 280 pts (Med Eng)
Liverpool – BBC–BBB 280–300 pts (Microbl Biotech)

Staffordshire – 280 pts (Foren Eng)
260 pts **Aston** – BCC–CCC (Biosci Tech)
Nottingham – BCC–CCC (Biotechnology)
Oxford Brookes – BCC **or** BCbc (Biotechnology)
Reading – 260 pts (Biotech; Biomed Eng Cyber)
Surrey – BCC (BEng Med Eng)
240 pts **Bradford** – 240 pts (BEng Med Eng; Med Tech Spo; Clin Tech)
City – CCC (BEng Biomed Eng)
London (QM) – 240 pts (BSc Biomed Mat Sci Eng)
Northumbria – 240 pts (Biotechnology)
Salford – 240 pts (Pros Orth)
Strathclyde – CCC (Pros Orth)
Ulster – CCC–DDD 240–180 pts (Biomed Eng)
220 pts **Liverpool John Moores** – 220 pts (Biotechnology)
Sheffield Hallam – 220 pts (Foren Eng)
200 pts **Aberdeen** – CDD 1st yr entry (Biotech (App Mol Biol))
Abertay Dundee – CDD (Biotechnology)
Hertfordshire – 200 pts (Biotech; Biotech Euro/N Am)
Napier – 200 pts (Microbiol Biotech)
180 pts **City** – DDD (BSc Biomed Eng App Phys)
160 pts **SAC (Scottish CAg)** – CC (App Biosci (Biotech))
Westminster – CC (Biotech; Biotech Med)
Wolverhampton – 160–220 pts (Biotechnology)
140 pts **Bell (Coll)** – CD 140 pts (App Biosci Biotech)
120 pts **Buckinghamshire Chilterns (UC)** – 120–180 pts (Med Tech)
Paisley – DD **or** bb (Phys Med Tech)

Alternative offers
IB offers Bath 36 pts; Birmingham 32–34 pts; City 25–28 pts; Glasgow 28 pts; Liverpool 28–32 pts;
London (QM) 30–32 pts; Manchester 32–35 pts; Newcastle 32–35 pts; Nottingham 24–30 pts; Reading
30 pts.
Scottish offers See **Chapter 7**.

OTHER HIGHER EDUCATION COURSES IN THE SUBJECT FIELD

Higher National Diploma courses
100 pts Oxford and Cherwell Valley (Coll); SAC (Scottish CAg); Sheffield Hallam; Wolverhampton. See
also **Biochemistry**, **Biological Sciences** and **Biology**.

CHOOSING YOUR COURSE (SEE ALSO CH.1)

Subject information Biotechnology is a multidisciplinary subject which can include chemistry,
biological sciences, microbiology, genetics and chemical engineering. Sandwich courses are available
and the work often focuses on medical, agricultural and food science areas. **Useful websites**
www.bbsrc.ac.uk; www.scienceyear.com.

Course variations Medical Engineering (Bath); Biomedical Engineering and Cybernetics (Reading);
Prosthetics and Orthotics (Salford); Biomaterials Science and Tissue Engineering (Sheffield). *NOW CHECK
PROSPECTUSES AND WEBSITES FOR ANY RECENT CHANGES.*

Universities and colleges teaching quality See www.tqi.ac.uk; www.qaa.ac.uk.

Sandwich degree courses Aberdeen; Aston; Bradford; Bristol; Cardiff; Hertfordshire; Manchester;
Napier; Reading; Sussex.

ADMISSIONS INFORMATION

Number of applicants per place (approx) Cardiff 4; Imperial London 4; Leeds 7; London (UCL) 4;
Strathclyde 4.

Advice to applicants and planning the UCAS personal statement See **Biological Sciences** and **Biochemistry**. See also **Appendix 2**.

Selection interviews **Yes** Leeds, Sheffield Hallam, Strathclyde, Surrey; **Some** Cardiff, Liverpool John Moores, Wolverhampton.

Interview advice and questions See **Biology** and **Biological Sciences**. See also **Chapter 6**.

AFTER-RESULTS ADVICE

Universities with vacancies in Clearing (2006) Aberdeen; Abertay Dundee; Aston; Birmingham; Imperial London; Leeds; Liverpool; Liverpool John Moores; Northumbria; Nottingham; Sheffield; Surrey; Warwick; Wolverhampton.

Offers to applicants repeating A-levels **Possibly higher** Nottingham; **Same** Cardiff, Leeds, Liverpool John Moores, Wolverhampton.

GRADUATE DESTINATIONS AND EMPLOYMENT (2005 HESA)
Graduates surveyed 10 **Employed** 5 **In further study** None **Assumed unemployed** None.

OTHER DEGREE SUBJECTS FOR CONSIDERATION
Agriculture; Biochemistry; Biological Sciences; Biology; Chemistry; Food Science; Health Studies; Materials Science and Technology; Microbiology; Pharmacology.

BUILDING

(including **Building Design, Building Services Engineering, Building Surveying, Construction, Fire Risk Engineering, Fire Safety Management; for Architectural Technology** see **Architecture;** see also **Property Management/Development)**

NB The points totals shown to the left of the institutions are for ease of reference only. It must not be assumed that tariff points are always used by institutions or that they can be substituted for an offer in grades. The level of an offer is not necessarily indicative of the quality of a course.

COURSE OFFERS INFORMATION
Subject requirements/preferences **GCSE** English, mathematics and science usually required. **AL** Physics and/or mathematics may be required for some courses.

Your target offers
340 pts **Manchester** – AAB–BBC (Blt Nat Env courses)
300 pts **London (UCL)** – BBB+AS (Proj Mgt Constr)
 Northumbria – 300 pts (MEng Bld Serv Eng)
 Ulster – 300 pts (Bld Surv)
280 pts **Loughborough** – 280–260 pts (Commer Mgt Quant Surv)
 Northumbria – 280 pts (Bld Surv)
 Nottingham Trent – 280 pts (Bld Surv)
 Ulster – 280 pts (Constr Eng Mgt)
270 pts **Glasgow Caledonian** – 270 pts (Bld Contr Surv; Bld Surv; Bld Serv Eng)
 Sheffield Hallam – 270 pts (Bld Surv)
260 pts **Anglia Ruskin** – 260 pts (Bld Surv)
 Aston – BCC–CCC 260–240 pts 3AL **or** 2AL+2AS (Constr Mgt; Constr Env Mgt; Constr Proj Mgt; Constr Hlth Sfty Mgt; Constr Trans Plan)
 Glasgow Caledonian – BCC (Fire Rsk Eng)
 Heriot-Watt – 260 pts 1st yr entry (Bld Surv; Constr Mgt; Constr Mgt (Bld Serv) (Proj Mgt))
 Loughborough – 260 pts (Constr Eng Mgt)
 Reading – 260–280 pts (3AL+AS) 260 pts (3AL) (Bld Constr Mgt; Bld Surv; Constr Mgt Surv)
 Salford – BCC 260 pts (Constr Mgt)

250 pts   **Kingston** – 250 pts (Bld Surv)
240 pts   **Anglia Ruskin** – 240 pts (Constr Mgt)
            Brunel – 240 pts (Mech Eng Bld Serv)
            Central Lancashire – 240 pts (Bld Serv Eng; Bld Surv; Constr Proj Mgt; Facil Mgt; Util Mgt)
            Glamorgan – 240 pts (Bld Serv Eng)
            Northumbria – 240 pts (Bld Des Mgt; Constr Mgt; Bld Serv Eng; Bld Proj Mgt)
            Nottingham – CCC (MEng Archit Env Des; Sust Blt Env)
            Salford – CCC 240 pts (Bld Surv)
230 pts   **Brighton** – 230 pts (Bld Surv)
            Bristol UWE – 230–260 pts (Bld Surv)
            Coventry – 230 pts (Bld Surv)
            Greenwich – 230 pts (Constr Bus Mgt (Bld Surv))
            Liverpool John Moores – 230 pts (Bld Surv)
            Napier – 230 pts (Bld Surv)
            Plymouth – 230 pts (Bld Surv Env)
            UCE Birmingham – 230 pts (Bld Surv)
            Wolverhampton – 230 pts (Bld Surv)
220 pts   **Bolton** – 220 pts (Constr Mgt; Bld Surv Prop Mgt; Constr)
            Brighton – 220 pts (Proj Mgt Constr)
            Coventry – 220 pts (Constr Mgt)
            Napier – 220 pts (Constr Proj Mgt)
            Nottingham Trent – 220 pts (Fin Proj Mgt Constr; Constr Mgt)
            Reading – 220 pts (Bld Surv – dist learn)
            Salford – CCD 220 pts (Constr Proj Mgt)
            Westminster – 220–240 pts (Bld Surv; Constr Surv; Bld Eng; Comm Mgt; Constr Mgt)
200 pts   **Napier** – 200 pts (Constr Eng)
            Oxford Brookes – BB (Constr Mgt)
            Plymouth – 200–220 pts (Constr Mgt Env)
            Sheffield Hallam – 200 pts (Constr Mgt; Constr Commer Mgt)
180 pts   **Anglia Ruskin** – 180–240 pts (Constr Econ Mgt; Prop Surv)
            Brighton – 180 pts (Bld St; Constr Mgt)
            Bristol UWE – 180–220 pts (Bld Serv Eng; Constr Commer Mgt; Constr Mgt; Constr Prop Mgt)
            Cardiff (UWIC) – 180 pts (Bld Mntnce Mgt)
            Glamorgan – 180 pts (Constr Mgt)
            Greenwich – 180 pts (Bld Surv; Des Constr Mgt)
            Kingston – 180 pts (Constr Mgt)
            Liverpool John Moores – 180 pts (Bld Des Tech Mgt; Constr Mgt)
            Portsmouth – 180–240 pts (Constr Eng Mgt)
            UCE Birmingham – 180 pts (Constr Mgt Econ; Prop Constr)
160 pts   **Bristol UWE** – 160 pts (Blt Nat Env)
            Central Lancashire – 160 pts (Fire Sfty Mgt)
            Derby – DDE–CD 160–140 pts (Constr Mgt)
            Glasgow Caledonian – CC (Bld Serv Eng)
            London South Bank – CC (Constr Mgt; Bld Serv Eng)
            Newport – 160 pts (Bld St)
            Oxford Brookes – DDE **or** DDdd (Building)
            Plymouth – 160 pts (Env Constr Surv)
            Robert Gordon – CC (Constr Des Mgt)
            Wolverhampton – 160–220 pts (Comp Aid Des Constr)
150 pts   **Napier** – 150 pts (Mntnce Surv)
120 pts   **Brighton** – 120 pts (Constr Tech)
            North East Wales (IHE) – 120 pts (Constr Mgt)

100 pts **Guildford (Coll)** – 100–80 pts (Construction)
Kingston – 100 pts (Fdn Constr Eng)
Southampton Solent – 100 pts (Constr Mgt)
Swansea (IHE) – 100 pts (Bld Cons Mgt; Proj Constr Mgt)
80 pts **Glasgow Met (Coll)** – 80 pts (Bld Surv; Bld Constr; Constr Mgt)
Guildford (Coll) – 80 pts (Building)
Nescot – EE (Constr Mgt; Facil Mgt)

Leeds Met – contact University

Alternative offers
IB offers Aston 29 pts; Brighton 28 pts; Bristol UWE 24–28 pts; London (UCL) 32 pts.
Scottish offers See **Chapter 7**.

OTHER HIGHER EDUCATION COURSES IN THE SUBJECT FIELD

Foundation degrees (contact the institutions for details) Anglia Ruskin; Barnfield (Coll); Barnsley (Univ Centre); Bedford (Coll); Bolton; Bolton (CmC); Brighton; Central Lancashire; Colchester (Inst); Derby; East Down (IFHE); East Lancashire (IHE); Glamorgan; Highbury (Coll); Kingston; Lambeth (Coll); London South Bank; Manchester (CAT); Mid-Kent (CFHE); North East Wales (IHE); North West London (Coll); Northumbria; Oldham (Coll); Peterborough (Coll); Portsmouth; St Helens (Coll); Sir Gar (Coll); Somerset (CAT); South Kent (Coll); Stockport (CFHE); Stoke on Trent (Coll); Swansea (IHE); West Nottinghamshire (Coll); Weymouth (Coll).

Higher National Diploma courses
120 pts and below
Adam Smith (Coll); Anglia Ruskin; Barking (Coll); Bell (Coll); Blackpool and Fylde (Coll); Bolton; Bradford (Coll); Brighton; Bromley (CFHE); Burton (Coll); Cardiff (UWIC); Central Lancashire; Colchester (Inst); Coventry; Creative Arts (UC); Derby; Doncaster (Univ Centre); Dudley (Coll); Dumfries and Galloway (Coll); Ealing, Hammersmith and West London (Coll); East Lancashire (IHE); Forth Valley (Coll); Glamorgan; Glasgow Caledonian; Glasgow Met (Coll); Gloucestershire; Gloucestershire (CAT); Greenwich (West Kent Coll); Grimsby (IFHE); Guildford (Coll); Hastings (Coll); Hertfordshire; Leeds Met; Liverpool John Moores; Llandrillo Cymru (Coll); London South Bank; Manchester (CAT) (HNC); Manchester Met; Menai (Coll); Mid-Kent (Coll); Napier EE; Nescot; Newport; North East London (Coll) (HNC); Northampton; Northumbria; Nottingham New (Coll); Nottingham Trent; Oxford Brookes; Pembrokeshire (Coll); Plymouth; Portsmouth; Preston (Coll); Robert Gordon; St Helens (Coll); Salford; Sheffield Hallam; Solihull (Coll); Somerset (CAT); South Birmingham (Coll); South Devon (Coll); Southend Campus Essex; Stockport (CFHE); Stoke on Trent (Coll); Swansea (IHE); Thames Valley; UCE Birmingham; UHI Millennium Inst; Wigan and Leigh (Coll); Willesden (CT); Wirral Met (Coll); Wolverhampton; Worcester (CT).

CHOOSING YOUR COURSE (SEE ALSO CH.1)

Subject information The building industry covers a wide range of activities and is closely allied to civil, municipal and structural engineering and quantity surveying. One branch of the industry covers building services engineering, a career which involves specialised areas such as heating, acoustics, lighting, refrigeration and air conditioning. Many Building courses include industrial placements. **Useful websites** www.ciob.org.uk; www.cibse.org; www.citb.org.uk.

Course variations Construction Health and Safety Management (Aston); Construction Commercial Management (Bristol UWE); Facilities Management (Central Lancashire); Building Services Engineering (Northumbria); Sustainable Built Environment (Nottingham); Building Surveying (Plymouth). *NOW CHECK PROSPECTUSES AND WEBSITES FOR ANY RECENT CHANGES.*

Universities and colleges teaching quality See www.tqi.ac.uk; www.qaa.ac.uk.

Top universities and colleges (Research) Loughborough; Reading; Salford.

Sandwich degree courses Aston; Bath; Bristol UWE; Brunel; Central Lancashire; Glamorgan; Kingston; Liverpool John Moores; London South Bank; Loughborough; Northumbria; Nottingham Trent; Oxford Brookes; Plymouth; Portsmouth; Sheffield Hallam; Ulster; Westminster; Wolverhampton.

ADMISSIONS INFORMATION

Number of applicants per place (approx) Bristol UWE (Constr Mgt) 5; Glamorgan 3; Glasgow Caledonian 6; Heriot-Watt 6; Kingston 4; London (UCL) 4; Loughborough 4; Napier 8; Northumbria 6; Salford (Bld Surv) 6; Sheffield Hallam (Bld Surv) 7; Strathclyde 5.

Advice to applicants and planning the UCAS personal statement Details of work experience with any levels of responsibility should be included. Make contact with any building organisation to arrange a meeting with staff to discuss careers in building. Building also covers civil engineering, surveying, quantity surveying etc and these areas should also be explored. **London South Bank** (Bld Serv Eng) Knowledge of the profession. **Loughborough** Ability to work in a team. **Salford** Personal achievement in technological areas, work experience. **UCE Birmingham** We look for evidence of work experience in the construction industry. See also **Appendix 2**.

Misconceptions about this course **Loughborough** Some students fail to realise that the degree includes law, finance, economics and management plus constructional technology.

Selection interviews **Yes** Bradford (Coll), Brunel, Derby, Glamorgan, Glasgow Caledonian, Greenwich, Kingston, Liverpool John Moores, London South Bank, Loughborough, Plymouth, Robert Gordon, Sheffield Hallam, Staffordshire, Westminster; **Some** Brighton, Central England, Salford.

Interview advice and questions Work experience in the building and civil engineering industries is important and you could be expected to describe any building project you have visited and any problems experienced in its construction. A knowledge of the range of activities to be found on a building site will be expected, for example the work of quantity and land surveyors and the various building trades. **Loughborough** The applicant should show an understanding of the role of the quantity surveyor. See also **Chapter 6**.

Reasons for rejection (non-academic) Inability to communicate. Lack of motivation. Indecisiveness about reasons for choosing the course. **Loughborough** Applicant more suited to hands-on rather than an academic course.

AFTER-RESULTS ADVICE

Universities with vacancies in Clearing (2006) Anglia Ruskin; Bolton; Bradford; Brighton; Bristol UWE; Central Lancashire; Derby; Glamorgan; Greenwich; Kingston; London South Bank; Napier; Northumbria; Nottingham; Nottingham Trent; Plymouth; Portsmouth; Reading; Salford; Sheffield Hallam; Southampton Solent; Thames Valley; UCE Birmingham; Westminster; Wolverhampton.

Offers to applicants repeating A-levels **Higher** Liverpool John Moores, Strathclyde; **Possibly higher** Bristol UWE; **Same** Bolton, Brighton, Coventry, Heriot-Watt, Huddersfield, Kingston, London (UCL), Loughborough, Northumbria, Robert Gordon, UCE Birmingham.

GRADUATE DESTINATIONS AND EMPLOYMENT (2005 HESA)

Graduates surveyed 845 Employed 620 In further study 15 Assumed unemployed 45.

OTHER DEGREE SUBJECTS FOR CONSIDERATION

Architecture; Civil Engineering; Quantity Surveying; Surveying.

BUSINESS COURSES

(Section A: Business and Management Courses; **Section B:** International and European Business and Management Courses, Business and Management Courses with Languages; **Section C:** Specialised Business and Management Courses including Advertising, E-Commerce, Entrepreneurship, Operations Management and Publishing; see also **Hospitality, Hotel and Catering Management, Human Resource Management, Leisure and Recreation Management/Studies, Marketing, Retail Management** and **Tourism)**

NB The points totals shown to the left of the institutions are for ease of reference only. It must not be assumed that tariff points are always used by institutions or that they can be substituted for an offer in grades. The level of an offer is not necessarily indicative of the quality of a course.

COURSE OFFERS INFORMATION
Subject requirements/preferences **GCSE** Mathematics and English often at grade A or B required. **Aberdeen, Belfast (Queen's), Dundee, Edinburgh, Glasgow, Nottingham** English, mathematics or science and a foreign language. **Bangor** Average of grade Bs. **Belfast (Queen's), Birmingham, Brighton, City, Dundee, East Anglia, Huddersfield, Lancaster, Leeds, London Met, Loughborough, Napier, Oxford Brookes, Portsmouth, Sheffield, Sheffield Hallam** (or grade C at A-level), **Southampton, Swansea, Warwick** All require mathematics at grade A or B. **Buckingham** Five grade Bs minimum. **De Montfort** Four subjects grade A–B. **European Bus Sch London** Five subjects at grade A preferred. **Exeter** Majority of subjects grade A*, A or B. **Hull** Three grade As, three grade Bs, three grade Cs preferred. **Kingston** Prefer mathematics grade B or higher. **London (LSE)** Grade A mathematics. **Warwick** Seven subjects grades A–B including English and mathematics. **AL** Mathematics required for some courses and a language will be stipulated for most courses in Section B. In some cases grades A, B or C may be required.

SECTION A: BUSINESS AND MANAGEMENT COURSES
(Refer to **Section B** and **Section C** for other Business courses)

Your target offers
360 pts **and above**
    Bath – AAA–AAB (Bus Admin)
    Cambridge – competitive entry after 2 or 3 yrs **or** another Cambridge Tripos course (Mgt St)
    Northumbria – 360 pts (Corp Mgt)
    Warwick – AABb **or** AAbbb (Management)
340 pts **Birmingham** – AAB–ABB (Bus Mgt courses)
    Bristol – AAB–BBB (Acc Mgt; Econ Mgt)
    City – AAB (Bus St; Mgt)
    Durham – AAB (Bus Econ)
    Exeter – AAB–BBB (Bus Acc; Bus Mgt; Bus Engl Lang; Mgt Ldrshp)
    Leeds – AAB (Management)
    London (King's) – AAB–ABB (Bus Mgt)
    London (LSE) – AAB **or** AAbbb (Management)
    Loughborough – 340–320 pts (Spo Sci Mgt)
    Manchester – AAB–BBB (Bus St; Mgt courses; Bus St Econ)
    St Andrews – AAB–ABB (Mgt courses)
    Southampton – AAB 340 pts (Mgt; Mgt Sci courses)
320 pts **Aston** – ABB–AAB 320–340 pts (Bus courses)
    Cardiff – ABB (Bus Mgt)
    Glasgow – ABB–AAA (Bus Mgt)
    Kent – 320 pts (MSci App Bus Mgt)
    Lancaster – ABB (Bus St (Acc) (Fin); Org St Psy; Org St Sociol; Bus St; Mgt)
    Leeds – ABB (Mgt Trans St)

198 | Business Courses

Liverpool – 320 pts (Bus St)
London (QM) – 320–300 pts (Bus Mgt; IT Org Mgt)
London (RH) – ABB (Mgt; Mgt Mark; Mgt Inf Sys; Mgt Acc; Mgt Econ)
Loughborough – ABB (Mgt Sci; Inf Mgt Bus St)
Newcastle – ABB (Bus Mgt; Agri-Bus Mgt)
Northumbria – 320 pts ABB (Bus St; Bus Mgt)
Nottingham – ABB (Mgt St)
Nottingham Trent – ABB 320 pts (Bus Mgt)
Reading – ABB (Mgt Bus Admin; Acc Mgt)
Sheffield – ABB–BBC (Mgt courses)
Surrey – 320 pts (Bus Mgt)
Sussex – ABB **or** 360 pts 3AL+AS (Bus Mgt St)
York – ABB (Mgt; Phys Bus Mgt; Mgt IT)

300 pts **Belfast (Queen's)** – BBB (Mgt; Mgt Inf Sys)
Bournemouth – 300 pts (Bus St)
East Anglia – BBB–BBC (Bus Mgt)
Edinburgh – BBB (Bus St; Bus St Acc; Bus St Econ; Bus St Geog; Bus St Law)
Hull – BBB–BBC (Mgt courses; Bus courses)
Keele – BBB–BCC 300–260 pts (Bus Admin courses)
Kent – 300 pts (BSc App Bus Mgt; Mgt Sci courses)
Leeds – BBB–BCC (Mgt Perf)
London (LSE) – BBB (Mgt Sci)
Manchester – BBB (Mgt Mark Tex)
Oxford Brookes – BBB (Bus Mgt; Bus Log; Bus Innov Ent; Bus Int Fin; Bus Fin Mgrs; Bus Mark Comm)

280 pts **Brunel** – 280 pts (Bus Mgt; Bus Mgt (Acc); Bus St Spo Sci)
De Montfort – 280 pts (Bus St)
Durham (Stockton) – BBC (Bus Fin; Bus)
Essex – 280 pts (Bus Mgt; Proj Mgt)
Kent – 280 pts (Bus Admin; Bus Admin (Mark) (Ind) (Comp); Bus Admin joint courses)
Leicester – 280–320 pts (Mgt St)
Liverpool – 280 pts (E-Business)
Loughborough – 280 pts (Geog Mgt; Maths Mgt; Phys Mgt)
Oxford Brookes – BBC (Bus Rl Est)
Strathclyde – BBC/AB (Tech Bus St; Mgt courses)
Westminster – 280 pts (Bus Mgt courses; Bus St courses; Bus courses)

260 pts **Aberystwyth** – 260 pts (Bus Mgt; Bus Econ; Bus Fin)
Bradford – 260 pts (Bus Econ)
Bristol UWE – 260–300 pts (Bus Prop)
Chester – 260 pts (Bus St; Mgt)
Coventry – 260 pts (Bus St; Bus Mgt; Bus Admin)
Heriot-Watt – BCC 260 pts (Bus Fin; Mgt; Mgt Bus Law; Mgt Ops Mgt; Mgt Mark; Bus Econ)
Hull – 260 pts (Bus Mark)
Imperial London – 260–300 pts (BSc App Bus Mgt)
Keele – 260–320 pts (Mgt Sci; Bus Admin)
Kent – BCC 260 pts (Mgt Sci; Mgt Sci Comp; Mgt Sci Yr Abrd/USA)
London (SOAS) – BCC (Mgt courses)
Richmond (Am Int Univ) – 260pts (Bus Admin (Fin))
Stirling – BCC (Mgt Sci; Bus St; Pblc Mgt Admin)
Stranmillis (UC) – BCC 260 pts (Bus St Educ)
Swansea – 260 pts (Bus Mgt; Bus Mgt (Acc) (Fin) (Mark); Mgt Sci; Mgt Sci (Acc) (Fin) (Mark))

240 pts **Aberdeen** – CCC **or** aabb (Mgt St)
Bangor – 240–280 pts (Bus St Fin; Bus St Fr/Ger/Ital/Span; Bus Soc Admin; Bus St Mark; Mgt Acc; Mgt Bank Fin; Admin Mgt; Bus Mgt Frsty)

Loughborough University
Business School

Loughborough University Business School runs outstanding degree programmes in business and management. From part-time programmes for working professionals to conversion programmes for non-business graduates, the Business School offers a wealth of career-enhancing courses to fuel your ambition.

"Loughborough offers so much: apart from degree courses, Loughborough holds one of the highest employability ratings for its graduates. Would I have chosen any other university? No."
Olusegun Cadmus, MSc in IM graduate

For high-flyers in business:
The Loughborough MBA

For non-business graduates:
MSc in Management
MSc in Business Analysis and Management
MSc in Finance and Management
MSc in International Management
MSc in Marketing and Management

For graduates seeking higher education:
Postgraduate Research Programmes

For working managers seeking career advancement:
Certificates, Diplomas and MSc's in Management

Invest in your future and transform your career prospects

www.lboro.ac.uk/businessschool

Loughborough University **Business School**
tel: +44 (0)1509 223140 (MBA & short courses),
223291 (MSc's) or 228276 (PhD)
email: pmdc@lboro.ac.uk **fax:** +44 (0)1509 223963

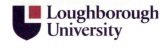
Loughborough University

Ref: **BS/4018**

200 | Business Courses

Bradford – 240 pts (Bus St Law; Bus Comp; Bus Mgt St 4 yrs)
Brighton – 240–260 pts (Bus St; Bus St E-Commer; Bus St Fin; Bus St Law; Bus St Mark; Bus Mgt courses)
Bristol UWE – 240–260 pts (Bus courses except under **260 pts**; Mgt)
Buckingham – 240 pts (Bus St; Bus Ent)
Chester (Warrington) – 240 pts (Bus courses; Mgt courses)
De Montfort – 240 pts (Acc Bus; Bus Mgt; Bus Mark; Bus Mgt Ent; E-Bus Mgt)
Hertfordshire – 240–200 pts (Bus St; Bus Admin; Mgt Sci)
Huddersfield – 240 pts (Bus St; Bus Mgt; Bus Psy; Bus Journal; E-Commer Tech; Bus Inf Mgt)
Kingston – 240–280 pts (Bus St; Bus Law; Bus Mgt Analys)
Lincoln – 240 pts (Bus St; Mgt)
Liverpool John Moores – 240 pts (Bus St)
Northumbria – 240 pts (Bus joint courses)
Nottingham Trent – 240–220 pts (Biol Bus; Bus Inf Sys)
Oxford Brookes – CCC (Bus Inf Sys)
Plymouth – 240–200 pts (Bus St; Bus Inf Comm Tech; Marit Bus)
Portsmouth – 240 pts (Bus Ent Dev; Bus Admin; Bus St)
Robert Gordon – CCC (Mgt; Mgt Fin; Mgt Econ; Mgt Mark)
Salford – 240–260 pts (Bus Decn Analys; Mgt Sci; Bus Mgt St; Bus Mgt St (Law) (Fin); Bus IT)
Sheffield Hallam – 240 pts (Bus courses except under **220 pts**)
Ulster – 240–200 pts (Bus courses)

220 pts **Abertay Dundee** – CCD (Bus St; Fin Bus Fin)
Anglia Ruskin – 220 pts (Bus Law)
Bolton – 220 pts (Bus St; E-Bus)
Gloucestershire – 220 pts (Mgt; Bus Mgt)
Heriot-Watt (Scottish Borders) – CCD (Bus Mgt Ind; Bus Admin; Bus Admin IT)
Kent – 220 pts (Bus St Yr Ind)
Liverpool Hope – 220 pts (Bus St)
Liverpool John Moores – 220 pts (Bus Admin; Bus Mgt Inf)
Manchester Met – 220–280 pts (Mgt Sys Comb Hons)
Oxford Brookes – CCD (Bus Stats; Bus Comb Hons)
Sheffield Hallam – 220 pts (Bus Tech; Mgt Comm Tech)
Westminster – 220–280 pts (Bus Mgt; Bus St)
Winchester – 220 pts (Bus Mgt courses)

200 pts **Anglia Ruskin** – 200 pts (Bus Mgt; Bus St; Bus Soc Pol)
Bath Spa – 200–240 pts (Bus Mgt)
Bournemouth – 200–240 pts (Bus IT)
Bradford – 200–220 pts (Bus Mgt St 3 yrs)
Central Lancashire – 200–260 pts (Bus Econ; Bus IT; Bus St)
De Montfort – 200 pts (Bus Mgt)
Edge Hill – 200 pts (Bus Mgt St; Bus Law)
Hertfordshire – 200–240 pts (Bus joint courses; Mgt Sci)
Hull (Scarborough) – 200–220 pts (Bus Mgt)
Kent (Medway) – 200 pts (Bus IT Yr Ind)
Liverpool John Moores – 200 pts (Bus Econ; Bus Fin; Bus Mgt; Bus PR; E-Bus)
Manchester Met – 200–260 pts (Bus Ent; Bus; Bus St)
Middlesex – 200–240 pts (Bus St; Bus Admin; Mgt)
Napier – 200 pts (Bus St)
Newport – 200 pts (E-Bus Mgt)
Nottingham Trent – 200 pts (Bus Comp Sci)
Plymouth – 200 pts (Marit Bus; Marit Bus Marit Law; Marit Bus Log)
Portsmouth – 200 pts (e Business)
Roehampton – 200 pts (Bus St; Inf Mgt; Bus Mgt)

Sunderland – 200–220 pts (Bus Mgt courses)

UCE Birmingham – 200–240 pts (Bus Psy Bus; Bus St; Mgt Comb)

Westminster – CDD (Inf Sys Bus Mgt)

180 pts **Cardiff (UWIC)** – BC 180 pts (Bus St courses)

Chichester – 180–220 pts (Bus St courses)

Lampeter – open admission policy (Bus Mgt)

Liverpool John Moores – 180 pts (Bus Econ; Bus Inf Sys)

Marjon (Coll) – 180–240 pts (Mgt courses)

Northampton – 180–220 pts (Bus; Bus St; Bus Bus Entre; Mgt)

Queen Margaret (UC) – 180 pts (Bus Mgt)

Staffordshire – 180–240 pts (Bus St; Bus Mgt; Bus Mgt Entre; Bus Comp)

160 pts **Canterbury Christ Church** – CC (Bus St joint courses; Bus St; Bus St Acc; Bus St Mark; Bus St Adv)

Central Lancashire – 160–180 pts (Bus Ent; Bus ICT; Bus Int Sys; Bus Mgt)

De Montfort – 160–200 pts (e-Commer Sys)

Derby – 160–200 pts (Bus Mgt; Bus St)

Doncaster (Univ Centre) – 160 pts (Bus courses)

East London – 160 pts (Bus St; Entre)

Farnborough (CT) – 160–200 pts (Bus Mgt; Bus Mgt Fin)

Glasgow Caledonian – CC (Bus Inf Mgt; Bus St)

Greenwich – 160 pts (Bus Admin; Bus St; Ops Log Mgt)

Harper Adams (UC) – 160–240 pts (Bus Mgt Mark)

Leeds Trinity and All Saints (Coll) – CC 160 pts (Bus Mgt; Bus)

London Met – 160 pts (Bus St; Bus Bus Ent; Bus Bus IT; Bus Admin)

Newman (CHE) – 160–240 pts (Mgt St courses)

Paisley – CC (Bus; Mgt)

Peterborough Reg (Coll) – 160 pts (Bus Sociol)

Regents Bus Sch London – check with School (Bus courses)

Roehampton – 160 pts (Bus St)

Royal (CAg) – 160 pts (Bus Mgt)

St Mary's (Coll) – 160–200 pts (Mgt St)

SAC (Scottish CAg) – 160 pts (Rur Bus Mgt)

Southampton Solent – 160 pts (Bus St; Bus Mgt; Bus Fin Mgt; Bus Soc Sci; Bus Psy)

Southend Campus Essex – 160 pts (Business)

Teesside – 160 pts (Bus Mgt; Bus St)

Thames Valley – 160 pts (Bus St)

Wolverhampton – 160–220 pts (Bus; Bus Mgt; Bus Inf Mgt)

Worcester – 160 pts (Bus Mgt)

Writtle (Coll) – 160 pts (Bus Mgt)

York St John – CC 160 pts (Bus Mgt)

140 pts **Bell (Coll)** – CD 140 pts (Bus St)

202 | Business Courses

Newport – 140–160 pts (Bus courses except under **200 pts**)
Trinity Carmarthen (Coll) – 140 pts (Inf Sys Mgt; Bus St)
120 pts **Bedfordshire** – 120–160 pts (Bus St courses)
Bradford (Coll) – 120 pts (Bus St; Bus Admin)
Buckinghamshire Chilterns (UC) – 120–180 pts (Bus Mgt courses)
London South Bank – DD–CC (Bus St; Bus Admin; Mgt Comb)
Northbrook (Coll) – 120 pts (Bus Admin)
100 pts **Suffolk (Univ Campus)** – 100–120 pts (Bus Mgt courses)
80 pts **Croydon (Coll)** – 80–100 pts (Bus courses)
Greenwich (Sch Mgt) – 80–120 pts (Bus Mgt IT)
Holborn (Coll) – 80 pts (Bus Admin)
Llandrillo Cymru (Coll) – 80 pts min (Mgt Bus)
London (Birk) – 80 pts under 21s (over 21 varies) (p/t Mgt)
North East Wales (IHE) – 80–160 pts (Bus Mgt; Bus Acc)
Norwich City (Coll) – 80 pts (Bus Mgt)
Swansea (IHE) – 80 pts (Bus St; Bus Psy; Mgt)
UHI Millennium Inst (IC) – 80 pts (Bus Mgt)
West Anglia (Coll) – 80 pts (Bus Mgt)
West Suffolk (Coll) – 80–160 pts (Bus Mgt)
60 pts **Colchester (Inst)** – 60 pts (Management)
Exeter (Coll) – 60 pts (Bus Mgt yr 3 entry option)
40 pts **Wigan and Leigh (Coll)** – D (Business)

Leeds Met – contact University
Open University – contact University

SECTION B: INTERNATIONAL AND EUROPEAN BUSINESS AND MANAGEMENT COURSES, BUSINESS AND MANAGEMENT COURSES WITH LANGUAGES
(Refer to **Section A** and **Section C** for other Business courses)

Your target offers
360 pts **and above**
Lancaster – AAA (Bus St N Am/Aus; Org St N Am/Aus; Mgt N Am/Aus; Bus Op Mgt; Int Bus (Econ) N Am/Aus)
Manchester – AAA (Int Mgt Am Bus St)
Warwick – AABb **or** AAbbb (Int Bus)
340 pts **Bath** – AAB 340 pts (Int Mgt Fr/Ger/Span)
Birmingham – AAB–ABB 320 pts (Int Bus Lang; Int Bus Comms)
Manchester – AAB (Int Bus Fin Econ)
Southampton – AAB 340 pts (Mgt Sci Fr/Ger/Span)
320 pts **Aston** – ABB 320–300 pts (Int Bus Mgt Fr/Ger; Int Bus Econ)
Cardiff – ABB–BBB (Int Mgt; Bus Mgt Euro Lang; Bus Mgt Jap)
Lancaster – ABB (Euro Mgt Fr/Ger/Ital/Span; Int Bus Econ)
Liverpool – 320 pts (Int Bus)
London (RH) – ABB 320 pts (Mgt Fr/Ger/Ital; Mgt Int Bus; Mgt Maths Euro; Mgt Lang)
Loughborough – ABB (Int Bus)
Newcastle – ABB–BBB (Modn Lang Mgt St; Bus St Fr/Ger/Span)
Nottingham – ABB (Mgt St Chin St/Fr/Ger/Span; Mgt Chin St/As St/Fr/Ger/Span; Int Bus – China campus)
Reading – ABB 320–350 pts (Int Mgt Bus Admin Fr/Ger/Ital)
Sheffield – ABB (Mgt Jap St; Kor St Mgt; E As St Mgt; Chin St Mgt; Fr/Ger/Russ Mgt)
300 pts **Belfast (Queen's)** – BBB–BCC (Mgt Fr/Ger/Span)
Dundee – 300 pts 4 yrs (Int Bus; Int Bus Fr/Ger/Span)
East Anglia – ABC (Lang Mgt St Fst Trk)

For information on how to read the Subject Tables, see **Chapter 7.**

Edinburgh – BBB (Bus St Fr/Ger/Span; Int Bus; Int Bus Arbc/Chin/Fr/Ger/Ital/Jap/
Russ/Span)
Essex – 300 pts (Bus Mgt Modn Lang)
Liverpool – BBB 300 pts (Bus St Fr/Ger/Ital; Bus St Hisp St)
Stirling – BBB 2nd yr entry (Bus St Fr/Span)
Strathclyde – BBB–ABC (Int Bus (Acc))
Surrey – BBB–BCC 300–260 pts (Bus Mgt Fr)

280 pts **Essex** – 280–260 pts (Lat Am St Bus Mgt)
Heriot-Watt – BBC 280 pts (Int Bus Langs)
Leicester – BBC (Modn Lang Mgt)
Northumbria – 280 pts (Int Bus Mgt)
Oxford Brookes – BBC (Int Bus Mgt)
Strathclyde – BBC (Int Bus Modn Lang)
Westminster – BBC 280 pts (Int Bus Arbc/Chin/Fr/Span; Int Bus; Euro Mgt)

260 pts **Brunel** – 260 pts (Int Bus)
Coventry – 260 pts (Int Bus Mgt)
East Anglia – BCC (Lang Mgt St Abrd)
Heriot-Watt – BCC 260 pts 1st yr entry (Int Mgt)
Kent – 260–320 pts (Bus Admin Ital/Span; Mgt Sci Fr/Ger/Ital/Span)
Richmond (Am Int Univ) – 260 pts (Bus Admin (Int Bus))
Swansea – 260–300 pts (Int Bus Mgt; Int Mgt Sci N Am/Euro; Int Mgt Sci Lang)

240 pts **Aberdeen** – CCC (Euro Mgt St)
Bradford – 240 pts (Int Bus Mgt)
Central Lancashire – 240–280 pts (Bus Mgt Chin)
De Montfort – 240 pts (Int Bus Glob; Int Mark Bus)
Dundee – 240 pts 3 yrs (Int Bus; Int Bus Fr/Ger/Span)
Hertfordshire – 240–200 pts (Int Bus)
Huddersfield – 240 pts (Int Bus; Int Bus Glob Pol)
Kingston – 240–280 pts (Int Bus; Int Bus Fr/Span)
Nottingham Trent – CCC 240 pts (Int Bus; Int Bus Admin)
Plymouth – 240 pts (Int Bus; Int Bus Lang)
Salford – 240–260 pts (Bus St Int Bus Mgt; Mgt Modn Lang; Mgt Sci N Am)
Sheffield Hallam – 240 pts (Int Bus St)
Stirling – CCC (Int Mgt St Int Cult St; Modn Lang Bus St)
Swansea – 240 pts (Bus St Fr/Ger)
UCE Birmingham – 240 pts (Int Bus)
Ulster – CCC (Bus St Int Pol)
Westminster – CCC/BB (Euro Mgt Fr/Ger/Span)

220 pts **Bournemouth** – 220 pts (Bus St Langs)
Brighton – 220 pts (Int Bus)
Glamorgan – 220 pts (Int Bus St)
Gloucestershire – 220 pts (Int Bus Mark; Int Bus Mgt)
Greenwich – 220–160 pts (Int Bus; Int Bus Chin)
Hull – 220–260 pts (Int Bus)

200 pts **Anglia Ruskin** – 200 pts (Int Bus; Bus Fr/Ger/Span; Int Mgt)
Lincoln – 200 pts (Euro Bus St)
Liverpool John Moores – 200 pts (Int Bus St Fr/Ger/Span)
Manchester Met – 200–260 pts (Int Bus)
Portsmouth – 200–240 pts (Int Bus St; Euro Bus)
Sheffield Hallam – 200 pts (Int Bus St Chin/Fr/Ger/Ital/Span; Int Bus St)

190 pts **London Met** – 190 pts (Int Bus; Int Bus Comb; Bus Law Int Bus)

180 pts **Cardiff (UWIC)** – 180 pts (Bus St Lang)
Derby – 180–200 pts (Int Bus Mgt)
Staffordshire – 180–240 pts (Int Bus Mgt)
Teesside – 180–220 pts (Int Bus)

160 pts **Canterbury Christ Church** – CC (Int Bus Mgt)
Central Lancashire – 160–220 pts (Int Bus Acc; Int Bus Mark; Int Bus)
East London – 160 pts (Int Bus courses)
Euro Bus Sch – CC 160 pts (Int Bus courses)
Glasgow Caledonian – CC (Int Bus)
London Met – 160–200 pts (Int Bus)
Middlesex – 160–200 pts (Mgt Fr/Ger)
Newport – 160 pts (Int Bus)
Royal (CAg) – 160 pts (Int Bus Mgt)
Southampton Solent – 160 pts (Int Bus Mgt; Int Bus Mgt Engl; Bus Euro St)
Wolverhampton – 160–220 pts (Int Bus Mgt)
140 pts **Cardiff (UWIC)** – CD 140 pts (Int Bus Mgt)
120 pts **Bedfordshire** – 120–160 pts (Int Bus St)
Buckinghamshire Chilterns (UC) – 120–180 pts (Int Mgt)
80 pts **Regents Bus Sch London** – check with Sch (Int Bus; Int Bus Des Mgt)

Leeds Met – contact University

SECTION C: SPECIALISED BUSINESS AND MANAGEMENT COURSES INCLUDING:

Advertising, Air Transport Management, Arts Management, Consumer and Product Management, E-Commerce, Entrepreneurship, Events Management, Fashion Management, Heritage Management, Industrial Relations, Operations Management, Public Relations, Publishing, Quality Management, Trading Standards, Transport Management.

(Refer to **Section A** and **Section B** for other Business courses)

Your target offers

340 pts **Cardiff** – AAB–CCC 340–260 pts (Ind Rel Sociol)
Southampton – AAB 340 pts (Mgt Entre)
Ulster – AAB 340 pts (Comm Adv Mark)
320 pts **Lancaster** – ABB (Adv Econ Mark; Ops Mgt N Am/Aus)
London (RH) – ABB (Mgt Hum Res)
Newcastle – ABB (Mark Mgt)
300 pts **Bournemouth** – 300 pts (PR; Adv Mark Comm)
Hull – 300 pts (Mgt Bus Econ; Mgt Mark)
Lancaster – BBB **or** AAac/bb **or** ABaa 300 pts (Adv Mark)
Loughborough – 300 pts (Air Trans Mgt; Trans Bus Mgt)
Manchester – ABC (Tex Tech (Bus Mgt))
Manchester – BBB–BCC (Mgt Leis)
Southampton – BBB (IT Org)
280 pts **Coventry** – 280 pts (Crea Ind Mgt)
De Montfort – 280 pts (Adv Mark Comm)
Liverpool – BBC–BBB (e-Business)
Loughborough – 280 pts (Pub Engl)
Surrey – 280 pts (Entre Tech IT Bus)
Swansea – 280 pts (Pblc Media Rel)
UCE Birmingham – 280 pts (Media Comm (PR))
260 pts **Arts London (CFash)** – BCC (Fash Mgt)
Aston – BCC–CCC (Log Mgt; Trans Mgt; Tech Ent Mgt)
Central Lancashire – 260–300 pts (Mgt PR)
Chester (Warrington) – 260 pts (Advertising)
Coventry – 260 pts (Adv Bus; Adv Mark)
Newcastle – BCC (Farm Bus Mgt)
Oxford Brookes – BCC **or** BCcc (Publishing)
Sunderland – 260 pts (PR)
240 pts **Aberdeen** – CCC (Entrepreneurship)
Bradford – 240 pts (Pharml Mgt)

Huddersfield – 240–320 pts (Adv Mark Comm; PR Media; Adv Media Des Mgt)
Lincoln – 240 pts (Adv Art Dir)
Manchester Met – 240 pts (Fash Buy)
Nottingham Trent – 240 pts (Fash Tex Mgt)
Portsmouth – 240 pts (Bus Ent Dev)
Robert Gordon – CCC (Publishing)
Sheffield Hallam – 240 pts (Bus Tech)
Strathclyde – CCC (Ent Tech Mgt)
Westminster – CCC (Fash Merch Mgt)
220 pts **Bangor** – 220–260 pts (Bus Soc Admin)
Central Lancashire – 220–260 pts (PR)
De Montfort – 220 pts (Arts Mgt)
Gloucestershire – 220 pts (Evnts Mgt)
Liverpool John Moores – 220 pts (Mgt Trans Log)
Southampton Solent – 220–240 pts (Wtrspo St Mgt)
200 pts **Central Lancashire** – 200–260 pts (Adv Mark Comm; Evnt Mgt; Fire Sfty Mgt; Fire Eng Mgt; Herit Mgt)
Coventry – 200–260 pts (Disas Mgt)
De Montfort – 200 pts (Des Mgt Innov)
Huddersfield – 200 pts (Evnts Mgt)
Lincoln – CDD 200 pts (PR; Adv)
London Met – 200 pts (Avn Mgt)
Manchester Met – 200–260 pts (Adv Mgt Brnd Mgt; Evnts Mgt)
Napier – 200 pts (Pub Media; Fstvl Evnts Mgt)
Plymouth – 200 pts (Marit Bus courses; Cru Op Mgt)
Portsmouth – 200–180 pts (e-Bus; Ent Prod Des; Ent Soft Dev)
Southampton Solent – 200 pts (Adv; PR Comm)
Staffordshire – 200 pts (Adv Brnd Mgt; Des Mgt)
UCE Birmingham – 200 pts (Bus Mark; Bus PR; Bus Adv)
180 pts **Birmingham (CFTCS)** – 180 pts (Fd Consum Mgt; Enter Mgt)
Bristol UWE – 180 pts (Bus Ent)
Glamorgan – 180–220 pts (Evnts Mgt)
Greenwich – 180 pts min (Evnts Mgt)
Liverpool (LIPA) – BC 180 pts (Arts Mus Enter Mgt)
Marjon (Coll) – 180–240 pts (PR)
Northampton – 180–220 pts (Bus Entre; Adv Des; Adv PR)
Queen Margaret (UC) – DDD (Evnts Mgt; PR Media; PR Mark)
Southampton Solent – 180 pts (Marit Bus; Evnts Mgt)
Swansea (IHE) – 180–120 pts (Trans Mgt; Mtspo Mgt; Sply Chn Mgt)
Teesside – 180–240 pts (PR; Bus Inf Sys; Disas Mgt)
Thames Valley – 180 pts (Airln Airpt Mgt; Bus Trav Tour)
160 pts **Bedfordshire** – 160 pts (Pblc Serv Mgt)
CAFRE – CC 160 pts (Sply Chn Mgt (Fd))
Central Lancashire – 160 pts (Org Bhv; Mgt Mark)
Derby – 160–200 pts (Evnts Mgt; Ent Mgt)
East London – 160 pts (Bus St (Entre))
Glasgow Caledonian – CC (Fash Bus; Enter Evnts Mgt)
Gloucestershire – 160–220 pts (Evnts Mgt)
London Met – 160 pts (Evnts Mgt; PR; Arts Mgt; Bus Ent; Adv Mark Commun)
London South Bank – CC (Arts Mgt)
Middlesex – 160–200 pts (Pub Media)
Paisley – CC (Ent St; Evnts Mgt)
Royal (CAg) – 160–240 pts (Bus Mgt (Agri Fd))
SAC (Scottish CAg) – CC (Rur Bus Mgt (Eqn) (Anim Sci))
Salford – 160 pts (Des Mgt Crea Ind)

For information on how to read the Subject Tables, see **Chapter 7**.

208 | Business Courses

Thames Valley – 160 pts (Adv; Evnts Mgt; PR)
Wolverhampton – 160–220 pts (PR)
140 pts **Cardiff (UWIC)** – CD 140 pts (Tr Stand)
Dartington (CA) – 140–160 pts (Mus Cult Entre)
Liverpool John Moores – 140 pts (Mar Bus Mgt)
Trinity Carmarthen (Coll) – 140 pts (Adv courses)
120 pts **Bedfordshire** – 120–160 pts (PR)
Buckinghamshire Chilterns (UC) – 120 pts (Bus Adv Mgt; Adv Prom Mgt; Airln Airpt Mgt; PR Mgt)
Grimsby (IFHE) – 120 pts (Bus Tour Mgt)
100 pts **Suffolk (Univ Campus)** – 100–120 pts (Evnts Mgt)
80 pts **and below**
Arts London (CComm) – 2AL contact admissions tutor (Publishing)
Creative Arts (UC) – (Adv Brnd Mgt)
Swansea (IHE) – 80 pts (Commer Mgt)

Leeds Met – contact University

Alternative offers
IB offers Aberdeen 30 pts; Aberystwyth 29 pts; Aston 34 pts; Bangor 28 pts; Bath 35 pts; Birmingham 34 pts; Brighton 28 pts; Bristol 32–36 pts; Bristol UWE 26–32 pts; Central Lancashire 34–36 pts; Chester 30 pts; Chichester 28 pts; City 35 pts; Coventry 24 pts; Dundee 29 pts; East Anglia 30–32 pts; Essex 32 pts; Exeter 32–35 pts; Glasgow 30 pts; Keele 28–32 pts; Kent 27–33 pts; Lancaster 34–36 pts; Leicester 30 pts; Liverpool 30–32 pts; London (LSE) 36 pts, (QM) 32 pts, (RH) 33 pts, (SOAS) 30 pts; Loughborough 36 pts; Manchester 33–35 pts; Manchester Met 24–28 pts; Newcastle 33–35 pts; Nottingham 32 pts; Reading 33 pts; St Andrews 32 pts; Salford 28–32 pts; Sheffield 30–32 pts; Southampton 35 pts; Staffordshire 26 pts; Stirling 28–30 pts; Sussex 34 pts; Warwick 36 pts; York 36 pts.
Scottish offers See **Chapter 7**.

OTHER HIGHER EDUCATION COURSES IN THE SUBJECT FIELD

Foundation degrees (contact the institutions for details) Abingdon and Witney (Coll); Amersham (Coll); Anglia Ruskin; Arts London (CComm); Askham Bryan (CAg); Barnet (Coll); Barnfield (Coll); Bath Spa; Bedfordshire; Bexley (Coll); Birmingham (CFTCS); Bishop Auckland (Coll); Blackpool and Fylde (Coll); Bolton; Bournemouth; Bournemouth and Poole (Coll); Bracknell (Coll); Bradford; Bridgend (Coll); Brighton; Bristol City (Coll); Bromley (CFHE); Buckinghamshire Chilterns (UC); Burnley (Coll); Central Lancashire; Central Sussex (Coll); Chesterfield (Coll); Colchester (Inst); Cornwall (Coll); Coventry; Coventry City (Coll); Craven (Coll); Croydon (Coll); Cumbria; De Montfort; Dearne Valley (Coll); Derby; Doncaster (Univ Centre); Duchy (Coll); Dunstable (Coll); Durham New (Coll); Ealing, Hammersmith and West London (Coll); East Devon (Coll); East Lancashire (IHE); Eccles (Coll); Edge Hill; Essex; Farnborough (CT); Glamorgan; Grantham (Coll); Guildford (Coll); Gwent (Coll); Halesowen (Coll); Harper Adams (UC); Hartpury (Coll); Hastings (Coll); Havering (Coll); Hertford Reg (Coll); Hertfordshire; Highbury (Coll); Huddersfield; Hugh Baird (Coll); Hull (Coll); Huntingdonshire Reg (Coll); Joseph Priestley (Coll); Kendal (Coll); Kensington Bus (Coll); Kingston; Kingston (Coll); Knowsley (Coll); Lakes (Coll); Leeds (CAD); Leeds (CAT); Leeds Met; Liverpool (CmC); Llandrillo Cymru (Coll); London (Birk); London Met; London South Bank; Loughborough (Coll); Macclesfield (Coll); Manchester (CAT); Manchester City (Coll); Manchester Met; Matthew Boulton (Coll); Merthyr Tydfll (Coll); Middlesbrough (Coll); Middlesex; Milton Keynes (Coll); Myerscough (Coll); Neath Port Talbot (Coll); Nelson and Colne (Coll); Newcastle (Coll); North Devon (Coll); North East Wales (IHE); North Herts (Coll); North Warwickshire (Coll); North West Kent (Coll); Northampton; Northumbria; Northbrook (Coll); Nottingham Trent; Oaklands (Coll); Oldham (Coll); Oxford Brookes; Park Lane Leeds (Coll); Plymouth; Plymouth (CFE); Portsmouth; Powys (Coll); Preston (Coll); Redcar (Coll); Richmond upon Thames (Coll); Riverside Halton (Coll); Royal (CAg); Runshaw (Coll); St Helens (Coll); Salford; Salisbury (Coll); Sheffield (Coll); Sheffield Hallam; Somerset (CAT); South Cheshire (Coll); South Devon (Coll); South Kent (Coll); Southampton Solent; Southend Campus Essex; Staffordshire Reg (Coll); Stockton Riverside (Coll); Suffolk (Univ Campus); Sunderland; Sunderland City (Coll); Teesside; Telford (CAT); Thames Valley; Thomas Danby (Coll); Thurrock (Coll); Trinity Carmarthen (Coll); Truro (Coll); Tyne Met (Coll); Wakefield (Coll); Warrington (Coll); Warwickshire (Coll); West Anglia

(Coll); West Herts (Coll); West Nottinghamshire (Coll); West Thames (Coll); Westminster Kingsway (Coll); Weymouth (Coll); Wigan and Leigh (Coll); Worcester; Worcester (CT); Worcestershire New (Coll); Writtle (Coll); Yeovil (Coll).

Higher National Diploma courses
140 pts and below
Aberdeen (Coll); Abertay Dundee; Aberystwyth; Accrington and Rossendale (Coll); Adam Smith (Coll); Anglia Ruskin; Arts London (CComm); Askham Bryan (Coll); Aylesbury (Coll); Ayr (Coll); Bangor; Barking (Coll); Barnsley (Univ Centre); Basingstoke (CT); Bath; Bedfordshire; Bell (Coll); Birmingham (CFTCS); Birmingham City (Coll); Blackpool and Fylde (Coll); Bolton; Boston (Coll); Bournemouth; Bradford (Coll); Bridgwater (Coll); Brighton; Bristol City (Coll); Bromley (Coll); Brooklands (Coll); Brunel; Buckinghamshire Chilterns (UC); Burton (Coll); Cambridge Reg (Coll); Canterbury Christ Church; Cardiff (UWIC); Carlisle (Coll); Carmarthenshire (Coll); Carshalton (Coll); Central Lancashire; Chesterfield (Coll); Chichester (Coll); Clydebank (Coll); Colchester (Inst); Coventry; Coventry City (Coll); Craven (Coll); Crawley (Coll); Croydon (Coll); Cumbria (IA); De Montfort; Dearne Valley (Coll); Derby; Dewsbury (Coll); Doncaster (Univ Centre); Dudley (Coll); Dumfries and Galloway (Coll); Dundee (Coll); Durham New (Coll); Ealing, Hammersmith and West London (Coll); East Lancashire (IHE); East London; Edge Hill; Enfield (Coll); Exeter (Coll); Fareham (Coll); Farnborough (CT); Filton (Coll); Forth Valley (Coll); Glamorgan; Glasgow Caledonian; Glasgow Met (Coll); Gloucestershire; Gloucestershire (CAT); Greenwich; Grimsby (IFHE); Guildford (Coll); Harper Adams (UC); Havering (Coll); Hendon (Coll); Henley (Coll); Herefordshire (CAD); Herefordshire (CT); Heriot-Watt; Hertfordshire; Highbury (Coll); Huddersfield; Inverness (Coll); Isle of Wight (Coll); Kent; Kilmarnock (Coll); Kingston; Kingston (Coll); Lakes (Coll); Leeds Met (contact University); Lincoln; Lincoln (Coll); Liverpool (CmC); Liverpool John Moores; Llandrillo Cymru (Coll); London Met; London South Bank; Loughborough (CT); Lowestoft (Coll); Macclesfield (Coll); Manchester (CAT); Manchester City (Coll); Manchester Met; Matthew Boulton (CFHE); Mid-Cheshire (Coll); Middlesex; Napier; Nescot; Newham (CFE); Newport; North East Wales (IHE); North Herts (CFE); North Nottinghamshire (Coll); Northampton; Northbrook (Coll); Northumbria; Norwich City (Coll); Nottingham New (Coll); Nottingham Trent; Oxford and Cherwell Valley (Coll); Oxford Brookes; Park Lane Leeds (Coll); Pembrokeshire (Coll); People's (Coll); Peterborough Reg (Coll); Plymouth; Plymouth (CFE); Portsmouth; Preston (Coll); Reid Kerr (Coll); Richmond-upon-Thames (Coll); Riverside Halton (Coll); Rotherham (CAT); Runshaw (Coll); SAC (Scottish CAg); St Helens (Coll); Salford; Salisbury (Coll); Sandwell (Coll); Sheffield (Coll); Sheffield Hallam; Shrewsbury (CAT); Solihull (Coll); Somerset (CAT); South Birmingham (Coll); South Devon (Coll); South Kent (Coll); South Leicestershire (CFE); South Trafford (Coll); Southampton Solent; Southport (Coll); Southwark (Coll); Stafford (Coll); Staffordshire; Stevenson (Coll); Stockport (CFHE); Stoke on Trent (Coll); Stratford-upon-Avon (Coll); Strode (Coll); Suffolk (Univ Campus); Sunderland; Sunderland City (Coll); Sutton Coldfield (Coll); Swansea (IHE); Swindon (Coll); Tameside (Coll); Teesside; Thames Valley; Thanet (Coll); Totton (Coll); Tresham (Inst); Tyne Met (Coll); UCE Birmingham; UHI Millennium Inst (IC) (LCC) (NHC); Ulster (Coll); Uxbridge (Coll); Wakefield (Coll); Walsall (Coll); Warrington (Coll); Warwickshire (Coll); West Anglia (Coll); West Herts (Coll); West Nottinghamshire (Coll); West Suffolk (Coll); West Thames (Coll); Weston (Coll); Wigan and Leigh (Coll); Wigston (CFE); Wiltshire (Coll); Winchester; Wirral Met (Coll); Wolverhampton; Worcester; Worcester (CT); Worcestershire New (Coll); Writtle (Coll); Wulfrun (Coll); York (Coll); Yorkshire Coast (CFHE); Ystrad Mynach (Coll).

HND Publishing courses Arts London (CComm); Blackpool and Fylde (Coll); Bournemouth (AI); Farnborough (CT); Gloucestershire (CAT); Napier; West Herts (Coll).

CHOOSING YOUR COURSE (SEE ALSO CH.1)
Subject information This subject attracts more applicants than any other degree course, with over 350,000 applying in 2006 to the wide range of programmes. It should be noted however, that a grade C in mathematics at GCSE is the minimum entry requirement although the majority of courses would expect a grade A, or even an AS or an A-level in the subject. This is because financial studies form part

of most courses, in addition to sales, marketing, human resources management and general management. Since this is a vocational subject, some work experience in the field is generally required prior to application. In Section C of the tables above, more specialised courses are listed including Advertising, Public Relations, and there are separate subject tables (to be used in conjunction with this table) for Retail Management and Human Resource Management programmes. Many courses offer industrial placements, in some cases in the USA, Australia and New Zealand and, for those students with an A-level in a language (and in some cases a good GCSE), placements abroad in Europe are possible. **Useful websites** www.faststream.gov.uk; www.bized.ac.uk; www.icsa.org.uk; www.oft.gov.uk; www.adassoc.org.uk; www.cipr.co.uk; www.ismm.co.uk; www.export.org.uk; www.mori.com; www.capitaras.co.uk; www.tax.org.uk; www.hmrc.gov.uk; www.camfoundation.com; www.shell-livewire.org/mentor; www.imc.co.uk; www.managers.org.uk; www.cipd.co.uk; www.iqps.org.

Course variations Fire Engineering Management, Public Relations (Central Lancashire); Emergency Disaster Management (Coventry); Business and Sports Management (De Montfort); Latin American Studies with Business Management (Essex); European Business Studies (Lincoln); Air Transport Management (Loughborough); Management Studies and Chinese Studies (Nottingham); Publishing (Oxford Brookes); Business Enterprise Development (Portsmouth); International Management with Intercultural Studies (Stirling); Business Travel and Tourism (Thames Valley); Fashion Merchandising Management (Westminster). *NOW CHECK PROSPECTUSES AND WEBSITES FOR ANY RECENT CHANGES.*

Universities and colleges teaching quality See www.tqi.ac.uk; www.qaa.ac.uk.

Top universities and colleges (Research) Aston; Bath; Cambridge; Cardiff; City; Imperial London; Lancaster*; Leeds; London (LSE); Manchester; Nottingham; Oxford; Reading; Warwick*.

Sandwich degree courses Abertay Dundee; Aberystwyth; Arts London; Aston; Bath; Bedfordshire; Belfast (Queen's); Birmingham (CFTCS); Bournemouth; Bradford; Brighton; Bristol UWE; Brunel; Central Lancashire; City; Coventry; De Montfort; Derby; East London; Glamorgan; Glasgow Caledonian; Gloucestershire; Greenwich; Harper Adams (UC); Hertfordshire; Huddersfield; Hull; Kingston; Lancaster; Leeds Met; Lincoln; Liverpool John Moores; London South Bank; Loughborough; Manchester Met; Middlesex; Napier; Newcastle; Northumbria; Nottingham Trent; Paisley; Plymouth; Portsmouth; Royal (CAg); Sheffield Hallam; Southampton Solent; Staffordshire; Sunderland; Surrey; Teesside; Thames Valley; UCE Birmingham; Ulster; Warwickshire (Coll); Westminster; Wolverhampton.

ADMISSIONS INFORMATION

Number of applicants per place (approx) Abertay Dundee (Bus St) 4; Aberystwyth 3; Anglia Ruskin 5; Aston (Bus Mgt) 12, (Int Bus) 6, (Mgt) 5, (Int Bus Econ) 8; Bangor 4; Bath (Bus Admin) 13, (Int Mgt Lang) 14; Birmingham 7; Birmingham (CFTCS) 5; Blackpool and Fylde (Coll) 2; Bolton 3; Bournemouth 30, (Adv) 20, (Rtl Mgt) 8, (PR) 10; Bradford 12; Bristol 28; Brunel 12; Canterbury Christ Church 20; Cardiff 8; Central Lancashire 15; City (Bus St) 17, (Mgt Sys) 6; Colchester (Inst) 2; De Montfort (Bus St) 5, (Adv Mark Comm) 6; Derby (Int Bus) 4; East Anglia (Bus Fin) 18; Edge Hill 4; Glasgow Caledonian 18; Heriot-Watt 5; Hertfordshire 10; Huddersfield 5; Hull (Bus St) 19, (Mgt) 10; Hull (Scarborough) 3; Kent 30; Kingston 50; Leeds 27, (Mgt St) 16; Leeds Trinity and All Saints (Coll) 3; Liverpool John Moores (Int Bus) 16; Llandrillo Cymru (Coll) 2; London (LSE) (Mgt) 23, (Mgt Sci) 19, (King's) 25, (RH) 9; London Met 10; London South Bank 4; Loughborough 5; Manchester Met (Bus St) 26, (Rtl Mark) 10, (Int Bus) 8; Mid-Kent (CFHE) 2; Middlesex 12; Napier (Pub) 7; Newcastle 27, (Euro Bus Mgt) 54, (Int Bus Mgt) 25, (Bus Mgt) 40; Northumbria 10; Oxford Brookes 40, (Rtl Mgt) 11; Paisley 5; Plymouth 4; Portsmouth 10; (Bus Admin) 7, (Bus St) 6, (Int Bus) 5, (Euro Bus) 3; Regents Bus Sch London 25; Robert Gordon 5; Salford (Bus St) 9, (Mgt Sci) 2; Sheffield Hallam (Int Bus) 6; Southampton Solent 13; Strathclyde 12, (Int Bus Lang) 6; Sunderland 20; Surrey (Bus Mgt) 6; Swansea (IHE) 7; Teesside (Bus St) 4; Thames Valley 4; Warwick 22; Westminster 12; Winchester 4; Wolverhampton 7; York 7; York St John 3.

Advice to applicants and planning the UCAS personal statement There are many different kinds of businesses and any work experience is almost essential for these courses. This should be described in detail: for example, size of firm, turnover, managerial problems, sales and marketing aspects, customers' attitudes. Any special interests in business management should also be included, for example, personnel work, purchasing, marketing. Give details of travel or work experience abroad and, for international courses, language expertise and examples of leadership and organising skills. Reference can be made to any particular business topics you have studied in the *Financial Times*, *The Economist* and the business sections in the weekend press. Don't say 'I enjoy socialising with my friends'. **Bournemouth** (Adv Mark Comm) Focus required on marketing. **Cardiff (UWIC)** Applicants need to be sociable, ambitious, team players. **Derby** (Int Bus) Interest in working outside the UK or with a multinational company. Students need an understanding of the objectives and practice of the EU. **Leeds** Mention your interests and ambitions. **Manchester Met** (Rtl Mgt) Evidence of working with people or voluntary work experience (department unable to assist with sponsorships). **Salford** Tell us why you are interested in the course, identify your academic strengths, your personal strengths and interests. **Staffordshire** Applicants with two A-levels contact the Business School. **Surrey** Further information could be obtained from the Chartered Institute of Public Relations, the Chartered Institute of Marketing and the Chartered Institute of Personnel and Development. **Warwick** One year preparatory courses for non-EU students failing to get the right grades. See **Appendix 2**; see also **Accountancy/Accounting**.

Misconceptions about this course **Aberystwyth** Students are unaware that the course addresses practical aspects of business. **Aston** (Int Bus Fr) Not two separate disciplines – the two subjects are integrated involving the study of language in a business and management context. **Loughborough** (Pub Engl) That this is a course in journalism: it is not! **Salford** (Mgt Sci) Students should appreciate that the courses are fairly mathematical. **York** A previous study of management, IT or languages at A-level is necessary.

Selection interviews **Yes** Abertay Dundee, Bradford, Carmarthenshire (Coll), Coventry, Doncaster (Univ Centre), Durham, Edge Hill, Euro Bus Sch London, Glamorgan, Glasgow Caledonian, Hull, Kent (mature and Access students), Lampeter, London Met, Middlesex, Northumbria, Nottingham Trent, Plymouth, Robert Gordon, Roehampton, Sheffield Hallam, Strathclyde, Swansea, Teesside, Thames Valley, UCE Birmingham, Warwick, West Thames (Coll), York; **Some** Aberystwyth, Anglia Ruskin, Bath, Blackpool and Fylde (Coll), Brighton, Buckingham, Cardiff (UWIC), Chichester, City, De Montfort, Derby (Int Bus), Greenwich, Kent, Leeds, Lincoln, Liverpool John Moores, Manchester Met, Salford, South Kent (Coll), Staffordshire, Stirling, Sunderland, Winchester, Wolverhampton.

Interview advice and questions Any work experience you describe on the UCAS form probably will be the focus of questions which could include topics covering marketing, selling, store organisation and management and customer problems. Personal qualities are naturally important in a career in business, so be ready for such questions as: What qualities do you have which are suitable and important for this course? Describe your strengths and weaknesses. Why should we give you a place on this course? Is advertising fair? What qualities does a person in business require to be successful? What makes a good manager? What is a cash-flow system? What problems can it cause? How could supermarkets improve customer relations? **Int Bus courses** Why can you be expected to be sent to China by your company when you only have French as a second language? Do you consider that knowing a foreign language makes you a good international manager? **Buckingham** Why Business? How do you see yourself in five years' time? Have you had any work experience? If so, discuss. **Loughborough** (Pub Engl) No tests at interview. We seek students with an interest in information issues within society. **Manchester Met** (Fash Buy) Be able to discuss in detail experience working with a fashion retailer. Knowledge of garment manufacture an advantage. **Wolverhampton** Mature students with no qualifications will be asked about their work experience. See also **Chapter 6**.

Applicants' impressions (A=Open day; B=Interview day) **Bath Spa** (A; Bus St Media Comm) There was a tour of the campus, a talk on student finance and a chance to talk to the subject lecturers. **Exeter** (A; Bus Mgt) The open day included a talk by a business expert. We then toured the campus and spoke to the students. **Portsmouth** (A; 1) There were no interviews, but a lot of good information on the induction course structure and good supporting information. (A; 2) I was sent a map of buildings and a plan of activities for the day. Most of the day was spent in the lecture theatre listening to talks, by the end of which everyone wanted to go home. It would have been useful to have a variety of activities and a tour of the campus. (A; 3) Coach tour round Portsmouth. Brief presentation. Tour of halls and departments. Free lunch and a chance to ask questions. (A; 4) A really good day with talks on the course, finance and the grades needed. There was also an opportunity to talk to current students. This was very encouraging and gave a better insight into the course and made it more appealing. **Reading** (A) The open day consisted of a talk about the course and a tour of the halls, facilities and union. **Surrey** (A) We met lecturers and were given an overview of the course and shown round the campus by a student. We didn't get to see the accommodation which would have been useful. **Warwickshire (Coll)** (B) There was an informal interview about my career plans and what the college expected of me. **Winchester** (A; Bus Media) We had a campus tour, a one-hour talk on finance and a meeting with subject tutors. There was a lot of friendly, good advice.

Reasons for rejection (non-academic) Hadn't read the prospectus. Lack of communication skills. Limited commercial interest. Weak on numeracy and problem-solving. Lack of interview preparation (no questions). Lack of outside interests. Inability to cope with a year abroad. The candidate brought his parent who answered all the questions. **Aberystwyth** Would have trouble fitting into the unique environment of Aberystwyth. Casual approach to learning. **Bournemouth** The Business Studies course is very popular. **Surrey** Hesitation about the period abroad. See also **Marketing**.

AFTER-RESULTS ADVICE

Universities with vacancies in Clearing (2006) Aberystwyth; Anglia Ruskin; Aston; Bangor; Birmingham; Bolton; Bournemouth; Bradford; Brighton; Bristol UWE; Brunel; Canterbury Christ Church; Central Lancashire; Chester; Chichester; Coventry; Cumbria; De Montfort; Derby; East London; Glamorgan; Gloucestershire; Greenwich; Heriot-Watt; Hertfordshire; Huddersfield; Hull; Keele; Kent; Kingston; Lampeter; Lincoln; London (QM); London Met; Manchester Met; Middlesex; Northampton; Northumbria; Nottingham Trent; Paisley; Plymouth; Portsmouth; Roehampton; Sheffield; Southampton; Southampton Solent; Staffordshire; Stirling; Sunderland; Swansea; UCE Birmingham; Ulster; Westminster; Winchester; Worcester; York St John.

Offers to applicants repeating A-levels **Higher** Bradford, Bristol UWE, Brunel, East Anglia, Greenwich, Hertfordshire, Kingston, Lancaster, Liverpool, Manchester Met, St Andrews, Sheffield, Strathclyde, Teesside; **Same** Aberystwyth, Anglia Ruskin, Aston, Bath, Blackpool and Fylde (Coll), Bournemouth, Brighton, Buckingham, Cardiff, Cardiff (UWIC), Chester, Chichester, De Montfort, Derby, Gloucestershire, Huddersfield, Hull, Kent, Leeds, Lincoln, Liverpool John Moores, Llandrillo Cymru (Coll), Loughborough, Northumbria, Oxford Brookes, Richmond (Am Int Univ), Robert Gordon, Roehampton, Royal (CAg), Salford, Sheffield Hallam, Staffordshire, Stirling, Sunderland, Surrey, Thames Valley, UCE Birmingham, Ulster, Winchester, Wolverhampton, Worcester, York, York St John; **Rare** Queen Margaret (UC), Warwick.

GRADUATE DESTINATIONS AND EMPLOYMENT (2005 HESA)
Graduates surveyed 15101 **Employed** 8935 **In further study** 975 **Assumed unemployed** 905. **Publishing graduates surveyed** 175 **Employed** 120 **In further study** 10 **Assumed unemployed** 10.

OTHER DEGREE SUBJECTS FOR CONSIDERATION
Accountancy; Banking; Business Information Technology; E-Business; Economics; Estate Management; Finance; Hospitality Management; Housing Management; Human Resource Management; Insurance; Leisure Management; Logistics; Marketing; Public Administration; Retail Management; Sports Management; Surveying; Transport Management; Tourism.

CHEMISTRY

NB The points totals shown to the left of the institutions are for ease of reference only. It must not be assumed that tariff points are always used by institutions or that they can be substituted for an offer in grades. The level of an offer is not necessarily indicative of the quality of a course.

COURSE OFFERS INFORMATION
Subject requirements/preferences **GCSE Birmingham** Nine subjects at grades A/B; also A/B in appropriate modern language. **Bradford** (Chem Pharm Foren Sci) Grade A or B in mathematics or

combined science. **Cambridge, Oxford** Grade A in most subjects preferred. **Cardiff** Good range of subjects including humanities. **Imperial London** Grade B in English, mathematics, physics or combined science. **Sheffield** Mathematics grade A or above if not offered at A-level; (Chem Euro) a language at grade A or above if not at A-level. **Southampton** Mathematics grade B. **Surrey** Four–five grade As, the rest grade Bs. **Swansea** Grade B in all subjects preferred. **AL** Two science subjects including chemistry required.

Your target offers

360 pts and above

Cambridge – AAA (Nat Sci (Chem))

Durham – AAA (Nat Sci (Chem))

Oxford – Offers vary eg AAA–AAB (Chemistry)

340 pts Bangor – 340–280 pts (MChem Chem courses)

Cardiff – AAB–BBB (MChem Chem; Chem Ind; Chem Abrd)

Edinburgh – AAB 2nd yr entry (Chem Phys Ind)

Manchester – AAB–ABC (Chem; Chem Ind Exp; Chem Euro/N Am; Chem Bus Mgt; Chem Pat Law; Medcnl Chem)

St Andrews – AAB (Chem Phys; Chem Maths)

Sheffield – AAB–ABB (Chem Aus; Chem USA; Chem Jap)

320 pts Durham – ABB–BBB (MChem Chem; Chem Ind; Chem Int)

East Anglia – ABB (MChem Chem N Am; Chem Ind; Chem Analyt Foren Sci; Chem Euro; Biol Medcnl Chem; Env Chem)

Imperial London – AAB–ABB (MSci/BSc Chem; Chem Rsch Abrd; Chem Mgt; Chem Cons Sci; Chem Fr; Chem Proc; Chem Medcnl Chem)

London (UCL) – ABB+AS–BBB+AS (Chem courses)

Nottingham – ABB (MSci Chem Mol Phys)

Nottingham – ABB–BBB (Chem Mgt St)

St Andrews – ABB 2nd yr entry (Chem courses)

Southampton – ABB–ABC (MChem Chem; Chem Medcnl Sci; Chem Ocn Earth Sci; Chem Maths)

Strathclyde – ABB–AAC (Foren Analyt Chem; App Chem Chem Eng; Chem Drug Dscvry)

Warwick – 320–350 pts (Chem; Chem Mgt; Chem Medcnl Chem; Biomed Chem; Chem Biol)

300 pts Aston – 300 pts (MChem Chem courses)

Bath – BBB–ABB 300–320 pts (Chem; Chem Mgt; Chem Drug Dscvry)

Belfast (Queen's) – BBB (MSci Chem; Medcnl Chem)

Birmingham – BBB–BBC (Chem; Chem Analyt Sci; Chem Bio-org Chem; Chem Fr; Chem Euro; Chem Abrd; Chem Bus Mgt; Chem Env Sci; Chem Pharmacol; Chem Psy)

Cardiff – BBB–BCC 260–300 pts (BSc Chem Ind; Chem Biosci; Chem)

East Anglia – BBB (BSc Chem; Chem N Am; Chem Analyt Sci; Biol Medcnl Chem; Env Chem; Chem Phys)

Leeds – BBB (Nanotech; Chem courses; Chem joint courses; Medcnl Chem)

Leicester – BBB (MChem: Chem; Chem Biol USA; Chem Euro; Chem Foren Sci; Pharm Chem)

London (UCL) – BBB+AS–BCC+AS (Chem; Chem Euro Lang; Chem Maths; Chem Mgt St; Medcnl Chem)

Newcastle – BBB–BBC (Chem courses)

Nottingham – BBB (Medncl Biol Chem; Chem Mol Phys)

Reading – 300 pts (MChem) 260–280 pts (BSc) (Chem; Chem Euro; Chem Ind; Chem Arch; Env Chem)

St Andrews – BBB 1st yr entry (Chem Geosci; Chem Comp Sci; Chem Fr/Ger/Span; Chem Sci)

Sheffield – BBB (Chem Inform; Chem Ent Mgt; Chem Ind; Chem Euro; Chem Maths; Chem Phys; Mat Chem; Biol Chem)

Southampton – BBB–BBC (BSc Chem; Chem Medcnl Sci; Chem Ocn Earth Sci)

Sussex – BBB–BBC 330–310 pts 3AL+AS (BSc Chem: Chem Am St; Chem Foren Sci)

York – BBB (Chem; Chem Biol Medicin Chem; Chem Mgt Ind; Chem Res Env)

280 pts **Bangor** – 280 pts (MChem courses)

Belfast (Queen's) – BBC (Medcnl Chem; BSc Chem)

Bristol – BBC–BCC (Chem; Chem Ind; Chem N Am; Chem Euro)

Edinburgh – BBC (Chem courses except under **340 pts**)

Glasgow – BBC–CCC (Chem; Chem Foren St; Chem Medcnl Chem; Chem Maths)

Lancaster – BBC–CCD 280–220 pts (MChem: Env Chem; Env Chem N Am; Env Chem Aus)

Leicester – BBC–CCC (BSc Chem courses)

Liverpool – 280 pts (Chem Nano; MChem Chem; Chem Bus St; Chem Ind; Medcnl Chem Pharmacol)

Loughborough – 280 pts (MChem: Chem Analyt Chem; Medcnl Pharm Chem; Chem Foren Analys; Chem Spo Sci; Chem IT)

Northumbria – 280 pts (MChem Chem)

Sheffield – BBC (Chem; Chem Inform; Chem Ent Mgt; Chem Maths)

Strathclyde – BBC (Chem; Chem Teach)

Surrey – BBC (Integ Sci)

260 pts **Aberdeen** – 260 pts (MChem Chem)

Aston – BCC–CCC (BSc Chem: Chem (Biotech) (Mgt St); Chem; App Chem)

Bradford – BCC 260 pts (Chem Pharm Foren Sci)

Dundee – 260 pts 2nd yr entry (Pharm Chem)

Heriot-Watt – BCC 2nd yr entry (Chem courses)

Plymouth – 260–300 pts (Analyt Chem)

Reading – 260–280 pts (BSc Chem courses see also **300 pts**)

Surrey – BCC–CCC 260–240 pts (MChem; Chem Foren Invstg; Medcnl Chem; Comp Aid Chem)

240 pts **Aberdeen** – CCC (BSc Chemistry)

Belfast (Queen's) – CCC/BC (BSc Chem; Chem Euro; Chem Ind; Medcnl Chem)

Cardiff – 240 pts contact admissions tutor (Prelim Yr to MChem/BSc Chem)

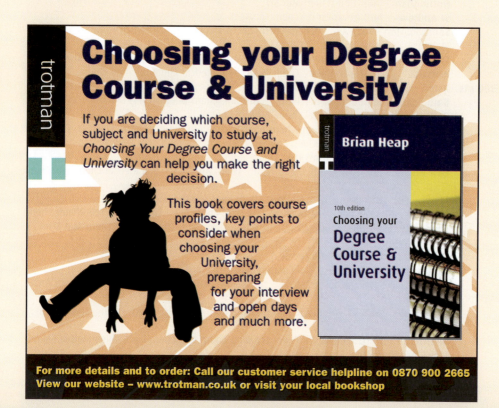

Hull – CCC–BBB 240–300 pts (Chem courses)
Keele – 240–260 pts (Chem; Medcnl Chem)
Leeds – CCC (App Chem; Col Poly Chem)
Liverpool – 240 pts (BSc Chem; Chem Ind; Medcnl Chem; Ocean Chem)
Loughborough – 240 pts (BSc Chem: Chem Analyt Chem; Chem Foren Analys; Chem Spo Sci; Medcnl Pharm Chem; Chem IT)
Northumbria – 240 pts (Chem Foren Chem; Chem Biomed Sci; Pharm Chem)

220 pts **Bangor** – 220–280 pts (BSc Chem; Env Chem; Mar Chem; Chem Euro; Chem Ind; Chem Comp Sci; Chem Biomol Sci)
Dundee – 220 pts 1st yr entry (Pharm Chem)
Glamorgan – 220–260 pts (Chem; Foren Chem)
Greenwich – 220 pts (MChem Chem)
Heriot-Watt – CCD 220 pts (MChem courses)
Lancaster – CCD (BSc Env Chem)
Liverpool John Moores – 220–240 pts (Medcnl Chem)
Nottingham Trent – 220 pts (Chem Int St; Chem Prof Prac; Chem Analyt Sci; Chem)
Plymouth – 220 pts (App Chem)

200 pts **Aberdeen** – CDD (Chemistry)
Huddersfield – 200 pts (Chem; Chem Ind)
Kingston – 200 pts (MChem Chem; Chem Ind; Foren Chem; App Chem; Chem Bus; Medcnl Chem)
Nottingham Trent – 200 pts (Chemistry)
Teesside – 200–260 pts (Foren Chem)

180 pts **Greenwich** – 180 pts (Chem; Pharm Chem; Analyt Chem)
Sunderland – 180 pts (Chem Pharm Sci)

160 pts **London Met** – 160 pts (Chem; Biol Medcnl Chem; Cos Sci)
Loughborough – CC (Chem Fdn)
Manchester Met – 160–220 pts (Chem; Chem Euro; Medcnl Biol Chem; Analyt Chem; Foren Chem)

120 pts **Paisley** – DD **or** bbc (Chem; Medicin Chem)
100 pts **Manchester Met** – 100–150 pts (Chem Sci; Pharm Chem)
80 pts **London (Birk)** – 80 pts under 21s (over 21s varies) (p/t Chemistry)
Manchester Met – 80 pts (Chem Ind Fdn)
60 pts **and below**
Eastleigh (Coll) – (Fdn Sci)

Alternative offers
IB offers Aberdeen 30 pts; Bath 34 pts; Birmingham 31 pts; Bristol 30 pts; Cambridge 38–42 pts; Cardiff 28 pts; East Anglia 32–33 pts; Glasgow 28 pts; Keele 26–28 pts; Lancaster 32–34 pts; Leicester 28–30 pts; Liverpool 28–32 pts; Loughborough 30 pts; Manchester 33–35 pts; Manchester Met 24 pts; Newcastle 32 pts; Nottingham 32 pts; Oxford 38–42 pts; St Andrews 31–34 pts; Sheffield 29–35 pts; Southampton 32–34 pts; Surrey 30 pts; Sussex 32 pts; Warwick 34 pts; York 32 pts.
Scottish offers See **Chapter 7**.

OTHER HIGHER EDUCATION COURSES IN THE SUBJECT FIELD

Higher National Diploma courses
100 pts Abertay Dundee; Adam Smith (Coll); Bangor (Access courses); Bell (Coll); Bradford (Coll); Coventry; Dudley (Coll); Forth Valley (Coll); Glamorgan; Glasgow Caledonian; Greenwich; Heriot-Watt (Scottish Borders); Hertfordshire; Huddersfield; Kingston; London Met; Manchester Met; Napier; North East Wales (IHE); Northampton; Nottingham Trent; Oldham (Coll); People's (Coll); Portsmouth; Riverside Halton (Coll); Robert Gordon; Stockport (CFHE); Sunderland; Teesside; Ulster; Westminster; Wolverhampton.

Note Eligible students on BTEC HND courses in Science (Chemistry) may elect to take an additional paper for Graduate Membership Part I of the Royal Society of Chemistry.

For information on how to read the Subject Tables, see **Chapter 7**.

CHOOSING YOUR COURSE (SEE ALSO CH.1)

Subject information There is a shortage of applicants for this subject despite the fact that it is the basis of a wide range of careers in the manufacturing industries. These focus on such areas as pharmaceuticals, medicine, veterinary science and health, agriculture, petroleum, cosmetics, plastics, the food industry, colour chemistry and aspects of the environment such as pollution and recycling. **Sheffield** Chemistry is a central science and this means that Chemistry graduates find a wide variety of occupations open to them which at first glance seem unusual. Excluding the obvious ones such as research scientists, graduates go into management, accountancy, finance, PR and publicity, information systems, marketing, journalism, politics (local and national), charities and pressure groups. In fact they go into any career where you need to gather information to be able to draw rational conclusions from information in order to construct an argument or hold a position. **Useful websites** www.rsc.org; www.chem.ox.ac.uk/vrchemistry.

Course variations Chemistry with Drug Discovery (Bath); Nanotechnology (Leeds); Medicinal Chemistry and Pharmacology (Liverpool); Chemistry with Patent Law (Manchester); Combined Studies (Newcastle); Chemistry in Australia, Europe, Japan, USA or Industry (Sheffield); Chemistry and Forensic Investigation (Surrey). *NOW CHECK PROSPECTUSES AND WEBSITES FOR ANY RECENT CHANGES.*

Universities and colleges teaching quality See www.tqi.ac.uk; www.qaa.ac.uk.

Top universities and colleges (Research) Bristol*; Cambridge*; Cardiff; Durham*; East Anglia; Edinburgh; Imperial London*; Leeds; Liverpool; London (UCL)*; Manchester; Nottingham; Oxford*; St Andrews; Sheffield; Southampton; Sussex; Warwick; York.

Sandwich degree courses Aston; Bangor; Bath; Belfast; Bradford; Cardiff; Coventry; Glamorgan; Huddersfield; Kingston; Leicester; Liverpool John Moores; Loughborough; Manchester; Northumbria; Nottingham Trent; Paisley; Plymouth; St Andrews; Surrey; Teesside.

ADMISSIONS INFORMATION

Number of applicants per place (approx) Bangor (Mar Chem) 3, (Chem) 6; Bradford (Chem Pharm Foren Sci) 10; Bristol 5; Durham 6; Edinburgh 5; Glasgow Caledonian 4; Heriot-Watt 6; Hull 7; Imperial London 3; Kingston 4; Leeds 3; London (QM) 3, (UCL) 5; Newcastle 5; Nottingham (Chem Mol Phys) 4, (Chem) 8; Oxford (success rate 63%); Southampton 12; Surrey 3; York 5.

Advice to applicants and planning the UCAS personal statement Extend your knowledge beyond your exam studies by reading scientific journals and keeping abreast of scientific developments in the news. Discuss any visits to chemical firms and laboratories, for example, pharmaceutical, food science, rubber and plastic, paper, photographic, environmental health. **Bath** We look for good communication skills, a positive personality and a mature outlook. **St Andrews** Reasons for choosing the course and evidence of interest. Sport and extra-curricular activities, positions of responsibility. **Sheffield** Some students feel that they should be doing a similar number of lectures as their friends doing Arts courses without realising just how much time Arts students are required to be in the library or studying at home. Some students are not prepared for the freedom they enjoy at university and, without the pressure of parents, they fall behind in their work. Often it is the ones who have had less parental pressure that perform the best because they are self-motivated. **Southampton** We value the individuality of students. The style of personal statement should reflect this. **Surrey** We look for work experience, language skills, travel, computing, business experience. See also **Appendix 2**.

Misconceptions about this course Many students do not fully appreciate the strengths of a chemistry degree for ANY career despite the fact that graduates regularly go into a diverse range of careers. **Durham** Students fail to realise that they require mathematics and that physics is useful.

Selection interviews **Yes** Bangor, Bath, Bristol, Cambridge, Coventry, Durham, East Anglia, Glasgow Caledonian, Greenwich, Huddersfield, Hull, Keele (mature students only), Kingston, London (UCL), London Met, London South Bank, Loughborough, Newcastle, Northumbria, Nottingham, Nottingham

Trent, Oxford (success rate 66%), Sheffield, Southampton, Surrey, Warwick; **Some** Aston, Cardiff, Dundee, Liverpool John Moores, Plymouth.

Interview advice and questions Be prepared for questions on your chemistry syllabus and aspects that you enjoy the most. In the past a variety of questions have been asked, for example: Why is carbon a special element? Discuss the nature of forces between atoms with varying intermolecular distances. Describe recent practicals. What is acid rain? What other types of pollution are caused by the human race? What is an enzyme? What are the general properties of benzene? Why might sciences be less popular among girls at school? What can a mass spectrometer be used for? What would you do if a river turned bright blue and you were asked how to test a sample? What would be the difference between metal and non-metal pollution? **Bath** Why Chemistry? Discuss the practical work you are doing. **Oxford** Evidence required of motivation and further potential and a capacity to analyse and use information to form opinions and a willingness to discuss them. **York** Discuss your favourite areas of chemistry, some of your extracurricular activities, your preferred learning styles – for example, small tutorials of four or fewer, lectures. See also **Chapter 6**.

Applicants' impressions (A=Open day; B=Interview day) **Aston** (A) We had a talk by members of staff, a tour of the campus with students and a group interview. **Bristol** (B) We had a short talk about the course, lunch, tour and an informal 15-minute interview. Quite useful. **London (UCL)** (B) Short tour and lunch, followed by an informal interview. It was useful to see the department. **Nottingham** (B) We had a tour of the campus and department, lunch, a talk on the course and an informal interview. **Nottingham Trent** (B) There was a tour of the department, interview and a chance to talk to students. **Southampton** (A) There was a tour and a very informal interview (really only a chance to ask questions). (B) A tour of department, halls, lunch, talk with current students, followed by an informal interview.

Reasons for rejection (non-academic) Didn't attend interview. Rude and unco-operative. Arrived under influence of drink. Poor attitude and poor commitment to chemistry. Incomplete, inappropriate, illegible, illiterate personal statements. **Southampton** Applicants called for interview are not normally rejected.

AFTER-RESULTS ADVICE
Universities with vacancies in Clearing (2006) Aberdeen; Aston; Bangor; Bath; Belfast; Birmingham; Bradford; Cardiff; East Anglia; Glamorgan; Glasgow; Greenwich; Heriot-Watt; Huddersfield; Keele; Kent; Kingston; Lancaster; Leeds; Leicester; Liverpool; Liverpool John Moores; London (QM); London Met; Loughborough; Manchester Met; Newcastle; Northumbria; Nottingham; Nottingham Trent; Paisley; Plymouth; Portsmouth; Reading; Sheffield; Sheffield Hallam; Southampton; Surrey; Teesside; Warwick; Westminster; York.

Offers to applicants repeating A-levels **Higher** Bangor, Dundee, Hull, Leeds, Loughborough, Northumbria, Nottingham, St Andrews, Warwick; **Possibly higher** Coventry, East Anglia, Edinburgh, Newcastle; **Same** Aston, Bath, Bristol (no offer if first-time grades are low), Cardiff, Derby, Durham, Greenwich, Heriot-Watt, Huddersfield, Keele, Kingston, Liverpool John Moores, London (UCL), London Met, Plymouth, Robert Gordon, Sheffield, Surrey.

GRADUATE DESTINATIONS AND EMPLOYMENT (2005 HESA)
Graduates surveyed 1880 **Employed** 700 **In further study** 650 **Assumed unemployed** 120.

OTHER DEGREE SUBJECTS FOR CONSIDERATION
Agriculture; Biochemistry; Biological Sciences; Biomedical Science; Chemical Engineering; Environmental Science; Forensic Science; Genetics; Materials Science; Medicine; Microbiology; Oceanography; Pharmacology; Pharmacy.

CHINESE

(including **Korean**; see also **Asia-Pacific Studies**, **Business Courses** and **Languages**)

NB The points totals shown to the left of the institutions are for ease of reference only. It must not be assumed that tariff points are always used by institutions or that they can be substituted for an offer in grades. The level of an offer is not necessarily indicative of the quality of a course.

COURSE OFFERS INFORMATION

Subject requirements/preferences **GCSE** A language is required. **AL** A modern language is usually required.

Your target offers

360 pts **and above**
    Cambridge – AAA (Orntl St (Chin St))
    Oxford – Offers vary eg AAA–AAB (Chinese)
320 pts **Newcastle** – ABB–BBB (Chin Cult St)
300 pts **Edinburgh** – BBB (Chinese)
    Manchester – BBB–BBC (Chin St)
    Sheffield – BBB–BBC (Chin St courses)
280 pts **Leeds** – BBC **or** Bbbcc (Chin courses)
    London (SOAS) – BBC 280 pts (Chin courses; Kor Chin)
    Nottingham – BBC (Contemp Euro St Chin)
240 pts **Central Lancashire** – 240–280 pts (Bus Mgt Chin)
    Westminster – 240–280 pts (Chin joint courses)
180 pts **Lampeter** – open admission policy (Chin St)
    Liverpool John Moores – 180–200 pts (Int Bus St Chin; App Langs (Fr Chin) (Span Chin); Tour Leis Chin)
160 pts **Central Lancashire** – 160 pts (Chin Comb courses)

    London (Birk) – check with admissions tutor (Chin Hist Art; Chin Ling)

Alternative offers
IB offers Cambridge 38–42 pts; London (SOAS) 32 pts; Manchester 33–35 pts; Newcastle 32 pts; Oxford 38–42 pts.
Scottish offers See **Chapter 7**.

CHOOSING YOUR COURSE (SEE ALSO CH.1)

Subject information Oriental languages are not necessarily difficult languages but they differ considerably in their writing systems which present their own problems for the new student. Even so, Chinese is not a language to be chosen for its novelty and students should have an interest in China and its people. It is a country with a high economic growth rate and there are good opportunities for graduates, an increasing number being recruited by firms based in East Asia. Other opportunities exist in diplomacy, aid work and tourism throughout China, Taiwan and Mongolia as well as most other non-scientific career areas in the UK. **Useful websites** www.cilt.org.uk; www.iol.org.uk; www.bbc.co.uk/languages; www.chinaonline.com; www.china.org.cn/english; www.languageadvantage.com; www.languagematters.co.uk; www.reed.co.uk/multilingual; www.chinadaily.com.cn.

Course variations Business management in China (Central Lancashire); Tourism and Leisure Studies and Chinese (Liverpool John Moores); Chinese and International Business Studies with Chinese (Liverpool John Moores); Chinese and the History of Art and Archaeology (London (SOAS)); Chinese and Cultural Studies (Newcastle). *NOW CHECK PROSPECTUSES AND WEBSITES FOR ANY RECENT CHANGES.*

Universities and colleges teaching quality See www.tqi.ac.uk; www.qaa.ac.uk.

Sandwich degree courses Westminster.

ADMISSIONS INFORMATION

Number of applicants per place (approx) Leeds 5; London (SOAS) 8; Westminster 18.

Advice to applicants and planning the UCAS personal statement It will be necessary to demonstrate a knowledge of China, its culture, political and economic background. Visits to the Far East should be mentioned, with reference to any features which have influenced your choice of degree course. See also **Appendix 2** under **Languages**.

Selection interviews **Yes** Cambridge, Leeds, London (SOAS), Oxford.

Interview advice and questions You will be expected to convince the admissions tutor why you wish to study the language. Your knowledge of Chinese culture, politics and society in general, and of Far Eastern problems, could also be tested. See also **Chapter 6**.

Reasons for rejection (non-academic) **Oxford** His language background seemed a little weak and his written work not as strong as that of other applicants. At interview he showed himself to be a dedicated hard-working young man but lacking in the imagination, flexibility and the intellectual liveliness needed to succeed on the course.

AFTER-RESULTS ADVICE

Universities with vacancies in Clearing (2006) Central Lancashire; Lampeter; Sheffield; Westminster.

Offers to applicants repeating A-levels **Higher** Leeds.

GRADUATE DESTINATIONS AND EMPLOYMENT (2005 HESA)

Graduates surveyed 50 Employed 25 In further study 10 Assumed unemployed 5.

OTHER DEGREE SUBJECTS FOR CONSIDERATION

Traditional Chinese Medicine; other Oriental languages.

CLASSICAL STUDIES/CLASSICAL CIVILISATION

(see also **Archaeology**, **Classics** and **History (Ancient)**)

NB The points totals shown to the left of the institutions are for ease of reference only. It must not be assumed that tariff points are always used by institutions or that they can be substituted for an offer in grades. The level of an offer is not necessarily indicative of the quality of a course.

COURSE OFFERS INFORMATION

Subject requirements/preferences **GCSE Birmingham** Modern language. **Bristol** Ancient or modern language. **Edinburgh**, **Glasgow**, **St Andrews** English, mathematics, foreign language. **Leeds** Grade B or better in five subjects. **AL** A modern language is required for joint language courses. Archaeology, Greek, Latin and ancient history are relevant subjects.

Your target offers
360 pts **Warwick** – AAB/ABBb (Phil Class Civ; Class Civ)
340 pts **Exeter** – AAB–ABB 340–320 pts (Class St Engl)
           Exeter – AAB–BBB 340–300 pts (Class St)
           St Andrews – AAB (Class St courses)
320 pts **Bristol** – ABB (Class St; Class St Euro; Class St Phil)
           Durham – ABB (Class Past; Class Past Euro St)
           Exeter – ABB–BBB (Class St Engl/Fr/Ger/Ital/Russ/Span; Class St Phil; Class St Theol)
           Glasgow – ABB–BBB (Class Civ)
           London (UCL) – ABB+AS (Anc Wrld St)
           Manchester – ABB–ABC (Class St; Class Civ Art Hist courses)
           Newcastle – ABB (Class St; Class St Engl)

Nottingham – ABB (Class Civ Engl St)

300 pts **Edinburgh** – BBB (Class St; Class Arch Gk)

Leeds – BBB (Class Civ; Rom Civ; Gk Civ)

London (King's) – BBB+AS **or** BBbbc (Class St courses)

London (RH) – BBB 300 pts (Class St; Class St Dr; Class St Ital)

Nottingham – ABC–BBB (Class Civ; Class Civ Fr/Ger; Class Civ Phil)

280 pts **Birmingham** – 280 pts (Class Lit Civ)

Liverpool – BBC 280 pts (Class St; Class St Modn Lang)

Reading – 280 pts (Class St courses)

260 pts **Kent** – 260–280 pts (Class Arch St; Class Arch St Compar Lit St; Class Arch St Comp; Class Arch St Dr; Class Arch St Engl Am Lit; Class Arch St Fr; Class Arch St Hist Phil Art; Class Arch St Relig St)

Swansea – 260–300 pts (Class Civ joint courses; Egypt Class Civ)

180 pts **Lampeter** – open admission policy (Class St courses)

Roehampton – 180–200 pts (Class Civ courses)

80 pts **London (Birk)** – 80 pts for under 21s (over 21s varies) (p/t Class St)

Alternative offers

IB offers Birmingham 32 pts; Bristol 34 pts; Exeter 30–34 pts; Glasgow 30 pts; Liverpool 30 pts; London (King's) 32 pts, (RH) 32 pts; Newcastle 32 pts; Reading 30 pts; St Andrews 36 pts; Warwick 32–36 pts.

Scottish offers See **Chapter 7**.

CHOOSING YOUR COURSE (SEE ALSO CH.1)

Subject information Classical Studies and Classical Civilisation courses cover the literature, history, philosophy and archaeology of Ancient Greece and Rome. A knowledge of Latin or Greek is not necessary for many courses. **Useful websites** www.british-museum.ac.uk; see also **History** and **History (Ancient)**.

Course variations Classical Past (European Studies) (Durham); Classical Archaeology and Greek (Edinburgh); Classical and Archaeological Studies with Drama (Kent); Classical Studies and a Modern Language (Liverpool); Classical Studies and Art History (St Andrews). *NOW CHECK PROSPECTUSES AND WEBSITES FOR ANY RECENT CHANGES.*

Universities and colleges teaching quality See www.tqi.ac.uk; www.qaa.ac.uk.

Top universities and colleges (Research) Bristol; Durham; Leeds; London (RH); Nottingham; Warwick.

ADMISSIONS INFORMATION

Number of applicants per place (approx) Birmingham 3; Bristol 10; Durham 15; Exeter 3; Lampeter 2; Leeds 7; London (RH) 4; Newcastle 8; Nottingham 10; Reading 10; Swansea 5; Warwick 23.

Advice to applicants and planning the UCAS personal statement Discuss any A-level work and what has attracted you to this subject. Describe visits to classical sites or museums and what impressed you. **Birmingham** (Class Lit Civ) The course is appropriate for students who enjoy books and the ideas behind them and who are fascinated by other cultures and different ways of observing the world. What do you most enjoy reading? **St Andrews** Reasons for choosing course. Evidence of interest. Sport/extra-curricular activities. Posts of responsibility.

Misconceptions about this course Birmingham (Class Lit Civ) A study of Classics at school is not necessary although while many people catch the classics bug by doing classical civilisation at A-level, others come to classics through reading the myths or seeing the plays and being fascinated by them. For others the interdisciplinary nature of the subject attracts them – literature, drama, history, politics and philosophy. **Exeter** (Class St) This is not a language degree. There is no requirement for either A-level Latin or Greek.

Selection interviews Yes Birmingham, Durham, Kent, Lampeter, London (RH), Newcastle, Nottingham, Warwick; **No** Bristol.

Interview advice and questions In the past questions have included: What special interests do you have in Classical Studies/Classics? Have you visited Greece, Rome or any other classical sites or museums and what were your impressions? These are the types of questions to expect, along with those to explore your knowledge of the culture, theatre and architecture of the period. **Birmingham** (Class Lit Civ) The programme includes some language study and, if applicants do not have a GCSE in a foreign language, we ask them to do a short language aptitude test. Interview questions are likely to focus on your reading interests (not necessarily classical texts!) and your own reflections on them. We are interested in your ability to think for yourself and we want to be sure that you are someone who will enjoy three years of reading and talking about books. **Swansea** Reasons for choosing the subject and how the student hopes to benefit from the course. See also **Chapter 6**.

Applicants' impressions (A=Open day; B=Interview day) Birmingham (A) A group talk about the course and tour was followed by individual interviews. **Exeter** (A) There was a lecture on gladiators, a tour, a lecture on the course and questions with current students and staff. **Warwick** (A) A talk about the course and finance, a tour of the campus and a question-and-answer session.

Reasons for rejection (non-academic) Birmingham Lukewarm interest in the subject. Lack of clear idea why they wanted to do this degree.

AFTER-RESULTS ADVICE

Universities with vacancies in Clearing (2006) Bradford; Kent; Lampeter; Leeds; London (RH); Newcastle; Reading; Roehampton.

Offers to applicants repeating A-levels Higher Nottingham, St Andrews, Warwick; **Same** Birmingham, Bristol, Durham, Exeter, Leeds, London (RH), Newcastle.

GRADUATE DESTINATIONS AND EMPLOYMENT (2005 HESA)

Graduates surveyed 530 **Employed** 225 **In further study** 145 **Assumed unemployed** 25.

OTHER DEGREE SUBJECTS FOR CONSIDERATION

Archaeology; Ancient History; Classics; Greek; History; History of Art; Latin; Philosophy.

For information on how to read the Subject Tables, see **Chapter 7**.

CLASSICS

(see also Classical Studies/Classical Civilisation, Greek and Latin)

NB The points totals shown to the left of the institutions are for ease of reference only. It must not be assumed that tariff points are always used by institutions or that they can be substituted for an offer in grades. The level of an offer is not necessarily indicative of the quality of a course.

COURSE OFFERS INFORMATION

Subject requirements/preferences **GCSE Cambridge**, **Oxford** Grade A in most subjects preferred. **Durham** Four grades A*, three grades A. **Edinburgh**, **St Andrews** English, mathematics and a foreign language. **Swansea** Greek if not at A-level, five grades A*, five grades B. **AL** Check courses for Latin/Greek requirements.

Your target offers

360 pts and above
    Cambridge – AAA (Class Gk Lat; Modn Mediev Langs (Class Lat) (Class Gk))
    Oxford – Offers vary eg AAA–AAB (Class Engl; Class Modn Langs)
340 pts **Bristol** – AAB–ABB (Class; Class Euro)
    St Andrews – AAB (Class courses)
320 pts **Durham** – ABB (Classics)
    London (UCL) – ABB+AS–BBB+AS (Class; Class Abrd)
    Newcastle – ABB–BBC (Classics)
    Warwick – ABB–BBBc **or** AB-BBbbc (Classics)
300 pts **Edinburgh** – BBB (Class; Class Engl Lang; Class Ling)
    Leeds – BBB (Classics)
    London (King's) – BBB+AS **or** BBbbc (Classics)
    London (RH) – BBB 300 pts (Classics)
    Manchester – BBB (Class; Class Anc Hist)
    Nottingham – ABC–BBB (Class (Gk) (Lat))
280 pts **Liverpool** – BBC 280 pts (Classics)
    Reading – 280 pts (Classics)
260 pts **Swansea** – 260–300 pts (Classics)
180 pts **Lampeter** – open admission policy (Classics)
80 pts **London (Birk)** – 80 pts for under 21s (over 21s varies) (p/t Classics)

Alternative offers
IB offers Bristol 33–34 pts; Cambridge 38–42 pts; Liverpool 30 pts; London (King's) 32 pts, (RH) 32 pts, (UCL) 34 pts; Manchester 32 pts; Newcastle 32 pts; Oxford 38–42 pts; Reading 30 pts; St Andrews 36 pts; Warwick 32–36 pts.
Scottish offers See **Chapter 7**.

CHOOSING YOUR COURSE (SEE ALSO CH.1)

Subject information Classics courses focus on a study of Greek and Latin but may also include topics related to ancient history, art and architecture, drama and philosophy. These subjects are also frequently offered in joint courses. **Useful websites** www.classicspage.com; www.classics.ac.uk; www.bbc.co.uk/history/ancient/greeks; www.bbc.co.uk/history/ancient/romans; www.cambridgescp.com.

Course variations Classical Past (Durham); Classics and Linguistics (Edinburgh); Classics and Ancient History (Manchester); Combined Honours (Liverpool); Classics and Management (St Andrews). *NOW CHECK PROSPECTUSES AND WEBSITES FOR ANY RECENT CHANGES.*

Universities and colleges teaching quality See www.tqi.ac.uk; www.qaa.ac.uk.

Top universities and colleges (Research) (including Ancient History and Modern Greek Studies) Bristol; Cambridge*; Durham; Exeter; London (King's)*, (RH), (UCL)*; Manchester; Oxford*; Reading; St Andrews; Warwick.

ADMISSIONS INFORMATION

Number of applicants per place (approx) Bristol 12; Cambridge 2; Durham (Class) 8, (Class Past) 10; Lampeter 5; Leeds 4; London (King's) 6, (RH) 6; Newcastle 14; Nottingham 10; Oxford 2; Swansea 6.

Advice to applicants and planning the UCAS personal statement Describe any visits made to classical sites or museums or literature which you have read and enjoyed. Discuss any significant aspects which impressed you. **Birmingham** Classics is an interdisciplinary subject and we are looking for people who are versatile, imaginative and independently minded, so all types of extra-curricular activities (drama, music, philosophy, creative arts, politics, other languages and cultures) will be relevant. See also under **Classical Studies/Classical Civilisation**.

Misconceptions about this course While Classics can appear irrelevant and elitist, universities aim to assist students to leave with a range of transferable skills that are of importance to employers.

Selection interviews Yes Cambridge, London (RH), (UCL), Newcastle, Oxford, Swansea; **No** Durham, Leeds, St Andrews.

Interview advice and questions What do you think it means to study Classics? Do you think Classics is still a vital and central cultural discipline? What made you apply to study Classics at this university? There are often detailed questions on the texts which the students have read, to find out how reflective they are in their reading. See also under **Classical Studies/Classical Civilisation**. See also **Chapter 6**.

Applicants' impressions (A=Open day; B=Interview day) Oxford (B; Classics and English) There were two interviewers and a 30-minute interview. I felt nervous but not pressurised, the interviewers were rather detached and not particularly friendly. The questions related to English Literature – the sources of Chaucer's *The Miller's Tale* and Shakespeare's *A Midsummer Night's Dream*. I was also asked to comment on an unseen poem and asked several questions about my personal statement. I was able to meet a number of undergraduates and discussed student life in detail. I also attended an unofficial 'open day' hosted by the students which covered these topics in more detail.

Reasons for rejection (non-academic) Failing to achieve grade B at Latin A-level. Did not demonstrate a clear sense of why they wanted to study Classics rather than anything else.

AFTER-RESULTS ADVICE

Universities with vacancies in Clearing (2006) Kent; Lampeter; Leeds; London (RH); Reading.

Offers to applicants repeating A-levels Higher Leeds, Nottingham, St Andrews; **Same** Durham, Newcastle; Swansea.

GRADUATE DESTINATIONS AND EMPLOYMENT (2005 HESA)
See **Classical Studies/Classical Civilisation**.

OTHER DEGREE SUBJECTS FOR CONSIDERATION
See **Classical Studies/Classical Civilisation**.

COMMUNICATION STUDIES/COMMUNICATIONS

(see also **Art and Design (General)**, **Business Courses (Section C)**, **Film, Radio, Video and TV Studies**, **Media Studies** and **Speech Pathology/Sciences/Therapy**)

NB The points totals shown to the left of the institutions are for ease of reference only. It must not be assumed that tariff points are always used by institutions or that they can be substituted for an offer in grades. The level of an offer is not necessarily indicative of the quality of a course.

COURSE OFFERS INFORMATION

Subject requirements/preferences GCSE English and mathematics grade A–C may be required. **AL** No specific subjects required.

Your target offers
340 pts Ulster – AAB (Comm Adv Mark)
320 pts London (Gold) – ABB (Media Comm)

300 pts **Birmingham** – BBB 300 pts approx (Cult Soty Comm (Euro); Comm Tech)
Bournemouth – 300 pts (Adv Mark Comm; PR)
Cardiff – BBB (ABB joint hons) (Comm; Engl Lang Comm)
Leeds – BBB (Comm St)
Leicester – BBB 300 pts (Comm Media Soty)
Loughborough – BBB **or** BBbb (Comm Media St)
Newcastle – BBB–BBC (Media Comm Cult St)
Sheffield – BBB (Hum Comm Sci)
Surrey – 300–260 pts (Cult Media Comm)
280 pts **Aberystwyth** – 280 pts (Media Comm St)
Bournemouth – BBC 280 pts (Comm Media)
De Montfort – 280 pts (Hum Comm (Sp Lang Thera))
Liverpool – 280–300 pts (Comm Media Pop Mus; Comm Bus St; Pol Comm St)
London (King's) – BBC (Engl Lang Comm)
London (RH) – BBC (Sci Comm courses)
Oxford Brookes – BBC (Comm Media Cult)
UCE Birmingham – 280 pts (Media Comm)
260 pts **Bristol** – BCC (Df St)
Brunel – 260 pts (Comm Media St)
Chester – 260 pts (Comm St)
Glasgow Caledonian – BCC (Comm Mass Media)
Lancaster – BCC (IT Media Comm; Comm Comp Sys)
Northumbria – BCC 260 pts (Communication)
Oxford Brookes – BCC (Publishing)
Sunderland – 260 pts (Media Cult Comm)
Ulster – BCC 260 pts (Communication)
240 pts **Abertay Dundee** – 240 pts (Corp Comm)
Brighton – 240 pts (Comm Dig Media; Comm Media St)
De Montfort – 240 pts (Adv Mark Comm)
Glamorgan – 240 pts (Comm St)
Nottingham Trent – 240 pts (Fash Mark Comm)
Robert Gordon – CCC (Corp Comm PR)
Sheffield Hallam – 240 pts (Comm St)
UCE Birmingham – 240–280 pts (Vis Comm)
220 pts **Huddersfield** – 220 pts (Adv Mark Comm)
Lincoln – 220–240 pts (Media Cult Comm courses)
200 pts **Buckingham** – 200–240 pts (Comm Bus St; Comm Media St)
Coventry – 200–260 pts (Comm Cult Media)
Hertfordshire – 200–240 pts (Engl Lang Comm courses; Multim Comm Comb Hons)
Southampton Solent – 200 pts (PR Comm)
180 pts **Anglia Ruskin** – 180–220 pts (Comm St; Intercult Comm courses)
Greenwich – 180 pts (Adv Mark Comm)
Hertfordshire – 180–280 pts (Multim Comm)
Sheffield Hallam – 180 pts (Bus Comm)
160 pts **Central Lancashire** – 160–200 pts (Fash Brnd Prom; Comm St courses)
East London – 160 pts (Comm St)
Greenwich – CC 160 pts (Media Cult Comm; Media Comm; Adv Mark Comm)
Huddersfield – 160 pts (Adv Media Des Mgt)
London Met – 160–200 pts (Mass Comm courses; Comm; Comm Vis Cult)
Manchester Met – 160 pts (Comm; Corp Comm; Hum Comm; Comm Cult Media)
Middlesex – 160–200 pts (Comm Engl Lang St; Journal Comm courses)
Napier – CC (Communication)
Portsmouth – 160 pts (Comm Des)
Wolverhampton – 160–220 pts (Media Comm St)
York St John – 160 pts (Communication)

140 pts   Richmond (Am Int Univ) – 140 pts (Crea Arts Comm)

Leeds Met – contact University

Alternative offers
IB offers Aberystwyth 28 pts; Brighton 30 pts; Chester 30 pts; Leicester 30 pts; Liverpool 30 pts.
Scottish offers See **Chapter 7**.

OTHER HIGHER EDUCATION COURSES IN THE SUBJECT FIELD

Foundation degrees (contact the institutions for details) Blackpool and Fylde (Coll); Derby; East Lancashire (IHE); Leicester; Oxford Brookes.

Higher National Diploma courses
100 pts and below
Aberdeen (Coll); Abertay Dundee; Adam Smith (Coll); Arts London; Bell (Coll); Bournemouth (AI); Cardiff (UWIC); Falmouth (UC); Forth Valley (Coll); Glamorgan; Glasgow (CC); Gloucestershire; Greenwich; Napier EE (also HND Journal); North Warwickshire (Coll); Northumberland (Coll); Ravensbourne (CDC); Reid Kerr (Coll); Robert Gordon; South Birmingham (Coll); Southampton Solent; UHI Millennium Inst; Warwickshire (Coll); Winchester; Wolverhampton; Worcester (CT). See also **Art and Design (Graphic Design)** and **Film, Radio, Video and TV Studies**.

CHOOSING YOUR COURSE (SEE ALSO CH.1)

Subject information Some courses combine academic and vocational studies, whilst others may be wholly academic or strictly vocational. The subject thus covers a very wide range of approaches concerning 'communication' which should be carefully researched before applying. **Useful websites** www.camfoundation.com; www.coi.gov.uk.

Course variations Culture, Society and Communication (Europe) (Birmingham); Advertising, Marketing and Communication (Bournemouth); Human Communication (Speech and Language Therapy) (De Montfort); Combined Honours (Liverpool); Science and Communication courses (London (RH)); Journalism and Communication Studies (Middlesex). *NOW CHECK PROSPECTUSES AND WEBSITES FOR ANY RECENT CHANGES.*

Universities and colleges teaching quality See www.tqi.ac.uk; www.qaa.ac.uk.

Top universities and colleges (Research) See **Media Studies**.

Sandwich degree courses Brighton; Brunel; De Montfort; London Met; Loughborough; Ulster.

ADMISSIONS INFORMATION

Number of applicants per place (approx) Brunel 9; Cardiff 6.

Advice to applicants and planning the UCAS personal statement Applicants should be able to give details of any work experience/work shadowing/discussions they have had in the media including, for example, in newspaper offices, advertising agencies, local radio stations or film companies (see also **Media Studies**). **Huddersfield** Critical awareness. Willingness to develop a range of communication skills including new technologies. **London (Gold)** Interest in a study in depth of media theory plus some experience in media practice. **Manchester Met** Motivation more important than grades.

Selection interviews Yes Brighton, Brunel, Buckingham, Coventry, Glamorgan, Glasgow Caledonian, Leicester, London Met, Manchester Met, Middlesex, Southampton Solent, Ulster; **Some** Anglia Ruskin, Cardiff, Chester, Huddersfield (rarely), London (Gold) (mature students), Sheffield Hallam (mature students).

Interview advice and questions Courses vary in this subject and, depending on your choice, the questions will focus on the type of course, either biased towards the media, or towards human communication by way of language, psychology, sociology or linguistics. See also separate subject tables. See also **Chapter 6**.

For information on how to read the Subject Tables, see **Chapter 7**.

Applicants' impressions (A=Open day; B=Interview day) Bournemouth (A) Applicants had a chance to wander round the campus (but not the accommodation since it was term time). There was a talk on Media and Communications courses, followed by questions and a guided tour with the students.

Reasons for rejection (non-academic) Unlikely to work well in groups. Poor writing. Misguided application, for example more practical work wanted. Poor motivation. Inability to give reasons for choosing the course. More practice needed in academic writing skills. Wrong course choice, wanted more practical work.

AFTER-RESULTS ADVICE
Universities with vacancies in Clearing (2006) Anglia Ruskin; Bournemouth; Cardiff; Central Lancashire; Chester; East London; Gloucestershire; Hertfordshire; Huddersfield; Kingston; Lincoln; London Met; Manchester Met; Middlesex; UCE Birmingham; Wolverhampton.

Offers to applicants repeating A-levels Possibly higher Coventry; **Same** Brunel, Cardiff, Chester, Huddersfield, Loughborough, Nottingham Trent, Richmond (Am Int Univ), Robert Gordon, Sheffield Hallam.

GRADUATE DESTINATIONS AND EMPLOYMENT (2005 HESA)
Graduates surveyed 205 **Employed** 135 **In further study** 15 **Assumed unemployed** 5.

OTHER DEGREE SUBJECTS FOR CONSIDERATION
Art and Design; Film, Radio, Video and TV Studies; Information Studies; Media Studies; Psychology.

COMMUNITY STUDIES
(see also **Health Sciences/Studies, Nursing and Midwifery** and **Social Work**)

NB The points totals shown to the left of the institutions are for ease of reference only. It must not be assumed that tariff points are always used by institutions or that they can be substituted for an offer in grades. The level of an offer is not necessarily indicative of the quality of a course.

COURSE OFFERS INFORMATION
Subject requirements/preferences GCSE English and mathematics grade A–C may be required at some institutions. **Other: North East Wales (IHE)** Minimum age 19 plus youth work experience. **AL** No specific subjects required.

Your target offers

240 pts **Bangor** – 240–280 pts (Commun Dev)
220 pts **Dundee** – 220 pts 2nd yr entry (Commun Educ)
Gloucestershire – 220 pts (Commun Dev)
200 pts **Coventry** – 200 pts (Soc Welf Commun St)
Manchester Met – 200 pts (Commun Arts)
Teesside – 200 pts (Yth St)
Ulster – 200 pts (Commun Yth Wk)
180 pts **Bolton** – 180 pts (Commun St)
Derby – 180 pts (App Commun Yth St)
Manchester Met – 180 pts (Yth Commun Wk)
160 pts **Cardiff (UWIC)** – 160 pts (Commun Educ)
Central Lancashire – 160 pts (Cr Commun Ctzn)
Cumbria – CC 160 pts approx (Chld Yng Pers Fam St Educ St)
De Montfort – 160 pts (Yth Commun Dev)
Greenwich – 160 pts min (Yth Commun St)
Liverpool John Moores – CC (App Commun Soc St; Commun Hlth Soc Welf)
London Met – 160 pts (Commun Sctr Mgt)
Newport – 160 pts (Yth Commun St)

Strathclyde – CC (Commun Arts; Commun Educ)
Sunderland – 160 pts (Commun Hlth)
150 pts **Dundee** – 150 pts 1ˢᵗ yr entry (Commun Educ)
140 pts **Marjon (Coll)** – 140–200 pts (Commun Prac courses; Commun Wk; Yth Commun Wk)
Trinity Carmarthen (Coll) – 140 pts (Chr Commun St; Yth Commun Wk)
120 pts **Huddersfield** – 120–140 pts (Hlth Commun St)
North East Wales (IHE) – 120–80 pts (Yth Commun)
100 pts **Bradford (Coll)** – 100–140 pts (Commun Wk; Yth Commun Dev)
80 pts **Oxford Brookes** – EE (Yth Commun Wk App Theol)

Alternative offers
IB offers Dundee 29 pts.
Scottish offers See **Chapter 7**.

OTHER HIGHER EDUCATION COURSES IN THE SUBJECT FIELD
Foundation degrees (contact the institutions for details) Bangor; Bradford; Bury (Coll); De Montfort; Derby; Glamorgan; Leeds Met; Newcastle (Coll); North East Wales (IHE); North Warwickshire (Coll); Truro (Coll); Winchester; Wolverhampton.

Higher National Diploma courses Cornwall (Coll); Dudley (Coll); East London; Havering (Coll); Llandrillo Cymru (Coll); Manchester Met; Plymouth; St Helens (Coll); South Devon (Coll); Truro (Coll); Worcester (CT).

CHOOSING YOUR COURSE (SEE ALSO CH.1)
Subject information These courses cover aspects of social problems, for example housing, food, health, the elderly, welfare rights and counselling. Work experience is very important. Most courses will give professional qualifications. **Useful website** www.csv.org.uk.

Course variations Child, Young Person and Family Studies (Cumbria); Community Sector Management (London Met); Community Arts (Manchester Met); Youth and Community Work with Applied Theology (Oxford Brookes); Community Health (Sunderland). *NOW CHECK PROSPECTUSES AND WEBSITES FOR ANY RECENT CHANGES.*

Universities and colleges teaching quality See www.tqi.ac.uk; www.qaa.ac.uk.

ADMISSIONS INFORMATION
Number of applicants per place (approx) Bradford (Coll) 5; Liverpool John Moores 2; Manchester Met 8; Marjon (Coll) 7; Strathclyde 6.

Advice to applicants and planning the UCAS personal statement You should describe any work you have done with people, particularly in a caring capacity, such as social work, or with the elderly or young children in schools, nursing, hospital work, youth work, community or charity work. You should also describe any problems arising when dealing with such people and how staff overcame these difficulties. **Derby** Experience and the ability to express oneself in written and spoken form. Relevant experience of work with the elderly or young people in the 11–25 age range. See **Appendix 2**.

Advice for overseas applicants **Marjon (Coll)** Strong multi-cultural policy. English as a Foreign Language teaching offered.

Selection interviews **Yes** Bradford (Coll), Derby, Huddersfield (in groups), Manchester Met, Strathclyde; **Some** Liverpool John Moores.

Interview advice and questions This subject has a vocational emphasis and work experience, or even full-time work in the field, will be expected. Community work varies considerably so, depending on your experiences, you could be asked about the extent of your work and how you would solve the problems which occur. **Derby** Take us through your experience of youth and community work. What are the problems facing young people today? See also **Chapter 6**.

Reasons for rejection (non-academic) Insufficient experience. Lack of understanding of community and youth work. Uncertain career aspirations. Incompatibility with values, methods and aims of the course. No work experience.

AFTER-RESULTS ADVICE
Universities with vacancies in Clearing (2006) Bangor; Bolton; De Montfort; Gloucestershire; Liverpool John Moores; London Met.

Offers to applicants repeating A-levels **Same** Bradford (Coll), Liverpool John Moores, Marjon (Coll).

GRADUATE DESTINATIONS AND EMPLOYMENT (2005 HESA)
See **Social Work**.

OTHER DEGREE SUBJECTS FOR CONSIDERATION
Communication Studies; Education; Nursing; Politics; Psychology; Social Policy and Administration; Social Work; Sociology; Youth Studies.

COMPUTER COURSES

(including **Artificial Intelligence, Business Information Systems, Computer Science, Digital Computing, E-Commerce, Information Technology, Technology, Virtual Reality** and **Web Management and Computer Networks;** see also **Engineering (Computer, Control, Software and Systems)** and **Technology)**

NB The points totals shown to the left of the institutions are for ease of reference only. It must not be assumed that tariff points are always used by institutions or that they can be substituted for an offer in grades. The level of an offer is not necessarily indicative of the quality of a course.

COURSE OFFERS INFORMATION
Subject requirements/preferences GCSE Aston, Belfast (Queen's), Leeds, Liverpool, London (Gold), Loughborough, Sheffield Hallam, Staffordshire, Warwick Mathematics grade A or B. Brunel Nine subjects at grade A–C. Buckingham English grade C, mathematics grade B. Cambridge, Oxford Grade As in most subjects preferred. Exeter Top seven GCSEs to equal 40 pts, with grade B mathematics if not taken at A/AS-level. Hull Three subjects grade A, three subjects grade B and three subjects grade C (average) preferred. Kingston Grade A or B in English, mathematics preferred. London (King's) Mathematics grade B. Surrey Eight subjects at grade B or better. Warwick Grade A/B in mathematics if not at A-level, B in English, seven subjects at grade B or better. York Six subjects at grade A. AL Mathematics, a science subject or computer science may be required for some courses.

Your target offers
360 pts **and above**
    Cambridge – AAA (Comp Sci)
    Durham – AAA (Nat Sci (Comp Sci))
    Imperial London – AAA (Maths Comp Sci)
    Manchester – AAA (MEng Comp Sci; Artif Intel)
    Nottingham – AAA–BBC (Comp Sci courses)
    Oxford – Offers vary eg AAA–AAB (Comp Sci)
    Southampton – 390 pts (MEng Comp Sci; Comp Sci Artif Intel; Soft Eng)
    Southampton – 370 pts (BSc/BEng Comp Sci; Comp Sci Artif Intel)
    Strathclyde – AAA 2nd yr entry (MEng Comp Sci)
    Warwick – AABb **or** AAbbb (Comp Sci; Comp Bus St; Comp Mgt Sci; Phil Comp Sci; Maths Comp)
340 pts **Bath** – AAB 340 pts (Comp Sci; Comp Inf Sys)
    Bristol – AAB (Comp Sci; Comp Sci Euro)
    Imperial London – AAB (Comp; Comp (Artif Intel) (Comput Mgt) (Euro) (Soft Eng))

Lancaster – AAB (Comp Sci Innov)

Manchester – AAB (Comp Sci Ind; Comp Sci; Artif Intel; Comp Sci Maths; Comp Sci Bus Mgt)

St Andrews – AAB (Comp Sci Econ; Comp Sci Phys; Intnet Comp Sci Phys)

York – AAB (Comp Sci; Comp Sci Maths)

320 pts **Aston** – ABB 320 pts (Bus Comp IT)

Birmingham – ABB–BBC (Comp Sci; Comp Sci Soft Eng; Comp Sci Bus Mgt; Artif Intel courses)

Cardiff – ABB–BBC (Comp Sci; Comp Sci (Comp Vis Comp Graph) (Knwl Inf Sys); Comp Phys; Comp Maths; Inf Sys)

East Anglia – ABB (Comp Sci N Am/Aus)

Exeter – ABB–BBC (IT Mgt Bus; Comp Sci)

Glasgow – ABB–BBB (BA Comp Sci)

Kent – 320 pts (Comp Sci courses)

Lancaster – ABB (Bus Comp Inf Sys)

Leeds – ABB (Artif Intel Phil; Artif Intel Phys; Artif Intel Maths; Artif Intel Mus; Inf Sys; Comp Sci courses)

Liverpool – ABB (Comp Multim Sys)

London (King's) – ABB **or** AAC **or** ABbb (Comp Sci; Comp Sci Mgt; Comp Sci Abrd; Comp Sci Ind)

London (QM) – ABB (IT Org Mgt)

London (UCL) – ABB+AS (Comp Sci; Comp Sci Int)

Manchester – ABB (Comp Bus Apps; IT NMedia; IT Mgt Bus; Intnet Comp)

Reading – 320–350 pts (MEng App Artif Intel Cyber)

St Andrews – ABB (Comp Sci Maths; Comp Sci Stats; Intnet Comp Sci Mgt)

Sheffield – ABB (MComp courses; Comp Sci; Artif Intel Comp Sci; Comp Bus Fin)

Southampton – ABB (Comp Sci; Comp Sci Artif Intel)

Sussex – ABB–BBB 360–340 pts (MComp IT E-Comm; Comp Sci; Comp Artif Intel; BA/BSc Comp Sci; Intnet Comp; Multim Dig Sys; Mus Inform)

300 pts **Aberdeen** – BBB (Comp Sci; Intnet Inf Sys; Comp E-Bus; Comp Sci (Biomed Comp))

Aston – BBB–BCC (Comp Sci; Comp Bus)

Bangor – 300–320 pts (MEng Comm Comp Sys)

Belfast (Queen's) – BBB (MEng Mgt Inf Sys; MEng Comp Sci; Bus IT; Comp Gms Des Dev; Comp IT)

Bournemouth – 300 pts (Comp Vis Animat)

Brunel – 300 pts (Multim Tech Des)

City – BBB–BBC (Comp Sci; Comp Sci Artif Intel; Comp Sci Dist Sys; Comp Sci Gms Tech; Comp Sci Mus Inform; Bus Comp Sys)

Dundee – BBB–CCC (App Comp; E-Comm Comp)

Durham – BBB–AAB (Comp Sci; Comp Sci Euro St)

East Anglia – BBB (Bus Inf Sys)

Choosing your university and degree course?

Why not contact **Brian Heap**, the author of *Degree Course Offers*, for a personal or telephone consultation for advice on issues such as:

- **choosing A-level subjects**
- **degree or diploma courses**
- **completing your UCAS form**
- **choosing the right university or college**

For details of services and consultation fees contact: The Higher Education Advice and Planning Service; phone 01386 859355 email heaps@dial.pipex.com

For information on how to read the Subject Tables, see **Chapter 7**.

Edinburgh – ABC–BBB (Comp Sci; Comp Sci Mgt Sci; Comp Sci Phys; Comp Sci Maths; Artif Intel Comp Sci; Comp Electron)

Essex – 300–280 pts (Comp Sci (Artif Intel) (Embd Sys Robot) (Soft Eng); Intnet Tech Bus)

Exeter – BBB–BCC (Intnet Comp; Intnet Eng)

Heriot-Watt – ABC 2nd yr entry (Comp Electron)

Kent – BBB (Comp Psy; Comp Sci)

Lancaster – BBB (Comp Sci; Comp Sci Maths; Comp Sci Mus; Comp Sci Multim Sys; Comp Euro Lang)

Leicester – 300–340 pts (Maths Comp Sci; Comp Sci; Comp Sci (Euro))

Liverpool – BBB 300 pts (MEng Comp Sci; Comp Inf Sys; Comp Sci; Intnet Comp; Electron Commer Comp; Artif Intel; Soft Dev)

London (Gold) – BBB (Crea Comp)

London (King's) – BBB–BBbb (Comp Sys Electron)

London (QM) – 300–260 pts (Comp Sci Bus Mgt; Fr/Ger/Russ Ling Comp Sci; Comp courses)

London (RH) – ABC–BBB 300 pts (Comp Sci; Comp Sci Artif Intel; Comp Sci Mgt; Comp Sci Fr; Comp Sci Maths; Comp Sci Phys; Comp Sci Bioinf)

Newcastle – ABC–BBB (Comp Sci courses; Inf Sys courses)

Reading – 300–340 pts (Comp Sci; App Comp Sci; IT courses)

St Andrews – BBB (Intnet Comp Sci)

Sheffield – BBB **or** ABbb/BBbb (BSc Comp Sci; Comp Sci Maths; Comp Sci Fr/Ger; Artif Intel Comp Sci)

Strathclyde – BBB–ABB 1st yr entry (Comp Sci; Bus Inf Sys; Comp Sci Law; MEng Des Comp; Intnet Comp)

Surrey – BBB (Comp IT; Comp Comm; Comp Mdl Simul; Comp Sci Eng)

Swansea – 300 pts (MEng Computing)

280 pts **Abertay Dundee** – BBC (Comp Arts; Comp Gms Tech)

Aberystwyth – 280 pts (Comp Sci; Comp Graph Vsn Gms; Comp Sci Artif Intel)

Brunel – BBC 280–300 pts (Comp Sci; Inf Sys; Interact Comp; Net Comp)

East Anglia – BBC (Comp Sci; App Comp; Intnet Comp)

Heriot-Watt – BBC 2nd yr entry (IT; Comp Sci)

Kent – 280 pts (Multim Tech Des)

Lancaster – BBC (IT Media Comm)

Leicester – 280–340 pts (Comp Sci Mgt)

Lincoln –280 pts (MComp Comp; Intnet Comp; Gms Comp; Comp Cyber)

Liverpool – 280 pts (Comp Multim Sys)

Reading – 280 pts (BSc Cyber courses)

St Andrews – BBC (Comp Sci courses except under **320/300 pts**)

Swansea – 280 pts (BSc Comp Sci; Comp Sci Lang; Comp Comm; E-Comm Tech; Intnet Tech; Maths Comp Sci; Mbl Comm)

Westminster – 280 pts (Bus IT)

260 pts **Aberystwyth** – 260 pts (Artif Intel Robot)

Aston – BCC–CCC (Multim Comp; Intnet Sys; Intnet Eng)

Belfast (Queen's) – BCC (BEng Comp Sci)

Bradford – 260–240 pts (Comp Animat Spec Efcts; Interact Sys Vid Gms Des; Intnet Prod Des)

Brunel – BCC 260 pts (Fin Comp; Mbl Comp)

Coventry – 260–280 pts (Crea Comp; Gms Tech)

Glasgow – BCC–CCC (BSc Comp Sci; Soft Eng)

Heriot-Watt – BCC 260 pts 2nd yr entry (Chem Comp Sci)

Kingston – 260 pts (Bus IT; Comp Sci courses; Mbl Comp; Intnet Comp; Bus IT)

Lancaster – BCC (Comm Comp Sys)

Leicester – 260–320 pts (Comp Comb courses)

London (Gold) – BCC (Comp Inf Sys; Comp Sci; Comp Des WWWeb; Intnet Comp; IT)

Loughborough – 260–340 pts (MComp Comp Sci; Comp Sci E-Bus; Comp Sci Artif Intel; BSc Comp Sci)

Napier – 260 pts (Comp; Comp Net Distr Sys; Hum Comp Sys; Inf Sys; IT Mgt; Intnet Comp; Multim Sys; Soft Eng)

Northumbria – 260 pts (Bus Inf Sys)

Richmond (Am Int Univ) – 260 pts (Comp Inf Sys)

Stirling – BCC (Bus Comp)

Swansea – 260 pts (Intnet Tech; E-Commer Tech; Mbl Comm Intnet Tech)

Ulster – 260–280 pts (Comp Sci; Comp; Comp Gms Dev)

240 pts **Abertay Dundee** – CCC (Gms Prod Mgt)

Bangor – 240–260 pts (Comp Sci; Comp Sys Bus St; Comp Sys Psy; Comm Comp Sys)

Bradford – 240 pts (Comp Sci; Comp Inf Sys; Intnet Comp; Bus Comp; Multim Comp; Cyber; ICT courses; Des Comp Gms)

Brighton – 240 pts (Comp; Comp Sci; Intnet Bus Comp; Bus Inf Sys; Interact Comp; Bus Soft Dev; Inftq DEST)

Bristol UWE – 240–260 pts (Comp Sci; Comp Inf Sys; Bus Inf Sys; Comp Scrty; Mbl Tech; Web Des; Comp Telecom)

Buckingham – 240 pts (Comp; Bus IT)

Chester – 240–260 pts (Net Comm Sys; Multim Tech; Intnet Tech; Inf Sys Mgt; Comp Sci; E-Bus; Bus Inf Sys)

Chester (Warrington) – 240 pts (Comp St Comb)

Coventry – 240 pts (Bus IT; Multim Comp; Net Mbl Comp)

De Montfort – 240 pts (Computing)

Glamorgan – 240 pts (Comp Foren; Comp Gms Dev; Comp Sys Scrty; Mbl Comp; Net Mgt Scrty)

Greenwich – 240 pts (BEng Comp Sys Soft Eng; Comp Net; Intnet Tech; Bus Comp)

Hertfordshire – 240 pts (Bus Inf Sys)

Hull – 240–300 pts (Comp Sci Gms Dev; Comp Sci Ind Exp; Comp Sci)

For information on how to read the Subject Tables, see **Chapter 7**.

Keele – 240–260 pts (Comp Sci; Inf Sys)

Kent – 240 pts (IT courses)

Lincoln – 240 pts (BSc Comp Inf Sys; Comp; Web Tech; Gms Prod)

London (St George's) – 240 pts (Biomed Inform)

Loughborough – 240 pts (Chem IT)

Northumbria – 240 pts (Multim Dig Enter; Intnet Comp; Comp Sci; Comp Gms Soft Eng; Comp Foren; Comp Bus; Intnet Comp)

Nottingham Trent – 240 pts (Comp Sci courses; Comp St; Comp Cyber; Hum Comp Interact; Inf Sys; Bus Inf Sys)

Oxford Brookes – CCC (Inf Sys; Comp; Comp Sci; Intel Sys)

Paisley – CCC (Comp Gms Tech; Comp Sci)

Plymouth – 240 pts (Comp Sys Net; Comp Inform)

Portsmouth – 240 pts (Bus Inf Sys; Inf Sys Net; Comp Net Mgt Des; Intnet Tech; Ent Comp Enter Tech)

Salford – 240 pts (Comp Sci; Comp Sci Inf Sys; Intel Sys; Intnet Comp; Mbl Comp)

Strathclyde – CCC (Des Comp)

Sunderland – 240 pts (BSc Net Comp; Comp)

220 pts **Abertay Dundee** – CCD (Comp; Comp Net)

Bangor – 220–260 pts (Intnet Sys E-Commer)

Glamorgan – 220–260 pts (Comp Sci; Inf Sys; IT; Intnet Comp)

Gloucestershire – 220 pts (Bus IT; Comp; IT; Dtbs Sys courses; Intnet Sys Dev; Multim; Net Comp; ICT)

Heriot-Watt – CCD 1st yr entry (Chem Comp Sci; Comp Sci)

Liverpool Hope – 220 pts (IT; Intnet Tech)

Manchester Met – 220–280 pts (Comp; Inf Sys; Multim Comp; Artif Intel; Intnet Comp; Comp Sys; Mbl Comp Tech; Comp Gms Tech; Comp Sci)

Salford – 220 pts (Multim Intnet Tech)
Stirling – CCD/BC (Comp Sci; Inf Sys)
Sunderland – 220 pts (Foren Comp)
Teesside – 220–260 pts (IT; Bus Inf Sys; Bus Comp; Comp Gms Des; Comp Gms Sci; Comp Gms Prog; Comp Graph Sci; Web Dev; Crea Multim; Comp St; Dig Foren)

200 pts **Abertay Dundee** – CDD (Inf Sys)
Aberystwyth – 200 pts (Intnet Comp)
Anglia Ruskin – 200 pts (Comp Sci; Bus Inf Sys)
Bolton – 200 pts (Multim Web Dev; Comp; Comp Gms Soft Dev; Bus Inf Sys; Comp Tech; Intnet Comm Net; Intnet Sys Dev)
Bournemouth – 200–240 pts (Comp; Mbl Sys; Intnet Comm Sys)
Bradford – 200 pts (Vrtl Des Innov; E-Comm Tech)
Central Lancashire – 200 pts (Comp Gms Dev; Inf Sys Mgt)
Coventry – 200–280 pts (Comp; Bus IT; Net Mbl Comp; Comp Sci; Dig Enter)
Derby – 200 pts (Comp Gms Mbl Animat; Comp Gms Prog)
Dundee – CDD 200 pts (App Comp without hons)
Edge Hill – 200 pts (Inf Sys; Comp; Bus IT; Soft Sys)
Glamorgan – 200–220 pts (Comp Law)
Hertfordshire – 200–240 pts (Inf Sys courses; Comp courses)
Huddersfield – 200–240 pts (Euro Comp Sci; Soft Dev; Intnet Sys; Comp Gms Des; Comp; Bus IT; Multim Des)
Hull – CDD–BBC 200–280 pts (Comp Bus Inform)
Hull (Scarborough) – 200–280 pts (Intnet Comp courses)
Liverpool John Moores – 200 pts (Comp St; Comp Tech; Multim Sys)
Manchester Met – 200–260 pts (Bus Inf Sys; Bus IT; Comp Gms Tech; Comp Sci)
Middlesex – 200–220 pts (Comp Sci; Bus Inf Sys; Comp Net; IT)
Napier – 200 pts (Bus Inf Sys)
Portsmouth – 200 pts (Mbl Comp Apps; Comp; e-Commer Intnet Sys)
Roehampton – 200 pts (Bus Inf Mgt)
Sheffield Hallam – 200 pts (Comp courses)

190 pts **London Met** – 190 pts (Bus IT Mgt; Bus IT; Multim Comm)

180 pts **Bournemouth** – 180–280 pts (Multim Comm Sys; Intnet Comm Sys; Dig Media Dev)
Bristol UWE – 180–240 pts (Computing)
Central Lancashire – 180–200 pts (Bus Inf Sys)
Chichester – 180–220 pts (IT Mgt Bus)
Derby – 180 pts (2AL) 200 pts (3AL) (Comp Net; Comp St)
Hertfordshire – 180 pts (Soft Sys; Arts Media)
Huddersfield – 180 pts (ICT)
Lampeter – open admission policy (Bus IT; IT)
Liverpool John Moores – 180 pts (Comp Gms Tech; Bus Inf Sys)
Newport – 180 pts (Bus IT)
Northampton – 180–220 pts (Bus Comp; Bus Inf Sys; Comp; Comp Comm; ICT courses)
Plymouth – 180 pts (Intnet Tech Apps; Multim Prod Tech)
Staffordshire – 180–240 pts (Comp Sci; Bus Comp; Bus IT; Intel Sys; Foren Comp; Intnet Tech courses; Mbl Comp; Net Comp; Comp Gms Prog)
Sunderland – 180–200 pts (Bus Comp; Comp; Multim Comp; Multim Gms)

160 pts **Anglia Ruskin** – 160 pts (Intnet Tech; Comp Aid Vis)
Bedfordshire – 160–120 pts (Comp Sci courses; Inf Sys Dev; Intnet Comp; Comp Gms Dev; Comp Graph)
Bradford – 160–180 pts (Fdn Comp)
Brunel – 160 pts (Fdn IT)
Canterbury Christ Church – CC (Comp; Dig Cult Arts Media Comp; Foren Comp; Intnet Comp)
Cumbria – CC 160 pts (Multim Des Dig Animat)
De Montfort – 160–240 pts (Bus Inf Sys; Comp Sci; Mbl Comm Sys; Intnet Comp; Foren Comp; Multim Comp; Comp Inf Mgt; Inf Sys Mgt)

Derby – 160–200 pts (Comp Inf Sys courses; Web Dev courses)
East London – 160 pts (Bus Inf Sys; IT; Comp Gms; Comp Net; Multim Tech)
Farnborough (CT) – 160–200 pts (Computing)
Glasgow Caledonian – CC (Comp; Gms Soft Dev; E-Bus; Intnet Soft Dev)
Liverpool John Moores – 160 pts (Comp St; Comp Gms Tech; Multim Sys)
London Met – 160 pts (Comp Sci; Comp courses; Bus IT; Comp Net; Comp Animat)
Loughborough – CC (Fdn Comp)
Manchester Met – 160–180 pts (App Comp)
Newman (CHE) – CC 160 pts (IT courses)
Newport – 160 pts (Intnet Net Tech; Comp Gms Des; Comp)
North East Wales (IHE) – 160 pts (Comp Net; Comp; Intnet Multim Comp; IT; Comp)
Paisley – CC–DD or cdd (Bus IT courses; Comp Animat; Intnet Tech; Comp Sci; Comp Gms Tech; Multim Tech; IT; Comp Net)
Robert Gordon – CC (Comp Sci; Comp Bus e-Commer; Comp Intnet Multim; Comp Mbl Apps; Comp Graph Animat)
Roehampton – 160–180 pts (Bus Comp courses; Intnet Multim Comp)
Salford – 160 pts (Fdn Intnet Comp)
Southend Campus Essex – 160–180 pts (Comp; Net Tech)
Swansea (IHE) – 160 pts (Comp Gms Dev)
Thames Valley – 160 pts (Bus Inf Sys; Comp Net Mgt; Comp Sci; Comp Inf Sys; Dig Animat)
UCE Birmingham – 160–180 pts (Comp; Comp Multim; Comp Net Tech; Bus IT; Inf Sys Multim; Inf Sys Net Tech)
Westminster – CC (Comp Sci; Comp; Bus Comp; Inf Sys; Comp Comm Net; Intnet Comm; Artif Intel; Multim Comp; Comp Gms Des Prog; Cog Sci; Comp Vis)
Wolverhampton – 160–220 pts (Comp Sci; Comp; Bus Comp; Bus Inf Sys; Comp (Multim); Comp Sci (Gms Dev); Web Comp)
Worcester – 160 pts (Bus Inf Sys; Comp)
York St John (Coll) – 160 pts (IT courses)

140 pts **Anglia Ruskin** – 140 pts (Comp Aid Prod Des)
Belfast (Queen's) – CD (Fdn Comp)
Bell (Coll) – CD 140 pts (App Comp)
Blackpool and Fylde (Coll) – 140 pts (Intnet Media Tech)
Cardiff (UWIC) – 140 pts (Bus Inf Sys courses)
Liverpool – 140 pts (Fdn Comp Inf Sys)
Marjon (Coll) – 140–200 pts (Comp IT courses)
Roehampton – 140 pts (Bus Comp; Intnet Multim Comp; Comp)
Sheffield Hallam – 140–160 pts (Inf Eng Bus)
Trinity Carmarthen (Coll) – 140 pts (Inf Sys courses; Tour Web Sys)

120 pts **Bradford** – 120 pts (Fdn courses except under **160 pts**)
Bradford (Coll) – 120 pts (Bus IT)
Buckinghamshire Chilterns (UC) – 120–180 pts (Bus IT; Mbl Comp; Gms Des Dev; Comp)
London South Bank – DD (Comp Sys Net; Comp; Bus IT; Prod Des Comp)
Peterborough Reg (Coll) – DD (Comp Inf Sys)
Richmond (Am Int Univ) – 120–260 pts (Comp Inf Sys)
Southampton Solent – 120 pts (Comp Net Web Des; Comp Vid Gms; Comp St; Bus IT; ICT; Mbl Comp; Intnet Comp)

100 pts **Suffolk (Univ Campus)** – 100 pts (Bus IT; Comp Gms Des; Comp Net; IT)
Swansea (IHE) – 100–160 pts (Bus IT; Comp Inf Sys; Comp Net)
Wolverhampton – 100–160 pts (Comp Aid Des (Constr)

80 pts **London (Birk)** – 80 pts for under 21s (over 21s varies) (p/t Inf Sys Mgt; Comp Biol/Chem)
Manchester Met – (Fdn Comp Sci)
UHI Millennium Inst (LCC) – (Computing)

Leeds Met – contact University
Open University – contact University (Comp; Comp Stats; Comp Sys; Inf Comm Tech)

Alternative offers
IB offers Aberdeen 30 pts; Aberystwyth 26–28 pts; Bath 35 pts; Birmingham 32–34 pts; Brighton 28 pts; Bristol 36 pts; Bristol UWE 28–30 pts; Brunel 28–30 pts; Cambridge 38–42 pts; Chester 30 pts; Chichester 28 pts; City 30 pts; Dundee 28 pts; East Anglia 30–32 pts; Essex 30–32 pts; Exeter 28–34 pts; Glasgow 28 pts; Keele 26–28 pts; Kent 28–32 pts; Lancaster 33–35 pts; Leicester 28–30 pts; London (Gold) 28 pts, (King's) 30–34 pts, (QM) 30 pts, (RH) 32 pts, (UCL) 34 pts; Loughborough 30–32 pts; Manchester 35–37 pts; Manchester Met 26 pts; Newcastle 30–32 pts; Nottingham 30 pts; Reading 33 pts; St Andrews 31–36 pts; Salford 25–30 pts; Sheffield 33 pts; Southampton 33 pts; Stirling 26–30 pts; Sussex 32 pts; Warwick 36 pts; York 36 pts.
Scottish offers See **Chapter 7**.

OTHER HIGHER EDUCATION COURSES IN THE SUBJECT FIELD
Foundation degrees (contact the institutions for details) Abingdon (Coll); Arts London; Barnet (Coll); Barnsley (Univ Centre); Bath; Bath City (Coll); Bath Spa; Bedford (Coll); Bedfordshire; Belfast (Queen's); Blackpool and Fyde (Coll); Bournemouth; Bournemouth and Poole (Coll); Bracknell (Coll); Bridgend (Coll); Brighton; Brighton City (Coll); Bristol City (Coll); Bromley (CFHE); Buckinghamshire Chilterns (UC); Burnley (Coll); Canterbury Christ Church; Castlereagh (CFE); Central Lancashire; Central Sussex (Coll); Colchester (Inst); Cornwall (Coll); Darlington (CAT); Derby (Coll); Dewsbury (Coll); Doncaster (Univ Centre); Dunstable (Coll); East Anglia; East Berkshire (Coll); East Lancashire (IHE); East London; Edge Hill; Enfield (Coll); Exeter (Coll); Farnborough (CT); Furness (Coll); Gateshead (Coll); Glamorgan; Hastings (Coll); Herefordshire (CAD); Huntingdonshire Reg (Coll); Isle of Man (Coll); Joseph Mason Sixth Form (Coll); Kidderminster (Coll); Kingston; Knowsley (CmC); Leeds (CAT); Leeds Met; Lewisham (Coll); Lincoln (Coll); Llandrillo Cymru (Coll); London (Birk); London Elect (Coll); London Met; London South Bank; Manchester (CAT); Mid-Cheshire (Coll); Mid-Kent (Coll); Nescot; Newbury (Coll); Newcastle (Coll); Newman (CHE); Newport; Newry (IFHE); North Devon (Coll); North East Wales (IHE); Northampton; Northbrook (Coll); Oldham (Coll); Omagh (CFE); Park Lane Leeds (Coll); Portsmouth; Powys (Coll); Preston (Coll); Ravensbourne (CDC); Riverside Halton (Coll); Runshaw (Coll); St Helens (Coll); Salford; Selby (Coll); Sheffield (Coll); Sheffield Hallam; Shrewsbury (Coll); Sir Gar (Coll); Skelmersdale (Coll); Somerset (CAT); South Birmingham (Coll); South Kent (Coll); Southend Campus Essex; Southampton Solent; Southport (Coll); Staffordshire; Staffordshire (Univ Fed); Stockton Riverside (Coll); Stoke on Trent (Coll); Stratford-upon-Avon (Coll); Strodes (Coll); Suffolk (Univ Campus); Sunderland; Sunderland City (Coll); Sussex Downs (Coll); Sutton Coldfield (Coll); Swansea (IHE); Thames Valley; Trinity Carmarthen (Coll); Truro (Coll); UCE Birmingham; Uxbridge (Coll); Wakefield (Coll); Warwickshire (Coll); West Cheshire (Coll); West Kent (Coll); West Thames (Coll); Weston (Coll); Wigan and Leigh (Coll); Wiltshire (Coll); Wolverhampton; Yeovil (Coll); Yorkshire Coast (CFHE).

Higher National Diploma courses
120 pts and below
Aberdeen (Coll); Abertay Dundee; Adam Smith (Coll); Anglia Ruskin; Ayr (Coll); Barking (Coll); Barnet (Coll); Barnsley (Univ Centre); Basingstoke (CT); Bath; Bedfordshire; Bell (Coll); Birmingham City (Coll); Blackpool and Fylde (Coll); Bolton; Boston (Coll); Bournemouth and Poole (Coll); Bournville (Coll); Bradford (Coll); Bridgwater (Coll); Brighton; Bristol City (Coll); Brooklands (Coll); Brunel; Buckinghamshire Chilterns (UC); Burnley (Coll); Burton (Coll); Cambridge Reg (Coll); Canterbury Christ Church; Cardiff (UWIC); Cardonald (Coll); Carlisle (Coll); Carmarthenshire (Coll); Carshalton (Coll); Central Lancashire; Chester; Chesterfield (Coll); Chichester (Coll); Colchester (Inst); Cornwall (Coll); Coventry; Coventry (Coll); Craven (Coll); Crawley (Coll); Croydon (Coll); Cumbria; De Montfort; Dearne Valley (Coll); Derby; Doncaster (Univ Centre); Dudley (Coll); Dumfries and Galloway (Coll); Durham New (Coll); East Berkshire (Coll); East Durham (CmC); East Lancashire (IHE); East London; Eastleigh (Coll); Edge Hill; Exeter; Falmouth (UC); Fareham (Coll); Farnborough (CT); Filton (Coll); Forth Valley (Coll); Glamorgan; Glasgow (Coll); Glasgow Caledonian; Glasgow Met (Coll); Gloucestershire; Gloucestershire (CAT); Greenwich; Grimsby (IFHE); Guildford (Coll); Hastings (CT); Havering (Coll); Henley (Coll); Herefordshire (CT); Heriot-Watt (Scottish Borders); Hertfordshire; Huddersfield; Isle of Wight (Coll); Kent; Kilmarnock (Coll); Kingston; Kingston (Coll); Lakes (Coll); Leeds Met; Leeds Park Lane (Coll); Lincoln; Lincoln (Coll); Liverpool (CmC); Liverpool

John Moores; Llandrillo Cymru (Coll); London Met; London South Bank; Loughborough (Coll); Manchester (CAT); Manchester City (Coll); Manchester Met; Mid-Cheshire (Coll); Middlesex; Napier; Neath Port Talbot (Coll); Nescot; Newbury (Coll); Newcastle (Coll); Newport; North East Wales (IHE); North East Warwickshire (Coll); North West Kent (Coll); Northampton; Northbrook (Coll); Northumbria; Norwich City (Coll); Nottingham New (Coll); Nottingham Trent; Oldham (Coll); Oxford and Cherwell Valley (Coll); Oxford Brookes; Pembrokeshire (Coll); People's (Coll); Peterborough Reg (Coll); Plymouth; Portsmouth; Preston (Coll); Reid Kerr (Coll); Riverside Halton (Coll); Robert Gordon; Runshaw (Coll); St Helens (Coll); Salford; Salisbury (Coll); Sheffield Hallam; Shrewsbury (CAT); Solihull (Coll); Somerset (CAT); South Birmingham (Coll); South Devon (Coll); South Kent (Coll); South Thames (Coll); South Tyneside (Coll); Southampton Solent; Southport (Coll); Staffordshire (Coll); Stevenson (Coll); Stoke-on-Trent (Coll) (mature students only); Stratford-upon-Avon (Coll); Strode (Coll); Suffolk (Univ Campus); Sunderland City (Coll); Sutton Coldfield (Coll); Swansea (Coll); Swansea (IHE); Swindon (Coll); Tameside (Coll); Teesside; Thames Valley; Thanet (Coll); Tile Hill (Coll); Truro (Coll); Tyne Met (Coll); UCE Birmingham; Ulster; Uxbridge (Coll); Wakefield (Coll); Walsall (CAT); Warwickshire (Coll); West Anglia (Coll); West Herts (Coll); West Nottinghamshire (Coll); West Suffolk (Coll); West Thames (Coll); Westminster; Weston (Coll); Weymouth (Coll); Wigan and Leigh (Coll); Wiltshire (Coll); Wirral Met (Coll); Wolverhampton; Worcester; Worcester (CT); Yeovil (Coll); York (Coll); Yorkshire Coast (CFHE).

CHOOSING YOUR COURSE (SEE ALSO CH.1)

Subject information Computer courses are extremely popular and provide graduates with very good career prospects. Courses vary in content and in the specialisations offered which may include software engineering, programming languages, artificial intelligence, data processing and graphics. Many universities offer sandwich placements in industry and commerce. **Useful websites** www.bcs.org.uk; www.intellectuk.org; www.e-skills.com; www.iap.org.uk.

Course variations Interactive Systems and Video Games Design (Bradford); Mobile Computing (Coventry); Computer Science in North America (East Anglia); Artificial Intelligence (Manchester); Business Information Systems (Northumbria); Computing Informatics (Plymouth); Cybernetics (Reading); Forensic Computing (Staffordshire); Web Development (Teesside). *NOW CHECK PROSPECTUSES AND WEBSITES FOR ANY RECENT CHANGES.*

Universities and colleges teaching quality See www.tqi.ac.uk; www.qaa.ac.uk.

Top universities and colleges (Research) Aston; Bristol; Cambridge*; Cardiff; Edinburgh; Glasgow; Imperial London; Lancaster; Leeds; Liverpool; London (RH), (UCL); Manchester; Newcastle; Nottingham; Oxford; Plymouth; St Andrews; Sheffield; Southampton*; Sussex; Warwick; York*.

Sandwich degree courses Aberystwyth; Aston; Bath; Belfast (Queen's); Bournemouth; Bradford; Brighton; Bristol UWE; Brunel; Central Lancashire; City; Coventry; De Montfort; Derby; East London; Glamorgan; Glasgow Caledonian; Gloucestershire; Hertfordshire; Huddersfield; Kent; Kingston; Leeds Met; Liverpool John Moores; London South Bank; Loughborough; Manchester; Manchester Met; Napier; Nescot; Northumbria; Nottingham Trent; Oxford Brookes; Paisley; Plymouth; Portsmouth; Reading; Sheffield Hallam; Southampton Solent; Staffordshire; Surrey; Teesside; Ulster; Westminster; Wolverhampton; York.

ADMISSIONS INFORMATION

Number of applicants per place (approx) Abertay Dundee 2; Aberystwyth 8; Aston (Bus Comp IT) 12; Bath 10; Birmingham 7; Bournemouth 8; Bradford 13; Bristol 9; Bristol UWE 4; Brunel 10; Buckingham 6; Cambridge 3; Cardiff 5; City 10; Coventry 10; Derby 3; Dundee 6; Durham 10; East Anglia (Comp Maths) 7; Edinburgh 4; Essex 2; Exeter 10; Glasgow Caledonian 8; Heriot-Watt 6; Hull (Comp Sci) 6; Imperial London 6; Kent 8; Kingston 10; Lampeter 1; Lancaster 5; Leeds 10; Leicester 22; Lincoln 5; Liverpool John Moores 3; London (King's) 20, (QM) 6, (RH) 5; Loughborough (CT) 2; Manchester Met 10, (Bus IT) 8; Newcastle 7; North East Wales (IHE) 3; Northumbria 4; Nottingham Trent 4; Oxford (success rate 23%); Oxford Brookes 18; Plymouth 12; Portsmouth 6; Queen Margaret (UC) 3; Richmond (Am Int Univ) 3; Robert Gordon 3; Roehampton 3; Sheffield Hallam 5; Southampton 9; Staffordshire 4; Stirling 6; Strathclyde 16; Surrey 9; Swansea 5; Teesside 4; Trinity Carmarthen (Coll) 2; Warwick 11; York 9.

Advice to applicants and planning the UCAS personal statement Your interest in, and use of computers, programming etc outside school or college should be described. It is also useful to give details of any visits, work experience and work shadowing relating to industrial or commercial organisations and their computer systems. (See **Appendix 2**.) **Birmingham** Little previous experience required, opportunity to study abroad or have a year in industry. **City** We are interested in applicants with an interest in the IT industry, the underlying principles and technology and how computers are applied to real world problems. **De Montfort** (Multim Comp) Interest in hardware and software. Prior experience should be included in the use of multimedia packages and your knowledge of computer usage and programming. **London (QM)** We are looking for applicants who are comfortable with formal reasoning and abstract concepts. This is more important than experience with computers. **Portsmouth** Evidence needed that applicants can work with people. Contact the British Computer Society for information. **St Andrews** Give reasons for choosing the course and evidence of interest and include details of sport and extra-curricular activities and positions of responsibility. **Sunderland** Provide an example of when you have worked as part of a team or met a deadline or worked on your own. **York** Be interested and articulate, think why you want to come to this University and why study Computer Science (have answers to these questions at interview).

Misconceptions about this course That anyone who plays computer games or uses a word processor can do a degree in Computer Studies. Some think Computing degrees are just about programming; in reality, programming is only one, albeit essential, part of computing. **Aston** (Bus Comp IT) 60% business, 40% computing and IT; compulsory placement year in industry. **City** (Bus Comp Sys) Some applicants think that it is a Business degree: it is a Computing degree focused on computing in business. **London (QM)** There are many misconceptions – among students, teachers and careers advisers – about what computer science entails. The main one is to confuse it with what schools call information and communication technology which is about the use of computer applications. Computer science is all about software – ie programming – and will generally only cover a limited study of hardware.

Selection interviews Yes Abertay Dundee, Bath, Bradford, Bristol, Bristol UWE, Brunel, Buckingham, Cambridge, Cardiff, City, Coventry, Cumbria, Durham, East Lancashire (IHE), Edinburgh, Glamorgan, Hertfordshire, Hull, Kingston, Liverpool Hope, London (Gold), (QM), (UCL), London South Bank, Loughborough, Newcastle, Newport, Northampton (UC), Northbrook (Coll), Nottingham, Oxford, Plymouth, Portsmouth, Sheffield Hallam, Southampton, Surrey, Thames Valley, Warwick, Wigan and Leigh (Coll), York; **Some** Aberystwyth, Anglia Ruskin, Blackpool and Fylde (Coll), Brighton, Chichester, Dundee, Exeter, Liverpool John Moores, London Met, Manchester Met, Napier, Salford, Staffordshire, Sunderland, UCE Birmingham.

Interview advice and questions Whilst A-level computer studies is not usually required, you will be questioned on your use of computers and aspects of the subject which interest you. How do you organise your homework/social life? What are your strengths and weaknesses? Do you have any idea of the type of career you would like? **City** The aim of the interview is to obtain a full picture of the applicant's background, life experiences etc, before making an offer. **York** No tests. Questions for discussion at the whiteboard are usually mathematical or are about fundamental computer science such as sorting. See also **Chapter 6**.

Applicants' impressions (A=Open day; B=Interview day) London (Imp) (B) There was a 45-minute talk on the College and the course structure and content with free refreshments. We were then split into small groups for a tour, followed by a brief interview. I had to demonstrate that I could understand simple mathematical problems clearly but there was no opportunity to ask questions. The offer was made after the interview. **Portsmouth** (A) I was sent a map and details of the open day. We had an interesting coach tour of the city, followed by lunch and then course talks, tea and coffee. At the end of the day students had private discussions with the staff.

Reasons for rejection (non-academic) Little practical interest in computers/electronics. Inability to work as part of a small team. Mismatch between referee's description and performance at interview. Unsatisfactory English. Can't communicate. Inability to convince interviewer of the candidate's worth. Incoherent, unmotivated, arrogant and without any evidence of good reason. **London (QM)** Misunderstanding of what computer science involves as an academic subject – especially in personal statements where some suggest that they are interested in a course with business and secretarial skills. Lack of sufficient mathematics. Computer science is a mathematical subject and we cannot accept applicants who are unable to demonstrate good mathematical skills. **Southampton** Lack of motivation; incoherence; carelessness.

AFTER-RESULTS ADVICE

Universities with vacancies in Clearing (2006) Abertay Dundee; Aberystwyth; Anglia Ruskin; Aston; Bangor; Bedfordshire; Belfast; Bolton; Bournemouth; Bradford; Brighton; Bristol UWE; Brunel; Canterbury Christ Church; Cardiff; Central Lancashire; Chester; City; Coventry; De Montfort; Derby; Dundee; East Anglia; East London; Edge Hill; Essex; Exeter; Glamorgan; Glasgow; Gloucestershire; Greenwich; Heriot-Watt; Hertfordshire; Huddersfield; Hull; Keele; Kent; Kingston; Lampeter; Lancaster; Leeds; Lincoln; Liverpool; Liverpool Hope; Liverpool John Moores; London (Gold), (QM), (RH); London Met; London South Bank; Loughborough; Manchester; Manchester Met; Middlesex; Napier; Northampton; Nottingham; Nottingham Trent; Oxford Brookes; Paisley; Plymouth; Portsmouth; Reading; Salford; Sheffield; Sheffield Hallam; Southampton; Southampton Solent; Staffordshire; Stirling; Strathclyde; Sunderland; Swansea; Teesside; Thames Valley; UCE Birmingham; Ulster; Warwick; Westminster; Wolverhampton; Worcester; York.

Offers to applicants repeating A-levels **Higher** Brighton, De Montfort, Greenwich, Kingston, St Andrews, Surrey, Sussex, Warwick, Wolverhampton; **Possibly higher** Bath, Bristol UWE, Durham, East Anglia, Edinburgh, Lancaster, Leeds, Newcastle, Oxford Brookes, Portsmouth, Sheffield, Teesside; **Same** Anglia Ruskin, Aston, Blackpool and Fylde (Coll), Brunel, Buckingham, Cardiff, Chichester, City, Derby, Dundee, Exeter, Farnborough (CT), Huddersfield, Hull, Kent, Lincoln, Liverpool, Liverpool John Moores, London (RH), (UCL), London South Bank, Loughborough, Manchester Met, Newman (CHE), Northumbria, Richmond (Am Int Univ), Robert Gordon, Salford, Sheffield Hallam, Staffordshire, Sunderland, Thames Valley, Ulster, Worcester, York.

GRADUATE DESTINATIONS AND EMPLOYMENT (2005 HESA)
Computer Science graduates surveyed 7440 **Employed** 4360 **In further study** 865 **Assumed unemployed** 825.

Software Engineering graduates surveyed 745 **Employed** 460 **In further study** 85 **Assumed unemployed** 65.

Information Systems graduates surveyed 2600 **Employed** 1565 **In further study** 220 **Assumed unemployed** 275.

Artificial Intelligence graduates surveyed 60 **Employed** 30 **In further study** 15 **Assumed unemployed** 5.

OTHER DEGREE SUBJECTS FOR CONSIDERATION
Business Studies; Communications Engineering; Computer Engineering; Electrical and Electronic Engineering; Geographical Information Systems; Information Studies; Mathematics; Physics; Software Engineering.

CONSUMER STUDIES/SCIENCES

(including **Consumer Product Design** and **Home Economics**; see also **Food Science/Studies and Technology** and **Hospitality and Hotel Management**)

NB The points totals shown to the left of the institutions are for ease of reference only. It must not be assumed that tariff points are always used by institutions or that they can be substituted for an offer in grades. The level of an offer is not necessarily indicative of the quality of a course.

COURSE OFFERS INFORMATION

Subject requirements/preferences GCSE Mathematics and English usually required. **AL** No specific subjects required.

Your target offers

260 pts	**Ulster** – BCC 260 pts (Consum St)
240 pts	**Coventry** – 240–200 pts (Consum Prod Des)
	Manchester Met – 240 pts (Consum Law; Law Tr Stand)
200 pts	**Abertay Dundee** – CDD 200 pts (Fd Consum Sci)
	Bath Spa – 200–240 pts (Fd Nutr Consum Prot)
	Manchester Met – 200 pts (Consum Prot)
180 pts	**Napier** – BC (Consum Prod Des)
	Queen Margaret (UC) – DDD/BC 180 pts (Consum St Mgt; Consum St Mark; Consum St Rtl)
160 pts	**Birmingham (CFTCS)** – 160 pts (Fd Consum Mgt)
	Liverpool John Moores – 160 pts (Consum St Mark)
140 pts	**Bolton** – 140 pts (Consum Prod Des)
	Cardiff (UWIC) – 140 pts approx (Fd Consum Sci; Consum Tr Stand)
120 pts	**London Met** – 120 pts (Hm Econ; Fd Consum St; Consum St)
80 pts	**Bolton** – 80–60 pts (Consum Prod Des 4 yrs)
	Leeds Met – contact University

Alternative offers
IB offers Birmingham (CFTCS) 24 pts; Cardiff (UWIC) 28 pts; Manchester Met 24 pts.
Scottish offers See **Chapter 7**.

OTHER HIGHER EDUCATION COURSES IN THE SUBJECT FIELD

Higher National Diploma courses
100 pts and below
Aberdeen (Coll); Adam Smith (Coll); Birmingham (CFTCS); Croydon (Coll); London Met; Manchester Met; UHI Millennium Inst.

CHOOSING YOUR COURSE (SEE ALSO CH.1)

Subject information Consumer Studies courses involve topics such as food and nutrition, shelter, clothing, community studies and consumer behaviour and marketing. It should be noted that the title 'Consumer Sciences' has recently replaced that of 'Home Economics'. **Useful websites** www.icsc.org.uk; www.which.co.uk .

Course variations Food, Nutrition and Consumer Protection (Bath Spa); Consumer Trading Standards (Cardiff (UWIC)); Consumer Product Design (Coventry, Bolton); Consumer Law (Manchester Met). *NOW CHECK PROSPECTUSES AND WEBSITES FOR ANY RECENT CHANGES.*

ADMISSIONS INFORMATION

Number of applicants per place (approx) Bath Spa 6; Birmingham (CFTCS) 2; Cardiff (UWIC) 5; Liverpool John Moores 3; London Met 5; Manchester Met 4; Queen Margaret (UC) 3.

Advice to applicants and planning the UCAS personal statement Relevant work experience or work shadowing in, for example, business organisations, restaurants, cafes, school meals service, would be useful and should be described. Visits to food factories should be mentioned. Good interpersonal and communication skills required. **Liverpool John Moores** Discuss consumer studies on your UCAS form. (See also **Hospitality, Hotel and Catering Management** and **Dietetics**.) Details may be obtained from the Institute of Consumer Sciences – see **Appendix 2**.

Selection interviews Bath Spa; **Some** Manchester Met.

Interview advice and questions Questions will stem from your special interests in this subject and in the past have included: What new developments are taking place in cooking techniques? What are the advantages and disadvantages? What is a home economist? What advice would you give to the designers of cookers? What is ergonomics? What interests you in current affairs? What world or national news has annoyed, pleased or upset you? What relevance do textiles and dress have to home economics? How would you react in a room full of fools? **Manchester Met** A general discussion – no tests. **Queen Margaret (UC)** Very informal interviews covering work experience and career aspirations. See also **Chapter 6**.

AFTER-RESULTS ADVICE
Universities with vacancies in Clearing (2006) Coventry; Liverpool John Moores; London Met; Manchester Met.

Offers to applicants repeating A-levels Same Bath Spa, Liverpool John Moores, Manchester Met, Queen Margaret (UC), Ulster.

GRADUATE DESTINATIONS AND EMPLOYMENT (2005 HESA)
No data available.

OTHER DEGREE SUBJECTS FOR CONSIDERATION
Biological Sciences; Business Studies; Dietetics; Environmental Health; Food Science; Health Studies; Hospitality Management; Marketing; Nutrition; Psychology; Retail Management.

DANCE/DANCE STUDIES
(see also **Drama (Performing Arts)**)

NB The points totals shown to the left of the institutions are for ease of reference only. It must not be assumed that tariff points are always used by institutions or that they can be substituted for an offer in grades. The level of an offer is not necessarily indicative of the quality of a course.

COURSE OFFERS INFORMATION
Subject requirements/preferences GCSE English usually required. Practical dance experience essential. **AL** No specific subjects required.

Your target offers
300 pts **Surrey** – BBB–BBC (Dance Cult; Dance Cult Prof Trg)
280 pts **Kingston** – 280–320 pts (Dance Glob Commun)
　　　　Leeds – BBC (Dance; Perf Des; Thea Perf)
　　　　Roehampton – 280 pts (Dance St courses)
260 pts **London (RAc Dance)** – BCC (Ballet Educ)
　　　　Northumbria – 260 pts (Dance Choreo)
240 pts **Chester** – 240 pts (Dance; Perf New Media Dance)
　　　　Dartington (CA) – 240–280 pts (Choreography)
　　　　Edge Hill – 240 pts (Dance)
　　　　Hull (Scarborough) – 240–260 pts (Thea Perf St Dance)
　　　　Oxford Brookes – CCC (Perf Arts)
　　　　Salford – CCC 240 pts (Perf Arts)
220 pts **Chichester** – 220–240 pts (Dance courses)

Liverpool Hope – 220 pts (Dance; Crea Perf Arts)
Middlesex – 220–240 pts (Perf Arts Dance Thea Prod))
Winchester – 220 pts (Choreo Dance St courses)
200 pts   **Bath Spa** – 200–240 pts (Dance; Crea St Engl Dance)
Cardiff (UWIC) – BB (Dance)
Coventry – 200–220 pts (Dance Thea; Dance Prof Prac)
Cumbria – 200 pts approx (Dance Tech Thea; Dance Mus Thea; Dance Dr; Dance Contemp Cult)
Liverpool John Moores – 200 pts (Dance St)
Manchester Met – 200 pts (Dance joint courses; Contemp Arts)
Middlesex – 200–240 pts (Dance St; Dance Perf Arts; Dance St Choreo; Dance St (Commun Dance) (Dance Sci))
Sunderland – 200 pts (Dance courses)
180 pts   **Bedfordshire** – 180 pts (Perf Arts)
Central Lancashire – 180 pts (Dance Perf Teach)
De Montfort – 180–200 pts (Dance)
Liverpool (LIPA) – BC 180 pts (Dance Perf Arts)
Northampton – 180–220 pts (Dance; Perf)
160 pts   **Derby** – 160 pts (Dance Mov St Thea; Dance Mov St Heal Arts; Dance Mov St Mark)
East London – 160 pts (Dance Perf Arts)
Laban – CC (Dance Thea – apply early)
London Met – 160 pts (Perf Arts)
Wolverhampton – 160–220 pts (Dance Prac Perf courses)
York St John – 160 pts (Perf Dance)
140 pts   **De Montfort** – 140–160 pts (Perf Arts)
80 pts   **and below**
Brighton – 80 pts (Fdn Art; Dance Vis Art; Thea Vis Art)
London (Arts Educ Sch) – (Mus Thea)
Northern (Sch Contemp Dance) – (Dance)

Alternative offers
IB offers Chester 30 pts; Chichester 28 pts; Manchester Met 28 pts; Surrey 28–30 pts.
Scottish offers See **Chapter 7**.

OTHER HIGHER EDUCATION COURSES IN THE SUBJECT FIELD

Foundation degrees (contact the institutions for details) Bristol City (Coll); Buckinghamshire Chilterns (UC); Coventry; Newcastle (Coll); London Studio; Truro (Coll).

Higher National Diploma courses
100 pts   and below
Accrington and Rossendale (Coll); Blackpool and Fylde (Coll); Bristol City (Coll); Chichester; De Montfort; Filton (Coll); Havering (Coll); Liverpool (CmC); Newcastle (Coll); Northbrook (Coll); Northern (Sch Contemp Dance); Nottingham New (Coll); Oldham (Coll); Plymouth; Salford; Southwark (Coll); Stratford-upon-Avon (Coll); Wakefield (Coll); West Thames (Coll); Wigan and Leigh (Coll).

CHOOSING YOUR COURSE (SEE ALSO CH.1)

Subject information Every aspect of dance can be studied in the various courses on offer as well as the theoretical, educational, historical and social aspects of the subject. **Useful websites** www.arts.org.uk; www.cdet.org.uk; www.ballet.co.uk; www.artscouncil.org.uk.

Course variations Dance and New Media Arts (Chichester); Dance and Professional Practice (Coventry); Dance and Music Theatre (Cumbria); Choreography and Technical Theatre (Dartington (CA)); Dance and Movement Studies and Healing Arts (Derby); Arts, Music and Entertainment Management (Liverpool (LIPA)); Dance Performance (Middlesex). *NOW CHECK PROSPECTUSES AND WEBSITES FOR ANY RECENT CHANGES.*

Universities and colleges teaching quality See www.tqi.ac.uk; www.qaa.ac.uk.

Top universities and colleges (Research) See under **Drama**.

ADMISSIONS INFORMATION

Number of applicants per place (approx) Birmingham 12; Chichester 6; De Montfort (Dance) 13, (Perf Arts) 9; Derby 12; Hull (Scarborough) 2; Laban 5; Liverpool John Moores 3; Liverpool (LIPA) 24; Middlesex 12, (Dance Perf Arts) 23; Northern (Sch Contemp Dance) 6; Roehampton 17; Surrey 5; York St John 3.

Advice to applicants and planning the UCAS personal statement Full details should be given of examinations taken and practical experience in contemporary dance or ballet. Refer to your visits to the theatre and your impressions. You should list the dance projects in which you have worked, productions in which you have performed and the roles. State any formal dance training you have had and the grades achieved. See **Appendix 2**. **De Montfort** (Perf Arts) A good balance of interests, both theoretical and practical; strengths in both dance and theatre. **Laban** We look for dedication, versatility, inventiveness and individuality. **Liverpool (LIPA)** Applicants should be educated to A-level standard with good communication and entrepreneurial skills and experience in dance projects/productions, and should give details of the roles they have played. **Surrey** Personal and intellectual maturity. Make sure you can demonstrate practical experience of dance, theoretical ability and language competency. **Winchester** Mature students with relevant experience considered.

Misconceptions about this course That Performing Arts is only an acting course: it also includes music. **Wolverhampton** The course focuses on the practical study of dance technique, performance and choreography with theoretical study and practical experience of teaching and community work.

Interview advice and questions All institutions will require auditions. The following scheme required by **Liverpool (LIPA)** may act as a guide:

1 Write a short essay (500 words) on your own views and experience of dance. You should take into account the following:
   * Your history and how you have developed physically and intellectually in your run-up to applying to LIPA.
   * Your main influences and what inspires you.
   * What you want to gain from training as a dancer.
   * Your ideas on health and nutrition as a dancer, taking into account gender and physicality.

2 All candidates must prepare **two** practical audition pieces:
   * The first piece must be a dance piece choreographed by the candidate. You are free to create whatever you like, in whatever style you wish, as long as the piece does not exceed two minutes (please note: panel will stop anyone exceeding this time-limit). There will be no pianist at this part of the session, so if you're using music please bring it with you on a cassette tape. This devised piece should be created through you and this means that you should feel comfortable with it and that it *expresses something personal about you*. You should wear your regular practice clothes for your presentation.
   * You must prepare a song of your own choice. An accompanist is provided, but you must provide the sheet music for your song, fully written out for piano accompaniment and in the key you wish to sing (the accompanist will **not** transpose at sight). **Important:** Do NOT choreograph your song. You should expect to sit on a high stool or stand when singing for the audition.

3 Additionally, all candidates will participate in a class given on the day of audition:
   * Please ensure that you are dressed appropriately for class with clothing you are comfortable in but allow your movement to be seen. In preparing the practical elements of the audition, please remember that audition panels are not looking for a 'polished' performance. The panel will be looking for candidates' ability to make a genuine emotional and physical connection with the material that they are presenting which shows clear intent and focus.

Remember that it is in your best interest to prepare thoroughly. Nerves inevitably play a part in any audition and can undermine even the best-prepared candidate. Your best defence is to feel confident in your preparation.

De Montfort (Perf Arts) Practical workshops in dance and theatre plus a written paper. **Salford** (Perf Arts) Audition and interview. **Surrey** Applicants invited to spend a day at the university for interview and a practical class to assess dance skills. An audition fee may be charged. **Wolverhampton** Audition in the form of a dance class. See also **Chapter 6**.

Reasons for rejection (non-academic) Applicants more suitable for an acting or dance school course than a degree course. No experience of dance on the UCAS application. Limited dance skills. **Surrey** Inadequate dance background. Had not seen/read about/done any dance.

AFTER-RESULTS ADVICE

Universities with vacancies in Clearing (2006) Brighton; Chester; De Montfort; Derby; East London; Liverpool Hope; Liverpool John Moores; Manchester Met; Northampton; Northumbria; Roehampton; Salford; Sunderland; Surrey; Wolverhampton; York St John.

Offers to applicants repeating A-levels **Same** Chester, Chichester, De Montfort (Perf Arts), Laban, Liverpool John Moores, Salford, Surrey, Winchester, Wolverhampton, York St John.

GRADUATE DESTINATIONS AND EMPLOYMENT (2005 HESA)

Graduates surveyed 375 **Employed** 180 **In further study** 65 **Assumed unemployed** 15.

OTHER DEGREE SUBJECTS FOR CONSIDERATION

Arts Management; Drama; Education (Primary); Performance Studies; Physical Education; Sport and Exercise Science.

DENTISTRY/DENTAL SURGERY

(including **Dental Technology, Dental Hygiene, Equine Dental Science** and **Oral Health Science**)

NB The points totals shown to the left of the institutions are for ease of reference only. It must not be assumed that tariff points are always used by institutions or that they can be substituted for an offer in grades. The level of an offer is not necessarily indicative of the quality of a course.

COURSE OFFERS INFORMATION

Subject requirements/preferences **GCSE Birmingham** Five subjects grade A/B including mathematics and English. **Bristol** Six subjects grade A. **Cardiff** Double award science grade BB. **Leeds** Substantial number of passes at a high standard including science subjects, mathematics and English. **London Dental Schools** Grade B in English, mathematics, physics and biology or double award or combined science. **London (King's)** Six subjects at grade A/B. **Sheffield** Grade A in English, chemistry, mathematics, biology and physics (dual science accepted). **Other Cardiff, Leeds and most dental schools** Evidence of non-infectivity or hepatitis-B immunisation required and all new dental students to be screened for hepatitis C. Completion of a criminal record disclaimer required and consent to police record check. **AL** Chemistry plus biology or a science subject usually required: see offers lines below. Some dental schools will use admissions tests (eg UKCAT) for 2007 entry **(see Chapter 6)**.

Your target offers
360 pts and above
    Belfast (Queen's) – AAAa (inc AL/AS chem A+1 subj from biol, maths, phys (must inc AS biol)) (Dentistry)
    Dundee – AAA +UKCAT (inc biol+2 subj from chem/phys/maths) (Dentistry)
    Liverpool – AAB+AS 390–340 pts (inc 2AL AA/AB inc chem/biol+1 subj from chem, biol, maths, phys, stats) (Dntl Srgy)
    London (King's) – ABBc **or** ABbbc +UKCAT (inc AL chem/biol) (Dentistry)
340 pts Birmingham – AAB–ABB 340–320 pts (inc 300 pts 3AL inc 2AL AB chem+biol) (Dentistry)
    Bristol – AAB–ABB (inc chem+biol pref+biol if 3rd AL is non-sci) (Dentistry A206)
    Bristol – AAB–ABB (inc 3 non-sci subjs **or** 1 sci+2 non-sci) (Dentistry A204)

Cardiff – AAB +UKCAT 340 pts +UKCAT (inc chem/biol+2 sci subj (5yr course); inc no more than one sci subj from chem/biol/phys (6yr course)) (Dentistry; Fdn Dentistry)
Leeds – AAB (inc AL chem, biol) (Dentistry)
London (QM) – AAB +UKCAT (inc 2ALs chem/biol/sci subj **or** chem/biol bb) (Dentistry)
Manchester – AAB +UKCAT (inc AL chem+biol+1 sci from phys/maths/comp sci) (Dentistry)
Newcastle – AAB +UKCAT (inc AL chem and/or biol) (Dentistry)
Sheffield – AAB **or** ABaa/ab +UKCAT (inc AL chem AB+1 sci B) (Dentistry)

320 pts **Glasgow** – ABB **or** AAbb +UKCAT (inc chem+phys/maths/biol) (Dentistry)
Manchester – ABB (2 arts+sci subj) (Dentistry pre-dental entry)

300 pts **London (QM)** – BBB–BCC (Dntl Mat)

280 pts **Birmingham** – BBC (Dntl Hyg Ther)

240 pts **Dundee** – 240 pts (Oral Hlth Sci)
Manchester – AA–CC (Oral Hlth Sci)

180 pts **Bristol UWE** – 180–220 pts (Eqn Dntl Sci)

160 pts **Manchester Met** – 160–220 pts (inc sci/tech) (Dntl Tech)
Portsmouth – 160–200 pts (Dntl Hyg Dntl Thera)

160 pts **Cardiff (UWIC)** – 160 pts (inc sci subj) (Dntl Tech)

Alternative offers
IB offers Birmingham 36 pts, (Dntl Hyg Ther) 30 pts; Bristol 36 pts; Dundee individual offer; Liverpool 36 pts; London (King's) 36 pts; Manchester 35 pts; Manchester Met 26 pts; Newcastle 35 pts; Sheffield 35 pts.
Scottish offers See **Chapter 7**.

OTHER HIGHER EDUCATION COURSES IN THE SUBJECT FIELD

Foundation degrees (contact the institutions for details) Cardiff (UWIC); De Montfort; Lambeth (Coll); Liverpool (CmC); Nottingham Castle (Coll).

Diploma courses
160 pts **Cardiff** – CC (Dntl Hyg; Dntl Thera)
London (King's) – CC (Dntl Hyg)

CHOOSING YOUR COURSE (SEE ALSO CH.1)

Subject information Courses in Dentistry cover the basic medical sciences, human disease, clinical studies and clinical dentistry. The amount of patient contact will vary between institutions but will be considerable in all dental schools. Intercalated courses in other science subjects are offered on most courses. **Useful websites** www.bda-dentistry.org.uk; www.bdha.org.uk; www.dla.org.uk; www.gdc-uk.org.

Mature students A-level standard necessary. Graduates require 2:1 degree plus A-level grades close to the normal requirement.

Course variations Equine Dental Science (Bristol UWE); Dental Technology (Cardiff (UWIC)); Oral Health Science (Manchester). *NOW CHECK PROSPECTUSES AND WEBSITES FOR ANY RECENT CHANGES.*

Universities and colleges teaching quality See www.tqi.ac.uk; www.qaa.ac.uk.

Top universities and colleges (Research) Bristol*; Dundee; Leeds; London (King's)*, (QM); Newcastle; Sheffield.

ADMISSIONS INFORMATION

Number of applicants per place (approx) Belfast (Queen's) 5; Birmingham 10; Bristol 16; Cardiff 14; Cardiff (UWIC) (Dntl Tech) 1; Dundee 8, (Pre-dental) 5; Glasgow 7; Leeds 11.5; Liverpool 15; London (King's) 162 places, (QM) 18, (300 interviewed and 200 offers made); Manchester 24; Manchester Met 16; Newcastle 12; Portsmouth 2; Sheffield 16 (interviews not held for non-EU students: 3 accepted each year). **International applicants** Birmingham 129 (no quota).

Number of applicants (a UK b EU (non-UK) c non-EU d mature) Bristol **ab**633 **c**83 **d**148; Glasgow **a**437 **b**45 **c**70 **d**79; Leeds **a**877 **b**42 **c**97 **d**158; Liverpool **a**704 **b**46 **c**73 **d**143; London (King's) **ab**137 **c**25; Manchester **a**1290 **b**81 **c**152 **d**331.

Advice to applicants and planning the UCAS personal statement UCAS applications listing four choices only should be submitted by 15 October. Applicants may add up to two alternative (non-Dentistry) courses. However, if they receive offers for these courses and are rejected for Dentistry, they will not be considered for Dentistry courses in Clearing if they perform better than expected in the examinations. Applicants for entry to some dental schools in 2007 and thereafter will be required to sit the United Kingdom Clinical Aptitude Test (UKCAT): see **Chapter 6**.

On your UCAS application show evidence of your manual dexterity, work experience and awareness of problems experienced by dentists. Details should be provided of discussions with dentists and work-shadowing in dental surgeries. Employment (paid or voluntary) in any field, preferably dealing with people in an environment widely removed from your home or school, could be described. Discuss any specialised fields of dentistry in which you might be interested. See also **Appendix 2**. **Cardiff** Expects students to have had work experience. Needs evidence of, and potential for, high academic achievement; a caring and committed attitude towards people; an understanding of the demands of dental training and practice; the ability to communicate effectively; a willingness to accept responsibility; evidence of broad social, cultural or sporting interests, good manual dexterity. **Cardiff (UWIC)** (Dntl Tech) Evidence of manual dexterity. **London (King's)** The personal statement is a significant factor in our assessment. We would expect that you will have undertaken some work experience in a caring environment. Communication skills and the ability to work in a team are important. Approximately 25% of applicants are invited to interview after initial UCAS screening.

Misconceptions about this course Cardiff (UWIC) (Dntl Tech) Some think that the course allows them to practise as a dentist. Some think the degree is entirely practical.

Selection interviews Birmingham (400–450 applicants and only 50% of applicants get through the initial sort); Bristol; Cardiff; Dundee; Glasgow; Leeds; London (King's), (QM); Newcastle; Sheffield.

Interview advice and questions Work shadowing in a dental surgery is essential and, as a result, questions will be asked on your reactions to the work and your understanding of the different types of treatment that a dentist can offer. In the past questions at interview have included: What is conservative dentistry? What does integrity mean? Do you think the first-year syllabus is a good one? What qualities are required by a dentist? What are prosthetics, periodontics, orthodontics? What causes tooth decay? Questions asked on the disadvantages of being a dentist, the future of dentistry and how you could show that you are manually dexterous. Other questions on personal attributes and spare time activities. What are the careers within the profession open to dentists? Questions on the future of dentistry (preventative and cosmetic dentistry), the problems facing dentists, the skills needed and the advantages and disadvantages of fluoride in water. How do you relax? How do you cope with stress? **Leeds** The interview assesses personality, verbal and communication skills and knowledge of dentistry. See also **Chapter 6**.

Applicants' impressions (A=Open day; B=Interview day) Cardiff (B) There were two interviewers (one male, one female). They were very helpful although I was not always sure whether they were smiling because they agreed with me or whether they were just being polite. It was a well organised interview but there was no opportunity to meet any students. **Sheffield** (A) The facilities looked impressive and the Dental School was quite new: it's a 15-minute walk from the city centre.

Reasons for rejection (non-academic) Lack of evidence of a firm commitment to dentistry. Lack of breadth of interests. Lack of motivation for a health care profession. Unprofessional attitude. Poor manual dexterity. Poor communication skills. Poor English. Lack of evidence of ability to work in groups. Not for the faint-hearted! More interested in running a business and making money than in caring for people. **Cardiff (UWIC)** (Dntl Tech) Target numbers need to be precise so the course fills at a late stage.

AFTER-RESULTS ADVICE
Offers to applicants repeating A-levels Higher Bristol (AAB), Cardiff (preference given to students who previously applied), Dundee, Leeds (Very few – AAB); **Same** Belfast (Queen's), Cardiff (UWIC) (Dntl Tech).

Universities with vacancies in Clearing (2006) **for other Dental courses** Bristol UWE; Cardiff (UWIC); Portsmouth.

GRADUATE DESTINATIONS AND EMPLOYMENT (2005 HESA)
Graduates surveyed 605 **Employed** 480 **In further study** 5 **Assumed unemployed** 5.
Medicine and Dentistry had the highest employment percentage (91.9%) of any subject.

OTHER DEGREE SUBJECTS FOR CONSIDERATION
Anatomy; Biochemistry; Biological Sciences; Chemistry; Medicine; Nursing; Optometry; Pharmacy; Physiology; Physiotherapy; Radiography; Speech Therapy/Sciences; Veterinary Medicine/Science.

DEVELOPMENT STUDIES

NB The points totals shown to the left of the institutions are for ease of reference only. It must not be assumed that tariff points are always used by institutions or that they can be substituted for an offer in grades. The level of an offer is not necessarily indicative of the quality of a course.

COURSE OFFERS INFORMATION
Subject requirements/preferences **GCSE** Mathematics, English and a foreign language may be required. **AL** Mathematics or economics may be required for some courses.

Your target offers
340 pts **Bath** – AAB (Econ Int Dev)
  Manchester – AAB–ABB (Dev St courses)
300 pts **Birmingham** – BBB–BBC (Af St Dev)
  East Anglia – BBB (Dev St; Dev St Langs; Dev St Ovrs Exp)
  Leeds – BBB (Int Dev)
  Liverpool – BBB 300 pts (Int Dev)
  St Andrews – BBB (BSc Sust Dev)
  Sussex – BBB 3AL+AS (Dev St)
280 pts **Bradford** – 280 pts (Dev Pce St)
  London (SOAS) – BBC (Dev St courses)
260 pts **London (King's)** – BCC–BBC **or** BCccc–BBccc (Dev Geog)
240 pts **Chester** – 240 pts (Int Dev St)
  Kingston – 240 pts (Dev Sust)
200 pts **London Met** – 200 pts (Dev St Int Rel)
  Middlesex – 200–240 pts (Dev St)
  Portsmouth – 200–280 pts (Lat Am Dev St)
160 pts **Central Lancashire** – 160 pts (Rce Eth St courses)
  East London – 160 pts (Third Wrld Dev NGO Mgt; Third Wrld Dev)
  Northampton – 160–200 pts (Third Wrld Dev courses)
140 pts **Derby** – 140–180 pts (Third Wrld Dev)

Alternative offers
IB offers Chester 30 pts; East Anglia 32 pts; London (SOAS) 31 pts; Manchester 32–34 pts.
Scottish offers See **Chapter 7**.

CHOOSING YOUR COURSE (SEE ALSO CH.1)
Subject information Development Studies courses are multi-disciplinary and cover a range of subjects including economics, geography, sociology, social anthropology, politics, natural resources, with special reference to countries overseas. **Useful websites** www.devstud.org.uk; www.dfid.gov.uk; see also **Politics**.

Course variations African Studies with Development (Bath); Development and Peace Studies (Bradford); Third World Development (East London); Development Geography (London (King's)); Latin

American Development Studies (Portsmouth). *NOW CHECK PROSPECTUSES AND WEBSITES FOR ANY RECENT CHANGES.*

Universities and colleges teaching quality See www.tqi.ac.uk; www.qaa.ac.uk.

Top universities and colleges (Research) East Anglia.

ADMISSIONS INFORMATION

Number of applicants per place (approx) Bradford 6; Derby 4; East Anglia 8; East London 8; Leeds 8; Swansea 9.

Advice to applicants and planning the UCAS personal statement Discuss aspects of development studies which interest you, for example in relation to geography, economics, politics. Interests in Third World countries should be mentioned. **Derby** Interest in politics, economics and the environment in less developed countries. **East Anglia** Knowledge of current events.

Misconceptions about this course **Swansea** Some students think that Development Studies has something to do with property, with plants or with childhood. It is none of these and is about international processes of change, development, progress and crisis.

Selection interviews **Yes** East London; **Some** Derby, Swansea.

Interview advice and questions Since this is a multi-disciplinary subject, questions will vary considerably. Initially they will stem from your interests and the information given on your UCAS application and your reasons for choosing the course. In the past, questions at interview have included: Define a Third World country. What help does the United Nations provide in the Third World? Could it do too much? What problems does the United Nations face in its work throughout the world? **Swansea** Why Development Studies? What will you do in your gap year, and what do you want to achieve? Is Swansea your first or second choice? See also **Chapter 6**.

AFTER-RESULTS ADVICE

Universities with vacancies in Clearing (2006) Bradford; Chester; Derby; East London.

Offers to applicants repeating A-levels **Same** Derby, East Anglia.

GRADUATE DESTINATIONS AND EMPLOYMENT (2005 HESA)

No data available.

OTHER DEGREE SUBJECTS FOR CONSIDERATION

Economics; Environmental Science/Studies; Geography; Government; International Relations; Politics; Sociology.

DIETETICS

(see also **Food Science/Studies and Technology** and **Nutrition**)

NB The points totals shown to the left of the institutions are for ease of reference only. It must not be assumed that tariff points are always used by institutions or that they can be substituted for an offer in grades. The level of an offer is not necessarily indicative of the quality of a course.

COURSE OFFERS INFORMATION

Subject requirements/preferences **GCSE** English, mathematics and science usually required. **AL** Biology and/or chemistry may be required.

Your target offers
300 pts **Nottingham** – BBB–BBC (Dietetics)
Surrey – BBB–BBC (Nutr Diet)
280 pts **London (King's)** – BBC+AS (Nutr Diet)
Plymouth – 280 pts (Dietetics)

240 pts **Coventry** – 240 pts (Dietetics)
220 pts **Cardiff (UWIC)** – 220 pts (App Hum Nutr; Hum Nutr Diet)
200 pts **Bath Spa** – 200–240 pts (Diet Hlth)
            London Met – 200 pts (Hum Nutr Diet)
180 pts **Queen Margaret (UC)** – 180 pts (Dietetics)
160 pts **Glasgow Caledonian** – CC (Hum Nutr Diet)
            Robert Gordon – CC (Nutr Diet)

            Leeds Met – contact University

Alternative offers
IB offers Surrey 30–32 pts.
Scottish offers See **Chapter 7**.

CHOOSING YOUR COURSE (SEE ALSO CH.1)

Subject information Dietitians are professionally trained to advise on diets and aspects of nutrition and many degree courses combine both subjects. They may work in the NHS as hospital dietitians collaborating with medical staff on the balance of foods for patients or in local health authorities working with GPs or in health centres or clinics dealing with infant welfare and ante-natal problems. In addition, dietitians advise consumer groups in the food industry and government and may be involved in research. Courses can lead to professional registration: check with admissions tutors and see **Appendix 2**. **Useful websites** www.eatright.org; www.bda.uk.com.

Course variations Diet and Health (Bath Spa); Human Nutrition and Dietetics (London Met). *NOW CHECK PROSPECTUSES AND WEBSITES FOR ANY RECENT CHANGES.*

Universities and colleges teaching quality See www.tqi.ac.uk; www.qaa.ac.uk.

Sandwich degree courses Cardiff (UWIC); Glasgow Caledonian; Surrey.

ADMISSIONS INFORMATION

Number of applicants per place (approx) Glasgow Caledonian 11; Queen Margaret (UC) 5; Surrey 1.

Advice to applicants and planning the UCAS personal statement Discuss the work with a hospital dietitian and describe fully work experience gained in hospital dietetics departments or with the schools meals services, and the problems experienced in working in these fields. Contact the British Dietetic Association (see **Appendix 2**).

Selection interviews All institutions.

Interview advice and questions Your knowledge of a career in dietetics will be fully explored and questions will be asked on your work experience and how you reacted to it. See also **Chapter 6**.

AFTER-RESULTS ADVICE

Universities with vacancies in Clearing (2006) Coventry; Plymouth; Robert Gordon.

Offers to applicants repeating A-levels **Possibly higher** Glasgow Caledonian.

GRADUATE DESTINATIONS AND EMPLOYMENT (2005 HESA)

No data available.

OTHER DEGREE SUBJECTS FOR CONSIDERATION

Biological Sciences; Biochemistry; Biology; Consumer Studies; Food Science; Health Studies; Hospitality Management; Nursing; Nutrition.

DRAMA

(including **Performing Arts/Studies, Theatre Arts, Theatre Studies** and **Theatre Design;**
see also **Art and Design (General))**

*NB The points totals shown to the left of the institutions are for ease of reference only. It must not
be assumed that tariff points are always used by institutions or that they can be substituted for an
offer in grades. The level of an offer is not necessarily indicative of the quality of a course.*

COURSE OFFERS INFORMATION

Subject requirements/preferences **GCSE** English usually required. **AL** English, drama, theatre studies
may be required or preferred.

Your target offers

360 pts and above
    Exeter – AAA–BBB (Drama)
    Warwick – ABBb–ABabb (Thea Perf St; Engl Thea St)
340 pts **Birmingham** – AAB–ABB (Dr Thea Arts)
    Manchester – AAB–ABB (Dr; Dr Engl Lit; Dr Scrn St)
320 pts **East Anglia** – ABB 320 pts (Engl Lit Dr; Dr; Script Perf)
    Glasgow – ABB–BBB (Thea St)
    Kent – 320 pts (Dr Thea St)
    Lancaster – ABB (Thea St Engl Lit)
    London (RH) – ABB 320 pts (Dr Thea St; Dr Mus; Dr Ger/Ital; Dr Crea Writ; Dr Engl; Class St
    Dr; Int Thea (Aus) (Fr))
    Loughborough – 320–300 pts (Dr; Dr Engl)
    Sussex – ABB **or** 360 pts 3AL+AS (Dr St courses)
300 pts **Belfast (Queen's)** – BBB **or** BBCb (Dr courses)
    Birmingham – BBB (Modn Langs Thea St)
    Bristol – BBB (Dr; Dr Engl; Dr Fr/Ger/Ital/Port/Span)
    Essex – 300 pts (Dr; Dr Lit)
    Hull – BBB–BBC 300–280 pts (Dr; Dr Engl; Dr Lang; Dr Mus; Dr Theol; Dr Hist Art; Dr Film St)
    Kent – 300 pts (Engl Am Lit Dr Thea St; Film St Dr Thea St)
    Lancaster – ABC–BBB (Thea St; Thea St Fr/Span)
    London (Gold) – BBB (Dr Thea Arts)
    London (QM) – 300–370 pts (Dr; Engl Dr; Fr Dr; Ger Dr; Russ Dr; Span Dr; Hisp St Dr; Film St
    Dr)
    Reading – 300 pts (TV Film Thea)
280 pts **Aberystwyth** – 280 pts (Dr; Perf St Dr; Scnograph St Dr)
    Bristol UWE – 280–300 pts (Dr; Dr joint courses)
    Brunel – 280 pts (Modn Dr St)
    Kent – 280 pts (Dr Hist; Dr Hist Phil Art; Dr Phil; Dr Relig St)
    Kingston – 280–320 pts (Dr courses)
    Leeds – BBC (Thea Perf; Perf Des)
    Liverpool John Moores – BBC (Drama)
    Queen Margaret (UC) – BBC (Thea Prod; Dr Thea Arts)
    Salford – 280 pts (Perf Arts)
260 pts **Kent** – 260 pts (Dr Fr/Ger/Ital; Dr Hisp St)
    London (Central Sch SpDr) – BCC (Dr App Thea Educ)
    Northumbria – BCC (Dr; Script Dr; Perf)
    Roehampton – 260–240 pts (Dr Thea Perf St courses)
    Salford – 260 pts (Contemp Thea Prac)
240 pts **Bangor** – 240–260 pts (Engl Thea St)
    Central Lancashire – 240 pts (Mus Thea; Actg)
    Chester – 240 pts (Dr Thea St; Perf New Media courses)

Chichester – 240–280 pts (Perf Arts)
Dartington (CA) – 240–280 pts (Theatre)
Edge Hill – 240 pts (Dr Physl Thea Dance)
Huddersfield – 240 pts (Dr; Mus Dr; Dr Engl; Dr Media)
Hull (Scarborough) – CCC 240–220 pts (Thea Perf St; Thea Perf St Dance; Thea Perf St Des Dig Media)
Nottingham Trent – 240 pts (Thea Des)
Oxford Brookes – CCC **or** CCcc (Perf Arts)
Portsmouth – 240–300 pts (Engl Dr)
Ulster – CCC 240 pts (Drama)

220 pts **Bangor** – 220–260 pts (Thea Media St)
Bath Spa – 220–260 pts (Dr St; Perf Arts (Actg); Dir)
Central Lancashire – 220 pts (Engl Thea St)
De Montfort – 220 pts (Dr St; Arts Mgt Dr St)
Edge Hill – 220–240 pts (Drama)
Glamorgan – 220–300 pts (Ltg Tech; Live Evnt Tech)
Lincoln – 220 pts (Drama)
Liverpool Hope – 220 pts (Dr Thea St; Crea Perf Arts)
Plymouth – 220 pts (Thea Perf)
Queen Margaret (UC) – CCD (Perf Prod Mgt; Cstm Des Constr)
Southampton Solent – 220 pts (Perf; Cmdy Writ Perf)
Winchester – 220–240 pts (Dr St courses)

200 pts **Anglia Ruskin** – 200 pts (Dr; Dr Engl; Dr Film St)
Coventry – 200–220 pts (Thea Prof Prac)
Cumbria – 200 pts (Dr Mus Thea; Dr Tech Thea; Mus Thea Tech Thea; Dr Crea Writ)
Glamorgan – 200–300 pts (Dr (Thea Media); Media Perf)
Manchester Met – 200 pts (Contemp Thea Perf)
Middlesex – 200–240 pts (Dr Thea Arts; Tech Thea Arts; Dr Thea St)
Newport – 200 pts (Dr App Thea Educ Commun; Perf Arts)
UCE Birmingham – CDD–BB (Engl Dr)

180 pts **Bedfordshire** – 180 pts (Perf Arts)
Central Lancashire – 180–160 pts (Thea Prac)
De Montfort – 180–200 pts (Dr St Engl)
Edge Hill – 180–220 pts (Educ St Dr)
Liverpool (LIPA) – BC 180 pts (Perf Arts (Actg); Commun Dr; Mus Thea Enter Mgt)
London (Central Sch SpDr) – 180 pts (Perf Arts; Stg Mgt; Pptry; Cstm Prod)
Northampton – 180–220 pts (Drama)
Staffordshire – 180–240 pts (Thea Arts Film St; Dr Perf Thea Arts; Thea St Script)

160 pts **Central Lancashire** – 160 pts (Dr Thea St)
Cumbria – CC 160 pts (Dr Crea Writ; Dr Mus Thea; Dr Tech Thea)

        East London – 160 pts (Perf Arts courses)
        Greenwich – 160 pts (Dr Comb courses)
        London (Central Sch SpDr) – CC (Actg courses)
        London Met – 160 pts (Perf Arts; Thea St courses)
        London South Bank – CC (Actg; Dr Perf St; Thea Prod)
        Manchester City (Coll) – 160 pts (Actg St; Stg Des Mgt St)
        Manchester Met – 160 pts (Acting)
        Newman (CHE) – CC 160 pts (Dr courses)
        Reading – 160 pts (Thea Arts Educ Df St)
        Rose Bruford (Coll) – 160 pts min approx; indiv interview/audition (Actg; Dir; Thea Des; Stg Mgt; Actr Mus; Am Thea Arts; Euro Thea Arts; Ltg Des; Scnc Arts; Cstm Prod)
        St Mary's (Coll) – 160–200 pts (Dr Perf St; Physl Thea courses)
        Wolverhampton – 160 pts (Dr Perf)
        Worcester – 160 pts (Dr Perf St)
        York St John – CC 160 pts (Perf Thea; Thea Engl Lit)
140 pts   **Bishop Grosseteste (Coll)** – 140–160 pts (Dr Commun; Educ St Dr)
        De Montfort – 140–160 pts (Perf Arts)
        Derby – 140–180 pts (Thea St Comb; Thea Arts)
        Marjon (Coll) – 140–200 pts (Dr courses)
        Queen Margaret (UC) – CD (Thea Prod; Actg Perf)
        Sunderland – 140–160 pts (Perf Arts St)
        Thames Valley – 140–160 pts (Acting)
120 pts   **Buckinghamshire Chilterns (UC)** – 120–180 pts (Dr courses)
        North East Wales (IHE) – 120–80 pts (Thea Perf)
        Peterborough Reg (Coll) – 120 pts (Perf Arts)
        Royal Welsh (CMusDr) – 120–200 pts (Actg; Stg Mgt; Thea Des)
        Suffolk (Univ Campus) – 120–180 pts (Perf Arts)
        Swansea (IHE) – 120 pts (Perf Arts Thea St)
        Trinity Carmarthen (Coll) – 120 pts (Thea St; Thea Des Prod; Actg)
100 pts   **Birmingham (Sch Actg)** – 100 pts (Actg; Actg (Musl Thea))
80 pts   **and below**
        Arts Educ London – entry by audition (Actg; Musl Thea)
        Arts London (Central Saint Martins CAD) – 80 pts audition (Actg; Dir; Thea; Des Perf)
        Arts London (CFash) – 80 pts (Cstm Mkup)
        Arts London (Wimbledon CA) – interview+portfolio (Thea Ltg Des Prac; Thea Set Des Stg Scrn; Tech Arts Spec Efcts)
        Bournemouth (AI) – 80 pts (Actg Thea Film TV)
        Brighton – 80 pts Fdn Art (Thea Vis Art)
        Carshalton (Coll) – (Commun Thea Educ)
        Essex – 80 pts+audition (Actg; Contemp Thea; Tech Thea St)
        Greenwich – 80 pts (Drama)
        GSA (Cons) – audition (Actg; Musl Thea)
        Laban – (Dance Thea)
        London (Arts Educ Sch) – (Acting)
        London Mountview (Ac Thea Arts) – audition (Musl Thea; Actg; Tech Thea)
        London (RADA) – audition (BA Dr)
        Royal Scottish (RSAMD) – 80 pts (Contemp Thea Prac; Actg; Tech Prod Arts)

Alternative offers

IB offers; Birmingham 34 pts; Bristol 32 pts; Bristol UWE 28–32 pts; Brunel 30 pts; Chester 30 pts; Chichester 28–30 pts; East Anglia 32 pts; Essex 32 pts; Exeter 32–36 pts; Keele 28–30 pts; Kent 28–34 pts; London (Gold) 32 pts, (QM) 32 pts, (RH) 32 pts; Loughborough 32–35 pts; Manchester 32–35 pts; Manchester Met 32–35 pts; Salford 28 pts; Warwick 36 pts.
Scottish offers See **Chapter 7**.

DRAMA CENTRE LONDON

BA (Hons) Acting Course
Accredited by the National Council for Drama Training

BA (Hons) Directing Course

Foundation in Performance
Subject to approval

MA in Performance
Screen Acting; Script Writing; Directing

MA in European Classical Acting

Information Office
Central Saint Martins College of Art & Design
Southampton Row
London
WC1B 4AP
Tel: +44 (0)20 7514 7022
E-mail: info@csm.arts.ac.uk
Website: www.csm.arts.ac.uk/drama

University of the Arts London Central Saint Martins

OTHER HIGHER EDUCATION COURSES IN THE SUBJECT FIELD

Foundation degrees (contact the institutions for details) Bath Spa; Bedfordshire; Bournemouth and Poole (Coll); Bridgwater (Coll); Brooklands (Coll); Burnley (Coll); Canterbury Christ Church; Coventry; Croydon (Coll); Cumbria; De Montfort; East Durham (CmC); East 15 Acting (Sch); Grimsby (IFHE); Guildford (Coll); Herefordshire (CAD); Hull (Coll); Leeds (CMus); Leeds Met; London Met; Nescot; Newcastle (Coll); North Devon (Coll); North East Wales (IHE); Northbrook (Coll); Nottingham New (Coll); Oldham (Coll); Oxford and Cherwell Valley (Coll); Preston (Coll); Rotherham (CAT); St Helens (Coll); Sheffield Hallam; Sheffield New (Coll); South Birmingham (Coll); South Cheshire (Coll); Stockton Riverside (Coll); Stratford-upon-Avon (Coll); Suffolk (Univ Campus); Sunderland; Teesside; Thames Valley; Truro (Coll); West Herts (Coll); West Kent (Coll); Weston (Coll); Weymouth (Coll); Worcestershire New (Coll); Yeovil (Coll).

Higher National Diploma courses

100 pts Accrington and Rossendale (Coll); Anglia Ruskin; Arts London (CFash); Bedfordshire; Birmingham City (Coll); Blackpool and Fylde (Coll); Bridgwater (Coll); Buckinghamshire Chilterns (UC); Burton (Coll); Central Lancashire; Chichester; Colchester (Inst); Coventry; De Montfort; Doncaster (Univ Centre); Dudley (Coll); East Berkshire (Coll); East London; Eastleigh (Coll); Fareham (Coll); Filton (Coll); Forth Valley (Coll); Glasgow (Coll); Gloucestershire (CAT); Great Yarmouth (Coll); Havering (Coll); Hertfordshire; Kidderminster (Coll); Leicester (Coll); Lewisham (Coll); Lincoln; Liverpool (CmC); Llandrillo Cymru (Coll); Matthew Boulton (CFHE); Nescot; Newcastle (Coll); Northbrook (Coll); Northampton; Nottingham New (Coll); Oldham (Coll); Peterborough Reg (Coll); Plymouth; St Helens (Coll); Salford; Salisbury (Coll); Shrewsbury (Coll); Somerset (CAT); South Birmingham (Coll); South Devon (Coll); Southend Campus Essex; Southwark (Coll); Stafford (Coll); Stratford-upon-Avon (Coll); Strode (Coll); Suffolk (Coll); Sutton Coldfield (Coll); Tameside (Coll); Teesside (Coll); Thames (Coll) (Perf Arts); Trinity Carmarthen (Coll); Tyne Met (Coll); UHI Millennium Inst; Wakefield (Coll);

Walsall (Coll); Warwickshire (Coll); West Anglia (Coll); West Thames (Coll); Weston (Coll); Wolverhampton; Worcester (CT); Worcestershire New (Coll); Wigan and Leigh (Coll); Yorkshire Coast (CFHE).

CHOOSING YOUR COURSE (SEE ALSO CH.1)

Subject information Drama courses are popular, with twice as many women as men applying each year. Lack of confidence in securing appropriate work at the end of the course, however, tends to encourage many applicants to bid for joint courses although these are usually far more competitive since there are fewer places available. Most schools of acting and drama provide a strong vocational bias whilst university drama departments offer a broader field of studies combining theory and practice. The choice of course will depend on personal preferences, either practical or theoretical, or a combination of both. **Useful websites** www.equity.org.uk; www.abtt.org.uk; www.thestage.co.uk; www.uktw.co.uk; www.netgain.org.uk; www.artscouncil.org.uk; www.stagecoach.co.uk.

Course variations Modern Drama Studies (Brunel); Contemporary Theatre (Essex); Theatre and Performance Studies (Hull); Theatre Studies and English Literature (Lancaster); Stage Management and Theatre Production (London (Central Sch SpDr)); Theatre Design (Nottingham Trent); Actor Musician (Rose Bruford); Comedy: Writing and Performance (Southampton Solent). *NOW CHECK PROSPECTUSES AND WEBSITES FOR ANY RECENT CHANGES.*

Universities and colleges teaching quality See www.tqi.ac.uk; www.qaa.ac.uk.

Top universities and colleges (Research) (including Dance and Performing Arts) Aberystwyth; Bristol*; Kent; London (RH); Manchester; Nottingham Trent; Reading; Warwick*.

ADMISSIONS INFORMATION

Number of applicants per place (approx) Aberystwyth 10; Arts London (Central Saint Martins CAD) (Actg) 32, (Dir) 10 (Wimbledon (CA) (Thea Des Perf) 2, (Tech Arts Spec Efcts) 3; Birmingham 15; Bishop Grosseteste (Coll) 4; Bristol 40; Brunel 9; Chester 14; Cumbria 4; Dartington (CA) 8; De Montfort (Perf Arts) 5; East Anglia 13; Edge Hill 8; Essex 15; Exeter 20; Glamorgan 6; Huddersfield 5; Hull 16; Hull (Scarborough) 2; Kent 24; Lancaster 18; Leeds 10; Liverpool (LIPA) (Perf Arts (Actg)) 48; Liverpool John Moores 10; London (Central Sch SpDr) (Thea Prac) 5, (Actg) 50; (Gold) 28, (RH) 10; London Met 20; London Mountview (Ac Thea Arts) (Mus Thea) 8; Loughborough 6; Manchester City (Coll) 10; Manchester Met 48; Middlesex 26; Northampton 3; Northumbria 25; Nottingham Trent 4; Queen Margaret (UC) 4; Reading 17; Roehampton 6; Royal Welsh (CMusDr) (Actg) 50, (Stg Mgt) 10; Warwick 18; Winchester (Dr) 6; Worcester 4; York St John 9.

Advice to applicants and planning the UCAS personal statement List the plays in which you have performed and specify the characters played. Indicate any experience in other areas of theatre, especially directing or writing. Add any information on projects you have initiated or developed or experienced in theatre craft, such as set design, costume design, lighting design, prop-making, scene painting. List any community arts projects such as work with youth clubs, hospital radio, amateur dramatics, music/drama workshops and voluntary work within the arts. **Arts London (Central Saint Martins CAD)** Only apply if you wish to pursue professional careers in acting or directing. **De Montfort** Strengths in both dance and theatre. **East Anglia** An all-round commitment to drama in all its aspects. **Leeds** Offers one, two or three-year diploma courses which provide an individually designed programme of study and do not have standard entry requirements. These give an opportunity for overseas students to work alongside honours degree students in a very rich arts context. **Liverpool (LIPA)** We look for communication and entrepreneurial skills; (Perf Arts (Actg)) Details of performance and specific characters played; **Loughborough** The course combines both theory and practice. **Nottingham Trent** Art portfolio required. See **Chapter 6** and also **Appendix 2**.

Misconceptions about this course That a Theatre Studies course is a training for the stage: it is not. **Arts London (Central Saint Martins CAD)** is a long-established classical conservatoire-type training for actors, and not a Theatre Studies or Performance Arts course. It is no longer a private school and home and EU students pay the standard degree fee. **De Montfort** (Perf Arts) Unaware that the course involves music. **Huddersfield** This is not a performing course. **Kent** This is not like an acting school. **Salford** (Contemp Thea Prac) This course does not include musical theatre. **Staffordshire** We stress to applicants that this is not a drama school course. **Sunderland** (Perf Arts St) Applicants often think the course only involves one subject but in fact they are required to study two. **Winchester** This is not an Acting course although practical work is involved. **York St John** This is not a course for intending actors.

Selection interviews **Yes** Most institutions, usually with auditions which are likely to involve solo and group tests; **Some** Chester, St Mary's (Coll).

Interview advice and questions **Arts London (Central Saint Martins CAD)** (Actg) Two three-minute speeches or scenes, one of which must be from the classical repertoire. (Dir) Interview and practical workshop which may involve directing actors. **Bristol** Assesses each case on its merits, paying attention to candidate's educational and cultural opportunities. Particularly interested in applicants who have already shown some evidence of commitment in their approach to drama in practical work, theatre-going, film viewing or reading. One fifth of applicants are called for interview and take part in practical sessions. They may present any art work, photography or similar material. (London Board Practical Music not acceptable for Drama/Music unless offered with theoretical music + one other A-level.) **Brunel** All applicants to whom an offer may be made will be auditioned, involving a practical workshop, voice, movement improvisation and a short prepared speech. Offers unlikely to be made to those with less than a grade B in drama or theatre studies. **De Montfort** (Perf Arts) What do you hope to gain on a three-year course in Performing Arts? Interviews involve practical workshops in drama and theatre and a written paper. **East Anglia** Looks for candidates with a sound balance of academic and practical skills. Applicants will be expected to analyse performance and to understand what is entailed in the production of a drama. **Hull** Interviews two groups of 18 for whole day which presents a mini-version of the course, with entire staff and number of current students present. Offers then made to about half. Selection process is all-important. More applicants for the joint honours courses with English, Theology, Classical Studies, American Studies or Modern Language who have a conventional half-hour interview. Drama/English is the most popular combination and the offer includes a B in English. **Kent** No single honours candidate accepted without interview. Emphasis equally on academic and practical abilities. Questions asked to probe the applicant's creative and analytical grasp of theatre. **Lancaster** (Thea St) Candidates invited for interview and should be prepared to take part in a workshop with other candidates. We are just as interested in backstage people as actors and now have an arts administration option. **Liverpool (LIPA)** (Perf Arts (Actg)) Applicants will be expected to perform one devised piece, one Shakespearean piece and a song plus a short review of a performance they have seen recently. **London (Central Sch SpDr)**, **Central Lancashire**, **De Montfort**, **London (RH)**. Written papers and/or tests. **London (RH)** At interview we look for students who are mentally agile and versatile who enjoy reading as well as taking part in productions. **London Mountview (Ac Thea Arts)** Voice, movement and singing sessions plus acting pieces. **Loughborough** Offers in terms of A-levels not set. Candidates judged as individuals. Applicants with unconventional subject combinations and mature students considered. Final selection based on interview and audition. Applicants ought to show experience of practical drama, preferably beyond school plays. **Royal Welsh (CMusDr)** Written papers and/or tests. BA Acting – audition; BA Stage Management – interview; BA Theatre Design – interview and portfolio presentation. All applicants are charged an audition/interview fee. **Warwick** Interview is important to assess academic potential and particularly commitment to, and suitability for, teaching; offers therefore variable. See also **Chapter 6**.

Applicants' impressions (A=Open day; B=Interview day) **London (Gold)** (B) There was one interviewer, who was fairly aggressive and forceful and who made me feel intimidated. I was asked what I thought about Goldsmiths, why I wanted to do Drama, would I rather go to a drama school and who was the most influential person of the 20th century? It was a well-organised visit. The teachers were very enthusiastic and the students thought it was a good course.

Reasons for rejection (non-academic) Poor ambition. Wrong expectations of the course. Several students clearly want a drama school acting training rather than a degree course. Not enough background reading. **Arts London (Central Saint Martins CAD)** Insufficient clarity about career aims.

De Montfort (Perf Arts) Candidate more suitable for a drama or dance school than for a degree course. No genuine engagement with the subject. Evidence of poor attendance at school.

AFTER-RESULTS ADVICE
Universities with vacancies in Clearing (2006) Aberystwyth; Anglia Ruskin; Bangor; Bristol; Bristol UWE; Brunel; Central Lancashire; Chester; Cumbria; De Montfort; Derby; East London; Edge Hill; Glamorgan; Greenwich; Huddersfield; Hull; Lincoln; Liverpool Hope; Liverpool John Moores; London (RH); Manchester Met; Northampton; Roehampton; Salford; Staffordshire; Teesside; Ulster; Wolverhampton; Winchester; York St John.

Offers to applicants repeating A-levels **Higher** Hull, Warwick; **Possibly higher** London (RH); **Same** Brunel, Chichester, De Montfort (Perf Arts), East Anglia, GSA (Cons), Huddersfield, Kent, Leeds (further audition required), Liverpool Hope (UC), Liverpool John Moores, Loughborough, Manchester City (Coll), Newman (CHE), Nottingham Trent, Roehampton, Royal Welsh (CMusDr), Staffordshire, Sunderland, Winchester, York St John.

GRADUATE DESTINATIONS AND EMPLOYMENT (2005 HESA)
Graduates surveyed 3230 **Employed** 1785 **In further study** 354 **Assumed unemployed** 240.

OTHER DEGREE SUBJECTS FOR CONSIDERATION
Art and Design (Costume Design, Stage Design); Arts Management; Dance; Education (Primary); English; Performance Studies.

ECONOMICS

NB The points totals shown to the left of the institutions are for ease of reference only. It must not be assumed that tariff points are always used by institutions or that they can be substituted for an offer in grades. The level of an offer is not necessarily indicative of the quality of a course.

COURSE OFFERS INFORMATION
Subject requirements/preferences **GCSE** Mathematics and occasionally English and a foreign language required. **Aberdeen, Dundee, Edinburgh, Glasgow, St Andrews** English, mathematics and a foreign language. **Aberystwyth** 50% grades A or B. **Bangor** Average grade B. **Bath** Majority of A or B grades including mathematics. **Belfast (Queen's), Birmingham** Mathematics grade B. **Bristol** Grade A or B in all subjects. **Cambridge, Oxford** Grade A in most subjects preferred. **City, Portsmouth, Surrey** Grade A or B in mathematics if not taken at A-level. **Durham** Minimum three As and four Bs, mathematics grade A if not taken at A-level. **Edinburgh** Mathematics grade B. **Essex** Eight As or Bs including mathematics and English. **Exeter** Mathematics and English at grade B or above plus a majority of As and Bs. **Hull** Three subjects grade A, three subjects grade B, three subjects grade C average preferred. **Keele** Mathematics grade B. **Lancaster** Mathematics grade B. **Leeds** Mathematics grade A. **Leicester** (Econ Law) Six subjects grade A or B. **Liverpool** Mathematics grade A/B. **London (LSE)** Grades A*, A and B. **London (RH)** A high proportion of As and Bs, mathematics grade B. **Newcastle** Mathematics grade B. **Nottingham** Six subjects at grade A including mathematics grade A or B. **Southampton** Good mathematics (grade B) and science; remaining subjects at grade A or B preferred; a good range of As and Bs. **Warwick** For GL11 course see under **Mathematics**. **York** Mainly As and Bs including mathematics. **AL** Mathematics, economics or business studies may be required or preferred.

Your target offers
360 pts **and above**
    Bristol – AAA–AAB (Econ; Econ Euro; Econ Fin; Econ Hist; Econ Maths; Econ Pol; Econ Sociol; Phil Econ; Econ Mgt)
    Cambridge – AAA (Econ; Land Econ (Env, Law, Econ))
    Durham – AAA (Nat Sci Econ)
    Lancaster – AAA (Econ N Am/Aus)

London (LSE) – AAA (Econ; Econ Econ Hist; Economet Mathem Econ; Env Pol Econ; Phil Econ)
London (UCL) – AAA+AS–AAB+AS (Econ; Econ Stats; Econ Geog; Phil Econ)
Nottingham – AAA–AABB (Econ courses; Int Econ)
Oxford – Offers vary eg AAA–AAB (Econ Mgt; Hist Econ; Mat Econ Mgt; Eng Econ Mgt; PPE)
Warwick – AABb (Econ; Ind Econ; Econ Pol Int St; Econ Econ Hist; Maths Econ; PPE)
340 pts **Aston** – 340 pts (2AL+2AS) **or** 320 pts (3AL) (Int Bus Econ)
Bath – AAB (Econ; Econ Pol; Econ Int Dev; Pol Econ)
Durham – AAB (Econ; Bus Econ; PPE; Econ Fr; Comb Soc Sci; Nat Sci Joint Hons)
Essex – 340–280 pts (PPE)
Exeter – AAB–BBB (Econ; Econ Fin; Econ Economet; Econ Pol; Bus Econ)
Manchester – AAB (Economics)
St Andrews – AAB (Econ Engl; App Econ; Econ Modn Hist; Econ Mid E St; Econ Span)
Southampton – AAB 340 pts (Econ; Econ Act Sci; Econ Economet; Econ Fin; Econ Mgt Sci; Maths Econ; Econ Phil; Econ Pol; Acc Econ)
York – AAB (Econ; Econ Fin; Econ Economet Fin; Econ Econ Hist; PPE)
320 pts **Aston** – 320 pts (Econ Mgt)
Belfast (Queen's) – ABB–BBBb (Econ Acc)
Birmingham – ABB (Mathem Econ Stats; Econ; Econ Lang; Pol Econ)
Cardiff – ABB (Bus Econ; Econ; Econ Mgt St; Econ Euro Lang; Bus Econ Euro Lang; Sociol Econ; Econ Fin)
Glasgow – ABB (Econ; Bus Econ)
Kent – 320 pts (Law Econ)
Lancaster – ABB (Econ; Econ Maths; Econ Geog; Adv Econ Mark; Int Bus (Econ); Fin Econ; Econ Lang)
Leeds – ABB (Econ; Econ Mgt; Econ Trans St; Bus Fin Econ; Bus Econ)
Leicester – ABB (BA Econ Law; Econ; Fin Econ; Bus Econ)
London (RH) – ABB–BBB (Econ; Fin Bus Econ; Econ Lang; Econ Mgt; Econ Maths; Econ Mus)
London (SOAS) – ABB (Econ; Dev Econ)
Loughborough – ABB–AAC (Econ; Bus Econ Fin; Int Econ; Econ Acc; Econ Pol; Econ Span; Econ Fr; Econ Ger; Econ Geog; Econ Soc Pol; Econ Sociol)
Manchester – ABB–BBB (BA Econ; Econ Pol; Econ Sociol; Econ Fin; Econ Crim; Econ Econ Soc Hist)
Newcastle – ABB–BBB (Econ courses)
Nottingham – ABB (Ind Econ; Ind Econ Ins)
Reading – 320 (3AL+AS) **or** 300 pts (3AL) (Econ; Bus Econ; Econ Economet)
Sheffield – ABB–BBB (Econ; Econ Geog; Econ Phil; Econ Pol; Econ Soc Pol; Econ Lang; Mgt Econ; Acc Fin Mgt Econ)
300 pts **Belfast (Queen's)** – BBB (Bus Econ; Econ Mgt; Econ Fin; Econ Lang; Econ)
City – 300–320 pts (Econ; Econ Acc)
Dundee – 300–220 pts (Bus Econ Mark courses; MA Econ; MA Fin Econ)
East Anglia – BBB–BBC (Econ; Econ Acc; Econ Phil; Bus Econ; Bus Fin Econ; PPE)
Edinburgh – BBB (Econ; Econ Acc; Econ Chin; Econ Law; Econ Econ Hist; Econ Pol; Econ Sociol; Econ Env St; Econ Mgt Sci)
Essex – BBB 300 pts (Econ; Econ Euro; Econ Fr/Ger/Ital/Span; Econ Pol; Econ Maths; Acc Econ; Econ Hist; Int Econ; Fin Econ)
Kent – 300 pts (PPE Euro; PPE)
Lancaster – BBB (Econ Int Rel; Econ Pol; PPE)
Leeds – BBB (Chin Econ)
Leicester – ABC (BSc Bus Econ; Econ; Fin Econ)
Liverpool – BBB–ABB 300–320 pts (Fin Econ; Econ; Bus Econ)
London (QM) – 300 pts (Econ courses)
London (UCL) – BBB+AS (Econ Bus E Euro St)
Strathclyde – ABC–BBB (Economics)
Surrey – 300 pts (Bus Econ Fin; Econ; Bus Econ)
Sussex – BBB **or** 340 pts 3AL+AS (Econ courses)

280 pts **Brunel** – 280–260 pts (Econ Bus Fin; Econ Mgt; Bus Econ)

Kent – BBC 280 pts (Econ; Econ Comp; Euro Econ (Fr) (Ger) (Span); Econ Pol; Soc Anth Econ; App Econ Sociol)

Westminster – 280 pts (Bus Econ)

260 pts **Aberystwyth** – 260 pts (Econ; Mark Econ; Bus Econ)

Bradford – 260 pts (Econ; Econ Dev St; Econ Int Rel; Econ Mark; Econ Sociol Psy; Econ Engl EFL; Econ Fr/Span; Int Econ; Bus Econ)

Coventry – 260–320 pts (Econ; Econ joint courses; Fin Econ; Bus Econ)

Heriot-Watt – BCC–CCC 260 pts (Econ courses)

Hull – 260 pts (Econ; Int Econ; Bus Econ courses)

Keele – 260–280 pts (Bus Econ; Econ courses)

Kingston – 260 pts (Econ; Bus Econ; Fin Econ; Glob Econ)

London (Gold) – BCC (Pol Econ; Econ Pol Pblc Pol)

Oxford Brookes – BCC–CCC (Econ courses; Bus Econ)

Richmond (Am Int Univ) – 260 pts (Economics)

Swansea – 260 pts (BSc Bus Econ; Fin Econ Comp)

240 pts **Aberdeen** – CCC (Econ courses)

Bangor – 240 pts (Bus Econ)

Dundee – 240 pts (Econ; Bus Econ Mark; Fin Econ; Econ joint courses)

Manchester Met – CCC 240 pts (Econ; Bus Econ)

Nottingham Trent – 240 pts (Econ; Bus Econ)

Portsmouth – 240–200 pts (Econ Fin Bank; Econ; Bus Econ; Bus Econ Bus Law; App Econ)

Robert Gordon – CCC (Mgt Econ)

Salford – 240–260 pts (Econ; Bus Econ; Bus Econ Gam St; Econ Spo Econ)

Stirling – CCC/BC (Econ; PPE)

Swansea – 240–300 pts (Econ; Fin Econ; Fin Econ Acc; Fin Econ Comp; Bus Econ; Bus Econ Acc)

Ulster – CCC 240 pts (Econ; Econ Govt)

230 pts **Buckingham** – 230 pts (Econ; Econ Bus Law; Econ Bus Journal; Econ Hist; Econ Inf Sys; Econ Pol; Econ Fr/Span)

220 pts **Glamorgan** – 220 pts (Bus Econ)

200 pts **Anglia Ruskin** – 200 pts (Bus Econ)

Bristol UWE – 200–240 pts (Int Bus Econ; Econ; Econ Mny Bank Fin)

Central Lancashire – 200–240 pts (Econ courses except under **160 pts**)

Hertfordshire – 200–240 pts (Econ; Bus Econ)

London Met – 200 pts (Econ; Econ St)

Middlesex – 200–240 pts (Econ courses)

Napier – 200 pts (Bus Econ)

Plymouth – 200 pts (Econ courses; Bus Econ courses)

UCE Birmingham – 200 pts (Acc Econ; Adv Econ; Bus Econ; Constr Mgt Econ; Econ Comp; Mark Econ; Econ Fin)

180 pts **Cardiff (UWIC)** – 180 pts (Acc Econ)

Northampton – 180–220 pts (Econ courses)

Staffordshire – 180–240 pts (Bus Fin Econ; Bus Econ)

160 pts **Central Lancashire** – 160 pts (Econ Acc; Econ Int Bus)

East London – 160 pts (Econ courses)

Glasgow Caledonian – CC (Bus Econ)

Greenwich – 160 pts (Bus Econ; Econ; Econ Int St)

Liverpool John Moores – 160–200 pts (Economics)

London Met – 160 pts (Econ Int Bus)

Paisley – CC–CD (Bus Econ App Econ; Econ)

80 pts **London (Birk)** – 80 pts for under 21s (over 21 varies) (p/t Econ Soc Pol; Fin Econ)

Leeds Met – contact University

Open University – contact University (Econ Maths Sci)

For a quick reference offers calculator, fold out the inside back cover.

Alternative offers
IB offers Bangor 28 pts; Bath 38 pts; Birmingham 34 pts; Bristol 34–38 pts; Bristol UWE 24–28 pts; Cambridge 38–42 pts; City 28–30 pts; Dundee 29 pts; Durham 36 pts; East Anglia 32–35 pts; Essex 32 pts; Exeter 32–35 pts; Glasgow 36 pts; Keele 28–30 pts; Kent 32 pts; Lancaster 34–36 pts; Leicester 32 pts; Liverpool 32 pts; London (LSE) 38 pts, (QM) 34 pts, (RH) 33–35 pts, (UCL) 36–39 pts; Loughborough 34 pts; Manchester 34 pts; Manchester Met 28 pts; Newcastle 33–35 pts; Nottingham 38 pts; Oxford 38–42 pts; St Andrews 34–36 pts; Salford 30 pts; Southampton 35 pts; Surrey 32 pts; Warwick 38 pts. **Scottish offers** See **Chapter 7**.

OTHER HIGHER EDUCATION COURSES IN THE SUBJECT FIELD
Higher National Diploma courses Anglia Ruskin; Plymouth.

CHOOSING YOUR COURSE (SEE ALSO CH.1)
Subject information Economics is about how society makes good use of the limited resources available. Degree courses cover all aspects of finance, taxation and monetary union between countries, aiming to equip the student to analyse economic problems in a systematic way and thus acquire an understanding of how economic systems work. Applicants without economics at A- or AS-level should be prepared for a study involving some mathematics and statistics depending on which course they choose. **Useful websites** www.bized.ac.uk; www.iea.org.uk; see also **Finance**.

Course variations PPE (Durham, East Anglia, Essex, Kent, Lancaster, Oxford, Stirling, Warwick and York); Economics and International Development (Bath); International and Financial Economics (Hull); Politics, Philosophy and Economics in Europe (Kent); Economics, Finance and Banking (Portsmouth); Business Economics and Gambling Studies (Salford); Business Economics (Westminster). *NOW CHECK PROSPECTUSES AND WEBSITES FOR ANY RECENT CHANGES.*

Universities and colleges teaching quality See www.tqi.ac.uk; www.qaa.ac.uk.

Top universities and colleges (Research) Aston; Cambridge; Essex*; Exeter; Leicester; London (LSE)*, (QM), (UCL)*; Nottingham; Oxford; Southampton; Warwick*; York.

Sandwich degree courses Abertay Dundee; Aberystwyth; Aston; Bath; Brunel; City; Hertfordshire; Kingston; Lancaster; Loughborough; Middlesex; Newcastle; Oxford Brookes; Paisley; Plymouth; Portsmouth; Reading; Staffordshire; Surrey; Swansea (IHE); Ulster; Westminster.

ADMISSIONS INFORMATION
Number of applicants per place (approx) Abertay Dundee 3; Aberystwyth 3; Anglia Ruskin 10; Aston 8; Bangor 4; Bath 12; Belfast (Queen's) 10; Birmingham 10; Bradford 5; Bristol 11; Brunel 12; Buckingham 4; Cambridge 7; Cardiff 8; Central Lancashire 5; City 18, (Econ Acc) 12; Coventry 10; Derby 3; Dundee 5; Durham (Econ) 10; East Anglia 15; Essex 6; Exeter 12; Greenwich 8; Heriot-Watt 4; Hull 15; Kent 11; Kingston 9; Lancaster 14; Leeds 16; Leicester 10; Liverpool 4; Liverpool John Moores 8; London (LSE) (Econ) 10, (Econ Econ Hist) 8, (Economet Mathem Econ) 20, (UCL) 12; Loughborough 15; Manchester Met 5; Middlesex (Econ) 8; Newcastle 11, (Econ Bus Mgt) 27, (Fin Bus Econ) 16; Northampton 8; Northumbria 16; Nottingham 15; Nottingham Trent 2; Oxford (success rate Econ Mgt 16%, PPE 29%); Oxford Brookes 51; Paisley 7; Plymouth 4; Portsmouth 6; St Andrews 5; Salford 6; Sheffield 10; Southampton 8; Staffordshire 4; Stirling 6; Sunderland 8; Surrey 5; Swansea 7; UCE Birmingham 16; Warwick 16; York 17.

Number of applicants (**a** UK **b** EU (non-UK) **c** non-EU **d** mature) Aston **a**300 **b**30 **c**50 **d**20; Leeds **a**433 **b**5 **c**70 **d**33.

Advice to applicants and planning the UCAS personal statement Visits, work experience and work shadowing in banks, insurance companies, accountants' offices etc should be described. Keep up-to-date with economic issues by reading *The Economist* and *Financial Times* and find other sources of information. Describe any particular aspects of economics which interest you – and why. Make it clear on the statement that you know what economics is and why you want to study it. **Hull** Interests and ambitions. **Kent** Take three A-levels and optionally one AS. **St Andrews** Evidence of interest and reasons for choosing the course. Sport/extracurricular activities. Positions of responsibility. Applicants should note that (a) it is not a disadvantage not to have studied economics and (b) an MA degree is not better than a BSc – they are both first degrees in the Scottish system. **Southampton** Clearly written statement of academic and non-academic strengths and interests. **York** We look for diligent, highly motivated students.

Misconceptions about this course Bradford That the course is very mathematical and that students will not get a good job, eg management. **Kent** That the course is mathematical, has a high failure rate and has poorer job prospects than business studies courses. **London (UCL)** Some think the Economics course is a Business course. **York** That PPE is a degree taken mainly by male students! That it is dry and overly abstract. Applicants should note that many courses will accept students without economics (check prospectuses and websites).

Selection interviews Yes Bristol, Bristol UWE, Brunel, Cambridge, Coventry, East London, Edinburgh, Essex, Keele, London (RH), (UCL), Manchester Met, Middlesex, Oxford, Southampton (Econ Acc) (interviews influence level of offer), Surrey; **Some** Aberystwyth, Anglia Ruskin, Bangor, Buckingham, Dundee, Kent, Leeds, London (LSE), London Met (mature students), Staffordshire, Swansea, York (PPE).

Interview advice and questions If you have studied economics at A-level or in other examinations, expect to be questioned on aspects of the subject. This is a subject which is constantly in the news, so keep abreast of developments and be prepared to be asked questions such as: What is happening to sterling at present? What is happening to the dollar? How relevant is economics today? What are your views of the Government's economic policy? Do you think that the family is declining as an institution? Discuss Keynesian economics. Is the power of the Prime Minister increasing? What is a recession? How would you get the world out of recession? What causes a recession? **Oxford** (Econ Mgt) Two samples of work required relating to economics or management (if studied at A-level). One-hour written test covering comprehension, writing, problem-solving skills. 'I was asked questions on a newspaper article I had been given to read 45 minutes beforehand, followed by a few maths problems and an economics question.' See also **Chapter 6**.

Applicants' impressions (A=Open day; B=Interview day) Bath (A) An informal day. We were able to pick and choose talks and tours. I went to talks about the course and student life and a tour of the campus and accommodation. **Birmingham** (B) There was a talk about the course, a free lunch and a tour of the campus. **Oxford** (B) All three interviewers were kind and helpful. They would re-route me if I went wrong and hint at the right answer. I was a bit apprehensive since I hadn't done any economics previously. The interview lasted 30 minutes.

Reasons for rejection (non-academic) Lack of knowledge about the course offered and the subject matter. Lack of care in preparing personal statement. Poor written English. The revelation on the statement that they want a course different from that for which they have applied! **Aberystwyth** Would have trouble fitting into the unique environment at Aberystwyth.

AFTER-RESULTS ADVICE

Universities with vacancies in Clearing (2006) Aberdeen; Aberystwyth; Aston; Bangor; Birmingham; Bradford; Bristol; Brunel; Buckingham; Central Lancashire; City; Coventry; Dundee; East Anglia; East London; Essex; Glasgow; Greenwich; Hertfordshire; Hull; Keele; Kent; Kingston; Lancaster; Leicester; London (QM), (RH); London Met; Manchester Met; Middlesex; Newcastle; Northampton; Northumbria; Nottingham Trent; Plymouth; Reading; Salford; Sheffield; Southampton; Staffordshire; Stirling; Swansea; UCE Birmingham; Westminster.

Offers to applicants repeating A-levels Higher Belfast (Queen's), City, Derby, East Anglia, Essex, Leeds, Newcastle, Northumbria, Nottingham, St Andrews, UCE Birmingham, Warwick, York; **Possibly higher** Bradford, Brunel, Durham, Lancaster, Nottingham Trent, Oxford Brookes; **Same** Aberystwyth, Anglia Ruskin, Bangor, Bath, Buckingham, Cardiff, Coventry, Dundee, East London, Heriot-Watt, Hull, Kingston, Liverpool, Liverpool John Moores, London (RH), London Met, Loughborough, Napier, Salford, Sheffield, Staffordshire, Surrey, Swansea, Ulster.

GRADUATE DESTINATIONS AND EMPLOYMENT (2005 HESA)

Graduates surveyed 3530 **Employed** 1825 **In further study** 475 **Assumed unemployed** 260.

OTHER DEGREE SUBJECTS FOR CONSIDERATION

Accountancy; Actuarial Studies; Administration; Banking; Business Studies; Development Studies; Estate Management; Financial Services; Government; Politics; Property Development; Quantity Surveying; Sociology; Statistics.

EDUCATION STUDIES AND TEACHER TRAINING

(see also **Social Studies/Science**)

NB The points totals shown to the left of the institutions are for ease of reference only. It must not be assumed that tariff points are always used by institutions or that they can be substituted for an offer in grades. The level of an offer is not necessarily indicative of the quality of a course.

COURSE OFFERS INFORMATION

Subject requirements/preferences GCSE English, mathematics and a science subject for those born after 1 September 1979. **Anglia Ruskin** Grade B or higher in English. **Aston** English and mathematics grades B/C. **Cambridge** (BA) Grade A in the majority of subjects. **Warwick** Eight subjects grade A–C. **AL** One A-level is usually required in the main subject of choice.

The following table is divided into two sections: **Education Studies** including Childhood Studies and **Teacher Training Courses**.

EDUCATION STUDIES

Your target offers

360 pts **and above**
Cambridge – AAA (Educ St courses)

340 pts **Cardiff** – AAB–BCC 340–260 pts (Educ joint courses)

320 pts **Durham** – ABB (Educ St (Biol Sci) (Engl St) (Geog) (Hist) (Psy) (Mus) (Maths))
Warwick – BBCc **or** BBccc (Ely Chld St)

300 pts **Bath** – BBB (Coach Educ Spo Dev)
Cardiff – BBB–BCC (Educ single hons)
Exeter – BBB–BCC (Educ St; Chld Yth St)

280 pts **Aston** – BBC–BCC (Audiology)
Birmingham – BBC 280 pts (Chld Cult Educ)
Bristol – BBC (Ely Chld St)
Glasgow – BBC (Commun Learn Dev)
Leeds – BBC (Chld Educ Cult)
Manchester – BBC–BCC (Learn Disab St)
Oxford Brookes – BBC (Ely Chld St; Educ Hum Dev)
York – BBC–BCC (Educ St courses)

260 pts **Aberystwyth** – 260 pts (Educ joint major courses)
Bristol – BCC–CCC (Df St)
Keele – 260–280 pts (Educ St)
London (Gold) – BCC (Educ Cult Soty)
Stranmillis (UC) – BCC (Ely Chld St)
Swansea – BCC 260 pts (Ely Chld St)

240 pts **Bristol UWE** – 240–280 pts (Ely Chld St courses; Educ courses)
Chester – 240 pts (Ely Chld St; Educ St)
Lincoln – 240 pts (Chld Yth St)
Plymouth – 240 pts (Ely Chld St)

220 pts **Bangor** – CCD 220–260 pts (Educ (Addysg; Astudiaethau Plentyndod joint hons))
Brighton – 220 pts (Education)

Dundee – 220 pts 2nd yr entry (Commun Educ)
Edge Hill – 220 pts (Educ St courses)
Glamorgan – 220 pts (Ely Yrs Dev Educ)
Hull – 220–280 pts (Educ St Psy)
Liverpool Hope – 220 pts (Ely Chld St; Educ St; Incln Educ courses)
Stirling – CCD (Cons Sci Educ; Env Sci Out Educ)
Winchester – 220 pts (Educ St courses)

200 pts **Bangor** – 200–240 pts (Chld St)
Bath Spa – 200–260 pts (Educ St; Ely Yrs)
Bolton – 200 pts (Educ St Comb courses)
Central Lancashire – 200 pts (Educ St Psy)
Cumbria – 200 pts (Educ St)
Gloucestershire – 200 pts (Ely Chld St)
Manchester Met – 200 pts (Ely Chld St; Chld Yth St)
Newport – 200 pts (Educ St)
Northumbria – 200 pts (Disab St Chld St; Chld St Prof Prac St; Cr Educ courses)
Nottingham Trent – 200 pts (Chld St)

180 pts **Bedfordshire** – 180 pts (Educ St; Educ St Engl; Chld Yth St)
Chichester – 180–220 pts (Chld St; Chld Yth Soty)
De Montfort – 180–200 pts (Educ St joint courses)
Derby – 180 pts (Ely Chld St)
Edge Hill – 180–220 pts (Chld Yth St Educ St; Ely Chld St courses)
Hertfordshire – 180 pts (Educ St)
Liverpool John Moores – 180 pts (Out Env Educ)
Middlesex – 180–200 pts (Educ St courses; Ely Chld St)
Northampton – 180–220 pts (Educ St courses; Ely Chld St)
Plymouth – 180 pts (Educ St)
Roehampton – 180 pts (Ely Chld St; Educ; Chld Soty)
Sheffield Hallam – 180 pts (Educ St; Educ Disab St)
Sunderland – 180 pts (Ely Chld St)

160 pts **Anglia Ruskin** – CC (Educ St; Ely Chld Educ Educ St)
Birmingham (CFTCS) – 160 pts (Ely Chld St)
Bishop Grosseteste (Coll) – 160 pts (Ely Chld St)
Canterbury Christ Church – CC (Ely Chld St; Infml Commun Educ)
Central Lancashire – 160 pts (Df St Educ; Df St Law; Educ Engl Lit; Educ Hist; Educ Sociol)
East London – 160 pts (Educ Commun Dev; Lang Educ; Ely Chld St; Spec Educ Nds)
Edinburgh – CC (Commun Educ)
Greenwich – 160 pts (Chld St; Educ St; Educ Chld Dev; Educ LD)
Hull – 160–220 pts (Educ St Urb Lrng)
Hull (Scarborough) – 160–220 pts (Educ St Ely Chld St; Educ St Env Sci; Educ St Engl St; Educ St ICT)
Leeds Trinity and All Saints (Coll) – 160–240 pts (Chld Yth St)
Liverpool John Moores – 160 pts (Child Adlscn St; Educ St courses)
London Met – 160 pts (Educ St)
Newman (CHE) – CC 160 pts (Ely Yrs Educ St; Educ St courses)
Reading – 160 pts (Thea Arts Educ Df St)
St Mary's (Coll) – CC 160 pts (Educ Emp courses)
Sheffield Hallam – 160 pts (Ely Chld St; Play)
Wolverhampton – 160–220 pts (Df St Educ St; Educ St joint courses; Cond Educ; Ely Chld St; Interp (Brit Sign Lang))
Worcester – 160 pts (Ely Chld St)
York St John – 160 pts (Educ St)

150 pts **Dundee** – 150 pts 1st yr entry (Commun Educ)
140 pts **Cardiff (UWIC)** – 140 pts (Educ St Ely Chld St; Educ St Hum; Educ St Welsh)
Guildford (Coll) – 140 pts (Ely Chld St)

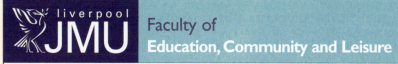

Marjon (Coll) – 140–200 pts (Educ St courses; Chld Wel Soty)
Trinity Carmarthen (Coll) – 140 pts (Ely Yrs Educ; Educ St courses)

120 pts **Bradford (Coll)** – 120 pts (Educ St)
North East Wales (IHE) – 120–80 pts (Ely Chld St courses; Educ St courses)
Suffolk (Univ Campus) – 120–180 pts (Ely Chld St)
UHI Millennium Inst (NHC) – 120 pts (Chld Yth St)
Worcester – 120 pts (Educ St)

100 pts **Cardiff (UWIC)** – 100 pts (Commun Educ)

80 pts **Newport** – 80 pts (Ely Yrs Educ)
Southend Campus Essex – 80 pts (Ely Yrs Educ; Spec Educ St)
Wigan and Leigh (Coll) – EE (Educ St)

Leeds Met – contact University
Open University – contact University (Chld Yth St)

TEACHER TRAINING

Subjects attracting the most applicants include Drama, History, Physical Education, Social Science, English and Art. Subjects attracting the fewest applicants include Modern Languages, Sciences, Craft Design and Technology, Music, Religious Education, Mathematics and Home Economics. The choice of subject will affect the level of the offer made. See also separate subject tables.

Subject requirements/preferences **GCSE** Grades A–C in English, mathematics and a science subject. **Cambridge** Majority of grade As. **Durham** English and mathematics at grade A or B. **Glasgow** Mathematics grade B. **London (Gold)** Grade A or B in design-related subject. **Worcester** Grade A in at least one curriculum subject. **AL** One subject is usually required in the main subject of choice.

Abbreviations P – Primary Teaching; S – Secondary Teaching; QTS – Qualified Teacher Status.

Your target offers

320 pts **Cambridge** – 320 pts ABB–BBB (BA Educ (Biol Sci) (Class) (Engl) (Engl Dr) (Geog) (Hist) (Maths) (Modn Langs) (Mus) (PE) (Relig St))
Stranmillis (UC) – ABB (Engl Educ; Geog Educ; Hist Educ; Relig St Educ)

300 pts **Sussex** – BBB–BBC **or** 340–310 pts 3AL+AS (Engl Lang Teach joint courses)
Stranmillis (UC) – BBB (Art Des Educ; PE Educ; Sci Educ)

280 pts **Durham (Stockton)** – 280 pts (BA/BSc P Teach Gen; P Teach ICT)
Edinburgh – BBC–BCC (BEd P; Des Tech BEd; PE BEd)
Northumbria – 280 pts (BA P)
Stirling – BBC–CCD (Educ Comb courses BA/BSc P S)
Stranmillis (UC) – BBC (Mus Educ)

260 pts **Nottingham Trent** – BCC 260 pts (BA P)
Stranmillis (UC) – BCC (Bus St Educ; Educ)

240 pts **Anglia Ruskin** – 240 pts (BA P (ITT))

Brunel – 240 pts (BSc S PE)
Chester – 240 pts (BEd P)
Glasgow – CCC (BEd P)
Glasgow (RSAMD) – AA–DD (Mus BEd)
Hertfordshire – 240 pts (BEd P)
Hull – 240 pts (BA P; BA P Engl)
Liverpool John Moores – 240 pts (BA Spo PE Dance; BA P S)
Manchester Met – CCC (BA P)
Oxford Brookes – CCC **or** CCcc (BA P Educ)
Roehampton – 240 pts (BA P Key Stgs 1 and 2)
Sheffield Hallam – 240 pts (Ely Yrs Educ QTS; BA P S)
Stranmillis (UC) – CCC (Tech Des Educ)

220 pts **Bedfordshire** – 220 pts (BA PE S)
Brighton – 220 pts (BA P QTS (3–7) (5–11); S Educ QTS; PE QTS; Des Tech Educ QTS)
De Montfort – 220–320 pts (BA PE QTS)
Edge Hill – 220 pts (BA P)
Glasgow – CCD (MA Relig Phil Educ S)
Hull (Scarborough) – 220–240 pts (BA P ICT)
Liverpool Hope – 220 pts (BA P QTS)
Paisley – CCD (BEd P)
Strathclyde – CCD/BB (BEd P)
Winchester – 220 pts (BA P)

200 pts **Bangor** – CDD 200–240 pts (BEd P; BSc Des Tech)
Bristol UWE – 200–260 pts (BA P ITE/Ely Yrs Educ)
Chichester – 200–240 pts (PE Educ S QTS; Educ (Maths) (ICT); BA P)
Cumbria – 200 pts (BA/BSc QTS S P)
Dundee – 200–230 pts (BEd P Educ)
Gloucestershire – 200–260 pts (BEd P Educ)
Liverpool John Moores – 200 pts (TESOL (Chin) (Engl) (Fr) (Ger) (Ital) (Jap) (Span); BA P; BA S PE)
Northampton – 200–220 pts (BA P Educ; Ely Yrs Educ)
Nottingham Trent – 200 pts (Des Tech Educ QTS)
Sunderland – 200 pts (BA P Educ)
Swansea (IHE) – 200 pts (BA P Educ)
UCE Birmingham – 200 pts (BA P)
Worcester – 200 pts (BA Ely Yrs P)

180 pts **Bedfordshire** – 180–260 pts (BA/BSc Spo PE)
Chichester – 180–220 pts (P Educ)
Coventry – DDD 180 pts (TEFL (Engl) (Fr) (Span))
Edge Hill – 180 pts (BSc S QTS (Des Tech) (ICT) (Maths) (Sci))
Huddersfield – 180–220 pts (BEd S (Des Tech))
Hull (Scarborough) – 180 pts (BSc Biol St)
Kingston – 180 pts (BA P QTS)
Newport – 180 pts (BA P St QTS)
Plymouth – 180–240 pts (Steiner-Waldorf Educ)
Reading – 180 pts (BEd Educ St P)
St Mary's (Coll) – 180 pts (BA ITT PE S)

160 pts **Bishop Grosseteste (Coll)** – CC (BA Educ St P)
Canterbury Christ Church – CC (BA QTS P Educ)
Cardiff (UWIC) – CC (BA P; BA S (Dr); 2yr Welsh/Mus/Modn Langs – applicants over 21)
Central Lancashire – 160–200 pts (Df St courses; TEFL (Fr) (Ger) (Span); Brit Sign Lang)
East London – 160 pts (Spec Educ Nds)
Edinburgh – CC (BEd Des Tech; PE; P Educ)
Glasgow – CC (Technol Educ)
Greenwich – 160 pts (Steiner-Waldorf Educ; BA S Des Tech Educ; BA P Educ)

For information on how to read the Subject Tables, see **Chapter 7**.

Leeds Trinity and All Saints (Coll) – 160–240 pts (BA P Educ)
London (Gold) – CC (Educ Des Tech – contact admissions office)
Manchester Met – CC 160 pts (BSc S Educ)
Middlesex – 160–200 pts (BA P Educ)
Newman (CHE) – 160–240 pts (BA/BEd P S (Art) (Biol) (Engl) (Geog) (Hist) (IT) (PE Spo Sci) (Theol))
Newport – 160–200 pts (BA S (Des Tech) (Maths ICT) (Maths Sci))
North East Wales (IHE) – 160 pts (BA P Educ)
Plymouth – 160–240 pts (BEd P)
St Mary's (Coll) – 160–200 pts (BA P Educ ITT)
Sheffield Hallam – 160 pts (BSc QTS S (Des Tech) (Sci) (Maths))
Sunderland – 160 pts (BA S (Engl Educ) (Geog Educ))
Wolverhampton – 160–220 pts (BEd P)

140 pts **Royal Welsh (CMusDr)** – 140 pts (BA S)
Trinity Carmarthen (Coll) – 140 pts (BA Educ P QTS; Out Educ courses)
York St John – 140–220 pts (BAP Educ)

120 pts **Aberdeen** – 120 pts (BEd P – check with admissions tutor)
Bradford (Coll) – 120 pts (BA P)
Liverpool John Moores – 120–140 pts (BA/BSc P (Maths) (PE))
Marjon (Coll) – 120–180 pts (BEd P S (Maths) (PE))

Leeds Met – contact University

Alternative offers

IB offers; Birmingham 32 pts; Brighton 28 pts; Bristol 28–30 pts; Bristol UWE 24–28 pts, (Ely Chld St) 26–32 pts; Cambridge (BA) 38–42 pts; Chester 30 pts; Chichester 26–28 pts; Durham 34 pts; Exeter 28–33 pts; Keele 28–30 pts; Manchester Met 28 pts; Warwick 30 pts.
Scottish offers See **Chapter 7**.

OTHER HIGHER EDUCATION COURSES IN THE SUBJECT FIELD

Foundation degrees (contact the institutions for details) Abingdon (Coll); Accrington and Rossendale (Coll); Anglia Ruskin; Bangor; Barnet (Coll); Barnsley (Univ Centre); Bath Spa; Bedfordshire; Beverley (CFE); Bicton (Coll); Birmingham (CFTCS); Birmingham City (Coll); Bishop Grosseteste (Coll); Blackpool and Fylde (Coll); Bolton; Bolton (CmC); Boston (Coll); Bournemouth and Poole (Coll); Bourneville (CFHE); Bracknell (Coll); Bradford; Bradford (Coll); Bridgwater (Coll); Brighton City (Coll); Bristol City (Coll); Burnley (Coll); Cambridge Reg (Coll); Canterbury Christ Church; Cardiff (UWIC); Carshalton (Coll); Central Lancashire; Chester; Cirencester (Coll); City and Islington (Coll); Colchester (Inst); Coventry City (Coll); Craven (Coll); Croydon (Coll); Cumbria; Darlington (CT); Derby; Dewsbury (Coll); Duchy (Coll); Dunstable (Coll); Ealing, Hammersmith and West London (Coll); East Antrim (IFHE); East Berkshire (Coll); East Lancashire (IHE); East London; Edge Hill; Evesham (Coll); Exeter (Coll); Farnborough (CT); Gateshead (Coll); Glamorgan; Gloucester (CAT); Gloucestershire; Grantham (Coll); Grimsby (IFHE); Hartlepool (CFE); Havering (CFHE); Herefordshire (CAD); Herefordshire (CT); Hertford Reg (Coll); Hertfordshire; Holy Cross (Coll); Hopwood Hall (Coll); Hugh Baird (Coll); Hull; Hull (Coll); Huntingdonshire Reg (Coll); Josiah Mason Sixth Form (Coll); Kendal (Coll); Kensington (Coll); Kent; Kingston; Kingston (Coll); Lambeth (Coll); Leeds Met; Leeds Trinity and All Saints (Coll); Leicester; Leicester (Coll); Lewisham (Coll); Liverpool (CmC); Liverpool Hope; Llandrillo (Coll); London Met; Macclesfield (Coll); Manchester Met; Mid-Kent (Coll); Middlesbrough (Coll); Milton Keynes (Coll); Myerscough (Coll); Nescot; Newcastle (Coll); Newman (CHE); Norland (Coll); North Devon (Coll); North East London (Coll); North East Wales (IHE); North Hertfordshire (Coll); North Lindsey (Coll); North Trafford (Coll); Northampton; Nottingham Castle (Coll); Nottingham Trent; Oaklands (Holl); Oldham (Coll); Open University; Peterborough Reg (Coll); Plymouth; Plymouth (CFE); Portsmouth; Preston (Coll); Redcar (Coll); Riverside Halton (Coll); Runshaw (Coll); St Helens (Coll); St Mary's (Coll); Selby (Coll); Sheffield (Coll); Sheffield Hallam; Shrewsbury (CAT); Solihull (Coll); Somerset (CAT); South Cheshire (Coll); South Devon (Coll); Southend Campus Essex; Southampton; Southampton Solent; Southport (Coll); Sparsholt (Coll); Spelthorne (Coll); Staffordshire Reg (Fed); Stamford (Coll); Stockport (CFHE); Stockton Riverside (Coll); Stratford-upon-Avon (Coll); Suffolk (Univ Campus); Sunderland; Swansea (IHE);

Swindon (Coll); Thames Valley; Thomas Danby (Coll); Thurrock (Coll); Trinity Carmarthen (Coll); Truro (Coll); Wakefield (Coll); Walsall (Coll); Warwick; West Anglia (Coll); West Cheshire (Coll); West Herts (Coll); West Kent (Coll); West Nottinghamshire (Coll); West Thames (Coll); Weymouth (Coll); Wigan and Leigh (Coll); Wiltshire (Coll); Winchester; Wolverhampton; Worcester; Worcester (CT); Worcestershire New (Coll); Yeovil (Coll); York St John.

Higher National Diploma courses (Childhood Studies and other courses)
100 pts   and below

Bath; Birmingham (CFTCS); Birmingham City (Coll); Blackpool and Fylde (Coll); Bradford (Coll); Bridgwater (Coll); Bristol City (Coll); Central Lancashire; Coventry (Coll); Croydon (Coll); Dearne Valley (Coll); Derby; Doncaster (Univ Centre); Exeter; Forth Valley (Coll); Grimsby (IFHE); Guildford (Coll); Halesowen (Coll); Henley (Coll); Herefordshire (Coll); Hertford Reg (Coll); Hopwood Hall (Coll); Isle of Wight (Coll); Kidderminster (Coll); Liverpool (CmC); Llandrillo Cymru (Coll); Manchester Met; Newcastle (Coll); Northbrook (Coll); Norwich City (Coll); Peterborough Reg (Coll); Runshaw (Coll); St Helens (Coll); Salford (Coll); Sheffield (Coll); Shrewsbury (Coll); Somerset (Coll); South Birmingham (Coll); Southend Campus Essex; Stockport (CFHE); Stratford-upon-Avon (Coll); Tameside (Coll); Thames Valley; Truro (Coll); Tyne Met (Coll); UCE Birmingham; UHI Millennium Inst (NHC); Wakefield (Coll); Walsall (Coll); Warwickshire (Coll); West Anglia (Coll); West Nottinghamshire (Coll); West Suffolk (Coll); Wigan and Leigh (Coll); Worcester; Worcester (CT); Worcestershire New (Coll); Yorkshire Coast (CFHE).

CHOOSING YOUR COURSE (SEE ALSO CH.1)

Subject information Early Childhood Studies has been introduced in recent years by a number of universities. The courses focus on child development, from birth to eight years of age, and the provision of education for children and their families. It is a multi-disciplinary subject and can cover social problems and legal and psychological issues. These courses do not train students to become teachers although it is possible to go on to teaching courses on graduation as well as embarking on other career routes such as social work, planning, law and administration. There are two types of degree courses in Education – those which cover the history, philosophy and theory of education but which are not necessarily teacher training courses, and those which prepare the student for a career in the teaching profession. Read prospectuses carefully. For the latter, candidates should be well-motivated towards teaching and education – the interview is important. Interview panels look for candidates with confidence in their own ability, a lively personality, patience and optimism. Experience of working with children is important. Students planning to follow a degree with a Postgraduate Certificate in Education (PGCE) are advised that problems may arise if their first degree subject is not a National Curriculum subject. Teacher training courses are offered in the following subject areas: Art and Design (P); Biology (P S); Business Studies (S); Chemistry (P S); Childhood (P); Computer Education (P); Creative and Performing Arts (P); Dance (P S); Design and Technology (P S); Drama (P S); English (P S); Environmental Science (P S); Environmental Studies (P); French (P S); General Primary; Geography (P S); History (P S); Home Economics (P S); Maths (P S); Music (P S); Physical Education/Movement Studies (P S); Religious Studies (P); Science (P S); Sociology (P); Textile Design (P); Welsh (P). Two-year BEd courses are also offered for holders of HND or equivalent qualifications (minimum age in some cases 23–25) in the following subject areas: Business Studies (S); Chemistry (S); Design and Technology (S); English (P); French (S); General Primary; German (S); Home Economics (S); Language Studies (P); Mathematics (S); Music (S); Physics (S); Science (S); Spanish (S); Welsh (S). For further information on teaching as a career see websites below and **Appendix 2** for contact details. Over 50 taster courses are offered each year to those considering teaching as a career. **Useful websites** www.tda.gov.uk; www.gtcs.org.uk; www.gttr.ac.uk.

Course variations Informal and Community Education (Canterbury Christ Church); Combined Social Sciences (Durham); Playwork and Youth Studies (East London); Education Studies and Special and Inclusive Needs (Liverpool John Moores); Learning and Disability Studies (Manchester); Education and Human Development (Oxford Brookes); Outdoor Education (Stirling, Trinity Carmarthen (Coll)); Conductive Education (Wolverhampton). *NOW CHECK PROPECTUSES AND WEBSITES FOR ANY RECENT CHANGES.*

Top teacher training providers See www.tda.gov.uk (England); www.shefc.ac.uk (Scotland); www.elwa.org.uk (Wales).

Top universities and colleges (Research) Aston (Audiology); Bath; Birmingham; Cambridge; Cardiff; Durham; Exeter; Lancaster; London (King's); Oxford; Sheffield; Sussex.

ADMISSIONS INFORMATION

Number of applicants per place (approx) Aberystwyth 6; Anglia Ruskin 1; Bangor 5; Bath 17; Bath Spa 5; Birmingham 8; Bishop Grosseteste (Coll) 12; Bristol (Df St) 2, (Ely Chld Dt) 9; Bristol UWE 20; Brunel (PE) 5; Cambridge 2.5; Canterbury Christ Church 15; Cardiff (Educ) 8; Cardiff (UWIC) 3; Central Lancashire 5; Chester 25; Chichester 12; Cumbria 5; De Montfort 10; Derby 13; Dundee 5; Durham 8; Edge Hill 17; Edinburgh (P) 3; Exeter 10, (S PE) 13; Gloucestershire 20; Greenwich 3; Hull 7; Hull (Scarborough) 4; Kingston 9; Leeds 4; Liverpool John Moores 3, (TEFL) 10; Liverpool Hope 5; London (Gold) 5, (Des Tech) 4; Manchester Met 23, (Maths) 4; Marjon (Coll) 5; Middlesex 7; Newman (CHE) (S Engl) 3, (Theol) 3, (Ely Yrs) 5, (Biol) 7, (Geog) 3, (PE) 6, (Sci) 1; North East Wales (IHE) 15; Northampton 7; Northumbria 8; Nottingham Trent 11; Oxford Brookes 6; Paisley 7; Plymouth 14; Roehampton 6; St Mary's (Coll) 19; Sheffield Hallam 7, (PE) 60; Strathclyde 7; Swansea (IHE) 10; Trinity Carmarthen (Coll) 10; Winchester 4; Wolverhampton 4; Worcester 21, (Engl) 51; York 3; York St John (Mus) 3, (Maths) 2, (Biol) 10, (Engl) 5, (Theol Relig St) 4, (Fr) 12, (Des Tech) 10, (IT) 4.

Advice to applicants and planning the UCAS personal statement Any application for teacher training courses requires candidates to have had experience of observation in schools and with children relevant to the choice of age range. Describe what you have learned from this. Any work with young people should be described in detail, indicating any problems which you may have seen which children create for the teacher. Applicants are strongly advised to have had some teaching practice prior to interview and should give evidence of time spent in primary school and give an analysis of activity undertaken with children. Give details of music qualifications, if any. **Anglia Ruskin** (Educ St) Experience of working with children. **De Montfort** (Educ St) Mature applicants welcome; the course is interdisciplinary and multidisciplinary. **Kingston** Precise, succinct, well-reasoned, well-written statement (no mistakes!). **Liverpool John Moores** (TESOL) We look for an interest in the language and culture of other countries. **Newman (CHE)** Classroom placements an advantage. Be prepared for hard work throughout the course. **Winchester** We look for students who are curious about the uses and abuses of educational processes. **York** (Educ St) Experience with children and young people useful but not essential. See also **Appendix 2**.

Misconceptions about this course That Childhood Studies is a childcare, child health or teaching course: it is not. That Educational Studies leads to a teaching qualification – it does not. **Bath Spa** (Educ St) Applicants should note that this is not a teacher training course – it leads on to PGCE teacher training (this applies to other Education Studies courses). **Newman (CHE)** That the Theology course only concentrates on the Christian/Catholic religions (all major religions are covered). **UHI Millennium Inst (NHC)** Candidates are unaware that on-line methods form a significant part of the course delivery.

Selection interviews **Yes** Bangor, Bishop Grosseteste (Coll), Brighton, Bristol, Bristol UWE, Cambridge, Chichester, Derby, Kingston, London (Gold), Manchester Met (group interviews), Nottingham Trent, Oxford Brookes, Plymouth, Stockport (CFHE), Worcester, York St John. Check all institutions. It is a requirement by the Department for Education and Skills that all candidates for teacher education are interviewed. Many institutions offering education studies also interview selected applicants. Additionally, candidates are asked to compose a short written statement on a given topic at interview in order to ensure an acceptable standard of written English; **Some** Cardiff, Dundee, Lincoln, Liverpool John Moores, Marjon (Coll), Paisley, Roehampton, Winchester, York.

Interview advice and questions Questions invariably focus on why you want to teach and your experiences in the classroom. In some cases you may be asked to write an essay on these topics. Questions in the past have included: What do you think are important issues in education at present? Discussion of course work will take place for Art applicants. **Bangor** (BEd P) No specific language or maths tests. **Bath Spa** Short essay on an aspect of education. **Brighton** 200-word essay. **Derby** Applicants are asked about an aspect of education. **Liverpool John Moores** (BA BSc P S Educ) Maths and English diagnostic tests are given on interview day. Discussion regarding any experience the applicant has had with children. **Nottingham Trent** English test. **Sunderland** (BA S Des Tech)

Applicants will be asked to complete a short piece of written work and to discuss their Des Tech curriculum. **Worcester** Interviewees are asked to write a statement concerning their impressions of the interview. **York St John** A short piece of written work is set on arrival for interview. See also **Chapter 6**.

Applicants' impressions (A=Open day; B=Interview day) **Brighton** (B) Talks on the course and the University were followed by individual interviews. **Bristol UWE** (B) There was a group interview and a tour of the campus and halls. Questions included 'What inspires you to become a teacher?' and 'What do you think you could contribute to the profession?' **Chichester** We had a group information session, individual interviews and a 30-minute essay test. **De Montfort** (B) There was a literacy test. Questions on health and safety and recent developments in education. **Gloucestershire** (B) There were individual interviews with maths and English tests, followed by a talk on the course and the University. **Nottingham Trent** (B) There was an English test, a talk on the University and the course, individual interviews and debate. **Plymouth** (B; Science) There was a group discussion and interviews in pairs, written and number tests and marking. (B) There were two literary tests and a numeracy test. There were group interviews in subject groups and questions on our understanding of the role of the subject teacher in a primary school. **Winchester** (B) There was a group information session, group interviews (eight students) with a 10-minute essay task. Then followed a tour of the accommodation.

Reasons for rejection (non-academic) Unable to meet the requirements of written standard English. Ungrammatical personal statements. Lack of research about teaching at primary or secondary levels. Lack of experience in schools. Insufficient experience of working with people; tendency to be racist.

AFTER-RESULTS ADVICE

Universities with vacancies in Clearing (2006) **(Education)** Aberystwyth; Bangor; Bath Spa; Bolton; Bristol; Bristol UWE; Canterbury Christ Church; Central Lancashire; Cumbria; De Montfort; Derby; East London; Edge Hill; Gloucestershire; Greenwich; Kingston; Reading; Worcester; **(Teacher Training)** Check all institutions.

Offers to applicants repeating A-levels **Higher** Oxford Brookes, Warwick; **Possibly higher** Cambridge, Cumbria; **Same** Anglia Ruskin, Aston, Bangor, Bishop Grosseteste (Coll), Brighton, Brunel, Canterbury Christ Church, Cardiff, Chester, Chichester, De Montfort, Derby, Dundee, Durham, Lincoln, Liverpool Hope, Liverpool John Moores, London (Gold), Manchester Met, Marjon (Coll), Newman (CHE), Northumbria, Roehampton, St Mary's (Coll), Sunderland, UHI Millennium Inst (NHC), Winchester, Wolverhampton, Worcester, York, York St John; **Not considered** Kingston.

GRADUATE DESTINATIONS AND EMPLOYMENT (2005 HESA)
Teacher graduates surveyed 4495 **Employed** 3470 **In further study** 105 **Assumed unemployed** 105.

Academic graduates surveyed 1770 **Employed** 780 **In further study** 475 **Assumed unemployed** 85.

OTHER DEGREE SUBJECTS FOR CONSIDERATION
Psychology; Social Policy; Social Sciences; Social Work.

ENGINEERING/ENGINEERING SCIENCES

(including **Engineering Product Design;** see also **Art and Design (Industrial/Product Design)** and **Technology)**

NB The points totals shown to the left of the institutions are for ease of reference only. It must not be assumed that tariff points are always used by institutions or that they can be substituted for an offer in grades. The level of an offer is not necessarily indicative of the quality of a course.

ENGINEERING COUNCIL UK (EC^UK) STATEMENT
Recent developments in the engineering profession and the regulations that govern registration as a professional engineer (UK-SPEC) mean that MEng and Bachelors degrees are the typical academic routes to becoming registered.

Chartered Engineers (CEng) develop solutions to engineering problems, using new or existing technologies, through innovation, creativity and change. They might develop and apply new technologies, promote advanced designs and design methods, introduce new and more efficient production techniques, marketing and construction concepts, and pioneer new engineering services and management methods.

The typical academic qualifications for CEng are a BEng (Hons) with subsequent 'further learning' or an integrated MEng degree.

Indicative entry requirements are:

MEng   GCE A-levels ABC–BBB
               (SQA Highers AABB; SQA Advanced Highers ABC–BBB; IB 30 pts; Irish Leaving
               Certificate AABB)

BEng (Hons) GCE A-levels CCC–BCD
               (SQA Highers BBBC; SQA Advanced Highers CCC–BCD; IB 26 pts; Irish Leaving Certificate
               BBBC)

All applicants should check the offers for MEng, BEng and BSc courses in each of the Engineering tables unless otherwise stated.

Incorporated Engineers (IEng) act as exponents of today's technology through creativity and innovation. They maintain and manage applications of current and developing technology, and may be involved in engineering design, development, manufacture, construction and operation.

Both Chartered and Incorporated Engineers are variously engaged in technical and commercial leadership and possess effective interpersonal skills.

The typical academic qualifications for IEng are an accredited Bachelor's degree.

Indicative entry requirements are: GCE A-levels CD/EE–DDE; SQA Highers BCC–CCCC; IB 24 pts; Irish Leaving Certificate BCC–CCC.

You should confirm with universities whether their courses are accredited for CEng or IEng by relevant professional engineering institutions. There are 21 institutions licensed by the EC[UK] to accredit engineering degree programmes.

To become a Chartered or Incorporated Engineer, you will have to demonstrate competence and commitment appropriate to the registration category. On top of your academic knowledge, you will also need to demonstrate your professional development and experience. Most of this will come after you graduate but placements in industry during your degree course are also available.

Both Chartered and Incorporated Engineers usually progress to become team leaders or to take other key management roles. Chartered Engineers earn an average salary of £53,067 (2005) and the top 10% over £80,000. Incorporated Engineers earn an average salary of £40,533 and the top 10% over £60,000.

More information on registering as a professional engineer can be found on the EC[UK] website www.engc.org.uk.

COURSE OFFERS INFORMATION
Subject requirements/preferences **GCSE** Grade A–C may be required in English, chemistry or a language for some courses. Mathematics essential. **Bath** Three subjects at grade A including mathematics A/B, grade A/B in language for French and German courses. **Brunel** Grade B in mathematics and English. **Cambridge, Oxford** Grade As in most subjects preferred. **Manchester Met, Portsmouth** Mathematics grade A or B, language grade B for European Studies courses. **AL** Mathematics and/or physics or another science usually required.

Your target offers
360 pts   and above
       Cambridge – AAA (Engineering)
       Oxford – Offers vary eg AAA–AAB (Eng Comp Sci; Eng; Eng Econ Mgt)

340 pts **Bath** – AAB (Innov Eng Des; Innov Eng Des Fr/Ger; Spo Eng)
Bristol – AAB–BBB (Eng Des)
Durham – AAB (MEng Gen Eng; New Renew Ener)
Leeds – AAB (Qntm Sci Eng)
Liverpool – AAB (MEng Eng; Lsr Eng; Eng Prod Des)
London (UCL) – AAB+AS–BBB+AS (Eng Bus Fin; Geoinf)
Sheffield – AAB (Eng (Civ Mat Mech) (Comp Electron Sys Contr))
Warwick – AAB–ABB (MEng Eng)

320 pts **Birmingham** – ABB–BBC (Eng Bus Mgt)
Bristol – ABB (Eng Maths)
Cardiff – ABB–BBB 320–300 pts (MEng Integ Eng)
Exeter – ABB–BBC (MEng Eng Mgt; Eng)
Lancaster – ABB–AAB (MEng Eng Yr in USA/Aus)
Leicester – 320 pts (MEng Gen Eng; Gen Eng Ind/Euro/USA)
Loughborough – 320 pts (Prod Des Manuf)
Newcastle – ABB–BBB (MEng Fdn Eng courses)
Nottingham – ABB–BCC (Integ Eng; Prod Des Manuf)
Sussex – ABB–BBB 360–330 pts (MEng Eng Des; Prod Des 4yr; Eng Soty)
Swansea – 320 pts (MEng Prod Des Eng)

300 pts **Aberdeen** – BBB 2nd yr entry (MEng Eng; Eng Sfty Rlblty Eng)
Bath – BBB (BEng Spo Eng)
Belfast (Queen's) – BBB (MEng Prod Des Dev)
Dundee – 300 pts 2nd yr entry (Innov Prod Des)
Durham – BBB (BEng Gen Eng)
Edinburgh – BBB (Engineering)
London (King's) – BBB+AS **or** BBbb (Eng Bus Mgt)
London (UCL) – BBB+AS (BEng Geoinform; Eng Bus Fin)
Strathclyde – BBB (MEng Eng Ent Mgt; Prod Des Eng)
Sussex – BBB–BBC (BEng Eng Des)
Ulster – 300 pts (MEng Eng)
Warwick – BBB–BBC (BEng/BSc Eng (Bus Mgt); Eng; Eng Bus St)

280 pts **Aberdeen** – BBC 1st yr entry (BEng Integ Eng Euro St; Integ Eng)
Aston – BBC–CCC 240 pts (3AL) **or** 280–240 pts (2AL+2AS) (Eng Prod Des; Prod Des Mgt; Des Eng; Ind Prod Des; Med Prod Des; Sust Prod Des; Auto Prod Des; Tech Ent Mgt)
Belfast (Queen's) – BBC (BEng Prod Des Dev)
Brighton – 280 pts (Prod Des; Des Tech Prof Prac)
Cardiff – BBC 280 pts (BEng Integ Eng)
City – 280 pts (Eng Ener Mgt)
Exeter – BBC–CCC (BEng Eng; Eng Mgt)
Heriot-Watt – BBC 2nd yr entry (Eng Mgt; Integ Prod Des)
Lancaster – BBC (BEng Eng; Eng N Am/Aus)
Liverpool – 280 pts (BEng Eng; Eng Prod Des)
Newcastle – BBB–BB (BEng Fdn Eng courses)
Sussex – BBC **or** 310 pts 3AL+AS (Prod Des 3yr)

260 pts **Brunel** – BCC 260 pts (Prod Des Eng; Vrtl Prod Des; Des Spo; Prod Des)
Coventry – 260 pts (Ind Prod Des; Disas Mgt Eng; Comp Aid Eng)
Glasgow – BCC 260 pts (MEng Prod Des Eng)
Leicester – BCC 260 pts (BEng Gen Eng; Gen Eng Ind/Euro/USA)
London (QM) – 260–340 pts (Eng Sci; Eng; Eng Bus Mgt; Des Innov; Spo Eng)
Loughborough – 260 pts (Prod Des Manuf)
Loughborough – 260–300 pts (Prod Des Tech; Ind Des Tech)
Staffordshire – 260 pts (Prod Des Tech; Des Tech)
Swansea – 260–300 pts (BEng Prod Des Eng)

240 pts **Bradford** – 240 pts (Eng Mgt; Ind Eng)
Dundee – 240 pts 1st yr entry (Innov Prod Des)

Glasgow – CCC 240 pts (BEng Prod Des Eng)
Greenwich – 240 pts (Ind Autom)
Hull – 240 pts (Med Prod Des)
Manchester Met – 240–220 pts (Eng; Eng IT; Vrtl Des Eng)
Middlesex – 240–260 pts (Eng Prod Des)
Northumbria – 240 pts (Prod Des Tech; Comp Aid Eng; Eng Bus St)
Nottingham Trent – 240 pts (Comp Aid Prod Des; Ind Des Innov)
Salford – 240 pts (Pros Orth)
Strathclyde – CCC (BEng Prod Des Eng; Pros Orth; Eng Ent Mgt)

220 pts **Aberdeen** – CCD 2nd yr entry (BEng Integ Eng Euro St)
Bournemouth – 220–300 pts (Prod Des)
Bristol UWE – 220–240 pts (Robot; Prod Des Innov; Crea Prod Des)
Central Lancashire – 220 pts (Comp Aid Eng)
Heriot-Watt – CCD 1st yr entry (Integ Prod Des; Eng Mgt; BSc Eng Mgt)
Hull – CCD–BBC 220–280 pts (Prod Innov)
Napier – 220 pts (Eng Mgt; Prod Des Eng)
Robert Gordon – CCD (Engineering)
Staffordshire – 220–280 pts (Foren Eng)
UCE Birmingham – 220–240 pts (Comp Aid Des)
Ulster – 220 pts (Eng Mgt)

200 pts **Bradford** – 200 pts (Ind Des; Tech Mgt; Vrtl Des Innov)
Coventry – 200 pts (Eng Bus Mgt; Vrtl Eng)
Greenwich – 200 pts (Prod Dev; Eng Prod Des)
Liverpool – 200 pts (Eng Prod Des)
Sheffield Hallam – 200 pts (Foren Eng)
Sunderland – 200 pts (Eng Des Manuf; Auto Eng Des)
Swansea – 200 pts (Fdn Prod Des Tech)

180 pts **Cardiff (UWIC)** – 180 pts (Prod Des courses)
Huddersfield – 180 pts (Prod Innov Des Dev)
Leicester – 180–240 pts (Fdn Eng)
Manchester Met – 180 pts (Robot Auto; Prod Des Tech)
Northampton – 180–220 pts (BSc Eng)

160 pts **Bell (Coll)** – contact admissions tutor (Eng Mgt)
Bournemouth – 160–220 pts (Des Eng)
Brunel – 160 pts (Fdn Eng)
Coventry – 160 pts (Eng St)
De Montfort – 160 pts (BSc Eng)
Derby – 160 pts (Prod Des Innov Mark)
East London – 160–180 pts (BSc Prod Des)
Greenwich – 160 pts (Eng Bus Mgt)
Harper Adams (UC) – 160–240 pts (Eng Des Dev)
Robert Gordon – CC (Eng Des)
Sheffield Hallam – 160 pts (Comp Aid Des Tech)

140 pts **Anglia Ruskin** – 140 pts (Comp Aid Prod Des)
Bell (Coll) – CD 140 pts (Prod Des; Prod Des Mtrspo)
Glamorgan – 140–180 pts (Eng Tech Mgt)
Kingston – 140 pts (Fdn Eng)
Sheffield Hallam – 140 pts (Eng Des Innov)
Swansea (IHE) – 140 pts (Comp Aid Prod Des; Ind Des)

120 pts **Aberdeen** – DD (BSc Eng Gen)
Bradford – 120 pts (Fdn Eng)
Brighton – 120 pts (Fdn Eng)
Huddersfield – 120 pts (Fdn Eng)
London South Bank – DD (Eng Prod Des; Prod Des Comp; Prod Des Env; Eng)
North East Wales (IHE) – 120–80 pts (Prod Des)
Paisley – DD (Prod Des Dev)
Southampton Solent – 120 pts (BEng Fdn; Eng Bus)
Ulster – 120 pts (Eng Integ Fdn Yrs)
Warwickshire (Coll) – 120 pts (Engineering)

100 pts **Bournemouth and Poole (Coll)** – 100 pts (Ext Eng)
Bristol UWE – 100 pts (Fdn Eng)
Coventry – 100 pts (Fdn Eng)
Plymouth – 100 pts (Fdn Eng)
Southampton Solent – 100 pts (BSc Fdn Des Tech; Prod Dev)

80 pts **City** – EE 80 pts (Fdn Eng)
Farnborough (CT) – 80 pts (BSc Eng)

Open University – contact University

Alternative offers
IB offers Aston 31–32 pts; Bath 36 pts; Birmingham 32–36 pts; Bristol 36 pts; Cambridge 38–42 pts; City 28–30 pts; Dundee 28 pts; Durham (MEng) 38 pts; Exeter (MEng) 30–34 pts, (BEng) 26–30 pts; Lancaster 32–34 pts; Leicester 30–32 pts; London (King's) 30 pts, (QM) 30–32 pts, (UCL) 34 pts; Manchester Met 26 pts; Newcastle 34 pts; Nottingham 33 pts; Oxford 38–42 pts; Salford 28 pts; Sheffield 29–32 pts; Warwick 35–37 pts.
Scottish offers See **Chapter 7**.

OTHER HIGHER EDUCATION COURSES IN THE SUBJECT FIELD
Foundation degrees (contact the institutions for details) Birmingham City (Coll); Bishop Auckland (Coll); Bradford (Coll); Central Lancashire; Exeter (Coll); Farnborough (CT); Harper Adams (UC); Lincoln (Coll); Loughborough (Coll); Newcastle (Coll); Newport; Northampton; Plymouth (CAD); Somerset (CAT); Suffolk (Univ Campus); Sutton Coldfield (Coll); Wakefield (Coll); Warwickshire (Coll); Wolverhampton; Yeovil (Coll).

For information on how to read the Subject Tables, see **Chapter 7**.

Choosing Your University And Degree Course... And Completing Your UCAS Form?

Why not contact Brian Heap, the author of *Degree Course Offers*, *Choosing Your Degree Course and University* and *University Scholarships, Awards and Bursaries* for a personal interview or a telephone consultation for advice on such issues as:

- Choosing A-level subjects (which are the best subjects and for which courses!)
- Degrees and Diploma courses (making the right choice from a list of thousands!)
- Completing your UCAS form (will the admissions tutor remember your personal statement?)
- Choosing the right university or college (the best ones for you and your courses)

For details of services and consultation fees contact: The Higher Education Advice and Planning Service

tel: 01386 859355 email: heaps@dial.pipex.com

Higher National Diploma courses

100 pts and below

Abertay Dundee; Adam Smith (Coll); Anglia Ruskin; Bedfordshire; Blackpool and Fylde (Coll); Bolton; Boston (Coll); Bradford (Coll); Brighton; Brooklands (Coll); Central Lancashire; Coventry; De Montfort; Derby; Durham New (Coll); East Lancashire (IHE); Epping Forest (Coll); Forth Valley (Coll); Glamorgan; Greenwich; Guildford (Coll); Harper Adams (UC); Havering (Coll); Huddersfield; Inverness (Coll); James Watt (Coll); Kingston; Liverpool (CmC); Liverpool John Moores; Llandrillo Cymru (Coll); Macclesfield (Coll); Mid–Cheshire (Coll); Motherwell (Coll); Napier; Newport; Northampton; Northbrook (Coll); Norwich City (Coll); Nottingham Trent; Oxford (CFE); Park Lane Leeds (Coll); Reading; Riverside Halton (Coll); Robert Gordon; St Helens (Coll); Sheffield Hallam; Solihull (Coll); Southend Campus Essex; Southampton Solent; Staffordshire; Stratford-upon-Avon (Coll); Swansea (IHE); Swindon (Coll); UHI Millennium Inst; Tameside (Coll); Wakefield (Coll); Walsall (Coll); Warwickshire (Coll); West Anglia (Coll); West Suffolk (Coll); Wiltshire (Coll); Wolverhampton; Worcester (CT); York (Coll).

CHOOSING YOUR COURSE (SEE ALSO CH.1)

Subject information Many of these courses enable students to delay their decision of their final engineering specialism. Mathematics and physics provide the basis of all Engineering courses although several universities and colleges now provide one-year Foundation courses for applicants without science A-levels. Many institutions offer sandwich courses and firms also offer sponsorships. Throughout prospectuses it will be noted that some courses are 'subject to approval'. The problem which can arise with Engineering courses is that the examinations taken may not be accepted by the professional body overseeing that particular branch of engineering and examinations set by these professional bodies (see **Appendix 2**) will have to be retaken so that the graduate can obtain Chartered Engineer status. **Useful websites** www.setwomenresource.org.uk; www.ergonomics.org.uk; www.scicentral.com; www.engc.org.uk; www.noisemakers.org.uk; www.yini.org.uk; www.enginuity.org.uk.

Course variations Sport Engineering (Bath); Industrial Design (Brunel); General Engineering (Leicester); Geoinformatics (London (UCL)); Applied Design, Production, Performance and Safety (Loughborough); Virtual Design in Engineering (Manchester Met); Integrated Engineering (Reading); Production Design (Sussex); Engineering Business Studies (Warwick). *NOW CHECK PROSPECTUSES AND WEBSITES FOR ANY RECENT CHANGES.*

Universities and colleges teaching quality See www.tqi.ac.uk; www.qaa.ac.uk.

Top universities and colleges (Research) Aston; Birmingham; Brunel; Cambridge*; Cardiff; Durham; Edinburgh; Glasgow; Leeds; Leicester; Liverpool John Moores; Manchester; Oxford*; Sheffield; Strathclyde; Sussex; Warwick.

Sandwich degree courses Aston; Bath; Belfast (Queen's); Bournemouth; Bradford; Brighton; Bristol; Cardiff; Coventry; De Montfort; Glamorgan; Hertfordshire; Huddersfield; Leeds Met; Leicester; London South Bank; Loughborough; Manchester Met; Northumbria; Sheffield Hallam; Sunderland; Surrey; Teesside; UCE Birmingham; Ulster; Wolverhampton.

ADMISSIONS INFORMATION

Number of applicants per place (approx) Aberdeen 6; Abertay Dundee 2; Aston 8; Bath 15; Blackburn (Coll) 1; Birmingham 6; Bournemouth 5; Bristol (Eng Des) 5; Brunel (Ind Des Eng) 10; Cambridge 4; Cardiff 5; City 3; Coventry 6, (Fdn) 2; Durham 9; Edinburgh 5; Exeter 6; Glasgow Caledonian 10; Hertfordshire 2; Hull 6; Kingston 5; Lancaster 15; Leicester 12; London (UCL) 5; Loughborough 9; Manchester Met 2; Northampton 3; Oxford (success rate 45%); Robert Gordon 2; Salford (Pros Orth) 3; Sheffield Hallam 6; Strathclyde 5; Warwick 10.

Advice to applicants and planning the UCAS personal statement Details of careers in the various engineering specialisms should be obtained from the relevant engineering institutions (see **Appendix**

2). This will enable you to describe your interests in various aspects of engineering. Contact engineers to discuss their work with them. Try to arrange a visit to an engineering firm relevant to your choice of specialism. **Bristol** (Eng Maths) Skills, work experience.

Selection interviews Bristol (Eng Maths), Brunel, Cambridge, Coventry, Durham, Lancaster, Leeds, Leicester, London (QM), (UCL), Loughborough, Manchester Met, Oxford, Oxford Brookes (English test for overseas students), Portsmouth, Robert Gordon, Salford, Sheffield Hallam, Strathclyde; **Some** Cardiff.

Applicants' impressions (A=Open day; B=Interview day) **Oxford** (B) I had two interviews, the first at Keble. They asked me why Engineering and why Oxford? How could you increase the force on a car without changing its acceleration or mass? I also had to work through equations to do with force on a whiteboard. They helped me along to work out what it was to do with – the grip of the tyres and the friction caused by the road surface. The second interview was at St Anne's, where they asked me an integration question and other topics such as graphic interpretations. However, the theme of the interview was aeronautics and they asked me a question about the fuel needed for an aircraft to take off from a given point at a certain speed and the pressure changes in the engine. Throughout the interview they were hinting a lot of things to me and so I felt I didn't do too well, but I must have done something right, because I got the offer!

Interview advice and questions Since mathematics and physics are important subjects, it is probable that you will be questioned on the applications of these subjects to, for example, the transmission of electricity, nuclear power, aeronautics, mechanics etc. Past questions have included: Explain the theory of an arch; what is its function? What is the connection between distance and velocity and acceleration and velocity? How does a car ignition work? **Nottingham Trent** What is Integrated Engineering? **Oxford** No written work required and no written test at interview. See also separate **Engineering** tables and **Chapter 6**.

Reasons for rejection (non-academic) Made no contribution whatsoever to the project discussions during the UCAS interview. Forged reference! Poor work ethic. Lack of motivation towards the subject area. Better suited to an alternative Engineering course. Failure to attend interview. Poor interview preparation. **Salford** (Pros Orth) Lack of sympathy with people with disabilities.

AFTER-RESULTS ADVICE

Universities with vacancies in Clearing (2006) Aberdeen; Anglia Ruskin; Aston; Belfast (Queen's); Birmingham; Bolton; Bradford; Brighton; Bristol UWE; Brunel; Central Lancashire; City; Coventry; De Montfort; Dundee; East London; Exeter; Glamorgan; Glasgow; Glasgow Caledonian; Greenwich; Heriot-Watt; Hertfordshire; Huddersfield; Hull; Imperial London; Kingston; Lancaster; Leeds; Leicester; Liverpool; Liverpool John Moores; London (King's), (QM); London South Bank; Loughborough; Manchester; Manchester Met; Napier; Newcastle; Northumbria; Nottingham; Nottingham Trent; Oxford Brookes; Paisley; Plymouth; Portsmouth; Reading; Robert Gordon; Salford; Sheffield; Sheffield Hallam; Southampton; Southampton Solent; Staffordshire; Strathclyde; Sunderland; Surrey; Swansea; Teesside; Thames Valley; UCE Birmingham; Warwick; Westminster; Wolverhampton; York.

Offers to applicants repeating A-levels **Higher** Loughborough, Warwick; **Possibly higher** Coventry, Durham, Edinburgh, Lancaster, Manchester Met, Robert Gordon, Sheffield Hallam; **Same** Brunel (good reasons needed for repeating), Cardiff, Derby, Exeter, Heriot-Watt, Huddersfield, Hull, Leeds, Liverpool, London (UCL), Napier, Nottingham Trent, UCE Birmingham.

GRADUATE DESTINATIONS AND EMPLOYMENT (2005 HESA)
Graduates surveyed 1070 **Employed** 630 **In further study** 125 **Assumed unemployed** 100.

OTHER DEGREE SUBJECTS FOR CONSIDERATION
Computer Science; Materials Science; Mathematics; Physics; Technology; all branches of Engineering (see also following **Engineering** tables).

ENGINEERING (ACOUSTICS)

(including **Audio and Sound Technology;** see also **Film, Radio, Video and TV Studies** and **Media Studies)**

NB The points totals shown to the left of the institutions are for ease of reference only. It must not be assumed that tariff points are always used by institutions or that they can be substituted for an offer in grades. The level of an offer is not necessarily indicative of the quality of a course.

Engineering Council Statement: See **Engineering/Engineering Sciences.**

COURSE OFFERS INFORMATION

Subject requirements/preferences See **Engineering/Engineering Sciences.**

Your target offers

340 pts **Surrey** – AAB (MEng Aud Media Eng)

320 pts **Southampton** – ABB 320 pts (MEng/BEng Acoust Eng)

300 pts **Southampton** – BBB 300 pts (Acoust Mus)
  Surrey – BBB (BEng Aud Media Eng)

260 pts **Glasgow** – BCC (Aud Vid Eng)
  London (QM) – 260 pts (Aud Sys Eng)

240 pts **Glamorgan** – 240–300 pts (Snd Eng)
  Lincoln – 240 pts (Aud Tech)
  Salford – 240 pts (Phys Acoust)

220 pts **Bristol UWE** – 220–240 pts (Mus Sys Eng; Mus Aud Tech)
  Glamorgan – 220–300 pts (Snd Tech)

200 pts **Newport** – 200 pts (Crea Snd Mus)
  Salford – 200 pts (Acoust; Aud Vid Broad Tech; Aud Tech)

180 pts **Derby** – 180 pts (Mus Tech Aud Sys Des)
  Liverpool (LIPA) – 180 pts (Snd Tech)
  Oxford Brookes – contact admissions tutor (Snd Tech Dig Mus)

160 pts **Anglia Ruskin** – 160 pts (Aud Mus Tech)
  De Montfort – 160–200 pts (Media Tech)
  London Met – 160 pts (Mus Tech (Aud Sys); Snd Media)
  London South Bank – CC (Snc Media)
  Southampton Solent – 160 pts (Aud Tech; Media Tech)

120 pts **North East Wales (IHE)** – 140 pts (Snd Broad Eng; Std Rec Perf Tech)

  Leeds Met – contact University

Alternative offers
IB offers London (QM) 30–36 pts; Salford 27 pts; Southampton 34 pts.
Scottish offers See **Chapter 7**.

OTHER HIGHER EDUCATION COURSES IN THE SUBJECT FIELD
Foundation degrees (contact the institution for details) Bolton; Glamorgan; North East Wales (IHE); Thames Valley.

Higher National Diploma courses
100 pts   and below
  Derby; Loughborough (Coll); People's (Coll); Salford; Sandwell (Coll).

CHOOSING YOUR COURSE (SEE ALSO CH.1)
Subject information Apart from the scientific aspect of sound, these courses also involve the measurement of sound, hearing, environmental health and legal aspects of sound and vibration. Acoustics topics are also included in some music and media technology courses. **Useful websites** www.ioa.org.uk; www.engc.org.uk; www.enginuity.org.uk.

Course variations Audio and Music Technology (Anglia Ruskin); Sound Engineering (Glamorgan); Physics and Acoustics (Salford); Acoustics and Music (Southampton); Audio Media Engineering (Surrey). *NOW CHECK PROSPECTUSES AND WEBSITES FOR ANY RECENT CHANGES.*

Universities and colleges teaching quality See www.tqi.ac.uk; www.qaa.ac.uk.

Top universities and colleges (Research) Southampton.

ADMISSIONS INFORMATION
Number of applicants per place (approx) Anglia Ruskin 5; Salford 4; Southampton 4–5.

Advice to applicants and planning the UCAS personal statement See **Engineering/Engineering Sciences**. See also **Appendix 2**.

Misconceptions about this course Anglia Ruskin Failure to appreciate the emphasis that the course gives to science and technology.

Selection interviews Salford, Southampton.

Interview advice and questions What interests you about Acoustics Engineering? What career do you have in mind on graduating? See also **Chapter 6**.

Reasons for rejection (non-academic) See **Engineering/Engineering Sciences**.

AFTER-RESULTS ADVICE
Universities with vacancies in Clearing (2006) Salford; Southampton.

Offers to applicants repeating A-levels Same Anglia Ruskin, Salford.

GRADUATE DESTINATIONS AND EMPLOYMENT (2005 HESA)
No data available.

OTHER DEGREE SUBJECTS FOR CONSIDERATION
Audiology; Broadcast Engineering; Communications Engineering; Computer Engineering; Computer Science; Media Technology; Music; Radio and TV; Technology; Telecommunications Engineering and Electronic Engineering.

ENGINEERING (AERONAUTICAL AND AEROSPACE)

NB The points totals shown to the left of the institutions are for ease of reference only. It must not be assumed that tariff points are always used by institutions or that they can be substituted for an offer in grades. The level of an offer is not necessarily indicative of the quality of a course.

Engineering Council statement: See **Engineering/Engineering Sciences**.

COURSE OFFERS INFORMATION
Subject requirements/preferences See **Engineering/Engineering Sciences**.

Your target offers
360 pts   and above
           Cambridge – AAA (Aerosp Aeroth Eng)
340 pts   Bath – AAB (Aerosp Eng; Aerosp Eng Fr; Aerosp Eng Ger)
           Bristol – AAB–BBB 340 pts (Avion Sys; Aero Eng; Aero Eng Euro)
           Brunel – AAB 340 pts (MEng Spc Eng; Aerosp Eng; Avn Eng; Avn Eng Plt St)
           Durham AAB (MEng Aeronautics)
           Imperial London – AAB 340 pts 3AL **or** 2AL+2AS (Aero Eng; Aero Eng Euro)
           Leeds – AAB–BBB (MEng/BEng Aero Aerosp Eng)
           Liverpool – 340 pts (MEng Aerosp Eng courses; Aerosp Eng Plt St; Avion Sys)
           Loughborough – AAB (MEng Aero Eng)

Sheffield – AAB 340 pts (MEng Aerosp Eng; Aerosp Eng Pvt Plt Instr)

Southampton – AAB–ABB 340 pts (Aero Astro; Aerosp Eng (Eng Mgt); Aerosp Eng Advnc Mat; Aerosp Eng Euro St; Spc Sys Eng)

Strathclyde – AAB (MEng Aero Mech Eng)

York – AAB–ABB (Avionics)

320 pts **Belfast (Queen's)** – ABB–BBB (MEng Aero Eng)

Brunel – ABB 320 pts (Avn Eng; Avn Eng Plt St)

Hertfordshire – 320 pts (MEng Aerosp Eng; Aerosp Sys Eng)

Imperial London – ABB (MEng Aerosp Mat)

Liverpool – 320 pts (MEng Avion Sys Plt St)

London (QM) – 320 pts (MEng Aerosp Eng; Avion Spc Sys)

Manchester – ABB (MEng Aerosp Eng; Aerosp Eng Ind; Aerosp Eng Mgt; Aerosp Eng Euro)

Sheffield – ABB 320 pts (BEng Aerosp Eng; Aerosp Eng Plt Instr)

Swansea – 320–360 pts (MEng Aerosp Eng; Aerosp Eng Mat; Aerosp Eng Mgt; Aerosp Eng Prplsn)

300 pts **Brunel** – BBB 300 pts (Mech Eng Aero)

City – 300 pts (MEng Aero Eng; Air Trans Eng)

Kingston – BBB 300 pts (MEng Aerosp Eng; Aerosp Eng Astnaut)

Leeds – BBB (Avn Tech Plt St; Avn Tech Mgt; BEng Aero Aerosp Eng)

Liverpool – 300 pts (BEng Aerosp Eng courses; Avion Sys Plt St)

Loughborough – BBB–ABC (BEng Aero Eng)

Manchester – BBB (BEng Aerosp Eng)

Salford – 300 pts (MEng Mech Eng Aerosp Eng)

Strathclyde – BBB (BEng Aero Mech Eng)

Surrey – BBB–BCC 300–260 pts (Aerosp Eng)

280 pts **Belfast (Queen's)** – BBC–BCC (BEng Aero Eng)

Brunel – BBC 280 pts (BEng Aerosp Eng; Aerosp Eng)

City – 280–240 pts (Air Trans Ops; Air Trans Eng; Aero Eng)

Glasgow – BBC (Aero Eng)

Liverpool – 280 pts (Aerosp Mats; Avion Sys Plt St)

Staffordshire – 280 (Aero Des Tech)

260 pts **Brunel** – BCC 260 pts (BEng Avn Eng; Avn Eng Plt St)

Coventry – 260 pts (Aerosp Sys Eng)

Hertfordshire – 260 pts (BEng Aerosp Eng; Aerosp Sys Eng)

Imperial London – BCC (BEng Aerosp Mat)

London (QM) – 260 pts (BEng Aerosp Eng)

Swansea – 260 pts (BEng Aerosp Eng; Aerosp Comm; Aerosp Eng Mat)

240 pts **Coventry** – 240 pts (Aerosp Tech; Avion Tech)

Kingston – 240 pts (BEng Aerosp Eng Astnaut; Aerosp Eng)

London (QM) – 240 pts (Avionics)

Salford – 240 pts (BEng Aero Eng; Aircft Eng Plt St; Mech Eng (Aerosp))

220 pts **Bristol UWE** – 220–260 (MEng/BEng Aerosp Sys Eng; Aerosp Manuf Eng)

200 pts **Glasgow** – BB 200 pts (Avionics)

Hertfordshire – 200 pts (Aerosp Tech Mgt; Aerosp Tech Plt St)

Staffordshire – 200–240 pts (Aero Robot Tech)

160 pts **Farnborough (CT)** – 160–200 pts (Aero Eng)

London Met – 160 pts approx (Avn Mgt)

Salford – 160 pts (BSc Aerosp Bus Sys; Avn Tech Plt St; Mech Eng (Aerosp))

140 pts **Coventry** – 140 pts (Fdn Aerosp Sys Eng)

Glamorgan – 140 pts (Aircrft Mntnc Eng; Aerosp Eng)

Kingston – 140 pts (BEng Aerosp Eng Des)

North East Wales (IHE) – 140 pts (Aero Eng (Avion); Aero Mech Eng; Aero Electron (Avion))

100 pts **Kingston** – 100 pts (Fdn Aerosp Eng; Aerosp Eng St)

80 pts **UHI Millennium Inst (PC)** – 80 pts (Aircrft Eng)

Alternative offers
IB offers Bath 36 pts; Bristol 36 pts; Bristol UWE 26–28 pts; Brunel 28–34 pts; Cambridge 38–42 pts; City 30 pts; Durham (MEng) 38 pts; Liverpool 30–33 pts; London (QM) 30–32 pts; Loughborough 30–36 pts; Manchester 34–36 pts; Nottingham 30–32 pts; Salford 27–32 pts; Sheffield 31–32 pts; Southampton 34 pts.
Scottish offers See **Chapter 7**.

OTHER HIGHER EDUCATION COURSES IN THE SUBJECT FIELD
Foundation degrees (contact the institutions for details) Bristol City (Coll); Farnborough (CT); Hertfordshire; Kingston; Macclesfield (Coll); North East Wales (IHE).

Higher National Diploma courses
100 pts **and below**
Anglia Ruskin; Bolton; Brooklands (Coll); City (Coll); Coventry; Farnborough (CT); Glamorgan; Hertfordshire; Loughborough (Coll); North East Wales (IHE); Northbrook (Coll); Norwich City (Coll); Solihull (Coll); Stockport (CFHE); UHI Millennium Inst (PC).

CHOOSING YOUR COURSE (SEE ALSO CH.1)
Subject information Courses cover the manufacture of military and civil aircraft, theories of mechanics, thermodynamics, electronics, computing and engine design. Avionics courses include flight and energy control systems, airborne computing, navigation, optical and TV displays, airborne communications, radar systems for navigation and power. **Useful websites** www.raes.org.uk; www.engc.org.uk; www.enginuity.org.uk.

Course variations Avionic Systems (Bristol); Aviation Engineering with Pilot Study (Brunel); Air Transport Engineering (City); Aircraft Maintenance Engineering (Glamorgan); Aerospace Engineering with Astronautics (Kingston); Aviation Technology with Pilot Study (Salford); Space Systems Engineering (Southampton); Aeronautical and Robotics Technology (Staffordshire). *NOW CHECK PROSPECTUSES AND WEBSITES FOR ANY RECENT CHANGES.*

Universities and colleges teaching quality See www.tqi.ac.uk; www.qaa.ac.uk.

Top universities and colleges (Research) See **Engineering (Mechanical)**.

Sandwich degree courses Bath; Belfast (Queen's); Brunel; City; Coventry; Glamorgan; Hertfordshire; Kingston; Liverpool; London (QM); Loughborough; Salford; Staffordshire; Surrey.

ADMISSIONS INFORMATION
Number of applicants per place (approx) Bath 13, (MEng) 18; Belfast (Queen's) 6; Bristol 11; Bristol UWE 4; City 17; Coventry 7; Farnborough (CT) 7; Hertfordshire 17; Imperial London 7; Kingston 9; London (QM) 8; Loughborough 10; North East Wales (IHE) 5; Salford 6; Southampton 10.

Advice to applicants and planning the UCAS personal statement **Bristol** Interest in engineering and aerospace. Work experience in engineering. Flying experience. Personal attainments. **London (QM)** Practical experience. Relevant hobbies. Membership of Air Training Corps. See also under **Engineering/Engineering Sciences**. See also **Appendix 2**.

Misconceptions about this course That Aeronautical Engineering is not a highly analytical subject: it is.

Selection interviews **Yes** Bristol, Cambridge, Farnborough (CT), Hertfordshire, Kingston, London (QM), Loughborough, Salford, Southampton.

Interview advice and questions Why Aeronautical Engineering? Questions about different types of aircraft and flight principles of helicopters. Range of interests in engineering. See also **Chapter 6**.

Reasons for rejection (non-academic) See **Engineering/Engineering Sciences**.

AFTER-RESULTS ADVICE

Universities with vacancies in Clearing (2006) Bath; Belfast (Queen's); Bristol; Brunel; City; Coventry; Glamorgan; Glasgow; Hertfordshire; Imperial London; Kingston; Leeds; Liverpool; London (QM); Salford; Sheffield; Southampton; Staffordshire; Surrey; Swansea.

Offers to applicants repeating A-levels Higher Belfast (Queen's), Bristol; **Possibly higher** Hertfordshire; **Same** Bath, City, Farnborough (CT), Kingston, Liverpool, Loughborough, Salford, Southampton, York.

GRADUATE DESTINATIONS AND EMPLOYMENT (2005 HESA)

Graduates surveyed 780 **Employed** 395 **In further study** 150 **Assumed unemployed** 70.

OTHER DEGREE SUBJECTS FOR CONSIDERATION

Astronomy; Astrophysics; Computer Science; Electronics and Systems Engineering; Materials Science; Mathematics; Naval Architecture; Physics.

ENGINEERING (CHEMICAL)

NB The points totals shown to the left of the institutions are for ease of reference only. It must not be assumed that tariff points are always used by institutions or that they can be substituted for an offer in grades. The level of an offer is not necessarily indicative of the quality of a course.

Engineering Council Statement: See **Engineering/Engineering Sciences**.

COURSE OFFERS INFORMATION

Subject requirements/preferences See **Engineering/Engineering Sciences**.

Your target offers

360 pts and above
> **Cambridge** – (Chem Eng 2nd yr entry only via Eng or Nat Sci)
> **Oxford** – Offers vary eg AAA–AAB (Chem Eng)

340 pts Imperial London – AAB–ABB (Chem Eng; Chem Eng Yr Abrd)
> **London (UCL)** – AAB+AS–BBB+AS (Chem Eng; Bioch Eng Bioproc Mgt; Chem Bioch Eng)

320 pts Birmingham – ABB–BBB 320–300 pts (Chem Eng; Chem Eng Bus Mgt; Chem Eng Int St; Chem Eng Ind)
> **Manchester** – ABB (MEng Chem Eng; Chem Eng Ind; Chem Eng Euro; Chem Eng Biotech; Chem Eng Chem; Chem Eng Env Tech; Chem Eng (Bus Mgt))
> **Newcastle** – ABB–BBB (MEng Chem Proc Eng)
> **Nottingham** – ABB (MEng/BEng Chem Eng; Chem Eng Env Eng; Chem Eng Modn Lang)
> **Sheffield** – ABB (MEng Chem Eng Chem)
> **Strathclyde** – ABB (MEng Chem Eng)

300 pts Aston – BBB–ABB 300–320 pts (MEng Chem Eng; Chem Eng App Chem)
> **Bath** – BBB–ABC 300 pts (MEng Chem Eng; Bioch Eng)
> **Belfast (Queen's)** – BBB (MEng Chem Eng)
> **Edinburgh** – BBB (BEng Chem Eng; Chem Eng Env Eng; Chem Eng Mgt)
> **Leeds** – BBB (Pharm Chem Eng; Chem Eng)
> **Loughborough** – 300–320 pts (MEng Chem Eng courses; Chem Eng Mgt)
> **Newcastle** – BBB–BBC (BEng Chem Proc Eng courses)
> **Sheffield** – BBB–BCC (BEng Chem Eng courses)
> **Surrey** – BBB–BBC 300–280 pts (Chem Eng; Chem Biosys Eng)
> **Swansea** – 300 pts (MEng Chem Bioproc Eng)

280 pts Aston – BBC–CCC (BEng Chem Eng; Chem Eng (Mgt St) (Comp Simul) (Ener Env); Chem Eng App Chem; Chem Tech Des)
> **Heriot-Watt** – BBC 2nd yr entry (Chem Eng courses)

Biochemical Engineering – *the challenge to sixth formers in creating health and wealth from new life science discoveries*

The discovery of penicillin was a momentous achievement. It took 15 years and an international effort to find a way to produce it in the quantities needed for medical treatment and led to the birth of the discipline of biochemical engineering.

The medicines of the future – human proteins, therapeutic vaccines and human tissue for repair – are even more complex than penicillin. They address previously intractable conditions and are generating many opportunities spanning the initial discovery, to point of care. Those who are numerate and have gained engineering team and leadership skills are translating these opportunities into new medicines. It is also such people who are managing the billions of pounds of investment required and who are dealing with the social and environmental issues that all big endeavours must address.

Those seeking a professional career in a subject that is demanding, and who want a life at the cutting edge that is highly rewarded, should consider the excitement of biochemical engineering as a degree option.

Information on courses can be found in UCAS guides both under biochemical engineering and chemical engineering and more information is on the web. Visits can be arranged to explore in more detail the A level requirements, the courses and the careers available.

Nottingham – BBC–BCC (Env Eng)
260 pts **Bath** – 260 pts (BEng Chem Eng; Chem Bioproc Eng)
Belfast (Queen's) – BCC (BEng Chem Eng)
Glasgow Caledonian – BCC (Fire Risk Eng)
Leeds – BCC (Fire Explsn; Ener Env Eng)
Loughborough – 260–280 pts (BEng Chem Eng; Chem Eng Env Prot)
Strathclyde – BCC (BEng Chem Eng; Chem Eng Proc Biotech)
Swansea – 260 pts (BEng Chem Bioproc Eng)
240 pts **Central Lancashire** – 240 pts (Fire Eng)
Heriot-Watt – CCC 2nd yr entry (Brew Distil)
Loughborough – 240 pts (Proc Tech Mgt)
Surrey – CCC (Fdn Chem Eng)
200 pts **Heriot-Watt** – CDD–CCD 1st yr entry (Chem Eng courses)
180 pts **Heriot-Watt** – DDD 1st yr entry (Brew Distil)
Huddersfield – DDD 180 pts (Chem Chem Eng)
Teesside – 180–240 pts (Chem Eng)
160 pts **Central Lancashire** – 160 pts (Fire Sfty)
London South Bank – CC (Chem Proc Eng; Petrol Eng)
Loughborough – CC (Fdn Chem Eng)
Newport – 160 pts (Fire Eng)
Swansea – 160 pts (Fdn Chem Bioproc Eng)
120 pts **London Met** – 120 pts (Poly Eng)
Paisley – DD **or** bbc (BSc Chem Eng)

Alternative offers
IB offers Birmingham 32–34 pts; Bristol 34 pts; Cambridge 38–42 pts; London (UCL) 32–36 pts; Loughborough 30–32 pts; Manchester 35 pts; Newcastle 30–34 pts; Nottingham individual offer; Oxford 38–42 pts; Sheffield 34 pts.
Scottish offers See **Chapter 7**.

OTHER HIGHER EDUCATION COURSES IN THE SUBJECT FIELD
Foundation degrees (contact the institutions for details) Teesside.

Higher National Diploma courses
100 pts **and below**
Adam Smith (Coll); Central Lancashire; Dudley (Coll); Farnborough (CT); Forth Valley (Coll); Glamorgan; Huddersfield; London South Bank; Riverside Halton (Coll); Teesside; Wirral Met (Coll).

CHOOSING YOUR COURSE (SEE ALSO CH.1)
Subject information Chemical Engineering is involved in many aspects of industry and scientific development. In addition to the oil and chemical-based industries, graduates enter a wide range of careers including the design and construction of chemical process plants, food production, pollution control, environmental protection, energy conservation, waste recovery and recycling, medical science, health and safety, and alternative energy sources. Courses vary and this is a subject for which sponsorship opportunities are available. **Useful websites** www.icheme.org; www.engc.org.uk; www.enginuity.org.uk; www.whynotchemeng.com.

Course variations Brewing and Distilling (Heriot-Watt); Fire and Explosion (Leeds); Polymer Engineering (London Met); Petroleum Engineering (London South Bank); Chemical Engineering with Environmental Protection (Loughborough); Chemical Engineering and Business Management (Manchester); Chemical and Process Engineering (Newcastle). *NOW CHECK PROSPECTUSES AND WEBSITES FOR ANY RECENT CHANGES.*

Universities and colleges teaching quality See www.tqi.ac.uk; www.qaa.ac.uk.

Top universities and colleges (Research) Aston; Birmingham*; Cambridge; Imperial London*; London (UCL)*; Newcastle; Surrey.

Sandwich degree courses Aston; Bath; Belfast (Queen's); London South Bank; Loughborough; Manchester; Paisley; Surrey; Teesside.

ADMISSIONS INFORMATION

Number of applicants per place (approx) Aston 4; Bath 6; Birmingham 8; Heriot-Watt 8; Huddersfield 7; Imperial London 4, (MEng) 4; Leeds 9; London (UCL) 8; Loughborough 7; Newcastle (MEng/BEng) 6; Nottingham 6; Sheffield 14; Strathclyde 6; Surrey 5; Swansea 3.

Misconceptions about this course Surrey That chemical engineering is chemistry on a large scale: physics is as applicable as chemistry.

Selection interviews Yes Bath, Cambridge, Leeds, London (UCL), London South Bank, Newcastle, Nottingham, Oxford, Surrey, Sussex, Teesside.

Interview advice and questions Past questions have included the following: How would you justify the processing of radioactive waste to people living in the neighbourhood? What is public health engineering? What is biochemical engineering? What could be the sources of fuel and energy in the year 2200? Discuss some industrial applications of chemistry. Regular incidents occur in which chemical spillage and other problems affect the environment. Be prepared to discuss these social issues. See also **Chapter 6**.

Reasons for rejection (non-academic) See **Engineering/Engineering Sciences**.

AFTER-RESULTS ADVICE

Universities with vacancies in Clearing (2006) Aston; Bath; Belfast (Queen's); Birmingham; Central Lancashire; Heriot-Watt; Huddersfield; Leeds; London South Bank; Loughborough; Newcastle; Nottingham; Sheffield; Southampton; Surrey; Swansea; Teesside.

Offers to applicants repeating A-levels Higher Swansea; **Possibly higher** Bath, Belfast, Leeds, London South Bank; **Same** Aston, Birmingham, Loughborough, Newcastle, Nottingham, Sheffield, Surrey, Teesside.

GRADUATE DESTINATIONS AND EMPLOYMENT (2005 HESA)

Graduates surveyed 410 **Employed** 235 **In further study** 75 **Assumed unemployed** 30.

OTHER DEGREE SUBJECTS FOR CONSIDERATION

Biochemistry; Biotechnology; Chemistry; Colour Chemistry; Cosmetic Science; Environmental Science; Food Science and Technology; Materials Science; Mathematics; Nuclear Engineering; Physics.

ENGINEERING (CIVIL)

(including **Environmental Engineering**)

NB The points totals shown to the left of the institutions are for ease of reference only. It must not be assumed that tariff points are always used by institutions or that they can be substituted for an offer in grades. The level of an offer is not necessarily indicative of the quality of a course.

Engineering Council statement See **Engineering/Engineering Sciences**.

COURSE OFFERS INFORMATION

Subject requirements/preferences See **Engineering/Engineering Sciences**.

Your target offers

360 pts **and above**
            Cambridge – AAA (Civ Struct Env Eng)
            Oxford – Offers vary eg AAA–AAB (Civ Eng)
            Southampton – ABBb 370 pts (MEng Civ Eng Ind; Civ Eng Euro St; Env Eng courses; Civ Eng Archit)
350 pts **Southampton** – BBBb 350 pts (BEng Civ Eng; Env Eng courses)

340 pts **Bath** – 340 pts AAB (MEng Civ Eng; Civ Archit Eng)
Durham – AAB (MEng Civ Eng)
Imperial London – AAB–BBB (Civ Eng; Civ Env Eng; Civ Eng Yr Abrd)
London (UCL) – AAB–BBB (MEng/BEng Civ Eng; Env Eng)
Sheffield – AAB–BBB **or** AAbb–BBbb (MEng Civ Eng; Struct Eng Archit; Civ Struct Eng; Civ Eng Modn Lang; Civ Eng Bus Mgt; Eng (Civ Mat Mech))
Warwick – AAB–ABB (MEng Civ Eng courses)

320 pts **Birmingham** – ABB–BBC (MEng Civ Eng courses; Disas Mgt Tech; Sust Tech)
Bristol – ABB–BBB (Civ Eng; Civ Eng Euro)
Cardiff – ABB 320–300 pts (MEng Civ Eng; Civ Env Eng; Archit Eng)
Dundee – 320–260 pts (MEng Civ Eng; Civ Eng Mgt; Civ Eng Des Mgt)
Edinburgh – ABB 2nd yr entry (Civ Eng; Civ Eng Constr Mgt; Struct Fire Sfty Eng; Struct Eng Archit; Civ Env Eng)
Exeter – ABB–BBC (MEng Civ Eng)
Heriot-Watt – 320 pts 2nd yr entry (MEng/BEng Civ Eng; Struct Eng Archit Des; Civ Env Eng)
Loughborough – 320 pts (MEng Civ Eng)
Manchester – ABB (MEng Civ Eng N Am))
Newcastle – ABB–BBB (MEng Civ Eng; Env Eng; Off Eng)
Nottingham – ABB–BBC (Civ Eng; Civ Eng Fr/Ger)
Swansea – 320 pts (MEng Civ Eng)

300 pts **Aberdeen** – BBB 2nd yr entry (MEng Civ Eng; Civ Struct Eng; Civ Eng Euro St; Civ Eng Mgt)
Bath – BBB (BEng Civ Eng)
Belfast (Queen's) – BBB (MEng Civ Eng; Env Civ Eng; Struct Eng Archit)
Bradford – 300 pts (MEng Civ Struct Eng)
Brighton – 300 pts (MEng Civ Eng)
Brunel – 300 pts (Mech Eng Bld Serv)
City – 300 pts (MEng Civ Eng; Civ Eng Surv; Civ Eng Archit)
Coventry – 300 pts (MEng Civ Eng)
Dundee – 300–240 pts (BEng Civ Eng; Civ Eng Mgt; Civ Eng Des Mgt)
East London – 300 pts (MEng Civ Eng)
Edinburgh – BBB 1st yr entry (Civ Eng; Civ Eng Constr Mgt; Struct Fire Sfty Eng; Struct Eng Archit; Civ Env Eng)
Glasgow – BBB (Civ Eng Archit)
Leeds – BBB (MEng Civ Struct Eng; Civ Env Eng; Civ Eng Constr Mgt; Civ Eng Trans; Archit Eng)
Liverpool – 300 pts (MEng Civ Env Eng; Civ Eng; Civ Marit Eng; Civ Struct Eng)
Liverpool John Moores – 300 pts (MEng Civ Eng)
Manchester – BBB (BEng Civ Eng; Civ Struct Eng)
Newcastle – BBB–BBC (BEng Civ Eng; Off Eng; Env Eng)
Nottingham – BBB–BCC (Archit Env Eng; Env Eng)
Plymouth – 300 pts (MEng Civ Eng; Civ Cstl Eng)
Portsmouth – 300 pts (MEng Civ Eng)
Salford – 300 pts (MEng Civ Eng)
Strathclyde – BBB (MEng Civ Eng; Civ Eng Euro St; Civ Eng Env Mgt; Archit Eng)
Surrey – ABC–BBB (MEng Civ Eng)
Warwick – BBB–BBC (BEng Civ Eng courses)

280 pts **Aberdeen** – BBC (BEng 2nd yr entry CCD 1st yr entry) (Civ Eng; Civ Eng Euro St; Civ Struct Eng; Civ Env Eng; Civ Eng Mgt)
Cardiff – BBC 280 pts (BEng Archit Eng; Civ Eng; Civ Env Eng)
Glasgow Caledonian – BBC (Fire Rsk Eng)
Nottingham Trent – 280 pts (BEng Civ Eng; Civ Struct Eng)

260 pts **Belfast (Queen's)** – BCC (BSc/BEng Civ Eng)
Coventry – 260 pts (BEng Civ Eng; Civ Eng Struct Eng)
Exeter – BCC–CCC (BEng Civ Eng)
Glasgow – BCC–CCC (Civ Eng; Civ Eng Archit)

Glasgow Caledonian – BCC (Env Civ Eng)

Heriot-Watt – BCC 260 pts 1st yr entry (MEng/BEng Civ Eng; Struct Eng; Struct Eng Archit Des; Civ Env Eng)

Liverpool – 260 pts (BEng Civ Eng)

Liverpool John Moores – 260 pts (BEng Civ Eng)

Loughborough – 260 pts (Constr Eng Mgt; Archit Eng Des Mgt; BEng Civ Eng)

Strathclyde – BCC (BEng Civ Eng; Civ Eng Env Mgt; Archit Eng)

Surrey – BCC (BEng Civ Eng; Fdn Civ Eng)

Swansea – 260 pts (BEng Civ Eng)

Ulster – BCC 260 pts (BEng Civ Eng; Env Eng)

240 pts **Anglia Ruskin** – 240 pts (Civ Eng)

Bradford – 240 pts (BEng Civ Struct Eng)

Brighton – 240 pts (BEng Civ Eng)

Glamorgan – 240 pts (BEng Civ Eng)

Greenwich – 240 pts (BEng Civ Eng; Civ Eng Proj Mgt; Civ Eng Wtr Env Mgt)

Plymouth – 240 pts ((BEng Civ Eng; Civ Cstl Eng)

Portsmouth – 240 pts (BEng Civ Eng)

Salford – 240 pts (BEng Civ Eng; Civ Eng Comp Sci; Struct Eng Comp Sci)

230 pts **City** – 230 pts (BEng Civ Eng; Civ Eng Surv; Civ Eng Archit)

Napier – 230 pts (BEng Civ Trans Eng; Archit Des Civ Eng)

220 pts **Brighton** – 220 pts (Civ Env Eng)

Dundee – 220–260 pts (BEng Civ Eng; Civ Eng Des Mgt)

East London – 220 pts (BEng Civ Eng)

Kingston – 220 pts (BEng Civ Eng)

Nottingham Trent – 220 pts (BSc Civ Eng St)

Swansea – 220 pts (BEng Civ Eng Mgt)

200 pts **Abertay Dundee** – CDD 200 pts (Civ Eng)

Coventry – 200 pts (BEng/BSc Civ Eng Constr; Civ Eng Des)

Liverpool – 200 pts (Fdn Civ Eng)

Napier – 200 pts (BSc Civ Eng; Constr Eng; Civ Tmbr Eng)

180 pts **Greenwich** – 180 pts (BSc Civ Eng)

Teesside – 180–240 pts (Civ Eng; Disas Mgt)

160 pts **Bristol UWE** – 160–200 pts (BEng Civ Eng)

East London – 160 pts (BEng Civ Eng; Civ Eng Surv)

London South Bank – CC (BEng/BSc Civ Eng; Archit Eng)

Loughborough – CC (Fdn Civ Eng)

Newport – 160 pts (Civ Constr Eng)

Paisley – DDE (BEng Civ Eng)

Plymouth – 160 pts (BSc Civ Eng; Civ Cstl Eng)

Salford – 160 pts (BSc Civ Eng)

Wolverhampton – 160–220 pts (Civ Eng; Civ Eng Mgt)

140 pts **Bolton** – 140 pts (Civ Eng)

Glamorgan – 140 pts (BSc Civ Eng; Civ Eng Int St)

120 pts **Aberdeen** – DD (BSc Civ Eng)

Bradford – 120 pts (Fdn Civ Eng)

East London – 120 pts (BSc Civ Eng)

Kingston – 120 pts (BSc Civ Eng)

Paisley – DD (BSc Civ Eng)

100 pts **Nottingham Trent** – 100 pts (Fdn Civ Eng)

80 pts **Swansea (IHE)** – 80 pts (Civ Eng Env Mgt)

Leeds Met – contact University

Alternative offers

IB offers Bath 35–36 pts; Birmingham 30–34 pts; Cambridge 38–42 pts; Durham (MEng) 38 pts; Dundee 28 pts; Exeter (MEng) 30–34 pts, (BEng) 26–30 pts; Leicester 30–32 pts; Liverpool 30 pts;

Loughborough 30–32 pts; Manchester 34–36 pts; Newcastle (MEng) 34–36 pts, (BEng) 30–32 pts; Nottingham 32 pts; Oxford 38–42 pts; Salford 27–32 pts; Sheffield 32–34 pts; Southampton 31–33 pts; Warwick 35–37 pts.

Scottish offers See **Chapter 7**.

OTHER HIGHER EDUCATION COURSES IN THE SUBJECT FIELD

Foundation degrees (contact the institutions for details) Bolton; Bristol UWE; Central Lancashire; Derby; East Lancashire (IHE); Glamorgan; Kent; Mid-Kent (Coll); Nottingham Trent; Suffolk (Univ Campus); Swansea (IHE).

Higher National Diploma courses
100 pts and below
>Abertay Dundee; Adam Smith (Coll); Anglia Ruskin; Bell (Coll); Bradford (Coll); Burton (Coll); Coventry; Derby; Glamorgan; Gloucestershire (CAT); Greenwich; Kingston; Leeds Met; Liverpool John Moores; Llandrillo Cymru (Coll); London South Bank; Loughborough (Coll); Menai (Coll); Mid-Kent (Coll); Napier; Nescot; Newport; Northampton; Nottingham Trent; Oxford Brookes; Plymouth; Portsmouth; St Helens (Coll); Sheffield Hallam; Somerset (CAT); Stockport (CFHE); Swansea (IHE); Teesside; West Anglia (Coll); Wiltshire (Coll); Wolverhampton.

CHOOSING YOUR COURSE (SEE ALSO CH.1)

Subject information Civil engineering is concerned with the science and art of large-scale projects. This involves the planning, design, construction, maintenance and environmental assessment of roads, railways, bridges, airports, tunnels, docks, offshore structures, dams, high rise buildings and other major works. Specialist courses may also involve water, drainage, irrigation schemes and waste engineering, traffic and public health engineering. **Useful websites** www.ice.org.uk; www.engc.org.uk; www.enginuity.org.uk.

Course variations Disaster Management Technology (Birmingham); Civil Engineering with Water and Environmental Management (Greenwich); Architectural Engineering and Design Management (Loughborough); Civil and Timber Engineering (Napier); Architectural and Environmental Engineering (Nottingham); Civil and Coastal Engineering (Plymouth); Civil and Structural Engineering (Sheffield). *NOW CHECK PROSPECTUSES AND WEBSITES FOR ANY RECENT CHANGES.*

Universities and colleges teaching quality See www.tqi.ac.uk; www.qaa.ac.uk.

Top universities and colleges (Research) (See also **Building**) Belfast (Queen's); Birmingham; Bristol*; Cardiff*; Dundee; Imperial London*; Leeds; London (UCL); Newcastle; Nottingham; Sheffield; Southampton*.

Sandwich degree courses Bath; Belfast (Queen's); Bradford; Brighton; Cardiff; City; Coventry; East London; Glamorgan; Kingston; London South Bank; Loughborough; Nottingham Trent; Paisley; Portsmouth; Salford; Surrey; Teesside; Ulster.

ADMISSIONS INFORMATION

Number of applicants per place (approx) Abertay Dundee 8; Bath 5; Belfast (Queen's) 6; Birmingham 6; Bradford (BEng) 5; Bristol 10; Brunel 4; Cardiff 5; City 11; Coventry 10, (Civ Eng) 11; Dundee 5; Durham 8; Glamorgan 6; Glasgow Caledonian 4; Greenwich 11; Heriot-Watt 7; Imperial London 4; Kingston 8; Leeds 10; Liverpool John Moores 16; London (UCL) 5; London South Bank 5; Loughborough 6; Napier 4; Newcastle 11, (Off Eng) 9; Nottingham 6; Nottingham Trent 11; Paisley 4; Plymouth 3; Portsmouth 3; Salford 5; Sheffield 7; Southampton 9; Strathclyde 4; Surrey 5; Swansea 3; Teesside 6; Wolverhampton 3.

Advice to applicants and planning the UCAS personal statement **Portsmouth** Evidence of mathematical skills. See **Engineering/Engineering Sciences**. Also read the magazine *The New Civil Engineer* and discuss articles which interest you on your application. See also **Appendix 2**.

Selection interviews **Yes** Bath, Belfast (Queen's), Brighton, Bristol, Brunel, Cambridge, Coventry, Durham, Glamorgan, Greenwich, Heriot-Watt, Kingston, Leeds, London (UCL), London South Bank,

Loughborough, Napier, Newcastle, Nottingham, Oxford, Southampton, Surrey, Sussex, Warwick; **Some** Cardiff, Dundee, Nottingham Trent, Salford.

Interview advice and questions Past questions have included: Why have you chosen Civil Engineering? Have you contacted the Institution of Civil Engineers? How would you define the difference between the work of a civil engineer and the work of an architect? What would happen to a concrete beam if a load was applied? Where would it break and how could it be strengthened? The favourite question: Why do you want to be a civil engineer? What would you do if you were asked to build a concrete boat? Do you know any civil engineers? What problems have been faced in building the Channel Tunnel? See also **Chapter 6**.

Reasons for rejection (non-academic) Lack of vitality. Lack of interest in buildings, the built environment or in civil engineering. Poor communication skills. See also **Engineering/Engineering Sciences**.

AFTER-RESULTS ADVICE
Universities with vacancies in Clearing (2006) Aberdeen; Abertay Dundee; Anglia Ruskin; Belfast (Queen's); Birmingham; Bolton; Bradford; Brighton; Bristol UWE; Brunel; Central Lancashire; City; Coventry; Dundee; East London; Exeter; Glamorgan; Glasgow; Greenwich; Kingston; Leeds; Manchester; Newcastle; Nottingham; Nottingham Trent; Plymouth; Portsmouth; Salford; Southampton; Surrey; Swansea; Teesside; Warwick; Wolverhampton.

Offers to applicants repeating A-levels Higher Belfast (Queen's), East London, Kingston, Liverpool John Moores, Nottingham, Teesside, Warwick; **Possibly higher** Durham, Portsmouth, Southampton; **Same** Bath, Birmingham, Bradford, Brighton, Bristol, Cardiff, City, Coventry, Dundee, Greenwich, Heriot-Watt, Leeds, London (UCL), London South Bank, Loughborough, Newcastle, Nottingham Trent, Salford, Sheffield.

GRADUATE DESTINATIONS AND EMPLOYMENT (2005 HESA)
Graduates surveyed 1185 **Employed** 845 **In further study** 80 **Assumed unemployed** 45.

OTHER DEGREE SUBJECTS FOR CONSIDERATION
Architecture; Building; Surveying; Town and Country Planning.

ENGINEERING (COMMUNICATIONS)
(Including **Mobile Communications;** see also **Engineering (Computer, Control, Software and Systems)** and **Engineering (Electrical and Electronic))**

NB The points totals shown to the left of the institutions are for ease of reference only. It must not be assumed that tariff points are always used by institutions or that they can be substituted for an offer in grades. The level of an offer is not necessarily indicative of the quality of a course.

Engineering Council Statement See **Engineering/Engineering Sciences**.

COURSE OFFERS INFORMATION
Subject requirements/preferences See **Engineering/Engineering Sciences**.

Your target offers
360 pts and above
    London (UCL) – AAA+AS–AAB+AS (Electron Eng Comm Eng)
    Strathclyde – AAA (Dig Comm Multim Sys)
    Warwick – AABc **or** ABbbb (MEng Electron Eng (Comm))
340 pts Bristol – AAB–BBC (Comm Multim Eng)
    Durham – AAB (MEng Comm Eng)
    Sheffield – AAB–ABB **or** ABab–BBaa (Electron Comms Eng; Data Comms Eng)
    Surrey – AAB (MEng Telecomm Sys)

320 pts   **Bath** – ABB (MEng Electron Comm Eng; Comp Electron Comm)
      Leeds – ABB–BBB (Electron Comm Eng; Comm Comp Eng Mgt)
      Leicester – 320 pts (MEng Comm Electron Eng courses)
      Liverpool – ABB 320 pts (MEng Electron Comm Eng; Wrls Comm 3G Tech)
      London (QM) – 320 pts (MEng Comm Eng)
      Newcastle – ABB (MEng Electron Comm)

300 pts   **Bangor** – 300–320 pts (MEng Comm Comp Sys Eng)
      Bath – BBB (BEng Electron Comm Eng; Comp Electron Comm)
      Birmingham – 300–340 pts (Comm Sys Eng; Comp Comm Sys Eng courses)
      Bradford – BBB 300 pts (MEng Electron Telecomm Intnet Eng)
      Dundee – 300 pts 2nd yr entry (Electron Comp (Comm Eng))
      Hertfordshire – 300 pts (Dig Comm Electron)
      London (King's) – BBB+AS **or** BBbb (Telecomm Eng; Telecomm Eng Ind)
      Loughborough – BBB 300 pts (Wrlss Comm Eng)
      Newcastle – BBB (BEng Electron Comm)
      Portsmouth – 300 pts (MEng Comm Sys Eng)
      Strathclyde – BBB (BEng Dig Comm Multim Sys)
      Surrey – BBB (BEng Telecomm Sys)
      Swansea – 300 pts (MEng Comm Sys)
      Warwick – BCCc **or** BCccc (BEng Electron Eng (Comm))

280 pts   **Aberdeen** – BBC (Electron Eng Comm)
      Essex – 280 pts (MEng Telecomm Eng; Comp Telecomm; Optoelectron Comm Sys)
      Hull – 280–300 pts (MEng Mbl Telecomm Tech)
      Lancaster – BBC–BCC 280–260 pts (Electron Sys Eng; Comp Sys Eng)
      Liverpool – BBC 280 pts (BEng Electron Comm Eng; Wrls Comm 3G Tech)
      Staffordshire – 280 pts (Mbl Comm courses)

260 pts   **Aston** – BCC–CCC 260–240 pts (Comm Eng)
      Bristol UWE – 260–240 pts (MEng Dig Sys Eng)
      Brunel – 260 pts (Electron Elec Eng Comm Sys)
      Glamorgan – 260 pts (Dig Comm Eng)
      Kent – 260 pts (Electron Comm Eng)
      Leicester – 260 pts (BEng Comm Electron Eng)
      London (QM) – 260 pts (BEng Telecommunications)
      Robert Gordon – BCC (Electron Comm Eng; Comm Comp Eng; Artif Intel Comm Eng)
      Swansea – 260 pts (BEng Comm Sys; Mbl Comm Intnet Tech)
      Westminster – BCC (Dig Comm Eng; Dig Sig Proc)

240 pts   **Bangor** – 240–260 pts (BEng Comm Comp Sys)
      Bradford – CCC 240 pts (BEng Electron Telecomm Intnet Eng)
      Brighton – 240 pts (Dig Electron Comp Comm)
      City – CCC (BEng Media Comm Sys; Multim Intnet Sys Eng; Comm)
      Greenwich – 240 pts (Comm Sys Soft Eng)
      Liverpool John Moores – 240 pts (Net Telecomm Eng)
      Northumbria – 240 pts (Comm Electron Eng)
      Plymouth – 240 pts (BEng Comm Eng)
      Portsmouth – 240 pts (BEng Comm Sys Eng)

220 pts   **East London** – 220 pts (Elec Electron Eng (Comm))
      Hertfordshire – 220 pts (BEng Dig Comm Electron)
      Hull – 220–280 pts (BEng Mbl Telecomm Tech)
      Napier – 220 pts (Electron Comm Eng)
      UCE Birmingham – 220–240 pts (Mgt Tech Comm Net)

200 pts   **Bristol UWE** – 200–240 pts (Comp Telecomm)
      Central Lancashire – 200 pts (Dig Comm; Dig Sgnl Imag Proc)
      Coventry – 200 pts (Comp Net Comm Tech; Comm Eng)
      Liverpool John Moores – 200 pts (Broad Tech)
      Manchester Met – 200–240 pts (Comm Electron Eng)

Oxford Brookes – CDD or CDdd (Telecommunications)
Portsmouth – 200 pts (BEng Comm Eng)
Westminster – 200–260 pts (Mbl Comm; Net Comm Eng)
180 pts **Bristol UWE** – 180–240 pts (BEng Dig Sys Eng)
Leicester – 180–240 pts (Fdn Eng)
Plymouth – 180 pts (Electron Comm Sys)
Sheffield Hallam – 180 pts (Electron Eng (Comm Eng))
160 pts **Kingston** – 160 pts (Comm Sys)
London Met – 160 pts (Comm Sys)
London South Bank – CC (Telecomm Comp Net Eng)
140 pts **Cardiff (UWIC)** – 140 pts (Electron Comm Sys)
Glasgow Caledonian – CD (Telecomm Eng)
120 pts **Paisley** – DD (Comm Tech; Comp Net)
80 pts **UHI Millennium Inst** – 80 pts (Eng (Telecomm))

Leeds Met – contact University

Alternative offers
IB offers Bath 32–34 pts; Birmingham 32–36 pts; City 28 pts; Durham (MEng) 38 pts; Leicester 32 pts;
London (King's) 30 pts, (QM) 30–36 pts; Manchester Met 26 pts; Newcastle 32–34 pts.
Scottish offers See **Chapter 7**.

OTHER HIGHER EDUCATION COURSES IN THE SUBJECT FIELD
Foundation degrees (contact the institutions for details) East Antrim (IFHE); East Lancashire (IHE);
Plymouth (CAD).

Higher National Diploma courses
100 pts **and below**
Bedfordshire; Bell (Coll); Blackpool and Fylde (Coll); Bristol City (Coll); Cardiff (UWIC);
Coventry (Coll); East Lancashire (IHE); East London; Glasgow (Coll); Kingston; Lincoln; Lincoln
(Coll); Liverpool (CmC); Liverpool John Moores; London Met; Nescot; Newport; North East
Wales (IHE); Plymouth; Portsmouth; Ravensbourne (CDC); St Helens (Coll); Southampton
Solent; Teesside; UCE Birmingham; UHI Millennium Inst; Walsall (Coll); West Thames (Coll).

CHOOSING YOUR COURSE (SEE ALSO CH.1)
Subject information Communications Engineering impacts on many aspects of the engineering and
business world. Courses overlap considerably with Electronic Engineering and provide graduates with
expertise in such fields as telecommunications, mobile communications and microwave engineering,
optoelectronics, radio engineering and internet technology. Sandwich courses and sponsorships are
offered by several universities. **Useful websites** See **Computer Courses** and **Engineering (Electrical
and Electronic)**.

Course variations Electronic, Telecommunications and Internet Engineering (Bradford); Multimedia
Communications (Hertfordshire); Wireless Communications and 3G Technology (Liverpool); Networks
and Telecommunications Engineering (Liverpool John Moores); Mobile Communication and Internet
Technology (Swansea). *NOW CHECK PROSPECTUSES AND WEBSITES FOR ANY RECENT CHANGES.*

Sandwich degree courses See under **Engineering (Electrical and Electronic)**.

ADMISSIONS INFORMATION
Number of applicants per place (approx) Bradford 9; Bristol 2; Coventry 7; Hull 8; London Met 5;
London South Bank 3; Northumbria 7; Plymouth 4.

Advice to applicants and planning the UCAS personal statement See **Engineering (Electrical and
Electronic)**. See also **Appendix 2**.

Selection interviews **Yes** Bradford, Bristol, Hertfordshire, Kent, London Met, London South Bank,
Sunderland.

Interview advice and questions See **Engineering (Electrical and Electronic)**.

Reasons for rejection (non-academic) See **Engineering (Electrical and Electronic)**.

AFTER-RESULTS ADVICE
Universities with vacancies in Clearing (2006) Bradford; Bristol UWE; City; Hertfordshire; Kingston; Leicester; Manchester Met; Plymouth; Portsmouth; Robert Gordon; Swansea; UCE Birmingham; Warwick; Westminster.

Offers to applicants repeating A-levels: **Same** Loughborough.

GRADUATE DESTINATIONS AND EMPLOYMENT (2005 HESA)
See **Engineering (Electrical and Electronic)**.

OTHER DEGREE SUBJECTS FOR CONSIDERATION
Computer Science; Engineering (Computer, Control, Electrical, Electronic Systems); Physics

---

ENGINEERING (COMPUTER, CONTROL, SOFTWARE AND SYSTEMS)
(see also **Computer Courses** and **Engineering (Electrical and Electronic)**)

NB The points totals shown to the left of the institutions are for ease of reference only. It must not be assumed that tariff points are always used by institutions or that they can be substituted for an offer in grades. The level of an offer is not necessarily indicative of the quality of a course.

Engineering Council statement See **Engineering/Engineering Sciences**.

COURSE OFFERS INFORMATION
Subject requirements/preferences See **Engineering/Engineering Sciences**.

Your target offers
360 pts **and above**
    Cambridge – AAA (Inf Comp Eng yrs 3 and 4 specialisation via Engineering Tripos)
    Imperial London – AAA (Inf Sys Eng; Inf Sys Eng Abrd)
    Manchester – AAA–AAB (Comp Eng; Soft Eng)
    Oxford – Offers vary between candidates (Eng Comp Sci; Inf Eng)
    Strathclyde – AAA (MEng Comp Electron Sys; Dig Comm Multim Sys)
340 pts **Bristol** – AAB (Comp Sys Eng; Comp Sys Eng Euro)
    Reading – 340 pts (MEng Comp Eng)
    Sheffield – AAB–ABB (Electron Contr Sys Eng; Sys Contr Eng; Med Sys Eng; Sys Eng)
    Southampton – AAB 340 pts (MEng/BEng Comp Eng; MEng Soft Eng)
    Surrey – AAB (MEng Dig Media Eng)
    Warwick – AAB–ABB (MEng Sys Eng; Comp Inf Eng)
    York – AAB (Comp Sys Soft Eng)
320 pts **Bath** – ABB (MEng Comp Electron Comm)
    Cardiff – ABB 320–300 pts (MEng Comp Sys Eng)
    Essex – 320–300 pts (4yr Electron Comp; Comp Eng)
    Lancaster – ABB (MEng Comp Sys Eng)
    Leeds – ABB (Comm Comp Eng Mgt)
    Leicester – 320 pts (MEng Embd Sys Eng)
    Liverpool – 320 pts (MEng Lsr Eng; Comp Sci Electron Eng)
    London (QM) – 320 pts (MEng Comp Eng; E-Commer Eng; Intnet Comp)
    Loughborough – ABB 320 pts (MEng Electron Comp Sys Eng; Sys Eng; Electron Soft Eng)
    Newcastle – ABB (MEng Comp Sys Eng)

Sheffield – ABB **or** ABbb (MEng Soft Eng; Soft Eng Bus; Soft Eng Mgt)
Sussex – ABB–BBB 360–330 pts (MEng Comp Sys Eng)
300 pts Bangor – 300–320 pts (MEng Comm Comp Sys Eng)
Bath – BBB (BEng Comp Electron Comm)
Birmingham – 300 pts (Comp Sys Eng courses; Comp Comm Sys Eng courses)
Bradford – 300–280 pts (Electron Telecomm Intnet Eng)
Brunel – BBB 300 pts (Multim Tech Des)
Dundee – 300 pts 2nd yr entry (Electron Comp)
Durham – BBB 300 pts check with admissions tutor (Comp Eng)
Edinburgh – BBB (Comp Sci Electron; Electron Soft Eng)
Essex – 300–280 pts (Comp Net; Comp Sci (Soft Eng) (Intnet Tech) (Embd Sys Robot); Comp Net Scrty; Comp Eng)
Heriot-Watt – ABC 2nd yr entry (Comp Electron Inf Sys Eng)
Hertfordshire – 300 pts (MEng Dig Sys Comp Eng)
Lancaster – BBB (BEng Comp Sys Eng)
London (King's) – BBB **or** BBbb (Comp Sys Electron courses)
Newcastle – BBB (BEng Comp Sys Eng)
Portsmouth – 300 pts (MEng Comp Eng)
Reading – 300 pts (BSc Comp Eng; Cyber Contr Eng; Sys Eng)
Sheffield – BBB **or** BBbb (BEng Soft Eng; Soft Eng Bus; Soft Eng Mgt)
Surrey – BBB–BBC (BEng Dig Media Eng; Comp Sci Eng)
Strathclyde – BBB (BEng Comp Electron Sys; Dig Comm Multim Sys)
Sussex – BBB–BBC (BEng Comp Sys Eng)
Warwick – BBB–BBC+AS (BEng Sys Eng; Comp Inf Eng)
280 pts Aston – 280 pts (Intnet Sys; Electron Eng Comp Sci; Multim Dig Sys)
Bath – BBC (Comp Electron Comm)
Bristol UWE – 280–300 pts (MEng/BEng Dig Sys Eng)
Cardiff – BBC 3AL pref 280 pts (BEng Comp Sys Eng)
East Anglia – BBC (Comp Sys Eng; Intnet Comp)
Exeter – BBC (Intnet Eng)
Liverpool – 280 pts (BEng Lsr Eng; Comp Sci Electron Eng)
Reading – 280 pts (Cyber Contr Eng)
260 pts Aberystwyth – 260–310 pts (Soft Eng)
Aston – BCC–CCC (Intnet Eng; Electron Eng Comp Sci)
Brunel – BCC 260 pts (Intnet Eng; Comp Sys Eng)
Glamorgan – 260 pts (Comp Sys Eng)
Glasgow – BCC (Electron Soft Eng; Microcomp Sys Eng)
Heriot-Watt – BCC 260 pts 1st yr entry (Comp Electron (Inf Sys Eng))
Huddersfield – 260–320 pts (Comp Contr Sys)
Kent – 260 pts (BEng Comp Sys Eng)
Leicester – 260 pts (BEng Embd Sys Eng)
London (QM) – 260–300 pts (BEng Comp Eng; Aud Sys Eng; Multim Sys Tech; Dig Aud Mus Sys Eng)
Loughborough – 260 pts (BEng Sys Eng)
Reading – 260 pts (Sys Eng)
Richmond (Am Int Univ) – 260 pts (Comp Aid Eng)
Robert Gordon – BCC 2nd yr entry (Artif Intel Comp Eng courses)
Westminster – 260 pts (Comp Sys Eng)
240 pts Bangor – 240–260 pts (BEng Comp Sys Eng)
Bradford – 240 pts (BEng Soft Eng)
Brighton – 240 pts (Dig Electron Comp Comm)
Bristol UWE – 240–260 pts (Comp Sys Eng)
Brunel – 240pts (App Comp Eng Soft Des)
City – CCC (BEng Sys Contr Eng; Multim Intnet Sys Eng; Comp Sys Eng)
Greenwich – 240 pts (Comp Sys Soft Eng; Contr Instr Eng)

For information on how to read the Subject Tables, see **Chapter 7**.

        Liverpool John Moores – 240 pts (Comp Eng)
        Manchester Met – 240 pts (Comp Electron Eng; Auto Contr)
        Northumbria – 240 pts (Comp Aid Eng)
        Oxford Brookes – CCC (Comp Sys)
        Plymouth – 240 pts (Robot Auto Sys; Comp Eng)
        Portsmouth – 240 pts (BEng Comp Eng)
        Ulster – 240 pts (Electron Comp Sys)

220 pts **Aberdeen** – CCD (Eng (Electron Soft Eng); Electron Comp Eng)
        East London – 220–180 pts (Comp Tech)
        Essex – 220–200 pts (Electron Comp)
        Glamorgan – 220 pts (Inf Sys Eng)
        Hertfordshire – 220 pts (Dig Sys Comp Eng; Aud Vid Broad Eng)
        Hull – 220–280 pts (Comp Sys Eng)
        Napier – 220 pts (Electron Comp Eng)
        Robert Gordon – CCD 1st yr entry (Artif Intel Comp Eng)
        Staffordshire – 220–280 pts (Comp Sys Net Eng; Net Comp; Comp Net Scrty; Soft Eng)
        UCE Birmingham – 220–240 pts (Soft Des Net; Comp Electron)

200 pts **Bolton** – 200 pts (Electron Comp Eng)
        Coventry – 200 pts (Comp Hard Soft Eng; Comp Net Comm Tech)
        Heriot-Watt – CDD (BEng Inf Sys Eng)
        Hertfordshire – 200 pts (Soft Eng)
        Liverpool John Moores – 200 pts (Soft Eng)
        Manchester Met – 200–240 pts (Comp Net Tech; Comp Electron Eng)

180 pts **Aberdeen** – BC (Eng (Electron Comp Eng))
        Anglia Ruskin – 180 pts (Comp Aid Eng)
        Central Lancashire – 180–200 pts (Comp Eng)
        Greenwich – 180 pts (Intnet Eng Web Mgt)
        Leicester – 180–240 pts (Fdn Eng)
        Sheffield Hallam – 180 pts (Comp Eng; Comp Aid Eng Des)
        Teesside – 180–240 pts (Comp Aid Des Eng; Soft Eng; Instr Contr Eng)

160 pts **Bournemouth** – 160–180 pts (Electron Comp Sys)
        East London – 160 pts (Soft Eng)
        Greenwich – CC (Contr Instr Eng)
        Kent – 160 pts (Fdn Comp Sys Eng)
        Loughborough – CC (Fdn Sys Eng)
        North East Wales (IHE) – 160 pts (Comp Net; Intnet Multim Comp)
        Westminster – CC (Comp Sys Tech; Mbl Comm)
        Wolverhampton – 160–220 pts (Comp Sci (Soft Eng))

140 pts **Cardiff (UWIC)** – 140 pts (Electron Contr Sys)
        Glasgow Caledonian – CD/DDE (Comp Eng)

120 pts **Bradford** – 120 pts (Fdn Cyber)
        London South Bank – DD (Intnet Multim Eng; Comp Aid Eng)

100 pts **Paisley** – DE (Comp Net; Intnet Tech)

80 pts **Swansea (IHE)** – 80 pts (Comp Sys Electron)

Alternative offers

IB offers Bath 34–36 pts; Birmingham 32–36 pts; Bristol 34 pts; Bristol UWE 28–30 pts; Brunel 28–30 pts; Cambridge 38–42 pts; City 25–28 pts; Lancaster 32–34 pts; London (QM) 30–36 pts; Manchester Met 26 pts; Newcastle 34 pts; Oxford 38–42 pts; Reading 30 pts; Sheffield 32–35 pts; Southampton 34 pts; Warwick 35–37 pts.

Scottish offers See **Chapter 7**.

OTHER HIGHER EDUCATION COURSES IN THE SUBJECT FIELD

Foundation degrees (contact the institutions for details) Ealing, Hammersmith and West London (Coll); Glamorgan; Hull (Coll); North East Wales (IHE); Preston (Coll).

Higher National Diploma courses

120 pts Manchester Met.

80 pts **and below**

Anglia Ruskin; Bedfordshire; Blackpool and Fylde (Coll); Bolton; Bournemouth; Bromley (CFHE); Cardiff (UWIC); Carmarthenshire (Coll); Central Lancashire; Coventry; Derby; Doncaster (Univ Centre); Dumfries and Galloway (Coll); Farnborough (CT); Gateshead (Coll); Glamorgan; Glasgow Caledonian; Greenwich; Herefordshire (CT); Hertfordshire; Highbury (Coll); Huddersfield; Isle of Man (Coll); Leeds (CAD); Lincoln; Liverpool John Moores; Llandrillo Cymru (Coll); London Met; London South Bank; Loughborough (Coll); Middlesex; Napier; Newcastle (Coll); Newport; North East Wales (IHE); Northumbria; Nottingham Trent; Oxford Brookes; People's (Coll); Plymouth; Portsmouth; Salford; Sandwell (Coll); St Helens (Coll); Sheffield Hallam; Staffordshire; Stockport (CFHE); Swansea (IHE); Teesside; Thames Valley; UHI Millennium Inst; West Herts (Coll); Westminster; Wigan and Leigh (Coll); Worcestershire New (Coll).

CHOOSING YOUR COURSE (SEE ALSO CH.1)

Subject information The design and application of modern computer systems is fundamental to a wide range of disciplines which will also include electronic, software and computer-aided engineering. Most courses give priority to reinforcing the essential 'transferable skills' consisting of management techniques, leadership skills, literacy, presentation skills, business skills and time management. At many universities Computer Engineering is offered as part of a range of Electronics degree programmes when the first- and even the second-year courses are common to all students who choose to specialise later. A year in industry is a common feature of many of these courses. Career opportunities extend right across the whole field of electronics, telecommunications, control and systems engineering. **Useful websites** See **Computer Courses** and **Engineering/Engineering Sciences**.

Course variations Computer Systems Engineering (Birmingham); Digital Systems Engineering (Bristol UWE); Computer Science (Embedded Systems and Robotics) (Essex); Laser Engineering (Liverpool); Internet and Multimedia Engineering (London South Bank). *NOW CHECK PROSPECTUSES AND WEBSITES FOR ANY RECENT CHANGES.*

Universities and colleges teaching quality See www.tqi.ac.uk; www.qaa.ac.uk.

Top universities and colleges (Research) See **Computer Courses**.

Sandwich degree courses See under **Engineering (Electrical and Electronic)**.

ADMISSIONS INFORMATION

Number of applicants per place (approx) Aberystwyth 6; Aston 6; Bangor 5; Birmingham 10; Bournemouth 3; Bradford 6; Bristol 4; Bristol UWE 12; Cardiff 6; Central Lancashire 12; Coventry 2; Durham 6; East Anglia 4; Edinburgh 3; Huddersfield 2; Imperial London 5; Kent 5; Lancaster 12; Liverpool John Moores 2; London South Bank 3; Loughborough 17; Sheffield 10; Sheffield Hallam 8; Southampton 4; Staffordshire 5; Stirling 7; Strathclyde 7; Suffolk (Univ Campus) 1; Surrey (MEng, BEng) 3; Swansea (IHE) 4; Teesside 3; UCE Birmingham 6; Westminster 5.

Advice to applicants and planning the UCAS personal statement **Exeter** (Intnet Eng) One of an increasing number of courses of interest to those aiming for careers in the Internet and related industries. See also **Computer Courses** and **Engineering (Electrical and Electronic)**. See also **Appendix 2**.

Selection interviews Aston, Bath, Bradford, Cardiff, Durham, East Anglia, Glamorgan, Hertfordshire, Huddersfield, Kent, Liverpool John Moores, London South Bank, Nottingham Trent, Sheffield Hallam, Swansea (IHE), Westminster, York; **Some** Aberystwyth, Exeter, Manchester.

Interview advice and questions **Southampton** (B; Soft Eng) Free transport was provided from the railway station and free refreshments. There was a 45-minute talk on the University and tariff points and a brief outline of the courses on offer. There was a brief tour with a member of staff, lunch and a tour with students. The interview was really an informal chat about the personal statement and the teacher's reference. See also **Computer Courses** and **Engineering (Electrical and Electronic)** and **Chapter 6**.

Reasons for rejection (non-academic) Lack of understanding that the course involves engineering. See also **Computer Courses** and **Engineering (Electrical and Electronic)**.

AFTER-RESULTS ADVICE

Universities with vacancies in Clearing (2006) Aberystwyth; Aston; Bangor; Bath; Birmingham; Bolton; Bradford; City; Coventry; Dundee; Essex; Glamorgan; Hertfordshire; Huddersfield; Hull; Kent; Liverpool; Loughborough; Manchester; Newcastle; Plymouth; Portsmouth; Reading; Sheffield; Southampton; Staffordshire; Teesside; UCE Birmingham; York.

Offers to applicants repeating A-levels Higher Bristol, Strathclyde, Warwick, York; **Possibly higher** City, Huddersfield, Sheffield; **Same** Aston, Bath, Birmingham, Coventry, East Anglia, Exeter, Lancaster, Liverpool John Moores, London South Bank, Salford, Teesside, Ulster.

GRADUATE DESTINATIONS AND EMPLOYMENT (2005 HESA)
Software Engineering graduates surveyed 8480 **Employed** 4870 **In further study** 1015 **Assumed unemployed** 985.

OTHER DEGREE SUBJECTS FOR CONSIDERATION
Computer Science; Computing; Engineering (Aeronautical, Aerospace, Communications, Electrical and Electronic); Mathematics; Physics.

ENGINEERING (ELECTRICAL AND ELECTRONIC)

NB The points totals shown to the left of the institutions are for ease of reference only. It must not be assumed that tariff points are always used by institutions or that they can be substituted for an offer in grades. The level of an offer is not necessarily indicative of the quality of a course.

Engineering Council statement See **Engineering/Engineering Sciences**.

COURSE OFFERS INFORMATION
Subject requirements/preferences See **Engineering/Engineering Sciences**.

Your target offers
360 pts **and above**
　　　　　Cambridge – AAA (Eng (Elec Inf Sci) (Elec Electron Eng))
　　　　　Imperial London – AAA (MEng/BEng Elec Electron Eng; Inf Sys Eng; Inf Sys Eng Yr Abrd; Elec Electron Eng Mgt; Elec Electron Eng Yr Abrd)
　　　　　London (UCL) – AAA+AS–AAB+AS (Electron Elec Eng; Electron Eng Comm; Electron Eng Comp Sci; Electron Elec Int; Electron Eng Nanotech)
　　　　　Oxford – Offers vary eg AAA–AAB (Elec Eng)
　　　　　Strathclyde – AAA (MEng Elec Mech Eng; Elec Ener Sys; Electron Dig Sys; Electron Elec Eng Euro)
340 pts **Bristol** – AAB (Electron Eng; Elec Electron Eng; Elec Electron Eng Euro; Electron Comm Eng; Elec Electron Mgt)
　　　　　Durham – AAB (MEng Electron Eng)
　　　　　Nottingham – AAB–BCC (MEng/BEng Elec Eng; Elec Electron Eng courses; Electron Eng courses)
　　　　　St Andrews – AAB 2nd yr entry (Microelectron Photon)
　　　　　Sheffield – AAB–ABB **or** ABab **or** BBaa (Elec Eng courses; Electron Eng courses)
　　　　　Southampton – AAB 340 pts (MEng Electron Eng courses)
　　　　　Surrey – AAB (MEng Electron Eng; Electron Comp Eng; Dig Media Eng; Aud Media Eng)
　　　　　Warwick – AAB–ABB (MEng Electron Eng)
　　　　　York – AAB–ABB (MEng Electron Eng; Electron Eng Bus Mgt; Electron Comm Eng; Electron Comp Eng; Electron Eng Media Tech; Electron Eng Mus Tech Sys; Rad Freq Eng)
320 pts **Aston** – ABB–BBB (MEng Electron Sys Eng Mgt St; Electron Sys Eng)

Bath – ABB (MEng Elec Electron Eng; Comp Electron Comm; Electron Comm Eng; Electron Spc Sci Tech)

Birmingham – ABB–BBC (Electron Eng; Electron Comp Eng; Electron Comm Eng; Electron Eng Bus Mgt; Electron Elec Eng Int St; Electron Elec Eng)

Cardiff – ABB–BBB 3AL pref 320–300 pts (MEng Elec Electron Eng; Electron Eng)

Dundee – 320–260 pts (MEng Electron Elec Eng; Electron Eng Mgt; Electron Eng Microcomp Sys; Electron Eng Phys)

Exeter – ABB–BBC (MEng Electron Eng)

Lancaster – ABB (MEng Electron Sys Eng; Mecha)

Leeds – ABB–BBB (MEng Electron Elec Eng; Electron Eng; Electron Comm Eng; Consum Electron; Nano)

Leicester – 320 pts (MEng Elec Electron Eng courses)

Liverpool – 320 pts (MEng Elec Eng Electron courses; Med Electron Instr)

Loughborough – 320 pts (Electron Soft Eng; Wrlss Comm Eng; Electron Elec Eng)

Manchester – ABB (MEng/BEng Elec Electron Eng; Electron Sys Eng)

Newcastle – ABB–BBB (MEng Electron Comm; Electron Sys Eng; Elec Electron Eng)

Reading – 320 pts (MEng Electron Eng courses; Cyber)

Southampton – ABB 320 pts (MEng/BEng Elec Eng; Electromech Eng)

Sussex – ABB–BBB 360–330 pts (MEng Elec Electron Eng; Electron Comm Eng; Electron Dig Tech)

300 pts **Aberdeen** – BBB 2nd yr entry (MEng Elec Electron Eng; Elec Electron Eng Euro St; Electron Eng Comm; Elec Electron Eng Contr; Elec Electron Eng Mgt; Electron Comp Eng)

Bangor – 300–320 pts (MEng Electron Eng)

Belfast (Queen's) – BBB (MEng Elec Electron Eng; Electron Soft Eng)

Bradford – 300 pts (MEng Elec Electron Eng; Electron Telecomm Intnet Eng)

City – 300–280 pts (MEng Elec Electron Eng)

Dundee – 300–240 pts (BEng Electron Elec Eng; Electron Eng Mgt; Electron Eng Microcomp Sys; Electron Eng Phys; Electron Comp)

Edinburgh – BBB (MEng/BEng Electron Elec Eng (Comm); Elec Eng; Electron; Electron Elec Mgt)

Essex – 300 pts (Telecomm Eng; Electron Eng; Optoelect Comm Sys)

Heriot-Watt – ABC 2nd yr entry (MEng Elec Electron Eng)

Hull – 300 pts (MEng Electron Eng)

Kent – 300 pts (MEng Electron Eng)

Lancaster – BBB (BEng Electron Sys Eng; Mecha)

London (King's) – BBB+AS **or** BBbb (Comp Sys Electron; Electron Eng)

London (QM) – 300–340 pts (MEng Electron Eng courses)

Newcastle – BBB–BBC (BEng Elec Electron Eng; Electron Comm)

Portsmouth – 300 pts (MEng Electron Elec Eng)

Robert Gordon – BBB (MEng Electron Elec Eng)

St Andrews – BBB 1st yr entry (Microelectron Photon)

Strathclyde – BBB–AAA 2nd yr entry (BEng Elec Ener Sys; Electron Dig Sys; Electron Elec Sys)

Sussex – BBB (BEng Elec Electron Eng; Electron Eng; Sat Comm Sp Sys)

Swansea – BBB (MEng Electron Elec Eng; Electron Comp Sci)

Warwick – BBB–BBC (BEng Electron Eng)

Westminster – 300 pts (MEng Electron Eng)

York – BBB–BBC (BEng Electron Eng)

280 pts **Aberdeen** – BBC 2nd yr entry (BEng Elec Electron Eng; Elec Electron Eng Euro St; Electron Eng Comm; Elec Electron Eng Contr; Electron Eng Soft Eng; Electron Eng Comp Eng; Electron Eng Mgt)

Bath – BBC **or** 2AL+2AS (BEng Elec Electron Eng; Electron Spc Sci Tech; Electron Comm Eng; Comp Electron Comm)

Brighton – 280 pts (Elec Electron Eng)

Cardiff – BBC 280 pts 3AL pref (BEng Electron Eng; Elec Electron Eng)

Exeter – BBC–CCC (BEng Electron Eng)

Glasgow – BBC (Electron Mus; Electron Elec Eng Euro; Electron Elec Eng Int)
Liverpool – 280 pts (BEng Elec Eng Electron; Med Electron Instr)
Reading – 280 pts (BEng Electron Eng courses)
Staffordshire – 280 pts (Electron Eng; Electron Sys Des)
Surrey – BBC–BBB (BEng Electron Eng; Electron Comp Eng; Dig Media Eng)

260 pts **Aberdeen** – BCC 1st yr entry (MEng Elec Electron Eng; Elec Electron Eng Euro St; Electron Eng Comm; Electron Eng Comp)
Aston – BCC–CCC (BEng Electron Elec Eng; Electron Eng Mgt St; Electron Eng Comp Sci; Electromech Eng; Multim Dig Intnet Sys; Electron Prod Des)
Belfast (Queen's) – BCC (BEng Elec Electron Eng; Electron Soft Eng)
Brunel – BCC 260 pts (Electron Elec Eng courses; Electron Microelec Eng)
Glamorgan – 260–220 pts (BEng Elec Electron Eng courses)
Glasgow – BCC (Electron Soft Eng; Electron Elec Eng)
Heriot-Watt – BCC 260 pts (Elec Electron Eng courses; Robot Cybertron; Comp Electron)
Huddersfield – 260–320 pts (MEng/BEng Electron Eng)
Kent – 260 pts (BEng Electron Comm Eng)
London (QM) – 260–300 pts (BEng Elec Electron Eng courses)
Leicester – 260 pts (BEng Elec Electron Eng)
Loughborough – 260 pts (BEng Electron Elec Eng)
Robert Gordon – BCC–CCC (BEng Electron Comm Eng; Electron Elec Eng; Electron Comp Eng; Artif Intel Electron Eng)
Swansea – BCC 260 pts (BEng Electron Elec Eng; Electron Comp Sci)
Ulster – 260 pts (Electron Comp Sys)
Westminster – BCC (BEng Electron Eng)

240 pts **Bangor** – 240–260 pts 2AL (BEng Electron Eng)
Bradford – 240 pts (BEng Elec Electron Eng; Electron Telecomm Intnet Eng)
Brighton – 240 pts (Dig Electron Comp Comm; Aud Electron)

For a quick reference offers calculator, fold out the inside back cover.

Schools of
Electronic Engineering
and Computer Science
University of Wales, Bangor

· PRIFYSGOL CYMRU ·
UNIVERSITY OF WALES
BANGOR
1884

Electronics and Computer Science at Bangor will provide you with the Science and Engineering training for the job you want. Our up-to-date courses are taught in a friendly and supportive atmosphere with well-equipped laboratories & teaching facilities, situated between the beaches of Anglesey and the mountains of Snowdonia.

Undergraduate Honours Courses:
MEng Electronic Engineering (4 years, H601)   BEng Electronic Engineering (3 years, H610)
MEng Communications and Computer Systems (4 years, H655)
BEng Communications and Computer Systems (3 years, H654)
BSc Creative Technologies (3 years, GW49)
BSc Computer Systems with Business Studies (3 years, H6N1)
BSc Computer Systems with Psychology (3 years, H6C8)
BSc Internet Systems and E-Commerce (3 years, NGC5)
BSc Computer Science with Mathematics (3 years, G4G1)
BSc Computer Science (3 years, G400)

NEW Courses, see www.seecs.bangor.ac.uk for further details:
3 year BSc Honours degrees in
   Electronics with Computer Science, Electronics with Finance, Electronics with Management

Further Information:
Please contact Admissions Tutor, Schools of Electronic Engineering and Computer Science, University of Wales, Bangor, Dean Street, Bangor, Gwynedd LL57 1UT.
Tel: 01248 382686   www.seecs.bangor.ac.uk
Email: admissions@informatics.bangor.ac.uk

City – CCC (Elec Electron Eng)
Greenwich – 240 pts (BEng Electron Eng; Elec Eng; Elec Electron Eng; Electron Comp Sys)
Hull – 240–300 pts (BEng Electron Eng; Electron Gmg Sys)
Liverpool John Moores – 240 pts (Elec Electron Eng; Broad Eng)
Manchester Met – 240 pts (Elec Electron Eng; Elec Electron Eng Euro; Comp Electron Eng)
Northumbria – 240 pts (Elec Electron Eng; Comm Electron Eng)
Plymouth – 240 pts (BEng Elec Electron Sys; Robot Auto Sys)
Portsmouth – 240 pts (BEng Electron Elec Eng)
Salford – 240 pts (Dig Electron Comp Sci)
Sheffield Hallam – 240 pts (Elec Electron Eng)
Strathclyde – CCC (BEng Electron Elec Eng courses)
Surrey – 240 pts (Fdn Electron Comp Eng)
220 pts **Bristol UWE** – 220–260 pts (Mus Sys Eng; Elec Electron Eng)
East London – 220–260 pts (BEng Elec Electron Eng; Elec Electron Eng (Contr) (Comm))
Glamorgan – 220–300 pts (Elec Electron St; Electron; Electron IT St; Electron Comm Eng)
Hertfordshire – 220 pts (Elec Electron Eng; Aud Vid Dig Broad Eng)
Huddersfield – 220–260 pts (Electron Des; Electron Mus Tech)
Napier – 220 pts (Electron Elec Eng; Mecha)
Oxford Brookes – CCD **or** CCcc (BEng Electron Sys Des)
Staffordshire – 220–280 pts (Electron Eng)
UCE Birmingham – 220 pts (Electron Eng; Electron Aud Eng)
Ulster – 220–180 pts (Electron Comms Soft)
200 pts **Anglia Ruskin** – 200 pts (Aud Tech Electron; Electron Comp Sci)
Central Lancashire – 200 pts (Electron Eng; Robot Mecha)
Coventry – 200 pts (Electron Eng)
De Montfort – 200–280 pts (Electron Eng)
Glasgow Caledonian – AC (BEng Electron)

Heriot-Watt – CDD 1st yr entry (BEng Elec Electron Eng courses; Electron Photon Eng; Robot Cybertron)
Liverpool – CDD 200 pts (Fdn Elec Eng Electron)
Liverpool John Moores – 200 pts (Broad Tech; Des Electron)
Oxford Brookes – CDD (BSc Electron Sys Des)
Portsmouth – 200 pts (BEng Electron Eng)
Reading – 200 pts (Fdn Electron Eng)
Westminster – CDD/EE (Dig Sig Proc; Electron Eng; Electron Comp)

180 pts **Derby** – 180 pts CC **or** DDee (Elec Electron Eng; Electron)
Glasgow Caledonian – BC (Elec Pwr Eng)
Leicester – 180–240 pts (Fdn Eng)
Plymouth – 180 pts (Electron Comm Sys)
Sheffield Hallam – 180 pts (Electron Eng)
Teesside – 180–240 pts (Elec Electron Eng)

160 pts **Bournemouth** – 160–240 pts (Electron Prod Des; Electron; Electron Contr Robot)
City – DDE (BSc Elec Electron Eng)
De Montfort – 160–240 pts (Electron Gms Tech)
Greenwich – 160 pts (Elec Electron Eng Tech)
Kent – 160 pts (Fdn Electron Eng)
London Met – 160 pts (Electron Comm Eng; Aud Electron)
London South Bank – CC (Elec Electron Eng)
Loughborough – CC (Fdn Elec Electron Eng)
Newport – 160 pts (Elec Eng; Electron Eng)

140 pts **Bolton** – 140–160 pts (Electron Comp Eng)
Cardiff (UWIC) – 140 pts (Electron Microcomp Sys; Electron Comm Sys)
Glasgow Caledonian – CD (BSc Electron Eng; Mecha)
North East Wales (IHE) – 140 pts (Elec Electron Eng; Aero Electron)
Robert Gordon – CD-CEE (BSc Electron Elec Eng)

120 pts **Aberdeen** – DD (BSc Electron courses)
Bradford – 120 pts (Fdn Cyber)
Southampton Solent – 120 pts (Electron Eng)
Swansea (IHE) – 120–180 pts (Comp Sys (Electron); Auto Electron Sys)

80 pts **Glamorgan** – 80–140 pts (Elec Electron Eng)
Greenwich – 80 pts (Ext Mecha)
Portsmouth – 80 pts (Ext Eng)
UHI Millennium Inst (IC) (NHC) – 80 pts (Elec Electron Eng)

Leeds Met – contact University

Alternative offers

IB offers Birmingham 32–36 pts; Brighton 30 pts; Bristol 36 pts; Bristol UWE 24–30 pts; Brunel 28 pts; Cambridge 38–42 pts; City 28–30 pts; Dundee 28 pts; Durham (MEng) 38 pts; Essex (BEng) 32–34 pts, (BSc) 24 pts; Exeter (MEng) 30–34 pts, (BEng) 26–30 pts; Kent 28 pts; Lancaster 32–34 pts; Leicester 30–32 pts; London (King's) 30 pts, (QM) 30–36 pts, (UCL) 34–38 pts; Loughborough 30–34 pts; Manchester 33 pts; Manchester Met 24 pts; Newcastle 32–34 pts; Nottingham 30–32 pts; Oxford 38–42 pts; Reading 29–32 pts; St Andrews 36 pts; Salford 30 pts; Sheffield 33 pts; Southampton 34 pts; Warwick 35–37 pts.

Scottish offers See **Chapter 7**.

OTHER HIGHER EDUCATION COURSES IN THE SUBJECT FIELD

Foundation degrees (contact the institutions for details) Birmingham City (Coll); Bolton; Bournemouth and Poole (Coll); Brighton City (Coll); Bristol City (Coll); De Montfort; East Lancashire (IHE); Farnborough (CT); Glamorgan; Hastings (Coll); Huddersfield; Leeds Met; London Electron (Coll); Mid-Kent (Coll); Newcastle (Coll); Northampton; Plymouth (CT); Portsmouth; Somerset (CAT); Southampton Solent; Staffordshire Reg (Fed); Thames Valley.

Higher National Diploma courses
100 pts and below

Abertay Dundee; Adam Smith (Coll); Anglia Ruskin; Barnsley (Univ Centre); Bath; Bedford (Coll); Bell (Coll); Blackpool and Fylde (Coll); Bolton; Bournemouth; Bradford (Coll); Bridgwater (Coll); Brighton; Bristol City (Coll); Bromley (CFHE); Brooklands (Coll); Burton (Coll); Canterbury Christ Church; Cardiff (UWIC); Carlisle (Coll); Central Lancashire; Chesterfield (Coll); Chichester (Coll); Coventry City (Coll); De Montfort; Derby; Doncaster (Univ Centre); Dudley (Coll); Dumfries and Galloway (Coll); Durham (Stockton); East Lancashire (IHE); East London; Exeter; Farnborough (CT); Forth Valley (Coll); Glamorgan; Glasgow Caledonian; Glasgow Met (Coll); Greenwich; Hastings (Coll); Havering (Coll); Hertfordshire; Huddersfield; James Watt (Coll); Kilmarnock (Coll); Kingston; Kingston (Coll); Lakes (Coll); Lincoln; Lincoln (Coll); Liverpool (CmC); Llandrillo Cymru (Coll); London Met; London South Bank; Loughborough (Coll); Manchester Met; Mid-Cheshire (Coll); Napier; Nescot; Newcastle (Coll); Newcastle under Lyme (Coll); Newport; North East Wales (IHE); North West London (Coll); Northampton; Northbrook (Coll); Northumbria; Oldham (Coll); Oxford Brookes; Oxford and Cherwell Valley (Coll); Pembrokeshire (Coll); People's (Coll); Plymouth; Portsmouth; Robert Gordon; Rotherham (CAT); St Helens (Coll); Salford; Salisbury (Coll); Sandwell (Coll); Sheffield Hallam; Shrewsbury (CAT); Solihull (Coll); Somerset (CAT); South Devon (Coll); Southampton Solent; Staffordshire; Stevenson (Coll); Stockport (CFHE); Stoke on Trent (Coll); Sunderland; Suffolk (Univ Campus); Swansea (IHE); Swindon (Coll); Tameside (Coll); Teesside; Thames Valley; UCE Birmingham; UHI Millennium Inst (IC), (NHC); Ulster; Uxbridge (Coll); Wakefield (Coll); Walsall (Coll); Warwickshire (Coll); West Suffolk (Coll); Westminster; Weymouth (Coll); Wigan and Leigh (Coll); Wolverhampton; York (Coll); Yorkshire Coast (CFHE).

CHOOSING YOUR COURSE (SEE ALSO CH.1)

Subject information Electrical and Electronic Engineering courses provide a sound foundation for those looking for a career in electricity generation and transmission, communications or control systems, including robotics. All courses cater for students wanting a general or specialist Engineering education and options should be considered when choosing degree courses. These could include optoelectronics and optical communication systems, microwave systems, radio frequency engineering and circuit technology. Many courses have common first years, allowing transfer in Year 2. Most universities and colleges have good industrial contacts and can arrange industrial placements, in some cases abroad. Useful websites www.theiet.org; www.engc.org.uk; www.enginuity.org.uk.

Course variations Electronics with Space Science Technology (Bath); Music, Audio and Electronic Systems (Cardiff (UWIC)); Consumer Electronics (Leeds); Medical Electronics and Instrumentation (Liverpool); Microelectronics and Photonics (St Andrews); Cybernetics (Southampton); Digital Media Engineering (Surrey); Satellite Communication and Space Systems (Sussex). *NOW CHECK PROSPECTUSES AND WEBSITES FOR ANY RECENT CHANGES.*

Universities and colleges teaching quality See www.tqi.ac.uk; www.qaa.ac.uk.

Top universities and colleges (Research) Aston; Belfast (Queen's); Birmingham; Bristol; Cardiff; Edinburgh*; Essex; Glasgow; Heriot-Watt; Imperial London; Leeds*; Liverpool; London (King's), (UCL); Loughborough; Newcastle; Reading; Sheffield*; Southampton*; Strathclyde; Surrey*; Ulster.

Sandwich degree courses Aston; Bath; Belfast (Queen's); Bournemouth; Bradford; Brighton; Bristol UWE; Brunel; Cardiff; Central Lancashire; City; Coventry; De Montfort; East London; Glamorgan; Glasgow Caledonian; Greenwich; Hertfordshire; Huddersfield; Kingston; Leicester; Liverpool John Moores; London Met; London South Bank; Loughborough; Manchester; Manchester Met; Middlesex; Northumbria; Nottingham Trent; Oxford Brookes; Plymouth; Portsmouth; Reading; Sheffield Hallam; Southampton Solent; Staffordshire; Surrey; Teesside; UCE Birmingham; Ulster; York.

ADMISSIONS INFORMATION

Number of applicants per place (approx) Abertay Dundee 3; Aston 6; Bath 8; Birmingham 7; Bolton 3; Bournemouth 3; Bradford (Electron Eng) 8; Bristol 5; Bristol UWE 8; Cardiff 7; Central Lancashire 4; City 10; Coventry 8; De Montfort 1; Derby 8; Dundee 5; Glamorgan 2; Glasgow Caledonian 5; Greenwich

10; Hertfordshire 7; Heriot-Watt 6; Huddersfield 5; Hull 8; Kent 5; Kingston 8; Leeds 15; Lancaster 7; Leicester 15; Lincoln 8; Liverpool John Moores 2; London (King's) 8, (UCL) 9; London South Bank 5; Manchester Met 5; Napier 8; Newcastle 9; North East Wales (IHE) 3; Northumbria 7; Nottingham 6, (Fdn courses) 6, (BEng/MEng) 8; Plymouth 22; Portsmouth 4; Robert Gordon 3; Salford 5; Sheffield 15; Sheffield Hallam 2; Southampton 10; Staffordshire 7; Strathclyde 7; Sunderland 6; Surrey (BEng) 6, (MEng) 3; Swansea 3; Teesside 4; UCE Birmingham 11; UHI Millennium Inst (IC) 1; Westminster 5; Warwick 8; York 5.

Advice to applicants and planning the UCAS personal statement **Liverpool John Moores** Enthusiasm for the subject, for example career ambitions, hobbies, work experience, attendance at appropriate events, competitions etc. **York** Our top priority is evidence of good ability in mathematics and also a scientific mind. Applicants should show that they can think creatively and have the motivation to succeed on a demanding course. See also **Engineering/Engineering Sciences** and **Appendix 2**.

Selection interviews Abertay Dundee, Aston, Bangor (Electron Eng only), Bath, Belfast (Queen's), Bournemouth, Bradford, Bristol, Bristol UWE, Cambridge, Central Lancashire, De Montfort, Derby, Durham, East Anglia (Electron Eng), Essex, Heriot-Watt, Hertfordshire, Huddersfield, Hull, Kingston, Lancaster, Liverpool, London (UCL), London South Bank, Loughborough, Newcastle, Nottingham, Oxford, Plymouth, Portsmouth, Southampton, Strathclyde, Sunderland, Surrey, Westminster, York; **Some** Anglia Ruskin, Brighton, Cardiff, Dundee, Kent, Leicester, Liverpool John Moores, Salford, Staffordshire.

Interview advice and questions Past questions have included: How does a combustion engine work? How does a trumpet work? What type of position do you hope to reach in five to ten years' time? Could you sack an employee? What was your last physics practical? What did you learn from it? What are the methods of transmitting information from a moving object to a stationary observer? Wire bending exercise – you are provided with an accurate diagram of a shape that could be produced by bending a length of wire in a particular way. You are supplied with a pair of pliers and the exact length of wire required and you are given 10 minutes to reproduce as accurately as possible the shape drawn. How does a transistor work? A three-minute talk had to be given on one of six subjects (topics given several weeks before the interview); for example, the best is the enemy of the good. Is there a lesson here for British industry? 'I was asked to take my physics file and discuss some of my conclusions in certain experiments.' Explain power transmission through the National Grid. How would you explain power transmission to a friend who hasn't done physics? **York** Questions based on a mathematical problem. See also **Chapter 6**.

Reasons for rejection (non-academic) Poor English. Inability to communicate. Frightened of technology or mathematics. Poor motivation and work ethic. Better suited to a less specialised engineering/science course. Some foreign applicants do not have adequate English. **Surrey** Can't speak English (it has happened!). See also **Engineering/Engineering Sciences**.

AFTER-RESULTS ADVICE

Universities with vacancies in Clearing (2006) Aberdeen; Aberystwyth; Anglia Ruskin; Aston; Bangor; Bath; Belfast (Queen's); Birmingham; Bolton; Bournemouth; Bristol; Bradford; Brunel; Central Lancashire; City; Coventry; De Montfort; Derby; Dundee; East London; Essex; Glamorgan; Glasgow; Glasgow Caledonian; Greenwich; Heriot-Watt; Hertfordshire; Huddersfield; Hull; Kent; Lancaster; Leeds; Leicester; Liverpool; Liverpool John Moores; London (King's), (QM), (RH); London South Bank; Loughborough; Manchester; Manchester Met; Newcastle; Northampton; Northumbria; Nottingham; Oxford Brookes; Plymouth; Portsmouth; Reading; Robert Gordon; Salford; Sheffield; Sheffield Hallam; Southampton; Southampton Solent; Staffordshire; Strathclyde; Surrey; Swansea; Thames Valley; UCE Birmingham; Warwick; Westminster; York.

Offers to applicants repeating A-levels **Higher** Belfast (Queen's), Brighton, Central Lancashire, Greenwich, Huddersfield, Kingston, Newcastle, Strathclyde, Warwick; **Possibly higher** Aston, City, De Montfort, Derby, Glasgow, Hertfordshire, North London, Portsmouth, Sheffield; **Same** Anglia Ruskin, Bangor, Bath, Birmingham, Bolton, Bradford, Cardiff, Coventry, Dundee, Hull, Kent, Leeds, Liverpool, Liverpool John Moores, London South Bank, Loughborough, Northumbria, Nottingham (usually), Robert Gordon, Salford, Southampton, Staffordshire, Surrey, York.

GRADUATE DESTINATIONS AND EMPLOYMENT (2005 HESA)
Graduates surveyed 2285 **Employed** 1315 **In further study** 295 **Assumed unemployed** 230.

OTHER DEGREE SUBJECTS FOR CONSIDERATION
Computer Science; Engineering (Aeronautical, Communications, Computer, Control); Mathematics; Physics.

ENGINEERING (MANUFACTURING)

NB The points totals shown to the left of the institutions are for ease of reference only. It must not be assumed that tariff points are always used by institutions or that they can be substituted for an offer in grades. The level of an offer is not necessarily indicative of the quality of a course.

Engineering Council statement See **Engineering/Engineering Sciences**.

COURSE OFFERS INFORMATION
Subject requirements/preferences See **Engineering/Engineering Sciences**.

Your target offers

360 pts **and above**
  Cambridge – AAA (Manuf Eng)
340 pts **Bath** – AAB (Manuf; Manuf Fr/Ger; Spo Eng)
  Durham – AAB (MEng Des Manuf Mgt)
  Warwick – AAB–ABB (MEng Manuf Mech Eng)
320 pts **Cardiff** – ABB (MEng Mech Manuf Eng)
  Loughborough – 320 pts (Innov Manuf Tech)
  Newcastle – ABB (Mech Manuf Eng)
  Nottingham – ABB–BCC (MEng Manuf Eng Mgt; Manuf Eng Mgt Fr/Ger/Ital/Jap/Span; Prod Des Manuf)
300 pts **Belfast (Queen's)** – BBB (MEng Manuf Eng; Mech Manuf Eng)
  London (QM) – 300 pts (Innov Entre Mgt Advnc Tech)
  Loughborough – BBB–BCC (MEng Prod Des Manuf; Manuf Eng Mgt)
  Strathclyde – BBB–CCC (Manuf Eng Tech courses)
  Warwick – BBB–BBC (BEng Manuf Mech Eng)
280 pts **Belfast (Queen's)** – BBC–BCC (BEng Manuf Eng)
  Cardiff – BBC (BEng Mech Manuf Eng)
  London (King's) – BBC–BCC (Eng Bus Mgt)
260 pts **Loughborough** – 260 pts (BEng Prod Des Manuf; Manuf Eng Mgt)
240 pts **Aston** – CCC (Eng Prod Des; Ind Prod Des; Prod Des Mgt; Sust Prod Des)
  Greenwich – 240 pts (BEng Manuf Sys Eng)
  Hertfordshire – 240–280 pts (Manuf Eng)
  Northumbria – 240 pts (Manuf Sys Eng)
220 pts **UCE Birmingham** – 220 pts (Mgt Manuf Sys)
180 pts **Glamorgan** – 180 pts (BSc Mech Manuf Eng)
  Glasgow Caledonian – BC (Manuf Sys Eng)
  Huddersfield – 180 pts (Manuf Ops Mgt)
  Teesside – 180–240 pts (Manuf Mgt)
160 pts **Portsmouth** – 160 pts (Mech Manuf Eng)
  Southampton Solent – 160 pts (Ycht Manuf Surv)
140 pts **Cardiff (UWIC)** – 140 pts (Manuf Sys Eng)
  Liverpool John Moores – 140 pts (Robotics)
100 pts **Greenwich** – 100 pts (Ext Manuf Sys Eng)
80 pts **Swansea (IHE)** – 80–340 pts (Mech Manuf Eng; Manuf Sys Eng)
  Leeds Met – contact University

Alternative offers
IB offers Aston 30–34 pts; Bath 36–34 pts; Cambridge 38–42 pts; Durham (MEng) 38 pts; Loughborough 34 pts; Warwick 35–37 pts.
Scottish offers See **Chapter 7**.

OTHER HIGHER EDUCATION COURSES IN THE SUBJECT FIELD

Foundation degrees (contact institutions for details) Bristol City (Coll); Darlington (CT); Derby (Coll); Glamorgan; Havering (Coll); Huddersfield; Huddersfield (CT); Swansea (IHE).

Higher National Diploma courses
100 pts Abertay Dundee; Anglia Ruskin; Barking (Coll); Bedford (Coll); Bedfordshire; Bell (Coll); Blackpool and Fylde (Coll); Bournemouth; Bradford (Coll); Brighton; Brighton and Hove City (Coll); Canterbury Christ Church; Cardiff (UWIC); Carlisle (Coll); Carmarthenshire (Coll); Central Lancashire; Coventry City (Coll); Derby; Dudley (Coll); East London; Farnborough (CT); Gateshead (Coll); Glamorgan; Gloucestershire (CAT); Greenwich; Hertfordshire; Huddersfield; Kingston; Leeds Met; Lincoln; Liverpool John Moores; Llandrillo Cymru (Coll); Manchester Met; Newbury (Coll); Newcastle (Coll); Nescot; Newport; North East Wales (IHE); Northbrook (Coll); Nottingham Trent; Oldham (Coll); Oxford Brookes; People's (Coll); Plymouth; Portsmouth; St Helens (Coll); Salford; Salisbury (Coll); Sheffield Hallam; Shrewsbury (CAT); Solihull (Coll); Somerset (CAT); Southampton Solent; Staffordshire; Stockport (CFHE); Stoke on Trent (Coll); Suffolk (Univ Campus); Swansea (IHE); Teesside; Thames Valley; UCE Birmingham; UHI Millennium Inst; Ulster; Warwickshire (Coll); Wigan and Leigh (Coll); Wirral Met (Coll); Wolverhampton; Yorkshire Coast (CFHE).

CHOOSING YOUR COURSE (SEE ALSO CH.1)

Subject information Manufacturing engineering is sometimes referred to as production engineering. It is a branch of the subject concerned with management aspects of engineering such as industrial organisation, purchasing, and the planning and control of operations. Courses are therefore geared to providing the student with a broad-based portfolio of knowledge in both the technical and business areas. **Useful websites** www.engc.org.uk; www.imeche.org.uk; www.enginuity.org.uk.

Course variations Manufacturing Systems Engineering (Greenwich); Manufacturing and Operations Management (Huddersfield); Innovative Manufacturing Technology (Loughborough); Manufacturing Engineering and Management with Japanese (Nottingham); Manufacturing and Mechanical Engineering (Warwick). *NOW CHECK PROSPECTUSES AND WEBSITES FOR ANY RECENT CHANGES.*

Universities and colleges teaching quality See www.tqi.ac.uk; www.qaa.ac.uk.

Top universities and colleges (Research) Aston; Bath*; Leeds*; London (King's), (QM); Loughborough; Nottingham; Strathclyde.

Sandwich degree courses See under **Engineering (Mechanical)**.

ADMISSIONS INFORMATION

Number of applicants per place (approx) Aston 6; Bath 18; Bristol UWE 3; Hertfordshire 1; Huddersfield 1; Loughborough 6; Northumbria 4; Nottingham 6; Sheffield Hallam 3; Strathclyde 8; Warwick 8.

Advice to applicants and planning the UCAS personal statement Work experience shadowing in industry should be mentioned. See **Engineering/Engineering Sciences**. See also **Appendix 2**.

Selection interviews Yes Cambridge, Coventry, Hertfordshire, Leeds, Loughborough, Nottingham, Oxford, Strathclyde.

Interview advice and questions Past questions include: What is the function of an engineer? Describe something interesting you have recently done in your A-levels. What do you know about careers in manufacturing engineering? Discuss the role of women engineers in industry. Why is a disc brake better than a drum brake? Would you be prepared to make people redundant to improve the efficiency of a production line? See also **Chapter 6**.

Reasons for rejection (non-academic) Mature students failing to attend interview are rejected. One applicant produced a forged reference and was immediately rejected. See also **Engineering/ Engineering Sciences**.

AFTER-RESULTS ADVICE

Universities with vacancies in Clearing (2006) Belfast (Queen's); Greenwich; Huddersfield; Loughborough; Newcastle; Nottingham; Portsmouth; Strathclyde; Ulster; Warwick.

Offers to applicants repeating A-levels Higher Strathclyde; **Possibly higher** Hertfordshire; **Same** Huddersfield, Nottingham.

GRADUATE DESTINATIONS AND EMPLOYMENT (2005 HESA)

Graduates surveyed 640 **Employed** 345 **In further study** 75 **Assumed unemployed** 65.

OTHER DEGREE SUBJECTS FOR CONSIDERATION

Business Studies; Computer Science; Engineering (Electrical, Mechanical); Physics; Technology.

ENGINEERING (MECHANICAL)

(including Agricultural Engineering, Automotive Engineering and Motorsport Engineering)

NB The points totals shown to the left of the institutions are for ease of reference only. It must not be assumed that tariff points are always used by institutions or that they can be substituted for an offer in grades. The level of an offer is not necessarily indicative of the quality of a course.

Engineering Council statement See **Engineering/Engineering Sciences**.

COURSE OFFERS INFORMATION

Subject requirements/preferences See **Engineering/Engineering Sciences**.

Your target offers

360 pts and above
> **Bristol** – AAA (Mech Eng; Mech Eng Euro)
> **Cambridge** – AAA (Eng (Mech Eng))
> **Oxford** – Offers vary eg AAA–AAB (Mech Eng)

340 pts Bath – AAB (Auto Eng; Mech Eng; Innov Eng Des; Auto Eng Fr/Ger; Mech Eng Fr/Ger; Innov Eng Des Fr/Ger; Spo Eng)
> **Brunel** – 340 pts (Mech Eng Auto Des)
> **Imperial London** – AAB 3AL **or** 2AL+2AS (MEng Mech Eng; Mech Eng Yr Abrd)
> **Liverpool** – AAB (MEng Mech Eng; Mech Sys Des Eng; Mecha Robot Sys; Mech Eng Bus)
> **London (UCL)** – AAB+AS–ABB+AS (MEng Mech Eng)
> **Loughborough** – 340 pts (MEng Auto Eng; Spo Tech; Mech Eng)
> **Nottingham** – AAB–BBB (MEng/BEng Mech Eng; Mech Eng Fr/Ger/Span; Mech Eng Mat Manuf; Mech Eng Maths; Mech Eng (Aerosp) (Auto) (Bioeng) (Bus))
> **Sheffield** – 340 pts (MEng Mech Eng; Mech Eng Ind Mgt; Mech Eng N Am; Mtrspo Eng Mgt; Spo Eng; Mech Eng Lang; Mech Sys Dig)
> **Southampton** – AAB 340 pts (MEng/BEng Mech Eng courses)
> **Strathclyde** – AAB (MEng Mech Eng; Mech Eng Aero; Mech Eng Int St)
> **Warwick** – AAB–ABB (MEng Mech Eng; Manuf Mech Eng; Auto Eng)

320 pts Belfast (Queen's) – ABB–BBB (MEng Mech Manuf Eng)
> **Birmingham** – ABB–BBC (MEng Mech Eng; Mech Eng Bus Mgt; Mech Auto Eng)
> **Cardiff** – ABB (MEng Mech Eng; Mech Manuf Eng)
> **City** – ABB–BBB (MEng Auto Mtrspo Eng; Mech Eng)
> **Durham** – ABB–AAC 3AL **or** 2AL+2AS (MEng Mech Eng)
> **Exeter** – ABB–BBC (MEng Mech Eng; Min Eng)

Glasgow – ABB (MEng Mech Eng (fast track); Mech Eng Aero; Mech Eng Euro; Mech Eng Des Eng)

Hertfordshire – 320 pts (MEng Auto Eng; Auto Eng Mtrspo)

Lancaster – ABB (MEng Eng (Mech); Mecha)

Leicester – 320 pts (MEng Mech Eng)

London (QM) – 320 pts (MEng Mech Eng courses; Spo Eng)

Manchester – ABB (MEng Mech Eng courses; Mecha Eng courses)

Newcastle – ABB (MEng Mech Eng courses)

Sheffield – 320 pts (BEng Mech Eng)

Sussex – ABB–BBB (MEng Auto Eng; Mech Eng)

Swansea – 320 pts (MEng Mech Eng)

300 pts **Aberdeen** – BBB (MEng Mech Eng courses)

Aston – BBB or 2AL+2AS (MEng Electromech Eng; Mech Eng)

Bradford – 300 pts (MEng Mech Eng; Med Eng; Mech Auto Eng)

Brunel – 300 pts (MEng Mech Eng Bld Serv; Mech Eng Auto Des; Mech Eng Aero; Mech Eng Auto Des; Mech Eng)

Dundee – 300–240 pts (BEng Mech Eng)

Edinburgh – BBB (Mech Eng; Mech Eng Mgt; Mech Eng Renew Ener; Elec Mech Eng)

Hull – 300 pts (MEng Mech Eng; Mech Med Eng)

Lancaster – BBB (BEng Eng (Mech); Mecha)

Leeds – BBB–BBC (Auto Eng; Mech Eng; Mecha; Med Eng)

London (King's) – BBB+AS or BBbb (Mecha; Mech Eng)

London (UCL) – BBB+AS–BBC+AS (BEng Mech Eng)

Loughborough – BBB–ABC 300 pts (BEng Auto Eng)

Manchester – BBB (BEng Mech Eng courses)

Oxford Brookes – BBB–DD (Mech Eng; Auto Eng; Mtrspo Eng)

Portsmouth – 300 pts (MEng Mech Eng)

Robert Gordon – BBB/ABC 300 pts (MEng Mech Eng)

Salford – 300 pts (MEng Mech Eng (Aerosp))

Sheffield – BBB–ABC 300 pts (Fdn Mech Eng; Mech Sys Eng; Mecha)

Sheffield Hallam – 300 pts (MEng Mech Eng)

Strathclyde – BBB (BEng Mech Eng; Mech Eng Int St)

Surrey – BBB (MEng Mech Eng; Sust Sys Eng)

Sussex – BBB–BBC (BEng Mech Eng; Auto Eng)

Warwick – BBB–BBC+AS (BEng Manuf Mech Eng; Mech Eng; Auto Eng)

280 pts **Aberdeen** – BBC 2nd yr entry (CCD 1st yr entry) (BEng Mech Eng; Mech Eng Comp Aid Eng; Mech Eng Contr; Mech Eng Euro St; Mech Eng Mgt; Mech Eng Oil Gas St)

Birmingham – 280–320 pts (BEng Mech Eng; Mech Mat Eng)

Brighton – 280 pts (MEng Mech Eng)

Brunel – 280 pts (BEng Mtrspo Eng)

Cardiff – BBC (BEng Mech Manuf Eng)

Exeter – BBC–CCC (BEng Mech Eng; Min Eng)

Harper Adams (UC) – 280–300 pts (Agric Eng; Off Rd Veh Des)

Heriot-Watt – BBC 2nd yr entry (Mech Eng; Mech Eng Comp Aid Eng; Mech Ener Eng; Auto Eng; Robot Cyber)

Liverpool – 280 pts (BEng Mech Eng; Mech Sys Des Eng; Mecha Robot Sys; Mech Eng Bus)

London (UCL) – BBC+AS–BCC+AS (BEng Mech Eng)

Newcastle – BBC (BEng Mech Eng courses)

Staffordshire – 280–200 pts (Mech Eng Spo Tech; Mecha; Mech Eng; Foren Comp Mech Eng)

260 pts **Aston** – BCC–CCC (BEng Mech Eng; Electromech Eng; Eng Prod Des)

Belfast (Queen's) – BCC–BBC (BEng Mech Eng)

Brighton – 260 pts (Mech Eng; Auto Eng)

Coventry – 260 pts (BEng Mech Eng; Auto Eng; Auto Eng Des)
Edinburgh – BCC (BEng Mech Eng courses)
Glasgow – BCC (BEng Prod Des Eng; Mech Eng; Mech Eng Aero; Mech Eng Euro; Mech Des Eng)
Heriot-Watt – BCC 2nd yr entry (Robot Cybertron)
Hertfordshire – 260 pts (BEng Auto Eng; Mech Eng; Auto Eng Mtrspo)
Huddersfield – 260 pts (MEng Auto Eng; Auto Des; Mech Eng; Eng Des (Mech); Mtrspo Eng)
Leeds – BCC (Min Miner Eng)
Leicester – 260 pts (BEng Mech Eng; Prod Des)
London (QM) – 260–340 pts (BEng Mech Eng courses; Spo Eng)
Loughborough – 260 pts (Mech Eng)
Robert Gordon – BCC (BEng Mech Eng; Mech Off Eng; Mech Env Eng; Mech Eng Ener Eng; Artif Intel Mech Eng)
Surrey – BCC (BEng Mech Eng)
Swansea – 260 pts (BEng Mech Eng courses)

240 pts **Bradford** – 240 pts (BEng Mech Eng; Mech Auto Eng; Med Eng)
Brunel – 240 pts (BEng Mech Eng Bld Serv; Mech Eng; Mech Eng Auto Des; Mech Eng Aero; Spo Tech)
Central Lancashire – 240 pts (Mtrspo Eng)
City – BCD–CCD (BEng Auto Mtrspo Eng; Mech Eng)
Glamorgan – 240–260 pts (BEng Mech Eng; Mecha Eng)
Glasgow – CCC (BEng Mech Eng; Mech Eng Aero; Mech Eng Euro; Prod Des Eng; Mech Des Eng)
Greenwich – 240 pts (BEng Mech Eng; Ind Autom; Mecha)
Hull – 240 pts (BEng Mech Eng; Prod Innov)
Kingston – 240 pts (BEng Mech Eng)
Liverpool John Moores – 240 pts (Mecha; Auto Eng; Mech Eng; Mech Mar Eng)
Northumbria – 240 pts (Mech Eng)
Plymouth – 240 pts (BEng Mech Eng)
Portsmouth – 240 pts (Mech Eng)
Salford – 240 pts (BEng Mech Eng (Aerosp))
Sheffield Hallam – 240 pts (Mech Comp Aid Eng)
Strathclyde – CCC (Spo Eng)
Surrey – CCC (BEng Mech Eng; Fdn Mech Eng)

220 pts **Bradford** – 220 pts (Auto Des Tech)
Bristol UWE – 220–260 pts (Mech Eng; Mtrspo Eng)
Heriot-Watt – CCD 1st yr entry (Mech Eng; Mech Eng Comp Aid Eng; Auto Eng; Mech Eng Ener Eng; Robot Cybertron)
Huddersfield – 220 pts (BEng Auto Des; Auto Eng; Eng Des Mech; Mech Eng; Mtrspo Eng)
Napier – 220 pts (Mech Eng; Mecha; Spo Tech)
UCE Birmingham – 220–240 pts (Mech Eng; Auto Eng)
Ulster – 220 pts (BEng Mech Eng)

200 pts **Belfast (Queen's)** – BB–BC (BSc Agric Tech)
Bolton – 200 pts (Autombl Eng; Mech Eng)
Coventry – 200–240 pts (Mtrspo Eng; Veh Des; Mtrspo Mtrcycl Eng; Auto Eng Des; Mtrspo Pwrtrn Eng)
Dundee – 200 pts (BEng Mech Eng without hons)
Hertfordshire – 200 pts (BSc Auto Tech Mgt; Mtrspo Tech)
Liverpool – 200 pts (BEng Fdn Mech Eng)
Manchester Met – 200–240 pts (Mech Eng; Autom Contr; Auto Eng)
Northumbria – 200 pts (Comp Aid Prod Des)
Portsmouth – 200 pts (Prod Des Innov; Prod Des Modn Mats)
Sheffield Hallam – 200 pts (Spo Equip Dev)
Sunderland – 200 pts (Auto courses; Mech Eng Des)

For information on how to read the Subject Tables, see **Chapter 7**.

Swansea – 200 pts (Fdn Mech Eng)
180 pts **Central Lancashire** – 180–200 pts (Mtrspo Ops; Robot Mecha)
Dundee – 180–200 pts (BSc Mech Eng)
Glamorgan – 180 pts (Mech Manuf Eng)
Glasgow Caledonian – 180 pts (Mech Electron Sys Eng)
Leicester – 180–240 pts (Fdn Eng)
Manchester Met – 180–220 pts (BSc Mech Eng; Mech Eng Tech Auth)
Sheffield Hallam – 180 pts (Mech Eng)
Teesside – 180–240 pts (Mech Eng)
160 pts **Blackpool and Fylde (Coll)** – 160 pts (Mech Prod Eng; Mecha)
Greenwich – 160 pts (Mech Eng Tech)
Harper Adams (UC) – 160 pts (Eng Des Dev; Agric Eng Mark Mgt; Agric Eng; Offrd Veh Des)
Plymouth – 160 pts (BSc Mech Des Manuf; Mech Des Manuf Bus St; Mech Eng Comp Aid Des)
Portsmouth – 160 pts (Mech Manuf Eng)
Salford – 160 pts (BSc Mech Eng (Aerosp))
Wolverhampton – 160–200 pts (Auto Sys Eng; Mech Eng; Mecha)
140 pts **Bolton** – 140 pts (Autombl Tech)
Cardiff (UWIC) – 140 pts (Mech Sys Eng)
Glamorgan – 140–180 pts (BSc Mech Manuf Eng)
Glasgow Caledonian – CD/DDE (Mechatronics)
Kingston – 140 pts (Mtrcycl Eng Des; Mech Eng Des; Auto Eng Des; Mtrspo Eng)
North East Wales (IHE) – 140 pts (Auto Electron Tech; Mtrspo Des Mgt; Perf Car Tech)
Paisley – CD (Mech Eng)
Robert Gordon – CD (BSc Mech Eng)
Sheffield Hallam – 140 pts (Auto Tech)
Swansea (IHE) – 140 pts (Auto Eng; Mech Manuf Eng; Mtrspo Eng Des)
120 pts **Aberdeen** – DD (BSc Mech Eng)
London South Bank – DD (Mech Eng; Mecha)
Southampton Solent – 120 pts (Mech Des)
100 pts **CAFRE** – 100 pts (Agric Tech)
Coventry – 100 pts (Fdn Mtrspo Eng)
Hull – 100 pts (BEng Mech Eng 4 yrs)
Kingston – 100 pts (Auto Eng St; Mech Eng St; Mtrcycl Eng St)
80 pts **Greenwich** – 80 pts (Ext Mech Eng)
Hertfordshire – 80 pts (BEng Eng Ext)
Stockport (CFHE) – 80 pts (Mech Eng)
UHI Millennium Inst (NHC) – (Mech Eng)

Alternative offers
IB offers Bath 36 pts; Birmingham 32–34 pts; Brighton 30 pts; Bristol 38 pts; Bristol UWE 24–30 pts; Brunel 28–30 pts; Cambridge 38–42 pts; City 28–30 pts; Dundee 28 pts; Exeter (MEng) 30–34 pts, (BEng) 26–30 pts; Lancaster 30 pts; Leicester 30–32 pts; Liverpool 29–32 pts; London (King's) 30 pts, (QM) 30–32 pts, (UCL) 34–36 pts; Loughborough 34 pts; Manchester 34–36 pts; Manchester Met 26 pts; Newcastle 30–34 pts; Nottingham 33 pts; Oxford 38–42 pts; Salford 27–32 pts; Sheffield 32 pts; Southampton 34 pts; Warwick 35–37 pts.
Scottish offers See **Chapter 7**.

OTHER HIGHER EDUCATION COURSES IN THE SUBJECT FIELD

Foundation degrees (contact the institutions for details) Blackpool and Fylde (Coll); Bolton; Bridgwater (Coll); Brighton City (Coll); Central Lancashire; Colchester (Inst); Coventry; Derby; East Lancashire (IHE); Farnborough (CT); Glamorgan; Hastings (Coll); Havering (Coll); Kingston; Myerscough (Coll); Newcastle (Coll); Northampton; Oxford Brookes; Sheffield Hallam; Somerset (CAT); Swansea (IHE); Tameside (Coll); Warwickshire (Coll); West Nottinghamshire (Coll). **Agricultural Engineering** Bicton (Coll); Harper Adams (UC).

Higher National Diploma courses
100 pts and below
Abertay Dundee; Accrington and Rossendale (Coll); Adam Smith (Coll); Anglia Ruskin; Bangor; Barnsley (Univ Centre); Bedford (Coll); Bedfordshire; Bell (Coll); Birmingham City (Coll); Blackpool and Fylde (Coll); Bolton; Bournemouth; Bradford (Coll); Bridgwater (Coll); Brighton; Bromley (CFHE); Brooklands (Coll); Burton (Coll); Cambridge Reg (Coll); Cardiff (UWIC); Carlisle (Coll); Carmarthenshire (Coll); Central Lancashire; Chesterfield (Coll); Coventry; Coventry City (Coll); Crawley (Coll); De Montfort; Derby; Doncaster (Univ Centre); Dudley (Coll); East Lancashire (IHE); Farnborough (CT); Forth Valley (Coll); Furness (Coll); Glamorgan; Glasgow (Coll); Gloucester (CAT); Glasgow Caledonian; Greenwich; Grimsby (IFHE); Guildford (Coll); Harper Adams (UC); Hastings (Coll); Hertfordshire; Highbury (Coll); Huddersfield; Kingston; Kingston (Coll); Lincoln; Liverpool (CmC); Liverpool John Moores; Llandrillo Cymru (Coll); Loughborough (Coll); Manchester Met; Mid-Kent (Coll); Myerscough (Coll); Newcastle (Coll); Newport; North East Wales (IHE); North Herts (Coll); Northampton; Northbrook (Coll); Northumbria; Norwich City (Coll); Oldham (Coll); Oxford Brookes; Oxford and Cherwell Valley (Coll); People's (Coll) Nottingham; Plymouth; Portsmouth; Robert Gordon; Rycotewood (Coll); St Helens (Coll); SAC (Scottish CAg); Sheffield Hallam; Shrewsbury (CAT); Solihull (Coll); Somerset (CAT); South Cheshire (Coll); Southampton Solent; Staffordshire; Stevenson (Coll); Stockport (CFHE); Stoke on Trent (Coll); Suffolk (Univ Campus); Sunderland; Swansea (IHE); Tameside (Coll); Teesside; Thames Valley; UCE Birmingham; UHI Millennium Inst (NHC); Ulster; Uxbridge (Coll); Warrington (Coll); Warwickshire (Coll); West Herts (Coll); West Suffolk (Coll); Westminster; Weymouth (Coll); Wigan and Leigh (Coll); Wiltshire (Coll); Wirral Met (Coll); Wolverhampton; Worcestershire New (Coll); Writtle (Coll); Yorkshire Coast (CFHE).

CHOOSING YOUR COURSE (SEE ALSO CH.1)
Subject information Mechanical Engineering is one of the most wide-ranging engineering disciplines. Mechanical engineers share interests such as structures and stress analysis with civil and aeronautical engineers as well as electronics and computing with electrical and software engineers. All courses involve the design, installation and maintenance of equipment used in industry. Several universities include a range of Engineering courses with a common first year allowing students to specialise from Year 2. Agricultural Engineering involves all aspects of off-road vehicle design and maintenance of other machinery used in agriculture. **Useful websites** www.imeche.org.uk; www.engc.org.uk; www.iagre.org.

Course variations Agricultural Technology (Belfast (Queen's)); Mechanical Engineering with Aeronautics (Brunel, Glasgow); Offroad Vehicle Design (Harper Adams); Mechatronics (Lancaster); Mechatronics and Robotic Systems (Liverpool); Automotive Engineering (Loughborough); Mechanical Engineering and Materials Manufacture (Nottingham); Motorsport Engineering Management (Sheffield); Mechanical Engineering with International Studies (Strathclyde). *NOW CHECK PROSPECTUSES AND WEBSITES FOR ANY RECENT CHANGES.*

Universities and colleges teaching quality See www.tqi.ac.uk; www.qaa.ac.uk.

Top universities and colleges (Research) (Engineering, including Aeronautical and Manufacturing Engineering) Aston; Bath*; Bristol; Brunel; Glasgow; Imperial London*; Leeds*; London (King's), (QM), (UCL); Loughborough; Manchester; Nottingham; Sheffield; Southampton; Strathclyde.

Sandwich degree courses Aston; Bath; Belfast (Queen's); Bradford; Brighton; Bristol UWE; Brunel; Cardiff; Central Lancashire; City; Coventry; East London; Glamorgan; Glasgow Caledonian; Greenwich; Harper Adams (UC); Hertfordshire; Huddersfield; Kingston; Leicester; Liverpool John Moores; London (QM); London South Bank; Loughborough; Manchester Met; Northumbria; Nottingham Trent; Oxford Brookes; Paisley; Plymouth; Portsmouth; Salford; Sheffield Hallam; Staffordshire; Sunderland; Surrey; Teesside; UCE Birmingham; Ulster.

ADMISSIONS INFORMATION
Number of applicants per place (approx) Abertay Dundee 4; Aston 8; Bath (MEng) 13; Birmingham 8; Blackpool and Fylde (Coll) 1; Bradford 4; Brighton 10; Bristol 8; Bristol UWE 17; Brunel 12; Cardiff 8;

Coventry 8; City 13; Dundee 5; Durham 8; Glamorgan 6; Hertfordshire 10; Heriot-Watt 9; Huddersfield 1; Hull 11; Kingston 8; Lancaster 8; Leeds 15; Leicester 11; Liverpool 6; Liverpool John Moores (Mech Eng) 2; London (King's) 8, (QM) 6; London South Bank 4; Loughborough 8, (Mech Eng) 12, (Auto Eng) 7; Manchester Met 6, (Mecha) 2, (Mech Eng) 6; Newcastle 10; North East Wales (IHE) 4; Northumbria 4; Nottingham 8; Plymouth 6; Portsmouth 6; Sheffield 10; Southampton 8; Staffordshire 6; Strathclyde 6; Surrey 9; Teesside 7; Warwick 8; Westminster 11.

Advice to applicants and planning the UCAS personal statement Cardiff Work experience; hands-on skills; self-starter. **Liverpool** An interest in solving mathematical problems related to physical concepts. Enjoyment in designing mechanical devices or components. Interest in engines, structures, dynamics or fluid flow and efficient use of materials or energy. **London (UCL)** We encourage applicants to apply for the Year in Industry Scheme (www.yini.org.uk) for placement. Scholarships are available to supplement the scheme. Students have the opportunity to work in industry for a year during their degree course. See **Engineering/Engineering Sciences**. See also **Appendix 2**

Misconceptions about this course Loughborough Although organised by the Wolfson School of Manufacturing and Mechanical Engineering, the degree does not include manufacturing.

Selection interviews Yes Aston, Belfast (Queen's), Birmingham, Bolton, Bradford, Brighton, Bristol, Brunel, Cambridge, Cardiff, Durham, Hertfordshire, Huddersfield, Kingston, Lancaster, Leeds, Leicester, Liverpool John Moores, London (QM), London South Bank, Loughborough, Manchester Met, Newcastle, Nottingham, Oxford, Sheffield, Sheffield Hallam, Strathclyde, Sunderland, Surrey, Sussex; **Some** Blackpool and Fylde (Coll), Dundee, Liverpool, Staffordshire.

Interview advice and questions Past questions include: What mechanical objects have you examined and/or tried to repair? How do you see yourself in five years' time? What do you imagine you would be doing (production, management or design engineering)? What engineering interests do you have? What qualities are required to become a successful mechanical engineer? Do you like sixth form work? Describe the working of parts on an engineering drawing. How does a fridge work? What is design in the context of mechanical engineering? What has been your greatest achievement to date? What are your career aspirations? **Hertfordshire** All interviewees receive a conditional offer. **Sunderland** Provide an example of working as part of a team, meeting a deadline, working on your own. See also **Engineering/Engineering Sciences**. See also **Chapter 6**.

Reasons for rejection (non-academic) See **Engineering/Engineering Sciences**.

AFTER-RESULTS ADVICE

Universities with vacancies in Clearing (2006) Aberdeen; Aston; Belfast (Queen's); Birmingham; Bolton; Bradford; Brighton; Bristol UWE; Brunel; Central Lancashire; City; Coventry; Derby; Dundee; Glamorgan; Glasgow; Glasgow Caledonian; Greenwich; Heriot-Watt; Hertfordshire; Huddersfield; Hull; Kingston; Lancaster; Leeds; Leicester; Liverpool; Liverpool John Moores; London (King's), (QM); London South Bank; Loughborough; Manchester; Manchester Met; Napier; Newcastle; Northumbria; Nottingham; Oxford Brookes; Plymouth; Portsmouth; Robert Gordon; Salford; Sheffield; Sheffield Hallam; Southampton; Staffordshire; Sunderland; Swansea; UCE Birmingham; Ulster; Warwick.

Offers to applicants repeating A-levels Higher Belfast (Queen's), Brighton, Dundee, Kingston, Loughborough, Newcastle, Swansea, Warwick; **Possibly higher** City, Durham, Huddersfield; **Same** Aston, Bath, Blackpool and Fylde (Coll), Bradford, Bristol, Brunel, Coventry, Derby, East London, Heriot-Watt, Leeds (usually), Lincoln, Liverpool, Liverpool John Moores, London South Bank, Manchester Met, Napier, Northumbria, Nottingham, Oxford Brookes, Sheffield, Sheffield Hallam, Southampton, Staffordshire, Sunderland, Surrey, Teesside.

GRADUATE DESTINATIONS AND EMPLOYMENT (2005 HESA)
Graduates surveyed 1855 **Employed** 1150 **In further study** 220 **Assumed unemployed** 155.

OTHER DEGREE SUBJECTS FOR CONSIDERATION
Engineering (Building, Manufacturing, Marine); Materials Science; Mathematics; Physics.

ENGLISH

(including **Creative Writing**)

NB The points totals shown to the left of the institutions are for ease of reference only. It must not be assumed that tariff points are always used by institutions or that they can be substituted for an offer in grades. The level of an offer is not necessarily indicative of the quality of a course.

COURSE OFFERS INFORMATION

Subject requirements/preferences GCSE A foreign language may be preferred. **Aberdeen, Dundee, Edinburgh, Glasgow, St Andrews** Mathematics and foreign language required. **Aberystwyth** English Literature grade B. **Birmingham** Five–six grades A*, A or B plus decent grade in mathematics (not applicable to mature students). **Cardiff** No fixed target, the higher the better. **Leeds** Good GCSEs sought. **Liverpool** Grade Bs are important. **Newman (CHE)** Five subjects grades A–C. **London South Bank** Five subjects minimum at grade A–C. **Reading** Seven subjects at grade A–C. **Swansea (IHE)** Three subjects minimum at grade A–C. **York** A good grade in another language. **AL** English with specific grades usually stipulated. Modern languages required for joint courses with languages.

Your target offers

360 pts **and above**
Bristol – AAA no pts offer (Engl; Engl Phil; Dr Engl; Engl Class St)
Cambridge – AAA (Engl; A-Sxn Nrs Celt)
Durham – AAA (Engl Lit; Engl Lit Hist)
Exeter – AAA–AAB (Engl; Engl Film St; Engl N Am)
London (UCL) – AAA+AS–AAB+AS (Engl; Engl Ger)
Oxford – Offers vary eg AAA–AAB (Engl Lang Lit; Class Engl; Engl Modn Langs; Hist Engl)
Warwick – AABb **or** AAaab (Engl Lit; Engl Am Lit; Engl Lit Crea Writ; Engl Fr Lit; Eng Ger Lit; Eng It Lit; Eng Lat Lit; Engl Lit Thea St)
York – AAA–AAB (Engl; Engl Educ; Engl Hist Art; Engl Pol; Engl Hist; Engl Phil; Engl Ling)

340 pts **Birmingham** – AAB (English)
Cardiff – AAB (Engl Lit courses; Engl Lang)
Durham – AAB (Engl Lit Phil; Engl Comb Hons)
East Anglia – AAB (Engl Lit Crea Writ; Engl Lit)
Exeter – AAB–ABB (Engl Fr/Ger/Ital/Russ/Span)
Leeds – AAB (Engl; Engl Lang; Engl Lang Lit; Engl Lang Lit Thea St)
Liverpool – AAB 340 pts (Engl Lang Lit; Engl Comm St; Engl Modn Hist; Engl Phil)
Manchester – AAB (Engl Lit Dr; Engl Lit)
Newcastle – AAB (Engl Lit; Engl Lang Lit)
Nottingham – AAB (Engl St)
Reading – 340 pts (3AL) 360 pts (3AL+AS) (Engl courses except under **300/280 pts**)
St Andrews – AAB (Engl courses)
Sheffield – AAB (Engl Hist; Engl Lit)
Southampton – AAB (English)
Sussex – AAB–ABB **or** 380–360 pts 3AL+AS (Engl courses; Engl Lang courses)

320 pts **Cardiff** – ABB (Cult Crit Engl Lit)
Durham – ABB (Educ St (Engl St))
East Anglia – ABB–BBB (Engl Am Lit; Engl Lit Dr)
Glasgow – ABB (Engl Lit; Engl Lang; Scot Lit)
Keele – 320 pts (Engl Am Lit)
Lancaster – ABB–BBB (Engl Lang courses; Engl Lit courses; Engl Lit Crea Writ)
Leeds – ABB–BBC (Engl joint courses)
London (King's) – ABB+AS (Engl Lang Lit; Engl Film)
London (RH) – ABB (Engl courses)
Loughborough – 320–300 pts (Engl; Engl N Am Lit Film; Pub Engl)
Manchester – ABB (Engl Lang Fr)

Manchester – ABB–BBB (Engl Lang)
Newcastle – ABB (Engl Lang)
Nottingham – ABB (Engl St courses except under **340/300 pts**)
Sheffield – ABB (Engl Fr; Engl Phil)
Southampton – ABB 320 pts (Engl courses except under **340 pts**)

300 pts **Belfast (Queen's)** – BBB (Engl courses)
Birmingham – BBB (Modn Langs Engl Lit; Mediev Engl Hist; Engl Lang Lit Educ; Engl courses)
Bournemouth – 300 pts (Scrptwr Film TV)
Chester – 300 pts (English)
Dundee – BBB–CCC (Engl courses)
East Anglia – BBB–BBC (Engl St; Engl Compar Lit; Cult Lit Pol)
Edinburgh – BBB (Engl Lang courses; Engl Lit courses; Scot Lit courses)
Essex – 300 pts (Engl Lit; Lit Myth; Crea Writ; Lit Hist Art; Compar Lit; Lit Sociol)
Exeter (Cornwall) – BBB–CCC (Engl Corn St)
Leicester – 300–320 pts (Engl; Engl Am St; Engl Hist)
London (Gold) – ABC–BBB (Engl; Media Modn Lit; Engl Am Lit; Engl Hist; Engl Compar Lit; Engl Dr)
London (QM) – 300–370 pts (Engl; Engl Ling; Engl Dr; Engl Hist; Engl Fr/Ger/Russ; Engl Hisp St)
Manchester – BBB (Engl Lit Chin/Ger/Ital/Port/Russ/Span; Engl Lang Ger/Ital/Span/Russ)
Nottingham – ABC (Engl St Russ; Engl St Serb Croat)
Oxford Brookes – BBB **or** BBbb (Engl St)
Reading – 300–340 pts (Engl Comb courses)
Sheffield – BBB (Bib St Engl; Engl Ger; Engl Mus; Engl Russ)
Swansea – 300 pts (Engl single hons courses)

280 pts **Aberystwyth** – 280 pts (Engl Lit; Crea Writ Engl)
Aston – 280–300 pts (Engl Lang joint courses)
Brighton – 280 pts (Engl Sociol)
Bristol UWE – 280–320 pts (Engl; Dr Engl; Film St Eng; Cult Media St Engl)
Brunel – 280 pts (Engl; Engl Film TV St; Engl Mus; Engl Crea Writ)
Essex – 280 pts (Engl Lang Ling; Engl Lang Lit)
Glasgow (Crichton) – BBC (Crea Cult St)
Kent – 280 pts (Engl Am Lit; Engl Lang St)
Liverpool – BBC (Engl Fr/Ger; Engl Hisp St)
London (King's) – BBC+AS **or** BBbb (Fr Engl; Ger Engl; Gk Engl; Hisp St Engl; Lat Engl; Port Braz St Engl)
Manchester Met – 280 pts (Engl see also under **220 pts**; Engl Crea Writ)
Northumbria – 280 pts (Engl; Engl Film St; Journal Engl; Engl Hist; Engl Crea Writ; Engl Sociol)

Nottingham – BBC (Vkng St)
Plymouth – 280 pts (Engl; Engl Crea Writ)
Reading – 280 pts (3AL) 300 pts (3AL+AS) (App Engl Lang St)
Sheffield Hallam – 280 pts (Engl St)
Strathclyde – BBC (Journal Crea Writ)

260 pts **Coventry** – 260 pts (Engl; Engl joint courses; Engl Journal St; TEFL)
Huddersfield – 260 pts (Engl St; Engl Lang courses; Engl Lit courses)
Hull – 260–300 pts (Engl Modn Lang; Engl Film St; Engl Hist; Engl Mus; Engl Phil; Engl Theol; Engl Hist Art; Engl Crea Writ; Engl Gndr St; Engl)
Keele – 260–320 pts (Engl courses)
Kent – 260–320 pts (Engl Lit)
Leicester – 260–320 pts (Engl Comb courses)
Lincoln – 260 pts (English)
Liverpool – 260 pts (Irish St Engl Lang Lit)
Liverpool John Moores – 260 pts (4AL) 220 pts (3AL) 160 pts (2AL) (Imgntv Writ; Engl; Engl Lit Crea Electron Tech)
Northumbria – 260 pts (Engl Art Hist; Engl Lang St)
Sheffield Hallam – 260 pts (Engl Hist)
Stirling – BCC (Engl St; Scot Lit)
Strathclyde – BCC/BB (English)
Swansea – 260–280 pts (Engl joint hons courses)
Ulster – BCC 260 pts (English)
Westminster – BCC (Engl courses)
Winchester – BCC/BC (Engl Lang courses; Engl Lit courses)

240 pts **Aberdeen** – CCC (Engl courses; Engl Scot Lit; Scot St)
Bangor – 240–280 pts (Engl; Engl Crea Writ; Engl Thea St; Engl Journal; Engl Lang Film St; Engl Lit Engl Lang; Engl Am Lit Cult)
Bournemouth – 240–280 pts (Engl Hist)
Bradford – 240 pts (Engl courses)
Brighton – 240 pts (Engl St Engl Lit; Engl Lang Engl Lit; Engl St Ling; Engl St Media)
Chester – 240 pts (Engl Comb courses; Crea Writ courses)
Hertfordshire – 240 pts (Engl Lit; Engl Lit Crea Writ)
Kingston – 240 pts (Crea Writ courses)
Nottingham Trent – 240–220 pts (Engl; Engl Crea Writ)
Oxford Brookes – CCC **or** CCcc (Engl Lang Ling)
Portsmouth – 240–300 pts (Engl Dr; Engl Am St; Engl Psy; Engl Crea Writ; Engl Media St; Engl Hist; Engl Lang Journal; Engl Lit Journal; Crea Writ Dr)
Roehampton – 240 pts (Engl Lit courses)
Ulster – CCC–CCD 240–220 pts (Engl Comb courses)

220 pts **Bath Spa** – 220–260 pts (Engl Lit; Crea St Engl)

For information on how to read the Subject Tables, see **Chapter 7**

Cardiff (UWIC) – 220 pts (Engl Pop Cult)
Chichester – 220–240 pts (Engl courses; Engl Crea Writ courses)
De Montfort – 220 pts (English)
Edge Hill – 220 pts (Crea Writ Media)
Falmouth (UC) – 220 pts (Engl Crea Writ; Engl Media St)
Glamorgan – 220–260 pts (Engl Lit; Crea Prof Writ; Engl St)
Gloucestershire – 220–280 pts (Engl Lit; Engl Lang Crea Writ)
Hull (Scarborough) – 220–240 pts (Educ St Engl St; Engl Thea Perf St)
Kingston – 220–320 pts (Engl Lang Comm; Engl Lit)
Liverpool Hope – 220 pts (Engl Lang courses; Engl Lit courses)
Manchester Met – 220–200 pts (Writing)
Nottingham Trent – 220 pts (Engl joint courses)
Salford – 220 pts (Engl Lit; Engl Lit Engl Lang; Engl Cult St; Engl Crea Writ; Engl Lang Ling)

200 pts **Anglia Ruskin** – 200–240 pts (Engl; Engl Comm St; Engl Film St)
Blackpool and Fylde (Coll) – 200 pts (Engl Lang Lit Writ)
Bolton – 200 pts (Crea Writ; Engl; Media Writ Prod)
Bristol UWE – 200–280 pts (Engl joint and EFL courses; Engl Lang)
Central Lancashire – 200–240 pts (Engl Lang St; Engl Lit; Engl Lang Lit)
Cumbria – 200 pts (Engl; Engl Am St; Engl Crea Writ; Engl Dr; Engl Hist)
Edge Hill – 200–240 pts (Engl Lang courses; Engl Lit courses; Crea Writ courses)
Middlesex – 200–240 pts (Engl Lit St; Crea Media Writ; Engl St)
Newport – 200 pts (Engl; Engl Crea Writ)
Roehampton – 200 pts (Engl Lang Ling)
Sunderland – 200 pts (Engl; Engl Lang Ling; Engl Educ; Engl Film; Engl Dr)
UCE Birmingham – 200 pts (Engl Lit; Engl Dr; Engl Lang; Engl Cult St)

190 pts **Buckingham** – 190 pts (Engl Lang; Engl Lit EFL; Engl Lit Fr; Engl Lit Hist; Engl Lit Multim Journal; Engl Lit Psy; Engl Lit Span; Engl St courses)

180 pts **Anglia Ruskin** – 180–220 pts (EFL; Int Bus Engl; Engl Lang Comm St; Eng Lang; Writ)
Bradford – 180–220 pts (Crea Writ Idnty)
Dartington (CA) – 180 pts (Writ courses)
De Montfort – 180–200 pts (English joint hons; Engl Film St; Crea Writ joint hons)
Derby – 180–220 pts (Engl courses; Crea Writ courses)
East Lancashire (IHE) – 180 pts (Engl Lang Lit St)
East London – 180 pts (Engl Lang)
Lampeter – open admission policy (Engl Lit; Engl Crea Writ; Engl Modn Lit St)
Northampton – 180–200 pts (Engl; Crea Writ courses)
Southampton Solent – 180 pts (Scrnwrit; Writ Fash Cult; Media Writ; Writ Pop; Cmdy Writ Perf)
Staffordshire – 180–240 pts (Engl Lit courses; Crea Writ)

160 pts **Bedfordshire** – 160 pts (Crea Writ courses; Engl Lang Bus)
Canterbury Christ Church – CC (English)
Doncaster (Univ Centre) – 160 pts (English)
East London – 160 pts (Engl Lit; Engl Lang; Ling Engl Lit)
Greenwich – 160 pts (Engl; Engl Lang Teach Ling; Crea Writ; Crea Ind Prof Writ)
Leeds Trinity and All Saints (Coll) – CC–CCC (Engl; Engl Hist; Engl Media; Engl Film St; Engl Writ)
London Met – 160 pts (Crea Writ; Engl Lang St; Engl Lit)
London South Bank – CC (Engl; Crea Writ Engl)
Newman (CHE) – 160–240 pts (Engl; Engl Lit courses)
Norwich City (Coll) – 160 pts (Engl courses)
St Mary's (Coll) – CC 160 pts (Engl courses)
Wolverhampton – 160–220 pts (Engl courses; Engl Lang; Crea Prof Writ courses; Lit St)
Worcester – 160 pts (Engl Lit St)
York St John – 160 pts (Engl Lit; Engl Lang Psy)

140 pts **Bishop Grosseteste (Coll)** – 140 pts (Engl Lit)

Marjon (Coll) – 140–200 pts (Engl Lit; Engl Lang Ling; Crea Writ courses)
Teesside – 140–160 pts (Engl St; Engl Media St; Engl Hist; Engl Sociol)
Trinity Carmarthen (Coll) – 140 pts (Engl; Crea Writ courses)
120 pts Buckinghamshire Chilterns (UC) – 120–240 pts (Crea Writ courses; Engl Lit courses)
Grimsby (IFHE) – 120 pts check with admissions tutor (Engl St; Prof Writ)
North East Wales (IHE) – 120–80 pts (English)
Suffolk (Univ Campus) – 120–180 pts (Engl; Engl Hist)
80 pts London (Birk) – 80 pts for under 21s (over 21s varies) (p/t English)
South Devon (Coll) – 80 pts check with Inst (Arts (Engl Hist))
Swansea (IHE) – 80 pts (Engl St; Engl St Film TV St; Engl St Sociol)

Leeds Met – contact University

Alternative offers
IB offers Aberystwyth 30 pts; Birmingham 34–36 pts; Brighton 28–30 pts; Bristol 38 pts; Bristol UWE 28–32 pts; Cambridge 38–42 pts; Chester 30 pts; Chichester 28 pts; Durham 34 pts; Essex 30–32 pts; Exeter 34–36 pts; Keele 30–32 pts; Kent 28–32 pts; Lancaster 33–34 pts; Leicester 32 pts; Liverpool 36 pts; London (QM) 32 pts, (RH) 34 pts, (UCL) 36–38 pts; Loughborough 32–35 pts; Manchester Met 28 pts; Nottingham 34–36 pts; Reading 31–32 pts; St Andrews 36 pts; Salford 31 pts; Sheffield 29–35 pts; Southampton 33–36 pts; Staffordshire 28 pts; Stirling 30 pts; Warwick 36 pts; Winchester 24–26 pts; York 36 pts.
Scottish offers See **Chapter 7**.

OTHER HIGHER EDUCATION COURSES IN THE SUBJECT FIELD
Foundation degrees (contact the institutions for details) Bedfordshire; North West Kent (Coll); St Helens (Coll); Truro (Coll).

CHOOSING YOUR COURSE (SEE ALSO CH.1)
Subject information English courses continue to be extremely popular and competitive. They are an extension of school studies in literature and language and may cover topics ranging from Anglo-Saxon literature to writing in the present day. Most courses, however, will focus on certain areas such as the Medieval or Renaissance periods of literature or English language studies. Admissions tutors will expect students to have read widely outside their A-level syllabus. **Useful websites** www.bl.uk; www.lrb.co.uk; www.literature.org; www.bibliomania.com.

Course variations Creative Writing and English (Aberystwyth); Medieval English and History (Birmingham); Anglo-Saxon, Norse and Celtic (Cambridge); Cultural Criticism and English Literature (Cardiff); English and Comparative Literature (East Anglia); Literature and Myth (Essex); Scottish Literature (Glasgow); Publishing with English (Loughborough); English, Writing and Performance (York). *NOW CHECK PROSPECTUSES AND WEBSITES FOR ANY RECENT CHANGES.*

Universities and colleges teaching quality See www.tqi.ac.uk; www.qaa.ac.uk.

Top universities and colleges (Research) Anglia Ruskin; Belfast (Queen's); Birmingham; Bristol; Cambridge*; Cardiff*; De Montfort; Durham*; East Anglia; Edinburgh*; Exeter; Glasgow*; Hull; Keele; Kent; Lampeter; Lancaster; Leeds*; Leicester; Liverpool*; London (Birk), (Gold), (QM), (RH), (UCL); Loughborough; Manchester; Newcastle; Nottingham; Nottingham Trent; Oxford*; Oxford Brookes; Reading; St Andrews*; Sheffield; Southampton; Stirling; Strathclyde; Sussex; Warwick*; York*.

Sandwich degree courses Brighton; East London; Glamorgan; Huddersfield; Lancaster; Loughborough; Nottingham Trent; Oxford Brookes; Westminster.

ADMISSIONS INFORMATION
Number of applicants per place (approx) Aberystwyth 7; Anglia Ruskin 5; Bangor 5; Bath Spa 8; Birmingham 7; Blackpool and Fylde (Coll) 2; Bristol 28, (Engl Dr) 45; Bristol UWE 4; Brunel 10; Buckingham 2; Cambridge (A-Sxn Nrs Celt) 2, (Engl) 4.9; Cardiff (Engl Lit) 6; Central Lancashire 10; Chester 20; Chichester 4; Cumbria 24; De Montfort 7; Derby 6; Dundee 6; Durham 20; East Anglia (Engl

Lit Dr) 22, (Engl Lit Crea Writ) 17, (Engl St) 12, (Engl Compar Lit) 13; Edge Hill (CHE) 4; Exeter 13; Glamorgan 8; Gloucestershire 35; Hertfordshire 6; Huddersfield 5; Hull 14; Hull (Scarborough) 1; Kingston 6; Lampeter 4; Lancaster 12; Leeds 10; Leeds Trinity and All Saints (Coll) 7; Leicester 7; Liverpool (Engl Comm St) 7; London (Gold) 9, (King's) 15, (QM) 9, (RH) 9, (UCL) 13; Loughborough 40; London South Bank 5; Manchester Met 7; Middlesex 8; Newman (CHE) 3; North East Wales (IHE) 2; Northampton 3; Nottingham 22; Nottingham Trent 21; Oxford (success rate 25%), (Magdalen) 15; Oxford Brookes 15; Portsmouth 8; Reading 11; Roehampton 5; Salford 12; Sheffield 12; Sheffield Hallam 4; Southampton 5; Stirling 9; Sunderland 10; Swansea (IHE) 4; Teesside 5; UCE Birmingham 9; Warwick 15, (Engl Thea) 26; Winchester 3; York 16; York St John 3.

Advice to applicants and planning the UCAS personal statement Applicants should read outside their subject. Details of any writing you have done (for example poetry, short stories) should be provided. Theatre visits and play readings are also important. Keep up to date by reading literary and theatre reviews in the national newspapers (keep a scrapbook of reviews for reference). Evidence is needed of a good writing style. **Birmingham** Independence of mind, wit! **Bristol** Very popular course – not enough places to make offers to all those whose qualifications are deserving of a place. **Bristol UWE** Favourite authors, spare-time reading. **Cardiff** (Engl Lit) Ability to write lucidly, accurately and succinctly. Evidence of literary enthusiasm. **Derby** We seek a literate and accurate statement. **Durham** Background reading about linguistics essential. **East Anglia** (Crea Writ) Aims and objectives in their own writing. (Engl Lit Dr) Commitment to drama in all its aspects. **Leeds** 'Tell me why you read and, more importantly, what you think about what you read.' **Liverpool** General interest in communications – verbal, visual, media. Intellectual curiosity. Read everything from the classics to contemporary literature and the daily newspaper. For non-EU students – limited places; English language competence essential. **London (Gold)** Some interests should reflect chosen course. **London (QM)** Evidence of commitment to literature; also for Dr Engl, evidence of acting and production experience. **Nottingham Trent** Ability to write accurately and clearly. **St Andrews** Evidence of interest and reasons for choosing the course. Sport/extracurricular activities. Posts of responsibility. **Sheffield Hallam** (Engl St) Applicants do not need previous experience in literature, language or creative writing. **Stirling** What has the student done between school and university? Literary and linguistic interests. **Warwick** Oxbridge decisions awaited before offers made. Reading beyond the syllabus. (Engl St Thea) Synopsis of theatre experience (viewing and/or practical).

Misconceptions about this course **Buckingham** Native speakers of English often do not realise that the EFL degree courses are restricted to non-native speakers of English. **East Anglia** (Engl Lit Crea Writ) This is not simply a creative writing course: English literature is the predominant element. **Liverpool** (Engl Comm St) The course is not a training in journalism, although some students go on to work in the press, radio or TV. **UCE Birmingham** The study of English language means descriptive linguistics – the course won't necessarily enable students to speak or write better English.

Selection interviews **Yes** Anglia Ruskin, Bangor (mature students), Brunel, Cambridge, Canterbury Christ Church, Exeter, Gloucestershire, Huddersfield, Hull, Hull (Scarborough), Kingston, Lampeter, Lancaster, Leeds Trinity and All Saints (Coll), London (Gold), (RH), London South Bank, Loughborough, Middlesex, Newcastle, Newport, Oxford, Portsmouth, Reading, Roehampton, Warwick; **Some** Aberystwyth, Bath Spa, Blackpool and Fylde (Coll), Bristol, Chester, De Montfort, Derby, Dundee, East Anglia, East Lancashire (IHE), Leeds, Liverpool (Engl Comm St), London (King's), London Met, Salford, Southampton, Swansea (IHE), Truro (Coll), UCE Birmingham, Wolverhampton.

Interview advice and questions Questions will almost certainly be asked on set A-level texts and any essays which have been submitted prior to the interview. You will also be expected to have read outside your A-level subjects and to answer questions about your favourite authors, poets, dramatists etc. Questions in the past have included: Do you think that class discussion plays an important part in your English course? What is the value of studying a text in depth rather than just reading it for pleasure? What is the difference between satire and comedy? Are books written by women different from those written by men? Why would you go to see a production of *Hamlet*? What are your views on the choice of novels for this year's Booker Prize? Short verbal tests and a précis may be set. **Buckingham** It is useful to know if there is any particular reason why students want a particular programme; for example, for the TEFL degree is a member of the family a teacher? **Cambridge** We look for interviewees who respond positively to ideas, can think on their feet, can intelligently engage with critical issues and sustain an argument. If they don't evince any of these we reject them. **East Anglia** (Am Lit Crea Writ) Compare your writing trends with other examples. How does a study of English literature contribute to your critical attitude to your own work? (Engl Lit Dr) How do you reconcile yourself to an academic interest in literature on the one hand and the belief in practical performance on the other? Interviews are accompanied by auditions. **Leeds** Academic ability; current reading interests. **Liverpool** (Engl Comm St) General questions only. Reading interests, general interests, career ambitions. **Roehampton** Samples of work taken to interview and discussed. **Warwick** We may ask students to sight-read or to analyse a text. See also **Chapter 6**.

Applicants' impressions (A=Open day; B=Interview day) Cambridge (B) There was one half-hour interview with questions on my A-level subjects and specific questions on English, plays and books I had read. It was a formal interview but not intimidating. (B) I was asked how I chose my reading material and to respond to a set poem. **Exeter** (B) There were three interviewers, all helpful, friendly, encouraging and welcoming. We had a comprehensive discussion on the areas which interest me, why I had applied to Exeter and what I felt it would offer me. **Lancaster** (A) There was a mini-lecture and tour. We were introduced to all the lecturers and had a talk and presentation on the social life of the university and of Lancashire. **Oxford** (B) I was asked to discuss a text I had mentioned in my personal statement and to comment on a set poem. **(St Hilda's)** (B) There were two interviewers, with the interview lasting 40 minutes. The questions were demanding but I was treated helpfully. There was a very friendly atmosphere and beautiful surroundings. I was able to meet students to discuss various problems concerning studying and living in college. Strongly recommended. **(Magdalen)** (B) There were two interviews, one of 15 minutes and the other of 30 minutes. The questioning was intense and I felt I had been 'laid bare'! The students were overwhelmingly friendly and there was a really happy atmosphere; pity I was rejected! The department was very high-powered and dynamic – the best of the best! But I wasn't aware that it was the most popular college! **Sussex** (A) The open day consisted of a talk on the course. It would be useful to have some questions prepared before you go. **Warwick** (B) (Engl Thea St) One 20-minute pressurised interview with one person. I was unable to meet the students. **York** (A) The open day consisted of a mini-lecture, an introduction to the lecturers and a campus tour.

Reasons for rejection (non-academic) Some are well-informed about English literature – others are not. Inability to respond to questions about their current studies. Lack of enthusiasm for the challenge of studying familiar subjects from a different perspective. Must be able to benefit from the course. Little interest in how people communicate with each other. They don't know a single thing about our course. **Bangor** We reject those who decline interviews. **Bristol** Not enough places to make offers to all those whose qualifications deserve one. **Cambridge** See **Interview advice and questions**. **Oxford** (1) The essay she submitted was poorly written, careless and reductive and, in general, lacking in attention to the subject. She should be encouraged to write less and think more about what she is saying. She seems to put down the first thing that comes into her head. (2) We had the feeling that he rather tended to dismiss texts which did not satisfy the requirements of his personal canon and that he therefore might not be happy pursuing a course requiring the study of texts from all periods. (3) In her essay on Brontë she took a phrase from Arnold which was metaphorical (to do with hunger) and applied it literally, writing at length about the diet of the characters. **East Anglia** (Am Engl Lit) Personal statement unconvincing in its commitment to American literature. (Other courses) Poor examples of work submitted. **Leeds** Unsuitable predictions. **Liverpool** (Engl Comm St) Student more suited to a practical course. Ungrammatical Personal Statement. **Reading** None. If they have reached the interview we have already eliminated all other factors. **Sheffield Hallam** Apparent lack of eagerness to tackle all three strands of the course (literature, language and creative writing). **Southampton** Insufficient or patchy academic achievement. Applicants coming from non-standard academic backgrounds are assessed in terms of their individual situations.

AFTER-RESULTS ADVICE

Universities with vacancies in Clearing (2006) Aberdeen; Aberystwyth; Anglia Ruskin; Aston; Bangor; Bath Spa; Bedfordshire; Bolton; Bradford; Bristol UWE; Brunel; Canterbury Christ Church; Central Lancashire; Chester; Chichester; Coventry; De Montfort; Derby; East Anglia; East London; Edge Hill; Exeter; Glamorgan; Gloucestershire; Greenwich; Hertfordshire; Huddersfield; Hull; Keele; Kent; Kingston;

Lampeter; Lancaster; Lincoln; Liverpool Hope; Liverpool John Moores; London (Gold), (QM), (RH); London South Bank; Manchester Met; Middlesex; Northampton; Nottingham Trent; Plymouth; Portsmouth; Reading; Roehampton; Salford; Sheffield Hallam; Southampton; Staffordshire; Stirling; Sunderland; Swansea; Teesside; UCE Birmingham; Ulster; Westminster; Wolverhampton; Winchester; York St John.

Offers to applicants repeating A-levels Higher Aberystwyth, Sheffield Hallam, Southampton (varies), Warwick; **Possibly higher** Lancaster, Newcastle, Oxford Brookes; **Same** Anglia Ruskin, Bangor, Blackpool and Fylde (Coll), Bristol, Cardiff, Chester, Chichester, Cumbria, De Montfort, Derby, Dundee, Durham, East Anglia, Edge Hill, Hull, Lampeter, Leeds, Leeds Trinity and All Saints (Coll), Liverpool, London (Gold), (RH), Loughborough (varies), Manchester Met, Newman (CHE), Newport, Nottingham, Portsmouth, Reading, Roehampton, Salford, Sheffield, Staffordshire, UCE Birmingham, Ulster, Winchester, Wolverhampton, York, York St John.

GRADUATE DESTINATIONS AND EMPLOYMENT (2005 HESA)
English graduates surveyed 7805 **Employed** 3710 **In further study** 1725 **Assumed unemployed** 495.

Creative Writing graduates surveyed 305 **Employed** 145 **In further study** 40 **Assumed unemployed** 30.

OTHER DEGREE SUBJECTS FOR CONSIDERATION
Communication Studies; Drama; Language courses; Linguistics; Literature; Media Studies.

ENVIRONMENTAL SCIENCE/STUDIES

(including **Conservation, Ecology, Environmental Health and Environmental Management;** see also **Biological Sciences, Geography** and **Geology/Geological Sciences**)

NB The points totals shown to the left of the institutions are for ease of reference only. It must not be assumed that tariff points are always used by institutions or that they can be substituted for an offer in grades. The level of an offer is not necessarily indicative of the quality of a course.

COURSE OFFERS INFORMATION
Subject requirements/preferences GCSE English, mathematics and a science (often chemistry) usually required. **Edinburgh** Biology or mathematics at grade B. **London (LSE)** Mathematics grade A. **Surrey** Grade A in chemistry or combined science if not at A-level. **York** Mathematics A or B. **AL** One or two science subjects are usually stipulated.

Your target offers
360 pts and above
    Cambridge – AAA (Ener Env; Lnd Econ; Nat Sci (Geol Sci))
    East Anglia – AAA–AAB (Env Sci N Am/Aus; Env Earth Sci N Am/Aus; Env Geog Int Dev; Meteor Ocean Aus/N Am)
    Leeds – AAA (MGeol Env Geol N Am)
340 pts East Anglia – AAB–ABB (Ecol Aus/N Am)
    Imperial London – AAB–ABB (Ecology)
    London (UCL) – AAB–BBB+AS (Env Biol)
    Manchester – AAB–BBC (Blt Nat Env courses)
    Reading – 340 pts (Meteor; Meteor Yr Okl)
320 pts Cardiff – ABB–BBB (Ecology)
    Durham – ABB (Ecology)
    East Anglia – ABB (Env Earth Sci Euro; Env Sci Euro; Env Chem; Meteor Ocean Euro)
    Imperial London – ABB (Env Geosci)
    Lancaster – ABB (Env Sci N Am/Aus; Env Biol N Am/Aus; Env Chem N Am/Aus; Earth Env Sci N Am/Aus)

St Andrews – ABB (MA Sust Dev)
Sheffield – ABB (MBioch Ecol; Env Sci)
Southampton – ABB 320 pts (MEnvSci Env Sci; Ocean courses)
Strathclyde – ABB (Enviro Mech Eng)

300 pts **Aberdeen** – BBB 300 pts 2nd yr entry (Env Sci; Ecol; Cons Biol)
Birmingham – BBB–BCC 300–260 pts (Env Geosci; Env Biol; Env Mgt; Env Sci; Env Sci Aus)
Bristol – BBB (Env Geosci)
Dundee – BBB–CCC 300–240 pts (Env Mgt; Env Sci; Env Sci Geog; Renew Ener)
Durham – BBB (Env Geosci; New Renew Ener)
Edinburgh – BBB (Ecol Sci; Ecol Sci (Cons Ecol Mgt) (Ecol) (Env Sci) (Frsty); Geog Env St)
Exeter (Cornwall) – BBB–BCC 300–260 pts (Renew Ener)
Leeds – BBB 300 pts (Ecol Env Biol)
London (LSE) – BBB (Env Pol Econ; Env Pol)
Manchester – ABC (Env Sci; Env Res Geol; Env St)
Reading – 300 pts (Env Biol)
St Andrews – BBB (Ecol Cons; Env Geosci; Sust Dev)
Sheffield – BBB **or** BBbb (BSc Ecology)
Southampton – BBB 300 pts (BSc Env Sci)
Stirling – BBB 2nd yr entry (Env Sci; Env Geog; Ecol; Cons Sci; Cons Mgt; Frshwtr Sci)
Sussex – BBB–BBC 330–310 pts (Ecol Cons; Env Sci)
York – BBB (Env Sci; Env Econ Ecol)

280 pts **Aberystwyth** – 280–300 pts (Env Sci; Env Earth Sci)
Belfast (Queen's) – BBC **or** BCCb (Env Arch; Env Plan)
Coventry – 280 pts (Cons Geog; Nat Haz)

East Anglia – BBC 280 pts (Env Sci; Env Sci Ind; Env Earth Sci; Meteor Ocean; Meteor Ocean Ind)

Edinburgh – BBC (Env Geosci)

Essex – 280–240 pts (Env Lf Hlth; Ecol)

Glasgow – BBC–CCC (Env Chem; Env Biogeochem)

Glasgow (Crichton) – BBC (Env St)

Lancaster – BBC (Env Sci)

Leeds – BBC (Env Biogeosci; Env Cons; BSc Env Geol; Env Bus; Env Trans Plan; Env Sci; Env Mgt; Env Sust)

Liverpool – BBC–BBB 280–300 pts (Env Biol)

London (QM) – 280–320 pts (Env Sci; Env Geog)

Loughborough – 280 pts (Chem Eng Env Prot)

Newcastle – BBC–BCC (Ecol; Env Sci)

Nottingham – BBC–BCC (Env Sci+Cert Euro St (Biosci))

Portsmouth – 280–240 pts (Env Sci; Env Haz)

Reading – 280 pts (Env Sci; Env Sci Prof Exp)

Sheffield – BBC (Env Sci)

Ulster – 280 pts (Env Hlth)

260 pts **Abertay Dundee** – BCC (Nat Res Mgt)

Aston – BCC–CCC 260 pts (Hlth Sfty Env Mgt; Constr Hlth Sfty Mgt; Constr Env Mgt; Geog Inf Env Sys; Env Sci Tech; Trans Env Plan)

Belfast (Queen's) – BCC/AB (Env Biol)

Coventry – 260 pts (Disas Mgt courses)

Kent – 260 pts (Biodiv Cons Mgt; Wldlf Mgt)

Lancaster – BCC (BSc Env Chem; Env Maths; Env Chem)

Leeds – BCC (Ener Env Eng)

Liverpool – BCC 280 pts (Env Plan)

Manchester – BCC (Env Mgt)

Nottingham – BCC (Env Biol+Cert Euro St; Env Biol)

Oxford Brookes – BCC (Env Sci courses)

Strathclyde – BCC (Env Hlth)

240 pts **Aberdeen** – CCC 1st yr entry (Env Sci; Ecol; Cons Biol)

Anglia Ruskin – 240 pts (Env Plan)

Bangor – 240–260 pts (Env Cons; Env Sci; Ecol Env; Env Mgt)

Bangor – 240–280 pts (Env Plan Mgt; Ecol; Sust Dev)

Bristol UWE – 240–300 pts (Env Sci)

Glamorgan – 240 pts (Env Sust)

Glasgow Caledonian – CCC (Env Mgt Plan)

Hertfordshire – 240 pts (Env St; Cons Mgt; Env Mgt)

Keele – CCC 240 pts (App Env Sci)

Kent – 240 pts (Env Soc Sci)

Kingston – 240–260 pts (Env Haz Disas Mgt; Env Sci; Env Mgt)

Manchester Met – 240 pts (Env Hlth)

Northumbria – 240 pts (Env Mgt; Env Hlth)

Nottingham Trent – 240 pts (Hlth Env)

Oxford Brookes – CCC or BCcc (Cits Env Des Dev)

Plymouth – 240 pts (Wldlf Cons)

Reading – 240–280 pts (Rur Env Sci)

SAC (Scottish CAg) – CCC (Env Prot)

Staffordshire – 240 pts (Hum Env Geog; Anim Biol Cons)

230 pts **Brighton** – 230 pts (Urb Cons Env Mgt)

Sheffield Hallam – 230 pts (Env Mgt; Env St)

220 pts **Bangor** – 220–280 pts (Env Foren; Env Chem)

Bradford – 220 pts (Env Sci; App Ecol; Geog Env Mgt)

Brighton – 220 pts (Civ Env Eng; Env Sci; Env Haz)

Central Lancashire – 220 pts (Env Mgt)
Gloucestershire – 220 pts (Env Mgt; Env Sci; Wtr Res Mgt)
Liverpool Hope – 220 pts (Env Mgt)
Liverpool John Moores – 220 pts (Env Sci; Wldlf Cons; Out Env Educ)
Nottingham Trent – 220 pts (Env Soc Just)
Stirling – CCD 1st yr entry (Env Sci; Cons Biol; Ecol; Frshwtr Sci)
Ulster – 220 pts (Env Sci)

200 pts **Bath Spa** – 200–240 pts (Env Sci)
Bradford – 200 pts (Wtr Lnd Mgt)
Bristol UWE – 200–240 pts (Env Sci joint courses)
Central Lancashire – 200–240 pts (Env Haz; Ener Sust Des; Env Mgt)
East London – 200 pts approx (Env Sci courses)
Hull (Scarborough) – 200–240 pts (Ecol; Env Sci; Cstl Mar Biol)
Kingston – 200 pts (Env St)
Manchester Met – 200–240 pts (Env St; Env Mgt; Ecol; Sust Dev; Env Ent)
Napier – 200 pts (Env Biol; Ecotour)
Nottingham Trent – 200 pts (Ecol Env Mgt)
Sheffield Hallam – 200 pts (Env Cons)

180 pts **Aberystwyth** – 180–210 pts (Sust Rur Dev; Cntry Cons)
Bristol UWE – 180–220 pts (Env Hlth; Env Biol; Hlth Sfty Env; Env Foren)
Manchester Met – 180–200 pts (Env Mgt; Env Sci; Env St; Sust Dev; Ecol; Ecol Cons; Env Ent)
Northampton – 180–200 pts (Env Mgt)
Nottingham Trent – 180 pts (Env Cons Cntry Mgt; Wldlf Cons Env Sci)
Portsmouth – 180–240 pts (Mar Env Sci; Env Biol; Env Haz; Env Foren Sci; Env Sci)
Salford – 180 pts (Env Mgt; Aqua Sci; Wldlf Prac Cons; Env St; Env Hlth)

160 pts **Bournemouth** – 160 pts (Env Prot; Env Cons Biol; Env Cstl Mgt)

Bristol UWE – 160–200 pts (Blt Nat Env)
Canterbury Christ Church – CC (Env Biol; Env Sci)
Cardiff (UWIC) – 160 pts (Hlth Sfty Env Prot)
Central Lancashire – 160 pts (Env Mgt Comb; Env Geog)
Derby – 160–180 pts (Env Mgt; Env Sci; Cons Cntry Mgt; Ecol)
Greenwich – 160–240 pts (Env Sci courses)
Harper Adams (UC) – 160–240 pts (Agric Env Mgt)
Middlesex – 160–200 pts (Env Hlth)
Plymouth – 160–240 pts (Env Sci; Env Sci (Biodiv Cons) (Env Chng) (Env Sust) (Env Hlth) (Mar Cons))
SAC (Scottish CAg) – CC (Sust Env Mgt; Env Prot)
Southampton Solent – 160–180 pts (Cstl Cons Mgt; Mar Env Sci)
Swansea (IHE) – 160 pts approx (Civ Eng Env Mgt)
Wolverhampton – 160–220 pts (Env Mgt; Env Sci; Wtr Sci Mgt; Ecol)

140 pts **Anglia Ruskin** – 140–200 pts (Ecol Cons; Nat Hist)
Bell (Coll) – contact admissions tutor (Env Sci Env Mgt)
Bolton – 140 pts (Env St)
Worcester – 140–120 pts (Env Mgt; Wtr Env Mgt)
Writtle (Coll) – 140–160 pts (Cons Env; Wldlf Mgt)

120 pts **North East Wales (IHE)** – 120–80 pts (Env St)
Paisley – DD (Env Biol)

80 pts **London (Birk)** – 80 pts for under 21s (over 21s varies) (p/t Env Cons; Env Sci; Env Mgt; Env Geol)
Swansea (IHE) – 80 pts (BA/BSc Env Cons)
UHI Millennium Inst (IC) (NHC) – 80 pts (Env Herit St)

Leeds Met – contact University
Open University – contact University

Alternative offers

IB offers Aberystwyth 30 pts; Birmingham 32 pts; Brighton 28 pts; Bristol UWE 24–26 pts; Dundee 26 pts; Essex 26–30 pts; Keele 26–28 pts; Kent 27 pts; Lancaster 32–34 pts; London (LSE) 32 pts, (QM) 30 pts, (UCL) 32–36 pts; Manchester Met 24–28 pts; Newcastle 28–30 pts; Nottingham 24–30 pts; Reading 31 pts; Salford 24 pts; Sheffield 30 pts; Southampton 31–32 pts; Stirling 26 pts; York 30 pts.
Scottish offers See **Chapter 7**.

OTHER HIGHER EDUCATION COURSES IN THE SUBJECT FIELD

Foundation degrees (contact the institutions for details) Blackpool and Fylde (Coll); Bournemouth; Cornwall (Coll); East Lancashire (IHE); Kingston Maurwood (Coll); Myerscough (Coll); Northampton; Nottingham Trent; Wigan and Leigh (Coll); Suffolk (Univ Campus); Swansea (IHE); Writtle (Coll).

Higher National Diploma courses
100 pts **and below**
Adam Smith (Coll); Anglia Ruskin; Askham Bryan (Coll); Bath; Bedfordshire; Blackpool and Fylde (Coll); Bournemouth; Bridgwater (Coll); Canterbury Christ Church; Cardiff (UWIC); Central Lancashire; Cornwall (Coll); Coventry; De Montfort; Derby; Exeter; Falmouth (UC); Farnborough (CT); Forth Valley (Coll); Glamorgan; Glasgow Met (Coll); Gloucestershire; Isle of Wight (Coll); Manchester Met; Nescot; Northampton; Park Lane Leeds (Coll); Pembrokeshire (Coll); Plymouth; Queen Margaret (UC); Riverside Halton (Coll); Rodbaston (Coll); St Helens (Coll); Salford; SAC (Scottish CAg); Stevenson (Coll); Stockport (CFHE); Teesside; UHI Millennium Inst (IC), (NHC); West Herts (Coll); Wiltshire (Coll); Wirral Met (Coll); Wolverhampton; Worcester; Writtle (Coll).

CHOOSING YOUR COURSE (SEE ALSO CH.1)

Subject information Environmental Science/Studies courses need to be considered with care as, depending on their content and specialisms, they lead to very different careers. Environmental Health courses usually lead to qualifying as an environmental health officer. Environmental Science, however, covers a range of subjects with options which may include biology, geography, geology, oceanography, chemistry, legal, social and political issues. **Useful websites** www.cieh.org; www.ends.co.uk; www.enn.com; www.iagre.org.uk; www.defra.gov.uk; www.socenv.org.uk; www.ies-uk.org.uk; www.noc.soton.ac.uk.

Course variations Water and Land Management (Bradford); Environmental Geoscience (Bristol); Environmental Protection (Bournemouth); Energy and the Environment (Cambridge); Environmental Geography and International Development (East Anglia); Ecology (Imperial London); Built and Natural Environment (Manchester); Ecology (Newcastle); Sustainable Development (St Andrews); Coastal Conservation Management (Southampton Solent); Environment, Economics and Ecology (York). *NOW CHECK PROSPECTUSES AND WEBSITES FOR ANY RECENT CHANGES.*

Universities and colleges teaching quality See www.tqi.ac.uk; www.qaa.ac.uk.

Top universities and colleges (Research) East Anglia*; Leeds; Reading*; Southampton.

Sandwich degree courses Aston; Bradford; Brighton; Bristol UWE; Coventry; Glamorgan; Glasgow Caledonian; Greenwich; Harper Adams (UC); Hertfordshire; Kingston; Liverpool John Moores; Loughborough; Manchester Met; Nottingham Trent; Oxford Brookes; Paisley; Plymouth; Reading; Salford; Staffordshire; Surrey; Ulster; Wolverhampton.

ADMISSIONS INFORMATION

Number of applicants per place (approx) Abertay Dundee 5; Aberystwyth 3; Aston 6; Bangor 3; Bath Spa 2; Birmingham 5; Bournemouth 4; Bradford 3; Bristol UWE 1, (Env Hlth) 7; Cardiff (UWIC) 4; Central Lancashire 10; Coventry 9; De Montfort 9; Dundee 6; Durham 5; East Anglia 7; East London 4; Edinburgh 1; Essex 3; Farnborough (CT) 2; Glamorgan 1; Glasgow Caledonian 1; Greenwich 2; Gloucestershire 11; Harper Adams (UC) 5; Hertfordshire 5; Hull 8; Kingston 3; Lampeter 3; Lancaster 11; Leeds (Env Sci Ener) 2; Liverpool John Moores 5; London (King's) 5, (LSE) 4, (RH) 8; Manchester Met (Env Mgt) 16, (Env Hlth) 6, (Env Sci) 5; North East Wales (IHE) 3; Northampton 4; Northumbria 8; Nottingham 6; Nottingham Trent 3, (Hlth Env) 8; Oxford Brookes 13; Plymouth 8; Portsmouth 5; Roehampton 3; Salford 8; Sheffield Hallam 8; Southampton 5; Stirling 10; Strathclyde 1; Trinity Carmarthen (Coll) 2; Ulster 16; Westminster 3; Wolverhampton 2; Worcester 7; York 3.

Advice to applicants and planning the UCAS personal statement 'We want doers, not just thinkers.' Describe any field courses which you have attended; make an effort to visit one of the National Parks. Discuss these visits and identify any particular aspects which impressed you. Outline travel interests. Give details of work as a conservation volunteer and other outside school activities. Strong communication skills, people-oriented work experience. **Bangor** Competence in science and watch your spelling and grammar! **Bath Spa** Evidence of a good science background and willingness to undertake fieldwork. **East Anglia** What sparked your interest in Environmental Science? Discuss your field trips. **Leeds** Give details of outside activities, career interests. **Nottingham Trent** (Hlth Env) A basic knowledge of environmental health as opposed to environmental sciences. Work experience in an environmental health department is looked upon very favourably. **Southampton** See http://www.envsci.soton.ac.uk/study/skills.htm. Problem-solving ability, resilience and self-management. See also **Appendix 2**.

Misconceptions about this course **Bangor** Students should note that only simple mathematical skills are required for this course. **Leeds** (Ener Env Sci) Note that the course is closer to environmental technology than to environmental science. **London (King's)** This course is not an easy option. **Manchester Met** Some believe that the course is mainly about food which is incorrect. **Nottingham Trent** (Hlth Env) Too many are influenced by what is shown on TV, for example some aspects of food safety, pest control and work in mortuaries! The work also involves health and safety, housing, public health and environmental management. **Southampton** This is not just a course for environmentalists, for example links with BP, IBM etc. **Wolverhampton** This is a course in Environmental Science, not Environmental Studies; there is a difference. **York** Some students worry that the economics part of the course will be too difficult which is not the case.

Selection interviews Yes Bradford, Bristol UWE, Cambridge, Coventry, Durham, Glamorgan, Gloucestershire, Greenwich, Harper Adams (UC) (advisory), Hertfordshire, Huddersfield, Kingston, Lampeter, London (RH), Manchester Met, Newcastle, Newport, Nottingham, Nottingham Trent, Oxford Brookes, Sheffield Hallam, Strathclyde, Sunderland, Surrey, Sussex, Warwick; **Some** Bangor, Bath Spa, Birmingham, Derby, Dundee, East Anglia, London (King's), Plymouth, Salford, Southampton, Staffordshire, York.

Interview advice and questions Environmental issues are constantly in the news, so keep abreast of developments. You could be asked to discuss any particular environmental problems in the area in which you live and to justify your stance on any environmental issues on which you have strong opinions. **Bath Spa** Questions on school work, current affairs and field courses. **East Anglia** Can you display an informed interest in any aspect of environmental science? See also **Chapter 6**.

Applicants' impressions (A=Open day; B=Interview day) Bangor (A) A very interesting open day with talks on the course content, a tour of the university and also a coach tour of the surrounding countryside, including glacial features, which made the day all the more interesting. **Bristol** (B) It was an informal interview with questions about my personal statement and an environmental problem near my home and how I thought it could be managed or prevented. **East Anglia** (A) There was a general talk on the University and the course content. Go to open days, they give a good idea of what to expect. **London (UCL)** (B Env Geosci) It was a hard interview. I was asked challenging questions on all the subjects I was studying.

Reasons for rejection (non-academic) Inability to be aware of the needs of others.

AFTER-RESULTS ADVICE

Universities with vacancies in Clearing (2006) Bangor; Bournemouth; Bristol UWE; Canterbury Christ Church; Central Lancashire; Chester; Derby; Glamorgan; Gloucestershire; Greenwich; Hertfordshire; Kingston; Lancaster; Liverpool Hope; London (QM); Manchester Met; Northampton; Nottingham Trent; Oxford Brookes; Plymouth; Portsmouth; Reading; Salford; Southampton; Southampton Solent; Stirling; Sunderland; Wolverhampton; Worcester.

Offers to applicants repeating A-levels Higher Greenwich, Lancaster, London (King's), Nottingham, Strathclyde, Swansea; **Possibly higher** Aberystwyth, Bradford, Northumbria; **Same** Aston, Bangor, Brighton, Cardiff (UWIC), Derby, Dundee, East Anglia, Leeds, Liverpool John Moores, London (RH), Manchester Met, Nottingham Trent, Plymouth, SAC (Scottish CAg), Salford, Southampton, Ulster, Wolverhampton.

GRADUATE DESTINATIONS AND EMPLOYMENT (2005 HESA)

No data available, but in 2004: **Graduates surveyed** 3410 **Employed** 1795 **In further study** 620 **Assumed unemployed** 210.

OTHER DEGREE SUBJECTS FOR CONSIDERATION

Biological Sciences; Biology; Chemistry; Environmental Engineering; Environmental Health; Geography; Geology; Ocean Sciences/Oceanography; Town and Country Planning.

EUROPEAN STUDIES

(see also **Business Courses, Languages** and **Russian and East European Studies**)

NB The points totals shown to the left of the institutions are for ease of reference only. It must not be assumed that tariff points are always used by institutions or that they can be substituted for an offer in grades. The level of an offer is not necessarily indicative of the quality of a course.

COURSE OFFERS INFORMATION

Subject requirements/preferences GCSE English for all courses and possibly mathematics. **Aberdeen**, **Dundee** English, mathematics or science, grade B in languages. **Leeds** Grade A*, A or B in eight–ten subjects. **Nottingham** Mathematics grade B. **AL** A modern language usually required.

Your target offers

360 pts **and above**
  London (UCL) – AAA+AS (Euro Soc Pol St)
340 pts **Durham** – AAB (Euro St courses)
320 pts **Bath** – ABB–BBB (Modn Lang Euro St)
  Cardiff – ABB–BCC (EU St)
  East Anglia – ABB–BBB (Euro St Pol; Euro St Lang)
  Leeds – ABB (Euro St Law)
  London (King's) – ABB+AS **or** ABaaa (Euro St courses)
  Southampton – ABB 320 pts (Contemp Euro)
300 pts **Belfast (Queen's)** – BBB (Euro St)
  Birmingham – 300 pts (Modn Langs Euro St (Soty Cult Hist))
  Dundee – BBB–CCC 300–240 pts (Euro St courses)
  Exeter – 300 pts (Int Rel Euro St; Sociol Euro St)
  Glasgow – BBB (Slav E Euro St; Cnt E Euro St)
  Hull – 300 pts (Euro Gov Pol)
  Leeds – BBB (Euro Pol)
  Lancaster – BBB (Euro St; Euro Pol Soty Cult)
  London (RH) – ABC–BBB (Euro St Fr/Ger/Ital/Span)
  London (UCL) – BBB+AS–BCC+AS (Dutch courses)
  Manchester – BBB (Euro St Fr/Ger/Ital/Span/Port/Russ)
  Nottingham – BBB–BBC (Modn Euro St)
  Sussex – BBB **or** 340 pts 3AL+AS (see 2nd subj) (Anth Contemp Euro St; Geog Contemp Euro St; Econ Contemp Euro St; Int Rel Contemp Euro St; Langs Contemp Euro St; Phil Contemp Euro St; Sociol Contemp Euro St; Ling Contemp Euro St)
280 pts **Aberystwyth** – 280 pts (Euro Lang; Euro Pol; Euro St joint courses)
  Aston – 280–300 pts (Euro St Fr/Ger/Span; Euro St Sociol; Euro St Engl Lang; Euro St Pblc Pol; Euro St Comp Sci)
  Newcastle – BBC (Gov EU St)
  Reading – 280 pts (Euro St; Engl Euro Lit Cult; Hist Euro Lit Cult)
  Stirling – BBC (Euro Film Media)
  Strathclyde – BBC (Archit St Euro St)
260 pts **Essex** – 260 pts (Euro St; Euro St Fr/Ger/Ital/Span; Euro St Cult Soty; Euro Pol)
  Kent – 260–280 pts (Euro St courses; Euro Cult Tht courses)
  Leicester – 260–300 pts (Euro St)
  London (Gold) – BCC (Euro St)
  London (QM) – 260 pts (Euro St courses)
  London (RH) – BCC (Euro Lit Cult)
  Northumbria – 260 pts (Euro Int Pol)
  Stirling – BCC (Euro Soc Pol)
  Swansea – 260 pts (Geog Euro St)
240 pts **Aberdeen** – CCC (Euro St)
  Aston – 240–280 pts (Euro St Comb)
  Loughborough – 240–300 pts (Euro St)
  Ulster – CCC–CCD 240 pts (Euro St courses)
  Westminster – CCC 240 pts (Comb Euro St)
220 pts **Nottingham Trent** – 220 pts (Euro St courses)
  Plymouth – 220 pts (Euro St; Euro St Fr/Ger/Span)
200 pts **Bristol UWE** – 200–280 pts (Euro St joint courses)
  Glamorgan – 200 pts (Modn Euro)
  Manchester Met – 200–280 pts (Euro St)
  Portsmouth – 200–280 pts (Euro St courses)
  Sunderland – 200 pts (Euro St courses)
180 pts **Liverpool John Moores** – 180–220 pts (Euro St Fr/Ger/Span)

For information on how to read the Subject Tables, see **Chapter 7**.

160 pts **London Met** – 160–200 pts (Euro Bank Fin)
London South Bank – CC (Euro Pol St)

Leeds Met – contact University

Alternative offers
IB offers Aberystwyth 29 pts; Bath 36 pts; Birmingham 32 pts; Bristol UWE 26–32 pts; Dundee 29 pts; Essex 32 pts; Kent 28–32 pts; Lancaster 33pts; Leicester 28–30 pts; London (RH) 32 pts, (UCL) 38 pts; Loughborough 30 pts; Manchester Met 26 pts; Reading 31 pts; Southampton 32 pts; Stirling 30 pts.
Scottish offers See **Chapter 7**.

OTHER HIGHER EDUCATION COURSES IN THE SUBJECT FIELD
Higher National Diploma courses East Lancashire (IHE) (Euro Leg St); Mid-Cheshire (Coll); Newport; West Herts (Coll).

CHOOSING YOUR COURSE (SEE ALSO CH.1)
Subject information European Studies is an increasingly popular subject and offers the language student an opportunity to study modern languages within the context of a European country (for example, economics, politics, legal, social and cultural aspects). In these courses there is usually a strong emphasis on the written and spoken word. Useful website www.europa.eu; see also **Languages**.

Course variations European Studies and Public Policy (Aston); Modern Languages and European Studies (Society, Culture and History) (Birmingham); International Relations with European Studies (Exeter); European Tourism (Lincoln); European Studies Combined Honours (Liverpool); European Literature and Culture (London (RH)); European Banking and Finance (London Met); European Film and Media (Stirling); Contemporary European Studies (Sussex). *NOW CHECK PROSPECTUSES AND WEBSITES FOR ANY RECENT CHANGES.*

Universities and colleges teaching quality See www.tqi.ac.uk; www.qaa.ac.uk.

Top universities and colleges (Research) Aston; Bath; Belfast (Queen's); Birmingham*; Cardiff; Glasgow*; Lancaster; London (UCL); Loughborough; Portsmouth; Southampton*.

ADMISSIONS INFORMATION
Number of applicants per place (approx) Aberystwyth 10; Aston 5; Cardiff 5; Dundee 6; Durham 2; East Anglia 11; Hull 6; Kent 11; Lancaster 9; Leicester 15; London (King's) 7, (UCL) 2; London Met 4; London South Bank 6; Loughborough 4; Northumbria 7; Nottingham 23; Nottingham Trent 12; Plymouth 9; Portsmouth 5.

Advice to applicants and planning the UCAS personal statement Try to identify an interest you have in the country relevant to your studies. Visits to that country should be described. Read the national newspapers and magazines and keep up to date with political and economic developments. Interest in the culture and civilisation of Europe as a whole. **Leeds** Motivation for choosing the course; personal achievements; future career plans, if any; travel. **Loughborough** Broad range of interests and experience. **Portsmouth** International awareness and perspective.

Selection interviews **Yes** Durham, East Anglia, Hull, London (Gold), London Met, London South Bank, Stirling, Sussex; **Some** Cardiff, Dundee, Kent (not usually), Liverpool John Moores, Loughborough, Portsmouth.

Interview advice and questions Whilst your interest in studying a language may be the main reason for applying for this subject, the politics, economics and culture of European countries are constantly in the news. You should keep up-to-date with any such topics concerning your chosen country and be prepared for questions. A language test may occupy part of the interview. **Loughborough** No tests. Interview designed to inform students about the course. See also **Chapter 6**.

Reasons for rejection (non-academic) Poor powers of expression. Lack of ideas on any issues. Lack of enthusiasm.

AFTER-RESULTS ADVICE
Universities with vacancies in Clearing (2006) Aberystwyth; Birmingham; Bristol UWE; Essex; London (QM), (RH); Manchester; Manchester Met; Nottingham Trent; Portsmouth; Southampton Solent; Sunderland; Swansea.

Offers to applicants repeating A-levels **Higher** Aberystwyth, East Anglia; **Same** Aston, Cardiff, Dundee, Liverpool John Moores, London Met, London South Bank, Loughborough, Plymouth.

GRADUATE DESTINATIONS AND EMPLOYMENT (2005 HESA)
No data available. See under separate **Language** tables.

OTHER DEGREE SUBJECTS FOR CONSIDERATION
Business and Management; History; International Relations; Politics; Language courses.

FILM, RADIO, VIDEO AND TV STUDIES

(see also **Communication Studies, Media Studies** and **Photography**)

NB The points totals shown to the left of the institutions are for ease of reference only. It must not be assumed that tariff points are always used by institutions or that they can be substituted for an offer in grades. The level of an offer is not necessarily indicative of the quality of a course.

COURSE OFFERS INFORMATION
Subject requirements/preferences **GCSE** English usually required. Courses vary, check prospectuses. **Bournemouth** Grade A/B profile. **Warwick** Grade B English literature. **Ancient Scottish universities** English, mathematics and foreign language. **AL** English may be stipulated for some courses.

Your target offers
360 pts **and above**
    Warwick – AABb **or** AAaab–BBBc (Film TV St; Film Lit)
340 pts **East Anglia** – AAB–ABB 340–320 pts (Film TV St; Film Engl St; Film Am St; Film Art Hist)
    St Andrews – AAB–ABB (Film St courses)
320 pts **Cardiff** – ABB (Journal Film Media; Journal Film Media joint courses)
    Exeter – ABB–BBB 320–300 pts (Film St (Cnma Prac); Film St Fr/Ger/Ital/Russ/Span)
    Glasgow – ABB (Film TV St courses)
    Kent – 320 pts (Film St)
    London (King's) – ABB+AS (Film Am St)
    Manchester – ABB–BBC (Film St courses)
    Nottingham – ABB–ABC/BBB (Film Am St)
    Southampton – ABB (3AL) 320 pts **or** ABBB (4AL) (Film courses)
    Sussex – ABB–BBB **or** 360 pts 3AL+AS see 2nd subj (Film St courses)
300 pts **Aberdeen** – BBB–BBC 2nd yr entry (Film St courses)
    Belfast (Queen's) – BBB (Film St)
    Bournemouth – 300 pts (Script Film TV; TV Prod)
    Essex – BBB–BBC 300–280 pts (Film St Hist Art; Film St; Hist Film St)
    Kent – 300 pts (Film St Hist)
    Lancaster – BBB (Film St Phil; Film Sociol; Film Cult St; Euro Lang Film St)
    Leeds – BBB (Cnma Photo TV St)
    London (QM) – 300–260 pts (Film St courses)
    Reading – 300 pts (TV Film Thea)
280 pts **Aberystwyth** – 280–310 pts (Film TV St courses; Scngrph St courses)
    Bristol UWE – 280–300 pts (Film St Engl; Dr Film St; Film St Media Cult St)
    Chester (Warrington) – 280–240 pts (Media (Rad Prod) (TV Prod); Film St Lit Film)
    Kent – 280–260 pts (Film St Fr/Ger/Ital/Hisp St; Film St Phil; Film St Hist Phil Art; Film St Phil; Film Contemp Arts)

Northumbria – 280 pts (Engl Film St)
Staffordshire – 280 pts (Film Prod Tech; Des Film Prod Tech)
Stirling – BBC (Film Media St; Euro Film Media)
UCE Birmingham – 280 pts (Media Comm (TV Vid))

260 pts **Brunel** – 260 pts (Film TV St courses)
Exeter – BCC (Film St Russ)
Leicester – BCC **or** 260–340 pts (Film St Vis Arts)
Liverpool – 260 pts (inc B/C lang) (Euro Film St Modn Lang)
Northumbria – 260 pts (Film TV St)
Oxford Brookes – BCC (Film St)
Roehampton – 260 pts (single hons) 220 pts (comb hons) (Film St; Film St Scrn Prac)
Sheffield Hallam – 260 pts (Film Lit; Film Hist; Film St (Hist Theor Crit))
Sunderland – 260 pts (Film Media St; Media Prod (TV Rad))
Winchester – 260 pts (Scrn Prod)

240 pts **Aberdeen** – CCC (Film St)
Bristol UWE – 240–300 pts (Film St Hist)
Central Lancashire – 240 pts (TV Prod)
Hertfordshire – 240 pts (Film Comb courses)
Kingston – 240–320 pts (TV St joint courses)
Lincoln – 240 pts (Contemp Lns Media)
Manchester Met – 240 pts (Film Media St)
Middlesex – 240–280 pts (TV Prod)
Northumbria – 240 pts (Film St Sociol)
Portsmouth – 240–300 pts (Film St; Film St Crea Writ; Film St Ent Tech; Film St Dr)
Swansea – 240 pts (Scrn St joint courses)
Westminster – CCC (Film TV Prod)
York St John – 240 pts BCC (Film TV Prod)

220 pts **Anglia Ruskin** – 220 pts (Film TV Prod; Film TV Thea Des)
Bangor – 220–260 pts (Hist Film St; Engl Film St; Fr/Ger Film St)
Brighton – 220 pts (Scrn St)
Central Lancashire – 220 pts (Film Media St)
Edge Hill – 220 pts (Film TV Prod)
Falmouth (UC) – 220 pts (Film St)
Glamorgan – 220 pts (Film Rad TV)
Kingston – 220 pts (Film St)
Liverpool Hope – 220 pts (Film St)
Queen Margaret (UC) – 220 pts (Film Media)
UCE Birmingham – 220–240 pts (TV Tech Prod)
Winchester – 220–240 pts (Film St courses; Cnma Tech courses except under **240 pts**)

200 pts **Barnsley (Univ Centre)** – 200 pts (TV Vid Efcts)
Bolton – 200 pts (Film Media St)

Bristol UWE – 200–280 pts (Film St; Film St Pol; Film St Sociol)
Creative Arts (UC) – 200 pts (Film Prod)
Gloucestershire – 200 pts (Film St courses)
Hertfordshire – 200 pts (Spec Efcts; Dig Film TV Prod; Dig Lns Media)
Liverpool John Moores – BB (Scrn St courses)
Manchester Met – CDD 200 pts (Film TV St Cult St; Writ Film TV)
Middlesex – 200–240 pts (Film St)
Napier – 200 pts (Photo Film Imag)
Newport – 200–300 pts (Film Vid; Doc Film TV)

180 pts **De Montfort** – 180–200 pts (Film St; Film Media St)
Derby – 180 pts (Film TV St; Film St)
Edge Hill – 180–220 pts (Film St)
Kingston – 180–240 pts (Film St joint courses)
Lampeter – open admission policy (Film Media; Film St)
Paisley – BC–CC (Scrn Prac; Cnma)
Southampton Solent – 180–160 pts (Film St; Film TV St)
Staffordshire – 180–240 pts (Film TV Rad St; Film St)

160 pts **Bedfordshire** – 160 pts (TV Prod)
Bournemouth – 160 pts (TV Prod)
Bournemouth (AI) – 160 pts (Film Prod; Animat Prod)
Canterbury Christ Church – CC (Film Rad TV St)
Cardiff (UWIC) – 160 pts (Broad Media Pop Cult)
Central Lancashire – 160 pts (Film Media St; Film Media Comb; TV Prod Comb)
East London – 160 pts (Film Hist; Film Vid)
Glamorgan – 160 pts (TV Film Set Des)
Leeds Trinity and All Saints (Coll) – 160–240 pts (Film St; Engl Film St)
London Met – 160–200 pts (Film St; Dig Media; Film Broad Prod)
London South Bank – CC (Film St; Dig Film Vid)
Manchester Met – 160–200 pts (Contemp Film Vid)
Portsmouth – 160–240 pts (Vid Prod)
St Mary's (Coll) – CC 160 pts (Film TV courses)
Thames Valley – 160 pts (Vid Prod; Film Vid Prod; Film St)
Wolverhampton – 160–220 pts (Film St; Lit St Film St)
Worcester – 160 pts (Film St)
York St John – 160 pts (Film St)

140 pts **Teesside** – 140 pts approx (TV Prod Prof Prac)
Trinity Carmarthen (Coll) – 140–100 pts (Film St; Film St Adv; Film St Crea Writ; Film St Engl; Film St Media St)

120 pts **Buckinghamshire Chilterns (UC)** – 120 pts (Film St courses; Vid Prod courses)
North East Wales (IHE) – 120–80 pts (Mov Imag (Des))
SAE (Inst) – 120–220 pts (Rec Arts)
Suffolk (Univ Campus) – 120–180 pts (Film Media St)

100 pts **Swansea (IHE)** – 100–340 pts (Engl St Film TV St)

80 pts **Accrington and Rossendale (Coll)** – 80 pts (Broad Film Comm)
Arts London – 80 pts (Film Vid)
Creative Arts (UC) – 80 pts (Film Prod; Dig Scrn Arts)
London (Birk) – 80 pts for under 21s (over 21s varies) (p/t Film Media)
Ravensbourne (CDC) – 80 pts (Mov Imag Des)
Royal Scottish (RSAMD) – 80 pts (Film TV)
Southend Campus Essex – 80–160 pts (TV Prod Scrn Media)

Leeds Met – contact University

Alternative offers
IB offers Aberystwyth 28 pts; Brighton 28 pts; Bristol UWE 28–32 pts; Brunel 28 pts; Essex 28–30 pts; Exeter 32–34 pts; Kent 28–34 pts; Lancaster 34 pts; Leicester 30 pts; London (QM) 32 pts; Manchester

For information on how to read the Subject Tables, see **Chapter 7**.

Met 28 pts; Reading 32 pts; St Andrews 32–36 pts; Southampton 33 pts; Staffordshire 28 pts; Stirling 32 pts; Thames Valley 28 pts; Warwick 36 pts; Winchester 24–26 pts.
Scottish offers See **Chapter 7**.

OTHER HIGHER EDUCATION COURSES IN THE SUBJECT FIELD

Foundation degrees (contact the institutions for details) Bournemouth and Poole (Coll); Cleveland (CAD); Farnborough (CT); Leeds Met; Newcastle (Coll); St Helens (Coll).

Higher National Diploma courses
100 pts and below
> Bournemouth; Buckinghamshire Chilterns (UC); Grimsby (IFHE); North East Wales (IHE); North Warwickshire (Coll); Northbrook (Coll); Norwich City (Coll); Plymouth (CAD); Salisbury (Coll); Staffordshire; Thames Valley; UHI Millennium Inst; Walsall (Coll); Warwickshire (Coll); Wolverhampton; Worcester.

CHOOSING YOUR COURSE (SEE ALSO CH.1)

Subject information A wide range of courses are on offer although applicants should be aware that many courses cover theoretical or historical aspects of the subject. Students wishing to follow courses with practical applications must check with the institution beforehand to determine how much time in the course is spent on actual film-making or video production. **Useful websites** www.bfi.org.uk; www.film.com; www.allmovie.com; www.bksts.com; www.imdb.com; www.fwfr.com; www.bafta.org; www.movingimage.us.

Course variations Scenographic Studies (Aberystwyth); Scriptwriting, Film and TV (Bournemouth); Journalism, Film and Media (Cardiff); Film History (East London); Television and Film Set Design (Glamorgan); Digital Film and Television Production (Hertfordshire); Film Studies and Visual Arts (Leicester); Television, Film and Theatre (Reading); Screen Production (Winchester); Literary Studies and Film Studies (Wolverhampton). *NOW CHECK PROSPECTUSES AND WEBSITES FOR ANY RECENT CHANGES.*

Universities and colleges teaching quality See www.tqi.ac.uk; www.qaa.ac.uk.

Top universities and colleges (Research) Warwick.

Sandwich degree courses See under **Media Studies**.

ADMISSIONS INFORMATION

Number of applicants per place (approx) Anglia Ruskin 3; Bournemouth 30; Bournemouth (AI) 9; Brunel 10; Canterbury Christ Church 50; Cardiff 11; Central Lancashire 5; East Anglia (Film Engl St) 7, (Film Am St) 5; Kent 30; Liverpool John Moores 17; London Met 7; Portsmouth 20; Ravensbourne (CDC) 9; Sheffield Hallam 60; Southampton 5; Southampton Solent 7; Staffordshire (Film TV Rad St) 31; Stirling 12; Warwick 18; Westminster 41; York St John 6.

Advice to applicants and planning the UCAS personal statement Any experience in film-making (beyond home videos) should be described in detail. Knowledge and preferences of types of films and the work of some producers should be included on the UCAS application. Read film magazines and other appropriate literature to keep informed of developments. Show genuine interest in film and be knowledgeable about favourite films, directors and give details of work experience or film projects undertaken. **De Montfort** A genuine interest in a range of film genres. **East Anglia** Applicants need to discuss the ways in which films relate to broader cultural phenomena, social, literary, historical. **Staffordshire** Are you fascinated by film, inspired by television or devoted to radio and keen to know more? See also **Appendix 2**.

Misconceptions about this course That an A-level film or media studies is required; it is not. That it's Film so it's easy! That the course is all practical work. Some applicants believe that these are Media courses. Some applicants believe that Film and TV Studies is a training for production work. **Bournemouth (AI)** (Animat Prod) This is not a Film Studies course but a course based on traditional animation with supported computer image processing. **De Montfort** Some believe that this is a course in practical film-making: it is not, it is for analysts and historians. **Winchester** That graduation automatically leads to a job in broadcasting!

Selection interviews Most institutions will interview some applicants in this subject. **Yes** Bournemouth, Bournemouth (AI), Brunel, Canterbury Christ Church, Chichester, Liverpool John Moores, Newport, York St John; **Some** Anglia Ruskin, East Anglia, Staffordshire, Wolverhampton.

Interview advice and questions Questions will focus on your chosen field. In the case of films be prepared to answer questions not only on your favourite films but on the work of one or two directors you admire and early Hollywood examples. **Anglia Ruskin** We ask for an original review of a film recently seen. **Bournemouth** (Script Film TV) Successful applicants will be required to submit a 20–page screenplay; (TV Prod) A good applicant will have the ability to discuss media issues in depth, to have total commitment to TV and video productions and will have attempted to make programmes. **Bournemouth (AI)** Written piece prior to interview. Questions at interview relevant to the portfolio/reel. **Staffordshire** We assess essay-writing skills. See also **Chapter 6**.

Reasons for rejection (non-academic) Not enough drive or ambition. No creative or original ideas. Preference for production work rather than practical work. Inability to articulate the thought process behind the work in the applicant's portfolio. Insufficient knowledge of media affairs. Lack of knowledge of film history. Wrong course choice, wanted more practical work.

AFTER-RESULTS ADVICE
Universities with vacancies in Clearing (2006) Aberystwyth; Anglia Ruskin; Bangor; Bournemouth; Bradford; Bristol UWE; Brunel; Canterbury Christ Church; Central Lancashire; Chester; De Montfort; Derby; East Anglia; East London; Edge Hill; Essex; Glamorgan; Gloucestershire; Hull; Kent; Kingston; Lampeter; Leicester; Lincoln; Liverpool Hope; Liverpool John Moores; London (QM), (RH); London Met; London South Bank; Manchester Met; Middlesex; Northampton; Northumbria; Nottingham; Portsmouth; Roehampton; Southampton; Southampton Solent; Staffordshire; Stirling; Sunderland; Thames Valley; Wolverhampton; Winchester; Worcester; York St John.

Offers to applicants repeating A-levels **Higher** Bournemouth (AI), Glasgow, Manchester Met; **Same** Anglia Ruskin, De Montfort, East Anglia, Staffordshire, Winchester, Wolverhampton, York St John.

GRADUATE DESTINATIONS AND EMPLOYMENT (2005 HESA)
Cinematics and Photography graduates surveyed 2010 **Employed** 1100 **In further study** 150 **Assumed unemployed** 260.

OTHER DEGREE SUBJECTS FOR CONSIDERATION
Communication Studies; Creative Writing; Media Studies; Photography.

FINANCE

(including **Banking, Financial Services, Insurance;** see also **Accountancy/Accounting**)

NB The points totals shown to the left of the institutions are for ease of reference only. It must not be assumed that tariff points are always used by institutions or that they can be substituted for an offer in grades. The level of an offer is not necessarily indicative of the quality of a course.

COURSE OFFERS INFORMATION
Subject requirements/preferences **GCSE** Most institutions will require English and mathematics grade C minimum. **Bangor** Average grade B. **Birmingham, Buckingham, De Montfort, East Anglia, Keele, Loughborough** and **Portsmouth** Grade B in mathematics. **City** Grade B in English and mathematics. **AL** Mathematics may be required or preferred.

Your target offers
360 pts **and above**
  Southampton – 390–340 pts (Acc Fin)
350 pts **Southampton** – 350–300 pts (Acc Econ)
340 pts **City** – AAB (Bank Int Fin; Invest Fin Risk Mgt; Rl Est Fin Invest; Risk Analys Ins)
  Newcastle – AAB (Fin Maths)

320 pts **Belfast (Queen's)** – ABB–BBB (Fin; Fin Fr/Ger/Span)
           Birmingham – ABB 320 pts (Mny Bank Fin)
           Heriot-Watt – ABB 320 pts 2nd yr entry (Fin Maths)
           Lancaster – ABB (Fin Econ; Fin Maths; Fin)
           London (QM) – 320 pts (Econ Fin Mgt)
           Loughborough – ABB (Bank Fin Mgt; Acc Fin Mgt)
           Manchester – ABB–ABC (Finance)
           Newcastle – ABB (Fin Bus Econ)
           Nottingham – ABB (Ind Econ Ins; Fin Acc Mgt)
           Reading – 320–360 pts (Invest Fin Prop; Int Scrts Inv Bank)

300 pts **Aberystwyth** – 300 pts (Fin Maths)
           Bristol – 300 pts (Econ Fin)
           Cardiff – BBB (Acc Fin; Bank Fin; Bank Fin Euro Lang)
           East Anglia – BBB–BBC (Acc Fin; Bus Fin Econ)
           Exeter – 300–320 pts (Econ Fin)
           Glasgow – BBB (Acc Fin)
           Heriot-Watt – ABC 1st yr entry (Fin Maths)
           Heriot-Watt – BBB 2nd yr entry (Econ Fin; Acc Fin; Fin Bus Law)
           Loughborough – 300 pts (Bus Econ Fin)
           Sheffield – BBB 300 pts (Acc Fin Mgt courses)
           Strathclyde – ABC–BBC (Finance)

280 pts **Abertay Dundee** – BBC 2nd yr entry (Fin Bus)
           Bournemouth – 280 pts (Fin Law; Fin Bus; Acc Tax; Acc Fin)
           Brunel – 280 pts (Fin Maths; Econ Bus Fin)
           Durham – BBC (Bus Fin)
           Essex – 280–260 pts (Fin Mgt; Fin; Fin Maths)
           Northumbria – BBC (Fin Inv Mgt)
           Swansea – 280 pts (Fin Econ Acc)
           Westminster – 280 pts (Bus Mgt (Fin) (Fin Serv))

260 pts **Coventry** – 260–320 pts (Fin Serv; Acc Fin; Bus Acc)
           Heriot-Watt – BCC 260 pts 1st yr entry (Econ Fin; Acc Fin; Fin Bus Law)
           Hull – 260 pts (Fin Mgt Econ; Fin Mgt)
           Keele – 260–320 pts (Fin courses)
           London Met – 260 pts (Euro Bank Fin)
           Salford – BCC–CCC (Fin Acc)

250 pts **Buckingham** – 250 pts (Fin Serv; Fin Inf Sys)

240 pts **Aberdeen** – CCC (Fin courses)
           Bangor – 240–280 pts (Bank Fin)
           De Montfort – 240–220 pts (Fin joint hons)
           Dundee – CCC 240 pts (Finance)
           Nottingham Trent – 240 pts (Acc Fin)
           Robert Gordon – CCC (Mgt Fin)
           Salford – 240–260 pts (Bus St Fin Mgt)
           Sheffield Hallam – 240 pts (Bank Fin; Bus Fin Serv)
           Staffordshire – 240 pts (Finance)
           Stirling – CCC (Fin; Mny Bank Fin)
           Ulster – 240 pts (Bus Fin Invest)

220 pts **Abertay Dundee** – CCD 1st yr entry (Fin Bus)
           Aberystwyth – 220–280 pts (Bus Fin; Acc Fin courses)
           Brighton – 220 pts (Int Fin Cap Mark St)
           Sunderland – 220 pts (Bus Mgt (Fin Mgt))

200 pts **Hertfordshire** – 200–240 pts (Finance)
           Lincoln – 200 pts (Fin courses)
           Liverpool John Moores – 200 pts (Int Bank Fin)
           London Met – 200 pts (Int Econ Fin)

For a quick reference offers calculator, fold out the inside back cover.

Manchester Met – 200–260 pts (Fin Serv; Fin Sctr Mgt)
Napier – 200 pts (Fin Serv; Fin Serv Bus Econ)
Portsmouth – 200 pts (Fin Bus; Int Fin Tr)
UCE Birmingham – 200 pts (Acc Fin; Bus Fin)
180 pts **Greenwich** – 180–220 pts (Fin Fin Inf Sys)
Northampton – 180–220 pts (Fin Inf Mgt; Fin Serv)
Regents Bus Sch London – DDD/CC (Int Fin Acc)
160 pts **Anglia Ruskin** – DDE 160–220 pts (Int Fin Mark; Acc Fin)
Buckinghamshire Chilterns (UC) – 160–240 pts (Fin courses)
East London – 160 pts (Fin Mny Bank; Bus Fin)
Farnborough (CT) – 160 pts (Bus Mgt Fin)
Glasgow Caledonian – CC (Fin Serv; Fin Maths; Rsk Mgt)
Huddersfield – 160–240 pts (Acc Fin)
London Met – 160–200 pts (Fin Maths; Fin Serv; Bank Fin; Ins)
London South Bank – CC (Acc Fin; Fin Mgt)
Middlesex – 160–200 pts (Mny Bank Fin)
Royal (CAg) – 160 pts (Bus Mgt (Fin))
Worcester – 160 pts (Bus Mgt (Fin Acc))
120 pts **East Lancashire (IHE)** – 120 pts (Bus Acc)
80 pts **London (Birk)** – 80 pts for under 21s (over 21s varies) (p/t Fin Econ)

Leeds Met – contact University

Alternative offers
IB offers Aberystwyth 29 pts; Birmingham 32–34 pts; Brunel 30 pts; City 35 pts; Dundee 29 pts; Durham 30 pts; Keele 28–30 pts; Leicester 32 pts; Reading 33 pts; Stirling 30 pts.
Scottish offers See **Chapter 7**.

OTHER HIGHER EDUCATION COURSES IN THE SUBJECT FIELD
Foundation degrees (contact the institutions for details) Bournemouth and Poole (Coll); Bromley (CFHE); Grimsby (IFHE); Leicester; London Met; North West Kent (Coll); Northampton (Coll); Stratford-upon-Avon (Coll); Sutton Coldfield (Coll); Swansea (IHE); Thames Valley; West Kent (Coll); Weymouth (Coll).

Higher National Diploma courses Anglia Ruskin; Bangor; Bath; Bell (Coll); Blackpool and Fylde (Coll); Bradford (Coll); Brighton; Buckinghamshire Chilterns (UC); Cardiff (UWIC); Carshalton (Coll); Chesterfield (Coll); Coventry City (Coll); De Montfort; Doncaster (Univ Centre); Dudley (Coll); Durham New (Coll); East Lancashire (IHE); East London; Exeter (Coll); Glamorgan; Gloucestershire; Guildford (Coll); Herefordshire (CT); Hertfordshire; Hopwood Hall (Coll); Kingston; Lakes (Coll); Llandrillo Cymru (Coll); London Met; Manchester City (Coll); Newcastle (Coll); Newport; Northampton; Northbrook (Coll); Norwich City (Coll); Oldham (Coll); Park Lane Leeds (Coll); Peterborough Reg (Coll); Riverside Halton (Coll); Salford; Sandwell (Coll); Sheffield (Coll); South Birmingham (Coll); Southampton Solent; Stockport (CFHE); Suffolk (Univ Campus); Swansea (Coll); Tameside (Coll); Teesside; UCE Birmingham; Walsall (Coll); West Herts (Coll); Westminster (Coll); Wigan and Leigh (Coll); Wolverhampton; Worcester (CT); Worcestershire New (Coll); see also **Accountancy/Accounting** and **Business Courses**.

CHOOSING YOUR COURSE (SEE ALSO CH.1)
Subject information Financial Services courses provide a comprehensive view of the world of finance and normally cover banking, insurance, investment, building societies, international finance, accounting and economics. These courses will not necessarily provide graduates with full exemptions from Institute of Banking qualifications (see **Appendix 2**). Major banks offer sponsorships for some of the specialised Banking courses. **Useful websites** www.cii.co.uk; www.sii.org.uk; www.fsa.gov.uk; www.efinancialnews.com; www.worldbank.org; www.ifslearning.com; www.ft.com.

Course variations International Finance and Capital Market Studies (Brighton); Banking and International Finance (City); Risk Analysis and Insurance (City); Finance, Money and Banking (East London); Industrial Economics with Insurance (Nottingham); International Finance and Trade

(Portsmouth); International Securities and Investment Banking (Reading); Business Finance and Investment (Ulster). *NOW CHECK PROSPECTUSES AND WEBSITES FOR ANY RECENT CHANGES.*

Universities and colleges teaching quality See www.tqi.ac.uk; www.qaa.ac.uk.

ADMISSIONS INFORMATION

Number of applicants per place (approx) Aberystwyth 4; Bangor 30; Birmingham 17; Bristol UWE 4; Buckingham 4; Cardiff 10; Central Lancashire 6; City 10; Dundee 5; Durham 4; Glamorgan 3; Loughborough 35; Middlesex 3; Northampton 3; Portsmouth 4; Sheffield Hallam 4; UCE Birmingham 13.

Advice to applicants and planning the UCAS personal statement Visits to banks or insurance companies should be described, giving details of any work experience or work shadowing done in various departments. Discuss any particular aspects of finance etc which interest you. **City** Give details of sport, voluntary work, skills etc. See also **Appendix 2**.

Misconceptions about this course Applicants should note that a number of graduates choose careers outside banking and finance.

Selection interviews **Yes** Buckingham (pref), Huddersfield; **Some** Anglia Ruskin, Dundee, Staffordshire, Stirling; **No** City.

Interview advice and questions Banking involves both high street and merchant banks, so a knowledge of banking activities in general will be expected. In the past mergers have been discussed and also the role of the Bank of England in the economy. The work of the accountant may be discussed. See also **Chapter 6**.

Reasons for rejection (non-academic) Lack of interest. Poor English. Lacking in motivation and determination to complete the course.

AFTER-RESULTS ADVICE

Universities with vacancies in Clearing (2006) Aberdeen; Abertay Dundee; Aberystwyth; Anglia Ruskin; Bangor; Bournemouth; Brunel; Dundee; Coventry; East London; Essex; Greenwich; Heriot-Watt; Hertfordshire; Huddersfield; Hull; Keele; Lincoln; Liverpool John Moores; London (QM); London Met; Manchester Met; Middlesex; Northampton; Portsmouth; Salford; Sheffield; Sheffield Hallam; Southampton; Stirling; Strathclyde; Swansea; UCE Birmingham; Westminster.

Offers to applicants repeating A-levels **Higher** Glasgow; **Possibly higher** Bangor; **Same** Anglia Ruskin, Birmingham, Bradford, Cardiff, City, Dundee, London Met, Loughborough, Napier, Northumbria, Stirling, UCE Birmingham.

GRADUATE DESTINATIONS AND EMPLOYMENT (2005 HESA)

Graduates surveyed 855 **Employed** 475 **In further study** 70 **Assumed unemployed** 45.

OTHER DEGREE SUBJECTS FOR CONSIDERATION

Accountancy; Actuarial Studies; Business Studies; Economics.

FOOD SCIENCE/STUDIES AND TECHNOLOGY

(see also **Agricultural Sciences/Agriculture, Consumer Studies, Dietetics and Nutrition**)

NB The points totals shown to the left of the institutions are for ease of reference only. It must not be assumed that tariff points are always used by institutions or that they can be substituted for an offer in grades. The level of an offer is not necessarily indicative of the quality of a course.

COURSE OFFERS INFORMATION

Subject requirements/preferences **GCSE** English, mathematics and a science. **Bournemouth** English, mathematics and double science at grade A–C. **Leeds** Mathematics grade B. **Newcastle** Chemistry or dual science if not at A-level; mathematics grade B. **Surrey** (Fd Sci Microbiol) Grades A or B in sciences if not offered at A-level. **AL** One or two science subjects; chemistry may be required.

Your target offers
300 pts **Leeds** – BBB (Fd Sci Microbiol)
　　　　Newcastle – BBB (Fd Hum Nutr)
　　　　Nottingham – BBB–BCD (Fd Sci)
　　　　Surrey – BBB–BBC (Fd Sci Microbiol; Nutr Fd Sci)
280 pts **Glasgow** – BBC–CCC (Physiol Spo Sci Nutr)
　　　　Leeds – BBC 280–260 pts (Fd St Nutr; Fd Sci; Fd Bioch Hlth; Fd Prod Proc Mgt)
260 pts **Belfast (Queen's)** – BCC/AB (Fd Qual Sfty Nutr)
　　　　Newcastle – BCC (Orgnc Fd Prod)
　　　　Reading – 260–280 pts (Fd Sci; Fd Sci Bus; Fd Tech; Fd Mark Bus Econ)
240 pts **Manchester Met** – 240 pts (Fd Nutr; Fd Mgt; Fd Tech)
　　　　Nottingham – CCC (Fd Microbiol)
　　　　Ulster – 240 pts (Fd Nutr)
220 pts **Brighton** – 220 pts (Vit Oeno)
200 pts **Abertay Dundee** – CDD (Fd Consum Sci; Fd Nutr Hlth; Fd Prod Des)
　　　　Bath Spa – 200–240 pts (Fd Nutr Consum Prot; Fd St)
　　　　Bournemouth – 200 pts (Fd Mark)
　　　　Glamorgan – 200–240 pts (Nutr Fd Techi Hlth)
　　　　Huddersfield – 200 pts (Fd Nutr Hlth; Fd Nutr)
　　　　Northumbria – 200 pts (Fd Sci Nutr)
　　　　Sheffield Hallam – 200 pts (Fd Nutr; Fd Mark)
　　　　Ulster – 200 pts (Culn Arts)
180 pts **Birmingham (CFTCS)** – 180 pts (Rtl Fd Mgt; Fd Consum Mgt; Culn Arts Mgt)
　　　　Glasgow Caledonian – DDD–CC (Fd Biosci)
　　　　Heriot-Watt – DDD–CCC (Fd Sci Tech Mgt; Brew Distil)
　　　　Oxford Brookes – BC–CDD (Pblc Hlth Nutr)
　　　　Teesside – 180–240 pts (Fd Nutr Hlth Sci)
160 pts **CAFRE** – CC 160 pts (Fd Tech; Sply Mgt (Fd))
　　　　Harper Adams (UC) – CC (Fd Rtl Mgt; Fd Qual Bus Mgt; Agri-Fd Mark Bus St; Fd Consum St; Frsh Prod Mgt)
　　　　Liverpool John Moores – 160 pts (Fd Nutr; Home Econ (Fd Des Tech); Consum St Mark)
　　　　London Met – 160 pts (Fd Consum St)
　　　　London South Bank – CC–EE (Biosci (Nutr); Orgnc Fd St; Fd Nutr)
　　　　Royal (CAg) – 160 pts (Bus Mgt (Agri-Fd))
　　　　SAC (Scottish CAg) – CC (Rur Bus Mgt (Fd Tech); Rur Bus Mgt Fd Tech)
　　　　Thames Valley – 160 pts (Hspty Mgt Fd St)
　　　　Wolverhampton – 160–220 pts (Fd Biol Hum Physiol; Bioch Fd Sci)
140 pts **Cardiff (UWIC)** – 140 pts (Nutr Fd Sci; Fd Sci Tech; Fd Consum Sci)

Alternative offers
IB offers Manchester Met 28 pts; Newcastle 32 pts; Nottingham 24–30 pts; Reading 30 pts; Surrey 30–32 pts.
Scottish offers See **Chapter 7**.

OTHER HIGHER EDUCATION COURSES IN THE SUBJECT FIELD

Foundation degrees (contact the institutions for details) Askham Bryan (Coll); Birmingham (CFTCS); Bridgwater (Coll); CAFRE; Hartpury (Coll); Pershore (Coll); Reaseheath (Coll).

Higher National Diploma courses
100 pts **and below**
　　　　Blackpool and Fylde (Coll); Brighton; Cardiff (UWIC); CAFRE; Central Lancashire; Harper Adams (UC); Leeds Thomas Danby (Coll); Manchester Met; SAC (Scottish CAg); Salford; UHI Millennium Inst; West Anglia (Coll); Wolverhampton; Worcester.

CHOOSING YOUR COURSE (SEE ALSO CH.1)

Subject information Biochemistry, microbiology, dietetics, human nutrition, food processing and technology are components of Food Science courses as well as being degree courses in their own right (and appropriate alternative courses). The study depends for its understanding on a secure foundation of several pure sciences – chemistry and two subjects from physics, mathematics, biology, botany or zoology. Only students offering subjects from these fields are likely to be considered. Food Technology covers the engineering aspects of food processing and management. A number of bursaries are offered by the food industry. Check with admissions tutors. See also **Appendix 2. Useful websites** www.iagre.org.uk; www.scienceyear.com; www.sofht.co.uk; www.ifst.org; www.defra.gov.uk; www.icsc.org.uk.

Course variations Food Quality Safety and Nutrition (Belfast (Queen's)); Viticulture and Oenology (Brighton); Fresh Produce Management (Harper Adams (UC)); Biosciences (Nutrition) (London South Bank); Food and Human Nutrition (Newcastle); Public Health and Nutrition (Oxford Brookes). *NOW CHECK PROSPECTUSES AND WEBSITES FOR ANY RECENT CHANGES.*

Universities and colleges teaching quality See www.tqi.ac.uk; www.qaa.ac.uk.

Top universities and colleges (Research) Leeds*; Nottingham; Reading.

Sandwich degree courses Belfast (Queen's); Birmingham (CFTCS); Bournemouth; Coventry; Glasgow Caledonian; Harper Adams (UC); Huddersfield; Leeds Met; London South Bank; Manchester Met; Newcastle; Northumbria; Reading; Sheffield Hallam; Surrey; Teesside; Ulster; Wolverhampton.

ADMISSIONS INFORMATION

Number of applicants per place (approx) Bath Spa 4; Belfast (Queen's) 10; Blackpool and Fylde (Coll) 1; Bournemouth 5; Cardiff (UWIC) 1; Dundee 3; Huddersfield (Fd Nutr Hlth) 4; Leeds 5; Liverpool John Moores 2; London Met 5; London South Bank 3; Manchester Met 3; Newcastle 13; Nottingham 7; Oxford Brookes 20; Robert Gordon 4; Sheffield Hallam 4; Surrey 17; Wolverhampton 4.

Advice to applicants and planning the UCAS personal statement Visits, work experience or work shadowing in any food manufacturing firm, or visits to laboratories, should be described on your UCAS application. Keep up-to-date with developments by reading journals relating to the industry. See also **Appendix 2**.

Misconceptions about this course Some applicants confuse Food Technology with Catering or Hospitality Management. Applicants under-estimate the job prospects. There are approximately 300 vacancies per month advertised by food manufacturers. **Leeds** (Fd Sci) Food Science is NOT food technology, catering or cooking. It aims to understand WHY food materials behave in the way they do, in order to improve the nutritive value, safety and quality of the food we eat.

Selection interviews Yes Belfast (Queen's), London South Bank, Nottingham (depends on application), Reading, Surrey; **Some** Bath Spa, Leeds (applicants with non-standard qualifications), Liverpool John Moores, Manchester Met, Salford.

Interview advice and questions This is a specialised field and admissions tutors will want to know your reasons for choosing the subject. You will be questioned on any experience you have had in the food industry. More general questions may cover the reasons for the trends in the popularity of certain types of food, the value of junk food and whether scientific interference with food is justifiable. **Leeds** Questions asked to ensure that the student understands, and can cope with, the science content of the course. See also **Chapter 6**.

Reasons for rejection (non-academic) Too immature. Unlikely to integrate well. Lack of vocational commitment.

AFTER-RESULTS ADVICE

Universities with vacancies in Clearing (2006) Abertay Dundee; Belfast (Queen's); Bournemouth; Heriot-Watt; Huddersfield; London South Bank; Manchester Met; Newcastle; Nottingham; Reading; Sheffield Hallam; Surrey; Wolverhampton.

Offers to applicants repeating A-levels **Higher** Leeds; **Possibly higher** Nottingham; **Same** Belfast (Queen's), Liverpool John Moores, Manchester Met, Salford, Sheffield Hallam, Surrey, Wolverhampton.

GRADUATE DESTINATIONS AND EMPLOYMENT (2005 HESA)
Graduates surveyed 320 **Employed** 200 **In further study** 45 **Assumed unemployed** 15.

OTHER DEGREE SUBJECTS FOR CONSIDERATION
Biochemistry; Biological Sciences; Biology; Biotechnology; Chemistry; Consumer Studies; Dietetics; Health Studies; Hospitality Management; Nutrition.

FORESTRY
(see also Agricultural Sciences/Agriculture)

NB The points totals shown to the left of the institutions are for ease of reference only. It must not be assumed that tariff points are always used by institutions or that they can be substituted for an offer in grades. The level of an offer is not necessarily indicative of the quality of a course.

COURSE OFFERS INFORMATION
Subject requirements/preferences GCSE Mathematics or science usually required. Check prospectuses. **Edinburgh** Biology or mathematics grade B. **AL** Two science subjects are usually stipulated which can include mathematics, geography or geology.

Your target offers
300 pts **Edinburgh** – BBB (Ecol Sci (Frsty))
240 pts **Aberdeen** – CCC (Frsty; Frsty Cons; Frsty Sci)
        Bangor – 240–280 pts (Cons Frsty Ecosys; Bus Mgt Frsty)
        Central Lancashire (Penrith) – 240 pts (Frsty Wdlnd Mgt; Frsty Env Mgt)
220 pts **Bangor** – 220–240 pts (Forestry)
120 pts **UHI Millennium Inst (IC)** – 120 pts (Arbor Urb Frsty; Frsty Cons)

Alternative offers
IB offers Bangor 28 pts.
Scottish offers See **Chapter 7**.

OTHER HIGHER EDUCATION COURSES IN THE SUBJECT FIELD
Foundation degrees (contact the institutions for details) Central Lancashire; Plumpton (Coll); Sparsholt (Coll).

Higher National Diploma courses Askham Bryan (Coll); Brighton; Capel Manor (Coll); East Durham and Houghall (CmC); Northampton; UHI Millennium Inst (IC); Warwickshire (Coll); Worcester.

CHOOSING YOUR COURSE (SEE ALSO CH.1)
Subject information Forestry is concerned with the establishment and management of forests for timber production, environmental, conservation and amenity purposes. **Useful websites** www.iagre.org.uk; www.forestry.gov.uk; www.rfs.org.uk; www.charteredforesters.org; www.iwsc.org.uk; www.british-trees.com; www.woodland-trust.org.uk.

Course variations Conservation and Forest Ecosystems (Bangor); Arboriculture and Urban Forestry (UHI Millennium Inst (IC)). *NOW CHECK PROSPECTUSES AND WEBSITES FOR ANY RECENT CHANGES.*

Universities and colleges teaching quality See www.tqi.ac.uk; www.qaa.ac.uk.

Sandwich degree courses Aberdeen; Bangor; Central Lancashire.

ADMISSIONS INFORMATION
Number of applicants per place (approx) Bangor 2; Edinburgh 9.

Advice to applicants and planning the UCAS personal statement Contact the Forestry Training Council and Commission and try to arrange visits to forestry centres, local community forests and nature trails. Discuss the work with forest officers and learn about future plans for specific forest areas and describe any visits made. **Bangor** Mention any experience of forestry or wood processing industries (for example, visits to forests and mills, work experience in relevant organisations). See **Appendix 2**.

Advice to overseas (non-EU) applicants **Bangor** Good proportion of overseas students on course.

Misconceptions about this course **Bangor** The course does not provide practical training in forestry (eg use of chainsaws and pesticides) or wood processing. It is intended to educate future managers, for example, not to train forestry or mill workers.

Selection interviews Most institutions.

Interview advice and questions Work experience or field courses attended are likely to be discussed and questions asked such as: What is arboriculture? On a desert island how would you get food from wood? How do you see forestry developing in the next hundred years? What aspects of forestry are the most important? **Bangor** Why are you interested in forestry/forest products? See also **Chapter 6**.

AFTER-RESULTS ADVICE

Universities with vacancies in Clearing (2006) Bangor; Central Lancashire.

Offers to applicants repeating A-levels **Same** Bangor.

GRADUATE DESTINATIONS AND EMPLOYMENT (2005 HESA)

Graduates surveyed 40 Employed 20 In further study 5 Assumed unemployed 5.

OTHER DEGREE SUBJECTS FOR CONSIDERATION

Agriculture; Biological Sciences; Countryside Management; Ecology; Environmental Sciences; Woodland and Wildlife Management.

FRENCH

(see also **European Studies** and **Languages**)

NB The points totals shown to the left of the institutions are for ease of reference only. It must not be assumed that tariff points are always used by institutions or that they can be substituted for an offer in grades. The level of an offer is not necessarily indicative of the quality of a course.

COURSE OFFERS INFORMATION

Subject requirements/preferences **GCSE Aberdeen, Dundee, Edinburgh, St Andrews** English, mathematics or science. **Bangor** Grade A* or A in French. **Exeter** As and Bs preferable in most subjects. **Hull** French grade A–B plus a range of As and Bs in other subjects. **Leeds** Grade A in languages, mathematics grade B for Mgt St. **Nottingham** French grade A–B. **Oxford** and **Cambridge** Usually majority of grade As. **Portsmouth** Three A grades, three B grades. **Sheffield** (Fr Bus) Mathematics grade B. **Sheffield Hallam** French grade B. **Swansea** Grade A in three subjects, grade B in three subjects. **AL** French is usually required at a specific grade and in some cases a second language may be stipulated.

Your target offers
360 pts **and above**
        Cambridge – AAA (Modn Mediev Lang (Fr))
        Oxford – Offers vary eg AAA–AAB (Modn Lang (Fr))
        Warwick – ABBb–BBBb (Fr courses)
340 pts **Cardiff** – AAB–BCC 340–260 pts (Educ Fr; Fr Sociol)
        Manchester – AAB (Fr Ger; Fr Ital; Fr Span; Fr Russ; Fr Chin)

St Andrews – AAB (Fr Psy)

320 pts   **Aston** – ABB 320 pts (Int Bus Fr)

Bath – ABB–BBB 3AL+AS (Modn Lang Euro St (Fr Ital) (Fr Russ) (Fr Ger) (Fr Span) (Fr Pol))

Bristol – ABB–BBB (Pol Fr; Dr Fr)

Cardiff – ABB–BBC (Fr; Fr joint courses; Fr Jap)

Durham – ABB (Fr Econ)

Exeter – ABB 320 pts (Fr courses)

Glasgow – ABB–BBB (French)

Kent – 320 pts (Fr Licence de Lettres)

Lancaster – ABB (Fr St Econ; Fr St Psy)

London (British Inst in Paris) – ABB (Fr St)

London (King's) – ABB+AS (Fr Maths; Fr Phil; Fr 3 yr)

London (UCL) – ABB+AS–BBB+AS (Fr courses)

Manchester – ABB (Fr Ling)

Newcastle – ABB–BBB (Fr; Fr Bus St; Fr Pol)

St Andrews – ABB–BBB (Fr courses except under **340 pts**)

Sheffield – ABB–BBB (Fr courses)

Southampton – ABB 320 pts (Fr courses)

300 pts   **Belfast (Queen's)** – BBB–BBC (Fr courses)

Birmingham – BBB–BBC (Fr St)

East Anglia – 300 pts (Interp Transl 2 Langs)

Edinburgh – BBB (Fr courses)

Exeter – BBB (Fr Russ)

Lancaster – BBB (Fr Comb courses except under **320 pts**)

Liverpool – BBB–ABB 300–320 pts (Fr Maths)

London (King's) – BBB+AS **or** BBbbb (Fr courses except under **320 pts**)

London (RH) – 300–320 pts (Fr courses)

Manchester – BBB (BA Fr Ger/Ital/Span/Port/Russ; Euro St Fr)

Newcastle – ABC–BBB (Ling Fr)

Nottingham – BBB–BBC (Fr courses)

Stirling – BBB–CCC (Fr courses)

Surrey – BBB–BCC 300–260 pts (Bus Mgt Fr)

Sussex – BBB (Fr courses)

York – BBB (Fr Ger; Fr Ling)

280 pts   **Aston** – 280–300 pts (Fr; Fr Ger/Span; Pol Fr; Sociol Fr; Fr Engl Lang; Fr Comb Hons; Transl St Fr)

Bristol – BBC (Fr; Cz Fr; Fr Ger/Ital/Lat/Port/Russ/Span)

Dundee – 280 pts (Law Fr)

Essex – BBC 280 pts (Econ Fr)

Heriot-Watt – 280–220 pts (Fr courses inc App Langs Transl)

Kent – 280–260 pts (Fr; Fr Ger/Hisp St/Ital; Fr Hist; Fr Hist Phil Art; Fr Phil; Fr Relig St)

Leeds – BBC (Fr courses)

Liverpool – BBC–BBB 280–300 pts (Fr; Fr Ger; Fr Hisp St)

London (King's) – BBC+AS **or** BBbbc (Fr 4 yr course; Fr Modn Gk; Fr Ger/Port; Fr Film; Fr Ling; Fr Hisp St)

Loughborough – 280 pts (Econ Fr)

Plymouth – 280 pts (Geog Fr)

Reading – 280 pts (Fr courses)

260 pts   **Aberystwyth** – 260 pts (Fr courses)

Keele – 260–280 pts (Fr courses)

Leicester – 260–300 pts (Fr Ger; Fr Ital; Fr Span)

Leicester – 260–320 pts (Fr Comb courses)

London (Gold) – 260 pts check with admissions tutor (MFL Fr Ling)

London (QM) – 260–300 pts (Fr courses)

Oxford Brookes – BCC (Fr St)

Strathclyde – BCC (French)

240 pts **Aberdeen** – CCC (Fr courses)

Bangor – 240–260 pts (Fr; Fr Ger/Ital/Span; Fr Crea Writ; Fr Film St; Fr Psy; Fr Tour; Fr Mark; Fr+2 Langs)

Bradford – 240 pts (Psy Fr; Sociol Fr; Phil Fr; Hist Fr; Fr Crim St; Fr Crea Writ; Fr Econ; Fr Lang)

Brighton – 240 pts (Fr St Engl Lit; Fr St Ling; Fr St Media)

Bristol UWE – 240–300 pts (Fr courses)

Chester – 240 pts (Fr courses)

Coventry – 240–280 pts (Fr Bus; Fr Mark; Fr Span; Fr Int Rel)

Hertfordshire – 240 pts (Fr; Fr Comb courses)

Salford – 240–300 pts (Modn Lang Transl Interp (Fr); Modn Lang Ling courses)

Swansea – 240–300 pts (Fr courses)

Ulster – 240–280 pts (Fr courses)

220 pts **Dundee** – 220 pts (Fr courses except under 280 pts)

Hull – 220–280 pts (Fr Film St; Fr Ger/Ital/Span; Fr Bus; Fr Gndr St; Fr Mgt; Fr Mark)

Nottingham Trent – 220 pts (Fr courses)

200 pts **Cardiff (UWIC)** – 200 pts (Tour Mgt Fr)

Kingston – 200–240 pts (Fr courses)

Middlesex – 200–240 pts (Fr courses)

Napier – 200 pts (Fr courses)

Northumbria – 200–340 pts (Fr courses)

Plymouth – 200 pts (Int Rel Fr)

Portsmouth – 200–280 pts (Fr St)

Sheffield Hallam – 200 pts (Int Bus Fr; Fr Mark; Fr Tour; Fr e-Commer)

180 pts **Anglia Ruskin** – 180–200 pts (Fr Comm St; Fr Film St; Fr Law)

Buckingham – 180–280 pts (Fr courses)

Liverpool John Moores – 180–200 pts (Euro St Fr; Int Bus St Fr; Tour Leis Fr; Fr Jap; Fr Chin)

Manchester Met – 180 pts (Fr St; Fr Cult St)

Northampton – 180–220 pts (Fr courses)

Roehampton – 180 pts (Fr courses)

160 pts **Buckinghamshire Chilterns (UC)** – 160–240 pts (Fr courses)

Canterbury Christ Church – CC (Fr joint courses)

Central Lancashire – 160 pts (Fr Bus Fr)

Greenwich – 160–240 pts (Fr courses)

London Met – 160 pts (Fr St courses)

Paisley – CC (French)

Southampton Solent – 160–120 pts (Fr subject to demand)

Westminster – CC (Arbc Fr; Chin Fr; Engl Lit Fr)

Wolverhampton – 160–220 pts (Fr courses)

80 pts **London (Birk)** – 80 pts for under 21s (p/t Fr Ger; Fr Span; Fr Mgt; Fr St)

Leeds Met – contact University

London (LSE) – optional course offered by the language centre: check with admissions tutor (Fr/Ger/Span/Russ)

Alternative offers

IB offers Aberystwyth 29 pts; Birmingham 32–34 pts; Brighton 28 pts; Bristol 30 pts; Bristol UWE 26–32 pts; Cambridge 38–42 pts; Chester 30 pts; Exeter 33–34 pts; Glasgow 30 pts; Keele 28–30 pts; Kent 28–34 pts; Lancaster 33–34 pts; Liverpool 30 pts; London (King's) 36 pts, (QM) 32–36 pts, (RH) 32 pts, (UCL) 36 pts; Manchester 32 pts; Manchester Met 26 pts; Newcastle 32 pts; Nottingham 30–32 pts; Reading 28 pts; St Andrews 32–36 pts; Sheffield 30–35 pts; Southampton 32 pts; Stirling 28 pts; Warwick 34–35 pts; York 34 pts.

Scottish offers See **Chapter 7**.

OTHER HIGHER EDUCATION COURSES IN THE SUBJECT FIELD

Higher National Diploma courses
80 pts   and below
Canterbury Christ Church.

CHOOSING YOUR COURSE (SEE ALSO CH.1)

Subject information Applicants should select courses according to the emphasis which they prefer. Courses could focus on literature or language (or both), or on the written and spoken word, as in the case of interpreting and translating courses, or on the broader study of French culture, political and social aspects to be found on courses as in European Studies. **Useful websites** www.europa.eu; www.visavis.org; www.bbc.co.uk/languages; www.languageadvantage.com; www.languagematters.co.uk; www.iol.org.uk; www.reed.co.uk/multilingual; www.cilt.org.uk; www.lemonde.fr; www.institut-francais.org.uk; www.academie-francaise.fr; www.institut-de-france.fr.

Course variations French and Creative Writing (Bradford); French Licence de Lettres (Kent); Combined Honours (Liverpool); French and Philosophy (London (King's)); Economics with French (Loughborough); French and Linguistics (Manchester); Modern Languages Translation and Interpreting (Salford); French and International Business (Sheffield Hallam). *NOW CHECK PROSPECTUSES AND WEBSITES FOR ANY RECENT CHANGES.*

Universities and colleges teaching quality See www.tqi.ac.uk; www.qaa.ac.uk.

Top universities and colleges (Research) Aberdeen*; Aston; Birmingham*; Bristol; Cambridge*; Durham; Edinburgh; Glasgow; Liverpool; London (King's), (QM), (RH)*, (UCL); Manchester; Nottingham; Oxford*; Oxford Brookes; Reading; Stirling; Warwick.

ADMISSIONS INFORMATION

Number of applicants per place (approx) Anglia Ruskin 7; Aston 6; Bangor 4; Birmingham 10; Bradford 3; Bristol 6; Cardiff 6; Central Lancashire 5; Durham 8; Exeter 8; Huddersfield 3; Hull 12; Kent 10; Kingston 4; Lancaster 7; Leeds (joint hons) 8; Leicester (Fr Ital) 5; Liverpool 5; Liverpool John Moores 8; London (British Inst in Paris) 9, (King's) 9, (RH) 5, (UCL) (Fr Phil) 7, (Fr Span) 8, (Fr Ital) 4, (Fr Hist Art) 8; Manchester Met 13; Middlesex 6; Newcastle (Fr) 17, (Fr minor) 16, (Fr Span) 22, (Fr Ger) 20; Northampton 3; Nottingham 16; Oxford Brookes 8; Portsmouth 20; Roehampton 5; Warwick 7; York 8.

Advice to applicants and planning the UCAS personal statement Visits to France (including exchange visits) should be described, with reference to any particular cultural or geographical features of the region visited. Contacts with French friends and experience in speaking the language are also important. Willingness to work/live/travel abroad. Interests in French life and culture. Read French newspapers and magazines and keep up-to-date with news stories etc. **Hull** We look for dynamism – students looking for a challenge. **Leeds** See **Languages**. **St Andrews** Evidence of interest and reasons for choosing the course. Sport/extra-curricular activities. Posts of responsibility. **Sheffield** Applicants should state if French is their first language. **Swansea** Applicants with AS French grades A or B will be considered for joint courses. We are interested to read about extra-curricular activities involving France and French culture. See also **Appendix 2**.

Misconceptions about this course **Leeds** See **Languages**. **Swansea** Some applicants are not aware of the range of subjects which can be combined with French in our flexible modular system. They sometimes do not know that linguistics and area studies options are also available as well as literature options in French.

Selection interviews **Yes** Bangor, Birmingham, Bradford, Cambridge, Canterbury Christ Church, Durham, East Anglia (after offer), Essex, Exeter, Heriot-Watt, Huddersfield, Hull, Kingston, Lancaster, Liverpool, Liverpool John Moores, London (RH), (UCL), London South Bank, Oxford, Portsmouth, Reading, Surrey, Sussex, Warwick; **Some** Brighton, Leeds.

Interview advice and questions Questions will almost certainly be asked on your A-level texts, in addition to your reading outside the syllabus – books, magazines, newspapers etc. Part of the interview may be conducted in French and written tests may be involved (see **Chapter 6**). **Leeds** See under **Languages**.

Applicants' impressions (A=Open day; B=Interview day) **London (Brit Inst in Paris)** (B) There were two interviewers, both nice and not intimidating. They explained about the course and the department. The interview started in English, then suddenly changed to French. The interview was in London. The course in Paris lasts three years with a small department of 30 students. No students' union as such and accommodation in Paris very expensive. It's a good course if you want to be independent and wish to become fluent quickly, but the student life is different from that in a large British university. **Manchester** (B; Fr Span) A well organised interview, very friendly and supportive. The department was impressive and well equipped. There was an opportunity to meet the students to discuss various aspects of student life. I was not interviewed in the foreign languages. (B; Fr Ital) The interview lasted 15 minutes with one interviewer. More like an informal chat, but there was no warning when he would start speaking French. Not impressed with the university buildings but the students recommended the department, the teaching and the facilities. **Oxford** (B; Modn Lang (Fr/Span)) Questions were asked in the target language. The French interview seemed fairly well organised and the interviewer seemed very sympathetic which made it feel more like a chat.

Reasons for rejection (non-academic) Unstable personality. Known alcoholism. Poor motivation. Candidate unenthusiastic, unmotivated, ill-informed about the nature of the course (had not read the prospectus). Not keen to spend a year abroad.

AFTER-RESULTS ADVICE
Universities with vacancies in Clearing (2006) Aberystwyth; Aston; Bangor; Birmingham; Bristol UWE; Buckingham; Canterbury Christ Church; Chester; Coventry; East Anglia; Essex; Greenwich; Hertfordshire; Hull; Keele; Kent; Kingston; Lancaster; Leicester; Liverpool; Liverpool John Moores; London (QM), (RH); London Met; Manchester Met; Middlesex; Northampton; Northumbria; Nottingham; Nottingham Trent; Plymouth; Portsmouth; Reading; Roehampton; Salford; Sheffield; Sheffield Hallam; Southampton; Stirling; Surrey; Swansea; Ulster; Westminster; Wolverhampton.

Offers to applicants repeating A-levels **Higher** Aberystwyth, Bristol (Fr), Glasgow, Leeds, Oxford Brookes, Warwick; **Possibly higher** Aston (Fr; Fr Ger); **Same** Aston, Bradford, Bristol (Phil Fr; Fr Lat), Brighton, Chester, Durham, East Anglia, Lancaster, Liverpool, London (RH), Newcastle, Nottingham (Fr Ger; Fr Lat), Roehampton, Sheffield, Surrey, Sussex, Ulster.

GRADUATE DESTINATIONS AND EMPLOYMENT (2005 HESA)
Graduates surveyed 1270 **Employed** 660 **In further study** 270 **Assumed unemployed** 70.

OTHER DEGREE SUBJECTS FOR CONSIDERATION
European Studies; International Business Studies; Literature; other language tables.

GENETICS

(see also **Biological Sciences)**

NB The points totals shown to the left of the institutions are for ease of reference only. It must not be assumed that tariff points are always used by institutions or that they can be substituted for an offer in grades. The level of an offer is not necessarily indicative of the quality of a course.

COURSE OFFERS INFORMATION
Subject requirements/preferences **GCSE Birmingham** Average of Bs in five relevant subjects. **Cambridge** Usually a majority of As. **Edinburgh** Mathematics grade B. **Leeds** Mathematics grade B. **AL** Chemistry and/or biology are usually required or preferred.

Your target offers

360 pts and above

Cambridge – AAA (Nat Sci (Genet))

350 pts **Warwick** – BBBb (Biol Sci (Mol Genet))

340 pts **London (UCL)** – AAB–BBB (Genet; Hum Genet)

Manchester – AAB–BBC (Genet; Genet Ind; Genet Modn Lang)

320 pts **Cardiff** – ABB–BBB (Genetics)

Leicester – ABB (Med Genet)

Newcastle – ABB–BBB (Hum Genet; Genet)

Nottingham – ABB–BBB (Genet; Hum Genet)

Sheffield – ABB **or** ABbb (Genet; Genet Microbiol; Genet Mol Cell Biol; Med Genet)

York – ABB (Genet; Genet Euro; Genet Ind)

300 pts **Dundee** – 300–240 pts (Mol Genet)

East Anglia – BBB–BBC (Genet Mol Biol)

Edinburgh – BBB (Genetics)

Leeds – 300 pts (Genet; Hum Genet)

Leicester – BBB (Biol Sci (Genet))

London (King's) – BBB+AS **or** BBbb (Mol Genet)

Sussex – BBB–BBC 330–300 pts (Mol Genet)

280 pts **Aberystwyth** – 280 pts (Genet Hum Hlth)

Birmingham – 280–300 pts (Biol Sci (Genet))

Brunel – BBC 280 pts (Biomed Sci (Genet))

Essex – 280–240 pts (Genetics)

Glasgow – BBC–CCC (Genetics)

Lancaster – BBC (Bioch Genet)

Liverpool – BBC–BBB 280–300 pts (Genet; Genet Ind; Genet Comb Hons)

London (QM) – 280–300 pts (Genet; Genet Microbiol)

Swansea – 280–300 pts (Genet; Med Genet)

260 pts **Belfast (Queen's)** – BCC/AB (Genetics)

Wolverhampton – 260–320 pts (Clin Genet)

240 pts **Aberdeen** – CCC (Genet; Genet (Immun))

200 pts **Huddersfield** – 200 pts (Med Genet)

Portsmouth – 200–240 pts (Gnm Sci)

180 pts **Bristol UWE** – 180–220 pts (App Genet)

Hertfordshire – 180–220 pts (Mol Biol Genet courses)

160 pts **Liverpool John Moores** – 160–220 pts (App Mol Biol Genet)

Westminster – CC (Mol Biol Genet)

Wolverhampton – 160–220 pts (Genet Mol Biol)

140 pts **Anglia Ruskin** – 140–200 pts (Genet Biomed Sci; Genet Microbiol)

Alternative offers
IB offers Aberystwyth 26 pts; Cambridge 38–42 pts; London (UCL) 32–36 pts; Nottingham 32 pts; Sheffield 33 pts.
Scottish offers See **Chapter 7**.

CHOOSING YOUR COURSE (SEE ALSO CH.1)

Subject information Over the years genetics has developed into a detailed and wide-ranging science. It involves, on the one hand, population genetics, and on the other, molecular interactions. Studies may therefore cover microbial, plant, animal and human genetics. **Useful websites** www.genetics.org; www.nature.com/genetics; see also **Biological Sciences**.

Course variations Genetics and Human Health (Aberystwyth); Human Genetics (Leeds); Combined Honours (Liverpool); Genetics in Industry (Manchester); Genome Science (Portsmouth); Medical Genetics (Swansea). *NOW CHECK PROSPECTUSES AND WEBSITES FOR ANY RECENT CHANGES.*

Universities and colleges teaching quality See www.tqi.ac.uk; www.qaa.ac.uk.

Top universities and colleges (Research) Cambridge; Leicester; Nottingham.

Sandwich degree courses Bristol UWE; Brunel; Cardiff; Huddersfield; Sussex; York; see also under **Biological Sciences**.

ADMISSIONS INFORMATION

Number of applicants per place (approx) Cardiff 8; Dundee 5; Leeds 7; Leicester (for all Biol Sci courses) 10; Newcastle 8; Nottingham 13; Swansea 7; Wolverhampton 4; York 9.

Advice to applicants and planning the UCAS personal statement See **Biological Sciences**.

Misconceptions about this course **York** Some fail to realise that chemistry (beyond GCSE) is essential to an understanding of genetics.

Selection interviews **Yes** Cambridge, Liverpool, Swansea; **Some** Cardiff, Dundee, Wolverhampton, York.

Interview advice and questions Likely questions will focus on your A-level science subjects, particularly biology, why you wish to study genetics and on careers in genetics. See also **Chapter 6**.

AFTER-RESULTS ADVICE

Universities with vacancies in Clearing (2006) Aberystwyth; Anglia Ruskin; Belfast (Queen's); Bristol UWE; Dundee; Essex; Hertfordshire; Huddersfield; Leeds; Leicester; Liverpool; Liverpool John Moores; London (QM); Nottingham; Portsmouth; Sheffield; Sussex; Swansea; Warwick; Westminster; Wolverhampton.

Offers to applicants repeating A-levels **Higher** Aberystwyth, Leeds, Newcastle, Nottingham, Swansea; **Same** Anglia Ruskin, Cardiff, Dundee, London (UCL), Wolverhampton, York.

GRADUATE DESTINATIONS AND EMPLOYMENT (2005 HESA)
Graduates surveyed 365 **Employed** 160 **In further study** 120 **Assumed unemployed** 20.

OTHER DEGREE SUBJECTS FOR CONSIDERATION
Anatomy; Biochemistry; Biological Sciences; Biology; Biotechnology; Human Sciences; Life Sciences; Medicine; Microbiology; Molecular Biology; Natural Sciences; Physiology; Plant Sciences.

GEOGRAPHY

(including **Meteorology**)

NB The points totals shown to the left of the institutions are for ease of reference only. It must not be assumed that tariff points are always used by institutions or that they can be substituted for an offer in grades. The level of an offer is not necessarily indicative of the quality of a course.

COURSE OFFERS INFORMATION

Subject requirements/preferences **GCSE** Mathematics often required for BSc courses. **Aberdeen, Dundee, Edinburgh, Glasgow, Nottingham, St Andrews** English, mathematics and a foreign language. **Bristol** (BSc), **Cambridge, Oxford** Usually a majority of grade As. **Durham** Grade A*, A and very few grade Cs. **Edinburgh** Mathematics grade B. **Exeter** Good range of grade A*, A or B. **Hull** (BSc) Grade B in geography and one science. **London (LSE)** (Geog Econ) Mathematics grade A. **London (QM)** (BSc) Seven grade As. **London (RH)** (BSc) Three grade As, six grade Bs. **Salford** (Env Geog) Grade B mathematics, grade C English. **Swansea** Balance of grade As. Most universities will require English and mathematics. **AL** Geography is usually required for most courses. In some cases the grade will also be stipulated.

Your target offers

360 pts **and above**

      Bristol – AAA–AAB (Geog; Geog Euro)

      Cambridge – AAA (Geography)

      Durham – AAA (Nat Sci Geog)

      East Anglia – AAA–AAB (Env Geog Int Dev; Meteor Ocean N Am/Aus)

      Lancaster – AAA (Physl Geog Aus)

      Nottingham – AAA–AAB (Geog; Geog Bus Env; Geog Chin S; Geog E Euro St)

      Oxford – Offers vary eg AAA–AAB (Geography)

340 pts **Durham** – AAB (BA/BSc Geog; Geog (Euro St); Geog Comb Soc Sci)

      Leeds – AAB (BA Geog)

      London (King's) – AAB (Geog Hist)

      London (UCL) – AAB+AS–ABB+AS (Geog; Env Geog; Anth Geog; Econ Geog)

      Manchester – AAB–BBC (Geog Geol)

      Manchester – AAB–ABB (Geography)

      Reading – 340 pts (Meteor Yr Okl)

      St Andrews – AAB (MA Geog courses)

      Southampton – AAB–ABB (BA Geog; BSc Geog Geol)

320 pts **Birmingham** – ABB–BBB 320–300 pts (Geography)

      Durham – ABB (Educ St (Geog))

      East Anglia – ABB (Meteor Ocean Euro)

      Exeter – ABB–ACC (Geog; Geog Euro)

      Glasgow – ABB–BBB (BA Geog)

      Lancaster – ABB–BBB (Geog; Physl Geog; Hum Geog)

      Leeds – ABB (BSc Geog)

      Liverpool – ABB 320 pts (Geog; Geog Mgt; Geol Physl Geog; Ocns Clim Physl Geog; Geog Arch)

      London (RH) – ABB 320 pts (Geog; Hum Geog; Physl Geog; Geog Arch; Physl Geog Sci Comm)

      London (SOAS) – ABB (Law Geog; S As St Geog)

      London (UCL) – ABB+AS–BCC+AS (Geoinform)

      Loughborough – 320–240 pts (Geog Spo Sci; Geog)

      Newcastle – ABB (BA Geog; Geog Maths; Geog Stats)

      Reading – 320 pts (Meteorology)

      St Andrews – ABB (BSc Geog courses)

      Sheffield – ABB **or** ABbb (BA Geog; Econ Geog; Geog Pol; Geog Sociol; Geog Plan)

      Southampton – ABB 320 pts (BSc Geog; Geog Ocean)

300 pts **Aberystwyth** – 300 pts (Physl Geog; Hum Geog)

      Belfast (Queen's) – BBB (BA Geog; Hum Geog)

      Birmingham – BBB–BCC (Geol Geog; Geog Urb Reg Plan)

      Cardiff – 300 pts BBB (Hum Geog Plan; Mar Geog)

      Dundee – 300 pts (Geog courses 3 yr)

      Edinburgh – BBB (MA Geog courses; BSc Geog courses)

      Exeter (Cornwall) – BBB–BCC 300–260 pts (Geog; Geog Earth Sys Sci; Geog Env Mgt; Geog Env Soty)

Leeds – BBB (Geog Trans Plan)
Leicester – BBB 260–320 pts (Geog; Geog Arch; Geog Geol; Physl Geog)
London (King's) – BBB+AS **or** BBbbc (Dev Geog; Geog; Geog Film)
London (LSE) – BBB (Geog; Geog Econ)
Loughborough – 300 pts (BSc Geog; Geog Econ; Geog Mgt; Geog Spo Leis Mgt)
Manchester – BBB (Geog Arch)
Newcastle – BBB–BCC (Geog Plan; Geog Inf Sci; Physl Geog; BSc Geog)
Reading – 300 pts (Hum Geog; Physl Geog; Hum Physl Geog; Geog Econ Reg Sci)
Southampton – BBB (Popn Sci)
Stirling – BBB 2nd yr entry (Env Geog)
Stranmillis (UC) – BBB (Geog Educ)
Sussex – BBB **or** 340 pts 3AL+AS (Geog courses)
Swansea – 300 pts (Geog courses)
280 pts **Belfast (Queen's)** – BBC **or** BCCb (Arch Palae Geog; Geog Euro; Geog)
Coventry – 280 pts (Geog; Geog Tour; Cons Geog; Nat Haz; Geog Nat Haz)
East Anglia – BBC (Meteor Ocean; Meteor Ocean Ind)
Glasgow – BBC–CCC (BSc Geog; Geog Chem Env)
Leeds – BBC (Meteor Atmos Sci)
Leicester – BBC (Hum Geog)
Liverpool – BBC–BBB 280–300 pts (Geog Arch; Geog Biol)
London (QM) – 280–320 pts (BA/BSc Geog; Hum Geog; Physl Geog; Env Geog; Geog Bus Mgt; Hisp St Geog; Russ Geog; Cits Econ Soc Ch; Geog Env Haz)
London (RH) – BBC (Physl Geog Geol)
Portsmouth – 280 pts (BA/BSc Geog; Hum Geog; Physl Geog; Geog Inf Sci)
270 pts **Sheffield Hallam** – 270 pts (Urb Lnd Econ)

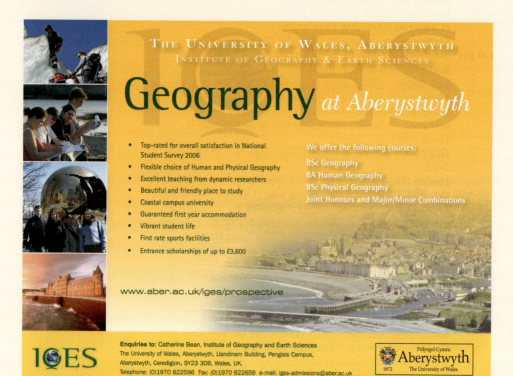

260 pts **Aston** – BCC–CCC (Geog Inf Sys)
Belfast (Queen's) – BCC–CCC (BSc Geog)
Birmingham – 260 pts (Geol Geog)
Bristol UWE – 260–300 pts (Geog; Geog Env Mgt; Geog Plan; Geog Trans)
Chester – 260 pts (Geog courses)
Hull – 260–300 pts (MPhysl Geog)
Keele – 260–280 pts (Geog; Hum Geog; Physl Geog)
Northumbria – 260 pts (Geog Spo St)
Plymouth – 260–280 pts (BA/BSc Geog; Hum Geog)
Sheffield Hallam – 260 pts (Hum Geog)
Strathclyde – BCC (Geography)
Ulster – 260 pts (Geography)
240 pts **Aberdeen** – CCC (BA/BSc Geog)
Bangor – 240–320 pts (Geog courses)
Bradford – 240 pts (Geog Arch)
Brighton – 240 pts (BA/BSc Geog)
Dundee – 240 pts (Geog courses 4 yr)
Hertfordshire – 240 pts (Geog courses)
Hull – CCC–BBC 240–280 pts (Geog Arch; Geog Ecol; Geog Spo Sci; BSc Physl Geog)
Kingston – 240–200 pts (Geog courses; Hum Geog courses; Geog Inf Sys courses)
Liverpool John Moores – 240 pts (Geography)
Northumbria – 240 pts (Geog; Geog Env Mgt)
Nottingham Trent – 240 pts (Engl Geog)
Oxford Brookes – CCC (Geography)
Sheffield Hallam – 240 pts (Geog Plan; Geog Trans)
Westminster – CCC (Hum Geog)
230 pts **Brighton** – 230 pts (Urb Cons Env Mgt)
Sheffield Hallam – 230 pts (Soty Cits)
220 pts **Bangor** – 220–260 pts (Cstl Wtr Res)
Bradford – 220 pts (Geog Env Mgt; Physl Env Geog)
Brighton – 220 pts (Biogeography)
Glamorgan – 220 pts (Geog Inf Sci)
Gloucestershire – 220 pts (Hum Geog; Geog; Physl Geog courses)
Liverpool Hope – 220 pts (Geog courses)
Liverpool John Moores – 220 pts (Physl Geog)
Manchester Met – 220 pts (Geog; Physl Geog; Geog Inf Sci)
Nottingham Trent – 220 pts (Hum Geog)
Oxford Brookes – CCD **or** CCdd (Physl Geog)
Stirling – CCD 1st yr entry (Env Geog)
Winchester – 220 pts (P Educ Geog)
200 pts **Bath Spa** – 200–240 pts (Geog; Geog Inf Sys; Geog Sociol; Dev Geog)
Central Lancashire – 200 pts (Geog courses except under **160 pts**)
Cumbria – 200 pts (Geography)
Glamorgan – 200 pts (Physl Geog courses)
Manchester Met – 200 pts (Physl Geog; Hum Geog; Comb Geog courses)
Plymouth – 200–240 pts (Physl Geog Geol)
180 pts **Edge Hill** – 180 pts (Geog; Hum Geog; Physl Geog)
Northampton – 180–220 pts (Hum Geog; Physl Geog; Geog)
Nottingham Trent – 180 pts (Physl Geog)
Salford – 180 pts (Env Geog; Aqua Sci; Geog)
Staffordshire – 180–240 pts (Geog; Physl Env Geog; Hum Env Geog; Geog Mntn Ldrshp; Geog joint courses)
160 pts **Bishop Grosseteste (Coll)** – 160 pts (Educ St Geog)
Bournemouth – 160 pts (App Geog)
Canterbury Christ Church – CC (Geography)

Central Lancashire – 160 pts (Geog Sociol; Geog Env Mgt; Geog Comb hons)
Derby – 160–180 pts (Geog courses)
East London – 160 pts (Geog Inf Sci)
Glamorgan – 160 pts (Modn Contemp Wls; Geog)
Greenwich – 160–240 pts (Geog; Geog Inf Sys)
Newman (CHE) – 160–240 pts (Geography)
St Mary's (Coll) – CC 160 pts (Geog courses)
Southampton Solent – 160 pts (Geog Env St; Mar Geog; Geog Tour)
Sunderland – 160 pts (Geog courses)
Wolverhampton – 160–220 pts (Geog courses)

140 pts **Marjon (Coll)** – 140–200 pts (Geog courses)
Worcester – 140–200 pts (Geog; Hum Geog; Physl Geog)

100 pts **Bristol UWE** – 100 pts (Fdn Geog)
Wigan and Leigh (Coll) – 100 pts (Geog Comb Hons)

80 pts **London (Birk)** – 80 pts for under 21s (over 21s varies) (p/t Geog Env)

Leeds Met – contact University

Alternative offers

IB offers Aberystwyth 30 pts; Birmingham 32–34 pts; Brighton 28 pts; Bristol 38 pts; Bristol UWE 26–32 pts; Cambridge 38–42 pts; Chester 30 pts; Exeter 30–34 pts; Glasgow 28–30 pts; Keele 26–28 pts; Leicester 30 pts; Liverpool 30 pts; London (King's) 32 pts, (LSE) 35 pts, (QM) 32 pts, (RH) 34 pts, (UCL) 34–36 pts; Loughborough 30 pts; Manchester 33–35 pts; Manchester Met 24 pts; Newcastle 30–38 pts; Nottingham 34–36 pts; Reading 28–31 pts, (Meteor) 33–34 pts; St Andrews 32–36 pts; Salford 24 pts; Sheffield 33 pts; Southampton 33 pts; Staffordshire 28 pts; Stirling 26 pts.
Scottish offers See **Chapter 7**.

OTHER HIGHER EDUCATION COURSES IN THE SUBJECT FIELD

Foundation degrees (contact the institutions for details) Truro (Coll).

Higher National Diploma courses Bournemouth; Derby; East London; Kingston; SAC (Scottish CAg); Worcester.

CHOOSING YOUR COURSE (SEE ALSO CH.1)

Subject information Students following BA and BSc Geography courses usually choose options from the same range of modules, but the choice of degree will depend on the arts or science subjects taken at A-level. The content and focus of courses will vary between universities and could emphasise the human, physical, economic or social aspects of the subject. **Useful websites** www.met-office.gov.uk; www.ccw.gov.uk; www.rgs.org; www.ordnancesurvey.co.uk; www.geographical.co.uk; www.nationalgeographic.com; www.cartography.org.uk; www.countryside.gov.uk; www.geography.org.uk; www.thepowerofgeography.co.uk; www.spatial-literacy.org; www.geographynetwork.com; www.gis.com.

Course variations Development Geography (Bath Spa; London (King's)); Biogeography (Brighton); Oceans, Climate and Physical Geography (Liverpool); Cities, Economies and Social Change (London (QM)); Anthropology and Environmental Geography (London (UCL)); Geography and Planning (Newcastle); Geography and Sport Studies (Northumbria); Geography, Business and the Environment (Nottingham); Meteorology (Reading); Geography and Transport (Sheffield Hallam); Geography and Mountain Leadership (Staffordshire). *NOW CHECK PROSPECTUSES AND WEBSITES FOR ANY RECENT CHANGES.*

Universities and colleges teaching quality See www.tqi.ac.uk; www.qaa.ac.uk.

Top universities and colleges (Research) Bristol*; Cambridge; Durham*; Edinburgh*; Hull; Leeds; London (LSE), (QM), (RH), (UCL)*; Loughborough; Newcastle; Nottingham; Sheffield; Southampton.

Sandwich degree courses Aberystwyth; Aston; Belfast (Queen's); Bradford; Cardiff; Coventry; Glamorgan; Hertfordshire; Kingston; Loughborough; Manchester Met; Nottingham Trent; Oxford Brookes; Plymouth; Salford; Ulster; Wolverhampton.

ADMISSIONS INFORMATION

Number of applicants per place (approx) Aberystwyth 3; Birmingham 6; Bristol 9; Bristol UWE 10; Cambridge 3; Cardiff 5; Central Lancashire 3; Chester 10; Coventry 12; Cumbria 5, (Comb) 10, (QTS) 11; Derby 4; Dundee 5; Durham 8; East Anglia (Meteor Ocean) 7; Edinburgh 8; Edge Hill 8; Exeter 10; Glamorgan 5; Gloucestershire 40; Greenwich 2; Hull 10; Kent 15; Kingston 7; Lancaster 13; Leeds 12; Leicester (BA) 19, (BSc) 17; Liverpool 3; Liverpool John Moores 6; London (King's) 5, (LSE) (Geog) 5 (Geog Econ) 4, (QM) 5, (RH) 7, (SOAS) 5; Loughborough 6, (Geog Spo Sci) 20; Newcastle 14; Newman (CHE) 2; Northampton 4; Northumbria 16; Nottingham 12; Oxford (success rate 41%); Plymouth 10; Portsmouth (Geog) 5; St Mary's (Coll) 4; Salford 3; Sheffield (BA) 13, (BSc) 10; Southampton (Geog) 7; Staffordshire 10; Strathclyde 8; Swansea 5; Wolverhampton 2; Worcester 5.

Advice to applicants and planning the UCAS personal statement Visits to, and field courses in, any specific geographical region should be fully described. Study your own locality in detail and get in touch with the area Planning Office to learn about any future developments. Read geographical magazines and describe any special interests you have – and why. **Durham** Interview essential for overseas students. **Liverpool** We look for evidence of interest in geography or at least in a particular part of the subject, for example field trips, travel, books or magazines read, and also for evidence of interests beyond academic work. **London (King's)** Awareness of world issues. **Loughborough** Geography interest, travel experience, voluntary work and, for the Geography and Sports Science course a very high level of sports experience. **St Andrews** Reasons for choosing course and evidence of interest; sport/extracurricular activities and posts of responsibility.

Misconceptions about this course **Birmingham** Some students think that the BA and BSc Geography courses are very different: in fact they do not differ from one another. All course options are available for both degrees. **East Anglia** (Meteor Ocean) Some applicants don't realise that the course is a very mathematical and physics subject. **Liverpool** Some applicants assume that a BSc course restricts them to physical geography modules. This is not so since human geography modules can be taken. Some students later specialise in human geography. **Southampton** (Popn Sci) No previous knowledge of population science is necessary for this course and we positively welcome applications from mature students with considerable flexibility in the entrance requirements for such candidates.

Selection interviews **Yes** Bristol UWE, Cambridge, Central Lancashire, Coventry, Durham (essential for overseas applicants), Edge Hill, Greenwich, Kingston, London (King's), (QM), (RH), (SOAS), (UCL), Manchester Met, Northumbria, Oxford, Warwick (BA QTS); **Some** Aston, Bath Spa, Bristol, Cardiff, Chichester, Dundee, East Anglia (Meteor Ocean), Liverpool, Loughborough, Newcastle, Nottingham, Salford, Southampton, Staffordshire.

Interview advice and questions Geography is a very broad subject and applicants can expect to be questioned on their syllabus and those aspects which they find of special interest. Some questions in the past have included: What fieldwork have you done? What are your views on ecology? What changes in the landscape have you noticed on the way to the interview? Explain in simple meteorological terms today's weather. Why are earthquakes almost unknown in Britain? What is the value of practical work in geography to primary school children? (BEd course) What do you enjoy about geography and why? Are there any articles of geographical importance in the news at present? Discuss the current economic situation in Britain and give your views. Questions on the Third World, on world ocean currents and drainage and economic factors world-wide. Expect to comment on local geography and on geographical photographs and diagrams. **Liverpool** Why students have chosen Geography and which aspects of the subject they enjoy. **Southampton** Applicants selected on academic ability only. See **Chapter 6**.

Applicants' impressions (A=Open day; B=Interview day) **Bath Spa** (B; Geog/Sociol) I had interviews with both heads of department followed by a tour of the university. **Cambridge (Emmanuel)** (B) There were two interviews, each with one interviewer. I was asked why Geography and why Emmanuel? I was also asked whether there was much of a distinction between human and physical geography. At the second interview the essays I had previously submitted were discussed. The visit was well organised. We were able to discuss life in Cambridge and in the college with some of the students. **Oxford (St Edmund Hall)** (B) There were two 20-minute interviews with two interviewers asking questions on physical geography and human geography respectively. I was asked why I wanted to do Geography, about the formation of hurricanes in Bermuda, about the geographical aspects of my holiday in Singapore and questions on my AS- and A-level coursework investigations. The interviews were well organised and although fairly informal, I felt under pressure. **Southampton** (B) There was an informal interview and a talk on the human and physical aspects of the courses. There was also a tour of the campus and halls.

Reasons for rejection (non-academic) Lack of awareness of the content of the course. Failure to attend interview. Poor general knowledge. Lack of geographical awareness. **Hull** (BSc) Usually insufficient science background. **Liverpool** Personal statement gave no reason for choosing geography.

AFTER-RESULTS ADVICE

Universities with vacancies in Clearing (2006) Aberystwyth; Bangor; Birmingham; Bradford; Brighton; Bristol UWE; Canterbury Christ Church; Central Lancashire; Chester; Derby; Dundee; East Anglia; Edge Hill; Exeter; Glamorgan; Gloucestershire; Hull; Keele; Kingston; Leicester; Liverpool; Liverpool Hope; Liverpool John Moores; London (QM); Manchester Met; Newcastle; Northampton; Nottingham Trent; Plymouth; Portsmouth; Reading; Salford; Southampton; Staffordshire; Sunderland; Swansea; Wolverhampton; Worcester.

Offers to applicants repeating A-levels **Higher** Bournemouth, Durham, Glasgow, Hull, Kingston, Nottingham, St Andrews, Sussex (Geog Lang); **Possibly higher** Edinburgh; **Same** Aberystwyth, Aston, Birmingham, Bradford, Brighton, Bristol, Cardiff, Chester, Chichester, Coventry, Cumbria, Derby, Dundee, East Anglia (Meteor Ocean), Edge Hill, Lancaster, Leeds (applicants consider which A-levels to resit for the BSc course), Liverpool, Liverpool John Moores, London (RH), (SOAS), Loughborough, Manchester Met, Newcastle, Newman (CHE), Newport, Northumbria, Oxford Brookes, Plymouth, Salford, Southampton, Staffordshire, Ulster, Wolverhampton.

GRADUATE DESTINATIONS AND EMPLOYMENT (2005 HESA)
Human and Social Geography graduates surveyed 2430 **Employed** 1250 **In further study** 470 **Assumed unemployed** 160.

OTHER DEGREE SUBJECTS FOR CONSIDERATION
Agriculture; Anthropology; Countryside Management; Development Studies; Environmental Science/Studies; Forestry; Geology; Surveying; Town Planning; Urban Land Economics; Urban Studies.

GEOLOGY/GEOLOGICAL SCIENCES

(including **Earth Sciences and Engineering (Mining), Geophysics and Geoscience**)

NB The points totals shown to the left of the institutions are for ease of reference only. It must not be assumed that tariff points are always used by institutions or that they can be substituted for an offer in grades. The level of an offer is not necessarily indicative of the quality of a course.

COURSE OFFERS INFORMATION
Subject requirements/preferences **GCSE** English and mathematics required. **Bristol** Majority of grades A and B. **Cambridge** Usually a majority of grade As. **Liverpool** French grade B. **AL** Two science subjects usually required.

Your target offers
360 pts   and above
    Birmingham – AAA–AAB (MSci Geol Int Yr; Res App Geol Int Yr; Env Geosci)
    Cambridge – AAA (Nat Sci (Geol Sci))
    Durham – AAA (Nat Sci (Earth Sci))
    East Anglia – AAA–AAB (Env Earth Sci N Am/Aus; Geophys Sci N Am/Aus)
    Leeds – AAA–BBB (MGeol/MSci Geol Sci courses; Geophys Sci courses; MGeol Env Geol)

London (UCL) – AAA–AAB+AS (Geol; Earth Sci; Geophys; Env Geosci; Pal; Planet Sci)

Oxford – Offers vary eg AAA–AAB (Earth Sci; Geol)

Southampton – AAA (MGeol Geol N Am; MGeophys N Am)

340 pts **Imperial London** – AAB (Geol; Env Geosci; Geol Geophys; Geophys; Geol Geophys Abrd)

Liverpool – AAB 340 pts (MSci Geophys N Am)

London (RH) – AAB (Geoscience)

320 pts **Cardiff** – 320 pts (MSci Explor Res Geol)

East Anglia – ABB (Geophys Sci Euro; Env Earth Sci Euro)

Liverpool – ABB 320 pts (MSci Geol; Geol Geophys)

St Andrews – ABB–BBB (Geosci courses)

300 pts **Birmingham** – BBB–BCC 300–260 pts (Geol; Geol Biol; Env Geosci; Res App Geol)

Bristol – BBB (Env Geosci; Geol Biol; Geol; Geol N Am/Euro; Env Geosci N Am/Euro; Palae Evol)

Durham – BBB (Geol; Earth Sci; Env Geosci; Geophys Geol)

Exeter (Cornwall) – BBB–BCC 300–260 pts (App Geol; Min Eng; Eng Geol Geotech)

Lancaster – 300 pts (Earth Sci N Am/Aus)

Leicester – BBB–ABB 300–320 pts (MGeol Geol courses; MGeol App Env Geol; MGeol Geol Geophys; Geol Pal; Earth Planet Sci)

Liverpool – BBB 300 pts (BSc Geol; Geophys; Geol Physl Geog; Geophys (Phys); Ocn Earth Sci; Ocn Clim St; Chem Ocean)

Manchester – ABC (Geol; Env Res Geol; Geol Planet Sci; Geochem; Earth Sci)

Southampton – BBB 300 pts (MGeol Geol; MGeophys Geophys courses)

280 pts **Cardiff** – BBC (BSc Geol; Explor Res Geol; Env Geosci)

East Anglia – BBC (Geophys Sci; Env Earth Sci)

Edinburgh – BBC (Geol; Env Geosci; Geol Physl Geog)

Leeds – BBC (Geol Sci; Earth Sys Sci; Env Geol; Geophys Sci)

Southampton – BBC 280 pts (BSc Geol; Geol Ocean; Geol Phys Geol; Geol Mar Biol; Geophys Sci)

260 pts **Edinburgh** – BCC (Geophysics)

Glasgow – BCC–CCC (Earth Sci; Env Biogeochem)

Lancaster – BCC (Earth Env Sci)

Leicester – BCC–BBC 260–280 pts (BSc Geol; App Env Geol; Geol Geophys; BSc Geol Pal; Geog Geol; Earth Planet Sci)

London (RH) – 260–280 pts (Geol courses; Env Geol courses; Env Geosci; Geosci)

240 pts **Aberdeen** – CCC (Geol Petrol Geol; Geosci)

Aberystwyth – CCC–CCD 240–220 pts (Env Earth Sci)

Bangor – 240–260 pts (Geol Ocean)

Brighton – 240 pts (Geology)

Derby – 240 pts (Earth Sys Sci; Geol; Glob Haz)

Keele – 240–260 pts (Geol; Earth Sys Sci)

Kingston – 240–260 pts (Earth Sys Sci; Earth Planet Sci; Geol)

Leeds – CCC (Min Miner Eng)

Plymouth – 240–280 pts (MGeol Geol)

220 pts **Liverpool John Moores** – 220 pts (Geol; Haz Geosci)

200 pts **Glamorgan** – 200–240 pts (Geology)

Plymouth – 200–240 pts (Ocn Sci; App Geol; Geol; Physl Geog Geol; Ocn Explor)

180 pts **Portsmouth** – 180–240 pts (Eng Geol Geotech; Earth Sci; Geol; Geol Haz; Pal Evol)

160 pts **Exeter** – 160 pts (Fdn Eng Geol Geotech)

Greenwich – 160–240 pts (Geol; Geol Geog Inf Sys)

Northampton – 160–200 pts (Earth Sci courses)

140 pts **Liverpool** – 140 pts (Fdn Earth Sci)

80 pts **Eastleigh (Coll)** – 80 pts (Fdn Sci)

London (Birk) – 80 pts for under 21s (over 21s varies) (p/t Geol; Env Geol; Earth Sci; dist learn)

For information on how to read the Subject Tables, see **Chapter 7**.

Alternative offers

IB offers Birmingham 30–32 pts; Brighton 28 pts; Bristol 32 pts; Cambridge 38–42 pts; Dundee 29 pts; Exeter 28–33 pts; Glasgow 28 pts; Keele 26–30 pts; Leicester 28–30 pts; Liverpool 31 pts; London (LSE) 34–38 pts, (RH) 35 pts; Newcastle 30–32 pts; St Andrews 30–32 pts; Southampton 30–38 pts.
Scottish offers See **Chapter 7**.

OTHER HIGHER EDUCATION COURSES IN THE SUBJECT FIELD

Higher National Diploma courses
100 pts   and below
   Adam Smith (Coll); Glamorgan; Sheffield Hallam.

CHOOSING YOUR COURSE (SEE ALSO CH.1)

Subject information Topics in Geology courses include the physical and chemical constitution of the earth, exploration geophysics, oil and marine geology (oceanography) and seismic interpretation. Earth Sciences cover geology, environmental science, physical geography and can also include business studies and language modules. No previous knowledge of geology is required for most courses. **Useful websites** www.geolsoc.org.uk; www.bgs.ac.uk; www.noc.soton.ac.uk; www.scicentral.com.

Course variations Geology and Petroleum Geology (Aberdeen); Palaeontology and Evolution (Bristol); Mining Engineering (Exeter); Earth and Planetary Science (Leicester); Mathematics, Ocean and Climate Studies (Liverpool); Hazard Geoscience (Liverpool John Moores); Ocean Exploration (Plymouth); Engineering Geology and Geotechnics (Portsmouth). *NOW CHECK PROSPECTUSES AND WEBSITES FOR ANY RECENT CHANGES.*

Universities and colleges teaching quality See www.tqi.ac.uk; www.qaa.ac.uk.

Top universities and colleges (Research) (including Environmental Sciences) Bristol*; Cambridge*; Cardiff; Edinburgh; Leeds; Liverpool; London (RH), (UCL); Manchester; Newcastle; Oxford*.

Sandwich degree courses Glamorgan; Greenwich; Kingston; Paisley.

ADMISSIONS INFORMATION

Number of applicants per place (approx) Aberystwyth 5; Bangor 4; Birmingham 4; Bristol 7; Cardiff 7; Derby 4; Durham 4; East Anglia 7; Edinburgh 5; Exeter 5; Greenwich 2; Kingston 19, (Earth Sys Sci) 3; Imperial London 5; Leeds 8; Liverpool 5; Liverpool John Moores 6; London (RH) 5, (UCL) 3; Northampton 7; Oxford 1.2; Plymouth 7; Portsmouth (Eng Geol Geotech) 2, (Geol) 2; Southampton 5.

Advice to applicants and planning the UCAS personal statement Visits to any outstanding geological sites and field courses you have attended should be described in detail. Apart from geological formations, you should also be aware of how geology has affected humankind in specific areas in the architecture of the region and artefacts used. Evidence of social skills could be given. **Bristol** Apply early. **Leeds** Solid maths and science background required. See also **Appendix 2**.

Misconceptions about this course **East Anglia** Many applicants fail to realise that Environmental Earth Science extends beyond geology to the links between the solid earth and its behaviour and society in general. **London (UCL)** Environmental geoscience is sometimes mistaken for environmental science; they are two different subjects.

Selection interviews **Yes** Birmingham, Cambridge, Durham, Edinburgh, Exeter, Greenwich, Kingston, Liverpool, London (RH), Oxford, Southampton, Sunderland; **Some** Aberystwyth (mature students only), Cardiff, Derby, East Anglia.

Interview advice and questions Some knowledge of the subject will be expected and applicants could be questioned on specimens of rocks and their origins. Past interviews have included questions on the field courses attended, and the geophysical methods of exploration in the detection of metals. How would you determine the age of this rock (sample shown)? Can you integrate a decay curve function and would it help you to determine the age of rocks? How many planes of crystallisation could this rock have? What causes a volcano? What is your local geology? **Oxford** (Earth Sci) Candidates may be asked to comment on specimens of a geological nature, based on previous knowledge of the subject. See **Chapter 6**.

Applicants' impressions (A=Open day; B=Interview day) **Bristol** (B) There was an overview of the course, a tour of the department and accommodation and an informal interview when I was asked questions about my personal statement.

Reasons for rejection (non-academic) Misconceptions about the course. **Exeter** Outright rejection uncommon but some applicants advised to apply for other programmes.

AFTER-RESULTS ADVICE

Universities with vacancies in Clearing (2006) Aberdeen; Aberystwyth; Birmingham; Brighton; Cardiff; Derby; East Anglia; Exeter; Glasgow; Greenwich; Imperial London; Keele; Kingston; Lancaster; Leeds; Leicester; Liverpool; London (RH); Manchester; Plymouth; Portsmouth; Southampton.

Offers to applicants repeating A-levels **Higher** Bristol, St Andrews; **Possibly higher** Portsmouth; **Same** Aberystwyth, Cardiff, Derby, Durham, East Anglia, Leeds, Liverpool John Moores, London (RH), Plymouth, Southampton.

GRADUATE DESTINATIONS AND EMPLOYMENT (2005 HESA)

Geology graduates surveyed 860 **Employed** 415 **In further study** 215 **Assumed unemployed** 75. **Mining Engineering graduates surveyed** 25 **Employed** 10 **In further study** 10 **Assumed unemployed** 5.

OTHER DEGREE SUBJECTS FOR CONSIDERATION

Archaeology; Civil and Mining Engineering; Environmental Science; Geography; Physics.

GERMAN

(see also **European Studies** and **Languages**)

NB The points totals shown to the left of the institutions are for ease of reference only. It must not be assumed that tariff points are always used by institutions or that they can be substituted for an offer in grades. The level of an offer is not necessarily indicative of the quality of a course.

COURSE OFFERS INFORMATION

Subject requirements/preferences **GCSE Aberdeen, Dundee, Edinburgh, Glasgow, St Andrews** English, mathematics or science and a foreign language. **Birmingham** German grade A–B. **Portsmouth** Three grade As, three grade Bs. Other universities require English and a foreign language. **AL** German required usually at a specified grade.

Your target offers

360 pts **and above**
        Birmingham – AAA (Law Ger)
        Cambridge – AAA (Modn Mediev Lang (Ger))
        London (UCL) – AAA+AS–BBB+AS (Ger courses)
        Oxford – Offers vary eg AAA–AAB (Modn Lang (Ger))
340 pts **Bath** – AAB (Int Mgt Ger)
        Cardiff – AAB–BBC (Ger Hum joint courses; Ger; Ger Jap)
        Durham – AAB (Hist Ger)
        London (King's) – AAB (Ger Hist; Ger Mus)
        Manchester – AAB–BBC (Ger courses)
        St Andrews – AAB–ABB (Ger courses)
        Sheffield – AAB–BBC (Ger courses)
320 pts **Aston** – ABB 320 pts (Int Bus Ger)
        Bath – ABB (Ger Pol)

Durham – ABB (Modn Lang)
East Anglia – ABB 320 pts (Law Ger; Law Lang)
Glasgow – ABB–BBB (Ger courses)
Lancaster – ABB (Ger St Econ; Ger St Mark; Ger St Psy; Ger St Engl Lit)
London (King's) – ABB+AS (Ger Phil)
Newcastle – ABB–BBB (Ger; Ger Bus St)
Nottingham – ABB (Ger Mus)
Southampton – 320–310 pts (Ger courses)

300 pts **Belfast (Queen's)** – BBB–BCCb (Ger courses)
Birmingham – BBB–BBC (Ger St courses; Ger courses except under **360 pts**)
Durham – 300–320 pts (Ger Comb Arts courses)
Edinburgh – BBB (Ger courses)
Exeter – BBB (Ger courses)
Lancaster – BBB (Ger St; Ger St courses except under **320 pts**)
London (LSE) – optional course offered by language centre (check with admissions tutor) (Fr/Ger/Russ/Span)
London (RH) – 300–320 pts (Ger courses)
Loughborough – 300 pts (Econ Ger)
Nottingham – BBB–BBC (Ger; Ger Hisp St; Ger Port; Ger Russ; Ger Hist; Film St Ger; Ger Pol; Modn Lang St; Modn Euro St; Modn Lang Bus)
Surrey – 300 pts (Law Ger Law)
Warwick – 300–340 pts (Ger courses)
York – BBB–BBC (Ger Ling; Fr Ger (Lang Ling))

280 pts **Aston** – 280–300 pts (Ger with Fr/Span; Ger Pol; Ger Int Rel; Ger Engl Lang)
Cardiff – BBC–BCC (Ger courses except under **340 pts**)
Essex – 280–260 pts (Ger courses)
Heriot-Watt – BBC (Ger courses except under **180 pts**)
Liverpool – BBC (Ger; Ger Hisp St)
London (King's) – BBC+AS **or** BBbbc (Ger; Ger Port; Ger Dig Hum; Ger Film; Ger Ling; Ger Modn Gk; Ger Hisp St; Ger Class St; Ger Engl)
Reading – 280 pts (Ger courses)

260 pts **Aberystwyth** – 260 pts (Ger courses)
Bristol – BCC (Ger courses)
Kent – 260–280 pts (Ger; Ger Hisp St; Ger Hist; Ger Ital; Ger Relig St)
Leeds – BCC (German)
Leicester – BCC 260–320 pts (Ital Ger; Span Ger; Fr Ger)
Liverpool – 260 pts (Ger Hisp St)
London (QM) – 260–300 pts (Ger courses)
Salford – 260–300 pts (Ger with 2nd Lang)
Strathclyde – BCC/BB (Arts Soc Sci (Ger))

240 pts **Aberdeen** – CCC (Ger courses)
Bangor – 240–260 pts (Ger; Ger Crea Writ; Ger Film St; Ger Ital/Span; Ger Mark; Ger Bus St; Ger Psy; Ger Tour; Ger +2 Langs)
Brighton – 240 pts (Ger St Engl Lit; Ger St Ling; Ger St Media)
Bristol UWE – 240–300 pts (Ger joint courses)
Chester – 240 pts (Ger courses)
Greenwich – 240 pts approx (Law Ger)
Swansea – 240–300 pts (Ger courses)
Ulster – 240 pts (Ger courses)

220 pts **Hull** – 220–280 pts (Ger Bus; Ger Film St; Ger Mark; Ger Mgt; Ger Gndr St; Ger Ital/Span; Ger St)
Nottingham Trent – 220 pts (Ger courses)

200 pts **Dundee** – 200 pts (Ger courses)
Hertfordshire – 200–240 pts (Ger courses)
Liverpool John Moores – 200 pts (Int Bus St Ger)

Middlesex – 200–240 pts (Ger courses)
Napier – 200 pts (Ger courses)
Northumbria – 200–240 pts (Ger courses)
Plymouth – 200–260 pts (Ger courses)
Portsmouth – 200–280 pts (Ger St)
Sheffield Hallam – 200 pts (Int Bus Ger)
180 pts **Anglia Ruskin** – 180–200 pts (Ger; Ger Film St)
Central Lancashire – 180–160 pts (Ger Bus Ger)
Greenwich – 180 pts (Int Bus Ger; Int Mark Ger)
Heriot-Watt – DDD (Chem Ger)
Heriot-Watt – BC (Maths Ger)
Liverpool John Moores – 180–200 pts (German)
Manchester Met – 180 pts (Ger courses)
Northampton – 180–220 pts (Ger courses)
160 pts **Wolverhampton** – 160–220 pts (Ger courses)
80 pts **London (Birk)** – 80 pts (p/t Ger Mgt; Modn Grmny St)

Leeds Met – contact University

Alternative offers
IB offers Aberystwyth 29 pts; Birmingham 32–34 pts; Brighton 28 pts; Bristol 29 pts; Bristol UWE 26–32 pts; Chester 30 pts; Exeter 32–33 pts; Glasgow 30 pts; Kent 28 pts; Liverpool 30 pts; London (King's) 32 pts, (QM) 32–36 pts, (RH) 32 pts, (UCL) 32–36 pts; Manchester 30–35 pts; Manchester Met 28 pts; Newcastle 32 pts; Nottingham 30–32 pts; Reading 28 pts; St Andrews 32–36 pts; Sheffield 32–35 pts; Southampton 32 pts; Warwick 34 pts; York 34 pts.
Scottish offers See **Chapter 7**.

OTHER HIGHER EDUCATION COURSES IN THE SUBJECT FIELD

Higher National Diploma courses (with Business Studies)
100 pts **and below**
Buckinghamshire Chilterns (UC).

CHOOSING YOUR COURSE (SEE ALSO CH.1)

Subject information Language, literature, practical language skills or a broader study of Germany and its culture (European Studies) are alternative study approaches. See also **Appendix 2** under **Languages**.
Useful websites www.cilt.org.uk; www.goethe.de; www.bbc.co.uk/languages; www.iol.org.uk; www.languageadvantage.com; www.languagematters.co.uk; www.reed.co.uk/multilingual; www.deutsch-online.com; www.faz.net; www.sueddeutsche.de; www.europa.eu.

Course variations German and Japanese (Cardiff); International Business and German (Greenwich); German Studies and Economics (Lancaster); German and Hispanic Studies (Liverpool); German and Digital Humanities (London (King's)); German and Music (Nottingham); English and German Literature (Warwick); Linguistics and German (Wolverhampton). *NOW CHECK PROSPECTUSES AND WEBSITES FOR ANY RECENT CHANGES.*

Universities and colleges teaching quality See www.tqi.ac.uk; www.qaa.ac.uk.

Top universities and colleges (Research) Aston; Birmingham*; Bristol; Cambridge; Edinburgh; Exeter*; Liverpool; London (King's)*, (QM), (RH)*, (UCL)*; Manchester*; Nottingham*; Oxford*; Swansea; Warwick.

ADMISSIONS INFORMATION

Number of applicants per place (approx) Aston 4, (Ger Journal) 22; Bangor 6; Birmingham 6; Bradford 6; Bristol 3; Cardiff 6; Central Lancashire 2; Durham 4; East Anglia 4; Exeter 4; Heriot-Watt 10; Hull 12; Kent 10; Lancaster 7; Leeds (joint hons) 8; Leicester 4; London (King's) 5, (QM) 6, (RH) 5, (UCL) 4; Newcastle 6; Nottingham 14; Portsmouth 5; Salford 5; Staffordshire 5; Stirling 6; Surrey 2; Swansea 4; Warwick (Ger Bus St) 16, (Ger) 8; York 6.

Advice to applicants and planning the UCAS personal statement Describe visits to Germany or a German-speaking country and the particular cultural and geographical features of the region. Contacts with friends in Germany and language experience should also be mentioned, and if you are bilingual, say so. Read German newspapers and magazines and keep up-to-date with national news. **Leeds** See **Languages**. **Nottingham** We are looking for a high degree of competence in using and understanding German, a genuine determination to develop skills in linguistic comprehension and analysis, a love of literature, an imaginative approach to it and a keen interest in German affairs. **Portsmouth** Experience of German-speaking countries not necessary. **St Andrews** Evidence of interest and reasons for choosing the course. **Swansea** We like students who have been to Germany or are planning to go.

Misconceptions about this course **Leeds** See **Languages**. **Swansea** Some students are afraid of the year abroad, which is actually one of the most enjoyable parts of the course.

Selection interviews **Yes** Bangor, Birmingham (short conversation in German), Bradford, Cambridge, Durham, East Anglia, Exeter, Heriot-Watt, Huddersfield, Hull, Kingston, Liverpool, Liverpool John Moores, London (RH), (UCL), Newcastle, Oxford, Sheffield, Southampton, Surrey (always); **Some** Cardiff, Leeds, Portsmouth, Staffordshire, Swansea.

Interview advice and questions Questions asked on A-level syllabus. Part of the interview may be in German. What foreign newspapers and/or magazines do you read? Questions on German current affairs, particularly politics and reunification problems, books read outside the course, etc. **Leeds** See **Languages**. See **Chapter 6**.

Reasons for rejection (non-academic) Unstable personality. Poor motivation. Insufficient commitment. Unrealistic expectations. Not interested in spending a year abroad.

AFTER-RESULTS ADVICE
Universities with vacancies in Clearing (2006) Aberdeen; Aberystwyth; Aston; Bangor; Bath; Birmingham; Chester; Essex; Greenwich; Hertfordshire; Hull; Kent; Lancaster; Leicester; Liverpool; London (QM), (RH); Manchester Met; Middlesex; Northampton; Northumbria; Nottingham; Nottingham Trent; Plymouth; Portsmouth; Reading; Salford; Sheffield; Southampton; Surrey; Swansea; Ulster; Wolverhampton.

Offers to applicants repeating A-levels **Higher** Birmingham, Glasgow, Leeds, Warwick; **Same** Aston, Bradford, Brighton, Cardiff, Chester, Durham, East Anglia, London (RH), Newcastle (not always), Nottingham, Salford, Staffordshire, Surrey, Swansea, Ulster, York.

GRADUATE DESTINATIONS AND EMPLOYMENT (2005 HESA)
Graduates surveyed 535 **Employed** 290 **In further study** 100 **Assumed unemployed** 25.

OTHER DEGREE SUBJECTS FOR CONSIDERATION
East European Studies; European Studies; International Business Studies.

GREEK
(see also **Classical Studies/Classical Civilisation and Classics**)

NB The points totals shown to the left of the institutions are for ease of reference only. It must not be assumed that tariff points are always used by institutions or that they can be substituted for an offer in grades. The level of an offer is not necessarily indicative of the quality of a course.

COURSE OFFERS INFORMATION
Subject requirements/preferences **GCSE** Mathematics usually required. **Edinburgh**, **Glasgow**, **St Andrews** English, mathematics or science and a foreign language. **Lampeter** Five to six subjects at grade A or B. **London (King's)** English, history, foreign language. **London (RH)** Good grade in Greek. **Oxford**, **Cambridge** Mostly grade As/Bs. **Swansea** Five A* or A, five Bs. **AL** Check requirements if any for Latin or Greek.

Your target offers
360 pts **and above**
  Cambridge – AAA (Modn Mediev Lang (Class Gk) (Modn Gk))
  Oxford – Offers vary eg AAA–AAB (Class; Modn Gk)
340 pts **St Andrews** – AAB (Gk courses)
320 pts **Glasgow** – ABB–BBB (Greek)
  London (UCL) – ABB+AS–BBB+AS (Gk Lat)
300 pts **Belfast (Queen's)** – BBB (Modn Gk)
  Durham – BBB (Class (Gk lang option))
  Edinburgh – BBB (Gk St; Class Arch Gk)
  Leeds – BBB (Gk Civ; Gk A/B)
  Manchester – BBB (Greek)
280 pts **London (King's)** – BBC (Modn Gk St Ling; Modn Gk Port; Modn Gk St; Modn Gk Dig Hum;
  Modn Gk Engl)
  London (RH) – BBC (Gk; Fr Gk; Ger Gk)
260 pts **Swansea** – 260–300 pts (Gk joint courses)
180 pts **Lampeter** – open admission policy (Gk Anc Hist; Gk Media St)

Alternative offers
IB offers Cambridge 38–42 pts; London (King's) 32 pts; St Andrews 36 pts.
Scottish offers See **Chapter 7**.

CHOOSING YOUR COURSE (SEE ALSO CH.1)
Subject information Courses are offered in Ancient and Modern Greek, covering the language and
literature from ancient times to present day. **Useful websites** www.greek-language.com;
www.arwhead.com/Greeks; www.greekmyth.org; www.fhw.gr; www.culture.gr;
www.greeklanguage.gr.

Course variations Classical Archaeology and Greek (Edinburgh); Greek and Media Studies (Lampeter);
Modern Greek with Digital Humanities (London (King's)). *NOW CHECK PROSPECTUSES AND WEBSITES FOR
ANY RECENT CHANGES.*

Top universities and colleges (Research) See **Classics**.

ADMISSIONS INFORMATION
Number of applicants per place (approx) Lampeter 1; Leeds 2; London (King's) 3.

Advice to applicants and planning the UCAS personal statement See **Classical Studies/Classical
Civilisation**.

Selection interviews **Yes** Cambridge, Lampeter, London (RH).

Interview advice and questions Questions asked on A-level syllabus. Why do you want to study Greek?
What aspects of this course interest you? (Questions will develop from answers.) See also **Chapter 6**.

Reasons for rejection (non-academic) Poor language ability.

AFTER-RESULTS ADVICE
Universities with vacancies in Clearing (2006) Lampeter; London (RH).

Offers to applicants repeating A-levels **Higher** St Andrews; **Same** Leeds.

GRADUATE DESTINATIONS AND EMPLOYMENT (2005 HESA)
No data available.

OTHER DEGREE SUBJECTS FOR CONSIDERATION
Ancient History; Classical Studies; Classics; European Studies; Philosophy.

HEALTH SCIENCES/STUDIES

(including **Audiology, Chiropractic and Osteopathy;** see also **Community Studies, Environmental Science/Studies, Nursing and Midwifery, Optometry, Physiotherapy, Podiatry, Radiography, Social Work** and **Sports Science/Studies)**

NB The points totals shown to the left of the institutions are for ease of reference only. It must not be assumed that tariff points are always used by institutions or that they can be substituted for an offer in grades. The level of an offer is not necessarily indicative of the quality of a course.

COURSE OFFERS INFORMATION

Subject requirements/preferences GCSE Mathematics and a science usually preferred. **Aston** English and mathematics grades B/C. **Bournemouth** Grade B mathematics. **British Sch Ost** Grade B in biology plus one other science subject. **Leeds** (Audiology) Five subjects. **Sheffield** Good science background. **AL** Mathematics or a science subject may be required for some courses.

Your target offers

350 pts **Southampton** – BBBb (Audiology)

300 pts **Bradford** – 300 pts (MEng Med Eng)
Essex – 300–260 pts (Hlth Hum Sci)
Glamorgan – 300–340 pts (Chiropractic)
Imperial London – ABC–BBB (Biomat Tiss Eng)
Leeds – BBB 300 pts (Med Sci)
Sheffield – BBB or BBbb (Orthoptics)

280 pts **Aberdeen** – BBC 2nd yr entry (Hlth Sci; Hlth Sci (Hlth Mgt) (Hlth Soty) (Hlth Spo) (Hlth Nutr); Hlth Serv Rsch)
Aston – BBC (Audiology)
Bangor – 280 pts (Hlth Soc Cr)
Brighton – 280 pts (Hlth Soc Cr)
Bristol – BBC (Audiology)
British Sch Ost – BBC (Osteopathy)
Glasgow (Crichton) – BBC (Hlth Soc St)
Hertfordshire – 280 pts (Paramed Sci)
Manchester – BBC (Audiology)
Queen Margaret (UC) – BBC 280 pts (Audiology)

260 pts **Aston** – BCC–CCC (Hlth Sfty Env Mgt)
Chichester – 260–300 pts (Spo Thera)
London (UCL) – BCC+AS (Audiology)
Oxford Brookes – BCC (Exer Hlth)
Sheffield – BCC (Hlth Hum Sci)
Ulster – BCC 260 pts (Hlth Soc Cr Pol)

240 pts **Aberdeen** – CCC 1st yr entry (Hlth Sci; Hlth Sci (Hlth Nutr) (Hlth Mgt) (Hlth Spo) (Hlth Soty); Hlth Serv Rsch)
Bradford – 240 pts (BEng Med Eng)
Bristol – CCC (Df St)
British Coll Ost Med – CCC 240 pts (Ost Med)
Brunel – CCC 240 pts pref (Hlth Prom; Hlth Serv Mgt Admin; Hlth Cr Law Eth; Hlth St)
De Montfort – 240 pts (Audiology)
Dundee – CCC (Oral Hlth Sci)
Glasgow – CCC–BBC (Spo Med)
Gloucestershire – 240 pts (Exer Hlth Sci courses)
Hertfordshire – 240 pts (Radiothera Onc)
Kent – 240–260 pts (Hlth Soc Cr Prac)
Leeds – CCC–CC (Audiology)
Manchester – AA–CC (Oral Hlth Sci)
Manchester Met – CCC (Hlth Soc Cr + Fdn Yr)

Northumbria – 240 pts (Hlth Soc Cr courses)
Nottingham Trent – 240 pts (Hlth Env)
Queen Margaret (UC) – BCD 240 pts (Hlth Psy)
Staffordshire – 240 pts (Biol Spo Hlth)
Strathclyde – CCC/BCD (Env Hlth; Pros Orth)
Swansea – 240 pts (Audiology)

220 pts **Central Lancashire** – 220 pts (Herb Med; Hom Med)
Coventry – 220 pts (Hlth Lfstl Mgt)
Liverpool Hope – 220 pts (Hlth Comb Hons)

200 pts **Abertay Dundee** – CDD (Hlth Sci; Mntl Hlth Cnslg)
Anglia Ruskin – 200 pts (Osteopathy)
Barnsley (Univ Centre) – 200–220 pts (Hlth Commun St)
Bath Spa – 200–240 pts (Diet Hlth; Hlth St courses)
Bournemouth Anglo Euro (Coll) – CDD 200 pts (Chiropractic – apply direct, not in UCAS scheme)
Huddersfield – 200–220 pts (Hlth Commun St; Hlth Soc Welf)
Kent – 200 pts (Hlth Soc Cr Prac)
Lincoln – 200 pts (Hlth St; Acpntr; Herb Med)
Manchester Met – CDD 200 pts (Env Hlth; Hlth St)
Middlesex – 200–240 pts (Env Hlth)
Napier – 200 pts (Complem Thera; Herb Med)
Nescot – BB 200 pts (Ost Med)
Plymouth – 200 pts (Hlth Soc Cr Mgt)
Sunderland – 200 pts (Hlth St)
Thames Valley – 200 pts (Hlth Sci)

180 pts **Brighton** – 180 pts (Osteopathy)

For information on how to read the Subject Tables, see **Chapter 7**.

Bristol UWE – 180–220 pts (Hlth Sfty Env)
Cardiff (UWIC) – 180 pts (Complem Thera)
Chichester – 180–220 pts (Exer Hlth Sci)
Greenwich – 180 pts (Pblc Hlth)
Liverpool John Moores – 180 pts (Commun Hlth Soc Welf)
Northampton – 180–220 pts (Hlth St courses)
Salford – 180–200 pts (Hlth Sci Soc Pol; Hlth Sci; Exer Hlth Sci; Trad Chin Med; Complem Med Hlth Sci)
Sheffield Hallam – 180 pts (Pblc Hlth Nutr)
Southampton Solent – 180 pts (Hlth Fit Mgt)

160 pts **Anglia Ruskin** – 160 pts (Complem Med (Aroma) (Rflxgy))
Bedfordshire – 160–240 pts (Hlth Soc Cr)
Bournemouth – 160 pts (Sfty Hlth Env)
Bradford (Coll) – 160 pts (Complem Thera)
Canterbury Christ Church – CC (Hlth St)
Central Lancashire – 160–200 pts (Hlth St Educ; Hlth St Soc Pol; Hlth St Sociol; Hlth St Psy; Exer Nutr Hlth)
De Montfort – 160–240 pts (Hlth Inform)
Derby – 160–180 pts (Complem Thera)
East London – 160 pts (Fit Hlth; Pblc Hlth; Hlth Prom; Hlth Serv Mgt; Complem Med; Herb Med)
European Sch Ost – CC 160–280 pts flexible approach (Osteopathy)
Greenwich – 160 pts (Hlth; Complem Thera; Pblc Hlth)
Liverpool John Moores – 160–180 pts (Pblc Hlth)
Manchester – CC (Oral Hlth Sci)
Manchester Met – 160 pts (Hlth Soc Cr)
Northumbria – 160 pts (Cr Educ (Ely Yrs Disab St) (Ely Yrs Prof Prac); Hlth Soc Cr)
St Mary's (Coll) – CC 160 pts (Hlth Exer)
Sheffield Hallam – 160 pts (Oprtg Dept Prac)
Sunderland – 160–180 pts (Hlth Soc Cr; Commun Hlth)
Westminster – CC (Hlth Sci (Complem Thera) (Herb Med) (Hom) (Nutr Thera) (Ther Bdwk); Trad Chin Med)
Wolverhampton – 160–220 pts (Complem Thera; Hlth St; Df St)

140 pts **Cardiff (UWIC)** – 140 pts (Hlth Sfty Env Prot)
Teesside – 140–200 pts (Fd Nutr Hlth Sci; Pblc Hlth)
Trinity Carmarthen (Coll) – 140–120 pts (Hlth Exer; Hlth Exer Out Educ; Hlth Exer Spo St)

120 pts **Bradford (Coll)** – DD 120 pts (Hlth Soc Welf)
Brighton – 120 pts check with admissions tutor (Acupuncture)
De Montfort – 120–140 pts (Hlth St)
Derby – 120 pts (Heal Arts courses)
Gloucestershire – 120 pts (Hlth Commun Soc Cr)
London Met – 120–140 pts (Hlth Prom; Herb Medicin Sci)
London South Bank – 120 pts (Hlth St; Hlth Prot)
Paisley – DD (Hlth Sci; Occ Sfty Hlth)
Roehampton – 120 pts (Hlth St; Nutr Hlth)
Suffolk (Univ Campus) – 120–180 pts (Nutr Hlth)
UCE Birmingham – 120 pts (Hlth St; Hlth Pol Mgt)

80 pts **Arts London (CFash)** – 80 pts (Cos Sci)
Cornwall (Coll) – 80 pts (Hlth Soc Cr Mgt)
Farnborough (CT) – 80 pts (Sci Mgt; Exer Hlth)
Kingston – 80 pts (Acupuncture)
North East Wales (IHE) – 80–120 pts (Occ Hlth Sfty Env Mgt; Trad Chin Med)
Oxford Brookes – 80 pts (Osteopathy)
Swansea (IHE) – 80 pts (Hlth St courses)
UHI Millennium Inst – 80 pts (Hlth St; Complem Thera)

Worcester – EE 80 pts (Hlth St; Hlth Sci)

Leeds Met – contact University
Middlesex – contact University (Trad Chin Med)
Open University – contact University

Alternative offers
IB offers Brighton 28 pts; Bristol (Aud) 30 pts; Bristol UWE 24–26 pts; Brunel 26 pts; Chichester 28 pts; Essex 28–30 pts; Kent 27 pts; London (RH) 30 pts; Salford 24–27 pts; Sheffield 29 pts; Southampton indiv merit; Thames Valley 30 pts.
Scottish offers See **Chapter 7**.

OTHER HIGHER EDUCATION COURSES IN THE SUBJECT FIELD

Foundation degrees (contact the institutions for details) (See also Social and Public Policy and Administration) Abingdon (Coll); Arts London (CFash); Barnet (Coll); Barnfield (Coll); Bath Spa; Bath City (Coll); Bedford (Coll); Bedfordshire; Bexley (Coll); Bishop Auckland (Coll); Bolton (CmC); Bournemouth and Poole (Coll); Bradford; Bradford (Coll); Brighton; Bristol City (Coll); Bristol UWE; Buckinghamshire Chilterns (UC); Bromley (Coll); Calderdale (Coll); Canterbury (Coll); Canterbury Christ Church; Cardiff (UWIC); Central Lancashire; Cirencester (Coll); City; Colchester (Inst); Coleg Sir Gar; Cornwall (Coll); Cumbria; Derby; Dewsbury (Coll); Dunstable (Coll); Durham New (Coll); East Berkshire (Coll); East London; Edge Hill; Exeter (Coll); Farnborough (CT); Gateshead (Coll); Gloucestershire (CAT); Great Yarmouth (Coll); Greenwich; Grimsby (IFHE); Hartpury (Coll); Herefordshire (CAT); Hopwood Hall (Coll); Hugh Baird (Coll); Hull (Coll); Kendal (Coll); Kingston; Kingston (Coll); Leeds Thomas Danby (Coll); Loughborough (Coll); Manchester (CAT); Manchester Met; Matthew Boulton (CFHE); Middlesex; Myerscough (Coll); Newcastle (Coll); Newman (CHE); North East Wales (IHE); Northumberland (Coll); Norwich City (Coll); Open University; Peterborough Reg (Coll); Plymouth (CT); Portsmouth; Preston (Coll); Redcar (Coll); Riverside Halton (Coll); St Helens (Coll); St Mary's (Coll); Salisbury (Coll); Sheffield (Coll); Shipley (Coll); Shrewsbury (CAT); Somerset (CAT); South Birmingham (Coll); South Downs (Coll); Southampton; Stratford-upon-Avon (Coll); Stockport (Coll); Stockton Riverside (Coll); Suffolk (Univ Campus); Sunderland City (Coll); Sussex Downs (Coll); Sutton Coldfield (Coll); Swindon New (Coll); Teesside; Telford (CAT); Thames Valley; Totton (Coll); Trinity Carmarthen (Coll); Truro (Coll); Tyne Met (Coll); Wakefield (Coll); Walsall (Coll); Warwickshire (Coll); West Anglia (Coll); West Kent (Coll); Weston (Coll); Weymouth (Coll); Wigan and Leigh (Coll); Wolverhampton City (Coll); Worcester; Worcester (CT); Yeovil (Coll); York St John.

Higher National Diploma courses Accrington and Rossendale (Coll); Anglia Ruskin; Arts London; Bangor; Birmingham (CFTCS); Blackpool and Fylde (Coll); Bradford (Coll); Bridgwater (Coll); Bristol City (Coll); Buckinghamshire Chilterns (UC); Burton (Coll); Cardiff (UWIC); Carlisle (Coll); Carmarthenshire (Coll); Central Lancashire; Chichester (Coll); Coventry City (Coll); Derby; Dudley (Coll); Dumfries and Galloway (Coll); East Lancashire (IHE); Farnborough (CT); Forth Valley (Coll); Glamorgan; Glasgow Met (Coll); Gloucestershire (CAT); Greenwich; Grimsby (IFHE); Herefordshire (CT); Henley (Coll); Hopwood Hall (Coll); Leeds Met; Llandrillo Cymru (Coll); London Met; Manchester Met; Middlesex; Neath Port Talbot (Coll); Newcastle (Coll); Oldham (Coll); Pembrokeshire (Coll); Plymouth; St Helens (Coll); Salford; Somerset (CAT); South Devon (Coll); Southend Campus Essex; Stockport (CFHE); Swansea (Coll); Teesside; UHI Millennium Inst; Uxbridge (Coll); Walsall (Coll); Waltham Forest (Coll); West Anglia (Coll); West Herts (Coll); Weston (Coll); Worcester.

Beauty courses are offered by Arts London (CFash); Blackpool and Fylde (Coll); Bradford (Coll); City (Coll); Cornwall (Coll); Gloucestershire (CAT); Leicester (Coll); Middlesex; Newcastle (Coll); Strode (Coll); Warwickshire (Coll); Wolverhampton; Worcester.

CHOOSING YOUR COURSE (SEE ALSO CH.1)

Subject information Health Sciences/Studies is a broad subject-field which offers courses covering both practical applications concerning health and well-being (some of which border on nursing) and also the administrative activities involved in the promotion of health in the community. Also included are some specialised careers which include **Chiropractic** involving the healing process by way of manipulation, mainly in the spinal region, and also **Osteopathy** in which joints and tissues are manipulated to correct abnormalities. **Audiology** is concerned with the treatment and diagnosis of hearing and balance disorders in humans of all ages. **Prosthetics and Orthotics** involves the provision and fitting of artificial limbs. **Useful websites** www.riph.org.uk; www.bmj.com; www.reflexology.org; www.baap.org.uk; www.chiropractic-uk.co.uk; www.osteopathy.org.uk; www.who.int; www.i-c-m.org.uk; www.csp.org.uk; www.scienceyear.com.

Course variations Acupuncture (Oriental Medicine) (Brighton); Deaf Studies (Bristol); Health Studies and Education (Central Lancashire); Paramedic Science (Hertfordshire); Public Health (Greenwich); Audiology (London (UCL)); Oral Health Science (Manchester); Traditional Chinese Medicine (Middlesex, Salford, Westminister, Wolverhampton). *NOW CHECK PROSPECTUSES AND WEBSITES FOR ANY RECENT CHANGES.*

Universities and colleges teaching quality See www.tqi.ac.uk; www.qaa.ac.uk.

Top universities and colleges (Research) Aston (Audiology).

ADMISSIONS INFORMATION

Number of applicants per place (approx) Bangor 2; Barnsley (Univ Centre) 2; Bath Spa 1; Bournemouth 4; Bournemouth Anglo Euro (Coll) 1; British Sch Ost 5; Brunel 2; Central Lancashire 6; Chester 6; Chichester 5; Cumbria 4; De Montfort 2; European (Sch Ost) 3; Huddersfield (Hlth Spo St) 4; Liverpool John Moores 10; London Met 7; Manchester Met 10; Middlesex 4; Northampton 3; Portsmouth 12; Roehampton 10; Salford 8; Southampton 4; Swansea 1; Worcester 3.

Advice to applicants and planning the UCAS personal statement You should describe any work you have done dealing with people, particularly in a caring capacity, for example, working with the elderly, nursing, hospital work. Give evidence of why you wish to study this subject. Evidence of people-orientated work experience. (Chiropractic) You should provide clear evidence of why you wish to follow this career. Give evidence of talking to a chiropractor and details of any work using your hands. (Osteopathy) Evidence required for motivation to study Osteopathy through work experience or general hobbies/activities, communication skills, a caring nature and people orientation. **Bangor** (Hlth Soc Cr) Applicants should be able to communicate and work in a group. They should also have an interest in the non-nursing side of health authorities. Evidence needed to indicate that applicants have an understanding of the NHS and health care systems. **European Sch Ost** Evidence of interest in the caring professions. Some work experience in an osteopathic practice preferable. **Liverpool John Moores** Information on relevant experience, reasons for wanting to do this degree and the types of careers sought would be useful.

Misconceptions about this course There is a mistaken belief that all courses cover nursing. **Bangor** (Hlth Soc Cr) This is an administration course, not a nursing course. **Brit Coll Ost Med** Some students think that we offer an orthodox course in medicine. **European Sch Ost** We do not teach in French although we do have a franchise with a French school based in St Etienne and a high percentage of international students. All lectures are in English. Applicants should note that cranial osteopathy – one of our specialisms – is only one aspect of the programme.

Selection interviews Yes Aston, Barnsley (Univ Centre), Bristol, Central Lancashire, Chichester, Coventry, De Montfort, European Sch Ost, Glamorgan, Middlesex, Nottingham Trent, Worcester **Some** Bath Spa, Canterbury Christ Church, Derby, Huddersfield (mature students), Liverpool John Moores, Salford, Swansea.

Interview advice and questions Courses vary considerably and you are likely to be questioned on your reasons for choosing the course at that university or college. If you have studied biology then questions are possible on the A-level syllabus and you could also be asked to discuss any work experience you have had. (Chiropractic) Interview questions are likely to arise about your reasons for choosing this career and your discussions with a chiropractor. Be aware of the differences between the work of chiropractors, osteopaths and physiotherapists. (Osteopathy) What personal qualities would you need to be a good osteopath? What have you done that you would feel demonstrates a sense of responsibility? What would you do if you were not able to secure a place on an Osteopathy course this year? International applicants will be verbally tested on their ability in spoken English at interview.

Liverpool John Moores Interviews are informal. It would be useful for you to bring samples of coursework to the interview. See **Chapter 6**.

Reasons for rejection (non-academic) Some students are mistakenly looking for a professional qualification in, for example, occupational therapy, nursing. Inability to be aware of the needs of others (in the environmental health field). **Coventry** Inadequate mathematics. **Salford** (Trad Chn Med) No experience of communicating with people. No knowledge of Chinese Medicine.

AFTER-RESULTS ADVICE

Universities with vacancies in Clearing (2006) Aberdeen; Abertay Dundee; Bournemouth; Bradford; Brunel; Canterbury Christ Church; Central Lancashire; De Montfort; Derby; Dundee; East London; Gloucestershire; Greenwich; Hertfordshire; Huddersfield; Leeds; Lincoln; London Met; Manchester Met; Middlesex; Northampton; Northumbria; Nottingham Trent; Paisley; Plymouth; Roehampton; Salford; Sheffield Hallam; Southampton; Sunderland; Swansea; Westminster; Wolverhampton; Worcester.

Offers to applicants repeating A-levels Same Aston, Bangor, Brighton, Chester, Derby, European Sch Ost, Huddersfield, Lincoln, Liverpool John Moores, Nottingham Trent (Hlth Env), Roehampton, Salford, Surrey, Swansea.

GRADUATE DESTINATIONS AND EMPLOYMENT (2005 HESA)
Complementary Medicine graduates surveyed 520 **Employed** 320 **In further study** 15 **Assumed unemployed** 20.

See also under **Dentistry**, **Medicine**, **Nursing and Midwifery**, **Nutrition**, **Optometry**, **Physiotherapy**, **Podiatry** and **Radiography**.

OTHER DEGREE SUBJECTS FOR CONSIDERATION
Audiology; Biological Sciences; Biology; Community Studies; Consumer Studies; Dentistry; Dietetics; Medicine; Nursing; Occupational Therapy; Optometry; Physiotherapy; Psychology; Podiatry; Radiography; Speech Therapy; Sport Science.

HISTORY

(including **Heritage Management and Medieval Studies;** see also **History (Ancient)**, **History (Economic and Social)** and **History of Art)**

NB The points totals shown to the left of the institutions are for ease of reference only. It must not be assumed that tariff points are always used by institutions or that they can be substituted for an offer in grades. The level of an offer is not necessarily indicative of the quality of a course.

COURSE OFFERS INFORMATION
Subject requirements/preferences GCSE Aberdeen, **Dundee**, **Edinburgh**, **Glasgow**, **Nottingham** (also IT preferred), **St Andrews** English, mathematics or science and a foreign language. **Birmingham**, **Durham** (mostly grades A* and A), **Exeter**, **Leicester**, **London (QM)**, **(RH)**, **(UCL)**, **Manchester**, **Southampton**, **Sussex**, **Ulster** Foreign language required. **Sheffield Hallam** Mathematics grade A–C. **London (Gold)** Six subjects grade A–C. **Manchester Met** Five subjects A–C minimum. **Oxford**, **Cambridge** Majority of grade As preferred. **AL** History usually required at a specified grade.

Your target offers
360 pts   and above

        Bristol – AAA–AAB (Hist St Fr/Ger; Econ Econ Hist)
        Cambridge – AAA (History)
        Durham – AAA (Hist; Hist Pol; Engl Lit Hist)
        Exeter – AAA–AAB 360–340 pts (Hist; Hist Pol; Hist Anc Hist; Hist Int Rel)
        London (King's) – AAA (History)
        London (UCL) – AAA–AAB+AS (Hist courses)
        Manchester – AAA–BBB (Hist courses)

Oxford – Offers vary eg AAA–AAB (Hist Econ; Anc Modn Hist; Hist Engl; Modn Hist Modn Lang; Hist Pol)

340 pts **Birmingham** – AAB (Hist Anc Mediev; Hist Soc Sci)

Cardiff – AAB (Hist; Hist Welsh Hist; Hist joint hons)

Durham – AAB (Anc Mediev Modn Hist; Hist Pol; Hist Comb Hons Soc Sci; Hist Langs; Anc Hist (Euro St))

East Anglia – AAB–ABB (Hist; Modn Hist; Hist Pol; Hist Land Arch; Euro Hist Lang; Hist Hist Med)

Exeter – AAB–ABB 340–320 pts (Hist Fr/Ger/Ital/Russ/Span; Hist Hist Arch)

Leeds – AAB (Hist; Int Hist Pol)

London (King's) – AAB (War St courses)

Newcastle – AAB (Hist; Pol Hist)

Nottingham – AAB (Hist; Hist Pol)

St Andrews – AAB (Mediev Hist courses; Modn Hist courses; Scot Hist courses; Mediev St)

Sheffield – AAB–BBB (Hist courses)

Warwick – AAB–ABBc (Hist (Modn) (Ren Modn); Hist Cult; Hist Pol; Hist Sociol)

York – AAB (Hist courses)

320 pts **Birmingham** – ABB 320 pts (Anc Mediev Hist)

Cardiff – ABB (Modn Hist Pol; Mediev Hist)

Durham – ABB (Educ St (Hist))

Exeter – ABB–BBB 320–300 pts (Hist Soty)

Glasgow – ABB–BBB (Hist; Scot Hist)

Lancaster – ABB (Hist; Mediev Ren St)

Leicester – ABB–BBB 320–300 pts (History)

Liverpool – ABB 340 pts (Hist; Modn Hist Pol)

London (King's) – ABB+AS (Hist Port Braz St)

London (LSE) – ABB (Hist; Gov Hist; Int Rel Hist)

London (QM) – 320 pts (Hist; Journal Contemp Hist; Film St Hist; Fr Hist; Hist Ger Lang; Modn Contemp Hist)

London (RH) – 320 pts ABB (Hist; Hist Span; Modn Hist Pol)

Southampton – ABB–BBB (Hist courses)

Sussex – ABB–BBB **or** 360–340 pts 3AL+AS (Hist; Hist Anth; Hist Film St; Hist Lang; Contemp Hist courses; Intlctl Hist)

300 pts **Aberystwyth** – 300 pts (Hist; Welsh Hist)

Belfast (Queen's) – BBB (Modn Hist; Byz St courses; Hist Sci)

Birmingham – BBB–BBC 300–280 pts (E Medit Hist; Anc Hist))

Chester – 300 pts (History)

Dundee – 300 pts 2nd yr entry (Hist; Scot Hist St)

Edinburgh – BBB (Hist; Hist Pol; Hist Scot Hist St; Hist Class; Hist Hist Art; Hist Sociol; Soc Archit Hist; Scot Hist St)

Essex – 300–260 pts (Hist; Modn Hist; Contemp Hist; Soc Cult Hist; Br Euro Hist; Hist Film St; Hist Econ; Hist Lit; Hist Modn Langs; Hist Sociol; Hist Crim; Hist Modn Hist Pol; Modn Hist Int Rel)

Exeter – BBB–BBC (Hist Corn St)

Hull – BBB–BBC (Hist courses except under **260 pts**)

Kent – 300–280 pts (Hist; War St)

Lancaster – BBB (Hist courses except under **320 pts**)

Leeds – BBB (Hist Phil Sci)

Leicester – BBB–BCC (Contemp Hist Pol)

Leicester – BBB (Hist Pol; Hist Arch; Int Rel Hist; Engl Hist)

London (Gold) – BBB–BBC (Hist; Hist Hist Ideas; Hist Sociol; Hist Anth)

Nottingham – ABC–BBB (Hist; Hist Contemp Chin St)

Oxford Brookes – BBB **or** BBbb **or** ABb (History)

Stranmillis (UC) – BBB (Hist Educ)

280 pts East Anglia – BBC–BCC (Am Hist Engl Hist; Am Hist Pol)

Glasgow (Crichton) – BBC (Scot St)

Huddersfield – 280 pts (Hist Law)

Kent – 280–260 pts (Hist joint courses; Hist Arch St)

Liverpool – BBC–BBB 320 pts (Hist (Soc Econ); Hist with Fr/Ger/Hisp St)

London (Gold) – BBC (Hist Pol)

Nottingham – BBC (Viking St)

Reading – 280–300 pts (3AL+AS) (Hist; Modn Hist Int Rel; Hist Euro Lit Cult; Modn Hist Pol)

260 pts Aberystwyth – 260 pts (Musm Gllry St)

Bristol UWE – 260–300 pts (Hist; Dr Hist; Film St Hist; Media Cult St Hist; Hist Engl)

Central Lancashire – 260 pts (Herit Mgt)

Gloucestershire – 260 pts (Herit Mgt)

Huddersfield – 260 pts (Hist; Hist Inf Sys; Hist Spo Hist; Hist Pol; Mus Hist; Hist Musm Herit St; Hist Sociol; Hist Journal)

Hull – 260–280 pts (20th Cent Hist)

Keele – 260–320 pts (Am St Hist; Hist)

Kent – 260 pts (Herit Sci)

Leicester – 260–320 pts BCC (Hist Comb courses)

Liverpool – BCC 260 pts (Irish St Hist)

London (SOAS) – BCC (Hist courses)

Northumbria – 260 pts (Br Am Cult; Hist; Hist Pol; Hist Sociol)

Oxford Brookes – BCC/AB **or** BCcc (Hist joint courses)

Richmond (Am Int Univ) – 260 pts (History)

Stirling – BCC (Hist courses; Scot Hist)

Strathclyde – BCC–BB (History)

Swansea – 260–300 pts (Mediev St courses; Hist courses)

240 pts Aberdeen – CCC (Hist; Scot St; Celt Civ courses)

Bradford – 240 pts (Hist Law; Hist Pol; Hist Phil; Hist Fr/Span; Modn Euro Hist)

Bristol UWE – 240–280 pts (Int Hist Int Pol)

Brunel – 240 pts (Hist; Pol Hist)

Cardiff (UWIC) – 240 pts (Modn Hist Pol; Modn Hist Pop Cult)

Chester – 240–260 pts (History)

Coventry – 240–260 pts (Hist; Hist joint hons)

Dundee – 240 pts 1st yr entry (Hist; Scot Hist St)

Glasgow Caledonian – 240 pts (History)

Hertfordshire – 240 pts (Hist courses)

Lincoln – 240 pts (Cons Restor; Musm Exhib Des)

Portsmouth – 240–300 pts (Hist; Am St Hist; Hist Pol; Int Rel Hist; Hist joint courses)

Sheffield Hallam – 240 pts (History)

Ulster – CCC 240 pts (Irish Hist; Hist; Irish Hist Pol)

Westminster – CCC (Modn Hist)

220 pts **Bangor** – 220–260 pts (Hist Arch; Hist Film St; Herit Arch Hist; Mediev Ely Modn Hist; Welsh Hist; Welsh Hist Arch; Herit Mgt; Hist Journal; Modn Contemp Hist; Hist)
Brighton – 220 pts (Cult Hist St)
Central Lancashire – 220 pts (Hist; Hist Comb; Modn Wrld Hist; Hist Musms Herit)
Chichester – 220–240 pts (Hist courses)
Gloucestershire – 220 pts (Hist courses; Herit Mgt Hist)
Kingston – 220–320 pts (Hist; Hist joint courses)
Lincoln – CCD 220 pts (History)
Liverpool Hope – 220 pts (Hist courses)
Manchester Met – 220 pts (Hist courses)
Nottingham Trent – 220 pts (History)
Winchester – 220 pts (Hist courses)

200 pts **Anglia Ruskin** – 200 pts (Hist; Hist Engl; Hist Pol; Hist Sociol)
Bath Spa – 200–240 pts (History)
Bolton – 200 pts (Hist courses)
Cumbria – 200 pts (Hist; Hist Am St)
Glamorgan – 200–160 pts (Hist; Modn Contemp Wales; Modn Euro)
Huddersfield – 200–280 pts (Pol Contemp Hist)
Newport – 200 pts (History)
Plymouth – 200 pts (History)
Staffordshire – 200 pts (History)

180 pts **Buckingham** – 180 pts (Engl Lit Hist)
De Montfort – 180–220 pts (Hist; Hist joint courses)
Derby – 180 pts (History)
Edge Hill – 180 pts (Hist Educ St)
Lampeter – open admissions policy (Hist; Mediev St; Modn Hist St; Welsh St; Ch Hist Anc Hist)
Northampton – 180–220 pts (Hist courses; Herit Mgt)
Roehampton – 180–200 pts (Hist courses)
Salford – 180–200 pts (Contemp Hist Pol; Contemp Mltry Int Hist)

160 pts **Bishop Grosseteste (Coll)** – 160 pts (Educ Hist St)
Bournemouth – 160 pts (Herit Cons)
Canterbury Christ Church – CC (Hist; Mediev Ren St)
Central Lancashire – 160–180 pts (Hist Am St; Hist Educ; Hist Engl Lit; Hist Film Media; Hist Law; Hist Pol; Hist Sociol)
East London – 160 pts (Hist; Hist Anth; Hist Pol; Hist Sociol)
Edge Hill – 160–180 pts (Hist; Hist Crea Writ; Hist Crim; Hist Engl; Hist Film St; Hist IT; Hist Mgt)
Greenwich – 160 pts (History)
Leeds Trinity and All Saints (Coll) – 160–240 pts (Hist; Engl Hist)
Liverpool John Moores – 160–200 pts (Hist courses)
London Met – 160 pts (Restor Cons; Hist)
Middlesex – 160–200 pts (Hist Art Archit courses)
Newman (CHE) – 160–240 pts (Hist; Hist Crea Writ)
Peterborough Reg (Coll) – 160 pts (Engl Hist; Hist Law; Hist Sociol)
SAC (Scottish CAg) – CC (Rur Recr Tour Mgt (Herit St))
St Mary's (Coll) – CC 160 pts (History)
Sunderland – 160 pts (History)
Winchester – 160 pts (Herit Mgt)
Wolverhampton – 160–220 pts (App Hist St; Hist; War St Hist)
Worcester – 160 pts (Hist courses)
York St John – 160 pts (Hist courses)

140 pts **Bishop Grosseteste (Coll)** – 140 pts (Herit St)
Marjon (Coll) – 140–200 pts (Hist courses)
Teesside – 140 pts (Hist; Modn Contemp Euro Hist; Soc Cult Hist; Hist Media St)

120 pts   **Bradford (Coll)** – 120 pts (Humanities)
          Suffolk (Univ Campus) – 120–180 pts (Hist courses)
100 pts   **West Suffolk (Coll)** – 100 pts (Hist Engl; Hist Sociol)
          Wigan and Leigh (Coll) – 100 pts (Hist Comb Hons)
80 pts   **London (Birk)** – 80 pts for under 21s (over 21s varies) (p/t Hist; Hist Arch)
          North East Wales (IHE) – 80–120 pts (History)
          South Devon (Coll) – 80 pts check with Coll (Arts (Engl Hist))
          UHI Millennium Inst – 80 pts (Hist Scot Hlnds and Isl)

          Leeds Met – contact University

Alternative offers
IB offers Aberystwyth 30 pts; Birmingham 32 pts; Brighton 28 pts; Bristol 36–38 pts; Bristol UWE 28–32 pts; Brunel 28 pts; Cambridge 38–42 pts; Chester 30 pts; Chichester 26 pts; Essex 28–32 pts; Exeter 34–35 pts; Glasgow 30 pts; Keele 28–30 pts; Kent 28–32 pts; Leicester 34 pts; Liverpool 33 pts; London (King's) 36–37 pts, (LSE) 36 pts, (QM) 30 pts, (SOAS) 32 pts, (UCL) 36–39 pts; Manchester 32–37 pts; Manchester Met 24–26 pts; Newcastle 35 pts; Reading 32 pts; St Andrews 36 pts; Sheffield 32–35 pts; Southampton 32 pts; Stirling 28 pts; Warwick 37–38 pts; Winchester 24–26 pts; York 37 pts.
Scottish offers See **Chapter 7**.

OTHER HIGHER EDUCATION COURSES IN THE SUBJECT FIELD
Foundation degrees (contact the institutions for details) Bishop Burton (Coll); Blackpool and Fylde (Coll); Cornwall (Coll); Northampton; Nottingham New (Coll); Truro (Coll).

CHOOSING YOUR COURSE (SEE ALSO CH.1)
Subject information Degrees in History cover a very broad field with many courses focusing on British and European history. However, specialised History degrees are available which cover other regions of the world and, in addition, all courses will offer a wide range of modules. **Useful websites** www.english-heritage.org.uk; www.historytoday.com; www.genhomepage.com; www.historynet.com; www.archives.org.uk; www.artefact.co.uk; www.rhs.ac.uk.

Course variations Museum and Gallery Studies; Welsh History (Aberystwyth); Heritage Management (Bangor); History and Journalism (Bradford); History and History of Medicine (East Anglia); History and International Relations (Exeter); History and Journalism (Huddersfield); Medieval and Renaissance Studies (Lancaster); Combined Studies (Leicester and Newcastle); Modern Contemporary History (London (QM)); Central and East European History (London (UCL)); Viking Studies (Nottingham); Scottish History (St Andrews); Contemporary Military and International History (Salford). *NOW CHECK PROSPECTUSES AND WEBSITES FOR ANY RECENT CHANGES.*

Universities and colleges teaching quality See www.tqi.ac.uk; www.qaa.ac.uk.

Top universities and colleges (Research) Belfast (Queen's); Birmingham; Cambridge*; Cardiff; Dundee; Durham*; East Anglia*; Edinburgh; Essex; Exeter; Glasgow; Hertfordshire; Huddersfield; Hull; Keele; Leeds; Leicester; Liverpool; London (King's)*, (LSE)*, (QM), (RH), (SOAS)*, (UCL); Manchester; Oxford; Oxford Brookes*; Roehampton; St Andrews; Sheffield; Sheffield Hallam; Southampton; Stirling; Teesside; Warwick; York.

Sandwich degree courses Bangor (workplace modules).

ADMISSIONS INFORMATION
Number of applicants per place (approx) Aberystwyth 6; Anglia Ruskin 4; Bangor 6; Bath Spa 6; Birmingham 7, (E Medit Hist) 3; Bournemouth (Herit Cons) 3; Bristol 25; Bristol UWE 6; Brunel 6; Buckingham 10; Cambridge 4; Cardiff 7; Central Lancashire 5; Chichester 4; Cumbria 5; De Montfort 10; Dundee 6; Durham 15; East Anglia 8; Edge Hill 8; Exeter 9; Gloucestershire 26; Huddersfield 4; Hull 5; Kent 12; Kingston 6; Lampeter 6; Lancaster 11; Leeds 12; Leeds Trinity and All Saints (Coll) 14; Leicester 7; Liverpool 6; London (Gold) 6, (King's) 10, (LSE) 10, (Gov Hist) 10, (QM) 5, (RH) 9, (UCL) 13; London Met 2; Manchester Met 8; Marjon (Coll) 3; Middlesex 10; Newcastle 13; Newman (CHE) 2; North East Wales (IHE) 2; Northampton 4; Nottingham 20; Oxford (success rate 39%); Oxford Brookes 25;

Portsmouth 5; Richmond (Am Int Univ) 2; Roehampton 3; St Mary's (Coll) 5; Sheffield Hallam 21; Southampton 12; Staffordshire 8; Stirling 2; Teesside 4; Warwick 17; York 10; York St John 3.

Advice to applicants and planning the UCAS personal statement Show your passion for the past! Visits to places of interest should be mentioned, together with any particular features which impressed you. Read historical books and magazines outside your A-level syllabus. Mention these and describe any special areas of study which interest you. (Check that these areas are covered in the courses for which you are applying!) **Bangor** Clear commitment to history/archaeological studies through, for example, work experience. Travel. **Birmingham** An interest in the past above and beyond school work. **London (King's)** History books read and enjoyed – why? **(UCL)** We are impressed by a genuine academic passion for the subject for which you are applying. We are looking for teachable, committed students who will contribute to class discussion. **Nottingham** Active engagement with history and enthusiasm for the subject. **Portsmouth** Write clearly and concisely. **St Andrews** Reasons for choosing the course. Evidence of interest. **Southampton** Demonstrate through the personal statement an enthusiasm to study a range of periods, approaches and geographical areas.

Misconceptions about this course Students sometimes under-estimate the amount of reading required. **Lincoln** Some students expect the subject to be assessed only by exams and essays. It is not – we use a wide range of assessment methods. **Liverpool John Moores** Some applicants think that they have to study ancient and medieval history as well as modern; we actually only cover post-1750 history. **Stirling** Some applicants think that we only teach British history. We also cover European, American, African and Environmental History.

Selection interviews Yes Bangor, Birmingham (Mediev St) (all), (E Medit Hist), Bishop Grosseteste (Coll), Brighton, Bristol, Brunel, Cambridge, Edge Hill, Essex, Hertfordshire, Hull, Lancaster, Leeds Trinity and All Saints (Coll), London, (King's), (QM), (RH), (UCL), London Met, London South Bank, Middlesex, Oxford, Oxford Brookes, Portsmouth, Roehampton, Sussex, Warwick; **Some** Anglia Ruskin, Bath Spa, Buckingham, Cardiff, Chichester, De Montfort, Dundee, Exeter, Huddersfield, Kent, Lampeter, Lincoln, Liverpool, London (LSE) (rarely), Salford, Sheffield Hallam, Southampton, Staffordshire, Winchester, Wolverhampton, York.

Interview advice and questions Questions are almost certain to be asked on those aspects of the history A-level syllabus which interest you. Examples of questions in previous years have included: Why did imperialism happen? If a Martian arrived on Earth what aspect of life would you show him/her to sum up today's society? Has the role of class been exaggerated by Marxist historians? What is the difference between power and authority and between patriotism and nationalism? Did Elizabeth I have a foreign policy? What is the relevance of history in modern society? Who are your favourite monarchs? How could you justify your study of history to the taxpayer? **Cumbria** Questions about interest in research, analysis, argument, information gathering, future plans after study, motivation. **De Montfort** Why History? Why is history important? **Oxford** Questions on submitted work and the capacity to think independently. **Swansea** We ask applicants to explain something – a hobby, an historical problem or a novel. The subject is less important than a coherent and enthusiastic explanation. See **Chapter 6**.

Applicants' impressions (A=Open day; B=Interview day) Bristol (A) The open day consisted of a tour of the city, accommodation and a talk to lecturers and current students. **Cardiff** (A) There was a tour of halls, the students' union and the History department. There was also a talk by staff and the opportunity to speak to the students. **Exeter** (A) There was a well-planned tour, a talk about the course and chance to speak to students. **Reading** (A) We were given a talk by the History department staff and a tour of the campus, halls and students' union. We also had the opportunity to speak to staff and students.

Reasons for rejection (non-academic) Personal statements which read like job applications, focusing extensively on personal skills and saying nothing about the applicant's passion for history. Poor use of personal statement combined with predicted grades. Little commitment and enthusiasm. No clear reason for choice of course. Little understanding of history. Absence or narrowness of intellectual pursuits. Deception or concealment on the UCAS application. His knowledge of 19th century history (his chosen subject) did not have any depth. Unwillingness to learn. Narrow approach to subject. Failure to submit requested information. **Birmingham** Commitment insufficient to sustain interest over three years. **London (King's)** Inability to think analytically and comparatively. **(UCL)** The vast majority of applications are of a very high standard, many applicants being predicted AAA grades. We view each application as a complete picture taking into account personal statement, reference and performance at any interview as well as actual and predicted academic performance. There is no single rule by which applicants are selected and therefore no single reason why they are rejected. **Nottingham** No discrimination against Oxbridge applicants.

AFTER-RESULTS ADVICE

Universities with vacancies in Clearing (2006) Aberdeen; Aberystwyth; Anglia Ruskin; Bangor; Bath Spa; Belfast (Queen's); Bolton; Bournemouth; Bradford; Bristol UWE; Buckingham; Canterbury Christ Church; Central Lancashire; Chester; Chichester; Coventry; Cumbria; De Montfort; Derby; East Anglia; East London; Edge Hill; Essex; Glamorgan; Gloucestershire; Greenwich; Hertfordshire; Huddersfield; Hull; Keele; Kent; Kingston; Lancaster; Leicester; Lincoln; Liverpool Hope; Liverpool John Moores; London (Gold), (QM), (RH); London Met; Manchester; Manchester Met; Northampton; Northumbria; Nottingham Trent; Plymouth; Portsmouth; Reading; Roehampton; Salford; Sheffield Hallam; Southampton; Staffordshire; Stirling; Sunderland; Swansea; Teesside; Ulster; Wolverhampton; Winchester; Worcester; York St John.

Offers to applicants repeating A-levels Higher East Anglia, Exeter, Glasgow, Huddersfield, Lampeter, Leeds, Liverpool, St Andrews, Warwick; **Possibly higher** Aberystwyth, Birmingham, Cambridge, Durham, Portsmouth; **Same** Anglia Ruskin, Bangor, Buckingham, Bristol, Cardiff, Chester, Chichester, De Montfort, Dundee, Edge Hill (CHE), Hull, Kent, Lancaster, Lincoln, Liverpool John Moores, London (QM), (RH), (SOAS), Newcastle, Newman (CHE), Newport, Oxford Brookes, Richmond (Am Int Univ), Roehampton, Staffordshire, Winchester, York, York St John.

GRADUATE DESTINATIONS AND EMPLOYMENT (2005 HESA)

Graduates surveyed 6970 **Employed** 825 **In further study** 1575 **Assumed unemployed** 485.

OTHER DEGREE SUBJECTS FOR CONSIDERATION

Ancient History; Anthropology; Archaeology; Economic and Social History; Government; History of Art; International Relations; Medieval History; Politics.

HISTORY (ANCIENT)

(see also **History**)

NB The points totals shown to the left of the institutions are for ease of reference only. It must not be assumed that tariff points are always used by institutions or that they can be substituted for an offer in grades. The level of an offer is not necessarily indicative of the quality of a course.

COURSE OFFERS INFORMATION

Subject requirements/preferences GCSE Birmingham, **Durham**, **London (RH) (UCL)** A foreign language or classical language required. **Cardiff** Evidence of linguistic ability an advantage. **Durham** Four or five A* grades, three or four As. **Lampeter** Five or six subjects at grade A or B. **Oxford** Majority of grade As preferred. **Scottish universities** See under **History**. **Swansea** Five A* or As, five Bs. **AL** History or classical civilisation may be preferred subjects.

Your target offers

360 pts	**and above**	
	London (UCL)	– AAA+AS–ABB+AS (Anc Hist; Anc Hist Egypt)
	Oxford	– Offers vary eg AAA–AAB (Anc Modn Hist; Class Arch Anc Hist)
340 pts	**Durham**	– AAB (Anc Mediev Modn Hist)
	St Andrews	– AAB (Anc Hist courses)
320 pts	**Durham**	– ABB (Anc Hist; Anc Hist (Euro St))
	Warwick	– ABB–BBBc (Anc Hist Class Arch)
300 pts	**Belfast (Queen's)**	– BBB–BBC (Anc Hist; Byz St)
	Bristol	– ABC (Anc Hist; Anc Hist Arch)

Durham – BBB (Anc Hist Arch)
Edinburgh – BBB (Anc Hist; Anc Hist Class Arch; Anc Hist Gk; Anc Hist Lat)
Exeter – BBB–BBC (Anc Hist; Anc Hist Arch)
Leicester – BBB 300–360 pts (Anc Hist Hist; Anc Hist Arch; Comb St)
London (King's) – BBB+AS (Anc Hist)
London (RH) – BBB (Anc Hist)
London (UCL) – ABC+AS (Anc Wrld St)
Manchester – BBB (Anc Hist courses)
Newcastle – BBB–BBC (Anc Hist courses)
Nottingham – ABC–BBB (Anc Hist; Anc Hist Arch; Anc Hist Hist; Anc Hist Lat)
280 pts **Birmingham** – BBC (Hist Anc Mediev; Anc Hist; Arch Anc Hist; Hist E Medit Lat)
Cardiff – BBC 280 pts (Anc Mediev Hist; Anc Hist)
Liverpool – BBC 280 pts (Anc Hist Arch; Anc Hist Comb Hons; Egypt; Arch Anc Civ; Egypt Arch)
Reading – 280 pts (Anc Hist)
260 pts **Swansea** – 260–300 pts (Anc Hist courses)
180 pts **Lampeter** – open admission policy (Anc Mediev Hist; Anc Hist Arch; Anc Hist)

Alternative offers

IB offers Birmingham 33–34 pts; Bristol 32 pts; London (King's) 32 pts; Reading 30 pts; St Andrews 36 pts.
Scottish offers See **Chapter 7**.

CHOOSING YOUR COURSE (SEE ALSO CH.1)

Subject information Ancient History covers the Greek and Roman world, the social, religious, political and economic changes taking place in the Byzantine period and the medieval era which followed. **Useful websites** www.rhs.ac.uk; www.guardians.net; www.arwhead.com/Greeks; www.ancientsites.com.

Course variations Ancient History (European Studies) (Durham); Ancient History and Classical Archaeology (Edinburgh; Oxford; Warwick); Combined Studies (Leicester); Egyptology; Archaeology of Ancient Civilisations (Liverpool); Ancient World Studies (London (UCL)); Ancient History and Latin (Nottingham). *NOW CHECK PROSPECTUSES AND WEBSITES FOR ANY RECENT CHANGES.*

Universities and colleges teaching quality See www.tqi.ac.uk; www.qaa.ac.uk.

Top universities and colleges (Research) See **Classics**.

ADMISSIONS INFORMATION

Number of applicants per place (approx) Birmingham 8; Bristol 11; Cardiff 4; Durham 12; Leicester 32; London (RH) 3; Newcastle 10; Nottingham 10; Oxford 2.

Advice to applicants and planning the UCAS personal statement Any information about experience of excavation or museum work should be given. Visits to Greece and Italy to study archaeological sites should be described. **Liverpool** (Egypt) Interest in Ancient Egypt developed through reading, TV, Internet. Course covers archaeology and the writings of Ancient Egypt. Be aware of the work of the career archaeologist, for example, sites and measurement officers, field officers and field researchers (often specialists in pottery, glass, metalwork). See also **History**.

Misconceptions about this course **Liverpool** (Egypt) Some students would have been better advised looking at V400 Archaeology or VV16 Ancient History and Archaeology, both of which offer major pathways in the study of Ancient Egypt.

Selection interviews **Yes** Birmingham, Durham, Leeds, London (RH), Oxford; **Some** Cardiff, Newcastle.

Interview advice and questions See **History**.

Applicants' impressions (A=Open day; B=Interview day) **Bristol** (A) There were sample lectures, a question-and-answer session and a tour of halls. **London (RH)** (B) I had a relatively informal interview followed by a session on finance and a talk about the course. **(UCL)** A 30-minute interview, quite intellectually demanding. **Swansea** (B) Nice interview. I was asked general questions, testing my knowledge, but it was mainly structured round my personal statement.

Reasons for rejection (non-academic) **Liverpool** (Egypt) Egyptology used to fill a gap on the UCAS application. Applicant misguided in choice of subject.

AFTER-RESULTS ADVICE

Universities with vacancies in Clearing (2006) Lampeter; Leicester; Manchester; Reading; Swansea.

Offers to applicants repeating A-levels **Same** Birmingham, Cardiff, Durham, Newcastle.

GRADUATE DESTINATIONS AND EMPLOYMENT (2005 HESA)
See **History**.

OTHER DEGREE SUBJECTS FOR CONSIDERATION
Anthropology; Archaeology; Classical Studies; Classics; Greek; History of Art; Latin.

HISTORY (ECONOMIC and SOCIAL)
(see also **History**)

NB The points totals shown to the left of the institutions are for ease of reference only. It must not be assumed that tariff points are always used by institutions or that they can be substituted for an offer in grades. The level of an offer is not necessarily indicative of the quality of a course.

COURSE OFFERS INFORMATION
Subject requirements/preferences **GCSE** Mathematics usually required. **London (LSE)** Grades A/B. **Manchester** A foreign language. **Scottish universities** See under **History**. **York** Spread of As and Bs. **AL** History usually preferred.

Your target offers
360 pts **and above**
    Bristol – AAA–AAB (Econ Hist; Sociol Econ Hist)
340 pts **Birmingham** – AAB (Econ Soc Hist)
    Glasgow – AAB (Econ Soc Hist)
    Warwick – AAB+AS (Econ Econ Hist)
320 pts **London (LSE)** – ABB (Econ Hist; Econ Hist Econ; Econ Econ Hist)
    York – ABB (Econ Econ Hist)
300 pts **Edinburgh** – BBB (Econ Hist; Econ Soc Hist; Econ Soc Hist Env St)
    Lancaster – BBB (Soc Hist)
    Manchester – ABC–ABB (Econ Soc Hist)
    Swansea – 300–260 pts (Econ Soc Hist courses)
280 pts **Essex** – 280 pts (Soc Cult Hist)
    Hull – 280 pts (Hist Soc Hist; Hist Econ Hist)
    Liverpool – BBC 320 pts (Hist (Soc Econ))
220 pts **Aberystwyth** – 220–280 pts (Econ Soc Hist; Econ Soc Hist Bus Mgt)
    Manchester Met – 220–280 pts (Sociol Econ Hist; Pol Soc Econ Hist)
140 pts **Teesside** – 140 pts (Soc Cult Hist)

Alternative offers
IB offers Aberystwyth 30 pts; Liverpool 30 pts; London (LSE) 36 pts; Manchester 34–32 pts.
Scottish offers See **Chapter 7**.

CHOOSING YOUR COURSE (SEE ALSO CH.1)
Subject information Economic and Social History is a study of societies and economies and explores the changes that have taken place in the past and the causes and consequences of those changes. The

study can cover Britain, Europe and other major powers. **Useful websites** www.rhs.ac.uk; see also **Economics** and **History**.

Course variations Economic and Social History (Aberystwyth); Social and Cultural History (Essex); Social History Combined Honours (Manchester Met); Social and Cultural History (Teesside). *NOW CHECK PROSPECTUSES AND WEBSITES FOR ANY RECENT CHANGES.*

Universities and colleges teaching quality See www.tqi.ac.uk; www.qaa.ac.uk.

Top universities and colleges (Research) Birmingham; Edinburgh; Glasgow; Hull; London (LSE).

ADMISSIONS INFORMATION
Number of applicants per place (approx) Birmingham 10; Bristol 3; Hull 4; Liverpool 3; London (LSE) (Econ Hist) 3, (Econ Hist Econ) 5; York 8.

Advice to applicants and planning the UCAS personal statement See **History**.

Selection interviews **Yes** Aberystwyth, Birmingham, Bristol, Liverpool, Warwick.

Interview advice and questions See **History**.

AFTER-RESULTS ADVICE
Universities with vacancies in Clearing (2006) Aberystwyth; Manchester Met; Swansea.

Offers to applicants repeating A-levels **Higher** Warwick, York; **Possibly higher** Liverpool; **Same** Hull.

GRADUATE DESTINATIONS AND EMPLOYMENT (2005 HESA)
See under **History**.

OTHER DEGREE SUBJECTS FOR CONSIDERATION
Economics; Government; History; Politics; Social Policy and Administration; Sociology.

HISTORY OF ART

NB The points totals shown to the left of the institutions are for ease of reference only. It must not be assumed that tariff points are always used by institutions or that they can be substituted for an offer in grades. The level of an offer is not necessarily indicative of the quality of a course.

COURSE OFFERS INFORMATION
Subject requirements/preferences **GCSE Cambridge** Usually grade As. **East Anglia** Modern language grade A–C preferred. **Nottingham** Modern language preferred grade A–C. **York** Good spread of A/B grades. **AL** History is preferred for some courses.

Your target offers
360 pts **and above**
       Bristol – AAA–BBC (Hist Art; Hist Art Yr Abrd; Hist Art Fr/Ger/Ital/Port/Russ/Span)
       Cambridge – AAA (Hist Art)
       Oxford – Offers vary eg AAA–AAB (Hist Art)
340 pts **Birmingham** – AAB–BBB (Hist Art Tech)
       East Anglia – AAB–BBB (Hist Art; Hist Art Aus/N Am; Hist Art Hist; Art Hist Phil; Hist Art Lit; Hist Art Hist Euro Lit; Arch Anth Art Hist)
       Essex – 340–280 pts (Hist Art; Hist Modn Contemp Art; Lit Hist Art; Film St Hist Art; Hist Art Modn Lang)
       London (UCL) – AAB+AS (Hist Art courses)
       Newcastle – AAB–ABB (Hist Art Comb St)
       St Andrews – AAB (Art Hist Class St; Art Hist; Art Hist Engl; Art Hist Gk; Art Hist Int Rel; Art Hist /Mediev Hist; Art Hist Modn Hist; Art Hist Psy)
       York – AAB (Hist Hist Art)

320 pts **Birmingham** – ABB–BBB 300–320 pts (Hist Art)
Glasgow – ABB–BBB (Hist Art)
Nottingham – ABB (Art Hist Engl St)
St Andrews – ABB (Art Hist courses except under **340 pts**)
Warwick – ABB–BBBc **or** AB/BBbbb (Hist Art; Hist Art Fr St)
York – ABB (Engl Hist Art)
300 pts **Edinburgh** – BBB (Hist Art; Hist Art Archit Hist; Hist Art Chin St; Hist Art Engl Lit; Hist Art Hist Mus)
Kent – 300 pts (Euro Arts (Hist Phil Art))
Leeds – BBB (Hist Art; Hist Art Musm St)
Manchester – BBB (Art Arch Anc Wrld; Hist Art)
Nottingham – BBB (Art Hist; Arch Art Hist; Art Hist Class Civ; Art Hist Ger)
Reading – 300–280 pts (Hist Art Archit; Art Hist Art; Anc Hist Hist Art; Arch Hist Art; Class St Hist Art; Engl Hist Art; Film Thea Hist Art; Hist Art Hist; Hist Art Fr/Ger/Ital; Typo Hist Art Archit)
Sussex – ABB–BBB **or** 340 pts 3AL+AS (Art Hist courses)
York – BBB (Hist Art)
280 pts **Hull** – BBC–BBB (Hist Hist Phil Art; Dr Hist Art)
Kent – 280–300 pts (Hist Phil Art; Euro Arts; Hist Phil Art)
London (Gold) – BBC (Hist Art)
Oxford Brookes – BBC **or** BCbb (Hist Art)
260 pts **Aberystwyth** – 260 pts (Art Hist; Art Hist Fine Art)
Leicester – BCC–BBC 260–340 pts (Hist Art)
London (SOAS) – BCC (Hist Art; Hist Art Arch)
Northumbria – 260 pts (Hist Modn Art Des Film; Vis Cult)
Reading – 260 pts (Art Hist Art)
240 pts **Aberdeen** – CCC 1st yr entry (Hist Art courses)
Manchester Met – 240 pts (Hist Art Des Prac)
UCE Birmingham – 240 pts (Hist Art Des)
220 pts **Brighton** – 220 pts (Hist Decr Arts Crfts; Hist Des Cult Soty; Vis Cult)
Kingston – 220 pts (Hist Art Des Film)
200 pts **Middlesex** – 200–240 pts (Hist Art Des)
180 pts **Greenwich** – 180 pts (Art Glry Herit Mgt)
Liverpool John Moores – 180–260 pts (Hist Art Musm St)
Northampton – 180 pts (Hist Art courses)
Sunderland – DDD–CDD 180–200 pts (Hist Art Des courses)
160 pts **Cardiff (UWIC)** – 160 pts (Art Art Hist)
Central Lancashire – 160 pts (Art Hist Vis Cult courses)
East London – 160 pts (Vis Theor)
London Met – 160 pts (Art Des Hist; Restor Cons)
Roehampton – 160–140 pts (Art Hist)
120 pts **Arts London (CFash)** – 120 pts check with admissions tutor (Fash Hist Theor)
Buckinghamshire Chilterns (UC) – 120–180 pts (Vis Cult)
Southampton Solent – 120 pts (Antiques)
80 pts **London (Birk)** – 80 pts for under 21s (over 21s varies) (p/t Hist Art)

Alternative offers
IB offers Aberystwyth 29 pts; Birmingham 34 pts; Brighton 28 pts; Bristol 32 pts; Cambridge 38–42 pts; Essex 32–36 pts; Kent 30–32 pts; Leicester 30 pts; London (SOAS) 30 pts; Manchester 32 pts; Reading 30 pts; St Andrews 32–36 pts; Warwick 32–34 pts; York 32–34 pts.
Scottish offers See **Chapter 7**.

CHOOSING YOUR COURSE (SEE ALSO CH.1)

Subject information History of Art and Design courses differ slightly between universities although most will focus on the history and appreciation of European art and architecture from the 14th to 20th centuries. Some courses also cover the Egyptian, Greek and Roman periods and, in the case of London

(SOAS), Asian, African and European Art. The history of all aspects of design and film can also be studied in some courses. There has been an increase in the popularity of these courses in recent years. **Useful websites** www.artchive.com; www.artcyclopedia.com; www.artguide.org; www.artefact.co.uk; www.fine-art.com; www.nationalgallery.org.uk; www.britisharts.co.uk; www.tate.org.uk.

Course variations History of Decorative Arts and Crafts (Brighton); Arts Gallery and Heritage Management (Greenwich); European Arts (History and Philosophy of Art) (Kent); History of Art and Museum Studies (Leeds); History of Modern and Contemporary Art (Manchester); History of Art Design and Practice (Manchester Met); Typography and History of Art and Architecture (Reading). *NOW CHECK PROSPECTUSES AND WEBSITES FOR ANY RECENT CHANGES.*

Universities and colleges teaching quality See www.tqi.ac.uk; www.qaa.ac.uk.

Top universities and colleges (Research) Birmingham; Cambridge; East Anglia; Essex; Glasgow; London (UCL); Manchester; Middlesex; St Andrews; Sussex; Warwick.

ADMISSIONS INFORMATION

Number of applicants per place (approx) Aberystwyth 9; Birmingham 6; Brighton 8; Bristol 10; Cambridge 4; East Anglia 7; Essex 5; Kent 3; Kingston 4; Leeds 29; Leicester 10; Liverpool John Moores 2; London (Gold) 10, (SOAS) 4; Manchester Met 10; Middlesex (Hist Art Archit) 16; Newcastle 23; Northampton (UC) 2; Nottingham 10; Portsmouth 8; York 6.

Advice to applicants and planning the UCAS personal statement Applicants for History of Art courses should have made extensive visits to art galleries, particularly in London, and should be familiar with the main European schools of painting. Evidence of lively interest required. Discuss your preferences and say why you prefer certain types of work or particular artists. You should also describe any visits to museums and any special interests in furniture, pottery or other artefacts (see also **Appendix 2**). **Aberystwyth** Attendance at evening classes in art history (if not at A-level). Related hobbies and interests, for example, reading, literature, music, cinema. **Kent** An interest in Modern Period (especially). An interest in all the arts. **London (Gold)** Art enthusiasms, influences, passions. **St Andrews** Reasons for choosing the course and evidence of interest. Sport/extra-curricular activities and positions of responsibility. **York** Visit art galleries, read books on the subject.

Misconceptions about this course **Kent** The History of Art is not a practical course in fine arts. **York** Students do not need a background in art or art history. It is not a course with a studio element in it.

Selection interviews **Yes** Brighton, Cambridge, East Anglia (majority), London (UCL), Manchester Met, Newcastle (also portfolio), Warwick; **Some** Bristol, Buckingham, Central England, Kent.

Interview advice and questions Some universities set slide tests on painting and sculpture. Those applicants who have not taken history of art at A-level will be questioned on their reasons for choosing the subject, their visits to art galleries and museums and their reactions to the art work which has impressed them. **Kent** Do they visit art galleries? Have they studied art history previously? What do they expect to get out of the degree? Sometimes they are given images to compare and discuss. See **Chapter 6**.

Applicants' impressions (A=Open day; B=Interview day) **East Anglia** (B) I had a 25-minute informal chat with one interviewer who made me feel at ease. It was a well-organised interview and she knew what she wanted to find out. It's a modern campus with a good art collection. Students took prospective students on tours round the campus and advised us on university life. I strongly recommend the course.

Reasons for rejection (non-academic) Poorly presented practical work. Students who do not express any interest or enthusiasm in contemporary visual arts are rejected.

AFTER-RESULTS ADVICE

Universities with vacancies in Clearing (2006) Aberystwyth; Brighton; East Anglia; Hull; Kent; Kingston; Leeds; Leicester; London (Gold); Manchester Met; Middlesex; Northampton; Northumbria; Nottingham; Roehampton; UCE Birmingham.

Offers to applicants repeating A-levels **Possibly higher** Oxford Brookes, St Andrews; **Same** Aberystwyth, Huddersfield, Kent, Leeds, Newcastle, UCE Birmingham, Warwick, York.

GRADUATE DESTINATIONS AND EMPLOYMENT (2005 HESA)
No data available for 2005, but in 2002, **Graduates surveyed** 655 **Employed** 275 **In further study** 175 **Assumed unemployed** 45.

OTHER DEGREE SUBJECTS FOR CONSIDERATION
Art; Archaeology; Architecture; Classical Studies; Photography.

HORTICULTURE
(including **Garden Design;** see also **Landscape Architecture**)

NB The points totals shown to the left of the institutions are for ease of reference only. It must not be assumed that tariff points are always used by institutions or that they can be substituted for an offer in grades. The level of an offer is not necessarily indicative of the quality of a course.

COURSE OFFERS INFORMATION
Subject requirements/preferences **GCSE** Mathematics sometimes required. **AL** A science subject may be required or preferred for some courses.

Your target offers
220 pts **Reading** – 220 pts (Horticulture)
180 pts **Gloucestershire** – 180–240 pts (Gard Des Land Des)
160 pts **Bristol UWE** – 160 pts (Amen Hort Mgt)
  Greenwich – 160 pts (Gard Des; Hort (Commer); Medcnl Hort)
  SAC (Scottish CAg) – CC (Hort Plntsmn; Hort)
140 pts **Writtle (Coll)** – 140 pts (Hort; Hort Bus Mgt; Land Amen Mgt; Int Hort; Gard Des Restor Mgt; Hort Crop Prod; Spo Turf Sci Mgt)
120 pts **Worcester** – DD 120 pts (Horticulture)
100 pts **Falmouth (UC)** – 100 pts (Gard Des Arts Env)

Alternative offers
IB offers Bristol UWE 28 pts; Reading 27 pts.
Scottish offers See **Chapter 7**.

OTHER HIGHER EDUCATION COURSES IN THE SUBJECT FIELD
Foundation degrees (contact the institutions for details) Askham Bryan (Coll); Bicton (Coll); Bishop Burton (Coll); Bournemouth; CAFRE; Duchy (Coll); Falmouth (UC); Hartpury (Coll); Moulton (Coll); Myerscough (Coll); Nottingham Trent; Pershore (Coll); Plumpton (Coll); SAC (Scottish CAg); Sparsholt (Coll); Warwickshire (Coll); Welsh Hort (Coll); Wolverhampton; Worcester; Writtle (Coll).

Higher National Diploma courses
100 pts and below
  Askham Bryan (Coll); Bangor; Bath; CAFRE; Capel Manor (Coll); Central Lancashire; Easton (Coll); Greenwich; Hertfordshire; Middlesex; Plymouth; SAC (Scottish CAg); Sunderland; UHI Millennium Inst; Warwickshire (Coll); West Anglia (Coll); Wiltshire (Coll); Wolverhampton; Worcester; Writtle (Coll).

CHOOSING YOUR COURSE (SEE ALSO CH.1)
Subject information Horticulture is a broad subject area which covers commercial horticulture and the provision of recreational and leisure facilities (amenity horticulture). **Useful websites** www.iagre.org; www.rhs.org.uk; www.horticulture.org.uk.

Course variations Amenity Horticultur Management (Bristol UWE); Horticulture with Plantsmanship (Glasgow/SAC (Scottish CAg)); Landscape, Garden Design and Landscape Design (Gloucestershire); Commercial Horticulture (Greenwich); Horticulture with Business Management; Sport Turf Science and Management; International Horticulture (Writtle (Coll)). *NOW CHECK PROSPECTUSES AND WEBSITES FOR ANY RECENT CHANGES.*

Sandwich degree courses Greenwich; Nottingham Trent.

ADMISSIONS INFORMATION
Number of applicants per place (approx) Greenwich 4; SAC (Scottish CAg) 1; Writtle (Coll) 3.

Advice to applicants and planning the UCAS personal statement Practical experience is important and visits to botanical gardens (the Royal Botanic Gardens, Kew or Edinburgh and the Royal Horticultural Society gardens at Wisley) could be described. Contact your local authority offices for details of work in parks and gardens departments. **Greenwich** An enthusiasm for horticulture, plants, science, technology and the land-based industries on a scale from worldwide to organic smallholdings. See also **Appendix 2**.

Misconceptions about this course **Greenwich** Students are unaware of the scope of this degree. The course covers commercial horticulture – plants, plant products, ornamentals, bedding plants, hardy trees and shrubs, salads, vegetables, fruit and organic crops from production to marketing.

Selection interviews **Yes** Greenwich, SAC (Scottish CAg), Worcester.

Interview advice and questions Past questions have included: How did you become interested in horticulture? How do you think this course will benefit you? Could you work in all weathers? What career are you aiming for? Are you interested in gardening? Describe your garden. What plants do you grow? How do you prune rose trees and fruit trees? Are there any EU policies at present affecting the horticulture industry? Topics relating to the importance of science and horticulture. See **Chapter 6**.

AFTER-RESULTS ADVICE
Universities with vacancies in Clearing (2006) Bournemouth; Greenwich; Nottingham Trent; Reading; Worcester.

Offers to applicants repeating A-levels **Same** Greenwich, SAC (Scottish CAg).

GRADUATE DESTINATIONS AND EMPLOYMENT (2005 HESA)
See under **Agricultural Sciences/Agriculture**.

OTHER DEGREE SUBJECTS FOR CONSIDERATION
Agriculture; Crop Science; Landscape Architecture; Plant Sciences.

HOSPITALITY AND HOTEL MANAGEMENT

(including **Events Management;** see also **Business Courses, Consumer Studies/Sciences, Food Science/Studies and Technology, Leisure and Recreation Management Studies** and **Tourism and Travel**)

NB The points totals shown to the left of the institutions are for ease of reference only. It must not be assumed that tariff points are always used by institutions or that they can be substituted for an offer in grades. The level of an offer is not necessarily indicative of the quality of a course.

COURSE OFFERS INFORMATION
Subject requirements/preferences **GCSE** English and mathematics usually required plus a foreign language for International Management courses. **Bournemouth** Average grades B. **Salford** Five subjects grade A–C including English and mathematics. **AL** No specified subjects.

Your target offers

280 pts **Surrey** – 280 pts (Int Hspty Mgt; Int Hspty Tour Mgt)
240 pts **Bournemouth** – 240 pts (Evnts Mgt)
 Brighton – 240 pts (Entre Hspty; Int Hspty Mgt; Hspty Evnt Mgt; Mgt Serv Ind; Mark Fd Drnk)
 Oxford Brookes – BCD (Hspty Mgt St; Htl Rstrnt Mgt; Int Hspty Mgt)
 Ulster – CCC–CCD (Int Hspty Mgt; Leis Evnts Cult Mgt; Int Hspty St Fr/Ger/Span; Int Htl Tour Mgt)
220 pts **Central Lancashire** – 220–240 pts (Hspty Mgt Int Hspty Mgt)
 Glamorgan – 220–260 pts (Evnt Mgt)
 Gloucestershire – 220 pts (Hspty Mgt; Int Hspty Mgt; Evnt Mgt)
 Strathclyde – CCD/BC (Htl Hspty Mgt)
 Winchester – 220 pts (Evnt Mgt)
200 pts **Central Lancashire** – 200–240 pts (Evnts Mgt)
 Manchester Met – 200 pts (Hspty Mgt; Hspty Mgt Tour; Hspty Mgt Culn Arts; Int Hspty Mgt; Hspty Lic Rtl Mgt; Evnts Mgt)
 Napier – 200 pts (Hspty Mgt courses; Festival Evnts Mgt)
 Plymouth – 200 pts (Hspty Mgt; Int Hspty Mgt; Hspty Tour Mgt; Cru Op Mgt; Evnts Mgt)
 Portsmouth – 200 pts (Hspty Mgt; Hspty Mgt Tour)
 Sheffield Hallam – 200 pts (Hspty Bus Mgt courses; Int Htl Mgt; Evnts Mgt courses)
180 pts **Birmingham (CFTCS)** – 180–200 pts (Hspty Bus Mgt; Hspty Fd Mgt; Hspty Tour Mgt; Culn Arts Mgt; Fd Consum Mgt; Hspty Leis Mgt; Mark Evnts Mgt; Mark Hspty Mgt; Hspty Lic Rtl Mgt)
 Bournemouth – 180 pts (Hspty Bus Dev; Hspty Mgt)
 Derby – 180 pts (Hspty Mgt; Hspty Lic Rtl Mgt; Evnts Mgt)
 East London – 180 pts (Evnts Mgt)
 Greenwich – 180 pts (Evnts Mgt)
 Huddersfield – 180–200 pts (Hspty Mgt Modn Lang; Hspty Mgt Tour Leis; Hspty Mgt; Evnts Mgt)
 Queen Margaret (UC) – BC/DDD (Hspty Tour Mgt; Int Hspty Mgt; Evnts Mgt)
160 pts **Glasgow Caledonian** – CC (Hspty Mgt; Enter Evnts Mgt)
 London Met – 160 pts (Evnts Mgt Spo Mgt; Int Hspty Mgt)
 Paisley – CC (Evnts Mgt)
 Robert Gordon – CC (Int Hspty Mgt)
 Thames Valley – 160–180 pts (Culn Arts Mgt; Hspty Mgt; Hspty Mgt Fd St; Hspty Evnts Mgt)
 Wolverhampton – 160–220 pts (Int Hspty Mgt; Evnts Vnu Mgt Leis Mgt)
140 pts **Blackpool and Fylde (Coll)** – DEE 140 pts approx (Hspty Mgt; Hspty Mgt (Int Htl Mgt); Hspty Mgt Tour)
 Bournemouth (AI) – 140 pts (Evnt Prod)
 Cardiff (UWIC) – CD 140 pts (Int Hspty Mgt; Hspty Mgt courses)
 Salford – CD 180 pts (Hspty Mgt; Hspty Tour Mgt; Hspty Leis Mgt)
 Southampton Solent – 140 pts (Evnt Mgt Spo/Tour)
120 pts **Buckinghamshire Chilterns (UC)** – 120 pts (Evnts Conf Mgt)
 Colchester (Inst) – DD 120 pts (Hspty Mgt)
 Llandrillo Cymru (Coll) – 120–80 pts (Htl Hspty Mgt)
100 pts **Suffolk (Univ Campus)** – 100–120 pts (Evnt Mgt; Hspty Mgt)

 Leeds Met – contact University

Alternative offers
IB offers Brighton 28 pts; Manchester Met 28 pts; Salford 26 pts; Surrey 30–32 pts; Thames Valley 28 pts.
Scottish offers See **Chapter 7**.

OTHER HIGHER EDUCATION COURSES IN THE SUBJECT FIELD
Foundation degrees (contact the institutions for details) Accrington and Rossendale (Coll); Bedford (Coll); Birmingham (CFTCS); Bishop Grosseteste (Coll); Blackpool and Fylde (Coll); Brighton City (Coll);

Bromley (CFHE); Buckinghamshire Chilterns (UC); Cirencester (Coll); Cornwall (Coll); Croydon (Coll); Darlington (CT); Derby; Doncaster (Univ Centre); Gloucestershire; Gloucestershire (CAT); Herefordshire (CAD); Kendal (Coll); Liverpool (CmC); Llandrillo Cymru (Coll); Loughborough (Coll); Manchester City (Coll); Middlesbrough (Coll); Newcastle (Coll); North Down and Ards (IFHE); North West Kent (Coll); Northbrook (Coll); Norwich City (Coll); Nottingham New (Coll); Oxford Brookes; Plymouth (CFE); Preston (Coll); Riverside Halton (Coll); Rose Bruford (Coll); Runshaw (Coll); Solihull (Coll); South Devon (Coll); Southampton Solent; Stratford-upon-Avon (Coll); Suffolk (Univ Campus); Thames Valley; Ulster; Westminster Kingsway (Coll); Worcestershire New (Coll); Yorkshire Coast (CFHE).

Higher National Diploma courses Anglia Ruskin; Bangor; Barnsley (Univ Centre); Bedfordshire; Birmingham (CFTCS); Blackpool and Fylde (Coll); Boston (Coll); Bradford (Coll); Brighton; Bristol City (Coll); Buckinghamshire Chilterns (UC); Canterbury Christ Church; Cardiff (UWIC); Central Lancashire; Colchester (Inst); Craven (Coll); Croydon (Coll); Darlington (CT); Derby (Coll); Doncaster (Univ Centre); Dumfries and Galloway (Coll); Farnborough (CT); Forth Valley (Coll); Gloucestershire; Greenwich; Grimsby (IFHE); Guildford (Coll); Hendon (Coll); Henley (Coll); Herefordshire (CT); Highbury (Coll); Huddersfield; Lancaster and Morecambe (Coll); Leeds Met; Leicester (Coll); Liverpool (CmC); Llandrillo Cymru (Coll); Loughborough (Coll); Manchester Met; Mid Cheshire (Coll); Middlesex; Neath Port Talbot (Coll); Nescot; Newcastle (Coll); Norwich City (Coll); Nottingham New (Coll); Oxford and Cherwell Valley (Coll); Peterborough Reg (Coll); Plymouth (CFE); Robert Gordon; St Helens (Coll); Salford; Sheffield Hallam; Shrewsbury (CAT); South Devon (Coll); Southampton Solent; Stratford-upon-Avon (Coll); Suffolk (Univ Campus); Sunderland City (Coll); Swansea (IHE); Swindon (Coll); Tameside (Coll); Thames Valley; UHI Millennium (Inst); Ulster; Walsall (CAT); West Anglia (Coll); West Herts (Coll); Westminster (Coll); Wigan and Leigh (Coll); Wirral Met (Coll); Wolverhampton; Worcester; Yorkshire Coast (CFHE).

CHOOSING YOUR COURSE (SEE ALSO CH.1)

Subject information These business-focused hospitality programmes open up a wide range of employment and career opportunities in both hospitality and other business sectors. The demand for employees is extremely high and the industry's professional body (Hotel, Catering and International Management Association (HCIMA)) (see **Appendix 2**) currently estimates that the demand for managers exceeds supply by a factor of eight. **Useful websites** www.baha.org.uk; www.cordonbleu.net; www.hcima.org.uk; www.people1st.co.uk.

Course variations Hospitality Business Development (Bournemouth); Entrepreneurship in Hospitality (Brighton); Entertainment and Event Management (Glasgow Caledonian); Events Management (London Met); Cruise Operations Management (Plymouth); Hospitality Management and Food Studies (Thames Valley); Leisure Events and Cultural Management (Ulster). *NOW CHECK PROPECTUSES AND WEBSITES FOR ANY RECENT CHANGES.*

Sandwich degree courses Birmingham (CFTCS); Bournemouth; Brighton; Cardiff (UWIC); Central Lancashire; Derby; Gloucestershire; Huddersfield; Leeds Met; London Met; Manchester Met; Oxford Brookes; Portsmouth; Plymouth; Sheffield Hallam; Surrey; Ulster; Wolverhampton.

ADMISSIONS INFORMATION

Number of applicants per place (approx) Blackpool and Fylde (Coll) 3; Bournemouth 9; Cardiff (UWIC) 12; Central Lancashire 8; London Met 10; Manchester Met (Hspty Mgt) 12, (Hspty Mgt Tour) 20; Middlesex 4; Napier 17; Oxford Brookes 9; Plymouth 5; Portsmouth 10; Robert Gordon 3; Strathclyde 8; Surrey 12.

Advice to applicants and planning the UCAS personal statement Experience in dealing with members of the public is an important element in this work which, coupled with work experience in cafes, restaurants or hotels, should be described fully. Admissions tutors are likely to look for experience in industry and for people who are ambitious, sociable and team players. **Bournemouth**, **London Met**, **Middlesex** (non-EU students) Ability required in spoken and written English. See also **Appendix 2**.

Misconceptions about this course **Cardiff (UWIC)** (Hspty Mgt) The course is not about cookery! We are looking to create managers, not chefs.

Selection interviews **Yes** Colchester (Inst), Manchester Met, Portsmouth, Robert Gordon, Surrey; **Some** Blackpool and Fylde (Coll), Salford.

Interview advice and questions What books do you read? What do you know about hotel work and management? What work experience have you had? What kind of job do you have in mind when you have qualified? How did you become interested in this course? Do you eat in restaurants? What types of restaurants? Discuss examples of good and bad restaurant organisation. What qualities do you have which make you suitable for management? All applicants are strongly recommended to obtain practical experience in catering or hotel work. See **Chapter 6**.

Reasons for rejection (non-academic) Lack of suitable work experience or practical training. Inability to communicate. Lack of awareness of work load, for example shift working, weekend work. **Cardiff (UWIC)** Students looking specifically for licensed trade courses or a cookery course. **Oxford Brookes** Lack of commitment to the hotel and restaurant industry.

AFTER-RESULTS ADVICE
Universities with vacancies in Clearing (2006) Bournemouth; Brighton; Central Lancashire; Derby; Gloucestershire; Manchester Met; Middlesex; Salford; Plymouth; Portsmouth; Thames Valley.

Offers to applicants repeating A-levels **Higher** Bournemouth, Huddersfield, Oxford Brookes, Surrey; **Same** Blackpool and Fylde (Coll), Brighton, Cardiff (UWIC), Manchester Met, Salford, Strathclyde, Surrey (BSc Ord), Ulster.

GRADUATE DESTINATIONS AND EMPLOYMENT (2005 HESA)
No data available for 2005, but in 2002: **Graduates surveyed** 2065 **Employed** 1405 **In further study** 115 **Assumed unemployed** 105.

OTHER DEGREE SUBJECTS FOR CONSIDERATION
Business; Consumer Studies; Dietetics; Food Science; Health Studies; Leisure and Recreation Management; Management; Tourism and Travel.

HOUSING

(see also **Building, Community Studies, Consumer Studies/Sciences, Property Management/Development** and **Town and Country Planning**)

NB The points totals shown to the left of the institutions are for ease of reference only. It must not be assumed that tariff points are always used by institutions or that they can be substituted for an offer in grades. The level of an offer is not necessarily indicative of the quality of a course.

COURSE OFFERS INFORMATION
Subject requirements/preferences **GCSE** English and mathematics required. **AL** No specified subjects.

Your target offers
230 pts **Sheffield Hallam** – 230 pts (Hous Prof St)
 UCE Birmingham – 230 pts (Rl Est)
220 pts **Ulster** – CCD 220 pts (Hous Mgt)
 Wolverhampton – 220–280 pts (Prop Ast Mgt)
200 pts **Anglia Ruskin** – 200 pts (Housing)
 Bristol UWE – 200–240 pts (Plan Hous Renew)
180 pts **Greenwich** – 180 pts min (Hous St)
160 pts **London South Bank** – CC–CD (Hous St)
 Middlesex – 160–200 pts (Housing)
140 pts **Cardiff (UWIC)** – CD 140 pts (Hous (Supptd) (Interprof St); Hous Pol Prac)
 North East Wales (IHE) – 140 pts (p/t Hous St)

 Bristol UWE – contact University (Hous Dev Mgt)

Leeds Met – contact University
UCE Birmingham – contact University (Prof Hous St)

Alternative offers
IB offers See **Chapter 7**.
Scottish offers See **Chapter 7**.

OTHER HIGHER EDUCATION COURSES IN THE SUBJECT FIELD
Foundation degrees (contact the institutions for details) Anglia Ruskin; Leeds Met; Middlesex; Swansea (IHE); UCE Birmingham.

Higher National Diploma courses
100 pts and below
Henley (Coll); Park Lane Leeds (Coll); Sheffield Hallam; Swansea (IHE); Worcester (CT).

CHOOSING YOUR COURSE (SEE ALSO CH.1)
Subject information These courses prepare students for careers in housing management although topics covered will also be relevant to other careers in business and administration. Modules will be taken in housing, law, finance, planning policy, public administration and construction. **Useful website** www.housingcorp.gov.uk.

Course variations Planning, Housing and Renewal (Bristol UWE); Housing Policy and Practice (Cardiff (UWIC)); Real Estate (UCE Birmingham); Property Asset Management (Wolverhampton). *NOW CHECK PROSPECTUSES AND WEBSITES FOR ANY RECENT CHANGES.*

ADMISSIONS INFORMATION
Number of applicants per place (approx) Anglia Ruskin 2; Bristol UWE 4; Cardiff (UWIC) 1; Greenwich 5; Northumbria 1; Sheffield Hallam 2.

Advice to applicants and planning the UCAS personal statement An interest in people, housing problems, social affairs and the built environment is important for this course. Contacts with local housing managers (through local authority offices or housing associations) are important. Describe any such contacts and your knowledge of the housing types and needs in your area. The planning department in your local council office will be able to provide information on the various types of developments taking place in your locality and how housing needs have changed during the past 50 years. See also **Appendix 2**.

Misconceptions about this course Applicants do not appreciate that the course is very close to social work/community work and is most suitable for those wishing to work with people.

Selection interviews **Yes** Liverpool John Moores; **Some** UCE Birmingham.

Interview advice and questions Since the subject is not studied at school questions are likely to be asked on reasons for choosing this degree. Other past questions include: What is a housing association? Why were housing associations formed? In which parts of the country would you expect private housing to be expensive and, by comparison, cheap? What is the cause of this? Have estates of multi-storey flats fulfilled their original purpose? If not, why not? What causes a slum? What is an almshouse? **Sheffield Hallam** An informal discussion of the course focusing on the student's interest in housing and any experience of working with the public. See **Chapter 6**.

Reasons for rejection (non-academic) Lack of awareness of current social policy issues.

AFTER-RESULTS ADVICE
Universities with vacancies in Clearing (2006) Anglia Ruskin; Greenwich; London South Bank; Sheffield Hallam; UCE Birmingham; Wolverhampton.

Offers to applicants repeating A-levels **Same** Bristol UWE, Cardiff (UWIC), London South Bank, Sheffield Hallam, UCE Birmingham.

GRADUATE DESTINATIONS AND EMPLOYMENT (2005 HESA)
No data available.

OTHER DEGREE SUBJECTS FOR CONSIDERATION
Architecture; Building; Business Studies; Community Studies; Environmental Planning; Estate Management; Property Development; Social Policy and Administration; Social Studies; Surveying; Town Planning; Urban Regeneration.

HUMAN RESOURCE MANAGEMENT
(see also **Business Courses**)

NB The points totals shown to the left of the institutions are for ease of reference only. It must not be assumed that tariff points are always used by institutions or that they can be substituted for an offer in grades. The level of an offer is not necessarily indicative of the quality of a course.

COURSE OFFERS INFORMATION

Subject requirements/preferences GCSE English and mathematics at C or above. **AL** No subjects specified.

Your target offers
340 pts **Manchester** – AAB–ABB (Mgt HR)
320 pts **Aston** – ABB 320 pts (HR Mgt)
        Bath – 320 pts (Sociol HR Mgt)
        Cardiff – ABB–BBB (Bus Mgt (HR); Ind Rel Sociol)
        Lancaster – ABB (Mgt Org (HR Mgt))
        Leeds – ABB (HR Mgt)
        London (LSE) – ABB (HR Mgt Emp Rel)
300 pts **Liverpool** – BBB (HR Mgt)
        Stirling – BBB 2nd yr entry (HR Mgt)
        Strathclyde – BBB–ABC (HR Mgt)
        Ulster – 300 pts (HR Mgt)
280 pts **Northumbria** – BBC (HR Mgt)
        Oxford Brookes – BBC 280 pts (HR Mgt Bus)
        Westminster – 280 pts (Bus HR Mgt)
260 pts **Coventry** – 260 pts (HR Mgt)
        Heriot-Watt – BCC 260 pts (Mgt HR Mgt)
        Keele – 260–280 pts (HR Mgt courses)
        Kent – 260–280 pts (Ind Rel HR Mgt courses)
        Stirling – BCC 1st yr entry (HR Mgt)
240 pts **Central Lancashire** – CCC (HR Mgt)
        De Montfort – 240 pts (HR Mgt courses)
        Kingston – 240 pts (HR Mgt)
        Middlesex – 240 pts (HR Mgt)
        Plymouth – 240 pts (Pers Mgt)
        Portsmouth – 240 pts (HR Mgt; HR Mgt Psy)
        Robert Gordon – 240 pts (Mgt HR Mgt)
        Salford – 240 pts (Bus St HR Mgt)
        Sheffield Hallam – 240 pts (Bus HR Mgt)
        Staffordshire – 240 pts (HR Mgt)
        Ulster – 240 pts (HR Mgt Mark; Bus HR Mgt)
220 pts **Bradford** – 220 pts (HR Mgt)
        Glamorgan – 220 pts (HR Mgt)
        Gloucestershire – 220 pts (HR Mgt courses)

Huddersfield – 220–200 pts (HR Mgt)
Liverpool John Moores – 220 pts (HR Mgt)
Sunderland – 220 pts (Bus Mgt (HR Mgt))
Teesside – 220 pts (HR Mgt)

200 pts **Bristol UWE** – 200–280 pts (Bus St HR Mgt)
Cumbria – 200 pts (Bus HR Mgt)
Hertfordshire – 200 pts (HR Mgt; HR courses)
Lincoln – CDD 200 pts (HR Mgt courses)
Manchester Met – 200–260 pts (HR Mgt courses)
Napier – 200 pts (HR Mgt; Hspty HR Mgt)
UCE Birmingham – 200 pts (Bus Psy HR Mgt; Bus law HR Mgt)

180 pts **Cardiff (UWIC)** – 180 pts (Bus St HR)
Derby – 180–200 pts (HR Mgt courses)
Greenwich – 180 pts (HR Mgt)
Northampton – 180–220 pts (HR Mgt courses)

160 pts **Anglia Ruskin** – 160–200 pts (HR Mgt)
Bedfordshire – 160–240 pts (HR Mgt)
Canterbury Christ Church – 160 pts (Bus Mgt (HR); Mark HR Mgt)
East London – 160 pts (HR Mgt)
Leeds Trinity and All Saints (Coll) – 160 pts (Bus HR Mgt)
London Met – 160–240 pts (HR Mgt courses; Int HR Mgt courses)
London South Bank – CC (HR Mgt – courses)
Paisley – 160 pts (HR Mgt)
Roehampton – 160 pts (HR Mgt)
Royal (CAg) – 160 pts (Bus Mgt HR)
Southampton Solent – 160 pts (HR Mgt courses)
Southend Campus Essex – 160 pts (Bus St (HR))
Thames Valley – 160 pts (Bus St HR Mgt)
Wolverhampton – 160 pts (Bus Law HR Mgt; Bus HR Mgt)

140 pts **Bolton** – 140 pts (HR Mgt courses)

120 pts **Buckinghamshire Chilterns (UC)** – 120 pts (HR Mgt; HR Mgt Fin; HR Mgt Law; HR Mgt Mark; HR Mgt Fr/Ital/Span)
North East Wales (IHE) – 120 pts (Bus St HR Mgt)
Swansea (IHE) – 120 pts (HR Mgt)

100 pts **Suffolk (Univ Campus)** – 100–120 pts (HR Mgt)

80 pts **Farnborough (CT)** – 80 pts (Bus Mgt HR Mgt)

Leeds Met – contact University

Alternative offers
IB offers Aston 35 pts; Bath 36 pts; Heriot-Watt 28–30 pts; Keele 28–30 pts; Kent 30 pts; Liverpool 32 pts; London (LSE) 36 pts; Oxford Brookes 28–30 pts; Stirling 30 pts; UCE Birmingham 28 pts.
Scottish offers See **Chapter 7**.

OTHER HIGHER EDUCATION COURSES IN THE SUBJECT FIELD

Foundation degrees (contact the institutions for details) Barry (Coll); Bridgend (Coll); Glamorgan; Gwent (Coll); Northampton; Powys (Coll); Truro (Coll); West Kent (Coll); Wolverhampton.

Higher National Diploma courses Bradford (Coll); Durham New (Coll); Greenwich; Llandrillo Cymru (Coll); London Met; Northampton; Norwich City (Coll); Southampton Solent.

CHOOSING YOUR COURSE (SEE ALSO CH.1)

Subject information See under **Business Courses**.

Course variations Industrial Relations with Sociology (Cardiff); Human Resource Management and Law (Buckinghamshire Chilterns (UC)); Human Resource Management and Tourism Management

(Gloucestershire); Human Resource Management with Languages (Hull); Human Resource Management and Employment Relations (London (LSE)); International Human Resource Management (London Met); Personnel Management (Plymouth); Human Resource Management with Psychology (Portsmouth). *NOW CHECK PROSPECTUSES AND WEBSITES FOR ANY RECENT CHANGES.*

Universities and colleges teaching quality See www.tqi.ac.uk; www.qaa.ac.uk.

Top universities and colleges (Research) Aston; Bath; Lancaster.

Sandwich degree courses Aston; Bath; Bradford; Central England; Coventry; De Montfort; East London; Glamorgan; Gloucestershire; Hertfordshire; Lincoln; Liverpool John Moores; London Met; Napier; Paisley; Plymouth; Portsmouth; Royal (CAg); Sheffield Hallam; Staffordshire; Sunderland; Swansea (IHE); Teesside; Ulster; Westminster.

ADMISSIONS INFORMATION
Number of applicants per place (approx) Aston 10; Anglia Ruskin 10; London (LSE) 13; see also under **Business Courses**.

Advice to applicants and planning the UCAS personal statement See under **Business Courses**.

Selection interviews **Yes** De Montfort; see also under **Business Courses**.

Interview advice and questions See under **Business Courses**.

Reasons for rejection (non-academic) See under **Business Courses**.

AFTER-RESULTS ADVICE
Universities with vacancies in Clearing (2006) Bolton; Bradford; Canterbury Christ Church; De Montfort; Derby; East London; Glamorgan; Gloucestershire; Greenwich; Hertfordshire; Hull; Keele; Kent; Kingston; Lincoln; London Met; London South Bank; Manchester Met; Middlesex; Northampton; Northumbria; Plymouth; Portsmouth; Roehampton; Salford; Staffordshire; Stirling; UCE Birmingham; Wolverhampton.

GRADUATE DESTINATIONS AND EMPLOYMENT (2005 HESA)
Graduates surveyed 600 **Employed** 405 **In further study** 40 **Assumed unemployed** 40.

OTHER DEGREE SUBJECTS FOR CONSIDERATION
Business Studies; Information Systems; Management Studies/Sciences; Marketing; Psychology; Retail Management; Sociology; Sports Management.

HUMAN SCIENCES/HUMAN STUDIES

NB The points totals shown to the left of the institutions are for ease of reference only. It must not be assumed that tariff points are always used by institutions or that they can be substituted for an offer in grades. The level of an offer is not necessarily indicative of the quality of a course.

COURSE OFFERS INFORMATION
Subject requirements/preferences **GCSE** Mathematics usually required. **Oxford** Mainly grade As. **Sheffield** Good GCSE science background. **AL** Chemistry or science subjects required or preferred for some courses.

Your target offers
360 pts **and above**
          Oxford – Offers vary eg AAA–AAB (Hum Sci)
340 pts **London (UCL)** – AAB+AS–ABB+AS (Hum Sci)
320 pts **Sussex** – ABB–BBB 360–340 pts (Hum Sci)
300 pts **Edinburgh** – BBB (Scot Ethnol courses)

Exeter – ABC (Hum Biosci)
London (King's) – BBB+AS **or** BBbb (Hum Sci)
260 pts **Durham** – BCC (Hum Sci)
Loughborough – 260 pts (Ergonomics)
Sheffield – BCC (Hlth Hum Sci)
200 pts **Bolton** – 200 pts (Hum Sci)
Thames Valley – 200 pts (Hum Sci – pre-Med Yr 1 optional transfer to Medicine at London (UCL))
180 pts **Bradford** – 180–220 pts (Interd Hum St)
160 pts **Roehampton** – 160–200 pts (Hum Biosci courses)

Alternative offers
IB offers London (UCL) 34–36 pts; Loughborough 30 pts; Oxford 38–42 pts; Sheffield 29 pts; Thames Valley 30 pts.
Scottish offers See **Chapter 7**.

CHOOSING YOUR COURSE (SEE ALSO CH.1)
Subject information Human Sciences is a multi-disciplinary study relating to biological and social sciences. Topics range from genetics and evolution to health, disease, social behaviour and industrial societies. **Useful websites** www.scienceyear.com; www.becominghuman.org; see also **Biology** and **Geography**.

Course variations Interdisciplinary Human Studies (Bradford); Scottish Ethnology (Edinburgh); Human Biosciences (Exeter); Ergonomics (Loughborough). *NOW CHECK PROSPECTUSES AND WEBSITES FOR ANY RECENT CHANGES.*

ADMISSIONS INFORMATION
Number of applicants per place (approx) Bradford 7; Oxford 4–5.

Advice to applicants and planning the UCAS personal statement See **Biology** and **Anthropology**. See also **Appendix 2**.

Selection interviews **Yes** London (UCL), Oxford.

Interview advice and questions Past questions have included: What do you expect to get out of a degree in Human Sciences? Why are you interested in this subject? What problems do you think you will be able to tackle after completing the course? Why did you drop PE as an A-level given that it's relevant to Human Sciences? How do you explain altruism, given that we are surely programmed by our genes to be selfish? How far is human behaviour determined by genes? What do you think are the key differences between animals and human beings? **Oxford** Two recent marked essays required relevant to human sciences. No written test. See **Chapter 6**.

AFTER-RESULTS ADVICE
Universities with vacancies in Clearing (2006) Bolton; Loughborough; Roehampton; Sheffield.

GRADUATE DESTINATIONS AND EMPLOYMENT (2005 HESA)
No data available for this subject area.

OTHER DEGREE SUBJECTS FOR CONSIDERATION
Anthropology; Biology; Community Studies; Environmental Sciences; Life Sciences; Psychology; Sociology.

INFORMATION MANAGEMENT

(including **Library Studies/Management**)

NB The points totals shown to the left of the institutions are for ease of reference only. It must not be assumed that tariff points are always used by institutions or that they can be substituted for an offer in grades. The level of an offer is not necessarily indicative of the quality of a course.

COURSE OFFERS INFORMATION

Subject requirements/preferences GCSE English, mathematics and occasionally a foreign language. **Sheffield** Mathematics grade A/B. **AL** No specified subjects.

Your target offers

320 pts	**London (UCL)** – ABB+AS (Inf Mgt)
	Sheffield – ABB (Bus Mgt Inf Mgt)
300 pts	**Loughborough** – 300 pts (Inf Mgt Bus St; Inf Mgt Comp)
	Sheffield – BBB (Inf Mgt)
280 pts	**Westminster** – 280 pts (Bus St (Inf Mgt))
260 pts	**Aberystwyth** – 260 pts (Musm Gllry St)
	Chester – 260 pts (Inf Sys Mgt)
	Northumbria – 260 pts (Inf St)
240 pts	**Bristol UWE** – 240 pts (Inf Analys)
	Robert Gordon – CCC (Inf Mgt)
	Westminster – CCC (Bus IT Mgt)
220 pts	**Wolverhampton** – 220–280 pts (Bus Inf Mgt)
200 pts	**Kingston** – 200 pts (Inf Sys)
	Manchester Met – 200 pts (Inf Lib Mgt; Inf Mgt; Inf Comm; Inf Archit)
	Napier – 200 pts (IT Mgt; Inf Sys)
180 pts	**Aberystwyth** – 180 pts (Inf Mgt; Inf Lib St)
	Brighton – 180 pts (Lib Inf St; Inf Mgt)
160 pts	**Glasgow Caledonian** – CC (Bus Inf Mgt)
	Paisley – CC (Inf Mgt)
	Leeds Met – contact University

Alternative offers
IB offers Aberystwyth 26 pts; Brighton 28 pts; London (UCL) 34 pts; Sheffield 33 pts.
Scottish offers See **Chapter 7**.

OTHER HIGHER EDUCATION COURSES IN THE SUBJECT FIELD

Higher National Diploma courses Bell (Coll); Gloucestershire (CAT).

CHOOSING YOUR COURSE (SEE ALSO CH.1)

Subject information Information Management and Library Studies covers the very wide field of information. Its organisation, retrieval, indexing, computer and media technology, classification and cataloguing are all included in these courses. **Useful websites** www.aslib.co.uk; www.ukoln.ac.uk; www.cilip.org.uk.

Course variations Museum and Gallery Studies (Aberystwyth); Information Analysis (Bristol UWE); Information Systems Management (Chester); Information and Library Management (Manchester Met). *NOW CHECK PROSPECTUSES AND WEBSITES FOR ANY RECENT CHANGES.*

Universities and colleges teaching quality See www.tqi.ac.uk; www.qaa.ac.uk.

Top universities and colleges (Research) Loughborough; Sheffield*.

Sandwich degree courses Loughborough; Napier; Paisley.

ADMISSIONS INFORMATION

Number of applicants per place (approx) Aberystwyth 4; London (UCL) 7; Loughborough 5; Manchester Met 4; Sheffield 30.

Advice to applicants and planning the UCAS personal statement Work experience or work shadowing in local libraries is important but remember that reference libraries provide a different field of work. Visit university libraries and major reference libraries and discuss the work with librarians. Describe your experiences on the form. **Loughborough** It might be helpful to have numerate ability. A-level business studies helpful but not a requirement. AS-level maths, physics, economics or biology could be useful. See also **Appendix 2**.

Misconceptions about this course Read the prospectus carefully. The course details can be confusing. Some courses have a bias towards the organisation and retrieval of information, others towards computing.

Selection interviews Yes London (UCL), Loughborough.

Interview advice and questions Past questions include: What is it about librarianship that interests you? Why do you think you are suited to be a librarian? What does the job entail? What is the role of the library in school? What is the role of the public library? What new developments are taking place in libraries? Which books do you read? How often do you use a library? What is the Dewey number for the history section in the library? (*Applicant studying A-level History.*) See **Chapter 6**.

AFTER-RESULTS ADVICE

Universities with vacancies in Clearing (2006) Aberystwyth; Brighton; Bristol UWE; Loughborough; Manchester Met; Sheffield; Westminster; Wolverhampton.

Offers to applicants repeating A-levels Higher Loughborough; **Same** Sheffield.

GRADUATE DESTINATIONS AND EMPLOYMENT (2005 HESA)

No data available, but in 2004: **Graduates surveyed** 190 **Employed** 115 **In further study** 10 **Assumed unemployed** 20.

OTHER DEGREE SUBJECTS FOR CONSIDERATION

Business Information Systems; Communication Studies; Computer Science; Geographic Information Systems; Media Studies.

INTERNATIONAL RELATIONS

(including **International Development, Peace Studies and War Studies;** see also **European Studies and Politics**)

NB The points totals shown to the left of the institutions are for ease of reference only. It must not be assumed that tariff points are always used by institutions or that they can be substituted for an offer in grades. The level of an offer is not necessarily indicative of the quality of a course.

COURSE OFFERS INFORMATION

Subject requirements/preferences GCSE English; a foreign language occasionally required. **London (LSE)** Grades A and B. **Sussex** Language grade A. **AL** No specified subjects.

Your target offers
360 pts and above
    Exeter – AAA–BBB (Int Rel Euro)
340 pts **Bath** – AAB (Econ Int Dev)
    Essex – 340 pts (Int Rel Pol)
    London (King's) – AAB+AS (War St courses)
    St Andrews – AAB (Int Rel courses)

Warwick – AAB (Int St Fr/Ger/Ital; Econ Pol Int St; Pol Int St)

320 pts **Birmingham** – ABB (Int Rel; Int St Lang; Int St Econ; Int St Pol Sci)

Cardiff – ABB–BBB (Euro Pol Int Rel)

Exeter – ABB–BBB (Int Rel Fr/Ger/Ital/Russ/Span)

Leeds – ABB–BBB (Int Rel courses; Int Dev)

Liverpool – ABB 320 pts (Int Dev)

London (LSE) – ABB (Int Rel; Int Rel Hist)

London (RH) – ABB (Int Rel Hist; Int Rel Geog)

Manchester – ABB (Pol Int Rel)

Southampton – ABB 320 pts (Int Rel courses)

Surrey – ABB 320 pts (Law Int St)

Sussex – ABB **or** 360 pts 3AL+AS (Int Rel courses)

300 pts **Aston** – 300 pts (Int Rel courses)

Belfast (Queen's) – BBB–BBCb (Int St)

Dundee – 300 pts 2nd yr entry (Int Rel courses)

East Anglia – BBB–BBC (Int St; Int St Abrd)

Edinburgh – BBB (Int Rel)

Hull – 300 pts (Glob Gov)

Lancaster – BBB **or** 2AL+2AS 280–260 pts (Int Rel Strat St)

Leicester – BBB (Int Rel Hist)

Sheffield – BBB (Int Rel Pol)

280 pts **Aberdeen** – BBC 2nd yr entry (Pol Int Rel)

Aberystwyth – 280 pts (Int Rel)

Bradford – 280 pts (Pce St; Cnflct Resoln; Dev Pce St; Int Rel Scrty St)

Leicester – BBC (Int Rel)

Liverpool – BBC 280 pts (Int Pol Pol)

Reading – 280–300 pts (War Pce Int Rel; Pol Int Rel)

Surrey – BBC 280 pts (Pol Int St)

260 pts **Kent** – BCC 260 pts (Int Rel Fr/Ger/Ital; Pol Int Rel; Cnflct Pce Scrty)

Loughborough – 260–300 pts (Int Rel; Euro St)

Richmond (Am Int Univ) – 260 pts (Soc Sci (Int Rel))

240 pts **Aberdeen** – CCC 1st yr entry (Pol Int Rel courses)

Bristol UWE – 240–280 pts (Int Rel)

Coventry – 240–260 pts (Int Rel Pol; Int Rel Engl/Fr/Span; Hist Int Rel)

Dundee – 240 pts 1st yr entry (Int Rel Pol)

Keele – 240–280 pts (Int Rel)

Kingston – 240–280 pts (Int St)

Oxford Brookes – CCC **or** CCc (Int Rel courses)

Plymouth – 240 pts (Int Rel)

Portsmouth – 240–280 pts (Int Rel Hist)

Salford – 240 pts (Int Rel Pol)

Swansea – 240–280 pts (Int Rel single hons courses; Int Rel joint courses)

230 pts **Buckingham** – 230 pts (Int St; Int St EFL; Int St Fr/Span; Journal Int St)

220 pts **Nottingham Trent** – 220 pts (Int Rel Glob Pol)

200 pts **Chester** – 200–240 pts (Int Dev St)

Huddersfield – 200–280 pts (Int St)

Lincoln – CDD 200 pts (Int Rel courses)

180 pts **De Montfort** – 180–220 pts (Int Rel courses)

160 pts **East London** – 160 pts (Int Dev)

Greenwich – 160 pts (Int St courses)

London Met – 160–190 pts (Int Rel; Int Rel Law; Int Rel Pce Cnflct St; Int Rel Mark; Int Rel Pol)

Middlesex – 160–200 pts (Pol Int St)

Wolverhampton – 160–220 pts (War St Pol; War St Phil)

For information on how to read the Subject Tables, see **Chapter 7**.

140 pts   Derby – 140–200 pts (Int Rel Glob Dev; Third Wrld Dev)

Leeds Met – contact University

Alternative offers
IB offers Aberystwyth 30 pts; Birmingham 34 pts; Bristol UWE 26–32 pts; Exeter 32–34 pts; Keele 28–30 pts; Liverpool 30 pts; London (LSE) 36 pts; Reading 31 pts; St Andrews 36 pts.
Scottish offers See **Chapter 7**.

CHOOSING YOUR COURSE (SEE ALSO CH.1)

Subject information A strong interest in international affairs is a pre-requisite for these courses which often allow students to focus on a specific area such as African, Asian, West European politics. **Useful websites** www.sipri.org; www.un.org; www.un.int; see also under **Politics**.

Course variations Economic and International Development (Bath); Peace Studies and Conflict Resolution (Bradford); International Relations and Politics (Essex); War and Security Studies (Hull); International Relations and Strategic Studies (Kent); International Relations and Global Politics (Nottingham Trent); War Studies (London (King's)); War, Peace and International Relations (Reading). *NOW CHECK PROSPECTUSES AND WEBSITES FOR ANY RECENT CHANGES.*

Top universities and colleges (Research) See **Politics**.

Sandwich degree courses Aston; Leeds Met; Loughborough; Nottingham Trent; Oxford Brookes; Plymouth; Portsmouth; Surrey.

ADMISSIONS INFORMATION

Number of applicants per place (approx) Aberystwyth 6; Birmingham 4; De Montfort 6; Derby 3; Exeter 8; Leeds 13; London (King's) 6, (LSE) (Int Rel) 17, (Int Rel Hist) 12; Portsmouth 2; Reading 5; Richmond (Am Int Univ) 5.

Advice to applicants and planning the UCAS personal statement Describe any special interests you have in the affairs of any particular country. Contact embassies for information on cultural, economic and political developments. Follow international events through newspapers and magazines. Give details of any voluntary work you have done. **London (King's)** Substantial experience in some area of direct relevance to War Studies. **St Andrews** Reasons for choice of course. Evidence of interest.

Misconceptions about this course Some students think that this degree will give direct entry into the Diplomatic Service. **Richmond (Am Int Univ)** Applicants should note that this is a UK/US validated degree.

Selection interviews **Yes** Birmingham, London (King's), London Met, Nottingham Trent; **Some** Buckingham, De Montfort, Kent, Wolverhampton.

Interview advice and questions Applicants are likely to be questioned on current international events and crises between countries. **Nottingham Trent** Be prepared to be challenged on your existing views! See **Chapter 6**.

AFTER-RESULTS ADVICE

Universities with vacancies in Clearing (2006) Aberystwyth; Bradford; Bristol UWE; Coventry; De Montfort; Hull; Keele; Kent; Lancaster; Leicester; London Met; Loughborough; Nottingham Trent.

Offers to applicants repeating A-levels **Same** Buckingham, Chester, De Montfort, Exeter, Lincoln, Richmond (Am Int Univ), Wolverhampton.

GRADUATE DESTINATIONS AND EMPLOYMENT (2005 HESA)

See under **Politics**.

OTHER DEGREE SUBJECTS FOR CONSIDERATION

Development Studies; Economics; European Studies; Government; Politics.

ITALIAN

(see also **Languages**)

NB The points totals shown to the left of the institutions are for ease of reference only. It must not be assumed that tariff points are always used by institutions or that they can be substituted for an offer in grades. The level of an offer is not necessarily indicative of the quality of a course.

COURSE OFFERS INFORMATION

Subject requirements/preferences GCSE English and a foreign language usually required. **Edinburgh, Glasgow** English, mathematics or science and a foreign language. **London (RH)** Six subjects grade A and B. **Oxford, Cambridge** Majority of grade As usually required. **AL** Italian may be required for some courses.

Your target offers

360 pts **and above**
　　　　Cambridge – AAA (Modn Mediev Lang (Ital))
　　　　Oxford – Offers vary eg AAA–AAB (Modn Lang)
340 pts **Cardiff** – AAB–BCC 340–260 pts (Educ Ital)
　　　　Manchester – AAB (MML Ital Chin/Russ/Span)
　　　　St Andrews – AAB–ABB (Ital courses)
　　　　Warwick – BBBc–Cbbc (Ital courses except below)
　　　　Warwick – BBBc (Engl Ital Lit)
320 pts **Bath** – ABB (Euro St Modn Lang)
　　　　Cardiff – ABB–BBB (Cult Crit Ital; Engl Lit Ital; Ital Mus; Ital Sociol; Ital Phil)
　　　　Exeter – ABB–BBB (Int Rel Ital; Ital Comb courses)
　　　　Glasgow – ABB–BBB (Italian)
　　　　Lancaster – ABB (Ital St Mark; Ital St Engl Lit; Ital St Econ; Ital St Geog; Ital St Psy)
　　　　London (RH) – ABB–BBB (Ital courses)
　　　　Manchester – ABB–BBB (Ital Ling)
300 pts **Bath** – BBB 3AL+AS (Modn Langs Euro St (Ital Fr/Ger/Span))
　　　　Edinburgh – BBB–BCC (Ital courses)
　　　　Lancaster – BBB (Ital courses except under **320 pts**)
　　　　London (UCL) – BBB+AS (Ital courses)
　　　　Manchester – BBB (BA Ital Span/Russ/Port)
　　　　Sussex – BBB (Ital courses)
280 pts **Bangor** – 280 pts (Law Ital)
　　　　Cardiff – BBC–BCC 280–260 pts (Ital Jap; Ital Pol; Ital Relig St; Ital Welsh)
　　　　Leicester – BBC (Ital Span; Fr Ital; Ger Ital)
　　　　Liverpool – BBC (Ital Comb Hons)
　　　　Manchester – BBC (Ital St)
　　　　Reading – 280 pts (4 subj) 260 pts (3 subj) (Italian)
260 pts **Birmingham** – BCC (Ital St)
　　　　Bristol – BCC (Ital; Ital Port/Russ/Span; Cz Ital; Fr Ital; Ger Ital)
　　　　Essex – 260 pts (Ital St)
　　　　Kent – 260 pts (Ital courses)
　　　　Leeds – BCC (Italian)
　　　　Strathclyde – BCC/BB (Italian)
240 pts **Bangor** – 240–280 pts (Bus St Ital; Ital Mark; Ital Span)
　　　　Hertfordshire – 240 (Ital joint courses)
　　　　Portsmouth – 240 pts (App Lang; Comb Modn Langs)
　　　　Salford – 240–300 pts (Mgt Ital; Ital Ling)
　　　　Swansea – 240–300 pts (Ital courses)
220 pts **Hull** – 220–280 pts (Ital Film; Ital Span; Ital Bus St; Ital Mgt; Ital Mark; Ital Gndr St)
　　　　Nottingham Trent – 220 pts (Ital courses)

200 pts   **European Bus Sch London** – CDD 200 pts (Int Bus Ital)
   Middlesex – 200–240 pts (Ital courses)
   Napier – 200 pts (Italian)
   Sheffield Hallam – 200 pts (Int Bus Ital; Int Bus St Ital)
180 pts   **Liverpool John Moores** – 180–200 pts (Ital courses)
   Manchester Met – 180 pts (Ital Cult St; Ital Intnet Mgt)
160 pts   **Central Lancashire** – 160 pts (Ital minor)
   Greenwich – 160–200 pts (Ital courses)
   Southampton Solent – 160 pts (Ital – subject to demand)

Alternative offers
IB offers Birmingham 30–32 pts; Bristol 29 pts; Cambridge 38–42 pts; Essex 28 pts; Glasgow 30 pts; Kent 28 pts; London (UCL) 32 pts, (RH) 32 pts; Manchester 30–35 pts; Manchester Met 26 pts; St Andrews 32–36 pts; Warwick 32 pts.
Scottish offers See **Chapter 7**.

OTHER HIGHER EDUCATION COURSES IN THE SUBJECT FIELD
Higher National Diploma courses **(with Business Studies)**
100 pts   and below
   Buckinghamshire Chilterns (UC).

CHOOSING YOUR COURSE (SEE ALSO CH.1)
Subject information The language and literature of Italy will feature strongly on most Italian courses. The majority of applicants have no knowledge of Italian. They will need to give convincing reasons for their interest and to show that they have the ability to assimilate language quickly. See also **Appendix 2** under **Languages**. **Useful websites** www.europa.eu; www.cyberitalian.com; www.italia.gov.it; www.bbc.co.uk/languages; www.languageadvantage.com; www.languagematters.co.uk; www.reed.co.uk/multilingual; see also **Languages**.

Course variations European Studies and a Modern Language (Bath); Cultural Criticism and Italian (Cardiff); Italian with International Relations (Exeter); Italian and Marketing (Lancaster); Translation (English and Italian) (Middlesex); International Business and Italian (Sheffield Hallam). *NOW CHECK PROSPECTUSES AND WEBSITES FOR ANY RECENT CHANGES.*

Universities and colleges teaching quality See www.tqi.ac.uk; www.qaa.ac.uk.

Top universities and colleges (Research) Birmingham*; Bristol; Cambridge*; Leeds*; London (UCL)*; Manchester; Oxford*; Reading*; Warwick.

ADMISSIONS INFORMATION
Number of applicants per place (approx) Birmingham 5; Bristol 4; Cardiff 3; Hull 8; Lancaster 8; Leeds 3; London (RH) 4.

Advice to applicants and planning the UCAS personal statement Describe any visits to Italy and experience of speaking the language. Interest in Italian art, literature, culture, society and architecture could also be mentioned. Read Italian newspapers and magazines. Bilingual background. **Leeds** See **Languages**. **St Andrews** Evidence of interest. Reasons for choosing the course. See also **Appendix 2** under **Languages**.

Misconceptions about this course **Leeds** See **Languages**.

Selection interviews **Yes** Birmingham (majority receive offers), Cambridge, London (RH), Oxford.

Interview advice and questions Past questions include: Why do you want to learn Italian? What foreign newspapers or magazines do you read (particularly if the applicant has taken A-level Italian)? Have you visited Italy? What do you know of the Italian people, culture, art? **Leeds** See **Languages**. See **Chapter 6**.

AFTER-RESULTS ADVICE
Universities with vacancies in Clearing (2006) Bangor; Birmingham; Essex; Greenwich; Hertfordshire; Hull; Kent; Lancaster; Leicester; London (RH); Manchester Met; Middlesex; Nottingham Trent; Portsmouth; Reading; Salford; Swansea.

Offers to applicants repeating A-levels **Higher** Birmingham, Glasgow, Warwick; **Same** Cardiff, Hull, Leeds.

GRADUATE DESTINATIONS AND EMPLOYMENT (2005 HESA)
Graduates surveyed 270 **Employed** 155 **In further study** 45 **Assumed unemployed** 15.

OTHER DEGREE SUBJECTS FOR CONSIDERATION
European Studies; International Business Studies; other languages.

JAPANESE
(see also **Asia-Pacific Studies, Business Courses** and **Languages**)

NB The points totals shown to the left of the institutions are for ease of reference only. It must not be assumed that tariff points are always used by institutions or that they can be substituted for an offer in grades. The level of an offer is not necessarily indicative of the quality of a course.

COURSE OFFERS INFORMATION
Subject requirements/preferences **GCSE Edinburgh** English, mathematics or science or a foreign language. **Oxford, Cambridge** Usually a majority of grade As. English often required at other universities, also mathematics for some joint courses. **AL** Modern language required for some courses.

Your target offers
360 pts and above
    Cambridge – AAA (Orntl St (Jap St))
    Oxford – Offers vary eg AAA–AAB (Orntl St (Jap))
340 pts **Birmingham** – AAB–ABB (Int Bus Jap; Econ Jap)
320 pts **Cardiff** – ABB–BBB (Bus St Jap)
    Newcastle – ABB–BBB (Jap Cult St)
300 pts **Cardiff** – ABC–BBC (Fr Jap; Ger Jap; Ital Jap; Jap Span)
    Edinburgh – BBB (Jap; Jap Ling)
    Leeds – BBB (Jap courses)
    Nottingham – BBB 300 pts (Manuf Eng Mgt Jap)
    Sheffield – BBB–BBC **or** BBcc (Jap St; Chin St Jap; Jap St Ger; Kor St Jap; Jap St Pol; Mgt Jap St; Russ Jap)
280 pts **London (SOAS)** – ABD–BCC (Jap courses)
260 pts **Oxford Brookes** – BCC **or** BCbc (Jap Lang Contemp Soty; Jap minor courses)
180 pts **Central Lancashire** – 180–160 pts (Jap Comb courses)
    European Bus Sch – DDD 180 pts (Int Bus Jap)
    Liverpool John Moores – 180–200 pts (Jap courses)

Alternative offers
IB offers Cambridge 38–42 pts.
Scottish offers See **Chapter 7**.

CHOOSING YOUR COURSE (SEE ALSO CH.1)
Subject information A strong interest in Japan and its culture is expected of applicants. A number of four-year joint courses are now offered, all of which include a period of study in Japan. Potential employers are showing an interest in Japanese. Students report that 'it is not a soft option'. They are expected to be firmly committed to a Japanese degree (for example, by listing only Japanese on the UCAS application), to have an interest in using their degree in employment and to be prepared for a lot of hard work. See **Appendix 2** under **Languages. Useful websites** www.cilt.org.uk;

392 | Landscape Architecture

www.iol.org.uk; www.bbc.co.uk/languages; www.languageadvantage.com; www.languagematters.co.uk; www.reed.co.uk/multilingual; www.japanese-online.com.

Course variations International Business with Japanese (Birmingham); Japanese with Linguistics (Edinburgh); Japanese and Cultural Studies (Newcastle); Manufacturing Engineering and Management with Japanese (Nottingham); *NOW CHECK PROSPECTUSES AND WEBSITES FOR ANY RECENT CHANGES.*

Universities and colleges teaching quality See www.tqi.ac.uk; www.qaa.ac.uk.

Sandwich degree courses Oxford Brookes.

ADMISSIONS INFORMATION

Number of applicants per place (approx) Cardiff 8; London (SOAS) 9; Sheffield 10.

Advice to applicants and planning the UCAS personal statement Discuss your interest in Japan and your reasons for wishing to study the language. Know Japan, its culture and background history. Discuss any visits you have made or contacts with Japanese nationals. **Leeds** See **Languages**. See also **Appendix 2** under **Languages**.

Misconceptions about this course Leeds See **Languages**.

Selection interviews Yes Cambridge, Oxford; **Some** Leeds.

Interview advice and questions Japanese is an extremely demanding subject and applicants are most likely to be questioned on their reasons for choosing this degree. They will be expected also to have some knowledge of Japanese culture, history and current affairs. See **Chapter 6**.

Reasons for rejection (non-academic) Insufficient evidence of genuine motivation.

AFTER-RESULTS ADVICE

Universities with vacancies in Clearing (2006) Central Lancashire; Liverpool John Moores; Nottingham; Sheffield.

GRADUATE DESTINATIONS AND EMPLOYMENT (2004 HESA)

Graduates surveyed 55 **Employed** 30 **In further study** 5 **Assumed unemployed** 5.

OTHER DEGREE SUBJECTS FOR CONSIDERATION

Asia-Pacific Studies; International Business Studies; Oriental Languages; South East Asia Studies.

LANDSCAPE ARCHITECTURE

(including **Garden Design and Landscape Design and Management;** see also **Art and Design (Industrial/Product Design)** and **Horticulture**)

NB The points totals shown to the left of the institutions are for ease of reference only. It must not be assumed that tariff points are always used by institutions or that they can be substituted for an offer in grades. The level of an offer is not necessarily indicative of the quality of a course.

COURSE OFFERS INFORMATION

Subject requirements/preferences GCSE English. Art and mathematics or science almost certainly required. **AL** Preferred subjects for some courses include biology, geography, environmental science.

Your target offers
340 pts **Sheffield** – AAB **or** AAbb (Archit Land)
320 pts **Kingston** – 320 pts (Land Archit; Land Plan; Land Geog Inf Sys)
           Reading – 320 pts (Lnd Mgt)
260 pts **Manchester** – BCC (Land Plan Mgt)
           Manchester Met – 260–300 pts (Land Archit)
           Sheffield – BCC–ABB (Land Archit Plan; Land Archit Ecol)

For a quick reference offers calculator, fold out the inside back cover.

240 pts **Edinburgh (CA)** – CCC (Land Archit)
      Nottingham Trent – 240 pts (Land Inter Des)
      UCE Birmingham – 240 pts (Land Archit)
230 pts **Greenwich** – 230 pts (Land Archit)
220 pts **Gloucestershire** – 220 pts (Gard Des Land Mgt; Land Archit; Gard Des; Land Mgt)
160 pts **Greenwich** – 160 pts (Land Mgt)
140 pts **Writtle (Coll)** – 140 pts (Land Gard Des; Gard Des Restor Mgt; Land Amen Mgt)
100 pts **Greenwich** – 100 pts (Gard Des)
80 pts **Falmouth (UC)** – EE–CC (Spat Des – Inter Land; Gard Des Arts Env)

      Leeds Met – contact University

Alternative offers
IB offers Edinburgh (CA) 30 pts; Kingston 28 pts; Manchester Met 24 pts; Sheffield 29–35 pts.
Scottish offers See **Chapter 7**.

OTHER HIGHER EDUCATION COURSES IN THE SUBJECT FIELD
Foundation degrees (contact the institutions for details) Bridgwater (Coll); Capel Manor (Coll); Myerscough (Coll); Plumpton (Coll); Reaseheath (Coll); SAC (Scottish CAg); Sparsholt (Coll); Welsh Hort (Coll); Writtle (Coll).

Higher National Diploma courses Askham Bryan (Coll); Brighton; Buckinghamshire Chilterns (UC); Capel Manor (Coll); Central Lancashire; Glamorgan; Gloucestershire; Greenwich; Guildford (Coll); Harper Adams (UC); SAC (Scottish CAg); Worcester; Writtle (Coll).

CHOOSING YOUR COURSE (SEE ALSO CH.1)
Subject information Landscape architecture is a specialised branch of architecture for which an ability in art and design is sought and for some of these courses a portfolio of art work may be required. Courses focus on the design of the environment and surrounding buildings. (It should not be confused with the work of a garden centre.) **Useful website** www.landscape.co.uk.

Course variations Landscape Planning and Management (Manchester); Landscapes, Interiors and Design (Nottingham Trent); Landscape Architecture and Ecology (Sheffield); Garden Design and Restoration Management (Writtle (Coll)). *NOW CHECK PROSPECTUSES AND WEBSITES FOR ANY RECENT CHANGES.*

Universities and colleges teaching quality See www.tqi.ac.uk; www.qaa.ac.uk.

Top universities and colleges (Research) Gloucestershire; Sheffield.

Sandwich degree courses Gloucestershire; Nottingham Trent; Writtle (Coll).

ADMISSIONS INFORMATION
Number of applicants per place (approx) Gloucestershire 9; Greenwich 3; Edinburgh (CA) 7; Kingston 4; Manchester Met 9; Writtle (Coll) 5.

Advice to applicants and planning the UCAS personal statement Knowledge of the work of landscape architects is important. Arrange a visit to a landscape architect's office and try to organise some work experience. Read up on historical landscape design and visit country house estates with examples of outstanding designs. Describe these visits in detail and your preferences. Membership of the National Trust could be useful. **Sheffield** Portfolio of work required. A-level art not necessary. See also **Appendix 2**.

Selection interviews **Yes** Gloucestershire, Greenwich, Manchester Met, Sheffield, Writtle (Coll); **Some** UCE Birmingham.

Interview advice and questions Applicants will be expected to have had some work experience and are likely to be questioned on their knowledge of landscape architectural work and the subject. Historical examples of good landscaping could also be asked for. See **Chapter 6**.

Reasons for rejection (non-academic) Lack of historical knowledge and awareness of current developments. Poor portfolio.

AFTER-RESULTS ADVICE

Universities with vacancies in Clearing (2006) Gloucestershire; Greenwich; Kingston; Manchester Met; Sheffield; UCE Birmingham.

Offers to applicants repeating A-levels Same Greenwich, Edinburgh (CA), Manchester Met, UCE Birmingham.

GRADUATE DESTINATIONS AND EMPLOYMENT (2005 HESA)

Graduates surveyed 125 **Employed** 80 **In further study** 15 **Assumed unemployed** 10.

OTHER DEGREE SUBJECTS FOR CONSIDERATION

Architecture; Art and Design; Environmental Planning; Forestry; Horticulture.

LANGUAGES

(including **Hebrew** and **Modern Languages;** see also **African and Caribbean Studies, Arabic and Near and Middle Eastern Studies, Asia-Pacific Studies, Chinese, English, French, German, Greek, Italian, Japanese, Latin, Linguistics, Russian and East European Studies, Scandinavian Studies, Spanish** and **Welsh (Cymraeg) and Celtic)**

NB The points totals shown to the left of the institutions are for ease of reference only. It must not be assumed that tariff points are always used by institutions or that they can be substituted for an offer in grades. The level of an offer is not necessarily indicative of the quality of a course.

COURSE OFFERS INFORMATION

Subject requirements/preferences GCSE Bath French or German at grade B. **Durham** Range of A* to B grades. **Cambridge, Oxford** Grade As in most subjects. **Oxford Brookes** Grade A in a language allows entry to a second language. **Sheffield Hallam** Grade B in a language. **AL** Language required for all courses.

Your target offers
360 pts **and above**
  Cambridge – AAA (Modn Mediev Lang; Orntl St; Heb)
  London (UCL) – AAA+AS–ABB+AS (Lang Cult; Modn Lang courses)
  Oxford – Offers vary eg AAA–AAB (Euro Mid E Lang; Class Modn Lang; Engl Modn Lang; Modn Langs; Ling Modn Lang; Phil Modn Langs; Modn Hist Modn Langs; Heb)
340 pts **Bristol** – AAB–BCC (see also separate language tables) (Fr; Ger; Ital; Russ; Span)
  Durham – AAB (Modn Langs Hist)
  Leeds – AAB–BCC (Modn Langs joint hons (see separate language tables))
  St Andrews – AAB–ABB (Modn Lang courses; Heb courses)
320 pts **Birmingham** – ABB 320 pts (Modn Langs)
  Cardiff – ABB (Lang Comm)
  Durham – ABB (Modn Langs; Modn Lang comb hons)
  Lancaster – ABB (Euro Lang Mgt St)
  London (RH) – ABB–BBB (Euro Lit Cult; Multiling St courses; Modn Lang courses)
  Manchester – ABB (Modn Lang Bus Mgt Fr; Lang St courses; Heb St; Heb Jew St)
  Newcastle – ABB (Modn Langs; Modn Lang Acc; Modn Lang Ling; Modn Lang Film St; Modn Lang Mgt St)
  Nottingham – ABB (Modn Langs Bus)
  Southampton – ABB 320 pts (Modn Langs; Lang Learn; Lang Soty)
  York – ABB (Engl Lang Ling)
300 pts **Bath** – BBB (Modn Lang Euro St Fr/Ger/Russ/Span)

Birmingham – BBB 300 pts (Modn Lang Euro St (Pol) (Soty Cult Hist))
East Anglia – ABC (Fst Trk: Modn Langs; Lang Mgt; Modn Lang St)
Edinburgh – BBB (Modn Euro Langs; Modn Euro Langs Euro St – 2 from Fr/Ger/Ital/Russ St/Scand St/Span)
Essex – 300–260 pts (Modn Lang; Lang St; Modn Lang Fr/Ger/Ital/Span)
Manchester – BBB (Modn Lang Bus Mgt Chin/Ger/Ital/Span/Port/Russ)
Nottingham – ABC–BBB (Modn Langs St; Modn Euro St)
Sheffield – BBB–BBC **or** BBbb (Modn Langs; Modn Langs Interp)
Surrey – 300–280 pts (Comb Langs; Bus Mgt Lang; Modn Lang Transl)
Sussex – BBB **or** 340 pts 3AL+AS (Fr/Ger/Ital/Span courses; Lang Cult St; Lang Contemp Euro St; Lang Ling; Lang Phil)
York – BBB–ABB (Modn Lang Ling; Lang Ling; Ling Lit; Ling Phil; Maths Ling)

280 pts **Aberystwyth** – 280 pts (Euro Lang)
Aston – 280–300 pts (Transl St Fr/Ger/Span; Modn Langs courses; Modn Lang Abrd)
East Anglia – BBC (Transl Interp (double Hons Langs))
Exeter – BBC–BCC (see separate language tables) (Comb Lang courses)
Heriot-Watt – BBC (Langs (App Transl) (Interp Transl) (For Langs Teach Engl (TESOL))
Lancaster – BBC (Euro Langs)
Leeds – BBC (Indo SE As St)
Liverpool – BBC–BBB 280–300 pts (Modn Euro Langs)
London (King's) – BBC+AS **or** BBcc (Modn For Lang Educ)
London (SOAS) – BBC–BCC (Amharic; Bengali; Burmese; Georgian; Gujarati; Hausa; Hindi; Indonesian; Jap; Korean; Nepali; Sanskrit; Sinhala; Swahili; Tamil; Thai; Tibetan; Turkish; Urdu; Vietnamese; Anc Nr E Langs; Heb Isrl St)
Strathclyde – BBC (Int Bus Modn Lang)

260 pts **East Anglia** – BCC (Lang(s) Mgt St; Modn Lang Yr Abrd)
Essex – 260 pts (Modn Lang courses)
Hull – 260–220 pts (Modn Lang St; 2 Modn Langs Bus/Mgt/Mark)
Leicester – 260–300 pts (Modn Lang St; Modn Lang Mgt)
London (QM) – 260 pts 3AL **or** 2AL+2AS (joint courses Modn Langs Fr/Ger/Russ; Modn Langs Hisp St)
Northumbria – 260 pts (Contemp Lang St; Modn Lang; Modn Lang Bus)
Salford – 260–300 pts (Euro Lang Fr/Ger/Ital/Span/Port)
Strathclyde – BCC (Modn Lang)
Ulster – 260 pts inc BC (Lang Ling; Langs Comm; Lang PR)
Westminster – BCC (Lang Soc Sci; Lang St; Modn Langs Arbc/Chin/Fr/Span)

240 pts **Aberdeen** – CCC (Euro Langs 20th Cent Cult; Lang Ling; Langs Lit Scot)
Bangor – 240–260 pts (3 Langs course Fr/Ger/Ital/Span; joint hons Lang)
Chester – 240 pts (Modn Langs)
Portsmouth – 240–300 pts (Comb Modn Lang; Langs Am St; Langs Crea Writ; Langs Euro St; Langs Film St; Langs Int Tr)
Salford – 240–300 pts (Modn Lang Transl Interpret courses (Fr/Ger/Ital/Port/Span); Modn Langs St; Media Lang Bus; Mgt Lang; Modn Lang Ling)
Stirling – CCC (Modn Lang (Fr/Ger/Span); Modn Lang Bus St; Modn Lang Int Pol; Modn Lang Mark)
Swansea – 240–280 pts (Lang courses)
Ulster – CCC 240 pts (Langs Bus Comp; Irish Lang Lit Irish St)

220 pts **Glamorgan** – 220 pts (Lang Comm)
Hull – 220–280 pts (Comb Langs)
Leo Baeck (Coll) – by interview (Heb Jew St)
Nottingham Trent – 220 pts (Modn Langs courses; Fr/Ger/Ital/Span courses)

200 pts **Bristol UWE** – 200–260 pts (Int Bus Modn Langs)
Cardiff (UWIC) – 200 pts (Tour Langs)
Cumbria – 200 pts (Lang St)
Hertfordshire – 200–300 pts (Langs (Comb Mod Schm))

For information on how to read the Subject Tables, see **Chapter 7**.

Lincoln – 200 pts (Bus Langs)
Liverpool John Moores – 200–180 pts (App Langs (Chin/Fr/Ger/Ital/Jap/Span); App Lang Euro)
Manchester Met – 200–280 pts (Comb Hons Langs)
Middlesex – 200–240 pts (Transl St Chin/Fr/Ger/Span)
Napier – 200 pts (Lang joint courses; Euro Bus Langs)
Plymouth – 200 pts (Modn Langs courses; Modn Lang St)
Sheffield Hallam – 200 pts (Langs (Fr/Ger/Ital/Span) Tour/Mark/Int Bus St/E-Commer)

180 pts   **Anglia Ruskin** – 180–220 pts (Intercult Comm)
Central Lancashire – 180 pts (Modn Lang 4yr course)
Coventry – 180 pts (Modn Langs)
Manchester Met – 180 pts (Langs Intnet Mgt)
Roehampton – 180 pts (Translation)

160 pts   **Anglia Ruskin** – 160–180 pts (Comb Langs (Fr/Ger/Span))
East London – 160 pts (Lang Educ)
London Met – 160 pts (App Transl)
Paisley – CC (Langs Fr/Ger/Span)
Wolverhampton – 160–220 pts (Interp (Brit Sign Lang))

Leeds Met – contact University

Alternative offers
IB offers Aberystwyth 29 pts; Birmingham 34 pts; Brighton indiv assessment; Cambridge 38–42 pts; Chester 30 pts; Essex 28 pts; Liverpool 30 pts; London (SOAS) 30 pts, (UCL) 32–38 pts; Manchester 28–30 pts; Newcastle 32 pts; St Andrews 32–36 pts; Salford 28 pts; Sheffield 30–33 pts; Stirling 28 pts; York 34 pts.
Scottish offers See **Chapter 7**.

OTHER HIGHER EDUCATION COURSES IN THE SUBJECT FIELD
Higher National Diploma courses Bell (Coll); Birmingham (CFTCS); South Devon (Coll). **For other HND courses see separate language tables.**

CHOOSING YOUR COURSE (SEE ALSO CH.1)
Subject information Modern Language courses usually offer three main options: a single subject degree commonly based on literature and language, a European Studies course, or two-language subjects which can often include languages different from those available at school (such as Scandinavian Studies, Russian and the languages of Eastern Europe, the Middle and Far East). See also **Appendix 2**. **Useful websites** www.iol.org.uk; www.iti.org.uk; www.europa.eu; www.cilt.org.uk; www.bbc.co.uk/languages; www.languageadvantage.com; www.languagematters.co.uk; www.reed.co.uk/multilingual; www.cactuslanguage.com; www.eurolingua.com; www.languagesabroad.co.uk; www.thelanguageshow.co.uk.

Course variations Modern Languages and Music (Durham); Interpreting and Translating with Double Honours Language (East Anglia); Hebrew and Jewish Studies (Manchester); Contemporary Language Studies (Northumbria); Linguistics and Literature (York). *NOW CHECK PROSPECTUSES AND WEBSITES FOR ANY RECENT CHANGES.*

Universities and colleges teaching quality See www.tqi.ac.uk; www.qaa.ac.uk.

Top universities and colleges (Research) See separate language tables.

ADMISSIONS INFORMATION
Number of applicants per place (approx) Aston 4; Bangor 5; Birmingham 8; Brighton 4; Bristol 15; Bristol UWE 4; Cambridge 3, (Orntl St) 3; Cardiff 6; Durham 6; East Anglia 15; Heriot-Watt 5; Huddersfield 12; Lancaster 10; Leeds (joint hons) 8; Leicester 5; Liverpool 5; Liverpool John Moores 12; Newcastle 22; Northumbria 4; Oxford (success rate 55%); Roehampton 3; Salford 6; Swansea 4; Wolverhampton 10.

Advice to applicants and planning the UCAS personal statement **Leeds** Many languages can be started from scratch. See separate language tables. **Oxford** Students can embark on language courses in which they have no previous knowledge (Italian, Portuguese, Modern Greek, Czech, Celtic, Russian). However, they would be expected to have done a considerable amount of language work on their own in their chosen language prior to starting the course. See also **Appendix 2**.

Misconceptions about this course **Leeds** (joint hons) Some applicants think that studying languages means studying masses of literature – wrong. At Leeds, generally speaking, it's up to you; you study as much or as little literature as you choose. Residence abroad does not inevitably mean a university course (except where you are taking a language from scratch). Paid employment is usually another option. **Liverpool John Moores** (App Langs) Applicants often assume that this course involves the study of literature.

Selection interviews **Yes** Aston, Cambridge, Coventry, Durham, East Anglia, Heriot-Watt, Hertfordshire, Huddersfield, Liverpool (open day invitation), Oxford (success rates (Euro Mid E Lang) 46%, (Modn Lang) 52%, (Modn Lang Ling) 27%, (Orntl St) 45%), Roehampton, Salford; **Some** Brighton, Bristol UWE, Leeds, Liverpool John Moores, Salford, Swansea.

Interview advice and questions **Leeds** (joint hons) Give an example of something outside your studies that you have achieved over the past year. See **Chapter 6**.

Reasons for rejection (non-academic) Lack of commitment to spend a year abroad. Poor references. Poor standard of English. No reasons for why the course has been selected. Poor communication skills. Incomplete applications, for example missing qualifications and reference.

AFTER-RESULTS ADVICE
Universities with vacancies in Clearing (2006) Aberdeen; Aberystwyth; Anglia Ruskin; Bangor; Bath; Birmingham; Bradford; Bristol UWE; Buckingham; Central Lancashire; Chester; Coventry; Cumbria; East Anglia; East London; Essex; Glamorgan; Greenwich; Heriot-Watt; Hertfordshire; Hull; Lancaster; Leeds; Leicester; Lincoln; Liverpool; Liverpool John Moores; London (QM), (RH), (SOAS); London Met; Manchester; Manchester Met; Middlesex; Napier; Northumbria; Nottingham; Nottingham Trent; Plymouth; Portsmouth; Reading; Roehampton; Salford; Sheffield; Sheffield Hallam; Southampton; Stirling; Surrey; Swansea; Ulster; Westminster; Wolverhampton. See also under separate language tables.

Offers to applicants repeating A-levels **Higher** Bristol UWE; **Possibly higher** Aston; **Same** Birmingham, Bristol, Leeds, Liverpool, Liverpool John Moores, Newcastle, Salford, York.

GRADUATE DESTINATIONS AND EMPLOYMENT (2005 HESA)
See separate language tables.

OTHER DEGREE SUBJECTS FOR CONSIDERATION
Communication Studies; Linguistics.

LATIN
(see also **Classical Studies/Classical Civilisation** and **Classics**)

NB The points totals shown to the left of the institutions are for ease of reference only. It must not be assumed that tariff points are always used by institutions or that they can be substituted for an offer in grades. The level of an offer is not necessarily indicative of the quality of a course.

COURSE OFFERS INFORMATION
Subject requirements/preferences **GCSE Cambridge**, **Oxford** Usually grade As. **Edinburgh**, **Glasgow**, **St Andrews** English, mathematics or science and a foreign language. **Lampeter** Five/six subjects at grade A or B. **AL** Check courses for Latin requirement.

Your target offers
360 pts and above
  Cambridge – AAA (Class; Modn Mediev Lang (Class Lat))
  Oxford – Offers vary between candidates (Classics)
340 pts St Andrews – AAB (Lat courses)
320 pts Exeter – ABB 320 pts (Latin)
  Glasgow – ABB–BBB (Latin)
  London (UCL) – ABB+AS–BBC+AS (Lat Gk)
300 pts Edinburgh – BBB (Lat St; Anc Hist Lat)
  Leeds – BBB (Latin)
  London (King's) – BBB+AS **or** BBbbc (Lat Engl)
  Manchester – BBB (Lat; Lat Fr/Ital/Span; Lat Engl Lit; Lat Ling)
  Nottingham – ABC–BBB (Anc Hist Lat; Lat; Engl St Lat)
  Warwick – BBB (Engl Lat Lit)
280 pts London (RH) – BBC (Latin)
260 pts Swansea – 260–300 pts (Lat joint courses)
180 pts Lampeter – open admission policy (Lat courses)

Alternative offers
IB offers Cambridge 38–42 pts; St Andrews 36 pts.
Scottish offers See **Chapter 7**.

CHOOSING YOUR COURSE (SEE ALSO CH.1)

Subject information Latin courses provide a study of the language, art, religion and history of the Roman world. This table should be read in conjunction with the **Classical Studies/Classical Civilisation** and **Classics** tables.

Useful website www.thelatinlibrary.com; www.minimus-etc.co.uk.

Course variations Classics (Cambridge); Latin and Greek (London (UCL)); Ancient History and Latin (Nottingham); English and Latin Literature (Warwick). *NOW CHECK PROSPECTUSES AND WEBSITES FOR ANY RECENT CHANGES.*

Universities and colleges teaching quality See www.tqi.ac.uk; www.qaa.ac.uk.

Top universities and colleges (Research) See **Classics**.

ADMISSIONS INFORMATION

Number of applicants per place (approx) Lampeter 3; Leeds 2; Nottingham 3.

Advice to applicants and planning the UCAS personal statement See **Classical Studies/Classical Civilisation** and **Classics**.

Selection interviews **Yes** Cambridge, Exeter, Lampeter, London (RH), (UCL), Nottingham, Oxford.

Interview advice and questions See **Classical Studies/Classical Civilisation** and **Classics**.

AFTER-RESULTS ADVICE

Universities with vacancies in Clearing (2006) Lampeter; London (RH); Swansea.

Offers to applicants repeating A-levels **Higher** Leeds, St Andrews, Warwick.

GRADUATE DESTINATIONS AND EMPLOYMENT (2005 HESA)

Graduates surveyed 15 **Employed** None **In further study** 5 **Assumed unemployed** None.

OTHER DEGREE SUBJECTS FOR CONSIDERATION

Ancient History; Archaeology; Classical Studies; Classics.

LATIN AMERICAN STUDIES

(including **Hispanic Studies;** see also **American Studies** and **Spanish**)

NB The points totals shown to the left of the institutions are for ease of reference only. It must not be assumed that tariff points are always used by institutions or that they can be substituted for an offer in grades. The level of an offer is not necessarily indicative of the quality of a course.

COURSE OFFERS INFORMATION

Subject requirements/preferences GCSE Aberdeen English, mathematics or science and a foreign language. English and a foreign language required by most universities. **AL** Spanish may be required for some courses

Your target offers

320 pts	**Glasgow** – ABB (Hisp St courses)
	London (UCL) – ABB+AS (Modn Iber Lat Am Reg St; Hisp St)
	Newcastle – ABB–BBB (Span Port Lat Am St)
	Southampton – ABB 320 pts **or** 400 pts 4AL (Span Lat Am St)
300 pts	**Essex** – 300 pts (Lat Am St Bus)
	Leeds – BBB (Hisp Lat Am St)
	London (King's) – BBB+AS **or** BBbbb (Port Braz St courses; Hisp St joint courses)
	Manchester – BBB (Am Lat Am St)
	Sheffield – BBB–BBC (Hisp St courses)
280 pts	**Birmingham** – 280–320 pts (Hisp St courses)
	Essex – 280–260 pts (Lat Am St; Lat Am St Hum Rts)
	Liverpool – BBC–BBB 280–300 pts (Lat Am St; Lat Am Hisp St)
	London (QM) – BBC–BCD (Hisp St Ling Comp Sci)
	Nottingham – BBC (Am St Lat Am St; Hisp St courses)
260 pts	**Kent** – 260 pts (Hisp St)
	London (King's) – BBC+AS **or** BBbbc (US Lat Am St)
240 pts	**Aberdeen** – CCC (Hisp St (Lat Am))
	Bristol UWE – 240–300 pts (Lat Am St; Lat Am St joint courses)
220 pts	**Hull** – 220–280 pts (Hisp St Gndr St)
200 pts	**Middlesex** – 200–240 pts (Lat Am St minor subj joint hons)
	Portsmouth – 200–280 pts (Lat Am Dev St; Span Lat Am St)
160 pts	**London Met** – 160 pts (Span Lat Am St)

Alternative offers

IB offers Bristol UWE 26–32 pts; Essex 28–30 pts; Liverpool 32 pts.
Scottish offers See **Chapter 7**.

CHOOSING YOUR COURSE (SEE ALSO CH.1)

Subject information In Latin American courses there will be an emphasis on the study of Spanish and of Latin American republics, covering both historical and present-day conditions and problems. Normally a year is spent in Latin America. **Useful websites** www.iol.org.uk; www.bbc.co.uk/languages; www.languageadvantage.com; www.languagematters.co.uk; www.reed.co.uk/multilingual; www.cilt.org.uk; www.latinworld.com; www.wola.org; www.latinamericalinks.com; see also **Languages** and **Spanish**.

Course variations Latin American Studies with Human Rights (Essex); Portuguese and Brazilian Studies (London (King's)); Modern Iberian and Latin American Regional Studies (London (UCL)); American and Latin American Studies (Manchester); Latin American Development Studies (Portsmouth). *NOW CHECK PROSPECTUSES AND WEBSITES FOR ANY RECENT CHANGES.*

Top universities and colleges (Research) Birmingham; Bristol.

ADMISSIONS INFORMATION

Number of applicants per place (approx) Essex 3; Liverpool 3; Newcastle 25; Portsmouth 5.

Advice to applicants and planning the UCAS personal statement Visits and contacts with Spain and Latin American countries should be described. An awareness of the economic, historical and political scene of these countries is also important. Information may be obtained from respective embassies.

Selection interviews **Yes** Newcastle; **Some** Portsmouth.

Interview advice and questions Past questions include: Why are you interested in studying Latin American Studies? What countries related to the degree course have you visited? What career are you planning when you finish your degree? Applicants taking Spanish are likely to be asked questions on their syllabus and should also be familiar with some Spanish newspapers and magazines. See **Chapter 6**.

AFTER-RESULTS ADVICE

Universities with vacancies in Clearing (2006) Bristol UWE; Essex; Liverpool; London Met; Middlesex; Portsmouth; Sheffield.

Offers to applicants repeating A-levels **Higher** Essex; **Same** Newcastle, Portsmouth.

GRADUATE DESTINATIONS AND EMPLOYMENT (2005 HESA)
No data available.

OTHER DEGREE SUBJECTS FOR CONSIDERATION
American Studies; Brazilian; Portuguese; Spanish.

LAW

(for **Criminology and Criminal Justice** courses see also under **Social Sciences**)

NB The points totals shown to the left of the institutions are for ease of reference only. It must not be assumed that tariff points are always used by institutions or that they can be substituted for an offer in grades. The level of an offer is not necessarily indicative of the quality of a course.

COURSE OFFERS INFORMATION

Subject requirements/preferences GCSE **Aberdeen**, **Dundee**, **Edinburgh**, **Glasgow** English, mathematics or science and a foreign language. **Birmingham** Grade A in approximately five subjects, with grade A or B in English. **Bristol UWE** Eight subjects, with some at grade A or B. **Brunel** Minimum of six subjects at grade A–C. **Cambridge** Majority of grade As. **Exeter** Four subjects at grade A* or A, usually none below B. **Hull** Six subjects (minimum) four As or Bs. **Kingston** Seven subjects, not more than two at grade C. **Leeds** Six subjects at grade B or above. **London (LSE)** A and B grades. **Manchester Met** Grade A or B in French or German for foreign language options. **Oxford** Mathematics required. **Robert Gordon** Six to eight subjects with grade A or B. **Warwick** Mathematics A for Law Bus St. **AL** Arts, humanities, social sciences and sciences plus languages for courses combined with a foreign language. The National Admissions Test for Law (LNAT) may be required by universities other than those listed below – CHECK UNIVERSITY WEBSITES AND PROSPECTUSES AND SEE ALSO **CHAPTER 6**.

Your target offers
360 pts **and above**

Belfast (Queen's) – AAA–AABa (Law; Law Acc; Law Pol)
Birmingham – AAA +LNAT (Law; Law Bus St)
Bristol – AAA–AAB +LNAT (Law; Law Fr/Ger; Chem Law)
Cambridge – AAA +LNAT (Law; Land Econ; Double Maitrise Cambridge/Paris)
Cardiff – AAA (Law; Law Crim)
Durham – AAA–AAB +LNAT (Law; Euro Leg St)
East Anglia – AAA (Law Am Law)
Exeter – AAA–AAB +LNAT (Law; Euro Law; Hist Law; Pol Law)
Lancaster – AAA (Law (Int))

Leeds – AAA (Law; Law Fr)
London (King's) – AABb–ABBb +LNAT (Law; Engl Law Fr Law)
London (LSE) – AAA–AAB (Law)
London (SOAS) – AAA (Law courses)
London (UCL) – AAA+AS +LNAT (Law; Law Advnc St; Law Fr Law; Law Ger Law; Law Ital Law; Law Hisp Law; Engl Fr Law; Engl Ger Law)
Manchester – AAA (Law; Engl Law Fr Law; Law Crim)
Newcastle – AAA (Law; Law Fr)
Nottingham – AAA–AAB +LNAT (Law; Law Fr; Law Ger)
Oxford – Offers vary eg AAA–AAB +LNAT (Law; Law Law St Euro)
Sheffield – AAA (Law; Euro Int Compar Law)
Southampton – AAA–AAB +LNAT 360 pts +LNAT (Law)
Warwick – AAAc–AAB +LNAT (Law 3yr/4yr)
Warwick – AABb–AAAc (Euro Law; Law Bus St)
Warwick – ABBc (Law Sociol)
340 pts **Aston** – AAB–ABB 340–320 pts (Law Mgt)
Cardiff – AAB–BBB joint hons (Law Pol; Law Sociol)
East Anglia – AAB (Law; Law Euro Leg Sys)
Essex – 340–320 pts (Law; Engl Fr Law; Law Phil; Law Pol; Law Hum Rts; Engl Euro Law)
Glasgow – AAB +LNAT (Law courses)
Lancaster – AAB (Law; Law Crim; Euro Leg St)
Leeds – AAB (Law Mgt; Law Fr)
Leicester – AAB 340–400 pts (Law; Law Fr Law Lang; LLB Maîtrise Engl Fr Law)
Liverpool – 340–390 pts (Engl Fr Law Fr; LLB Law)
London (King's) – AAB–AAA +LNAT **or** AAbbb–ABaab +LNAT (Engl Law Ger Law)
Manchester – AAB (Law Pol)
Reading – AAB (Law; Law Leg St Euro)

For information on how to read the Subject Tables, see **Chapter 7**.

Sheffield – AAB (Law Fr; Law Ger; Law Span)
Strathclyde – AAB (Law; Law Modn Lang)
Sussex – AAB–ABB **or** 360 pts 3AL+AS (Law courses)
Westminster – AAB (Commer Law)

320 pts **Aberystwyth** – 320 pts (Law; Law joint courses)
Brunel – ABB–AAC 320 pts (Law)
City – ABB 320 pts (Law; Law Prop Val; Engl Fr Law)
East Anglia – ABB (Law Fr Law Lang)
Kent – 320 pts (Law; Engl Fr Law; Engl Ger Law; Engl Ital Law; Engl Span Law; Law joint courses; Euro Leg St)
Kingston – 320–300 pts (Law; Commer Law; Int Law; Law Fr Law)
Leeds – ABB (Law Acc)
London (QM) – ABB–BBB (Law; Engl Euro Law; Law Ger)
Northumbria – ABB 320 pts (Law (exempting courses))
Oxford Brookes – ABB–CCD (Law Comb hons)
Swansea – 320 pts (Law courses)
Westminster – ABB/AA (Euro Leg St; LLB Law; Law Fr))

300 pts **Aberdeen** – BBB (Law; Law Acc; Law Econ; Law Mgt; Law Lang; Law Belg Law; Law Fr Law; Law Ger Law; Law Span Law)
Aston – 300 pts (Pol Law)
Bradford – 300 pts (Law)
Bristol UWE – 300–340 pts (Law; Commer Law; Euro Int Law; Law Fr/Ger/Span/EFL)
Cardiff – BBB (Law Ger/Fr/Welsh)
Chester – 300 pts (Law)
Dundee – BBB 300 pts (Scots Law; Law (Engl NI); Law Fr/Ger/Span)
Edinburgh – BBB (Law courses)
Glasgow Caledonian – BBB (LLB Law)
Hull – BBB 320 pts (Law; Law Fr Law Lang; Law Ger Law Lang; Law Crim; Law Phil; Law Pol)
Keele – 300–320 pts (Law; Law courses)
Kent – 300 pts (Law Fr/Ger)
Liverpool – 300 pts (Leg Bus St)
London (LSE) – BBB (Anth Law)
Manchester Met – BBB 300 pts +LNAT (Law; Law Fr)
Oxford Brookes – BBB **or** BBbb (Law)
Portsmouth – 300 pts (Law Crim)
Surrey – 300 pts (Law; Law Fr Law; Law Ger Law; Law Russ Law; Law Span Law; Law Int St)

280 pts **Bangor** – 280 pts (Law)
Bournemouth – 280 pts (Law; Law Tax; Acc Law)
Central Lancashire – BBC (Law)
Coventry – 280–320 pts (Law; Law Bus; Law Fr/Span)
De Montfort – 280 pts (Law Crim Just)
Derby – 280 pts (Law; Law Crim; Law (Bus Law) (Int Law) (Soc Pblc Law))
Glamorgan – 280 pts (Law; Commer Law; Euro Law; Law Crim)
Kingston – 280 pts (Law Fr St)
Liverpool John Moores – 280 pts (Law)
Nottingham Trent – 280 pts (Law)
Salford – 280 pts (Law)
Strathclyde – BBC (Bus Law)
UCE Birmingham – 280 pts (Law; Law Am Leg St; Law Crim; Law Leg Prac)
Ulster – BBC (Law Econ; Law Gov; Law Pol; Law Fr/Ger/Irish/Span)

260 pts **Abertay Dundee** – BCC (LLB Hons Law)
East Lancashire (IHE) – 260 pts (Law)
Gloucestershire – 260 pts (Law)
Heriot-Watt – BCC (Mgt Bus Law)

Plymouth – 260 pts (Law)
Sheffield Hallam – 260 pts (Law; Law Crim; Law Psy; Law Maîtrise Fr; Law Bus)
Strathclyde – BCC (BA Law)
240 pts **Aberdeen** – CCC (Leg St courses)
Bolton – 240–200 pts (Law courses)
Bradford – 240 pts (Bus St Law; Intnet Law Soty; Hist Law; ICT Law; Pharm Sci Law)
Brighton – 240 pts (Law Bus)
Bristol UWE – 240–300 pts (Law joint hons)
Brunel – 240 pts (Hlth Cr Law Eth)
Buckingham – 240–280 pts (Law; Law Fr; Law Bus Fin; Law Econ; Law Engl Lang St (EFL); Law Mgt St; Law Pol; Law Span)
Chester – 240 pts (Law courses except under **300 pts**)
De Montfort – 240 pts (Law; Law Hum Rts Soc Just)
Edge Hill – 240 pts (Law; Law Crim)
Glamorgan – 240–280 pts (Bus Law; Crim Crim Just)
Greenwich – 240 pts (Law; Law joint courses)
Hertfordshire – 240 pts (Law; Law joint courses)
London South Bank – CCC (Law courses)
Manchester Met – 240 pts (Consum Law; Law Tr Stand)
Middlesex – 240–280 pts (Law)
Napier – 240–200 pts (LLB Law)
Portsmouth – 240–280 pts (Law Acc; Law Bus; Law Int Rel; Law Fr; Law Euro St)
Robert Gordon – CCC (Law; Law Mgt)
Stirling – CCC (Bus Law courses)
Teesside – 240 pts (Law)
Thames Valley – 240 pts (Law)
220 pts **Anglia Ruskin** – 220–260 pts (Law Crim)
Brighton – 220 pts (Law Acc)
Central Lancashire – 220–200 pts (Law Crim; Law Psy)
Huddersfield – 220–240 pts (Law Bus Law Euro Leg St; Law Acc)
Lincoln – CCD 220 pts (Law)
Liverpool Hope – 220 pts (Law)
Northampton – 220–240 pts (LLB Law)
Sunderland – 220 pts (Law)
200 pts **East London** – 200–180 pts (Law; Crim Law; Acc Law; Bus St Law)
London Met – 200 pts (LLB Soc Just; Law; Bus Law Int Bus; Int Law Int Pol)
Napier – 200 pts (BA Law)
Northampton – 200–240 pts (BA/BSc Law)
Plymouth – 200–220 pts (Law joint courses)
Salford – 200 pts (Bus Mgt St Law)
Staffordshire – 200–300 pts (LLB; LLB (Crim) (Hum Rts) (Bus Law) (Spo Law))
UCE Birmingham – 200 pts (Bus Bus Law; Bus Law joint courses)
190 pts **London Met** – 190 pts (Bus Law)
180 pts **Bradford (Coll)** – BC–CC 180–160 pts (LLB Law)
Derby – 180–220 pts (Law Comb)
Glasgow Caledonian – BC (Bus Law)
Southampton Solent – 180–160 pts (Law; Commer Law)
Thames Valley – 180 pts (Crim Law)
160 pts **Bedfordshire** – 160–240 pts (Law; Acc Law)
Canterbury Christ Church – CC (Leg St courses)
Central Lancashire – 160 pts (Law Bus; Law Engl Lit; Law Pol)
Leeds Trinity and All Saints (Coll) – CC (Bus Law)
London Met – 160–200 pts (Leg Econ St)
London South Bank – CC (Law Comb)
Paisley – CC (Law; Law Pol)

         St Mary's (Coll) – CC 160 pts (Bus Law courses)
         Staffordshire – 160–200 pts (Advc Wk Law)
         Wolverhampton – 160–220 pts (LLB Law; BA Law; Bus Law; Soc Welf Law Sociol)
140 pts   **Bell (Coll)** – 140 pts (Leg St)
         Newport – CD 140 pts (Crim Commun Just)
120 pts   **Buckinghamshire Chilterns (UC)** – 120–180 pts (Law; Bus Law)
         Grimsby (IFHE) – 120 pts (Law)
         North East Wales (IHE) – 120 pts (Law Bus)
         Peterborough Reg (Coll) – 120 pts (Bus Law)
100 pts   **Bradford (Coll)** – 100–140 pts (Acc Law; Mark Law)
80 pts   **Croydon (Coll)** – 80 pts (Law)
         Holborn (Coll) – 80 pts (Law)
         Lansdowne (Coll) – 80 pts (Law)

         Leeds Met – contact University
         London (Birk) – degree reqd (not Law) interview+reasoning test (p/t Accelerated Law)
         London Regents Bus Sch – (Law, check with admissions tutor)
         Open University – contact University

Alternative offers

IB offers Aberdeen 36 pts; Aberystwyth 32 pts; Birmingham 38 pts; Brighton 26–28 pts; Bristol 36–38 pts; Bristol UWE 30–34 pts; Brunel 34 pts; Cambridge 38–42 pts; Chester 30 pts; City 32 pts; Essex 34–36 pts; Exeter 35–36 pts; Glasgow 36 pts; Keele 32 pts; Kent 32–33 pts; Leicester 32 pts; Liverpool 32–35 pts; London (King's) 38 pts, (LSE) 38 pts; (QM) 36 pts, (SOAS) 38 pts, (UCL) 40 pts; Manchester 35–37 pts; Manchester Met 30 pts; Newcastle 38 pts; Nottingham 38 pts; Reading 34 pts; Salford 31 pts; Sheffield 35–37 pts; Southampton 36 pts; Staffordshire 28 pts; Stirling 30 pts; Thames Valley 30–36 pts; Warwick 36–38 pts.

Scottish offers See **Chapter 7**.

OTHER HIGHER EDUCATION COURSES IN THE SUBJECT FIELD

Foundation degrees (contact the institutions for details) Bradford; Croydon (Coll); Kingston; Peterborough Reg (Coll); Portsmouth; Shrewsbury (Coll); Truro (Coll); Walsall (Coll); Weston (Coll).

Higher National Diploma courses

140 pts   **and below** Bedfordshire; Bell (Coll); Bradford (Coll); Buckinghamshire Chilterns (UC); Burton (Coll); Croydon (Coll); Doncaster (Univ Centre); East Lancashire (IHE); Exeter; Glasgow Caledonian; Henley (Coll); Llandrillo Cymru (Coll); Newport; Plymouth; South Birmingham (Coll); Teesside; Truro (Coll); UCE Birmingham; Worcester (CT).

CHOOSING YOUR COURSE (SEE ALSO CH.1)

Subject information Law courses are usually divided into two parts. Part I occupies the first year and introduces the student to criminal and constitutional law and the legal process. Thereafter many different specialised topics can be studied in the second and third years. The course content is very similar for most courses. Applicants are advised to check with universities as to their current policies, in particular Belfast (Queen's), Brunel, Cambridge (colleges), De Montfort, Edinburgh, Greenwich, Kingston, London (LSE), (QM), (UCL), Newcastle, Oxford (colleges) and UCE Birmingham. **NB** See **Chapter 6** for details of admissions tests for some Law courses at some universities including LNAT. See also **Appendix 2**. **Useful websites** www.barcouncil.org.uk; www.ilex.org.uk; www.lawcareers.net; www.lawsociety.org.uk; www.cps.gov.uk; www.hmcourts.gov.uk; www.lawscot.org.uk; www.lawsoc-ni.org; www.rollonfriday.com.

Course variations Pharmaceutical Science with Law (Bradford); Commercial Law (Bristol UWE); Law and Taxation (Bournemouth); Law and Criminology (Cardiff); Law and Property Valuation (City); European Legal Studies (Durham); International Law (Kingston); Anthropology and Law (London (LSE)); English and European Law (London (QM)); Law and Legal Studies in Europe (Reading). *NOW CHECK PROSPECTUSES AND WEBSITES FOR ANY RECENT CHANGES.*

Universities and colleges teaching quality See www.tqi.ac.uk; www.qaa.ac.uk.

Top universities and colleges (Research) Aberdeen; Belfast (Queen's); Birmingham; Bristol; Brunel; Cambridge*; Cardiff; City; Dundee; Durham*; East Anglia; Edinburgh; Essex; Exeter; Glasgow; Hull; Keele*; Kent; Lancaster; Leeds; Leicester; London (King's), (LSE)*, (QM)*, (SOAS), (UCL)*; Manchester; Newcastle; Nottingham; Oxford*; Reading; Sheffield; Southampton*; Strathclyde; Ulster; Warwick; Westminster.

Sandwich degree courses Aston (compulsory); Bournemouth; Bradford; Brighton; Brunel; City; Coventry; De Montfort; Hertfordshire; Huddersfield; Lancaster; Nottingham Trent; Oxford Brookes; Plymouth; Portsmouth; Staffordshire; Surrey; Teesside; UCE Birmingham; Westminster.

ADMISSIONS INFORMATION

Number of applicants per place (approx) Abertay Dundee 3; Aberystwyth 8; Anglia Ruskin 10; Aston 10; Bangor 3; Birmingham 7; Bournemouth 9; Bradford (Coll) 2; Bristol 20; Bristol UWE 27; Brunel 2; Buckingham 3; Cambridge 7; Cardiff 12; Central Lancashire 36; City 23; Coventry 15; De Montfort 6; Derby 7; Dundee 6; Durham 14; East Anglia 14; East London 13; Edinburgh 5; Essex 26; Exeter 15; Glamorgan 3; Glasgow 8; Glasgow Caledonian 10; Huddersfield 10; Hull 15; Kent 11; Kingston 25; Lancaster 8; Leeds 15; Leicester 14; Liverpool 10; Liverpool John Moores 10; London (King's) 14, (LSE) 14, (QM) 17, (SOAS) 8, (UCL) 21; London Met 13; London South Bank 4; Manchester Met 21; Middlesex 25; Napier 7; Newcastle 13; Northampton 4; Northumbria 12; Nottingham 25; Nottingham Trent 15; Oxford (success rate 25%, (Law Law St Euro) 10%); Oxford Brookes 18; Plymouth 14; Robert Gordon 4; Sheffield 16; Sheffield Hallam 6; Southampton 8; Southampton Solent 5; Staffordshire 16; Strathclyde (Law) 10; Sussex 10; Teesside 3; Thames Valley 18; UCE Birmingham 20; Warwick 20; Westminster 29; Wolverhampton 12.

Advice to applicants and planning the UCAS personal statement Visit the law courts and take notes on cases heard. Follow leading legal arguments in the press. Read the law sections in the *Independent*, *The Times* and the *Guardian*. Discuss the career with lawyers and, if possible, obtain work shadowing in lawyers' offices. Describe these visits and experiences and indicate any special areas of law which interest you. (Read *Learning the Law* by Glanville Williams.) **All universities** Applicants offering art and music A-levels should check whether these subjects are acceptable. **Birmingham** We look for commitment to the study of law as an academic discipline (not necessarily to taking up a career in it) and for a commitment to study in Birmingham. When writing to admissions tutors, especially by e-mail, take care to present yourself well. Text language is not acceptable. You should use communication as an opportunity to demonstrate your skill in the use of English. Spelling mistakes, punctuation errors and bad grammar suggest that you will struggle to develop the expected writing ability (see **Misconceptions about this course**) and may lead to your application being rejected. When writing to an admissions tutor do not demand an answer 'immediately' or 'by return' or 'urgently'. If your query is reasonable the tutor will respond without such urging. Adding these demands is bad manners and suggests that you are doing everything at the last minute and increases your chances of a rejection. **Bournemouth** Good command of English required. **Bristol** Make sure you submit a detailed statement which includes evidence that you have researched what the study of law entails. **Brunel** Intermediate London External LLB may enable direct entry to year 2. **Glamorgan** Fluency in English required. **Oxford** Criteria for admission: motivation and capacity for sustained and intense work; the ability to analyse and solve problems using logical and critical approaches; the ability to draw fine distinctions, to separate the relevant from the irrelevant; the capacity for accurate and critical observation, for sustained and cogent argument; creativity and flexibility of thought and lateral thinking; competence in English; willingness and the ability to express ideas clearly and effectively, to listen and to be able to give considered responses. (It should be assumed that these criteria will also apply to other Law courses.) **Oxford Brookes** Work experience very important, particularly for mature students. **Sheffield Hallam** Experience with a law firm, strong academic profile and interest in current affairs. **Southampton** Evidence that the applicant has given serious thought to the career; reading, work experience, court visits. See also **Appendix 2**.

Misconceptions about this course Aberystwyth Some applicants believe that all Law graduates enter the legal profession – this is incorrect. **Birmingham** Applicants do not necessarily have to be predicted to obtain the grades in our standard offer in order to receive an offer; after all, predictions are frequently inaccurate. Students tend to believe that success in the law centres on the ability to learn information. Whilst some information does necessarily have to be learnt, the most important skills involve (a) developing an ability to *select* the most relevant pieces of information and (b) developing the ability to write tightly argued, persuasively reasoned essays on the basis of such information. **Bristol** Many applicants think that most of our applicants have been privately educated: the reverse is true. **Derby** Many applicants do not realise the amount of work involved to get a good degree classification.

Selection interviews Approximately four well-qualified candidates apply for every place on undergraduate Law courses in the UK and the National Admission Test for Law (LNAT) has now been introduced (see **Chapter 6**). Only candidates performing well in this test will be called for interview at universities requiring LNAT, but a good performance in this test, however, does not guarantee an interview or admission (see www.lnat.ac.uk). **Yes** Aberystwyth, Bangor, Belfast (Queen's), Bristol, Bristol UWE, Buckingham, Cambridge, Central Lancashire, Coventry, Durham, East London, Essex, Glasgow, Lancaster, Liverpool, Liverpool John Moores, London (UCL), London South Bank, Napier, Northumbria, Nottingham, Oxford, Southampton Solent, Surrey, Teesside, Warwick; **Some** Anglia Ruskin, Birmingham, Cardiff, Derby, Dundee, Exeter, Huddersfield, Kent (mature/Access students), Nottingham Trent (mature students), Oxford Brookes (mature students), Sheffield Hallam, Southampton (mature students), Staffordshire, Sunderland; **No** Sussex.

Interview advice and questions Law is a highly competitive subject and applicants will be expected to have a basic awareness of aspects of law and to have gained some work experience, on which they are likely to be questioned. It is almost certain that a legal question will be asked at interview and applicants will be tested on their responses. Questions in the past have included: What interests you in the study of law? What would you do to overcome the problem of prison overcrowding if you were (a) a judge (b) a prosecutor (c) the Prime Minister? What legal cases have you read about recently? What is jurisprudence? What are the causes of violence in society? A friend bought a bun which, unknown to him, contained a stone. He gave it to you to eat and you broke a tooth. Could you sue anyone? Have you visited any law courts? What cases did you see? A person arrives in England unable to speak the language. He lights a cigarette in a non-smoking compartment of a train. Can he be charged and convicted? What should be done in the case of an elderly person who steals a bar of soap? What, in your opinion, would be the two basic laws in Utopia? Describe, without using your hands, how you would do the butterfly stroke. What would happen if there were no law? Should we legalise euthanasia? If you could change any law, what would it be? How would you implement the changes? If a person tries to kill someone using black magic, are they guilty of attempted murder? If a jury uses a ouija board to reach a decision, is it wrong? If so, why? Jane attends an interview. As she enters the building she sees a diamond brooch on the floor. She hands it to the interviewer who hands it to the police. The brooch is never claimed. Who is entitled to it? Jane? The interviewer? The police? The university authorities? The Crown? Mr Grabbit who owns the building? **Cambridge** *Logic Questions* If I returned to the waiting room and my jacket had been taken and I then took another one, got home and actually discovered it was mine, had I committed a crime? If the interviewer pulled out a gun and aimed it at me, but missed as he had a bad arm, had he committed a crime? If the interviewer pulled out a gun and aimed it at me, thinking it was loaded but, in fact, it was full of blanks and fired it at me with the intention to kill, had he committed a crime? Which of the three preceding situations are similar and which is the odd one out? If a law is immoral, is it still a law and must people abide by it? For example, when Hitler legalised the systematic killing of Jews, was it still law? For joint courses: what academic skills are needed to succeed? Why a joint degree? See **Chapter 6**.

Applicants' impressions (A=Open day; B=Interview day) Brunel (A) Tour of the campus, a sample lecture and a chat with the tutors. **Kent** (A) The open day included a tour of the campus, talks on the course, finance and accommodation. **Reading** (A) We attended a lecture and a seminar, toured the halls and had lunch. **Southampton** (A) We were set a series of tasks, followed by talks, and visited halls of residence.

Reasons for rejection (non-academic) 'Dreams' about being a lawyer! Poorly informed about the subject. Badly drafted application. Under-estimate of work load. Poor communication skills. **Manchester Met** Some were rejected because they were obviously more suited to Psychology.

AFTER-RESULTS ADVICE

Universities with vacancies in Clearing (2006) Aberystwyth; Anglia Ruskin; Bangor; Bolton; Bournemouth; Bradford; Brighton; Bristol UWE; Buckingham; Canterbury Christ Church; Central Lancashire; Chester; Coventry; De Montfort; Derby; East London; Essex; Glamorgan; Glasgow Caledonian; Greenwich; Hertfordshire; Huddersfield; Hull; Keele; Kent; Kingston; Lancaster; Lincoln; Liverpool Hope; Liverpool John Moores; London Met; London South Bank; Manchester Met; Middlesex; Northampton; Nottingham Trent; Plymouth; Portsmouth; Sheffield Hallam; Southampton Solent; Staffordshire; Stirling; Sunderland; Surrey; Swansea; Teesside; Thames Valley; UCE Birmingham; Westminster; Wolverhampton.

Offers to applicants repeating A-levels Higher Aberystwyth, Belfast (Queen's), Bristol UWE, Coventry, Dundee, Essex, Glamorgan, Glasgow, Hull, Leeds, London Met, Manchester Met, Newcastle, Nottingham, Oxford Brookes, Sheffield, Sheffield Hallam, Strathclyde, Warwick; **Possibly higher** Durham, Liverpool; **Same** Anglia Ruskin, Bangor, Birmingham, Brighton, Bristol, Brunel, Cardiff, De Montfort, Derby, Huddersfield, Kingston, Lincoln, Liverpool John Moores, Northumbria, Staffordshire, Sunderland, Surrey, Wolverhampton.

GRADUATE DESTINATIONS AND EMPLOYMENT (2005 HESA)

Graduates surveyed 7820 **Employed** 2380 **In further study** 3520 **Assumed unemployed** 320.

OTHER DEGREE SUBJECTS FOR CONSIDERATION

Criminology; Economics; Government; History; International Relations; Politics; Social Policy and Administration; Sociology.

LEISURE AND RECREATION MANAGEMENT/STUDIES

(see also **Sports Sciences/Studies** and **Tourism and Travel**)

NB The points totals shown to the left of the institutions are for ease of reference only. It must not be assumed that tariff points are always used by institutions or that they can be substituted for an offer in grades. The level of an offer is not necessarily indicative of the quality of a course.

COURSE OFFERS INFORMATION

Subject requirements/preferences GCSE Normally English and mathematics grades A–C. **Portsmouth** Subject grades A–C including English and mathematics. **AL** No specified subjects.

Your target offers

320 pts	**Loughborough** – 320–300 pts (Spo Leis Mgt; Geog Spo Leis Mgt)
280 pts	**Manchester** – BBC (Mgt Leis)
260 pts	**Brighton** – 260 pts (Spo Leis Mgt)
	Oxford Brookes – BCC–CCC **or** CCcc (Leis Tour Plan; Leis Plan)
240 pts	**Bangor** – 240–280 pts 2AL (Leis Tour Res Mgt; Leis Mgt; Leis Env)
	Coventry – 240 pts (Leis Mgt)
	Hull – 240 pts (Spo Leis Mgt)
	Ulster – CCC 240 pts (Leis Evnts Cult Mgt)
220 pts	**Bournemouth** – 220 pts (Leis Mark)
	Cumbria – 220–200 pts (Advntr Recr Mgt; Out St)
	Gloucestershire – 220 pts (Leis Spo Mgt courses; Advntr Leis Mgt)
	Liverpool Hope – 220 pts (Leis comb hons)
	Staffordshire – CCD 220 pts (Spo Leis Mgt)
200 pts	**Cardiff (UWIC)** – BB 200 pts (Leis Spo Mgt; Leis Mgt courses)
	Central Lancashire – 200–240 pts (Leis Mgt)
	Edge Hill – 200 pts (Leis Tour Mgt)
	Gloucestershire – 200–280 pts (Advntr Leis Mgt courses)

Manchester Met – 200 pts (Leis St joint hons)

Napier – 200 pts (Leis Fstvl Mgt courses)

180 pts **Birmingham (CFTCS)** – 180 pts (Enter Mgt; Hspty Leis Mgt)

Chichester (UC) – 180–220 pts (Advntr Educ)

Liverpool John Moores – 180 pts (Tour Leis Lang)

Portsmouth – 180–200 pts (Leis Mgt Mark)

Salford – 180 pts (Leis Tour Mgt)

Teesside – 180–220 pts (Leis Mgt; Leis Tour Mgt)

160 pts **Bedfordshire** – 160–200 pts (Leis Mgt)

Central Lancashire – 160–180 pts (Out Ldrshp courses)

Glasgow Caledonian – CC (Enter Evnts Mgt; Advntr Recr Mgt)

Harper Adams (UC) – 160 pts (Advntr Recr)

Liverpool John Moores – CC 160 pts (Tour Leis Mgt)

Manchester Met – 160 pts (Leis Mgt; Leis Mgt (Out Actvts))

SAC (Scottish CAg) – CC (Advntr Tour Out Prsts; Rur Recr Tour Mgt)

Strathclyde – CC (Out Educ)

Winchester – 160–220 pts (Leis Mgt courses)

Wolverhampton – 160–220 pts (Leis Mgt; Leis Tour Mgt)

140 pts **Blackpool and Fylde (Coll)** – 140 pts (Leis Evnts Enter Mgt)

Cardiff (UWIC) – 140 pts (Leis Mgt courses)

Marjon (Coll) – 140–200 pts (Out Advntr courses)

Writtle (Coll) – 140 pts (Leis Mgt Spo Mgt; Leis Tour Mgt; Advntr Tour; Out Recr Cons)

120 pts **Buckinghamshire Chilterns (UC)** – 120–180 pts (Spo Leis Mgt; Spo Leis Mgt Out St)

Southampton Solent – 120 pts (Out Advntr Mgt)

Swansea (IHE) – 120–180 pts (Leis Mgt)

100 pts **Suffolk (Univ Campus)** – 100–120 pts (Leis Mgt)

Leeds Met – contact University

Alternative offers

IB offers Chichester 28 pts; Manchester Met 28 pts; Salford 26 pts.

Scottish offers See **Chapter 7**.

OTHER HIGHER EDUCATION COURSES IN THE SUBJECT FIELD

Foundation degrees (contact the institutions for details) (see also under **Tourism**) Bicton (Coll); Blackpool and Fylde (Coll); Chichester; Cornwall (Coll); Cumbria; Derby; Harper Adams (UC); Kingston Maurward (Coll); Leeds Park Lane (Coll); Liverpool (CmC); Newcastle (Coll); Oxford Brookes; Sheffield (Coll); Shuttleworth (Coll); South Birmingham (Coll); West Nottinghamshire (Coll); Weymouth (Coll); Wolverhampton City (Coll); Writtle (Coll); Yorkshire Coast (Coll).

Higher National Diploma courses (in Business Studies)

100 pts **and below**

Anglia Ruskin; Bangor; Barking (Coll); Barnsley (Univ Centre); Bath; Bedfordshire; Birmingham (CFTCS); Bishop Burton (Coll); Blackpool and Fylde (Coll); Bournemouth; Bradford (Coll); Bristol UWE; Brockenhurst (Coll); Broxtowe (Coll); Buckinghamshire Chilterns (UC); Cardiff (UWIC); Central Lancashire; Chelmsford (Coll); Colchester (Inst); Cornwall (Coll); Crawley (Coll); De Montfort; Dearne Valley (Coll); Derby; Doncaster (Univ Centre); Dumfries and Galloway (Coll); East Durham (CmC); East Lancashire (IHE); Easton (Coll); Fareham (Coll); Farnborough (CT); Forth Valley (Coll); Glamorgan; Gloucestershire; Greenwich; Grimsby (IFHE); Guildford (Coll); Havering (Coll); Herefordshire (CT); Hertfordshire; Highbury (Coll); Isle of Wight (Coll); Kent; Lakes (Coll); Leeds Met; Lincoln; Liverpool (CmC); Llandrillo Cymru (Coll); London Met; Loughborough (Coll); Manchester City (Coll); Manchester Met; Nescot; Newcastle (Coll); North East Wales (IHE); Norwich City (Coll); Nottingham New (Coll); Oldham (Coll); Park Lane Leeds (Coll); Pembrokeshire (Coll); Peterborough Reg (Coll); SAC (Scottish CAg); Salford; Sheffield Hallam; Solihull (Coll); Somerset (CAT); South Devon (Coll);

Southampton Solent; Southport (Coll); Sparsholt (Coll); Strode (Coll); Suffolk (Univ Campus); Swansea (IHE); Swansea (Coll); Swindon (Coll); Teesside; Tresham (IFHE); UHI Millennium Inst; Walsall (Coll); Warrington (Coll); Warwickshire (Coll); West Anglia (Coll); West Herts (Coll); Westminster (Coll); Wigan and Leigh (Coll); Wirral Met (Coll); Wolverhampton; Worcester; Worcester (CT); Worcestershire New (Coll); Writtle (Coll); Yorkshire Coast (CFHE).

CHOOSING YOUR COURSE (SEE ALSO CH.1)

Subject information The courses cover various aspects of leisure and recreation. Specialist options include recreation management, tourism and countryside management, all of which are offered as individual degree courses in their own right. There is also an obvious link with Sports Studies and Physical Education courses. See also **Appendix 2**. **Useful websites** www.ilam.co.uk; www.bized.ac.uk; www.leisuremanagement.co.uk; www.baha.org.uk; www.leisureopportunities.co.uk; www.recmanagement.com; www.isrm.co.uk; www.uksport.gov.uk; www.london2012.org.

Course variations Outdoor Leadership (Central Lancashire); Adventure Leisure Management (Gloucestershire); Sport and Leisure Management (Loughborough); Leisure and Festival Management (Napier); Leisure, Tourism and Planning (Oxford Brookes); Rural Recreation and Tourism Management (SAC (Scottish CAg)). *NOW CHECK PROSPECTUSES AND WEBSITES FOR ANY RECENT CHANGES.*

Sandwich degree courses Brighton; Gloucestershire; Loughborough; Ulster.

ADMISSIONS INFORMATION

Number of applicants per place (approx) Brighton 10; Brunel 8; Cardiff (UWIC) 3; Coventry 14; Gloucestershire 7; Hull 3; Liverpool John Moores 3; Loughborough 25; Portsmouth 3; SAC (Scottish CAg) 4; Swansea (IHE) 8; Writtle (Coll) 8.

Advice to applicants and planning the UCAS personal statement Work experience, visits to leisure centres and national park centres and any interests you have in particular aspects of leisure should be described, for example, art galleries, museums, countryside management, sport. An involvement in sports and leisure as a participant or employee is an advantage. See also **Appendix 2**.

Misconceptions about this course The level of business studies in leisure management courses is higher than many students expect.

Selection interviews **Yes** Coventry, Writtle (Coll); **Some** Blackpool and Fylde (Coll), Lincoln, Liverpool John Moores, Salford.

Interview advice and questions In addition to sporting or other related interests, applicants will be expected to have had some work experience and can expect to be asked to discuss their interests. What do you hope to gain by going to university? See **Chapter 6**.

Reasons for rejection (non-academic) Poor communication or presentation skills. Relatively poor sporting background or knowledge.

AFTER-RESULTS ADVICE

Universities with vacancies in Clearing (2006) Central Lancashire; Gloucestershire; Hull; Southampton Solent.

Offers to applicants repeating A-levels **Same** Blackpool and Fylde (Coll), Cardiff (UWIC), Liverpool John Moores, Salford.

GRADUATE DESTINATIONS AND EMPLOYMENT (2005 HESA)

No data available.

OTHER DEGREE SUBJECTS FOR CONSIDERATION

Business Studies; Hospitality Management; Sports Studies; Tourism.

LINGUISTICS

(see also **English**)

NB The points totals shown to the left of the institutions are for ease of reference only. It must not be assumed that tariff points are always used by institutions or that they can be substituted for an offer in grades. The level of an offer is not necessarily indicative of the quality of a course.

COURSE OFFERS INFORMATION

Subject requirements/preferences GCSE Lancaster Mathematics and foreign language grade A–B. **Oxford**, **Cambridge** Mainly grade As. **Sussex** Language grade A–B; Modn Lang courses: grade A. **AL** English may be required or preferred for some courses.

Your target offers

360 pts **and above**

Cambridge – AAA (Ling (Part II subject, taken after Part I in another (usually language-related) subj))

London (QM) – AAA–BCC (Compar Lit Ling; Engl Ling)

Oxford – AAA–AAB (Modn Lang Ling)

340 pts **St Andrews** – AAB (Engl Ling)

330 pts **Southampton** – 330 pts (Lang Soty; Lang Learn)

320 pts **Lancaster** – ABB (Ling; Socioling; Ling Psy; Ling N Am; Engl Lang Ling)

London (UCL) – ABB+AS–BBB+AS (Ling courses)

Manchester – ABB–BBB (Ling; Ling Sociol; Ling Soc Anth; Ling Span; Ling Port; Ling Russ; Ling Mid E Lang; Engl Lit Ling; Fr/Ital Ling)

St Andrews – ABB–BBC (Ling courses except under **340 pts**)

Sheffield – ABB–BBB (Ling courses)

Sussex – ABB–BBB 360–340 pts 3AL+AS (Ling courses)

York – ABB–BBB (Engl Ling; Fr Ling; Ger Ling; Langs Ling; Phil Ling; Maths Ling)

300 pts **Belfast (Queen's)** – BBB–BBCb (Ling courses)

Edinburgh – BBB (Ling; Ling Artif Intel; Ling Soc Anth; Ling Modn Lang)

Lancaster – BBB (Ling Phil)

Leeds – BBB (Ling Phon)

Newcastle – ABC–BBB (Ling courses)

280 pts **Essex** – 280 pts (Engl Lang Ling; Ling; Psyling; Socioling; Ling St)

London (King's) – BBC (Ling courses)

London (QM) – 280 pts (Ling Comp Sci Fr/Ger/Russ)

260 pts **Leeds** – BCC (Ling Russ Civ)

London (SOAS) – BCC (Ling courses)

Oxford Brookes – BCC–CCD (Engl Lang Ling courses)

Reading – 260 pts (App Engl Lang St)

Ulster – 260 pts (Ling Sci; Ling Adv; Ling Comm; Ling PR)

240 pts **Aberdeen** – CCC (Lang Ling courses)

Bangor – 240–260 pts (Ling; Ling Engl Lang; Ling Engl Lit)

Bristol UWE – 240–300 pts (Ling joint courses)

Salford – 240–300 pts (Ling Fr/Ger/Ital/Port/Span)

220 pts **Brighton** – CCD 220 pts (Engl Lang St Ling; Fr Ling; Ger Ling)

Nottingham Trent – 220–240 pts (Ling courses)

160 pts **East London** – 160 pts (App Ling)

Greenwich – 160 pts (Linguistics)

Roehampton – 160–200 pts (Engl Lang Ling courses)

Sunderland – 160 pts (Ling courses)

Westminster – CC (Ling courses)

Wolverhampton – 160–220 pts (Ling courses)

120 pts   Marjon (Coll) – 120–140 pts (Engl Lang Ling courses)
80 pts   London (Birk) – no A-level reqs (p/t Ling Lang)

Alternative offers
IB offers Bristol UWE 26–32 pts; Cambridge 38–42 pts; London (QM) 32 pts, (UCL) 32–34 pts;
Manchester 32–33 pts; Newcastle 32 pts; Southampton 32 pts.
Scottish offers See **Chapter 7**.

CHOOSING YOUR COURSE (SEE ALSO CH.1)

Subject information Linguistics covers the study of language in general and also includes areas such
as children's language, slang, language handicap, advertising language, styles of language and the
learning of foreign languages. **Useful websites** www.iol.org.uk; www.cal.org;
http://web.mit.edu/linguistics/www; www.applij.oxfordjournals.org; www.aclweb.org; www.lsadc.org;
www.lingsoft.fi.

Course variations Linguistics and Artificial Intelligence (Edinburgh); Psycholinguistics and
Sociolinguistics (Essex); Linguistics and Social Anthropology (Manchester); Language and Society
(Southampton). *NOW CHECK PROSPECTUSES AND WEBSITES FOR ANY RECENT CHANGES.*

Top universities and colleges teaching quality See www.tqi.ac.uk; www.qaa.ac.uk.

Top universities and colleges (Research) Cambridge*; Edinburgh; Essex; Lancaster; London (QM)*,
(UCL)*; Manchester; Newcastle; Oxford*; Westminster; York.

ADMISSIONS INFORMATION

Number of applicants per place (approx) Bangor 3; East London 3; Essex 1; Lancaster 12; Leeds 12;
York 11.

Advice to applicants and planning the UCAS personal statement Give details of your interests in
language and how it works, and about your knowledge of languages and their similarities and
differences.

Selection interviews **Yes** Brighton, Cambridge, East London, Essex, Lancaster, Newcastle, Reading;
Some Salford, Sheffield.

Interview advice and questions Past questions include: Why do you want to study Linguistics? What
does the subject involve? What do you intend to do at the end of your degree course? What answer do
you give to your parents or friends when they ask why you want to study the subject? How and why
does language vary according to sex, age, social background and regional origins? See **Chapter 6**.

Reasons for rejection (non-academic) Lack of knowledge of linguistics. Hesitation about the period to
be spent abroad.

AFTER-RESULTS ADVICE

Universities with vacancies in Clearing (2006) Aberdeen; East London; Lancaster; London (QM), (RH),
(SOAS); Nottingham Trent; Roehampton; Salford; Sheffield; Southampton; Sunderland; Westminster;
Wolverhampton.

Offers to applicants repeating A-levels **Higher** Essex, Sussex; **Same** Brighton, Leeds, Newcastle,
Salford, York.

GRADUATE DESTINATIONS AND EMPLOYMENT (2005 HESA)
Graduates surveyed 495 Employed 255 In further study 105 Assumed unemployed 30.

OTHER DEGREE SUBJECTS FOR CONSIDERATION
Communication Studies; English; Speech Sciences.

LITERATURE

(including **Literature Studies** and **Literary Studies;** see also **English)**

NB The points totals shown to the left of the institutions are for ease of reference only. It must not be assumed that tariff points are always used by institutions or that they can be substituted for an offer in grades. The level of an offer is not necessarily indicative of the quality of a course.

COURSE OFFERS INFORMATION

Subject requirements/preferences GCSE English and a foreign language usually required. **AL** English may be required or preferred for some courses.

Your target offers

360 pts and above
  Warwick – AABb (Film Lit)
320 pts Glasgow – 320 pts ABB–BBB (Scot Lit courses; Compar Lit)
  London (King's) – ABB+AS (Compar Lit; Compar Lit Film St)
  Manchester – ABB–BBC (Lit St courses)
  York – ABB–BBB (Ling Lit)
300 pts East Anglia – BBB–BBC (Cult Lit Pol; Engl Compar Lit; Am Engl Lit)
  Edinburgh – BBB (Scot Ethnol Scot Lit)
  Essex – BBB–BBC 300–280 pts (Compar Lit; Lit Myth; Engl US Lit; Engl Lit; Lit Sociol; Lit Hist Art; Lit Hist; Lit Phil; Lit Modn Lang; Lit Dr)
  London (Gold) – BBB (Engl Compar Lit)
  Reading – 300–340 pts (Euro Lit Cult courses)
280 pts Liverpool – BBC–BBB 280–300 pts (Compar Lit Cult St)
260 pts Chester – 260 pts (Lit Film)
  Kent – 260 pts (Compar Lit St courses)
  London (RH) – BCC (Euro Lit Cult St)
  Sheffield Hallam – 260 pts (Film Lit)
  Stirling – BCC 1st yr entry (Scot Lit)
240 pts Aberdeen – CCC (Engl Scot Lit; Lang Lit Scot)
  Ulster – 240 pts (Irish Lang Lit)
200 pts Sunderland – 200 pts (Compar Lit minor)
180 pts Lampeter – open admission policy (Welsh St; Engl Modn Lit)
160 pts Wolverhampton – 160–220 pts (Lit Film Thea St; Lit St)
  Worcester – 160 pts (Engl Lit St courses)

Alternative offers
IB offers Chester 30 pts; Essex 32 pts; Kent 28 pts; Liverpool 30 pts; London (King's) 35 pts.
Scottish offers See **Chapter 7.**

CHOOSING YOUR COURSE (SEE ALSO CH.1)

Subject information This is a very broad subject introducing many aspects of the study of literature and aesthetics. Courses will vary in content. Degree courses in English and foreign languages will also include a study of literature. **Useful websites** www.lrb.co.uk; www.literature.org; www.bibliomania.com.

Course variations English and Comparative Literature (East Anglia); Scottish Ethnology and Scottish Literature (Edinburgh); Literature and Myth (Essex); Irish Language and Literature (Ulster); Literature, Film and Theatre Studies (Wolverhampton). *NOW CHECK PROSPECTUSES AND WEBSITES FOR ANY RECENT CHANGES.*

ADMISSIONS INFORMATION

Number of applicants per place (approx) East Anglia 12; Essex 4.

Advice to applicants and planning the UCAS personal statement **Kent** Interest in literatures other than English. See **English**.

Misconceptions about this course **Kent** Some students think that a foreign language is required – it is not.

Selection interviews **Yes** Lampeter.

Interview advice and questions **Kent** Which book would you take on a desert island, and why? What is the point of doing a Literature degree in the 21st century? See **English**. See also **Chapter 6**.

Reasons for rejection (non-academic) **Kent** Perceived inability to think on their feet.

AFTER-RESULTS ADVICE
Universities with vacancies in Clearing (2006) Anglia Ruskin; Chester; Essex; Kent; Lampeter; London (Gold); Reading; Stirling; Worcester.

GRADUATE DESTINATIONS AND EMPLOYMENT (2004 HESA)
Graduates surveyed 175 **Employed** 90 **In further study** 35 **Assumed unemployed** 10.

OTHER DEGREE SUBJECTS FOR CONSIDERATION
Arts; English; Linguistics; Welsh and Celtic Studies.

MARINE/MARITIME STUDIES
(including **Oceanography;** see also **Naval Architecture**)

NB The points totals shown to the left of the institutions are for ease of reference only. It must not be assumed that tariff points are always used by institutions or that they can be substituted for an offer in grades. The level of an offer is not necessarily indicative of the quality of a course.

COURSE OFFERS INFORMATION
Subject requirements/preferences **GCSE** Mathematics and science are required for several courses. Check prospectuses. **AL** Science or mathematics will be required or preferred for some courses.

Your target offers
360 pts **East Anglia** – AAA–ABB (Meteor Ocean courses except under **280 pts**)
340 pts **Southampton** – AAB 340 pts (MOcean Ocean N Am)
320 pts **Newcastle** – ABB (MEng Mar Tech; Mar Eng; Off Eng; Nvl Archit; Sml Crft Tech)
300 pts **Aberdeen** – BBB (Mar Cstl Res Mgt; Mar Biol)
 Liverpool – BBB 300 pts (Ocean Chem; Ocn Earth Sci; Ocn Clim Physl Geog)
 Newcastle – BBB–BBC (Mar Biol)
 Southampton – BBB 300 pts (MOcean Ocean; Ocean Fr; Ocn Earth Sys Sci)
 Strathclyde/Glasgow – BBB (Advnc Mar Des)
280 pts **East Anglia** – BBC (Meteor Ocean)
 Essex – 280–240 pts (Mar Frshwtr Biol)
 Liverpool – 280–320 pts (Mar Biol)
 London (QM) – 280 pts (Mar Frshwtr Biol)
 Newcastle – BBC (BEng Mar Tech; Mar Eng; Off Eng; Nvl Archit; Sml Crft Tech)
 Plymouth – 280 pts (Mar Biol; Mar Biol Cstl Ecol; Mar Biol Ocean)
 St Andrews – BBC (Mar Biol)
 Southampton – BBC 280 pts (BSc Ocean; Ocean Physl Geog; Ocean Geol; Ocn Phys; Ocn Chem)
 Swansea – 280–300 pts (Mar Biol)
260 pts **Bangor** – 260–320 pts (App Mar Biol; Mar Biol Zool; Mar Biol Ocean)
 Belfast (Queen's) – BCC/AB (Mar Biol)
 Cardiff – BCC–CCC (Mar Geog)

414 | Marine/Maritime Studies

240 pts **Bangor** – 240–280 pts (Mar Env St)
Hull – 240–260 pts (Aqua Zool; Mar Frshwtr Biol)
Plymouth – 240 pts (BEng Mar Tech)
Portsmouth – 240–280 pts (Mar Biol)
Southampton Solent – 240 pts (Ycht Pwrcrft Des)
Strathclyde/Glasgow – CCC–DD (Naut Sci)

220 pts **Bangor** – 220–260 pts (Ocn Sci; Geol Ocean; Ocean Comp; Cstl Geog; Geol Ocean; Mar Chem)
Hull – 220–280 pts (Cstl Mar Biol)
Stirling – CCD (Mar Biol)

200 pts **Anglia Ruskin** – 200 pts (Mar Biol)
Coventry – 200–240 pts (Boat Des)
Liverpool John Moores – 200 pts (Marit St; Marit Bus Mgt; Navig Mar Tech; Naut Sci)
Napier – 200 pts (Mar Frshwtr Biol)
Plymouth – 200 pts (Ocn Explor; Surf Sci Tech; Marit Bus; Marit Bus Log; Marit Bus Marit Law; Ocn Sci; App Mar Spo Sci; Mar St (Ocn Ycht) (Navig); Mar St; Cru Op Mgt)
Portsmouth – 200 pts (Mar Spo Tech)

180 pts **Heriot-Watt** – DDD (App Mar Biol)
Kingston – 180 pts (Mar Frshwtr Biol)
Portsmouth – 180–240 pts (Mar Env Sci)

160 pts **Bournemouth** – 160 pts (Mar Arch; Env Cstl Mgt)
Glamorgan – 160–180 pts (Boat Des)
Plymouth – 160 pts (Mar Spo Tech; Env Sci (Mar Cons); Mar Cmpste Tech)
Southampton Solent – 160 pts (Ycht Manuf Surv)

140 pts **Blackpool and Fylde (Coll)** – 140 pts (Cstl Cons Mar Biol)
Bournemouth – 140 pts (Cstl Cons Mar Biol)

120 pts **Essex** – 120 pts (Mar Frshwtr Biol 4 yrs)
Southampton Solent – 120 pts (Mar Env Sci; Cstl Cons Mgt; Marit Bus; Marit St; Mar Ship Ops; Mar Geog; Wtrspo St Mgt)

100 pts **Hull (Scarborough)** – 100 pts (Fdn Cstl Mar Biol)
Pembrokeshire (Coll) – 100 pts (Cstl Zn Mar Env St)

80 pts **and below**
Eastleigh (Coll) – (Fdn Sci)
UHI Millennium Inst (NHC) – check with admissions tutor (Mar Sci)

Alternative offers
IB offers Cardiff 30 pts; Liverpool 31 pts; Newcastle 35 pts; Stirling 26 pts.
Scottish offers See **Chapter 7**.

OTHER HIGHER EDUCATION COURSES IN THE SUBJECT FIELD

Foundation degrees (contact the institutions for details) Blackpool and Fylde (Coll); Bournemouth; Cornwall (Coll).

Higher National Diploma courses Blackpool and Fylde (Coll); Glasgow (Coll Naut St) (Mar St); Liverpool John Moores; Pembrokeshire (Coll); UHI Millennium Inst (NHC).

CHOOSING YOUR COURSE (SEE ALSO CH.1)

Subject information Marine and Maritime Studies can involve a range of subjects such as marine business, technology, navigation, nautical studies, underwater rescue and transport. **Useful websites** www.bized.ac.uk; www.british-shipping.org; www.uk-sail.org.uk; www.rya.org.uk; www.royal-navy.mod.uk; www.sstg.org; www.noc.soton.ac.uk; www.nautinst.org; www.mcsuk.org; www.nmm.ac.uk; www.imo.org; www.mcga.gov.uk.

Course variations Environmental Studies (Bangor); Marine Archaeology (Bournemouth); Meteorology and Oceanography in North America (East Anglia); Coastal Marine Biology (Hull); Marine Technology (Newcastle); Marine Business with Logistics (Plymouth); Surf Science and Technology (Plymouth);

tuition fees from just £1500*

FALMOUTH MARINE SCHOOL

YOUR UNIVERSITY COURSE IS CLOSER THAN YOU THINK

Study courses that will challenge, inspire and motivate you, in a unique location.

Cornwall College offers you a solution to the 'work or study?' dilemma, with a two-year university-level course that combines academic and practical study, based at Falmouth Marine School.

Apply now for one of our foundation degrees in:

- Boat Design and Production
- Marine Leisure Management
- Marine Science
- Marine Environmental Management
- Marine Sports Science

Developed with employers, a foundation degree, approved by the University of Plymouth, will give you the skills and knowledge that employers are looking for, as a fast track to a great career.

Upon graduation you could progress onto the final year of a related honours degree at the University of Plymouth

Call today for more information:
01209 616161
enquiries@cornwall.ac.uk
www.cornwall.ac.uk

*£2000 tuition fees with £500 fee waiver

College Mission "Creating opportunities for all through high quality education and training."

COMBINED UNIVERSITIES IN CORNWALL

UNIVERSITY OF PLYMOUTH • COLLEGES
CORNWALL COLLEGE

 Part of The **CORNWALL COLLEGE** GROUP

416 | Marketing

Oceanography (Southampton); Yacht and Powercraft Design (Southampton Solent). *NOW CHECK PROSPECTUSES AND WEBSITES FOR ANY RECENT CHANGES.*

Universities and colleges teaching quality See www.tqi.ac.uk; www.qaa.ac.uk.

Sandwich degree courses Liverpool John Moores; Plymouth; Southampton Solent.

ADMISSIONS INFORMATION

Number of applicants per place (approx) Glasgow 2; Liverpool John Moores (Marit St) 3.

Advice to applicants and planning the UCAS personal statement This is a specialised field and, in many cases, applicants will have experience of marine activities. Describe these experiences, for example, sailing, snorkelling, fishing. **UHI Millennium Inst (NHC)** Small intake, high staff/student ratio. Mature students welcome. See also **Appendix 2**.

Selection interviews Yes UHI Millennium Inst (NHC).

Interview advice and questions Most applicants will have been stimulated by their studies in science or will have strong interests or connections with marine activities and are likely to be questioned on their reasons for choosing the course. See **Chapter 6**.

AFTER-RESULTS ADVICE

Universities with vacancies in Clearing (2006) Aberdeen; Bangor; Bournemouth; Hull; Liverpool John Moores; Newcastle; Plymouth; Portsmouth; Southampton; Southampton Solent; Stirling; Strathclyde.

Offers to applicants repeating A-levels Same Bangor, Liverpool John Moores, Plymouth, UHI Millennium Inst (NHC).

GRADUATE DESTINATIONS AND EMPLOYMENT (2005 HESA)

Maritime Technology graduates surveyed 95 **Employed** 60 **In further study** 5 **Assumed unemployed** 5.

Ocean Sciences graduates surveyed 170 **Employed** 75 **In further study** 35 **Assumed unemployed** 15.

OTHER DEGREE SUBJECTS FOR CONSIDERATION

Biology; Civil Engineering; Environmental Studies/Sciences; Marine Engineering; Marine Transport; Naval Architecture; Oceanography.

MARKETING

(see also Art and Design (Fashion), Business Courses, and Food Sciences/Studies and Technology)

NB The points totals shown to the left of the institutions are for ease of reference only. It must not be assumed that tariff points are always used by institutions or that they can be substituted for an offer in grades. The level of an offer is not necessarily indicative of the quality of a course.

COURSE OFFERS INFORMATION

Subject requirements/preferences GCSE English and mathematics. **Lancaster** Mathematics grade B. **Oxford Brookes** Mathematics grade B. **AL** No specified subjects required.

Your target offers

360 pts and above
　　　　Lancaster – AAA (Mark N Am/Aus)
340 pts Lancaster – AAB (Mark Mgt; Adv Mark)
　　　　Manchester – AAB (Mgt (Mark))
　　　　Ulster – 340 pts (Comm Adv Mark)

320 pts **Aston** – ABB 320 pts (Marketing)
Cardiff – ABB (Bus Mgt (Mark))
Lancaster – ABB (Marketing)
Liverpool – 320 pts (Marketing)
London (RH) – 320–340 pts (Mgt Mark)
Newcastle – ABB (Mark; Mark Mgt)
Northumbria – ABB–BBC (Mark Mgt)
300 pts **Bournemouth** – 300 pts (Adv Mark Comm)
Manchester – BBB (Fash Tex Mark)
Stirling – BBB 2nd yr entry (Rtl Mark)
280 pts **Bournemouth** – 280–260 pts (Mark; Int Mark)
De Montfort – 280 pts (Mark; Int Mark Bus; Adv Mark Comm)
Oxford Brookes – BBC (Mark Mgt)
Strathclyde – BBC/ABC (Mark; Mark Modn Langs)
Swansea – 280 pts (Bus Mgt (Mark); Mgt Sci (Mark))
Ulster – 280 pts (Marketing)
260 pts **Aberystwyth** – 260 pts (Mark courses)
Brunel – 260 pts (Bus Mgt (Mark))
Coventry – 260 pts (Mark Mgt; Bus Mark; Fr Mark; Span Mark; Mark Acc)
Gloucestershire – 260–240 pts (Mark Adv Comms)
Heriot-Watt – BCC (Mgt Mark)
Huddersfield – 260 pts (Mark Innov)
Hull – 260 pts (Mark; Mark (Int) (Prof Exp); Mark Bus Econ)
Keele – 260–320 pts (Mark courses)
Kent – 260 pts (Bus St Mark)
Oxford Brookes – BCC (Mark Mgt Comb hons)
Plymouth – 260 pts (Marketing)
Richmond (Am Int Univ) – 260 pts (Bus Admin (Mark))
Stirling – BCC 2nd yr entry (Mark; Rtl Mark)
240 pts **Bournemouth** – 240 pts (Leis Mark)
Bradford – 240–300 pts (Marketing)
Brighton – 240 pts (Rtl Mark; Bus Mgt Mark; Mark Fd Drink)
Bristol UWE – 240–300 pts (Mark joint hons)
Chester – 240–260 pts (Marketing)
Derby – 240–260 pts (Mark Mgt)
Dundee – CCC (Bus Econ Mark)
Huddersfield – 240–160 pts (Mark; Mark Mgt; Int Mark; Dig Mark)
Kingston – 240–280 pts (Mark Mgt)
Liverpool John Moores – 240 pts (Marketing)
Manchester Met – 240 pts (Consum Mark)
Northumbria – CCC (Mark Lang)
Nottingham Trent – 240 pts (3AL **or** Art Fdn) (Fash Mark Comm)
Portsmouth – 240–200 pts (Mark; Mark Psy; Mark joint courses)
Reading – 240 pts (Fd Mark Bus Econ)
Robert Gordon – 240 pts (Mgt Mark)
Salford – 240–300 pts (Bus St Mark Mgt)
Sheffield Hallam – 240 pts (Bus Mark)
Staffordshire – 240 pts (Mark Mgt)
Stirling – CCC (Modn Lang Mark)
UCE Birmingham – 240 pts (Mark; Mark Adv PR; Int Mark)
Westminster – CCC (Bus Mark Mgt; Mark Comm; Glob Mark)
Winchester – 280–240 pts (Mark PR Mgt)
220 pts **Abertay Dundee** – CCD (Mark Bus)
Bangor – 220–280 pts 2AL (Mark Fr/Ger/Ital/Span)

Bournemouth – 220 pts (Fd Mark; Leis Mark)
Glamorgan – 220–180 pts (Marketing)
Gloucestershire – 220 pts (Mark Mgt Brnd; Int Bus Mark)
Lincoln – CCD 220 pts (Mark Media Cult Comm)
Liverpool Hope – 220 pts (Marketing)
Roehampton – 220–160 pts (Mark; Mgt Mark Fr/Span)
Sunderland – 220 pts (Bus (Mark Mgt))

200 pts **Anglia Ruskin** – 200 pts (Marketing)
Bristol UWE – 200–280 pts (Marketing)
Buckingham – 200–220 pts (Mark Fr/Span; Mark Media Comm; Mark Psy)
Central Lancashire – 200–160 pts (Mark; App Intnet Mark)
Coventry – 200–260 pts (Adv Mark)
Edge Hill – 200 pts (Marketing)
Hertfordshire – 200–240 pts (Marketing)
Lincoln – 200 pts (Marketing)
Manchester Met – 200 pts (Fd Mark; Int Fash Mark; Rtl Mark Mgt; Mark Mgt)
Middlesex – 200–240 pts (Mark; Mgt Mark; Mark Comm)
Napier – 200 pts (Mark Mgt)
Sheffield Hallam – 200 pts (Fd Mark; Int Fd Mark)
UCE Birmingham – 200 pts (Mark joint courses)

180 pts **Birmingham (CFTCS)** – 180 pts (Mark Mgt; Mark Evnts Mgt; Mark Tour Mgt; Mark Hspty Mgt)
Cardiff (UWIC) – 180 pts (Mark; Bus St Mark)
Newport – 180 pts (Marketing)
Northampton – 180–220 pts (Mark; Dig Mark; Mark Psy; Enter Mark; Fash Mark; Rtl Mark)
Queen Margaret (UC) – 180 pts (Mark courses)

160 pts **Bedfordshire** – 160–240 pts (Mark; Adv Mark Comm; Mark Media Prac)
Canterbury Christ Church – CC (Marketing)
Central Lancashire – 160 pts (Mark Bus; Mark Int Bus; Mark Mgt; Mark PR)
Creative Arts (UC) – 160 pts (Des Brnd Mark)
Cumbria – 160–200 pts (Bus Mark)
Doncaster (Univ Centre) – 160–240 pts (Bus Mark)
East London – 160 pts (Mark; Fash Des Mark)
Farnborough (CT) – 160–200 pts (Mark courses)
Glasgow Caledonian – CC (Mark; Fash Mark; Mark Media)
Greenwich – 160 pts (Mark Comm; Int Mark; Int Mark Langs; Mark)
Leeds Trinity and All Saints (Coll) – 160–240 pts (Mark; Media Mark; Bus Mark)
London Met – 160 pts (Mark; Mark Bus Mgt)
London South Bank – CC (Mark; Mark Comb courses)
North East Wales (IHE) – 160 pts (Marketing)
Paisley – CC (Mark Int Mark)
Roehampton – 160 pts (Marketing)
Royal (CAg) – 160 pts (Bus Mgt (Mark))
Southend Campus Essex – 160–180 pts (Bus St (Mark))
Southampton Solent – 160 pts (Mark Mgt; Mark Adv Mgt)
Teesside – 160 pts (Mark; Mark Rtl Mgt; Mark Adv Mgt; Mark PR; Des Mark)
Thames Valley – 160 pts (Mark Adv; Mark Bus)
Wolverhampton – 160–220 pts (Marketing)
Worcester – 160 pts (Bus Mgt (Mark))

140 pts **Arts London** – 140 pts check with admissions tutor (Fash Prom)
Bolton – 140 pts (Marketing)
Harper Adams (UC) – 140–280 pts (Agri-Fd Mark Bus St; Agric Mark)
Newport – 140 pts (Marketing)

For a quick reference offers calculator, fold out the inside back cover.

Writtle (Coll) – 140 pts (Mark Sply Chn Mgt)
120 pts **Bradford (Coll)** – 120 pts (Mark Sls; Mark Law)
Buckinghamshire Chilterns (UC) – 120–180 pts (Mark courses)
Cleveland (CAD) – 120 pts (Fash Ent)
Southampton Solent – 120 pts+Art Fdn (Prod Des Mark)
Swansea (IHE) – 120 pts (Marketing)
100 pts **Northbrook (Coll)** – 100 pts (Bus Admin Mark)
Suffolk (Univ Campus) – 100–120 pts (Mark Mgt)
80 pts **and below**
Arts London (CComm) – 80 pts (Mark Adv; PR)
Arts London (CFash) – 2AL contact admission tutor (Mark Adv)
Croydon (Coll) – 80 pts (Bus (Mark))
European Bus Sch London – 80 pts (Int Mark)
Regents Bus Sch London – 80 pts (Int Mark)

Leeds Met – contact University

Alternative offers
IB offers Aberystwyth 29 pts; Brighton 28 pts; Bristol UWE 24–28 pts; Chester 30 pts; Liverpool 32 pts;
Manchester Met 24–28 pts; Stirling 30 pts; Winchester 26 pts.
Scottish offers See **Chapter 7**.

OTHER HIGHER EDUCATION COURSES IN THE SUBJECT FIELD
Foundation degrees (contact the institutions for details) Arts London (CComm); Barry (Coll);
Bournemouth and Poole (Coll); Gwent (Coll); Merthyr Tydfil (Coll); Newcastle (Coll); Northampton.

Higher National Diploma courses (in Business Studies)
140 pts **and below**
Arts London; Askham Bryan (Coll); Bath; Bedfordshire; Birmingham (CFTCS); Blackpool and
Fylde (Coll); Bournemouth (AI); Bradford (Coll); Brighton; Buckinghamshire Chilterns (UC);
Carshalton (Coll); Central Lancashire; Chesterfield (Coll); Coventry City (Coll); Croydon (Coll);
Dearne Valley (Coll); Doncaster (Univ Centre); Dudley (Coll); Durham New (Coll); East
Lancashire (IHE); East London; Exeter (Coll); Farnborough (CT); Glamorgan; Gloucestershire;
Greenwich; Grimsby (IFHE); Guildford (Coll); Harper Adams (UC); Herefordshire (CT);
Hertfordshire; Llandrillo Cymru (Coll); London Met; London South Bank; Loughborough;
Manchester City (Coll); Manchester Met; Mid-Cheshire (Coll); Newcastle (Coll); North East
(IHE); Northampton; Northbrook (Coll); Norwich City (Coll); Oldham (Coll); Park Lane Leeds
(Coll); Salford; Sandwell (Coll); Sheffield (Coll); Solihull (Coll); South Birmingham (Coll);
Southampton Solent; Stockport (CFHE); Suffolk (Univ Campus); Swansea (IHE); Swindon (Coll);
Tameside (Coll); Teesside; Thames Valley; Walsall (Coll); West Herts (Coll); West Thames
(Coll); Westminster (Coll); Wigan and Leigh (Coll); Worcester (CT); Worcestershire New (Coll).

CHOOSING YOUR COURSE (SEE ALSO CH.1)
Subject information Marketing courses are very popular and applications should include evidence of
work experience or work shadowing. Marketing is a subject also covered in most Business Studies
courses and in specialist (and equally relevant) courses such as Textile Marketing and Food Marketing
for which lower offers are often made. Most courses offer the same subject content. **Useful websites**
www.adassoc.org.uk; www.cim.co.uk; www.mori.com; www.camfoundation.com; www.oft.gov.uk;
www.ipa.co.uk.

Course variations Leisure Marketing (Bournemouth); Applied Internet Marketing (Central Lancashire);
Agriculture and Marketing (Harper Adams (UC)); Advertising and Marketing (Lancaster); Fashion and
Textiles Marketing (Manchester); Consumer Marketing (Manchester Met); Creative Design and
Marketing (Northampton); Marketing and Public Relations (Teesside); Marketing and Supply Chain
Management (Writtle (Coll)). *NOW CHECK PROSPECTUSES AND WEBSITES FOR ANY RECENT CHANGES.*

Universities and colleges teaching quality See www.tqi.ac.uk; www.qaa.ac.uk.

Top universities and colleges (Research) Aston.

Sandwich degree courses Aston; Bournemouth; Bradford; Brighton; Bristol UWE; Brunel; Central England; Central Lancashire; Coventry; De Montfort; East London; Glamorgan; Glasgow Caledonian; Gloucestershire; Greenwich; Harper Adams (UC); Hertfordshire; Huddersfield; Hull; Lancaster; Leeds Met; Liverpool John Moores; London South Bank; Manchester; Manchester Met; Middlesex; Napier; Northumbria; Oxford Brookes; Paisley; Plymouth; Portsmouth; Royal (CAg); Sheffield Hallam; Staffordshire; Sunderland; Swansea (IHE); Teesside; Westminster.

ADMISSIONS INFORMATION
Number of applicants per place (approx) Abertay Dundee 6; Aberystwyth 3; Anglia Ruskin 5; Aston 9; Birmingham 4; Bournemouth 10; Brunel 10; Central England 15; Central Lancashire 13; De Montfort 3; Derby 5; Glasgow Caledonian 15; Harper Adams (UC) 3; Huddersfield 7; Lancaster 28; Lincoln 3; London Met 10; Northampton 4; Northumbria 8; Nottingham Trent 2; Plymouth 12; Portsmouth 4; Staffordshire 6; Stirling 10; Teesside 3.

Advice to applicants and planning the UCAS personal statement See **Business Courses.** See also **Appendix 2**.

Selection interviews **Yes** Harper Adams (UC) (advisory), Manchester Met, Middlesex, Northbrook (Coll), Norwich City (Coll), Writtle (Coll); **Some** Aberystwyth, Anglia Ruskin, Aston, Buckingham, De Montfort, Queen Margaret (UC), Staffordshire.

Interview advice and questions Past questions include: What is marketing? Why do you want to take a Marketing degree? Is sales pressure justified? How would you feel if you had to market a product which you considered to be inferior? **Buckingham** What job do you see yourself doing in five years' time? See **Chapter 6**.

Reasons for rejection (non-academic) Little thought of reasons for deciding on a Marketing degree. Weak on numeracy and problem-solving. Limited commercial awareness. Poor inter-personal skills. Lack of leadership potential. No interest in widening their horizons, either geographically or intellectually. 'We look at appearance and motivation and the applicant's ability to ask questions.' Not hungry enough. Limited understanding of the career. No clear reasons for wishing to do the course.

AFTER-RESULTS ADVICE
Universities with vacancies in Clearing (2006) Aberystwyth; Bangor; Bedfordshire; Bolton; Bournemouth; Bradford; Brighton; Bristol UWE; Canterbury Christ Church; Central Lancashire; Chester; Coventry; De Montfort; Derby; East London; Glamorgan; Gloucestershire; Greenwich; Hertfordshire; Huddersfield; Hull; Keele; Kingston; Lancaster; Lincoln; Liverpool Hope; Liverpool John Moores; London (RH); London Met; London South Bank; Manchester Met; Middlesex; Northampton; Northumbria; Nottingham Trent; Plymouth; Portsmouth; Roehampton; Salford; Sheffield Hallam; Southampton Solent; Teesside; UCE Birmingham; Westminster.

Offers to applicants repeating A-levels **Same** Aberystwyth, Anglia Ruskin, Aston, Buckingham, De Montfort, Lincoln, Manchester Met, Queen Margaret (UC), Staffordshire.

GRADUATE DESTINATIONS AND EMPLOYMENT (2005 HESA)
Graduates surveyed 2120 Employed 1470 In further study 75 Assumed unemployed 155.

OTHER DEGREE SUBJECTS FOR CONSIDERATION
Advertising; Art and Design; Business Studies; Communications; Graphic Design; Psychology; Public Relations.

MATERIALS SCIENCE/METALLURGY

(including **Polymer Engineering**)

NB The points totals shown to the left of the institutions are for ease of reference only. It must not be assumed that tariff points are always used by institutions or that they can be substituted for an offer in grades. The level of an offer is not necessarily indicative of the quality of a course.

COURSE OFFERS INFORMATION

Subject requirements/preferences GCSE Science/mathematics subjects. **Swansea** Eight A*, A and B grades. **AL** Mathematics, physics and/or chemistry required for most courses.

Your target offers

360 pts   and above
   Cambridge – AAA varies between colleges (Nat Sci (Mat Sci Metal))
   Oxford – Offers vary eg AAA–AAB (Mat Sci; Mat Econ Mgt)
340 pts   Manchester – AAB–ABC (Mat Sci Eng; Biomed Mat Sci)
   Sheffield – AAB **or** AAbb (MEng Eng (Civ Mat Mech))
   Southampton – AAB 340 pts (MEng Mech Eng Advnc Mat)
320 pts   Imperial London – ABB (MEng Mat Sci Eng; Biomat Tiss Eng; Aerosp Mat)
   Liverpool – ABB 320 pts (MEng Mat Eng)
   Newcastle – ABB–BBB (MEng Mech Mat Eng; Mat Proc Eng)
   Nottingham – ABB (MEng Mech Des Mat Manuf)
   St Andrews – ABB 2nd yr entry (Mat Sci)
   Sheffield – ABB **or** ABbb (MEng Mat Sci Eng courses; Metal; Biomat Sci Tiss Eng)
300 pts   Birmingham – BBB–BBC (Mech Mat Eng; Mat Sci Tech; Metal Mat Eng; Biomed Mat Sci; Spo Sci Mat Tech; Mat Sci Eng Bus Mgt)
   Leeds – BBB 3AL (MEng Mat Sci Eng)
   London (QM) – 300 pts (MEng Aerosp Mat Tech; Des Mat; Env Mat Tech; Mat Foren Sci; Mat Bus; Biomat; Biomed Mat Sci Eng; Mat Eng Med; Spo Mat)
   Loughborough – 300 pts (MEng Mat Eng; Auto Mat)
   Newcastle – BBB–BBC **or** BBcc (BEng Mech Mat Eng; Mat Proc Eng)
   Nottingham – BBB (Biomed Mat Sci)
   St Andrews – BBB (Mat Sci)
   Sheffield – BBB **or** BBbb (Mat Chem)
   Swansea – 300 pts (Mat Sci Eng)
280 pts   Aberdeen – BBC 280 pts 2nd yr entry (Eng (Mech Mat))
   Imperial London – BBC (BEng Mat Sci Eng; Mat Yr Abrd; Mat Mgt; Mat Mgt Yr Abrd)
   Liverpool – BBC 280 pts (BEng Mat Sci Eng; Mat Sci Mgt St; Mat Des Manuf; Biomat Sci Eng; Aerosp Mat)
   Sheffield – BBC (BEng Mat Sci Eng; Metal; Biomat Sci Tiss Eng; Aerosp Mat; Mat Sci Eng Modn Lang)
260 pts   London (QM) – 260 pts (BEng Biomed Mat Sci Eng; Mat Sci Eng; Mat For Sci; Env Mat Tech; Mat Bus; Aerosp Mat Tech; Poly Tech; Mat Eng Med; Biomat; Dntl Mat; Spo Mat)
   Nottingham – BCC (BSc Mech Des Mat Manuf)
240 pts   Leeds – CCC (BEng Mat Sci Eng; Biomat; Spo Mat Tech)
   London (QM) – 240 pts (BSc Biomat; Mat Sci Eng; Mat Eng Med)
   Loughborough – 240 pts (BEng Mat Eng; Mat Mgt St; Auto Mat; App Des (Prod Perf Sfty))
   Swansea – 240 pts (BEng Mat Sci Eng)
220 pts   Aberdeen – CCD 1st yr entry (Eng (Mech Mat))
   Napier – 220 pts (Poly Eng)
200 pts   Liverpool – CDD 200 pts (BEng Fdn Mat Sci)
160 pts   Manchester Met – 160–280 pts (varies with subj choices) (Mat Sci courses; Plas Rbr Mat)
   Plymouth – 160 pts (Mar Cmpste Tech)
120 pts   London Met – 120 pts (Poly Eng)

Alternative offers
IB offers Birmingham 30 pts; London (QM) 26–32 pts; Manchester 32–35 pts; Nottingham 30–32 pts; Sheffield 30–33 pts.
Scottish offers See **Chapter 7**.

OTHER HIGHER EDUCATION COURSES IN THE SUBJECT FIELD

Foundation degrees (contact the institution for details) Bradford (Coll); Capel Manor (Coll); Staffordshire (Reg Fed); West Nottinghamshire (Coll).

Higher National Diploma courses
100 pts and below

Arts London; Bradford (Coll); Capel Manor (Coll); Glamorgan; Leeds Met; Leicester (Coll); London Met; Manchester Met; Sandwell (Coll); Somerset (CAT); Swindon (Coll); West Herts (Coll).

CHOOSING YOUR COURSE (SEE ALSO CH.1)

Subject information Materials Science is a subject which covers physics, chemistry and engineering at one and the same time! From its origins in metallurgy, materials science has now moved into the processing, structure and properties of materials – ceramics, polymers, composites and electrical materials. Materials science and metallurgy are perhaps the most misunderstood of all careers and applications for degree courses are low with very reasonable offers. Valuable bursaries and scholarships are offered by the Institute of Materials, Minerals and Mining (check with Institute – see **Appendix 2**). Polymer Science is a branch of materials science and is often studied in conjunction with Chemistry and covers such topics as polymer properties and processing relating to industrial applications with, for example, plastics, paints, adhesives. As with other careers in which there is a shortfall of applicants, graduate employment and future prospects are good. See also **Appendix 2**.
Useful websites www.scienceyear.com; www.uksteel.org.uk; www.iom3.org.uk; www.noisemakers.org.uk; www.imm.org; www.gchq.gov.uk/codebreaking.

Course variations Biomedical Materials Science (Birmingham); Aerospace Materials (Imperial London); Biomaterials (Leeds); Sports Materials Technology (Leeds); Dental Materials (London (QM)); Polymer Engineering (London Met); Automotive Materials (Loughborough); Materials, Economics and Management (Oxford). *NOW CHECK PROSPECTUSES AND WEBSITES FOR ANY RECENT CHANGES.*

Universities and colleges teaching quality See www.tqi.ac.uk; www.qaa.ac.uk.

Top universities and colleges (Research) Birmingham*; Cambridge*; Imperial London; Liverpool; Manchester*; Oxford*; Sheffield*.

Sandwich degree courses Plymouth.

ADMISSIONS INFORMATION

Number of applicants per place (approx) Birmingham 8; Imperial London 3; Liverpool 3; Manchester Met 7; Nottingham 7; Oxford (success rate 62%); Swansea 4.

Advice to applicants and planning the UCAS personal statement Read scientific and engineering journals and describe any special interests you may have. Try to visit chemical or technological installations (rubber, plastics, glass etc) describing any such visits. See also **Appendix 2**.

Misconceptions about this course Students are generally unaware of what this subject involves or the opportunities within the industry.

Selection interviews **Yes** Birmingham, Oxford; **Some** Leeds.

Interview advice and questions Questions are likely to be based on A/AS-level science subjects. Recent examples include: Why did you choose Materials Science? How would you make each part of this table lamp (on the interviewer's desk)? Identify this piece of material. How was it manufactured? How has it been treated? (Questions related to metal and polymer samples.) What would you consider the major growth area in materials science? **Birmingham** We try to gauge understanding; for example, an applicant would be unlikely to be questioned on specific facts, but might be asked what they have understood from a piece of coursework at school. **Oxford** Tutors look for an ability to apply logical reasoning to problems in physical science and an enthusiasm for thinking about new concepts in science and engineering. See **Chapter 6**.

AFTER-RESULTS ADVICE

Universities with vacancies in Clearing (2006) Imperial London; Liverpool; London (QM); Loughborough; Manchester; Sheffield; Swansea.

Offers to applicants repeating A-levels **Higher** Swansea; **Same** Birmingham, Leeds, Liverpool, Manchester Met.

GRADUATE DESTINATIONS AND EMPLOYMENT (2005 HESA)

Materials Science graduates surveyed 30 **Employed** 10 **In further study** 10 **Assumed unemployed** none.

Metallurgy graduates surveyed 15 **Employed** 5 **In further study** 10 **Assumed unemployed** none.

Polymer Science/Engineering graduates surveyed 185 **Employed** 125 **In further study** 15 **Assumed unemployed** 15.
Materials Technology graduates surveyed 255 **Employed** 105 **In further study** 60 **Assumed unemployed** 25.

OTHER DEGREE SUBJECTS FOR CONSIDERATION

Aerospace Engineering; Biotechnology; Chemistry; Engineering Sciences; Mathematics; Mechanical Engineering; Plastics Technology; Physics; Product Design and Materials; Sports Technology.

MATHEMATICS

(including **Applied/Applicable Mathematics** and **Mathematical Sciences/Studies**)

NB The points totals shown to the left of the institutions are for ease of reference only. It must not be assumed that tariff points are always used by institutions or that they can be substituted for an offer in grades. The level of an offer is not necessarily indicative of the quality of a course.

COURSE OFFERS INFORMATION

Subject requirements/preferences **GCSE** English often required. **Aberdeen**, **Edinburgh**, **St Andrews** English and a foreign language required. **Brunel** (Fin Maths) English/mathematics at grade A or B; (Maths Lang) French or German at grade A or B. **City** Two subjects at grade A, three subjects at grade B, grade A mathematics, grade B English. **London (LSE)** A*, A and B grades. **Oxford**, **Cambridge** Usually grade As. **Strathclyde** (Maths Stats Acc) English language and literature grades AA–BB. **Warwick** A* mathematics plus five As. **AL** Mathematics, in some cases with a specified grade, required for all courses.

Your target offers
360 pts and above
        Bath – AAA (Maths; BSc Maths; Mathem Sci; Maths Stats; Comp Sci Maths; Maths Phys)
        Bristol – AAA–AAB (Maths; Maths Stats; Maths Euro; Maths Comp Sci; Maths Phil; Maths Phys; Biol Maths; Econ Maths)
        Cambridge – AAA+STEP varies between colleges (Mathematics)
        Cambridge – AAA (Maths Educ St; Maths Comp Sci; Maths Phys)
        Durham – AAA (Nat Sci (Maths))
        Imperial London – AAA (Maths Comp Sci)
        London (LSE) – AAA–AAB (Bus Maths Stats)
        London (QM) – 360 pts (MSci Maths courses)
        London (UCL) – AAA+AS–AAB+AS (Maths courses)

Oxford – Offers vary eg AAA–AAB (Maths; Maths Phil; Maths Comp Sci; Maths Stats)
Sheffield – AAA (Maths Aus/N Am)
Southampton – AAA 360 pts (MMaths Maths)
Warwick – AAA–AABa (Maths; Maths Bus St; Maths Econ; Maths Phil; Maths Comp; Maths Phys; MORSE)

340 pts **Aberystwyth** – 340 pts (MMaths Maths)
Birmingham – AAB–ABB 320 pts (Mathem Sci; Mathem Eng; Maths (Euro); Maths Bus Mgt; Maths Arts subjs)
Durham – AAB; AAA joint hons (Maths; Maths (Euro St); Maths; Maths Educ; Comb Arts)
East Anglia – AAB–AAC (MMaths Maths N Am/Aus/Euro)
Kent – 340 pts (MMaths courses)
Imperial London – 340 pts (MSci/BSc Maths; Maths Euro; Maths Stats; Maths Stats Fin; Maths App Maths; Maths Mathem Comput)
Lancaster – AAB (Maths N Am/Aus; Maths Stats OR)
Leeds – AAB (Maths; Maths Fin)
London (King's) – AAB–ABB+AS (Maths courses)
London (LSE) – AAB (Maths Econ)
Manchester – AAB (Maths; Maths Bus Mgt; Maths Fin Maths; Maths Stats OR; Maths Modn Lang; Maths Phil; Maths Appl; Maths Mgt)
Newcastle – AAB–ABB (MMaths Maths; MMaths Maths Stats; Maths Mgt; Maths Stats; Fin Maths; Fin Maths Mgt)
Nottingham – AAB–AAA (Maths; Mathem Sci; Mathem Phys; Maths Comp Sci; Maths Econ; Maths Mgt St; Maths Phil)
Reading – 340 pts (Maths Psy)
St Andrews – AAB–ABB (Maths courses)
Sheffield – AAB (Fin Maths)
Southampton – AAB 340 pts (BSc Maths)
Surrey – AAB (MMaths Maths)
Sussex– AAB–ABB (Maths courses)
York – AAB–ABB (Maths courses)

320 pts **Belfast (Queen's)** – ABB–ABC (MSci Maths courses)
Birmingham – ABB–ACC 300 pts (Maths Comp Sci; Maths Phil; Maths Psy; Maths Spo Sci)
Bristol – ABB (Eng Maths Abrd)
Cardiff – ABB–ABC 300 pts (Maths; Maths App; Maths OR Stats; Phys Maths; Comp Maths; Maths Hum courses)
East Anglia – ABB (BSc Maths; Maths Meteor; Maths Mgt St; Maths Econ; Maths Env Sci; Maths Stats; Maths Comp)
Exeter – ABB–BBB (Maths; Maths Phys; Maths Comp Sci; Maths Acc; Maths Econ; Maths Fin; Maths Mgt)
Glasgow – ABB–BBB (BA Maths)
Lancaster – ABB (Mathematics)
Leicester – 320–420 pts (MMaths Maths; MMaths Maths USA; Comput Maths; Maths Astron)
London (RH) – ABB–ABC (Maths courses)
Loughborough – 320 pts (Maths Spo Sci)
Newcastle – ABB (Mathem Sci; Comp Sci Maths; Econ Maths; Geog Maths; Acc Maths; Maths Psy)
Nottingham – ABB (Maths Eng)
Reading – 320 pts (MMaths courses)
St Andrews – ABB (Maths courses except under **340 pts**)
Sheffield – ABB (Geog Maths; Env Maths; Maths Phil)
Southampton – ABB 320 pts (Mathem St; Maths Fr/Ger; Maths Act St; Maths Astron; Maths Mus; Maths Mgt Sci)
Strathclyde – ABB–BBB 2nd yr entry (MSci/BSc Maths courses)
Surrey – ABB (BSc Maths; Maths Stats; Maths Comp Sci; Maths Mus; Fin Maths)

Swansea – ABB 320 pts (MMaths courses)
300 pts **Aberystwyth** – 300 pts (BSc Maths; PMaths; App Maths joint courses; Fin Maths)
Aston – BBB 300 pts (Maths; Maths Comb; Comp Sci Maths)
Brunel – 300 pts (Mathematics)
City – BBB (Maths Fin)
Dundee – BBB 300 pts 2nd yr entry (Maths courses)
Edinburgh – ABC (Maths; PMaths; Maths Stats; Maths Mgt; Maths Phys; Maths Bus St; Maths Mus)
Glasgow – BBB–BCC (BSc Maths; App Maths; Maths Stats)
Heriot-Watt – BBB–ABC 2nd yr entry (Maths; Act Maths Stats; Fin Maths; Maths Comp Sci; Maths Econ; Maths Fin; Maths Phys; Maths Stats; Maths Lang; Maths Educ; Maths Mgt)
Lancaster – BBB (Maths Phil)
Leeds – BBB–ABC (Mathem St)
Leicester – 300–400 pts (Maths courses except under **320 pts**)
Liverpool – BBB–ABB 300–320 pts (Maths; Mathem Sci; PMaths; Maths Stats; Maths joint courses)
Loughborough – BBB–ABC 300 pts (BSc Maths; Maths Econ; Maths Comp; Maths Acc Fin Mgt; Maths Mgt; Fin Maths)
Reading – 300 pts (BSc Maths; Maths App Stats; Maths Meteor; Comput Maths)
Sheffield – BBB–BBC (Chem Maths; Comp Sci Maths; Econ Maths; Mgt Maths; Acc Fin Mgt Maths)
Stranmillis (UC) – BBB (Maths Educ)
Surrey – ABC 300 pts (BSc Maths Bus St; Maths Mgt)
Swansea – BBB 300 pts (Maths courses except under **320 pts**)
280 pts **Aberdeen** – BBC 2nd yr entry (BSc Maths)
Belfast (Queen's) – BBC–BCC (BSc Maths; Maths Euro; Comput Maths; App Maths Phys; Maths Stats OR)
Brunel – 280 pts (Fin Maths)
Central Lancashire – BBC (Maths Stats; Maths)
Essex – 280 pts (Maths; Maths USA; Acc Maths; Maths Comp; Maths Econ; Fin Maths; Mgt Maths; Maths Crypt Net Scrty)
Lancaster – BBC (Maths Stats)
London (QM) – BBC 280 pts (BSc Maths courses)
London (RH) – BBC (BSc Maths courses)
260 pts **Brighton** – 260 pts (Maths; Maths Stats; Maths Fin; Maths Bus; Maths Comp)
Brunel – 260 pts (Maths Comp; Mathem Mgt St; Maths Stats Mgt)
Chester – 260 pts (Mathematics)
City – BCC (Mathem Sci; Mathem Sci Comp Sci)
Coventry – 260 pts (Fin Maths)
Keele – 260–300 pts (Mathematics)
Kent – 260 pts (MMaths/BSc/BA Maths; Bus Maths; Fin Maths; Maths Stats; App Quant Fin)
Kingston – 260 pts (Mathem Sci; Maths Bus Mgt; Act Maths Stats; Maths Med Stats)
Lancaster – BCC (Env Maths)
Northumbria – 260 pts (Maths; Maths Bus)
Strathclyde – BCC–BBC (Maths courses)
240 pts **Aberdeen** – CCC (BA Maths)
Bristol UWE – 240–260 pts (Maths; Euro St Maths; Lat Am St Maths; Intnet Sys Maths)
Central Lancashire – 240 pts (Maths Astron; Maths Psy)
Coventry – 240 pts (BSc Maths)
Dundee – 240 pts 1st yr entry (Maths courses)
Glamorgan – 240–280 pts (Maths; Maths Educ QTS)
Heriot-Watt – CCC 1st yr entry (Maths courses)
Nottingham Trent – 240–220 pts (Maths courses)
Portsmouth – 240 pts (Maths; Maths Stats; Maths Fin Mgt; Maths Comp)

Reading – 240 pts (BSc Mathem St)
230 pts **Bolton** – 230 pts (Mathematics)
220 pts **Aberdeen** – CCD 1st yr entry (BSc Maths)
Edge Hill – 220 pts (Maths Educ)
Liverpool Hope – 220 pts (Educ St (Maths))
Manchester Met – 220–280 pts (BA/BSc Bus Maths Comb courses)
Staffordshire – 220 pts (Comp Maths)
Stirling – CCD (Maths Apps)
Winchester – 220 pts (Maths P Educ)
200 pts **Central Lancashire** – 200 pts (Maths Bus Inf Sys; Maths Educ St)
Coventry – 200–260 pts (Mathem Sci courses)
Cumbria – 200 pts (Maths courses)
Heriot-Watt – CCE (Gen Maths)
Manchester Met – 200–260 pts (Mathematics)
Napier – 200 pts (Bus Maths)
Plymouth – 200 pts (Maths courses)
Sheffield Hallam – 200 pts (Maths; Maths Comp Apps; Maths Stats)
UCE Birmingham – 200 pts (Maths Educ)
180 pts **Glasgow Caledonian** – DDD 180 pts (Maths Comp; Fin Maths; Maths Bus Analys)
Greenwich – 180–220 pts (Maths; Maths Stats Comp)
Hertfordshire – 180 pts (Maths; Maths Comb St)
Northampton – 180–220 pts (Maths courses)
160 pts **Bishop Grosseteste (Coll)** – 160 pts (Educ St Maths Tech)
Canterbury Christ Church – CC (Maths Educ QTS)
Chichester – DDE 160 pts (Maths Educ QTS)

For a quick reference offers calculator, fold out the inside back cover.

Derby – 160–180 pts (Mathem St; Mathem St Educ; Mathem Comp St)
Liverpool John Moores – 160 pts (Maths Stats Comp; Bus Maths)
London Met – 160 pts (Fin Maths)
Manchester Met – 160–280 pts (BA/BSc Maths Comb hons)
Marjon (Coll) – 160–120 pts approx (Maths Educ)
Oxford Brookes – CC (Mathem Sci)

140 pts **Wolverhampton** – 140–220 pts (Mathem Sci; Mathem Bus Analys; Mathem Sci Spo St)

120 pts **London Met** – 120 pts (Mathematics)
Paisley – DD **or** bbc (Mathem Sci courses)

100 pts **Sheffield Hallam** – 100 pts (Fdn Sci Maths)

80 pts **Aberystwyth** – 80 pts (Maths Ord)
London (Birk) – 80 pts for under 21s (over 21s varies) (p/t Maths Stats)

Open University – contact University

Alternative offers

IB offers Aberystwyth 29–33 pts; Aston 31 pts; Birmingham 32–34 pts; Brighton 28 pts; Bristol 34 pts; Bristol UWE 24–26 pts; Brunel 30–32 pts; Cambridge 38–42 pts; Chester 30 pts; Essex 30 pts; Exeter 30–34 pts; Keele 26–30 pts; Kent 28 pts; Liverpool 33 pts; London (King's) 35 pts, (LSE) 36 pts, (QM) 32 pts, (UCL) 36–38 pts; Loughborough 32 pts; Manchester 33 pts; Manchester Met 24–28 pts; Newcastle 32 pts; Nottingham 35 pts; Reading 27–31 pts; Sheffield 32–33 pts; Southampton 34 pts; Stirling 26 pts; Strathclyde 28 pts; Warwick 36 pts; York 34 pts.
Scottish offers See **Chapter 7**.

OTHER HIGHER EDUCATION COURSES IN THE SUBJECT FIELD

Foundation degrees (contact the institution for details) Nottingham Trent.

Higher National Diploma courses
140 pts and below
Bell (Coll); De Montfort; Greenwich; London Met; Ulster.

CHOOSING YOUR COURSE (SEE ALSO CH.1)

Subject information Mathematics at degree level is an extension of A-level mathematics, covering pure and applied mathematics, statistics, computing, mathematical analysis and mathematical applications. Mathematics is of increasing importance and is used in the simplest of design procedures and not only in applications in the physical sciences and engineering. It also plays a key role in management, economics, medicine and the social and behavioural sciences. **York** Mathematics offers the pleasure of problem-solving, the satisfaction of a rigorous argument and the most widely employable non-vocational degree subject. A student's view: 'Maths trains you to work in the abstract, to think creatively and to come up with concrete conclusions'. These transferable skills are much sought-after by employers. Employment prospects are excellent with high salaries. **Useful websites** www.ima.org.uk; www.gchq.gov.uk/codebreaking/index; www.orsoc.org.uk; www.scienceyear.com; www.m-a.org.uk; www.mathscareers.org.uk; www.imo.math.ca; wwwbmoc.maths.org; www.mathcomp.leeds.ac.uk.

Course variations Engineering Mathematics (Bristol); Mathematics and Music (Edinburgh); Mathematics, Cryptography and Network Security (Essex); Mathematics and Mathematical Computing (Imperial London); Environmental Mathematics (Lancaster); Financial Mathematics (Newcastle); Mathematics and Meteorology (Reading); Mathematics, Operational Research, Statistics and Economics (Warwick). *NOW CHECK PROSPECTUSES AND WEBSITES FOR ANY RECENT CHANGES.*

Universities and colleges teaching quality See www.tqi.ac.uk; www.qaa.ac.uk.

Top universities and colleges (Research) Aberdeen; Bath*; Birmingham; Bristol*; Brunel; Cambridge*; Cardiff; Dundee; Durham*; East Anglia; Edinburgh*; Exeter; Glasgow; Heriot-Watt; Imperial London*; Keele; Kent; Leeds; Leicester; Liverpool; London (King's), (QM), (RH), (UCL); Manchester; Newcastle; Nottingham; Oxford*; St Andrews; Sheffield; Southampton; Strathclyde; Surrey; Warwick*; York.

Sandwich degree courses Aston; Bath; Belfast (Queen's); Brighton; Brunel; Cardiff; Coventry; Derby; Glamorgan; Glasgow Caledonian; Greenwich; Hertfordshire; Kent; Kingston; Lancaster; Liverpool John Moores; Loughborough; Manchester Met; Northumbria; Nottingham Trent; Oxford Brookes; Paisley; Portsmouth; Reading; Sheffield Hallam; Staffordshire; Surrey; Wolverhampton; York.

ADMISSIONS INFORMATION

Number of applicants per place (approx) Aberystwyth 8, (App Maths) 5; Anglia Ruskin 6; Aston 8; Bangor 4; Bath 10; Birmingham 7; Bristol 7; Brunel 5; Cambridge 4; Cardiff 5; Central Lancashire 7; City 6; Coventry 8; Cumbria 9; Derby 4; Dundee 5; Durham 5; East Anglia 5; East London 2; Edinburgh 4; Exeter 6; Glamorgan 3; Greenwich 2; Hertfordshire 9; Heriot-Watt 5; Kent 8; Lancaster 12; Leeds (Maths) 5, (Maths Fin) 4; Leicester 8; Liverpool 5; London (Gold) 5, (King's) 8, (LSE) (Maths Econ) 10, (Bus Maths Stats) 10, (QM) 5, (RH) 8, (UCL) 8; London Met 3; Manchester Met 3; Middlesex 5; Newcastle 7; Northumbria 7; Nottingham 15; Oxford (success rate 43%); Oxford Brookes 21; Plymouth 8; Portsmouth 7; Sheffield 5; Sheffield Hallam 3; Southampton 8; Strathclyde 6; Surrey 7; Warwick 6; Westminster 3; York 10.

Advice to applicants and planning the UCAS personal statement Any interests you have in careers requiring mathematical ability could be mentioned – for example, engineering, computers (hardware and software) and business applications. Show determination, love of mathematics and an appreciation of the rigour of the course. **Bristol** (Eng Maths) Skills, work experience, positions of responsibility. **Coventry** (for non-EU students) Fluency in oral and written English required. **St Andrews** Reasons for course choice. Evidence of interest. **Southampton** A variety of non-academic interests to complement the applicant's academic abilities. See also **Appendix 2**.

Misconceptions about this course London (QM) Some believe that a study of mechanics is compulsory – it is not. **Surrey** Maths is not just about calculations, it focuses on reasoning, logic and applications. **York** Further maths is not required for this course.

Selection interviews Yes Aberystwyth, Bath, Birmingham, Bishop Grosseteste (Coll), Bristol UWE, Brunel, Cambridge, Cardiff, Central Lancashire, City, Coventry, Durham, East London, Essex, Exeter, Glamorgan, Heriot-Watt, Kent, Kingston, Lancaster, Leeds, Liverpool, Liverpool John Moores, London (Gold), (King's), (RH), (UCL), London Met, Manchester Met, Newcastle, Northampton, Northumbria, Nottingham, Oxford, Reading, Salford, Sheffield, Southampton, Sussex, Warwick, York; **Some** Brighton, Bristol, Greenwich, London (LSE) (rarely), Loughborough.

Interview advice and questions Questions are likely to be asked arising from the information you have given in your UCAS application and about your interests in the subject. Questions in recent years have included: How many ways are there of incorrectly setting up the back row of a chess board? A ladder on a rough floor leans against a smooth wall. Describe the forces acting on the ladder and give the maximum possible angle of inclination possible. There are three particles connected by a string; the middle one is made to move – describe the subsequent motion of the particles. What mathematics books have you read outside your syllabus? Why does a ball bounce? Discuss the work of any renowned mathematician. Balance a pencil on your index fingers and then try to move both towards the centre of the pencil. Explain what is happening in terms of forces and friction. **Southampton** Personal statements generate discussion points. Our interviews are informal chats and so technical probing is kept low key. See **Chapter 6**.

Applicants' impressions (A=Open day; B=Interview day) Cambridge (B) The first interview (five minutes) was relaxed with a very helpful interviewer. The second interview (10 minutes) was intimidating, almost aggressive, and I felt under a lot of pressure. The course is very theoretical and the professors seemed very distant. There was no real chance to talk to the students. **Exeter** (B) There was one informal interview of 30 minutes with one interviewer. General questions were asked on why I wanted to study maths, what aspects of the subject interested me the most and questions on my personal statement. It is a pleasant campus, with the library and shops all fairly central. A friendly male-dominated department. We had a chance to meet and talk to students about the course and the University. **Oxford (St Hugh's)** (B) There were two interviews of 20 minutes, each with one interviewer. Very few questions were asked about why I wanted to study the subject and my extra-curricular activities. Most of the questions related to maths problems. The interviewers were friendly and helped me when I had difficulty with a problem. I felt under pressure but they helped me relax. The College is spacious and the buildings and grounds attractive. The small community atmosphere about the college impressed me. Being a student there would be a challenging and beneficial experience. No chance to talk to any students.

Reasons for rejection (non-academic) Usually academic reasons only. Lack of motivation. We were somewhat uneasy about how much mathematics he will remember after a gap year running a theatre in South Africa. **Birmingham** A poorly written and poorly organised personal statement.

AFTER-RESULTS ADVICE
Universities with vacancies in Clearing (2006) Aberystwyth; Aston; Belfast (Queen's); Birmingham; Bolton; Brunel; Central Lancashire; Chester; City; Coventry; Cumbria; Derby; Dundee; East Anglia; Exeter; Glamorgan; Glasgow; Greenwich; Heriot-Watt; Hertfordshire; Keele; Kent; Kingston; Lancaster; Leicester; London (King's), (QM), (RH); London Met; Loughborough; Manchester; Manchester Met; Newcastle; Northampton; Nottingham; Nottingham Trent; Oxford Brookes; Plymouth; Portsmouth; Reading; Sheffield; Southampton; Staffordshire; Stirling; Surrey; Swansea; Wolverhampton; York.

Offers to applicants repeating A-levels Higher Brighton, Coventry, Essex, Glasgow, London Met, Salford, Strathclyde, Swansea, Surrey, Warwick; **Possibly higher** Cambridge (Hom), Durham, Lancaster, Leeds, Newcastle, Sheffield; **Same** Aberystwyth, Aston, Bath, Birmingham, Bristol, Brunel, Chester, East Anglia, Liverpool, London (RH), Loughborough (usually), Manchester Met, Nottingham, Nottingham Trent, Oxford Brookes, Sheffield Hallam, Southampton, Ulster, York.

GRADUATE DESTINATIONS AND EMPLOYMENT (2005 HESA)
Mathematics graduates surveyed 3050 **Employed** 1365 **In further study** 705 **Assumed unemployed** 205.

Operational Research graduates surveyed 70 **Employed** 45 **In further study** 5 **Assumed unemployed** none.

OTHER DEGREE SUBJECTS FOR CONSIDERATION
Accountancy; Actuarial Studies; Astronomy; Astrophysics; Computer Science; Economics; Engineering Sciences; Operational Research; Physics; Statistics.

MEDIA STUDIES

(including **Broadcasting and Journalism;** see also **Art and Design (General), Communication Studies/Communications, Computer Courses, Engineering (Acoustics)** and **Film, Radio, Video and TV Studies)**

NB The points totals shown to the left of the institutions are for ease of reference only. It must not be assumed that tariff points are always used by institutions or that they can be substituted for an offer in grades. The level of an offer is not necessarily indicative of the quality of a course.

COURSE OFFERS INFORMATION

Subject requirements/preferences **GCSE** English and mathematics often required. **Bangor** Grade C in Welsh. **Bradford** Grade C in mathematics, combined science, physics and English. **Cardiff** Grade A or B in English. **London South Bank** Two subjects grade A, two at grade B, English grade A or B. **Nottingham Trent** Majority grades A/B. **Sheffield Hallam** Majority of grades A and B; grade B minimum in double science, mathematics, English. **AL** No specified subjects required.

Your target offers

340 pts **Surrey** – AAB (MEng Media Eng)
York – AAB–BBB (Media Tech)

320 pts **Cardiff** – ABB 320 pts (Journal Film Media; Journal Film Media Cult Crit; Journal Film Media Soc Pol; Journal Film Media Sociol)
City – ABB (Journal Contemp Hist: apply via London (QM))
East Anglia – ABB–BBB (Script Perf)
Glasgow – ABB–BBB (Arts Media Inform)
London (Gold) – ABB (Media Comm)
London (QM) – 320 pts (Journal Contemp Hist)
London (RH) – ABB (Media Arts)
Sussex – ABB–BBB **or** 360–340 pts 3AL+AS (Media Prac Theor; Media St Fr/Ger/Ital/Span; Media St Anth; Media Cult St)

300 pts **Birmingham** – BBB (Media Cult Soty courses)
Bournemouth – 300 pts (Interact Media Prod; Multim Journal; Comm Media Script Film TV)
Brighton – 300 pts (Spo Journal)
Brunel – 300 pts (Multim Tech Des)
Central Lancashire – BBB 300 pts (Journalism)
City – BBB (Journal Sociol; Journal Psy; Journal Econ)
Dundee – 300 pts 2nd yr entry (Interact Media Des)
East Anglia – BBB–BBC (Soty Cult Media; Pol Media)
Lancaster – BBB (Media Cult St)
Leeds – BBB (Broad Journal; Broad; Comm St; New Media)
Leicester – BBB (Comm Media Soty)
London (Gold) – BBB (Media Modn Lit)
Manchester – BBB (Media Cult Soc)
Newcastle – BBB (Media Comm Cult St)
Nottingham Trent – 300 pts (Broad Journal)
Sheffield – BBB **or** ABbb **or** BBbb (Journal St; Journal Gerc St; Journal Fr/Russ; Journal Hisp St)
Strathclyde – BBB–BBC (Journal Crea Writ)
Surrey – BBB (BEng Media Eng)
Surrey – 300–260 pts (Cult Media Comm)

280 pts **Aberystwyth** – 280 pts (Media Comm St)
Bristol UWE – 280–320 pts (Media Cult St; Media Cult St Dr; Media Cult St Film St; Media Cult St Hist; Media Cult St Engl)
Chester – 280–240 pts (Media Prod courses; Media St; Multim Tech; Journal)
De Montfort – 280 pts (Journal St)
Essex – 280–300 pts (Sociol Media St)

Huddersfield – 280–260 pts (Media (Prt Journal) (Rad Journal) (TV Journal) (Spo Journal) (Mus Journal))

Keele – BBC–BCC 280–320 pts (Media Comm Cult courses)

Kingston – 280–320 pts (Journalism)

Lancaster – BBC (IT Media Comm)

Lincoln – BBC 280 pts (Media Prod)

Liverpool John Moores – BBC 280–180 pts (Journal; Int Journal; Media Cult St courses)

London (Gold) – BBC (Int Media; Media Sociol)

Loughborough – 280 pts (Comm Media St)

Northumbria – 280 pts (Journal; Journal Engl; Media Journal)

Salford – BBC 280 pts (Journal Des St; Journal Engl Lit; Journal Pol; Journal Sociol; Journal Broad joint courses; Media Perf; TV Rad)

Sheffield Hallam – 280 pts (Media St)

Stirling – BBC (pre-application experience req) (Journal St)

Swansea – 280 pts (3AL) 200 pts (2AL) (Media St courses)

UCE Birmingham – 280 pts (Media Comm (Mus Ind) (Journal) (Multim) (Rad Prod) (PR) (Media Photo) (TV) (Web NMedia))

260 pts **Bradford** – 260 pts (Crea Media Tech; Media Tech Prod)

Brunel – 260 pts (Comm Media St)

Edge Hill – 260 pts (Journalism)

Glasgow Caledonian – BCC (Journal; Media Comm)

Lincoln – 260 pts (Journalism)

Northumbria – 260 pts (Mass Comm; Media Cult Soty)

Ulster – 260 pts (Media St)

Wolverhampton – 260–320 pts (Journal Edit Des)

240 pts **Bangor** – 240–260 pts (Cyfathrebu a' Cyfryngau; Comm Media; Journal Media St; Thea Media St)

Bradford – 240 pts (Media St courses)

Brighton – 240 pts (Comm Dig Media; Comm Media St)

Bristol UWE – 240–280 pts (Media Cult St Pol; Media Cult St Sociol; Media Cult St EFL; Media Cult St Fr/Ger/Span; Media Cult St Lat Am St; Media Cult St Crim; Media Cult St Phil)

Buckingham – 240 pts (Comm Media St; Journal Comm St; Engl Lit St Journal; Journal Int St)

Cardiff (UWIC) – CCC (Broad Media Pop Cult)

Central Lancashire – 240–220 pts (TV Prod; Journal Comb; Media Prod Tech; Dig Journal Prod; Int Journal)

City – CCC (BEng Media Comm Sys)

Coventry – 240–280 pts (Comm Cult Media; Journal Engl; Journal Media)

Dundee – 240 pts 1st yr entry (Interact Media Des)

Edge Hill – 240 pts (Media (Adv) (Film TV))

Glamorgan – 240 pts (Journal; Media Crim Cult)

Hertfordshire – 240 pts (Journal Comb St; Media Cult Comb St; Media Prac Mgt)
Kingston – 240–320 pts (Media Cult St)
Lincoln – 240 pts (Media Tech)
Liverpool John Moores – 240 pts (Media Cult St Mark)
Middlesex – 240 pts (Crea Media Writ; Media Cult St; Journal Comm St; Pub Media)
Napier – 240 pts (Journalism)
Nottingham Trent – 240 pts (Media Cult St courses)
Oxford Brookes – CCC **or** CCcc (Comm Media Cult)
Plymouth – 240–220 pts (Media Prac Soty; Sci Media)
Portsmouth – 240–300 pts (Media St joint courses; Dig Media)
Robert Gordon – CCC (Pub Journal)
Roehampton – 240 pts (Media Cult; Journal News Media)
Salford – 240 pts (Media Lang Bus; Media Tech)
Staffordshire – 240–280 pts (Journal; Broad Journal; Spo Journal)
Ulster – CCC–CCD 240–220 pts (Media St Comb)
Winchester – 240–220 pts (Media Prod; Journal)
220 pts **De Montfort** – 220–240 pts (Media St)
Edge Hill – 220 pts (Media (Dig Media Des))
Falmouth (UC) – CCD 220 pts (Broad; Engl Media St; Journal)
Glamorgan – 220–260 pts (Media Prod; Media Prod (Rad); Media St; Multim Tech; Media Tech Prod)
Lampeter – CCD–CDD 220–200 pts (Media St; Media Prod)
Lincoln – 220 pts (Media Cult Comm)
Liverpool Hope – 220 pts (Media courses)
Manchester Met – 220–280 pts (Multim Tech)
Middlesex – 220 pts (Journalism)
Queen Margaret (UC) – 220 pts (Media; Media Cult; PR Media)
Southampton Solent – 220 pts (Spo Writ; Spo Media)
Staffordshire – 220 pts (TV Rad Doc)
UCE Birmingham – 220–240 pts (Multim Tech; Multim Dev)
Winchester – 220 pts (Media St Comb courses)
200 pts **Barnsley (Univ Centre)** – 200 pts (Adv Media Rel)
Bath Spa – 200–240 pts (Media Comm courses)
Central Lancashire – 200 pts (Aud Vis Media Journal; Media Prod Tech)
Coventry – 200–220 pts (Media Prod)
Creative Arts (UC) – 200 pts (Arts Media)
Glamorgan – 200–240 pts (Media Pol Comm)
Gloucestershire – 200 pts (Prt Journal)
Huddersfield – 200–180 pts (Cult Media Soc)
Kingston – 200–260 pts (Media Tech)
Liverpool John Moores – BB (Media Prof St; Multim Arts; Broad Tech)
Napier – 200 pts (Pub Media; Cult Media Soty)
Oxford Brookes – CDD **or** CDdd (Media Tech)
Roehampton – 200 pts (Media Cult; Journal News Media)
Southampton Solent – 200–180 pts (Journal; Mag Journal FtreWrit; Media Comm; Media Cult St)
Sunderland – 200 pts (Broad Journal; Media Cult Comm; Media Prod; Journal courses)
180 pts **Anglia Ruskin** – 180–220 pts (Comm St courses)
Bolton – 180 pts (Media Writ Prod)
Chichester – 180–240 pts (Media St; Media Prod Media St)
De Montfort – 180–200 pts (Journal joint courses; Media St joint courses)
Lampeter – open admission policy (Media St; Media Prod; Film Media)
Marjon (Coll) – 180–240 pts (Writ Media; Media courses; Crea Media Prac; Contemp Cult Media Soty)
Northampton – 180–220 pts (Media St; Journal)

Paisley – BC–CC (Media)
Staffordshire – 180–240 pts (Media St courses; Mus Broad)
Teesside – 180–240 pts (Media Mus Tech; Crea Multim)
160 pts **Abertay Dundee** – CC (Media Cult Soty)
Arts London – 160 pts (Journal; Media Cult St)
Bedfordshire – 160–240 pts (Media Prod; Media Prac; Journal)
Bell (Coll) – CC (Journalism)
Canterbury Christ Church – CC (Film Rad TV St; Media Cult St joint courses)
Central Lancashire – 160–200 pts (Aud Vis Media courses except under **200 pts**; Media Prod Tech Aud Vis Media)
Cumbria – CC 160 pts (Media Prod; Journa; Multim Des Dig Animat; Crea Writ)
De Montfort – 160–240 pts (Media Tech; Broad Tech)
Derby – 160–180 pts (Broad Media; Media Apps courses; Media St)
East London – 160 pts (Media St; Journal; Media Crea Ind)
Farnborough (CT) – 160–200 pts (Media Tech)
Greenwich – 160 pts (Journal PR Mark)
Leeds Trinity and All Saints (Coll) – 160–240 pts (Spo Journal; Media; Engl Media; Media Mark; Spo Hlth Leis Media)
London Met – 160 pts (Media St; Dig Media courses; Mass Comm courses)
London South Bank – CC (Media Soty; Writ Media Arts; Media Comb)
Paisley – CC–DD (Multim Tech)
Portsmouth – 160 pts (Dig Media)
St Mary's (Coll) – CC (Media Arts; Prof Crea Writ Media Arts)
Southend Campus Essex – 160–180 pts (Journal; Dig Imag Interact Media)
Southampton Solent – 160 pts (Media Tech)
Swansea (IHE) – 160 pts (Multimedia)
Thames Valley – 160–180 pts (Media Arts; Journal courses; Multim; NMedia; Journal courses)
Trinity Carmarthen (Coll) – CC (Media St courses)
Wolverhampton – 160–220 pts (Media Comm St; Media Cult St; Dig Media)
Worcester – 160 pts (Media Cult St; Crea Dig Media)
York St John – 160 pts (Media (Interact Media))
140 pts **Liverpool John Moores** – 140–220 pts (Broad Tech)
London Met – 140 pts approx (Snd Media)
Teesside – 140–160 pts (Media Prod Prof Prac; Media St; TV Prod Prof Prac)
120 pts **Buckinghamshire Chilterns (UC)** – 120–180 pts (Media St courses; Journal courses; Media Cult Soty)
London Met – (Journal via Fdn course only)
North East Wales (IHE) – 120–80 pts (Media St courses; Media Comm Writ; Rad Prod Media Comm)
80 pts **Bristol UWE** – Fdn Art (Media Prac)
Creative Arts (UC) (M) – 80 pts (Vid Media Arts)
Creative Arts (UC) (F) – (Journal; Fash Jounal)
Northbrook (Coll) – 80 pts (Dig Journal; Media Arts)
Northumbria – 80 pts Fdn Art (Contemp Photo Prac)
Portsmouth – Fdn Art (Media St)
Suffolk (Univ Campus) – 80–120 pts (Film Media St courses)
Wirral Met (Coll) – 80 pts (Media St)

Leeds Met – contact University

Alternative offers
IB offers Aberystwyth 28 pts; Birmingham 32–34 pts; Brighton 28 pts; Bristol UWE 28–32 pts; Chester 30 pts; Chichester 28 pts; City indiv assessment; Keele 28–32 pts; London (RH) 34 pts; Newcastle 30–32 pts; Salford 31 pts; Staffordshire 28 pts; Stirling 32 pts; Surrey 32–35 pts; Winchester 24–26 pts.
Scottish offers See **Chapter 7**.

OTHER HIGHER EDUCATION COURSES IN THE SUBJECT FIELD

Foundation degrees (contact institutions for details) Arts London (CComm); Barnet (Coll); Barnfield (Coll); Barnsley (Univ Centre); Bedfordshire; Bradford (Coll); Brighton; Cornwall (Coll); Croydon (Coll); Darlington (Coll); Lambeth (Coll); Liverpool John Moores; Llandrillo Cymru (Coll); London (Birk); London Met; Milton Keynes (Coll); Nescot; Newham (Coll); Peterborough Reg (Coll); Plymouth (CAD); Ravensbourne (CDC); Solihull (Coll); South Devon (Coll); Teesside; Truro (Coll); Wolverhampton.

Higher National Diploma courses
140 pts and below

Anglia Ruskin; Barnet (Coll); Basingstoke (Coll); Bath; Bedfordshire; Blackpool and Fylde (Coll); Buckinghamshire Chilterns (UC); Burton (Coll); Carmarthenshire (Coll); Cleveland (CAD); Cornwall (Coll); Crawley (Coll); Dudley (Coll); East Berkshire (Coll); East Lancashire (IHE); Farnborough (CT); Glasgow Met; Gloucestershire (CAT) (NCJT course); Grimsby (IFHE); Guildford (Coll); Ealing, Hammersmith and West London (Coll); Havering (Coll); Henley (Coll); Hertfordshire; Huddersfield; Leeds Met; Lincoln; Liverpool (CmC); Llandrillo Cymru (Coll); Middlesex; Neath Port Talbot (Coll); Nescot; Pembrokeshire (Coll); Peterborough Reg (Coll); Plymouth (CAD); St Helens (Coll); Salisbury (Coll); Sheffield (Coll); Solihull (Coll); South Birmingham (Coll); South Devon (Coll); South Kent (Coll); South Nottingham (Coll); Staffordshire; Stoke on Trent (Coll); Stratford-upon-Avon (Coll); Sutton Coldfield (Coll); Thames Valley; Truro (Coll); Wakefield (Coll); West Herts (Coll); West Nottinghamshire (Coll); Weymouth (Coll); Worcester; Worcestershire New (Coll).

CHOOSING YOUR COURSE (SEE ALSO CH.1)

Subject information Intending Media applicants need to check course details carefully since this subject area can involve graphic design, illustration and other art courses as well as the media in the fields of TV, radio and journalism. Courses in Journalism include block and day release, pre-academic year, pre-entry calendar year, evening/weekend magazine journalism, and photo-journalism. Full details can be obtained by referring to www.nctj.com/courses. **Useful websites** www.bbc.co.uk; www.newspapersoc.org.uk; www.ppa.co.uk; www.reuters.com/careers; www.arts.org.uk; www.nctj.com; www.ipa.co.uk; www.camfoundation.com; www.mediastudies.com.

Course variations Sports Journalism (Brighton); Fashion Journalism (Creative Arts (UC)); Arts and Media (Creative Arts (UC)); Media, Crime and Culture (Glamorgan); Media, Politics and Communication (Glamorgan); Public Relations and Media (Queen Margaret (UC)); Science and the Media (Plymouth); Magazine Writing and Features Journalism (Southampton Solent); TV and Radio Documentary (Staffordshire); Media and Communications (Web and New Media) (UCE Birmingham). *NOW CHECK PROSPECTUSES AND WEBSITES FOR ANY RECENT CHANGES.*

Universities and colleges teaching quality See www.tqi.ac.uk; www.qaa.ac.uk.

Top universities and colleges (Research) (including Communication and Cultural Studies) Birmingham; Bristol UWE; East Anglia; East London; London (Gold), (RH); Stirling; Sussex; Westminster.

Sandwich degree courses Bradford; Brunel; Huddersfield; UCE Birmingham; Ulster.

ADMISSIONS INFORMATION

Number of applicants per place (approx) Birmingham 10; Bournemouth (Interact Media Prod) 24, (Multim Journal) 30; Bradford 13; Bristol UWE 20; Canterbury Christ Church 23; Cardiff 11; Cardiff (UWIC) 3; Central Lancashire 33; Chichester 6; City 50; Creative Arts (UC) 3; Cumbria 4; De Montfort 11; East London 27; Falmouth (UC) 4; Gloucestershire 25; Greenwich 12; Lincoln 4; London (Gold) 13, (RH) 11; London South Bank 11; Marjon (Coll) 33; Newport 12; Northampton 4; Northumbria 14; Nottingham Trent 5; Paisley 6; Portsmouth 5; Sheffield Hallam 56; Southend Campus Essex 10; Southampton Solent (Journal) 20, (Media Tech) 6; Swansea (IHE) 5; Teesside 33; Winchester (Film St Media Prod) 7; Westminster 44.

Advice to applicants and planning the UCAS personal statement Work experience or work shadowing is important. Contact local newspaper offices to meet journalists and to discuss their work. Contact local radio stations and advertising agencies, read newspapers (all types) and be able to describe the different approaches of newspapers. Watch TV coverage of news stories and the way in which the interviewer deals with politicians or members of the public. Give your opinions on the various forms of media. School magazine and/or any published work should be mentioned. **Bournemouth** (Non-EU students) Fluency in written and spoken English required. **Staffordshire** Creativity, problem-solving, cultural awareness, communication skills and commitment. **UCE Birmingham** A balance of academic and practical skills. See also **Communication Studies/Communications** and **Appendix 2**.

Misconceptions about this course **Cardiff (UWIC)** Some applicants believe that the course will automatically lead to a job in the media – it won't. This depends on the student developing other employment skills and experience. **Cumbria** This is not a Media Studies course: it is a highly practical media production course. **Lincoln** (Media Prod) BTEC applicants may think that this is a technology-based course. **UCE Birmingham** That Media courses are soft options: they are not!

Selection interviews **Yes** Bournemouth, Brunel, Creative Arts (UC), East Anglia, Glamorgan, Huddersfield, Liverpool John Moores, London (Gold), (RH), London South Bank, Marjon (Coll), Portsmouth, Sheffield Hallam, Solihull (Coll), South East Essex (Coll), Staffordshire, Swansea (IHE), Thames Valley, Wakefield (Coll), York; **Some** Cardiff, Cardiff (UWIC), Chichester, City, Nottingham Trent, Salford, Sunderland, West Herts (Coll), Wolverhampton.

Interview advice and questions Past questions include: Which newspapers do you read? Discuss the main differences between the national daily newspapers. Which radio programmes do you listen to each day? Which television programmes do you watch? Why do you think that ITV needs to spend £32 million advertising itself? Should the BBC broadcast advertisements? What do you think are the reasons for the popularity of *EastEnders*? Film or video work, if required, should be edited to a running time of 15 minutes unless otherwise stated. **Cardiff (UWIC)** What is your favourite area in respect of popular culture? Are you considering taking up the work placement module? If so where would you plan to go? **Cumbria** Role of journalism in society. What is today's main news story? Who is Rupert Murdoch? **Lincoln** Give a written or verbal critique of a media product. See **Chapter 6**.

Reasons for rejection (non-academic) No clear commitment (to Broadcast Journalism) plus no evidence of experience (now proving to be essential). Mistaken expectations of the nature of the course. Can't write and doesn't work well in groups. Too specific and narrow areas of media interest, for example, video or script-writing. Lack of knowledge of current affairs. **Cardiff (UWIC)** Lack of experience in the field. Application arrived too late. **City** Inadequate English language.

AFTER-RESULTS ADVICE

Universities with vacancies in Clearing (2006) Bolton; Bradford; Bristol UWE; Canterbury Christ Church; Central Lancashire; Chester; Cumbria; Derby; East Anglia; East London; Edge Hill; Glamorgan; Gloucestershire; Greenwich; Hertfordshire; Huddersfield; Keele; Kingston; Lampeter; Lancaster; Lincoln; Liverpool Hope; Liverpool John Moores; London (Gold), (QM), (RH); London Met; London South Bank; Manchester Met; Middlesex; Northampton; Nottingham Trent; Plymouth; Portsmouth; Roehampton; Sheffield Hallam; Southampton Solent; Staffordshire; Stirling; Sunderland; Swansea; Teesside; Thames Valley; Ulster; UCE Birmingham; Westminster; Wolverhampton; Winchester; Worcester; York St John.

Offers to applicants repeating A-levels **Same** Cardiff, Cardiff (UWIC), Chester, Chichester, City, De Montfort, Huddersfield, Lincoln, Loughborough, Manchester Met, Nottingham Trent, Salford, Southend Campus Essex, Staffordshire, Sunderland, UCE Birmingham, Winchester, Wolverhampton.

GRADUATE DESTINATIONS AND EMPLOYMENT (2005 HESA)

Graduates surveyed 3935 **Employed** 2390 **In further study** 235 **Assumed unemployed** 345. **Journalism graduates surveyed** 910 **Employed** 585 **In further study** 75 **Assumed unemployed** 55.

OTHER DEGREE SUBJECTS FOR CONSIDERATION

Advertising; Communications; English; Film, Radio and TV Studies; Journalism; Photography; Public Relations.

MEDICINE

(see also **Medical Sciences** under **Health Sciences/Studies)**

NB The points totals shown to the left of the institutions are for ease of reference only. It must not be assumed that tariff points are always used by institutions or that they can be substituted for an offer in grades. The level of an offer is not necessarily indicative of the quality of a course.

Applicants for places in Medicine may select only four universities or medical schools.

COURSE OFFERS INFORMATION

Subject requirements/preferences **GCSE Brighton and Sussex MS** Mathematics and English grade B. **Dundee** Biology. **East Anglia** Five subjects grade A/B. **Keele** English language, mathematics, science grade B if not offered at A/AS-level; four–five grade As. **Imperial London, Leeds** AAABB from chemistry, mathematics, physics, biology, English. **London (King's), (St George's)** Grade B in mathematics, English, physics, double science if not at A/AS-level. **London (QM)** Six subjects grade A/B. **London (UCL)** English language, mathematics grade B. **Manchester** Five subjects grade A including science subject, English language grade B. **Newcastle, Durham** (Stockton) Grades AAAAB including English, mathematics, biology, chemistry, physics, double science. **Nottingham** Six subjects grade A including chemistry, biology, physics and grade B English and mathematics. **Oxford** Mathematics, biology, physics or double science. **Peninsula (MS)** Seven subjects grade A/B including English, mathematics, double science or biology if not at A/AS-level. **Southampton** Seven subjects at grade A and B including mathematics, English, double science or equivalent. **AL** See **Your target offers** below.

NB Home and EU–funded students applying for entry to Medicine are required by many universities to sit either the UKCAT or BMAT tests before applying. See Your target offers below, Chapter 5 and Chapter 6 for further information.

Your target offers

360 pts **and above**

Belfast (Queen's) – AAAa (inc AL chem+sci; AS biol b min) (Medicine)

Cambridge – AAA +BMAT (inc AL chem+1 sci; 4AS in yr 12; some colleges may require 3 sci ALs) (Medicine)

Dundee – AAA +UKCAT (inc chem+sci) (Medicine)

Edinburgh – AAAb +UKCAT (inc AL chem+1 from maths/phys/biol; AS biol min) (Medicine 5/6 yrs)

Imperial London – AABb +BMAT (3AL) AABC +BMAT (4AL) (inc AL biol/chem+sci/maths) (Medicine)

Liverpool – AABb 390 pts (inc 2 sci BB, sci subjs to inc chem+biol at AL/AS) (Medicine)

London (King's) – AABc +UKCAT **or** ABbbc +UKCAT (inc AL chem/biol **or** AS b chem/biol) (Medicine)

London (King's) – ABBc +UKCAT **or** ABbbc +UKCAT (Nat Sci Fdn Med)

London (St George's) – AABb +UKCAT (BBCb for schools with AL average 245 pts and below) (inc AL chem/biol **or** AS chem/biol b) (Medicine)

London (UCL) – AABa +BMAT (inc AL chem; 1 AL maths subj only req; 4AS in yr 12 inc biol+chem) (Medicine)

Newcastle and Durham – AAA +UKCAT (inc AL chem/biol pref 1 non-sci at AL/AS) (Medicine)

Oxford – AAA +BMAT (inc AL chem+1 from biol/phys/maths) (Medicine)

Peninsula (MS) – 370–400 pts +UKCAT (max 3AL inc 1 sci) (Medicine)

340 pts **Aberdeen** – AAB +UKCAT (chem desirable+1 from biol/maths/phys+1 other) (Medicine)

Birmingham – AAB 340–360 pts (inc AL chem+1 from biol/maths/phys; AS biol min) (Medicine)

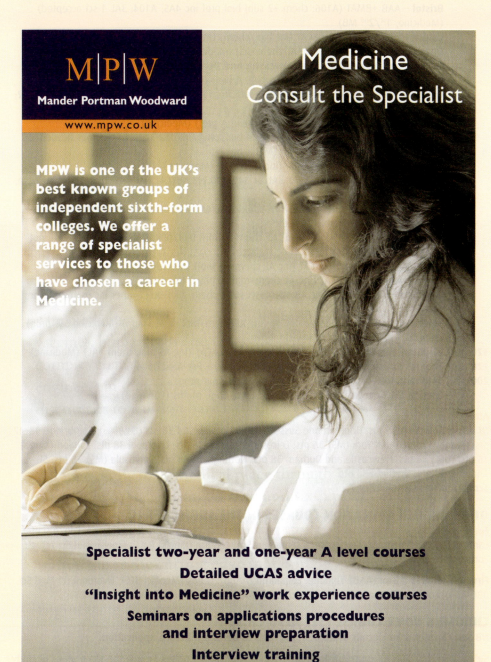

case in a family and social context as well as in the hospital), who treat patients and colleagues with respect, dignity and sensitivity, are skilled at teamwork and prepared for continual learning. These aims in several ways reflect the qualities which selectors will seek when interviewing applicants. In all cases, close attention will be paid to the confidential report on the UCAS application to judge the applicant's personality, communication skills, academic potential and commitment to a medical career. Whilst there is a core curriculum of knowledge, the first three years integrate scientific and clinical experience, and there are fewer formal lectures than before and more group and individual work. For outstanding students without science A-levels, some pre-medical courses are available. Thereafter for all, a period of pre-clinical studies leads on to clinical studies. Intercalated courses of one year leading to a BSc are also offered and elective periods abroad in the final years can sometimes be taken. **Useful websites** www.scicentral.com; www.ipem.org.uk; www.bmj.com; www.bmat.org.uk; www.gmc-uk.org; www.nhscareers.nhs.uk.

Course variations Six-year Pre-Medicine courses: Bristol; Cardiff (Fdn); Dundee; Edinburgh; London (King's) (Fdn in Nat Sci); Manchester; Sheffield (Fdn yr); Southampton (Widening access route).

Universities and colleges teaching quality See www.tqi.ac.uk; www.qaa.ac.uk.

Top universities and colleges (Research) Belfast (Queen's); Cardiff; Dundee*; Liverpool; London (King's)*; Liverpool; Newcastle*.

ADMISSIONS INFORMATION
Number of applicants per place and places (**a** UK **b** EU (non-UK) **c** non-EU **d** mature). Note that numbers quoted of applicants per place are approximate, and that all medical schools have a limited quota of places for non-EU applicants.

Aberdeen ab1513 for 162 places; **c**270 for 13 places (preference given to applicants from countries unable to provide a medical training); **Belfast (Queen's) a**4 **c**(a small number of places are allocated); **Birmingham a**5, **c**25 Grad entry 12; **Brighton and Sussex (MS) a**10; **Bristol** 16 (**ab**2683 **c**383 **d**1100: total places 246); **Cambridge a**5; **Cardiff a**20 (6-year course) **c**22 (preference given to applicants from countries not providing a medical training); **Dundee a**7 (Pre-Med yr 11); **East Anglia a**7; **Edinburgh a**11 (international applicants not normally called for interview); **Glasgow a**6, **c**20; **Hull York (MS) a**13; **Imperial London a**7 **c**25; **Leeds a**2156 **b**97 **c**352 **d**488; **Leicester Warwick a**7; **Liverpool a**8; **London (King's) ab**311 places **c**25 places; **London (QM) a**8 **c**20; **London (St George's)** 19 (**a**3200 **b**250 **c**260 **d**1950: total places 292; **London (UCL) a**8 **c**14; **Manchester a**8 **c**10; **Newcastle and Durham a**10 (Pre-Med yr 27; **c**14; **Nottingham a**9 **c**15; **Oxford a**26% success rate **c**10; **Peninsula (MS) a**9; **St Andrews a**8; **Sheffield a**17.

Admissions tutors' advice Policies adopted by all medical schools are very similar. However, a brief outline of the information provided by admissions tutors is given below. Further information should be

obtained direct from institutions. Applicants wishing to contact medical schools should do so either by letter or by telephone and not by e-mail.

Aberdeen Interviews for some applicants. Overseas applicants may be interviewed abroad. Interviews last about 15 minutes. Most offers made in March. Points equivalent results not accepted. Re-sits not normally accepted. International students English language entry requirement (or equivalent): IELTS 7.0. Minimum age on entry 17 years 5 months. Clinical teaching and patient contact in Year 2.

Belfast (Queen's) Majority of applicants are school-leavers; 95% from Northern Ireland. Aptitude tests under consideration for 2007. A proportion of candidates will be called for interview. Interviews last about 15 minutes. A small number of places are allocated to non-EU applicants. Offer for repeating applicants AAA. Number of places restricted for re-sit applicants who must have narrowly missed an offer at Queens. Clinical experience from Year 1.

Birmingham Non-academic interests and extra-curricular activities noted in addition to academic factors. General studies not accepted, but points equivalent results may be accepted. Interviews last about 15 minutes with three interviewers, a GP, a surgeon and a student. Approximately 1000 called for interview. 10% take a year off which does not jeopardise the chances of an offer but candidates must be available for interview. Re-sit candidates who failed by a small margin are only considered in exceptional circumstances. Transfers of undergraduates from other medical schools not considered. Clinical studies from Year 3.

Brighton and Sussex (MS) General studies not accepted. No offers without an interview. Interviews last about 15 minutes with three selectors. Students are members of both universities. Years 3–5 take place in the new Medical Education Centre at the Royal Sussex Hospital in Brighton. Clinical experience from Year 1.

Bristol Selection in stages. Top 10% of applicants called for interview, remainder grouped into three categories: 'high reserve', 'hold' and 'unsuccessful' – some from the first two categories will be interviewed. Widening participation panel considers appropriate candidates, 50 of whom will be interviewed. Criteria for selection – realistic and academic interest in medicine; commitment to helping others; wide range of interests; contribution to school/college activities; personal achievements. Interview criteria – reasons for wanting to study medicine; awareness of current developments; communication skills; self-confidence; enthusiasm and determination to study; ability to cope with stress; awareness of the content of the course and career. Gap year acceptable but applicants must be available for interview. Points equivalent results not accepted. International students English language requirement (or equivalent): IELTS 7.0. Clinical practice from Year 4.

Cambridge Some colleges insist on three science/maths subjects. Normally two interviews each of 20 minutes each. Films of interviews on www.cam.ac.uk/admissions/undergraduate/interviews. Gap year acceptable but for positive reasons. Clinical studies from Year 4. 50% of students continue at the Cambridge Clinical School (Addenbrooke's Hospital).

Cardiff Great emphasis placed on evidence of a caring nature and exposure to hospital/health environments. Applicant's comment: 'Two interviewers and a 15-minute interview. Mainly questions on "Why medicine". Very helpful students'. Points equivalent results not accepted. Clinical studies from Year 1.

Dundee Preference given to candidates who achieve the right grades at the first sitting. Interviews – 20 minutes. Deferred entry acceptable. Clinical attachments in Year 4.

Durham (see also **Newcastle**) The medical course is offered in partnership with Newcastle University. Study is at Queen's Campus, Stockton. Preference given to applicants with relevant work experience in caring environment, hospital, voluntary capacity or through previous employment. Particular interest in recruiting local students, either school leavers or mature students. Interviews at Stockton with two selectors; may include a written personal qualities assessment test (PQA). Applicants from non-EU countries must apply to Newcastle where there is a quota of places for overseas students. Clinical contact begins in Year 1.

East Anglia Screening of applications done by two selectors. Criteria include academic requirements, capacity to cope with self-directed learning, team work, responsibility, motivation. Interview regarded as the acid test; lasts 30–45 minutes including two scenarios (examples online at www.med.uea.ac.uk/mbbs/mbbs_application). Clinical experience from Year 1.

Edinburgh All examination grades must be achieved at the first sitting; only in extenuating circumstances will re-sits be considered. Equal weighting given to academic and non-academic criteria. Non-academic criteria score based on personal qualities and skills, evidence of career exploration prior to application, breadth and level of non-academic achievements and interests. Work experience and work shadowing viewed positively but the admissions panel recognise that not all applicants have equal opportunities to gain such experience. Most school-leaving applicants interviewed, also short-listed graduate and mature applicants. International applicants not normally called for interview. Clinical experience from Year 1.

Glasgow Formal work experience expected. (Work experience scheme operated by staff at Monklands Hospital, Lanarkshire.) All interviews held in Glasgow including those for overseas students. Interviews assess candidates' performance on five points (i) knowledge of the medical course and experience of self-directed learning, (ii) experience of teamwork, (iii) communication skills, (iv) understanding of a medical career, (v) enthusiasm and commitment to medicine. Only in extenuating circumstances (family illness etc) will second-time applications be considered. Points equivalent results not accepted. Feedback available to all candidates who fail to achieve admission. Transfers from other medical schools not accepted. Clinical experience from Year 1.

Hull York (MS) Students allocated places at Hull or York by ballot in Years 1 and 2. Non-EU applicants English language (or equivalent requirement) IELTS 7.0. Transfers from other medical schools not accepted. Disabilities listed on UCAS application do not affect the assessment of the application.

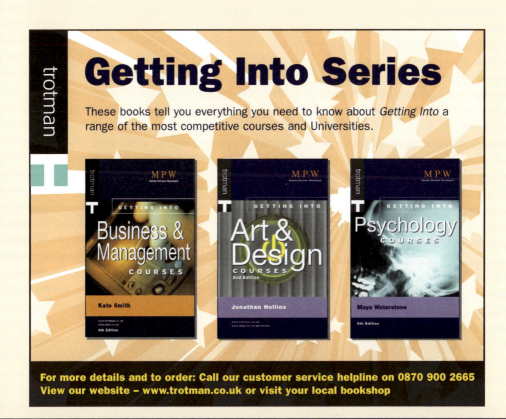

For information on how to read the Subject Tables, see **Chapter 7**.

444 | Medicine

Formally structured Interviews exploring academic ability, motivation, understanding of healthcare issues, communication skills, conscientiousness, empathy, tolerance and maturity. Questions are drawn from a bank of possible topics (available online prior to interview). Re-sits acceptable but with higher grades. Feedback to unsuccessful candidates not possible. Clinical placements from Year 1.

Imperial London Fifteen–minute interviews with panel of 4–5 selectors. Not aimed at being an intimidating experience – an evaluation of motivation, capacity to deal with stress, evidence of working as a leader and team member, ability to multitask, likely contribution to university life, communication skills and maturity. Admissions tutor's comment: 'We look for resourceful men and women with wide interests and accomplishments, practical concern for others and those who will make a contribution to the life of the school and hospital.' Results within two weeks. Re-sit candidates must have applied to Imperial School of Medicine previously, have achieved at least CCC and have predictions of AAA in the winter re-sit examinations and have extenuating circumstances to explain previous failure in the referee's statement. Candidates may also write directly to the School. Clinical contact in Year 1.

Keele (see also **Manchester**) Keele is in partnership with the Manchester Medical School. Years 1 and 2 take place in Manchester, Years 3–5 in Keele. All applications are submitted to Manchester showing one of three study preferences – Manchester, Keele or either.

Leeds Admissions tutors' comment: 'Consider your motivation carefully – we do!' Good verbal, non-verbal and presentational skills required. Candidates should: be able to report on some direct experience of what a career in medicine is about; show evidence of social activities on a regular basis (eg, part-time employment, organised community experiences); show evidence of positions of responsibility and interests outside medical and school activities. Gap years encouraged but candidates must be available for interview. 20% of all applicants interviewed. Points equivalent results not accepted. International students English language requirement (or equivalent): IELTS 7.5. Re-applications from students who have achieved the right grades accepted. Re-sits only considered in exceptional circumstances and with good supporting evidence; offer AAA. Transfers from other medical schools not encouraged. Clinical practice commences in Year 4.

Leicester Warwick Students resident in Leicester. Final award is a combined degree from both universities. Interview lasts 20 minutes with two selectors (one doctor and one final-year medical student; both have had interview training). Interview not an academic test. Selectors each score independently on motivation, communication skills and suitability for a career in medicine. Gap years acceptable. Re-sits considered only in exceptional circumstances; offer AAA. Transfers from other medical schools not accepted. Clinical work commences in Year 1.

Liverpool Gap years acceptable for positive reasons but applicants must be available for interview. Gap year not possible for overseas students. First year Foundation programme offered for under-qualified international students. English language requirement (or equivalent): IELTS 7.5. Clinical contact from Year 1.

London (King's) Personal statement a significant factor in selection. Emphasis placed on appreciation of academic, physical and emotional demands of the course, commitment, evidence of working in a caring environment, communication skills and interaction with the general public. Approximately 1200 applicants (35%) called for interview. Foundation course available. Clinical contact in Year 1.

London (QM) Personal statement a significant factor in selection. 'You are expected to write your own, with an honest reflection of your strengths and interests and you will be closely questioned on this statement at interview. We don't want people who are simply good at science. High grades are no guarantee of a place.' Interview of 15–20 minutes. Re-sits only considered in exceptional cases; offer AAA. Clinical experience from Year 1.

London (St George's) Applicants must be taking A-level chemistry and biology (or one to A-level and the other to AS-level). They will be required to complete their A-levels within two years of study and be predicted between BBC and AAA and have taken a 4th distinct AS-level in which they have achieved (or are predicted) a B. If not your application will be unsuccessful. However if you are predicted AABb and have at least 416 pts from 8 subjects at GCSE including mathematics, English and dual award science (ie average of grade A) then you will be called for interview. All applicants expected to have undertaken work experience in a medical environment. No offers without an interview – predicted grades important in selecting candidates for interview. Four selectors and an interview of 15–20 minutes. Some students who are not predicted to get the grades of our offer are also interviewed and considered for a place. (Fdn Med) This course is for mature non-graduate students only. Transfers from other medical schools rare. Foundation year offered for under-qualified applicants. International students English language requirement (or equivalent): IELTS 7.0. Clinical experience commences in Year 3.

London (UCL) Three selectors interview applicants, each interview lasting 15–20 minutes. Qualities sought include motivation, awareness of scientific and medical issues, ability to express and defend opinions, maturity and individual strengths. 30% of applicants interviewed. Deferred entry for good reason is acceptable. Repeat applications only considered if candidate has previously received and held a firm offer from Royal Free or University College Medical School. Minimum age of entry: 18 years. Transfers from other medical schools not accepted. International students may take the University Preparation Certificate for Science and Engineering (UPCSE) which is the minimum entry requirement for entry to medicine. Clinical attachments commence in Year 3.

Manchester (see also **Keele**) 341 places at Manchester/ 55 places at Keele. Minimum age of entry 17 years. Interviews with three selectors last about 15 minutes. If you feel unwell before the interview inform the admissions tutor and the interview will be re-scheduled; pleas of infirmity cannot be accepted after the interview! Candidates should be aware of the advantages and disadvantages of problem-based learning and opinions may be asked. Ethical questions may be raised. Decisions will be made by the end of March. Re-sit offers only made to applicants who received an offer after interview the previous year and who marginally failed to achieve the required grades; increasingly such offers are only made in the light of extenuating circumstances. Clinical attachments from Year 3.

Newcastle (see also **Durham**) 220 places at Newcastle; 95 places at Durham. Applicants' comments (Durham): 'Two interviewers and a 25 minute interview. Very relaxed interview. Stockton campus small. Good community spirit but some way from Durham'; (Newcastle): 'I had an interview with two selectors who had a gentle, helpful manner. I didn't feel under pressure but felt stretched'. Retakes not considered except in special circumstances. Deferred entry accepted. Consideration given to candidates who have overcome significant disadvantages (eg caring for parents with ill health). Clinical experience from Year 3.

Nottingham Candidates receive preliminary online questionnaire to be completed. Interviews 15 minutes with two selectors. Re-sit applicants who have previously applied will be reconsidered but only in extenuating circumstances. Deferred entry acceptable. International students English language requirement (or equivalent): IELTS 7.0. No transfers accepted from other medical schools. Clinical experience from Year 1.

Oxford Applicants called for interview on the basis of academic performance, test score and information on the application form. Ratio of interviewees to places: approximately 2.5 to 1. No student admitted without an interview. All colleges use a common set of selection criteria. Candidates comment (Lincoln College): 'Two interviewers and two interviews. Questions covered my hobbies and social life, and scientific topics to test my logical train of thought. A great university, but it's not the be-all and end-all if you don't get in'. Clinical experience commences in Year 4.

Peninsula (MS) In the first two years students will be based at either the Universities of Exeter or Plymouth, selection taking place on a random basis. Qualities sought on the application and at interview – integrity and honesty; motivation and commitment; empathy and non-judgemental attitudes; communication and listening skills; teamwork; ability to cope with stress; problem-solving skills; awareness of one's strengths and weaknesses; reflectiveness; suitable approach to life and people. Applicant's comment: 'I was asked to stand in the middle of the room and to demonstrate my commitment to medicine in one minute! They then asked me to write my responses to a series of questions.' Written questionnaire at interview. Clinical skills training commences in the first year.

446 | Medicine

St Andrews Medical Science students take full three-year programme leading to BSc (Hons), followed by clinical studies at Manchester University. Interviews last about 20 minutes with two or three selectors. Special attention given to international students and those who achieve qualifications at more than one sitting. As far as possible the interview panel will reflect the gender and ethnic distribution of candidates for interview.

Sheffield Applications processed between October and end of March. Candidates may send additional information concerning extenuating circumstances or health problems. Interviews last 20 minutes with up to three selectors. Candidates re-sitting for the first time may be considered: offer AAA. Gap year acceptable; medicine-related work very helpful. Clinical experience from Year 1.

Southampton In the personal statement and at interview applicants should be able to demonstrate that they are (i) self-motivated and have initiative, (ii) literate and articulate, (iii) able to interact successfully with others, (iv) able to demonstrate that they have learnt from their experiences with people in health and social care settings. Interviews normally last 20 minutes with two selectors. Deferred entry accepted. Candidates who wish to change their year of entry should submit requests before mid-March. Patient contact from Year 1.

Warwick – See under **Leicester Warwick**

Advice to applicants and planning the UCAS personal statement (See also **Admissions Tutors' advice**).

NB Nearly all universities now require either the new UKCAT or BMAT entry tests to be taken before applying for Medicine. Check websites (www.ukcat.ac.uk; www.bmat.org.uk) for details of test dates and test centres and with universities for their requirements. The medical admission process is changing fast and it is essential that you check for the latest information before applying and that you give yourself plenty of time to make arrangements for sitting these tests (see also **Chapter 6**).

Four Medicine choices only may be listed on the UCAS application which must be submitted by 15 October. Applicants may add up to two alternative courses. However, if they receive offers for these courses and perform better than expected, they will not be able to request medical schools to reconsider their application in Clearing. 'Don't rush around doing things just for your CV. If you are a boring student be an incredibly well-read boring student! You can play netball, rugby, hockey, make beautiful music and paint with your feet, but if you fail to get the grades you'll be rejected.' Some 13,000 applications are submitted for Medicine each year with approximately 4,700 candidates being successful. Admissions tutors obviously look for certain personal qualities and these will emerge in your personal statement, at the interview and on your school or college reference. There should be evidence of scientific interest, commitment, enthusiasm, determination, stability, self-motivation, ability to organise your own work, interest in the welfare of others, communication skills, modesty (arrogance and over-confidence could lead to rejection!), breadth of interest, leadership skills, stamina, good physical and mental health.

Some kind of first-hand experience in a medical setting is almost obligatory for those applying for Medicine (see also under **Admissions tutors' advice**). Depending on your personal contacts in the medical profession, this could include observing operations (for example, orthopaedic surgery), working in hospitals and discussing the career with your GP. Remember that your friends and relatives may have medical conditions that they would be willing to discuss with you – and all this will contribute to your knowledge and show that you are informed and interested. Read medical and scientific magazines and keep up-to-date with important current issues – AIDS, avian 'flu, euthanasia, abortion. Community work, clubs, societies, school and social activities should be mentioned. Show that you have an understanding of the role of health professionals in society and the social factors that influence health and disease.

Misconceptions about this course **Liverpool** Some applicants think that three science subjects at A-level are required to study Medicine. **London (St George's)** That you should be white, middle class and male: 60% of medical students are now female and 53% of our students are not white.

Selection interviews See **Admissions tutors' advice**. See also **Chapter 6**.

Interview advice and questions Questions will vary between applicants, depending on their UCAS statements and their A/AS-level subjects. Questions are likely to relate to A-level specific subjects, general medicine topics and unconnected topics (see also under **Admissions tutors' advice**). The following questions will provide a guide to the range of topics covered in past interviews. Outline the structure of DNA. What is meant by homeostasis? Is a virus a living organism? What has been the most important advance in biology in the last 50 years? What interests you about (i) science, (ii) biology, (iii) chemistry? Why did you choose the particular AS/A-level subjects you are doing? Why do you want to study Medicine/become a doctor? Do you expect people to be grateful? Why do you want to study here? Why should we take you? Do you agree with the concept of Foundation hospitals? Do you think NHS doctors and staff should be able to take private patients? If you were in charge of finances for a large health authority, what would be your priorities for funding? If you had to decide between saving the life of a young child and that of an old person, what would you do? Would you treat lung cancer patients who refuse to give up smoking? What do you understand by 'gene therapy'? Can you give any examples? In your opinion what is the most serious cause for concern for the health of the UK? What do you want to do with your medical degree? What do you think the human genome project can offer medicine? Should we pay for donor organs? Where do you see yourself in 15 years' time? What was the last non-technical book you read? What is your favourite piece of classical music? List your top five novels. What is your favourite play? What politician do you admire the most? Who made the most valuable contribution to the 20th century? Why do you think research is important? Why is teamwork important? What do you think about the NHS's problems? What do you think about euthanasia, cloning, etc? Do you think that sport is important? What did you gain from doing work experience in a nursing home? What were the standards like? How does the medical profession deal with social issues? What societies will you join at university? How could you compare your hobby of rowing with medicine? Do you agree that it is difficult to balance the demands of being a doctor with those of starting a family? In doing a medical course, what would you find the most emotionally challenging aspect? How would you cope with emotional strain? What do you think about going to war with Iraq? Who should have priority for receiving drugs in an avian 'flu epidemic/pandemic? How would you deal with the death of a patient? What are stem cells? Why are they controversial? How is cloning done? What constitutes a human being? Describe an egg. How can you measure intelligence? How do we combat genetic diseases? How are genes actually implanted? What do you want to talk about? If you were a cardio-thoracic surgeon, would you perform a heart by-pass operation on a smoker? What are the negative aspects of becoming a doctor? At some interviews essays may be set, eg (i) a scientific education is a good basis for a medical degree: discuss, (ii) only drugs that are safe and effective should be prescribed to patients. Occasionally applicants at interview may be given scenarios to discuss (see **East Anglia** under **Admissions tutors' advice**). See **Chapter 6**.

Applicants' impressions See under **Admissions tutors' advice**.

Reasons for rejection (non-academic) Insufficient vocation demonstrated. No steps taken to gain practical experience relevant to medicine. Doubts as to the ability to cope with the stress of a medical career. Not enough awareness about the career. Lack of knowledge about the course. Applicant appears dull and lacking in enthusiasm and motivation. Lacking in a caring, committed attitude towards people. No evidence of broad social, cultural or sporting interests or of teamwork. Poor or lack of communication skills. Uncaring attitude. Arrogance. Over-confident at interview. Unrealistic expectations about being a doctor.

Age at entry Applicants must be 17 years old on 30 September of the year of entry. However, some medical schools stipulate 17 years 6 months, and a small number stipulate 18 years. Those considering entry at 17 would probably be advised to take a gap year.

Health requirements Medical schools require all students to have their immunity status for hepatitis B, tuberculosis and rubella checked on entry. Offers are usually made subject to satisfactory health screening for hepatitis B. In line with advice from the General Medical Council, students will not be admitted to courses who are found to be e-antigen positive when screened within the first week of the course. Candidates accepting offers should assure themselves of their immunity status. **Dyslexia** Applicants with dyslexia should contact the admissions office prior to application. It is expected that most students will have successfully adapted to their medical condition. Whilst some medical schools may allow a limited amount of extra time for purely academic examinations, eg essays and multiple choice questions, the British Dyslexia Association and medical schools generally take the view that absolutely no concessions should be made in the conduct of clinical examinations.

Advice to mature students Medical schools usually accept a small number of mature students each year. However, several, if not the majority, reject applicants over 30 years of age. Some medical schools accept non-graduates although A-level passes at high grades are usually stipulated. The majority of applicants accepted are likely to be graduates with a first or upper second honours degree. **Birmingham**, **Bristol**, **Leeds** Maximum age at entry is 30 years. **Leeds** Applicants should hold the required A-level grades or a high class science degree; 15–20 places. **Southampton** 36 places available, maximum age 40; GCSE mathematics, physics, biology or double science required. Applicants with nursing qualifications should hold two grade B A-levels including chemistry. Mature students taking Access courses must achieve 70% in A2 chemistry.

Advice to graduate applicants Graduate applicants are considered by all medical schools. At some medical schools the Graduate Australian Medical Schools Admission Test (GAMSAT) and the Medical Schools Admissions Test (MSAT) are now being used to assess the aptitude of prospective applicants. Applicants, for example, at **Peninsula (MS)**, are selected on the basis of three criteria (i) an honours degree at 2.2 or above, (ii) the GAMSAT score, (iii) performance at interview. All applicants must be EU students. **London (St George's)** Some students think that science graduates are the only ones to do well in GAMSAT: 40% of those on the course do not have a science degree or A-levels; however, work experience is essential.

GRADUATE DESTINATIONS AND EMPLOYMENT (2005 HESA)
Graduates surveyed 3960 **Employed** 2735 **In further study** 5 **Assumed unemployed** 5.

OTHER DEGREE SUBJECTS FOR CONSIDERATION
Anatomy; Biochemistry; Biological Sciences; Biology; Biomedical/Medical Materials Science; Biology; Biotechnology; Clinical Sciences; Dentistry; Dietetics; Genetics; Health Sciences; Medical Physics; Medical Sciences; Midwifery; Nursing; Nutrition; Occupational Therapy; Optometry; Pharmacology; Pharmacy; Physiology; Physiotherapy; Psychology; Radiography; Speech Sciences – and Law! (The work of doctors and lawyers is similar in that both are required to identify the relevant information – symptoms or legal issues!)

MICROBIOLOGY

(including **Immunology;** see also **Biological Sciences, Biology, Biotechnology** and **Genetics**)

NB The points totals shown to the left of the institutions are for ease of reference only. It must not be assumed that tariff points are always used by institutions or that they can be substituted for an offer in grades. The level of an offer is not necessarily indicative of the quality of a course.

COURSE OFFERS INFORMATION
Subject requirements/preferences GCSE English and mathematics. **Edinburgh** Mathematics grade B. **Leeds** Mathematics grades A–C. **Leicester** Chemistry grade A–C if not taken at A/AS-level. **Reading** Mathematics grade B. **Surrey** Chemistry grade A if not offered at A/AS-level. **AL** One or two science subjects required, usually including chemistry.

Your target offers
360 pts Warwick – ABBc (Microbiol Virol)
340 pts Imperial London – AAB–ABB 340–320 pts (Microbiology)
　　　　　Manchester – AAB–BBB (Microbiol; Microbiol Ind; Microbiol Modn Lang)

---

320 pts **Birmingham** – ABB–BBC (Biol Sci (Microbiol))
Cardiff – ABB–BBB (Microbiology)
Newcastle – ABB–BBB (Med Microbiol Immun)
Sheffield – ABB (Microbiol courses)

300 pts **Bristol** – BBB (Path Microbiol; Med Microbiol)
Dundee – 300 pts 2nd yr entry (Microbiology)
East Anglia – BBB–BBC (Microbiology)
Edinburgh – BBB (Microbiol Infec)
Leeds – BBB–BBC (Microbiol; Med Microbiol; Microbiol Immun; Microbiol Virol)
Leicester – BBB (Biol Sci (Microbiol))
London (QM) – BBB–BCC 300–260 pts (Bioch Microbiol; Genet Microbiol)
Nottingham – BBB (Microbiology)
Surrey – BBB–BCC (Microbiol; Microbiol (Med); Microbl Genet; Fd Sci Microbiol; Bioch (Tox))

280 pts **Aberdeen** – BBC 2nd yr entry (Microbiology)
Aston – BBC 280 pts (Infec Immun)
Liverpool – BBC–BBB 280–300 pts (Microbiol; Microbl Biotech)
Reading – 280 pts (Med Microbiol)
Strathclyde – BBC (Bioch Microbiol; Immun Microbiol)

260 pts **Belfast (Queen's)** – BCC/AB (Microbiology)
Bradford – 260 pts (Med Microbiol)
Glasgow – BCC–CCC (Microbiology)
Nottingham – BCC–CCC (Fd Microbiol)

240 pts **Aberdeen** – CCC 1st yr entry (Microbiology)
Aberystwyth – CCC **or** CCcc 240 pts (Microbiology)
Dundee – 240 pts 1st yr entry (Microbiology)
Portsmouth – 240–260 pts (Microbiology)
Staffordshire – CCC–DDD 240–180 pts (Bioch Microbiol)

220 pts **Liverpool John Moores** – 220 pts (Microbiol; App Microbiol)

200 pts **Anglia Ruskin** – 200 pts (Microbiology)
Huddersfield – 200 pts (Microbl Sci)
Manchester Met – 200 pts (Med Env Microbiol)
Napier – 200 pts (Microbiol Biotech)
Nottingham Trent – 200 pts (Microbiol courses)

180 pts **Bristol UWE** – 180–220 pts (App Microbiol)
Glamorgan – 180–220 pts (Microbiology)
Glasgow Caledonian – DDD (Microbiology)
Heriot-Watt – DDD (Microbiology)
Hertfordshire – 180–200 pts (Microbiology)

160 pts **London Met** – 160 pts (Microbiology)
London South Bank – CC (Biosci (Microbiol))
Middlesex – 160 pts (Biol Sci Microbiol)
Westminster – CC (Microbiology)
Wolverhampton – 160–220 pts (Microbiol; Biotech Microbiol)

Alternative offers
IB offers Cambridge 38–42 pts; Manchester 32–35 pts; Newcastle 32–35 pts; Nottingham 24–30 pts; Reading 30 pts; Sheffield 33 pts; Surrey 30–32 pts.
Scottish offers See **Chapter 7**.

OTHER HIGHER EDUCATION COURSES IN THE SUBJECT FIELD

Foundation degrees (contact the institution for details) St Helens (Coll).

Higher National Diploma courses East London; Hertfordshire; Wolverhampton.

For information on how to read the Subject Tables, see **Chapter 7**.

CHOOSING YOUR COURSE (SEE ALSO CH.1)

Subject information Microbiology is a branch of biological science specialising in the study of micro-organisms: bacteria, viruses and fungi. The subject covers the relationship between these organisms and disease and industrial applications such as food and drug production, waste-water treatment as well as future biochemical uses. **Useful websites** www.scienceyear.com; www.sgm.ac.uk; see also under **Biochemistry**, **Biological Sciences** and **Biology**.

Course variations Pathology and Microbiology (Bristol); Immunology with Medical Microbiology (East London); Microbiology and Infection (Edinburgh); Genetics with Microbiology (London (QM)); Medical Microbiology and Immunity (Newcastle); Medical Food Science and Microbiology (Surrey); Microbiology and Virology (Warwick). *NOW CHECK PROSPECTUSES AND WEBSITES FOR ANY RECENT CHANGES.*

Universities and colleges teaching quality See www.tqi.ac.uk; www.qaa.ac.uk.

Top universities and colleges (Research) Leeds; see also **Biological Sciences**.

Sandwich degree courses Aston; Bristol; Bristol UWE; Cardiff; Glamorgan; Leeds; Liverpool John Moores; London South Bank; Nottingham Trent. See also **Biochemistry** and **Biological Sciences**

ADMISSIONS INFORMATION

Number of applicants per place (approx) Aberystwyth 5; Bradford 6; Bristol 6; Cardiff 4; Dundee 5; Leeds 7; Liverpool 3; Strathclyde 10; Surrey 4; Swansea 5; Wolverhampton 4.

Advice to applicants and planning the UCAS personal statement Relevant experience, particularly for mature students. See **Biological Sciences**. See also **Appendix 2**.

Selection interviews Yes Bristol, London South Bank, Nottingham (depends on application), Surrey, Swansea; **Some** Aberystwyth (mature applicants only), Cardiff, Leeds, Liverpool John Moores, Wolverhampton.

Interview advice and questions Examples of past questions include: Is money spent on the arts a waste? How much does the country spend on research and on the armed forces? Discuss reproduction in bacteria. What do you particularly like about your study of biology? What would you like to do after your degree? Do you have any strong views on vivisection? Discuss the differences between the courses you have applied for. What important advances have been made in the biological field recently? How would you describe microbiology? Do you know anything about the diseases caused by micro-organisms? What symptoms would be caused by which particular organisms? See **Chapter 6**.

AFTER-RESULTS ADVICE

Universities with vacancies in Clearing (2006) Aberdeen; Aberystwyth; Belfast (Queen's); Birmingham; Bradford; Bristol UWE; Dundee; East Anglia; Glasgow; Huddersfield; Leicester; Liverpool; Nottingham; Reading; Sheffield; Surrey; Warwick.

Offers to applicants repeating A-levels Higher Bristol, Strathclyde, Swansea, Warwick; **Possibly higher** East Anglia, Nottingham; **Same** Aberystwyth, Anglia Ruskin, Bradford, Cardiff, Leeds, Liverpool, Wolverhampton.

GRADUATE DESTINATIONS AND EMPLOYMENT (2005 HESA)

Graduates surveyed 490 **Employed** 220 **In further study** 140 **Assumed unemployed** 35.

OTHER DEGREE SUBJECTS FOR CONSIDERATION

Animal Sciences; Biochemistry; Biological Sciences; Biology; Biotechnology; Genetics; Medical Sciences; Medicine; Pharmacology; Physiology.

MUSIC

NB The points totals shown to the left of the institutions are for ease of reference only. It must not be assumed that tariff points are always used by institutions or that they can be substituted for an offer in grades. The level of an offer is not necessarily indicative of the quality of a course.

COURSE OFFERS INFORMATION

Subject requirements/preferences GCSE Bangor Music grade A or B. **Colchester (Inst)** Five subjects at grade A–C. **Edinburgh** Five–eight A–B grades including a foreign language. **Glasgow** English, mathematics or science and a foreign language. **Leeds** Eight subjects mostly A*, A or B grades. **London (RH)** A good range of As and Bs preferred. **Oxford**, **Cambridge** A good range of grades A and B. **AL** Music plus an instrumental grade usually required.

NB Some applications are made through the Conservatoires Admissions Service (CUKAS): see **Chapter 5** for details.

Music examinations Additional points will be awarded for Music examinations from the Associated Board of the Royal Schools of Music (ABRSM), the Guildhall School of Music and Drama, the London College of Music Examinations (LCMM) and Trinity College of Music music examinations at grades 6, 7, 8 (D=Distinction; M=Merit; P=Pass).

Practical:	Grade 6 – D 45 pts; M 40 pts; P 25 pts.
	Grade 7 – D 60 pts; M 55 pts; P 40 pts.
	Grade 8 – D 75 pts; M 70 pts; P 55 pts.
Theory:	Grade 6 – D 15 pts; M 10 pts; P 5 pts.
	Grade 7 – D 20 pts; M 15 pts; P 10 pts.
	Grade 8 – D 30 pts; M 25 pts; P 20 pts.

Music examinations Additional points will be awarded for Music examinations from the Associated Board of the Royal Schools of Music (ABRSM), the Guildhall School of Music and Drama, the London College of Music Examinations (LCMM) and Trinity College of Music music examinations at grades 6, 7, 8 (D=Distinction; M=Merit; P=Pass).

Your target offers

360 pts and above
    Cambridge – AAA (Music)
    Imperial London – AAA (Phys St Musl Perf)
    Manchester – AAA–AAB (Mus; Mus Dr)
    Oxford – Offers vary eg AAA–AAB (Music)

340 pts Birmingham – AAB–ABB (Mus courses)
    Cambridge (Hom) – AAB–ABB (BA Mus Educ St)
    Durham – AAB (Mus Comb Arts)
    London (King's) – AAB+AS **or** AAaab (Mus; Mus Dig Hum; Ger Mus)
    Nottingham – AAB (Mus; Mus Phil)
    Surrey – AAB (inc gr 7) (Mus Snd Rec (Tonmeister))
    Sussex – 340 pts (Mus Inform)
    York – AAB–ABB (Mus Tech Sys)

320 pts Bristol – 320 pts ABB (inc ABRSM gr 5 piano) (Mus; Mus Fr/Ger/Ital)
    Cardiff – ABB–BBC gr 8 theor+gr 8 prac (BA/BMus courses)
    Durham – ABB (Mus; Mus Educ)
    Glasgow – ABB (+ gr 8 for BMus) (Music)

Liverpool – ABB 320 pts (Mus; Mus Pop Mus; Pop Mus)
London (RH) – ABB (inc gr 7 instr) (Mus Fr/Ger/Ital/Span; Mus Mgt; Mus Pol St)
Newcastle – ABB (BA Mus/BMus Folk Trad Mus; Pop Contemp Mus)
Sheffield – ABB–BBC (Mus courses)
Southampton – ABB 320 pts (Mus courses)
Sussex – ABB–BBB 3AL+AS (inc gr 7) (Mus; Mus Cult St; Mus Film St; Mus Fr/Ger/Ital/Span)
York – ABB (Music)

300 pts **Belfast (Queen's)** – BBB–BBCb (Mus; Ethnomus)
East Anglia – ABC (Mus Maths)
Edinburgh – BBB (Mus; Mus Tech)
Huddersfield – 300 pts (Mus; Mus Journal; Mus Lang; Mus Dr; Mus Engl; Mus Hist)
Lancaster – BBB–BBC (Mus; Musicol; Mus Tech)
Leeds – ABC (inc ABRSM gr 5 not prac mus/mus tech) (Music)
London (Gold) – BBB (Mus; Pop Mus St)
York – BBB–BBC (BEng Mus Tech)

280 pts **Brunel** – 280 pts (inc gr 6/7 instr/vocal) (Engl Mus; Dr Mus; Film TV St Mus; Crea Mus Tech)
City – BBC–BCC (inc gr 7) (Wrld Mus St)
Coventry – 280 pts (Mus Tech)
East Anglia – BBC–BCC (Mus; Mus Comp)
Hull – BBC–BBB (inc gr 7 or above on 1st study instr/voice) (Mus Fr/Ger/Ital/Span)
Kent – 280 pts (Mus Tech)
Leeds – BBC (Mus Multim Electron; Pop Wrld Mus)
Liverpool – BBC–BBB 280–300 pts (Comm Media Pop Mus)
Staffordshire – 280 pts (Crea Mus Tech; Mus Tech Mgt)
Surrey – BBC (Mus; Mus Comp Snd Des)
UCE Birmingham – 280 pts (Media Comm (Mus Ind))

260 pts **Bangor** – 260–280 pts (Music)
Cardiff – BCC (Phys Mus)
Huddersfield – 260–320 pts (Mus Tech courses; Pop Mus Prod; Vid 3D Pop Mus)
Keele – 260–320 pts (Mus; Mus Tech)
Liverpool (LIPA) – BCC (Music)
London (SOAS) – BCC/BB (Mus courses)
Royal Welsh (CMusDr) – 260–180 pts (Mus (gr 8 principal instrument); Pop Mus; Perf Prod; apply direct)
Stranmillis (UC) – BCC (Mus Educ)
Ulster – BCC 260 pts (Music)
Winchester – 260 pts (Perf Arts Mus Thea)

240 pts **Aberdeen** – CCC/BB (BMus Mus; Mus St courses)
Chester – 240–260 pts (Media (Commer Mus Prod); Pop Mus; Perf New Media Pop Mus)
Glasgow – AA–DD (Mus BEd)

Hertfordshire – 240 pts+pts from graded mus exams (inc gr 5 theor) (Mus Cmpsn Tech; Snd Des Tech; Mus Tech; Mus Enter Ind Mgt)
Hull – 240–300 pts (BA/BMus Mus)
Hull (Scarborough) – CCC–BBB 240–300 pts (Crea Mus Tech; Crea Mus Tech Bus Mgt; Crea Mus Tech Dance)
Leeds (CMus) – 240 pts (Mus; Jazz; Pop Mus St; Mus Prod)
Liverpool John Moores – 240 pts (3AL) 180 pts (2AL) (Pop Mus St)
Portsmouth – 240 pts (Mus Snd Tech)

220 pts **Bath Spa** – 220 pts (Crea Mus Tech)
Bristol UWE – 220–240 pts (Mus Sys Eng; Crea Mus Tech)
Chichester – 220 pts (Perf Arts Mus)
De Montfort – 220 pts (Mus Tech Innov)
Glamorgan – 220 pts (Snd Tech)
Liverpool Hope – 220 pts (Mus; Mus Tech)
London (RAcMus) – AB–BC (BMus Mus)
Staffordshire – 220 pts (Mus Broad)
Sunderland – 220–180 pts (Mus courses)
Swansea (IHE) – 220 pts (Mus Tech)
UCE Birmingham – 220–240 pts (Mus Tech; Snd Multim Tech)
Winchester – 220 pts (Perf Arts Theol Relig St)

200 pts **Anglia Ruskin** – 200–240 pts (Mus; Mus Dr; Mus Engl; Crea Mus Tech; Crea Mus Tech Mus)
Barnsley (Univ Centre) – 200 pts (Mus Media Prom)
Bath Spa – 200–240 pts (+ gr 8) (Mus; Crea Arts)
Coventry – 200–220 pts (Mus Prof Prac; Mus Cmpsn Prof Prac)
Glamorgan – 200 pts (Pop Mus)
Hull – 200–280 pts (Mus Tech Comp; Crea Mus Tech)
Lincoln – 200 pts (Aud Tech)
Manchester Met – 200 pts (Mus; Pop Mus; Snc Arts)
Middlesex – 200–240 pts (Mus; Mus Arts Mgt; Jazz; Snc Arts; Mus Commun)
Napier – 200 pts (Mus; Pop Mus)
Oxford Brookes – CDD **or** CDdd/CDE (joint hons)) (Mus; Snd Tech Dig Music)
Salford – 160–200 pts (Mus; Pop Mus Rec)
Teesside – 200–240 pts (Media Mus Tech; Dig Mus Crea; Crea Dig Media)

190 pts **London Met** – 190 pts (Mus Media Mgt)

180 pts **Barnsley (Univ Centre)** – 180 pts (Pop Mus)
Bridgwater (Coll) – 180 pts (Crea Mus Tech)
Central Lancashire – 180–220 pts+audition (Mus Prac)
Derby – 180 pts (Multim Tech Mus Prod; Mus Tech Aud Sys Des; Pop Mus Prod; Pop Mus Mus Tech; Snd Lt Live Evnt Tech; Crea Expr Thera)
Kingston – 180–320 pts (Mus joint courses)
Liverpool (LIPA) – BC 180 pts (Snd Tech; Mus Arts Enter Mgt)
Northampton – 180–220 pts (Crea Dig Mus courses)
Plymouth – 180 pts (Mus; Mus Educ St)
Reading – 180 pts (Educ St Mus)
Roehampton – 180 pts (Music)
Southampton Solent – 180 pts (Pop Mus Rec Prod)

160 pts **Bedfordshire** – 160 pts (Mus Tech)
Bishop Grosseteste (Coll) – DDE 160 pts (Educ St Mus)
Brighton – 160 pts (Dig Mus)
Canterbury Christ Church – CC (Music)
Chichester – 160–200 pts/gr 8+C (Mus; Mus joint courses)
Colchester (Inst) – BD 160 pts (Music)
Cumbria – CC 160 pts (Educ Mus; Mus QTS Spec; Musl Thea)
Dartington (CA) – 160–200 pts (Mus (Cmpsn); Mus (Perf))
East London – 160 pts (Mus Cult (Theor Prod); Perf Arts)
Kingston – 160 pts (Music)

For information on how to read the Subject Tables, see **Chapter 7**.

London Met – CC 160 pts (Mus Tech (Aud Sys); Mark Musl Instr; Mus Media Mgt; Mus Educ)
Newcastle (Coll) – 160 pts (BMus Pop Jazz Commer Mus)
Paisley – CC (Commer Mus)
Southend Campus Essex – 160 pts (Mus Prod)
Southampton Solent – 160 pts (Aud Tech)
Strathclyde – CC (App Mus)
Thames Valley – 160 pts (Mus Perf Comp; Mus Tech; Pop Mus Perf)
Truro (Coll) – 160 pts (Contemp Wrld Jazz)
Westminster – CC (Commer Mus; Commer Mus Perf)
Wolverhampton – 160–220 pts (Mus; Mus Tech Pop Mus; Pop Mus)
York St John – 160 pts (Perf Mus; Mus)

140 pts **Barnsley (Univ Centre)** – 140–180 pts (Crea Mus Tech Snd Rec)
Bath Spa – 140 pts (Commer Mus)
Cardiff (UWIC) – 140 pts (Mus Aud Electron Sys)
Doncaster (Univ Centre) – DEE 140 pts (Crea Mus Tech)
Thames Valley – 140 pts (Mus Media; Mus Evnt Mgt)

120 pts **Buckinghamshire Chilterns (UC)** – 120–180 pts (Mus Ind Mgt)
North East Wales (IHE) – EEE 120 pts (Std Rec Perf Tech)
Paisley – DD (Mus Tech)
RCMus – 120 pts (Music)
Southampton Solent – 120 pts (Aud Tech Fdn)

100 pts **and below**
Arts Educ (Sch) – 2AL (Mus Thea)
Arts London – 80 pts (Snd Arts Des)
Arts London (CComm) – 100 pts (Music)
Barnsley (Univ Centre) – 100 pts (Mus Ext)
Birmingham (Consv) – 80 pts+audition (BMus; BMus Jazz)
Glamorgan – 80–140 pts (Mus Tech)
Grimsby (IFHE) – 100 pts check with admissions tutor (Crea Mus)
Guildhall (Sch Mus Dr) – 100 pts (Mus; Thea)
Herefordshire (CAD) – 100 pts (Perf Arts)
Manchester (RNCM) – 80–120 pts (BMus; Mus)
Northbrook (Coll) – 100 pts (Mus Cmpsn Prof Media)
Rose Bruford (Coll) – 100 pts individual interview/audition (Act Mus; Mus Tech)
Royal Scottish (RSAMD) – (Mus; BA Scot Mus; Scot Mus Piping)
Royal Welsh (CMD) – 100 pts min+ABRSM gr 8+gr 5 theory (Mus; Pop Mus min age 20)
SAE (Inst) – EE 80 pts (Rec Arts)
Southend Campus Essex – 80 pts (Mus Prod)
TrCMus – (inc gr 8) (BMus (Perf); MMus (Perf St))
UCE Birmingham/Birmingham Consv – 80 pts (Mus; Jazz)
UHI Millennium Inst (PC) – (Mus Perf)
Weston (Coll) – 80 pts **or** mus tech qual (Crea Mus Tech)

Leeds Met – contact University

Alternative offers
IB offers Aberdeen 30 pts; Birmingham 34 pts; Bristol 34 pts; Bristol UWE 26–28 pts; Brunel 30 pts; Cambridge 38–42 pts; Chester 30 pts; Chichester 26 pts; City indiv assessment; Keele 28–30 pts; Kent 28 pts; Liverpool 31 pts; London (King's) 36 pts, (RH) 35 pts, (SOAS) 30 pts; Manchester 35–37 pts; Manchester Met 28 pts; Newcastle 34 pts; Nottingham 30–32 pts; Salford 28 pts; Sheffield 30–32 pts; Southampton 33 pts; Surrey 30 pts; York 34 pts.
Scottish offers See **Chapter 7**.

OTHER HIGHER EDUCATION COURSES IN THE SUBJECT FIELD
Foundation degrees (contact institutions for details) Barnsley (Univ Centre); Bath Spa; Bedfordshire; Bournemouth and Poole (Coll); Burnley (Coll); Chichester; Colchester (Inst); Coventry; Cumbria; Durham

New (Coll); Farnborough (CT); Gateshead (Coll); Glamorgan; Hull (Coll); Isle of Wight (Coll); Kendal (Coll); London Met; Manchester City (Coll); Newcastle (Coll); North Devon (Coll); North East London (Coll); Northbrook (Coll); Peterborough Reg (Coll); Plymouth; Preston (Coll); RNCB; St Helens (Coll); South Thames (Coll); Teesside; Thames Valley; Truro (Coll); West Anglia (Coll); West Kent (Coll); Westminster City (Coll); Weymouth (Coll); York St John.

Higher National Diploma courses

140 pts   and below

Accrington and Rossendale (Coll); Bath Spa; Bournemouth and Poole (Coll); Bridgwater (Coll); Brighton; Cambridge Reg (Coll); Cardiff (UWIC); Derby; Doncaster (Univ Centre); Eastleigh (Coll); Filton (Coll); Forth Valley (Coll); Great Yarmouth (Coll); Havering (Coll); Herefordshire (CAD); London Met; Manchester City (Coll); Nelson and Colne (Coll); Newcastle (Coll); Northbrook (Coll); Nottingham New (Coll); People's (Coll); Salford; Salisbury (Coll); South Downs (Coll); Southend Campus Essex; Strode (Coll); UHI Millennium Inst (PC); Wakefield (Coll); Worcester (CT); Worcester.

CHOOSING YOUR COURSE (SEE ALSO CH.1)

Subject information Theory and practice are combined to a greater or lesser extent in most Music courses. The menu of options is varied – choose with care! See also **Appendix 2**. **Useful websites** www.arts.org.uk; www.communitymusic.org; www.ism.org; www.bpi-med.co.uk; www.royalopera.org; www.nyo.org.uk; www.bbc.co.uk/youngmusican

Course variations Combined Arts (Durham); Creative Music Technology (Hull (Scarborough)); Musicology (Lancaster); Popular and World Musics (Leeds); Music Technology (Liverpool Hope); Folk and Traditional Music (Newcastle); Popular Music Recording (Salford); Music and Sound Recording (Surrey); Music Informatics (Sussex). *NOW CHECK PROSPECTUSES AND WEBSITES FOR ANY RECENT CHANGES.*

Universities and colleges teaching quality See www.tqi.ac.uk; www.qaa.ac.uk.

Top universities and colleges (Research) Bangor; Belfast (Queen's); Birmingham*; Bristol; Cambridge*; Cardiff; City*; Huddersfield; Hull; London (Gold), (King's), (RH), (SOAS); Manchester*; Newcastle*; Nottingham*; Oxford*; Sheffield; Southampton*; Sussex; York.

Sandwich degree courses Brunel; Hertfordshire; Huddersfield; Leeds Met; London Met; Staffordshire; Surrey; Teesside; UCE Birmingham.

ADMISSIONS INFORMATION

Number of applicants per place (approx) Aberystwyth 5; Anglia Ruskin 5; Bangor (BA) 4; Bath Spa 8; Belfast (Queen's) 6; Birmingham 12; Bristol 8; Brunel 7; Cambridge 3; Cambridge (Hom) 4; Cardiff 6; Chichester 4; City 7; Colchester (Inst) 4; Cumbria 7; Dartington (CA) 8; Durham 5; East Anglia 12; Edinburgh 11; Glasgow 4; Huddersfield 2; Hull 21; Kingston 18; Lancaster 8; Leeds 18; Liverpool 9; Liverpool (LIPA) 12; London (Gold) 7, (King's) 10, (RH) 7, (RAcMus) 7, (SOAS) 4; London Met 10; Manchester (RNCM) 8; Middlesex 23; Napier 3; Newcastle 24; Northampton 3; Northern (Coll) 3; Northumbria 12; Nottingham 35; Oxford (success rate 61%); Oxford Brookes 12; Roehampton 4; Rose Bruford (Coll) 15; RCMus 10; Royal Scottish (RSAMD) 6; Salford 5, (Pop Mus Rec) 8; Southampton 5; Strathclyde 15; Surrey average 6, (Tonmeister) 12; TrCMus 4; Ulster 8; Worcester 8; York 11; York St John 2.

Interview advice and questions Anglia Ruskin In addition to A-levels, we also require Grade 7 (good pass, first study) plus Grade 5 minimum keyboard standard. **Bangor** Offer depends on proven ability in historical or compositional fields plus acceptable performance standard. Options include music therapy, recording techniques, jazz. **Bath Spa** Some candidates interviewed. Required to perform and sight-read on main instrument, and given aural and critical listening tests. Discussion of previous performing, composing and academic experience. (Fdn Commer Mus) All applicants must submit a self-composed audio prior to interview. **Bristol** (Mus Modn Lang) No in-depth interviews; candidates invited to open days. **Cambridge (St Catharine's)** At interview candidates may have to undergo some simple keyboard or aural tests (such as harmonisation of an unseen melody or memorisation of a rhythm). More importantly, they will have to comment on some unseen musical extracts from a stylistic and analytical point of view. Candidates are also asked to submit some samples of work before the interview, from the fields of harmony and counterpoint, history, and analysis; they are also encouraged to send any other material such as compositions, programme notes or an independent essay on a subject of interest to the candidate. (Taking the STEP examination is not a requirement for admission.) Above all this, though, the main pre-requisite for reading Music at St Catharine's is an *academic* interest in the subject itself. **Cambridge (Hom)** Tests will also include busking accompaniments to children's songs on keyboard. Questions on stylistic features of piece performed. **Canterbury Christ Church** Associated Board examinations in two instruments (or one instrument and voice); keyboard competence essential, particularly for the BEd course. **Colchester (Inst)** Great stress laid on candidate's ability to communicate love of the subject. **Cumbria)** Admission by live performance or on tape. QTS applicants interviewed for teaching suitability. See **Chapter 6**.

Durham We also require Grade 6 piano (Associated Board) and a foreign language (GCSE grade A–C), A-level music grade B. **East Anglia** Only unusual and mature candidates are interviewed. Applicants are expected to perform music with insight and show genuine intellectual curiosity about music and its cultural background. At interview candidates will be asked to perform on their principal instrument. Those who play orchestral instruments or sing will also be expected to play simple music on the piano. At interview we look for applicants with proficiency in instrumental or vocal performance (preferably at Grade 8 standard or above), range of experience of music of many types and an intelligent attitude towards discussion. **Edinburgh** Most candidates are called for interview, although very well qualified candidates may be offered a place without interview. All are asked to submit samples of their work. Associated Board Grade 7 on piano is usually expected. **Glasgow** The BA (Mus Educ) course is for students aiming at a career in school music and is largely keyboard-orientated. The BA (Music Performance) course is for those wanting a career in professional performance (Instrument and Voice). **Huddersfield** Have an open and inquisitive outlook with regard to all aspects of music from performing to composing, musicology to listening. Candidates auditioned on their principal instrument or voice. They will be asked about playing technique, interpretation and interests. **Hull** Good instrumental grades can improve chances of an offer and of confirmation in August. Students are not normally required to attend an audition/interview. Decisions will be made according to the information supplied on the UCAS application. Successful applicants will be invited to attend a departmental open day. We welcome applications from mature students and those with unconventional qualifications: in such cases an interview may be required. **Kingston** Associated Board Grade 8 on main instrument is required, with at least Grade 4 on a keyboard instrument (where this is not the main instrument). Audition and interview may be required. Candidates with non-standard qualifications are interviewed and asked to bring samples of written work.

Lancaster Grade 8 Associated Board required on an instrument or voice and some keyboard proficiency (grade 6) usually expected. We do not accept candidates without interview. For the Music degree, instrumental or vocal skills equivalent to Grade 8 required (not required for Musicology). For Music Technology, applicants should hold music theory grade 5 or be able to demonstrate the ability to read a score. Applicants wishing to take practical studies will need instrumental or vocal skills equivalent to Grade 8. **Leeds** Intending students should follow an academic rather than practical-oriented A-level course. The University is experimenting with abandoning the formal interview in favour of small group open days for those holding offers made on the UCAS information, to focus on a practical exchange of information relevant to the applicant's decision to accept or reject the offer. Grade 8 Associated Board on an instrument is a normal expectation. **Leeds (CMus)** There will be an audition and an essay on music theory. **Liverpool** At interview each candidate is required to take a piano sight-reading test (Associated Board Grade 6) and a series of simple aural tests. They will be asked to play a prepared piece on the piano or on their main instrument (required standard approximately Grade 8), and to enter into a musical discussion on a topic of interest to them. Great importance is attached to performing and composing achievement prior to interview and to potential for future development (intellect, motivation and enthusiasm). **Liverpool (LIPA)** In addition to performing in orchestras etc, give details of any compositions you have completed (the number and styles). Instrumentalists (including vocalists) should describe any performance/gig experience together with any musical instrument grades achieved. **(Mus)** Candidates should prepare two pieces of contrasting music to play on their chosen instrument. Candidates who have put song-writing/composition as either first or second choice should have a cassette, CD or minidisc of their work to play to the panel. (Snd Tech) Applicants must prepare a critical review of a sound recording of their choice which highlights the technical and production values that they think are the most important. Examples of recorded work they have undertaken should also be available at interview eg on CD, cassette or DAT.

London (Gold) The interview will include an aural discussion of music and the personal interests of the applicant. **London (RAcMus)** All candidates are called for audition, and those who are successful are called for a further interview; places are offered later, subject to the minimum GCSE requirements being achieved. **London (RH)** Candidates are tested with an aural test, a harmony/counterpoint test, a conceptual essay, and a *viva* at which they are asked questions and asked to perform. On the basis of the results in these tests we make offers. There is a tradition of caring for each individual and we strive to give each applicant a fair hearing. Musicality, a good intellect and real enthusiasm are the qualities we look for. **London (SOAS)** Candidates are judged on individual merits. Applicants are expected to have substantial practical experience of musical performance, but not necessarily Western music. **RCMus** All UK and Eire candidates are required to attend for audition in person but tapes are acceptable from overseas applicants. It must be stressed, however, that personal audition is preferable and those students offered places on the basis of a tape audition may be required to take a confirmatory audition on arrival. Candidates are required to perform on the principal study instrument as well as undertaking sight-reading, aural tests and paperwork. There is also an interview. Potential scholars sometimes proceed to a second audition, usually on the same day. The academic requirement for the BMus (RCM) course is two A-levels at pass grades. Acceptance is ultimately based on the quality of performance at audition, performing experience and perceived potential as a performer. As a guide, applicants should be of at least Grade 8 distinction standard. **TrCMus** Applicants for the BMus degree must attend an audition and show that they have attained a certain level of competence in their principal and second studies, musical subjects and in musical theory. Grade 8 practical and theory can count as one A-level, but not if the second A-level is in music. Overseas applicants may submit a tape recording in the first instance when a place may be offered for one year. Thereafter they will have to undergo a further test. They must also show evidence of good aural perception in musical techniques and musical analysis.

Manchester (RNCM) All applicants are called for audition. Successful applicants proceed to an academic interview which will include aural tests and questions on music theory and history. Student comment: 'A 45-minute interview with a panel of three. Focus was on portfolio of compositions sent in advance. Prior to interview was asked to harmonise a short passage and study an orchestral excerpt followed up at interview. Aural test waived.' **Newcastle** We expect a reasonable background knowledge of musical history, basic harmony and counterpoint and keyboard skills of approximately Grade 8 standard; if the main instrument is not piano or organ – Grade 5. While practical skills are important, academic ability is the primary requisite. Practical Music or Music Technology accepted in place of Music. **Nottingham** A high standard of aural ability is expected. Interviewees take two short written papers, intellectual enquiry and attainment are looked for, together with a good range of knowledge and sense of enterprise. No places are offered without interview – each offer is tailored to the student at interview: we do not just use the points system. Only borderline/mature students are interviewed, successful applicants are invited to an open day. **Nottingham Trent** Music students require Grade 6 on two instruments. Candidates submit a marked sample of harmony and/or counterpoint and two marked essays on any areas or aspects of music. Candidates may also submit a portfolio of compositions if they wish, but it is not possible to return any copies. Candidates will take the following tests at interview: (i) A one-hour harmony or counterpoint written test (candidates will not have access to a piano); there is no composition option; (ii) A 40-minute aural test in three parts: dictation of a Bach chorale (bass given)/melodic dictation, and identification of errors heard in a two-part piece; (iii) Performance of a prepared piece on the candidate's principal instrument or voice (organists, percussionists and candidates requiring an accompanist should inform the Faculty in advance of the interview period); (iv) Keyboard skills in three parts: score reading of a string quartet; keyboard harmony; and sight-reading (sight-reading examples will take into account candidates' keyboard proficiency). **Oxford** One marked sample of harmony and/or counterpoint and two marked essays on aspects of music required (see also above). Success rate 56%. **Royal Welsh (CMus Dr)** All UK and Eire applicants are called to audition in person; overseas candidates may audition by tape.

Candidates are required to perform on their sight-reading ability. Candidates who are successful in the audition proceed to interview in which there will be a short aural test. Candidates for the BA (Music) course are required to bring recent examples of harmony, counterpoint and essays. **Surrey** (Music) Applicants may expect to be questioned in the interview about their musical experience, enthusiasm and any particular compositions they have studied. They will also be asked to perform on their first instrument. (Mus Snd Rec) Applicants can expect to be questioned about their recording interests and motivation and show an ability to relate A-level scientific knowledge to simple recording equipment. They may be asked to perform on their first instrument. **Wolverhampton** The audition will involve playing/singing a piece of own-choice music (up to five minutes – no longer). Accompanists may be brought along or the department may be able to provide one if requested in advance. Candidates will be requested to produce a short piece of written work. It would be helpful to see any music certificates and a Record of Achievement if available, together with examples of recent work in music (an essay, harmony, composition etc).

Advice to applicants and planning the UCAS personal statement In addition to your ability and expertise with your chosen musical instrument(s), it is also important to know your composers and to take a critical interest in various kinds of music. Reference should be made to these, visits to concerts listed and any special interests indicated in types of musical activity, for example, opera, ballet. Work with orchestras, choirs and other musical groups should also be included and full details given of any competitions entered and awards obtained. **London (Gold)** We encourage students to bring examples of their written and creative work. **Royal Welsh (CMus Dr)** Evidence of performance-related experience, eg youth orchestras, solo work, prizes, scholarships etc. Our course is a conservatoire course as opposed to a more academic university course. We offer a very high standard of performance tuition balanced with academic theory modules. **Surrey** (Music Snd Rec (Tonmeister)) Demonstration of motivation towards professional sound recording. See also **Appendix 2**.

Misconceptions about this course **Cardiff** Some mistakenly think that the BMus scheme is either performance-based or something inferior to the principal music-based degree. **Leeds (CMus)** (Mus St) This is not a performing course: it is a classical performance degree. No pop music on any of our courses. **SAE (Inst)** Some applicants think that this is only a practical course – there is a strong theoretical element. That contemporary music means pop. **Salford** (Pop Mus Rec) This is not a specialised music technology degree, it is a music degree with specialisation in music technology and production. Specialisation can be significant in Year 3. BTEC Popular Music students must be prepared for the rigours of an academic degree. Some students expect the course to make them famous! **Surrey** Some believe that the Music course is exclusively performance-based (the course includes substantial academic and compositional elements).

Selection interviews **Yes** Most institutions, plus audition to include a performance of a prepared piece (or pieces) on main instrument or vocal study; **Some** Anglia Ruskin, Bath Spa, Cardiff, Liverpool (LIPA), Staffordshire (Mus Tech Mgt), Surrey. Details of interview requirements for individual institutions are given in **Chapter 6**.

Applicants' impressions (A=Open day; B=Interview day) **Bath Spa** (B) A formal interview, an audition and a tour of the campus. **Bristol** (A) On the open day we were split into small groups for the talk and tour which included the accommodation. **Cardiff** (B) There was a tour, a 45-minute examination, an audition, but no formal interview (the audition and interview are combined). **Chichester** (B) I had a short informal interview, an audition on one instrument and a course talk. I didn't see the accommodation. **Salford** (B; Mus Tech) There was a performance, theory test and interview. **Southampton** (A) On the open day we had a course talk, a tour of the department and halls and a short chat with head of department. **York** (B) There was one interviewer and one interview of 25 minutes which seemed to be a little haphazard although quite friendly. I was asked questions about my special interests and future career options and also where else I had applied and what was the likelihood of me accepting a place! The course looks good as does the department. Go to the open day or interview before deciding whether or not to accept an offer.

Reasons for rejection Usually academic (auditions, practical, aural/written test). Dull, unenthusiastic students, ignorant about their subject, showing lack of motivation and imagination. **Cambridge** Her harmony was marred by elementary technical errors and her compositions lacked formal and stylistic focus. **Coventry** Proforma used prior to interview (some students rejected at this stage). **London (King's)** Apparent lack of interest, performance not good enough, lack of music history knowledge. Foreign students: language skills inadequate. **Royal Welsh (CMus Dr)** Performing/technical ability not of the required standard.

AFTER-RESULTS ADVICE
Universities with vacancies in Clearing (2006) Aberdeen; Anglia Ruskin; Bangor; Bath Spa; Birmingham; Bristol UWE; Brunel; Canterbury Christ Church; Central Lancashire; Chester; Chichester; Derby; East London; Hertfordshire; Huddersfield; Hull; Keele; Kingston; Lancaster; Liverpool Hope; London (RH), (SOAS); Manchester Met; Middlesex; Roehampton; Staffordshire; Sunderland; Surrey; Thames Valley; Ulster; UCE Birmingham; Westminster; Wolverhampton; York St John.

Offers to applicants repeating A-levels Higher Aberystwyth, Leeds; **Possibly higher** Cambridge (Hom); **Same** Anglia Ruskin, Bath Spa, Bristol, Cardiff, City, Colchester (Inst), De Montfort, Durham, East Anglia, Huddersfield, Hull, Kingston, Leeds (CMus), London Guildhall (Sch Mus), London (RAcMus), (RH), Nottingham, Rose Bruford (Coll), Royal Welsh (CMus Dr), SAE (Inst), Salford, Staffordshire, Surrey, York, York St John.

GRADUATE DESTINATIONS AND EMPLOYMENT (2005 HESA)
Graduates surveyed 2445 **Employed** 1050 **In further study** 585 **Assumed unemployed** 145.

OTHER DEGREE COURSES FOR CONSIDERATION
Acoustics; Drama; Musical Theatre; Performance Arts.

NATURAL SCIENCES
(see also **Biological Sciences** and **Science**)

NB The points totals shown to the left of the institutions are for ease of reference only. It must not be assumed that tariff points are always used by institutions or that they can be substituted for an offer in grades. The level of an offer is not necessarily indicative of the quality of a course.

COURSE OFFERS INFORMATION
Subject requirements/preferences GCSE Cambridge Mainly grade As. **AL** Science subjects required.

Your target offers
360 pts **and above**
        Bath – AAA (Nat Sci; Nat Sci Yr Ind; Nat Sci Yr Abrd)
        Cambridge – AAA (Nat Sci)
        Durham – AAA (Nat Sci courses)
        London (King's) – ABBc **or** ABbbc (Fdn Nat Sci (Dntstry) (Med))
        London (UCL) – AAA+AS–ABB+AS (Nat Sci)
340 pts **Birmingham** – AAB–ABB (Nat Sci; Nat Sci Euro)
        Leeds – AAB (Nat Sci)
320 pts **East Anglia** – ABB (Nat Sci)
        Lancaster – ABB (Nat Sci N Am)
        Newcastle – ABB (Nat Sci)
        Reading – ABB–BBB (Nat Sci)
280 pts **Lancaster** – BBC (Nat Sci)
        Strathclyde – BBC–CCC (BSc Hons Nat Sci)
200 pts **UHI Millennium Inst** – 200 pts check with admissions tutor (Nat Sci)
180 pts **Bristol UWE** – 180–220 pts check with admissions tutor (Nat Sci)
        Strathclyde – DDD/CC (BSc Pass Nat Sci)
        Liverpool John Moores – check with admissions tutor (Fdn Nat Sci)

Alternative offers
IB offers Bath 36 pts; Birmingham 34 pts; Cambridge 38–42 pts; London (UCL) 34–38 pts; Newcastle 34 pts; Reading 32–34 pts.
Scottish offers See **Chapter 7**.

OTHER HIGHER EDUCATION COURSES IN THE SUBJECT FIELD
Foundation degrees (contact institution for details) Liverpool John Moores.

Higher National Diploma courses Anglia Ruskin.

CHOOSING YOUR COURSE (SEE ALSO CH.1)
Subject information Natural Sciences degrees allow the student to obtain a broad view of the origins and potential of science in general, and then to focus on one specialist area of scientific study. **Useful website** www.scienceyear.com; see also **Biology**, **Chemistry** and **Physics**.

Course variations Natural Sciences with a Year in Industry (Bath); Natural Sciences with a Year in Europe (Birmingham); Natural Sciences with a Year in North America (Lancaster); Foundation Natural Sciences for Dentistry and Medicine (London (King's)). *NOW CHECK PROSPECTUSES AND WEBSITES FOR ANY RECENT CHANGES.*

Sandwich degree courses Bath.

ADMISSIONS INFORMATION
Number of applicants per place (approx) Bath 8; Birmingham 11; Cambridge 3; Durham 5.

Advice to applicants and planning the UCAS personal statement See **Biology**, **Chemistry** and **Physics**. See also **Appendix 2**.

Selection interviews **Yes** Bath, Cambridge.

Interview advice and questions **Cambridge** Questions are dependent on subject choices and studies at A-level and past questions have included the following: Discuss the setting up of a chemical engineering plant and the probabilities of failure of various components. Questions on the basic principles of physical chemistry, protein structure and functions and physiology. Questions on biological specimens. Comment on the theory of evolution and the story of the Creation in Genesis. What are your weaknesses? Questions on electro-micrographs. What do you talk about with your friends? How would you benefit from a university education? What scientific magazines do you read? Questions on atoms, types of bonding and structures. What are the problems of being tall? What are the differences between metals and non-metals? Why does graphite conduct? Questions on quantum physics and wave mechanics. How could you contribute to life here? What do you see yourself doing in five years' time? Was the Second World War justified? If it is common public belief that today's problems, for example industrial pollution, are caused by scientists, why do you wish to become one? Questions on the gyroscopic motion of cycle wheels, the forces on a cycle in motion and the design of mountain bikes. What do you consider will be the most startling scientific development in the future? What do you estimate is the mass of air in this room? See **Chapter 6**.

Applicants' impressions (A=Open day; B=Interview day) **Cambridge** I was asked why Cambridge? And why I had chosen their college? I had an interview with the Biology professors. They asked me questions on my personal statement and on biology and what were my views on genetic engineering. I was also asked to design a mammal – challenging but fun! It was a great experience – even though I didn't get an offer!

AFTER-RESULTS ADVICE
Universities with vacancies in Clearing (2006) Liverpool John Moores; Strathclyde.

GRADUATE DESTINATIONS AND EMPLOYMENT (2005 HESA)
See separate science subjects.

OTHER DEGREE SUBJECTS FOR CONSIDERATION

Anatomy; Anthropology; Archaeology; Astrophysics; Biochemistry; Biological Sciences; Biology; Chemistry; Earth Sciences; Ecology; Genetics; Geology; History and Philosophy of Science; Neuroscience; Pharmacology; Physics; Plant Sciences; Psychology; Zoology.

NAVAL ARCHITECTURE

(including **Marine Engineering and Ship Science;** see also **Marine/Maritime Studies**)

NB The points totals shown to the left of the institutions are for ease of reference only. It must not be assumed that tariff points are always used by institutions or that they can be substituted for an offer in grades. The level of an offer is not necessarily indicative of the quality of a course.

COURSE OFFERS INFORMATION

Subject requirements/preferences GCSE Grades A–C in mathematics and physics are normally required. **AL** Mathematics and physics usually required.

Your target offers

320 pts **London (UCL)** – ABB+AS (MEng Nvl Archit Mar Eng)
 Newcastle – ABB (MEng Mar Tech; Mar Eng; Off Eng; Nvl Archit; Sml Crft Tech)
 Southampton – ABB 320 pts (MEng Ship Sci Nvl Archit; Ship Sci Advnc Mats; Ship Sci Mar Sys Eng; Ship Sci Ycht Sml Crft; Ship Sci Eng Mgt; BEng Ship Sci)

300 pts **Strathclyde/Glasgow** – BBB (MEng Nvl Archit Mar Eng; Nvl Archit; Nvl Archit Ocn Eng; Nvl Archit Sml Crft Eng)

280 pts **London (UCL)** – BBC+AS (BEng Nvl Archit Mar Eng)
 Newcastle – BBC (BEng Mar Tech; Mar Eng; Nvl Archit; Off Eng; Sml Crft Tech)

260 pts **Liverpool** – 260 pts (Civ Marit Eng)
 Strathclyde/Glasgow – BCC (BEng Nvl Archit Mar Eng; Nvl Archit Ocn Eng; Nvl Archit Sml Crft Eng)

240 pts **Liverpool John Moores** – 240 pts (Mech Mar Eng)

200 pts **Coventry** – 200–240 pts (Boat Des)
 Greenwich – 200 pts (Naut Sci Tech)

160 pts **Plymouth** – 160 pts (BSc Mar Spo Tech; Mar Cmpste Tech)
 Southampton Solent – 160 pts (Ycht Manuf Surv; Ycht Pwrcrft Des)

Alternative offers
IB offers London (UCL) 34 pts.
Scottish offers See **Chapter 7**.

OTHER HIGHER EDUCATION COURSES IN THE SUBJECT FIELD

Foundation degrees (contact the institutions for details) Cornwall (Coll); Plymouth (CFE); Southampton Solent.

Higher National Diploma courses
100 pts and below
 Cornwall (Coll); Glamorgan; Pembrokeshire (Coll); Southampton Solent.

CHOOSING YOUR COURSE (SEE ALSO CH.1)

Subject information There is a shortage of applicants for Naval Architecture and Ship Science courses and a shortage of well qualified naval architects. Naval Architecture is also an option at **Newcastle** in the Marine Technology course. Studies involve marine structures, transport and operations, design, propulsion and mathematics. Ship design has many similarities to the design of aircraft. See **Appendix 2**. **Useful website** www.rina.org.uk.

Course variations Boat Design (Coventry); Naval Architecture and Marine Engineering (London (UCL)); Offshore Engineering (Newcastle); Marine Composites Technology (Plymouth); Ship Science (Southampton); Yacht and Powercraft Design (Southampton Solent); Small Craft Technology (Strathclyde/Glasgow). *NOW CHECK PROSPECTUSES AND WEBSITES FOR ANY RECENT CHANGES.*

Top universities and colleges (Research) Southampton.

ADMISSIONS INFORMATION
Number of applicants per place (approx) Newcastle 9; Southampton 6.

Advice to applicants and planning the UCAS personal statement Special interests in this subject area should be described fully. Visits to shipyards and awareness of ship design from the *Mary Rose* in Portsmouth to modern speed boats should be fully explained and the problems noted. See also **Engineering/Engineering Sciences** and **Marine/Maritime Studies**. See also **Appendix 2**.

Selection interviews Yes Newcastle, Southampton.

Interview advice and questions Because of the highly vocational nature of this subject, applicants will naturally be expected to discuss any work experience and to justify their reasons for choosing the course. See **Chapter 6**.

AFTER-RESULTS ADVICE
Universities with vacancies in Clearing (2006) Newcastle; Plymouth; Southampton; Southampton Solent; Strathclyde.

Offers to applicants repeating A-levels Higher Newcastle.

GRADUATE DESTINATIONS AND EMPLOYMENT (2005 HESA)
Graduates surveyed 35 **Employed** 20 **In further study** none **Assumed unemployed** 5.

OTHER DEGREE SUBJECTS FOR CONSIDERATION
Aeronautical Engineering; Civil Engineering; Electrical/Electronic Engineering; Geography; Marine Biology; Marine Engineering; Marine/Maritime Studies; Marine Technology; Mechanical Engineering; Oceanography; Physics; Shipping Operations; Transport Management.

NURSING and MIDWIFERY
(including **Paramedic Science;** see also **Biological Sciences, Community Studies** and **Health Sciences/Studies)**

NB The points totals shown to the left of the institutions are for ease of reference only. It must not be assumed that tariff points are always used by institutions or that they can be substituted for an offer in grades. The level of an offer is not necessarily indicative of the quality of a course.

APPLICATIONS FOR NURSING AND MIDWIFERY
UCAS now handles applications for degree courses: see **Chapter 5** for information about applications for diploma courses

COURSE OFFERS INFORMATION
Subject requirements/preferences GCSE English and a science subject. Mathematics required at **East Anglia, Bristol UWE, City, Glasgow Caledonian, Hertfordshire, Hull, Liverpool, Manchester, Northumbria, Robert Gordon, Sheffield Hallam, Southampton, Staffordshire, Surrey, Ulster. Edinburgh** Mathematics and science grade B. **AL** Science subjects required for some courses.

Other requirements All applicants holding firm offers will require an occupational health check and Criminal Records Bureau clearance and are required to provide documentary evidence that they have not been infected with hepatitis B.

Choosing Your University And Degree Course... And Completing Your UCAS Form?

Why not contact Brian Heap, the author of *Degree Course Offers*, *Choosing Your Degree Course and University* and *University Scholarships, Awards and Bursaries* for a personal interview or a telephone consultation for advice on such issues as:

- Choosing A-level subjects (which are the best subjects and for which courses!)
- Degrees and Diploma courses (making the right choice from a list of thousands!)
- Completing your UCAS form (will the admissions tutor remember your personal statement?)
- Choosing the right university or college (the best ones for you and your courses)

For details of services and consultation fees contact: The Higher Education Advice and Planning Service

tel: 01386 859355 email: heaps@dial.pipex.com

For information on how to read the Subject Tables, see **Chapter 7**.

Abbreviations used in the following table A Adult; C Child; LD Learning Disability; MH Mental Health.

Your target offers

320 pts **Southampton** – 320 pts (Midwifery)

300 pts **Edinburgh** – BBB (Nursing)
Cumbria – 300 pts (Nurs A)
Southampton – BBB–BBC 300–280 pts (Nurs A/C/MH/LD)

280 pts **Bradford** – 280 pts (Midwif St; Midwif Prac)
Hertfordshire – 280–320 pts (Paramed Sci)
Hull – 280 pts (Nurs C)
Leeds – BBC (Midwifery)
Manchester – BBC–BBB (Nurs; Midwif)

260 pts **Birmingham** – BCC–CCC 260–240 pts (Nursing)
Coventry – 260 pts check with admissions tutor (Midwifery)
East Anglia – BCC 260 pts (Nurs A/C/LD/MH; Midwif)
Liverpool – 260 pts (Nursing)
Northumbria – 260 pts (Midwif St)
Nottingham – BCC (Nurs Sci A/C/MH)
Oxford Brookes – BCC (Nurs C; Midwif)
Surrey – BCC **or** 300 pts (Midwif St; Nurs St A/C/MH)
Ulster – 260–180 pts (Nurs A/MH)
York – BCC/CCC (Nurs Prac A/C/LD/MH)

240 pts **Bangor** – 240–200 pts 2AL (Nurs A/C/MH/LD – check with admissions tutor)
Belfast (Queen's) – CCC/BB (Nurs A/C/MH/LD; Midwif)
Cardiff – CCC 240 pts (Nurs A/C/MH; Midwif)
Central Lancashire – 240–220 pts (Nurs; Midwif; Paramed Prac)

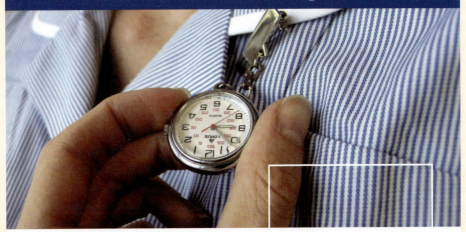

Ever considered a career in nursing or midwifery?

School of
Nursing and Midwifery

It's not just a qualification...
and much more than just a uniform

- ↘ **No tuition fees**
- ↘ **Get paid up to £6,000 per year to study**
- ↘ **Study in Basingstoke, Isle of Wight, Portsmouth, Southampton or Winchester**
- ↘ **Choose adult, child, learning disability or mental health nursing as well as midwifery**
- ↘ **Mature students welcomed – no age limit**

Call us now for a prospectus and for details of our open days so that you can see what it's all about

University
of Southampton

www.nursingandmidwifery.com
T e l : 0 2 3 8 0 5 9 5 5 0 0

Chester – 240 pts (Nurs; Midwif)
Coventry – 240 pts (Nurs A/C/LD/MH)
De Montfort – 240–260 pts (Nurs A/C/MH; Midwif)
Glasgow – CCC (Nurs A/C/LD/MH)
Huddersfield – 240 pts (Midwif St)
Hull – CCC 240 pts (Nurs A/MH/LD)
Leeds – CCC (Nurs A/C)
London (King's) – CCC+AS **or** BCccc (Nurs St A/C/MH)
Northumbria – 240 pts (Nurs St A/C/MH/LD)
Oxford Brookes – CCC (Nurs A)
Robert Gordon – CCC (Nurs A/C/MH)
Salford – 240 pts (Midwifery)
Staffordshire – 240 pts (Midwif Prac)
Swansea – 240 pts (Nurs C; Midwif)

220 pts Bournemouth – 220 pts (Midwifery)
Brighton – 220 pts (Nursing)
City (St Bartholomew's) – 220 pts (Nurs A/C/MH; Midwif)
Edge Hill (CHE) – 220 pts (Nurs A/C/MH/LD; Midwif)
UCE Birmingham – 220 pts (Midwifery)

210 pts Kingston (London St George's) – 210 pts (Nurs A)

200 pts Abertay Dundee – CDD (Mntl Hlth Cnslg)
Bristol UWE – 200–240 pts (Midwif; Nurs A/C/MH/LD)
Cumbria – 200 pts (Nurs MH)
Glamorgan – 200–240 pts (Nurs A/C/LD/MH; Midwif)
Hertfordshire – 200 pts (Midwif; Nurs LD Soc Wk; Nurs A/C/MH)
Huddersfield – 200–240 pts (Nurs A/C/MH)
Lincoln – 200 pts (Nurs A)
Liverpool John Moores – 200 pts (Nurs A/C/MH; Midwif)
Plymouth – 200 pts (Midwif; Nurs A/C/MH)
Queen Margaret (UC) – CDD (Nursing)
Staffordshire – 200 pts (Nurs Prac A/C/MH)
Swansea – 200 pts (Nurs A/MH)
Teesside – 200 pts (Midwif; Nurs St A/C/MH)
UCE Birmingham – BB 200 pts (Nursing)
Wolverhampton – 200–260 pts (Nurs; Midwif)

180 pts Bournemouth – 180 pts (Nurs A/MH/LD/C)
Brighton – 180 pts (Midwifery)
Napier – 180 pts (Nurs A/C/MH/LD; Midwif)
Northampton – 180–220 pts (Midwif St; Nurs A/C/MH/LD)
Sheffield Hallam – 180 (Nurs St A/C/MH; App Nurs Soc Wk LD)

160 pts Abertay Dundee – CC (Nursing)
Anglia Ruskin – 160–180 pts (Nurs A/C/LD/MH; Midwif)
Bedfordshire – 160–240 pts (Nurs A/C/MH; Midwif)
Canterbury Christ Church – CC (Nurs A/C/MH; Midwif)
Glasgow Caledonian – CC (Nurs St A/LD/MH; Midwif)
Greenwich – 160 pts min (Nurs A/C/MH; Midwif)
Keele – 160 pts (Nurs A/C/MH/LD; Midwif)
London South Bank – CC (Nurs St A/C/MH/LD; Nurs Soc Wk St (LD); Midwif)
Middlesex – 160–200 pts (Nurs A/C/MH; Midwif)
North East Wales (IHE) – 160 pts (Nursing)
Salford – CC 160 pts (Nurs A/C/MH)
Sheffield Hallam – 160 pts (Oprtg Dpt Prac)
Suffolk (Univ Campus) – 160 pts (Nurs A)

Worcester – CC–EE (Midwifery)
140 pts **Oxford Brookes** – CD (Nurs LD/MH)
Trinity Carmarthen (Coll) – 140 pts (Nursy Mgt)
120 pts **Buckinghamshire Chilterns (UC)** – 120 pts (Nurs A/C/MH)
Robert Gordon – DD (Midwifery)
Salford – 120–180 pts (Prof St Nurs Soc Wk)
80 pts **and below**
Dundee – contact admissions tutor (Nurs; Midwif)
Gloucestershire – (Commun Nurs; spec prac 1 yr top-up for nurses)
Sunderland – contact University (Nursing)
UCE Birmingham – contact admissions tutor (p/t BSc Nurs St)

Leeds Met – contact University

Alternative offers
IB offers Bristol UWE 24 pts; Chester 30 pts; Liverpool 30 pts; London (King's) 28 pts; Nottingham 30 pts; Salford 26 pts; Staffordshire 26 pts.
Scottish offers See **Chapter 7**.

OTHER HIGHER EDUCATION COURSES IN THE SUBJECT FIELD
Foundation degrees (contact institutions for details) Halton Riverside (Coll).

Higher National Diploma courses Greenwich.

CHOOSING YOUR COURSE (SEE ALSO CH.1)
Subject information Nursing and Midwifery courses are designed to equip students with the scientific and caring skills demanded by medical science in the 21st century. Courses follow a similar pattern with an introductory programme of study covering clinical skills, nursing practice and the behavioural and social sciences. Thereafter, specialisation starts in adult, child or mental health nursing, or with patients with learning disabilities. Throughout the three-year course students gain extensive clinical experience in hospital wards, clinics, accident and emergency and high-dependency settings. **Useful websites** www.scicentral.com; www.nmas.ac.uk; www.nhscareers.nhs.uk; www.nursingtimes.net; see also **Health Sciences/Studies** and **Medicine**.

Course variations Mental Health and Counselling (Abertay Dundee); Paramedic Science (Hertfordshire); Applied Nursing and Social Work (Sheffield Hallam); Operating Department Practice (Sheffield Hallam). *NOW CHECK PROSPECTUSES AND WEBSITES FOR ANY RECENT CHANGES.*

Universities and colleges teaching quality See www.tqi.ac.uk; www.qaa.ac.uk.

Top universities and colleges (Research) Manchester; Newcastle; Sheffield; York.

ADMISSIONS INFORMATION
Number of applicants per place (approx) Abertay Dundee 10; Anglia Ruskin 10; Bangor 10; Birmingham 8; Bournemouth 9; Brighton 3; Bristol UWE 27; Cardiff 12, (non-EU) 6; Central Lancashire (Midwif) 14; City (Nurs MH) 4, (Nurs C) 8, (Midwif) 5; Cumbria 8; De Montfort 10; Glasgow Caledonian 12; Huddersfield (Midwif) 10; Hull 10; Leeds (Midwif) 12; Liverpool John Moores (Nurs) 5; London (King's) 4; London South Bank 16; Middlesex 10; North East Wales (IHE) 4; Northampton 17; Northumbria 16; Queen Margaret (UC) 3; Salford 10, (Midwif) 11; Sheffield Hallam 8; Staffordshire (Midwif) 10; Surrey 10; Swansea 10; UCE Birmingham 15; York (Nurs) 6, (Midwif) 2.

Advice to applicants and planning the UCAS personal statement Nursing experience – for example in hospitals, old people's homes, children's homes – is important. Describe these experiences and what you have learned from them. Read nursing journals in order to be aware of new developments in the treatment of illnesses. Note, in particular, the various needs of patients and the problems they experience. Try to compare different nursing approaches with, for example, children, people with learning disabilities, old people and terminally ill people. If you under-performed at GCSE, provide mitigating circumstances if possible. Describe your social skills and your commitment to working with people. If you have had work experience or a part-time job, describe how your skills have developed, for example responsibility, communication, team-building, organisational skills. How do you spend your spare time? Explain how your interests help with stress and pressure. **City** (Midwif) Some experience of care is very valuable (paid or voluntary). **De Montfort** A financially demanding course (37 hours per week) with no time for part-time work. See also **Appendix 2**. Admission is subject to eligibility for an NHS bursary. Contact NHS Student Grants Unit, tel 01253 655655.

Misconceptions about this course That Nursing programmes are not demanding. Midwives and nurses don't do shift work and are not involved in travelling! **City** Midwives are not only involved at the birth stage but ante-natal, post-natal, in education and support.

Selection interviews Yes Most institutions, Birmingham, Bournemouth (Midwif), Cardiff, City, Hertfordshire, Sheffield Hallam, Swansea; **Some** Salford.

Interview advice and questions Past questions have included: Why do you want to be a nurse? What experience have you had in nursing? What do you think of the nurses' pay situation? Should nurses go on strike? What are your views on abortion? What branch of nursing most interests you? How would you communicate with a foreigner who can't speak English? What is the nurse's role in the community? How should a nurse react in an emergency? How would you cope with telling a patient's relative that the patient was dying? Admissions tutors look for communication skills, team interaction and the applicant's understanding of health/society related subjects. (Some applicants have difficulty with maths – multiplication and division – used in calculating dosage for medicines.) **London South Bank** What do you understand by equal opportunities? **Swansea** What is your perception of the role of the nurse? What qualities do you have that would be good for nursing? See **Chapter 6**.

Applicants' impressions (A=Open day; B=Interview day) Bournemouth (B) Talk on the course. My reasons for choosing adult nursing and aspects of my current studies (AVCE). **Nottingham** (B) I was interviewed by two members of staff who asked me why I thought I would make a good nurse and what I would find the most challenging part of the work. They were obviously looking for real commitment and were particularly interested in my attitude and personality. We were taken round the medical centre by a student and I would strongly recommend students to apply here. The only problem seemed to be the difficulty of changing from children's to adults' nursing.

Reasons for rejection (non-academic) Insufficient awareness of the roles and responsibilities of a midwife or nurse. Lack of motivation. Poor communication skills. Lack of awareness of nursing developments through the media. (Detailed knowledge of the NHS or nursing practice not usually required.) Failed medical. Unsatisfactory health record. Not fulfilling the hepatitis B requirements or police check requirements. Poor preparation for the interview. Too shy. Only wants nursing as a means to something else, for example commission in the armed forces. Too many choices on the UCAS application, for example Midwifery, Physiotherapy, Occupational Therapy. No care experience. **Birmingham** No work experience. **De Montfort** No insight as to nursing as a career or the various branches of nursing. **Swansea** Poor communication skills.

AFTER-RESULTS ADVICE

Universities with vacancies in Clearing (2006) Anglia Ruskin; Bedfordshire; Bristol UWE; Canterbury Christ Church; Chester; City; Coventry; Cumbria; Edge Hill; Greenwich; Hertfordshire; Hull; Keele; Kingston; Lincoln; Liverpool John Moores; London (King's); London South Bank; Manchester; Middlesex; Oxford Brookes; Plymouth; Roehampton; Sheffield Hallam; Southampton; Staffordshire; Sunderland; Surrey; Swansea; UCE Birmingham; Wolverhampton.

Offers to applicants repeating A-levels Higher Bristol UWE, Cardiff, Hull, Liverpool John Moores (Midwif); **Same** De Montfort, Huddersfield, Liverpool John Moores, London South Bank, Queen Margaret (UC), Salford, Staffordshire, Surrey, Swansea.

GRADUATE DESTINATIONS AND EMPLOYMENT (2005 HESA)

Graduates surveyed 4723 **Employed** 3505 **In further study** 35 **Assumed unemployed** 65.

OTHER DEGREE SUBJECTS FOR CONSIDERATION

Audiology; Biological Sciences; Biology; Community Studies; Dietetics; Education; Health Studies; Medicine; Nutrition; Occupational Therapy; Optometry; Pharmacology; Pharmacy; Physiotherapy; Podiatry; Psychology; Radiography; Social Policy and Administration; Social Work; Sociology; Speech Therapy; Veterinary Nursing.

NUTRITION

(see also **Dietetics** and **Food Science/Studies and Technology**)

NB The points totals shown to the left of the institutions are for ease of reference only. It must not be assumed that tariff points are always used by institutions or that they can be substituted for an offer in grades. The level of an offer is not necessarily indicative of the quality of a course.

COURSE OFFERS INFORMATION

Subject requirements/preferences **GCSE** Mathematics and science usually required. **Surrey** Good science grade. **AL** Science subjects required.

Your target offers

300 pts	**London (King's)** – BBB (Nutr Diet)
	Newcastle – BBB (Fd Hum Nutr)
	Surrey – 300–260 pts (Nutr Fd Sci; Nutr Diet)
280 pts	**Chester** – 280 pts (Nutr Diet)
	Leeds – BBC 280 pts (Fd St Nutr)
	London (King's) – BBC+AS (Nutrition)
	Nottingham – BBC (MNutr Nutr+Diet St Reg)
260 pts	**Belfast (Queen's)** – BCC–CCC (Fd Qual Sfty Nutr)
	Chester – 260 pts (Hum Nutr)
	Glasgow – BCC (Physiol Spo Sci Nutr)
	London Met – 260 pts (Hum Nutr Diet)
	Nottingham – BCC–BCD (Nutr; Nutr Fd Sci Euro St)
	Oxford Brookes – BCC (Nutr; Pblc Hlth Nutr)
	Reading – 260–280 pts (Nutr Fd Sci)
240 pts	**Chester** – 240 pts (Nutr courses; Hum Nutr courses)
	Manchester Met – 240 pts (Hum Nutr)
	Northumbria – 240 pts (Hum Nutr; Fd Sci Nutr)
	Ulster – CCC 240 pts (Hum Nutr; Fd Nutr)
220 pts	**Cardiff (UWIC)** – 220 pts (App Hum Nutr; Hum Nutr Diet)
	Liverpool Hope – 220 pts (Nutr Comb courses)
	Liverpool John Moores – 220 pts (Nutrition)
200 pts	**Aberdeen** – CDD (Hlth Sci (Hlth Nutr))
	Bath Spa – 200 pts (Fd Nutr Consum Prot)
	Cardiff (UWIC) – 200 pts (Spo Biomed Nutr)
	Central Lancashire – 200 pts (Exer Nutr Hlth)
	Glamorgan – 200 pts (Nutr Fd Tech Hlth)
	Huddersfield – 200 pts (Fd Nutr; Fd Nutr Hlth; Nutr Pblc Hlth)
	Kingston – 200–240 pts (Nutrition)
	Manchester Met – 200 pts (Fd Nutr)
	Sheffield Hallam – 200 pts (Fd Nutr; Pblc Hlth Nutr)
180 pts	**Abertay Dundee** – 180–160 pts (Fd Nutr Hlth)
	Bournemouth – 180 pts (Nutrition)
	Greenwich – 180 pts (Hum Nutr)
	Queen Margaret (UC) – 180–160 pts (Nutr; Diet)

Staffordshire – 180–240 pts (Spo Exer Nutr)

160 pts Glasgow Caledonian – CC (Hum Nutr Diet)

Leeds Trinity and All Saints (Coll) – CC–CCC (Nutr Hlth Psy)

London Met – 160 pts (Nutr Exer Hlth; Hum Nutr)

London South Bank – CC–EE (Fd Nutr; Biosci (Nutr))

Robert Gordon – CC (Nutr; Nutr Diet + Diet St Reg)

Roehampton – 160 pts (Exer Nutr Hlth)

St Mary's (Coll) – CC 160 pts (Hlth Exer Nutr courses; Nutr courses)

Westminster – CC (Hum Nutr; Hlth Sci (Nutr Thera))

140 pts Cardiff (UWIC) – 140 pts (Fd Nutr Hlth Sci; Nutr Fd Sci)

Teesside – 140–200 pts (Fd Nutr Hlth Sci)

120 pts Roehampton – 120 pts (Nutr Hlth)

Suffolk (Univ Campus) – DD (Spo Sci Nutr Hlth)

80 pts and below

Eastleigh (Coll) – (Fdn Sci)

Leeds Met – contact University

Alternative offers

IB offers Chester 30 pts; Manchester Met 30 pts; Newcastle 32 pts; Nottingham 24–30 pts; Reading 30 pts; Surrey 30–32 pts.

Scottish offers See **Chapter 7**.

OTHER HIGHER EDUCATION COURSES IN THE SUBJECT FIELD

Higher National Diploma courses Bridgwater (Coll); Manchester Met.

CHOOSING YOUR COURSE (SEE ALSO CH.1)

Subject information Nutrition attracts a great deal of attention in society and whilst controversy, claim and counter-claim seem to focus daily on the merits and otherwise of food and its value, it is, nevertheless, a scientific study in itself. It involves topics relating to diet, health, nutrition and food policy and courses are designed to prepare students to enter careers as specialists in nutrition and dietetics. **Useful websites** www.nutrition.org.uk; see also under **Dietetics**.

Course variations Health Sciences (Health and Nutrition) (Aberdeen); Food Quality, Safety and Nutrition (Belfast (Queen's)); Sports Biomedicine and Nutrition (Cardiff (UWIC)); Nutrition and Dietetics (Chester); Physiology, Sports Science and Nutrition (Glasgow); Public Health Nutrition (Sheffield Hallam); Nutrition and Food Science (Surrey). *NOW CHECK PROSPECTUSES AND WEBSITES FOR ANY RECENT CHANGES.*

Top universities and colleges (Research) London (King's).

Sandwich degree courses Belfast (Queen's); Cardiff (UWIC); Glasgow Caledonian; Leeds Met; London South Bank; Manchester Met; Northumbria; Oxford Brookes; Reading; Sheffield Hallam; Surrey; Teesside; Ulster.

ADMISSIONS INFORMATION

Number of applicants per place (approx) Cardiff (UWIC) 5; Glasgow Caledonian 8; Liverpool John Moores 10; London (King's) 6; London Met 9; London South Bank 5; Newcastle 5; Robert Gordon 4; Suffolk (Univ Campus) 1; Surrey 5.

Advice to applicants and planning the UCAS personal statement **Liverpool John Moores** Information on relevant experience, reasons for wanting to do the degree and careers sought would be useful. **Surrey** Overseas students not eligible for Nutrition and Dietetics course. See also **Dietetics** and **Appendix 2**.

Misconceptions about this course Some applicants do not realise that this is a science course.

Selection interviews **Yes** London Met, London South Bank, Nottingham (depends on application), Robert Gordon, Surrey, Sussex; **Some** Liverpool John Moores, Roehampton.

Interview advice and questions Past questions have focused on scientific A-level subjects studied and aspects of subjects enjoyed by the applicants. Questions then arise from answers. Extensive knowledge expected of nutrition as a career and candidates should have talked to people involved in this type of work, for example dietitians. They will also be expected to discuss wider problems such as food supplies in developing countries and nutritional problems resulting from famine. **Liverpool John Moores** Interviews are informal. It would be useful for you to bring samples of coursework to the interview. See **Chapter 6.**

AFTER-RESULTS ADVICE

Universities with vacancies in Clearing (2006) Abertay Dundee; Bournemouth; Central Lancashire; Chester; Glamorgan; Greenwich; Huddersfield; Kingston; Leeds; Liverpool Hope; Liverpool John Moores; London (King's); London Met; Manchester Met; Newcastle; Northumbria; Nottingham; Reading; Roehampton; Staffordshire; Surrey; Teesside; Westminster.

Offers to applicants repeating A-levels **Possibly higher** Nottingham; **Same** Liverpool John Moores, Manchester Met, Roehampton, Surrey.

GRADUATE DESTINATIONS AND EMPLOYMENT (2005 HESA)

Graduates surveyed 405 **Employed** 250 **In further study** 45 **Assumed unemployed** 30.

OTHER DEGREE SUBJECTS FOR CONSIDERATION

Biological Sciences; Biology; Consumer Studies; Dietetics; Food Sciences; Health Studies/Sciences.

OCCUPATIONAL THERAPY

NB The points totals shown to the left of the institutions are for ease of reference only. It must not be assumed that tariff points are always used by institutions or that they can be substituted for an offer in grades. The level of an offer is not necessarily indicative of the quality of a course.

COURSE OFFERS INFORMATION

Subject requirements/preferences **GCSE** English, mathematics and science grade A–C. **Brunel** At least four subjects including biology, human biology, chemistry, art and design. **Cardiff** Five subjects minimum grades A–C at one sitting including English or Welsh and a science. **Coventry** Five subjects grades A–C. **AL** Science subjects required or preferred for most courses.

Your target offers

300 pts	**Cumbria** – 300 pts (Occ Thera)
	Southampton – BBB 300 pts (Occ Thera)
	Ulster – BBB 300 pts (Occ Thera)
280 pts	**Bristol UWE** – 280–320 pts (Occ Thera)
260 pts	**Brunel** – 260 pts (Occ Thera)
	Cardiff – BCC 260 pts (Occ Thera)
	East Anglia – BCC (Occ Thera)
	Northumbria – 260 pts (Occ Thera)
	Robert Gordon – BCC (Occ Thera)
240 pts	**Bradford** – 240 pts (Occ Thera)
	Coventry – 240 pts (Occ Thera)
	Derby – CCC **or** CCcc 240 pts (Occ Thera)
	Huddersfield – CCC (Occ Thera)
	Liverpool – 240 pts (Occ Thera)

Northampton – 240 pts (Occ Thera)
Oxford Brookes – CCC **or** CCcc (Occ Thera)
Salford – 240 pts CCC (Occ Thera)
Sheffield Hallam – 240 pts (Occ Thera)
Teesside – CCC 240 pts (Occ Thera)
York St John – CCC 240 pts (Occ Thera)
220 pts **Bournemouth** – 220 pts (Occ Thera)
Queen Margaret (UC) – 220 pts (Occ Thera)
180 pts **Plymouth** – 180 pts check with admissions tutor (Occ Thera)
160 pts **Canterbury Christ Church** – CC (Occ Thera)
Glasgow Caledonian – CC (Occ Thera)
80 pts **Colchester (Inst)** – 80 pts check with admissions tutor (Occ Thera 4 yr p/t)
Brighton – check with admissions tutor (Occ Thera)

Alternative offers
IB offers Bristol UWE 28–32 pts; Brunel 28 pts; Liverpool 26 pts; Salford 24 pts; Southampton 28 pts.
Scottish offers See **Chapter 7**.

OTHER HIGHER EDUCATION COURSES IN THE SUBJECT FIELD

Foundation degrees (contact the institutions for details) Salford.

Higher National Diploma courses Stevenson (Coll).

CHOOSING YOUR COURSE (SEE ALSO CH.1)

Subject information Occupational Therapy is not an art career although art and craftwork may be involved as a therapeutic exercise. Occupational therapists (who work mostly in hospital departments) are involved in the rehabilitation of those who have required medical treatment and involve the young, aged and, for example, people with learning difficulties. Most courses include psychology, sociology and psychiatry. Selectors look for maturity, initiative, enterprise, tact, sound judgement and organising ability. All applicants need to pass an occupational health check and obtain Criminal Records Bureau (CRB) clearance. **Useful websites** www.cot.co.uk; www.otdirect.co.uk.

Universities and colleges teaching quality See www.tqi.ac.uk; www.qaa.ac.uk.

ADMISSIONS INFORMATION

Number of applicants per place (approx) Brunel 3; Canterbury Christ Church 5; Cardiff 10; Coventry 15; Cumbria 20; Derby 5; East Anglia 5; Northampton 4; Northumbria 4; Oxford Brookes 12; Queen Margaret (UC) 7; Robert Gordon 6; Salford 5; Sheffield Hallam 7; Southampton 7; Ulster 13; York St John 5.

Advice to applicants and planning the UCAS personal statement Contact your local hospital and discuss this career with the occupational therapists. Try to obtain work shadowing experience and make notes of your observations. Describe any such visits in full (see **Reasons for rejection**). Applicants are expected to have visited two occupational therapy departments, one in a physical or social services setting, one in the mental health field. Good interpersonal skills. **Brunel** Breadth and nature of health-related work experience. Also skills, interests (for example, sports, design). **Sheffield Hallam** Applicants should have a high standard of communication skills and experience of working with people with disabilities. **York St John** Contact with the profession essential; very competitive course. See also **Appendix 2**.

Selection interviews East Anglia; most institutions.

Interview advice and questions Since this a vocational course, work experience is nearly always essential and applicants are likely to be questioned on the types of work involved and the career. See **Chapter 6**.

Reasons for rejection (non-academic) Poor communication skills. Lack of knowledge of occupational therapy. Little evidence of working with people. Uncertain about their future career. Lack of maturity. Indecision regarding the profession. **Salford** Failure to function well in groups and inability to perform practical tasks.

AFTER-RESULTS ADVICE

Universities with vacancies in Clearing (2006) Brunel; Canterbury Christ Church; Coventry; Cumbria; Derby; East Anglia; Hertfordshire; Liverpool; Sheffield Hallam; Southampton; Teesside.

Offers to applicants repeating A-levels **Same** Derby, Salford, York St John.

GRADUATE DESTINATIONS AND EMPLOYMENT (2005 HESA)

See **Physiotherapy**.

OTHER DEGREE SUBJECTS FOR CONSIDERATION

Audiology; Community Studies; Dietetics; Education; Health Studies/Sciences; Nursing; Nutrition; Physiotherapy; Podiatry; Psychology; Radiography; Social Policy and Administration; Social Work; Sociology; Speech Sciences.

OPTOMETRY (OPHTHALMIC OPTICS)

(including **Ophthalmic Dispensing** and **Orthoptics**)

NB The points totals shown to the left of the institutions are for ease of reference only. It must not be assumed that tariff points are always used by institutions or that they can be substituted for an offer in grades. The level of an offer is not necessarily indicative of the quality of a course.

COURSE OFFERS INFORMATION

Subject requirements/preferences **GCSE** English usually required. **Aston** English, mathematics, physics, double science preferred at grade B. **Bradford** A/B grades. **AL** Science subjects required for all Optometry courses. Mathematics usually acceptable.

Your target offers
340 pts   **Aston** – AAB–AAA (Optometry)
             Cardiff – AAB (Optometry)
             City – AAB (Optometry)
             Ulster – AAB 340 pts (Optometry)
320 pts   **Anglia Ruskin** – ABB (Optometry)
             Bradford – 320 pts (Optometry)
             Glasgow Caledonian – ABB (Optometry)
             Manchester – ABB (Optometry)
300 pts   **Sheffield** – BBB or BBbb (Orthoptics)
240 pts   **Liverpool** – CCC 240 pts (Orthoptics)
200 pts   **Anglia Ruskin** – 200–160 pts (Oph Disp)
120 pts   **Bradford (Coll)** – 120 pts (Oph Disp Mgt)
             Glasgow Caledonian – DD (Oph Disp)

Alternative offers
IB offers City 33 pts; Liverpool 26 pts; Sheffield 32 pts.
Scottish offers See **Chapter 7**.

OTHER HIGHER EDUCATION COURSES IN THE SUBJECT FIELD

Foundation degrees (contact institution for details) Anglia Ruskin; City and Islington (Coll).

Higher National Diploma courses Bradford (Coll).

CHOOSING YOUR COURSE (SEE ALSO CH.1)
Subject information **Optometry** courses lead to qualification as an optometrist (previously known as an ophthalmic optician). Courses provide training in detecting defects and diseases in the eye and in prescribing treatment with, for example, spectacles, contact lenses and other appliances to correct or improve vision. Optometry has become an increasingly popular course. **Orthoptics** includes the study of general anatomy, physiology and normal child development and leads to a career as an orthoptist. This involves the investigation, diagnosis and treatment of binocular vision and other eye conditions. Most of orthoptists' work is with children and the elderly in areas of public health and education. The main components of degree courses include the study of the eye, the use of diagnostic and measuring equipment and treatment of eye abnormalities. See also **Appendix 2**. **Useful websites** www.assoc-optometrists.org; www.optical.org; www.college-optometrists.org; www.orthoptics.org.uk.

Course variations Optical Management (Anglia Ruskin); Ophthalmic Dispensing with Management (Bradford (Coll)); Orthoptics (Liverpool; Sheffield). *NOW CHECK PROSPECTUSES AND WEBSITES FOR ANY RECENT CHANGES.*

Universities and colleges teaching quality See www.tqi.ac.uk; www.qaa.ac.uk.

Top universities and colleges (Research) Aston; City.

ADMISSIONS INFORMATION

Number of applicants per place (approx) Anglia Ruskin 12; Aston 7; Bradford 6; Cardiff 13; City 11; Glasgow Caledonian 9.

Number of applicants (a UK b EU (non-UK) c non-EU d mature) Anglia Ruskin **ab**431; Aston **a**700 **b**50 **c**70 **d**10; Bradford **ab**600 **c**90; Glasgow Caledonian **a**548 **c**23

Advice to applicants and planning the UCAS personal statement For Optometry courses contact with optometrists is essential, either work shadowing or gaining some work experience. Make notes of your experiences and the work done and report fully on the UCAS application on why the career interests you. See also **Appendix 2**.

Selection interviews **Yes** Bradford, City, Glasgow Caledonian; **Some** Anglia Ruskin, Aston, Cardiff.

Interview advice and questions Optometry is a competitive subject requiring applicants to have had some work experience on which they will be questioned. **Anglia Ruskin** Why will you make a good optometrist? Describe the job. See **Chapter 6**.

AFTER-RESULTS ADVICE
Universities with vacancies in Clearing (2006) Anglia Ruskin (Ophthalmic Dispensing); Bradford (Optometry); Sheffield (Orthoptics).

Offers to applicants repeating A-levels **Higher** City; **Possibly higher** Aston; **Same** Anglia Ruskin, Cardiff.

GRADUATE DESTINATIONS AND EMPLOYMENT (2005 HESA)
Optometry graduates surveyed 519 **Employed** 335 **In further study** 15 **Assumed unemployed** 10.

OTHER DEGREE SUBJECTS FOR CONSIDERATION
Health Studies; Nursing; Occupational Therapy; Physics; Physiotherapy; Radiography; Speech Studies.

PHARMACOLOGY

(including **Toxicology;** see also **Biological Sciences, Health Sciences/Studies** and **Pharmacy**)

NB The points totals shown to the left of the institutions are for ease of reference only. It must not be assumed that tariff points are always used by institutions or that they can be substituted for an offer in grades. The level of an offer is not necessarily indicative of the quality of a course.

COURSE OFFERS INFORMATION

Subject requirements/preferences **GCSE** English and mathematics. **Cambridge** Grade A in most subjects preferred. **Edinburgh, Leeds** Mathematics grade B. **Portsmouth** Chemistry essential, biology preferred. **Sheffield** Biology grade B/C. **AL** Chemistry and/or biology required for most courses.

Your target offers

360 pts **and above**
 Cambridge – AAA (Nat Sci (Pharmacol))
340 pts **Bath** – AAB–BBB (Pharmacology)
 Manchester – AAB–ABB (Pharmacol Physiol Ind)
 Manchester – AAB–BBC (Pharmacol; Pharmacol Ind; Pharmacol Modn Lang)
 Sheffield – AAB **or** ABaa (Physiol Pharmacol)
320 pts **Cardiff** – ABB–BBB 320–300 pts (Biomed Sci (Pharmacol))
 London (UCL) – ABB–BBB+AS (Pharmacology)
300 pts **Aberdeen** – BBB 2nd yr entry (Pharmacology)
 Bristol – BBB (Pharmacol; Pharmacol Ind)
 Dundee – 300–240 pts 2nd yr entry (Pharmacol; Bioch Pharmacol; Pharmacol Physiol Sci)
 Edinburgh – BBB (Pharmacology)
 Leeds – BBB 300 pts (Pharmacology)
 Leicester – BBB 300 pts (Biol Sci (Physiol Pharmacol))
 London (King's) – BBB+AS **or** BBbb **or** ACab (Pharmacol; Pharmacol Mol Gnm; Physiol Pharmacol)
 Middlesex – 300–240 pts (Trad Chin Med)
 Newcastle – BBB–BBC (Pharmacology)
 St Andrews – ABC–BCC (Chem Pharmacol)
 Southampton – BBB 300 pts (Pharmacol; Pharmacol Yr Ind)
 Ulster – 300 pts (Pharmacology)
280 pts **Birmingham** – BBC 280 pts (Chem Pharmacol)
 Liverpool – BBC–BBB 280–300 pts (Pharmacol; Medcnl Chem Pharmacol)
 Strathclyde – BBC (Bioch Pharmacol; Immun Pharmacol)
260 pts **Bradford** – 260 pts (Pharmacology)
 Glasgow – BCC–CCC (Pharmacology)
 Surrey – BCC 260 pts (Bioch (Pharmacol) (Tox))
240 pts **Aberdeen** – CCC 1st yr entry (Pharmacology)
 Sunderland – CCC (Pharmacology)
220 pts **Dundee** – 220 pts 1st yr entry (Pharmacol; Bioch Pharmacol; Pharmacol Physiol Sci)
 Middlesex – 220–180 pts (Herb Med)
 Napier – 220 pts (Tox; Immun Tox)
200 pts **Kingston** – 200–240 pts (Pharmacology)
 Nottingham Trent – 200 pts (Physiol Pharmacol; Pharmacol Neuro)
 Portsmouth – 200–280 pts (Pharmacology)
180 pts **Bristol UWE** – DDD–CCD 180–220 pts (App Physiol Pharmacol)
 Glasgow Caledonian – DDD (Pharmacology)
 Hertfordshire – 180–220 pts (Pharmacol courses)
 Sunderland – 180 pts (Pharmacology)
160 pts **Manchester Met** – 160–200 pts (Physiol Pharmacol St)
 Queen Margaret (UC) – 160 pts (App Pharmacol)
 Westminster – CC (Physiol Pharmacol; Hlth Sci (Hom))

For information on how to read the Subject Tables, see **Chapter 7.**

Wolverhampton – 160–200 pts (Pharmacol; Pharmacol Hum Phsyiol)
120 pts **East London** – 120 pts (Pharmacology)
London Met – 120 pts (Pharmacol; Herb Medicin Sci)
80 pts **and below**
Eastleigh (Coll) – (Fdn Sci)
Southampton – (Fdn Pharmacol)
Sunderland – (Fdn Pharmacol)
Westminster – (Fdn Physiol Pharmacol)

Leeds Met – contact University

Alternative offers
IB offers Bristol 32 pts; Cambridge 38–42 pts; London (King's) 32 pts, (UCL) 32–34 pts.
Scottish offers See **Chapter 7**.

OTHER HIGHER EDUCATION COURSES IN THE SUBJECT FIELD
Higher National Diploma courses Coventry; De Montfort; East London; Greenwich; Hertfordshire; Huddersfield; Kingston; South Birmingham (Coll); Wolverhampton.

CHOOSING YOUR COURSE (SEE ALSO CH.1)
Subject information Pharmacology is the study of drugs and medicines and courses focus on physiology, biochemistry, toxicology, immunology, microbiology and chemotherapy. Pharmacologists are not qualified to work as pharmacists. Toxicology involves the study of the adverse effects of chemicals on living systems. See also **Appendix 2** under **Pharmacy**. **Useful websites** www.thebts.org; www.scienceyear.com.

Course variations Pharmacology and Molecular Genomics (London (King's)); Physiology and Pharmacology (London (UCL)); Pharmacology with Industrial Experience (Manchester); Herbal Medicine (Middlesex); Toxicology (Napier); Immunology and Pharmacology (Strathclyde); Biochemistry (Toxicology) (Surrey). *NOW CHECK PROSPECTUSES AND WEBSITES FOR ANY RECENT CHANGES.*

Universities and colleges teaching quality See www.tqi.ac.uk; www.qaa.ac.uk.

Top universities and colleges (Research) Cambridge; Liverpool; London (UCL)*.

Sandwich degree courses (including **Pharmaceutical Sciences**, **Pharmacology** and **Pharmacy**) Bath (Pharmacol); Bradford (Pharm); Bristol (Pharmacol); Bristol UWE (Pharm Sci); Cardiff (Pharmacol); Coventry (Pharm Sci); De Montfort (Pharm Sci); East London (Pharmacol); Greenwich (Pharm Sci); Hertfordshire (Pharm Sci); Huddersfield (Pharm Sci); Kingston (Pharm Sci; Pharmacol); London Met (Pharmacol); Manchester (Pharmacol); Manchester Met (Physiol Pharmacol St); Napier (Tox); Nottingham Trent (Physiol Pharmacol); Salford (Pharm Sci); Sheffield Hallam (Pharm Sci); Southampton (Pharmacol); Sunderland (Pharmacol).

ADMISSIONS INFORMATION
Number of applicants per place (approx) Bath 12; Birmingham 6; Bradford 20; Bristol 8; Cardiff 8; Dundee 5; East London 4; Hertfordshire 10; Leeds 7; Liverpool 5; London (King's) 6; Portsmouth 4; Southampton 8; Strathclyde 10; Sunderland 12, Wolverhampton 4.

Advice to applicants and planning the UCAS personal statement Contact with the pharmaceutical industry is important in order to be aware of the range of work undertaken. Read pharmaceutical journals (although note that Pharmacology and Pharmacy courses lead to different careers). **Bath** Interests outside A-level studies. Evidence that there is more to the student than A-level ability. **Bristol** Be aware that a Pharmacology degree is mainly biological rather than chemical although both are important. See also **Pharmacy**.

Misconceptions about this course Mistaken belief that Pharmacology and Pharmaceutical Sciences is Pharmacy and that a Pharmacology degree will lead to work as a pharmacist.

Selection interviews **Yes** Bath, Birmingham (Don't be anxious – this is an opportunity for you to see us!), Cambridge, Newcastle; **Some** Cardiff, Dundee, Sunderland.

Interview advice and questions Past questions include: Why do you want to do Pharmacology? Why not Pharmacy? Why not Chemistry? How are pharmacologists employed in industry? What are the issues raised by anti-vivisectionists on animal experimentation? Questions relating to the A-level syllabus in chemistry and biology. See **Chapter 6**.

Reasons for rejection (non-academic) Confusion between Pharmacology, Pharmacy and Pharmaceutical Sciences. One university rejected two applicants because they had no motivation or understanding of the course (one had A-levels at AAB!). Insurance against rejection for Medicine. Lack of knowledge about pharmacology as a subject.

AFTER-RESULTS ADVICE
Universities with vacancies in Clearing (2006) Aberdeen; Bath; Birmingham; Bristol UWE; Dundee; Glasgow; Hertfordshire; Kingston; Leeds; Liverpool; Manchester Met; Nottingham Trent; Portsmouth; Sheffield; Southampton; Sunderland; Surrey; Westminster; Wolverhampton.

Offers to applicants repeating A-levels Higher Bristol, Glasgow, Leeds; **Same** Bath, Bradford, Cardiff, Dundee, Portsmouth, Sunderland.

GRADUATE DESTINATIONS AND EMPLOYMENT (2005 HESA)
Pharmacology, Toxicology and Pharmacy graduates surveyed 1655 **Employed** 1050 **In further study** 195 **Assumed unemployed** 45.

OTHER DEGREE SUBJECTS FOR CONSIDERATION
Biochemistry; Biological Sciences; Biology; Biotechnology; Chemistry; Life Sciences; Microbiology; Natural Sciences; Pharmaceutical Sciences; Pharmacy; Physiology; Toxicology.

PHARMACY

(including **Herbal Medicine, Pharmaceutical Management** and **Pharmaceutical Sciences**)

NB The points totals shown to the left of the institutions are for ease of reference only. It must not be assumed that tariff points are always used by institutions or that they can be substituted for an offer in grades. The level of an offer is not necessarily indicative of the quality of a course.

Not all courses lead to qualification as a pharmacist; check prospectuses and websites.

COURSE OFFERS INFORMATION
Subject requirements/preferences GCSE English, mathematics and a science subject. **Aston** Ideally grades A or B. **Bath** Grade A or B in mathematics preferred and at least grade C in English. **Cardiff** A*, A and Bs in chemistry, a biological science and mathematics. **Manchester** English and mathematics grade B. **Robert Gordon** Grade B in mathematics if not at A-level. **AL** Chemistry and another science required for most courses.

Your target offers
350 pts **London (King's)** – BBBb–ABB (MPharm Pharm)
340 pts **Belfast (Queen's)** – AAB–ABBb (MPharm Pharm)
Manchester – AAB–ABB (MPharm)
320 pts **Aston** – ABB 320 pts (MPharm Pharm)
Cardiff – ABB–BBB (MPharm Pharm)
East Anglia – ABB (MPharm Pharm)
Hertfordshire 320 pts (MPharm Pharm)
Liverpool John Moores – ABB–BBC 320–280 pts (MPharm Pharm)
Nottingham – ABB–BBB (MPharm Pharm)
Reading – 320 pts (Pharm)
300 pts **Bath** – BBB–ABC (MPharm Pharm)
Brighton – 300 pts (MPharm Pharm)
Dundee – 300–240 pts (Pharml Chem)

East Anglia – BBB (Pharml Chem)
Keele – BBB (MPharm Pharm)
Kent (Medway Sch Pharm) – 300 pts (MPharm Pharm)
Kingston – 300 pts (MPharm Pharm)
London (Sch Pharm) – BBB (MPharm Pharm)
Portsmouth – BBB 300 pts (MPharm Pharm)
Robert Gordon – BBB (MPharm Pharm)
Strathclyde – BBB (MPharm Pharm)

280 pts **Bradford** – 280 pts (MPharm Pharm)
De Montfort – 280–300 pts (MPharm Pharm)
Sunderland – 280 pts (MPharm)

240 pts **Bradford** – 240 pts (Pharm Mgt; Pharm Sci Law; Chem Pharm Foren Sci)
Hull – 240 pts (Pharml Sci)
Liverpool John Moores – 240–280 pts (Pharml Sci Biol Chem; Pharml Sci Clin Rsch; Pharml Analys)
Northumbria – 240 pts (Pharml Chem)

220 pts **Middlesex** – 220–180 pts (Herb Med)

200 pts **Brighton** – 200 pts (Pharml Chem Sci)
Hertfordshire – 200 pts (Pharml Sci)
Huddersfield – 200 pts (Pharml Sci)
Kingston – 200 pts (Pharml Sci)
Nottingham Trent – 200–220 pts (Pharml Medicin Sci)
Portsmouth – 200–280 pts (Pharm Sci)

180 pts **Bristol UWE** – 180–220 pts (Pharml Sci)
De Montfort – 180 pts (Pharml Sci (Drug Del) (Cosmet Prod))
Greenwich – 180 pts (Pharml Sci)
Sheffield Hallam – 180 pts (Pharml Sci)
Sunderland – 180 pts (Chem Pharml Sci)

160 pts **Westminster** – CC (Hlth Sci (Herb Med) (Hom))
Wolverhampton – 160–220 pts (Pharml Sci)

120 pts **London Met** – 120 pts (Pharml Sci; Herb Medicin Sci)
Paisley – DD (Pharml Sci)
Liverpool John Moores – Individual offers, depending on aptitude test, interview and A-levels. Contact admissions tutor (MPharm Pharm)

Alternative offers
IB offers Bath 34 pts; Brighton 28–30 pts; Bristol UWE 24–26 pts; Keele 32 pts; London (King's) 32 pts; Manchester 33–35 pts; Nottingham 34 pts.
Scottish offers See **Chapter 7**.

OTHER HIGHER EDUCATION COURSES IN THE SUBJECT FIELD

Foundation degree (contact institutions for details) Aston; Kingston; Matthew Boulton (CFHE); Merton (Coll); Preston (Coll).

CHOOSING YOUR COURSE (SEE ALSO CH.1)

Subject information Pharmacy is the science of medicines, involving research into chemical structures and natural products of possible medicinal value, the development of dosage and the safety testing of products. This table also includes information on courses in Pharmaceutical Science (which should not be confused with Pharmacy) which is a multi-disciplinary subject covering chemistry, biochemistry, pharmacology and medical issues. Pharmaceutical scientists apply their knowledge of science and the biology of disease to the design and delivery of therapeutic agents. **Note** All courses leading to MPharm are now four years. Recommended reading: *Pharmacy: Effective Caring* Royal Pharmaceutical Society, 1 Lambeth High Street, London SE1 7JN. See also **Appendix 2**. **Useful websites** www.askyourpharmacist.co.uk; www.pharmweb.net; www.scienceyear.com; www.pharmacy.org; www.dotpharmacy.com.

Course variations Pharmaceutical Science (Drug Delivery) (Cosmetic Products) (De Montfort); Herbal Medicinal Science (London Met); Pharmaceutical and Medicinal Sciences (Nottingham Trent); Health Sciences (Homeopathy) (Westminster). *NOW CHECK PROSPECTUSES AND WEBSITES FOR ANY RECENT CHANGES.*

Universities and colleges teaching quality See www.tqi.ac.uk; www.qaa.ac.uk.

Top universities and colleges (Research) Aston; Bath*; Cardiff; London (King's), (Sch Pharm); Manchester*; Nottingham; Strathclyde.

Sandwich degree courses See **Pharmacology**.

ADMISSIONS INFORMATION

Number of applicants per place (approx) Aston 10; Bath 6; Bradford 10; Brighton 24 (apply early); Cardiff 5; De Montfort 14; Liverpool John Moores (Pharm) 7, (Pharm Sci Biol Chem) 2; London (King's) 15, (Sch Pharm) 6; Nottingham 11; Portsmouth 20; Robert Gordon 11; Strathclyde 10; Sunderland 20.

Number of applicants (**a** UK **b** EU (non-UK) **c** non-EU **d** mature) Aston **a**1400 **b**100 **c**300 **d**180; Bradford **ab**1200 **c**200.

Advice to applicants and planning the UCAS personal statement Work experience and work shadowing with a retail and/or hospital pharmacist is important. Read pharmaceutical journals, extend your knowledge of well known drugs and antibiotics. Read up on the history of drugs. Attendance at open days or careers conference. See also **Appendix 2**.

Misconceptions about this course That a degree in Pharmaceutical Science is a qualification leading to a career as a pharmacist. It is not: it is a course which concerns the application of chemical and biomedical science to the design, synthesis and analysis of pharmaceuticals for medicinal purposes. See also **Pharmacology**.

Selection interviews **Yes** Bath, Bradford, Brighton, Bristol, De Montfort, Liverpool John Moores, London (Sch Pharm), Nottingham, Robert Gordon, Strathclyde; **Some** Aston, Cardiff.

Interview advice and questions Work experience is essential for Pharmacy applicants and relevant questions could include: Why do you want to study Pharmacy? What types of work do pharmacists do? What interests you about the Pharmacy course? What branch of pharmacy do you want to enter? Name a drug – what do you know about it (formula, use etc)? Name a drug from a natural source and its use. Can you think of another way of extracting a drug? Why do fungi destroy bacteria? What is an antibiotic? Can you name one and say how it was discovered? What is insulin? What is its source and function? What is diabetes? What type of insulin is used in its treatment? What is a hormone? What drugs are available over the counter without prescription? What is the formula of aspirin? What is genetic engineering? **Bath** Informal and relaxed; 400 approx selected for interview – very few rejected at this stage. **Cardiff** Interviews cover both academic and vocational aspects; candidates must reach a satisfactory level in both areas. **Liverpool John Moores** What are the products of a reaction between an alcohol and a carboxylic acid? See **Chapter 6**.

Applicants' impressions (A=Open day; B=Interview day) **Nottingham** (B) I had a 20–30 minute interview with two interviewers. They asked me why Pharmacy? And why is geography (one of my A-level subjects) useful for pharmacy? I felt the interview intimidating but I would strongly recommend to others to apply. They regarded their course very highly.

Reasons for rejection (non-academic) Poor communication skills. Poor knowledge of pharmacy and the work of a pharmacist.

AFTER-RESULTS ADVICE

Universities with vacancies in Clearing (2006) Bradford; East Anglia; Hertfordshire; Keele; Kent (Medway); Liverpool John Moores; London (Sch Pharm); Portsmouth; Sunderland; Wolverhampton.

Offers to applicants repeating A-levels **Higher** Belfast (Queen's), Bradford, Cardiff, De Montfort, Liverpool John Moores, London (Sch Pharm), Nottingham (offers rarely made), Portsmouth, Strathclyde; **Possibly higher** Aston, Robert Gordon; **Same** Bath, Brighton, Sunderland.

GRADUATE DESTINATIONS AND EMPLOYMENT (2005 HESA)
See under **Pharmacology**.

OTHER DEGREE SUBJECTS FOR CONSIDERATION
Biochemistry; Biological Sciences; Biology; Biotechnology; Chemistry; Life Sciences; Microbiology; Natural Sciences; Pharmacology; Physiology.

PHILOSOPHY

NB The points totals shown to the left of the institutions are for ease of reference only. It must not be assumed that tariff points are always used by institutions or that they can be substituted for an offer in grades. The level of an offer is not necessarily indicative of the quality of a course.

COURSE OFFERS INFORMATION

Subject requirements/preferences **GCSE** English and mathematics. **Aberdeen**, **Dundee**, **Edinburgh**, **Glasgow**, **St Andrews** English, mathematics or science and a foreign language. **London (LSE)** Grade B in mathematics. **Nottingham** Grade B/C mathematics. **Oxford**, **Cambridge** Grade A in most subjects preferred. **Sussex** Grade B in a foreign language. **AL** No specific subjects except for joint courses.

Your target offers

360 pts **and above**

Cambridge – AAA (Philosophy)

Durham – AAA (Nat Sci (Phil); Phil Psy)

Exeter – AAA–ABB (Phil Hist)

London (King's) – AAA–AAB (Phil; War St Phil; Relig Phil Eth; Ger Phil; Maths Phil; Phil Hisp St)

London (LSE) – AAA (Phil Econ)

Oxford – Offers vary eg AAA–AAB (Maths Phil; PPE; Phil Theol; Psy Phil; Phil Modn Lang; Physiol Phil)

Warwick – AABb (Phil; Phil Lit; Phil Class Civ; Phil Comp Sci; Phil Psy; PPE)

340 pts **Durham** – AAB (PPE)

Durham – AAB–ABB (Phil; Phil Pol; Phil Theol)

London (LSE) – AAB (Phil Lgc Sci Meth)

London (UCL) – AAB+AS–ABB+AS (Phil; Phil Gk; Phil Econ; Phil Hist Art; Fr Phil)

Manchester – AAB–BBC (Phil Sci Psy; Phil Class Civ Art Hist; Phil Relig St Compar Relig; Phil Jew St; Phil Ling Engl Lang; Phil Langs; Phil Blt Nat Env; Phil Pol)

St Andrews – AAB (Phil Scot Hist; Phil Psy; Lgc Phil Sci Phys)

Sheffield – AAB–BBB (Phil courses)

York – AAB–ABB (Phil courses)

320 pts **Birmingham** – ABB–BBB (Philosophy)

Bristol – ABB–BBB (Phil joint courses)

East Anglia – ABB–BBB (PPE)

East Anglia – ABB–ABC (Philosophy)

Exeter – ABB 320 pts (Phil Fr/Ger/Ital/Russ/Span; Phil Pol; Phil Sociol; Phil Theol)

Glasgow – ABB–BBB (BA Philosophy)

Kent – 320 pts (PPE Euro)

Lancaster – ABB (Engl Lit Phil)

Leeds – ABB (Phil Sociol)

Liverpool – ABB 320 pts (Phil; Phil Pol)

Manchester – ABB (PPE)

Nottingham – ABB (Mus Phil)

St Andrews – ABB (Phil Langs)

Southampton – ABB 320 pts (Phil; Econ Phil; Phil Maths; Phil Pol; Phil Sociol)

Sussex – ABB **or** 360 pts 3AL+AS (Phil courses)

300 pts **Belfast (Queen's)** – BBB–BBCb (Phil courses; Schlstc Phil courses)
Cardiff – BBB (Phil; Hist Ideas Phil; Hist Ideas Hum courses)
Dundee – BBB 2nd yr entry (Philosophy)
East Anglia – BBB–BBC (Phil Hist; Phil Pol)
Edinburgh – BBB (Phil courses)
Lancaster – BBB 300 pts (Phil; Phil Pol; Phil Relig St; Film St Phil; Phil Fr/Ger/Span/Ital;
Hist Phil; Ling Phil; Eth Phil Relig)
Leeds – BBB–BBC (Phil courses except under **320 pts**)
London (UCL) – BBB+AS (Hist Phil Sci)
Manchester – BBB (Philosophy)
Newcastle – ABC–BBB (Phil St)
Nottingham – ABC–BBC (Phil; Phil Theol)
Reading – 300–320 pts (Phil; Art Phil)
280 pts **Hull** – BBC 280 pts (Phil; Phil Film St; Phil Crea Writ; Phil Lang; Phil Sociol; Phil Pol; Phil Psy;
Phil Gndr St)
Kent – 280 pts (Phil; Phil Yr Abrd; Phil Pol; Phil Relig St; Phil Soc Anth; Phil Soc Bhv; Phil
Sociol)
Liverpool – BBC 280 pts (Phil Fr/Ger; Phil Hisp St)
Oxford Brookes – BBC (Phil courses)
260 pts **Essex** – 260–300 pts (Phil; Phil Hist; Phil Lit; Phil Pol; Phil Sociol; Phil Law)
Keele – 260–320 pts (Phil courses)
240 pts **Aberdeen** – CCC (Phil courses)
Bradford – 240 pts (Phil courses)
Dundee – 240 pts 1st yr entry (Philosophy)
London (Hey) – 240 pts (Phil; Phil Relig Eth; Phil Theol; Psy Phil)
Manchester Met – 240 pts (Philosophy)
Stirling – CCC (Phil; Comp Sci Phil; Phil Psy; PPE)
220 pts **Gloucestershire** – 220 pts (Relig Phil Eth)
Kingston – 220–260 pts (Hist Ideas courses)
Liverpool Hope – 220 pts (Phil Eth courses)
200 pts **Anglia Ruskin** – 200 pts (Phil; Phil Dr; Phil Engl; Phil Film St)
Bristol UWE – 200–280 pts (Phil courses)
Central Lancashire – 200–160 pts (Phil courses)
Hertfordshire – 200–240 pts (Phil (mod schm); Phil Comb courses)
London Met – 200 pts (PPE)
Staffordshire – 200 pts (Phil courses)
180 pts **Glamorgan** – 180–240 pts (Phil courses)
Greenwich – 180 pts (Phil courses)
Lampeter – 180–220 pts open admissions policy (Philosophy)
Roehampton – 180 pts (Phil courses)

For information on how to read the Subject Tables, see **Chapter 7**.

160 pts **Cumbria** – 160 pts (Phil Eth)

Glamorgan – 160–200 pts (Phil Contemp Tht)

London Met – 160 pts (Philosophy)

Middlesex – 160–200 pts (Phil courses)

Newman (CHE) – 160 pts (Phil Relig Eth; Phil Theol courses)

Newport – 160 pts (Relig St Phil courses)

Northampton – 160–220 pts (Phil courses)

St Mary's (Coll) – 160–200 pts (Phil courses)

Wolverhampton – 160–220 pts (Phil courses)

140 pts **Bolton** – 140 pts (Philosophy)

Marjon (Coll) – 140–200 pts (Phil courses)

80 pts **London (Birk)** – 80 pts for under 21s (over 21s varies) (p/t Philosophy)

Leeds Met – contact University

Open University – contact University

Alternative offers

IB offers Birmingham 32–34 pts; Bristol 34–36 pts; Bristol UWE 26–32 pts; Cambridge 38–42 pts; Essex 28–32 pts; Exeter 32–34 pts; Keele 28–30 pts; Kent 30 pts; Lancaster 32–33 pts; Liverpool 34 pts; London (LSE) 38 pts, (UCL) 36–38 pts; Manchester 34 pts; Manchester Met 28 pts; Newcastle 32 pts; Oxford 38–42 pts; St Andrews 32–36 pts; Sheffield 32–35 pts; Warwick 36–38 pts; York 34–36 pts. *Scottish offers:* See **Chapter 7**.

CHOOSING YOUR COURSE (SEE ALSO CH.1)

Subject information Philosophy is one of the oldest and most fundamental disciplines which examines the nature of the universe and humanity's place in it. It seeks to discover the essence of the mind, language and physical reality and discusses the methods used to investigate these topics. **Useful websites** www.iep.utm.edu; www.philosophypages.com; see also **Religious Studies**.

Course variations PPE (Durham, East Anglia, Essex, Hull, Kent, London Met, Manchester, Oxford, Warwick, York); Scholastic Philosophy (Belfast (Queen's)); Religion, Philosophy and Ethics (Gloucestershire); Philosophy, Logic and Scientific Method (London (LSE)); Philosophy and Religious Studies (Manchester); Music and Philosophy (Nottingham); Physiology and Philosophy (Oxford). *NOW CHECK PROSPECTUSES AND WEBSITES FOR ANY RECENT CHANGES.*

Universities and colleges teaching quality See www.tqi.ac.uk; www.qaa.ac.uk.

TOP UNIVERSITIES AND COLLEGES (RESEARCH) Bristol; Cambridge; Durham; East Anglia; Edinburgh*; Essex; Leeds; London (King's), (LSE)*, (UCL); Middlesex; Nottingham; Oxford*; Reading; St Andrews; Sheffield; Stirling; Warwick; York.

ADMISSIONS INFORMATION

Number of applicants per place (approx) Birmingham 6; Bradford 7; Bristol 20; Cambridge 6; Cardiff 8; Dundee 6; Durham 14 (all courses); East Anglia 6; Hull 19; Kent 9; Lampeter 4; Lancaster 6; Leeds 10; Liverpool 5; London (Hey) 4, (King's) 6, (LSE) (Phil Lgc Sci Meth) 4, (Phil Econ) 32; London Met 3; Middlesex 8; Northampton 3; Nottingham 11; Oxford (success rate 44%, (PPE) 29%); Sheffield 6; Southampton 7; Staffordshire 8; Warwick 9; York 11.

Advice to applicants and planning the UCAS personal statement Read Bertrand Russell's *Problems of Philosophy*. Refer to any particular aspects of philosophy which interest you (check that these are offered on the courses for which you are applying). Since Philosophy is not a school subject, selectors will expect applicants to have read around the subject. **Bristol** Explain what you know about the nature of studying philosophy. **East Anglia** (non-EU students) Pre-sessional courses in English and study skills. **Lampeter** Books which have influenced you. **Staffordshire** We look for an interest in some of the most basic and universal questions about human nature and our experience of the world. **York** Say what you have read in philosophy and give an example of a philosophical issue that interests you. We do not expect applicants to have a wide knowledge of the subject, but evidence that you know what the subject is about is important.

Misconceptions about this course Applicants are sometimes surprised to find what wide-ranging Philosophy courses are offered. **York** That PPE is a degree taken only by male students and that it is dry and overly abstract!

Selection interviews **Yes** Bangor, Birmingham, Bristol (mature students), Cambridge, Durham, Kingston, Lampeter, Lancaster, Leeds, Liverpool, London (Hey), (UCL), Newcastle, Oxford, Southampton, Staffordshire, Warwick; **Some** Cardiff, Dundee, Hull, London (LSE) (rare), York.

Interview advice and questions Philosophy is a very wide subject and initially applicants will be asked for their reasons for their choice and their special interests in the subject. Questions in recent years have included: Is there a difference between being tactless and being insensitive? Can you be tactless and thin-skinned? Define the difference between knowledge and belief. Was the vertical distortion of El Greco's paintings a product of a vision defect? What is the point of studying philosophy? What books on philosophy have you read? Discuss the work of a renowned philosopher. What is a philosophical novel? Who has the right to decide your future – yourself or another? What do you want to do with your life? What is a philosophical question? John is your husband, and if John is your husband then necessarily you must be his wife; if you are necessarily his wife then it is not possible that you could not be his wife; so it was impossible for you not to have married him – you were destined for each other. Discuss. What is the difference between a man's entitlements, his deserts and his attributes? What are morals? A good understanding of philosophy is needed for entry to degree courses, and applicants are expected to demonstrate this if they are called to interview. As one admissions tutor stated, 'If you find Bertrand Russell's *Problems of Philosophy* unreadable – don't apply!' **Leeds** 500 word essay. **Oxford** (PPE) Tutors are not so much concerned with what you know as how you think about it. Evidence required concerning social and political topics and the ability to discuss them critically. **York** Do human beings have free will? Do we perceive the world as it really is? See also **Chapter 6**.

Applicants' impressions (A=Open day; B=Interview day) **London (UCL)** (B) There were no individual interviews. All candidates were given a lecture on free will problems and had 30 minutes in which to write an essay on the subject. **Oxford** (PPE; B) There were interviews with one–four interviewers lasting 20 to 30 minutes. The more interviewers present, the less intimidating the interviews; the one-to-one interviews were quite intense. In Politics, I was questioned on current affairs, and for Economics I was given a sheet with questions and was asked to prepare the answers. In Philosophy I was asked 'If God is all-powerful could He create a rock too heavy for Him to lift?' The whole process was tough but it was worth it and was good experience. **(Magdalen)** (B) I had three separate interviews, each lasting about 15 minutes and each with one interviewer. In Philosophy I had a question on time travel and in Economics I was asked which part of my A-level course I enjoyed the most and was given a topic to discuss. For Politics I had to answer questions on political parties and on power and expertise.

Reasons for rejection (non-academic) Evidence of severe psychological disturbance, criminal activity, drug problems (evidence from referees' reports). Lack of knowledge of philosophy. **Oxford** He was not able to explore his thoughts deeply enough or with sufficient centrality. **York** No evidence of having read any philosophical literature.

AFTER-RESULTS ADVICE

Universities with vacancies in Clearing (2006) Aberdeen; Anglia Ruskin; Birmingham; Bolton; Bradford; Bristol UWE; Cardiff; Cumbria; Dundee; East Anglia; Essex; Glamorgan; Glasgow; Gloucestershire; Greenwich; Hertfordshire; Hull; Keele; Kent; Lampeter; Lancaster; London (Hey), (King's), (RH); London Met; Manchester Met; Middlesex; Northampton; Nottingham; Reading; Roehampton; Southampton; Staffordshire; Stirling; Wolverhampton.

Offers to applicants repeating A-levels **Higher** Bristol (Phil Econ), Essex, Glasgow, Leeds, Nottingham (in some cases), Warwick, York (PPE); **Same** Bangor, Birmingham, Bristol, Cardiff, Dundee, Hull, Newcastle, Newport, Nottingham (for previous applicants), Southampton, Staffordshire, York.

GRADUATE DESTINATIONS AND EMPLOYMENT (2005 HESA)
Graduates surveyed 1445 **Employed** 660 **In further study** 330 **Assumed unemployed** 125.

OTHER DEGREE SUBJECTS FOR CONSIDERATION
Divinity; History of Art; History and Philosophy of Science; Human Sciences; Psychology; Religious Studies; Science; Theology.

PHOTOGRAPHY

(see also **Film, Radio, Video and TV Studies** and **Media Studies**)

NB The points totals shown to the left of the institutions are for ease of reference only. It must not be assumed that tariff points are always used by institutions or that they can be substituted for an offer in grades. The level of an offer is not necessarily indicative of the quality of a course.

Applicants should note that there are two pathways for those applying for some of these courses (Route A or Route B or both): see **Chapter 5** for details.

COURSE OFFERS INFORMATION

Subject requirements/preferences **GCSE** Art and/or a portfolio usually required. **AL** One or two subjects may be required including an art/design or creative subject.

Your target offers

300 pts **Leeds** – BBB 300 pts (Cnma Photo TV St)

280 pts **Bournemouth** – 280 pts (PhotoM (Photo Film TV Multim))

260 pts **Chester** – 260–240 pts (Photo Comb courses)

240 pts **De Montfort** – 240 pts (Photo Vid)
Great Yarmouth (Coll) – 240 pts (Photo Dig Media)
Lincoln – 240 pts (Contemp Lns Imag Media)
Nottingham Trent – 240 pts (Photo Photo Euro)
UCE Birmingham – 240 pts (Photography)

220 pts **Glamorgan** – 220 pts (Media Prod (Photo))
Robert Gordon – CCD (Photo Electron Media)

200 pts **Bristol UWE** – 200 pts (Photography check with admissions tutor)
Creative Arts (UC) – 200 pts (Photography)
Gloucestershire – 200–240 pts (Photojrnl; Photo Edit Adv)
Napier – 200 pts (Photo Film Imag)
Newport – 200 pts (Doc Photo; Photo Art; NMedia Pub; Doc Film TV)
Northumbria – 200 pts 2AL Fdn art+portfolio (Contemp Photo Prac)
Sunderland – 200 pts (Media Prod (TV Rad) (Vid NMedia); Photo joint hons)

180 pts **Anglia Ruskin** – 180 pts (Photography)
East London – 180 pts (Photography)
Northampton – 180 pts (Photo Prac)
Portsmouth – 180–240 pts Fdn art (Photo; Vid Prod)
Southampton Solent – 180 pts (Photography)

160 pts **Blackpool and Fylde (Coll)** – 160 pts (Photo; Wldlf Photo)
Central Lancashire – 160–200 pts (Photo; Photo Journal; Photo Aud Vis Media; Photo Fash Brnd Prom)
Creative Arts (UC) – 160 pts (Photo Media Arts; Vid Photo)
Cumbria – CC 160 pts (Photography)
Derby – 160 pts (Photography)
Grimsby (IFHE) – 160 pts (Photography)
Hertfordshire – 160 pts (Dig Lens Media)
London South Bank – CC (Dig Film Vid; Dig Photo)
Manchester Met – 160 pts+Fdn art (Photography)
Middlesex – 160 pts (Photography)

Roehampton – 160 pts (Photo courses)
Southend Campus Essex – 160–180 pts (Photography)
Staffordshire – 160–120 pts (Photography)
Sunderland – 160–140 pts (Journal Photo; Photo Vid Dig Imag)
Thames Valley (London CMusMedia) – 160 pts (Photo Dig Imag; Photo St)
Westminster – CC (Photo Arts)
Wolverhampton – 160–220 pts (Photo; Vid)
140 pts **Bolton** – 140 pts (Photo Vid)
Edinburgh (CA) – DEE 140 pts (Vis Comm (Photo))
120 pts **Bournemouth (AI)** – 120 pts (Photography)
Dewsbury (Coll) – DD (Contemp Photo Arts)
Glasgow (SA) – DD (Fine Art (Photo))
Southampton City (Coll) – 120 pts (Photography)
Southampton Solent – 120 pts (Fash Photo)
Stockport (CFHE) – 120–240 pts (Doc Fine Art Photo)
Swansea (IHE) – 120–180 pts (Photojrnl; Photo Arts; Vid)
100 pts **Arts London (CComm)** – contact Univ (Photography)
80 pts **Bedfordshire** – contact Univ (Dig Photo Vid Art)
Brighton – 80 pts (Edit Photo)
Carmarthenshire (Coll) – 80 pts (Photography)
Cleveland (CAD) – 80–120 pts (Photography)
Croydon (Coll) – 80 pts (Photomedia)
Falmouth (UC) – EE (Photo; Press Photo; Mar Nat Hist Photo)
Kingston – EE (Graph Photo)
Robert Gordon – EE (Photography)

Leeds Met – contact University

Alternative offers
IB offers Manchester Met 26 pts.
Scottish offers See **Chapter 7**.

OTHER HIGHER EDUCATION COURSES IN THE SUBJECT FIELD
Foundation degrees (contact institutions for details) Anglia Ruskin; Bournemouth (AI); Derby; Dewsbury (Coll); Dunstable (Coll); East Lancashire (IHE); Farnborough (CT); Herefordshire (CAD); Hull (Coll); Leeds (CAD); Leicester (Coll); Nescot; Newcastle (Coll); Plymouth (CAD); St Helens (Coll); South Nottingham (Coll); Truro (Coll); Westminster City (Coll).

Higher National Diploma courses
100 pts **and below**
Arts London; Barking (Coll); Bournemouth; Bradford (Coll); Bristol City (Coll); Buckinghamshire Chilterns (UC); Carmarthenshire (Coll); City and Islington (Coll); Cornwall (Coll); Doncaster (Univ Centre); East Lancashire (IHE); East Surrey (Coll); Glamorgan; Great Yarmouth (Coll); Greenwich; Grimsby (IFHE); Hull (Coll); Leeds (CAD); Leicester (Coll); Liverpool (CmC); Llandrillo Cymru (Coll); Manchester City (Coll); Mid Cheshire (Coll); Nescot; Newcastle (Coll); North East Wales (IHE); Northampton; Plymouth (CAD); St Helens (Coll); Salisbury (Coll); Sandwell (Coll); Sheffield (Coll); Solihull (Coll); Southend Campus Essex; South Nottingham (Coll); Staffordshire; Stoke on Trent (Coll); Tameside (Coll); Teesside; Thames Valley; Truro (Coll); Warwickshire (Coll); West Thames (Coll).

CHOOSING YOUR COURSE (SEE ALSO CH.1)
Subject information Photography courses offer a range of specialised studies involving commercial, industrial and still photography, portraiture and film, digital and video work. Increasingly this subject is featuring in Graphic Design courses. See also **Appendix 2**. **Useful websites** www.the-aop.org; www.rps.org; www.bjphoto.co.uk.

Course variations Photomedia (Photography, Film and TV with Multimedia) (Bournemouth); Visual Communication (Photography) (Edinburgh (CA)); Marine and Natural History Photography (Falmouth (UC)); Photojournalism (Gloucestershire); Digital Photography and Video Art (London South Bank); Documentary and Fine Art Photography (Stockport (CFHE)). *NOW CHECK PROSPECTUSES AND WEBSITES FOR ANY RECENT CHANGES.*

Universities and colleges teaching quality See www.tqi.ac.uk; www.qaa.ac.uk.

Sandwich degree courses Portsmouth; Staffordshire; UCE Birmingham.

ADMISSIONS INFORMATION

Number of applicants per place (approx) Arts London 10; Blackpool and Fylde (Coll) 3; Bournemouth (AI) 7; Cleveland (CAD) 2; Croydon (Coll) 15; Derby 20; Falmouth (UC) 3; Napier 33; Newport 2; Nottingham Trent 4; Plymouth 2; Plymouth (CAD) 7; Portsmouth 4; Staffordshire 3; Stockport (CFHE) 6; Swansea (IHE) 12; UCE Birmingham 6.

Advice to applicants and planning the UCAS personal statement Discuss your interest in photography and your knowledge of various aspects of the subject, for example, digital, 35mm, video, landscape, medical, wildlife and portrait photography. Read photographic journals to keep up-to-date on developments, particularly in photographic technology. You will also need first-hand experience of photography and be competent in basic skills. **Croydon (Coll)** Broad range of interests. **Derby** (Non-EU students) Fluency in written and spoken English important. Portfolio of work essential. See also **Appendix 2**.

Misconceptions about this course Some believe that all courses are all practical work with no theory. **Cumbria** They didn't realise the facilities were so good! **Dewsbury (Coll)** Some applicants think that it's a traditional photography course. It's as digital as the individual wants it to be.

Selection interviews **Yes** Most institutions will interview applicants and expect to see a portfolio of work.

Interview advice and questions Questions relate to the applicant's portfolio of work which, for these courses, is of prime importance. Who are your favourite photographers? What is the most recent exhibition you have attended? Have any leading photographers influenced your work? Questions regarding contemporary photography. Written work sometimes required. See **Chapter 6**.

Reasons for rejection (non-academic) Lack of passion for the subject. Lack of exploration and creativity in practical work. Poorly presented portfolio.

AFTER-RESULTS ADVICE

Universities with vacancies in Clearing (2006) Bolton; Bournemouth; Bristol UWE; Central Lancashire; Chester; Cumbria; De Montfort; Derby; Gloucestershire; Northampton; Nottingham Trent; Roehampton; Southampton Solent; Staffordshire; Sunderland; Thames Valley; UCE Birmingham; Westminster; Wolverhampton.

Offers to applicants repeating A-levels **Same** Blackpool and Fylde (Coll), Chester, Cumbria, Dewsbury (Coll), Manchester Met, Nottingham Trent, Plymouth, Staffordshire, UCE Birmingham.

GRADUATE DESTINATIONS AND EMPLOYMENT (2005 HESA)

See under **Film, Radio, Video and TV Studies**.

OTHER DEGREE SUBJECTS FOR CONSIDERATION

Animation; Art and Design; Film, Radio, Video and TV Studies; Media Studies; Moving Image.

PHYSICAL EDUCATION

(see also **Sports Sciences/Studies**)

NB The points totals shown to the left of the institutions are for ease of reference only. It must not be assumed that tariff points are always used by institutions or that they can be substituted for an offer in grades. The level of an offer is not necessarily indicative of the quality of a course.

Abbreviations: P – Primary Teaching; S – Secondary Teaching; QTS – Qualified Teacher Status.

COURSE OFFERS INFORMATION

Subject requirements/preferences **GCSE** English and mathematics. **AL** PE, sports studies and science are preferred subjects and for some courses one of these may be required.

Your target offers
300 pts **Belfast (Queen's)** – BBB (PE Educ)
280 pts **Hull** – 280 pts (PE Spo Sci Mgt; PE Spo Sci Psy)
260 pts **Birmingham** – 260 pts (Spo PE Commun St)
　　　　 Brunel – 260 pts (Spo Sci PE)
　　　　 Chester – 260 pts (PE Spo Exer Sci courses)
　　　　 Hull – 260 pts (PE Spo Sci)
　　　　 Manchester Met – BCC 260 pts (PE)
　　　　 Sheffield Hallam – 260 pts (PE Yth Spo)
　　　　 Stirling – BCC (Spo St PE)
240 pts **Bangor** – 240 pts (Spo Hlth PE)
　　　　 Brighton – 240 pts (PE QTS)
　　　　 Brunel – 240 pts (PE S)
　　　　 Edinburgh – CCC–BBC (BEd PE)
　　　　 Liverpool John Moores – 240 pts (Spo Dev PE; PE P S; Physl Actvt Exer Hlth)
220 pts **Edge Hill** – 220 pts (PE)
　　　　 Winchester – 220 pts (P PE QTS)
200 pts **Chichester** – 200–240 pts (PE QTS S; Advntr Educ)
　　　　 Cumbria – 200 pts (PE courses)
　　　　 De Montfort – 200 pts (BA PE QTS S; Spo PE)
　　　　 Leeds Trinity and All Saints (Coll) – CDD 200 pts (P PE)
　　　　 Manchester Met – 200 pts (Educ St Spo; Coach Spo Dev)
　　　　 Worcester – CDD 200 pts (PE Spo Coach Sci; PE)
　　　　 York St John – CDD–DDD 200–180 pts (Spo St PE)
180 pts **Canterbury Christ Church** – 180 pts (PE QTS)
　　　　 Liverpool Hope – DDD 180–160 pts (Educ St Spo St)
　　　　 Marjon (Coll) – 180–240 pts (Coach PE)
　　　　 St Mary's (Coll) – 180–200 pts (BA QTS S PE)
　　　　 Trinity Carmarthen (Coll) – 180 pts (PE)
160 pts **Greenwich** – 160 pts (PE Spo; BEd P PE)
　　　　 Newman (CHE) – 160 pts (Educ St Spo St; PE P Spo St)
　　　　 Plymouth – 160–200 pts (PE P)
　　　　 Roehampton – 160 pts (P Educ (PE) QTS)
　　　　 St Mary's (Coll) – 160–200 pts (PE Commun)
　　　　 Wolverhampton – 160–220 pts (PE non-QTS; Physl Actvt Exer Hlth)
120 pts **North East Wales (IHE)** – 120 pts (PE)

　　　　 Leeds Met – contact University

Alternative offers
IB offers Birmingham 32 pts; Chichester 28 pts.
Scottish offers See **Chapter 7**.

CHOOSING YOUR COURSE (SEE ALSO CH.1)

Subject information Physical Education courses are very popular and unfortunately restricted in number. Ability in gymnastics and involvement in sport are obviously important factors. See also **Appendix 2**. **Useful websites** www.afpe.org.uk; www.uksport.gov.uk; see also under **Education**.

Course variations Sport, Physical Education and Community Studies (Birmingham); PE, Sports Science and Psychology (Hull); Coaching and Sport Development (Manchester Met); PE and Youth Sport (Sheffield Hallam); Physical Activity, Exercise and Health (Wolverhampton). *NOW CHECK PROSPECTUSES AND WEBSITES FOR ANY RECENT CHANGES.*

Top universities and colleges (Research) See under **Sports Sciences/Studies**.

ADMISSIONS INFORMATION

Number of applicants per place (approx) Bangor 19; Birmingham 5; Brunel 10; Chichester 5; De Montfort 7; Edge Hill 40; Leeds Trinity and All Saints (Coll) 33; Liverpool John Moores 4; Marjon (Coll) 18; Newman (CHE) 5; St Mary's (Coll) 9; Sheffield Hallam 60; Worcester 31.

Advice to applicants and planning the UCAS personal statement Ability in gymnastics, athletics and all sports and games is important. Full details of these activities should be given on the UCAS application – for example, teams, dates and awards achieved, assisting in extra-curricular activities. Involvement with local sports clubs, health clubs, summer camps, gap year. Relevant experience in coaching, teaching, community and youth work. **Liverpool John Moores** Commitment to working with children and a good sports background.

Selection interviews Yes Most institutions. In most cases, applicants will take part in physical education practical tests and games/gymnastics, depending on the course. The results of these tests could affect the level of offers. See **Chapter 6**.

Interview advice and questions The applicant's interests in physical education will be discussed, with specific questions on, for example, sportsmanship, refereeing, umpiring and coaching. Questions in the past have also included: What qualities should a good netball goal defence possess? How could you encourage a group of children into believing that sport is fun? Do you think that physical education should be compulsory in schools? Why do you think you would make a good teacher? What is the name of the education minister? **Liverpool John Moores** Questions on what the applicant has gained or learned through experiences with children.

Reasons for rejection (non-academic) Poor communication and presentational skills. Relatively poor sporting background or knowledge. Lack of knowledge about the teaching of physical education and the commitment required. Lack of ability in practicalities, for example, gymnastics, dance when relevant. Poor self-presentation. Poor writing skills.

AFTER-RESULTS ADVICE

Universities with vacancies in Clearing (2006) Bangor; Birmingham; Brunel; Canterbury Christ Church; Cumbria; Greenwich; Hull; Liverpool John Moores; York St John.

Offers to applicants repeating A-levels Same Liverpool John Moores, Newman (CHE).

NEW GRADUATE DESTINATIONS AND EMPLOYMENT (2005 HESA)
No data available.

OTHER DEGREE SUBJECTS FOR CONSIDERATION
Coach Education; Exercise and Fitness; Exercise Physiology; Human Biology; Leisure and Recreation; Physiotherapy; Sport and Exercise Science; Sport Health and Exercise; Sport Studies/Sciences; Sports Development; Sports Engineering; Sports Psychology; Sports Therapy.

PHYSICS

(see also **Astronomy/Astrophysics**)

NB The points totals shown to the left of the institutions are for ease of reference only. It must not be assumed that tariff points are always used by institutions or that they can be substituted for an offer in grades. The level of an offer is not necessarily indicative of the quality of a course.

COURSE OFFERS INFORMATION

Subject requirements/preferences **GCSE** Grade A–C in English. **Belfast (Queen's)**, **Exeter** Grade B in French or German for language courses. **Durham** (MPhys, BSc) Grade A in three subjects, grade B in three subjects. **Hertfordshire**, **Paisley** Grade A–C in English. **London (QM)** Average of grade B across all subjects. **London (RH)** Good proportion of grades A and B. **Surrey** Six subjects at grade B or better including science and mathematics. **Swansea** Three/four grades A* or A, three/four grade Bs. **York** Grade B in physics and mathematics. **AL** Physics and mathematics are required for most courses.

Your target offers

360 pts   **and above**
   Cambridge – AAA (Nat Sci (Phys Expmntl Theor) (Physl Sci); Astro)
   Durham – AAA (Nat Sci Phys)
   Durham – AAA–AAB (Phys; Phys Astron; Theor Phys)
   Oxford – Offers vary eg AAA–AAB (Phys; Phys Phil)
   Warwick – AAA–AAB (Maths Phys)

340 pts   **Bath** – AAB (Maths Phys)
   Birmingham – AAB–ABB (Phys; Theor Phys; Phys Astro; Phys Bus Mgt; Phys Astro Int; Phys Spc Rsch; Phys Prtcl Phys Cosmo; Phys Nano)
   Edinburgh – AAB 2nd yr entry (Astro; Phys; Comput Phys; Phys Meteor; Phys Mus)

Durham University

Department of Physics

B.Sc. and M.Phys/M.Sci. degrees in Physics, Physics & Astronomy, Theoretical Physics and Mathematics & Physics, Chemistry & Physics and E-science & Physics

One of the top departments in the Times League Table in recent years

Supportive college system

Optional courses, including particle physics, cosmology and photonics

Excellent laboratory facilities including 4 modern telescopes

For more information see
www.dur.ac.uk/physics/undergraduate or
to arrange a visit ring the admissions secretary
on 0191 334 3726

Imperial London – AAB (Phys; Phys St Musl Perf; Phys Yr Euro; Phys Theor Phys)
London (UCL) – AAB+AS–BBB+AS (Phys; Chem Phys; Theor Phys; Med Phys)
Manchester – AAB–BBB (Phys; Phys Euro; Phys Technol Phys; Phys Astro; Phys Bus Mgt; Phys Phil)
St Andrews – AAB 2nd yr entry (Phys courses)
Warwick – AAB–ABB (Phys; Phys Bus St)

320 pts **Bath** – ABB (MPhys Phys; Maths Phys)
Belfast (Queen's) – ABB (MSci Phys; Phys Euro)
Bristol – ABB–BBB (Cheml Phys; Cheml Phys Ind Exp; Phys courses)
Cardiff – ABB (MPhys Astro; Phys Astron; Phys; Phys Mus; Theor Comput Phys)
Durham – ABB (MSci Phys Astron)
East Anglia – ABB (Cheml Phys Ind; Cheml Phys N Am)
Glasgow – ABB–BBB (BA Phys)
Lancaster – ABB–BBB (MPhys Phys; MSci Phys N Am; Phys Astro Cosmo; Phys Med Phys; Phys (Comput Phys) (Theor Phys); Theor Phys Maths)
Leeds – ABB (MPhys Phys; Phys Astro; Phys Nano; Theor Phys)
Leicester – ABB 320 pts (MPhys Phys; Phys Astro; Phys Spc Sci Tech; Phys Nano Tech; Phys Planet Sci)
Liverpool – ABB 320 pts (MPhys Phys; Mathem Phys; Phys Maths; Astro; Theor Phys; Phys Maths)
London (King's) – ABB+AS–BBB+AS **or** ABbbb (Phys; Phys Phil; Phys Mgt; Phys Med Apps; Phys Mol Biophys)
Nottingham – ABB–BBB (Chem Mol Phys; Mathem Phys; Phys; Phys Euro Lang; Phys Astron; Phys Med Phys; Phys Theor Astro; Phys Theor Phys))
Sheffield – ABB–ABC (MPhys Theor Phys; Phys Aus/N Am; Phys Phil)
Southampton – ABB 320 pts (Phys; Phys Astron; Phys Nano; Phys Photon; Phys Spc Sci)
Sussex – ABB (MPhys Phys; Phys Astro; Phys Foren Sci; Theor Phys)
York – ABB (MPhys) (Phys; Phys Astro; Phys Bus Mgt; Maths Phys; Phys Phil courses)

300 pts **Bath** – ABC (BSc Maths Phys; Phys Comp)
Birmingham – ABC–BBC (Phys; Phys Prctl Cosmo; Phys Bus Mgt; Theor Phys App Maths)
Durham – ABC (BSc Phys Astro; Theor Phys; Phys)
East Anglia – BBB (Cheml Phys)
Exeter – BBB (Phys Euro/Aus/N Am/NZ; Phys Astro; Phys Med Phys; Phys Qntm Las Tech)
Glasgow – BBB–BBC (BSc Phys; Astron Phys; Cheml Phys)
Lancaster – BBB (BSc Phys; Phys Med Phys; Theor Phys; Phys Astro Cosmo)
Liverpool – BBB (BSc Phys Ocn Clim St; Mathem Phys; Phys Med Appl; Phys Astron)
London (RH) – 300–320 pts (MSci Phys; App Phys; Theor Phys; Phys Mus; Phys Prtcl Phys; Phys Mgt; Phys Astro)
Loughborough – 300 pts (MPhys Eng Phys; Phys Maths)
Strathclyde – BBB–BBC (Biophys; App Phys; Phys Mathem Fin; Phys Vis Simul; Lsr Phys Optoel; Phys)
Surrey – BBB (MPhys Phys; Phys Fin; Phys Med Phys; Phys Nclr Astro; Phys Sat Tech)
Swansea – 300–320 pts (Theor Phys; Phys joint hons)
York – BBB (BSc Phys courses)

280 pts **Aberdeen** – BBC 2nd yr entry (Phys; Physl Sci)
Aberystwyth – 280 pts (Spc Sci Robot)
Cardiff – BBC (BSc Phys Astron; Astro; Phys Med Phys)
Central Lancashire – BBC (MPhys Phys; App Phys)
Exeter – BBC (BSc Phys courses; Qntm Sci Lsr)
Kent – BBC–BCC (MPhys/BSc Phys; Phys Foren Sci; Phys Spc Sci Sys; Phys Astro)
Leeds – BBC (BSc Phys; Phys Astro; Phys Nano)
Leicester – BBC 280 pts (BSc Phys; Phys Astro; Phys Spc Sci Tech; Phys Nano Tech; Phys Planet Sci)
Liverpool John Moores – BBC 280 pts (Phys Astron; Astro)
London (QM) – 280 pts (Phys; Phys Comp; Phys Comp Sci; Phys Env; Phys Bus Mgt)

London (RH) – BBC (Phys Sci Comm)
Loughborough – 280 pts (BSc Phys; Phys Comp; Phys Mgt; Spo Sci Phys; Phys Maths; Eng Phys)
Sussex – BBC **or** 310 pts 3AL+AS (BSc Phys; Phys Astron; Phys Foren Sci; Theor Phys)
Swansea – 280 pts (Phys courses except under **300 pts**)

260 pts **Belfast (Queen's)** – BCC (BSc Phys; Theor Phys)
Hull – 260–300 pts (MSci Phys Med Tech; Phys Lsr Phot; Phys Astro; Phys; App Phys)
London (RH) – BCC–BBC (BSc Phys courses)
Surrey – BCC (BSc Phys; Phys Med Phys; Phys Nclr Astro; Phys Astro; Phys Sat Tech; Phys Fin)

240 pts **Aberdeen** – CCC (Nat Phil (Phys))
Aberystwyth – 240 pts (MPhys Phys courses; BSc Phys courses)

physics
AT BRISTOL

▶▶ Live and study in one of the most
dynamic and exciting cities in the UK

▶▶ Choose from programmes in Physics, Physics & Astrophysics,
Mathematics & Physics, and Physics & Philosophy

▶▶ Enjoy excellent teaching with world-class researchers and facilities -
15 new lecturers and £10M new teaching lab

    Central Lancashire – 240 pts (Phys Maths)
    Dundee – 240–300 pts (Phys courses)
    Edinburgh – CCC 1st yr entry (Phys; Comput Phys; Phys Meteor; Phys Mus)
    Heriot-Watt – AA+AS 2nd yr entry (MPhys courses)
    Hertfordshire – 240–280 pts (Phys Sci Comp)
    Hull – 240–280 pts (BSc App Phys; Phys Astro; Phys Lsr Phot; Phys Med Tech; Phys Phil)
    Keele – 240–260 pts (Physics)
    Lancaster – CCC (Phys St)
    Salford – CCC (Phys; Phys N Am; Phys Acoust; Phys Euro; Phys Avn St; Phys Lang; Phys Spc Tech)
    Sheffield – CCC (Fdn Phys)
    Surrey – CCC (Fdn Phys)
220 pts **City** – 220–280 pts (Biomed Eng App Phys)
    Dundee – 220 pts 1st yr entry (BSc Phys 4 yr; MSci Phys 5 yr)
    Nottingham Trent – 220–240 pts (Phys; Phys Astro; Astron Phys)
200 pts **Aberdeen** – CDD 1st yr entry (Physics)
    Central Lancashire – 200 pts (Phys Media Prod Tech; Phys Mgt; Phys Mark; Phys Phil)
    Heriot-Watt – BB+AS 2nd yr entry (BSc Phys courses)
160 pts **Central Lancashire** – 160–200 pts (Phys courses except under **280/240 pts**)
    Heriot-Watt – CC+AS 1st yr entry (BSc Phys courses)
    Loughborough – CC (Fdn Phys)
    Strathclyde – CC (Phys QTS)
140 pts **Liverpool** – 140 pts flexible entry reqs (Phys New Tech)
120 pts **Paisley** – DD **or** bbc (Phys courses)
100 pts **London (Birk)** – 100 pts (p/t Phys)
80 pts **Aberystwyth** – 80 pts (Phys Ord)
    Salford – 80 pts (Fdn Phys)

For a quick reference offers calculator, fold out the inside back cover.

Alternative offers

IB offers Aberystwyth 29–30 pts; Bath 32–35 pts; Bristol 30 pts; Cambridge 38–42 pts; Essex 32–33 pts; Keele 26–28 pts; Kent 30 pts; Lancaster 28–33 pts; Leicester 28–34 pts; Liverpool 32–33 pts; London (King's) 32 pts, (QM) 30–32 pts, (UCL) 36–38 pts; Loughborough 30 pts; Manchester 33–37 pts; Nottingham 36 pts H665; St Andrews 36 pts; Salford 27 pts; Sheffield 32–33 pts; Surrey 30 pts; Warwick 36–38 pts; York 32–34 pts.
Scottish offers See **Chapter 7**.

OTHER HIGHER EDUCATION COURSES IN THE SUBJECT FIELD

Foundation degrees (contact institutions for details) Hull; Nottingham Trent.

Higher National Diploma courses

100 pts   and below
People's (Coll).

CHOOSING YOUR COURSE (SEE ALSO CH.1)

Subject information There is a considerable shortage of applicants for Physics courses. Many courses have flexible arrangements to enable students to follow their own interests and specialisations, for example circuit design, microwave devices, cosmology, medical physics, solid state electronics. **Useful websites** www.scienceyear.com; www.scicentral.com; www.ipem.org.uk; www.iop.org; www.noisemakers.org.uk.

Course variations Natural Philosophy (Physics) (Aberdeen); Physics with Particle Physics and Cosmology (Birmingham); Physics with Space Research (Birmingham); Chemical Physics (East Anglia); Quantum Science and Lasers (Exeter); Physics with a Year in Australia, Europe, New Zealand or North America (Exeter); Sports Science and Physics (Loughborough); Physics with Forensic Science (Southampton; Sussex); Physics with Mathematical Finance (Strathclyde); Physics with Satellite Technology (Surrey). *NOW CHECK PROSPECTUSES AND WEBSITES FOR ANY RECENT CHANGES.*

Universities and colleges teaching quality See www.tqi.ac.uk; www.qaa.ac.uk.

Top universities and colleges (Research) Belfast (Queen's); Birmingham; Bristol; Cambridge*; Cardiff; Durham; Edinburgh; Exeter; Glasgow; Imperial London*; Lancaster*; Leeds; Leicester; Liverpool; London (QM), (RH), (UCL); Manchester; Nottingham; Oxford*; St Andrews; Sheffield; Southampton; Surrey; Sussex; Swansea; Warwick.

Sandwich degree courses Aston; Bath; Bristol; Loughborough; Nottingham Trent; Salford; Surrey.

ADMISSIONS INFORMATION

Number of applicants per place (approx) Bath 8; Birmingham 6; Bristol 9; Cardiff 4, (Phys Astron) 6; Dundee 5; Durham 6; Edinburgh 9; Exeter 5; Heriot-Watt 5; Hull 7; Imperial London 3; Kent 8; Lancaster 8; Leeds 7; Leicester 7; Liverpool 4; London (King's) 7, (QM) 6, (RH) 9, (UCL) 6; Loughborough 6; Nottingham 9; Oxford (success rate 46%); Salford 5; Southampton 5; Strathclyde 5; Surrey 5; Swansea 3; Warwick 8; York 9.

Advice to applicants and planning the UCAS personal statement Work experience should be mentioned, together with interests in maths and physics. Admissions tutors look for potential, enthusiasm and interest in the subject. The Institute of Physics can provide information on the work of the physicist. An awareness of the range of careers in which physics is involved should also be mentioned on the UCAS application, together with an explanation of any particular interests and details of books read on physics or mathematics (not science fiction!), and attendance at courses on physics or engineering. See **Appendix 2**.

Selection interviews Yes Aston, Bath, Birmingham, Cambridge, Durham, Exeter, Heriot-Watt, Hull, Lancaster, Liverpool, London (QM), (RH), Loughborough, Nottingham, Oxford, Sheffield, Strathclyde, Surrey, Swansea, Warwick, York; **Some** Cardiff, Dundee, Salford.

Interview advice and questions Questions will almost certainly focus on those aspects of the physics A/AS-level course which the student enjoys. **Bristol** Why Physics? Questions on mechanics, physics and pure maths. Given paper and calculator and questions asked orally; best to take your own calculator. Tutors seek enthusiastic and highly motivated students and the physicist's ability to apply basic principles to unfamiliar situations. See **Chapter 6**.

Applicants' impressions (A=Open day; B=Interview day) Bath (B) We had a tour of the campus and department, followed by an informal interview with questions based on my personal statement. **Bristol** (B) There was a tour of the city, the department and accommodation. A formal interview followed. **London (RH)** (Phys Astron; B) There was a tour of the campus with an opportunity to see the telescope. The interviewer asked questions about star gazing and web design and some ideas about the solar system. **London (UCL)** (B) There was a tour and talk about the course. I was asked oral questions only on physics during the interview. **Oxford** (B) I had a formal physics interview, going through problems and explaining points which I had mentioned in my personal statement. **Southampton** (Phys Astron; A) The open day consisted of a tour of the campus and labs and talks about the course. Seems a really good university. **Warwick** (B) No interview as such, just small group discussions.

AFTER-RESULTS ADVICE

Universities with vacancies in Clearing (2006) Aberdeen; Aberystwyth; Bath; Belfast (Queen's); Cardiff; Dundee; East Anglia; Glasgow; Heriot-Watt; Hertfordshire; Hull; Keele; Kent; Lancaster; Leeds; Leicester; Liverpool; London (King's), (QM), (RH); Loughborough; Nottingham; Nottingham Trent; Salford; Sheffield; Southampton; Strathclyde; Surrey; Swansea; York.

Offers to applicants repeating A-levels Higher Bristol, Glasgow, St Andrews, Warwick; **Possibly higher** Aberystwyth, Hull, Leeds, Loughborough, York; **Same** Birmingham, Cardiff, Dundee, Exeter, Lancaster, Leicester, Liverpool, Salford, Swansea.

GRADUATE DESTINATIONS AND EMPLOYMENT (2005 HESA)

Graduates surveyed 1670 **Employed** 610 **In further study** 585 **Assumed unemployed** 145.

OTHER DEGREE SUBJECTS FOR CONSIDERATION

Astronomy; Astrophysics; Computer Science; Earth Sciences; Engineering subjects; Geophysics; Materials Science and Metallurgy; Mathematics; Meteorology; Natural Sciences; Oceanography; Optometry; Radiography.

PHYSIOLOGY

(see also **Animal Sciences**)

NB The points totals shown to the left of the institutions are for ease of reference only. It must not be assumed that tariff points are always used by institutions or that they can be substituted for an offer in grades. The level of an offer is not necessarily indicative of the quality of a course.

COURSE OFFERS INFORMATION

Subject requirements/preferences GCSE Science and mathematics at grade A. **Bristol** Biology grade A–C. **Cardiff** Minimum of six grade Bs or above. **Edinburgh** Mathematics grade B. **Newcastle** Biology and mathematics if not offered at A-level. 75% grade A or above. **AL** Two science subjects are usually required; chemistry and biology are the preferred subjects.

Your target offers

360 pts and above
    Cambridge – AAA (Nat Sci (Physiol))
    Oxford – Offers vary eg AAA–AAB +BMAT (Physiol Sci; Physiol Psy; Physiol Phil)
340 pts **Manchester** – AAB–BBB (Physiol; Physiol Ind; Physiol Modn Lang)
320 pts **Cardiff** – ABB–BBB 320–300 pts (Biomed Sci (Physiol))
    Leicester – ABB (Med Physiol)
300 pts **Birmingham** – BBB (Med Sci)
    Bristol – BBB (Physiol Sci)
    Dundee – 300 pts 2nd yr entry (Physiol Sci; Physiol Spo Biomed; Bioch Physiol Sci)
    Edinburgh – BBB (Physiology)
    Glasgow – BBB–BCC (Physiol; Physiol Spo Sci; Physiol Psy)
    Leeds – BBB 300 pts (Hum Physiol)
    London (King's) – BBB+AS **or** BBbb **or** ACac (Physiol; Physiol Pharmacol)
    Newcastle – BBB (Physiol Sci)
    St Andrews – BBB (Physiology)
280 pts **Aberdeen** – BBC 2nd yr entry (Physiology)
    Glasgow – BBC (Physiology)
    London (RH) – 280–300 pts (Zool Physiol)
    Sheffield – BBC **or** BBbb **or** ABbb (Physiol Pharmacol)
260 pts **Belfast (Queen's)** – BCC–CCCc (Physiology)
    Essex – 260–240 pts (Clin Physiol (Cardio))
    Liverpool – BCC–BBC 260–280 pts (Physiology)
    Wolverhampton – 260–320 pts (Hum Physiol joint hons)
240 pts **Dundee** – 240 pts 1st yr entry (Physiol Sci; Physiol Spo Biomed; Bioch Physiol Sci)
    Leeds – CCC (Clin Physiol (Cardio))
    Swansea – 240 pts (Clin Physiol Rsprty Physiol; Clin Physiol Med Phys; Clin Physiol Cardiol)
    Ulster – 240 pts (Clin Physiol)
200 pts **Aberdeen** – CDD 1st yr entry (Physiology)
    Central Lancashire – 200 pts (Hum Physiol)
    Manchester Met – 200–240 (Physiol Pharmacol)
    Salford – 200 pts (Physiol Bioch)
180 pts **Bristol UWE** – 180–220 pts (App Physiol Pharmacol)
    Hertfordshire – 180–220 pts (Physiology)
    Nottingham Trent – 180 pts (Physiol Pharmacol)
    Sunderland – DDD–DDE 180–160 pts (Physiol courses)

160 pts **Westminster** – CC (Physiol Pharmacol)
Wolverhampton – 160–200 pts (Pharmacol Hum Physiol)
80 pts **and below**
Eastleigh (Coll) – (Fdn Sci)

Leeds Met – contact University

Alternative offers
IB offers Bristol 32 pts; Bristol UWE 32–34 pts; Cambridge 38–42 pts; London (King's) 32 pts;
Manchester 32–35 pts; Oxford 38–42 pts.
Scottish offers See **Chapter 7.**

OTHER HIGHER EDUCATION COURSES IN THE SUBJECT FIELD
Foundation degrees (contact institution for details) Nescot.

Higher National Diploma courses Central Lancashire; People's (Coll); Wolverhampton.

CHOOSING YOUR COURSE (SEE ALSO CH.1)
Subject information Physiology is a study of body function. Courses in this wide-ranging subject will
cover the central nervous system, special senses and neuro-muscular mechanisms, and body-regulating
systems such as exercise, stress and temperature regulation. **Oxford** (Physiol Sci) Applicants take the
BioMedical Admissions Test (BMAT) (see **Chapter 6**). **Useful websites** www.scienceyear.com;
www.physoc.org; see also **Biological Sciences**.

Course variations Physiology with Sports Biomedicine (Dundee); Medical Physiology (Leicester);
Physiology with Pharmacology (Nottingham Trent); Physiology with Biochemistry (Salford); Clinical
Physiology with Cardiology (Swansea). *NOW CHECK PROSPECTUSES AND WEBSITES FOR ANY RECENT
CHANGES.*

Universities and colleges teaching quality See www.tqi.ac.uk; www.qaa.ac.uk.

Top universities and colleges (Research) Aberdeen; Leeds; Liverpool*; Newcastle; Oxford.

Sandwich degree courses Bristol UWE; Coventry; Hertfordshire; London (King's); Nottingham Trent;
Salford; Southampton.

ADMISSIONS INFORMATION
Number of applicants per place (approx) Birmingham 9; Bristol 8; Cardiff 8; Dundee 5; Leeds 4;
Liverpool 10; London (King's) 5; Newcastle 6; Nottingham Trent 3; Oxford (success rate 41%);
Sheffield 25.

Advice to applicants and planning the UCAS personal statement See **Anatomical
Science/Anatomy** and **Biological Sciences**.

Selection interviews **Yes** Birmingham, Cambridge, Leeds, Newcastle, Nottingham Trent, Oxford,
Sheffield; **Some** Bristol, Cardiff, Dundee.

Interview advice and questions Past questions include: What made you decide to do a Physiology
degree? What experimental work have you done connected with physiology? What future career do
you have in mind? What is physiology? Why not choose Medicine instead? What practicals do you do at
school? **Cardiff** Interviewer expects to see outside interests and ability to mix with people as well as
an interest in biological sciences. **Oxford** Over 85% of applicants interviewed. See **Chapter 6**.

AFTER-RESULTS ADVICE
Universities with vacancies in Clearing (2006) Aberdeen; Bristol; Central Lancashire; Dundee; Essex;
Glasgow; Hertfordshire; Leicester; Salford; Sheffield; Sunderland; Swansea.

Offers to applicants repeating A-levels **Higher** Bristol, Glasgow, Leeds, Leicester, Newcastle, St
Andrews, Sheffield; **Same** Cardiff, Dundee.

GRADUATE DESTINATIONS AND EMPLOYMENT (2005 HESA)
(including **Anatomy/Anatomical Science**)
Graduates surveyed 2545 **Employed** 1545 **In further study** 625 **Assumed unemployed** 150.

OTHER DEGREE SUBJECTS FOR CONSIDERATION

Anatomy; Biochemistry; Biological Sciences; Biotechnology; Dentistry; Genetics; Health Studies; Medicine; Microbiology; Nursing; Optometry; Pharmacology; Radiography; Sports Science.

PHYSIOTHERAPY

NB The points totals shown to the left of the institutions are for ease of reference only. It must not be assumed that tariff points are always used by institutions or that they can be substituted for an offer in grades. The level of an offer is not necessarily indicative of the quality of a course.

COURSE OFFERS INFORMATION

Subject requirements/preferences GCSE English, mathematics and science subjects. **Birmingham** Seven subjects grades A–B including English, mathematics and science taken at one sitting. **Bradford** Seven subjects at good grades taken at one sitting. **Brighton** Eight grade Bs or better at one sitting. **Bristol UWE** Minimum of five subjects grades A–C. **Brunel** Six subjects grades A–C at one sitting. **Cardiff** Seven subjects grades A–C including English/Welsh, mathematics and science. **Coventry** Seven subjects grades A–C including English and mathematics. **Glasgow Caledonian** Two sciences. **Hertfordshire** Grade B in mathematics, English and sciences. **Huddersfield** Six–eight grades A–C. **Liverpool** Six subjects including two sciences. **London (King's)** All subjects grade B. **Manchester Met** Grades A–C in six subjects including mathematics and a science, five at one sitting. **Northumbria** Six subjects at grades A–B (for applicants under 21 years). **Nottingham** Grades A–B in six–eight subjects including mathematics, English and science; biology grade B. **Robert Gordon** Grades A*–B. **Salford** Grade B in eight subjects. **Southampton** Five (minimum) grades A–C. **Ulster** Three sciences. **AL** One or two science subjects are required.

Your target offers

360 pts **and above**
　　　　Southampton – ABBb 370 pts (Physiotherapy)
　　　　Ulster – AAA–AAB (Physiotherapy)
340 pts **Cardiff** – AAB (Physiotherapy)
320 pts **Birmingham** – ABB 320 pts (Physiotherapy)
　　　　Brighton – 320 pts (Physiotherapy)
　　　　Queen Margaret (UC) – ABB (Physiotherapy)
300 pts **Bradford** – 300 pts (Physiotherapy)
　　　　Central Lancashire – BBB (Physiotherapy)
　　　　Coventry – 300 pts (Physiotherapy)
　　　　Cumbria – 300 pts (Physiotherapy
　　　　East Anglia – BBB (Physiotherapy)
　　　　East London – 300 pts (Physiotherapy)
　　　　Glasgow Caledonian – BBB (Physiotherapy)
　　　　Hertfordshire – BBB–ABB (Physiotherapy)
　　　　Keele – BBB (Physiotherapy)
　　　　Liverpool – 300 pts (Physiotherapy)
　　　　London (King's) – BBB–BBC (Physiotherapy)
　　　　London (St George's) – 300 pts (Physiotherapy)
　　　　Manchester Met – BBB (Physiotherapy)
　　　　Northumbria – 300 pts (Physiotherapy)
　　　　Nottingham – BBB (Physiotherapy)
　　　　Oxford Brookes – BBB **or** BBbb (Physiotherapy)
　　　　Plymouth – 300 pts (Physiotherapy)
　　　　Robert Gordon – BBB (Physiotherapy)
　　　　Salford – BBB 300 pts (Physiotherapy)
　　　　Sheffield Hallam – 300 pts (Physiotherapy)
　　　　Teesside – BBB (Physiotherapy)
　　　　York St John – 300 pts (Physiotherapy)

280 pts **Bristol UWE** – 280–340 pts (Physiotherapy)
Brunel – 280–300 pts (Physiotherapy)
Kingston/London (St George's) – 280–300 pts (Physiotherapy)

260 pts **Bournemouth** – 260 pts (Physiotherapy)
Huddersfield – BCC 260 pts (Physiotherapy)

160 pts **and below**
Colchester (Inst) – part-time; contact Inst (Physiotherapy)
London South Bank – min age 21 (Physiotherapy)
York St John – Part-time courses for physiotherapy assistants, min age 21; A-levels or equiv reqd.

Leeds Met – contact University

Alternative offers
IB offers Birmingham 34 pts; Brighton 32 pts; Bristol UWE 32–34 pts; Brunel 30 pts; Keele 32 pts; London (King's) 32 pts; Manchester Met 32 pts; Nottingham 32 pts; Salford 32 pts.
Scottish offers See **Chapter 7**.

OTHER HIGHER EDUCATION COURSES IN THE SUBJECT FIELD
Foundation degrees (contact institution for details) Salford.

CHOOSING YOUR COURSE (SEE ALSO CH. 1)
Subject information Physiotherapists work as part of a multi-disciplinary team with other health professionals and are involved in the treatment and rehabilitation of patients of all ages and with a wide variety of medical problems. On successful completion of the three-year course, graduates are eligible for State Registration and Membership of the Chartered Society of Physiotherapy. (See **Appendix 2**) **Useful websites** www.csp.org.uk; www.thephysiotherapysite.co.uk; www.nhscareers.nhs.uk; www.physiotherapy.co.uk.

Universities and colleges teaching quality See www.tqi.ac.uk; www.qaa.ac.uk.

Sandwich degree courses Glasgow Caledonian.

ADMISSIONS INFORMATION
Number of applicants per place (approx) Birmingham 15; Bradford 22; Brighton 30 (6 places for overseas candidates); Bristol UWE 12; Brunel 11; Cardiff 17; Coventry 15; East Anglia 14; East London 10; Glasgow Caledonian 12; Hertfordshire 13; Huddersfield 18; Liverpool 20; London (King's) 16, (Kingston/St George's) 9; Manchester 18; Northumbria 37; Nottingham 48; Queen Margaret (UC) 11; Robert Gordon 13; Salford 28; Sheffield Hallam 12; Southampton 20; Teesside 33; Ulster 12.

Advice to applicants and planning the UCAS personal statement Visits to, and work experience in, hospital physiotherapy departments are important although many universities publicly state that this is not necessary. However, with the level of competition for this subject I would regard this as doubtful (see **Reasons for rejection**). Applicants must demonstrate a clear understanding of the nature of the profession. Give details of voluntary work activities. Take notes of the work done and the different aspects of physiotherapy. Explain your experience fully on the UCAS application. Outside interests and teamwork are considered important. Good communication skills. Observation placement within a physiotherapy department. **Manchester Met** We need to know why you want to be a physiotherapist. We also look for work shadowing a physiotherapist or work experience in another caring role. Evidence is also required of good communication skills, ability to care for people and of teamwork and leadership. **Salford** Essential for applicants to seek experience in as wide a range of settings as possible. See also **Appendix 2**.

Advice to overseas (non-EU) applicants Places for students from overseas are limited and applicants must be able to read, speak and write English fluently. Information on the minimum educational qualifications required by overseas students and details concerning grants and funding are available from the Chartered Society of Physiotherapy (see **Appendix 2**). **Brunel, Glasgow Caledonian**

Proficiency in English essential. **Queen Margaret (UC)** Several overseas students recruited each year. **Ulster** Exams and continuous assessment.

Misconceptions about this course Some applicants think that physiotherapy has a sports bias.

Selection interviews **Yes** Most institutions including Birmingham, Bradford, Brighton, Coventry, East London, Huddersfield, Nottingham, Robert Gordon, Salford, Sheffield Hallam; **Some** Brunel (mature students), Cardiff (mature students), London (Kingston/St George's), Queen Margaret (UC), Southampton (mature students, who are asked to write about life experience).

Interview advice and questions Physiotherapy is one of the most popular courses at present and work experience is very important, if not essential. A sound knowledge of the career, types of treatment used in physiotherapy and some understanding of the possible problems experienced by patients will be expected. Applicants will require an occupational health check and Criminal Records Bureau (CRB) clearance. Past interview questions include: How does physiotherapy fit into the overall health care system? If one patient was a heavy smoker and the other not, would you treat them the same? What was the most emotionally challenging thing you have ever done? Give an example of teamwork in which you have been involved. Why should we make you an offer? What is chiropractic? What is osteopathy? See **Chapter 6**.

Applicants' impressions (A=Open day; B=Interview day) **Nottingham** (B) The interviewers were helpful and not aggressive. It was a modern department with good facilities. There was no chance to talk to the students.

Reasons for rejection (non-academic) Lack of knowledge of the profession. Failure to convince the interviewers of a reasoned basis for following the profession. Failure to have visited a hospital physiotherapy unit. Lack of awareness of the demands of the course. Other subjects listed on the UCAS application. **Birmingham** Poor communication skills. Lack of career insight. **Bristol UWE** Applicants re-sitting A-levels are not normally considered. **Cardiff** Lack of knowledge of physiotherapy; experience of sports injuries only.

AFTER-RESULTS ADVICE
Universities with vacancies in Clearing (2006) Brunel; Keele; Northumbria.

Offers to applicants repeating A-levels **Higher** Bristol UWE (candidates who fail at interview will not normally be reconsidered), East London, Glasgow Caledonian, London (Kingston/St George's), Teesside; **Same** Coventry, Queen Margaret (UC), Salford, Southampton.

GRADUATE DESTINATIONS AND EMPLOYMENT (2005 HESA)
No data available.

OTHER DEGREE SUBJECTS FOR CONSIDERATION
Anatomy; Audiology; Biological Sciences; Health Studies; Leisure and Recreation; Nursing; Occupational Therapy; Osteopathy; Physical Education; Psychology; Sport Science/Studies.

PLANT SCIENCES
(including **Botany**; see also **Biological Sciences** and **Biology**)

NB The points totals shown to the left of the institutions are for ease of reference only. It must not be assumed that tariff points are always used by institutions or that they can be substituted for an offer in grades. The level of an offer is not necessarily indicative of the quality of a course.

COURSE OFFERS INFORMATION
Subject requirements/preferences GCSE Mathematics if not offered at A-level. **Birmingham** Grade B in five relevant subjects. **Cambridge** Grade As in most subjects preferred. **Edinburgh** Mathematics grade B. **AL** One or two science subjects are usually required.

Your target offers

360 pts **and above**
        Cambridge – AAA (Nat Sci (Plnt Sci))
340 pts **Manchester** – AAB–BBC (Plnt Sci; Plnt Sci Modn Lang; Plnt Sci Ind)
320 pts **Birmingham** – ABB–BBC (Biol Sci (Plnt Biol))
        Bristol – ABB–BBB (Botany)
        Durham – ABB (Plnt Sci; Plnt Sci Ind)
        Sheffield – ABB (MBS Plnt Sci)
300 pts **East Anglia** – BBB–BBC (Plnt Biol)
        Edinburgh – BBB (Plnt Sci)
        Glasgow – BBB–BCC (Plnt Sci)
        Sheffield – BBB (BSc Plnt Sci)
280 pts **Aberdeen** – BBC 2nd yr entry (Plnt Biol; Plnt Soil Sci)
        Nottingham – BBC–CCC (Plnt Sci; Plnt Sci Euro St)
260 pts **Reading** – 260 pts (Bot Zool; Bot)
240 pts **Bangor** – 240 pts (Plnt Biol Cons)
220 pts **Aberystwyth** – 220 pts (Plnt Biol)
200 pts **Aberdeen** – CDD 1st yr entry (Plnt Biol; Plnt Soil Sci)
180 pts **Nottingham Trent** – 180 pts (Microbiol Plnt Sci)
160 pts **SAC (Scottish CAg)** – CC (App Biosci (Plnt Sci))
        Wolverhampton – 160–220 pts (Plnt Biol)
120 pts **Worcester** – 120 pts (Ecol Plnt Sci; Plnt Sci courses)

Alternative offers

IB offers Bristol 34–36 pts; Cambridge 38–42 pts; Manchester 32–35 pts; Reading 30 pts; Sheffield 32–34 pts.
Scottish offers See **Chapter 7**.

OTHER HIGHER EDUCATION COURSES IN THE SUBJECT FIELD

Higher National Diploma courses
100 pts **and below**
        Bath; SAC (Scottish CAg); Worcester; Writtle (Coll); see also **Biological Sciences** and **Biology**.

CHOOSING YOUR COURSE (SEE ALSO CH.1)

Subject information Plant Sciences cover such areas as plant biochemistry, plant genetics, plant conservation and plant geography. Botany encompasses all aspects of plant science and also other subject areas including agriculture, forestry and horticulture. Botany is basic to these subjects and others including pharmacology and water management. As with other biological sciences, some universities introduce Plant Sciences by way of a common first year with other subjects. **Useful websites** www.rbgkew.org.uk; www.anbg.gov.au; www.scienceyear.com; www.botany.net.

Course variations Plant and Soil Science (Aberystwyth); Botany (Bristol); Botany and Zoology (Reading); Ecology and Plant Science (Worcester). *NOW CHECK PROSPECTUSES AND WEBSITES FOR ANY RECENT CHANGES.*

Top universities and colleges (Research) Aberdeen; Cambridge; Reading; see also **Biological Sciences**.

Sandwich degree courses Bangor; Durham; Glasgow; Manchester; Wolverhampton.

ADMISSIONS INFORMATION

Number of applicants per place (approx) Bangor 4; Bristol 5; Edinburgh 6; Glasgow 4; Nottingham 5; Reading 3; Sheffield 5; Wolverhampton 4.

Advice to applicants and planning the UCAS personal statement Visit botanical gardens. See **Biological Sciences**. See also **Appendix 2**.

Selection interviews **Yes** Cambridge, Durham, Nottingham (depends on application); **Some** Wolverhampton.

Interview advice and questions You are likely to be questioned on your biology studies, your reasons for wishing to study Plant Sciences and your ideas about a possible future career. In the past questions have been asked about Darwin's theory of evolution, photosynthesis and DNA and the value of gardening programmes on TV! See **Chapter 6**.

AFTER-RESULTS ADVICE
Universities with vacancies in Clearing (2006) Aberdeen; Aberystwyth; Birmingham; Bristol; East Anglia; Glasgow; Nottingham; Nottingham Trent; Reading; Sheffield; Wolverhampton; Worcester.

Offers to applicants repeating A-levels **Possibly higher** Nottingham; **Same** Birmingham, Sheffield, Wolverhampton.

GRADUATE DESTINATIONS AND EMPLOYMENT (2005 HESA)
Graduates surveyed 40 **Employed** 15 **In further study** 15 **Assumed unemployed** None.

OTHER DEGREE COURSES FOR CONSIDERATION
Agriculture; Biochemistry; Biological Sciences; Biology; Crop Science (Agronomy); Food Science; Forestry; Herbal Medicine; Homeopathy; Horticulture; Landscape Architecture; Traditional Chinese Medicine.

PODIATRY (CHIROPODY)

NB The points totals shown to the left of the institutions are for ease of reference only. It must not be assumed that tariff points are always used by institutions or that they can be substituted for an offer in grades. The level of an offer is not necessarily indicative of the quality of a course.

COURSE OFFERS INFORMATION
Subject requirements/preferences **GCSE** Mathematics and science subjects. **AL** Biology usually required or preferred.

Your target offers
300 pts **Southampton** – BBB (Podiatry)
240 pts **Ulster** – BCD 240 pts (Podiatry)
        Salford – 240 pts (Podiatry)
220 pts **Huddersfield** – 220 pts (Podiatry)
200 pts **Brighton** – 200 pts (Podiatry)
        East London – 200 pts (Pod Med)
180 pts **Cardiff (UWIC)** – 180 pts (Podiatry)
        Durham New (Coll) – 180 pts (Podiatry)
160 pts **Glasgow Caledonian** – CC (Podiatry)
        Northampton – 160 pts (Podiatry)
        Plymouth – 160 pts (Podiatry)
        Queen Margaret (UC) – DDE (Podiatry)
80 pts **Matthew Boulton (CFHE)** – EE (Podiatry)
        Sunderland – contact Univ (Podiatry – course is run in association with the Durham School of Podiatric Medicine at New College Durham)

Alternative offers
IB offers Brighton 28 pts; Salford 24 pts.
Scottish offers See **Chapter 7**.

OTHER HIGHER EDUCATION COURSES IN THE SUBJECT FIELD
Foundation degrees (contact institution for details) Salford.

CHOOSING YOUR COURSE (SEE ALSO CH.1)

Subject information Students on health-related courses are required to have Criminal Records Bureau clearance. A pre-existing record could prevent a student from participating in the placement component of the course and prevent the student from gaining state registration. Students are also required to be immunised against hepatitis B, tuberculosis and tetanus. Podiatry is a relatively new term for chiropody and courses lead to state registration and some work shadowing prior to application is preferred by admissions tutors. **Useful website** www.feetforlife.org; www.nhscareers.nhs.uk.

Universities and colleges teaching quality See www.tqi.ac.uk; www.qaa.ac.uk.

ADMISSIONS INFORMATION

Number of applicants per place (approx) Cardiff (UWIC) 8; Huddersfield 2–3; Matthew Boulton (CFHE) 4; Northampton 2; Salford 3; Southampton 3.

Advice to applicants and planning the UCAS personal statement Visit a podiatrist's clinic to gain work experience/work shadowing experience. Discuss your knowledge of the work fully on your UCAS application. **Cardiff (UWIC)** Applicants need the ability to communicate with all age ranges, to work independently, to be resourceful and to possess a focussed approach to academic work. **Huddersfield** Admissions tutors look for evidence of an understanding of podiatry, some work experience, good people skills, and effective communication. Mature applicants must include an academic reference (not an employer reference). See also **Appendix 2**.

Misconceptions about this course Cardiff (UWIC) Prospective students are often not aware of the demanding requirements of the course: 1000 practical clinical hours augmented by a rigorous academic programme. Whilst the elderly are a significant sub-population of patients with a variety of foot problems, increasingly the role of the podiatrist is the diagnosis and management of biomechanical/developmental disorders as well as the management of the diabetic or rheumatoid patient and those who require surgical intervention for nail problems. **Huddersfield** Many people think that podiatry is limited in its scope of practice to treating toe nails, corns and calluses – FALSE. As professionals, we do treat such pathologies but the scope of practice is much wider. It now includes surgery, biomechanics, sports injuries, treating children and high risk patients. Because offers are low it is considered an easier course than, for example, Physiotherapy – FALSE. The course is academically demanding in addition to the compulsory clinical requirement.

Selection interviews Yes Most institutions; Huddersfield, Southampton; **Some** Cardiff (UWIC).

Interview advice and questions Past questions include: Have you visited a podiatrist's surgery? What do your friends think about your choice of career? Do you think that being a podiatrist could cause you any physical problems? With which groups of people do podiatrists come into contact? What are your perceptions of the scope of practice of podiatry? What transferable skills do you think you will need? **Cardiff (UWIC)** What made you consider podiatry as a career? Have you researched your career choice and where did you find the information? What have you discovered and has this altered your original perception of podiatry? What personal characteristics do you think you possess which might be useful for this work? See **Chapter 6**.

Reasons for rejection (non-academic) Unconvincing attitude; poor communication and inter-personal skills; lack of motivation; medical condition or physical disabilities which are incompatible with professional practice; no knowledge of chosen profession; lack of work experience.

AFTER-RESULTS ADVICE

Universities with vacancies in Clearing (2006) East London; Glasgow Caledonian; Northampton; Plymouth; Salford.

Offers to applicants repeating A-levels Same Cardiff (UWIC), Huddersfield, Salford.

GRADUATE DESTINATIONS AND EMPLOYMENT (2005 HESA)

No data available.

OTHER DEGREE SUBJECTS FOR CONSIDERATION
Audiology; Biological Sciences; Health Studies; Nursing; Occupational Therapy; Osteopathy; Physiotherapy.

POLITICS

(including **Government;** see also **Development Studies** and **International Relations)**

NB The points totals shown to the left of the institutions are for ease of reference only. It must not be assumed that tariff points are always used by institutions or that they can be substituted for an offer in grades. The level of an offer is not necessarily indicative of the quality of a course.

COURSE OFFERS INFORMATION
Subject requirements/preferences GCSE Bath Majority of A*, A or B grades. **Belfast (Queen's)**, **Bristol UWE, London (LSE), London South Bank, Newcastle, Plymouth** Mathematics required. **Bristol UWE, Brunel, London Met, London South Bank, York** Grade B English required. **Cambridge, Oxford** Grade A in most subjects preferred. **Durham** High proportion of grades A and B and at least one humanities subject at grade A or B. **Glasgow, Lincoln, Newcastle, Swansea** (Euro Pol) Foreign language required. **London South Bank** Six subjects, majority grade B. **AL** No subjects specified; history useful.

Your target offers
360 pts **and above**
    Belfast (Queen's) – AAA (Law Pol)
    Bristol – AAA–BCC (Pol courses)
    Cambridge – AAA (Soc Pol Sci)
    Durham – AAA (Hist Pol)
    London (UCL) – AAA+AS (Euro Soc Pol St)
    Oxford – Offers vary eg AAA–AAB (Hist Pol; PPE)
    Warwick – ABBb (Pol; Pol Int St; Pol Fr)
340 pts **Durham** – AAB (Pol; Pol (Euro St); PPE; Econ Pol; Hist Pol; Phil Pol; Comb Soc Sci)
    Essex – 340–280 pts (Pol; Pol Hum Rts; Econ Pol; Pol Sociol; Int Rel Pol; PPE)
    London (King's) – AAB+AS **or** AAbb (War St courses)
    St Andrews – AAB (Int Rel courses)
    Sheffield – AAB (Politics)
    York – AAB–ABB (Hist Pol; Engl Pol; PPE; Econ Pol; Pol Sociol; Pol Soc Pol)
320 pts **Bath** – ABB (Pol Econ)
    Birmingham – ABB 320 pts (Pol Sci; Pol Econ; Pol Sci Int)
    Durham – ABB (Pol Sociol)
    East Anglia – ABB–BBB–BBC (Pol; Pol Sociol Contemp Cult; Pol Media)
    Exeter – ABB–BBB 320–300 pts (Pol; Pol Fr/Ger/Ital/Russ/Span; Pol Sociol)
    Glasgow – ABB–BBB (Pol courses)
    Hull – 320 pts (Pol Int Rel; War Scrty St)
    Kent – 320 pts (PPE Euro)
    Lancaster – ABB (Pol N Am)
    Leeds – ABB (Pol Parl St; Pol St)
    London (LSE) – ABB (Gov; Gov Econ; Gov Hist; Int Rel; Int Rel Hist)
    London (RH) – ABB (Pol courses)
    London (SOAS) – 320 pts (Pol courses)
    London (UCL) – ABB (Pol E Euro St)
    Loughborough – ABB–AAC (Econ Pol)
    Manchester – ABB–BBB (Pol Sociol; Pol Econ Soc Hist; Pol Crim)
    Newcastle – ABB–BBB (Pol courses)
    Nottingham – ABB–BBB (Fr Pol; Ger Pol; Hist Pol; Euro Pol; Pol Am St)
    Sheffield – ABB (Pol Phil; Int Hist Int Pol)
    Southampton – ABB–BBB (Pol courses)
    Sussex – ABB **or** 360 pts 3AL+AS (Pol courses)

300 pts **Aston** – BBB 300 pts (Pol courses)
Belfast (Queen's) – BBB–BBCb (Politics)
Cardiff – BBB–BCC 300–260 pts (Pol; Euro Pol Int Rel; Modn Hist Pol; Pol Econ; Pol Sociol)
Dundee – BBB 2nd yr entry (Pol; Euro Pol courses; Int Rel Pol)
East Anglia – BBB–BBC (Pol Econ)
Edinburgh – BBB (Pol; Pol Econ Soc Hist; Geog Pol)
Hull – 300 pts (Pol; PPE; Glob Gov; Euro Gov Pol)
Kent – 300 pts (Pol Int Rel Jap)
Lancaster – BBB (Pol; Pol Int Rel; Glob Pol; Pce St Int Rel; Euro Pol Soty Cult; Pol St)
Leicester – BBB (Hist Pol)
London (LSE) – BBB (Soc Pol Gov)
London (QM) – 300 pts (Pol courses)
Reading – 300 pts (3AL+AS) 280 pts (3AL) (Pol Econ; Pol Int Rel; War Pce Int Rel)
Sheffield – BBB–BBC (Pol courses except under **340/320 pts**)
280 pts **Aberystwyth** – 280 pts (Pol St; Int Pol; Euro Pol; Int Pol Intel St)
Bradford – 280 pts (Pol Law)
Kent – 280 pts (Pol; Pol Int Rel courses except under **300 pts**)
Leeds – BBC (Pol Russ; Pol Russ Civ; Pol Span; Pol Parl St)
Leicester – BBC 280–340 pts (Politics)
Liverpool – BBC 280 pts (Pol; Int Pol Pol; Pol Int Bus; Pol Comm St)
Sheffield – BBC **or** BBcc (Ger Pol; Russ Pol)
Surrey – 280 pts (Pol; Pol Int St; Pol Citz St; Pol Pol St)
Ulster – BBC–CCC (Law Gov)
260 pts **Brunel** – 260 pts (Int Pol; Pol courses)
Gloucestershire – 260 pts (Lcl Pol)
Keele – BCC–BBC 260–280 pts (Pol courses)
Kingston – 260–320 pts (Pol courses)
London (Gold) – BCC (Pol; Pol Econ; Econ Pol Pblc Pol; Int St)
Northampton – 260 pts (Pol courses)
Richmond (Am Int Univ) – 260 pts (Soc Sci (Int Rel) (Pol Sci))
Strathclyde – BCC (Politics)
Swansea – 260–300 pts (Pol joint courses; War Soty; Fr Euro Pol)
240 pts **Aberdeen** – CCC 240 pts (Pol courses; Pol Int Rel)
Bradford – 240 pts (Pce St; Pol Pce St)
Bristol UWE – 240–300 pts (Pol courses)
Cardiff (UWIC) – 240 pts (Politics)
City – 240–260 pts (Int Pol; Int Pol Sociol)
Coventry – 240–260 pts (Pol courses)
Dundee – 240 pts 1st yr entry (Pol courses; Euro Pol courses; Int Rel Pol)
Kent – 240 pts (Brit Am Pol St)
Loughborough – 240–300 pts (Pol with minor subj)
Oxford Brookes – CCC **or** CCcc (Politics)
Plymouth – 240 pts (Law Pol)
Portsmouth – 240–300 pts (Pol; Pol Sociol)
Robert Gordon – CCC (Pol Mgt)
Stirling – CCC (PPE; Pol; Int Pol Lang)
Ulster – CCC 240 pts (Pol; Int Pol courses; Econ Gov)
Westminster – CCC/BC (Politics)
230 pts **Buckingham** – 230 pts (Pol Econ Law)
220 pts **Bangor** – 220–260 pts (Pol Soc Sci)
Liverpool Hope – 220 pts (Politics)
Nottingham Trent – 220 pts (Pol; Pol Geog; Pol Hist; Pol Int Rel)
Salford – CCD (Pol; E W Euro Pol St; Crim Pol)
Sunderland – CCD–DDD 220–180 pts (Pol courses)
200 pts **Anglia Ruskin** – 200 pts (Pol courses)
Huddersfield – 200–240 pts (Pol; Pol Contemp Hist; Pol Media)

Lincoln – CDD 200 pts (Politics)
London Met – 200 pts (PPE; Pol Sociol; Pol Soc Pol)
180 pts De Montfort – 180–200 pts (Pol joint courses)
Greenwich – 180 pts min (Politics)
Liverpool John Moores – 180–240 pts (Pol courses)
160 pts Canterbury Christ Church – CC (Politics)
Central Lancashire – 160 pts (Pol; Pol Phil; Pol Soc Pol; Pol Hist)
East London – 160 pts (Int Pol)
Glamorgan – 160–200 pts (Pol courses)
London Met – 160 pts (Pol courses)
London South Bank – CC (Int Pol courses)
Manchester Met – 160 pts (Pol courses; Int Pol courses)
Middlesex – 160–200 pts (Pol Int St)
Westminster – CC (Politics)
Wolverhampton – 160–220 pts (War St Pol)
140 pts Paisley – CD (Politics)
120 pts Roehampton – 120–220 pts (Hum Rts courses)
80 pts London (Birk) – 80 pts for under 21s (over 21s varies) (p/t Pol Soc; Pol Phil Hist)

Leeds Met – contact University
Open University – contact University

Alternative offers
IB offers Aberystwyth 30 pts; Aston 31–32 pts; Birmingham 34 pts; Bristol 34–38 pts; Bristol UWE 24–28 pts; Brunel 28 pts; Cambridge 38–42 pts; City 26 pts; Essex 30–36 pts; Exeter 30–34 pts; Keele 28–30 pts; Kent 32 pts; Lancaster 32–33 pts; Leicester 28 pts; Liverpool 30 pts; London (Gold) 28 pts, (King's) 36 pts, (LSE) 38 pts, (QM) 30–34 pts, (RH) 34 pts, (SOAS) 38 pts, (UCL) 34 pts; Loughborough 30 pts; Manchester 35 pts; Manchester Met 26 pts; Newcastle 32 pts; Nottingham 34 pts; Salford 29 pts; Sheffield 30–33 pts; Surrey 27–30 pts; York 37 pts.
Scottish offers See **Chapter 7**.

CHOOSING YOUR COURSE (SEE ALSO CH.1)
Subject information Politics is often described as the study of 'who gets what, where, when and how'. Courses have become increasingly popular in recent years and usually cover the politics and government of the major powers. Because of the variety of degree courses on offer, it is possible to study the politics of almost any country in the world. **Useful websites** www.europa.eu; www.fco.gov.uk; www.psa.ac.uk; www.parliament.uk; www.whitehouse.gov; www.amnesty.org; www.gov.uk; www.un.org; www.un.int; www.ukpolitics.org.uk; www.bbc.co.uk/politics.

Course variations PPE (Durham, East Anglia, Essex, Hull, Kent, London Met, Manchester, Oxford, Warwick, York); Politics with Media (East Anglia); Globalisation and Governance (Hull); British and American Policy Studies; Conflict, Peace and Security (Kent); Government (London (LSE)); Politics with East European Studies (London (UCL)); Government and European Union Studies (Newcastle); War Studies and Politics (Wolverhampton). *NOW CHECK PROSPECTUSES AND WEBSITES FOR ANY RECENT CHANGES.*

Universities and colleges teaching quality See www.tqi.ac.uk; www.qaa.ac.uk.

Top universities and colleges (Research) Aberystwyth*; Belfast (Queen's); Birmingham; Bradford; Bristol; De Montfort; Essex*; Exeter; Glasgow; Hull; Keele; London (King's) (War St)*, (LSE); Manchester; Newcastle; Oxford*; Reading; St Andrews; Sheffield*; Strathclyde; Sussex; Warwick; York.

Sandwich degree courses Aston; Brunel; De Montfort; Lancaster; Loughborough; Oxford Brookes; Plymouth; Surrey.

ADMISSIONS INFORMATION
Number of applicants per place (approx) Aberystwyth 4; Aston 4; Bath 2; Birmingham 6; Bradford 10; Bristol 18; Brunel 5; Buckingham 2; Cambridge (Soc Pol Sci) 5; Cardiff 14; Cardiff (UWIC) 3; De

Montfort 6; Dundee 6; Durham 11 (all courses); East Anglia 15; Exeter 8; Hull 11, (PPE) 20; Kent 14; Lancaster 14; Leeds 18; Leicester 10; Liverpool 9; Liverpool John Moores 6; London (LSE) (Gov) 17, (Gov Econ) 10, (Gov Hist) 17, (QM) 10, (SOAS) 5; London Met 5; Loughborough 4; Newcastle 9; Northampton 4; Nottingham 12; Nottingham Trent 3; Oxford (PPE) 7; Oxford Brookes 12; Portsmouth 6; Salford 7; Southampton 10; Staffordshire 10; Stirling 9; Swansea 3; Warwick 10; York 8.

Advice to applicants and planning the UCAS personal statement Study the workings of government in the UK, Europe and other areas of the world, such as the Middle East, the Far East, America and Russia. Describe visits to the Houses of Commons and Lords and the debates taking place. Attend council meetings – county, town, district, village halls. Describe these visits and agendas. Read current affairs avidly. Be aware of political developments in the major countries (UK, Europe, USA, China, Korea, and Russia and the Commonwealth of Independent States). Keep abreast of developments in theatres of war. Explain your interests in detail. **Aberystwyth** We look for degree candidates with a strong interest in political and social issues and who want to inquire into the way in which the world is organised politically, socially and economically. **De Montfort** Demonstration of active interest in current affairs and some understanding of how politics affects our daily lives.

Misconceptions about this course Aberystwyth Many students believe that they need to study politics at A-level for Politics courses – this is not the case. **Cardiff (UWIC)** Some consider that politics is a narrow subject, only relevant to those who want a political career. **De Montfort** Some applicants believe that a Politics course only covers the mechanics of government and parliament.

Selection interviews Yes Bath (mature students), Birmingham, Cambridge, Durham, Exeter, Huddersfield, Hull, Leeds (Pol Parl St), Leicester, Liverpool, London (Gold), (SOAS), London Met, London South Bank, Nottingham, Oxford, Portsmouth, Sheffield, Sussex, Swansea, Ulster, Warwick; **Some** Aberystwyth, Bristol, Cardiff (UWIC), De Montfort, Dundee, Liverpool John Moores, London (LSE), Loughborough, Salford, Staffordshire, York.

Interview advice and questions Questions may stem from A/AS-level studies but applicants will also be expected to be up-to-date in their knowledge and opinions of current events. Questions in recent years have included: What constitutes a 'great power'? What is happening at present in the Labour Party? Define capitalism. What is a political decision? How do opinion polls detract from democracy? Is the European Union a good idea? Why? What are the views of the present government on the European Union? What is a 'spin doctor'? Are politicians hypocrites? **De Montfort** Why Politics? What political issues motivate your interests eg environmentalism, human rights? **London (Gold)** Essays required from A/AS-level current course. See **Chapter 6**.

Applicants' impressions (A=Open day; B=Interview day) Cardiff (Modn Hist Pol; A) We were shown a video of the University and visited the departments of politics and history and the students' union. It was very informative and interesting. **Exeter** (A) A very well-organised day with lunch and a detailed and well-presented guided tour. **Nottingham** (A) A well-organised and informative open day. **Oxford (Keble)** (B) I had three one-to-one interviews. In the Politics interview I was asked to name the positions of ten current and former politicians. I also had a difficult written examination with questions based on a specific test, whilst in Philosophy I had to answer questions on work I had previously submitted.

AFTER-RESULTS ADVICE

Universities with vacancies in Clearing (2006) Aberystwyth; Aston; Birmingham; Bradford; Bristol UWE; Buckingham; Canterbury Christ Church; Central Lancashire; City; Coventry; De Montfort; East Anglia; East London; Essex; Glamorgan; Greenwich; Huddersfield; Hull; Keele; Kent; Kingston; Lancaster; Leicester; Lincoln; Liverpool; Liverpool Hope; Liverpool John Moores; London (Gold), (QM), (RH); London Met; London South Bank; Loughborough; Manchester Met; Middlesex; Northampton; Northumbria; Nottingham Trent; Plymouth; Portsmouth; Reading; Salford; Sheffield; Southampton; Stirling; Sunderland; Surrey; Swansea; UCE Birmingham; Ulster; Westminster; Wolverhampton; Worcester.

Offers to applicants repeating A-levels Higher East Anglia, Essex, Glasgow, Leeds, Newcastle, Nottingham, Warwick, York; **Possibly higher** Hull, Lancaster, Oxford Brookes, Swansea; **Same** Aberystwyth, Birmingham, Bristol, Buckingham, Cardiff (UWIC), De Montfort, Dundee, Durham,

Lancaster, Lincoln, Liverpool John Moores, London (SOAS), London Met, London South Bank, Loughborough, Portsmouth, Richmond (Am Int Univ), Salford, Staffordshire, Sussex.

GRADUATE DESTINATIONS AND EMPLOYMENT (2005 HESA)
Graduates surveyed 3350 **Employed** 1675 **In further study** 660 **Assumed unemployed** 225.

OTHER DEGREE SUBJECTS FOR CONSIDERATION
Development Studies; Economics; Government; History; International Relations; Public Policy and Administration; Social Policy and Administration; Sociology.

PROPERTY MANAGEMENT/DEVELOPMENT

(including **Estate, Land and Valuation Surveying;** see also **Building Surveying** (under **Building), Housing** and **Quantity Surveying)**

NB The points totals shown to the left of the institutions are for ease of reference only. It must not be assumed that tariff points are always used by institutions or that they can be substituted for an offer in grades. The level of an offer is not necessarily indicative of the quality of a course.

COURSE OFFERS INFORMATION
Subject requirements/preferences **GCSE** English and mathematics required and for some institutions, a science subject (for Chartered Surveyor registration). **Newcastle** (Surv Map Sci) Mathematics grade B if not at AL/AS. **Nottingham Trent** Two subjects grade A, three subjects grade B, three subjects grade C including mathematics and English language. **AL** No subjects specified.

Your target offers
360 pts **Cambridge** – AAA (Lnd Econ)
340 pts **City** – AAB (Rl Est Fin Invest; Law Prop Val)
320 pts **Reading** – 320 pts 3AL **or** 350 pts 3AL+AS (Lnd Mgt)
300 pts **Ulster** – 300 pts (Prop Invest Dev)
280 pts **Newcastle** – BBC–BCC (Surv Map Sci)
          Northumbria – 280 pts (Est Mgt; Plan Dev Surv)
          Nottingham Trent – 280 pts (Rl Est Mgt; Plan Prop Dev)
          Oxford Brookes – BBC (Rl Est Mgt)
270 pts **Sheffield Hallam** – 270 pts (Bus Prop Mgt; Prop Dev; Urb Lnd Econ)
260 pts **Anglia Ruskin** – 260 pts (Rl Est Mgt)
          Bristol UWE – 260–300 pts (Bus Prop; Prop Mgt Invest; Prop Dev Plan)
          Glasgow Caledonian – BCC (Prop Mgt Val)
          Heriot-Watt – 260 pts (Rl Est Mgt; Plan Prop Dev)
          Kingston – 260 pts (Rl Est Mgt; Prop Lnd Inf Sys; Prop Plan Dev)
240 pts **Aberdeen** – CCC (Prop Surv)
          London South Bank – 240 pts (Surveying)
          Robert Gordon – CCC (Surveying)
          Salford – 240 pts (Prop Mgt Invest)
230 pts **Liverpool John Moores** – 230 pts (Prop Mgt; Rl Est Mgt; Rl Est Mgt Bus)
          Napier – 230 pts (Prop Dev Val)
          Portsmouth – 230–270 pts (Prop Dev; Prop Dev Quant Surv)
          Reading – 230 pts (Est Mgt – distance learning)
          UCE Birmingham – 230 pts (Rl Est – subject to review)
220 pts **Royal (CAg)** – 220–240 pts (Prop Agncy Mark)
          Westminster – 220–230 pts (Urb Est Mgt; Leis Prop; Prop Bus)
200 pts **Anglia Ruskin** – 200 pts (Prop Surv)
180 pts **Bristol UWE** – 180–220 pts (Rl Est (Val Mgt))
          Glamorgan – 180 pts (Surveying)
          Portsmouth – 180–240 pts (Prop Mark Des Dev)

UCE Birmingham – 180 pts (Plan Constr – subject to review)
160 pts **East London** – 160 pts (Surv Map Sci)
Wolverhampton – 160–220 pts (Prop Ast Mgt; Surv)
140 pts **Harper Adams (UC)** – 140–280 pts (Rur Ent Lnd Mgt)
120 pts **North East Wales (IHE)** – 120–80 pts (Est Agncy; Est Mgt)
Aberdeen – Advanced entry individual assessment (Property)

Alternative offers
IB offers Bristol UWE (Prop) 26–32 pts, (Rl Est) 24 pts; City 32 pts.
Scottish offers See **Chapter 7**.

OTHER HIGHER EDUCATION COURSES IN THE SUBJECT FIELD

Foundation degrees (contact institutions for details) Glamorgan; Moulton (Coll); North East Wales (IHE); Northampton; Northumbria.

Higher National Diploma courses Anglia Ruskin; Askham Bryan (Coll); Liverpool John Moores; Luton; Northumbria; Royal (CAg); Sheffield Hallam.

CHOOSING YOUR COURSE (SEE ALSO CH.1)

Subject information Property degree courses cover a wide range of subjects relevant to careers in managing, planning and implementing the development of property and regeneration of cities. Surveying is also a very broad subject (and career) and includes several specialisms, for example building surveying, quantity surveying, land valuation, surveying and architecture: this table focuses on degrees in general surveying, land and valuation surveying. **Useful website** www.rics.org/careers.

Course variations Law, Property and Valuation (City); Rural Enterprise and Land Management (Harper Adams (UC)); Surveying and Mapping Science (Newcastle); Real Estate Management (Nottingham Trent); Property Management and Investment (Salford); Urban Land Economics (Sheffield Hallam); Leisure Property (Westminster). *NOW CHECK PROSPECTUSES AND WEBSITES FOR ANY RECENT CHANGES.*

Universities and colleges teaching quality See www.tqi.ac.uk; www.qaa.ac.uk.

Top universities and colleges (Research) Cambridge.

Sandwich degree courses Bristol UWE; Glasgow Caledonian; Heriot-Watt; Kingston; Northumbria; Portsmouth; Salford; Sheffield Hallam; UCE Birmingham.

ADMISSIONS INFORMATION

Number of applicants per place (approx) Bristol UWE 11; Cambridge 4; City 20; Glamorgan 6; Harper Adams (UC) 4; Heriot-Watt 6; Kingston 22; Liverpool John Moores 15; London South Bank 2; Newcastle 6; North East Wales (IHE) 3; Northumbria 17; Nottingham Trent 3; Portsmouth 5; Royal (CAg) 3; Salford 3; Sheffield Hallam 5; UCE Birmingham 28; Westminster 10.

Advice to applicants and planning the UCAS personal statement There are different specialisms in this subject area. If you have any special interests, list and discuss them. Give details of all the contacts you have made, especially with, for example, property developers or surveying practices in your locality. Discuss the careers and try to arrange work experience or work shadowing. **Nottingham Trent** Candidates should demonstrate that they have researched the employment opportunities in the property and construction sectors and should have sought some practical experience. **Oxford Brookes** (Non-EU students) Written and spoken English must be good.

Misconceptions about this course Students under-estimate the need for numerical competence.

Selection interviews **Yes** Bristol UWE, Cambridge, De Montfort, Exeter, Glamorgan, Greenwich, Harper Adams (UC), Heriot-Watt, Newcastle, Royal (CAg); **Some** East London, Nottingham Trent, Salford, UCE Birmingham.

Applicants' impressions (A=Open day; B=Interview day) **Cambridge** (Land Econ; B) The interview was well organised but I felt under pressure with difficult taxing questions followed by a debate. I didn't meet any students.

Interview advice and questions Some work experience will be expected and questions will be asked on the applicants' course and career interests. **Cambridge** Questions on subsidies and the euro, economics, dynamic efficiency. **UCE Birmingham** Who employs surveyors? What roles could a surveyor undertake? What do you expect to be doing five years after graduating? See **Chapter 6**.

Reasons for rejection (non-academic) **Nottingham Trent** Incoherent and badly written application forms.

AFTER-RESULTS ADVICE
Universities with vacancies in Clearing (2006) Anglia Ruskin; Bristol UWE; Glasgow Caledonian; Heriot-Watt; Kingston; Liverpool John Moores; London South Bank; Northumbria; Nottingham Trent; Portsmouth; Reading; Royal (CAg); Salford; Sheffield Hallam; Westminster; Wolverhampton.

Offers to applicants repeating A-levels **Same** Nottingham Trent, Salford, UCE Birmingham.

GRADUATE DESTINATIONS AND EMPLOYMENT (2005 HESA)
No data available.

OTHER DEGREE SUBJECTS FOR CONSIDERATION
Architecture; Building Surveying; Civil Engineering; Construction; Estate Management; Housing; Quantity Surveying; Town Planning; Urban Studies.

PSYCHOLOGY

(including **Behavioural Science, Cognitive Sciences, Counselling** and **Neuroscience;** see also **Biological Sciences)**

NB The points totals shown to the left of the institutions are for ease of reference only. It must not be assumed that tariff points are always used by institutions or that they can be substituted for an offer in grades. The level of an offer is not necessarily indicative of the quality of a course.

COURSE OFFERS INFORMATION
Subject requirements/preferences **GCSE** Most universities require mathematics grade A–C. **Aston** English and mathematics grades A–C. **Bangor** Biology grades A–C desirable. **Bath** Mainly A* and As. **Bath Spa (UC)** Mathematics grade C. **Birmingham, Derby, Essex, Hull, Plymouth, Portsmouth, Swansea, York** English and mathematics grade A–C. **Buckingham** Five grade Bs or Cs minimum. **Exeter, Glasgow Caledonian, Lancaster, Lincoln, London (Gold), (RH), (UCL), Manchester Met, Newcastle** Biology. **Greenwich, Nottingham Trent** Mathematics grade A/B. **Leeds** Majority of A*, A or Bs, mathematics grade B. **Leicester** Mathematics and biology. **Northumbria** Mathematics grade B or above, science grade B or above preferred. **Oxford** Seven subjects at grade A. **Portsmouth** Seven subjects grade A–C. **Sheffield** Grade C mathematics plus two sciences. **Warwick** Seven subjects grade B or above including mathematics grade B or AS-level grade C. **York** Mathematics grade B. **AL** A science subject is usually required.

Your target offers
360 pts   and above
    Bath – AAAb–AAA (Psychology)
    Cambridge – AAA (Nat Sci (Psy))
    Cardiff – AAA (Psy; App Psy; Psy Crim; Educ Psy)
    Durham – AAA (Nat Sci (Psy))
    Exeter – AAA–AAB (Psychology)
    Oxford – Offers vary eg AAA–AAB (Expmtl Psy; Psy Phil; Physiol Psy)
    Reading – AAA–AAB (Psy Chld Age; Psy Mntl Phys Hlth)
    Warwick – AABb (Psy; Phil Psy)
340 pts   Birmingham – AAB–ABB (Psychology)
    Bristol – AAB–ABB (Psy; Psy Phil; Psy Zool)

Durham – AAB (Psy Comb Soc Sci; Comb Arts; Psy; Phil Psy)
Leeds – AAB–ABB (Psy; Cog Sci)
Leicester – AAB–ABB (Psychology)
London (RH) – AAB–ABB (Psy; Maths Psy; Mus Psy; Biol Psy; Bioch Psy)
London (UCL) – AAB (Psychology)
Loughborough – AAB (Psy; Psy Ergon)
Manchester – AAB–ABB (Psychology)
Newcastle – AAB–ABB (Psy; Psy Stats; Maths Psy)
Nottingham – AAB (Psy; Psy Phil; Psy Cog Neuro)
Reading – 340 pts (Psy; Art Psy; Psy Phil; Psy Biol; Maths Psy)
St Andrews – AAB (Psy courses)
Sheffield – AAB (Psy; Phil Psy)
Southampton – AAB 340 pts (Psychology)
Strathclyde – AAB–BBB (Biomed Sci Psy)
Sussex – AAB–ABB (Psy; Psy Am St; Psy Cog Sci; Psy Sociol; Psy Neuro)
York – AAB–ABB (Psychology)

320 pts **Aston** – ABB 320 pts (Psy Bus)
Belfast (Queen's) – ABB–BBBb (Psychology)
Cardiff – ABB (Physiol Psy)
Durham – ABB (Educ St (Psy))
Glasgow – ABB–BBB (BA Psy)
Kent – 320 pts (App Soc Psy Clin Psy; App Psy Clin Psy; Psy Clin Psy; Soc Psy Clin Psy)
Lancaster – ABB–BBB (Psy; Psy Educ; Fr St Psy; Ger St Psy; Ital St Psy; Span St Psy; Org St Psy)
Leeds – ABB (Psy Sociol)
Leicester – ABB–BBB (Psy Sociol)
Liverpool – ABB 320 pts (Psychology)
London (LSE) – ABB approx (Soc Psy – optional subject, check with admissions tutor)
Loughborough – ABB (Soc Psy)
Oxford Brookes – ABB offers vary depending on 2nd subj (Psy Comb courses)
Surrey – ABB (Psychology)

300 pts **Aston** – BBB 300 pts (Psy courses except under **320 pts**)
Bangor – 300–260 pts (Psy; Psy Neuropsy; Psy Clin Hlth Psy; Psy Chld Lang Dev; Psy joint courses)
Brighton – 300 pts (App Psy Sociol; Crim App Psy)
Bristol – BBB (Neuroscience)
Brunel – 300 pts (Psy; Psy Soc Anth; Psy Sociol)
City – BBB–ABB (Psychology)
Dundee – BBB 300 pts (MA Psy 3 yr; BSc Psy 3 yr; App Psy)
Durham (Stockton) – BBB (App Psy)
East Anglia – BBB (Psysoc Sci)
Edinburgh – BBB (Psy; Psy Bus St; Psy Ling)
Essex – 300 pts (Psy; Dev Psy)
Keele – BBB **or** 300 pts (Psy courses)
Kent – BBB 300 pts (Psy; Euro Soc Psy; App Psy; App Soc Psy; Psy (Euro); Soc Psy; Psy Soc Anth)
Lancaster – BBB (Biol Psy; Psy Stats)
Leeds – BBB (Neuroscience)
Leicester – BBB–BBC (Psy Neuro; Psy Biol)
London (Hey) – 300–340 pts (Psy Phil)
Manchester Met – 300 pts (Psy Sp Path)
Oxford Brookes – BBB **or** BBbb (Psychology)
Portsmouth – 300 pts (Psy; Psy Crim)
Sheffield Hallam – 300 pts (Psychology)
Stirling – BBB 2nd yr entry (Psychology)

Surrey – BBB–BBC (App Psy Sociol)
Swansea – 300–320 pts (Psy courses)
280 pts **Bradford** – 280 pts (Psychology)
Coventry – 280 pts (Psychology)
Glasgow – BBC–BCC (BSc Psy; Neuro)
Hertfordshire – 280 pts (Psychology)
Hull – BBC–BCC 280–260 pts (Psy; Psy Cnslg; Psy Crim; Psy Phil; Psy Sociol; Psy Spo Sci)
Lincoln – BBC 280 pts (Psychology)
London (Gold) – BBC (Psychology)
Manchester Met – 280 pts (Psychology)
Northumbria – 280 pts (Psy; Psy Spo Sci)
Nottingham Trent – BBC 280 pts (Psy; Psy Crim; Psy Educ Dev; Psy Sociol)
Southampton – 280–330 pts (App Soc Sci (Crim Psy St))
Sheffield – BBC–BB+bc (Hum Comm Sci)
Ulster – 280 pts (Psy courses; Soc Psy)
260 pts **Bournemouth** – 260 pts (Spo Psy Coach Sci)
Bristol UWE – 260–300 pts (Psychology)
Central Lancashire – 260 pts (Psy; App Psy; Neuropsy)
Chester – 260 pts (Psy; Cnslg Sk Psy)
Coventry – 260 pts (Psy joint courses)
Keele – 260–320 pts (Psychology)
Kingston – BCC 260 pts (Psychology)
Liverpool John Moores – 260 pts (App Psy)
London (Hey) – 260–300 pts (Psy Theol)
Richmond (Am Int Univ) – 260 pts (Soc Sci (Psy))
Stirling – BCC (Psy courses)
Strathclyde – BCC/BB (Psy (Arts Soc (Psy)))

240 pts **Aberdeen** – CCC (Neuro Psy)
Bolton – 240 pts (Psy; Cnslg Psy; Crim Foren Psy; Spo Exer Psy)
Bradford – 240 pts (Psychology)
Bristol UWE – 240–300 pts (Psy Hlth; Psy Foren Sci; Psy joint hons)
Buckingham – 240 pts (Psy; Psy Bus St; Psy Engl Lang St (EFL); Psy Engl Lit; Psy Fr; Psy Inf Sys; Psy Mark; Psy Media Comm; Psy Socio Leg St; Psy Span)
Central Lancashire – 240 pts (Psy Crim; Psy Foren Sci)
De Montfort – 240 pts (Psy courses)
Dundee – CCC 240 pts (MA Psy 4 yr; BSc Psy 4 yr)
Edge Hill – 240 pts (Psychology)
Glasgow Caledonian – CCC (Psy courses)
Gloucestershire – 240 pts (Psychology)
Greenwich – 240 pts (Psychology)
Heriot-Watt – CCC 240 pts (Spo Exer Sci Psy)
Huddersfield – 240 pts (Psy; Spo Exer Sci Psy; Psy Cnslg; Bhv Sci)
Keele – 240–260 pts (Neuroscience)
Lincoln – 240 pts (Neuroscience)
London Met – 240 pts (Psy; App Psy)
Nottingham Trent – 240 pts (Psy Spo Sci)
Portsmouth – 240–300 pts (Engl Psy; Mark Psy; HR Mgt Psy)
Queen Margaret (UC) – CCC 240 pts (Hlth Psy; Psy)
Salford – 240 pts (Psy; Psy St Cnslg St; Psy St Hlth Sci)
Sheffield Hallam – 240 pts (Psy Sociol)
Staffordshire – 240 pts (Psy; Soc Psy; Psy Spo Exer)
Swansea – 240–300 pts (Psy joint courses)
Thames Valley – 240 pts (Psychology)
Westminster – CCC (Psy; Psy Neuro)
Winchester – 240–220 pts (Psy courses)
Wolverhampton – 240–300 pts (Psy; Cnslg Psy; Ling Psy)
220 pts **Anglia Ruskin** – 220–260 pts (Psy courses)
Glamorgan – 220–260 pts (Psychology)
Hertfordshire – 220–260 pts (Cog Sci)
Kingston – 220–280 pts (Psy joint courses)
Liverpool Hope – 220 pts (Psychology)
Liverpool John Moores – 220 pts (Psy Biol; Psy Foren Sci)
Nottingham Trent – 220 pts (Eqn Spo Sci (Eqstrn Psy))
Plymouth – 220–280 pts (3AL) 220 pts (2AL) (Psy courses)
Queen Margaret (UC) – CCD 220 pts (Psy Media; Psy Sociol; PR Psy)
Southampton Solent – 220 pts (Psychology)
Sunderland – 220 pts (Psychology)
Winchester – 220 pts (Psy Comb courses)
200 pts **Abertay Dundee** – 200–180 pts (Psy; Bhv Sci; Foren Psychobiol)
Anglia Ruskin – 200 pts (Psysoc St)
Bath Spa – 200–240 pts (Psychology)
Bristol UWE – 200–240 pts (Psy Spo Biol)
Cardiff (UWIC) – 200 pts (Psy Nutr Consum Chc)
Central Lancashire – 200 pts (Psy Educ; Psy Hlth St; Psy Law; Psy Bus)
Chichester – 200–260 pts (Spo Exer Psy)
Dundee – BB (BSc Psy)
Huddersfield – 200 pts (Bhv Sci)
Manchester Met – 200 pts (Psy Spo Exer)
Middlesex – 200–220 pts (Psychology)
Napier – 200 pts (Psy; Psy Sociol)
Newport – 200 pts (Engl Psy; Psy Cnslg St)
UCE Birmingham – 200 pts (Bus Psy courses)

Wolverhampton – 200–260 pts (Psy joint courses)
190 pts **London Met** – 190–240 pts (App Sociol Psy)
180 pts **Bournemouth** – 180–240 pts (Psy Comp)
Bristol UWE – 180–220 pts (Psy Foren Sci)
Bradford – 180–220 (Psy Crim; Psy Mgt; Psy Fr/Span; Psy Engl EFL)
De Montfort – 180 pts (Psy joint courses)
Derby – 180–220 pts (App Psy; Psy St; Psy Cnslg St)
East London – 180 pts (Psy; Psy Crim; Psy Hlth St)
Heriot-Watt – DDD (App Psy)
Northampton – 180–200 pts (Psy joint courses)
Teesside – 180 pts (Psy; Foren Psy; Hlth Psy; Spo Exer Psy; Psy Crim)
York St John – 180 pts (Psychology)
160 pts **Barnsley (Univ Centre)** – 160 pts (Psy St)
Bedfordshire – 160–240 pts (Psy; App Psy; Hlth Psy; Psy Crim Bhv; Psy St)
Canterbury Christ Church – CC (Psy courses)
Cumbria – 160 pts (App Psy)
East London – 160 pts (Psysoc St)
Leeds Trinity and All Saints (Coll) – 160–240 pts (Psy courses)
London South Bank – CC **or** Ccc (Psy courses)
Manchester Met/Manchester (CAT) – CC (p/t Psy course)
Middlesex – 160–200 pts (Psy joint courses)
Newman (CHE) – CC 160 pts (Psy courses; Soc App Psy courses)
Norwich City (Coll) – 160–240 pts (Psy courses)
Roehampton – 160–180 pts (Psy Cnslg; Psy; Psy Hlth)
St Mary's (Coll) – 160–200 pts (Psy courses)
Swansea (IHE) – 160–140 pts approx (Cnslg Psy)
Westminster – CC (Cog Sci; Psy Neuro)
Worcester – 160–120 pts (Psy courses)
York St John – 160–180 pts (Cnslg St Psy)
140 pts **Paisley** – CD–DD (Psychology)
120 pts **Bradford (Coll)** – 120 pts (Psy Mgt; Cnslg Psy Commun Set)
Buckinghamshire Chilterns (UC) – 120–240 pts (Psy; Crimin Psy)
Cardiff (UWIC) – 120 pts (Psy Hum Biol; Psy)
Grimsby (IFHE) – 120–240 pts (Sociol Psy; Bus Psy)
North East Wales (IHE) – 120 pts (Psychology)
Suffolk (Univ Campus) – 120–180 pts (Psy Sociol)
West Anglia (Coll) – 120 pts (Psysoc St)
100 pts **Swansea (IHE)** – 100 pts (Hlth Psy; Psy Sociol)
80 pts **London (Birk)** – 80 pts for under 21s (over 21s varies) (p/t Psychology)
Matthew Boulton (CFHE) – (Fdn Psy)
West Suffolk (Coll) – 80–160 pts (Psy courses)

Leeds Met – contact University
Open University – contact University

Alternative offers
IB offers Aston 33–34 pts; Bath 36 pts; Birmingham 34 pts; Brighton 30 pts; Bristol 34–36 pts; Bristol UWE 28–32 pts; Brunel 32 pts; Cambridge 38–42 pts; Chichester 30 pts; City 35 pts; Essex 32 pts; Exeter 36–38 pts; Keele 32 pts; Kent 33–35 pts; Lancaster 33–34 pts; Leicester 32–34 pts; Liverpool 30 pts; London (Gold) 30 pts, (RH) 34–36 pts, (UCL) 36 pts; Loughborough 34 pts; Manchester 33–38 pts; Newcastle 34 pts; Nottingham 36 pts; Oxford 38–42 pts; St Andrews 36 pts; Sheffield 35 pts; Surrey 32–34 pts; Warwick 36 pts; York 36 pts.
Scottish offers See **Chapter 7**.

OTHER HIGHER EDUCATION COURSES IN THE SUBJECT FIELD
Foundation degrees (contact institutions for details) Bedford (Coll); Leicester; Milton Keynes (Coll); North Devon (Coll).

Higher National Diploma courses Truro (Coll); Wolverhampton.

CHOOSING YOUR COURSE (SEE ALSO CH.1)

Subject information Psychology is a very popular subject, with the number of applications rising by 40,000 in the last ten years. The study attracts three times more women than men. It covers studies in development, behaviour, perception, memory, language, learning, personality as well as social relationships and abnormal psychology. Psychology is a science and you will be involved in experimentation and statistical analysis. The degree is usually offered as a BSc or a BA course and there are many similarities between them. The differences are in the elective subjects which can be taken in the second and third years. It is not a training to enable you to psycho-analyse your friends – psychology is not the same as psychiatry! To qualify as a chartered psychologist (for which a postgraduate qualification is required) it is necessary to obtain a first degree (or equivalent) qualification which gives eligibility for both Graduate Membership (GM) **and** the Graduate Basis for Registration (GBR) of the British Psychological Society (BPS). A full list of courses accredited by the British Psychological Society can be viewed at www.bps.org.uk/careers/accredited-courses/accredited-courses_home.cfm. The Society also publishes a booklet *So You Want to be a Psychologist?* which can be downloaded from www.bps.org.uk/careers/careers_home.cfm. Full details about careers in psychology can also be obtained from the British Psychological Society (see **Appendix 2**). Behavioural Science covers the study of animal and human behaviour and offers an overlap between Zoology, Sociology, Psychology and Biological Sciences. Psychology, however, also crosses over into Education, Management Sciences, Human Resource Management, Counselling, Public Relations, Advertising, Artificial Intelligence, Marketing, Sales and Social Studies. **Useful websites** www.psychology.org; www.bps.org.uk; www.socialpsychology.org; www.psych-central.com.

Course variations Psychology with Child Language Development (Bangor); Sports Psychology and Coaching Sciences (Bournemouth); Psychology and Social Anthropology (Brunel; Kent); European Social Psychology (Kent); French Studies and Psychology (Lancaster); Psychology with Speech Pathology (Manchester Met); Marketing with Psychology (Portsmouth); Psychology with Public Relations (Queen Margaret (UC)); Psychology and Forensic Science; Psychology, Childhood and Ageing (Reading); Psychology and Cognitive Science (Sussex). *NOW CHECK PROSPECTUSES AND WEBSITES FOR ANY RECENT CHANGES.*

Universities and colleges teaching quality See www.tqi.ac.uk; www.qaa.ac.uk.

Top universities and colleges (Research) Aston; Bangor*; Birmingham*; Bristol*; Cambridge*; Cardiff*; Durham; Edinburgh; Essex; Exeter; Glasgow*; Lancaster; Leeds; London (Birk), (RH), (UCL)*; Manchester; Newcastle*; Nottingham; Oxford*; Plymouth; Reading*; St Andrews*; Sheffield; Southampton; Stirling; Surrey; Sussex; Warwick; York*.

Sandwich degree courses Aston; Bath; Bournemouth; Bristol UWE; Brunel; Cardiff; Hertfordshire; Huddersfield; Kent; Lancaster; London Met; Loughborough; Manchester; Manchester Met; Middlesex; Oxford Brookes; Paisley; Portsmouth; Queen Margaret (UC); Surrey; UCE Birmingham; Ulster; Wolverhampton.

ADMISSIONS INFORMATION

Number of applicants per place (approx) Abertay Dundee 5; Aston 6; Bangor 5; Bath 4; Birmingham 9; Bolton 5; Bournemouth 4; Bradford 14; Bradford (Coll) 2; Bristol 17; Bristol UWE 12; Brunel 20; Buckingham 1; Cardiff 10; Cardiff (UWIC) 5; Central Lancashire 13; Chester 20; City 6; Coventry 7; De Montfort 10; Derby 6; Dundee 6; Durham 20; East Anglia (Psysoc St) 6; Exeter 14; Glamorgan 6; Glasgow Caledonian 15; Gloucestershire 50; Greenwich 8; Hertfordshire 22; Huddersfield 3; Hull 14; Kent 15; Lancaster 20; Leeds 12; Leeds Trinity and All Saints (Coll) 13; Leicester 22; Liverpool 21; Liverpool John Moores 10; London (RH) 10, (UCL) 15; London South Bank 7; Loughborough 8; Manchester Met 27; Manchester Met/Manchester (CAT) (Psy p/t) 2; Middlesex 10; Napier 6; Newcastle 20; Newman (CHE) 3; Northampton 4; Northumbria 2; Nottingham 27; Nottingham Trent 3; Oxford (success rate 23%); Oxford Brookes 29; Plymouth 5; Portsmouth 10; Roehampton 7; Salford 4; Sheffield 12; Sheffield Hallam 10; Southampton 10; Staffordshire 6; Stirling 9; Surrey 10; Sussex 5; Swansea 7; Teesside 10; Warwick 13; Westminster 6; Worcester 9; York 9; York St John 3.

Number of applicants (**a** UK **b** EU (non-UK) **c** non-EU **d** mature) Aston **a**800 **b**100 **c**70 **d**90; Bradford **ab**200 **c**20; Bristol **ab**1421 **c**91 **d**156; Derby **a**407 **b**152 **c**5; Leeds **a**1758 **b**36 **c**37 **d**165; Manchester Met/Manchester (CAT) **abc**14 **d**14; Swansea **ab**800 **c**50.

Advice to applicants and planning the UCAS personal statement Psychology is heavily over-subscribed so prepare well in advance by choosing suitable AS- and A-level subjects. Contact the Education and Social Services departments in your local authority office to arrange meetings with psychologists to gain a knowledge of the work. Make notes during those meetings and of any work experience gained and describe these fully on the UCAS application. English language courses available for non-EU students. **Bangor** Evidence of interest in caring-type work including voluntary or paid experience. **Birmingham** A science subject is desirable but not required. **East Anglia** (Psysoc St) For students wishing to study psychology as a research-based discipline, but not wishing to become psychologists. **Keele** Reference to introductory reading in psychology (many students have a distorted image of it). **Liverpool John Moores** Applicants studying AS psychology are more likely to receive an offer but must achieve grade C. **Manchester Met** Use UCAS application section 10 well. (Psy Sp Path) Observations with speech therapists working with children and adults. **St Andrews** Evidence of interest. Reasons for choosing the course. **Sheffield Hallam** Interest in psychology, preferably demonstrated through voluntary or other work experience. See also **Appendix 2**.

Misconceptions about this course Some believe a Psychology course will train them as therapists or counsellors – it will not. **Bath** They think that they are going to learn about themselves. **Birmingham** Some applicants underestimate the scientific nature of the course. **Exeter** It's scientific! **Lincoln** Applicants should be aware that this is a science-based course. Academic psychology is an empirical science requiring research methodologies and statistical analysis. **Reading** Not all applicants are aware that it is a science-based course and are surprised at the high science and statistics content. **Sussex** Applicants should note that the BSc course is not harder than the BA course. Many students mistakenly believe that psychology consists of counselling and that there is no maths. Psychology is a science. **York** Some students think psychology means Freud which it hasn't done for 50 years or more. They do not realise that psychology is a science in the same vein as biology, chemistry or physics. Only 20 per cent of Psychology graduates become professional psychologists. This involves taking a postgraduate degree in a specialist area of psychology.

Selection interviews Yes Blackpool and Fylde (Coll), Bolton, Brunel, Buckingham, Cambridge, Durham, Glamorgan, Glasgow Caledonian, Leeds Trinity and All Saints (Coll), London (UCL), London Met, London South Bank, Middlesex, Newcastle, Northampton, Norwich City (Coll), Oxford, Oxford Brookes, Plymouth, Swansea; **Some** Aston, Bangor, Bristol, Cardiff, Derby (non-standard applications), Dundee, Exeter (mature students), Huddersfield (mature students), Keele, Leeds (mature students), Liverpool John Moores, Nottingham Trent (for non-standard applications), Roehampton, Salford, Sunderland.

Interview advice and questions Although some applicants will have studied the subject at A-level and will have a broad understanding of its coverage, it is still essential to have gained some work experience or to have discussed the career with a professional psychologist. Questions will be asked relevant to this experience and in previous years these have included: What have you read about psychology? What do you expect to gain by studying psychology? What are your parents' and teachers' views on your choice of subject? Are you interested in any particular branch of the subject? Is psychology an art or a science? Do you think you are well suited to this course? Why? Do you think it is possible that if we learn enough about the functioning of the brain we can create a computer that is functionally the same? What is counselling? Is it necessary? Know the differences between the various branches of psychology and discuss any specific interests, for example, in clinical, occupational, educational, criminal psychology and cognitive, neuro-, social or physiological psychology. What influences young children's food choices? What stereotypes do we have of people with mental illness? **Oxford** Ability to evaluate evidence and to have the capacity for logical and creative thinking. See **Chapter 6**.

Reasons for rejection (non-academic) Lack of background reading and lack of awareness of psychology; poor communication skills; misunderstanding of what is involved in a degree course. Poor personal statement. Poor grades, especially in GCSE maths. **Exeter** Competition for places – we can select those with exceptional grades. **Sheffield** Poor predicted grades. **Surrey** Inarticulate; **Warwick** (BSc) Lack of science background.

AFTER-RESULTS ADVICE

Universities with vacancies in Clearing (2006) Anglia Ruskin; Aston; Bangor; Bath Spa; Bolton; Bournemouth; Bradford; Bristol UWE; Brunel; Buckingham; Canterbury Christ Church; Central Lancashire; Chester; De Montfort; Derby; Dundee; East London; Essex; Glamorgan; Gloucestershire; Greenwich; Hertfordshire; Hull; Keele; Kent; Kingston; Lancaster; Lincoln; Liverpool Hope; Liverpool John Moores; London (Hey), (RH); London Met; London South Bank; Manchester Met; Middlesex; Northampton; Nottingham Trent; Plymouth; Portsmouth; Reading; Roehampton; Salford; Sheffield Hallam; Staffordshire; Stirling; Sunderland; Teesside; Thames Valley; UCE Birmingham; Ulster; Wolverhampton; Winchester; Worcester; York St John.

Offers to applicants repeating A-levels **Higher** Birmingham, City, Loughborough, Newcastle, Portsmouth, Southampton, Swansea, Warwick, York; **Possibly higher** Aston, Northampton; **Same** Aston (Comb Hons), Bangor, Blackpool and Fylde (Coll), Bolton, Brunel, Cardiff, Cardiff (UWIC), Chester, Derby, Dundee, East Anglia, Huddersfield, Hull, Lincoln, Liverpool John Moores, London (RH), London South Bank, Manchester Met, Newman (CHE), Nottingham, Nottingham Trent, Oxford Brookes, Roehampton, Salford, Sheffield Hallam, Staffordshire, Sunderland, Surrey, Ulster, York St John.

GRADUATE DESTINATIONS AND EMPLOYMENT (2005 HESA)
Graduates surveyed 7695 **Employed** 3390 **In further study** 1170 **Assumed unemployed** 460.

OTHER DEGREE SUBJECTS FOR CONSIDERATION
Anthropology; Behavioural Science; Cognitive Sciences; Education; Health Studies; Neuroscience; Sociology.

QUANTITY SURVEYING

NB The points totals shown to the left of the institutions are for ease of reference only. It must not be assumed that tariff points are always used by institutions or that they can be substituted for an offer in grades. The level of an offer is not necessarily indicative of the quality of a course.

COURSE OFFERS INFORMATION
Subject requirements/preferences **GCSE** English and mathematics grade A–C. **AL** No subjects specified; mathematics useful.

Your target offers
280 pts **Loughborough** – 280 pts (Commer Mgt Quant Surv)
270 pts **Glasgow Caledonian** – 270 pts (Quant Surv)
  Sheffield Hallam – 270 pts (Quant Surv)
260 pts **Anglia Ruskin** – 260 pts (Quant Surv; Constr Econ Mgt)
  Heriot-Watt – 260 pts (Quant Surv courses)
  Kingston – 260 pts (Quant Surv)
  Nottingham Trent – 260 pts (Quant Surv Constr Commer Mgt)
  Reading – 260 pts (Quant Surv)
  Ulster – 260 pts (Quant Surv)
240 pts **Central Lancashire** – 240 pts (Commer Mgt Quant Surv)
  Northumbria – 240 pts (Quant Surv)
  Robert Gordon – CCC (Surv (Quant Surv))
  Salford – 240 pts (Quant Surv)
  Westminster – CCC (Quant Surv)

230 pts   **Bristol UWE** – 230–290 pts (Quant Surv Commer Mgt)
           Liverpool John Moores – 230 pts (Quant Surv)
           Napier – 230 pts (Quant Surv)
           Portsmouth – 230–270 pts (Prop Dev Quant Surv)
           Reading – 230 pts (d/l Quant Surv)
           UCE Birmingham – 230 pts (Quant Surv)
220 pts   **Bolton** – 220 pts (Quant Surv Commer Mgt)
           Nottingham Trent – 220 pts (Quant Surv)
           Wolverhampton – 220–280 pts (Commer Mgt Quant Surv)
180 pts   **Glamorgan** – 180 pts (Quant Surv)
           Greenwich – 180 pts min (Quant Surv)
           UCE Birmingham – 180 pts (Constr Quant Surv)

           Leeds Met – contact University

Alternative offers
IB offers See **Chapter 7**.
Scottish offers See **Chapter 7**.

OTHER HIGHER EDUCATION COURSES IN THE SUBJECT FIELD

Foundation degrees (contact institutions for details) Bolton; Manchester (CAT); Northumbria; Swansea (IHE).

Higher National Diploma courses
140 pts **and below**
        Bell (Coll); Bradford (Coll); Brighton; Luton; Northumbria; Robert Gordon; UHI Millennium Inst; Wigan and Leigh (Coll).

CHOOSING YOUR COURSE (SEE ALSO CH.1)

Subject information Quantity Surveying is a specialised field of surveying which focuses on the costing of the built environment. Students are introduced to construction studies, measurement cost studies, economics and law. The work is similar, in some aspects, to the work of an accountant and requires the same attention to detail. See also **Architecture**, **Building** and **Surveying** courses. **Useful website** www.rics.org/careers.

Course variations Construction Economics and Management (Anglia Ruskin); Commercial Management and Quantity Surveying (Bolton, Bristol UWE, Central Lancashire, Loughborough, Wolverhampton); Quantity Surveying and Construction Commercial Management (Nottingham Trent); Property Development and Quantity Surveying (Portsmouth). *NOW CHECK PROSPECTUSES AND WEBSITES FOR ANY RECENT CHANGES.*

Universities and colleges teaching quality See www.tqi.ac.uk; www.qaa.ac.uk.

Top universities and colleges (Research) Salford.

Sandwich degree courses Glasgow Caledonian; Greenwich; Kingston; Leeds Met; Napier; Nottingham Trent; Plymouth; Robert Gordon; Salford; Sheffield Hallam; UCE Birmingham; Ulster; Wolverhampton.

ADMISSIONS INFORMATION

Number of applicants per place (approx) Anglia Ruskin 2; Glamorgan 4; Glasgow Caledonian 3; Greenwich 11; Kingston 13; Liverpool John Moores 10; Loughborough 9; Napier 2; Northumbria 11; Nottingham Trent 10; Robert Gordon 5; Salford 16; Sheffield Hallam 7; UCE Birmingham 14; Wolverhampton 6.

Advice to applicants and planning the UCAS personal statement Surveyors work with architects and builders as well as in their own consultancies and these organisations should be approached to discuss quantity surveying or to obtain work experience. Explain your interests fully. Read *The Chartered Quantity Surveyor* magazine. See also **Appendix 2**.

Selection interviews **Yes** Glamorgan, Glasgow Caledonian, Heriot-Watt, Kingston, Liverpool John Moores, Nottingham Trent, Robert Gordon, UCE Birmingham, Ulster.

Interview advice and questions Past questions have included: What is quantity surveying? What is the scope of the work? How do you qualify to do this work? Have you spoken to a quantity surveyor or spent any time in a quantity surveyor's office? See **Chapter 6**.

AFTER-RESULTS ADVICE
Offers to applicants repeating A-levels **Higher** Bolton, Nottingham Trent; **Possibly higher** Glamorgan, Liverpool John Moores; **Same** Salford.

GRADUATE DESTINATIONS AND EMPLOYMENT (2005 HESA)
No data available.

OTHER DEGREE SUBJECTS FOR CONSIDERATION
Architectural Technology; Architecture; Building; Civil Engineering; Construction Management; Surveying.

RADIOGRAPHY

(including **Medical Imaging** and **Radiotherapy; see also Health Sciences/Studies**)

NB The points totals shown to the left of the institutions are for ease of reference only. It must not be assumed that tariff points are always used by institutions or that they can be substituted for an offer in grades. The level of an offer is not necessarily indicative of the quality of a course.

COURSE OFFERS INFORMATION
Information on courses is also available from the Society of Radiographers (see **Appendix 2**).

Subject requirements/preferences **GCSE** Five subjects including English, mathematics and a science subject (usually at one sitting). **Bangor** Grade A–E English, mathematics. **London (St George's)/Kingston** Six subjects at grade C or higher. **AL** Sciences required; mathematics may be acceptable.

Your target offers

300 pts	**Cumbria** – 300 pts (Diag Radiog)
	Ulster – BBB 300 pts (Radiography)
280 pts	**Salford** – 280 pts (Diag Radiog)
260 pts	**Cardiff** – BCC (Radiog (Diag Imag); Radiothera Onc)
	Glasgow Caledonian – BCC (Rdtn Onc Sci; Diag Imag Sci)
240 pts	**Bradford** – 240 pts (Diag Radiog)
	Exeter – CCC 240 pts (Med Imag (Diag Radiog))
	Leeds – CCC (Radiog (Diag))
	Liverpool – 240 pts (Diag Radiog; Radiothera)
220 pts	**Bangor** – CCD 220–240 pts (Diag Radiog Imag)
	Hertfordshire – 220–240 pts (Diag Radiog Imag; Radiothera Onc)
	London (St George's)/Kingston – 220–240 pts (Diag Radiog; Ther Radiog)
	Portsmouth – 220 pts (Radiog (Diag) (Ther))
200 pts	**Derby** – 200 pts (Diag Radiog)
	London South Bank – BB–CC (Diag Imag (Radiog))
180 pts	**Anglia Ruskin** – 180–220 pts (Radiog (Diag Imag))
	City – BC (Radiog (Diag) (Ther))

Queen Margaret (UC) – 180 pts (Diag Radiog; Ther Radiog)
Sheffield Hallam – 180 pts (Diag Radiog; Radiothera Onc)
Teesside – 180–240 pts (Diag Radiog)
160 pts **Bristol UWE** – 160–200 pts (Diag Imag; Radiothera)
Canterbury Christ Church – CC (Med Imag (Radiog))
Robert Gordon – CC (Diag Radiog)
Suffolk (Univ Campus) – 160–180 pts (Diag Radiog; Onc Radiothera Tech)
UCE Birmingham – 160 pts (Radiothera; Diag Radiog)

Alternative offers
IB offers Bristol UWE 24 pts; City indiv offer; Liverpool 26 pts; Salford 30 pts.
Scottish offers See **Chapter 7**.

OTHER HIGHER EDUCATION COURSES IN THE SUBJECT FIELD
Foundation degrees (contact institutions for details) Anglia Ruskin; Leicester; Liverpool John Moores; Portsmouth; Salford.

CHOOSING YOUR COURSE (SEE ALSO CH.1)
Subject information Many institutions offer both Diagnostic and Therapeutic Radiography but applicants should check this, and course entry requirements, before applying. Information on courses is also available from the Society of Radiographers (see **Appendix 2**). **Diagnostic Radiography** The demonstration on film (or other imaging materials) of the position and structure of the body's organs using radiation or other imaging media. **Therapeutic Radiography** The planning and administration of treatment for patients suffering from malignant and non-malignant disease using different forms of

radiation. Courses lead to state registration. **Useful websites** www.sor.org; www.radiographycareers.co.uk; www.nhscareers.nhs.uk .

Course variations Diagnostic Imaging (Bristol UWE; London South Bank); Radiotherapy (Bristol UWE; Liverpool; UCE Birmingham); Medical Imaging (Radiography) (Canterbury Christ Church). *NOW CHECK PROSPECTUSES AND WEBSITES FOR ANY RECENT CHANGES.*

Universities and colleges teaching quality See www.tqi.ac.uk; www.qaa.ac.uk.

ADMISSIONS INFORMATION

Number of applicants per place (approx) Bangor 7; Bradford 8; Cardiff 3; Derby 6; Glasgow Caledonian 7; Hertfordshire (Diag Radiog Imag) 8, (Radiother) 50; Leeds 10; Liverpool 13; London (St George's)/Kingston 7; London South Bank 9; Portsmouth 10; Robert Gordon 5; Salford 10; Sheffield Hallam 8, (Radiother Onc) 3; Southampton 5; Suffolk (Univ Campus) 3; Teesside 10; UCE Birmingham (Radiother) 8.

Advice to applicants and planning the UCAS personal statement Contacts with radiographers and visits to the radiography departments of hospitals should be discussed in full on the UCAS application. Applicants required to have an occupational health check and a Criminal Records Bureau (CRB) clearance. **Liverpool** Decision to choose between therapeutic and diagnostic pathways should be made before applying. **Salford** Communication skills, teamwork, work experience in public areas. **UCE Birmingham** Evidence needed of a visit to at least one imaging department or oncology (radiotherapy) department before completing UCAS application. Evidence of good research into career. See also **Appendix 2**.

Misconceptions about this course There is often confusion between radiotherapy and diagnostic imaging and between diagnostic and therapeutic radiography.

Selection interviews Yes Bangor, Cardiff, City, Derby, Hertfordshire, London South Bank, Queen Margaret (UC), Salford, Sheffield Hallam, UCE Birmingham; **Some** London (St George's)/Kingston.

Interview advice and questions All applicants should have discussed this career with a radiographer and visited a hospital radiography department. Questions follow from these contacts. Where does radiography fit into the overall health care system? See **Chapter 6**.

Reasons for rejection (non-academic) Lack of interest in people. Poor communication skills. Occasionally students may be unsuitable for the clinical environment, for example, they express a fear of blood and needles; poor grasp of radiography as a career. Unable to meet criteria for employment in the Health Service, for example, health factors, criminal convictions, severe disabilities.

AFTER-RESULTS ADVICE

Universities with vacancies in Clearing (2006) Bangor; Bradford; Bristol UWE; City; Derby; Hertfordshire; Liverpool; London (St George's)/Kingston; London South Bank; Portsmouth; Robert Gordon; Sheffield Hallam.

Offers to applicants repeating A-levels Higher London (St George's)/Kingston; **Same** Derby, Salford.

GRADUATE DESTINATIONS AND EMPLOYMENT (2005 HESA)

No data available.

OTHER DEGREE SUBJECTS FOR CONSIDERATION

Audiology; Health Studies; Medical Physics; Nursing; Occupational Therapy; Physics; Podiatry; Speech Sciences.

RELIGIOUS STUDIES

(including **Biblical Studies, Divinity, Jewish Studies** and **Theology**)

NB The points totals shown to the left of the institutions are for ease of reference only. It must not be assumed that tariff points are always used by institutions or that they can be substituted for an offer in grades. The level of an offer is not necessarily indicative of the quality of a course.

COURSE OFFERS INFORMATION

Subject requirements/preferences GCSE Aberdeen, **Edinburgh** English and mathematics or science and a foreign language. *For teacher training* English and mathematics and science. **Cambridge**, **Oxford** Grade A in most subjects preferred. **Cardiff** (Theol) English language plus a foreign language. **London (SOAS)** Six subjects grade A–C minimum. **AL** Religious studies or theology may be required or preferred for some courses.

Your target offers

360 pts **and above**

  Cambridge – AAA (Theol Relig St)

  Cambridge (Hom) – AAA (BA Relig St Educ)

  Oxford – Offers vary eg AAA–AAB (Theology)

340 pts **Cardiff** – AAB–BBC 340–260 pts (Relig joint courses)

  Durham – AAB (Theol Comb Arts)

  St Andrews – AAB–ABB (Theol St courses; Bib St courses)

320 pts **Durham** – ABB (Phil Theol; Theol; Theol (Euro St))

  London (King's) – ABB–BBB (Relig St; Theol; Relig Phil Eth)

  Manchester – ABB (St Relig Theol; Compar Relig Soc Anth; St Relig Theol (Jew St) (Bib St) (Relig Soty) (S As St))

300 pts **Belfast (Queen's)** – BBB–BBCb (Theol; Div)

  Birmingham – BBB–BBC (Theology)

  Bristol – BBB–CCC; BBC for joint courses (Theol Relig St; Phil Theol; Theol Pol; Theol Sociol)

  Edinburgh – BBB (Relig St; Div)

  Exeter – BBB–BBC 300–280 pts (Theol St; Class St Theol; Phil Theol)

  Glasgow – BBB 2nd yr entry (Theol Relig St)

  Lancaster – BBB/ABC (Engl Lit Relig St; Hist Relig St)

  Leeds – BBB (Theol Relig St)

  London (UCL) – BBB–BBC (Heb Jew St; Jew Hist)

  Nottingham – ABC (Theol; Phil Theol)

  St Andrews – ABC (MTheol Theol)

  Sheffield – BBB (Bib St Engl; Bib St Phil; Bib St Ling)

280 pts **Cardiff** – BBC (Relig Theol St)
Kent – 280 pts (Relig St courses)
Lancaster – BBC–BCC (Relig St; Relig St Sociol; Anth Relig; Eth Phil Relig; Phil Relig St)
Oxford Brookes – BBC (Relig Cult Eth)
Sheffield – BBC–BCC **or** BBbb/BBcc/BCcc (Bib St; Bib St Ger; Bib St Mus)
260 pts **Hull** – BCC 260 pts (Theol; Theol Crea Writ; Theol Film St; Theol Sociol; Theol Hist Art; Mrl Relig St)
Leo Baeck (Coll) – BCC (Heb Jew St)
London (Hey) – BCC (Theol; Phil Theol; Phil Relig Eth; Ab Religs Islam Chr Jud)
London (SOAS) – BCC (St Relig)
Stranmillis (UC) – BCC (Relig St Educ)
240 pts **Aberdeen** – CCC (Div; Relig St)
Bangor – 240–280 pts (Relig St; Bib St; Theol)
Birmingham – CCC (Islam St)
Chester – 240–260 pts (Theol Relig St courses)
Oxford Brookes – CCC **or** CCcc (Relig St; Theol courses)
Stirling – CCC/BC (Relig St courses)
220 pts **Glasgow** – CCD 1st yr entry (Theol Relig St; Relig Phil Educ)
Gloucestershire – 220 pts (Relig Phil Eth)
Liverpool Hope – 220 pts (Theol Relig St)
Winchester – 220 pts (Theol Relig St)
200 pts **Bath Spa** – 200–240 pts (St Relig)
180 pts **Chichester** – 180–220 pts (Theology)
Lampeter – open admission policy (Theol; Relig St; Islam St; Relig Hist; Div)
York St John – 180 pts (Theol Relig St)
160 pts **Bishop Grosseteste (Coll)** – 160 pts (Educ St Theol)
Canterbury Christ Church – CC (Theol courses; Relig St courses)
Cumbria – CC 160 pts (Relig St)
Greenwich – 160 pts (Theol Relig courses)
Leeds Trinity and All Saints (Coll) – CC–CCC 160–240 pts (Theology)
Middlesex – 160–200 pts (Relig Cntxt courses)
Newman (CHE) – 160–240 pts (Theol Educ St)
Newport – 160 pts (Relig St Phil)
Roehampton – 160 pts (Theol Relig St)
St Mary's (Coll) – 160–200 pts (Theol Relig St; Theol)
Wolverhampton – 160–220 pts (Relig St courses)
140 pts **Trinity Carmarthen (Coll)** – 140 pts (Relig St courses; Relig Educ; Chr Commun St)
120 pts **Cliff (Coll)** – 120–240 pts (Theology)
80 pts **Oxford Brookes** – 80 pts (Yth Commun Wk App Theol)
UHI Millennium Inst (HTC) – 80 pts (Theol St)

Brighton – contact University (BA Relig Educ St)

Alternative offers
IB offers Aberdeen 29 pts; Birmingham 30–32 pts; Bristol 32 pts; Cambridge (BA) 38–42 pts, (BEd) 36 pts; Chichester 26 pts; Kent 31 pts; Lancaster 32–33 pts; London (King's) 33 pts; Manchester 32–33 pts; Nottingham 32 pts; Oxford 38–42 pts; St Andrews 32–36 pts.
Scottish offers See **Chapter 7**.

OTHER HIGHER EDUCATION COURSES IN THE SUBJECT FIELD
Foundation degrees (contact institution for details) York St John.

CHOOSING YOUR COURSE (SEE ALSO CH.1)

Subject information Religious Studies courses cover four degree course subjects: Religious Studies, Divinity, Theology and Biblical Studies. The subject content of these courses varies and students should check prospectuses carefully. They are not intended as training courses for church ministry; an adherence to a particular religious denomination is not a necessary qualification for entry. (Religious studies is an acceptable second or third A-level for any non-scientific degree course.) **Useful websites** www.guardian.co.uk/religion; www.cwmission.org.uk; www.miraclestudies.net; www.academicinfo.net/religindex.html; www.theologywebsite.com; www.jewishstudies.org; www.jewishstudies.virtualave.net; www.jewfaq.org; www.virtualreligion.net; www.jis.oxfordjournals.org.

Course variations Divinity (Belfast (Queen's)); Edinburgh; Theology and Politics (Bristol); Moral and Religious Studies (Hull); Religion, Philosophy and Ethics (London (King's)); Comparative Religion and Social Anthropology (Manchester). *NOW CHECK PROSPECTUSES AND WEBSITES FOR ANY RECENT CHANGES.*

Universities and colleges teaching quality See www.tqi.ac.uk; www.qaa.ac.uk.

Top universities and colleges (Research) (including Theology and Divinity) Aberdeen; Birmingham; Bristol; Cambridge; Cardiff*; Durham; Edinburgh; Exeter; Glasgow; Lampeter; Lancaster; London (King's), (SOAS); Manchester*; Nottingham*; Oxford*; St Andrews; Sheffield; Stirling.

ADMISSIONS INFORMATION

Number of applicants per place (approx) Bangor 5; Birmingham 4; Bristol 7; Cambridge 2; Cambridge (Hom) 4; Chichester 6; Cumbria 12; Durham 6; Edinburgh 3; Exeter 7; Glasgow 4; Greenwich 10; Hull (Theol) 10; Kent 13; Lampeter 7; Lancaster 6; Leeds 4; Leeds Trinity and All Saints (Coll) 4; Liverpool Hope 6; London (Hey) 4, (King's) 6, (SOAS) 1; Middlesex 4; Newman (CHE) 2; Nottingham 10; Oxford (success rate 60%); Sheffield 7; Roehampton 2; Winchester 6; York St John 2.

Advice to applicants and planning the UCAS personal statement An awareness of the differences between the main religions is important as is any special research undertaken. Interests in the religious art and architecture of various periods and styles should be noted. Applicants should have an open-minded approach to studying a diverse range of religious traditions. **Bristol** Early application recommended. **St Andrews** Give evidence of interest and reasons for choosing the course.

Misconceptions about this course Some students think that you must be religious to study Theology – in fact, people of all faiths and none study the subject. A study of religions is not Christian theology. **Leeds** Some applicants are not aware of the breadth of the subject. We offer modules covering New Testament, Christian theology, Islamic studies, Hinduism, Buddhism, Sikhism, Christian ethics, sociology of religion.

Selection interviews **Yes** Aberystwyth, Cambridge, Chester, Durham, Edinburgh, Glasgow, Hull, Lampeter, Lancaster, Leeds, Leeds Trinity and All Saints (Coll), London (Hey), (SOAS), Nottingham, Oxford, Oxford Brookes, Roehampton, Sheffield, Winchester; **Some** Bristol, Cardiff, Southampton.

Interview advice and questions Past questions have included: Why do you want to study Theology/Biblical Studies/Religious Studies? What do you hope to do after obtaining your degree? Questions relating to the A-level syllabus. Questions on current theological topics. Do you have any strong religious convictions? Do you think that your religious beliefs will be changed at the end of the course? Why did you choose Religious Studies rather than Biblical Studies? How would you explain the miracles to a 10-year-old? (BEd course). Do you agree with the National Lottery? How do you think you can apply theology to your career? **Oxford** Ability to defend one's opinions and willingness to engage in a lively dialogue. See **Chapter 6**.

Reasons for rejection (non-academic) Students not attending open days may be rejected. Too religiously conservative. Failure to interact. Lack of motivation to study a subject which goes beyond A-level. **Cardiff** Insufficiently open to an academic study of religion. **Leo Baeck (Coll)** Inability to fit into life of the College, bearing in mind that its main aim is to train rabbis for the Jewish community.

AFTER-RESULTS ADVICE

Universities with vacancies in Clearing (2006) Aberdeen; Bangor; Birmingham; Canterbury Christ Church; Cardiff; Chester; Chichester; Cumbria; Glasgow; Greenwich; Hull; Kent; Lampeter; Lancaster; Liverpool Hope; London (Hey), (SOAS); Manchester; Middlesex; Nottingham; Roehampton; Stirling; Wolverhampton; Winchester; York St John.

Offers to applicants repeating A-levels Higher Durham, Hull, Manchester, St Andrews; **Possibly higher** Cambridge (Hom); **Same** Bangor, Birmingham, Cardiff, Chester, Glasgow, Greenwich, Lampeter, Lancaster, Leeds, London (SOAS), Nottingham, Roehampton, Sheffield, Winchester, York St John.

GRADUATE DESTINATIONS AND EMPLOYMENT (2005 HESA)

Graduates surveyed 990 **Employed** 390 **In further study** 285 **Assumed unemployed** 60.

OTHER DEGREE SUBJECTS FOR CONSIDERATION

Community Studies; Education; History; Philosophy; Psychology; Social Policy and Administration; Social Work.

RETAIL MANAGEMENT

NB The points totals shown to the left of the institutions are for ease of reference only. It must not be assumed that tariff points are always used by institutions or that they can be substituted for an offer in grades. The level of an offer is not necessarily indicative of the quality of a course.

COURSE OFFERS INFORMATION

Subject requirements/preferences GCSE English and mathematics at grade C or above. **AL** No subjects specified.

Your target offers

320 pts **Loughborough** – ABB (Rtl Mgt)
300 pts **Manchester** – BBB (Fash Tex Rtl; Des Mgt Fash Rtl)
  Stirling – BBB 2nd yr entry (Rtl Mark)
  Surrey – 300 pts (Rtl Mgt)
280 pts **Oxford Brookes** – BBC (Rtl Bus Mgt)
260 pts **Stirling** – BCC 1st yr entry (Rtl Mark)
240 pts **Bournemouth** – 240 pts (Rtl Mgt)
  Brighton – 240 pts (Rtl Mgt; Rtl Mark)
  De Montfort – 240 pts (Rtl Buy)
  Manchester Met – 240 pts (Rtl Mark Mgt; Fash Buy)
  Robert Gordon – CCC (Rtl Mgt)
  UCE Birmingham – 240 pts (Fash Rtl Mgt)
  Westminster – 240 pts (Fash Mrchnds Mgt)
220 pts **Huddersfield** – 220 pts (Rtl Mgt)
  Teesside – 220 pts (Retailing)
200 pts **Central Lancashire** – 200–260 pts (Rtl Mgt Buy; Rtl Mgt Fash; Rtl Mgt Mark; Rtl Mgt)
180 pts **Birmingham (CFTCS)** – 180 pts (Lic Rtl Mgt; Rtl Fd Mgt)
  Cardiff (UWIC) – 180 pts (Rtl Mgt)
  Queen Margaret (UC) – 180 pts (Consum St Rtl; Rtl Bus)
  Roehampton – 180–160 pts (Rtl Mgt Mark)
160 pts **Arts London** – 160 pts (Rtl Mgt)
  Canterbury Christ Church – 160 pts (Bus St Rtl Mgt)
  Central Lancashire – 160 pts (Rtl Mgt Comb hons)

Glasgow Caledonian – 160 pts (Retailing)
Northampton – 160 pts (Rtl Mark)
Wolverhampton – 160–220 pts (Rtl Mark)

Leeds Met – contact University

Alternative offers
IB offers Surrey 32 pts; see also under **Business Courses**.
Scottish offers See **Chapter 7**.

OTHER HIGHER EDUCATION COURSES IN THE SUBJECT FIELD

Foundation degrees (contact institutions for details) Arts London (CComm); Birmingham (CFTCS); Canterbury Christ Church; London Met; Nottingham New (Coll); Plymouth (CFE); Preston (Coll); Wolverhampton.

Higher National Diploma courses Bell (Coll); Cardiff (UWIC); Greenwich; Solihull (Coll); Swansea (IHE); Worcester (CT).

CHOOSING YOUR COURSE (SEE ALSO CH.1)

Subject information See under **Business Courses**. **Useful websites** See **Business Courses**.

Course variations Retail and Food Management (Birmingham (CFTCS)); Retail Management with Buying (Central Lancashire); Design Management for Fashion Retailing (Manchester); Consumer Studies and Retailing (Queen Margaret (UC)); Fashion Merchandise Management (Westminster). *NOW CHECK PROSPECTUSES AND WEBSITES FOR ANY RECENT CHANGES.*

Universities and colleges teaching quality See www.tqi.ac.uk; www.qaa.ac.uk.

Top universities and colleges (Research) See **Business Courses**.

ADMISSIONS INFORMATION

Number of applicants per place (approx) See **Business Courses**.

Advice to applicants and planning the UCAS personal statement See **Business Courses**.

Misconceptions about this course See **Business Courses**.

Selection interviews See **Business Courses**.

Interview advice and questions See **Business Courses**.

Reasons for rejection (non-academic) See **Business Courses**.

AFTER-RESULTS ADVICE

Universities with vacancies in Clearing (2006) Birmingham (CFTCS); Brighton; Canterbury Christ Church; Cardiff (UWIC); Central Lancashire; De Montfort; Huddersfield; Manchester Met; Robert Gordon; Roehampton; Stirling; Teesside; UCE Birmingham; Ulster; Westminster.

Offers to applicants repeating A-levels See **Business Courses**.

GRADUATE DESTINATIONS AND EMPLOYMENT (2005 HESA)

See under **Business Courses**.

OTHER DEGREE SUBJECTS FOR CONSIDERATION

Business Studies; Consumer Sciences/Studies; E-Commerce; Human Resource Management; Psychology; Supply Chain Management.

RUSSIAN AND EAST EUROPEAN STUDIES

(including **Bulgarian, Czech, Finnish, Hungarian, Polish, Romanian, Russian** and **Serbo-Croat;** see also **European Studies** and **Languages)**

NB The points totals shown to the left of the institutions are for ease of reference only. It must not be assumed that tariff points are always used by institutions or that they can be substituted for an offer in grades. The level of an offer is not necessarily indicative of the quality of a course.

COURSE OFFERS INFORMATION

Subject requirements/preferences **GCSE Edinburgh** English, mathematics or science and a foreign language. **Oxford**, **Cambridge** Grade A in most subjects preferred. **AL** One or two modern languages may be stipulated.

Your target offers

360 pts   and above
  Cambridge – AAA (Russ; Modn Mediev Lang (Russ))
  Oxford – Offers vary eg AAA–AAB (Modn Langs (Russ+2nd Lang) (Cz Slov+2nd Lang); Engl Modn Langs (Russ))

340 pts   Durham – AAB (Modn Langs (Russ) Hist)
  St Andrews – AAB–ABB (Russ courses)

320 pts   Bath – ABB (Modn Lang – Euro St courses; Russ Pol)
  Bristol – ABB–BBB (Cz Fr/Ger/Ital/Port/Russ/Span)
  Durham – ABB (Russ Comb Hons)
  Exeter – ABB–BBB (Int Rel Russ; Pol Russ)
  Glasgow – ABB–BBB (Cnt E Euro St; Cz; Russ; Polh; Slav St)

300 pts   Birmingham – BBB 300 pts (Russ St joint courses)
  Bristol – BBB–BCC (Russ courses)
  Edinburgh – BBB (Russ St Bus St; Russ St Ling; Russ St Euro Hist; Russ St Phil; Russ St Pol; Russ St Hist Art)
  London (LSE) – check with admissions tutor (Lang St (Russ))
  London (UCL) – BBB+AS (E Euro St; E Euro St Bulg/Cz/Finn/Hung/Slov/Polh/Romn/Serb/Cro/Ukr; Russ St; Russ Hist)
  Manchester – BBB (Russ St; Russ Chin)
  Sheffield – BBB–BBC (Russ courses)
  Surrey – 300–260 pts (Modn Langs; Law Russ Law)

280 pts   Exeter – BBC (Russ courses)
  Leeds – BBC–BCC (Russ St A and B courses; Russ joint hons; Russ Civ courses; Russ St; Pol Russ)
  London (QM) – 280–320 pts (Russ Geog)
  London (SOAS) – BBC (Georgian)
  Westminster – 280 pts (Russ courses)

260 pts   Birmingham – BCC 260 pts (Russ St)
  London (QM) – 260 pts (Russ courses except under **280 pts**)
  Nottingham – BCC (Russ St courses; Serb Cro St)

200 pts   European Bus Sch London – CDD 200 pts approx (Int Bus (Russ))

Alternative offers
IB offers Birmingham 32 pts; Bristol 29–32 pts, (Czech) 30–34 pts; Cambridge 38–42 pts; Exeter 30–31 pts; London (UCL) 32 pts; Manchester 32–33 pts; Nottingham 28–30 pts; St Andrews 32–36 pts; Sheffield 30–32 pts.
Scottish offers See **Chapter 7**.

CHOOSING YOUR COURSE (SEE ALSO CH.1)

Subject information East European Studies cover a wide range of the less popular language courses and should be considered by anyone with a love of and gift for languages. Many natural linguists often devote themselves to one of the popular European languages studied up to A-level, when their language skills could be extended to the more unusual languages, thereby increasing their future career opportunities. **Useful websites** www.basees.org.uk; www.iol.org.uk; www.bbc.co.uk/languages; www.languageadvantage.com; www.languagematters.co.uk; www.reed.co.uk/multilingual; www.cilt.org.uk.

Course variations Russian and Politics (Bath); Russian Combined Honours Arts (Durham); Central and East European Studies (Glasgow); Russian Civilisation and Sociology (Leeds); Russian with Geography (London (QM)); Georgian (London (SOAS)). *NOW CHECK PROSPECTUSES AND WEBSITES FOR ANY RECENT CHANGES.*

Universities and colleges teaching quality See www.tqi.ac.uk; www.qaa.ac.uk.

Top universities and colleges (Research) Birmingham; Bristol; Cambridge; Exeter; London (QM); Nottingham; Oxford*; Sheffield*; Surrey.

ADMISSIONS INFORMATION

Number of applicants per place (approx) Birmingham 3; Bristol 3; Durham 7; Leeds 3; London (UCL) (E Euro St Bulg) 1; Nottingham 5; Surrey 3.

Advice to applicants and planning the UCAS personal statement Visits to Eastern Europe should be mentioned, supported by your special reasons for wishing to study the language. A knowledge of the cultural, economic and political scene would also be important. **Leeds** Fluent English important for non-EU students. See also **Languages**. **St Andrews** Evidence of interest, reasons for choosing the course. **Surrey** Evidence of wide reading, travel and residence abroad. Fluent English important. See also **Appendix 2** under **Languages**.

Selection interviews Yes Cambridge, Durham, Exeter, London (UCL), Oxford, Surrey; **Some** Nottingham.

Interview advice and questions Since many applicants will not have taken Russian at A-level, questions often focus on their reasons for choosing a Russian degree, and their knowledge of, and interest in, Russia. Those taking A-level Russian are likely to be questioned on the course and on any reading done outside A-level work. East European Studies applicants will need to show some knowledge of their chosen country/countries and any specific reasons why they wish to follow the course. **Leeds** See **Languages**. See **Chapter 6**.

Reasons for rejection (non-academic) Lack of perceived commitment for a demanding *ab initio* subject.

AFTER-RESULTS ADVICE

Universities with vacancies in Clearing (2006) Bath; Birmingham; London (QM); Nottingham; Sheffield; Surrey.

Offers to applicants repeating A-levels Higher Bristol, Glasgow, Leeds, St Andrews, Surrey (if candidate is re-sitting 2 A-levels); **Same** Durham.

GRADUATE DESTINATIONS AND EMPLOYMENT (2005 HESA)

Graduates surveyed 110 **Employed** 50 **In further study** 15 **Assumed unemployed** 15.

OTHER DEGREE SUBJECTS FOR CONSIDERATION

Economics; European Studies; International Relations; Linguistics; Politics; other languages.

SCANDINAVIAN STUDIES

NB The points totals shown to the left of the institutions are for ease of reference only. It must not be assumed that tariff points are always used by institutions or that they can be substituted for an offer in grades. The level of an offer is not necessarily indicative of the quality of a course.

COURSE OFFERS INFORMATION

Subject requirements/preferences GCSE Foreign language preferred for all courses. **Cambridge** Grade A in most subjects preferred. **Edinburgh** English, mathematics or science and a foreign language preferred. **AL** A modern language may be required.

Your target offers

360 pts and above
Cambridge – AAA varies between colleges (A-Sxn Nrs Celt)

300 pts Edinburgh – BBB (Scand St (Dan Norw Swed); Scand St Class; Scand St Euro Hist; Scand St Hist Art; Scand St Ling; Scand St Phil; Scand St Pol; Scand St Soc Pol; Scand St Scot Ethnol; Scand St Bus St)

280 pts London (UCL) – BBC+AS (Scand St (Dan) (Norw) (Swed); Scand St Hist; Ice; Vkg St)
Nottingham – BBC (Vkg St)

Alternative offers
IB offers London (UCL) 32 pts; see also **Chapter 7**.
Scottish offers See **Chapter 7**.

CHOOSING YOUR COURSE (SEE ALSO CH.1)

Subject information Scandinavian Studies provides those students who enjoy languages with the opportunity to extend their language expertise to learn a modern Scandinavian language – Danish, Norwegian or Swedish – from beginner's level to honours level in four years, including a year in Scandinavia. The three languages are very similar to each other and a knowledge of one makes it possible to easily access the literature and cultures of the other two. Viking Studies includes Old Norse, runology and archaeology. **Useful websites** www.cilt.org.uk; www.iol.org.uk; www.bbc.co.uk/languages; www.languageadvantage.com; www.languagematters.co.uk; www.reed.co.uk/multilingual; www.scandinaviahouse.org.

Course variations Anglo Saxon, Norse and Celtic (Cambridge); Scandinavian Studies (Danish) (Norwegian) (Swedish) (Edinburgh; London (UCL)); Icelandic (London (UCL)); Viking Studies (London (UCL); Nottingham). *NOW CHECK PROSPECTUSES AND WEBSITES FOR ANY RECENT CHANGES.*

Universities and colleges teaching quality See www.tqi.ac.uk; www.qaa.ac.uk.

Top universities and colleges (Research) Cambridge; Edinburgh; London (UCL).

ADMISSIONS INFORMATION

Number of applicants per place (approx) London (UCL) 3.

Advice to applicants and planning the UCAS personal statement Visits to Scandinavian countries could be the source of an interest in studying these languages. You should also be aware of cultural, political, geographical and economic aspects of Scandinavian countries. Knowledge of these should be shown in your statement.

Selection interviews Yes Cambridge.

Interview advice and questions Applicants in the past have been questioned on why they have chosen this subject area, on their visits to Scandinavia and on their knowledge of the country/countries and their people. Future career plans are likely to be discussed. See **Chapter 6**.

Reasons for rejection (non-academic) One applicant didn't know the difference between a noun and a verb.

GRADUATE DESTINATIONS AND EMPLOYMENT (2005 HESA)

No data available but in 2004: **Graduates surveyed** 15 **Employed** 5 **In further study** none **Assumed unemployed** 5.

OTHER DEGREE SUBJECTS FOR CONSIDERATION

Archaeology; History; European History/Studies; other modern languages, including, for example, Russian and East European languages.

SCIENCE

(including **Combined and General Science;** see also **Biological Sciences** and **Natural Sciences**)

NB The points totals shown to the left of the institutions are for ease of reference only. It must not be assumed that tariff points are always used by institutions or that they can be substituted for an offer in grades. The level of an offer is not necessarily indicative of the quality of a course.

COURSE OFFERS INFORMATION

Subject requirements/preferences GCSE Science/mathematics subjects. *Teacher Training courses* English, mathematics. **Cambridge** Grade A in most subjects preferred. **AL** One or two sciences may be required.

Your target offers

360 pts and above
  Cambridge – AAA (Nat Sci; Hist Phil Sci)
  Oxford – Offers vary eg AAA–AAB (Hum Sci)
350 pts Belfast (Queen's) – BBBb–BBCb (Hist Sci courses)
340 pts Durham – AAB (Nat Sci)
  London (UCL) – AAB+AS–ABB+AS (Hum Sci)
320 pts Lancaster – ABB (Nat Sci N Am; Comb Sci N Am)
  Leicester – 320 pts (MSci Interd Sci)
  London (UCL) – ABB+AS (Hist Phil Sci; Hist Phil Soc St Sci; Sci Comm Pol)
  Reading – ABB–BBB 320 pts (Nat Sci)
  Sussex – ABB (Hum Sci)
300 pts Birmingham – BBB–BBC (Nat Sci courses)
  East Anglia – BBB (Nat Sci)
  Lancaster – BBB (Sci Tech Soty)
  Leeds – BBB (Hist Phil Sci)
  St Andrews – BBB (Lgc Phil Sci (Comp Sci) (Maths) (Phys) (Stats); Intnet Comp Sci Lgc Phil Sci)
  Stranmillis (UC) – BBB (Sci Educ)
280 pts Lancaster – BBC (Nat Sci)
  Liverpool – BBC–ABB 280–320 pts (Sci Comb hons)
  Liverpool John Moores – 280–300 pts (Sci Ftbl)
260 pts Bath – BCC–BBB 260–300 pts (Nat Sci)
  Bristol – BCC–BBD (Soc Sci)
  Lancaster – BCC (Comb Sci)
  Leicester – 260 pts (BSc Interd Sci)
  London (RH) – 260 pts (Bioch Sci Comm; Biol Sci Comm; Physl Geog Sci Comm; Geol Sci Comm; Phys Sci Comm)
  Oxford Brookes – BCC **or** BCbb (Sci Soty)
  St Andrews – BCC (Sci Gen Deg)
240 pts Paisley – CCC–EE (Science)
220 pts Bradford – 220 pts (BSc Comb St)
  Winchester – 220 pts (Sci P Educ)
200 pts Glamorgan – 200 pts (Sci Rgby; Out Learn Sci Advntr; Sci Fict Cult)

Plymouth – 200 pts (Sci Media)
Reading – 200 pts (Fdn Sci)
180 pts **Heriot-Watt** – DDD 180 pts (BSc Comb St)
160 pts **Bishop Grosseteste (Coll)** – 160 pts (Sci Educ St)
Canterbury Christ Church – CC (Integ Sci; Sci QTS)
Glamorgan – 160 pts (Comb Sci)
London South Bank – CC (App Sci)
Nottingham Trent – 160 pts (Interd Sci courses)
Teesside – 160 pts (App Sci Foren Invstg; Crime Sc Sci)
140 pts **Bath Spa** – CD (Comb awards)
120 pts **Bradford** – 120 pts (Fdn Sci)
Huddersfield – 120 pts (App Sci)
Wolverhampton – 120–160 pts (Analyt Sci)
100 pts **Bristol UWE** – 100–140 pts (Fdn Sci)
Sheffield Hallam – 100 pts (Fdn Sci Maths)
80 pts **Coventry** – 80 pts (Fdn Sci)
Eastleigh (Coll) – 80 pts (Fdn Sci)
Farnborough (CT) – 80–120 pts (Sci Mgt Exer Hlth)
Huddersfield – 80 pts (Fdn Sci)
Leicester – 80 pts (Fdn Sci)
UHI Millennium Inst – 80 pts (App Sci)

Open University – contact University

Alternative offers
IB offers Bristol 28 pts; Cambridge 38–42 pts.
Scottish offers See **Chapter 7**.

OTHER HIGHER EDUCATION COURSES IN THE SUBJECT FIELD
Foundation degrees (contact institutions for details) Central Lancashire.

Higher National Diploma courses
100 pts and below
Bristol UWE; Cardiff (UWIC); Coventry; Derby; Paisley; Portsmouth; Riverside Halton (Coll); Robert Gordon; Stockport (CFHE).

CHOOSING YOUR COURSE (SEE ALSO CH.1)
Subject information This table includes a range of specialised and general science degree subjects. Courses in the History and Philosophy of Science may not necessarily require a science subject at A-level. **Useful websites** www.planet-science.com; www.scicentral.com; www.noisemakers.org.uk; see also **Biology**, **Chemistry** and **Physics**.

Course variations Integrated Science (Canterbury Christ Church); Science of Football (Glamorgan); History and Philosophy of Science (Leeds); Science Communication (London (RH)); Interdisciplinary Science (Nottingham Trent); Logic and Philosophy of Science (St Andrews); Human Science (Sussex). *NOW CHECK PROSPECTUSES AND WEBSITES FOR ANY RECENT CHANGES.*

ADMISSIONS INFORMATION
Number of applicants per place (approx) Bristol UWE 3; Coventry 2; Glamorgan 9; Heriot-Watt 2; Lancaster 7; Liverpool John Moores (Sci Ftbl) 10; Paisley 4.

Advice to applicants and planning the UCAS personal statement **Liverpool John Moores** (Sci Ftbl) This is a lab-based course examining physical stress. See **Biology, Biological Sciences, Chemistry, Physics**. See also **Appendix 2**.

Misconceptions about this course **Liverpool John Moores** (Sci Ftbl) Some applicants believe that scientific ability is not needed for the course: this is not true. Both scientific and practical ability are essential.

Selection interviews Yes Bristol UWE, Cambridge, London (UCL).

Interview advice and questions Past applicants have been questioned on their A-level work and aspects they particularly enjoyed. See **Chapter 6**.

Reasons for rejection (non-academic) (Mainly academic) Lack of an active interest in scientific issues.

AFTER-RESULTS ADVICE
Universities with vacancies in Clearing (2006) Check all institutions and see under separate subject tables.

GRADUATE DESTINATIONS AND EMPLOYMENT (2005 HESA)
No data available for 2005 but in 2002:

History of Science and Philosophy graduates surveyed 15 **Employed** 5 **In further study** 5 **Assumed unemployed** None.

General Science graduates surveyed 1120 **Employed** 480 **In further study** 350 **Assumed unemployed** 90.

OTHER DEGREE SUBJECTS FOR CONSIDERATION
Biochemistry; Biological Sciences; Biology; Health Sciences; Life Sciences; Natural Sciences; Physics; Sports Sciences.

SOCIAL AND PUBLIC POLICY AND ADMINISTRATION

(see also **Community Studies** and **Social Work**)

NB The points totals shown to the left of the institutions are for ease of reference only. It must not be assumed that tariff points are always used by institutions or that they can be substituted for an offer in grades. The level of an offer is not necessarily indicative of the quality of a course.

COURSE OFFERS INFORMATION
Subject requirements/preferences GCSE English and mathematics normally required. **Edinburgh** Mathematics grade A or AS grade B. **London (LSE)** A* to B grades, mathematics grade C or better. **Southampton** Grade B mathematics. **AL** No subjects specified.

Your target offers
340 pts **Cardiff** – AAB–BCC (Soc Pol joint courses)
320 pts **York** – ABB (Pol Soc Pol)
300 pts **Belfast (Queen's)** – BBB–BBCb (Soc Pol)
          Bristol – BBB–BCC (Soc Pol Sociol)
          Cardiff – BBB–BCC (Soc Pol single hons)
          Edinburgh – BBB (Soc Pol Soc Econ Hist; Soc Pol Sociol; Soc Pol Law; Soc Pol Pol)
          Hull – 300 pts (Pblc Pol)
          Liverpool – BBB (Sociol Soc Pol)
          London (LSE) – BBB (Soc Pol; Soc Pol Crim; Soc Pol Gov; Soc Pol Sociol; Soc Pol Econ)
          Nottingham – ABC–BBB (Soc Pol Admin; Soc Cult St)
          Sheffield – BBB–BBC (Soc Pol Crim)
          Stirling – BBB 2nd yr entry (Sociol Soc Pol)
          York – BBB–BBC (Soc Pol; Sociol Soc Pol)
280 pts **Aston** – BBC–BBB 280-300 pts (Pblc Pol Mgt)
          Bangor – BBC 280-260 pts (Soc Pol Psy)

Bath – BBC (Soc Pol Admin; Sociol Soc Pol)
Birmingham – BBC–BCC 260–280 pts (Soc Pol; Pblc Soc Pol Mgt; Soc Pol Pol Sci; Soc Pol Sociol; Pblc Pol Gov Mgt)
Brighton – 280 pts (Soc Pol; Crim Soc Pol; Sociol Soc Pol)
Leeds – BBC (Soc Pol Sociol; Soc Pol Theol Relig St; Soc Pol Span)
Southampton – BBC 280 pts (Soc Pol Admin)

260 pts **Bangor** – 260–300 pts (Law Soc Pol)
Bristol – BCC–BBD (Soc Pol)
Leeds – BCC (Soc Pol)
Loughborough – 260–280 pts (Crim Soc Pol)
Northumbria – 260 pts (Pol Soc Pol)
Stirling – BCC (Pblc Mgt Admin)
Stirling – BCC 1st yr entry (Soc Pol Sociol)
Warwick – BCC (Sociol Soc Pol)

240 pts **De Montfort** – 240 pts (Pblc Pol joint courses)
Kent – 240 pts (Soc Pol Pblc Sctr Mgt)
Sheffield Hallam – 240 pts inc 2AL (Soc Pol; Soc Pol Sociol)
Swansea – CCC–BCC 240–260 pts (Soc Pol courses)

220 pts **Anglia Ruskin** – 220–260 pts (Soc Pol Crim; Soc Pol Law)
Bangor – 220–260 pts (Soc Pol)
Gloucestershire – 220 pts (Lcl Pol)
Hull – 220–280 pts (Soc Pol Gndr St; Soc Pol Pblc Sctr Mgt)
UCE Birmingham – 220 pts (Sociol Pol St)
Ulster – 220 pts (Soc Pol; Soc Pol Gov)

200 pts **Anglia Ruskin** – 200 pts (Soc Pol Sociol; Bus Soc Pol)
Lincoln – CDD 200 pts (Soc Pol)
Middlesex – 200–240 pts (Soc Pol courses)

180 pts **Bradford** – 180–220 pts (Soc Pol Sociol)
Derby – 180 pts (Pblc Serv Mgt courses)
Northampton – 180 pts (Soc Welf)
Salford – 180–200 pts (Soc Pol; Cnslg Soc Pol; Hlth Sci Soc Pol)

160 pts **Central Lancashire** – 160 pts (Soc Pol Comb courses)
Glamorgan – 160 pts (Pblc Soc Pol)
Wolverhampton – 160–220 pts (Soc Pol)

140 pts **Anglia Ruskin** – 140 pts (Soc Pol)
London South Bank – CD–CC (Soc Pol courses; Euro Pol St courses; Int Soc Pol)
Paisley – CD (Soc Sci (Soc Pol))

120 pts **Llandrillo Cymru (Coll)** – 120–180 pts (Pblc Soc Pol)
Manchester Met – 120 pts (Pblc Serv)
Roehampton – 120 pts (Soc Pol Admin)
Swansea (IHE) – 120–80 pts (Pblc Serv)
Worcester – 120 pts (Soc Welf courses)

Leeds Met – contact University

Alternative offers
IB offers Bath 30–32 pts; Birmingham 30–32 pts; Brighton 28 pts; Kent 27 pts; London (LSE) 36 pts; (RH) 30 pts; Salford 24 pts; Sheffield 35–30 pts; Stirling 30 pts; Swansea 30 pts; York 30–34 pts.
Scottish offers See **Chapter 7**.

OTHER HIGHER EDUCATION COURSES IN THE SUBJECT FIELD

Foundation degrees (contact institutions for details) Anglia Ruskin; Barnfield (Coll); Bath; Bournemouth and Poole (Coll); Bradford; Bristol City (Coll); City; City and Islington (Coll); Cornwall (Coll); Derby; Durham New (Coll); Exeter (Coll); Hull (Coll); Leeds Park Lane (Coll); Newman (CHE); Plymouth (CFE); St Helens (Coll); Suffolk (Univ Campus); Sussex Downs (Coll); Truro (Coll); Walsall (Coll); West Anglia (Coll); Westminster Kingsway (Coll); Weymouth (Coll); Worcester; York St John.

Higher National Diploma courses See **Social Studies/Science**.

CHOOSING YOUR COURSE (SEE ALSO CH.1)

Subject information Social Policy is a multi-disciplinary degree that combines elements from sociology, political science, social and economic history, economics, cultural studies and philosophy. It is a study of the needs of society and how best to provide such services as education, housing, health and welfare services. **Useful website** www.lga.gov.uk; www.ippr.org.uk; www.swap.ac.uk; www.socialpolicy.net.

Course variations Psychology and Social Policy (Bangor); Public Policy, Government and Management (Birmingham); Local Policy (Gloucestershire); Social Policy and Government (London (LSE)); European Policy Studies; International Social Policy (London South Bank); Criminology and Social Policy (Loughborough); Health Sciences and Social Policy (Salford). *NOW CHECK PROSPECTUSES AND WEBSITES FOR ANY RECENT CHANGES.*

Universities and colleges teaching quality See www.tqi.ac.uk; www.qaa.ac.uk.

Top universities and colleges (Research) Bath; Bristol; Kent*; Leeds; London (LSE)*; Sheffield; York.

Sandwich degree courses Aston; Bath; De Montfort; Glamorgan; Loughborough; Middlesex.

ADMISSIONS INFORMATION

Number of applicants per place (approx) Aston 8; Bangor 6; Bath 6; Birmingham 3; Bristol 4; Cardiff 4; Central Lancashire 6; De Montfort 5; Glamorgan 5; Hull 9; Kent 5; Leeds 10; London (LSE) (Soc Pol) 6, (Soc Pol Sociol) 8, (Soc Pol Econ) 7, (Soc Pol Gov) 14; Loughborough 5; Manchester Met 4; Middlesex 12; Nottingham 3; Roehampton 4; Sheffield Hallam 4; Southampton 6; Stirling 11; Swansea 6; York 3.

Advice to applicants and planning the UCAS personal statement Careers in public and social administration are covered by this subject; consequently a good knowledge of these occupations and contacts with the social services should be discussed fully on your UCAS application. Gain work experience if possible. **Aston** The course is specially tailored for students aiming for careers in NHS management, the civil service and local government. **Bangor** Ability to communicate and work in a group. **Sheffield Hallam** Interest in current affairs and contemporary issues. Details of work experience, paid or unpaid. **York** Work experience, including voluntary work relevant to social policy. (See **Appendix 2** for contact details of some relevant organisations.)

Misconceptions about this course York Some applicants imagine that the course is vocational and leads directly to social work – it does not. Graduates in this field are well placed for a wide range of careers.

Selection interviews Yes Birmingham, London (LSE), Swansea; **Some** Anglia Ruskin, Bangor, Bath (mature applicants), Cardiff, Kent, Leeds (mature students), Loughborough, Salford, Sheffield Hallam, Southampton, York.

Interview advice and questions Past questions have included: What relevance has history to social administration? What do you understand by 'public policy'? What advantage do you think studying social science gives when working in policy fields? How could the image of public management of services be improved? Applicants should be fully aware of the content and the differences between all the courses on offer, why they want to study Social Policy and their career objectives. See **Chapter 6**.

Reasons for rejection (non-academic) Some universities require attendance when they invite applicants to open days (check). Lack of awareness of current social issues. **Bath** Applicant really wanted Business Studies: evidence that teacher, careers adviser or parents are pushing the applicant into the subject or higher education. See also **Social Work**.

AFTER-RESULTS ADVICE

Universities with vacancies in Clearing (2006) Anglia Ruskin; Aston; Bangor; Bath; Birmingham; Brighton; Central Lancashire; Derby; De Montfort; Glamorgan; Gloucestershire; Hull; Kent; Lincoln;

London South Bank; Manchester Met; Middlesex; Roehampton; Salford; Sheffield; Sheffield Hallam; Southampton; Stirling; Swansea; UCE Birmingham; Wolverhampton; Worcester; York.

Offers to applicants repeating A-levels Higher Glasgow, Leeds, Newcastle; **Same** Anglia Ruskin, Bangor, Bath, Birmingham, Brighton, Cardiff, Loughborough, Roehampton, Salford, Sheffield Hallam, Southampton, York.

GRADUATE DESTINATIONS AND EMPLOYMENT (2005 HESA)
Graduates surveyed 860 **Employed** 450 **In further study** 125 **Assumed unemployed** 65.

OTHER DEGREE SUBJECTS FOR CONSIDERATION
Behavioural Science; Community Studies; Criminology; Economics; Economic and Social History; Education; Government; Health Studies; Human Resource Management; Law; Politics; Psychology; Social Work; Sociology; Women's Studies.

SOCIAL STUDIES/SCIENCE

(including **Criminology, Criminal Justice and Human Rights;** see also under specific subject tables in the Social Sciences field **(eg Anthropology, Politics, Psychology, Social and Public Policy and Administration** and **Sociology), Community Studies** and **Health Sciences/Studies)**

NB The points totals shown to the left of the institutions are for ease of reference only. It must not be assumed that tariff points are always used by institutions or that they can be substituted for an offer in grades. The level of an offer is not necessarily indicative of the quality of a course.

COURSE OFFERS INFORMATION
Subject requirements/preferences GCSE Usually English and mathematics; a science may be required. **Durham** Science grade A or B. **AL** No subjects specified.

Your target offers

360 pts **and above**
 Cambridge – AAA (Soc Pol Sci)
340 pts **Birmingham** – AAB 340 pts (Hist Soc Sci)
 Durham – AAB (Comb Soc Sci)
 Lancaster – AAB (Law Crim)
320 pts **Aberystwyth** – 320 pts (Crim courses)
 Cardiff – ABB–BBB 320 pts (Crim joint courses)
 Kent – 320 pts (Law Crim)
 Manchester – ABB–BBC (Soc Sci Phil; Soc Sci Sci Psy; Soc Sci Class Civ Art Hist; Soc Sci Relig St Compar Relig; Crim Soc Pol; Soc Sci Jew St; Soc Sci Blt Nat Env; Crim; Crim Soc Pol)
300 pts **Aston** – BBB 300 pts (Soty Gov)
 Bath – BBB (Soc Sci)
 Belfast (Queen's) – BBB–BBCb (Gndr St)
 Brighton – 300 pts (Crim App Psy)
 Cardiff – 300–260 pts (Crim; Soc Sci)
 Dundee – 300 pts 2nd yr entry (Arts Soc Sci)
 East Anglia – BBB (Psysoc Sci)
 East Anglia – BBB–BBC (Soty Cult Media)
 Edinburgh – BBB (MA Soc Sci)
 Essex – 300–280 pts (Sociol Crim; Law Hum Rts; Phil Hum Rts; Sociol Hum Rts; Soc Sci Theor Methl)
 Lancaster – BBB–BBC (Crim; Crim Sociol; Cnsltncy Indep Rsch)
 Leeds – BBB 300 pts (Crim Just Crim; Soc Sci)
 Nottingham – ABC–BBB (Soc Cult St)
 Southampton – BBB–BBC 300 pts (App Soc Sci (Crim))

Staffordshire – 300 pts (Criminology)
- York – BBB–BBC (App Soc Sci (Child Yng Ppl) (Hlth) (Crm))
280 pts Brighton – 280–240 pts (Crim Soc Pol; Crim Sociol)
Glasgow – BBC–BCC (Scot St)
Glasgow (Crichton) – BBC (Hlth Soc St)
Loughborough – 280 pts (Crim Soc Pol)
Ulster – 280 pts (Crim Crim Just)
260 pts Brighton – 260 pts (App Soc Sci)
Central Lancashire – 260 pts (Plc Crim Invstg)
Coventry – 260 pts (Crim Law; Crim Psy; Crim Sociol St)
Essex – 260 pts (Crim Am St)
Glasgow Caledonian – BBD (Criminology)
Keele – 260–320 pts (Criminology)
Kent – 260 pts (Crim Soc Pol; Crim Sociol)
Liverpool – BCC–ABB (Comb Hons Soc Sci)
Northumbria – 260 pts (Crim; Crim Sociol)
Richmond (Am Int Univ) – 260 pts (Soc Sci)
Sheffield Hallam – 260 pts (Crim; Crim Psy; Crim Sociol; Crim Soc Pol)
Stirling – BCC (Criminology)
Strathclyde – BCC (Arts Soc Sci)
Swansea – BCC–CCC 260–240 pts (Crm Law Pol; Crim Psy)
240 pts Aberdeen – CCC 1st yr entry (Soc Rsch; Gndr St)
Bangor – 240 pts (Crim Crim Just)
. Bristol – CCC (Df St)
Bristol UWE – 240–300 pts (Crim joint courses)
Chester – 240–260 pts (Yth Wk)
Glamorgan – 240–280 pts (Plc Sci)
Kent – 240 pts (Env Soc Sci)
Lincoln – 240 pts (Chld Yth St)
Liverpool John Moores – 240 pts (Crim Scrty St; Crim Urb Cult)
Nottingham Trent – 240 pts (Crim; Hum Serv; Yth St)
Portsmouth – 240–300 pts (Crim Crim Just; Crim Foren St)
Salford – 240 pts (Crim Pol; Crim Sociol; Crim Cult St)
Sheffield Hallam – 240 pts (App Soc St)
Westminster – CCC/BC (Soc Sci; Crim Just)
230 pts Sheffield Hallam – 230 pts (Soty Cits)
220 pts Anglia Ruskin – 220–260 pts (Crim; Crim Sociol)
Central Lancashire – 220 pts (Crim Crim Just)
Dundee – 220 pts 1st yr entry (Arts Soc Sci)
Edge Hill – 220 pts (Crim courses)
Glamorgan – 220–260 pts (Crim Crim Just)
Glasgow Caledonian – CCD (Soc Sci)
Hull – 220–300 pts (Crim courses)
Kingston – 220–280 pts (Crim courses; Hum Rts)
Lincoln – 220–200 pts (Crim courses)
Liverpool Hope – 220 pts (Criminology)
Sheffield Hallam – 220–200 pts (Soc Cult St Spo)
200 pts Central Lancashire – 200 pts (Df St Psy)
Coventry – 200pts (Soc Welf Commun St)
Cumbria – 200 pts (Soc Sci; Chld Yng Per Fam St; Soc Sci Educ St; Soc Sci Crim; Soc Sci IT; Soc Sci Bus Mgt St)
Derby – CDD 200 pts (Crim Comb St)
East Lancashire (IHE) – 200–220 pts (Soc Sci)
Huddersfield – 200–240 pts (Criminology)
Kent – 200 pts (Soc Sci)

For information on how to read the Subject Tables, see **Chapter 7**.

Lincoln – 200 pts (Soc Sci)
London Met – 200 pts (Crim Law)
Manchester Met – 200 pts (Crim; Crm St)
Napier – 200 pts (Soc Sci)
Plymouth – CDD (Crim Just St Soc Rsch)

190 pts London Met – 190 pts (Crim Law; Crim Psy)

180 pts Bradford – 180–220 pts (App Crim Just St)
Chichester – 180–220 pts (Child Yth Soty)
De Montfort – 180–220 pts (App Crim; App Crim Foren; App Crim Psy)
Derby – 180–200 pts (App Soc Cult St)
Havering (Coll) – 180 pts (Soc St)
East London – 180 pts (Crim courses)
Liverpool John Moores – 180 pts (App Soc St)
Manchester Met – 180 pts (Crim Contemp Cult; Crim Sociol)
Northampton – 180 pts (Criminology)

160 pts Abertay Dundee – CC (Crimin St)
Canterbury Christ Church – CC (App Crim)
Central Lancashire – 160–180 pts (Df St; Rce Ethnic St courses; Crim Phil; Crim Soc Pol; Crim Sociol)
Doncaster (Univ Centre) – CC 160 pts (Law Crim; App Soc Sci)
East London – 160 pts (Psysoc St)
Glamorgan – 160–200 pts (Soc Sci)
Greenwich – 160 pts (Yth Commun St)
Lampeter – open admissions policy (Vol Sctr St)
London South Bank – CC 160 pts (Crim; Crim Comb courses; Citzn St courses)
Manchester Met – CC 160 pts (App Soc St; Yth Commun Wk St)
Middlesex – 160–200 pts (Soc Sci; Crim)
Newport – 160 pts (Cnslg St Soty; Soc Welf; Crim Commun Just; Yth Commun St)
Peterborough Reg (Coll) – 160 pts (Comb St)
Robert Gordon – CC (App Soc Sci)
Roehampton – 160–120 pts (Hum Rts; Crim)
Southend Campus Essex – 160–180 pts (BSc Soc St)
Sunderland – 160 pts (Criminology)
Teesside – 160–200 pts (Crim; Crim Sociol; Crm Scn Sci; Invstg St)
Thames Valley – 160–180 pts (Crim Sociol; Crim Psy)
Winchester – 160 pts (Soc Cr St)
Wolverhampton – 160–220 pts (Crim Just; Soc Cr Df St; Interp (Br Sign Lang))

140 pts Bell (Coll) – CD (Crim Just)
Paisley – CD (Soc Sci)

120 pts Bell (Coll) – 120 pts (Soc Sci)
Buckinghamshire Chilterns (UC) – 120 pts (Ctzn; Plc St; Crim Psy)
Marjon (Coll) – 120–180 pts (Yth Commun Wk)
Roehampton – 120–160 pts (Child Soty)
South Devon (Coll) – 120–180 pts (Soc Sci)
Suffolk (Univ Campus) – 120–180 pts (Yth St; Crim)
Teesside – 120 pts (Yth St)
Trinity Carmarthen (Coll) – 120 pts (Yth Commun Wk)

100 pts UHI Millennium Inst (IC) – 100 pts (Soc Sci)

80 pts Bradford (Coll) – 80 pts (Soc Welf Law)
Cornwall (Coll) – 80–120 pts (Comb Soc Sci)
London (Gold) – EE contact admissions tutor (App Soc Sci Commun Dev Yth Wk; Sociol Cult St)
North East Wales (IHE) – 80–120 pts (Soc Sci; Sbstnc Use St; Crim Just)
Wigan and Leigh (Coll) – EE (Crim Crim Just)

Leeds Met – contact University
Open University – contact University

Alternative offers
IB offers Aberystwyth 32 pts; Brighton 28 pts; Cambridge 38–42 pts; Keele 32 pts; Kent (Soc Sci) 27 pts, (Crim) 30–33 pts; Lancaster 32–35 pts; Loughborough 32 pts; Manchester Met 24–28 pts; York 30–32 pts.
Scottish offers See **Chapter 7**.

OTHER HIGHER EDUCATION COURSES IN THE SUBJECT FIELD

Foundation degrees (contact institutions for details) (see also under **Social and Public Policy and Administration**) Barnfield (Coll); Bath; Bedford (Coll); Bedfordshire; Blackpool and Fylde (Coll); Bicton (Coll); Boston (Coll); Bournemouth; Bradford; Brighton; Bristol City (Coll); Canterbury Christ Church; Carshalton (Coll); Central Lancashire; Coleg Sîr Gar (Coll); Cumbria; Derby; Dunstable (Coll); Grantham (Coll); Grimsby (IFHE); Hartlepool (CFE); Hertford Reg (Coll); Huddersfield; Hull (Coll); Huntingdonshire Reg (Coll); Leeds Park Lane (Coll); Leicester; Leicester (Coll); Liverpool Hope; London Met; Merthyr Tydfll (Coll); Newcastle (Coll); Newman (CHE); Newport; Northbrook (Coll); Nottingham Castle (Coll); Nottingham Trent; Oaklands (Coll); Oxford Brookes; Open University; Oxford and Cherwell Valley (Coll); Peterborough Reg (Coll); Plymouth; Portsmouth; Ruskin (Coll); Staffordshire Reg Fed; Stratford-upon-Avon (Coll); Sunderland City (Coll); Sussex Downs (Coll); Teesside; Truro (Coll); West Anglia (Coll); Worcester; Worcestershire New (Coll); Winchester; York St John; Yorkshire Coast (Coll)

Higher National Diploma courses Anglia Ruskin; Bedfordshire; Blackpool and Fylde (Coll); Bradford (Coll); Burton (Coll); Carmarthenshire (Coll); Central Lancashire; Cornwall (Coll); Craven (Coll); Derby; Dewsbury (Coll); Dudley (Coll); East Lancashire (IHE); Gloucestershire (CAT); Greenwich; Grimsby (IFHE); Herefordshire (CT); Kent; Llandrillo Cymru (Coll); Newcastle (Coll); Oldham (Coll); South Birmingham (Coll); Southend Campus Essex; Swansea (IHE); Swansea (Coll); Teesside; UHI Millennium Inst (IC); Walsall (Coll); Wigan and Leigh (Coll); Winchester; Worcester (CT); Worcestershire New (Coll).

CHOOSING YOUR COURSE (SEE ALSO CH.1)

Subject information Most Social Studies/Science courses take a broad view of aspects of society, for example, economics, politics, history, social psychology and urban studies. Applied Social Studies usually focuses on practical and theoretical preparation for a career in social work. These courses are particularly popular with mature students and some universities and colleges offer shortened degree courses for those with relevant work experience. **Useful websites** www.police.uk; www.csv.org.uk; www.intute.ac.uk.

Course variations Criminology and Applied Psychology (Brighton); Police and Criminal Investigation (Central Lancashire); Social Welfare and Community Studies (Coventry); Police Sciences (Glamorgan); Environmental Social Science (Kent); Human Rights (Kingston); Crime, Security and the State (Liverpool John Moores); Criminal Justice Studies and Social Research (Plymouth); Applied Social Studies (Sheffield Hallam); Crime, Law and Policy (Swansea). *NOW CHECK PROSPECTUSES AND WEBSITES FOR ANY RECENT CHANGES.*

Universities and colleges teaching quality See www.tqi.ac.uk; www.qaa.ac.uk.

Top universities and colleges (Research) Bradford.

Sandwich degree courses Bath; Gloucestershire.

ADMISSIONS INFORMATION

Number of applicants per place (approx) Abertay Dundee 1; Aston 5; Bangor 2; Bath 6; Bath Spa 4; Bradford 15; Cambridge 7; Cornwall (Coll) 2; Coventry 7; Cumbria 4; De Montfort 1; Durham 3; East London 10; East Anglia (Psysoc Sci) 4; Edge Hill 5; Glasgow Caledonian 9; Hull 5; Kingston 5; Liverpool 13; London (King's) 5, (LSE) (all progs) 14; London South Bank 3; Manchester Met 10; Middlesex 26; Northampton 5; Nottingham 16; Nottingham Trent 2; Paisley 5; Portsmouth 3; Roehampton 6; Salford 12; Sheffield Hallam 7; Southampton 2; Staffordshire 2; Strathclyde 9; Sunderland 11; Swansea 8; Westminster 14; Winchester 3.

Advice to applicants and planning the UCAS personal statement The Social Studies/Science subject area covers several topics (see **Subject information**). Focus on these (or some of these) and state your main areas of interest, outlining your work experience, personal goals and motivation to follow the course. See under separate subject headings, for example, **Social and Public Policy and Administration**, **Sociology**, **Geography**, **Economics**, **Politics** for further information. **Bristol** Evidence of a bright, lively mind. **East Anglia** (Psysoc Sci) This course is designed for those keen to study psychology as a research-based discipline but not wishing to become psychologists. **London (LSE)** Most students take a quarter of their studies outside their main subject area. We have a preference for 'traditional' academic subjects. **Nottingham Trent** GCSE grade C maths may be waived for mature applicants or those taking Access courses who can demonstrate equivalent competence in these areas. **Sheffield Hallam** Interest in current affairs. Details of work experience, paid or unpaid.

Misconceptions about this course Cornwall (Coll) That students transfer to Plymouth at the end of year 1: this is a three-year course in Cornwall.

Selection interviews Yes Anglia Ruskin, Birmingham, Brunel, Cambridge, Coventry, Cumbria, Doncaster (Univ Centre), Durham, East London, Edge Hill, Essex, Glasgow Caledonian, Hull, Kingston, Lampeter, London South Bank, Newcastle, Newport, Oxford, Roehampton, Salford, Sunderland, Westminster; **Some** Bath (mature students), Bristol, Cornwall (Coll), Robert Gordon, Staffordshire, Winchester, York.

Interview advice and questions Past questions have included: Define democracy. What is the role of the Church in nationalistic aspirations? Does today's government listen to its people? Questions on current affairs. How would you change the running of your school? What are the faults of the Labour Party/Conservative Party? Do you agree with the National Lottery? Is money from the National Lottery well spent? Give examples of how the social services have failed. What is your awareness of the social origins of problems? **Cambridge (Robinson)** 'The main interview is to assess potential. Achievement is measured far more by school reports and the details on the Preliminary Application Form. The interview consists of three main elements. Firstly, the applicant is asked to think about issues which raise questions relating to the four topics in Part I of the course. He or she has to think about and discuss a current political issue, an anthropological question about ritual or how psychology experiments are carried out, for example. The applicant's views are not assessed, merely their ability to discuss their views in a serious and academic way. Next, the applicant is asked to discuss an unfamiliar and difficult text – handed out prior to interview – in order that interpretation and comprehension skills may be assessed. Lastly, we ask the applicant to bring with them an appropriate school essay.' See also **Chapter 6**.

Reasons for rejection (non-academic) Stated preference for other institutions. Incompetence in answering questions.

AFTER-RESULTS ADVICE

Universities with vacancies in Clearing (2006) Anglia Ruskin; Aston; Bangor; Bath; Bolton; Bradford; Bristol UWE; Buckinghamshire Chilterns (UC); Canterbury Christ Church; Chester; Cumbria; Derby; East Anglia; East London; Glamorgan; Gloucestershire; Greenwich; Huddersfield; Hull; Keele; Kent; Kingston; London (Gold); Manchester Met; Middlesex; Oxford Brookes; Northampton; Northumbria; Nottingham Trent; Plymouth; Roehampton; Southampton; Staffordshire; Sunderland; Westminster; Worcester.

Offers to applicants repeating A-levels Higher Aston, Essex, Glasgow, Salford (possibly), Swansea; **Same** Anglia Ruskin, Bangor, Bath Spa, Bradford, Chester, Cornwall (Coll), Coventry, Cumbria, Durham, East Anglia, Gloucestershire, Leeds, Liverpool, London Met, London South Bank, Manchester Met, Newport, Roehampton, Sheffield Hallam, Staffordshire, Winchester.

GRADUATE DESTINATIONS AND EMPLOYMENT (2005 HESA)
See **Social and Public Policy and Administration**, **Social Work** and **Sociology**.

OTHER DEGREE SUBJECTS FOR CONSIDERATION
Business Studies; Community Studies; Economics; Education; Geography; Government; Health Studies; Law; Politics; Psychology; Public Administration; Social Policy; Social Work; Sociology; Urban Studies.

SOCIAL WORK

(see also **Community Studies and Social and Public Policy and Administration**)

NB The points totals shown to the left of the institutions are for ease of reference only. It must not be assumed that tariff points are always used by institutions or that they can be substituted for an offer in grades. The level of an offer is not necessarily indicative of the quality of a course.

COURSE OFFERS INFORMATION

Subject requirements/preferences GCSE English and mathematics usually required. **AL** No subjects specified.

Your target offers

320 pts **Belfast (Queen's)** – ABB (Soc Wk)
East Anglia – ABB–BBC (Soc Wk)
300 pts **Edinburgh** – BBB (Soc Wk)
Glasgow – BBB (Soc Wk)
Manchester – BBB (Soc Wk)
Sussex – BBB+AS **or** 340 pts (3AL) (Soc Wk)
Ulster – BBB 300 pts (Soc Wk)
280 pts **Bath** – BBC (Soc Wk App Soc St)
Birmingham – entry reqs vary according to age and education (Soc Wk)
Lancaster – BBC (Soc Wk)
Leeds – BBC (Soc Wk)
London (Gold) – BBC (Soc Wk)
Sheffield – BBC (Soc Wk)
Strathclyde – BBC (Soc Wk)
York – BBC (Soc Wk)
260 pts **Bradford** – 260 pts (Soc Wk)
Hull – 260 pts (Soc Wk)
Keele – BCC–BBC 260–280 pts (Soc Wk)
London (RH) – 260 pts (Soc Wk)
Reading – 260 pts (3AL) 280 pts (4AL) (Soc Wk)
Stirling – BCC (min age 18) (Soc Wk)
240 pts **Brunel** – 240 pts (Soc Wk)
Chester (Warrington) – 240 pts (Soc Wk)
Coventry – 240–220 pts (Soc Wk)
Gloucestershire – 240 pts (Soc Wk)
Kingston – 240 pts (Soc Wk)
Northumbria – 240 pts (Soc Wk)
Nottingham Trent – 240 pts (Soc Wk)

Southampton – CCC 240 pts (Soc Wk St)
Swansea – 240 pts (Soc Wk)
220 pts **Bangor** – 220–260 pts (Soc Wk)
Huddersfield – 220 pts (min age 19 on 1 July) (Soc Wk)
Winchester – 220 pts (Soc Cr St Comb courses)
200 pts **Anglia Ruskin** – 200 pts (Soc Wk)
Coventry – 200 pts (Soc Welf Commun St)
Cumbria – 200 pts (Soc Wk)
Kent – 200 pts (Soc Wk)
Lincoln – 200 pts (Soc Wk)
Liverpool Hope – 200 pts (Soc Wk)
Staffordshire – BB 200 pts (Soc Wk)
180 pts **Bournemouth** – 180 pts (Soc Wk)
Chichester – 180–220 pts (Soc Wk)
Edge Hill – 180–220 pts (Soc Wk St)
Liverpool John Moores – 180 pts (Soc Wk)
Liverpool (CmC) – 180 pts (Soc Wk)
160 pts **Bedfordshire** – 160–240 pts (Soc Wk)
Bristol UWE – 160–180 pts (Soc Wk)
Canterbury Christ Church – 160 pts (Soc Wk)
Cardiff (UWIC) – 160 pts (Soc Wk)
Central Lancashire – 160 pts (Soc Wk)
Derby – 160–120 pts (App Soc Wk)
Dundee – CC (Soc Wk)
East London – 160 pts (Soc Wk)
Essex (Southend Campus) – 160 pts (Soc Wk)
Glasgow Caledonian – CC (Soc Wk)
Greenwich – 160 pts (Soc Wk)
Hertfordshire – 160 pts (Soc Wk)
London Met – 160 pts (min age 21) (Soc Wk)
London South Bank – CC-EE (Soc Wk)
Middlesex – 160–200 pts check with Univ (Soc Wk)
Newport – 160 pts (Soc Wk)
Northampton – 160–180 pts (Soc Welf; Soc Wk)
Oxford Brookes – CC (Soc Wk)
Plymouth – 160 pts (Soc Wk)
Portsmouth – 160 pts (Soc Wk)
Robert Gordon – CC (Soc Wk)
Sheffield Hallam – 160 pts (Soc Wk St)
Suffolk (Univ Campus) – 160–120 pts (Soc Wk)
Sunderland – 160 pts (Soc Wk)
UCE Birmingham – CC 160 pts (Soc Wk)
Winchester – 160 pts (Soc Cr St)
Wolverhampton – 160–220 pts (Soc Wk; Soc Cr)
140 pts **Manchester Met** – 140–180 pts (Soc Wk)
Paisley – CD (Soc Wk)
Southampton Solent – 140 pts (Soc Wk St)
120 pts **Bradford (Coll)** – 120 pts (Soc Wk)
Brighton – 120 pts contact admissions tutor (Soc Wk)
Cardiff (UWIC) – 120 pts (Hlth Soc Cr)
Manchester Met – 120 pts (Soc Wk)
Salford – 120–180 pts (Soc Wk St)
Teesside – 120–240 pts (Soc Wk; Soc Wk Nurs LD/MH)
Worcester – 120 pts (Soc Welf courses)
80 pts **De Montfort** – 80 pts (Soc Wk)

Durham New (Coll) – check with admissions tutor (Soc Wk)
Havering (Coll) – 80 pts check with admissions tutor (Soc Wk)
North East Wales (IHE) – 80–120 pts (Soc Wk)
Norwich City (Coll) – EE (Soc Wk)
Stockport (CFHE) – 80 pts check with admissions tutor (Soc Wk)
Wiltshire (Coll) – 80 pts check with admissions tutor (Soc Wk)

Leeds Met – contact University

Alternative offers
IB offers Brunel 28 pts; Chichester 28 pts; City 26 pts; Keele 26–28 pts; Kent 27 pts; Lancaster 32 pts; Manchester 28 pts; Manchester Met 24 pts; Salford 24 pts.
Scottish offers See **Chapter 7**.

OTHER HIGHER EDUCATION COURSES IN THE SUBJECT FIELD
Foundation degrees (contact institution for details) Chichester. See also **Social and Public Policy and Administration**.

Higher National Diploma courses See **Social Studies/Science**.

CHOOSING YOUR COURSE (SEE ALSO CH.1)
Subject information Social Work courses (which lead to careers in social work) have similarities to those in Applied Social Studies, Social Policy and Administration and Community Studies and Health Studies. If you are offered a place on a Social Work course which leads to registration as a social worker, you must undergo the Criminal Records Bureau (CRB) disclosure check. You will also have to provide health information and certification. Check for full details of training and careers in social work with the General Social Care Council (see **Appendix 2**). **Useful websites** www.gscc.org.uk; www.swap.ac.uk; www.ace.org.uk; www.samaritans.org; www.ccwales.org.uk; www.sssc.uk.com; www.niscc.info; www.socialworkcareers.co.uk.

Course variations Social Work and Applied Social Studies (Bath); Social Welfare and Community Studies (Coventry); Social Work and Nursing (Learning Disabilities) (Mental Health) (Teesside). *NOW CHECK PROSPECTUSES AND WEBSITES FOR ANY RECENT CHANGES.*

Universities and colleges teaching quality See www.tqi.ac.uk; www.qaa.ac.uk.

Top universities and colleges (Research) Bristol*; East Anglia; Huddersfield; Kent*; Lancaster; Stirling; Swansea; Warwick; York.

Sandwich degree courses Bath.

ADMISSIONS INFORMATION
Number of applicants per place (approx) Bangor 2; Bath 11; Bradford 10; Coventry 22; Dundee 6; London Met 27; Northampton 7; Nottingham Trent 6; Sheffield Hallam 4; Staffordshire 3.

Advice to applicants and planning the UCAS personal statement The statement should show motivation for social work, relevant work experience, awareness of the demands of social work and give relevant personal information, for example disabilities. Previous relevant experience in social work preferred in most cases. **Lincoln** Applicants must have had some voluntary or work experience working with people. **Salford** Applicants must be over 19 years on application. **Staffordshire** Awareness of the origins of personal and family difficulties, commitment to anti-discriminatory practice. See also **Social and Public Policy and Administration**. See also **Appendix 2**.

Selection interviews **Yes** Most courses; Bradford, Chichester, Coventry, Nottingham Trent, Salford, Sheffield Hallam, Staffordshire; **Some** Dundee.

Interview advice and questions What qualities are needed to be a social worker? What use do you think you will be to society as a social worker? Why should money be spent on prison offenders? Your younger brother is playing truant and mixing with bad company. Your parents don't know. What would you do? See also **Social and Public Policy and Administration** and **Chapter 6**.

Reasons for rejection (non-academic) Criminal convictions.

AFTER-RESULTS ADVICE

Universities with vacancies in Clearing (2006) Bangor; Bath; Bedfordshire; Bradford; Brighton; Brunel; Central Lancashire; Chester; Chichester; De Montfort; Dundee; East Anglia; East London; Edge Hill; Gloucestershire; Greenwich; Hertfordshire; Hull; Liverpool Hope; Liverpool John Moores; London (RH); London South Bank; Manchester Met; Nottingham Trent; Plymouth; Sunderland; UCE Birmingham; Wolverhampton; Worcester.

Offers to applicants repeating A-levels Same Lincoln, Salford, Staffordshire.

GRADUATE DESTINATIONS AND EMPLOYMENT (2005 HESA)

Graduates surveyed 1750 Employed 1130 In further study 115 Assumed unemployed 95.

OTHER DEGREE SUBJECTS FOR CONSIDERATION

Community Studies; Conductive Education; Criminology; Economics; Education; Health Studies; Law; Psychology; Public Sector Management and Administration; Social Policy; Sociology; Youth Studies.

SOCIOLOGY

(see also Social and Public Policy and Administration and Social Studies/Science)

NB The points totals shown to the left of the institutions are for ease of reference only. It must not be assumed that tariff points are always used by institutions or that they can be substituted for an offer in grades. The level of an offer is not necessarily indicative of the quality of a course.

COURSE OFFERS INFORMATION

Subject requirements/preferences GCSE English and mathematics usually required. Bath Majority of A*, A and B grades. Edinburgh Mathematics grade A or AS-level grade b. Leeds Mathematics. London (LSE) A*, A and B grades. AL No subjects specified.

Your target offers
360 pts and above
  Cambridge – AAA (Soc Pol Sci)
340 pts Cardiff – AAB–BCC 340–260 pts (Sociol joint courses; offers vary with 2nd subj)
320 pts Durham – ABB (Sociol Law; Pol Sociol)
  Exeter – ABB–BBC (Sociol; Sociol Fr/Ger/Ital/Russ/Span)
  Lancaster – ABB (Org St Sociol)
  Warwick – BBCc–BBBc (Sociol; Sociol Soc Pol; Sociol Gndr St; Sociol Cult St; Sociol Rsch Meth; Hist Sociol; Law Sociol; Fr Sociol)
300 pts Aston – BBB 300 pts (Sociology)
  Belfast (Queen's) – BBB–BBCb (Sociol courses)
  Birmingham – BBB–BBC (Sociology)
  Bristol – BBB (Sociol; Sociol Econ Hist; Sociol Phil; Pol Sociol; Soc Pol Sociol; Theol Sociol)
  Cardiff – BBB–BCC (Sociol single hons)
  Durham – BBB (Sociology)
  East Anglia – BBB–BBC (Pol Sociol Contemp Cult; Soty Cult Media)
  Edinburgh – BBB (Sociol; Sociol Pol; Sociol Soc Econ Hist; Sociol Anth; Sociol S As St)
  Essex – 300–280 pts (Sociol; Sociol Crim; Sociol Media St)
  Glasgow – BBB (Sociology)
  Lancaster – BBB (Sociol courses except under 280/320 pts)
  Leeds – BBB (Sociol Span; Sociol Theol Relig St)
  Liverpool – BBB 300 pts (Sociol; Sociol Soc Pol; Crim Sociol)
  London (LSE) – BBB (Sociol; Soc Pol Sociol)
  Manchester – BBB (Sociol; Sociol Crim; Dev St Sociol; Bus St Sociol; Econ Sociol)

Newcastle – BBB (Sociol; Pol Sociol)
Nottingham – ABC–BBB (Sociol; Sociol Soc Pol)
Sheffield – BBB (Sociology)
Surrey – BBB–BBC 300–280 pts (Sociol; Sociol Soc Rsch; Sociol Cult Media)
Sussex – BBB **or** 340 pts 3AL+AS (Sociol courses)
York – BBB (Sociol Soc Pol; Sociol; Sociol Educ)

280 pts   **Aston** – BBC–BBB 280–300 pts (Sociol; Sociol Econ; Bus Admin Sociol; Sociol Pblc Pol; Int Rel Sociol; Fr/Ger/Span Sociol)
Bath – BBC (Sociol; Sociol Soc Pol; Sociol HR Mgt)
Brighton – 280 pts (Sociol Soc Pol)
Durham – BBC (Anth Sociol)
Lancaster – BBC (Relig St Sociol)
Leeds – BBC (Sociol; Soc Pol Sociol)
London (Gold) – BBC (Sociol Cult St)
Loughborough – 280 pts (Sociol; Econ Sociol)
Salford – 280 pts (Journal Sociol)
Southampton – BBC–ABB (Sociol courses)

260 pts   **Brighton** – 260 pts (Sociol Spo Leis; Sociol PE)
Brunel – 260 pts (Sociol; Psy Sociol; Soc Anth Sociol; Sociol Media St)
Chester – 260 pts (Sociology)
Coventry – 260 pts (Sociol; Sociol Psy; Sociol Crim)
Keele – 260–320 pts (Sociol courses)
Leicester – 260–320 pts (Sociol; Psy Sociol; Comb St)
London (Gold) – BCC (Sociol; Sociol Pol)
Northumbria – 260 pts (Sociol courses)
Oxford Brookes – BCC **or** BCcc (Sociology)
Richmond (Am Int Univ) – 260 pts (Soc Sci (Sociol))
Stirling – BCC (Sociol courses)
Strathclyde – BCC/BB (Sociology)

240 pts   **Aberdeen** – CCC (Sociol courses)
Bolton – 240 pts (Sociol courses)
Cardiff (UWIC) – 240 pts (Sociol Pop Cult)
City – CCC–BCC (Sociol; Sociol Econ; Sociol Media St; Sociol Psy)
Gloucestershire – 240 pts (Sociol courses)
Kent – 240–260 pts (Sociol; Sociol Yr Abrd; Sociol Ital)
Nottingham Trent – 240–280 pts (Sociol courses)
Portsmouth – 240–300 pts (Sociol; Sociol Crim; Sociol Media St; Sociol Psy)
Salford – 240 pts (Sociol Crim)
Sheffield Hallam – 240 pts (Sociology)
Ulster – 240–220 pts (Sociol; Sociol Ir Hist; Sociol Soc Pol)
Westminster – CCC/BC (Sociology)

220 pts   **Bangor** – 220–260 pts (Sociology)
Hull – 220–280 pts (Sociol; Sociol Anth Gndr St; Sociol Soc Anth Span)
Kingston – 220–280 pts (Sociol courses)
Liverpool Hope – 220 pts (Sociology)
Manchester Met – 220–280 pts (Sociol joint courses)
Queen Margaret (UC) – CCD 220 pts (Sociol Cult)
Salford – 220 pts (Sociol; Sociol Cult St)
UCE Birmingham – 220 pts (Sociol; Sociol Crim; Sociol Psy; Sociol Cult St)

200 pts   **Anglia Ruskin** – 200 pts (Sociology)
Bath Spa – 200–240 pts (Sociol; Sociol Comb courses)
Bristol UWE – 200–260 pts (Sociology)
De Montfort – 200–260 pts (Sociology)
Glamorgan – 200 pts (Sociology)
Huddersfield – 200 pts (Sociol; Sociol Crim)

For information on how to read the Subject Tables, see **Chapter 7**.

Napier – 200 pts (Psy Sociol)
Plymouth – 200 pts (Sociol courses)
Staffordshire – 200 pts (Sociology)
180 pts **Bangor** – 180–220 pts (Sociol Soc Pol (Welsh medium only))
Bradford – 180–220 pts (Sociol Psy; Sociol Engl (EFL); Sociol Fr/Span; Interd Hum St)
Derby – 180 pts (Sociol Comb Hons)
Edge Hill – 180–220 pts (Sociol; Sociol Soc Wk St)
Greenwich – 180 pts min (Sociology)
Manchester Met – 180 pts (Sociol; Cult St Sociol)
Northumbria – 180 pts (Sociol Soc Pol; Sociol)
160 pts **Abertay Dundee** – CC (Sociology)
Canterbury Christ Church – 160 pts (Sociology)
Central Lancashire – 160 pts (Sociol courses)
East London – 160 pts (Sociol courses)
Glasgow Caledonian – CC–DD 160 pts (Hum Biol Sociol Psy)
Liverpool John Moores – 160–240 pts (Sociol courses)
London Met – 160 pts **or** Access course (Sociol; App Sociol)
London South Bank – CC (Sociology)
Middlesex – 160–200 pts (Sociology)
Northampton – 160–200 pts (Sociology)
Norwich City (Coll) – 160 pts (Sociol courses)
St Mary's (Coll) – 160–200 pts (Sociol courses)
Sunderland – 160 pts (Sociology)
Teesside – 160 pts (Sociology)
Thames Valley – 160 pts (Sociol Hlth St; Sociol Hum Sci; Sociol NMedia Journal; Sociol Lang)
Wolverhampton – 160–220 pts (Sociology)
Worcester – 160 pts (Sociology)
140 pts **Marjon (Coll)** – 140–200 pts (Sociol courses)
Paisley – CD (Soc Sci (Sociol))
120 pts **Bell (Coll)** – 120 pts (Soc Sci)
Bradford (Coll) – 120 pts (Sociol Comb St)
Buckinghamshire Chilterns (UC) – 120–240 pts 2AL (Sociology)
Grimsby (IFHE) – 120 pts (Sociol Psy)
North East Wales (IHE) – 120–80 pts (Sociol courses)
Roehampton – 120 pts (Sociol courses)
Suffolk (Univ Campus) – 120–140 pts (Sociol courses)
100 pts **Swansea (IHE)** – 100 pts (Engl St Sociol)
West Suffolk (Coll) – 100 pts (Sociol courses)

Leeds Met – contact University

Alternative offers
IB offers Birmingham 32 pts; Brighton 28 pts; Bristol UWE 28 pts; Brunel 28 pts; City 26 pts; Essex 30–32 pts; Keele 30 pts; Kent 27 pts; Lancaster 32–33 pts; Leicester 28–30 pts; Liverpool 30 pts; London (Gold) 28 pts, (LSE) 36 pts; Manchester 32 pts; Manchester Met 24–28 pts; Newcastle 32 pts; Nottingham 30–32 pts; Salford 27 pts; Surrey 30–32 pts; Warwick 32–33 pts; York 34 pts.
Scottish offers See **Chapter 7**.

OTHER HIGHER EDUCATION COURSES IN THE SUBJECT FIELD
Foundation degree courses (contact the institutions for details) Bradford; Cornwall (Coll); East Lancashire (IHE); London Met; Winchester.

CHOOSING YOUR COURSE (SEE ALSO CH.1)
Subject information Sociology is not a training course for social workers, although some graduates take additional qualifications to qualify in social work. Elective subjects offered often include industrial

behaviour, crime and deviance, health and illness. **Useful websites** www.britsoc.co.uk; www.sociologyonline.co.uk; www.sociology.org.uk; www.sociology.org.

Course variations Sociology and Social Policy (Welsh medium) (Bangor); Sociology of Sport and Leisure (Brighton); Sociology and South Asian Studies (Edinburgh); Sociology and Anthropology with Gender Studies (Hull); Development Studies and Sociology (Manchester); Journalism and Sociology (Salford); Sociology with Social Research (Surrey); Sociology with Irish History (Ulster). *NOW CHECK PROSPECTUSES AND WEBSITES FOR RECENT CHANGES.*

Universities and colleges teaching quality See www.tqi.ac.uk; www.qaa.ac.uk.

Top universities and colleges (Research) Aberdeen; Belfast (Queen's); Bristol; Brunel; Cambridge; Cardiff; Edinburgh; Essex*; Exeter; Lancaster*; London (Gold)*, (LSE); Loughborough*; Manchester*; Surrey*; Warwick; York.

Sandwich degree courses Aston; Bath.

ADMISSIONS INFORMATION

Number of applicants per place (approx) Aston 8; Bangor 1; Bath 6; Birmingham 8; Bristol 8; Brunel 24; Cardiff 5; Cardiff (UWIC) 4; City 11; De Montfort 10; Durham 13; East Anglia 15; East London 8; Exeter 5; Gloucestershire 8; Greenwich 5; Hull 11; Kent 10; Kingston 9; Lancaster 12; Leeds 14; Leicester 6; Liverpool 9; Liverpool John Moores 10; London (Gold) 5, (LSE) 6; London Met 3; Loughborough 10; Marjon (Coll) 13; Northampton 3; Northumbria 18; Nottingham 7; Plymouth 9; Portsmouth 12; Roehampton 4; Sheffield Hallam 7; Southampton 8; Staffordshire 10; Sunderland 5; Surrey 6; Swansea 8; UCE Birmingham 12; Warwick 20; Worcester 5; York 5.

Advice to applicants and planning the UCAS personal statement Show your ability to communicate and work as part of a group and your curiosity about issues such as social conflict and social change between social groups. **Birmingham** Discuss your interests in sociology on the personal statement. **Cardiff (UWIC)** (Non-EU students) Good command of written and spoken English required. **Liverpool John Moores** We look for intellectual curiosity about sociology and social problems. **London Met** Realistic awareness of the needs of living and studying in university conditions. **Northumbria** (Non-EU students) Fluency in English is required. See **Social Studies/Science**.

Misconceptions about this course Some applicants believe that all sociologists want to become social workers. **Birmingham** Students with an interest in crime and deviance may be disappointed that we do not offer modules in this area. **London Met** That it is the stamping ground of student activists and has no relevance to the real world.

Selection interviews Yes Aston, Brunel, Cambridge, City, Derby, Durham, East London, Exeter, Hull, Lancaster, Leeds, Leicester, Liverpool, Liverpool Hope, London (Gold), Loughborough, Newcastle, Nottingham, Portsmouth, St Mary's (Coll), Surrey, Swansea, UCE Birmingham, Warwick; **Some** Bath (mature applicants), Bath Spa, Birmingham (mature applicants), Bristol, Cardiff, Kent, Liverpool John Moores, London Met, Nottingham Trent, Salford, Sheffield Hallam, Southampton, Staffordshire.

Interview advice and questions Past questions have included: Why do you want to study Sociology? What books have you read on the subject? How do you see the role of women changing in the next 20 years? **Leeds** Copy of written work requested. **London Met** Questions will focus on existing level of interest in the subject and the applicant's expectations about studying. Where appropriate we offer applicants separate tests in comprehension and mathematical skills that will be used to help us reach a decision. See also **Chapter 6**.

Reasons for rejection (non-academic) Evidence of difficulty with written work. Non-attendance at open days (find out from your universities if your attendance will affect their offers). In the middle of an interview for Sociology a student asked us if we could interview him for Sports Studies instead! **Durham** No evidence of awareness of what the course involves. **London Met** References which indicated that the individual would not be able to work effectively within a diverse student group; concern that the applicant had not put any serious thought into the choice of subject for study. See also **Social and Public Policy and Administration**.

AFTER-RESULTS ADVICE

Universities with vacancies in Clearing (2006) Aberdeen; Aston; Bangor; Bath; Bath Spa; Bristol UWE; Brunel; Canterbury Christ Church; Central Lancashire; Chester; Cumbria; De Montfort; Derby; East Anglia; East London; Essex; Glamorgan; Gloucestershire; Greenwich; Huddersfield; Hull; Keele; Kent; Kingston; Lancaster; Leicester; Liverpool Hope; Liverpool John Moores; London (Gold); London Met; London South Bank; Manchester Met; Middlesex; Northampton; Northumbria; Nottingham; Nottingham Trent; Plymouth; Portsmouth; Roehampton; Salford; Sheffield; Sheffield Hallam; Southampton; Staffordshire; Stirling; Sunderland; Teesside; Thames Valley; UCE Birmingham; Ulster; Wolverhampton; Worcester.

Offers to applicants repeating A-levels Higher Brunel, East London, Essex, Glasgow, Hull, Newcastle, Nottingham Trent, Swansea, Warwick, York; **Possibly higher** Leeds, Liverpool, Portsmouth; **Same** Aston, Bangor, Bath, Birmingham, Bristol, Cardiff, Coventry, Derby, Durham, Gloucestershire, Kingston, Lancaster, Liverpool John Moores, London Met, Loughborough, Northumbria, Roehampton, Salford, Sheffield Hallam, Southampton, Staffordshire, UCE Birmingham.

GRADUATE DESTINATIONS AND EMPLOYMENT (2005 HESA)

Graduates surveyed 4070 **Employed** 2170 **In further study** 565 **Assumed unemployed** 275.

OTHER DEGREE SUBJECTS FOR CONSIDERATION

Anthropology; Economics; Economic and Social History; Education; Geography; Government; Health Studies; History; Law; Politics; Psychology; Social Policy; Social Work.

SPANISH

(including **Hispanic Studies** and **Portuguese;** see also **Languages** and **Latin American Studies**)

NB The points totals shown to the left of the institutions are for ease of reference only. It must not be assumed that tariff points are always used by institutions or that they can be substituted for an offer in grades. The level of an offer is not necessarily indicative of the quality of a course.

COURSE OFFERS INFORMATION

Subject requirements/preferences GCSE Edinburgh, **St Andrews** English, mathematics or science and a foreign language. **Oxford**, **Cambridge** Grade A in most subjects usually preferred. **AL** Spanish required for most courses.

Your target offers

360 pts **and above**
    Cambridge – AAA (Modn Mediev Langs (Span))
    London (UCL) – AAA–AAB (Span Mgt St; Span Lat; Span Hist Art)
    Oxford – Offers vary eg AAA–AAB (Modn Lang (Port) (Span))
    Warwick – AABc–ABBc (Hist Cult (Span))
340 pts **Bristol** – AAB–BBC (Span; Span Port/Russ; Hisp St)
    Lancaster – AAB (Euro Mgt Span)
    St Andrews – AAB–BBB (Span courses)
320 pts **Aston** – ABB 320 pts (Int Bus Span)
    Bath – ABB–BBB (Span Ital/Russ; Fr Span)
    Bristol – ABB–BBB (Port courses)
    Cardiff – ABB–BBC (Span courses)
    Glasgow – ABB–BBB (Hisp St)
    Lancaster – ABB (Span St Econ; Span St Engl Lit; Span St Psy; Span St Mark)
    Manchester – ABB–BBB (Span Port Lat Am St; Span Chin)
    Newcastle – ABB–BBB (Span; Span Bus St; Span Pol; Span Port Lat Am St)
    Southampton – ABB 320 pts (Span courses; Port courses)
300 pts **Belfast (Queen's)** – BBB–BBCb (Span Port St)
    Birmingham – BBB–BBC (Port courses; Hisp St courses)

East Anglia – ABC (Transl Media Span)
Edinburgh – BBB (Span courses)
Exeter – BBB (Span Arbc; Span Maths)
Lancaster – BBB (Span courses except under **320 pts**)
Leeds – BBB–BBC (Port joint courses)
Leeds – BBB (Span; Hisp Lat Am St)
London (King's) – BBB+AS **or** BBbbb (Port Braz St courses)
London (LSE) – optional subj check with admissions tutor (Fr/Ger/Russ/Span)
London (RH) – ABC–BBB (Span courses)
London (UCL) – BBB+AS–BBC+AS (Hisp St; Modn Iber Lat Am Reg St)
Sheffield – BBB–BBC (Hisp St courses)
Stirling – BBB 2nd yr entry (Span courses)
Surrey – BBB–BCC 300–260 pts (Law Span Law)

280 pts **Aston** – 280–300 pts (Span courses)
East Anglia – BBC–BCC (Span Lang Int Dev)
Heriot-Watt – BBC (App Langs Transl (Fr Span) (Ger Span))
Kent – 280–260 pts (Span courses)
Leicester – BBC–BCC (Span Ger/Fr/Ital)
Liverpool – BBC–BBB 280–300 pts (Hisp St courses)
London (King's) – BBC+AS **or** BBbcc (Hisp St Modn Gk; Hisp St Engl; Hisp St Ling; Hisp St Port)
Loughborough – 280–300 pts (Econ Span)
Nottingham – BBC (Hisp St; Hisp St Russ; Hisp St Hist; Port Russ; Port Span)
Westminster – 280 pts (Span courses)

260 pts **Aberystwyth** – 260 pts (Span courses)
Bradford – 260 pts (Econ Span)
Essex – 260 pts (Span St Modn Langs)
Kent – 260 pts (Hisp St)
London (Gold) – BCC (MFL (Span) Ling – see www.goldsmiths.ac.uk/ug)
London (QM) – 260 pts (Hisp St courses)
Strathclyde – BCC/BB (Spanish)

240 pts **Aberdeen** – CCC (Hisp St courses; Span courses)
Bradford – 240 pts (Span courses except under **260 pts**)
Bristol UWE – 240–300 pts (Span courses)
Chester – 240 pts (Span courses)
Coventry – 240 pts (Span courses)
Salford – 240–300 pts (Modn Langs Span)
Stirling – CCC 1st yr entry (Span courses)
Swansea – 240–300 pts (Span courses)
Ulster – CCC–CCD 240–220 pts (Span courses)

220 pts **Bangor** – 220–260 pts (Span Fr/Ger/Ital; Acc Span; Mgt Span; Span Tour)
Dundee – CCD–BCC 220–300 pts (Span courses)
Hull – 220–280 pts (Span courses)
Nottingham Trent – 220 pts (Span courses)

200 pts **Hertfordshire** – 200–240 pts (Span courses)
Napier – 200 pts (Tour Mgt Span)
Northumbria – 200–280 pts (Span courses)
Plymouth – 200–280 pts (Span courses)
Portsmouth – 200–280 pts (Span Lat Am St; Span St)
Sheffield Hallam – 200 pts (Int Bus Span; Span Mark; Span Tour)

180 pts **Anglia Ruskin** – 180–200 pts (Span courses)
Buckingham – 180–240 pts (Span courses)
European Bus Sch London – DDD (Int Bus Span)
Heriot-Watt – DDD (Chem Span)
Liverpool John Moores – 180–220 pts (Span courses)

For information on how to read the Subject Tables, see **Chapter 7**.

160 pts **Buckinghamshire Chilterns (UC)** – 160–180 pts (Span courses)
Central Lancashire – 160–180 pts (Span Bus Span)
Greenwich – DDE–BCC 160–260 pts (Span courses)
Manchester Met – 160–180 pts (Span courses)
Middlesex – 160–200 pts (Span courses)
London Met – 160 pts (Span Lat Am St)
Roehampton – 160 pts (Span courses; Transl Span)
Wolverhampton – 160–220 pts (Span courses)
80 pts **Kingston** – 80 pts (Span minor subj – lang req)
London (Birk) – 80 pts (p/t Span Lat Am St; Span Port)

Leeds Met – contact University

Alternative offers
IB offers Aston 30–31 pts; Birmingham 24 pts; Bristol 30–33 pts; Bristol UWE 26–32 pts; Cambridge
38–42 pts; Kent 28 pts; Lancaster 33 pts; Liverpool 30 pts; London (King's) 32 pts, (QM) 32 pts, (UCL)
34 pts; Manchester 32–33 pts; Newcastle 32 pts; Nottingham 30 pts; St Andrews 32–36 pts; Sheffield
30–35 pts.
Scottish offers See **Chapter 7**.

OTHER HIGHER EDUCATION COURSES IN THE SUBJECT FIELD
Higher National Diploma courses (with Bus St)
140 pts **and below**
Northumbria; Sheffield Hallam; Thames Valley.

CHOOSING YOUR COURSE (SEE ALSO CH.1)
Subject information Spanish can be studied by focusing on the language and literature of Spain,
although broader courses in Hispanic Studies are available which also include Portuguese and Latin
American studies. See also **Appendix 2** under **Languages**. **Useful websites** www.donquijote.co.uk;
www.europa.eu; www.cilt.org.uk; www.iol.org.uk; www.bbc.co.uk/languages;
www.languageadvantage.com; www.languagematters.co.uk; www.reed.co.uk/multilingual;
www.studyspanish.com; see also under **Latin American Studies**.

Course variations International Business with Spanish (Aston; Sheffield Hallam); Spanish and
Portuguese Studies (Belfast (Queen's)); Translation, Media and Spanish (East Anglia); Portuguese and
Brazilian Studies (London (King's)); Economics and Spanish (Loughborough); Spanish, Portuguese and
Latin American Studies (Newcastle); Hispanic Studies (Sheffield); History and Culture (Spanish)
(Warwick). *NOW CHECK PROSPECTUSES AND WEBSITES FOR ANY RECENT CHANGES.*

Universities and colleges teaching quality See www.tqi.ac.uk; www.qaa.ac.uk.

Top universities and colleges (Research) (Iberian and Latin American Languages) Birmingham;
Cambridge*; Edinburgh; London (King's)*, (QM)*; Manchester*; Newcastle; Nottingham*; Oxford; St
Andrews; Sheffield; Swansea.

ADMISSIONS INFORMATION
Number of applicants per place (approx) Birmingham 9; Bristol 3; Cardiff 3; Exeter 5; Hull 14; Leeds
10; Liverpool 3; London (Gold) 6, (King's) 6, (QM) 5, (UCL) 6; Middlesex 2; Newcastle 12; Nottingham
16; Portsmouth 4; Salford 5.

Advice to applicants and planning the UCAS personal statement Visits to Spanish-speaking
countries should be discussed. Study the geography, culture, literature and politics of Spain (or
Portugal) and discuss your interests in full. Further information could be obtained from embassies in
London. **St Andrews** Give evidence of interest and your reasons for choosing the course. See also
Appendix 2 under **Languages**.

Selection interviews **Yes** Cambridge, Huddersfield, Hull, London (Gold), (RH), (UCL), Nottingham,
Oxford; **Some** Cardiff, Leeds, Roehampton, Swansea.

Applicants' impressions (A=Open day; B=Interview day) **Exeter** (A) The open day consisted of a presentation about the University and the department and then an interview with the course tutor followed by a tour of the campus and halls. **London (UCL)** (Hisp St; B) The interview was followed by a brief talk and a Spanish TV programme.

Interview advice and questions Candidates offering A-level Spanish are likely to be questioned on their A-level work, their reasons for wanting to take the subject and on their knowledge of Spain and its people. Interest in Spain important for all applicants. Mostly questions about the literature I had read and I was given a poem and asked questions on it. Questions were asked in the target language. There were two interviewers for the Spanish interview; they did their best to trip me up and to make me think under pressure by asking aggressive questions. See **Chapter 6**.

AFTER-RESULTS ADVICE
Universities with vacancies in Clearing (2006) Aberdeen; Aberystwyth; Aston; Bangor; Bath; Birmingham; Bradford; Bristol UWE; Buckingham; Central Lancashire; Chester; Coventry; East Anglia; Essex; Greenwich; Hertfordshire; Hull; Kent; Kingston; Lancaster; Leicester; Liverpool; London (QM), (RH); London Met; Manchester Met; Middlesex; Northumbria; Nottingham; Nottingham Trent; Plymouth; Portsmouth; Salford; Sheffield; Sheffield Hallam; Southampton; Stirling; Swansea; Ulster; Westminster; Wolverhampton.

Offers to applicants repeating A-levels **Higher** Glasgow, Leeds; **Same** Cardiff, Chester, Hull, Liverpool, London (RH), Newcastle, Nottingham, Roehampton, Swansea.

GRADUATE DESTINATIONS AND EMPLOYMENT (2005 HESA)
Graduates in Spanish surveyed 710 **Employed** 370 **In further study** 125 **Assumed unemployed** 30.

Graduates in Portuguese surveyed 35 **Employed** 20 **In further study** 5 **Assumed unemployed** none.

OTHER DEGREE SUBJECTS FOR CONSIDERATION
International Business Studies; Latin American Studies; Linguistics; see other **Language** tables.

SPEECH PATHOLOGY/SCIENCES/THERAPY

NB The points totals shown to the left of the institutions are for ease of reference only. It must not be assumed that tariff points are always used by institutions or that they can be substituted for an offer in grades. The level of an offer is not necessarily indicative of the quality of a course.

COURSE OFFERS INFORMATION
Subject requirements/preferences **GCSE Manchester** Six subjects including English language, modern foreign language and biology/dual award science at grade B or above. **Manchester Met** Biology grade A–C. **Newcastle** Mathematics. **Sheffield** Strong profile including mathematics, English and science. **UCE Birmingham** At least five subjects at grade A or B. **AL** At least one science subject; biology may be stipulated.

Your target offers
340 pts **London (UCL)** – AAB–BBB +AS (Sp Sci)
320 pts **Manchester** – ABB (Sp Lang Thera)
     Newcastle – ABB (Sp Lang Sci)
     Queen Margaret (UC) – ABB (Sp Lang Thera)
     Sheffield – ABB or ABbb (Sp Sci)
300 pts **Cardiff (UWIC)** – BBB (Sp Lang Thera)
     City – BBB (Sp Lang Thera)
     East Anglia – BBB (Sp Lang Thera)
     Manchester Met – BBB (Sp Path Thera; Psy Sp Path)
     Reading – 300–320 pts (Sp Lang Thera)

Sheffield – BBB–BBC (Hum Comm Sci)
Strathclyde – BBB (Sp Lang Path)
Ulster – BBB (Sp Lang Thera)
280 pts **De Montfort** – BBC (Hum Comm (Sp Lang Thera))
Marjon (Coll) – BBC 280 pts (Sp Lang Thera))
260 pts **UCE Birmingham** – BCC–BBC 260–280 pts (Sp Lang Thera)

Leeds Met – contact University

Alternative offers
IB offers City 30 pts; London (UCL) 32–34 pts; Manchester 33 pts; Manchester Met 32 pts; Newcastle 35 pts; Reading 33 pts; Sheffield 33 pts.
Scottish offers See **Chapter 7**.

CHOOSING YOUR COURSE (SEE ALSO CH.1)

Subject information Speech Pathology/Sciences/Therapy is the study of speech defects which may be caused by accident, disease or psychological trauma. Courses lead to qualification as a speech therapist. This is one of many medical courses. See also **Medicine** (**Subject information**) and **Appendix 2**. **Useful website** www.rcslt.org.

Course variations Speech Communication (London (UCL)); Psychology and Speech Pathology (Manchester Met); Human Communication Science (Sheffield); Speech and Language Pathology (Strathclyde). *NOW CHECK PROSPECTUSES AND WEBSITES FOR ANY RECENT CHANGES.*

Universities and colleges teaching quality See www.tqi.ac.uk; www.qaa.ac.uk.

Top universities and colleges (Research) London (UCL); Manchester.

ADMISSIONS INFORMATION

Number of applicants per place (approx) Cardiff (UWIC) 10; City 16; De Montfort 5; London (UCL) 9; Manchester Met 21; Newcastle 23; Queen Margaret (UC) 12; UCE Birmingham 28.

Advice to applicants and planning the UCAS personal statement Contact with speech therapists and visits to their clinics is an essential part of the preparation for this career. Discuss these contacts in full, together with details of any work experience or work shadowing you have done and your interest in helping people to communicate, giving evidence of good 'people skills'. **Cardiff (UWIC)** Observation of speech and language therapists. Relevant work experience. **Manchester Met** Observation of speech therapists working with children and adults. (Non-EU students) Good English required because of placement periods. See also **Appendix 2** and **Chapter 6**.

Misconceptions about this course Some students fail to differentiate between speech therapy, occupational therapy and physiotherapy. They do not realise that to study speech and language therapy there are academic demands, including the study of linguistics, psychology, medical sciences and clinical dynamics, so the course is intensive. **Cardiff (UWIC)** Some are under the impression that good grades are not necessary, that it is an easy option and one has to speak with a standard pronunciation.

Selection interviews Yes De Montfort, London (UCL), Manchester Met, Marjon (Coll), Queen Margaret (UC), Sheffield.

Interview advice and questions Have you visited a speech therapy clinic? What made you want to become a speech therapist? What type of speech problems are there? What type of person would make a good speech therapist? Interviews often include an ear test (test of listening ability). What did you see when you visited a speech and language therapy clinic? **Cardiff (UWIC)** Interviewees must demonstrate an insight into communication problems and explain how one speech sound is produced. See also **Chapter 6**.

Reasons for rejection (non-academic) Insufficient knowledge of speech and language therapy. Lack of maturity. Poor communication skills. Written language problems.

AFTER-RESULTS ADVICE
Universities with vacancies in Clearing (2006) De Montfort; Leeds Met.

Offers to applicants repeating A-levels Higher Cardiff (UWIC), UCE Birmingham; **Possibly higher** Manchester Met; **Same** City, De Montfort, Newcastle, Ulster.

GRADUATE DESTINATIONS AND EMPLOYMENT (2005 HESA)
No data available.

OTHER DEGREE SUBJECTS FOR CONSIDERATION
Audiology; Communication Studies; Deaf Studies; Education; Health Studies; Linguistics; Psychology.

SPORTS SCIENCES/STUDIES
(see also **Physical Education**)

NB The points totals shown to the left of the institutions are for ease of reference only. It must not be assumed that tariff points are always used by institutions or that they can be substituted for an offer in grades. The level of an offer is not necessarily indicative of the quality of a course.

COURSE OFFERS INFORMATION
Subject requirements/preferences GCSE English, mathematics and, often, a science subject; check prospectuses. **Bath** Grade B in English, mathematics and science. **Leeds** Mainly grade Bs or better; minimum grade B in mathematics, science and English. **Loughborough** (Spo Tech) Mathematics grade A or AS-level grade c. **AL** Science required for Sport Science courses. PE required for some Sport Studies courses.

Your target offers

360 pts or above
- **Bath** – AAA (Spo Exer Sci; Spo Eng)
- **Loughborough** – AAA–AAB (Spo Exer Sci)

340 pts **Loughborough** – 340–320 pts (Spo Sci Mgt)

320 pts **Bath** – ABB (Coach Educ Spo Dev courses)
- **Birmingham** – ABB–BBB 320–300 pts (Spo Sci Mat Tech; Spo Exer Sci; App Glf Mgt St; Spo PE Commun St)
- **Durham** – ABB (Spo Comb Soc Sci Spo)
- **Exeter** – ABB–BBB 320–300 pts (Exer Spo Sci)
- **Loughborough** – 320–340 pts (Spo Sci Maths; Spo Leis Mgt; Spo Tech)

300 pts **Aberdeen** – 300 pts 2nd yr entry (BSc Spo Exer Sci; Spo St)
- **Brighton** – 300 pts (Spo Journal)
- **Central Lancashire** – BBB (Spo Journal)
- **Dundee** – 300 pts 2nd yr entry (Spo Biomed)
- **Edinburgh** – BBB (App Spo Sci; Spo Recr Mgt)
- **Glasgow** – BBB (Spo Sci; Spo Med)
- **Hertfordshire** – 300 pts (Spo Thera)
- **Leeds** – BBB (Spo Sci Physiol; Spo Sci (Out Actvts); Spo Exer Sci)
- **Salford** – 300 pts (Spo Rehab)
- **Sheffield** – BBB–BBC (Spo Eng)
- **Staffordshire** – 300 pts (Spo Journal)

280 pts **Brighton** – 280 pts (Spo Exer Sci)
- **Brunel** – 280 pts (Spo Tech)
- **Chichester** – 280–320 pts (Spo Thera)
- **Durham** – BBC 280 pts (Sport)
- **Gloucestershire** – 280 pts (Spo Educ; Spo Dev)

Heriot-Watt – BBC 2nd yr entry (Spo Exer Sci; Spo Exer Sci Psy)
Hertfordshire – 280 pts (Spo Exer Sci)
Liverpool John Moores – 280–300 pts (Sci Ftbl; Spo Sci; Phys Actvt Exer Hlth)
Loughborough – 280 pts (Spo Sci Phys)
Manchester Met – 280 pts (Spo Exer Coach Sci)
Northumbria – 280 pts (App Spo Exer Sci; Spo Mgt; Spo Dev Coach; Psy Spo Sci; Psy Spo Sci)
Sheffield Hallam – 280 pts (Exer Sci; Spo Exer Sci; Spo Sci Coach)
Southampton – 280–300 pts (Spo Mgt Ldrshp; Spo St)
Staffordshire – 280 pts (Ftbl Tech; Spo Tech Mgt; Spo Tech)
Swansea – BBC 280 pts (Spo Sci)
Ulster – BBC–CCC 280–240 pts (Spo Exer Sci)

260 pts **Aberystwyth** – BCC 260 pts (Spo Exer Sci)
Bangor – 260 pts (Spo Hlth PE; Spo Sci; Spo Psy Sci; Spo Sci (Out Actvt))
Bournemouth – 260 pts (Spo Dev Coach Sci; Spo Psy Coach Sci)
Brighton – 260 pts (Spo Leis Mgt)
Brunel – 260–240 pts (Spo Sci; Bus St Spo Sci; Spo Sci (Admin Dev) (Coach) (Exer Fit) (PE))
Central Lancashire – 260 pts (Spo Psy)
Essex – 260–300 pts (Spo Exer Sci; Spo Sci Biol)
London (QM) – 260–340 pts (Spo Eng; Spo Mat)
Middlesex – 260 pts (Spo Rehab Injry Prvntn)
Northumbria – 260 pts (Geog Spo St)
Oxford Brookes – BCC (Exer Hlth; Spo Coach St)
Portsmouth – 260 pts (Wtr Spo Sci; Spo Sci)
Sheffield Hallam – 260 pts (Spo Dev Coach)
Stirling – BCC (Spo St courses; Spo Exer Sci)

240 pts **Aberdeen** – 240 pts 1st yr entry (BSc Spo Exer Sci; Spo St)
Abertay Dundee – CCC (Spo Coach Dev)
Bournemouth – 240–260 pts (Spo Mgt (Glf); Spo Mgt)
Brighton – 240 pts (Spo Tech)
Central Lancashire – 240–260 pts (Spo Sci; Spo Thera)
Chester – 240–260 pts (Spo Exer Sci)
Chester (Warrington) – 240 pts (Spo Dev)
Coventry – 240 pts (Spo Mgt; Spo Exer Hlth Sci; Spo Mgt; Spo Mark)
Dundee – 240 pts 1st yr entry (Spo Biomed)
Gloucestershire – 240 pts (Spo Exer Sci; Spo Sci; Exer Hlth Sci)
Greenwich – 240 pts (Spo Sci (Prof Tns Coach) (Prof Ftbl Coach))
Heriot-Watt – CCC 1st yr entry (Spo Exer Sci; Spo Exer Sci Psy)
Hertfordshire – 240 pts (Spo St)
Huddersfield – 240 pts (Spo Thera; Spo Exer Sty)
Hull – 240–280 pts (Spo Coach Perf; Spo Exer Sci; Spo Rehab; Spo Geog Sci)
Kent – 240 pts (Spo Hlth Fit (Spo Thera))
Leeds – CCC (Spo Mat Tech)
Manchester Met – 240 pts (Coach Spo Dev)
Newport – 240 pts (Spo St)
Nottingham Trent – 240 pts (Spo Sci Mgt; Spo Exer Sci)
Portsmouth – 240 pts (Spo Dev)
Robert Gordon – CCC (Spo Exer Sci)
Salford – CCC 240 pts (App Spo Sci; Econ Spo Econ)
Staffordshire – 240 pts (Spo St; Spo Leis Mgt; Spo Exer Sci; Spo Cult Media)
Strathclyde – CCC (Spo Eng; Spo Exer Sci)

220 pts **Central Lancashire** – 220 pts (Spo Tech; Spo Tech (Glf Ops))
Chester (Warrington) – 220 pts (Spo Mgt)

Chichester – 220–260 pts (Spo Coach Sci; Spo Exer Sci)
De Montfort – 220–280 pts (Spo Exer Sci; Spo PE; Spo Media Cult; Spo St)
Edge Hill – 220 pts (Spo Exer Sci; Spo Dev; Spo Thera; Coach Perf Dev; Spo St)
Gloucestershire – 220 pts (Spo Tour Mgt; Spo Exer Sci; Leis Spo Mgt courses)
Huddersfield – 220 pts (Spo Prom Mark)
Liverpool Hope – 220 pts (Spo St; Spo Dev)
Liverpool John Moores – 220–260 pts (Spo Dev PE)
Napier – 220 pts (Spo Exer Sci; Spo Tech)
Nottingham Trent – 220 pts (Eqn Spo Sci courses; Spo Sci Maths; Spo Sci IT; Spo Sci Mgt)
Sheffield Hallam – 220–200 pts (Spo Tech)
Sunderland – 220 pts (Spo Exer Dev; Spo Exer Sci; Spo St)
Winchester – 220 pts (Spo St; Spo Dev courses; Spo Sci)
York St John – 220 pts (Spo St; Spo Exer Sci)

210 pts **Anglia Ruskin** – 210 pts (Spo Hlth Exer; Spo Sci; Coach Sci)

200 pts **Birmingham (CFTCS)** – 200 pts (Spo Thera)
Bolton – 200 pts (Spo Leis Mgt; Spo Dev; Spo Sci Coach; Spo Rehab)
Bradford – 200 pts (BSc Med Tech Spo)
Bristol UWE – 200–260 pts (Psy Spo Biol; Spo Bus Mgt; Spo Cndtng Coach)
Buckinghamshire Chilterns (UC) – 200–240 pts (Spo Psy)
Cardiff (UWIC) – BB (Spo Coach; Spo Dev; Spo Exer Sci; Spo PE; Spo Biomed Nutr)
Cumbria – 200 pts (Spo St; Spo St Spo Dev; Spo St Spo Hist)
Glamorgan – 200–260 pts (Sci Rgby; Spo Exer Sci; Spo Psy)
Huddersfield – 200 pts (Spo Biol)
Lincoln – CDD 200 pts (Eqn Spo Sci; Spo Dev Coach (Glf); Spo Exer Sci (Glf))

Liverpool John Moores – 200 pts (Spo Tech)
London Met – 200–240 pts (Spo Thera)
Manchester Met – 200 pts (Psy Spo; Out St)
Middlesex – 200–240 pts (Spo Exer Sci Spo Rehab)
Plymouth – 200 pts (App Mar Spo Sci; Srf Sci Tech)
Sheffield Hallam – 200 pts (Soc Cult St Spo; Spo Equip Dev; Spo Leis Mgt; Spo Mgt)
Strathclyde – BB-AC (Spo Physl Actvt)
Teesside – 200–240 pts (Spo Exer courses; Spo Thera)
Worcester – 200 pts (Spo Coach Sci; Spo St; Spo Exer Sci)

180 pts **Birmingham (CFTCS)** – 180 pts (Spo Mgt)
Bristol UWE – 180–220 pts (Spo Biol)
Central Lancashire – 180–220 pts (Mtr Spo; Mtr Spo Ops; Spo Coach; Spo Mgt; Spo St; Out Ldrshp courses)
Chichester – 180–220 pts (Exer Hlth Sci; Spo Fit Mgt; Spo St (Spo Dev))
Derby – 180 pts (Out Actvts Mgt)
Glamorgan – 180 pts (Spo St)
Greenwich – 180 pts (Fit Sci; Spo Sci)
Hull – 180–200 pts (Spo Leis Mgt courses)
Kingston – 180–220 pts (Spo Sci courses)
Marjon (Coll) – 180–240 pts (Spo Dev courses)
Northampton – 180 pts (Spo Exer Sci)
St Mary's (Coll) – BC 180 pts (Spo Rehab; Spo Sci; Strg Condit)
Salford – 180–200 pts (Exer Hlth Sci)
Salford – 180 pts+Fdn Art (Spo Equip Des)

160 pts **Bedfordshire** – 160–240 pts (Spo Exer Sci; Spo Thera; Spo Mgt)
Canterbury Christ Church – CC (Spo Exer Sci; Spo Exer Sci Psy)
Central Lancashire – 160 pts (Comb Hons: Ftbl Soty; Spo)
East London – 160 pts (Spo Coach; Spo Exer Sci; Spo Dev)
Glasgow Caledonian – CC (Spo Mgt)
Glamorgan – 160–200 pts (Out Learn Sci Advntr)
Hertfordshire – 160–240 pts (Spo St Comb St)
Leeds Trinity and All Saints (Coll) – 160–240 pts (Spo Hlth Exer Nutr; Spo Dev Mark; Spo Exer Psy; Spo Dev PE; Spo Hlth Leis Media)
London Met – 160 pts (Spo Mgt Spo Sci; Spo Sci Coach)
London South Bank – CC (Spo Exer Sci)
Loughborough – CC (Fdn Spo Tech)
Manchester Met – 160–200 pts (Bus Spo)
Marjon (Coll) – 160–120 pts (App Spo Sci Coach)
Newman (CHE) – CC 160 pts (Spo St courses)
Northampton – 160 pts (Spo St)
Newport – 160 pts (Spo St courses)
Plymouth – 160 pts (Mar Spo Tech)
Roehampton – 160 pts (Spo Exer Sci)
St Mary's (Coll) – 160 pts (Spo Hlth Exer Sci; Spo Sci)
Salford – 160 pts (Spo Equip Des)
Southampton Solent – 160 pts (Spo St Bus; Spo Dev Mark; Ftbl St; Wtrspo St Mgt; Out Advntr Mgt)
Teesside – 160 pts (Spo Tech)
Thames Valley – 160–180 pts (Spo Hlth Fit Mgt)
Westminster – CC (Spo Exer Sci)
Wolverhampton – 160–220 pts (Spo Coach; Spo St; Spo Exer Sci courses)

140 pts **Bell (Coll)** – CD (Spo Dev; Spo Mgt; Spo Coach)
Trinity Carmarthen (Coll) – 140 pts (Out Educ Spo St)

Writtle (Coll) – 140 pts (Spo Exer Perf)

120 pts **Buckinghamshire Chilterns (UC)** – 120–180 pts (Spo Leis Mgt; Spo Mgt Glf St; Spo Mgt Rgby St; Spo Coach Mgt; Int Ftbl Mgt; Spo Mgt Ftbl)

Essex – 120 pts (4yr Spo Exer Sci; Spo Sci Biol)

Huddersfield – 120 pts (Spo Coach)

London Met – 120 pts (Spo Psy Perf)

North East Wales (IHE) – 120 pts (Spo Sci; Spo Exer Mgt; Spo St)

Salford – 120 pts (Spo Leis Mgt)

Suffolk (Univ Campus) – 120–180 pts (Spo Sci courses)

Swansea (IHE) – 120 pts (Spo Recr Mgt)

100 pts **North East Wales (IHE)** – 100 pts (App Spo Exer Sci; Commun Spo Dev)

UHI Millennium Inst (NHC) – 100 pts approx (Glf Mgt)

80 pts **Southend Campus Essex** – 80 pts (Spo St)

West Suffolk (Coll) – 80 pts (Spo Hlth Exer)

Leeds Met – contact University

Alternative offers

IB offers Aberystwyth 26 pts; Bath 35–36 pts; Birmingham 32–34 pts; Brighton 30 pts; Bristol UWE 30 pts; Brunel 28 pts; Chichester 28–30 pts; Essex 28–32 pts; Exeter 32–34 pts; Loughborough 32–34 pts; Manchester Met 28 pts; Salford 29 pts.

Scottish offers See **Chapter 7**.

OTHER HIGHER EDUCATION COURSES IN THE SUBJECT FIELD

Foundation degrees (contact institutions for details) Arts London (CComm); Barnfield (Coll); Bath; Bath City (Coll); Bedfordshire; Birmingham (CFTCS); Bishop Burton (Coll); Blackpool and Fylde (Coll); Bridgwater (Coll); Buckinghamshire Chilterns (UC); Burnley (Coll); Central Lancashire; Cornwall (Coll); Derby; Dunstable (Coll); Durham New (Coll); East Durham (CmC); Exeter (Coll); Farnborough (CT); Gateshead (Coll); Hartpury (Coll); Hastings (Coll); Herefordshire (CAD); Hertfordshire; Huddersfield; Kingston (Coll); Lancaster and Morecambe (Coll); Lincoln (Coll); London South Bank; Loughborough (Coll); Manchester (CAT); Middlesex; Milton Keynes (Coll); Myerscough (Coll); Newcastle (Coll); Nescot; Newport; North Devon (Coll); North Herefordshire (Coll); Nottingham Trent; Oaklands (Coll); Park Lane Leeds (Coll); Pembrokeshire (Coll); Penwith (Coll); Peterborough Reg (Coll); Plymouth (CFE); Preston (Coll); Reaseheath (Coll); Richmond upon Thames (Coll); St Helens (Coll); St Mary's (Coll); Sheffield (Coll); Somerset (CAT); South Cheshire (Coll); South Devon (Coll); Southampton Solent; Southport (Coll); Suffolk (Univ Campus); Sunderland; Sunderland City (Coll); Sussex Downs (Coll); Swindon New (Coll); Thames Valley; Truro (Coll); Warwickshire (Coll); West Herts (Coll); West Suffolk (Coll); Wolverhampton; Worcester (CT); Writtle (Coll); Yeovil (Coll).

Higher National Diploma courses

140 pts **and below**

Anglia Ruskin; Aylesbury (Coll); Bangor; Barnsley (Univ Centre); Bath; Bedfordshire; Bell (Coll); Berkshire (CAg); Birmingham (CFTCS); Blackpool and Fylde (Coll); Boston (Coll); Bradford (Coll); Bridgwater (Coll); Bristol UWE (Hartpury); Buckinghamshire Chilterns (UC); Cambridge Reg (Coll); Carmarthenshire (Coll); Central Lancashire; Chelmsford (Coll); Cornwall (Coll); Coventry; De Montfort; Derby; Doncaster (Univ Centre); Duchy (Coll); Dumfries and Galloway (Coll); Durham New (Coll); East Berkshire (Coll); East Lancashire (IHE); Eastleigh (Coll); Easton (Coll); Exeter; Glamorgan; Gloucestershire; Greenwich; Grimsby (IFHE); Guildford (Coll); Harper Adams (UC); Hendon (Coll); Henley (Coll); Herefordshire (CT); Lancaster and Morecambe (Coll); Lincoln; Llandrillo Cymru (Coll); Loughborough (CT); Manchester Met; Mid Cheshire (Coll); Middlesex; Neath Port Talbot (Coll); Newcastle (Coll); North East Wales (IHE); Northampton; Northumberland (Coll); Nottingham New (Coll); Park Lane Leeds (Coll); Pembrokeshire (Coll); Plymouth (Coll); Riverside Halton (Coll); Runshaw (Coll); Sheffield (Coll); Sheffield Hallam; Solihull (Coll); Somerset (CAT); South Birmingham (Coll); South Devon (Coll); South Nottingham (Coll); South Tyneside (Coll); Southwark (Coll);

Staffordshire; Stockport (CFHE); Stoke on Trent (Coll); Stourbridge (Coll); Strode (Coll); Sutton Coldfield (Coll); Swansea; Swansea (IHE); Teesside; Thomas Danby (Coll); Truro (Coll); UHI Millennium Inst (NHC); Wakefield (Coll); Warwickshire (Coll); West Anglia (Coll); West Nottinghamshire (Coll); West Suffolk (Coll); Wigan and Leigh (Coll); Wiltshire (Coll); Wolverhampton; Worcester; Worcester (CT); Yeovil (Coll); York (Coll); Yorkshire Coast (CFHE).

CHOOSING YOUR COURSE (SEE ALSO CH.1)

Subject information In addition to the theory and practice of many different sporting activities, Sports Sciences/Studies students will also cover the psychological aspects of sports and business administration. The geography, economics and sociology of recreation may also be included. **Centres of Cricketing Excellence** The England and Wales Cricket Board has introduced the Universities Centres of Cricketing Excellence scheme (UCCE). The scheme is open to male cricketers with potential to play first class cricket and to female cricketers of senior county standard irrespective of their choice of degree subject. Details can be obtained from the following centres of excellence: Bradford (Univ) tel 01274 234867; Bradford (Coll) tel 01274 753291; Leeds (Univ) tel 0113 233 5096; Leeds Met (Univ) tel 0113 282 3113; Cambridge (Univ) tel 01223 336580; Anglia Ruskin (Univ) tel 01223 363271; Cardiff (Univ) tel 029 2087 4045; Cardiff (UWIC) tel 029 2041 6590; Glamorgan (Univ) tel 01443 482577; Durham (Univ) 0191 374 3463; Loughborough (Univ) tel 01509 223283; Oxford (Univ) tel 01865 245869; Oxford Brookes (Univ) tel 01865 483166. See also **Appendix 2**. **Useful websites** www.isrm.co.uk; www.uksport.gov.uk; www.worldsport.com; www.wsf.org.uk; www.sta.co.uk; www.sportscotland.org.uk; www.baha.org.uk; www.planet-science.com; www.london2012.org.

Course variations Sports Psychology and Coaching Science (Bournemouth); Medical Technology in Sport (Bradford; Bristol UWE); Business Studies and Sport Science (Brunel); Sport Technology (Golf Operations) (Central Lancashire); Sports Biomedicine (Dundee); Sports Science with Professional Tennis Coaching (Greenwich); Sports Promotion and Marketing (Huddersfield); Sports Rehabilitation and Injury Prevention (Middlesex); Equine Sports Science (Nottingham Trent); Watersports Science (Portsmouth); Sport Equipment Design (Salford). *NOW CHECK PROSPECTUSES AND WEBSITES FOR ANY RECENT CHANGES.*

Top universities and colleges (Research) Bangor; Birmingham*; Exeter; Glasgow*; Liverpool John Moores*; Manchester Met*.

Sandwich degree courses Bath; Bournemouth; Brighton; Bristol UWE; Brunel; Buckinghamshire Chilterns (UC); Coventry; Glamorgan; Gloucestershire; Greenwich; Hertfordshire; Huddersfield; Kingston; London Met; Loughborough; Northumbria; Oxford Brookes; Paisley; Sheffield Hallam; Sunderland; Swansea (IHE); Teesside; Ulster; Warwickshire (Coll); Wolverhampton; Writtle (Coll).

ADMISSIONS INFORMATION

Number of applicants per place (approx) Aberystwyth 5; Bangor 15; Bath (Coach Educ Spo Dev) 3; Birmingham 7; Brunel 6; Canterbury Christ Church 30; Cardiff (UWIC) 10; Chichester 4; Cumbria 14, (Spo St) 6; De Montfort 11; Durham 6; Edinburgh 11; Exeter 23; Gloucestershire 8; Kingston 13; Leeds 25; Leeds Trinity and All Saints (Coll) 35; Liverpool John Moores 4; Loughborough 20; Manchester Met 16; Northampton 4; Northumbria 30; Nottingham Trent 8; Portsmouth 12; Roehampton 8; St Mary's (Coll) 4; Salford 30; Sheffield Hallam 7; Southend Campus Essex 1; Staffordshire 12; Stirling 10; Strathclyde 28; Sunderland 2; Swansea 6; Teesside 15; Winchester 5; Wolverhampton 4; Worcester 10; York St John 4.

Advice to applicants and planning the UCAS personal statement **Cardiff (UWIC)** A strong personal statement which clearly identifies current performance profile and indicates a balanced lifestyle. **Salford** Previous experience in a sporting environment will be noted. Previous study in biology/human biology, physics, chemistry, physical education/sports studies. Psychology is preferred. **Other comments** (Coach Sci) For these courses applicants must have proven coaching skills to gain a place. (Spo Sci) These are lab-based courses examining the physical stress of sport on the human body. A sound scientific aptitude is required. Although professional sporting qualifications and high level practical experience cannot take the place of scientific entry qualifications, they will be considered in any borderline applicants holding a conditional offer. Comment on any coaching or competitive experience. See also **Physical Education**. See also **Appendix 2**.

Misconceptions about this course Bath (Spo Exer Sci) This is not a sports course with a high component of practical sport: it is a science programme with minimal practical sport. (Coach Educ Spo Dev) This is not necessarily a course for elite athletes. **Birmingham** (App Glf Mgt St) Applicants do not appreciate the academic depth required across key areas (it is, in a sense, a multiple honours course – business management, sports science, coaching theory, materials science). **Sheffield Hallam** (Spo Tech) Some applicants expect an engineering course! **Swansea** (Spo Sci) Applicants underestimate the quantity of maths on the course. Many applicants are uncertain about the differences between Sports Studies and Sports Science.

Selection interviews Yes Bath, Birmingham, Bristol UWE, Cumbria, Durham, Edinburgh, Leeds, Leeds Trinity and All Saints (Coll), Southend Campus Essex, Swansea; **Some** Cardiff (UWIC), Chichester, Derby, Liverpool John Moores, Roehampton, St Mary's (Coll), Salford, Sheffield Hallam, Staffordshire, Wolverhampton.

Applicants' impressions (A=Open day; B=Interview day) Essex (Spo Exer Sci; B) There were two interviewers, the interview lasted 10–15 minutes. It was well organised and very friendly. A tour of the campus followed but there was no chance to talk to students. I would recommend the university, but you need to talk to students to get a good idea of the course. **Leeds Met** (A) It was a worthwhile open day. It cost a lot to get there but good to see the accommodation available.

Interview advice and questions Applicants' interests in sport and their sporting activities are likely to be discussed at length. Past questions include: How do you strike a balance between sport and academic work? How many, and which, sports do you coach? For how long? Have you devised your own coaching programme? What age-range do you coach? Do you coach unsupervised? **Loughborough** A high level of sporting achievement is expected. See **Chapter 6**.

Reasons for rejection (non-academic) Not genuinely interested in outdoor activities. Poor sporting background or knowledge. Personal appearance. Inability to apply their science to their specialist sport. Illiteracy. Using the course as a second option to physiotherapy. Arrogance. Expectation that they will be playing sport all day. When the course is explained to them some applicants realise that a more arts-based course would be more appropriate.

AFTER-RESULTS ADVICE

Universities with vacancies in Clearing (2006) Aberystwyth; Bangor; Bedfordshire; Bolton; Bournemouth; Bristol UWE; Brunel; Canterbury Christ Church; Central Lancashire; Chester; Cumbria; Derby; East London; Edge Hill; Glamorgan; Gloucestershire; Greenwich; Hertfordshire; Huddersfield; Hull; Kent; Kingston; Leeds; Lincoln; Liverpool Hope; Liverpool John Moores; London Met; Manchester Met; Middlesex; Napier; Northampton; Nottingham Trent; Oxford Brookes; Roehampton; Southampton Solent; Staffordshire; Strathclyde; Sunderland; Swansea; Wolverhampton; Winchester; York St John.

Offers to applicants repeating A-levels Higher Swansea; **Same** Cardiff (UWIC), Chichester, Derby, Dundee, Lincoln, Liverpool John Moores, Loughborough, Plymouth, Roehampton, Salford, Sheffield Hallam, Southend Campus Essex, Staffordshire, Sunderland, Winchester, York St John.

GRADUATE DESTINATIONS AND EMPLOYMENT (2005 HESA)
Graduates surveyed 4280 **Employed** 2265 **In further study** 660 **Assumed unemployed** 200.

OTHER DEGREE SUBJECTS FOR CONSIDERATION
Anatomy; Biology; Human Movement Studies; Leisure and Recreation Management; Nutrition; Physical Education; Physiology; Physiotherapy.

STATISTICS

(see also **Business Courses** and **Mathematics**)

NB The points totals shown to the left of the institutions are for ease of reference only. It must not be assumed that tariff points are always used by institutions or that they can be substituted for an offer in grades. The level of an offer is not necessarily indicative of the quality of a course.

COURSE OFFERS INFORMATION

Subject requirements/preferences GCSE English and mathematics. **Exeter** Reasonable spread of grades A*, A and B. **Greenwich**, **Kingston**, **Sheffield Hallam** Mathematics grade A or B. **AL** Mathematics required for all courses.

Your target offers

360 pts **and above**
  Bath – AAA (Stats; Maths Stats)
  London (UCL) – AAA–AAB+AS (Econ Stats; Stats Sci (Int))
  Oxford – Offers range AAA–AAB (Maths Stats)
  Southampton – ABBb 370 pts (Maths Stats)
  Warwick – AAA–AABa/b (Maths OR Stats Econ; Maths Stats)

340 pts **Bristol** – AAB (Maths Stats)
  Imperial London – AAB (Maths Stats)
  Lancaster – AAB (Stats N Am/Aus)
  Leeds – AAB (Stats courses)
  London (LSE) – AAB–BBB (Bus Maths Stats)
  London (UCL) – AAB–ABB+AS (BSc Stats; Stats Euro Lang; Stats OR Mgt St; Stats Comp OR Econ; Stats OR Econ Euro Lang)

320 pts **East Anglia** – 320 pts (Maths Stats)
  Edinburgh – ABB–ABC (Maths Stats)
  Lancaster – ABB (Statistics)
  Manchester – ABB (Maths Stats)
  Newcastle – ABB–ABC (Stats courses)
  St Andrews – ABB (Stats courses)
  Sheffield – ABB–BBC (Econ Stats)
  York – ABB–ABC (Maths Stats)

300 pts **Aberystwyth** – 300 pts (Stats joint courses)
  Birmingham – BBB (Mathem Econ Stats)
  Cardiff – BBB–BBC 300–280 pts (Maths OR Stats)
  Glasgow – BBB (Statistics)
  Liverpool – BBB–ABB (Maths Stats)

280 pts **Brunel** – 280 pts (Maths Stats Mgt)
  Lancaster – BBC (Maths Stats)
  London (QM) – 280 pts (Statistics)
  London (RH) – 280–320 pts (Maths Stats)
  Reading – 280–300 pts (Maths App Stats; Maths Stats; Bus Stats; App Stats; Stats)
  Strathclyde – BBC (Maths Stats Acc)
  Surrey – BBC (Maths Stats)

260 pts **Brighton** – 260 pts (Maths Stats)
  City – BCC 260 pts (Mathem Sci Stats)
  Kent – BCC (Maths Stats)
  Kingston – 260 pts (Stats Bus Mgt; Med Stats; Stats joint courses; Act Maths Stats)

240 pts **Bristol UWE** – 240–260 pts (Stats joint courses)
  Dundee – 240 pts (Stats courses)
  Heriot-Watt – BCD (Statistics)
  Oxford Brookes – CCC–CD (Bus Stats courses)

For information on how to read the Subject Tables, see **Chapter 7**.

220 pts **Central Lancashire** – CCD (Maths Stats)
Glamorgan – 220–260 pts (Stats joint courses)
200 pts **Coventry** – 200 pts (Maths Stats)
Hertfordshire – 200–260 pts (Stats courses)
Plymouth – 200 pts (App Stats courses)
Portsmouth – 200 pts (Maths Stats)
180 pts **Bristol UWE** – 180–220 pts (Statistics)
Sheffield Hallam – 180 pts (Maths Stats)
160 pts **Greenwich** – 160–200 pts (Stats Comb courses)
Liverpool John Moores – 160 pts (Maths Stats Comp)
Middlesex – 160–200 pts (Stats courses)
140 pts **Wolverhampton** – 140–200 pts (Stats Sci courses)
120 pts **London Met** – 120 pts (Stats joint courses)
80 pts **London (Birk)** – 80 pts for under 21s (over 21s varies) (p/t Stats Econ; Stats Mgt)

Alternative offers
IB offers Aberystwyth 29 pts; Bath 36 pts; Bristol UWE 28–30 pts; London (UCL) 36–38 pts; Newcastle 32–36 pts; St Andrews 32 pts; Warwick 36 pts.
Scottish offers See **Chapter 7**.

OTHER HIGHER EDUCATION COURSES IN THE SUBJECT FIELD

Higher National Diploma courses
100 pts and below
Coventry; East Lancashire (IHE); Glamorgan; Greenwich; Hertfordshire; Leeds Met; Manchester Met; Sheffield Hallam.

CHOOSING YOUR COURSE (SEE ALSO CH.1)

Subject information Statistics has mathematical underpinnings but is primarily concerned with the collection, interpretation and analysis of data. Statistics are used to analyse and solve problems in a wide range of areas, particularly in the scientific, business, government and public services. **Useful website** www.rss.org.uk.

Course variations Mathematics, Statistics and Management (Brunel); Mathematics, Operational Research and Statistics (Cardiff); Medical Statistics (Kingston); Statistics with a Year in North America or Australia (Lancaster); Business Mathematics and Statistics (London (LSE)). *NOW CHECK PROSPECTUSES AND WEBSITES FOR ANY RECENT CHANGES.*

Universities and colleges teaching quality See www.tqi.ac.uk; www.qaa.ac.uk.

Top universities and colleges (Research) (including Operational Research) Bath; Bristol*; Cambridge*; Glasgow; Heriot-Watt; Kent*; Imperial London; Lancaster*; Leeds; London (QM), (UCL); Newcastle; Oxford*; Sheffield; Southampton; Surrey; Warwick*.

Sandwich degree courses Bath; Brighton; Coventry; Hertfordshire; Kingston; Liverpool John Moores; Portsmouth; Reading; Sheffield Hallam; Surrey; Wolverhampton.

ADMISSIONS INFORMATION

Number of applicants per place (approx) Bath 10; Bristol UWE 2; Cardiff 3; Coventry 3; East London 3; Heriot-Watt 6; Lancaster 11; Liverpool John Moores 6; London (UCL) 9; Newcastle 5; Sheffield Hallam 2; York 5.

Advice to applicants and planning the UCAS personal statement Love mathematics, don't expect an easy life. See **Mathematics**. See also **Appendix 2**.

Selection interviews **Yes** Bath, Birmingham, Liverpool, Liverpool John Moores, London (UCL), Newcastle, Sheffield, Sheffield Hallam; **Some** Greenwich.

Interview advice and questions Questions could be asked on your A-level syllabus (particularly in mathematics). Applicants' knowledge of statistics and their interest in the subject are likely to be tested, together with their awareness of the application of statistics in commerce and industry. See Chapter 6.

AFTER-RESULTS ADVICE

Universities with vacancies in Clearing (2006) Aberystwyth; Bristol UWE; Brunel; Cardiff; City; Dundee; East Anglia; Glamorgan; Glasgow; Greenwich; Heriot-Watt; Hertfordshire; Kent; Kingston; Lancaster; Leeds; Liverpool John Moores; London (QM), (RH); London Met; Middlesex; Newcastle; Oxford Brookes; Plymouth; Portsmouth; Reading; Sheffield; Sheffield Hallam; Southampton; Strathclyde; Surrey; Wolverhampton; York.

Offers to applicants repeating A-levels **Higher** Kent, Leeds, Liverpool, Liverpool John Moores, Newcastle, Swansea; **Same** Birmingham.

GRADUATE DESTINATIONS AND EMPLOYMENT (2005 HESA)
Graduates surveyed 240 **Employed** 125 **In further study** 45 **Assumed unemployed** 15.

OTHER DEGREE SUBJECTS FOR CONSIDERATION
Accountancy; Actuarial Sciences; Business Information Technology; Business Studies; Computer Science; Economics; Financial Services; Mathematics.

TECHNOLOGY

(see also **separate technologies, eg Architecture, Broadcast, Business Information, Communications, Design, Fashion, Food, Information, Internet, Materials, Media, Music, Sound** and **Sport** under relevant subject tables)

NB The points totals shown to the left of the institutions are for ease of reference only. It must not be assumed that tariff points are always used by institutions or that they can be substituted for an offer in grades. The level of an offer is not necessarily indicative of the quality of a course.

COURSE OFFERS INFORMATION
Subject requirements/preferences **GCSE** English and mathematics required. **AL** Mathematics and/or a science may be required.

Your target offers

300 pts **Birmingham** – BBB 300 pts (Comm Tech; Tech; Sust Tech; Disas Mgt Tech)
Exeter – BBB–BBC 300–280 pts (Phys Qntm Lsr Tech)
London (QM) – 300 pts (MEng Innov Entre Mgt Advnc Tech)
Warwick – BBB–BBC+AS (BEng Comb Tech)

280 pts **Coventry** – 280 pts (Mus Tech)
Staffordshire – 280 pts (Spo Tech Mgt; Ftbl Tech; Tech Teach Lrng; Film Prod Tech; Mbl Dvc Tech)
Strathclyde – BBC (Tech Bus St (Acc) (Fin))
Surrey – 280 pts (Entre Tech IT Bus)

260 pts **Aston** – BCC–CCC **or** 2AL+2AS (Tech Ent Mgt; Chem Tech Des)
Chester – 260–240 pts (Multim Tech courses)
Lancaster – BCC (Comb Tech)
London (QM) – 260 pts (Poly Tech)
Surrey – BCC (Phys Sat Tech)

240 pts **Bradford** – 240 pts (Med Tech Spo; Clin Tech)
De Montfort – 240 pts (Tech joint courses; Fash Tech)
Portsmouth – 240 pts (Intnet Tech; Crea Comp Tech; Mus Snd Tech; Dig Vid Tech)
Strathclyde – CCC (Tech Bus St courses except under **280 pts**)

220 pts **Glasgow Caledonian** – CCD/CC (Multim Tech)
          Huddersfield – 220 pts (Tech Bus Mgt)
          Manchester Met – 220–280 pts (Comp Gms Tech)
          Sheffield Hallam – 220 pts (Spo Tech)
          UCE Birmingham – 220–240 pts (Inf Comm Tech)
          Ulster – 220 pts (Tech Des)
200 pts **Bradford** – 200 pts (Tech Mgt; Med Tech Spo; E-Commer Tech; IT Mgt)
          De Montfort – 200–240 pts (Aud Rec Tech)
          Glamorgan – 200–300 pts (Dig Media Broad Tech)
          Glasgow – BB (Tech Mgt)
          Portsmouth – 200 pts (Mar Spo Tech)
180 pts **Derby** – 180 pts (Snd Lt Lv Evnt Tech)
160 pts **De Montfort** – 160–240 pts (Electron Gms Tech; Mus Tech Innov)
          Derby – 160–180 pts (Des Tech)
          Glasgow – CC (Technol Educ)
          Manchester Met – 160 pts (Des Tech courses)
140 pts **Glamorgan** – 140–180 pts (Archit Tech; Eng Tech Mgt)
120 pts **Oxford Brookes** – DD–CCC (Tech Mgt)
          Paisley – DD (Technol Phys; Phys Med Tech)

          Open University – contact University

Alternative offers
IB offers Birmingham 32 pts; Staffordshire 27 pts.
Scottish offers See **Chapter 7**.

OTHER HIGHER EDUCATION COURSES IN THE SUBJECT FIELD

Foundation degrees (contact the institutions for details) Accrington and Rossendale (Coll); Leeds Met; Manchester Met.

Higher National Diploma courses Arts London; Barking (Coll); Bolton; Birmingham City (Coll); Cornwall (Coll); Dudley (Coll); Farnborough (CT); Glamorgan; Glasgow Met (Coll); Leicester (Coll); Llandrillo Cymru (Coll); Loughborough (Coll); North East Wales (IHE); Northampton; Nottingham Trent; Plymouth (CAD); Sheffield (Coll); South Nottingham (Coll); Staffordshire; Stockport (CFHE); Teesside; Thames Valley; West Herts (Coll); Wolverhampton.

CHOOSING YOUR COURSE (SEE ALSO CH.1)

Subject information Technology covers a wide range of activities and is commonly associated with the engineering industries although there are also scientific and artistic applications. See individual subject tables. **Useful website** www.techreview.com.

Course variations Disaster Management and Technology (Birmingham); Medical Technology in Sport (Bradford); Audio and Recording Technology (De Montfort); Architectural Technology (Glamorgan); Multimedia Technology (Glasgow Caledonian); Marine Sports Technology (Portsmouth); Mobile Device Technology (Staffordshire). *NOW CHECK PROSPECTUSES AND WEBSITES FOR ANY RECENT CHANGES.*

Sandwich degree courses Aston; Bradford; Coventry; De Montfort; Huddersfield; Oxford Brookes; Portsmouth.

ADMISSIONS INFORMATION

Number of applicants per place (approx) Aston 6.

Advice to applicants and planning the UCAS personal statement See **Engineering** courses and **Physics**.

Selection interviews Yes Aston, Glasgow, Staffordshire.

Interview advice and questions See **Engineering/Engineering Sciences** and **Chapter 6**.

AFTER-RESULTS ADVICE

Universities with vacancies in Clearing (2006) Aston; Birmingham; Bradford; Derby; London South Bank; Manchester Met; Oxford Brookes; Portsmouth; Strathclyde; Surrey.

Offers to applicants repeating A-levels **Same** Aston, Bradford, Staffordshire.

GRADUATE DESTINATIONS AND EMPLOYMENT (2005 HESA)

See **Engineering/Engineering Sciences**.

OTHER DEGREE SUBJECTS FOR CONSIDERATION

Biotechnology; Design Technology; Engineering Sciences; Materials Science and Technology; Mechanical Engineering.

TOURISM AND TRAVEL

(see also **Business Courses, Hospitality and Hotel Management** and **Leisure and Recreation Management/Studies)**

NB The points totals shown to the left of the institutions are for ease of reference only. It must not be assumed that tariff points are always used by institutions or that they can be substituted for an offer in grades. The level of an offer is not necessarily indicative of the quality of a course.

COURSE OFFERS INFORMATION

Subject requirements/preferences GCSE English and mathematics required. **AL** No subjects specified.

Your target offers

300 pts	**Strathclyde** – BBB–BBC/AB (Tourism)
280 pts	**Aberystwyth** – 280 pts (Tour Mgt)
	Glasgow (Crichton) – BBC (Tour Herit)
	Northumbria – BBC (Trav Tour Mgt)
	Surrey – 280 pts (Tour Mgt)
260 pts	**Oxford Brookes** – BCC (Int Tour Mgt; Tour Mgt courses)
240 pts	**Bangor** – 240–280 pts (Langs Tour)
	Brighton – 240 pts (Int Tour Mgt; Int Trav Mgt; Entre Trav Tour; Trav Tour Mark)
	Bristol UWE – 240–300 pts (Tour; Tour Env Mgt)
	Chester – 240 pts (Tour courses)
	Coventry – 240–220 pts (Tour Mgt; Tour Mark; Tour Fr/Span; Trav Mgt)
	Manchester Met – 240 pts (Tour Mgt)
	Northumbria – 240 pts (Bus Tour)
	Staffordshire – 240 pts (Trav Tour Mgt)
	Ulster – CCC 240 pts (Int Htl Tour Mgt)
220 pts	**Glamorgan** – 220–260 pts (Tour Mgt; Tour Mark; Trans Leis Tour Mgt)
	Gloucestershire – 220 pts (Tour Mgt; Int Tour Mgt; Spo Tour Mgt)
	Kent – 220 pts (Tour Mgt; Tour Mgt Ind)
	Liverpool Hope – 220 pts (Tour courses)
	Stirling – CCD (Tour Mgt; Int Tour Mgt)
	Westminster – 220 pts (Tour Bus; Tour Plan)
	Winchester – 220–160 pts (Tour Herit Mgt; Tour Mgt Bus Mgt; Tour Mgt)
200 pts	**Anglia Ruskin** – 200 pts (Tour St)
	Bath Spa – 200–240 pts (Tour Mgt)
	Birmingham (CFTCS) – 200 pts (Tour Mgt)
	Bolton – 200 pts (Tour Mgt; Int Tour Mgt)
	Bournemouth – 220 pts (Tour Mgt)
	Cardiff (UWIC) – 200 pts (Tour Mgt courses; Tour St Fr/Ger/Span)
	Hertfordshire – 200 pts (Tourism)

Lincoln – 200 pts (Euro Tour; Int Tour; Tour)

Napier – 200 pts (Tour Mgt; Ecotour)

Plymouth – 200 pts (Hspty Tour Mgt; Bus (Tour); Int Tour Mgt; Tour Mgt; Cru Ops Mgt)

Salford – 200 pts (Tour Mgt)

Sheffield Hallam – 200 pts (Tour Mgt; Tour Mgt Arts Enter; Tour Hspty Bus Mgt)

190 pts **Aberystwyth** – 190–220 pts (Cntry Recr Tour)

180 pts **Birmingham (CFTCS)** – 180 pts (Tour Bus Mgt; Mark Tour Mgt; Hspty Tour Mgt; Int Hspty Tour Bus St; Advntr Tour Mgt)

Central Lancashire – 180–200 pts (Tour Leis Mgt; Tour Mgt; Trav Journal)

Chichester – 180–220 pts (Tour Mgt courses)

Derby – 180–200 pts (Trav Tour Mgt)

Greenwich – 180 pts (Tour Mgt; Tour Mgt Fr/Ger/Span)

Hull – 180–200 pts (Tour Mgt courses)

Liverpool John Moores – 180 pts (Tour Leis courses)

Northampton – 180–220 pts (Tour courses)

160 pts **Anglia Ruskin** – 160 pts (Tour Mgt)

Bedfordshire – 160–240 pts (Trav Tour; Spo Tour; Int Tour Mgt)

Canterbury Christ Church – CC (Tour Leis St; Tour Mgt; Tour Mark)

Glasgow Caledonian – CC (Tour Mgt; Int Trav Mgt Tour)

Greenwich – 160 pts (Tour Mgt courses; Trav Tour Mgt)

Huddersfield – 160 pts (Tour Leis Mgt)

Liverpool John Moores – 160–180 pts (Advntr Tour; Tour Leis Chin/Fr/Ger/Jap/Span)

London Met – 160 pts (Int Tour Mgt; Tour Mgt; Tour Env)

London South Bank – CC 160 pts (Tour Hspty; Tour courses)

Middlesex – 160–200 pts (Int Tour Mgt)

Paisley – CC (Tourism)

Queen Margaret (UC) – CC (Hspty Tour Mgt; Tour Mgt)

Robert Gordon – CC (Tour Int Mgt)

SAC (Scottish CAg) – CC 160 pts (Rur Recr Tour Mgt; Advntr Tour Out Prsts)

St Mary's (Coll) – CC 160 pts (Tour courses)

Sunderland – 160 pts (Tour Dev; Tour Mgt; Tour Ent)

Teesside – 160 pts (Tour Mgt; Leis Tour Mgt)

Thames Valley – 160 pts (Trav Tour Mgt; Airln Airpt Mgt)

Wolverhampton – 160–220 pts (Tour Mgt courses)

140 pts **Blackpool and Fylde (Coll)** – 140 pts (Hspty Mgt Tour; Int Tour Rsrt Mgt)

Harper Adams (UC) – 140–200 pts (Tour Bus Mgt)

Trinity Carmarthen (Coll) – 140 pts (Advntr Tour)

Writtle (Coll) – 140 pts (Advntr Tour)

120 pts **Buckinghamshire Chilterns (UC)** – 120–180 pts (Air Trav Mgt; Int Trav Tour Mgt)

Southampton Solent – 120 pts (Tour Mgt; Tour Mgt Out Advntr)

100 pts **Arts London** – 100 pts check with admissions tutor (Int Trav Tour)

Northbrook (Coll) – 100 pts (Bus Admin Trav Tour)

80 pts **Greenwich (Sch Mgt)** – 80–120 pts (Bus Mgt Trav Tour – 2 yrs)

Havering (Coll) – 80 pts (Trav Mgt; Tour)

Llandrillo Cymru (Coll) – 80 pts min (Trav Tour Mgt)

Suffolk (Univ Campus) – 80–120 pts (Bus Mgt Tour Mgt)

Swansea (IHE) – 80–340 pts (Int Trav Tour Mgt; Tour Mgt)

UHI Millennium Inst (PC) – 80 pts (Tourism)

Leeds Met – contact University

Alternative offers

IB offers Aberystwyth 28 pts; Brighton 28 pts; Bristol UWE 26–30 pts; Kent 27 pts; Salford 26 pts; Surrey 30–32 pts.

Scottish offers See **Chapter 7**.

OTHER HIGHER EDUCATION COURSES IN THE SUBJECT FIELD

Foundation degrees (contact the institutions for details) Arts London (CComm); Bath Spa; Bedfordshire; Birmingham (CFTCS); Bournemouth and Poole (Coll); Bridgwater (Coll); Brighton; Brighton and Hove City (Coll); Buckinghamshire Chilterns (UC); Canterbury Christ Church; Central Lancashire; Cornwall (Coll); Croydon (Coll); De Montfort; Derby; Durham New (Coll); Ealing, Hammersmith and West London (Coll); Edge Hill; Grimsby (IFHE); Harper Adams (UC); Herefordshire (CAD); Hugh Baird (Coll); Hull (Coll); Liverpool (CmC); Llandrillo (Coll); London Met; Loughborough (Coll); Mid-Kent (Coll); Myerscough (Coll); Newcastle (Coll); Northampton; Northampton (Coll); Northbrook (Coll); Norwich City (Coll); Nottingham Castle (Coll); Park Lane Leeds (Coll); Pembrokeshire (Coll); Pershore (Coll); Plymouth; Plymouth (CFE); Preston (Coll); Riverside Halton (Coll); Runshaw (Coll); Somerset (CAT); South Devon (Coll); Southport (Coll); Sunderland; Sunderland City (Coll); Trinity Carmarthen (Coll); Westminster Kingsway (Coll); Weston (Coll); Writtle (Coll).

Higher National Diploma courses
120 pts and below

Aberystwyth; Anglia Ruskin; Arts London; Aylesbury (Coll); Barnsley (Univ Centre); Basingstoke (Coll); Bath; Bedfordshire; Bell (Coll); Birmingham (CFTCS); Bishop Burton (Coll); Blackpool and Fylde (Coll); Bolton; Bournemouth and Poole (Coll); Bradford (Coll); Bridgwater (Coll); Brighton; Brockenhurst (Coll); Buckinghamshire Chilterns (UC); Cambridge Reg (Coll); Cardiff (UWIC); Cardonald (Coll); Central Lancashire; Chelmsford (Coll); Cornwall (Coll); Coventry City (Coll); Craven (Coll); Croydon (Coll); Dearne Valley (Coll); Derby; Doncaster (Univ Centre); Dudley (Coll); Dumfries and Galloway (Coll); East Lancashire (IHE); Farnborough (CT); Filton (Coll); Glamorgan; Gloucestershire (CAT); Greenwich; Grimsby (IFHE); Guildford (Coll); Hammersmith (Coll); Havering (Coll); Hendon (Coll); Henley (Coll); Herefordshire (CT); Highbury (Coll); Isle of Wight (Coll); Kent; Lancaster and Morecambe (Coll); Leeds Met; Lincoln; Llandrillo Cymru (Coll); London Met; Loughborough (Coll); Manchester Met; Manchester City (Coll); Mid Cheshire (Coll); Newcastle (Coll); Northbrook (Coll); Northampton; Norwich City (Coll); Nottingham New (Coll); Oaklands (Coll); Oldham (Coll); Park Lane Leeds (Coll); Pembrokeshire (Coll); Peterborough Reg (Coll); Plymouth; Portsmouth; Runshaw (Coll); Rutland (Coll); St Helens (Coll); SAC (Scottish CAg); Salisbury (Coll); Salford; Sandwell (Coll); Sheffield Hallam; Sheffield (Coll); Shrewsbury (CAT); Somerset (CAT); South Cheshire (Coll); South Devon (Coll); South Downs (Coll); South Nottingham (Coll); Southampton Solent; Southport (Coll); Staffordshire; Stockport (CFHE); Stoke on Trent (Coll); Stratford-upon-Avon (Coll); Suffolk (Univ Campus); Sunderland City (Coll); Sutton Coldfield (Coll); Swansea (IHE); Swansea (Coll); Teesside; Thames Valley; Tyne Met (Coll); UHI Millennium Inst (PC); Wakefield (Coll); Warwickshire (Coll); West Herts (Coll); West Thames (Coll); Wigan and Leigh (Coll); Wirral Met (Coll); Wolverhampton; Worcester; Worcester (CT); Worcestershire New (Coll); York (Coll); Yorkshire Coast (CFHE).

CHOOSING YOUR COURSE (SEE ALSO CH.1)

Subject information Tourism and Travel courses are popular; some are combined with Hospitality Management which provides students with specialisms in two areas. Courses involve business studies and a detailed study of tourism and travel. Industrial placements are frequently involved and language options are often included. See also **Appendix 2**. **Useful websites** www.wttc.org; www.abta.com; www.baha.org.uk.

Course variations Countryside Recreation and Tourism (Aberystwyth); International Tourism Resort Management (Blackpool and Fylde (Coll)); Entrepreneurship in Travel and Tourism (Brighton); Travel Journalism (Central Lancashire); European Tourism (Lincoln); Ecotourism (Napier); Cruise Operations Management (Plymouth); Adventure Tourism and Outdoor Pursuits (SAC (Scottish CAg)); Airline and Airport Management (Thames Valley). *NOW CHECK PROSPECTUSES AND WEBSITES FOR ANY RECENT CHANGES.*

Sandwich degree courses Aberystwyth; Bedfordshire; Birmingham (CFTCS); Bournemouth; Brighton; Bristol UWE; Central Lancashire; Glamorgan; Gloucestershire; Harper Adams (UC); Hertfordshire;

Huddersfield; Hull; Leeds Met; London Met; London South Bank; Manchester Met; Northumbria; Oxford Brookes; Paisley; Plymouth; Sheffield Hallam; Staffordshire; Sunderland; Surrey; Swansea (IHE); Ulster; Writtle (Coll).

ADMISSIONS INFORMATION

Number of applicants per place (approx) Aberystwyth 3; Bath Spa 5; Birmingham (CFTCS) 10; Bournemouth 16; Derby 4; Glamorgan 8; Glasgow Caledonian 30; Liverpool John Moores 10; Northumbria 6; Sheffield Hallam 12; Sunderland 2; Winchester 3.

Advice to applicants and planning the UCAS personal statement Work experience in the travel and tourism industry is important – in agencies, in the airline industry or hotels. This work could be described in detail. Any experience with people in sales work, dealing with the public – their problems and complaints – should also be included. Travel should be outlined, detailing places visited. Genuine interest in travel, diverse cultures and people. Good communication skills required. See also **Appendix 2**.

Misconceptions about this course Bath Spa The course is not purely vocational and operational: it also involves management issues. **Wolverhampton** Some applicants are uncertain whether or not to take a Business Management course instead of Tourism Management. They should be aware that the latter will equip them with a tourism-specific knowledge of business.

Selection interviews Yes Brighton, Derby, Glasgow Caledonian, Sunderland; **Some** Lincoln, Liverpool John Moores, Salford.

Interview advice and questions Past questions have included: What problems have you experienced when travelling? Questions on places visited. Experiences of air, rail and sea travel. What is marketing? What special qualities do you have that will be of use in the travel industry? See **Chapter 6**.

Applicants' impressions (A=Open day; B=Interview day) Bournemouth (A) A good tour of the University. The course was well explained. **Winchester** It was a very well organised open day. There were talks about the University and the course, followed by an informal talk with the tutor.

Reasons for rejection (non-academic) Wolverhampton English language competence.

AFTER-RESULTS ADVICE

Universities with vacancies in Clearing (2006) Aberystwyth; Anglia Ruskin; Bournemouth; Brighton; Bristol UWE; Canterbury Christ Church; Central Lancashire; Chester; Chichester; Derby; Gloucestershire; Greenwich; Hertfordshire; Huddersfield; Kent; Lincoln; Liverpool Hope; Liverpool John Moores; Manchester Met; Middlesex; Northumbria; Plymouth; Sheffield Hallam; Southampton Solent; Sunderland; Westminster; Winchester.

Offers to applicants repeating A-levels Same Birmingham (CFTCS), Chester, Derby, Lincoln, Liverpool John Moores, Manchester Met, Northumbria, Salford, Winchester, Wolverhampton.

GRADUATE DESTINATIONS AND EMPLOYMENT (2005 HESA)
Graduates surveyed 1375 **Employed** 910 **In further study** 55 **Assumed unemployed** 100.

OTHER DEGREE SUBJECTS FOR CONSIDERATION
Business Studies; Events Management; Heritage Management; Hospitality Management; Leisure and Recreation Management; Travel Management.

TOWN AND COUNTRY PLANNING

(including **Environmental Planning** and **Urban Studies;** see also **Development Studies, Environmental Science/Studies, Housing** and **Transport Management and Planning)**

NB The points totals shown to the left of the institutions are for ease of reference only. It must not be assumed that tariff points are always used by institutions or that they can be substituted for an offer in grades. The level of an offer is not necessarily indicative of the quality of a course.

COURSE OFFERS INFORMATION

Subject requirements/preferences GCSE English and mathematics required. **AL** No subjects specified.

Your target offers

300 pts **Birmingham** – BBB–BBC 300–280 pts (Urb Reg Plan courses)
Cardiff – 300 pts (Geog (Hum) Plan)
Dundee – BBB 300 pts 2nd yr entry (Twn Reg Plan; Geog Plan)
Newcastle – BBB–BBC (Twn Plan; Geog Plan)
Sheffield – BBB (Urb St Plan)

280 pts **Belfast (Queen's)** – BBC–BBB (Env Plan)
Liverpool – 280–260 pts (Twn Reg Plan; Env Plan; Urb Regn Plan)
London (QM) – 280–320 pts (Cts Econ Soc Chng)
London (UCL) – BBC+AS (Urb St; Urb Plan Des Mgt)

260 pts **Cardiff** – BCC 260 pts (Cty Reg Plan)
Heriot-Watt – 260 pts (Urb Reg Plan)
Leeds – BCC (Env Trans Plan)
Manchester – BCC (Cty Reg Dev; Land Plan Mgt; Twn Cntry Plan)
Northumbria – 260 pts (Plan Dev Surv)

240 pts **Aberdeen** – CCC (Spat Plan)
Anglia Ruskin – 240 pts (Env Plan)
Bangor – 240–280 pts (Env Plan Mgt)
Brighton – 240 pts (Urb St courses)
Bristol UWE – 240–280 pts (Prop Dev Plan; Plan Hous Renew; Plan Trans; Twn Cntry Plan)
Chester – 240 pts (Urb St)
Dundee – 240 pts CC+AL/2AS 1st yr entry (Twn Reg Plan; Geog Plan)
Kent – 240 pts (Urb St Soc Pol)
Oxford Brookes – CCC/BC **or** CCCc (Cty Reg Plan; Cits Env Des Dev)

230 pts **Sheffield Hallam** – 230 pts (Plan; Plan Trans; Urb Regn; Soty Cits)

180 pts **Liverpool John Moores** – 180 pts (Urb Plan)
UCE Birmingham – 180 pts (Plan Dev)

160 pts **London South Bank** – CC (Urb Env Plan)

Leeds Met – contact University

For information on how to read the Subject Tables, see **Chapter 7.**

Alternative offers
IB offers Birmingham 30–32 pts; Bristol UWE 26–30 pts; Manchester 28 pts; Newcastle 28 pts; Sheffield 30–33 pts.
Scottish offers See **Chapter 7**.

OTHER HIGHER EDUCATION COURSES IN THE SUBJECT FIELD

Foundation degrees (contact the institutions for details) Lambeth (Coll); London (Birk); North East Wales (IHE).

Higher National Diploma courses
100 pts   and below
Henley (Coll); Park Lane Leeds (Coll); Sheffield Hallam.

CHOOSING YOUR COURSE (SEE ALSO CH.1)

Subject information Town and Country Planning courses are very similar and some lead to qualification or part of a qualification as a member of the Royal Town Planning Institute (RTPI). Further information from the RTPI (see **Appendix 2**). **Useful websites** www.rtpi.org.uk; www.townplanningreview.org.

Course variations Urban Regional Planning (Birmingham); Environmental Planning (Liverpool); Landscape Planning and Management (Manchester); Planning and Development Surveying (Northumbria); Cities, Environment, Design and Development (Oxford Brookes); Urban Regeneration (Sheffield Hallam). *NOW CHECK PROSPECTUSES AND WEBSITES FOR ANY RECENT CHANGES.*

Universities and colleges teaching quality See www.tqi.ac.uk; www.qaa.ac.uk.

Top universities and colleges (Research) Cardiff*; Leeds*; Newcastle; Sheffield.

ADMISSIONS INFORMATION

Number of applicants per place (approx) Birmingham 2; Bristol UWE 6; Cardiff 6; Dundee 5; London (UCL) 6; London South Bank 3; Newcastle 9; Sheffield Hallam 6; UCE Birmingham 8.

Advice to applicants and planning the UCAS personal statement Visit your local planning office and discuss the career with planners. Know plans and proposed developments in your area and any objections to them. Study the history of town planning worldwide and the development of new towns in the United Kingdom during the 20th century, for example Bourneville, Milton Keynes, Port Sunlight, Welwyn Garden City, Cumbernauld, and the advantages and disadvantages which became apparent. See also **Appendix 2**.

Selection interviews **Yes** Bristol UWE, London (UCL), London South Bank, Newcastle; **Some** Cardiff, Dundee, UCE Birmingham.

Interview advice and questions Since Town and Country Planning courses are vocational, work experience in a planning office is relevant and questions are likely to be asked on the type of work done and the problems faced by planners. Questions in recent years have included: If you were re-planning your home county for the future, what points would you consider? How are statistics used in urban planning? How do you think the problem of inner cities can be solved? Have you visited your local planning office? See **Chapter 6**.

Reasons for rejection (non-academic) Lack of commitment to study for a professional qualification in Town Planning.

AFTER-RESULTS ADVICE

Universities with vacancies in Clearing (2006) Anglia Ruskin; Brighton; Bristol UWE; Heriot-Watt; Sheffield.

Offers to applicants repeating A-levels **Higher** Bristol UWE, Newcastle; **Same** Cardiff, Dundee, London South Bank, Oxford Brookes, UCE Birmingham.

GRADUATE DESTINATIONS AND EMPLOYMENT (2005 HESA)

Graduates surveyed 560 Employed 320 In further study 85 Assumed unemployed 25.

OTHER DEGREE SUBJECTS FOR CONSIDERATION

Architecture; Countryside Management; Environmental Studies; Geography; Heritage Management; Housing; Public Administration; Sociology; Surveying; Transport Management.

TRANSPORT MANAGEMENT AND PLANNING

(including **Supply Chain Management;** see also **Business Courses, Engineering/Engineering Sciences** and **Town and Country Planning**)

NB The points totals shown to the left of the institutions are for ease of reference only. It must not be assumed that tariff points are always used by institutions or that they can be substituted for an offer in grades. The level of an offer is not necessarily indicative of the quality of a course.

COURSE OFFERS INFORMATION

Subject requirements/preferences GCSE English and mathematics required. **Birmingham** Mathematics grade B. **AL** No subjects specified.

Your target offers

320 pts **Cardiff** – 320 pts (Bus Mgt (Log Ops))
300 pts **Leeds** – BBB (Mgt Trans St; Econ Trans St)
Loughborough – 300–260 pts (Trans Bus Mgt; Air Trans Mgt)
280 pts **Northumbria** – 280 pts+portfolio (Trans Des)
260 pts **Aston** – BCC–CCC (Trans Mgt; Log Mgt; Trans Plan GIS; Trans Env Plan; Constr Trans Plan)
240 pts **Bristol UWE** – 240–280 pts (Plan Trans)
Northumbria – 240 pts (Bus Sply Chn Mgt)
230 pts **Sheffield Hallam** – 230 pts inc 2AL (Plan Trans)
220 pts **Ulster** – CCD 220 pts (Trans Sply Chn Mgt)
200 pts **Coventry** – 200–240 pts (Trans Des; Trans Des Fut)
Liverpool John Moores – 200 pts (Mgt Trans Log)
London Met – 200 pts (Avn Mgt)
180 pts **Huddersfield** – 180–240 pts (Trans Log Mgt; Air Trans Log Mgt; Log Sply Chn Mgt; Log; Euro Log Mgt)
160 pts **Coventry** – 160–240 pts (Trans Prod Des)
140 pts **Bolton** – 140 pts (Log Sply Chn Mgt; Mtr Veh Trans)
120 pts **Buckinghamshire Chilterns (UC)** – 120–180 pts (Air Trans Plt Trg; Air Trav Mgt)
London Met – 120 pts (Transport)
100 pts **Bristol UWE** – 100 pts (Fdn Trans)
Loughborough – 100 pts (Fdn Trans Mgt)
80 pts **Swansea (IHE)** – 80–340 pts (Trans Mgt; Sply Chn Mgt; Mtrspo Mgt)

Alternative offers
IB offers Aston 30–31 pts; Bristol UWE 28–24 pts.
Scottish offers See **Chapter 7**.

OTHER HIGHER EDUCATION COURSES IN THE SUBJECT FIELD

Foundation degrees (contact institutions for details) Anglia Ruskin; Buckinghamshire Chilterns (UC); London Met; Myerscough (Coll); Newcastle (Coll); Thurrock (Coll).

Higher National Diploma courses (in Business Studies)
100 pts   and below
Glamorgan; Northumbria; Plymouth; Swansea (IHE); Worcestershire New (Coll).

CHOOSING YOUR COURSE (SEE ALSO CH.1)

Subject information Transport Management and Planning is a specialised branch of business studies with many applications on land, sea and air. It is not as popular as the less specialised Business Studies courses but is just as relevant and will provide the student with an excellent introduction to management and its problems. **Useful websites** www.cilt-international.com; www.transportweb.com; www.nats.co.uk; www.ciltuk.org.uk.

Course variations Transport Planning (Aston); Air Transport and Pilot Training (Buckinghamshire Chilterns (UC)); Business Management (Logistics Operations) (Cardiff); Transport and Product Design (Coventry); Aviation Management (London Met); Air Transport Management (Loughborough); Supply Chain Management (Northumbria). *NOW CHECK PROSPECTUSES AND WEBSITES FOR ANY RECENT CHANGES.*

Sandwich degree courses Aston; Huddersfield; Loughborough.

ADMISSIONS INFORMATION
Number of applicants per place (approx) Aston 5; Coventry 5; Huddersfield 5; Loughborough 11.

Advice to applicants and planning the UCAS personal statement Air, sea, road and rail transport are the main specialist areas. Contacts with those involved and work experience or work shadowing should be described in full. See also **Appendix 2**.

Selection interviews Yes Huddersfield, Loughborough; **Some** Aston.

Interview advice and questions Some knowledge of the transport industry (land, sea and air) is likely to be important at interview. Reading around the subject is also important, as are any contacts with management staff in the industries. Past questions have included: What developments are taking place to reduce the number of cars on the roads? What transport problems are there in your own locality? How did you travel to your interview? What problems did you encounter? How could they have been overcome? See **Chapter 6**.

AFTER-RESULTS ADVICE
Universities with vacancies in Clearing (2006) Aston; Bristol UWE; Coventry; Huddersfield; Leeds; Liverpool John Moores; London Met; Northumbria; Sheffield Hallam; Ulster.

Offers to applicants repeating A-levels Same Aston.

GRADUATE DESTINATIONS AND EMPLOYMENT (2005 HESA)
See under **Tourism and Travel**.

OTHER DEGREE SUBJECTS FOR CONSIDERATION
Environmental Studies; Marine Transport; Town and Country Planning; Urban Studies.

VETERINARY SCIENCE/MEDICINE
(including **Veterinary Nursing**)

NB The points totals shown to the left of the institutions are for ease of reference only. It must not be assumed that tariff points are always used by institutions or that they can be substituted for an offer in grades. The level of an offer is not necessarily indicative of the quality of a course.

NB For places in Veterinary Science/Medicine, applicants may select only four universities. Applicants to the University of Bristol Veterinary School, the University of Cambridge Veterinary School and the Royal Veterinary College, University of London are required to sit the BioMedical Admissions Test (BMAT) (see Chapter 6).

COURSE OFFERS INFORMATION
Subject requirements/preferences GCSE Grade B English, mathematics, physics, dual science if not at A-level. **Bristol, Glasgow** Grade A or B in physics. **Bristol** Grade A in five or six subjects. **Liverpool** English, mathematics, physics, dual science grade B if not at A-level. **AL** See offers below. A science subject may be required for Nursing courses.

Your target offers
360 pts and above
　　　　Bristol – AAA +BMAT (Vet Sci)

Cambridge – AAA +BMAT (inc AL chem+1 from phys/biol/maths) (Vet Med)
Liverpool – AAB+AL/AS 390 pts (Vet Sci)
London (RVC) – AAA–AAB +BMAT (inc AL chem+1 from biol/phys/maths) (Vet Med)
340 pts **Edinburgh** – AAB (inc A chem+2AL from biol/maths/phys) (Vet Med)
Glasgow – AAB (inc A chem+biol+phys/maths AB/BA) (Vet Med)
Nottingham – AAB (Vet Med Vet Srgy)
300 pts **Bristol** – BBB **or** BBbbb (inc AL chem+1 sci inc 4AS inc 1 non-sci) (Vet Pathogen)
Liverpool – BBB 300 pts (inc biol+sci) (Biovet Sci)
London (RVC) – BBB (BSc Vet Sci 3yrs – **not** a qualification to practise as a veterinary surgeon)
Nottingham – BBB (inc biol/chem/maths/phys) (Pre-Vet Sci (Univ Cert) 5 places. Direct entry to St George's Grenada, West Indies)
220 pts **Central Lancashire** – 220 pts (Vet Nurs)
200 pts **Anglia Ruskin** – 200 pts (Vet Nurs Sci)
Bristol UWE (Hartpury) – 200–240 pts (inc biol) (Biovet Sci; Vet Nurs Sci; Vet Prac Mgt; Eqn Dntl Sci)
Middlesex – 200–220 pts (Vet Nurs)
Napier – 200 pts (Vet Nurs)
160 pts **Bristol** – CC (inc AL sci, biol pref inc 2AS sci inc biol) (Vet Nurs)
Harper Adams (UC) – 160–240 pts (Biovet Sci; Vet Nurs Prac Mgt)
London (RVC) – CC–AA (Vet Nurs)
120 pts **Sparsholt (Coll)** – DD (inc sci) (Vet Nurs Sci)

Alternative offers

IB offers Bristol (Vet Sci) 38 pts, (Vet Path) 32 pts, (Vet Nurs) 26 pts; Bristol UWE 26 pts; Cambridge 38–42 pts; Liverpool 32–38 pts; Nottingham 38 pts.
Scottish offers See **Chapter 7**.

OTHER HIGHER EDUCATION COURSES IN THE SUBJECT FIELD

Foundation degrees (contact institutions for details) Askham Bryan (Coll); Cornwall (Coll); Harper Adams (UC); Hartpury (Coll); Kingston Maurward (Coll); London (RVC); Myerscough (Coll); Nottingham Trent; Rodbaston (Coll); Sparsholt (Coll); Warwickshire (Coll).

Higher National Diploma courses Barony (Coll); Bristol UWE (Hartpury); Central Lancashire; Northampton; Plymouth.

CHOOSING YOUR COURSE (SEE ALSO CH.1)

Subject information Veterinary Medicine/Science degrees enable students to acquire the professional skills and experience to qualify as veterinary surgeons. Courses follow the same pattern and combine a rigorous scientific training with practical experience. The demand for these courses is considerable (see above) and work experience is essential prior to application. See also **Appendix 2**. **Useful websites** www.vetweb.co.uk; www.rcvs.org.uk; www.bmat.org.uk; www.bvna.org.uk; www.spvs.org.uk.

Author's note Veterinary Science/Medicine is the most intensely competitive subject and, as in the case of Medicine, one or two offers and three rejections are not uncommon. As a result, the Royal College of Veterinary Surgeons has raised a number of points which are relevant to applicants and advisers:

(a) Every candidate for a Veterinary Medicine/Sciences degree course should be advised to spend a suitable period with a veterinarian in practice.

(b) A period spent in veterinary work may reveal a hitherto unsuspected allergy or sensitivity following contact with various animals.

(c) Potential applicants should be under no illusions about the difficulty of the task they have set themselves . . . five applicants for every available place . . . with no likelihood of places being increased at the present time.

(d) There are so many candidates who can produce the necessary level of scholastic attainment that other considerations have to be taken into account in making the choice. In most cases, the number of GCSE grade As will be crucial. This is current practice. Headteachers' reports and details of applicants' interests, activities and background are very relevant and are taken fully into consideration . . . applicants are reminded to include details of periods of time spent with veterinary surgeons.

(e) Any applicant who has not received an offer but who achieves the grades required for admission ought to write as soon as the results are known to the schools and enquire about the prospects of entry at the Clearing stage. All courses cover the same subject topics.

Course variations Veterinary Pathogenesis (Bristol); Equine Dental Science; Veterinary Practice Management (Bristol UWE (Hartpury)); Veterinary Nursing (Central Lancashire); Bioveterinary Science (Harper Adams (UC)); Pre-Veterinary Science course (Nottingham). *NOW CHECK PROSPECTUSES AND WEBSITES FOR ANY RECENT CHANGES.*

Universities and colleges teaching quality See www.tqi.ac.uk; www.qaa.ac.uk.

Top universities and colleges (Research) Bristol; Cambridge; Edinburgh; Glasgow; Liverpool; London (RVC).

ADMISSIONS INFORMATION

Number of applicants per place (approx) Bristol (Vet Sci) 16, (Vet Nurs) 4, (Vet Pathogen) 4; Cambridge 5; Edinburgh 17; Glasgow 20; Liverpool 12; London (RVC) 5.

Numbers of applicants (a UK **b** EU (non-UK) **c** non-EU **d** mature) London (RVC) **a**759 **b**71 **c**156 **d**172.

Advice to applicants and planning the UCAS personal statement Applicants for Veterinary Science must limit their choices to four universities and submit their applications by 15 October. They may add up to two alternative courses. However, if they receive and accept offers, and then perform better than expected, they will not be able to request vet schools to reconsider their applications. Work experience is essential for all applicants so discuss experiences in full, giving information about the size and type of practice and the type of work in which you were involved. **Bristol** Evidence of wide veterinary animal experience; evidence of initiative. The Veterinary Nursing course is a possible route to the BVSc degree. **Liverpool** The selection process involves three areas: academic ability to cope with the course; knowledge of vocational aspects of veterinary science acquired through work experience in veterinary practice and working with animals; personal attributes that demonstrate responsibility and self-motivation. **London (RVC)** Six weeks' hands-on experience needed: two weeks in a veterinary practice; two weeks with large domestic animals; two weeks with other animals, for example riding school, zoo, kennels. See also **Appendix 2**.

Misconceptions about this course Bristol UWE (Hartpury) (Vet Nurs Sci) Students think that the degree qualifies them as veterinary nurses but RCVS assessment/training is additional. **Liverpool** (Biovet Sci) Some applicants think that the course allows students to transfer to Veterinary Science: it does not.

Selection interviews All institutions.

Interview advice and questions Past questions have included: Why do you want to be a vet? Have you visited a veterinary practice? What did you see? Do you think there should be a Vet National Health

Service? What are your views on vivisection? What are your views on intensive factory farming? How can you justify thousands of pounds of taxpayers' money being spent on training you to be a vet when it could be used to train a civil engineer? When would you feel it your responsibility to tell battery hen farmers that they were being cruel to their livestock? What are your views on vegetarians? How does aspirin stop pain? Why does it only work for a certain length of time? Do you eat beef? Outline the BSE problem and European attitudes. Questions on A-level science syllabus. **Glasgow** Applicants complete a questionnaire prior to interview. Questions cover experience with animals, reasons for choice of career, animal welfare, teamwork, work experience, stressful situations. See **Chapter 6**.

Applicants' impressions (A=Open day; B=Interview day) Bristol UWE (Hartpury) (Vet Nurs Sci; B) I had a 15-minute interview. The department was very well equipped.

Reasons for rejection (non-academic) Failure to demonstrate motivation. Lack of basic knowledge or understanding of ethical and animal issues.

AFTER-RESULTS ADVICE
Universities with vacancies in Clearing (2006) Bioveterinary Science and Veterinary Nursing courses had vacancies
Liverpool All hopeful candidates, with or without the required grades in August, should contact the faculty office in writing or by email for advice about future prospects. They should do this before accepting an alternative course.

Offers to applicants repeating A-levels Higher London (RVC); **Same** Bristol UWE (Hartpury) (Vet Nurs Sci), Liverpool (candidates achieving the necessary grades are welcome to reapply); **Not acceptable** Edinburgh, Glasgow.

GRADUATE DESTINATIONS AND EMPLOYMENT (2005 HESA)
Graduates surveyed 315 **Employed** 280 **In further study** 15 **Assumed unemployed** 10.

OTHER DEGREE SUBJECTS FOR CONSIDERATION
Agricultural Science; Agriculture; Animal Sciences; Biological Sciences; Biology; Dentistry; Equine Dental Science; Equine Management; Equine Studies; Medicine; Zoology.

WELSH (CYMRAEG) and CELTIC
(including **Gaelic** and **Irish Studies**)

NB The points totals shown to the left of the institutions are for ease of reference only. It must not be assumed that tariff points are always used by institutions or that they can be substituted for an offer in grades. The level of an offer is not necessarily indicative of the quality of a course.

COURSE OFFERS INFORMATION
Subject requirements/preferences GCSE A foreign language or Welsh may be required. **AL** Welsh may be required for some courses.

Your target offers
360 pts **and above**
        Cambridge – AAA varies between colleges (A-Sxn Nrs Celt)
300 pts **Aberystwyth** – 300 pts (Modn Welsh St; Welsh Hist)
        Belfast (Queen's) – BBB–BBCb (Irish Celt courses)
        Edinburgh – BBB (Celt; Celt Arch; Celt Ger; Celt Ling; Celt Scand St; Celt Scot Hist St; Scot Lit; Celt Engl Lang; Celtic Engl/Scot Lit)
        Glasgow – BBB (Celt; Celt Civ)
280 pts **Cardiff** – BBC–BCC (Welsh; Anrhydedd; Cydanrhydedd)
        Swansea – 280–300 pts (Welsh courses)
260 pts **Bangor** – 260–220 pts (Welsh courses (taught in Welsh medium))
        Liverpool – BCC (Irish St Engl Lang Lit; Ir St Hist)

Stirling – BCC (Scot Lit)
240 pts **Aberdeen** – CCC (Celt Civ courses; Celt St; Gael St; Scot St)
Aberystwyth – 240 pts (Celt St; Ir Lang Lit; Welsh)
Liverpool – CCC 240 pts (Irish St)
Ulster – CCC–CCD 240–220 pts (Ir Lang Lit Ir St; Ir; Ir Lang)
220 pts **Bangor** – 220–200 pts (Cymraeg)
180 pts **Lampeter** – open admission policy (Welsh St; Cymraeg; Welsh Transl Subtit; Welsh Subtit)
UHI Millennium Inst – DDD 180 pts (Gael; Gael Lang Cult; Gael N Atlan St; Gael Media St)
160 pts **Glamorgan** – 160 pts (Modn Contemp Wls)
St Mary's (Coll) – 160–200 pts (Ir St)
140 pts **Glamorgan** – 140–160 pts (Prof Welsh courses)
Trinity Carmarthen (Coll) – 140 pts (Welsh biling prac)

Alternative offers
IB offers Cambridge 38–42 pts; Liverpool 32 pts.
Scottish offers See **Chapter 7**.

CHOOSING YOUR COURSE (SEE ALSO CH.1)

Subject information Irish, Scottish, Gaelic, Welsh, Breton, Manx, Cornish, Gaulish and Celtiberian are all included in this subject area. Courses may also include the history and civilisation of the Celtic peoples. **Useful websites** www.bwrdd-yr-iaith.org.uk; www.wales.gov.uk; www.bbc.co.uk/wales; www.daltai.com.

Course variations Irish Language and Literature (Aberystwyth); Celtic and Linguistics (Edinburgh); Modern and Contemporary Wales (Glamorgan); Welsh, Translating and Sub-titling (Lampeter). *NOW CHECK PROSPECTUSES AND WEBSITES FOR ANY RECENT CHANGES.*

Universities and colleges teaching quality See www.tqi.ac.uk; www.qaa.ac.uk.

Top universities and colleges (Research) Aberystwyth*; Belfast (Queen's); Bangor*; Cambridge*; Cardiff; Edinburgh; Swansea.

ADMISSIONS INFORMATION

Number of applicants per place (approx) Aberystwyth 6; Bangor 8; Cambridge 2; Cardiff 2; Lampeter 3; St Mary's (Coll) 3; Swansea 7.

Advice to applicants and planning the UCAS personal statement Interests in this field largely develop through literature, museum visits or archaeology which should be fully described in the UCAS application.

Selection interviews **Yes** Aberystwyth, Lampeter; **No** St Mary's (Coll).

Interview advice and questions Past questions have included: Why do you want to study this subject? What specific areas of Celtic culture interest you? What do you expect to gain by studying unusual subjects? See **Chapter 6**.

AFTER-RESULTS ADVICE

Universities with vacancies in Clearing (2006) All institutions.

Offers to applicants repeating A-levels **Same** Aberystwyth, Bangor, Cardiff, Lampeter, Swansea.

GRADUATE DESTINATIONS AND EMPLOYMENT (2005 HESA)

No data available but in 2004: **Graduates surveyed** 180 **Employed** 65 **In further study** 65 **Assumed unemployed** 5.

OTHER DEGREE SUBJECTS FOR CONSIDERATION

Anthropology; Archaeology; History.

ZOOLOGY

(see also **Agricultural Sciences/Agriculture, Animal Sciences** and **Biology**)

NB The points totals shown to the left of the institutions are for ease of reference only. It must not be assumed that tariff points are always used by institutions or that they can be substituted for an offer in grades. The level of an offer is not necessarily indicative of the quality of a course.

COURSE OFFERS INFORMATION

Subject requirements/preferences **GCSE Bristol** Grade A or B in chemistry and mathematics if not at A-level. **Edinburgh** Mathematics grade B. **Swansea** Majority of grade Bs or better. **AL** One or two sciences will be required.

Your target offers
360 pts and above
    Cambridge – AAA (Nat Sci (Zool))
340 pts Imperial London – AAB–ABB (Zoology)
320 pts Bristol – ABB–BBB (Zoology)
    Cardiff – ABB–BBB (Zoology)
    Durham – ABB (Zool; Zool Ind)
    London (RH) – ABB–BBB (Zool; Zool Physiol)
    London (UCL) – ABB+AS (Zoology)
    Manchester – ABB–BBB (Zool; Zool Ind; Zool Modn Lang)
    Newcastle – ABB (Zoology)
    Nottingham – ABB–AAB (Zoology)
    Sheffield – ABB (MBiol Sci Zool)
300 pts Aberdeen – 300 pts 2nd yr entry (Zoology)
    Birmingham – BBB 300 pts (Biol Sci (Anim Biol))
    Dundee – 300 pts 2nd yr entry (Zoology)
    Edinburgh – BBB (Zoology)
    Glasgow – BBB (Zoology)
    Leeds – BBB 300 pts (Zool; Zool (Anim Sci))
    Leicester – BBB (Biol Sci (Zool))
    Reading – 300 pts (Zoology)
    St Andrews – BBB (Zoology)
    Sheffield – BBB (BSc Zool)
    Southampton – BBB 300 pts (Zoology)
280 pts Liverpool – BBC–BBB 280–300 pts (Zool; Zool Evol Psy)
    London (QM) – 280 pts (Zoology)
    Swansea – 280–300 pts (3AL) 220–200 pts (2AL) (Zoology)
260 pts Aberdeen – BCC 1st yr entry (Zoology)
    Belfast (Queen's) – BCC–AB (Zoology)
    Reading – 260 pts (Bot Zool)
240 pts Bangor – 240–280 pts (Zool; Zool Cons; Zool Mar Biol; Mar Biol Zool; Mar Vrtbrt Zool)
    Dundee – 240 pts 1st yr entry (Zoology)
    Hull – 240–260 pts (Aqua Zool)
220 pts Aberystwyth – 220–280 pts (Zool; Zool Microbiol)
    Liverpool John Moores – 220 pts (Zoology)
    Stirling – CCD (Anim Biol)
200 pts Anglia Ruskin – 200 pts (Zool; Wldlf Biol; Nat Hist courses)
    Napier – 200 pts (Anim Biol)
180 pts Salford – 180 pts (Wldlf Prac Cons; Wldlf Cons Zoo Biol)
    Staffordshire – 180 pts check with admissions tutor (Anim Biol Cons)
160 pts Blackpool and Fylde (Coll) – 160 pts (Sci Nat Hist Illus)
    Derby – 160–180 pts (Zoology)
    Roehampton – 160–200 pts (Zoology)
    Wolverhampton – 160–200 pts (Anim Biol courses)

120 pts Paisley – DD (Biol Zool)
80 pts and below
Eastleigh (Coll) – (Fdn Sci)

Alternative offers
IB offers Cambridge 38–42 pts; London (UCL) 32–36 pts; Manchester 32–35 pts; Newcastle 32–35 pts;
St Andrews 31 pts; Salford 24 pts; Sheffield 35 pts.
Scottish offers See **Chapter 7**.

OTHER HIGHER EDUCATION COURSES IN THE SUBJECT FIELD

Foundation degrees (contact institutions for details) (See also **Animal Sciences**) Cornwall (Coll);
Sparsholt (Coll).

CHOOSING YOUR COURSE (SEE ALSO CH.1)

Subject information Zoology courses have a biological science foundation and could cover animal
ecology, marine and fisheries biology, animal population, development and behaviour and, on some
courses, wildlife management and fisheries. **Useful websites** www.scienceyear.com;
www.zoo.cam.ac.uk/ioz; www.zsl.org; www.academicinfo.net/zoo.html.

Course variations Zoology with Microbiology (Aberystwyth); Zoology with Conservation, Marine
Vertebrate Zoology (Bangor); Scientific and Natural History Illustration (Blackpool and Fylde (Coll));
Aquatic Zoology (Hull); Natural History (Kingston); Wildlife Conservation and Zoo Biology (Salford). *NOW
CHECK PROSPECTUSES AND WEBSITES FOR ANY RECENT CHANGES.*

Universities and colleges teaching quality See www.tqi.ac.uk; www.qaa.ac.uk.

Top universities and colleges (Research) Cambridge*.

Sandwich degree courses Cardiff; Durham; Manchester; Paisley.

ADMISSIONS INFORMATION

Number of applicants per place (approx) Aberystwyth 8; Bangor 3; Bristol 13; Cardiff 8; Durham 11;
Leeds 7; Liverpool John Moores 6; London (RH) 6, (UCL) 8; Newcastle 15; Nottingham 9; Swansea 6.

Advice to applicants and planning the UCAS personal statement Interests in animals should be
described, together with any first-hand experience gained. Visits to zoos, farms, fish farms etc and field
courses attended should be described, together with any special points of interest that you noted.

Selection interviews **Yes** Cambridge, Durham, Hull, Liverpool, London (RH), Newcastle; **Some** Cardiff,
Derby, Dundee, Roehampton, Swansea.

Interview questions Past questions have included: Why do you want to study Zoology? What career do
you hope to follow on graduation? Specimens may be given to identify. Questions usually asked on the
A-level subjects. See **Chapter 6**.

AFTER-RESULTS ADVICE

Universities with vacancies in Clearing (2006) Aberdeen; Aberystwyth; Bangor; Belfast (Queen's);
Birmingham; Cardiff; Derby; Dundee; Glasgow; Hull; Leeds; Leicester; Liverpool; Liverpool John Moores;
London (QM), (RH); Napier; Newcastle; Nottingham; Reading; Salford; Sheffield; Southampton; Stirling;
Swansea.

Offers to applicants repeating A-levels **Higher** Bristol, Hull, Leeds, Swansea; **Same** Aberystwyth,
Bangor, Cardiff, Derby, Dundee, Durham, Liverpool, Liverpool John Moores, London (RH), Roehampton,
Swansea.

GRADUATE DESTINATIONS AND EMPLOYMENT (2005 HESA)

Graduates surveyed 690 **Employed** 315 **In further study** 140 **Assumed unemployed** 50.

OTHER DEGREE SUBJECTS FOR CONSIDERATION

Animal Sciences; Aquaculture; Biological Sciences; Biology; Ecology; Fisheries Management; Marine
Biology; Parasitology; Veterinary Science.

9 | INFORMATION FOR INTERNATIONAL STUDENTS

The choice of a subject to study (from over 50,000 degree courses) and of a university or college (from more than 300 institutions) is a major task for students living in the United Kingdom (UK). For overseas and European Union (EU) applicants it is even greater, and the decisions that have to be made need much careful planning, preferably beginning two years before the start of the course.

SELECTION POLICIES

The first reason for making early contact with your preferred institution is to check their requirements for your chosen subject and their selection policies for overseas applicants. For example, for all Art and some Architecture courses you will have to present a portfolio of work or slides. For Music courses your application often will have to be accompanied by a recording you have made of your playing or singing and, in many cases, a personal audition will be necessary. Attendance at an interview in this country is compulsory for some universities and for some courses. At other institutions the interview may take place either in the UK or with a university or college representative in your own country.

The ability to speak and write good English is essential and many institutions require evidence of competence, for example scores from the International English Language Testing System (IELTS) or from the Test of English as a Foreign Language (TOEFL) (see www.ielts.org and www.ets.org/toefl). For some institutions you may have to send examples of your written work. Each institution provides information about its English language entry requirements and a summary of this is given for each university listed below.

In **Chapter 2** of this book you will find a directory of universities and colleges in the UK, together with their contact details. Most universities and colleges in the UK have an overseas student adviser who can advise you on these and other points you need to consider, such as passports, visas, entry certificates, evidence of financial support, medical certificates, medical insurance, and the numbers of overseas students in the university from your own country. All these details are very important and need to be considered at the same time as choosing your course and institution.

The subject tables in **Chapter 8** provide a comprehensive picture of courses on offer and of comparative entry levels. However, before making an application, other factors should be considered such as English language entry requirements (see above), the availability of English language teaching, living costs, tuition fees and any scholarships or other awards which might be offered. Detailed information about these can be obtained from the international offices in each university or college, from British higher education fairs throughout the world and from the British Council offices abroad and from websites: see www.britishcouncil.org; www.education.org.

Below is a brief summary of the arrangements made by each university in the UK for students aiming to take a full-time degree programme. The information is presented as follows:

* Institution.
* International student numbers.
* English language entry requirements for degree programmes shown in either IELTS or TOEFL scores. These vary between universities and courses. For the IELTS, scores can range from 5.5 to 7.5, and for

the TOEFL computer-based test, scores can range from a minimum of 213; for the written TOEFL the usual minimum entry level is 5.0. For full details contact the university or college.

* Arrangements for English tuition.
* International Foundation courses.
* Annual tuition fees for degree courses (approximate). Tuition fees also usually include fees for examinations and graduation. These figures are approximate and are subject to change each year. EU students pay 'home student' fees, except for those from the Channel Islands and the Isle of Man; also, from 2007/8 students from the British Overseas Territories will be treated as home students for fee purposes at universities and other institutions of higher education.
* Annual living costs. These are approximate and represent the costs for a single student over the year. The living costs shown cover university accommodation (usually guaranteed for the first year only), food, books, clothing and travel in the UK, but not travel to or from the UK. (Costs are likely to rise year by year in line with the rate of inflation in the UK, currently around 3% per year.) Overseas students are normally permitted to take part-time work for a period of up to 20 hours per week.
* Scholarships and awards for non-EU students (most universities offer awards for EU students).

UNIVERSITY INFORMATION FOR INTERNATIONAL STUDENTS

Aberdeen International students 14%, 115 nationalities; *English language entry requirement (or equivalent):* IELTS 6.0; for Medicine 7.0. Four-week English course available in August before the start of the academic year. *Fees:* Arts subjects £9000, Science subjects £11,500, Medicine £21,000. *Living costs:* £6000. Some scholarships and grants.

Abertay Dundee International students 10%; *English language entry requirement (or equivalent):* IELTS 5.5. Pre-sessional English course available, also full-time English course September to May and free English tuition throughout degree course. *Fees:* all courses £8000. *Living costs:* £5000. Several scholarships available, including special awards for students from India and from some countries in the Far East and the USA.

Aberystwyth A large number of international students. *English language entry requirement (or equivalent):* IELTS 6.5. Full-time tuition in English available. *Fees:* Arts subjects £7500, Science subjects £9800, joint courses £9000. *Living costs:* £6000. Awards for students from the Far East.

American InterContinental There are 91 overseas students currently following courses at the University. *Living costs:* £10,000 (minimum).

Anglia Ruskin International students 21%. *English language entry requirement (or equivalent):* IELTS 5.5. A one-year International Foundation programme available. *Fees:* Arts subjects £7750, Science subjects £8750, Optometry £9800, Nursing £13,000. *Living costs:* £6800.

Arts London A large number of international students. *English language entry requirement (or equivalent):* IELTS 6.5. Courses in Fashion Promotion, Acting, Directing require IELTS 7.5. Language Centre courses in academic English for 12, 24, 34 or 36 weeks. *Fees:* degree courses £10,500. *Living costs:* £10,000.

Aston Over 1000 students from over 80 countries, with 15% of the total student population from overseas. International Orientation programme at the beginning of the academic year. *English language entry requirement (or equivalent):* IELTS 6.0–6.5. International Foundation programme offered as a bridge to the degree courses. Pre-sessional English classes also available of five and ten weeks duration. *Fees:* non-Science programmes £8500, Engineering and Science courses £10,500. *Living costs:* £7000. Scholarships offered, including bursaries for Engineering and Science subjects.

Bangor International students 10% from 70 countries. Lower cost of living than many other UK cities. *English language entry requirement (or equivalent):* IELTS 6.0. Pre-study English course starting

September, January or April depending on level of English proficiency, leads to International Foundation course. One-month or two-month courses before starting degree course also offered. *Fees:* £8500. *Living costs:* £5500. Scholarships available.

Bath 1500 international students from around 100 countries. *English language entry requirement (or equivalent):* IELTS 6.0. Pre-degree language courses offered, ranging from one month to one year. *Fees:* Arts and Social Science subjects £9000, Science and Engineering courses £11,250. *Living costs:* £7500. Scholarships and awards available, including residential awards for applicants from the Far East and Kenya.

Bath Spa A new university (2005). Students from 40 countries. *English language entry requirement (or equivalent):* IELTS 5.5 for subjects supported by the Undergraduate Course for International Students (UCIS). Foundation courses available for students below this score. Subjects not supported by UCIS, entry level IELTS 6.0. *Fees:* £8000–£9500 (plus studio fees £150–£250 for Art and Design courses). *Living costs:* £6500.

Bedfordshire 3000 EU and international students. *English language entry requirement (or equivalent):* IELTS 6.0. General English programmes are offered, including a summer school. *Fees:* One-year International Foundation course and English language course £6300, one-semester course £3500; Arts degree courses £7500, Science degree courses £8300. *Living costs:* £6000.

Belfast (Queen's) 2400 international students from over 60 countries. *English language entry requirement (or equivalent):* IELTS 6.0–6.5. Special English language summer schools and pre-university language courses are provided, also weekly language courses. Three-day orientation programme held before the start of the academic year. *Fees:* classroom subjects £8000, laboratory/workshop subjects £9800, Medicine/Dentistry pre-clinical £11,200, clinical £20,000. *Living costs:* £7500. Awards available.

Birmingham 4000 international students from 152 countries. *English language entry requirement (or equivalent):* IELTS 6.0. Six, ten and 20-week English language programmes available, depending on language proficiency, ranging from IELTS 4.5 to 5.5. *Fees:* non-laboratory subjects £8700, laboratory subjects £10,900, clinical programmes £20,200. *Living costs:* £7500. International Foundation programme available. Awards are offered by some subject departments including Bioscience, Computer Science, Earth Sciences, Law, Psychology; there are also Engineering scholarships for students from Malaysia.

Bolton 70 countries represented. *English language entry requirement (or equivalent):* IELTS 6.0. Courses start in September, some in February. Pre-sessional and in-session English tuition. *Fees:* £8000. *Living costs:* £5500.

Bournemouth A large number of international students. *English language entry requirement (or equivalent):* IELTS 6.0. Preparatory English programme offered, starting in January, April or July depending on applicant's level of English (entry IELTS 4.5/5.0/5.5). Several language schools in the town (see www.englishuk.com.uk or www.baselt.org.uk). Pre-sessional study skills programme also offered. *Fees:* £7400–£8400. *Living costs:* £8000. Some subject awards available.

Bradford Over 100 countries represented. *English language entry requirement (or equivalent):* IELTS 6.0. Some students may be admitted to Year 2, depending on qualifications. *Fees:* Science and Engineering courses £8500, other courses £8000 (lower fees for students taking a sandwich year – see **Chapter 1**). *Living costs:* £7500. Ten scholarships to cover the duration of the course.

Brighton 2000 international students from over 100 countries. *English language entry requirement (or equivalent):* IELTS 6.0 (or 5.5 for less linguistically demanding subjects). New four-year degree programme (UK4) includes preparatory year. *Fees:* £8000. Fixed fees possible. *Living costs:* £8000. Links with other nationals at Brighton. Merit scholarships for students from some countries in the Far East, Africa and Norway.

Bristol Students from over 100 countries. *English language entry requirement (or equivalent):* IELTS 6.5 (possibly lower for some Science and Engineering subjects). *Fees:* Arts subjects £8500, Science subjects £12,000, Clinical subjects £21,000. *Living costs:* £6000–£8500. Some bursaries and scholarships for one year from some subject departments including Law, Medicine, Dentistry and Veterinary Science.

Bristol UWE More than 1750 international students. *English language entry requirement (or equivalent):* IELTS 6.0. English language preparatory and pre-sessional courses offered. English modules can also be taken throughout your degree. *Fees:* classroom-based subjects £7000, laboratory subjects £7500. *Living costs:* £6000–£8000. Some partial fee scholarships available in Computing, Mathematics and Engineering, and Law scholarships for students from the Far East, South Africa, the West Indies and North America.

Brunel 2000 international students from over 110 countries. *English language entry requirement (or equivalent):* IELTS 6.0 for science/technology subjects, 7.0 for Law, 6.5 for other subjects. English language tuition offered during and before the course but only to improve existing skills. *Fees:* non-laboratory subjects £8400, laboratory subjects £10,900. *Living costs:* £8000. Twenty bursaries offered.

Buckingham 80 nationalities represented at this small university. *English language entry requirement (or equivalent):* IELTS 6.0. *Fees:* £32,500 (total for two-year courses). *Living costs:* £7500. Tuition fee discount for students from the Bahamas, Bulgaria and India. Some scholarships for students from the Far East, Russia and Eastern Europe.

Cambridge 1000 international undergraduate students. *English language entry requirement (or equivalent):* IELTS 7.0 overall, with minimum of 6.0 in each element. TOEFL (written) 600 (minimum) and at least 5.0 in TOEFL test of written English. *Fees:* classroom-based subjects £9700, laboratory-based subjects £11,300, clinical subjects £20,500; College fees (average) £3800. *Living costs:* £7000. Awards available, also scholarships for students from Hong Kong.

Canterbury Christ Church A new university (2005). *English language entry requirement (or equivalent):* IELTS 6.0. *Fees:* £7500. *Living costs:* £7000.

Cardiff 3500 international students from 100 countries. *English language entry requirement (or equivalent):* IELTS 6.5. Comprehensive selection of pre-sessional language courses from three weeks to nine months. Induction course for all students. International Foundation courses for Business, Law, Engineering, Computer Science and Health and Life Sciences. *Fees:* £8700. *Living costs:* £7700. Law scholarships offered on the basis of academic merit.

Central Lancashire Large international student population from many countries. *English language entry requirement (or equivalent):* IELTS 6.0. Competence in written and spoken English required on application. *Fees:* classroom subjects £7700, laboratory subjects £8800. *Living costs:* £6500.

Chester A new university (2005). English language entry requirement (or equivalent): IELTS 6.0. International Foundation year available for Business Studies students. Fees: £7500. Living costs: £7500.

Chichester A new university (2005). International students from several countries. *English language entry requirement (or equivalent):* IELTS 6.0. *Fees:* £7500–£9000. *Living costs:* £8000.

City A large international community. *English language entry requirement (or equivalent):* IELTS 6.0 (6.5 for Business, Law and Journalism). August and September pre-sessional English language courses, and in-session English workshops. International Foundation programmes in Law, Business, Engineering and Management. *Fees:* Arts-based programmes £8000, Business programmes £9700, Engineering programmes £8800, Science-based programmes £10,300. *Living costs:* £9500. Scholarships available for applicants for Actuarial Science, Engineering (Cypriot applicants only) and Law.

Coventry 2500 international students. *English language entry requirement (or equivalent):* IELTS 6.0. *Fees:* £7700. *Living costs:* £7200. Scholarships available.

Cumbria A new university (2007). *English language entry requirement (or equivalent):* IELTS 6.0. *Fees:* Undergraduate £7175. English language programmes: 1 month £825, 2 months £1650, 3 months £2475. *Living costs:* £6500.

De Montfort Over 1000 international students from over 100 countries. *English language entry requirement (or equivalent):* IELTS 6.5 (lower for some faculties). In-session English tuition in some degree courses. One-year International Foundation Certificate courses in Business and Law. Orientation programme in September for all students. *Fees:* classroom subjects £8900, laboratory subjects £9900. *Living costs:* £8000. Some scholarships for overseas students.

Derby Students from 70 countries. *English language entry requirement (or equivalent):* IELTS 6.0. Courses offered to those needing tuition in English language. Foundation courses (£5200) and pre-sessional intensive English tuition (£2000), and also language support whilst studying for degree. *Fees:* £7700. *Living costs:* £6800. International scholarships available for applicants from some countries in the Far East.

Dundee Students from 83 countries. *English language entry requirement (or equivalent):* IELTS 6.0. Foundation courses in English and for Business and Art and Design courses. *Fees:* classroom-based courses £8300, laboratory-based courses £10,300, clinical courses £20,200. *Living costs:* £7000. Some awards for overseas students in Arts and Social Sciences, Law, Accountancy, Science and Engineering and Art and Design.

Durham 1600 international students from over 120 countries. *English language entry requirement (or equivalent):* IELTS 6.5. Three-day induction programme before the start of the academic year. Intensive English language course if required if standard of English does not meet the required level. *Fees:* Clinical Medicine £18,900, Science, Engineering and Technology courses £10,900, all other courses £8800. *Living costs:* £5000, plus college fees (Durham); £2800 (Stockton). Scholarships for nationals from some Far Eastern countries.

East Anglia 2000 international students from 120 countries. *English language entry requirement (or equivalent):* IELTS 6.0 (higher for some courses). Four, eight and twelve-week pre-sessional courses in English and tuition during degree courses. *Fees:* classroom-based subjects £8500, laboratory-based subjects £10,500. *Living costs:* £570 per month. Scholarships available including awards, based on academic merit, cover part of the cost of tuition fees.

East London 3300 international students from 120 countries. *English language entry requirement (or equivalent):* IELTS 6.0. One-year full-time preparatory English course available. Fees: £7500–£9500. Living costs: £9500.

Edge Hill This new university near Liverpool has a small number of international students. *English language entry requirement (or equivalent):* IELTS 6.5. *Fees:* £6800. *Living costs:* £5500.

Edinburgh 4000 international students from 120 countries. *English language entry requirement (or equivalent):* IELTS 6.0–6.5. English language support. *Fees:* £9800–£12,500, Clinical Medicine £22,300. *Living costs:* £7500. Awards include two India scholarships.

Essex International students from over 125 countries. *English language entry requirement (or equivalent):* IELTS 6.0–6.5. English language courses available before entry to degree course. *Fees:* non-Science courses £8700, laboratory courses £10,900. *Living costs:* £7700. Some funding available for students in need.

Exeter Over 1500 international students from 120 countries. *English language entry requirement (or equivalent):* IELTS 6.5. Full-time Foundation programme in English, with opportunity to specialise in Physical Sciences, Computer Science, Business, Politics, History, Sociology or Law. Also pre-sessional courses in English starting in July, August or September as well as in-session support. *Fees:* non-Science programmes £8900, Science and Engineering programmes £10,800. *Living costs:* £7000. Awards available, including some subject and South East Asian scholarships.

Glamorgan 1500 international students from 60 different countries. *English language entry requirement (or equivalent):* IELTS from 5.0. Pre-sessional course offered in English, and also a 10–14-week English language skills programme. An International Foundation programme is also offered. *Fees:* £8800. *Living costs:* £7500.

Glasgow Over 2000 international students. *English language entry requirement (or equivalent):* IELTS 6.0 (higher for some courses). The English as a Foreign Language Unit offers intensive five-week pre-sessional language courses in Foundation programme covering English language and study skills. *Fees:* classroom-based subjects £8900, Engineering, Sciences, Nursing £10,900, Clinical Medicine and Dentistry £19,300, Veterinary Medicine £15,900. *Living costs:* £7000. Fee-waiver scholarships and automatic Fourth Year scholarships available (not for Dentistry, Medicine or Veterinary Science).

Glasgow Caledonian Students from 70 countries. *English language entry requirement (or equivalent):* IELTS 6.0. English language programmes available. *Fees:* £7700–£8500. *Living costs:* £7000.

Gloucestershire *English language entry requirement (or equivalent):* IELTS 5.5. English language support and mentor scheme with other international students. *Fees:* £8500–£9200. *Living costs:* £6700.

Greenwich 4500 international students (including those from European countries). *English language entry requirement (or equivalent):* IELTS 6.0. Pre-sessional English courses, Access and International Foundation programmes. *Fees:* classroom-based subjects £8500, laboratory-based subjects £9500. *Living costs:* from £8000. Scholarships open to applicants from 25 countries.

Heriot-Watt Twenty-three per cent of the student population comes from over 90 countries. *English language entry requirement (or equivalent):* IELTS 6.5, and 6.8 for language courses. Several English language courses are offered; these range in length depending on students' requirements. *Fees:* £7900–£10,900. *Living costs:* £6300. Some international scholarships are available worth £1500–£2000 for one year.

Hertfordshire Students from over 90 countries are at present studying at the University. *English language entry requirement (or equivalent):* IELTS 6.0. English language tuition is offered in the one-year International Foundation course, in a course for the Foundation Certificate in English for Academic Purposes, and in a pre-sessional intensive English course held during the summer months. *Fees:* £9200–£10,000. *Living costs:* £6500.

Huddersfield International students from over 80 countries. *English language entry requirement (or equivalent):* IELTS 6.0. English language courses available and a one-year International Foundation course in English language with options in Business, Computing, Engineering, Mathematics and Music. Students guaranteed entry to Huddersfield courses on completion. *Fees:* classroom-based subjects £7500, laboratory-based subjects £8400, Foundation programme £6700. *Living costs:* £5700.

Hull Ten per cent of students from outside the EU. *English language entry requirement (or equivalent):* IELTS 6.0. English summer study programme through the three months before the start of the academic year. In-session study in English also available. Foundation programmes for Business and Management degrees. *Fees:* non-Science-based courses £8500, Science-based programmes £10,500, for the year in industry courses and for year-abroad courses £4500–£5500. *Living costs:* £6500. Hull has one of the best overseas scholarship provision of any British university, including full-tuition and 30 partial-tuition awards (50% of fees).

Imperial London 2200 international students from over 110 countries. *English language entry requirement (or equivalent):* IELTS 6.0–7.0. *Fees:* Mathematics and Computer Science £10,700, Chemistry £15,000, Computing £15,500, Pre-clinical Medicine £13,900, Clinical Medicine £22,500, other courses £14,300. *Living costs:* £10,000 (minimum). Scholarships available.

Keele Large number of overseas students. *English language entry requirement (or equivalent):* IELTS 6.0–6.5. English language summer school before the start of degree course. International Foundation year degree programmes (entry IELTS 4.5). *Fees:* classroom-based subjects £8500, Foundation year £8000, Science-based subjects £9500 (one science) £10700 (two sciences), Science Foundation year £10,300. *Living costs:* £9000. Some bursaries valued at £1300 per annum.

Kent Comprehensive English language support service. *English language entry requirement (or equivalent):* IELTS 5.5. Foundation programmes (entry IELTS 5.0) to prepare students for Arts, Business, Science, Engineering and Law courses. Non-degree courses also offered for one year or less. *Fees:* laboratory courses £11,400, non-laboratory courses £9000. *Living costs:* £8500. Certificate of chest X-ray required. Limited number of scholarships available and some general scholarships for students from Hong Kong and Singapore.

Kingston 2000 international students from over 70 countries. *English language entry requirement (or equivalent):* IELTS 6.5. Foundation level Science and Technology courses. Pre-sessional English language courses and free English support during degree studies. *Fees:* classroom-based subjects £8500, studio-based subjects (including Design and some Computing and Science subjects) £9400, and most laboratory-based subjects £10,000. *Living costs:* £9000.

Lampeter International students represented at this small distinctive university. *English language entry requirement (or equivalent):* IELTS 6.0. International Foundation programme. Accommodation possible for each year at university. *Fees:* £7500. *Living costs:* £5500.

Lancaster Twenty per cent of student population from over 100 countries. *English language entry requirement (or equivalent):* IELTS 5.5–6.0. Pre-sessional and in-session English language courses cover reading, writing, listening and speaking skills. On-campus accommodation throughout your degree course. *Fees:* £9000–£11,000. *Living costs:* £6500.

Leeds 4000 students from outside the UK. *English language entry requirement (or equivalent):* IELTS 6.0. *Fees:* Arts and Social Sciences £9000, for Engineering and Science subjects £11,500 and for Clinical Medicine and Dentistry £20,900. *Living costs:* £9000. Partial scholarships offered.

Leeds Metropolitan 2500 international students from 110 countries. *English language entry requirement (or equivalent):* IELTS 6.0 (IELTS 4.0 or 5.0 for the International Foundation programme, starting September or February). Also general English courses. *Fees:* £8100–£9500. *Living costs:* £9000. Small number of scholarships.

Leicester Fourteen per cent of full-time students are from outside the UK. *English language entry requirement (or equivalent):* IELTS 6.0 (IELTS 6.5 for Law, Medicine, Arts and Social Science programmes, 5.5 for the Foundation year). English language preparatory programmes and on-going support Foundation programme. *Fees:* £8900–£9900, Medicine £20,400. *Living costs:* £7500. Scholarships and bursaries awarded in a range of subjects, with special awards for students from India and Singapore.

Lincoln 2000 students from over 40 countries. *English language entry requirement (or equivalent):* IELTS 6.0. *Fees:* classroom-based subjects £8200, laboratory-based subjects £8700. *Living costs:* £7500.

Liverpool 2600 international students from over 100 countries. *English language entry requirement (or equivalent):* IELTS 6.0–6.5. International Foundation course (IELTS 5.0–5.5). *Fees:* Arts subjects £8800, Engineering and Science £10,900, Dentistry and Medicine £16,700, Veterinary Science £15,700. *Living costs:* £8800. Scholarships available, including special awards for students from Hong Kong and Singapore.

Liverpool Hope A new university (2005). 700 international students. *English language entry requirement (or equivalent):* IELTS 6.0. Language courses available. *Fees:* £8800. *Living costs:* £8800.

Liverpool John Moores A large number of overseas students. *English language entry requirement (or equivalent):* IELTS 6.0. Pre-sessional and in-session English tuition available. *Fees:* classroom-based subjects £8200, laboratory-based subjects £8700. *Living costs:* £8800. Some awards available.

London (Central School of Speech and Drama) International students from over 40 countries are currently following courses. *Fees:* from £10,000. *Living costs:* £10,000.

London (Goldsmiths) Large number of overseas students. *English language entry requirement (or equivalent):* IELTS 6.5; IELTS 5.5 for Extension degrees and IELTS 5.0 for entry to the one-year Foundation course. Certificate course in Language and Contemporary Culture or pre-sessional programmes available. *Fees:* classroom-based subjects £8600, Art and Design, Computer Science, Drama, European Studies, Media and Communications and Social Work £11,400. *Living costs:* £10,000.

London (Heythrop College) A small college; students can take part in activities in any of the colleges belonging to London University. *English language entry requirement (or equivalent):* IELTS 6.0. *Fees:* £8900. *Living costs:* £10,000.

London (King's College) A large number of international students. *English language entry requirement (or equivalent):* IELTS 6.5 for Engineering, Nursing, Science courses, 7.0 for Dentistry, Law, Medicine, Physiotherapy and 7.5 for Humanities, Social Sciences. Pre-sessional summer courses and a one-year Foundation course available. *Fees:* classroom-based subjects £11,100, laboratory-based subjects £13,900, clinically based subjects £24,700. *Living costs:* £10,000. Awards available, including Hong Kong scholarships.

London (Queen Mary) Large number of international students. *English language entry requirement (or equivalent):* IELTS 6.5. International Foundation course covering English language tuition and specialist courses in Business, Management, Economics, Mathematics, Spanish, Geography and European Studies. The course guarantees progression to linked degree courses including Law. *Fees:* Arts, Social Studies, Law £9500, Engineering and Science £11,500, Medicine Years 1 and 2 £14,500, Years 3–5 £21,500, Dentistry Years 1 and 2 £12,800, Years 3–5 £22,000. *Living costs:* £10,000. Several departments operate scholarship schemes for overseas students.

London (Royal Holloway) Twenty per cent of students from over 120 countries. *English language entry requirement (or equivalent):* IELTS 4.0–5.5 for English language programmes. Ten-month Foundation course with studies in English language and introduction to specialist studies in a range of degree subjects. *Fees:* Foundation course £8500, classroom-based subjects £11,500, laboratory-based subjects £12,700, Computer Science and Media Arts £13,900. *Living costs:* £10,000. International student scholarships offered.

London (Royal Veterinary College) *Fees:* £16,500. *Living costs:* £10,000. Contact for further information tel 020 7468 5000; Fax 020 7388 2342.

London (St George's) *Fees:* BSc programmes £15,900, MBBS Years 1 and 2 £14,000, MBBS Years 3–5 £23,700. *Living costs:* £10,000.

London (School of Economics) 150 countries represented. *English language entry requirement (or equivalent):* TOEFL 627 (paper test). Language Centre courses available. *Fees:* £10,900. *Living costs:* £10,000.

London (School of Oriental and African Studies) Large number of international students. *English language entry requirement (or equivalent):* IELTS 7.0. A one-year Foundation programme and English language courses available with an entry requirement of IELTS 4.0. Three-day International Students' Orientation programme. *Fees:* £10,500. *Living costs:* £10,000.

London (School of Pharmacy) *English language entry requirement (or equivalent):* IELTS 6.5. *Living costs:* £10,000. For further information tel 020 7753 5831; Fax 020 7753 5829.

London (University College) Some 6460 students (34% of the total student body) are from countries outside the UK. *English language entry requirement (or equivalent):* Science and Engineering IELTS 6.5, Arts courses 7.0, Speech Science and Law 7.5. *Fees:* Arts and Social Sciences £10,900, Science, Engineering,

Archaeology, Fine Art, Built Environment, Architecture £14,000, Law £11,000, Medicine £20,800. *Living costs:* £10,000. Scholarships available, including awards for students from Hong Kong and China.

London Metropolitan Over 4000 students from 147 countries. *English language entry requirement (or equivalent):* IELTS 5.5. One-year International Foundation programme (IELTS entry requirement 4.5). Full range of English courses. *Fees:* £7700, Foundation programme £5500. *Living costs:* £10,000.

London South Bank 2500 international students, including 1300 from the EU. *English language entry requirement (or equivalent):* IELTS 6.0. Pre-study English course and a University Foundation course for overseas students. *Fees:* £7300–£7700. *Living costs:* £10,000.

Loughborough 800 students from outside the UK. *English language entry requirement (or equivalent):* IELTS 6.5. Special courses offered by the English Language Study Unit. One-week residential course for international students before the start of the academic year. *Fees:* Arts courses £9500, Science and Engineering courses £11,900. *Living costs:* £6500. Eight merit-based scholarships offered.

Manchester A high proportion of international students. *English language entry requirement (or equivalent):* IELTS 6.0–7.5, depending on the high linguistic demands of courses eg Law, Management and Medicine. Foundation Year programme in Informatics, Engineering, Science and Biological Sciences. English language courses are also offered. *Fees:* Arts courses £9200, Science or studio-based courses £11,500, clinical courses in Medicine and Dentistry £20,400. *Living costs:* £8500. Some scholarships and bursaries are available.

Manchester Metropolitan A large number of international students. *English language entry requirement (or equivalent):* IELTS 6.0. English language courses in January, April and July. *Fees:* £8000–£8500, Architecture £11,000. *Living costs:* £8500.

Middlesex International students from 30 countries around the world. *English language entry requirement (or equivalent):* IELTS 6.0. Foundation course (IELTS entry requirement 4.5). Extended English language course from September to July. International summer school. *Fees:* International Foundation course £6300, degree courses £8900–£9400. *Living costs:* £9000–£10,000.

Napier Large intake of international students. *English language entry requirement (or equivalent):* IELTS 5.5. English language programmes in September and January; English language support through Foundation programmes. *Fees:* £7900–£9000. *Living costs:* £7000.

Newcastle 2500 students from outside the UK. *English language entry requirement (or equivalent):* IELTS 6.5 (7.0 for English, Law and Medicine). English language support and Foundation programmes in Arts and Social Sciences, Business and Finance, Computing, Science and Engineering. *Fees:* Tuition fees vary between courses: classroom-based subjects £8400, laboratory, studio and pre-clinical Medicine £11,300, Clinical Medicine and Dentistry courses £20,500. *Living costs:* £7600. Some awards available.

Newport International students from 50 countries. *English language entry requirement (or equivalent):* IELTS 6.0. *Fees:* £7500–£8500. *Living costs:* £5,500.

Northampton 700 students from over 100 countries are enrolled on courses at this new (2005) university. *English language entry requirement (or equivalent):* IELTS 6.0. English language courses available. *Fees:* £7500. *Living costs:* £6500.

Northumbria 2500 international students from over 80 countries. *English language entry requirement (or equivalent):* IELTS 5.5–6.5. English language and Foundation courses. *Fees:* classroom-based courses £7400, laboratory-based courses £8000. *Living costs:* £7600. Country scholarships for students from over 15 countries; some merit-based course scholarships.

Nottingham Students from over 130 countries. *English language entry requirement (or equivalent):* IELTS 6.0–6.5 (7.5 for Medicine). *Fees:* Arts, Law and Social Sciences £9500–£12,500, Science and

Engineering £12,500–£13,300, Medicine £20,500. *Living costs:* £7000. Scholarships for siblings and science applicants.

Nottingham Trent Large number of overseas students. *English language entry requirement (or equivalent):* IELTS 6.5. English language courses (19, 10 and 5 weeks duration) available. *Fees:* classroom-based subjects £8500, laboratory-based subjects £9500. *Living costs:* £7000. Discounted overseas fees for some applicants for Art and Design courses.

Open University Courses are open to students throughout the world with study on-line or by way of educational partners. Tutorial support is by telephone, fax, computer conferencing or email. Non-EU students' fees vary depending on courses.

Oxford Large proportion of international students. *English language entry requirement (or equivalent):* IELTS 7.5 (minimum), TOEFL 650 (275 in the computer-based TOEFL). *Fees:* Arts subjects and Mathematics £8800, Science subjects, Music and Fine Art £11,300, Clinical Medicine £20,300. *Living costs:* £8500. University and college scholarships and awards.

Oxford Brookes Large number of international students. *English language entry requirement (or equivalent):* IELTS scores for Engineering and Construction 5.5; for Business, Social Sciences, Computing and Humanities 6.0; for Law and Psychology 6.5. Large number of English language support courses from two weeks to two years offered by the Centre for English Language Studies. Fees: £8700. Living costs: £8000. Engineering scholarships and family awards.

Paisley 700 international students. *English language entry requirement (or equivalent):* IELTS 6.0. English language Foundation course available. *Fees:* classroom-based courses £7900, laboratory-based courses £8700. *Living costs:* £7000. Some first-year scholarships.

Plymouth *English language entry requirement (or equivalent):* IELTS 6.5. 'English for University' courses available with IELTS entry requirement of 4.5. *Fees:* £7900–£8500, depending on subject. *Living costs:* £7,500. Scholarships for applicants from Malaysia.

Portsmouth Students from over 100 countries. *English language entry requirement (or equivalent):* IELTS 6.0 (5.5 for Foundation-level study). Induction, academic skills and language courses available. *Fees:* £8500–£9500. *Living costs:* £7500. Scholarships for first-year students.

Reading 3000 students from 135 countries. *English language entry requirement (or equivalent):* IELTS 6.5–7.0. International Foundation programme offering English language tuition and specialist studies in a choice of 14 subjects. Other pre-sessional English courses offered. *Fees:* £8600 for International Foundation programme, £8400–£9400 non-laboratory courses, £10,500 for courses with a significant laboratory content. *Living costs:* £6000. Some scholarships offered.

Richmond, The American International University in London Contact the Admissions Officer for details of entry requirements for all countries. Qualifications gained under education systems outside the American high school grading system will be assessed for equivalence. Students holding advanced qualifications (for example French Baccalaureate, GCE A-levels, the German Abitur) may be awarded course credit towards the Bachelor's degree. *Living costs:* £7500–£8500.

Robert Gordon 500 international students from over 50 countries. *English language entry requirement (or equivalent):* IELTS 6.0. Pre-entry English programme requirement IELTS 5.0 or above. *Fees:* £8500–£10,300. *Living costs:* £4500. Partial scholarship scheme.

Roehampton *English language entry requirement (or equivalent):* IELTS 5.5–6.0. *Fees:* £7900. *Living costs:* £7500.

St Andrews Twenty-six per cent of students from overseas. *English language entry requirement (or equivalent):* IELTS 6.5. Pre-entry English and study skills programmes and Foundation courses specialising in Arts, Science or Social Science subjects. *Fees:* Arts, Divinity and Sciences £11,300, Medicine £14,500. *Living costs:* £7500. Scholarships available.

Salford 1500 international students. *English language entry requirement (or equivalent):* IELTS 6.0. English study programmes and a very comprehensive International Foundation year. *Fees:* International Foundation courses £7300–£7900, classroom-based courses £8000, laboratory-based degree courses £10,200. *Living costs:* £7000.

Sheffield 3700 international students. *English language entry requirement (or equivalent):* IELTS 6.0. Preparatory English courses (one–nine months) and an international summer school with English classes. *Fees:* Arts and Social Sciences £10,100, Architecture £10,300, Law £9900, Science £10,300, Engineering £11,700, Medicine £20,800. *Living costs:* £7000. Scholarships available for applicants from Africa and the Far East, for siblings and alumni.

Sheffield Hallam 3000 international students from over 80 countries. *English language entry requirement (or equivalent):* IELTS 6.0. English language tuition available on four, eight and twelve week courses (£810, £1700 and £2200 respectively and IELTS entry requirement 4.5). *Fees:* Arts subjects £7800, Science subjects £8800, Engineering £10,700. *Living costs:* £7000.

Southampton 2000 international students. *English language entry requirement (or equivalent):* IELTS 6.0–6.5. English courses offered and also an International Foundation course covering Arts, Humanities, Social Sciences and Law. *Fees:* Arts-based subjects £8800, Science-based subjects and Pre-clinical Medicine £11,300, Clinical Medicine £20,800. *Living costs:* £7500. Awards available in Computer Science, Electronics, Law, Mathematics and Science.

Southampton Solent A new university (2005). Students from over 50 countries. *English language entry requirement (or equivalent):* IELTS 6.0. Induction programme and language tuition available. *Fees:* Contact +44 (0)23 8031 9129; e-mail international@solent.ac.uk. *Living costs:* £7500.

Staffordshire Students from over 70 countries. *English language entry requirement (or equivalent):* IELTS 5.5–6.0. English tuition available. *Fees:* £7800. *Living costs:* £7500.

Stirling Thirteen per cent overseas students from 70 nationalities. *English language entry requirement (or equivalent):* IELTS 6.0. English language tuition available. *Fees:* classroom-based subjects £8400, laboratory-based subjects £10,300. *Living costs:* £5500. Some scholarships for students from South East Asia.

Strathclyde Students from 90 countries. *English language entry requirement (or equivalent):* IELTS 6.5. Pre-entry and pre-sessional English tuition available. *Fees:* Science and Engineering courses £10,700, Law, Arts and Social Sciences £8600, Education and Business £8700. *Living costs:* £6000.

Sunderland A large number of international students. *English language entry requirement (or equivalent):* IELTS 5.5–6.0. English language tuition available. *Fees:* Arts subjects £8400, Science subjects £8600. *Living costs:* £5500.

Surrey A large international community with 43% from the Far East. *English language entry requirement (or equivalent):* IELTS 6.0. English language courses and summer courses offered. *Fees:* Arts courses £8700–£9900, Science, Engineering and Management courses £11,100. *Living costs:* £6500. Scholarships and bursaries offered, including awards for students on Civil Engineering courses.

Sussex 2500 international students. *English language entry requirement (or equivalent):* IELTS 6.5. English language and study skills courses available. International Foundation courses offered, covering English language tuition and a choice from Humanities, Law, Media Studies, Social Sciences and Cultural Studies and Science and Technology. *Fees:* International Foundation courses £7500–£8800, classroom-based subjects £9400, laboratory-based subjects £11,800. *Living costs:* £7000. Forty international scholarships.

Swansea Students from over 100 countries. *English language entry requirement (or equivalent):* IELTS 6.0. Pre-sessional English language courses available and on-going support during degree courses. *Fees:* Arts-based courses £8400, Science-based courses £11,000. *Living costs:* £5500. Some overseas scholarships and prizes.

Teesside Students from over 75 countries. *English language entry requirement (or equivalent):* IELTS 6.5 for Law, English and Humanities, 5.5 for Engineering, Science Technology and Computing courses and 6.0 for all other courses. Free English courses available throughout the year while following degree programmes. International summer school available. *Fees:* classroom-based courses £7400, laboratory-based courses £8400. *Living costs:* £5500.

Thames Valley A large number of international students. *English language entry requirement (or equivalent):* IELTS 5.0 for the International Foundation programme and 5.5 for undergraduate courses. English language support available and also pre-sessional courses. *Fees:* Arts-based courses £7800, Science-based courses £4500. *Living costs:* £9000.

UCE Birmingham Large number of international students. *English language entry requirement (or equivalent):* IELTS 6.0. Pre-sessional language courses and in-session language support. Orientation programme for all students. Fees: £8000–£9700. Living costs: £7000. Music bursaries.

Ulster Students from over 40 countries. *Fees:* £7800 for degree and diploma courses, Foundation course £5400. *Living costs:* £5500.

Warwick 3500 international students. *English language entry requirement (or equivalent):* IELTS 6.0 for Science courses, 6.5 for Arts courses, 6.5 for MORSE courses, and 7.0 for Social Studies and Business courses. English support available. *Fees:* Arts courses £8800, Science courses £11,100, Medical School Year 1 £10,800, Years 2–4 £19,900. *Living costs:* £6500. Over 20 awards available for overseas students.

Westminster Students from 148 countries (51% Asian). *English language entry requirement (or equivalent):* IELTS 6.0. International Foundation certificate courses available focusing on the Built Environment, Mathematics and Computing or Social Sciences and Literature. *Fees:* classroom-based subjects £8500, laboratory-based subjects £8900. *Living costs:* £9400.

Winchester A new university (2005). 150 international students from 30 countries. *English language entry requirement (or equivalent):* IELTS 6.0. Language courses available. *Fees:* £7000–£9000. *Living costs:* £7500.

Worcester A new university (2005). *English language entry requirement (or equivalent):* IELTS 6.0. *Fees:* £7000–£8000. *Living costs:* £6000.

Wolverhampton A large number of international students. *English language entry requirement (or equivalent):* IELTS 6.0. English courses available over one or two months or longer. International student programme. *Fees:* undergraduate courses £7900, £6800 for the international student programme. *Living costs:* £6000. Twenty Scholarships for Excellence offered.

York Fifteen per cent of students from outside the UK. *English language entry requirement (or equivalent):* IELTS 6.0. Six-month and pre-sessional English language courses. Intensive vacation courses. *Fees:* sciences £11,500, other courses £8900. *Living costs:* £6300. Several scholarships for overseas students.

York St John *English language entry requirement (or equivalent):* IELTS 6.0 (3 year degree course or 4 year course including Foundation year). *Fees:* £7900, 10-week English language course £1900, Pre-sessional 4-week course £760. *Living costs:* £6500.

BRITISH OVERSEAS TERRITORIES STUDENTS

Proposals have been announced which will mean that from 2007/2008 students from British Overseas Territories will be treated as home students for fee purposes at universities and other institutions of higher education in the UK. The territories to which these changes will apply are:

British Overseas Territories Anguilla, Bermuda, British Antarctic Territory, British Indian Ocean Territory, British Virgin Islands, Cayman Islands, Falkland Islands, Montserrat, Pitcairn Islands, South Georgia and the South Sandwich Islands, St Helena and its Dependencies, Turks and Caicos Islands.

Overseas Territories of other EU member states Greenland, Faroe Islands (Denmark), Netherlands Antilles (Bonaire, Curacao, Saba, St Eustatius, St Marten), Aruba (Netherlands), New Caledonia, French Polynesia, Wallis and Futura, Mayotte, St Pierre et Miquelon (France).

APPENDIX 1
INTERNATIONAL QUALIFICATIONS

Universities in the UK accept a range of international qualifications and those which normally satisfy the minimum general entrance requirements are listed below. However, the specific levels of achievement or grades required for entry to degree courses with international qualifications will vary, depending on the popularity of the university or college and the chosen degree programme. (The subject tables in **Chapter 8** provide a guide to the levels of entry to courses.) Students not holding the required qualifications should consider taking an International Foundation course.

International students whose mother tongue is not English and/or who have not studied for their secondary education in English will be required to pass an English test such as IELTS (International English Language Testing System) or TOEFL (the Test of English as a Foreign Language). Entry requirements vary between universities and courses. For the IELTS, scores can range from 5.5 to 7.5, for the TOEFL computer-based test scores can range from a minimum of 213, and for the TOEFL written test the minimum entry score is 500 (see www.ielts.org and www.ets.org/toefl).

Algeria Baccalaureate de l'Enseignement Secondaire
Argentina Completion of Year One of Licenciado/Professional Title
Australia Completion of Year 12 certificates
Austria Reifazeugnis/Maturazeugnis
Bahrain Two-year diploma or associate degree
Bangladesh Bachelor of Arts, Science and Commerce
Belgium Certificat d'Enseignement Secondaire Superieur
Bermuda Diploma of Arts and Science
Bosnia-Herzegovina Secondary School Leaving Diploma
Brazil Completion of Ensino Medio and a good pass in the Vestibular
Brunei Brunei GCE A-level
Bulgaria Diploma za Zavarshino Sredno Obrazovanie (Diploma of Completed Secondary Education)
Canada Completion of Grade 12 secondary/high school certificate or equivalent
Chile Completion of secondary education and a good pass in the Prueba de Conocimientos Especificos
China Completion of one year of a Bachelor degree from a recognised university with good grades
Croatia Matura (Secondary school leaving diploma)
Cyprus Apolytirion/Lise Bitirme Diploma with good grades
Czech Republic Vysvedceni o Maturitni Zkousce/Maturita
Denmark Studentereksamen (HF), (HHX), (HTX)
Egypt Completion of year one of a Bachelor degree or two-year Diploma
Finland Ylioppilastutkinoto/Studentexamen (Matriculation certificate)
France French Baccalaureate
Gambia West African Examinations Council Advanced Level
Georgia Successful completion of Year One of a Bachelor degree
Germany Abitur
Ghana West African High School Certificate/A-levels
Greece Apolytirion of Eniaio Lykeio (previously Apolytirion of Lykeio)
Hong Kong A-levels
Hungary Erettsegi/Matura

Iceland Studentsprof
India High grades from Standard XII School Leaving examinations from certain examination boards
Ireland Irish Leaving Certificate Higher Level
Israel Bagrut
Italy Diploma Conseguito con l'Esame di Stato (formerly the Diploma di Matura) with good grades
Japan Junior College Diploma
Kenya Cambridge Overseas Higher School Certificate
Lebanon Successful completion of year one of Licence
Malaysia Sijil Tinggi Persekolahan Malaysia (STPM, Malaysia Higher School Certificate)
Mauritius Cambridge Overseas Higher School Certificate or A-levels
Mexico Successful completion of year one of Licenciado
Netherlands Voorbereidend Wetenschappelijk Onderwijs (VWO)
Nigeria Successful completion of year one of a Bachelor degree
Norway Diploma of a completed 3-year course of upper secondary education
Pakistan Bachelor degree
Poland Matura/Swiadectwo Dojrzalosci
Portugal Certificado di Fim de Estudos Secundarios with good grades
Russian Federation Diploma of completed Specialised Secondary Education or successful completion of first year of Bakalav
Saudi Arabia Successful completion of first year of a Bachelor degree
Singapore Polytechnic Diploma or A-levels
South Korea Junior College Diploma
Spain Curso de Orientacion Universitaria (COU) with good grades
Sri Lanka A-levels
Sweden Fullstandigt Slutbetyg fran Gymnasieskolan
Taiwan Junior College Diploma
Thailand Successful completion of year one of a Bachelor degree
Turkey Devlet Lise Diplomasi (State High School Diploma) with good grades
Uganda East African Advanced Certificate of Education
Ukraine Successful completion of year one of Bakakavre
USA Good grades from the High School Graduation Diploma with SAT and/or APT
Yugoslavia (**Serbia** and **Montenegro**) Secondary School Leaving Diploma

APPENDIX 2
PROFESSIONAL ASSOCIATIONS

Professional associations vary in size and function and many offer examinations to provide members with vocational qualifications. However, many of the larger bodies do not conduct examinations but accept evidence provided by the satisfactory completion of appropriate degree and diploma courses. When applying for courses in vocational subjects, therefore, it is important to check whether your chosen course is accredited by a professional association, since membership of such bodies is usually necessary for progression in your chosen career after graduation.

Information about careers, which you can use as background information for your UCAS application, can be obtained from the organisations below listed under the subject table headings used in **Chapter 8**. Full details of professional associations, their examinations and the degree courses accredited to them are published in *British Qualifications* (see **Appendix 3**).

Some additional organisations that can provide useful careers-related information are listed below under the subject table headings and other sources of relevant information are indicated in the subject tables of **Chapter 8** and in **Appendix 3**.

Accountancy/Accounting
Association of Accounting Technicians www.aat.org.uk
Association of International Accountants www.aia.org.uk
Association of Chartered Certified Accountants www.accaglobal.com
Chartered Institute of Public Finance and Accountancy www.cipfa.org.uk
Chartered Institute of Management Accountants www.cimaglobal.com
Institute of Accounting Technicians in Ireland www.iati.ie
Institute of Chartered Accountants in England and Wales www.icaew.co.uk
Institute of Chartered Accountants of Scotland www.icas.org.uk
Institute of Chartered Accountants in Ireland www.icai.ie
Institute of Financial Accountants www.ifa.org.uk
Institute of Internal Auditors www.iia.org.uk

Actuarial Science/Studies
Faculty of Actuaries www.actuaries.org.uk
Institute of Actuaries www.actuaries.org.uk

Agricultural Sciences/Agriculture
Royal Agricultural Society of England www.rase.org.uk

Animal Sciences
British Horse Society www.bhs.org.uk
British Society of Animal Science www.bsas.org.uk

Anthropology
Association of Social Anthropologists of the UK and Commonwealth www.theasa.org

Archaeology
Council for British Archaeology www.britarch.ac.uk
Institute of Field Archaeologists www.archaeologists.net

Architecture
Chartered Institute of Architectural Technologists www.ciat.org.uk
Royal Incorporation of Architects in Scotland www.rias.org.uk
Royal Institute of British Architects www.riba.org

Art and Design
Arts Council England www.artscouncil.org.uk
Association of Illustrators www.theaoi.co
Association of Photographers www.the-aop.org
British Association of Art Therapists www.baat.org.
British Association of Paintings Conservator-Restorers www.bapcr.org.uk
British Institute of Professional Photography www.bipp.com.
Chartered Society of Designers www.csd.org.uk
Crafts Council www.craftscouncil.org.uk
Design Council www.designcouncil.org.uk
Institute of Professional Goldsmiths www.ipgold.org.uk
National Society for Education in Art and Design www.nsead.org
Professional Accreditation of Conservator-Restorers www.pacr.org.uk
Royal British Society of Sculptors www.rbs.org.uk
Scottish Arts Council www.scottisharts.org.uk

Astronomy/Astrophysics
Royal Astronomical Society www.ras.org.uk

Biochemistry (see also Chemistry)
Association of Clinical Biochemistry www.acb.org.uk

Biological Sciences/Biology
British Society for Human Genetics www.bshg.org.uk
Genetics Society www.genetics.org.uk
Institute of Biology www.iob.org

Building
Chartered Institute of Building www.ciob.org.uk
Chartered Institution of Building Services Engineers www.cibse.org
Construction Industry Training Board (CITB) www.citb.org.uk

Business Courses
Chartered Institute of Personnel and Development www.cipd.co.uk
Chartered Institute of Public Relations www.ipr.org.uk
Chartered Management Institute www.managers.org.uk
Communication, Advertising and Marketing Education Foundation (CAM Foundation) www.camfoundation.com
Council for Administration www.cfa.uk.com
Institute of Administrative Management www.instam.org
Institute of Chartered Secretaries and Administrators www.icsa.org.uk
Institute of Export www.export.org.uk
Institute of Practitioners in Advertising www.ipa.co.uk
Institute of Qualified Professional Secretaries www.iqps.org
Institute of Sales and Marketing Management www.ismm.co.uk

Chemistry
Royal Society of Chemistry www.rsc.org
Institute of Nanotechnology www.nano.org.uk

Computer Courses
British Computer Society www.bcs.org
Institute of Information Technology Training www.iitt.org.uk
Institution of Analysts and Programmers www.iap.org.uk
Institute for the Management of Information Systems www.imis.org.uk

Consumer Studies/Sciences
Institute of Consumer Sciences (incorporating Home Economics) www.institute-consumer-sciences.co.uk

Dance
Council for Dance Education and Training www.cdet.org.uk

Dentistry
British Association of Dental Nurses www.badn.org.uk
British Association of Dental Therapists www.badt.org.uk
British Dental Association www.bda.org
British Dental Hygienists' Association www.bdha.org.uk
Dental Technicians Association www.dta-uk.org
General Dental Council www.gdc-uk.org

Dietetics
British Dietetic Association www.bda.uk.com

Drama
National Council for Drama Training www.ncdt.co.uk

Education and Teacher Training
Department for Education and Skills www.dfes.gov.uk
General Teaching Council for Scotland www.gtcs.org.uk
Training and Development Agency for Schools www.tda.gov.uk

Engineering/Engineering Sciences
Energy Institute www.energyinst.org.uk
Engineering Council UK www.engc.org.uk
Institute of Acoustics www.ioa.org.uk
Institute for Manufacturing www.ifm.eng.cam.ac.uk
Institute of Marine Engineering, Science and Technology www.imarest.org
Institution of Agricultural Engineers www.iagre.org
Institution of Civil Engineers www.ice.org.uk
Institution of Engineering and Technology www.theiet.org
Institution of Mechanical Engineers www.imeche.org.uk
Institution of Nuclear Engineers www.inuce.org.uk
Royal Aeronautical Society www.raes.org.uk

Environmental Science/Studies
Chartered Institute of Environmental Health www.cieh.org
Chartered Institution of Wastes Management www.ciwm.co.uk
Chartered Institution of Water and Environmental Management www.ciwem.org
Environment Agency www.environment-agency.gov.uk
Institute of Ecology and Environmental Management www.ieem.org.uk
Institution of Environmental Sciences www.ies-uk.org.uk
Institution of Occupational Safety and Health www.iosh.co.uk
Royal Environmental Health Institute of Scotland www.rehis.org
Society for the Environment www.socenv.org.uk

Film, Radio, Video and TV Studies
British Film Institute www.bfi.org.uk
Skillset (The Sector Skills Council for the Audio Visual Industries) www.skillset.org

Finance (*including Banking and Insurance*)
Chartered Institute of Bankers in Scotland www.ciobs.org.uk
Chartered Institute of Loss Adjusters www.cila.co.uk
Chartered Insurance Institute www.cii.co.uk
Financial Services Skills Council www.fssc.org.uk
Institute of Financial Services www.ifslearning.com
Personal Finance Society www.thepfs.org
Securities and Investment Institute www.securities-institute.org.uk

Food Science/Studies and Technology
Institute of Food Science and Technology www.ifst.org

Forestry
Institute of Chartered Foresters www.charteredforesters.org
Institute of Wood Science www.iwsc.org.uk
Royal Forestry Society www.rfs.org.uk.

Geography
British Cartographic Society www.cartography.org.uk
Royal Geographical Society www.rgs.org
Royal Meteorological Society www.rmets.org

Geology/Geological Sciences
Geological Society www.geolsoc.org.uk

Health Sciences/Studies
British Academy of Audiology www.baaudiology.org
British Association of Prosthetists and Orthotists www.bapo.com
British Chiropractic Association www.chiropractic-uk.co.uk
British and Irish Orthoptic Society www.orthoptics.org.uk
British Occupational Hygiene Society www.bohs.org
British Osteopathic Association and General Osteopathic Council www.osteopathy.org.uk
Institute for Complementary Medicine www.i-c-m.org.uk
Institution of Occupational Safety and Health www.iosh.co.uk
Society of Homeopaths www.homeopathy-soh.org

History
Royal Historical Society www.rhs.ac.uk

Horticulture
Institute of Horticulture www.horticulture.org.uk

Hospitality and Hotel Management
Hotel and Catering International Management Association www.hcima.org.uk
People 1st www.people1st.co.uk

Housing
Chartered Institute of Housing www.cih.org

Human Resource Management
Chartered Institute of Personnel and Development www.cipd.co.uk

Information Management
Chartered Institute of Library and Information Professionals www.cilip.org.uk

Landscape Architecture
Landscape Institute www.l-i.org.uk

Languages
Chartered Institute of Linguists www.iol.org.uk
Institute of Translation and Interpreting www.iti.org.uk

Law
Bar Council www.barcouncil.org.uk
Faculty of Advocates www.advocates.org.uk
Law Society www.lawsociety.org.uk
Law Society of Northern Ireland www.lawsoc-ni.org
Law Society of Scotland www.lawscot.org.uk

Leisure and Recreation Management/Studies
Institute of Leisure and Amenity Management www.ilam.co.uk

Linguistics
Royal College of Speech and Language Therapists www.rcslt.org

Marine/Maritime Studies
Nautical Institute www.nautinst.org

Marketing
Chartered Institute of Marketing www.cim.co.uk
Institute of Sales and Marketing Management www.ismm.co.uk

Materials Science/Metallurgy
Institute of Materials, Minerals and Mining www.iom3.org

Mathematics
Council for Mathematical Sciences www.cms.ac.uk
Institute of Mathematics and its Applications www.ima.org.uk
London Mathematical Society www.lms.ac.uk
Mathematical Association www.m-a.org.uk

Media Studies
British Broadcasting Corporation www.bbc.co.uk/jobs
National Council for the Training of Journalists www.nctj.com
Skillset (The Sector Skills Council for the Audio Visual Industries) www.skillset.org
Society of Authors www.societyofauthors.net
Society for Editors and Proofreaders www.sfep.org.uk

Medicine
British Medical Association www.bma.org.uk
General Medical Council www.gmc-uk.org
Institute for Complementary Medicine www.i-c-m.org.uk

Microbiology (see Biological Sciences)

Music
Incorporated Society of Musicians www.ism.org.
Institute of Musical Instrument Technology www.imit.org.uk

Naval Architecture
Royal Institution of Naval Architects www.rina.org.uk

Nursing and Midwifery
Community Practitioners' and Health Visitors' Association www.amicustheunion.org/~cphva
Northern Ireland Practice and Educational Council for Nursing and Midwifery www.n-i.nhs.uk
Nursing and Midwifery Council www.nmc-uk.org
Royal College of Midwives www.rcm.org.uk
Royal College of Nursing www.rcn.org.uk

Nutrition (see *Dietetics*)

Occupational Therapy
British Association/College of Occupational Therapists www.cot.co.uk

Optometry
Association of British Dispensing Opticians www.abdo.org.uk
British and Irish Orthoptic Society www.orthoptics.org.uk
College of Optometrists www.college-optometrists.org
General Optical Council www.optical.org

Pharmacology
British Toxicology Society www.thebts.org
Royal Pharmaceutical Society of Great Britain www.rpsgb.org.uk

Pharmacy
Royal Pharmaceutical Society of Great Britain www.rpsgb.org.uk

Photography
Association of Photographers www.the-aop.org
British Institute of Professional Photography www.bipp.com
Royal Photographic Society www.rps.org

Physical Education (see *Education* and *Sports Studies/Sciences*)

Physics
Institute of Physics www.iop.org
Institute of Physics and Engineering in Medicine www.ipem.org.uk

Physiotherapy
Association of Chartered Physiotherapists in Animal Therapy www.acpat.org.uk
Chartered Society of Physiotherapy www.csp.org.uk

Plant Sciences (see *Biological Sciences*)

Podiatry
Society of Chiropodists and Podiatrists www.feetforlife.org

Property Management/Development
Chartered Institute of Building www.ciob.org.uk
Chartered Surveyors Training Trust www.cstt.org.uk
National Association of Estate Agents www.naea.co.uk
Royal Institution of Chartered Surveyors www.rics.org

Psychology
British Psychological Society www.bps.org.uk

Quantity Surveying
Chartered Institute of Building www.ciob.org.uk
Royal Institution of Chartered Surveyors www.rics.org

Radiography
Society and College of Radiographers www.sor.org

Social Work
Care Council for Wales www.ccwales.org.uk
General Social Care Council www.gscc.org.uk
Northern Ireland Social Care Council www.niscc.info
Scottish Social Services Council www.sssc.uk.com

Speech Pathology/Therapy
Royal College of Speech and Language Therapists www.rcslt.org

Sports Sciences/Studies
British Association of Sport and Exercise Sciences www.bases.org.uk
English Institute of Sport www.eis2win.co.uk
Institute of Sport and Recreation Management www.isrm.co.uk
Scottish Institute of Sport www.sisport.com
Society of Sports Therapists www.society-of-sports-therapists.org
Sport England www.sportengland.org
Sport Scotland www.sportscotland.org.uk
Sports Council for Wales www.sports-council-wales.co.uk
Sports Institute Northern Ireland www.sini.co.uk
UK Sport www.uksport.gov.uk.

Statistics
Royal Statistical Society www.rss.org.uk

Tourism and Travel
Institute of Leisure and Amenity Management www.ilam.co.uk
Institute of Travel and Tourism www.itt.co.uk
TTC Training www.ttctraining.co.uk

Town and Country Planning
Royal Town Planning Institute www.rtpi.org.uk

Transport Management and Planning
Chartered Institute of Logistics and Transport www.cilt-international.com.

Veterinary Science/Medicine/Nursing
Association of Chartered Physiotherapists in Animal Therapy www.acpat.org.uk
British Veterinary Nursing Association www.bvna.org.uk
Royal College of Veterinary Surgeons www.rcvs.ac.uk
Royal Veterinary College www.rvc.ac.uk

Zoology
Royal Entomological Society www.royensoc.co.uk
Zoological Society of London www.zsl.org

APPENDIX 3
BOOKLIST AND USEFUL WEBSITES

Unless otherwise stated, the publications in this list are all available from Trotman Publishing (www.trotman.co.uk / 0870 900 2665).

STANDARD REFERENCE BOOKS
British Qualifications, 37th edition, Kogan Page Ltd
British Vocational Qualifications, 9th edition, Kogan Page Ltd
The UCAS Directory 2008, UCAS
The Big Guide 2008 – The official universities and colleges entrance guide for 2008 entry, UCAS
The Scottish Guide 2008, UCAS

OTHER BOOKS AND RESOURCES
Choosing Your Degree Course and University, 11th edition, Brian Heap, Trotman Publishing
Critical Choices: Applying to University, Trotman Publishing
Destinations of Leavers from Higher Education, Higher Education Statistics Agency Services (available from www.hesa.ac.uk)
Disabled Students' Guide to University, 3rd edition, Trotman Publishing
The Educational Grants Directory 2007/8, 8th edition, Directory of Social Change
Experience Erasmus 2007 – The UK Guide to Socrates/Erasmus Programmes, ISCO
A Guide to Financial Support for Higher Education Students in 2007/2008, Department for Education (available from www.dfes.gov.uk/studentsupport)
How to Complete Your UCAS Application for 2008 entry to University and College, Trotman Publishing
Making the Most of University, Kate van Haeften, Trotman Publishing
The Mature Students' Directory, 4th edition, Trotman Publishing
MPW Getting Into course guides: American Universities, Art and Design Courses, Business and Management Courses, Dental School, Law, Medical School, Oxford and Cambridge, Physiotherapy Courses, Psychology Courses, Veterinary School, Trotman Publishing
The Push Guide to Which University 2008, Johnny Rich, Hodder Arnold
Sixthformer's Guide to Visiting Universities and Colleges 2006, ISCO
The Times Good University Guide 2008, John O'Leary, Times Books
Student Book 2008, 29th edition, Klaus Boehm and Jenny Lees-Spalding, Trotman Publishing
Students' Money Matters 2007, 13th edition, Trotman Publishing
Taking a Year Off, 5th edition, Margaret Flynn, Trotman Publishing
The Times Good University Guide 2008, John O'Leary, Times Books
The Ultimate University Ranking Guide, Catherine Harris, Trotman Publishing
Trotman's Green Guide 2007, Trotman Publishing
University Scholarships, Awards and Bursaries, 2006, Brian Heap, Trotman Publishing
The Virgin Alternative Guide to British Universities 2007, Piers Dudgeon, Virgin
Which Degree? 2007, Trotman Publishing
You Want to Study Where?!, Philip Dring, Barbara Lynn and Jim O'Brien, Trotman Publishing

USEFUL WEBSITES

Education, course and applications information
www.aimhigher.ac.uk
www.coursediscover.co.uk
www.direct.gov.uk/studentfinance
www.hero.ac.uk
www.opendays.com (information on university and college open days)
www.tqi.ac.uk (teaching quality information)
www.ucas.com

Careers information
www.armyjobs.mod.uk
www.careers.co.uk
www.careers.manchester.ac.uk
www.careerseurope.co.uk
www.enginuity.org.uk
www.insidecareers.co.uk
www.isco.org.uk
www.milkround.com
www.nhscareers.nhs.uk
www.prospects.ac.uk
www.rgu.ac.uk/careers
www.socialworkcareers.co.uk
www.surrart.ac.uk/careers
www.tda.gov.uk
www.trotman.co.uk
www.york.ac.uk/careers

Gap years
www.gapyear.com
www.gap-year.com
www.yini.org.uk (Year in Industry)

Study overseas
www.acu.ac.uk
www.fulbright.co.uk
www.allaboutcollege.com

APPENDIX 4
CAMBRIDGE PRE-U DIPLOMA: A NEW QUALIFICATION

Readers may wish to be alerted to details of this new non-modular examination which is at present under development and consultation with schools and universities. The examination is equivalent to A-levels and the IB and will be offered by some schools from September 2008.

Cambridge Pre-U is a new post-16 qualification being developed by the University of Cambridge International Examinations (CIE). It aims to prepare students from across the world with the skills and knowledge required to make a success of their subsequent studies at university. Representatives from higher education have been involved in writing the syllabi and universities have shown great interest in the qualification.

Students can take **individual Cambridge Pre-U subjects** and build them up into a portfolio that suits their interests and ambitions. The structure of each Cambridge Pre-U syllabus is *linear*, and this differentiates it from AS and A-levels. All the assessment takes place at the end of the two-year course. Students can take a Cambridge Pre-U subject at Subsidiary level (in other words after one year) although the result would not count towards the full (Principal) qualification.

Twenty-four syllabi will be available from 2008: Mathematics, Further Maths, Economics, Chemistry, Physics, Biology, English, History, Geography, Business Studies, German, French, Spanish, Classical Heritage, Mandarin Chinese, Art History, Sport Science, Greek, Latin, Art and Design, Comparative Government and Politics, Psychology, Music, and Philosophy and Ethics.

Results will be reported for individual subjects on a scale of 1 to 10, with a separate grade for the full Diploma.

For the full **Cambridge Pre-U Diploma** students will offer at least three Principal subjects (some will want to offer more). The distinguishing feature is that students will have *complete freedom of choice* in their subjects, in other words they can specialise in, say, the natural sciences. To qualify for the full Diploma, students offer a programme that includes a core course in **Global Perspectives** – giving students the opportunity to engage with issues that will face every young person, wherever in the world they live and work.

Cambridge Pre-U will be taught from September 2008, with the first examinations in 2010.

You can find out more about Cambridge Pre-U at www.cie.org.uk/cambridgepreu.

COURSE INDEX

INDEX OF ADVERTISERS